AMERICAN PERIODICALS 1741-1900

An Index to the Microfilm Collections:

American Periodicals 18th Century

American Periodicals 1800–1850

American Periodicals 1850–1900, Civil War and Reconstruction

Edited by
Jean Hoornstra and Trudy Heath

University Microfilms International
Ann Arbor, Michigan 48106
1979

Library of Congress Cataloging in Publication Data

Hoornstra, Jean.
    American periodicals, 1741-1900.

    1. American periodical series, eighteenth century—Indexes.
2. American periodical series, 1800-1850—Indexes. 3. American
periodical series, 1850-1900—Indexes.   I. Heath, Trudy, 1953-
joint author. II. American periodical series, eighteenth century.
III. American periodical series, 1800-1850. IV. American
periodical series, 1850-1900. V. Title.

Z6951.H65 [PN4877]   016.051   79-63165
ISBN 0-8357-0374-6

Manufactured in the United States of America

University Microfilms International
300 N. Zeeb Road
Ann Arbor, Michigan 48106

P.O. Box 91
London WC1R 4EG, England

CONTENTS

COOPERATING LIBRARIES vii

INTRODUCTION xiii

TITLE INDEX 1

SUBJECT INDEX 233

EDITOR INDEX 265

REEL NUMBER INDEX 289

    American Periodicals—18th Century (APS I) 289

    American Periodicals—1800-1850 (APS II) 291

    American Periodicals—1850-1900,
        Civil War and Reconstruction (APS III) 332

ACKNOWLEDGEMENTS

University Microfilms International wishes to thank all the cooperating libraries for making their resources available for inclusion in this collection.

COOPERATING LIBRARIES

ATT	Tuskegee Institute Library, Tuskegee, Alabama
AU	University of Alabama Library, University, Alabama
C	California State Library, Sacramento, California
C-S	California State Library, Sutro Branch, San Francisco, California
CCC	Claremont College Library, Claremont, California
CL	Los Angeles Public Library, Los Angeles, California
CLCo	Los Angeles County Public Library, Los Angeles, California
CLM	Los Angeles County Medical Association Library, Los Angeles, California
CLSM	Southwest Museum, Los Angeles, California
CMenSP	St. Patrick's Seminary Library, Menlo Park, California
CS	Sacramento City–County Library, Sacramento, California
CSmH	Henry E. Huntington Library and Art Gallery, San Marino, California
CSt	Stanford University Libraries, Stanford, California
CSt-Law	Stanford University Law Library, Palo Alto, California
CU	University of California, Berkeley, California
Co	Colorado State Library, Denver, Colorado
CoCC	Charles Leaming Tutt Library, Colorado College, Colorado Springs, Colorado
CoGrS	Colorado State College Library, Greeley, Colorado
Ct	Connecticut State Library, Hartford, Connecticut
CtHT	Trinity College Library, Hartford, Connecticut
CtHT-W	Trinity College, Watkinson Library, Hartford, Connecticut
CtHi	Connecticut Historical Society Library, Hartford, Connecticut
CtW	Wesleyan University Library, Middletown, Connecticut
CtY	Yale University Library, New Haven, Connecticut
CaOLU	University of Western Ontario Library, London, Canada
DBRA	Bureau of Railway Economics Library of the Association of American Railroads, Washington, D.C.
DCU	Catholic University of America Libraries, Washington, D.C.
DHEW	U.S. Department of Health, Education, and Welfare Library, Washington, D.C.
DHU	Howard University Library, Washington, D.C.
DI-GS	Geological Survey Library, U.S. Department of the Interior, Washington, D.C.
DLC	U.S. Library of Congress, Washington, D.C.
DNAL	U.S. National Agricultural Library, Beltsville, Maryland
DNLM	U.S. National Library of Medicine, Bethesda, Maryland
DSI	Smithsonian Institution, Washington, D.C.
DeU	University of Delaware Library, Newark, Delaware
DeWI	Wilmington Institute Free Library and the New Castle County Free Library, Wilmington, Delaware
EP	Edinburgh Public Libraries, Edinburgh, Scotland
FDS	Stetson University Library, Deland, Florida
FJ	Jacksonville Public Library System, Jacksonville, Florida
FTaSU	Florida State University Library, Tallahassee, Florida
FU	University of Florida Library, Gainesville, Florida
GA	Atlanta Public Library, Atlanta, Georgia
GDS	Agnes Scott College Library, Decatur, Georgia
GEU	Emory University Libraries, Atlanta, Georgia
GEU-M	A. W. Calhoun Medical Library, Emory University, Atlanta, Georgia
GHi	Georgia Historical Society Library, Savannah, Georgia

GMiW	Georgia College Library at Milledgeville, Georgia	KHi	Kansas State Historical Society, Topeka, Kansas
GU	University of Georgia Libraries, Athens, Georgia	KKc	Kansas City Public Library, Kansas City, Kansas
IC	Chicago Public Library, Chicago, Illinois	KMK	Kansas State University of Agriculture and Applied Science Library, Manhattan, Kansas
ICAC	American College of Surgeons, Chicago, Illinois		
ICHi	Chicago Historical Society Library, Chicago, Illinois	KPT	Kansas State College of Pittsburg Library, Pittsburg, Kansas
ICJ	John Crerar Library, Chicago, Illinois	KU	University of Kansas Libraries, Lawrence, Kansas
ICMe	Meadville Theological School Library, Chicago, Illinois	KyBB	Berea College Library, Berea, Kentucky
ICN	Newberry Library, Chicago, Illinois	KyLo	Louisville Free Public Library, Louisville, Kentucky
ICRL	Center for Research Libraries, Chicago, Illinois		
ICRM	Rush Medical College Library, Chicago, Illinois	KyLoS	Southern Baptist Theological Seminary Library, Louisville, Kentucky
ICS	American College of Surgeons Library, Chicago, Illinois	KyLxCB	Lexington Theological Seminary, Lexington, Kentucky
ICT	Chicago Theological Seminary Library, Chicago, Illinois		
ICU	University of Chicago Library, Chicago, Illinois	L	British Museum Library, London, England
ICham	Public Library, Champaign-Urbana, Illinois	LN	New Orleans Public Library, New Orleans, Louisiana
IEG	Garrett Theological Seminary Library, Evanston, Illinois	LNHT	Tulane University Library, New Orleans, Louisiana
IGK	Knox College Library, Galesburg, Illinois	LNL	Loyola University Library, New Orleans, Louisiana
IMunS	St. Mary of the Lake Seminary Library, Mundelein, Illinois		
IU	University of Illinois at Urbana-Champaign Library, Urbana, Illinois	LU	Louisiana State University Library, Baton Rouge, Louisiana
IU-M	Medical Sciences Library, University of Illinois, Chicago, Illinois	M	Massachusetts State Library, Boston, Massachusetts
Ia-T	Iowa State Traveling Library, Des Moines, Iowa	MA	Amherst College Library, Amherst, Massachusetts
IaDL	Luther College Library, Decorah, Iowa	MB	Boston Public Library, Boston, Massachusetts
IaDm	Des Moines Public Library, Des Moines, Iowa	MBAt	Boston Atheneum, Boston, Massachusetts
IaDmD	Drake University Library, Des Moines, Iowa	MBC	American Congregational Association Library, Boston, Massachusetts
IaU	University of Iowa Library, Iowa City, Iowa		
IdU	University of Idaho Library, Moscow, Idaho	MBtS	Saint John's Seminary Library, Brighton, Massachusetts
In	Indiana State Library, Indianapolis, Indiana		
InCW	Wabash College Library, Crawfordsville, Indiana	MChB	Boston College Library, Chestnut Hill, Massachusetts
InFC	Franklin College of Indiana Library, Franklin, Indiana	MH	Harvard University Library, Cambridge, Massachusetts
InGrD	De Pauw University Library, Greencastle, Indiana	MH-AH	Harvard University, Andover-Harvard Theological Library, Cambridge, Massachusetts
InI	Indianapolis-Marion County Public Library, Indianapolis, Indiana		
		MH-BA	Graduate School of Business Administration Library, Harvard University, Cambridge, Massachusetts
InLP	Purdue University Libraries, Lafayette, Indiana		
InNU	Memorial Library, University of Notre Dame, Notre Dame, Indiana	MMeT	Tufts University Libraries, Medford, Massachusetts
InNhW	Workingmen's Institute Library, New Harmony, Indiana	MMeT-Hi	Tufts University, Universalist Historical Society Library, Crane Theological School, Medford, Massachusetts
InRE	Earlham College Library, Richmond, Indiana		
InS	South Bend Public Library, South Bend, Indiana	MNF	Forbes Library, Northampton, Massachusetts
InStme	Saint Meinrad's College and Seminary Library, Saint Meinrad, Indiana	MU	University of Massachusetts Library, Amherst, Massachusetts
InTI	Indiana State University Library, Terre Haute, Indiana	MWA	American Antiquarian Society, Worcester, Massachusetts
InU	Indiana University Libraries, Bloomington, Indiana	MWC	Clark University Library, Worcester, Massachusetts
K	Kansas State Library, Topeka, Kansas		
KAS	Saint Benedict's College Library, Atchison, Kansas		

MWelC	Wellesley College Library, Wellesley, Massachusetts	NBuG	Grosvenor Reference Division, Buffalo and Erie County Public Library, Buffalo, New York
MWiW	Williams College Library, Williamstown, Massachusetts	NBuU	State University of New York at Buffalo Libraries, Buffalo, New York
MdBE	Enoch Pratt Free Library, Baltimore, Maryland	NCH	Hamilton College Library, Clinton, New York
MdBM	Medical and Chirurgical Faculty Library of the State of Maryland, Baltimore, Maryland	NCaS	Saint Lawrence University Library, Canton, New York
MdBP	Peabody Institute Library, Baltimore, Maryland	NHC	Colgate University Library, Hamilton, New York
MdBPS	Paulist Fathers Preparatory Seminary Library, Baltimore, Maryland	NHi	New York Historical Society, New York, New York
Me	Maine State Library, Augusta, Maine		
MeB	Bowdoin College Library, Brunswick, Maine	NIC	Cornell University Library, Ithaca, New York
MeBa	Bangor Public Library, Bangor, Maine	NJQ	Queens Borough Public Library, Jamaica, New York
MeLB	Bates College Library, Lewiston, Maine		
MeU	University of Maine Library, Orono, Maine	NN	New York Public Library, New York, New York
Mi	Michigan State Library, Lansing, Michigan		
MiD	Detroit Public Library, Detroit, Michigan	NNC	Columbia University Library, New York, New York
MiD-B	Burton Historical Collection, Detroit Public Library, Detroit, Michigan	NNC-T	Teachers College Library, Columbia University, New York, New York
MiDU	University of Detroit Library, Detroit, Michigan		
MiEM	Michigan State University Library, East Lansing, Michigan	NNG	General Theological Seminary of the Protestant Episcopal Church, New York, New York
MiGr	Grand Rapids Public Library, Grand Rapids, Michigan	NNM	American Museum of Natural History, New York, New York
MiHM	Michigan College of Science and Technology Library, Houghton, Michigan	NNNAM	New York Academy of Medicine Library, New York, New York
MiKW	Western Michigan University Library, Kalamazoo, Michigan	NNU-H	New York University, Heights Library, New York, New York
MiU	The University of Michigan Library, Ann Arbor, Michigan	NNUT	Union Theological Seminary Library, New York, New York
MiU-C	Clements Library, The University of Michigan, Ann Arbor, Michigan	NPV	Vassar College Library, Poughkeepsie, New York
MiYEM	Eastern Michigan University Library, Ypsilanti, Michigan	NR	Rochester Public Library, Rochester, New York
MnCS	Saint John's University Library, Collegeville, Minnesota	NRAB	Samuel Colgate Baptist Historical Library of the American Baptist Historical Society, Rochester, New York
MnM	Minneapolis Public Library, Minneapolis, Minnesota		
MnNC	Carleton College Library, Northfield, Minnesota	NRCR	Colgate-Rochester Divinity School Library, Rochester, New York
MnS	Saint Paul Public Library, Saint Paul, Minnesota		
MnSRM	Ramsey County Medical Society Library, Saint Paul, Minnesota	NRSB	Saint Bernard's Seminary and College Library, Rochester, New York
MnU	University of Minnesota Library, Minneapolis, Minnesota	NRU	University of Rochester Library, Rochester, New York
MoK	Kansas City Public Library, Kansas City, Missouri	NSchU	Union College Library, Schenectady, New York
MoS	St. Louis Public Library, St. Louis, Missouri	NSySU-M	State University of New York, Upstate Medical Center Library, Syracuse, New York
MoU	University of Missouri Library, Columbia, Missouri	NSyU	Syracuse University Library, Syracuse, New York
Ms-Ar	Mississippi Department of Archives and History, Jackson, Mississippi	NbO	Omaha Public Library, Omaha, Nebraska
MtBC	Montana State University at Bozeman Library, Bozeman, Montana	NbU	University of Nebraska Library, Lincoln, Nebraska
N	New York State Library, Albany, New York	NbU-M	University of Nebraska, College of Medicine Library, Omaha, Nebraska
NB	Brooklyn Public Library, Brooklyn, New York	NcD	Duke University Library, Durham, North Carolina
NBP	Pratt Institute, Brooklyn, New York		
NBu	Buffalo and Erie County Public Library, Buffalo, New York	NcGU	University of North Carolina at Greensboro Library, Greensboro, North Carolina

NcGuG	Guilford College Library, Guilford, North Carolina	PCC	Crozier Theological Seminary Library, Chester, Pennsylvania
NcMHi	Historical Foundation of the Presbyterian and Reformed Churches Library, Montreat, North Carolina	PCaD	Dickinson College Library, Carlisle, Pennsylvania
NcU	University of North Carolina Libraries, Chapel Hill, North Carolina	PHC	Haverford College Library, Haverford, Pennsylvania
NdU	University of North Dakota Library, Grand Forks, North Dakota	PHi	Historical Society of Pennsylvania, Philadelphia, Pennsylvania
Nh	New Hampshire State Library, Concord, New Hampshire	PHuJ	Juniata College Library, Huntingdon, Pennsylvania
NhD	Dartmouth College Library, Hanover, New Hampshire	PLF	Franklin and Marshall College Library, Lancaster, Pennsylvania
NhHi	New Hampshire Historical Society, Concord, New Hampshire	PLeB	Bucknell University Library, Lewisburg, Pennsylvania
NjMD	Drew University Library, Madison, New Jersey	PP	Free Library of Philadelphia, Philadelphia, Pennsylvania
NjP	Princeton University Libraries, Princeton, New Jersey	PPC	College of Physicians of Philadelphia Library, Philadelphia, Pennsylvania
NjPT	Princeton Theological Seminary Library, Princeton, New Jersey	PPJ	Jefferson Medical College Library, Philadelphia, Pennsylvania
NjR	Rutgers, The State University Library, New Brunswick, New Jersey	PPL	Library Company of Philadelphia, Philadelphia, Pennsylvania
OAU	Ohio University Library, Athens, Ohio	PPPrHi	Presbyterian Historical Society, Philadelphia, Pennsylvania
OC	Public Library of Cincinnati and Hamilton County, Cincinnati, Ohio	PPi	Carnegie Library of Pittsburgh, Pittsburgh, Pennsylvania
OCA	Cincinnati Art Museum Library, Cincinnati, Ohio	PR	Reading Public Library, Reading, Pennsylvania
OCHP	Cincinnati Historical Society Library, Cincinnati, Ohio	PSC	Swarthmore College Library, Swarthmore, Pennsylvania
OCLoyd	Lloyd Library and Museum, Cincinnati, Ohio	PSt	Pennsylvania State University Libraries, University Park, Pennsylvania
OCU	University of Cincinnati Library, Cincinnati, Ohio	PU	University of Pennsylvania Libraries, Philadelphia, Pennsylvania
OCX	Xavier University Library, Cincinnati, Ohio	RP	Providence Public Library, Providence, Rhode Island
OCl	Cleveland Public Library, Cleveland, Ohio	RPB	Brown University Library, Providence, Rhode Island
ODW	Ohio Wesleyan University Library, Delaware, Ohio	RPJCB	John Carter Brown Library, Providence, Rhode Island
ODa	Dayton and Montgomery County Public Library, Dayton, Ohio	ScC	Charleston Library Society, Charleston, South Carolina
OFH	Rutherford B. Hayes Library, Fremont, Ohio	ScCM	Medical College of the State of South Carolina Library, Charleston, South Carolina
OMC	Dawes Memorial Library, Marietta College, Marietta, Ohio	ScCleU	Clemson University Library, Clemson, South Carolina
OMidU	Gardner-Harvey Library, Miami University, Middletown Campus, Middletown, Ohio	ScU	University of South Carolina Library, Columbia, South Carolina
OMtsjC	College of Mount Saint Joseph-on-the-Ohio Library, Mount Saint Joseph, Ohio	T	Tennessee State Library, Nashville, Tennessee
OO	Oberlin College Library, Oberlin, Ohio	TKL	Public Library of Knoxville and Knox County, Knoxville, Tennessee
OOxM	Miami University Library, Oxford, Ohio	TNJ	Joint University Libraries, Nashville, Tennessee
OT	Toledo Public Library, Toledo, Ohio	TNJ-P	Joint University Libraries, George Peabody College, Nashville, Tennessee
OU	Ohio State University Library, Columbus, Ohio	TNJ-R	Joint University Libraries, Vanderbilt School of Religion, Nashville, Tennessee
OWoC	College of Wooster Library, Wooster, Ohio	TU	University of Tennessee, Knoxville, Tennessee
OkT	Tulsa Public Library, Tulsa, Oklahoma	TxDN	North Texas State University Library, Denton, Texas
OkU	University of Oklahoma Library, Norman, Oklahoma		
OrU	University of Oregon Library, Eugene, Oregon		
PBL	LeHigh University Library, Bethlehem, Pennsylvania		
PBm	Bryn Mawr College Library, Bryn Mawr, Pennsylvania		

TxDaM	Southern Methodist University Library, Dallas, Texas	ViW	College of William and Mary Library, Williamsburg, Virginia
TxH	Houston Public Library, Houston, Texas	VtMiM	Middlebury College Library, Middlebury, Vermont
TxHR	Rice University Library, Houston, Texas		
TxU	University of Texas Library, Austin, Texas	VtNN	Norwich University Library, Northfield, Vermont
TxWB	Baylor University Libraries, Waco, Texas		
UU	University of Utah Library, Salt Lake City, Utah	VtU	University of Vermont and State Agricultural College Library, Burlington, Vermont
VRU	University of Richmond Library, Richmond, Virginia	WHi	Wisconsin State Historical Society Library, Madison, Wisconsin
Vi	Virginia State Library, Richmond, Virginia	WaS	Seattle Public Library, Seattle, Washington
ViBlbV	Virginia Polytechnic Institute Library, Blacksburg, Virginia	WaU	University of Washington Library, Seattle, Washington
ViNeM	Mariners' Museum, Newport News, Virginia	WvU	West Virginia University Library, Morgantown, West Virginia
ViU	University of Virginia Libraries, Charlottesville, Virginia		

Ladies Home Journal: Vol. 23, no. 2; Jan. 1906

INTRODUCTION

University Microfilms International's three collections of American periodicals on microfilm together include more than 1100 periodicals with publishing dates ranging from 1741 to 1900. This cumulative index provides easy access by title, subject, editor, and reel number to all three collections.

ABOUT THE COLLECTIONS

Although periodicals are recognized by historians as valuable source materials for the study of American ideas and social patterns, it was difficult in the past for libraries to acquire complete files of eighteenth- and nineteenth-century magazines because they were rare and costs were prohibitive. In 1941, a microfilm project, sponsored by the William L. Clements Library and the Department of English of the University of Michigan, was launched to make rare eighteenth-century periodicals available to libraries and was later extended to include nineteenth-century periodicals as well. This resulted in the creation of UMI's three American periodicals collections: APS I, APS II, and APS III.

American Periodicals, 18th Century (APS I)

The APS I collection, which contains 88 periodicals on 33 reels of microfilm, provides basic source materials for the study and understanding of eighteenth-century American society in all its phases. Selected by R. E. Booth, APS I traces the evolution of the American magazine from two short-lived publications of 1741 by Andrew Bradford and Benjamin Franklin through the increased magazine activity after the Revolution. Four of the era's most important and longest-lived periodicals—the *Columbian Magazine* and the *American Museum*, both of Philadelphia, the *Massachusetts Magazine* of Boston, and the *New-York Magazine*, are included in this collection.

American Periodicals, 1800-1850 (APS II)

APS II consists of 1,966 reels of microfilm and contains 923 periodicals published in America between 1800 and 1850. The spirit of nationalism and of westward expansion is reflected in the magazines of this prolific period, which marked the beginnings of a distinctly American literature. The years between 1825 and 1850 are sometimes called the "golden age of periodicals," because there was an extraordinary outburst of magazine activity during these years. Religious periodicals, and

magazines for women and children were numerous during this time; many of these can be found in the APS II collection. *Godey's Lady's Book,* the *Juvenile Port-Folio,* the *Saturday Evening Post,* and the *New-York Mirror* were a few of the more significant periodicals of the time.

American Periodicals 1850-1900, Civil War and Reconstruction (APS III)

APS III is made up of 117 American periodicals published between 1850 and the turn of the century. Through these magazines, readers can trace the philosophical, social, and literary background of the Civil War and Reconstruction eras. Because the variety and scope of periodical literature enlarged during this time, the magazines make fascinating reading. In addition, the earliest published works of many outstanding American writers are to be found in abundance in this collection. Some significant periodicals which were begun during this period were *Putnam's Monthly Magazine, Vanity Fair,* and *Ladies' Home Journal.*

HOW TO USE THE INDEX

To allow the user maximum access to the periodicals, this guide is arranged in four sections: Title Index, Subject Index, Editor Index, and Reel Number Index.

Title Index

The Title Index is a cumulated alphabetical listing of all titles in the three collections. Each entry provides complete bibliographical information, such as complete title, beginning and ending volumes and dates, and publisher, and usually provides additional information, such as title variations, editors, volumes included on the film, etc. Following this is an annotation describing the periodical. The location of the periodical is given at the right, including the abbreviation for the collection (APS I, APS II, or APS III), and the reel numbers, along with volumes and inclusive dates on each reel. It should be noted that a few periodicals appear in more than one collection. If a title varied, each title which is included in the microfilm edition is given in bold type, with appropriate volumes, dates, and reel numbers listed beneath each title. Notes on the microfilm edition, including information on missing or damaged volumes or issues, appear next in the entry, followed by the abbreviations for source libraries from which the microfilm copy was obtained. The list of libraries with corresponding abbreviations is given on page vii. "See Also" references are given at the end of the entry for related titles which are also in the collection; i.e., periodicals which succeeded or preceded the title listed. Cross-references are also provided in the Title Index for all title variations referring the user back to the cataloged title.

SAMPLE ENTRY

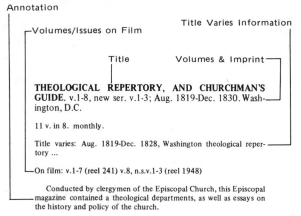

Annotation

Title Varies Information

Volumes/Issues on Film

Title   Volumes & Imprint

THEOLOGICAL REPERTORY, AND CHURCHMAN'S GUIDE. v.1-8, new ser. v.1-3; Aug. 1819-Dec. 1830. Washington, D.C.

11 v. in 8. monthly.

Title varies: Aug. 1819-Dec. 1828, Washington theological repertory ...

On film: v.1-7 (reel 241) v.8, n.s.v.1-3 (reel 1948)

Conducted by clergymen of the Episcopal Church, this Episcopal magazine contained a theological departments, as well as essays on the history and policy of the church.

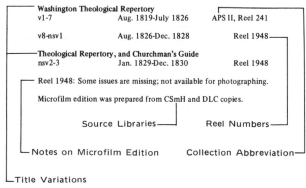

Washington Theological Repertory
v1-7   Aug. 1819-July 1826   APS II, Reel 241

v8-nsv1   Aug. 1826-Dec. 1828   Reel 1948

Theological Repertory, and Churchman's Guide
nsv2-3   Jan. 1829-Dec. 1830   Reel 1948

Reel 1948: Some issues are missing; not available for photographing.

Microfilm edition was prepared from CSmH and DLC copies.

Source Libraries   Reel Numbers

Notes on Microfilm Edition   Collection Abbreviation

Title Variations

○ **Finding the Title on the Film**—The APS II and APS III collections were compiled in random order as material for filming became available and released in units (formerly called "years") of approximately 100,000 pages each; for this reason, various segments of a periodical may not appear on the same reel but may appear in several units. The Title Index lists all reels for each periodical, but does not indicate in which unit each reel is included. If unit number information is needed, refer to page 288 for a listing of inclusive reels for each unit of APS II and APS III.

There may be several titles on one reel, or one title may occupy several reels of film. Although the Title Index does not give a position for each title on the film, most reels contain a "title sheet" photographed at the beginning of the reel which lists its contents.

For information on the position of the title on the reel, the user should refer to the Reel Number Index beginning on page 289. By going to the appropriate section (APS I, II, or III) and then finding the correct reel number, the user can quickly determine the sequence of the titles on the film.

Subject Index

The collections can be accessed by subject by referring to the Subject Index, which is an alphabetical listing of the Library of Congress subject headings assigned to each title during cataloging. Titles are arranged alphabetically within each subject category. Short titles only are given, followed by collection abbreviation and reel number identifying the location of the title in the microfilm collections.

Editor Index

The Editor Index provides an alphabetical listing of editors' names for many of the periodicals, with titles arranged in alphabetical order under each editor's name. Entries include short title, collection abbreviation, and reel numbers on which the periodical can be found. For further information, such as dates of editorship, refer to the complete entry in the Title Index.

Reel Number Index

The Reel Number Index is useful in determining the order in which the titles are arranged on the film reel and also serves as a convenient guide for the user who is not searching for a particular title, but is just browsing through the film. Entries in the Reel Number Index are arranged in the order in which they appear in the microfilm collections; thus, the index is divided into three sections, one for each collection. APS II and APS III are further divided into units. Information given includes inclusive reel numbers, which appear in columnar form to the left of each entry, as well as short title, and inclusive volumes and publication dates in the microfilm collection. In cases where the title of the periodical varies, all titles have been listed in boldface type under the initial title, along with the reel number, volumes, and dates which correspond to each title. Note that the title which appears on the microfilm "title sheet" may not match the initial title, but may be one of the title variations listed below the initial title.

ADDITIONAL ACCESS TOOLS AND BIBLIOGRAPHIC SOURCES

Access Tools

○ **Poole's Index to Periodical Literature**—Nearly one hundred of the periodicals in the APS II and APS III collections are at least partially indexed in *Poole's*

Index to Periodical Literature; thus *Poole's Index* can be used to access these periodicals by topic. Titles which are indexed in *Poole's Index* are indicated in the American Periodicals Title Index by an asterisk preceding the title. After an article has been selected from *Poole's Index,* the user should check the Title Index to determine whether or not the desired magazine is included in UMI's collections. If the title is listed and is preceded by an asterisk, check the list of volumes to see if the desired volume is available. If so, the correct reel of film can then be searched for the appropriate volume, page number and article.

○ **19th Century Readers' Guide to Periodical Literature, 1890-1899**—This two-volume set provides indexing to 51 periodicals for the years 1890-1899, with author, subject and illustrator access. A number of the periodicals in the American Periodicals collections are indexed in this publication; some of these are the *New Englander and Yale Review, Catholic World, Critic, Dial, Arena,* and *Bookman.*

Bibliographic Sources

○ **A History of American Magazines** (Frank Luther Mott): This five-volume set covers the years from 1741 to 1930 and provides extensive coverage of American periodicals, as well as a cumulative index in volume 5, which lists titles, editors, contributors, and topics.

○ **A History and Bibliography of American Magazines, 1810-1820** (Neal L. Edgar). As indicated by its title, this publication includes a section on the history of American magazines from 1810 to 1820 plus a section of bibliography, with descriptions of each periodical. Following these sections are a chronological list of magazines; a register of printers, publishers, editors, and engravers; and an index.

TITLE INDEX

McClure's Magazine: Vol. 33, Sept. 1909 issue

TITLE INDEX

THE —————————. By Nonius Nondescript. v.1, no.1-8; Feb. 18-May 18, 1826. Washington, P. Thompson, 1826.

96 p. biweekly.

Cover title.

Edited by "Nonius Nondescript, Esq.," this satirical magazine poked fun at Congress, both the House and the Senate, and included other political material and poetry.

v1, no.1-8 Feb. 18-May 18, 1826 APS II, Reel 333

Microfilm edition was prepared from NN copy.

ABOLITION INTELLIGENCER AND MISSIONARY MAGAZINE. v.1, no.1-12; May 7, 1822-Apr. 1823. Shelbyville, Ky.; J.F. Crow.

1 v. monthly.

Edited by J. F. Crow.

Film incomplete: no. 8-9, 12 wanting.

Edited by John Finley Crowe, this monthly anti-slavery magazine published minutes and other important documents of abolition and manumission societies. Comments on slavery came in the form of anecdotes, articles, and letters to the editor and were based on humanitarian, though somewhat sentimentalized, feelings. Like other anti-slavery magazines it was religiously motivated and contained a section on missionary efforts and the history of missions all over the world. It was published for one year, under the aegis of the Kentucky Abolition Society.

v1, no.1-7, 10-11 May 7, 1822-Mar. 1823 APS II, Reel 47

THE ABOLITIONIST; or, Record of the New England anti-slavery society. Edited by a committee. v.1; Jan.-Dec. 1833. Boston. Printed by Garrison and Knapp [1833]

192 p. pl. monthly.

Cover title.

"William Lloyd Garrison was the principal editor."–Sabin, Dict. of books relating to America, v.20, p. 73.

Published by the New England Anti-Slavery Society, this monthly antislavery journal was concerned with promoting the immediate abolition of slavery and with improving the condition of free blacks in the U.S. In addition to articles on slavery in the U.S. and the West Indies, this 16-page paper published proceedings of meetings and annual reports of the New England Anti-Slavery Society, as well as material on the American Colonization Society and various other antislavery societies. Some letters and poetry were also included.

v.1 Jan.-Dec. 1833 APS II, Reel 362

Microfilm edition was prepared from DLC and NN copies.

THE ACADEMICIAN, containing the elements of scholastic science, and the outlines of philosophic education,

predicated on the analysis of the human mind, and exhibiting the improved methods of instruction. By Albert Picket, and John W. Picket. v.1; Feb. 7, 1818-Jan. 29, 1820. New York, Printed by C.N. Baldwin, 1820.

iv, 399 p. semimonthly (irregular)

The *Academician* was an educational magazine edited by Albert and John W. Picket, who were partners in the management of the Incorporated Society of New York Teachers and also conducted a school. Its varied contents included comment on such educators as Pestalozzi, Fellenberg, Lancaster, and Bell, reports of educational conditions in various parts of the U.S., reviews of textbooks, an abstract of the *Outlines of Philosophical Education*, by Prof. George Jardine of Glasgow University, and advice on teaching methods. In addition, there were departments of philology, geography, and arithmetic, along with biographical sketches and some poetry and criticism.

v.1, nos.1-25 Feb. 7, 1818-Jan. 29, 1820 APS II, Reel 47

THE ADVISER; or, Vermont evangelical magazine. v.1-7 Jan. 1809-Dec. 1815. Middlebury [Vt.] H.G. Hooker, 1809-15.

7 v. in 4. monthly.

Editors: Jan. 1809-Dec. 1814, Asa Burton and others.–Jan.-Dec. 1815, John Hough.

The *Adviser* was conducted by a number of editors appointed by the General Convention of Congregational and Presbyterian ministers, except for the last volume, which was conducted by John Hough, a professor at Middlebury College. It published religious news, both foreign and domestic, including news of missions, revivals, ordinations, and the activities of Bible societies, along with religious essays, reviews of religious books, lists of new publications, poetry and anecdotes, and some biography.

v1 Jan.-Dec. 1809 APS II, Reel 1
v2-7 Jan. 1810-Dec. 1815 Reel 47

Microfilm edition was prepared from DLC copies.

THE ADVOCATE FOR THE TESTIMONY OF GOD, as it is written in the books of nature and revelation. Edited by John Thomas. v.1-5, no.12, May 1, 1834-Apr. 1839. Amelia Co., Va.

5 v.

Title varies: 1834-April 1837 as Apostolic advocate.

A religious magazine which fought against the "corruptions of Christianity," defended the Scripture, and presented prophecy. Contents included sermons, addresses, dialogues, letters, anecdotes, and articles on doctrine, religious history, and the various religions.

Apostolic Advocate
v1-3 May 1, 1834-Apr. 1837 APS II, Reel 767
Advocate for the Testimony of God
v4-5 May 1837-Apr. 1839 Reel 767

---

*Indicates titles which are indexed in *Poole's Index to Periodical Literature.* Note that the asterisk may refer to one or more of the variant titles listed below the initial title.

Vol. 1: Index and table of contents are lacking. Vol. 2: Article "Future of punishment" bound and photographed at the end of the volume. Vols. 3-4: Best copy available for photographing. Print is extremely light. Vol. 5: Best copy available for photographing. Many pages are badly stained, with some loss of print. Some pages are torn.

Microfilm edition was prepared from PPPrHi, TxU and Vi copies.

ADVOCATE OF PEACE. *SEE* World Affairs.

ADVOCATE OF PEACE AND CHRISTIAN PATRIOT. v.1, nos.1-12; Sept. 1828-June 1829. Philadelphia, 1828-1829.

96 p.

This short-lived magazine advocated the peace movement by publishing articles on peace, reports on the activities of peace societies, addresses to peace societies, and poetry.

no.1-12   Sept. 1828-June 1829   APS II, Reel 584

Microfilm edition was prepared from NHi copy.

ADVOCATE OF PEACE AND UNIVERSAL BROTHERHOOD. *SEE* World Affairs.

THE ADVOCATE OF SCIENCE. v.1; Feb. 18, 1833-Feb. 20, 1834. Philadelphia, W.P. Gibbons.

192 p. Weekly (irregular) Feb.-Mar. 1833; semimonthly, Apr. 1833-Feb. 1834.

Superseded in Aug. 1834 by the Advocate of science, and annals of natural history.

This scientific journal, published by William P. Gibbons, emphasized geology and meteorology and also contained a series of articles on botany and natural history. Meteorological tables are included.

v1   Feb. 18, 1833-Feb. 20, 1834   APS II, Reel 532

Title page and index are missing. Pagination is irregular. Pages 1-2 stained; 14-15 cropped with loss of text.

Microfilm edition was prepared from PHi and PWcS copies.

SEE ALSO Advocate of Science, and Annals of Natural History.

THE ADVOCATE OF SCIENCE, and annals of natural history. Conducted by W.P. Gibbons. vol.1, no.1-9; Aug. 1834-Apr. 1835. Philadelphia, W.P. Gibbons [1834-35]

illus. monthly.

Basically a continuation of the old Advocate of Science, this magazine presented articles on botany and geology, zoology, proceedings of various learned societies in the U.S., notices of new books, and answers to queries from readers. Some illustrations appeared and meteorological data and miscellaneous material were also included.

v1   Aug. 1834-Apr. 1835   APS II, Reel 532

Title page and index are missing. Pagination is irregular. Some pages are tightly bound with loss of text.

Microfilm edition was prepared from CLU and ICJ copies.

THE AERONAUT; a periodical paper. v.1-13; May 18, 1816-1822. New York.

13v. irregular.

Vols. 1-9 contain papers numbered 1-195 and dated May 18, 1816-Sept. 30, 1822; most later issues are unnumbered and undated.

This journal of general literature was based on the essays prepared by various members of a New York City gentleman's club which met for weekly discussions. A great variety of subjects were discussed and written about including philosophy, fashion, poetry, short stories, superstition and popular culture. The essays were usually five to ten pages long, though were sometimes quite extensive.

v 1-6   May 18, 1816-Oct. 4, 1817   APS II, Reel 48
v 7-13   Oct. 6, 1817-1822   Reel 49

THE AESCULAPIAN REGISTER. Ed. by several physicians. v.1; June 17-Dec. 9, 1824. Philadelphia, R. Desilver, 1824.

204 p. weekly.

Edited by several physicians, this bimonthly medical magazine published articles on medicine, warnings of and cures for diseases, household hints and cautions, and a monthly series of meteorological observations. The topics discussed were of popular interest and included medical ethics, the history of medicine, mental alienation, and even vampyrism. Serious and satirical poems were also included. A list of the number of deaths and their causes for major cities in the U.S. was published monthly.

v1   June 17-Dec. 9, 1824   APS II, Reel 49

THE AFRICAN INTELLIGENCER. v.1; July 1820. Washington, J. Ashmun, 1820.

32 p.

Proposed to be a regular journal of the proceedings of the American Colonization Society, this periodical published the Society's history, official documents, correspondence extracts and general interest papers for only one issue. It also included general articles about the people and land of Africa and the history, consequences, and means of suppressing the slave trade.

v1, no.1   July 1820   APS II, Reel 49

THE AFRICAN REPOSITORY. Published by the American Colonization Society. v.1-67, 68 no.1; Mar. 1825-Jan. 1892. Washington, 1826-92.

68 v. in 56. illus., plates, maps. Monthly, 1825-74 (Feb. 1839-Feb. 1842, semimonthly); quarterly, 1875-92 (July 1880-June 1881, monthly) Index: 1-10 in 10

From 1824-74 (v.1-50) a t.-p, and index were issued for each volume. Beginning with 1875 a t.-p, and index were issued at the end of every third year for the three preceding years.
Vols. 1-25 have title: The African repository and colonial journal.

Edited by R.R. Gurley and others.

From its beginning in 1825, the *African Repository* denounced the slavery of Negroes in the Southern states. Published by the American Colonization Society, it was the oldest colonization periodical, and gave an accurate account of the society's work to resettle the American Negro in Africa, in addition to publishing reports and records of that organization.

African Repository and Colonial Journal

v1, nos. 1-10	Mar.-Dec. 1825	APS II, Reel 49
v1-8	1825-1832	Reel 641
v9-15	1833-1839	Reel 642
v16-22	1840-1846	Reel 643
v23-25	1847-1849	Reel 644

African Repository

v26	1850	APS II, Reel 644
v27-30	Jan. 1851-Dec. 1854	Reel 881
v31-40	Jan.1855-Dec. 1864	Reel 882
v41-49	Jan. 1865-Dec. 1873	Reel 883
v50-68	Jan. 1874-Jan. 1892	Reel 884

Pagination is irregular. Some pages are stained or have print missing. Cumulative indexes are bound with vols. 51, 54, 57, 60, 63 and 66. These indexes cover the volume listed and the following two volumes. Vol. 68, page 29 lacking; not available for photographing.

Microfilm edition was prepared from DLC, MiU, NjPT copies.

AFRICAN REPOSITORY AND COLONIAL JOURNAL. *SEE* African Repository.

THE AGRICULTURAL MUSEUM: designed to be a repository of valuable information to the farmer and manufacturer, and to the mean of a free communication of sentiment, and general interchange of ideas, on the important subjects of their occupations. v. 1-2, no. 11; July 4, 1810-May 1812. Georgetown, Ca.; Printed by W.A. Rind.

2v. Semimonthly, July 4, 1810-June 9, 1811; monthly, July 1811-May 1812.

Begun in 1810 by the Rev. David Wiley, the Agricultural Museum was apparently the first periodical to be mainly devoted to agriculture. Designed to be "a convenient appendage to the Columbian Agricultural Society," it published the Society's Constitution and proceedings, along with the proceedings of other societies, essays on agriculture, manufacturing and the arts, and a variety of selected material. Along with his duties as a minister, editor, and secretary of the agricultural society, Wiley also served as postmaster, superintendent of the turnpike, merchant, miller, and mayor of his town.

v1-2, no.11	July 4,1810-May 1812	APS II, Reel 49

AGRICULTURAL REVIEW OF NEW YORK. *SEE* Debow's Review.

AGRICULTURIST, and journal of the state and county societies. *SEE* Tennessee Farmer.

ALBANY BOUQUET AND LITERARY SPECTATOR. v.1, no. 1-12; April 18-Sept. 19, 1835. Albany, N.Y., 1835.

96 p.

An eight-page biweekly devoted entirely to miscellaneous reading material—some serious reading, and some light material and humorous articles. Contents were made up of contributions, selections from popular periodicals, and some original material, and included popular tales, biography, travel sketches, poetry, anecdotes, short moral essays, articles on natural history, and brief reviews of magazines, books, and the theater.

v1	April 18-Sep. 19, 1835	APS II, Reel 767

Microfilm edition was prepared from N copy.

THE ALBANY LAW JOURNAL; A weekly record of the law and the lawyers. v. 1-70; Jan. 8, 1870-Dec. 1908. Albany, Weed, Parsons [etc.]

70v. illus.; ports. Weekly, 1870-1900; monthly, 1901-08.

Subtitle varies.
Editors: 1870-June 1879, I.G. Thompson.—July 1879-June 1893, I. Browne.
Supplements accompany v.44; v.56, no. 26; and v. 57, no. 17-23.
Film includes v. 1-70 and cumulative indexes to v. 1-20 and 21-34.

Founded during the postbellum period, the *Albany Law Journal* was one of the most widely circulated legal periodicals of the seventies.

Cumulative index 1-20	1870-1879	
v1-7	Jan. 1870-June 28, 1873	APS III, Reel 570
v8-14	July 5, 1873-Dec. 20, 1876	Reel 571
v15-20	Jan. 6, 1877-Dec. 27, 1879	Reel 572
Cumulative index 21-34	1880-1886	
v21-26	Jan. 3, 1880-Dec. 30, 1882	Reel 573
v27-32	Jan. 6, 1883-Dec. 26, 1885	Reel 574
v33-38	Jan. 2, 1886-Dec. 29, 1888	Reel 575
v39-44	Jan. 5, 1889-Dec. 26, 1891	Reel 576
v45-51	Jan. 2, 1892-June 29, 1895	Reel 577
v52-58	July 6, 1895-Dec. 31, 1898	Reel 578
v59-65	Jan. 7, 1899-Dec. 1903	Reel 579
v66-70	Jan. 1904-Dec. 1908	Reel 580

Several volumes have misdated title pages. Some pages creased, stained or torn. Several pages have print faded with some loss of text. Volumes 44, 56, and 57 include supplements.

Microfilm edition was prepared from C, InU, MnU, Nh, and NjP copies.

THE ALBION, a journal of news, politics, and literature. v. 1-11, 1822-32; n.s., v.1-6, 1833-38; [s.3] v.1-3, 1839-41; [s.4] v.1-15, 1842-56; v.35-54, 1857-76. New York [J.S. Bartlett] 1822-

weekly.

Subtitle varies slightly.
Caption title: 1822-56, The Albion; or, British, colonial, and foreign weekly gazette; 1857-58, The Albion, a British, colonial, and foreign weekly gazette.

Editors: 1822, J.C. Fisher.—1823-Apr. 1848, J.S. Bartlett.—May 1848-William Young.

A basically eclectic New York weekly which was devoted chiefly to the reprinting of articles from the English journals, and whose position was not very loyal to the North during the war.

v1-4	1822-1825	APS II, Reel 50
v5-7	June 17, 1826-June 6, 1829	Reel 706
v8-11	June 13, 1829-Dec. 29, 1832	Reel 707
nsv1-3	Jan. 5, 1833-Dec. 26, 1835	Reel 708

nsv4-6	Jan. 2, 1836-Dec. 29, 1838	Reel 709
nsv1-3 [s3]	Jan. 5, 1839-Dec. 25, 1841	Reel 710
nsv1-2 [s4]	Jan. 1, 1842-Dec. 30, 1843	Reel 711
nsv3-4 [s4]	Jan. 6, 1844-Dec. 27, 1845	Reel 712
nsv5-6[s4]	Jan. 3, 1846-Dec. 25, 1847	Reel 713
nsv7-8 [s4]	Jan. 1, 1848-Dec. 29, 1849	Reel 714
nsv9-10 [s4]	Jan. 5, 1850-Dec. 27, 1851	Reel 715
nsv11-12 [s4]	Jan. 3, 1852-Dec. 31, 1853	Reel 716
nsv13-14 [s4]	Jan. 1, 1854-Dec. 29, 1855	Reel 717
nsv15 [s4]	Jan. 5-Dec. 27, 1856	Reel 718
v35-37	Jan. 3, 1857-Dec. 31, 1859	Reel 1263
v38-40	Jan. 7, 1860-Dec. 27, 1862	Reel 1264
v41-43	Jan. 3, 1863-Dec. 30, 1865	Reel 1265
v44-46	Jan. 6, 1866-Dec. 26, 1868	Reel 1266
v47-48	Jan. 2, 1869-Dec. 31, 1870	Reel 1267
v49-50	Jan. 7, 1871-Dec. 28, 1872	Reel 1268
v51-52	Jan. 4, 1873-Dec. 26, 1874	Reel 1269
v53-54	Jan. 2, 1875-Dec. 23, 1876	Reel 1270

Best copy available for photographing. Several volumes have creased, torn, or stained pages with some loss of text. Some volumes have misnumbered or tightly bound pages. Vol.41: Index and title page is missing. Vol.44: Issue 1 is misnumbered as volume 45. Vol.45-54: Indexes are not available for photographing. Vol.45: Issues 33 and 37 are missing. Issue 38 is bound between 35 and 36. Vol.48: Contents pages for issues are photographed at beginning of volume. Vol.50: Pages 171-72 and issues 28-38 are missing. Vol.51: Issue 17 is missing. Vol.53: Issue 8 is missing. Issue 52, pages 2-3 are missing. Vol.54: Issues 38, 47, 49, and 51 are missing. Issue 12, pages 14-15 are missing.

Microfilm edition was prepared from CaOLU, CtY, DLC, GHi, MH, MWA, N, RPB, and WHi copies.

SEE ALSO: Anglo-American.

ALBUM AND LADIES' WEEKLY GAZETTE. *SEE* Philadelphia Album and Ladies' Literary Port Folio.

THE ALDINE, the art journal of America. v.1-9; Sept. 1868-1879. New York, Sutton, Bowne, 1868-74; Aldine Pub. Co. [1875-79]

9 v. in 7. illus., plates (part col.) ports monthly.

Title varies: 1868-70, The Aldine press: a typographic art journal. 1871-73, The Aldine, a typographic art journal. (Caption title: The Adline) 1874-79, The Aldine, the art journal of America.

Film incomplete: v.1-2 wanting.

Aldine was founded as a house organ of Sutton, Browne, and Company, New York printers, and later became a subscription magazine. Emphasis was on graphic arts, with reproductions of Gustav Dore's illustrations from *Don Quixote* and the Bible. W.H. Ingersoll and others wrote on art subjects. Richard Henry Stoddard was editor from 1871-1876.

Aldine Press: A Typographic Art Journal
v3	1870	APS III, Reel 239

Aldine, A Typographic Art Journal
v4-6	1871-73	APS III, Reel 239

Aldine, The Art Journal of America
v7-8	1874-1877	APS III, Reel 239
v9	1878-1879	Reel 240

ALDINE PRESS: A Typographic Art Journal. *SEE* Aldine, the Art Journal of America.

ALETHIAN CRITIC, or error exposed. v.1, Apr. 1804-[1806] Lexington, 1804.

72 p.

Projected as quarterly, only one issue in April reached the public.

The *Alethian Critic, or Error Exposed,* by Abel M. Sarjent, reflected the religious views of the Millenium Church. Although the title page projected it as a quarterly, only one issue in April (?) reached the public.

v1	April 1804-1806	APS II, Reel 945

Microfilm edition prepared from MMeT copy.

ALL OUTDOORS. *SEE* Outing; Sport, Adventure, Travel, Fiction.

THE ALMONER, a periodical religious publication. v.1; Apr. 1814-May, 1815. Lexington, Ky., T.T. Skillman [1815]

304 p. Issues at irregular intervals

The first periodical center in the new West was Lexington, Kentucky. In 1812, Thomas Skillman began a series of three distinctly polemical religious periodicals, none of which lived long enough to win an important place. One of these, *The Almoner,* which followed *The Evangelical Record and Western Review* (1812-13) and preceded the *Christian Register* (1822-23), included general instructive articles, scriptural lessons, reports of Bible societies and foreign missions, book reviews, and sketches of Christian martyrs.

v1, no.1-6	Apr. 1814-May 1815	APS II, Reel 51

THE AMARANTH. A semi-monthly publication, devoted to polite literature, science, poetry and amusement. v.1, no.1--18; Feb. 20-Dec. 11. 1847. Ashland, O. [R.V. Kennedy] 1847.

72 p.

R.V. Kennedy, editor.

The publishers of this four-page literary magazine hoped to foster and encourage "Western" talent and genius rather than relying on Eastern magazines and writers, as had been done up to that time. The magazine was intended to be instructive and amusing, presenting "gems" of prose and poetry but no news. Contents included original and selected poetry, original tales, moral essays, a "Ladies' Column," and a humor column of riddles and anecdotes.

v1	Feb. 20-Dec. 11, 1847	APS II, Reel 784

Index and table of contents are lacking.

Microfilm edition was prepared from DLC copy.

THE AMARANTH; or, Masonic garland. v.1-2, no.7; Apr. 1828-Oct. 1829. Boston.

2 v. pl. monthly.

Editor: 1828- C. W. Moore.

Aimed at bringing useful, instructive and interesting articles about Masonry into all Masonic homes, the periodical used little original material. Detailed historical accounts, anecdotes on Masonry, notes of elections, meeting notices and descriptions of ceremonies filled the pages. Occasional detailed illustrations of Masonic halls were printed. Poems were often of Masonic themes although other subject matter was included.

v1-2   Apr. 1828-Oct. 1829   APS II, Reel 404

Microfilm edition was prepared from MH and NN copy.

AMARANTH; or, token of remembrance. Boston [and] New York, 1847-1855.

9v.

Women's magazine which published much sentimental fiction and poetry. Plates embellished the text.

                    1847-1855   APS II, Reel 813

Indexes are lacking.

Microfilm edition was prepared from DLC and MiU copies.

AMERICAN ACADEMY OF ARTS AND SCIENCES, BOSTON. MEMOIRS of the American Academy of Arts and Sciences. v.1-4; new ser., v.1- Boston, 1785-19- .

v. illus., plates (part col.) maps, facsims.

Imprint varies: v.1-v.2. pt.1, Boston, 1785-93.—v.2, pt.2, Charlestown, 1804.—v.3-new ser., v.2, Cambridge, 1809-46.—new ser., v.3-9, pt.1, v.10, pt.1, Cambridge and Boston, 1848-68; new ser., v.9, pt.2, v.10, pt.2- Cambridge, 1873-

Vol.1 contains memoirs dating from the foundation of the academy in 1780 to the end of the year 1783.
No memoirs in quarto were published 1874-1881. Vol.10, no.3 (embryology of the Ctenophora by Alexander Agassix) was printed in August 1874, but was not distributed by the author. When publication was resumed in 1881, the paper of Mr. Agassix was overlooked, its paging being duplicated and the volume completed and distributed without it. In 1885 it was distributed as a supplement to v.10, pt.2, together with a new table of contents. cf. "Note" following table of contents of v.10, pt.2.
Vol.11, pt.1, "Centennial volume", includes full list of officers and members of the academy, 1780-1881.
On film: v.1-4 and new ser., v.1-12.

This publication consisted of scholarly papers, many accompanied by illustrations and diagrams, on a variety of scientific topics, including anthropology, astronomy, math, biology, and bacteriology, as well as some articles on languages and other subjects, and proceedings of the Academy. A series on the fish of Massachusetts ran through many issues.

v1-nsv1   1785-1833   APS II, Reel 363
nsv2-4   1846-1850   Reel 364

nsv5-9   1855-1867   Reel 1364
nsv10-12   1868-1902   Reel 1365

Pagination is irregular.

Microfilm edition was prepared from DLC, MiD and OU copies.

AMERICAN ACADEMY OF ARTS AND SCIENCES, BOSTON. PROCEEDINGS. v.1-May 1846- . Boston, 1848-19- .

v. illus., plates (part col.)

Vols. 1-8 published also at Cambridge.
Vols.9-31 numbered also new ser. v.1-23. v.1-85 as the Academy's Proceedings; now known as Daedelus.
On film: issues for May 1846-May 1906.

This file affords the selected records, meetings, and papers presented to the Academy. Published in Cambridge for two decades, it became the chief vehicle for the contributions of the Chemical, Physical, and Botanical Departments of Harvard University, occupying many pages. Occasionally, Harvard's Medical Department supplied material.
Asa Gray, Samuel Scudder, John Trowbridge, Frederic Charles Moulton, Henry Taber, and Charles F. Mabery were found in the extensive list of well-known contributors.

v1-7   May 1846-May 1868   APS III, Reel 141
v8-14   May 1868-May 1879   Reel 142
v15-20   May 1879-May 1885   Reel 143
v21-27   May 1885-May 1892   Reel 144
v28-33   May 1892-May 1898   Reel 145
v34-37   May 1898-May 1902   Reel 146
38-41   May 1902-May 1906   Reel 147

Vol.7: lacks title page. Page 432 is misnumbered.

Microfilm edition prepared from MiU and MiHM copies.

AMERICAN ADVOCATE OF PEACE. *SEE* World Affairs.

AMERICAN ADVOCATE OF PEACE. (HARTFORD). *SEE* World Affairs.

AMERICAN AGRICULTURIST. v.1-, April 1842-. New York, Saxton & Miles, etc.

illus. monthly.

On film: v1-9, April 1842-Dec. 1850.

Established by A.B. and Richard L. Allen in 1842, the *American Agriculturist* was one of the most important of the American farm journals. It attempted to be national in scope, paying attention to the South and West as well as to the East, and to planters as well as farmers. There were departments for ladies and for boys; and some rhymes, though little poetry. One of the leading contributors was Solon Robinson, who was an assistant editor and traveling correspondent in 1851. Orange Judd, who became co-editor with A.B. Allen in September, 1853, almost at once made the *Agriculturist* a valuable contribution to scientific farming, claiming a circulation of 100,000 by the end of 1864. While under his direction it reached what was perhaps the most distinguished position ever held by an American agricultural journal. In 1864 Judd turned the editorship over to Professor George Thurber. In the 70's the competition of the sectional farm papers caused its circulation to drop and between this time and 1921, when it finally recovered its identity and its original name, the *Agriculturist* underwent a number of changes in location, name, and periodicity. In 1888 it was purchased by the owners of the *New England Homestead* of Springfield, Massachusetts, and in 1894 it was made a weekly. It printed articles by Asa Gray on insect and plant fertilization, George E. Waring's Ogden Farm papers, and Frank G. Carpenter's series on farming in eastern countries. Joseph Harris's "Walks and Talks" and the Rev. William Clift's "Timothy Bunker" papers were valuable features. From the beginning of Herbert Myrick's editorship in 1891 much attention was given to political discussion.

v1-4	Apr. 1842-Dec. 1845	APS II, Reel 364
v5-9	Jan. 1846-Dec. 1850	Reel 365

Vol.5: pgs. 10-11 are torn.

Microfilm edition was prepared from NN copy.

SEE ALSO: American Farmer; American Farmer's Magazine; Farmers Cabinet and American Herd Book; *and* Genesee Farmer.

** **THE AMERICAN ALMANAC AND REPOSITORY OF USEFUL KNOWLEDGE,** for 1830-61, v.1-32. Boston, Gray and Bowen, 1829-61.

32v. fold. maps.

Vol.1 has title: The American almanac and repository of useful knowledge ... comprising a calendar for the year; astronomical information; miscellaneous directions, hints, and remarks; and statistical and other particulars ...

Indexes for the years 1830-39, 1840-49, 1850-59, in v.10, 20, and 30, respectively.
"The volume for 1830 was edited by Jared Sparks; from 1831 to 1842 the work was conducted by J.E. Worcester; from 1843 to 1847 by Francis Bowen, subsequently by G.P. Sanger ... This valuable work ... terminated in 1862."-Sabin.
Mr. Ainsworth R. Spofford states that the work ceased publication with 1861.

A yearly publication containing useful and interesting information, including a calendar for the year, astronomical and meteorological data, statistical material and tables on a variety of topics—information on the U.S. and foreign countries, including a register of national and state governments, facts about the executive and legislative branches and the judiciary; listings of patents and copyrights; and statistics on commerce, educational and literary institutions, and population of the U.S. It also included tables on agriculture, manufacturing, and foreign trade, a chronicle of events, and much miscellaneous material.

v1-10	1830-1839	APS II, Reel 810
v11-20	1840-1849	Reel 811
v21-32	1850-1861	Reel 812

Microfilm edition was prepared from MiU copy.

AMERICAN ANNALS OF EDUCATION. v.1-4, Jan. 1826-Dec. 1829; new ser., v.1, no.1-5, Jan.-July 1830; 3d ser., v.1-9, Aug. 1830-Dec. 1839. Boston, Wait, Greene, 1826-38.

13 v. in 14. illus., plates, port., plan, facsims. Monthly (1829-Mar. 1830, bimonthly; 1882, semimonthly)

Absorbed the Education reporter in 1831.
From Jan. 1826-July 1830 title reads: American journal of education: In Aug. 1830 the title was changed to American annals of education and under this later title (as 3, ser., v.1, no.1-4) and under the title American journal and annals of education and instruction, new ser., v.1, no.6-9.
The numbers for Jan-Dec. 1831 form the second part of v.1 of the 3d ser. They are preceded by 24 pages ("Editor's address" and "Sketches of Hofwyl," reprinted from the numbers for Aug-Dec. 1830) In 1838 the title was shortened to American annals of education.

Editors: 1826-29, William Russell.—1830-37, W.C. Woolbridge,—1837-38, W.A. Alcott.

Though not the first of the educational periodicals in America,

"Russell's *Journal of Education,*" as it was called, was the first really important American magazine in the field of education. Edited by William Russell, it emphasized physical and moral training, and advocated education for women and physical education for both boys and girls. It was chiefly devoted to early or elementary education. After two years, it was turned over to S.G. Goodrich, who kept it for about a year; it was then purchased by James Gordon Carter, a pioneer advocate of normal schools. In 1830, the *Journal of Education* began to devote much space to the lyceums and became, to an extent, the organ of the lyceum movement. From 1831 on, the magazine published much commentary on foreign education theory; the writings of foreign educators, official reports, the Paris and London *Journals of Education,* and other sources from abroad were drawn upon as well as older writings like those of Plato, Bacon, Ascham, and Locke. Articles on education in foreign countries were written by such students of foreign education as William H. Prescott, George Ticknor, and Thomas H. Gallaudet; as well as Goold Brown, Thomas S. Grimke, and others. Book reviews were well done, and there was much educational news.

American Journal of Education

v1-nsv1, no.5	Jan. 1826-July 1830	APS II, Reel 293

American Journal, and Annals of Education and Instruction

nsv1, no.6-9	Aug. 1830-Dec. 1830	APS II, Reel 293

American Annals of Education

s3v1, no.1-12	Aug. 1830-Dec.1831	APS II, Reel 293
s3v2-s3v9	Jan. 1832-Dec. 1839	Reel 294

Vol.3: pagination is irregular.

Microfilm edition was prepared from MiU copy.

AMERICAN ANTIQUARIAN: A Quarterly Journal, Devoted to Early American History, Ethnology and Archaeology. *SEE* American Antiquarian and Oriental Journal.

THE AMERICAN ANTIQUARIAN AND ORIENTAL JOURNAL. v.1-35, v.36, no.1; Apr. 1878-Jan. 1914. Chicago, Jameson Morse, 1878-1914.

36v. illus., plates, ports., maps. quarterly (bimonthly: 1884-1909, 1912-Mar. 1913)

Vols.1-2 have title: The American antiquarian: a quarterly journal, Imprint varies: 1878-1908, Chicago, Jameson & Morse [etc.] (v.1, no.1-3, pub. in Cleveland, O., by Brooks, Schinkel & co.)—1909-10. Salem, Mass., S.D. Peet.—1911-12, Benton Harbor, Mich., The Antiquarian Publishing Co. (Incorporated)—1913-14, Toledo, O., The Antiquarian publishing company of Benton Harbor, Mich. Absorbed the Oriental and Biblical journal in Jan. 1881, Biblia in Jan. 1906.

The *American Antiquarian and Oriental Journal* was edited by Stephen Peet. Its chief interest was in American archaeology.

American Antiquarian: A Quarterly Journal Devoted to Early American History, Ethnology and Archaeology

v1-2	Apr. 1878-June 1880	APS III, Reel 54

American Antiquarian and Oriental Journal

v3-10	Oct. 1880-Nov. 1888	APS III, Reel 54
v11-18	Jan. 1889-Nov. 1896	Reel 55
v19-26	Jan. 1897-Nov. 1904	Reel 56
v27-36, no.1	Jan. 1905-Jan. 1914	Reel 57

Vol.1-31: Indexes lacking. Please refer to Tables of Contents. Pagination is irregular. Some pages creased, stained, or have print missing. Vol.28: pages 229-238 missing. Best copy available for photographing.

Microfilm edition was prepared from C, MiD, N, and NjP copies.

AMERICAN ANTI-SLAVERY REPORTER. v.1, no.1-8; Jan.-Aug. 1834. [New York] 1834.

128 p. monthly.

Caption title.

Published by the American Anti-Slavery Society.
Preceded by Anti-slavery reporter (June-Nov. 1833)

The *American Anti-Slavery Reporter,* which superseded the *Anti-Slavery reporter,* was published in New York by the American Anti-Slavery Society and provided coverage of the activities of that society and of the American Colonization Society. In addition, it published articles, essays, and letters dealing with the slavery question and with recent events concerning slavery in the U.S. and other countries, as well as some biography and poetry.

v1   Jan.-Aug. 1834   APS II, Reel 725

Microfilm edition was prepared from DLC copy.

SEE ALSO: Anti-Slavery Reporter.

THE AMERICAN APOLLO. v.1, no.1-39; Jan. 6-Sept. 28, 1792. Boston, Printed at the Apollo Press by Belknap and Hall.

3v. weekly.

Vols.2-3, 1793-94 (published as a newspaper) not issued in this series.
Issued in 2 pts: pt.1, Containing the publications of the Massachusetts Historical Society.—pt.2, Containing essays, moral, political and poetical, and the daily occurrences in the natural, civil and commercial world.

A post-Revolutionary weekly octavo which presented coverage of both American and foreign current events and the U.S. Congress, as well as shipping news, vital statistics, poetry, and other miscellaneous material.

v1   Jan. 6-Sept. 28, 1792   APS I, Reel 1

Microfilm edition was prepared from the MiU-C copy.

AMERICAN ARCHITECT. *SEE* American Architect and Architecture.

AMERICAN ARCHITECT AND THE ARCHITECTURAL REVIEW. *SEE* American Architect and Architecture.

* **THE AMERICAN ARCHITECT AND ARCHITECTURE.** v.1-152 (no.1-2666); Jan. 1, 1876-Feb. 1938. Boston, J.R. Osgood [etc.]

152v. illus., maps, plans, plates. Weekly, Jan. 1876-Apr. 1921; May 1921-Feb. 1938, frequency varies.

Published in New York by American Architect, Nov. 1904-Feb. 1938.
Title varies: Jan. 1876-Dec. 1908, The American architect and building news; Jan. 1909-Aug. 17, 1921, The American architect; Aug. 31, 1921-Dec. 1924, The American architect and the architectural review; Jan. 1925-May 1936, The American architect.
Besides the regular edition, the following were issued with additional plates: Gelatine ed., Nov. 28, 1885-88(?); Imperial ed., Mar. 1886-Dec. 1889; International ed., 1890-1908 (?)

Absorbed the Inland architect in Jan. 1909; the Architectural Review in Aug. 1921; Architecture in June 1936.
Merged into the Architectural record.
Supplements accompany some numbers.
Microfilm edition includes v.1-152 with an index to the illustrations.

Founded by the famous Boston publishing firm of James R. Osgood and Company under the editorship of William P.P. Longfellow, the *American Architect* was one of the most successful of the building and architecture journals. Begun in Boston in 1876, it was moved to New York in 1905 and was acquired by W.R. Hearst's International Publishing Company in 1929. The publishers of this weekly journal of architecture, construction, and interior decoration promised that it would be national in scope and would furnish a full record of important news in architecture and building in the country and, when possible, in foreign countries. The *Architect* dealt with all aspects of building—construction, mechanics, building laws, drainage, sanitary systems, studies of European and ancient architecture, and much more. It contained many full-page illustrations of both private homes and public buildings, with designs for them, and an advertising section listing builders' supplies and names of architects painters, and other tradesmen. In the 1930's the magazine adopted a more modern format, and had less text and more pictures and advertisements than before.

American Architect and Building News		
Decennial Index	1876-1885	APS III, Reel 600
v1-2	Jan. 1, 1876-Dec. 29, 1877	Reel 600
v3-5	Jan. 5, 1878-Jun. 28, 1879	Reel 601
v6-8	Jul. 5, 1879-Dec. 25, 1880	Reel 602
v9-11	Jan. 1, 1881-Jun. 24, 1882	Reel 603
v12-14	Jul. 1, 1882-Dec. 29, 1883	Reel 604
v15-17	Jan. 5, 1884-Jan. 27, 1885	Reel 605
v18-19	Jul. 4, 1885-Jun. 26, 1886	Reel 606
v20-21	Jul. 3, 1886-Jun. 25, 1887	Reel 607
v22-23	Jul. 2, 1887-Jun. 30, 1888	Reel 608
v24-25	Jul. 7, 1888-Jun. 29, 1889	Reel 609
v26-28	Jul. 6, 1889-Jun. 28, 1890	Reel 610
v29-31	Jul. 5, 1890-Mar. 28, 1891	Reel 611
v32-34	Apr. 4-Dec. 26, 1891	Reel 612
v35-37	Jan. 2-Sept. 24, 1892	Reel 613
v38-41	Oct. 1, 1892-Sept. 30, 1893	Reel 614
v42-46	Oct. 7, 1893-Dec. 29, 1894	Reel 615
v47-50	Jan. 5-Dec. 28, 1895	Reel 616
v51-54	Jan. 4-Dec. 26, 1896	Reel 617
v55-59	Jan. 2, 1897-Mar. 26, 1898	Reel 618
v60-65	Apr. 2, 1898-Sept. 30, 1899	Reel 619
v66-70	Oct. 7, 1899-Dec. 29, 1900	Reel 620
v71-75	Jan. 5, 1901-Mar. 29, 1902	Reel 621
v76-80	Apr. 5, 1902-Jun. 1903	Reel 622
v81-85	Jul. 4, 1903-Sept. 24, 1904	Reel 623
v86-88	Oct. 1, 1904-Dec. 30, 1905	Reel 624
v89-90	Jan. 6-Dec. 29, 1906	Reel 625
v91-92	Jan. 5-Dec. 28, 1907	Reel 626
v93-94	Jan. 4-Dec. 30, 1908	Reel 627
American Architect		
v95-96	Jan. 6-Dec. 29, 1909	APS III, Reel 628
v97	Jan. 5-Jun. 29, 1910	Reel 629
v98-99	Jul. 6, 1910-Jun. 28, 1911	Reel 630
v100-102	Jul. 5, 1911-Dec. 25, 1912	Reel 631
v103-104	Jan. 1-Dec. 31, 1913	Reel 632
v105-106	Jan. 7-Dec. 30, 1914	Reel 633
v107-108	Jan. 6-Dec. 29, 1915	Reel 634
v109-110	Jan. 5-Dec. 27, 1916	Reel 635
v111-112	Jan. 3-Dec. 26, 1917	Reel 636
v113-114	Jan. 2-Dec. 25, 1918	Reel 637
v115-116	Jan. 1-Dec. 31, 1919	Reel 638
v117-118	Jan. 7-Dec. 29, 1920	Reel 639
v119-120	Jan. 5-1921-Aug. 17, 1921	Reel 640
American Architect and the Architectural Review		
v121	Aug. 31, 1921-Jun. 21, 1922	APS III, Reel 640
v122-124	Jul. 5, 1922-Dec. 19, 1923	Reel 641
v125-126	Jan. 2-Dec. 31, 1924	Reel 642

American Architect

v127-129	Jan. 14, 1925-Jun. 20, 1926	APS III, Reel 643
v130-132	Jul. 5, 1926-Dec. 20, 1927	Reel 644
v133-135	Jan. 5, 1928-Jun. 20, 1929	Reel 645
v136-139	Jul. 5, 1929-Jun. 1931	Reel 646
v140-143	Jul. 1931-Nov. 1933	Reel 647
v144-148	Jan. 1934-May, 1936	Reel 648

American Architect and Architecture

v148	June 1936	APS III, Reel 648
v149-152	Jul. 1936-Feb. 1938	Reel 649

AMERICAN ARCHITECT AND BUILDING NEWS. *SEE* American Architect and Architecture.

THE AMERICAN ATHENAEUM: a repository of belles lettres, science, and the arts. v.1 (no.1-44); Apr. 21, 1825-Mar. 2, 1826. [New York] G. Bond.

weekly.

Caption title.

Merged into the New York literary gazette.
Film covers: v.1, no.1-36, Apr. 21-Dec. 29, 1825.

A miscellany of polite literature including book reviews, poetry, tales, anecdotes, biographical sketches, original essays and excerpts from other magazines such as the *London Quarterly Review.* This merged into the *New York Literary Gazette,* which later became the *Literary Gazette and American Athenaeum.*

v 1, nos.1-36	Apr. 21-Dec. 29, 1825	APS II, Reel 51

SEE ALSO: Literary Gazette and American Athenaeum.

AMERICAN BAPTIST MAGAZINE. *SEE* Baptist Missionary Magazine.

AMERICAN BAPTIST MAGAZINE AND MISSIONARY INTELLIGENCER. *SEE* Baptist Missionary Magazine *and* Massachusetts Baptist Missionary Magazine.

*****AMERICAN BIBLICAL REPOSITORY.** *SEE* Biblical Repository and Classical Review *and* Quarterly Christian Spectator.

AMERICAN BOY. *SEE* Youth's Companion.

THE AMERICAN CATHOLIC HISTORICAL RE-SEARCHES. v.1-21, July 1884-Oct. 1904; v.22-29 (new ser., v.1-8), Jan. 1905-July 1912. Pittsburgh, Myers, Shingle, 1884-86; Philadelphia, M. I.J. Griffin [1887-1912]

29v. in 36. illus.; plates, ports., facsims. quarterly. Index covering volumes I-XXIX, July, 1884-July, 1912. Philadelphia, American Catholic Historical Society, 1916.

Title varies: July 1884-Apr. 1885, Historical researches in western Pennsylvania, principally Catholic. July 1885-Oct. 1886, Catholic historical researches. Jan. 1887-July 1912, The American Catholic historical researches.

Editors: July 1884-Oct. 1886, A.A. Lambing.—Jan. 1884-Oct. 1911, M.I.J. Griffin.—Jan.- July 1912, W.I.J. Griffin.
Absorbed Griffin's journal in Oct. 1900.

Merged into Records of the American Catholic historical society.

American Catholic Historical Researches contained articles giving documentary information about the clergy and people of the Roman Catholic Church in America.

Cumulative Index 1-29	July 1884-July 1912	APS III, Reel 201

Historical Researches in Western Pennsylvania, Principally Catholic.

v 1	July 1884-Apr. 1885	APS III, Reel 201

Catholic Historical Researches.

v 2-3, no.2.	July 1885-Oct. 1886	APS III, Reel 201

American Catholic Historical Researches.

v 3, no.3-21	Jan. 1887-Oct. 1904	APS III, Reel 201
nsv1-8	Jan. 1905-July 1912	Reel 202

Vols.1-21: The contents for some issues are photographed at the end of the volume. Vol.6: The index is misnumbered as Vol.11. Vol.15: Some pages smeared. Vol.17: Pgs.113-122 missing (advertising pages). Vol.19: Pgs.180-181 and 184-185 faded print. Vol.20: Pgs.18-31 have blurred print. New Series Vol.8: Only has 3 issues.

Microfilm edition was prepared from MChB, MnCS, NRSB and OCX copies.

*****THE AMERICAN CATHOLIC QUARTERLY REVIEW ...** v.1-49 (no.1-193); Jan. 1876-Jan. 1924. Philadelphia, Hardy and Mahony; [etc., etc.]

49 v. illus.

Editors: 1876-89, J. A. Corcoran.—1890-1911, P. J. Ryan.— 1912-14, E. F. Prendergast.
Microfilm edition includes separately published general index for vol. I-XXV; Jan. 1876-Oct. 1900.

James A. Corcoran, who had been editor of the *United States Catholic Miscellany,* was the first editor of the *American Catholic Quarterly Review,* established in Philadelphia in 1876; he was followed in the editorship by Archbishop Patrick John Ryan. Leading church dignitaries contributed much of the material; among extensive contributors were Cardinals Manning and Gibbons, Archbishops Seghers, Keane, and Lynch, and Bishops O'Conor, Becker, Spalding, and Chatard. This journal claimed to present "a complete Catholic chronicle" of half a century; religion and ecclesiastical policy were given much attention, as were the missions to the Indians in Michigan and elsewhere. But the contents were not confined to theological subjects; literature, education, art, science, history, philosophy, and politics were given attention, and there were also book reviews and advertisements.

Cumulative Index v.1-25	Jan. 1876-1900	APS III, Reel 650
v 1-4	Jan. 1876-Oct. 1879	Reel 650
v 5-8	Jan. 1880-Oct. 1883	Reel 651
v 9-12	Jan. 1884-Oct. 1887	Reel 652
v 13-16	Jan. 1888-Oct. 1891	Reel 653
v 17-20	Jan. 1892-Oct. 1895	Reel 654
v 21-24	Jan. 1896-Oct. 1899	Reel 655
v 25-28	Jan. 1900-Oct. 1903	Reel 656
v 29-33	Jan. 1904-Oct. 1908	Reel 657
v 34-38	Jan. 1909-Oct. 1913	Reel 658
v 39-44	Jan. 1914-Oct. 1919	Reel 659
v 45-49	Jan. 1920-Jan. 1924	Reel 660

Vol.16: issue 61 is misnumbered. Some pages are torn and taped. Vol.44: October issue is misnumbered as vol.45.

Microfilm edition was prepared from DLC, InStme, MiDU, MiGr, NhD, and NjPT copies.

*****AMERICAN CHURCH REVIEW.** *SEE* Church Review.

THE AMERICAN CRITIC AND GENERAL REVIEW. v.1, no.1-2; Apr. 1-29, 1820. [Washington, J. Wright]

32 p.

A magazine of general articles in literature, science and the arts whose purpose was to encourage virtue and talent and censure vice. It also reviewed new publications throughout the world. Only two numbers were published.

v 1, no.1-2   Apr. 1-29, 1820   APS II, Reel 51

AMERICAN CULTIVATOR. v.1-77, no.15; Jan. 1839- Sept. 1915. Boston.

12 v. weekly. Vol.2, no.50-51 misnumbered as 49-50.

Title varies: 1839-1876, Boston cultivator.

On film: v.1-12; Jan. 1839-Dec. 1850. Scattered issues missing.

Begun as the *Boston Cultivator,* the *American Cultivator* was the leading New England farm journal at the end of the Civil War, and maintained a considerable circulation for many years afterwards. About one-fourth of its space was devoted to farming interests and the mechanical arts; this included articles on livestock, labor-saving machines, and the best methods of cultivation. In addition, there were sections devoted to trade and commerce, moral and religious pieces, listing of marriages and deaths, proceedings of the Massachusetts legislature and Congress, and after 1843, a Young Men's Department, and a Ladies' Department, which featured tales and items on marriage. The *Cultivator* also published news, prices, serialized tales, poetry, an editor's column, notices of new publications, and some illustrations, mainly of machinery, plants and animals, and designs for homes. There was much original material as well as selections from the best English and American periodicals.

Boston Cultivator.
v 1-6	Jan. 1839-Dec. 1844	APS II, Reel 465
v 7-10	Jan. 1845-Dec. 1848	Reel 466
v 11-12	Jan. 1849-Dec. 1850	Reel 467

Several issues are missing; not available for photographing. Several pages are creased, stained and have faded print with some loss of text.

Microfilm edition was prepared from M, MB, MH, MiU-C, MWA, and RPB copies.

AMERICAN EAGLE MAGAZINE; a journal, dedicated to science, art, and literature. v.1, no.2; June-July 1847. New York.

60 p.

Edited by Thomas C. Dudley, John J. Schoolcraft, and D.W.C. Morris, this monthly literary miscellany was to contain no political or religious material, but did devote some attention to science. In addition to poetry, book reviews, and travel and historical sketches, it published essays and articles on miscellaneous topics. Some illustrations were included.

v1, no.1-2   June-July 1847   APS II, Reel 365

Microfilm edition was prepared from CSmH copy.

* **THE AMERICAN ECLECTIC;** or, selections from the periodical literature of all foreign countries. v.1-4; Jan. 1841-Nov. 1842. New York, W.R. Peters; Boston, Whipple & Damrell, 1841-42.

4 v. port. bimonthly.

At head of title: The literature of the world.
Editors: 1841-Jan. 1842, A. Peters, S.B. Treat.—Mar.-July, 1842, A. Peters, J.H. Agnew.—Sept.-Nov. 1842, J.H. Agnew.
United with the Museum of foreign literature to form the Eclectic museum of foreign literature.

Conducted by Absalom Peters and Selah B. Treat, this bimonthly magazine was compiled principally from foreign journals and reviews, encompassing a wide variety of topics—history, current events, exploration, recent discoveries in science and the arts, education, anthropology, philosophy, and literature of various countries. It also published poetry and bibliographical notices.

v1-4   Jan. 1841-Nov. 1842   APS II, Reel 295

Microfilm edition was prepared from MiU copy.

SEE ALSO: Eclectic Museum of Foreign Literature, Science and Art.

AMERICAN ECONOMIC ASSOCIATION. PUBLICATIONS. v.1-11, Mar. 1886-Aug. 1896; new ser., v.1-2, Dec. 1897-Mar. 1899; 3d ser., v.1-11, Feb. 1900-Dec. 1910; 4th ser., v.1, no.1-4 [i.e., 1-6] Mar.-Dec. 1911. Baltimore.

25 v.

6 no. a year, 1886-1895, 1911; quarterly, 1896-1910.
Imprint varies: 1886-1895, Baltimore, American Economic Association.—1896-1907, New York, Macmillan.—1908-1911, Cambridge, American Economic Association.
General index to v.1-3d ser., v.11; 1886-1910 precedes v.1 on film.

The *Publications of the American Economic Association* was a bimonthly serial founded in 1886 by Richard T. Ely, secretary of the A.E.A. The file constitutes a series of monographs, supplemented by the proceedings of the association.

Index	1886-1910	APS III, Reel 494
General Contents		
and Index, v1-11	1886-1896	Reel 494
v1-6	Mar. 1886-Nov. 1891	Reel 494
v7-11	Jan. 1892-Aug. 1896	Reel 495
nsv1-s3v2	Dec. 1897-Nov. 1901	Reel 496
s3v3-5	Feb. 1902-Nov. 1904	Reel 497
s3v6-8	Feb. 1905-Nov. 1907	Reel 498
s3v9-11	Feb. 1908-Dec. 1910	Reel 499
s4v1	Mar. 1911-Dec. 1911	Reel 500

Several volumes have stained pages. Vol.5: Issue 5, Pg. 64 misnumbered. Vol.10 and third series vol.9: Supplement precedes text. Third series vol.8: Supplement follows issue 2. Third series vol.10: Pagination is irregular.

Microfilm edition was prepared from CtW, MiU, MnU, NBuG, and NjP copies.

AMERICAN ECONOMIC REVIEW. *SEE* American Economic Association. Publications.

THE AMERICAN EDUCATIONAL MONTHLY; a magazine of popular instruction and literature. v.1-13; Jan. 1864-Dec. 1876. New York, Schermerhorn, Bancroft.

13 v. illus., plates.

Title varies: Jan. 1864-Sept. 1867, American educational monthly (subtitle varies) Oct.-Dec. 1867, American educational monthly, and New York teacher. Jan. 1868-Dec. 1869, The New York teacher and

American educational monthly. 1876, Schermerhorn's monthly.

Absorbed the New York teacher in Oct. 1867.

The *American Educational Monthly* was of some importance as an educational magazine. It served at times as the vehicle of various state organizations.

American Educational Monthly
v 1-4, no.9	Jan. 1864-Sept. 1867	APS III, Reel 171

American Educational Monthly, and New York Teacher
v 4, nos.10-12	Oct.-Dec. 1867	APS III, Reel 171

The New York Teacher and American Educational Monthly
v 5-6	Jan. 1868-Dec. 1869	APS III, Reel 171

The American Educational Monthly
v 7-8	Jan. 1870-Dec. 1871	APS III, Reel 171
v 9-12	Jan. 1872-Dec. 1875	Reel 172

Schermerhorn's Monthly
v 13	Jan.-Dec. 1876	APS III, Reel 172

Some pages are torn or stained. Vols.12-13: Indexes and Tables of Contents not available for photographing. Although *Union List of Serials* reports August 1876 as the final issue, this microfilm copy includes the September-December 1876 issues also.

Microfilm edition was prepared from C, IaU, InTI, KyBB, MiU, NBu, and NNC-T copies.

AMERICAN EDUCATIONAL MONTHLY, AND NEW YORK TEACHER. *SEE* American Educational Monthly; A Magazine of Popular Instruction and Literature.

AMERICAN EXPOSITOR. v.1, no.1; May 1850. Mt. Vernon, Ohio, 1850.

16 p.

Edited by John A. Reed, this very short-lived magazine was concerned with religion and morality and was reformative in character—it published moral essays and articles on religion and morality and on gambling, slavery, and other vices. In addition, it included material dealing with education, politics, agriculture, and horticulture, as well as news, poetry, and many short items.

v 1, no.1	May 1850	APS II, Reel 365

Microfilm edition was prepared from OHi copy.

AMERICAN FARMER AND RURAL REGISTER. *SEE* American farmer; Devoted to Agriculture, ...

THE AMERICAN FARMER; devoted to agriculture, horticulture and rural life. v.1-15, Apr.2, 1819-Mar. 7, 1834; [2d ser.] v.1-6, May 9, 1834-May 22, 1839; new [3d] ser., v.1-6, May 29, 1839-June 1845; [4th] ser., v.1-14, July 1845-1859; 5th ser., v.1-3, July 1859-Dec. 1861; 6th ser., v.1-4, July 1866-Dec. 1869; 7th ser., v.1- Jan. 1870- ; new [8th] ser., v.1- Jan. 1872- . Baltimore, S. Sands 1820-

v. illus., plates, ports, diagrs. Weekly, Apr. 2, 1819- ; monthly, July 1845-

Publication suspended from [Jan.?] 1862 to June 1866, inclusive.
Vol.2: 3ded., rev. and cor.
Many issues are incorrectly numbered or dated.
Title varies: Apr. 2, 1819-Mar. 7, 1834, The American farmer, containing original essays and selections on rural economy and internal improvements, with illustrative engravings and prices current of country produce (varies slightly). May 9, 1834-Apr. 28, 1839, The Farmer and gardener, and live-stock breeder and manager ... (Later The Farmer & gardener, containing original essays ...) May 29, 1839-June 1850, The American farmer, and spirit of the agricultural journals of the day ... July 1850- The American farmer: a monthly magazine of agriculture and horticulture (varies slightly). Jan. 1872-Dec. 1873. The American farmer and rural register. Jan. 1874-Dec. 1880, The American farmer. Jan 1881-. The American farmer; devoted to agriculture, horticulture etc.

Editors: Apr. 2, 1819-Aug. 27, 1830, J.S. Skinner.—Sept. 3, 1830-Sept. 27, 1833, G.B.Smith.—Oct. 4, 1833-Apr. 28, 1835, I.I. Hitchcock.—May 5, 1835-Apr. 23, 1839, E.P. Roberts.—May 29, 1839-Aug. 18, 1841, J.S. Skinner.—Aug. 25, 1841-Dec. 1854, Samuel Sands.—Jan. 1855?-N.B. Worthington.—Jan. 1872- Samuel Sands, W.B.Sands.
Published in Baltimore by J.S. Skinner, Apr. 2, 1819-Aug. 27, 1830; I.I. Hitchcock & co., Sept. 3, 1830-Apr. 28, 1835; Sinclair & Moore and R. Sinclair, Jr., May 5, 1835-Nov. 22, 1836; S. Sands & son [etc.] Nov. 29, 1836-.
4th ser., v.4-14 include the Proceedings of the 1st-11th annual meetings (1848-58) of the Maryland state agricultural society.
Absorbed the Rural register, Jan. 1872. Merged into American agriculturalist in 1897?

The *American Farmer* was one of the most successful of the early farm papers and had the endorsement of such men as Jefferson, Madison, and Pickering. Founded by John S. Skinner, a postmaster at Baltimore, this partly eclectic magazine began as an eight-page quarto devoted to "rural economy, internal improvements, news, prices current," and ran through a dozen series to its end in 1897. It was illustrated throughout its long life, and contained news on agriculture, horticulture, and livestock, market prices, and activities of agricultural societies. The first series featured a ladies' department and a "Sporting Olio"; with Skinner's departure, both columns disappeared but the ladies' department reappeared, along with foreign intelligence, when he returned in 1839. The volume for 1891 included a juvenile column, and short stories and humor appeared between 1893 and 1897. Gideon B. Smith, J. Irvine Hitchcock, Edward P. Roberts, Samuel Sands, and William B. Sands followed Skinner as editors.

American Farmer, Containing Original Essays ...
v 1, nos.1-52	Apr. 2, 1819-Mar. 24, 1820	APS II, Reel 51
v 1-7, no.41	**Apr. 2, 1819-Dec. 30, 1825**	Reel 52
v 7-13	Mar. 25, 1825-Mar. 9, 1832	Reel 1062
v 14-15	Mar. 16, 1832-Mar. 7, 1834	Reel 1063

Farmer and Gardener ...
2sv 1-6	May 9, 1834-May 22, 1839	APS II, Reel 1063

American Farmer, and Spirit of the Agricultural Journals ...
3sv 1-5	May 29, 1839-May 15, 1844	APS II, Reel 1064
3sv 6-4sv 5	May 22, 1844-June 1850	Reel 1065

American Farmer, a Monthly Magazine ...
4sv 6	July 1850-June 1851	APS II, Reel 1065
4sv 7-13	July 1851-Jan. 1858	Reel 1066
4sv 14-6sv 4	July 1858-Dec. 1869	Reel 1067
7sv 1, no. 1-7	Jan.-July 1870	Reel 1068

American Farmer and Rural Register
8sv 1-2	Jan. 1872-Dec. 1873	APS II, Reel 1068

American Farmer
8sv 3-4	Jan. 1874-Dec. 1875	APS II, Reel 1068
8sv 5-9	Jan. 1876-Dec. 1880	Reel 1069

American Farmer; Devoted to Agriculture ...
8sv10-9sv3; 10sv10-11sv1	Jan. 1881-Dec. 15, 1892	APS II, Reel 1070
ns, nos. 25-90	Jan. 1, 1893-Feb. 1897	Reel 1071

Pagination is irregular. Some pages are stained. Series 2 Vols.2-3: Indexes bound and photographed at end. Series 2 Vol.6: Index and Contents not available for photographing. This volume continues through May 22 rather than May 5 as reported in *Union List of Serials*. Series 3 Vol.5: Pgs. 322-325 bound and photographed out of order. Series 3 Vol.6: Index and Contents were not available for photographing. Suspended May 21-June 30, 1845. Series 4 Vol.5:

Many pages tightly bound; pages 421-426 bound following page 430; pages 431-434 bound following page 440. May and June issues contain Supplements. Series 4 Vols.9-10: Many pages are tightly bound. Series 4 Vol.11: Contains Supplement following page 256. Series 4 Vol.13: Tightly bound. July issue contains Supplement. Series 5 Vol.3: Contains six issues only rather than the usual twelve. A discrepancy between the *Union List of Serials* and our microfilm edition arises in Series 6 and 7. Series 6 contains only four volumes rather than five, dated July 1866-December 1869. Series 7 contains one volume as reported, but the volume is dated January-December 1870. No 1871 issues were located. Series 7 Vol.1: Index, June, and August-December issues were not available for photographing. Series 8 Vol.1-10: Indexes bound and photographed at end of volumes. Series 9 Vol.1: June 15, September 15, and December 15 issues not available for photographing. Series 9 Vol.2: January 1, 15, April 1, May 1, August 15 and December 15 issues not available for photographing. Series 9 Vol.3: January 1, March 15, April 1, May 15, June 1, July 1, and August 1 issues not available for photographing. Series 9 Vols.4-9: Not available for photographing. Series 10 Vol.10: Index and Contents not available for photographing. Issue 24 also known as 73rd year. New Series Numbers 25-90: Also known as 74th-78th years.

Microfilm edition was prepared from CtHT, DNAL, DLC, ICRL, KMK, MU, MdBE, MiD, MiEM, N, NcD, NcU, NjR, OU, PSt, ScU, TU, TxU, Vi, ViW, and WHi copies.

AMERICAN FARMER'S MAGAZINE. v.1-12; 1848-59. Philadelphia [and] New York, 1848-59.

12 v.

Supersedes Journal of agriculture. Vols.1-10, 1848-57 as Plough, the loom and the anvil. Merged into American agriculturalist.

Though mainly concerned with agriculture and related industries, the *American Farmer's Magazine* also gave attention to the needs of the farmer's family. Throughout its pages can be found discussions of household problems, child-rearing, cooking methods and recipes, and manners. Also included are the usual informative articles, many accompanied by illustrations and diagrams, on farming methods, implements, crops, animals, horticulture, the wool trade, manufacturing, and other miscellaneous topics.

Plough, the Loom and the Anvil.

v.1	July 1848-June 1849	APS II, Reel 503
v2-4	July 1849-June 1852	Reel 504
v5-7	July 1852-June 1855	Reel 505
v8-10	July 1855-Dec. 1857	Reel 506
American Farmer's Magazine		
v11-12	Jan. 1858-June 1859	APS II, Reel 507

Vols.5-7: Some issues are misnumbered Vol.11: Pagination is irregular.

Microfilm edition was prepared from DLC, MiEM, and NN copies.

AMERICAN GEOGRAPHICAL SOCIETY OF NEW YORK. BULLETIN of the American Geographical and Statistical Society. v.1-2; 1852-57. New York, For the Society, 1852-1857.

2 v. maps.

Not to be confused with the Bulletins which from 1859-1900 formed the annual volumes of the "Journal" of the society, and since 1901 form the annual volumes of the "Bulletin". No more published.

The American Geographical and Statistical Society was formed in 1851 with the purposes of collecting and disseminating the most valuable geographical and statistical information, cooperating with foreign consuls on geographical and statistical information of their respective countries, corresponding with missionaries and explorers, entertaining speakers, and publishing a bulletin to be sent to interested people in the U.S. and elsewhere. This *Bulletin* published the transactions and papers of the society from 1852-1857. Transactions included lists of officers and members, the Society's charter and by-laws, reports of general meetings and committee activities and foreign correspondence. Papers read before the Society comprised the second part of the *Bulletin* and included such topics as the topography of New Jersey and the agricultural features of the census in 1850.

v.1-2	Aug. 1852-1857	APS III, Reel 708

Best copy available for photographing. Indexes are lacking. Several pages are stained. Vol.1: part III, pages 1-2 are missing number only.

Microfilm edition was prepared from C and NhD copies.

AMERICAN GEOGRAPHICAL SOCIETY OF NEW YORK. BULLETIN. (formerly Journal) of the American Geographical Society of New York. v.1-47; 1859-1915. New York, For the Society.

47 v. illus., maps. Frequency varies. Suspended 1860-1870.

Title varies: v.1-2 Journal of the American Geographical and Statistical Society, v.3-32, Journal of the American Geographical Society of New York.

"From 1859 to 1900 the Bulletins, when bound, were called the Journal [v.1-32]"—Letter of librarian of the society, May, 1904.
This Bulletin is not to be confused with "Bulletin of the American Geographical and Statistical Society," 1852-56.
Superseded by Geographical Review.
Includes Index, 1852-1915. By Arthur A. Brooks. (New York, American Geographical Society, 1918).

First begun as the *Journal of the American Geographical and Statistical Society* in 1859, this was for over 30 years the only American periodical devoted to scientific geography. Known variously as the Society's *Bulletin* or *Journal,* it contained records of much of the most important exploration and research done in the U.S. during that time and probably contained more geographic material than all other publications with the exception of government documents. Many important early government surveys such as the Pacific Railroad Surveys of 1872-3 and those of other Western or Arctic territories are recorded in the *Bulletin.* The official report of the Northwestern Boundary Survey of 1857-1861, which carried out the privisions of the treaty settling the Oregon question and separating American from British territory in the West, was lost. A report for the *Bulletin.* written by George Gibbs, the official geologist of the American party of the survey, serves as the only presently existing American account of the survey.

Although its strengths lie in the articles on the Western Hemisphere, some extremely valuable materials from other explorations can be found. Some of the first letters written by David Livingston from his mission in central Africa are included, as well as articles by other eminent explorers of that time.

Though the publication changed names and formats during its history, its basic organization was the same as that of the Society's earlier publication, the *Bulletin of the American Geographical and Statistical Society.* Records of the Society's transactions including membership and officers lists, charter and records of meetings comprised the first part of the Journal. Selected papers read before or contributed to the Society comprised the second part. Beginning in 1872, these were issued in an annual volume. In later years, only the papers of the Society were bound in the annual volume.

Cumulative Index	1852-1915	APS III, Reel 708
Journal of the American Geographical and Statistical Society		
v1-2	Jan 1859-1872	APS III, Reel 708

Journal of the American Geographical Society of New York

v3-7	1873-1875	APS III, Reel 708
v8-17	1876-1885	Reel 709
v18-23	1886-1891	Reel 710
v24-29	1892-1897	Reel 711
v30-32	1898-1900	Reel 712

Bulletin (formerly Journal) of the American Geographical Society of New York.

v33-35	1901-1903	APS III, Reel 712
v36-39	1904-1907	Reel 713
v40-42	1908-1910	Reel 714
v43-45	1911-1913	Reel 715
v46-47	1914-1915	Reel 716

THE AMERICAN GLEANER AND VIRGINIA MAGAZINE. v.1, no.1-18; Jan. 24-Dec. 26, 1807. Richmond.

288 p.

Irregular. Film incomplete: parts of no.7 and 9 wanting.

This Richmond literary miscellany published a good deal of selected material. Contents included essays on literature and other topics, poetry, anecdotes, memoirs, and speeches.

v1, no.1-18	Jan.-Dec. 1807	APS II, Reel 1

Microfilm edition was prepared from Vi copy.

THE AMERICAN HISTORICAL MAGAZINE. v.1 (no.1-6); Jan.-June 1836. [New Haven, W. Storer]

1 v. monthly.

The object of the *American Historical Magazine* was to create an authentic record of important events in the nation's history, and to take note of its founders. It included biographies of historical figures, histories of various cities, such as Concord and New York, revolutionary papers, poetry, occasional reviewers of literary and scientific publications, and articles on such widely diversified subjects as silk culture, gold mines, and fine arts.

v1	Jan.-June 1836	APS II, Reel 767

Microfilm edition was prepared from DLC, ICU and MWA copies.

* **AMERICAN HISTORICAL RECORD.** *SEE* Potter's American Monthly.

THE AMERICAN HISTORICAL REGISTER and monthly gazette of the historic, military and patriotic-hereditary societies of the United States of America. v.1-5; Sept. 1894-May 1897. Philadelphia, Historical Register Publ. Co. 1895-97.

5 v illus., plates (part col.) ports, facisms.

Editors: Sept. 1894-May 1896, C.H. Browning.—June 1896-May 1897, F.B. Philbrook.
v.5 also called new ser. v.1.

Edited successively by Charles Henry Downing and Frederick B. Philbrook, the *American Historical Register* furnished history and genealogy to its readers. Information on American patriotic societies was prominent.

v1-ns1	Sept. 1894-May 1897	APS III, Reel 58

vol.2: preliminary pgs. 613-620, 717-724, 827-842, 926-938, 1135-1150 and 1344-1362 are missing. Best copy available for photographing. Vol.4: pg. 602 misnumbered. New Series Vol.1: Index missing. Please refer to the Table of Contents following May issue.

Microfilm edition was prepared from C-S, MiD, and N copies.

AMERICAN ILLUSTRATED MAGAZINE. *SEE* American Magazine.

AMERICAN JOURNAL AND ANNALS OF EDUCATION AND INSTRUCTION. *SEE* American Annals of Education.

* **THE AMERICAN JOURNAL OF EDUCATION.** Ed. by Henry Barnard, v.1-32; Aug. 1855-1882. Hartford, F.C. Brownell, 1856-82.

32 v. illus., plates, ports. quarterly (irregular)

On back: Barnard's American journal of education.

Vol.1, no.1-2, entitled "The American journal of education and college review," were edited by Henry Barnard and Absalom Peters and were published in New York by N.A. Calkins.
Vols.11-16 are called also "New ser., v.1-6." Vols. 17-24 form the National series and include the circulars, reports and documents issued by the editor as commissioner of education (v. 18 is the American yearbook and register for 1869; v.19, Special report on education in the District of Columbia)
Vol.25 is the report of the commissioner of education for 1880; v.29, report for 1877. Vols.26-31 form the International series, v.1-6.
Vol.26, no.1 contains a classified index to v.1-16 (also given in v.17, p. [17]-40) a general index to v.17-24, special volume indexes, etc. "American text books [a bibliography by H. Barnard]" v.13-15.

Edited by Henry Barnard, the *American Journal of Education* became the leader of the numerous educational journals appearing prior to the War.
The storehouse of information contained in this periodical overwhelms the reader with its completeness. The history of education in the United States was covered extensively, including the appearance of biographies. A running account of the progress of education (college, normal, and criminal), architectural design, translations from foreign educational journals, physical education, the education of women, and proceedings of educational societies were all included in the scope of this journal.
Because of the lack of popular appeal, and perhaps because of being poorly printed, the journal was in serious financial difficulty much of the time. More than once it required personal sacrifices by the editor or monetary assistance from its supporters to assure publication.

v1-5	Aug. 1855-Sept. 1858	APS III, Reel 85
v6-11	Mar. 1859-June 1862	Reel 86
v12-16	Sept. 1862-Dec. 1866	Reel 87
v17-20	Sept. 1867-1870	Reel 88
v21-24	1870-1873	Reel 89
c25-28	1874-1878	Reel 90
v29-32	1878-1882	Reel 91

Vol.1: Number 4 contains Supplement. Vol.6: Index covers only issues 16-17. Vol.16: pg. 385 stained. Vol.20: pgs. 738-740 repeated in number only. Vol.26: pgs. 195-424 repeated in number only.

Contains: 1) Classified Index. 2) General Index to National Series Volumes 16-24. 3) Special Volume Indexes. Best copy available for photographing.

Microfilm edition was Prepared from NhD, NPV, MiEM, and MiU copies.

SEE ALSO: American Annals of Education.

THE AMERICAN JOURNAL OF HOMEOPATHY ... v.1 (no.1-6); Aug. 1838-July 1839. Philadelphia, W.L.J. Kiderlen.

1 v. bimonthly (irregular)

Film includes a reissue dated 1839 with title: Miscellanies on homeopathy ...
Edited by an association of homeopathic physicians.

Edited by an association of homeopathic physicians, this journal published articles on the principles and methods of homeopathy, described homeopathic treatments for various ailments, reviewed addresses and lectures, and also included general news on homeopathy and publication notices of recent books.

v1, no.1-6	Aug. 1838-July 1839	APS II, Reel 295
Miscellanies on Homeopathy		
1 vol	1839	APS II, Reel 295

Microfilm edition was prepared from NNN copy.

THE AMERICAN JOURNAL OF HOMOEOPATHIA. v.1 (no.1-4); Feb.-Aug. 1835. [New York]

4 no. bimonthly.

This homeopathic journal contained a variety of material on the medical practice of homeopathy, including a description of, and the history of homeopathy, accounts of treatments using homeopathy, coverage of its advancement in foreign countries, and short news items.

v1, no.1-4	Feb.-Aug. 1835	APS II, Reel 365

Microfilm edition was prepared from MiU copy.

THE AMERICAN JOURNAL OF HOMOEOPATHY. v.1-9, no.4; Apr. 25, 1846-Aug. 1854. New York, editor [etc.]

9 v. Semimonthly, Apr. 25, 1846-Apr. 15, 1848, monthly; May 1, 1848-Aug. 1854.

Editors: Apr. 25, 1846-Apr 1848, S.R. Kirby and R.A. Snow.-May 1, 1848-Aug. 1854, S.R. Kirby.

This biweekly homeopathic journal was devoted to promoting the practice of homeopathy, recording its achievements, and describing important cases. It was popularly written, and included discussions of homeopathy and other approaches to medicine, articles describing cures for disease, and accounts of cases in which the homeopathic method was used.

v1-9, no.4	Apr. 25, 1846-Aug. 1854	APS II, Reel 365

Pagination is irregular.

Microfilm edition was prepared from MiU copy.

THE AMERICAN JOURNAL OF THE MEDICAL SCIENCES. v.1-26, Nov. 1827-Aug. 1840; new ser. v.1-Jan. 1841-   Philadelphia, Lea & Febiger.

illus. (part col.) Quarterly, 1827-87; monthly, 1888-19-

Supersedes the Philadelphia journal of the medical and physical sciences.
On film: v.1-new ser. v.168.

This medical journal contained articles on medical jurisprudence, monographs on disease, medical news and cases, proceedings of medical societies, reviews, and some plates and woodcuts. Prominent physicians and professors were regular contributors. "The Periscope," which was devoted to a survey of developments in medicine at home and abroad, became an important department. The founding editor, Dr. Isaac Hays, held that position for 52 years, and was succeeded by his son, Dr. I. Minis Hays and others. In later years more foreign medical news was included. The file of early years provides a valuable source for the study of the history of American medicine.

v1-2	Nov. 1827-Aug. 1828	APS II, Reel 368
v3-9	Nov. 1828-Feb. 1832	Reel 369
v10-15	May 1832-Feb. 1835	Reel 370
v16-21	May 1835-Feb. 1838	Reel 371
v22-nsv1	May 1838-Apr. 1841	Reel 372
nsv2-8	July 1841-Oct. 1844	Reel 373
nsv9-15	Jan. 1845-Apr. 1848	Reel 375
nsv16-20	July 1848-Oct. 1850	Reel 275
nsv21-25	1851-1852	Reel 1125
nsv26-32	1853-1856	Reel 1126
nsv33-38	1857-1859	Reel 1127
nsv39-45	1860-1863	Reel 1128
nsv46-52	1863-1866	Reel 1129
nsv53-58	1867-1869	Reel 1130
nsv59-63	1870-1872	Reel 1131
nsv64-70	1872-1875	Reel 1132
nsv71-76	1876-1878	Reel 1133
nsv77-82	1879-1881	Reel 1134
nsv83-88	1882-1884	Reel 1135
nsv89-94	1885-1887	Reel 1136
nsv95-99	1888-1890	Reel 1137
nsv100-104	1890-1892	REel 1138
nsv105-109	1893-1895	Reel 1139
nsv110-114	1895-1897	Reel 1140
nsv115-119	1898-1900	Reel 1141
nsv120-123	1900-1902	Reel 1142
nsv124-126	1902-1903	Reel 1143
nsv127-129	1904-1905	Reel 1144
nsv130-132	1905-1906	Reel 1144
nsv133-136	1907-1908	Reel 1146
nsv137-140	1909-1910	Reel 1147
nsv141-143	1911-1912	Reel 1148
nsv144-146	1913-1914	Reel 1149
nsv147-150	1915-1916	Reel 1150
nsv151-153	1916-1917	Reel 1151
nsv154-156	July 1917-Dec. 1918	Reel 1152
nsv157-159	Jan. 1919-June 1920	Reel 1153
nsv160-162	July 1920-Dec. 1921	Reel 1154
nsv163-164	Jan. 1922-Dec. 1922	Reel 1155
nsv165-166	Jan. 1923-Dec. 1923	Reel 1156
nsv167-168	Jan. 1924-Dec. 1924	Reel 1157

Microfilm edition was prepared from DLC, FTaSU, GEU, GEU-M, ICAC, ICN, ICRL, ICS, MH, MiU, MnSRM, and N copies.

SEE ALSO: American Medical Recorder *and* Philadelphia Journal of the Medical and Physical Sciences.

AMERICAN JOURNAL OF MUSIC AND MUSICAL VISITOR. v.1-5, no.2, June 1, 1840-Aug. 28, 1846. Boston.

5 v.

Volumes 1-2 as musical visitor; 3 as Boston musical visitor.

On film: v.1-5; July 17, 1840-Oct. 20, 1846.

This journal for both adult and juvenile readers was devoted to vocal and instrumental music. Its most interesting feature was the great number of musical pieces it published—one volume contained as many as 150 sacred and moral tunes, 50 pages of piano music, and 40 pages of other instrumental music; most was of a religious nature. It also furnished courses of instruction for several instruments. In addition to providing coverage of events in the music world, it published articles on theory and on music-related subjects, some religious and moral articles, notices of musical and literary works, and poetry.

Musical Visitor.
v1-2	July 17, 1840-July 2, 1842	APS II, Reel 725

Boston Musical Visitor.
v3	Aug. 8, 1842-Oct. 8, 1844	APS II, Reel 725

American Journal of Music and Musical Visitors.
v4-5	Aug. 29, 1844-Oct. 20, 1846	APS II, Reel 725

Best copy available for photographing. Several pages are torn, stained and have faded print with some loss of text. Vols.1 and 4-5: Indexes are missing. Vol.1: Microfilm edition includes issue 13, July 17, 1840, and issue 23, January 6, 1841. Vol.2: Supplement follows September 24 and October 16 issues. Page 152 appears to be missing in number only. Pg. 155 is misnumbered. Vol.4: Pgs. 25-32, 65-73, and 169-76 are missing. Vol.4, new series numbers 10-11 and vol.5, new series number 1 are bound and photographed at end of vol.4. Vol.5: Microfilm edition includes new series numbers 1-2, August 5-October 20, 1846.

Microfilm edition was prepared from DLC and NNC copies.

AMERICAN JOURNAL OF PHARMACY. v.1, no.1-4, 1825-1827; new ser. v.1-6, 1829-1835; new ser. v.1-18, 1836-1852; 3d ser. v.1-18, 1853-1870; 4th ser. v.1-24, 1871-1895; v.68-79, 1896-1907. Philadelphia, 1829-

82 v. illus. quarterly.

Published by authority of the Philadelphia College of Pharmacy. Title varies: Apr. 1829-Jan. 1835, Journal of the Philadelphia college of pharmacy.

On film: Reels 366-368 include v.1, no.1-4, 1825-1827; [whole no.] v.1-24, 1829-1852; and General index for years 1830-1850, Reels 1707-1716 include [whole no.] v.25-79, 1853-1907.
Editors: Apr. 1829-Jan. 1831, Benjamin Ellis.—Apr. 1831-Jan. 1836, R.E. Griffith.—Apr. 1836-Jan. 1850, Joseph Carson.—1851- William Proctor.—1871-1893, J.M. Malach.—1894- Henry Trimble. —1898- Henry Kraemer.

Founded in 1825, the *American Journal of Pharmacy* is said to be the oldest pharmaceutical journal in the English language and for some years was the only one in the United States. The fourth editor, William Procter, Jr., one of the founders of the American Pharmaceutical Association, contributed more than 500 articles to the *Journal* and his active and scholarly work gave his periodical high standing all over the world. For many years, the *Journal* published the proceedings of the American Pharmaceutical Association, though it was not an official organ. In 1852 an advertising department was introduced and in 1917, under the editorship of George M. Beringer, the magazine increased in size. While giving some attention to the commercial aspects of pharmacy, the *Journal* has always had a strong inclination toward the scientific side of pharmacy. Issues of the early 1900's offered articles on drugs, on chemistry, and on the chemical makeup of various foodstuffs, such as tea and flavoring extracts, as well as a "Progress in Pharmacy" section.

Journal of the Philadelphia College of Pharmacy
v1, nos.1-4	Dec. 1825-Nov. 1827	APS II, Reel 366
nsv1-6	Apr. 1829-Jan. 1835	Reel 366

American Journal of Pharmacy
nsv7-8 (nsv1-2)	Apr. 1835-Jan. 1837	APS II, Reel 366
nsv9-18 (ns3-12)	Apr. 1837-Jan. 1847	Reel 367
nsv19-24 (13-18)	Apr. 1847-Oct. 1852	Reel 368
v25-30	Jan. 1853-Nov. 1858	Reel 1707
v31-36	Jan. 1859-Nov. 1864	Reel 1708
v37-42	Jan. 1865-Nov. 1870	Reel 1709
v43-48	Jan. 1871-Dec. 1876	Reel 1710
v49-53	Jan. 1877-Dec. 1881	Reel 1711
v54-58	Jan. 1882-Dec. 1886	Reel 1712
v59-63	Jan. 1887-Dec. 1891	Reel 1713
v64-68	Jan. 1892-Dec. 1896	Reel 1714
v69-73	Jan. 1897-Dec. 1901	Reel 1715
v74-79	Jan. 1902-Dec. 1907	Reel 1716

Pagination is irregular.

Microfilm edition was prepared from MiU and NNN copy.

THE AMERICAN JOURNAL OF PHILOLOGY. v.1- (whole no.1-); Feb. 1880- Baltimore, New York and London, Macmillan, 1880-19-

v. illus., plates, facsims., tables.

"Four numbers constitute a volume, one volume each year."
Each number includes "Reviews and book notices."
Editors: Feb. 1880- B.L. Gildersleeve (with C.W.E. Miller Oct. 1915-) Imprint varies: 1880-97, Baltimore, The editor: New York and London, Macmillan & co.; [etc., etc.]—1898-19 Baltimore, The Johns-Hopkins press; London, K. Paul, Trench, Trubner & co.; [etc., etc.] "Indices volumes I-X. Prepared by W. Muss-Arnolt, Ph.D.": v.10, p. [515]-558.
List of contributions to v.11-20, 21-30, 31-40 are included in v.20, 30 and 40 respectively.
On film: issues for Feb. 1880-1910.
Index: 1-10 in 10; 11-20 in 20; 21-30 in 30; 31-40 in 40.

This influential quarterly was edited at Johns Hopkins University by Basil L. Gildersleeve who was also among the contributors. The emphasis was on the classical languages but there were also short reviews and editorial comment.

v1-5	1880-1884	APS III, Reel 424
v6-10	1885-1889	Reel 425
v11-15	1890-1894	Reel 426
v16-20	1895-1899	Reel 427
v21-25	1900-1904	Reel 428
v26-31	1905-1910	Reel 429

Some pages are torn or stained.

Microfilm was prepared from MiU copy.

AMERICAN JOURNAL OF POLITICS. *SEE* American Magazine of Civics.

* **THE AMERICAN JOURNAL OF SCIENCE.** v.1-50 [July 1818]-1845; v.[51]- 100 (2d ser., v.1-50) 1846-70; v.101-150 (3d ser., v.1-50) 1871-95; v.151-200 (4th ser., v.1-50) 1896-1920; v.201-236 (5th ser., v.1-36) 1921-1938. New Haven, etc., S. Converse, etc.

Editors: 1866-69, J.C. Ropes, J.C. Gray.—1870-73, O.W. Holmes, A.G. Sedgwick.—Oct. 1876-July 1879, M. Storey, S. Hoar.—Jan. 1881-Dec. 1882, C.E. Grinnell.—Jan. 1883-Oct. 1904, S.D. Thompson (with L. Eaton, Jan. 1883-Dec. 1889; L.A. Jones, Jan. 1885 -Oct. 1904)— Nov. 1904-Dec. 1906, L.A. Jones (with H. Taylor, 1906)

Imprint varies: 1866-82, Boston, Little, Brown & Co. Microfilm edition includes v.1-40 and a separately published index to v.1-13.

Begun in Boston in 1866, the *American Law Review* was one of the most brilliant legal periodicals of this period. It was edited by such men as Arthur G. Sedgwick, Oliver Wendell Holmes, Jr., Moorfield Storey, Samuel Hoar, and Charles E. Grinnell, In 1883, it was moved to St. Louis, where it was published for nearly half a century. In 1929, it became the *U.S. Law Review* and was moved to New York. It became the *New York Law Review* in 1940 during its final year of publication.

Cumulative Index	1866-79	
v1-5	Oct. 1866-July 1871	APS III, Reel 463
v6-10	Oct. 1871-July 1876	Reel 464
v11-14	Oct. 1876-Dec. 1880	Reel 465
v15-18	Jan. 1881-Dec. 1884	Reel 466
v19-22	Jan. 1885-Dec. 1888	Reel 467
v23-26	Jan. 1889-Dec. 1892	Reel 468
v27-30	Jan. 1893-Dec. 1896	Reel 469
v31-34	Jan. 1897-Dec. 1900	Reel 470
v35-38	Jan. 1901-Dec. 1904	Reel 471
v39-40	Jan. 1905-Dec. 1906	Reel 472

Several volumes have stained pages. Vol.19: Pagination is irregular. Vol.40: pgs. 581-82 are torn.

Microfilm edition was prepared from InU, NhD, and PPi copies.

THE AMERICAN LAWYER. v.1-16, no.7; 1893-July 1908. New York, Stumpf & Steurer, 1893-1908.

illus. monthly.

"The news-Magazine of the American Bar" was the subtitle for this periodical.

v1-4	Jan. 1893-Dec. 1896	APS III, Reel 240
v5-9	Jan. 1897-Dec. 1901	Reel 241
v10-14	Jan. 1902-Dec. 1906	Reel 242
v15-16	Jan. 1907-July 1908	Reel 243

Pagination irregular. Some pages creased, torn, or have print missing.

Microfilm edition was prepared from DLC, InU, Me, MiU copies.

AMERICAN LITERARY GAZETTE AND PUBLISHERS' CIRCULAR. v.1-8, Sept. 1855-Dec. 1862; new ser., v.1, Jan.-Apr. 1863; octavo ser., v.1-18, May 1863-Jan. 15, 1872. New York, Book Publishers' Association, 1855-63; Philadelphia, G.W. Childs, 1863-72.

27 v. Weekly, Sept 1855-June 1861; monthly, July 1862-Dec. 1862, semi-monthly, 1863-72.

Title varies: Sept. 1855-Oct. 1863, The American publishers' circular and literary gazette. Nov. 1863-Jan. 1872, American literary gazette and publishers circular. C.R. Rode, editor, July 1856-Apr. 1863. Supersedes Norton's literary gazette and publishers' circular (earlier called Norton's literary advertiser) 1851-55.

Merged into the Publishers' and stationers' weekly trade circular (later called the Publishers' weekly)

In 1855 George W. Childs of Philadelphia bought what had previously been *Norton's Literary Gazette and Publishers' Circular* and converted it to the *American Publishers' Circular and Literary Gazette,* which was used as an advertising medium by publishers and was designed primarily for book sellers. The *Criterion* was merged with it in 1856 and Charles R. Rode, editor of that literary journal, became editor of the *Circular.* In 1863, the *Circular* became more a journal of literary notes, changing its title to *American Literary Gazette and Publishers' Circular.* It was purchased by Frederick Leypoldt in 1872 and absorbed into his weekly.

American Publishers' Circular and Literary Gazette
v1-2	Sept. 1, 1855-Dec. 27, 1856	APS II, Reel 780
v3-7	Jan. 3, 1857-Dec. 5, 1861	Reel 781
v8	Jan.-Dec.1862	Reel 782

American Literary Gazette and Publishers' Circular
nsv1-s3v9	Jan. 1863-Oct. 15, 1867	APS II, Reel 782
s3v10-18	Nov. 1, 1867-Jan. 15, 1872	Reel 783

Some pages are discolored, with very light print. Vols.1-8, New Series Vol.1: Index and table of contents are lacking. Series 3, Vol.2: pgs.213-14 are cropped. Pgs. 185-86 are stained. Pgs. 387-90 are torn.

Microfilm edition was prepared from MiU and RPB copies.

* THE AMERICAN LITERARY MAGAZINE. Monthly. By T. Dwight Sprague. v.1-5, no.2; July 1847-Aug. 1849. Albany, Printed by J. Munsell, 1847-48; Hartford, etc. Printed by J.G. Wells, 1848-

5 v. plates, ports.

Imprint on cover of v.1-2; New York, Burgess, Stringer & co.

Edited by Timothy Dwight Sprague, *American Literary Magazine* published much material on good manners and appropriate dress. Frequent contributors included Mrs. Lydia Huntley Sigourney, Alfred B. Street, and C.A. Goodrich as well as various Yale professors. A portrait engraved on steel embellished each number.

v1-5	July 1847-Aug. 1849	APS II, Reel 787

Vol.1: Pgs. 259-68 are missing in number only.

Microfilm edition was prepared from MiD, MiU and WHi copies.

THE AMERICAN MAGAZINE. v.1-162, no.2; Jan. 1876-Aug. 1956. New York, Frank Leslie [etc.]

162 v. illus., facims., plates, ports. monthly.

Title varies: 1876-Feb. 1904, Frank Leslie's popular monthly.—Mar. 1904-Aug. 1905, Leslie's monthly magazine.—Sept. 1905-May 1906, American illustrated magazine.
Absorbed the Pocket magazine, Jan. 1902.—cf. Union list of serials.

Editor: 1876-80, F. Leslie.—1898-99, Mrs. F. Leslie.—1900-06, E. Sedgwick.—cf. Mott, Hist. of Amer. magazines, v.3.
Supplement accompanies v.54, no.3.
On film: v.1-62, Jan. 1876-Oct. 1906.

Begun in January, 1876 by Frank Leslie, the *Popular Monthly* survived until 1956. Its well-illustrated pages contained much miscellaneous material—serialized stories, short stories, a little poetry, essays in science, art, literature, and anthropology, and plenty of jokes and anecdotes. Travel articles gave attention to various foreign countries as well as to the World's Fair and such U.S. cities as Chicago, St. Louis, and New York. Joaquin Miller contributed the

Monthly's first serial, *The Pink Countess,* and other contributors included Amelia E. Barr, Jane G. Austin, Harriet Prescott Spofford, and Horatio Alger, along with several popular magazinists. Brander Matthews wrote on drama, Lady Blanche Murphy on European society, and Evert A. Duyckinck and Sarah K. Bolton on contemporary literature.

When Leslie died in 1880 his widow took over until 1900 when she turned the editorship over to Ellery Sedgwick. Under Sedgwick, *Leslie's Monthly,* as it was renamed in 1904, gave more attention to public events than before but did not yet participate in muckraking. There was some emphasis on wit and humor, and fiction was furnished by Stephen Crane, Frank R. Stockton, Samuel Merwin, Stewart Edward White and Emerson Hough. A series on "The American Woman in Action" and new book notices were also included. In the fall of 1905 its name was changed to the *American Illustrated Magazine* and the word *Illustrated* was dropped in June, 1906.

In the fall of 1906 a group of the leading contributors to *McClure's Magazine,* headed by John S. Phillips, seceded from *McClure's* and bought the *American.* These writers, who were among the best-known in the country, were Ida M. Tarbell, Lincoln Steffens, Ray Stannard Baker, Finley Peter Dunne, and William Allen White, and perhaps because the first three were outstanding in the muckraking campaign, the *American* published a good deal on muckraking for about four years. Around 1910, however, public taste changed and the magazine shifted its emphasis, displaying an interest in the affairs of the average man and woman, and in civic reform; but human interest became the dominant theme when the magazine was sold to the Crowell Company in 1915 and John M. Siddall became editor. Siddall's policies were continued by his successor, Merle Crowell, but when Sumner Blossom took over in 1929 the *American* became more sophisticated, displaying movie stars and bathing beauties. After a year or two, however, it returned to a more traditional policy. The later *American Magazine* published features on public affairs, personality articles, and a long detective story in each issue.

Frank Leslie's Popular Monthly

v1-4	Jan. 1876-Dec. 1877	APS III, Reel 675
v5-8	Jan. 1878-Dec. 1879	Reel 676
v9-12	Jan. 1880-Dec. 1881	Reel 677
v13-16	Jan. 1882-Dec. 1883	Reel 678
v17-20	Jan. 1884-Dec. 1885	Reel 679
v21-24	Jan. 1886-Dec. 1887	Reel 680
v25-28	Jan. 1888-Dec. 1889	Reel 681
v29-32	Jan. 1890-Dec. 1891	Reel 682
v33-36	Jan. 1892-Dec. 1893	Reel 683
v37-40	Jan. 1894-Dec. 1895	Reel 684
v41-44	Jan. 1896-Dec. 1897	Reel 685
v45-48	Jan. 1898-Oct. 1899	Reel 686
v49-53	Nov. 1899-Apr. 1902	Reel 687
v54-57, no.4	May 1902-Feb. 1904	Reel 688

Leslie's Monthly Magazine

v57, no.5-v58	Mar. 1904-Oct. 1904	APS III, Reel 688
v59-60, no.4	Nov. 1904-Aug. 1905	Reel 689

American Illustrated Magazine

v60, no.5-v.62, no.1	Sept. 1905- May, 1906	APS III, Reel 689

American Magazine

v62, no.2-6	June-Oct. 1906	APS III, Reel 689

Pagination is irregular. Several pages are torn, taped, stained, and have print faded or blurred with some loss of text. Volumes 1-4 and 52 lack indexes. Volumes 47, 48, 52, 56, and 57 lack title pages. Volume 54, issue 3 has supplement. Volume 61: pages 489-90 are missing.

Microfilm edition was prepared from IU, MiD, MiU, MnU, NBu, NcD, and OU copies.

THE AMERICAN MAGAZINE; a monthly miscellany devoted to literature, science, history, biography, and the arts. v.1, no.1-12; June 1815-May 1816. Albany, Printed by E. & E. Hosford.

443 p. illus.

This miscellany included articles of general interest, essays, poetry, biographies, and reviews of new publications but paid particular attention to practical agriculture and new and useful inventions and discoveries. It also included state papers but avoided engaging in discussions of party politics. Some of the great variety of topics included were a history of Albany, coins, poetry, storms in New York, medical tips, preserving fruit, and touring France.

v1, no.1-12	June 1815-May 1816	APS II, Reel 53

THE AMERICAN MAGAZINE AND HISTORICAL CHRONICLE. v.1-3; Sept. 1743-Dec. 1746. Boston, Rogers and Fowle, 1743-46.

3 v. map. monthly.

An important early periodical modeled after the *London Magazine.* Most of the contents dealt with English and American politics and war.

v1-3	Sept. 1743-Dec. 1746	APS I, Reel 1

Microfilm edition was prepared from MWA copy.

THE AMERICAN MAGAZINE AND MONTHLY CHRONICLE FOR THE BRITISH COLONIES. vol.I. containing from October 1757 to October 1758 inclusive. By a society of gentlemen. Philadelphia, Printed by William Bradford [1757-58]

1 p.1., 654 + p.

Incomplete. Sabin gives collation 656(6) p.

Ed. by Rev. William Smith, first provost of the College of Philadelphia.

An attempt to inform Britain about the colonies. Outspoken in criticism of the French and Quakers, the magazine also published much poetry and humorous and scientific articles.

v1	Oct. 1757-Oct. 1758	APS I, Reel 2

Some pages are missing.

SEE ALSO: New American Magazine.

THE AMERICAN MAGAZINE, and repository of useful literature. Devoted to science, literature, and arts, and embellished with numerous engravings. Ed. by John S. Wood, and Barnabas Wood. Assisted by several literary gentlemen. v.1, [v.2, no.1-3] July 1841-Mar./Apr. 1842. Albany, B. Wood, 1841-[42]

2 v. in 1. illus., plates, port. monthly.

In the area of science, this literary and scientific magazine published a summary of science news and articles on astronomy, geology, animals, and birds, and on other science topics as well. In the literary area, it published book reviews, essays on literature, and poetry, including some by Mrs. Mary E. Hewitt and Alfred B. Street. Political and religious news were also given coverage, and a ladies' department was added during the second volume. Numerous illustrations were included.

v1-2, no.3	July 1841-Mar./Apr. 1842	APS II, Reel 376

Microfilm edition was prepared from DLC copy.

THE AMERICAN MAGAZINE, containing a miscellaneous collection of original and other valuable essays in prose and verse, and calculated both for instruction and amusement. no. [1]-12; Dec. 1787-Nov. 1788. New York, Printed by S. and J. Loudon.

882 p. monthly.

Edited by N. Webster.

Articles on education, national affairs, and women's interests were published along with fiction, literary criticism, and book reviews.

no.[1]-12   Dec. 1787-Nov. 1788   APS I, Reel 2

Some pages are missing.

Microfilm edition was prepared from MiU-C copy.

AMERICAN MAGAZINE OF CIVICS. v.1-9, no. 6, July 1892-Jan. 1897. New York, American Institute of Civics, 1892-1897.

9 v.

Vols.1-5, 1892-1894 as American journal of politics. Merged into Arena.

The *American Magazine of Civics* was founded as the *American Journal of Politics* by Andrew J. Palm. It was liberal and non-partisan and had a list of contributors which contained many prominent politicians. There were articles on free trade, labor, political corruption, pacifism, and women's rights. This periodical became the organ of the American Institute of Civics in 1894 and changed its name to *American Magazine of Civics* the next year. It finally merged with *Arena,* another periodical interested in political reform, in 1897.

American Journal of Politics.
v 1-4   July 1892-June 1894   APS III, Reel 203
v 5   July 1894-Dec. 1894   Reel 204
American Magazine of Civics.
v 6-9   Jan. 1895-Jan. 1897   APS III, Reel 204

Pagination is irregular. Vol.9: Title page and index not published. Pg. 74 has print missing.

Microfilm edition was prepared from MiD copy.

SEE ALSO: Arena.

THE AMERICAN MAGAZINE OF USEFUL AND ENTERTAINING KNOWLEDGE. v.1-3; Sept. 1834-Sept. 1837. Boston, Boston Bewick Co., 1835-37.

3 v. illus. monthly.

Vols.2-3 were published by J. L. Sibley, etc.
Nos.7-12, v.2, March-August 1836, were edited anonymously by Hawthorne, who with his sister, Elizabeth, wrote or revised almost the entire contents. cf. N.E. Browne. Bibl. of Nathaniel Hawthorne.

Edited by Freeman Hunt, this magazine is interesting for its examples of Nathaniel Hawthorne's early work as a literary hack, and for the great number of woodcuts it contained. It also included music., It was published by the American Engraving and Printing Company, and later by the Boston Bewick Company, which was ruined by fire losses in 1836, causing the magazine to be suspended the following year.

v1-3   Sept. 1834-Sept. 1837   APS II, Reel 768

Microfilm edition was prepared from MiD and MiU copies.

THE AMERICAN MAGAZINE OF WONDERS AND MARVELLOUS CHRONICLE. v.1-2; 1809. New York, Printed by Southwick and Pelsue.

2 v. plates.

Edited by D. Fraser.

According to its subtitle, the *American Magazine of Wonders,* conducted by Donald Fraser, was intended to be "a record of accounts of the most extraordinary productions, events, and occurrences in providence, nature, and art, that have been witnessed at any time in Europe and America." This unusual magazine described dwarfs, giants, "monsters," and other oddities of nature, and gave accounts of murders, strange events, unusual customs, and scientific phenomena, along with much other interesting material.

v1-2   1809   APS II, Reel 1

Microfilm edition was prepared from DLC copy.

THE AMERICAN MAGAZINE; or, General repository. Jan.-Sept. 1769. Philadelphia, Printed by W. and T. Bradford.

328 p. Monthly.

Edited by L. Nicola. Cf. Sabin. Bibliotheca americana.

The first and foremost magazine during the third quarter of the eighteenth century to represent adequately American scientific thought. It published the Transactions of the American Philosophical Society and other scientific articles as well as articles on politics and religion and much sentimental fiction.

Jan.-Sept. 1769   APS I, Reel 2

Some pages are missing.

Microfilm edition was prepared from MiU-C and MH copies.

THE AMERICAN MAGAZINE; or, A monthly view of the political state of the British colonies. Jan.-Mar. 1741. Philadelphia, A. Bradford.

viii, 120 p. Monthly.

Edited by J. Webbe.

The first American magazine. Articles dealt mostly with the government of Pennsylvania, New York, New Jersey, and Maryland.

v1   Jan.-Mar. 1741   APS I, Reel 2

Microfilm edition was prepared from DLC and NHi copies.

THE AMERICAN MASONIC REGISTER, and ladies and gentlemen's magazine. v.1-2, no.7; Sept. 1820-June 1823. New York, B. Bolmore.

2 v. illus. monthly (irregular)

S.W. Conrad, 1818. (24 p.)

Edited by L. Pratt.

This periodical consisted primarily of records of the origins, constitutions, duties, procedures, elections of officers, and lectures of the Free Masons of the U.S. The religious bases of this organization were reflected in the regular feature "Christian Mason." Being also a literary magazine, it included articles, poetry, tales, biographies, and anecdotes.

v1-2, no.7   Sept. 1820-June 1823   APS II, Reel 54

AMERICAN MASONIC REGISTER AND LITERARY COMPANION. v.1-8; Aug. 31, 1839-Oct. 1847. Albany, N.Y. [L.G. Hoffman]

8 v. weekly.

The *American Masonic Register* was devoted to the freemasons. The paper, printed and published by L.G. Hoffman, sold for $1.50 a year. Later, the subscription was raised to $2.00. In addition to masonry news, there appeared tales, original poetry and local news. In the October 1847 issue, subscribers were advised that they would receive the *Cincinnati Review* in place of the *Register* due to Mr. Hoffman's involvement in other matters.

v1-4   Aug. 31, 1839-Aug. 26, 1843   APS II, Reel 915
v5-8   Nov. 1843-Oct. 1847   Reel 916

Best copy available for photographing. Pagination is irregular. Vol.1: lacks Index and Table of Contents. Vol.2: June 26 and July 3 issues lacking. Vol.3: many pages stained or faded. Pgs. 129-30 and 257-58 torn. Pg. 137 repaired. Pgs. 298, 314 and 337, print missing. Vol. 4: lacks Index. Please refer to the Table of Contents.

Microfilm edition was prepared from DLC, NN, WHi, N, MWA, Ia, NSchU, NjR, and RPB copies.

AMERICAN MASONICK RECORD. *SEE* Escritoir; or, Masonic and Miscellaneous Album.

AMERICAN MECHANICS' MAGAZINE: containing useful original matter, on subjects connected with manufactures, the arts and sciences: as well as selections from the most approved domestic and foreign journals. Conducted by associated mechanics. v.1-2; Feb. 5, 1825-Feb. 11, 1826. New York, J.V. Seaman, 1825-26

2 v. in 1. illus. weekly.

Superseded by the Franklin journal and American mechanics' magazine (called later "Journal of the Franklin institute")

Thomas P. Jones, professor of mechanics at the University of Pennsylvania, founded the *American Mechanics' Magazine* in 1825 on the model of the *London Mechanics' Magazine*. It soon became a strong, well-illustrated periodical devoted to the interests of American students of science and mechanics, containing descriptions of recently invented products and manufacturing processes, articles on miscellaneous scientific topics, and meteorological tables.

v1-2, no.40   Feb. 5-Dec. 24, 1825   APS II, Reel 54
v2, nos.41-45   Dec. 31, 1825-Feb. 11, 1826   Reel 763

Several pages are stained and torn.

Microfilm edition was prepared from MiU copy.

SEE ALSO: Franklin Institute, Philadelphia. Journal ... Devoted to Science ...

THE AMERICAN MEDICAL AND PHILOSOPHICAL REGISTER; or, Annals of medicine, natural history, agriculture, and the arts. Conducted by David Hossack, and John W. Francis, v.1-4, July 1810-Apr. 1814. New York, C.S. Van Winkle, 1814.

4 v. illus., plates, port. quarterly.

Vol.1: 2nd ed. Vol.3 wanting.

This was originally an anonymous journal but with the second edition was published by Drs. David Hosack and John W. Francis. It consisted of original materials dealing with medicine in general and epidemical diseases like yellow fever in particular, chemistry, agriculture, natural history, botany and the useful arts, reviews of new publications in the medical field, accounts of literary and humane associations, proceedings of learned societies, reports of public hospitals. Lengthy case studies were often included and later issues utilized engravings.

v1-2, 4   July 1810-Apr. 1814   APS II, Reel 54

AMERICAN MEDICAL DIGEST. *SEE* Medical Times and Register.

THE AMERICAN MEDICAL INTELLIGENCER. A concentrated record of medical science and literature. v.1-4, Apr. 1, 1837-Mar. 15, 1841; new ser. v.1, July 1841-June 1842. Philadelphia, A. Waldie, 1838-41; J.J. Haswell, 1842.

5 v. illus., pl.

Semimonthly, Apr. 1837-Mar. 1841; monthly, July 1841-June 1842.
Edited by Robley Dunglison.
A prospectus with title "The American medical library and intelligencer", edited by G. S. Pattison and Robley Dunglison, was issued in November 1836.
Superseded by the Medical news and library.

This monthly medical journal presented information on the various aspects of medicine—reports on medical colleges and medical associations, hospital reports, general articles on medicine, and articles describing various cases and treatments and covering a variety of medical and surgical problems. It kept abreast of medical literature, publishing lists of books received and bibliographical notices.

v1-4   Apr. 1, 1837-Mar. 15, 1841   APS II, Reel 296
nsv1   July 1841-June 1842   Reel 296

Microfilm edition was prepared from MiU copy.

SEE ALSO: Medical News.

THE AMERICAN MEDICAL RECORDER. Conducted by several respectable physicians of Philadelphia. v.1-16, no.2 (no. 1-[46]); Jan. 1818-[Apr.] 1829. Philadelphia, J. Webster; New York, T. & J. Swords, 1818-29.

Title varies: 1818 (v.1) The American medical recorder. 1819-27 (v.2-12) The American medical recorder, of original papers and intelligence in medicine and surgery. 1828-29 (v.13-15) The American medical recorder.

Vols.2-6 edited by John Eberle and others; v.7-10 by Samuel Colhoun and others; v.11-15 by James Webster and others. Merged into American journal of the medical sciences. Vol.4, no.1 and v.16, p. 166-168 wanting. Vol.14 omitted in numbering.

A medical journal which published the most recent knowledge and information in the medical field. In addition to articles and case studies on various diseases and their treatments, which were illustrated by diagrams and figures, it included reviews of recent books and American medical journals, analysis of foreign journals, coverage of medical societies, and small news items.

v1-5	Jan. 1818-Oct. 1822	APS II, Reel 55
v6-8	Jan. 1823-Oct. 1825	Reel 56
v9-16	Jan. 1826-Apr. 1829	Reel 645

Several pages are stained. Individual issues following the title page numbered volume 14 are numbered as volume 15. The next volume is printed as volume 16. Vols.15 and 16: Irregular paging throughout. Vol.16: Volume number on title page and issues has been altered. Best copy available for photographing.

Microfilm edition was prepared from DLC and MiU copies.

SEE ALSO: Journal of Foreign Medical Science and Literature

THE AMERICAN MEDICAL REVIEW, and journal of original and selected papers in medicine and surgery. v.1-3; June 1824-Aug. 1826. Conducted by John Eberle, Nathan R. Smith, and assisted by an association of physicians & surgeons. Philadelphia, A. Sherman, 1824-26.

3 v. plates. quarterly.

Vol. 1 has title The Medical review, and analectic journal ... Conducted by John Eberle, M. D. ... and George M'Clellan, M.D. ...

The *American Medical Review* provided reviews and original papers on medicine along with selections from medical news sources for members of the medical profession. John Eberle and George McClellan, both doctors, conducted the first volume of this medical journal, called *The Medical Review, and Analectic Journal,* but the second volume had two additional editors, Nathan Smith and Nathan R. Smith.

Medical Review and Analectic Journal		
v1	June 1824-Apr. 1825	APS II, Reel 57
v1	June 1824-Apr. 1825	Reel 944
American Medical Review, and Journal of ...		
v2	Sept.-Dec. 1825	APS II, Reel 57
v3	Apr.-Aug. 1826	Reel 846
v2-3	Sept. 1825-Aug. 1826	Reel 944

Microfilm edition was prepared from PU copy.

AMERICAN MEDICAL TIMES. *SEE* New York Journal of Medicine.

AMERICAN METEOROLOGICAL JOURNAL. A monthly review of meteorology and allied branches of study. v.1-12, 1884-96. Boston, 1884-96

12 v.

The *American Meteorological Journal* was edited first in Ann Arbor by Mark W. Harrington, director of the astronomical observatory at The University of Michigan. It was one of the earliest meteorological journals carrying scientific and scholarly articles.

v1-4	May 1884-April 1888	APS III, Reel 314
v5-9	May 1888-April 1893	Reel 315
v10-12	May 1893-April 1896	Reel 316

Vol.1: Title page is missing. Pgs. i-ii are missing. Vol.4: Index is

found in Vol.5 after P. 48. Some pages are tightly bound. Vol.5: Index for Vol.4 follows after P. 48. Supplement follows after pgs. 384 and 576. Vol.6: Supplement follows after P. 48. Vol.7: Best copy available for photographing. Supplement follows after P. 480.

Microfilm edition was prepared from KMK, MiD, MiU, NBuG, and MWC copies.

THE AMERICAN METROPOLITAN MAGAZINE. v.1, no. 1-2; Jan.-Feb. 1849. New York, I. Post [1849]

112 p. illus., plates. monthly.

Includes songs with piano accompaniment.

Edited by William Landon.

Edited by William Landon, the *American Metropolitan Magazine* was devoted to American literature and art and featured stories, poetry, musical pieces, and engravings as well as contributions from such eminent writers as Mrs. Caroline H. Butler, Mrs. E.F. Ellet, W. Gilmore Simms, Mrs. Ann S. Stephens, T.S. Arthur, Miss Catherine M. Sedgwick, L. Marie Child, and Mrs. Emma C. Embury.

v1, no.1-2	Jan.-Feb. 1849	APS II, Reel 333

Pagination is irregular.

Microfilm edition was prepared from NNHi copy.

THE AMERICAN MILLENARIAN AND PROPHETIC REVIEW, a monthly periodical, published in the city of New York, by Rev. I.P. Labagh. v.1-2, no.11, 1842-Apr. 1844. New York, Printed for I. P. Labagh, 1842-

v. pl., maps.

I.P. Labagh, editor. Film incomplete: v.1 wanting

American Millenarian and Prophetic Review was a religious monthly edited and published by Isaac P. Labagh

v2	June 1, 1843-April 1844	APS II, Reel 1093

Microfilm edition was prepared from DLC copy.

THE AMERICAN MINERALOGICAL JOURNAL: being a collection of facts and observations tending to elucidate the mineralogy and geology of the United States of America. Conducted by Archibald Bruce. v.1 (no.1-4); 1810-1814. New York, Printed by Collins

1 v. plates.

Edited by Archibald Bruce, the *American Mineralogical Journal,* which was concerned with mineralogy, geology, and chemistry, both in the U.S. and abroad, was one of the first specialized scientific periodicals in America. Its contents consisted mainly of reports of scientific observations in various parts of the U.S., many written by such leading contributors as Col. George Gibbs, Dr. W. Meade, Dr. Samuel Akerly, and Professors Benjamin Silliman and Benjamin S. Barton; and of extracts from various printed sources, including the *Transactions* of the American Philosophical Society, the *Philosophical Magazine* of London, and the *Journal de Physique* of Paris.

v1, no.1-4	Jan. 1810-1814	APS II, Reel 57

AMERICAN MISSIONARY *SEE* Missionary Herald at Home and Abroad.

THE AMERICAN MONITOR: or, The Republican magazine. v.1, no.1; Oct. 1785. Boston, E. Russell.

16 p.

The first magazine in the U.S. with a definitely commercial appeal, it was more like a newspaper in every respect but form. Only one number was published; it contained 3 pages of advertisements, excerpts from plays, shipping news, proceedings of a meeting, and other local news.

v1, no.1   Oct. 1785   APS I, Reel 3

Microfilm edition was prepared from MWA copy.

AMERICAN MONTHLY. *SEE* Knickerbocker.

AMERICAN MONTHLY KNICKERBOCKER. *SEE* Knickerbocker.

THE AMERICAN MONTHLY MAGAZINE. Ed. by James M'Henry. v.1-2; Jan.-Dec. 1824. Philadelphia, J. Palmer, 1824.

2 v. plates, ports.

The editor of this short-lived but notable general magazine was Dr. James McHenry, an Irish-born poet and physician of Philadelphia, who later became a leading poetry reviewer for the *American Quarterly.* Like the *United States Literary Gazette,* the *American Monthly* encouraged the youthful Longfellow, publishing some of his early writings, along with tales, biographical sketches, book reviews, literary and scientific news, poetry and anecdotes, and some political material. McHenry wrote some of the poetry himself.

v1-2   Jan.-Dec. 1824   APS II, Reel 57

THE AMERICAN MONTHLY MAGAZINE v.1-3; Apr. 1829-July 1831. Boston, Pierce and Williams

3 v.

Ed. by N.P. Willis. Absorbed by the New York mirror in Sept. 1831.

Nathaniel Parker Willis, who at 23 had already attracted widespread attention for his writing, modeled his *American Monthly Magazine* after Thomas Campbell's *New Monthly Magazine* of London. Filled with essays, stories and sketches, criticism, poetry, and humor, it was one of the most readable and entertaining magazines that had yet appeared in America. Willis wrote a large share of the magazine himself, including the travel sketches which were later to be so popular with his readers, and much literary criticism, especially of the current American poetry. His "Editor's Table" was reminiscent of *Blackwood's* "Noctes Ambrosianae." Contributors included J.L. Motley and Richard Hildreth, and poets Rufus Dawes, George Lunt, Mrs. Lydia Sigourney, and Albert Pike. Boston was not very friendly to the *American Monthly,* however; many were offended by its affectation, its praise of champagne, and its conceited airs, and Williams himself was excommunicated from his sedate Boston church for attending the theater. The magazine was not a success financially, either, and in July 1831 Willis gave it up. In spite of its problems, however, the *American Monthly* provided a pleasant change from the usually dull writing of the times.

v1   April 1829-March 1830   APS II, Reel 468
v2-3   April 1830-July 1831   Reel 469

Several pages are stained with some loss of text. Pagination is irregular.

Microfilm edition was prepared from MB and NIC copies.

SEE ALSO: New-York Mirror.

* **THE AMERICAN MONTHLY MAGAZINE** v.1-6, Mar. 1833-Feb. 1836; new ser., v.1-6, Jan. 1836-Oct. 1838. New York, G. Dearborn.

12 v.

New series v.1-6 also numbered as v.7-17.

Absorbed the New England magazine, Jan. 1836.

In 1833, Henry William Herbert, assisted by A.D. Patterson, began publication of the *American Monthly Magazine,* which was a rival for the *Knickerbocker.* Its prospectus promised moral essays, poetry, biography, and travel. The early numbers were written largely by Herbert; he wrote on the theater, art exhibitions, and on concerts, and also contributed a serial novel, "The Brothers, a Tale of the Fronde." Other contributors were James K. Paulding, Gulian Verplanck, and James Hall. In 1836 Charles Fenno Hoffman and Park Benjamin took over the editorship, and although greatly improved in variety and attractiveness, it did not make money. There was much on travel, much interest in German literature, and "Letters from Arkansas" by Albert Pike and other articles about the West and the Indians. Theater was given some attention, book reviews were regular, and short stories and "nouvellettes" added variety. Special attention was also given to the reports of the American Lyceum. Alfred B. Street, Arthur Cleveland Coxe, and Grenville Mellen were among the poets. After Hoffman left the *Monthly* in 1837, Benjamin increased the political content, but it still published other material as well.

v1-nsv6(v1-12)   Mar. 1833-Oct. 1838   APS II, Reel 377

Pagination is irregular.

Microfilm edition was prepared from NN copy.

SEE ALSO: New-England Magazine

THE AMERICAN MONTHLY MAGAZINE AND CRITICAL REVIEW. v.1-4; May 1817-Apr. 1819. [New York, Pub. for H. Biglow by Kirk & Mercein] 1817-18.

4 v.

"Vol. I was edited by H. Biglow; II. and III. by H. Biglow and O.L. Holley; IV, by O.L. Holley. De Witt Clinton, Dr. Mitchell, J.K. Paulding, and other eminent men, contributed to this magazine."—Sabin's Dict. of books relating to America. v.1.

Edited by H. Biglow and Orville Luther Holley, the *American Monthly Magazine* devoted most of its space to reviews, but also contained literary and religious news, a summary of current events, a list of "proposed publications," reports of medical cases, and a theatrical review. Prominent contributors included Dr. Samuel L. Mitchell, James K. Paulding, DeWitt Clinton, and Professor C.S. Rafinesque, who edited the "Museum of Natural Sciences" department.

v1-4   May 1817-Apr. 1819   APS II, Reel 58

* **THE AMERICAN MONTHLY REVIEW** v.1-4; Jan. 1832-Dec. 1833. Cambridge, Hilliard and Brown; Boston, Hilliard, Gray, 1832-33.

Merged into the New England magazine.

A well-printed and scholarly periodical edited by Sidney Willard which published such material as addresses, lectures, treatises, translated material, and articles on language and literature, chemistry, math, and history. Also included book reviews, poetry, essays, and biography.

v1-4   Jan. 1832-Dec. 1833   APS II, Reel 768

Vol.3: Lacks table of contents. Vol.4: Lacks title page and table of contents.

Microfilm edition was prepared from MiD copy.

THE AMERICAN MONTHLY REVIEW; or, Literary journal. With an appendix. v.1-3; Jan.-Dec. 1795. Philadelphia, S.H. Smith, 1795-96

3 v.

A literary miscellany which published articles on European affairs, travel, religion, science, and philosophy in addition to novels, poetry, and plays. Included much reprinted and translated material.

v1-3   Jan.-Dec. 1795   APS I, Reel 3

Microfilm edition was prepared from NHi copy.

THE AMERICAN MORAL & SENTIMENTAL MAGAZINE, consisting of a collection of select pieces, in prose and verse, from the best authors, on religious, moral, and sentimental subjects, calculated to form the understanding and improve the heart. v.1-2; July 3, 1797-May 21, 1798. New York, Printed by the editor, 1797-[98]

2 v. in 1. biweekly.

Paged continuously. Page 384 numbered 370. Thomas Kirk, editor.

Sentimental treatment of many subjects, including slavery and religion.

v1-2   July 3, 1797-May 21, 1798   APS I, Reel 3

Microfilm edition was prepared from MiU-C copy.

AMERICAN MUSEUM, and repository of arts, and sciences, as connected with domestic manufactures and national industry. (v.1, pt.1) Also, a list of all the patents granted by the United States up to the end of the year 1821 [continued by supplements to Apr. 1823] With a list of all the books that have been deposited in the Department of State, for securing their copy right according to law. Washington, Printed by S. Elliott, Pub. by J. Milligan, Georgetown, D.C., 1822-[23]

3 p. 1, 60, 72, xxiv, 13, 6, [9]-16 p. 4 pl.

The "American museum and repository of arts and sciences" and "List of patents" have also separate title pages.

This consisted of a list of new inventions with short descriptions, an alphabetical list of patents granted by the U.S. up to the end of the year 1821, and an alphabetical list of patentees including places of residence and dates patents were secured. Also included were a list of books in the Department of State for securing copyrights from January 1796-January 1822 which was continued by a supplement to April 1823, a list of the acts passed by Congress on the subject of patents, and a list of books, magazines and charts.

v1, pt.1   1822   APS II, Reel 58

THE AMERICAN MUSEUM OF LITERATURE AND THE ARTS. A monthly magazine. Ed. by N.C. Brooks and J. Evans Snodgrass. v.1-2; Sept. 1838-June 1839. Baltimore, Brooks & Snodgrass, 1838-39.

2 v. pl., port.

Title of v.1: "The American museum of science, literature, and the arts."

Originally the *North American Quarterly,* it was converted into a general monthly magazine by Nathan Brooks in 1838, but lasted only 10 months. Edgar Allan Poe was among the contributors.

American Museum of Science, Literature, and the Arts.
v1   Sept.-Dec. 1838   APS II, Reel 646
American Museum of Literature and the Arts.
v2   Jan.-June 1839   APS II, Reel 646

Microfilm edition was prepared from DLC copy.

AMERICAN MUSEUM OF SCIENCE, LITERATURE, AND THE ARTS. *SEE* American Museum of Literature and the Arts.

THE AMERICAN MUSEUM, OR, UNIVERSAL MAGAZINE, containing, essays on agriculture—commerce—manufactures—politics—morals—and manners. Sketches of national characters—natural and civil history—and biography. Law information—public papers— intelligence. Moral tales—ancient and modern poetry. v. 1-[12] Jan. 1787-Dec. 1792. Philadelphia, Printed by Mathew Carey.

12 v. illus., plates, map. monthly.

Title varies: 1787-1788, The American museum; or, Repository of ancient and modern fugitive pieces, &c. prose and poetical.

Mathew Carey, editor.

One of the first successful American magazines. The first half of the run consisted of reprints of Revolutionary pamphlets and belles-lettres. Beginning in 1790, original short fiction and poetry made up a large part of the contents.

American Museum; or, Repository of Ancient and Modern Fugitive Pieces, &c. Prose and Poetical
v1-4   Jan. 1787-Dec. 1788   APS I, Reel 4
American Museum, or, Universal Magazine.
v5   Jan. 1789-June 1789   APS I, Reel 4
v6-12   July 1789-Dec. 1792   Reel 5

Some pages are missing.

Microfilm edition was prepared from MWA copy.

AMERICAN MUSICAL JOURNAL. v.1, no.1-12; Oct. 1834-Nov. 1835. New York, 1834-1835.

1 v. (various pagings.)

A monthly magazine providing literature on music as well as a separate section of vocal and instrumental music. It included essays and extracts from standard works, biographical memoirs of composers, historical sketches of the music of various countries, articles on musical instruments, reviews of important musical publications, and lists of new music. The foriegn musical report gave a general view of the state and progress of the musical arts abroad, while the domestic musical report gave accounts of the theater, opera, oratorios, and concerts in the principal U.S. cities.

v1   Oct. 1834-Nov. 1835   APS II, Reel 769

Microfilm edition was prepared from DLC copy.

THE AMERICAN MUSICAL MAGAZINE. v.1, no.1-12; May 1786-Sept. 1787. New Haven, A. Doolittle & D. Read.

49 p.

Contained printed music.

v1, no.1-12   May 1786-Sept. 1787   APS I, Reel 6

Microfilm edition was prepared from CtY copy.

THE AMERICAN MUSICAL MAGAZINE v.1, no.1-2; Oct. 1800-Jan. 1801. [Northampton, Mass.]

48 p.

Film incomplete: v.1, no.1 (p. 1-24) wanting.

This short-lived magazine consisted entirely of musical pieces. Each issue presented both words and music for several religious songs.

v1, no.2   Jan. 1801   APS II, Reel 2

Microfilm edition was prepared from NN copy.

AMERICAN NATIONAL PREACHER. *SEE* National Preacher and Village Pulpit.

AMERICAN PENNY MAGAZINE. *SEE* Dwights American Magazine, and Family Newspaper.

AMERICAN PEOPLE'S JOURNAL OF SCIENCE, LITERATURE, AND ART. v.1, nos.1-2, Jan.-Feb. 1850. New York, 1850.

96 p.

S.B. Brittan was allied with Thomas Lake Harris and Carlos D. Stuart in the editorship of this Swedenborgian paper which focused mainly on science, literature, and art. The literary department featured letters from Europe by Carlos D. Stuart and a series of twelve mythic stories by Fanny Green, as well as essays, biography, historical and dramatic sketches, and original poetry. In addition, there were accounts of discoveries and inventions, and articles on psychology, physiology, art, architecture, and on applications of mechanical laws to manufacturing.

v1, nos.1-2   Jan.-Feb. 1850   APS II, Reel 333

Microfilm edition was prepared from NNHi copy.

AMERICAN PHRENOLOGICAL JOURNAL. *SEE* Phrenological Journal and Science of Health.

THE AMERICAN PIONEER; a monthly periodical, devoted to the objects of the Logan historical society; or, to collecting and publishing sketches relative to the early settlement and successive improvement of the country. v.1-2; Jan. 1842-Oct. 1843. Cincinnati, J.W. Williams, 1842-43.

2 v. illus., plates, plans.

Vol.1, 2d ed. J.S. Williams, editor.

Edited and published by John S. Williams, this monthly historical magazine was the organ of the Logan Historical Society of Ohio, and was devoted to the objects of the society—to preserve documents and other information relating to the early exploration, settlement, and development of the country. There is much on Ohio, but attention is also given to Pennsylvania, Michigan, Virginia, Massachusetts, and other southern and eastern states, and to the cities of Cincinnati, Cleveland, and Pittsburgh. Included are biographies; descriptions, with pictures, of many forts and buildings; and articles describing life in the early days and giving information on the Indians, and on battles, attacks, and massacres.

v1-2   Jan. 1842-Oct. 1843   APS II, Reel 297

Microfilm edition was prepared from MiU copy.

AMERICAN PRESBYTERIAN AND THEOLOGICAL REVIEW. *SEE* American Presbyterian Review.

* **THE AMERICAN PRESBYTERIAN REVIEW.** v.1-4, Jan. 1859-Oct. 1862; new ser., v.1-6, Jan. 1863-Oct. 1868; new ser., v.1-3, Jan. 1869-[1871] New York, C. Scribner, 1859-[71]

13 v. ports. quarterly.

Absorbed the Presbyterian quarterly review in Jan. 1863. Title varies: 1859-62, The American theological review. 1863-68, The American Presbyterian and theological review. 1869-71, The American Presbyterian review.

Editors: 1859-71, H.B. Smith (with J.M. Sherwood and others, 1863-71) Imprint varies: 1858-62, New York, C. Scribner; Boston, Moore, Munroe.—1863-71, New York, J.M. Sherwood.
Merged into the Biblical repertory and Princeton review which continued as the Presbyterian quarterly and Princeton review (later the Princeton review)

In 1859, the *American Presbyterian Review* was founded as the *American Theological Review*. It was intended to represent New England Calvinism, while bringing about a union between Congregationalism and Presbyterianism; however, New Yorkers took it over, and under Henry B. Smith of the Union Theological Seminary, it became a leading religious periodical.

In 1863, the *Presbyterian Quarterly Review* of Philadelphia, which also favored uniting old and new factions of the church, merged into this publication, becoming the *American Presbyterian and Theological Review*. In 1869 the title was shortened to *American Presbyterian Review*. In 1871 the publisher, James Sherwood, purchased the *Princeton Review* into which the *American Presbyterian Review* merged.

American Theological Review
v1-4   1859-1862   APS III, Reel 205
American Presbyterian and Theological Review
nsv1-5   Jan. 1863-Oct. 1867   APS III, Reel 206
nsv6   Jan.-Oct. 1868   Reel 206
American Presbyterian Review
ns(s3) v1-3   Jan. 1869-Oct. 1871   APS III, Reel 207

Some pages are stained, torn, or have print missing.

Microfilm edition was prepared from DLC, MnU and NCH copies.

AMERICAN PUBLISHERS' CIRCULAR AND LITERARY GAZETTE. *SEE* American Literary Gazette and Publishers' Circular.

AMERICAN QUARTERLY CHURCH REVIEW. *SEE* Church Review.

AMERICAN QUARTERLY CHURCH REVIEW, AND ECCLESIASTICAL REGISTER *SEE* Church Review.

* **THE AMERICAN QUARTERLY OBSERVER.** v.1-3; July 1833-Oct. 1834. Boston, Perkins & Marvin, 1833-34.

3 v.

B.B. Edwards, editor. Merged into the Biblical repository in Jan. 1835.

Edited by Bela B. Edwards, the Andover scholar, the *American Quarterly Observer* dealt with literary, political, social, theological, philosophical, and scientific subjects. Among its varied contents were writings on Hume and John Milton, reviews, biographies, literary news, and articles discussing the periodical press, public affairs, law, and moral reform. Contributors included C.C. Felton, Jacob Abbott, and Richard H. Dana

v1-3   July 1833-Oct. 1834   APS II, Reel 297

Microfilm edition was prepared from MiU copy.

SEE ALSO: Biblical Repository and Classical Review.

* **THE AMERICAN QUARTERLY REGISTER** v.1-18; July 1827-May 1846. Boston, American education society [etc., etc.]

18v. pl., ports, map.

Title varies: July 1827-Oct. 1828, The Quarterly journal of the American education society. –Jan. 1829-May 1830, The Quarterly register and journal of the American education society.– Aug. 1830-May 1831, The Quarterly register of the American education society.–Aug. 1831-May 1843, The American quarterly register, (caption title, Aug. 1831-May 1837: The Quarterly register)-Aug. 1843-May 1846, Quarterly journal of the American education society.

Editors: July 1827-1830, E. Cornelius, B.B. Edwards.–1831-May 1837, B.B. Edwards.–Aug. 1837-May 1841, B.B. Edwards, W. Cogswell.–Aug. 1841-May 1842, B.B. Edwards, S.H. Riddell.–Aug. 1842-May 1843, S.H. Riddel.–Aug. 1843-May 1846, unable to be ascertained. Imprint varies: July 1827-May 1830, Andover, Flagg and Gould.–Aug. 1830-May 1834, Boston, Perkins & Marvin; Aug. 1834-May 1846, American education society (1893 as the Congregational education society) May 1843, the American quarterly

register was discontinued. Publication of the Quarterly journal, which had been printed with the American Quarterly register and also in a separate form, was continued The American quarterly register, v.15, p.iii-iv. Advertisement. Includes a General index to the first ten volumes of the American quarterly register, from July, 1827 to May, 1838. Boston, Printed by Perkins & Marvin, 1839. On film: General index with v.1 and 11.

Edited by Bela B. Edwards and others, this was one of the most important periodicals devoted to education. Although interested primarily in the education of candidates for the ministry and mission fields, it also touched on more general topics in the education field. Contents included statistical material, such as listings of churches and ministers, activities of the American (later Congregational) Education Society, much biography, histories of universities, and essays and discussions pertaining to the ministry and to education. Beginning in 1836 a steel portrait was included in each number.

Quarterly Journal of the American Education Society
v1, no.1-6   July 1827-Oct. 1828   APS II, Reel 532
Quarterly Register and Journal of the American Education Society
v1,no.7-v2   Jan. 1829-May 1830   APS II, Reel 532
Quarterly Register of the American Education Society
v3   Aug. 1830-May 1831   APS II, Reel 532
American Quarterly Register
v4-6   Aug. 1831-May 1834   APS II, Reel 532
v7-12   Aug. 1834-May 1840   Reel 533
v13-15   Aug. 1840-May 1843   Reel 534
Quarterly Journal of the American Education Society
v16-18   Aug. 1843-May 1846   APS II, Reel 534

Vol.4: Pg. 352 is misnumbered. Vol.5: Pg. 211 is stained. Vol.6: Issue 3 is bound and photographed before issue 2. Vol.7: Pg. 184 has print missing. Vol.8: Pgs. 176 and 182 have faded print. Index for vols. 1-10 is bound and photographed at end of vol.11. Vol.12: Pgs. 401-08 are missing in number only Vols. 16-18: Indexes and tables of contents are missing; not available for photographing.

Microfilm edition was prepared from CtY, MH, and MiU copies.

AMERICAN QUARTERLY REGISTER AND MAGAZINE. *SEE* Stryker's American Register and Magazine.

* **THE AMERICAN QUARTERLY REVIEW** v.1-22; Mar. 1827-Dec. 1837. Philadelphia, Carey, Lea & Carey [1827]-37

22 v.

Robert Walsh, editor.

Begun by Robert Walsh in 1827, the *American Quarterly Review* was called dull by most critics, and certainly was not inviting in appearance, consisting almost entirely of reviews, one after another, with nothing to break up the pages of small type. It was also criticized for its reviewing of poetry and for its rather naive nationalism. There was much variety, however; geography and travel, astronomy, history, biography, law education, European literature, the classics, and the fine arts were among the subjects treated. There were some good articles on the West and American drama was occasionally discussed. Dr. James McHenry, an Irish born poet and physician of Philadelphia, was a leading poetry reviewer; and other contributors included George Bancroft, who wrote on history and general literature; James Kirk Paulding, who wrote on varied subjects; Professor James Renwick of Columbia, who contributed reviews of scientific books; Judge Joseph Hopkinson, who wrote on legal works; and Mrs. E.F. Ellet, who wrote papers on European belles-lettres.

v1-6   Mar. 1827-Dec. 1829   APS II, Reel 298
v7-12   Mar. 1830-Dec. 1832   Reel 299

v13-18	Mar. 1833-Dec. 1835	Reel 300
v19-22	Mar. 1836-Dec. 1837	Reel 301

Microfilm edition was prepared from MiU copy.

AMERICAN RAILROAD JOURNAL. *SEE* Mechanics Magazine, and Journal of the Mechanics Institute.

AMERICAN RAILWAY TIMES. *SEE* Railway Times

AMERICAN REGISTER AND INTERNATIONAL JOURNAL. *SEE* Niles' National Register.

THE AMERICAN REGISTER; or, general repository of history, politics and science. v.1-7; 1806/7-1810. Philadelphia, C. & A. Conrad; Baltimore, Conrad, Lucas, 1807-11.

7 v.

Editors: v.1-5, C.B.Brown.–v.6-7, R. Walsh.

In 1806 Charles Brockden Brown began a semiannual publication called the *American Register or General Repository of History, Politics, and Science,* which he conducted until his death in 1810. Each issue of this encyclopedia of current information contained five hundred pages, most of them devoted to "annals" of Europe and America, abstracts of laws, state papers, a section of news, and registers of deaths. There were also catalogs of British and American publications, some miscellaneous articles, and a little poetry. Robert Walsh edited the last two volumes of the *Register,* the second of them devoted to 1810 but issued the following year.

v1-5	1806-09	APS II, Reel 2
v6-7	1810	Reel 59

Vol.3: pages 177-280 are missing in number only.

Microfilm edition was prepared from DLC copy.

THE AMERICAN REGISTER; or, Summary review of history, politics, and literature. Philadelphia, Published by Thomas Dobson, William Fry, Printer, 1817.

2 v.

R. Walsh, editor.

This was the second *American Register* to be edited by Robert Walsh; he had previously served as editor for Brown's *American Register* during its last year. The new *American Register* published articles on the literature of Europe, including Italian and Spanish literature, miscellaneous literary and scientific news, debates of the British Parliament, interesting law cases and decisions, and a finance section.

v1-2	1817	APS II, Reel 59

THE AMERICAN REPERTORY OF ARTS, SCIENCES, AND MANUFACTURES. Ed. by James J. Mapes. v.1-4; Jan. 1840-Jan. 1842. New York, W.A. Cox; Boston, Weeks, Jordan.

4 v. pl., diagr. monthly.

Provided comprehensive coverage of the latest developments in the various areas of science and manufacturing, emphasizing metallurgy, and mechanical, industrial, and chemical engineering. Articles, often accompanied by diagrams and figures, described engines, new equipment, and methods for manufacturing a variety of products. Also included were reviews of new publications, a section describing advances in science made in foreign countries, and humorous anecdotes. At the end was a description of recent American patents, and a listing of English patents.

v1-4	Jan. 1840-Jan. 1842	APS II, Reel 646

Microfilm edition was prepared from DI-GS and DLC copies.

THE AMERICAN REPERTORY OF ARTS, SCIENCES, AND USEFUL LITERATURE. v.1-3, no.8; 1830-July 1832. By M.T.C. Gould. Philadelphia, M.T.C. Gould, 18-

v. monthly.

Film covers issues for Aug. 2, 1830-Apr. 1832.

The object of this work was to furnish a miniature encyclopedia giving a concise view of the most interesting topics of the age by condensing and systematizing useful material. Included are: "The Art of Shorthand Writing," "Dr. Locke's Method for a Commonplace Book," abstracts of the Constitution of the U.S. and of some states, an outline of the U.S. government, a classical dictionary, and encyclopedic-type listings of various areas of study–history, philosophy, chemistry, geography, optics, and geology.

v1-3	August 2, 1830-April 1832	APS II, Reel 734

No Indexes. Best copy available for photographing. Vol.1: Supplement precedes text. Pg. 23 has print missing. Vol.3: Microfilm edition includes nos.3-4, March-April 1832.

Microfilm edition was prepared from DI-GS and DLC copies.

AMERICAN REVIEW. *SEE* Bookman; A Review of Books and Life.

AMERICAN REVIEW: A WHIG JOURNAL ... *SEE* American Whig Review.

THE AMERICAN REVIEW, AND LITERARY JOURNAL, for 1801-1802. v.1-2. New-York, T. & J. Swords. 1801-02.

2 v. quarterly.

Edited by Charles Brockden Brown and others. Preceded by the Monthly magazine, and American review.

At the beginning of 1801, Charles Brockden Brown's *Monthly Magazine, and American Review* became the quarterly *American Review, and Literary Journal.* Also edited by Brown, the *American Review* was intended to "comprehend a survey of the state of literature, arts, and science in America," but although it gave much attention to science and mechanics it was less interesting than its predecessor. The first section was devoted to reviews of new books, with special attention being given to American literary works. The second section contained news of new patents, new inventions and discoveries, and new publications.

v1-2	1801-1802	APS II, Reel 3

Microfilm edition was prepared from DLC copy.

SEE ALSO: Monthly Magazine, and American Review.

* **THE AMERICAN REVIEW OF HISTORY AND POLITICS,** and general repository of literature and state papers. v.1-4; Jan. 1811-Oct. 1812. Philadelphia, Printed for Farrand and Nicholas, 1811-12.

4 v. fold. tables. quarterly.

In each volume the appendix, consisting of state papers, etc., has separate pagination. Robert Walsh, editor.

Founded in 1811 by Robert Walsh and edited by him through 1811 and 1812, the *American Review* was the first standard quarterly review in America. Although it proclaimed an interest in both politics and literature, it was largely devoted to politics, particularly to the difficulties with Napoleon, giving comparatively little space to belles-lettres. Each number consisted of 200 pages and an appendix of state papers. Except for a few extracts from English and French periodicals, Walsh wrote most of the *Review* himself.

v1-4   Jan. 1811-Oct. 1812   APS II, Reel 60

THE AMERICAN SOCIALIST. Devoted to the enlargement and perfection of home. v.1-4; Mar. 30, 1876-Dec. 25, 1879. Oneida, N.Y., 1876-79.

4 v. weekly.

Editors: J.H. Noyes, W.A. Hinds. Supersedes the Oneida circular (1851-76)

Published by the Oneida group, the *American Socialist* contained articles on communism, the Oneida brand of spirtualism, and free love.

v1-4   March 1876-Dec. 25, 1879   APS III, Reel 243

Vol.4: Pg. 170 print missing, readable.

Microfilm edition was prepared from WHi copy.

SEE ALSO: Oneida Circular.

AMERICAN SOCIETY FOR PROMOTING THE CIVILIZATION AND GENERAL IMPROVEMENT OF THE INDIAN TRIBES IN THE UNITED STATES. The first annual report of the American society for promoting the civilization and general improvement of the Indian tribes in the United States. Communicated to the society, in the city of Washington, with the documents in the appendix, at their meeting, Feb. 6, 1824. New Haven, S. Converse, 1824.

74 p., 11.

Appendix included "Indian languages", p. [47]-65.

Edited by Jedidiah Morse.

This publication was devoted entirely to the subject of the American Indian. In addition to the constitution of the society, it contained such material as articles on the Indian languages and histories of some of the tribes.

no.1   1824   APS II, Reel 534

Index is missing.

Microfilm edition was prepared from MiU copy.

THE AMERICAN SUNDAY SCHOOL MAGAZINE. v.1-8; July 1824-Jan. 1832. Philadelphia, American Sunday School Union.

8 v. illus., ports. Monthly, July 1824-Dec. 1830; quarterly, Apr. 1831-Jan. 1832.

Vol.8 also called new ser., v.1. Title varies: Apr. 1831-Jan. 1832, The Quarterly Sunday school magazine. Other slight variations in title.

The *American Sunday-School Magazine* was devoted mainly to promoting the Sunday school movement and to keeping the reader up to date concerning the activities of Sunday school unions and societies in various states. It also included much Sunday school-related news, lessons for Sunday school teachers, and articles on religious instruction for children, as well as some book reviews and occasional poetry and anecdotes.

American Sunday School Magazine
v1-7   July 1824-Dec. 1830   APS II, Reel 305
Quarterly Sunday School Magazine
v8   Apr. 1831-Jan. 1832   APS II, Reel 305

Microfilm edition was prepared from MBC copy.

SEE ALSO: American Sunday-School Teachers' Magazine and Journal of Education.

AMERICAN SUNDAY-SCHOOL TEACHERS' MAGAZINE AND JOURNAL OF EDUCATION. v.1, nos.1-12; Dec. 1823-Nov. 1824. Philadelphia, 1823-1824.

380 p.

Merged into American Sunday school magazine, later Quarterly Sunday school magazine.

A short-lived magazine published in Philadelphia, the center of the early Sunday-school movement.

v1   Dec. 1823-Nov. 1824   APS II, Reel 1158

Vol.1: P. 88 has print faded, pgs. 225-34 are missing in number only.

Microfilm edition was prepared from DeU copy.

AMERICAN THEOLOGICAL REVIEW. *SEE* American Presbyterian Review.

AMERICAN TURF REGISTER AND SPORTING MAGAZINE. v.1-15; Sept. 1829-Dec. 1844. New York.

15 v. illus., plates. monthly.

Published in Baltimore, 1829-38.

The first of its kind in the United States, the *American Turf Register* was founded and edited for the first ten years by John S. Skinner. According to the *Knickerbocker* it had no "superior in any country, for various merits, sporting, literary and pictorial." Illustrations were sporting pictures usually involving animals, such as diagrams of horses. The editor felt there was a great need for an authentic record of the performances and pedigrees of bred horses. However, the periodical was not devoted to the turf alone as it also featured material on shooting, hunting, fishing and other outdoor sports.

v1-3	Sept. 1829-Aug. 1832	APS II, Reel 404
v4-8	Sept. 1832-Nov. 1837	Reel 405
v9-12	Jan. 1838-Dec. 1841	Reel 406
v13-15	Jan. 1842-Dec. 1844	Reel 407

Vols.6-7: Pagination is irregular.

Microfilm edition was prepared from DLC and NN copy.

THE AMERICAN UNIVERSAL MAGAZINE. v.1-4; Jan. 2, 1797-Mar. 7, 1798. Philadelphia, R. Lee, [1797-98]

4 v. plates, ports.

Weekly, Jan. 2-23, 1797; biweekly, Feb. 1797-Mar. 1798.

Generally eclectic in character.

v1-2	Jan. 2, 1797-June 13, 1797	APS I, Reel 6
v 3-4	July 10, 1797-Mar. 7, 1798	Reel 7

Several pages are missing.

Microfilm edition was prepared from MWA and WHi copy.

* THE AMERICAN WHIG REVIEW. v.1-6, Jan. 1845-Dec. 1847; v.7-16 (new ser., v.1-10) Jan. 1848-Dec. 1852. New York, Wiley and Putnam, 1845-52.

16 v. ports. monthly.

Title varies: 1845-47, The American review: a Whig journal of politics, literature, art and science. 1848-Apr. 1850, The American review: a Whig journal devoted to politics and literature. (Title-pages for Jan.-June 1850 reads: The American Whig review; single numbers, Jan.-Apr. 1850, have title: The American review) May 1850-52, The American Whig review.

Editors: 1845-47, G.H. Colton.–1848-49? J.D. Whelpley.

One of the chief purposes of the *American Whig Review* was to help elect Henry Clay to the presidency, but after his defeat, party leaders felt they needed an organ of opinion to correspond to their opponents' *Democratic Review*. The *Whig Review* featured politics, much of it written by the chief political writer, Daniel D. Barnard. Also included were tales by Mrs. E.F. Ellet, translations of German and French poetry, vigorous literary criticism, comment upon American plays, and many articles about the arts in New York. The *Review* was famous for its biographies of statesmen, illustrated by engraved plates, and another specialty was its defense of American literature against attacks at home and abroad. It also included "Critical Notices," reports of current event, and proceedings of Congress. The editors and associate editors wrote much of the material, and contributors included Poe, Lowell, Daniel Webster, Edward Everett, John Calhoun, Horace Greeley, Henry Raymond, and a trio of notable critics—Henry T. Tuckerman, Grant White and "Carl Benson."

American Review: A Whig Journal ...

v1-6	Jan. 1845-Dec. 1847	APS II, Reel 302
v7-11, no.4	Jan. 1848-Apr. 1850	Reel 303

American Whig Review

v11, no.5-6	May-June 1850	APS II, Reel 303
v12-16	July 1850-Dec. 1852	Reel 304

Microfilm edition was prepared from MiU copy.

* THE ANALECTIC MAGAZINE. Comprising original reviews, biography, analytical abstracts of new publications, translations from French journals, and selections from the most esteemed British reviews. v.1-14, 1813-19; new ser.,

v. 1-2, 1820. Philadelphia, M. Thomas, 1813-20.

16 v. illus., plates (part col.) ports., plans, facsim. monthly. Added t.-p., engraved.

A.H. Smyth in his "Philadelphia magazines" states that Washington Irving was editor 1813-14. Title varies: 1813-15, The Analectic magazine, containing selections from foreign reviews and magazines. 1816, The Analectic magazine, and naval chronicle. 1817-19 The Analectic magazine ... Comprising original reviews, biography [etc.]

Preceded by Select reviews of literature. Continued as the Literary gazette; or, Journal of criticism, science, and the arts.

The *Analectic Magazine,* a new series of *Select Reviews* edited by Washington Irving, devoted most of its space to selections from British periodicals. There were also some original reviews, by contributors Gulian C. Verplanck and J.K. Paulding, and others, as well as by Irving himself, along with "literary and scientific intelligence" and biographies of naval heroes. When Thomas Isaac Wharton succeeded Irving as editor, the number of original contributions increased. In 1815 a history of the U.S. Navy was begun, followed by a department called "The Naval Chronicle." By 1817 the magazine had lost most of its eclectic character, while retaining its reviews and travel and science articles. Illustration was one of the magazine's chief distinctions.

v1-5	1813-June 1815	APS II, Reel 61
v6-9	July 1815-Feb. 1817	Reel 62
v9-14	Mar. 1817-Dec. 1819	Reel 63
nsv1-2	1820	Reel 64

SEE ALSO: Literary Gazette *and* Select Reviews of Literature, and Spirit of Foreign Magazines.

THE ANALYST; or Mathematical museum. Containing new elucidations, improvements and discoveries, in the various branches of mathematics. v.1, 1808; new ser. v.1, 1814. Philadelphia, W.P. Farrand.

2 v.

Title varies slightly.

Edited by R. Adrain.

Conducted by R. Adrain, a professor at Columbia College, New York, this math magazine was to contain "new elucidations, discoveries and improvements, in various branches of the mathematics." Each issue contained one or two articles on mathematics theory, and sections of problems sent in by readers, with their solutions.

v1	1808	APS II, Reel 3
nsv1	1814	Reel 64

Microfilm edition was prepared from CtY copy.

THE ANDOVER REVIEW; a religious and theological monthly. v.1-19; Jan. 1884- Dec. 1893. Editors, Egbert C. Smyth, William J. Tucker, J.W. Churchill, George Harris, Edward Y. Hincks, professors in Andover theological seminary, with the assistance of their colleagues in the faculty. Boston, New York, Houghton, Mifflin, 1884-93.

19 v. monthly, 1884-92; bimonthly, 1893.

Vol. 10 contains index to the first 10 volumes.

After *Bibliotheca Sacra* moved its publishing quarters to Oberlin, Ohio, the faculty at the Andover Theological Seminary began publishing its new journal, entitled the *Andover Review*. The first issue is by far the most important, overshadowing perhaps the entire file. In it, the guideline of the journal was set—that of a more liberal and modern view toward religion. It was this leaning toward liberalism which later led to the famous "Andover trials". These trials, more than the excellence of the magazine itself, gained for the *Review* its greatest fame. It was not long after the trials ended that the *Review* ceased publication. In the *Review,* readers may trace the advance of the church from the older Calvinism to the more modern religious views.

Cumulative Index, v1-10	1884-1888	APS III, Reel 1
v1-5	Jan. 1884-June 1886	Reel 1
v6-10	July 1886-Dec 1888	Reel 2
v11-15	Jan. 1889-June 1891	Reel 3
v16-19	July 1891-Dec 1893	Reel 4

Microfilm edition was prepared from MiD, MiEM, and ICM copies.

THE ANGLO AMERICAN, a journal of literature, news, politics, the drama, fine arts, etc. Edited by A.D. Paterson. v.1-9, v.10, no.1-4; Apr. 29, 1843-Nov. 13, 1847. New York, E.L. Garvin [1843-47]

10 v. in 7. 1 illus. weekly.

Absorbed Smith's weekly volume in April 1846. Merged into the Albion.

A literary miscellany which provided coverage of literature, fine arts, and drama with a variety of material—reviews of art exhibitions and plays, literary criticism, poetry, anecdotes, and biography. Also included were many short pieces and narratives, foreign and shipping news, and articles dealing with science and inventions, natural history, and travel.

v1-4	April 29, 1843-April 19, 1845	APS II, Reel 647
v5-8	April 26, 1845-April 17, 1847	Reel 648
v9-10	April 24-Nov. 13, 1847	Reel 649

Vols.1-2: Indexes appear at the ends of the volumes. Vols.7 and 10: Indexes are lacking.

Microfilm edition was prepared from DLC, MH and NNC copies.

SEE ALSO: Albion.

ANGLO-AMERICAN MAGAZINE. Feb.-July, 1843. Boston, 1843.

312 p. illus., port. monthly.

The *Anglo-American Magazine* was a mainly eclectic literary magazine, selecting most of its material from British periodicals, including *Bentley's Miscellany, Blackwood's Magazine, Dublin University Magazine,* and *Tait's Magazine.* It contained poetry, tales, some in serial form, illustrations, and articles on a wide variety of topics.

v1	Feb.-July 1843	APS II, Reel 378

Microfilm edition was prepared from DLC copy.

ANNALES PHILOSOPHIQUES, POLITIQUES ET LITTERAIRES. no.1. Philadelphia, 1807.

128 p.

This French-language publication gave much attention to history and geography; there were numerous articles on the history of the American continent, and on various areas of the U.S., Canada, and South America, as well as items on various islands throughout the world, and particularly in the Caribbean. In addition, there was some material on philosophy, sociology, and medicine.

no.1	1807	APS II, Reel 3

Microfilm edition was prepared from ICN copy.

ANNALS OF BENEFICENCE. no.1-2; Oct. 16-31, 1823. Philadelphia.

2 no.

This short-lived journal listed examples of charitable deeds to inspire virtuous actions in its readers.

no.1-2	Oct. 16-31, 1823	APS II, Reel 64

ANNALS OF NATURE; or, Annual synopsis of New Genera and species of animals in North America. v.1, 1820. Lexington, Ky., 1820.

16 p.

This issue by C.S. Rafinesque of Transylvania University consisted of listings of new genera and species of animals and plants of North America. Both listings were organized by class and species and included short descriptions and locations. Though it was to be an annual listing, only one was published.

v1	1820	APS II, Reel 64

ANNUAL LAW REGISTER OF THE UNITED STATES, by William Griffith. v.3-4; 1821-22. Burlington, N.J., D. Allinson, 1822.

2 v.

Paged continuously. Vols.1-2 never published.

These various issues by lawyer William Griffith described the state laws and regulations as of 1822 of Alabama, Connecticut, Delaware, Georgia, Indiana, Illinois, Kentucky, Louisiana, Maine, Maryland, Massachusetts, Mississippi, Missouri, New Hampshire, New Jersey, New York, North Carolina, Ohio, Pennsylvania, Rhode Island, South Carolina, Tennessee, Virginia, and Vermont. Also included were lists of national and state officers with judicial department connections, the times and places of circuit and district courts, and names of judges, attornies and counsellors.

v3-4	1821-1822	APS II, Reel 65

THE ANTI-MASONIC REVIEW, AND MAGAZINE; pub. monthly in the city of New York. Intended to take note of the origin and history, of the pretensions and character, and of the standard works and productions, of free masonry. By Henry Dana Ward, a renouncing mason. v.1-2; Jan. 1828-Dec. 1830. New York, H.D. Ward.

Superseded by New York register and antimasonic review.

A monthly periodical published by Henry Dana Ward, a former Mason and opponent of Free Masonry. The magazine's sole purpose was to oppose and destroy the Masons by publishing a variety of material about the order—information on its origin and history, its "pretensions" and character, and a record of the events which led to investigation and criticism of it. It also covered the various anti-

Masonic activities—conventions, speeches, etc., and included histories of various lodges and discussions of their rules, songs, and customs.

v1-2   Jan. 1828-Dec. 1830   APS II, Reel 769

Table of contents appears at the end of each volume.

Microfilm edition was prepared from MH copy.

THE ANTI-SLAVERY EXAMINER. New York, American Anti-Slavery Society (nos.1-14); 1836-45.

14 nos.

Several of the numbers have been issued in three or more editions. No.7 has supplement, entitled: The Anti-slavery examiner—Extra, separately paged.

Started as periodical with volume numbering of first two numbers, vol.I. no.1-2; August-September 1836. With no.3, volume number was dropped and each publication took form of monograph with separate title-page.

Published by the American Anti-Slavery Society, the *Anti-Slavery Examiner* appealed to the people of the United States to unite with the Society in maintaining common and unquestioned political rights. Appeals were made to Christian women of the South through Biblical quotations to join the cause of the Society. Speeches and letters on anti-slavery were reprinted. Testimony from slaveholders and other material taken mainly from slave state newspapers endeavored to present slavery as it was. Longer articles such as "The Bible Against Slavery", "Emancipation in the West Indies." and correspondence between a South Carolina Congressman and one of the secretaries of the American Anti-Slavery Society pointed out the moral and political arguments against slavery.

nos.1-14   1836-1845   APS II, Reel 408

Pagination is irregular.

Microfilm edition was prepared from NIC copy.

THE ANTI-SLAVERY RECORD. v.1-3; Jan. 1835-Dec. 1837. New York, American Anti-Slavery Society, 1835-38.

3 v. illus. monthly.

This small monthly journal of the American Anti-Slavery Society, which was established by William Lloyd Garrison, was filled with stories of the suffering of slaves. Almost every issue had a woodcut on the first page pointing out this inequity. All articles, poems and anecdotes carried the slavery theme. Meeting notices and detailed lists of receipts and funds of the Society were printed. Later whole issues were devoted to one article such as "Intellect of Colored Men" and "Are Slaveholders Mansteaters?"

v1-3   Jan. 1835-Dec. 1837   APS II, Reel 408

Microfilm edition was prepared from DLC and MiU copy.

ANTI-SLAVERY REPORTER. A periodical. v.1(no.1-6); June-Nov. 1833. New York, 1833.

96 p. monthly.

Superseded by the American anti-slavery reporter, (Jan.-Aug. 1834,1 v.) Contents.—no. 1. A letter to Thomas Clarkson, by J. Cropper: and Prejudice vincible ... by C. Stuart.—no.2. Three months in Jamaica ... by H. Whitely, correspondence on the Colonization society, &c.—no. 3. Extracts from Clarkson's thoughts on the

practicability ... of the emancipation of the slaves, &c.—no. 4. Justice and expediency ... By J.G. Whittier.—no. 5. Address of the New York city anti-slavery society, &c.—no. 6. Review of the law of retribution: "Union of colonizationists and abolitionists," &c.

This antislavery publication was little more than an antislavery tract sent out to clergymen and others. Each issue was generally devoted to only one or two lengthy items; contents included essays on slavery, an address of the New York City Antislavery Society, and news items on the progress being made against slavery, as well as poetry and book reviews.

v1, no.1-6   June-Nov. 1833   APS II, Reel 378

Microfilm edition was prepared from DLC copy.

SEE ALSO: American Anti-Slavery Reporter.

* APPLETONS' JOURNAL: a magazine of general literature. v.1-15; Apr. 3, 1869- June 3, 1876; new ser., v.1-11; July 1876-Dec. 1881. New York, D. Appleton, 1869-[81]

26 v. illus., plates. Weekly, Apr. 1869-June 1876; monthly, July 1876-Dec. 1881.

Title varies: Apr. 1869-June 1876, Appletons' journal of literature, science, and art. July 1876-Dec. 1878, Appletons' journal: a monthly miscellany of popular literature. 1879-81, Appletons' journal: a magazine of general literature.

Appletons' Journal, published by D. Appleton and Company, presented a vivid picture of post-Civil War America. It contained serial publications of novels, short articles on art, drama, education, travel, popular science, and biography. Many famous authors were published in its pages.

Appletons' Journal of Literature, Science and Art

v1-4	Apr. 3, 1869-Dec. 31, 1870	APS III, Reel 244
v5-8	Jan. 7, 1871-Dec. 28, 1872	Reel 245
v9-12	Jan. 1, 1873-Dec. 26, 1874	Reel 246
v13-15	Jan. 2, 1875-June, 1876	Reel 247

Appleton's Journal

nsv1-2	July, 1876-June, 1877	APS III, Reel 247
nsv3-9	July, 1877-Dec. 1880	Reel 248
nsv10-11	Jan.-Dec. 1881	Reel 249

Some pages are torn or have faded print.

Microfilm was prepared from MiD, OWoC copies.

APPLETON'S JOURNAL OF LITERATURE, SCIENCE AND ART. See Appleton's Journal: A Magazine of General Literature.

ARCHITECTURAL RECORD. See American Architect and Architecture.

ARCHITECTURAL REVIEW. SEE American Architect and Architecture.

ARCHITECTURE. SEE American Architect and Architecture.

ARCHIVES OF USEFUL KNOWLEDGE, a work devoted to commerce, manufactures, rural and domestic economy,

agriculture, and the useful arts. By James Mease. v.1-3, July 1810-April 1813. Philadelphia; Published by David Hogan, Thomas T. Stiles, Printer.

3 v. illus., pl. quarterly.

A quarterly work devoted to commerce, manufactures, rural and domestic economy, agriculture and the useful arts, edited by Dr. James Mease, secretary to the Agricultural Society of Philadelphia. It included general overviews of commerce throughout the world as well as detailed articles on various, generally agricultural, trades. Some biographies were also included.

v 1-3   July 1810-Apr. 1813   APS II, Reel 65

ARCTURUS, A journal of books and opinion. v.1-3; Dec. 1840-May 1842. New York, B.G. Trevett, 1841-42.

3 v. pl., port. monthly.

C. Mathews and E.A. Duyckinck, editors.

A general monthly magazine, founded in 1840 by Cornelius Mathews, which had a civilizing and cultural influence in America during its short life. Designed to have the mixed character of a review and a magazine, it presented literary criticism, a review of life in New York, and a fine arts department which treated painting and theater. Famous contributors included Hawthorne, Lowell, and Longfellow. A political satire, "The Career of Puffer Hopkins," ran serially through most of the magazine. Combined with the *Boston Miscellany* in 1842.

v1-3   Dec. 1840-May 1842   APS II, Reel 734

Microfilm edition was prepared from CSmH and DLC copies.

THE ARENA. v.1-41 (no. 233); Dec. 1889-Aug. 1909. Boston, Arena Pub. Co.

41 v. illus., plates, ports., maps, facsims. Monthly, forming 2 vols. annually (except Dec. 1894-Nov. 1895. 4 v.)

No numbers were issued from Apr. to June 1909. Editors: 1889-96, B.O. Flower—1897-Sept. 1898, J.C. Ridpath.—Oct. 1898-Sept. 1899, Paul Tyner.—Oct. 1899-Jan. 1900. J.E. McLean.—Feb.-Oct. 1900. N.O. Fanning.—Nov. 1900-Mar. 1904, C.B. Patterson, B.O. Flower and others.—Apr. 1904-Aug. 1909, B.O. Flower. Imprint varies: Dec. 1889-Sept. 1899, Boston, The Arena publishing company.—Oct. 1899-Mar. 1904, New York, The Alliance publishing company [etc.]—Apr. 1904-Aug. 1909, Trenton, N.J. and Boston, A. Brandt. Absorbed the Journal of practical metaphysics, the New time and the Temple in Dec. 1898; the Coming age in Nov. 1900. Merged into Christian work.

Of the social and political reform magazines that found birth in the 1890's, the news-minded *Arena* was one of the most active. Indeed, the title itself was an indication of the material to be found on its pages. Created by Benjamin O. Flower, the son of a clergyman, the *Arena's* pages were open to honest controversy including religious issues, unemployment, child labor, poverty, sweatshops, municipal government, prison reform, psychic phenomena, unionism, women's rights, dress reform, and tax reform.
A distinguished editor, Flower had the ability to arouse both pulpit and press with numerous exposes. A unique feature of the *Arena* was the pursuit of various causes at the same time.
The list of contributors reflects the variety and scope covered. Helen Campbell, N.P. Gilman, Frank Parson, W.T. Stead, Edward Bellamy, Hamlin Garland, Minot J. Savage, Richard Hodgson, M.D. Conway and Edmund Gosse were but a few.
The *Arena's* circulation was around 25,000 copies for the most part. Although this figure was impressive in view of the *Arena's*

competition with *Forum, Century, Harper's* and the *Atlantic Monthly,* it was never enough to show prosperity. The *Arena* was sold time after time, suspended for short periods, and finally merged into *Christian Work.*

v1-5	Dec. 1889-May 1892	APS III, Reel 92
v6-9	June 1892-May 1894	Reel 93
v10-14	June 1894-Nov. 1895	Reel 94
v15-19	Dec. 1895-June 1898	Reel 95
v20-25	July 1898-June 1901	Reel 96
v26-32	July 1901-Dec. 1904	Reel 97
v33-38	Jan. 1905-Dec. 1907	Reel 98
v39-41	Jan. 1908-Aug. 1909	Reel 99

Several volumes have faded or missing print, or some stained pages. Volumes 8-17 have supplements. Volumes 20-30, and 41 are missing indexes. Please refer to table of contents.

Microfilm edition prepared from MiD, MiGr, NbO, NPV, NR, C, CCC, Mi, ATT, OU, and Nh copies.

ARGOSY. *SEE* Peterson Magazine.

THE ARIEL. A semimonthly literary and miscellaneous gazette. v.1-6; May 5, 1827-Nov. 24, 1832. Philadelphia, E. Morris.

6 v. in 4. illus., plates.

Nos. 1-11 of v.1 were published by E. Walter. Vol. 1 has title: The Ariel. A literary gazette; v.2: The Ariel. A literary and critical gazette. Preliminary issue dated Apr. 14, 1827.

Apparently, there was a preliminary issue which was dated April 14, 1827. It explained the purpose of the periodical as devoted to "original and selected tales, essays, biographies of distinguished females, and of eminent individuals, reviews of new books, literary notices, poetry, original and selected anecdotes, and a choice selection of miscellaneous reading calculated to raise the genius and to mend the heart."*Ariel* was published by Edmund Morris and after six volumes, had to be discontinued because of "delinquency on the part of subscribers which is disgraceful to human nature."

v1-6   April 14, 1827-Nov. 24, 1832   APS II, Reel 839

In vol.1, Pgs. 49-50, 99 and 207 are missing. In vol.5, Pgs. 273-274 appear to be missing in number only. In vol.6, Pgs. 209-212 and 241-242 have some print missing. Best copy available.

Microfilm edition was prepared from DLC, CTW, NBuG and PHi copies.

ARISTIDEAN: A magazine of reviews, politics, and light literature. v.1, nos.1-6; March-Dec. 1845. New York, 1845.

476 p.

May-August 1845 never published.

This general monthly, edited by Dr. Thomas Dunn English, published one volume in 1845. Its contents were made up of tales and poetry, book reviews, biographical sketches, travel sketches, including a series on "Travels in Texas," and articles on literature and politics. Contributors included Walt Whitman, Edgar Allan Poe, Mrs. Elizabeth Ellet, Mayne Reid, Herman S. Saroni, and others. Some illustrations appeared in its pages.

v 1, no.1-6   Mar.-Dec. 1845   APS II, Reel 378

Microfilm edition was prepared from NN copy.

THE ARMINIAN MAGAZINE: consisting of extracts and original treatises on general redemption. v.1-2; Jan. 1789-Dec. 1790. Philadelphia, Prichard & Hall, 1789- 90.

2 v. monthly.

Sold by John Dickins, 1789-90. Edited by Thomas Coke and Francis Asbury.

The first American sectarian magazine.

| v1-2 | Jan. 1789-Dec. 1790 | APS I, Reel 8 |

Microfilm edition was prepared from MiU-C and MWA copy.

ARMY AND NAVY CHRONICLE. v.1-12, v.13, no.1-18; Jan. 3, 1835-May 21, 1842. Washington, B. Homans [1835-42]

13 v. in 12 pl. weekly.

Benjamin Homans, editor. Vol. 1 includes a specimen number issued June 30, 1834. Called "New series" beginning with v.2. Absorbed the Military and naval magazine of the United States in 1836. Continued as the Army and navy chronicle and scientific repository (v.1-3; Jan. 1843-June 1844)

As indicated by its title, this Washington weekly, edited by B. Homans, dealt primarily with army-and navy-related material, publishing articles on history, ships, battles, appointments, army pay, infantry tactics, and proceedings in Congress relative to the Army and Navy. In addition, it included a scientific column, poetry and some stories, coverage of events in Washington, foreign and domestic news, selections from other magazines, and articles on voyages and travel, intemperance, and other topics.

v1-2	Jan. 1835-July 1836	APS II, Reel 469
v3-8	July 1836-June 1839	Reel 470
v9-13	July 1839-May 1842	Reel 471

Vols. 3 and 9-13 lack title page and indexes. Vol. 12: Pgs. 17-272 are missing, not available for photographing. Vol. 13: Pgs. 195-267 are missing, not available for photographing. Several pages are stained with some loss of text. Pagination is irregular.

Microfilm edition was prepared from DLC, MB, N, and NjP copies.

SEE ALSO: Army and Navy Chronicle, and Scientific Repository; *and* Military and Naval Magazine of the United States.

THE ARMY AND NAVY CHRONICLE, AND SCIENTIFIC REPOSITORY. Being a continuation of Homans' "Army and navy chronicle". By Wm. Q. Force. v.1-3; Jan. 12, 1843-June 27, 1844. Washington, 1843-44.

3 v. in 1. illus. weekly.

This periodical was to replace Homans' *Army and Navy Chronicle* and was to contain news relative to the Army, Navy, and Militia in addition to any other material of interest to the military or of scientific value. It published articles on naval, military, and scientific subjects; selections from both American and foreign publications; notices of new publications and inventions; proceedings of Congress and state legislatures; and some poetry; in addition to such detailed information as orders, appointments, removals, resignations, changes of station, movement of troops, etc.

| v1-3 | Jan. 1843-June 1844 | APS II, Reel 472 |

Pagination is irregular. Several pages are stained with some loss of text.

Microfilm edition was prepared from the DLC copy.

SEE ALSO: Army and Navy Chronicle.

THE ART AMATEUR; a monthly journal devoted to art in the household. v, 1-49, no.4; June 1879-Sept. 1903. New York, M. Marks.

49 v. illus., facims., plates.

Caption title varies slightly. Editor and publisher: 1879-June(?) 1897, M. Marks.– July(?) 1897-Sept. 1903, J.W. Van Oost. A supplement of designs and plates accompanies each issue.

One of the few magazines of the period devoted specifically to fine arts, the *Art Amateur* maintained a circulation of as much as ten thousand.

v1-6	June 1879-May 1882	APS III, Reel 580
v7-16	June 1882-May 1887	Reel 581
v17-24	June 1887-May 1891	Reel 582
v25-32	June 1891-May 1895	Reel 583
v33-40	June 1895-May 1899	Reel 584
v41-49	June 1899-Sept. 1903	Reel 585

Best copy available for photographing. Several pages are stained, misnumbered or tightly bound. Some volumes have pages missing.

Microfilm edition was prepared from C, CL, CoGrS, ICRL, IU, InLP, MiD, MoS, NBuG, OU, and EP copies.

ARTHUR'S HOME MAGAZINE. v.1-67, Oct. 1852-Dec. 1898. Philadelphia, T.S. Arthur [etc.]

67 v. monthly.

Title varies: Oct. 1852-Dec. 1856, Home magazine.–1857-60, Lady's home magazine.–1861- 70, Arthur's home magazine.–1871-72, Arthur's lady's home magazine.–1873-79, Arthur's illustrated home magazine. Caption title varies slightly.

Absorbed Lady's friend, 1873, continuing its serial stories in a supplement incl. in a special edition for Lady's friend subscribers. Supplement follows v.41 on film. Unnumbered and undated supplement follows v.40. Suspended Feb. 1896-Jan. 1897. Vol. 67 wanting on film.

Arthur's Home Magazine began in October 1852 as a monthly reprint of the weekly *T.S. Arthur's Home Gazette.* It seemed to flourish better than its sister publication and at the end of *1854* the *Gazette* was abandoned and efforts were concentrated on *Home Magazine.*

The periodical was chiefly a women's and children's magazine with sections devoted to fashions, music and concert notes, a "Boys' and Girls' Treasury," an editor's department, book reviews, and so forth. It contained highly moral stories and features, written chiefly by Virginia F. Townsend. *Arthur's Home Magazine* never attained a large circulation, but it was cheap to produce except for illustration. Woodcuts adorned its pages and for a few years before the war it offered handcolored fashion plates. During the eighties, it offered free dress patterns as a circulation inducement, as did its major competitors.

Arthur died in 1885 and his son continued the magazine until 1891 when it was sold to E. Stanley Hunt. Subscription rates were lowered to meet the competition, but did not succeed in stopping a steady decline. Roderic Penfield bought it in 1894 and although he improved it, he could not put it back on its feet. After a suspension in 1896-97, it ended in 1898.

Arthur's Home Magazine succeeded during its existence of nearly half a century in making many devoted friends who liked precisely what it gave them—fashions, patterns, miscellany, and mildly sentimental verse and fiction at a low price.

Home Magazine
v1-6	Oct. 1852-Dec. 1855	APS III, Reel 533
v7-8	Jan. 1856-Dec. 1856	Reel 534

Lady's Home Magazine
v9-14	Jan. 1857-Dec. 1859	APS III, Reel 534
v15-16	Jan. 1860-Dec. 1860	Reel 535

Arthur's Home Magazine
v17-21	Jan. 1861-June 1863	APS III, Reel 535
v22-28	July 1863-Dec. 1866	Reel 536
v29-36	Jan. 1867-Dec. 1870	Reel 537

Arthur's Lady's Home Magazine
v37-40	Jan. 1871-Dec. 1872	APS III, Reel 538

Arthur's Illustrated Home Magazine
v41	Jan. 1873-Dec. 1873	APS III, Reel 538
v42-44	Jan. 1874-Dec. 1876	Reel 539
v45-47	Jan. 1877-Dec. 1879	Reel 540

Arthur's Home Magazine
v48-50	Jan. 1880-Dec. 1882	APS III, Reel 541
v51-53	Jan. 1883-Dec. 1885	Reel 542
v54-57	Jan. 1886-June 1888	Reel 543
v58-60	July 1888-Dec. 1890	Reel 544
v61-62	Jan. 1891-Dec. 1892	Reel 545
v63-64	Jan. 1893-Dec. 1894	Reel 546
v65-66	Jan. 1895-Sept. 1897	Reel 547

Best copy available for photographing. Several pages are stained, torn, taped, and have print show-through. Some advertisement pages are missing. Several pages are tightly bound. Many issues lack tables of contents and indexes. Vol.65 October issue is missing. Microfilm edition ends with September 1867.

ARTHUR'S ILLUSTRATED HOME MAGAZINE. *SEE* Arthur's Home Magazine.

ARTHUR'S LADIES' MAGAZINE OF ELEGANT LITERATURE AND THE FINE ARTS. *SEE* Arthur's Magazine.

ARTHUR'S LADY'S HOME MAGAZINE. *SEE* Arthur's Home Magazine.

ARTHUR'S MAGAZINE. v.1-5, no.4; Jan. 1844-April 1846. Philadelphia, 1844-1846.

5 v.

Supersedes Miss Leslie's magazine. Title varies: v.1 as Ladies' magazine of literature, fashion and fine arts. v2-4 as Arthur's Ladies' magazine of elegant literature and the fine arts. Merged into Godey's lady's book, later Godey's magazine.

T.S. Arthur was editor of this famous ladies' magazine, which superseded *Miss Leslie's Magazine* and was christened *Ladies' Magazine of Literature, Fashion and the Fine Arts* in February, 1844. Arthur was an active editor, writing much material himself, and bringing many of the better known magazinists of the times into his pages. Nathaniel Parker Willis, Park Benjamin, J.G. Percival, and A.J.H. Duganne were occasional contributors. Miss S.A. Hunt furnished sentimental short stories, and Mrs. Elizabeth Ellet sent many translations from the German. Longfellow's "The Village Blacksmith" appeared in the August, 1844 issue. Fashion plates were featured, and other illustrations appeared as well.

Ladies' Magazine of Literature, Fashion and Fine Arts
v1	Jan-June 1844	APS II, Reel 378

Arthur's Ladies' Magazine of Elegant Literature and the Fine Arts
v2-4	July 1844-Dec. 1845	APS II, Reel 378

Arthur's Magazine
v5	Jan-Apr. 1846	APS II, Reel 378

Pagination is irregular.

Microfilm edition was prepared from DLC copy.

THE ARTIST; a monthly lady's book. v.1-[2]; Sept. 1842-May 1843. New York, F. Quarre, 1842.

2 v. in 1. plates (part col.)

A monthly magazine for women which devoted itself exclusively to literature, arts, and fashion. It featured fashion plates with accompanying descriptions, and articles describing the latest modes, costumes, and colors for the fashionable woman. Much sentimental fiction and poetry as well as several musical pieces and illustrations also appeared. In 1843 it was bought by Charles Peterson and combined with the *Ladies' National Magazine,* later *Peterson Magazine.*

Sept. 1842-May 1843	APS II, Reel 649

Microfilm edition was prepared from CtY and DLC copies.

SEE ALSO: Peterson Magazine.

ARTIST AND LADY'S WORLD. *SEE* Peterson Magazine.

THE ATHENAEUM. v.1, no.1-15; Feb. 12-Aug. 6, 1814. Yale-college. [New Haven, Printed by O. Steele, 1814]

120 p. irregular.

Caption title.

"Under the immediate direction of the senior class."

The stated purpose of this bimonthly journal was to aid students of Yale College in improving their skills in literary composition by achieving the proper union of sense and elegance in writing. The journals contained essays, poetry, short stories, biographical works, and jokes but nothing controversial.

v1, nos1-15	Feb. 12-Aug. 6, 1814	APS II, Reel 65

THE ATHENEUM; or, spirit of the English magazines. v.1-14, Apr. 1, 1817-Mar. 15, 1824; 2d ser., v. 1-9, Apr. 1, 1824-Sept. 15, 1928; 3d ser., v. 1-5, Oct. 1, 1928- Mar. 15, 1931; 4th ser., v.1-4, Apr. 1, 1931-Mar. 1933. Boston.

32 v. illus. semimonthly.

Complete title on v. only. In masthead, issues give subtitle only. Subtitle varies: 4th ser., v. 2, Spirit of English literature and fashion; v.4, Journal of English literature and the fine arts.

Imprint varies: v.1-2d ser., v.2, Munroe and Francis.—2d ser., v.3-3d ser ser.(?). John Cotton.—4th ser.(?), Kane. Film incomplete: 4th ser., v. 3 wanting.

A Boston weekly begun in 1817, the *Atheneum* consisted largely of extracts from British periodicals.

v1-6, no.6	Apr. 1, 1817-Dec. 15, 1819	APS II, Reel 66
v6, no.7-v10, no.6	Jan. 1, 1820-Dec. 15, 1821	Reel 67

v10, no. 7-v13	Jan. 1, 1822-Sept. 15, 1823	Reel 68
v14-18	Oct. 1, 1823-Dec. 15, 1825	Reel 69
v19-21	Apr. 1826-Oct. 1827	Reel 1365
v22-29	Oct. 1827-Oct. 1831	Reel 1366
v30-32	Oct. 1831-Mar. 1833	Reel 1367

Several pages are stained, marked, tightly bound, and misnumbered. Some volumes have pages missing. Volume 26: Issues 1, 2, 9, and 10 are missing Volume 27: issue 3 is missing. Volume 28: Issues 6 and 12 are missing. Volume 31 is not available for photographing.

Microfilm edition was prepared from DLC, PCarlD and WHi copies.

ATKINSON'S CASKET. *SEE* Graham's American Monthly Magazine of Literature, Art, and Fashion.

ATKINSON'S SATURDAY EVENING POST. *SEE* Saturday Evening Post.

ATLANTIC JOURNAL, AND FRIEND OF KNOWLEDGE. In eight numbers. Containing about 160 original articles and tracts on natural and historical sciences, the description of about 150 new plants, and 100 new animals or fossils. Many vocabularies of languages, historical and geological facts, &c. By C.S. Rafinesque. [v. 1, nos. 1-8; Spring 1832-Winter 1833] Philadelphia, 1832-33.

212 p. front. (tab.) illus. quarterly.

Caption title: nos. 1-4, Atlantic journal, and friend of knowledge; a cyclopedic journal and review of universal science and knowledge: historical, natural, and medical arts and sciences ... –nos. 5-8, Atlantic journal and friend of knowledge; a quarterly journal of historical and natural sciences, useful knowledge, &c. ...

Professor Constantine S. Rafinesque wrote notable articles for the *American Monthly Magazine and Critical Review* and was a valuable contributor to the *Western Review and Miscellaneous Magazine.* He even published one issue of the *Western Review.* But, he longed to have a magazine of his own and in 1832, he came out with the spring issue of the journal here represented. it was devoted to scientific information with emphasis on the natural sciences.

v1	Spring 1832-Winter 1833	APS II, Reel 839

Pgs. 37-38 appear to be missing in number only.

Microfilm edition was prepared from the NNC copy.

THE ATLANTIC MAGAZINE. v. 1-2; May 1824-Apr. 1825. New York, E. Bliss & E. White, 1824-25.

2 v. monthly.

R.C.Sands, editor. Continued as the New York review and Atheneum magazine.

Robert C. Sands, a young lawyer with some distinction as a poet, founded the *Atlantic Magazine* in New York in May, 1824, and undoubtedly wrote much of the material himself. Contributors were Dr. D.L.M. Peixotto, a well-known New York physician, a Dr. McKay, the Reverend Manton Eastburn, and Thatcher Paine. The *Atlantic Magazine* printed a few excellent stories, along with reviews, scientific and literary news, and poetry. Early in 1825 Henry J. Anderson, a professor at Columbia, took over the editorship. Within a few months he had formed a partnership with William Cullen Bryant, and they decided to discontinue the *Atlantic Magazine* and begin a new series called the *New-York Review, and*

Atheneum Magazine.

v1-2	May 1824-Apr. 1825	APS II, Reel 70

SEE ALSO: New York Review and Atheneum Magazine.

ATLANTIC MONTHLY. *SEE* Galaxy. A Magazine of Entertaining Reading.

THE ATLANTIC SOUVENIR; A Christmas and New Year's offering. 1826-1832. Philadelphia, H.C. Carey & I. Lea [etc.]

7 v. illus., plates. annual.

Title varies: 1830-32, The Atlantic souvenir for MDCCCXXX-MDCCCXXXII.

This annual publication was to contain "light" literature and "specimens of art" done by American writers and artists. The engravings, which were mainly of scenery, included some by James Barton Longacre and other well-known engravers, and among the famous people whose writings appeared were Washington Irving, Henry Longfellow, Sarah J. Hale, Mrs. Sigourney, and Emma C. Embury. Contents included a good deal of poetry, tales of a sentimental nature, and travel and biographical sketches.

1826-1832		APS II, Reel 1367

Many pages are stained, torn or creased.

Microfilm edition was prepared from NN and ViU copies.

AURORA. v.1; July 4, 1834-Apr. 25, 1835. Philadelphia [W. Duane] 1834-35.

416 p.

Irregular, July 4-Aug. 22, 1834; semiweekly, Aug. 27, 1834-Jan. 17, 1835; irregular, Mar. 14-Apr. 25, 1835. William Duane, editor.

A political magazine with the stated purpose of discussing "all topics which concern the interest and happiness of society." Contents provided coverage of foreign news, events in Canada, activities of Parliament, and ward meetings, and of such topics as social problems, education, elections, and banks. Although most material was political in nature, poetry, miscellaneous essays, and some pieces on geography were also included.

v1	July 4, 1834-April 25, 1835	APS II, Reel 769

Index is lacking.

Microfilm edition was prepared from DLC copy.

BACHELOR'S JOURNAL. *SEE* Yankee and Boston Literary Gazette.

BALANCE AND COLUMBIAN REPOSITORY. *SEE* Balance and State Journal.

THE BALANCE, AND STATE JOURNAL. v.1-7, Jan. 5, 1802-Dec. 27, 1808; new ser., v.1-2, Jan. 4, 1809-Dec. 1810; new ser., v.1, Jan. 1-Dec. 24, 1811. Albany, etc., Croswell.

Title varies: Balance and Columbian repository; Balance, etc.

Harry Croswell, editor.

Begun in Hudson, New York and later moved to Albany, this weekly miscellany resembled a newspaper, having large-size pages and many advertisements. Among its varied contents were a section of moral and religious essays called "The Monitor," a section of poetry titled "The Wreath," articles on women's education and manners, an agriculture section, and literary notices. In addition there was some political material, including a section of speeches and addresses, proceedings of the state legislature and Congress, brief news items, and legal notices.

Balance and Columbian Repository

v1-2	Jan. 5, 1802-Dec. 27, 1803	APS II, Reel 3
v3-6	Jan. 3, 1804-Dec. 29, 1807	Reel 4

Balance

v7	Jan. 5-Dec. 27, 1808	APS II, Reel 5

Balance, and New-York State Journal; Balance and State Journal

nsv1	Jan. 4-Dec. 29, 1809	APS II, Reel 5
nsv2-s3v1	Jan. 2, 1810-Dec. 24, 1811	Reel 70

Vol. 4, issue 53 missing; vol. 7, issue 13 is missing.

Microfilm edition was prepared from MWA copy.

BALLOU'S DOLLAR MONTHLY MAGAZINE. *SEE* Ballou's Monthly Magazine.

BALLOU'S MONTHLY MAGAZINE. vols. 1-77; Jan. 1855-June 1893. Boston, Ballou.

77 v. illus.

Title varies: v.1-16, Ballou's dollar monthly magazine.–v. 17-22, Dollar monthly magazine.

Published by Thomes and Talbot, 1872-1885; by G.W.Studley, 1886-1893. Microfilm edition lacks v.19, no. 1-2; v.63, no.1, 4-5; v.64, no.2-4.

This magazine was one of the numerous and often inexpensive monthlies that flourished in the second half of the 19th century. Founded by Maturin M. Ballou in 1855, it was meant to have "such pleasant and readable tales, sketches, miscellany, and poems, with records of all that is new and curious, as to make the *Dollar Monthly* a charming and acceptable visitor, and still prove it to be, what it really is, the cheapest magazine in the world." Many short stories and poems carried romantic themes of coquetry, courtship and marriage. Miscellaneous facts of local and foreign scenes might include, on the same page, a report of a Paris printing press that printed the Lord's Prayer in 300 different languages, notice of the death of an eminent public figure or a listing of important dates from the Crimean War. The word "Dollar" was dropped from the title when the price was raised to $1.50 in 1866. It was sold to Thomes and Talbot in 1872, and to George W. Studley in 1886.

Ballou's Dollar Monthly Magazine

v1-2	Jan.-Dec. 1855	APS III, Reel 716
v3-8	Jan. 1856-Dec. 1858	Reel 717
v9-14	Jan. 1859-Dec. 1861	Reel 718
v15-16	Jan.-Dec. 1862	Reel 719

Dollar Monthly Magazine

v17-21	Jan. 1863-June 1865	APS III, Reel 719
v22	July-Dec. 1865	Reel 720

Ballou's Monthly Magazine

v23-28	Jan. 1866-Dec. 1868	APS III, Reel 720
v29-34	Jan. 1869-Dec. 1871	Reel 721
v35-40	Jan. 1872-Dec. 1874	Reel 722
v41-46	Jan. 1875-Dec. 1877	Reel 723
v47-52	Jan. 1878-Dec. 1880	Reel 724
v53-57	Jan. 1881-June 1883	Reel 725
v58-62	July 1883-Dec. 1885	Reel 726
v63-69	Feb. 1886-June 1889	Reel 727
v70-76	July 1889-Dec. 1892	Reel 728
v77	Jan.-June 1893	Reel 729

Several pages are torn, tightly bound, taped, and have print faded or show-through with some loss of text. Several pages are missing. Pagination is irregular.

Microfilm edition was prepared from DLC, IC, InI, InU, KKc,KyBB, MH, MeB, MiU, MnU, MoS, MoU, N, NjR, RPB, TxU, and WHi copies.

BALLOU'S PICTORIAL DRAWING-ROOM COMPANION. v.1-17; May 3, 1851-Dec. 24, 1859. Boston, F. Gleason, 1851-[59]

17 v. illus., port., maps, facsim. weekly.

Title varies: 1851-54, Gleason's pictorial drawing-room companion. 1855-59, Ballou's pictorial drawing-room companion. M.M. Ballou, editor.

Absorbed the New York Illustrated news in December 1853. The continuation of the periodical as the Welcome guest is announced in the last number of Ballou's pictorial.

Published by Frederick Gleason 1851-54 and Maturin M. Ballou 1854-59, this well-illustrated and well-printed miscellany was edited throughout by Ballou. It was initially modeled after the *London Illustrated News* but was very American in content. Woodcuts, stories, poems, serial romances, moral tales, travel series, and early Horatio Alger made up a very successful magazine.

Gleason's Pictorial Drawing-Room Companion

v1-4	May 3, 1851-June 25, 1853	APS III, Reel 249
v5-7	July 2, 1853-Dec. 30, 1854	Reel 250

Ballou's Pictorial Drawing-Room Companion

v8-10	Jan. 6, 1855-June 28, 1856	APS III, Reel 250
v11-16	July 5, 1856-June 24, 1859	Reel 251
v17	July 2,-Dec. 24, 1859	Reel 252

Several pages creased, stained, or tightly bound. Volumes 8-9 have some pages bound out of order.

Microfilm edition was prepared from M, NBuG, NjP, OU copies.

THE BALTIMORE LITERARY AND RELIGIOUS MAGAZINE. Conducted by Robert J. Breckinridge, and Andrew B. Cross. v.1-7; 1835-41. Baltimore, Printed by R.J. Matchett [1835]-41.

7 v. monthly.

Succeeded by the Spirit of the XIX century.

This "thoroughly protestant" religious monthly devoted much space to the controversy between Protestants and Roman Catholics —its articles, sermons, speeches, and letters attempted to discredit Roman Catholic doctrines and practices. Other religious matters were dealt with as well, and poetry and anecdotes were included.

v1-5	Jan. 1835-Dec. 1839	APS II, Reel 585
v6-7	Jan. 1840-Dec. 1841	Reel 586

Microfilm edition was prepared from DLC copy.

SEE ALSO: Spirit of the XIX Century.

THE BALTIMORE LITERARY MONUMENT, ed. by J.N. McJilton and T.S. Arthur. v.1-2; Oct. 1838-Oct. 1839. Baltimore, T.S. Arthur, 1839.

2 v. illus., plates, ports. monthly.

Engraved t.-p. Vol. 1 has caption title: Baltimore monument.

No number was issued in Jan. 1839. Preceded by the Baltimore monument. A weekly journal, devoted to polite literature, science, and the fine arts.

John N. McJilton and T.S. Arthur were editors of this monthly literary magazine, which featured steel or wood engravings and music in each issue, and published sentimental tales and poetry. Arthur, William H. Carpenter, Park Benjamin, Anna H. Dorsey, and Mrs. Lydia Jane Pierson were leading contributors, though much of the material was selected.

v1-2   Oct. 1838-Oct. 1839   APS II, Reel 379

Paging is irregular.

Microfilm edition was prepared from DLC copy.

SEE ALSO: Baltimore Monument.

THE BALTIMORE MAGAZINE. July 1807. [Baltimore] 28 p.

Only one issue of this literary magazine was published; included in its contents are several essays, a section of poetry, some dramatic criticism and a little fiction.

             July 1807   APS II, Reel 6

Microfilm edition was prepared from NNS copy.

THE BALTIMORE MEDICAL AND PHILOSOPHICAL LYCAEUM, by Nathaniel Potter. v.1 (no.1-4); Jan./Feb./Mar.-Oct./Nov./Dec., 1811. Baltimore, Published by George Hill.

1 v. double pl. quarterly.

Because of the high cost and unavailability of the latest medical magazine, this quarterly was founded to summarize important articles from the best European periodicals. It included case studies, experiments, remedies and reports by eminent physicians.

v1, no.1-4   Jan./Mar.-Oct./Dec. 1811   APS II, Reel 71

THE BALTIMORE MEDICAL AND PHYSICAL RECORDER; conducted by Tobias Watkins. v.1-2, no.1; Apr. 1808-Aug. 1809. Baltimore, Printed by S. Magill, 1809.

2 v. in 1. quarterly.

Caption title: Medical and physical recorder.

This medical journal conducted by Tobias Watkins provided a variety of information concerning the field of medicine—there were descriptions of cases, remedies and cures for various ailments, literary notices and reviews of medical books, and news about various medical schools in the U.S.

v1-2, no.1   Apr. 1808-Aug. 1809   APS II, Reel 6

Vol.2: issues 2-4 are lacking.

Microfilm edition was prepared from DLC copy.

BALTIMORE MEDICAL AND SURGICAL JOURNAL AND REVIEW. Supported by an association of physicians and surgeons. Edited by E. Geddings. v.1-2; [Oct. 1833-Sept. 1834] Baltimore, W.R. Lucas, 1833-34.

2 v. illus., plates (1 fold.) quarterly.

Vol. 2 published by Carey, Hart & co. Superseded by North American archives of medical and surgical science.

This Baltimore medical journal was intended to be national and even international in scope. It published papers on various diseases and on medical and surgical treatments, gave summaries of medical news, both American and foreign, and included book reviews and notices of new publications. Diagrams illustrated some of the articles.

v1-2   Oct. 1833-Sept. 1834   APS II, Reel 379

Microfilm edition was prepared from MiU copy.

SEE ALSO: North American Archives of Medical and Surgical Science.

THE BALTIMORE MONTHLY JOURNAL OF MEDICINE AND SURGERY. v.1; Feb. 1830-Jan. 1831. Baltimore, Printed by Bailey & Francis.

512 p.

Edited by N.R. Smith.

This medical journal proposed to enable readers to keep pace with the progress of medical science. It contained papers, written by physicians, describing cases and treatments; these were occasionally accompanied by illustrations or diagrams. Contents also included brief articles on recent developments, reviews of medical publications, and a monthly summary of foreign and domestic medical news.

v1, no.1-12   Feb. 1830-Jan. 1831   APS II, Reel 534

General index follows issue 12. Several pages are stained and have print show-through. P. 366 is misnumbered.

Microfilm edition was prepared from CtY and DNLM copies.

THE BALTIMORE MONTHLY VISITER. v.1, no. 1; Apr. 1842. [Baltimore, n.d.]

32 p. illus.

The 32-page single issue of the *Visiter* contained very romantic poetry, fiction and articles, profusely illustrated. Also featured were essays and literary notices of current books.

v1, no.1   Apr. 1842   APS II, Reel 408

Microfilm edition was prepared from MdBE copy.

THE BALTIMORE MONUMENT. A weekly journal, devoted to polite literature, science, and the fine arts. v.1-2; Oct. 8, 1836-Sept. 29, 1838. Baltimore, D. Creamer.

2 v. illus., plates.

Editors: 1836-38, J.N. M'Jilton and D. Creamer. Continued as the Baltimore literary monument.

Founded by T.S. Arthur, the *Baltimore Monument* was considered one of the best literary periodicals of the period. It contained original tales, poetry, critical notices, and recipes, and was embellished with engravings and music.

v1-2   Oct. 8, 1836-Sept. 29, 1838   APS II, Reel 769

Microfilm edition was prepared from MdBP and WHi copies.

SEE ALSO: Baltimore Literary Monument.

THE BALTIMORE PHILOSOPHICAL JOURNAL AND REVIEW. no.1; July 1823. Baltimore, J. Robinson.

199 p. illus.

Edited by J. B. Davidge.

The purposes of this periodical were to review important articles published in the European medical capitals of London, Paris, Edinburgh, and Vienna and to distribute this information widely into the Western and Southern States, not only the eastern United States. Only one issue was published.

no1   July 1823   APS II, Reel 71

BALTIMORE PHOENIX AND BUDGET. v.1, no.1-12; April 1841-March 1842. Baltimore, 1841-1842.

476 p.

This monthly magazine consisted largely of a number of serialized tales, several usually appearing in each issue. One of these was Joseph Holt Ingraham's *The Juvenile Genius.* Also included were reviews, geographical descriptions, miscellaneous essays, and a fair amount of poetry.

v1   Apr. 1841-March 1842   APS II, Reel 770

Index and table of contents are lacking.

Microfilm edition was prepared from NcU copy.

THE BALTIMORE REPERTORY OF PAPERS ON LITERARY AND OTHER TOPICS, including a selection of English dramas. v.1, no.1-6; Jan.-June 1811. Baltimore, J. Robinson.

334, 72 p. monthly.

A miscellany including a selection of English dramas, short stories, poems, translations, anecdotes, essays, and proceedings of Congress. Among the various topics included in the short run of this magazine were slavery in the U.S., mineralogy, a comparison of poet and painter, and drama.

v1, nos.1-6   Jan.-June 1811   APS II, Reel 71

THE BALTIMORE WEEKLY MAGAZINE COMPLETE IN ONE VOLUME. Containing a variety of entertaining, instructive, and useful productions, original and selected, making in the whole a collection of upwards of two hundred different tales suited to the palates of the moralist, lovers of sentiment, poetry or anecdotes: v.1, Apr. 26, 1800-May 27, 1801. Baltimore, W. Pechin.

1 p. 1., 312 p.

J.B. Colvin, editor.

The *Baltimore Weekly Magazine* ran for a little over a year under the editorship of John B. Colvin. It published a wide variety of material, including sentimental prose and poetry, much of it selected, moral essays, reviews of plays performed in Baltimore theaters, lists of new publications, and news items.

v1   Apr. 26, 1800-May 27, 1801   APS II, Reel 6

Microfilm edition was prepared from CtY and DLC copy.

* THE BANKERS MAGAZINE. v.1-146; July 1846-June 1943. Cambridge, Mass., The Bankers [etc.] 1847-1943.

146 v. illus. maps, plates, ports. monthly.

Vols. 6-20 also called new ser., v.1-15; v.21-49 also called ser. 3, v. 1-29. Supersedes the Bankers' weekly circular and statistical record (Oct. 1845-May 1846). Title varies: July 1846-June 1849, The Bankers' magazine and state financial register. July 1849-Nov. 1894, The Bankers' magazine and statistical register. Dec. 1894-June 1895, The Bankers' magazine. July-Dec. 1895, Rhodes' journal of banking and the Bankers' magazine consolidated. Absorbed Rhodes' journal of banking in July 1895.

Editors: July 1846-June 1861, I.S. Homans.—July 1861-June 1863, I.S. Homans, Jr.—July 1863-June 1874, I.S. Homans.—July 1874-June 1880, Benjamin Homans.—Sept. 1882-Oct. 1894, A.S. Bollas.—Nov. 1894-June 1895, J.G. Floyd.—July 1895-1903, Bradford Rhodes.—E.H. Youngman. Absorbed by the Banking law journal in July 1943.

Founded by I. Smith Homans in Baltimore in 1846, and later moved to Boston and New York, the *Bankers Magazine* was a leading banking periodical and had a high standing from its beginning. Bank statistics were a main feature; thus the contents include many statistical tables, as well as information on the histories of banks, on coinage and currency of various countries, on life insurance, trade, and stocks, legal decisions affecting banking, and articles by many prominent financiers and economists. William B. Greene was a leading contributor through the nineties.

After the turn of the century, departments were added which covered the financial situation abroad, investment and finance, and general banking news, and offered lists of books for bankers and digests of significant articles from other magazines. Articles dealt with banking and commercial law, modern banking methods, and banking and finance in general.

Bankers' Magazine and State Financial Register

v1-3	July 1846-June 1849	APS II, Reel 587

Bankers' Magazine and Statistical Register

v4-5	July 1849-June 1851	APS II, Reel 588
v6-8	July 1851-June 1854	Reel 1648
v9-12	July 1854-June 1858	Reel 1649
v13-16	July 1858-June 1862	Reel 1650
v17-20	July 1862-June 1866	Reel 1651
v21-24	July 1870-June 1874	Reel 1652
v25-28	July 1870-June 1874	Reel 1653
v29-32	July 1874-June 1878	Reel 1654
v33-36	July 1878-June 1882	Reel 1655
v37-40	July 1882-June 1886	Reel 1656
v41-44	July 1886-June 1890	Reel 1657
v45-48	July 1890-June 1894	Reel 1658
v49	July 1894-Nov. 1894	Reel 1659

Bankers' Magazine

v50	Dec. 1894-June 1895	APS II, Reel 1659

Rhodes' Journal of Banking and the Bankers' Magazine Consolidated

v51	July-Dec. 1895	APS II, Reel 1659

Bankers' Magazine

v52	Jan.-June 1896	APS II, Reel 1659
v53-56	July 1896-June 1898	Reel 1660
v57-59	July 1898-Dec. 1899	Reel 1661
v60-62	Jan. 1900-June 1911	Reel 1662
v63-65	July 1901-Dec. 1902	Reel 1663
v66-68	Jan. 1903-June 1904	Reel 1664
v69-71	July 1904-Dec. 1905	Reel 1665
v72-74	Jan. 1906-June 1907	Reel 1666
v75-77	July 1907-Dec. 1908	Reel 1667
v78-80	Jan. 1909-June 1910	Reel 1668
v81-84	July 1910-June 1912	Reel 1669
v85-89	July 1912-Dec. 1914	Reel 1670
v90-93	Jan. 1915-Dec. 1916	Reel 1671
v94-97	Jan. 1917-Dec. 1918	Reel 1672
v98-101	Jan. 1919-Dec. 1920	Reel 1673
v102-104	Jan. 1921-June 1922	Reel 1674
v105-107	July 1922-Dec. 1923	Reel 1675
v108-110	Jan. 1924-June 1925	Reel 1676
v111-114	July 1925-June 1927	Reel 1677
v115-118	July 1927-June 1929	Reel 1678
v119-122	July 1929-June 1931	Reel 1679
v123-127	July 1931-Dec. 1933	Reel 1680
v128-132	Jan. 1934-June 1936	Reel 1681
v133-139	July 1936-Dec. 1939	Reel 1682
v140-146	Jan. 1940-June 1943	Reel 1683

Vol.3: p. 384 is missing in number only.

Microfilm edition was prepared from DLC, InU, MiU, MoS, and TxU copies.

THE BANNER OF THE CONSTITUTION. Devoted to general politics, political economy, state papers, foreign and domestic news, &c. Ed. by Condy Raguet. v.1-3; Dec. 5, 1829-Dec. 31, 1832. Washington & Philadelphia, 1829-32.

3 v. in 2. weekly.

Successor of the Free trade advocate and journal of political economy.

This political magazine summarized foreign and domestic political news and news of inventions and advances in industry. It recorded the proceedings and debates of Congress, messages of the President, and decisions of the Supreme Court. In addition, it contained state papers, political articles and essays, statistical documents and tables, and extracts from foreign reviews.

v1-3	Dec. 5, 1829-Dec. 31, 1832	APS II, Reel 586

Several pages are stained, tightly bound, and have faded print. Vol.3: Pgs. 433-34 are missing in number only.

Microfilm edition was prepared from DLC copy.

BAPTIST BOARD OF FOREIGN MISSIONS FOR THE UNITED STATES. *SEE* Latter Day Luminary.

BAPTIST COMMONWEALTH. *SEE* Watchman-Examiner.

BAPTIST HOME MISSION MONTHLY. *SEE* Baptist Missionary Magazine.

BAPTIST MISSIONARY MAGAZINE. v.1-89; Jan. 1817-Dec. 1909. Boston, American Baptist Missionary Union.

89 v. in 83. illus., ports. Frequency varies. Vols. 1-6 called new ser.

Supersedes Massachusetts Baptist missionary magazine. Title varies: v.1-4, The American Baptist magazine and missionary intelligencer.—v.5-15, The American Baptist magazine.—v.30-52, The Missionary magazine.

Issued 1817-26 by the Massachusetts Baptist Convention under its earlier name: Baptist Missionary Society in Massachusetts; 1827-1909 by the American Baptist Foreign Mission Society (called 1827-45, Baptist General Convention; 1846-1909, American Baptist Missionary Union) United with Baptist home mission monthly and Good work to form Missions. Cf. Union list of serials.

The *Baptist Missionary Magazine* was the chief representative in the field of missions, ministering to the immense interest of the time in missionary activity, and for many years was the only Baptist periodical work in America. Missionary articles, chiefly about missions in India, were especially prominent and there was also some coverage of home missions in the West. Besides the pages which marked it as an official organ, there was a variety of religious reading: church records and proceedings, memoirs, obituaries, news, reviews of sermons and other religious literature, accounts of revivals, and some poetry and selected miscellany. It printed many articles about foreign lands, all of which lent themselves well to illustration. The new series had a few rude woodcuts in its earliest numbers, and woodcuts reappeared in the '70's. Half-tone illustrations increased after 1890.

American Baptist Magazine and Missionary Intelligencer

v1-2, no.6	Jan. 1817-Nov. 1819	APS II, Reel 71
v2, no.7-v4	Jan. 1820-Nov. 1824	Reel 72

American Baptist Magazine

v5	Jan.-Dec. 1825	APS II, Reel 72
v6-11	1826-1831	Reel 535
v12-15	Jan. 1832-Dec. 1835	Reel 536

Baptist Missionary Magazine

v16-17	Jan. 1836-Dec. 1837	APS II, Reel 536
v18-23	1838-1843	Reel 537
v24-28	1844-1848	Reel 538
v29	Jan.-Dec. 1849	Reel 539

Missionary Magazine

v30	Jan.-Dec. 1850	APS II, Reel 539
v31-33	Jan. 1851-Dec. 1853	Reel 830
v34-41	Jan. 1854-Dec. 1861	Reel 831
v42-49	Jan. 1862-Dec. 1869	Reel 832
v50-52	Jan. 1870-Dec. 1872	Reel 833

Baptist Missionary Magazine

v53-57	Jan. 1873-Dec. 1877	APS II, Reel 833
v58-65	Jan. 1878-Dec. 1885	Reel 834
v66-73	Jan. 1886-Dec. 1893	Reel 835
v74-79	Jan. 1894-Dec. 1899	Reel 836
v80-83	Jan. 1900-Dec. 1903	Reel 837
v84-89	Jan. 1904-Dec. 1909	Reel 838

Several pages are stained with some loss of text. Pagination is irregular. Vols. 7-16: Index follows volume. Vol. 17: Lacks title page and index.

Microfilm edition was prepared from C, DLC, and MiU copy.

SEE ALSO: Massachusetts Baptist Missionary Magazine.

* THE BAPTIST QUARTERLY. v.1-11; Jan. 1867-Oct. 1877.

Philadelphia, American Baptist Publication Society, 1867-77.

11 v.

Superseded by Baptist review, later Baptist quarterly review.

Edited by H.G. Weston.

| v1-2 | Jan. 1867-Oct. 1868 | APS III, Reel 4 |
| v3-11 | Jan. 1869-Oct. 1877 | Reel 5 |

Title pages for Vol.1 and the April, July, and October issues of Vols. 2-11 are not available. Best copy available for photographing.

Microfilm edition was prepared from MiD copy.

SEE ALSO: Baptist Quarterly Review.

THE BAPTIST QUARTERLY REVIEW. v.1-14; 1879-92.
Cincinnati, J.R. Baumes, 1879-84; New York, Baptist Review Association; London, Trubner.

14 v.

No numbers issued for April and July, 1891. Title varies: 1879-81, The Baptist review.

Editors: 1879-84, J.R.Baumes.—1885-89, R.S. MacArthur, H.C. Vedder.—1890-92, H.C. Vedder. Supersedes Baptist quarterly.

Beginning in Cincinnati in 1879, the *Baptist Quarterly Review* was one of the better, flourishing Baptist papers. The theological contents were supplied by David J. Hill, Albion W. Small, Daniel Coit Gilman and other prominent men.

Baptist Review.
| v1-3 | Jan. 1879-Dec. 1881 | APS III, Reel 59 |

Baptist Quarterly Review.
| v4-7 | Jan. 1882-Dec. 1885 | APS III, Reel 59 |
| v8-14 | Jan. 1886-Oct. 1892 | Reel 60 |

Vol. 2: p. 437 print missing. Vols. 6-14: Indexes missing. Please refer to the Table of Contents. Vol. 9: Pgs. 161-62 are stained. Vol. 13: April and July issues suspended.

Microfilm edition was prepared from InFC, MiGr, NjPT, and NRCR copies.

SEE ALSO: Baptist Quarterly.

BAPTIST REVIEW. *SEE* Baptist Quarterly Review.

THE BARBER'S SHOP, kept by Sir David Razor [pseud.] no.1-4. [Salem, 1807-08]

64 p.

Edited by I. Story.

This comic periodical by "Sir David Razor" published a good deal of satire, attacking the British and the morals and manners of the time, and also provided much humorous material, including anecdotes, poetry, and gibes at other comic magazines.

| no.1-4 | 1807-1808 | APS II, Reel 6 |

Microfilm edition was prepared from NN copy.

BARNARD'S AMERICAN JOURNAL OF EDUCATION.
SEE American Journal of Education.

BEADLE'S MONTHLY, a magazine of today. v.1-3; Jan. 1866-June 1867. New York, Beadle, 1866-67.

3 v. illus.

Closely copying the style of *Harper's Magazine,* Erastus Beadle founded *Beadle's Monthly.* Only the English serials, so popular in many magazines of the day, were lacking in the new monthly. Contributions included short stories by Harriet E. Prescott, John Neal, Frank R. Stockton, and Caroline Chesbrough. Kate Putnam Osgood and A.B. Street occasionally provided poetry.

| v1-3 | Jan. 1866-June 1867 | APS III, Reel 26 |

Vol. 3 lacks Index. Please refer to the Table of Contents.

Microfilm edition was prepared from MiU copy.

THE BEAUTIES OF THE EVANGELICAL MAGAZINE.
v.1-2. Philadelphia, W.W. Woodward, 1802-03.

2 v.

Edited by W. W. Woodward. Selections from the Evangelical magazine and missionary chronicle, London. Cf. Union list of serials.

The contents of this religious magazine were mainly made up of selections from the British *Evangelical Magazine and Missionary Chronicle;* the rest of the contents were also selected.

| v1-2 | 1802-1803 | APS II, Reel 6 |

Microfilm edition was prepared from DLC copy.

BELFORD'S MAGAZINE. *SEE* Belford's Monthly.

BELFORD'S MONTHLY. v. 1-7 (no.1-39), June 1888-Aug. 1891; [new ser.] v.1, Sept. 1891-Feb. 1892; v.8-10, v. 11, no. 1-2, Mar. 1892-July 1893. Chicago, New York [etc.] Belford, Clarke [etc.]

12 v. illus., ports. monthly.

Title varies: June 1888-Aug. 1891, Belford's magazine; Sept. 1891-Mar. 1892, Belford's monthly and Democratic review.

Vol. 8, no. [1-2] also called new ser. v. 2, no.1-2. Don Piatt, editor, June 1888-July 1889.

While devoted largely to Democratic party matters such as free trade, this Chicago magazine printed much fiction, together with poetry, book reviews, science items, and notes on the theatre. During its first three years, it printed a novel in each number. During *Belford's* later years writers such as Richard Henry Stoddard, Kate Field, Edgar Fawcett, Julian Hawthorne, and Hamlin Garland were among its contributors. Belford, Clarke & Company, the book publishers who issued the magazine, gave it up during the panic of 1893.

Belford's Magazine
v1-4	June 1888-May 1890	APS III, Reel 586
v5-6	June 1890-May 1891	Reel 587
v7	June 1891-Aug. 1891	Reel 588

Belford's Monthly and Democratic Review.
v8   Sept. 1891-May 1892   APS III, Reel 588

Belford's Monthly.
v9   June 1892-Nov. 1892   APS III, Reel 588
v10-11   Dec. 1892-July 1893   Reel 589

Some advertisement pages are missing. Vol.3: P. 22 is stained. Vol.4: Pagination is irregular. Vol.6: P. 816 is stained. Vol.8: p. 86 has print show-through.

Microfilm edition was prepared from DLC, KyLo, MiU, and MoS copies.

BELFORD'S MONTHLY AND DEMOCRATIC REVIEW. *SEE* Belford's Monthly.

BELLES-LETTRES REPOSITORY, AND MONTHLY MAGAZINE. *SEE* New-York Literary Journal.

THE BEREAN. A religious publication. v.1-3, Feb. 23, 1824-July 24, 1827; [new ser., v.1, Oct. 1827-Sept 1828] Wilmington, Del., Printed by Mendenhall & Walters.

4 v. biweekly.

Articles in this religious magazine dealt with doctrine, education, missionaries, and such reform topics as slavery and temperance. Contents also included selected material, occasional reviews, essays, biography, and poetry.

v1-2   Feb. 23, 1824-June 1826   APS II, Reel 72
v3-nsv1   July 1826-Sept. 1828   Reel 539

Some pages are tightly bound with loss of text. Several pages are stained; pagination is irregular.

Microfilm edition was prepared from DLC copy.

BEREAN; or Scripture-searcher. v.1-2, 1802-1810. Boston, Printed by S.G. Snelling, etc., 1802-1810.

2 v.

Title varies.

Film covers: v.1 (no.1-6) 1802-1809; v.2, no.2, 1810.

Published by the Berean Society of Universalists, this religious periodical emphasized study of the Scriptures. Articles usually dealt with a particular passage or verse of Scripture, and were occasionally contined through two or more numbers. Each number contained several items; sermons and some poetry accompanied the Bible studies.

v1, nos.1-6   1802-[1809]   APS II, Reel 6
v2, no.2   1810   Reel 72

Microfilm edition was prepared from MHi copy.

THE BIBELOT, a reprint of poetry and prose for book lovers, chosen in part from scarce editions and sources not generally known. v.1-21; Jan. 1895-1925. Portland, Me., T.B. Mosher.

21 v. plates (part col.) monthly. General index, volumes i to xx inclusive (1895-1914) comp. by Milton James Ferguson. Portland, Me., T.B. Mosher, 1915.

T.B. Mosher, editor.

Thomas Bird Mosher was founder and editor of the *Bibelot*. It published reprints of old but neglected poems, poem sequences, prose poems, and dramas. This monthly was cheap (since the authors were not paid) but well done. Contents varied greatly including Swinburne, Theocritus, William Morris, Blake, Villon, Yeats, and many others. Mosher was a good anthologist, and his publication was useful for self-education.

Cumulative Index 1-20   1895-1925   APS III, Reel 252
v1-10   1895-1904   Reel 252
v11-21   1905-1925   Reel 253

Microfilm edition was prepared from OU copy.

BIBLIA. *SEE* American Antiquarian and Oriental Journal.

BIBLICAL REPERTORY. *SEE* Princeton Review.

BIBLICAL REPERTORY AND PRINCETON REVIEW. *SEE* Princeton Review.

BIBLICAL REPERTORY AND THEOLOGICAL REVIEW. *SEE* Princeton Review.

BIBLICAL REPOSITORY. *SEE* American Quarterly Observer.

* **THE BIBLICAL REPOSITORY AND CLASSICAL REVIEW.** v.1-12, 1831-38; v. [13-24] 2d ser., v. 1-12, 1839-44; v. [25-30] 3d ser., v. 1-6, 1845-50. Andover [Mass., etc.] 1831-36; New York, 1837-50.

30 v. illus., pl., maps. quarterly.

Title varies: 1831-34, The Biblical repository. 1835-36, The Biblical repository and quarterly observer. 1837-38, The American Biblical repository. 1839-44. The American Biblical repository, devoted to Biblical and general literature, theological discussion, the history of theological opinions, etc. 1845-50, The Biblical repository and classical review.

Editors: 1831-34, E. Robinson.—1835-37, B.B. Edwards.—1838-42. A. Peters.—1840-41, S.B. Treat.—1842-46, J.H. Agnew.—1846-47, W.H. Bidwell.—1848-50, J.M. Sherwood. Absorbed the American quarterly observer in Jan. 1835, the Quarterly Christian spectator in Jan. 1839. Merged into Bibliotheca sacra in Jan. 1851.

The pages of the *Biblical Repository,* with their Hebrew and Greek, as well as English, indexes, are far from inviting. This Congregationalist magazine contained articles and essays on the Bible, doctrine, and theology, along with selections from the theological literature of England and other European countries. It also kept the reader up to date on the state of theology, education, and literature in other countries, and listed new publications in the U.S. and foreign countries.

Biblical Repository
v1-4   Jan. 1831-Oct. 1834   APS II, Reel 306

Biblical Repository and Quarterly Observer

v5-6	Jan.-Oct 1835	APS II, Reel 306
v7-8	Jan.-Oct. 1836	Reel 307

American Biblical Repository

v9-12	Jan. 1837-Oct. 1838	APS II, Reel 307

American Biblical Repository, Devoted To Biblical and General Literature

s2v1-3	Jan. 1839-Apr. 1840	APS II, Reel 307
s2v4-10	July 1840-Oct. 1843	Reel 308
s2v11-12	Jan.-Oct. 1844	Reel 309

Biblical Repository and Classical Review

s3v1-4	Jan. 1845-Oct. 1848	APS II, Reel 309
s3v5-6	Jan. 1849-Oct. 1850	Reel 310

Microfilm edition was prepared from MiU copy.

THE BIBLICAL WORLD. v.1-15, Apr. 1882-Dec. 1892; new ser., v. 1-54, Jan. 1893-Nov. 1920. Chicago, University of Chicago Press, 1882-[1920]

69 v. illus., plates, ports., maps, facsims. Monthly, Apr.-July 1882; monthly (except July and Aug.) Sept. 1882-June 1889; monthly, July 1889-June 1918; bimonthly, July 1918-Nov. 1920. Published by the University of Chicago, 1893-1920.

Title varies: v. 1-2 (Apr. 1882-June 1883) The Hebrew student: a monthly journal in the interests of Old Testament literature and interpretation. v. 3-8 (Sept. 1883-June 1889) The Old Testament student. (Vol. 8 includes New Testament supplement) v. 9-15 (July 1889- Dec. 1892) The Old and New Testament student. New ser. (Jan. 1893-Nov. 1920) The Biblical world.

Editors: Apr. 1882-Dec. 1905, W.R. Harper.—Jan. 1906-Dec. 1912, E.D. Burton.—Jan. 1913-Nov. 1920, Shaller Mathews. Imprint varies: Apr. 1882-Feb. 1887, Chicago E.B. Meredith; Mar. 1887-Mar. 1889, New Haven, Old Testament Student; Apr.-Dec. 1889, New York, C.V. Patterson Pub. Co.; Jan. 1890-Dec. 1892, Hartford, Student Pub. Co.; Jan 1893-Nov. 1920, Chicago, University Press of Chicago. Vols. 11-14 of new series include "Theological and Semitic literature; a bibliographical supplement to the American journal of theology, the American journal of Semitic languages and literatures, and the Biblical World. By W. Muss-Arnoit", 1898-99. "Books for New Testament study ... [By] Clyde Weber Votaw"; new ser., v. 26, p. 271-320; new ser., v.37, p. 289-352. "Books for Old Testament study. [By] John Merlin Powis Smith", new ser., v.30, p. 135-160, 302-320, 383-400. "Index to the Biblical world, vols. I-XXVII, 1893-1906"; new ser., v. 28, p. [433]-526. (United with the American journal of theology to form the Journal of religion.)

Biblical World was first edited by William Rainey Harper, president of The University of Chicago. It was generally philological in the beginning but later broadened to include articles on social questions, science and religion, and Sunday school reform.

Hebrew Student: a Monthly Journal in the Interests of Old Testament Literature and Interpretation

v1-2	Apr. 1882-June 1883	APS III, Reel 254

Old Testament Student

v3-8	Sept. 1883-June 1889	APS III, Reel 254

Old and New Testament Student

v9-15	July 1889-Dec. 1892	APS III, Reel 255

Biblical World

nsv 1-6	Jan. 1893-Dec. 1895	APS II, Reel 256
nsv 7-12	Jan. 1896-Dec. 1898	Reel 257
nsv 13-18	Jan. 1899-Dec. 1901	Reel 258
nsv 19-24	Jan. 1902-Dec. 1904	Reel 259
nsv 25-30	Jan. 1905-Dec. 1907	Reel 260
nsv 31-36	Jan. 1908-Dec. 1910	Reel 261
nsv 37-42	Jan. 1911-Dec. 1913	Reel 262
nsv 43-49	Jan. 1914-June 1917	Reel 263
nsv 50-54	July 1917-Nov. 1920	Reel 264

Vol.5: Pgs. 99-100 torn. Pgs. 139-140 missing. Vol.12: Pgs. 390-391 misnumbered. Vol.14: Pgs. 385-386 missing in number only. New Series Vol. 32: Pg 392 has print missing (readable).

Microfilm edition was prepared from MiU, NRCR copies.

BIBLIOTHECA SACRA. nos. 1-3; Feb., May, Dec. 1843. Robinson, N.Y. [and] London, 1843.

3 no.

Superseded by Bibliotheca sacra and theological review, later Bibliotheca sacra.

Edited by Edward Robinson, the *Bibliotheca Sacra* was a religious review which served as the mouthpiece of the Andover theologians, and thus represented orthodox Calvinism and opposed Unitarianism. After issuing only three numbers, Robinson turned it over to his friend Professor Bela B. Edwards of Andover and thus it was superseded by the *Bibliotheca Sacra and Theological Review*.

no. 1-3	Feb., May, Dec. 1843	APS II, Reel 379

Microfilm edition was prepared from DLC copy.

SEE ALSO: Biblical Repository and Classical Review *and* Christian Review.

BIBLIOTHECA SACRA AND THEOLOGICAL REVIEW. *SEE* Bibliotheca Sacra.

THE BOOKMAN; a review of books and life. v. 1-76, no.3; Feb. 1895-Mar. 1933. New York, Dodd, Mead [1895-1933]

76 v. illus. (incl. facsims.) plates (part col.) ports. monthly.

Subtitle varies.

Published by Dodd, Mead and company, Feb. 1895-Aug. 1918; George H. Doran company, Sept. 1918-Aug. 1927; Bookman publishing co., inc., Sept. 1927-Mar. 1933. Superseded by the American review.

The *Bookman* stands as an impressive file of honest, impartial criticism and as an excellent source for selected literature. The most notable volumes were the early ones edited by Harry Thurston Peck. His major contribution was the first "best seller" list published in America. His subeditor, James MacArthur, graduated to the helm of *Bookman* after Peck's retirement in 1907. He was followed in succession by Arthur Bartlett Maurice, G.G. Wyant, Robert Cortes Holliday, Henry L. West, John Farrar, Burton Rascoe, and Seward Collins. In addition to Peck, Maurice and Farrar were the best editors guiding the *Bookman* throughout its career. They both had the ability to forge their personalities into the review's pages.

Many prominent critics and authors enriched the entire series, whether or not the trend of the present editor was conservative (as under Collins), or bouncy (as under Peck). In addition to the reviewing of books, serials and special articles were included. The special articles included essays on important newspapers, authors, critics, illustrators, and notes on the theater.

v1-5	Feb. 1895-Aug. 1897	APS III, Reel 112
v6-9	Sept. 1897-Aug. 1899	Reel 113
v10-13	Sept. 1899-Aug. 1901	Reel 114
v14-17	Sept. 1901-Aug. 1903	Reel 115
v18-21	Sept. 1903-Aug. 1905	Reel 116
v22-25	Sept. 1905-Aug. 1907	Reel 117
v26-29	Sept. 1907-Aug. 1909	Reel 118
v30-33	Sept. 1909-Aug. 1911	Reel 119
v34-37	Sept. 1911-Aug. 1913	Reel 120
v38-41	Sept. 1813-Aug 1915	Reel 121
v42-45	Sept. 1915-Aug. 1917	Reel 122
v46-49	Sept. 1917-Aug. 1919	Reel 123
v50-54	Sept. 1919-Feb. 1922	Reel 124
v55-58	March 1922-Feb. 1924	Reel 125
v59-62	March 1924-Feb. 1926	Reel 126
v63-66	March 1926-Feb. 1928	Reel 127
v67-70	March 1928-Feb. 1930	Reel 128
v71-74	March 1930-March 1932	Reel 129
v75-76	April 1932-March 1933	Reel 130

Several volumes have advertising pages missing or torn. Volume 1, 47, and 71 have pages torn or stained. Vol. 56: tightly bound. Best copy available for photographing.

Microfilm edition was prepared from DLC, NcD, C, NPV, InGrD, CCC, and inLP copies.

BOSTON CULTIVATOR. *SEE* American Cultivator.

THE BOSTON JOURNAL OF PHILOSOPHY AND THE ARTS, intended to exhibit a view of the progress of discovery in natural philosophy, mechanics, chemistry, geology and mineralogy, natural history, comparative anatomy and physiology, geography, statistics, and the fine and useful arts. v.1-3; May 1823-Dec. 1826. Boston, Cummings, Hilliard, 1824-26.

3 v. plates,

Editors: 1823-23, John Ware, J. W. Webster, Daniel Treadwell. –1824-26, J.W. Webster, Daniel Treadwell.

This quarterly science magazine was for a short time a Harvard competitor of Yale's *American Journal of Science.* It provided a complete record of the state of science in the U.S. and Europe, along with original articles on American science, and selections from European magazines. In addition, there were frequent biographical sketches, and a "General Intelligence" section.

v1-3	May 1823-Dec. 1826	APS II, Reel 73

BOSTON LITERARY GAZETTE. *SEE* Yankee and Boston Literary Gazette.

THE BOSTON LITERARY MAGAZINE. v.1, no. 1-12; May 1, 1832-Apr. 1833. Boston, Clapp and Hull, 1833.

1 v. monthly.

This literary periodical published sentimental tales and poetry, book reviews, sketches of American scenery, biographical sketches, historical tales, essays, and anecdotes, listed new publications, and gave coverage to literature, travel, and art.

v1, no.1-12	May 1, 1832-Apr. 1833	APS II, Reel 379

Microfilm edition was prepared from NN copy.

THE BOSTON LYCEUM. v. 1-2 (no.1-11) Jan.-Nov. 1827. [Boston] 1827.

2 v. in 1. monthly.

Caption title. Nos. 9-11 have title: The Lyceum.

Primarily a literary magazine, the *Boston Lyceum* offered departments of poetry and drama, reviews of both American and foreign publications, biographical sketches, tales, essays, and brief political summaries.

v1-2, no.1-11	Jan.-Nov. 1827	APS II, Reel 379

Pagination is irregular.

Microfilm edition was prepared from DLC copy.

THE BOSTON MAGAZINE. v. 1-3, Oct. 30, 1802-Oct. 19, 1805; [new ser.] v. 1; Oct. 26, 1805-Apr. 26, 1806. Boston, Gilbert and Dean, 1803-06.

4 v. in 3. weekly.

Title varies: Oct. 30, 1802-Oct. 19, 1805, The Boston weekly magazine; devoted to morality, literature, biography, history, the fine arts, agriculture, &c. &c. (Vol.2, nos.1-13 have title: Boston weekly magazine: or, Ladies' and gentlemen's miscellany) Superseded by Emerald.

Oct. 26, 1805-Apr. 26, 1806, The Boston magazine. A notice in the number for Apr. 26, 1806, states that "the proprietors ... intend to issue their future numbers on a new and enlarged plan".

Begun in October, 1802 by Samuel Gilbert and Thomas Dean, this four-page miscellany was designed chiefly for "fashionable females" and contained occasional paragraphs on London and Paris fashions. It is important for its attention to fiction and richness in theatrical comment; serial novels, "fragments," and short stories are plentiful, and a "Thespian Department" begun in December 1803 provided reviews of productions at the Boston Theater. It also contained two or three essay series, some scientific miscellany, a "monitorial" department, a section of "amusement," poetry, and current events. In January 1804 the magazine suffered a serious loss by fire but nevertheless continued publication for nearly two more years, selling out in October 1805 to Joshua Belcher and Samuel T. Armstrong, who changed the title to "The Boston Magazine."

Boston Weekly Magazine; devoted to ...
v1-3	Oct. 30, 1802-Oct. 19, 1805	APS II, Reel 6

Boston Magazine
nsv1	Oct. 26, 1805-Feb. 22, 1806	APS II, Reel 6

Several issues are missing; not available for photographing. Film ends Feb. 22, 1806.

Microfilm edition was prepared from DLC and MiU-C copy.

SEE ALSO: Emerald.

THE BOSTON MAGAZINE, containing, a collection of instructive and entertaining essays, in the various branches of useful, and polite literature. Together with, foreign and domestick occurrences, anecdotes, observations on the weather, & c., & c. v.1-3; Oct. 1783-Nov./Dec. 1786. Boston, Greenleaf and Freeman.

3 v. plates, ports., map. monthly.

A well-illustrated miscellany which included much original material and some music.

v1-3   Oct. 1783-Nov./Dec. 1786   APS I, Reel 9

Some pages are missing.

Microfilm edition was prepared from DLC copy.

BOSTON MASONIC MIRROR. v. 1-3, Nov. 27, 1824-1827; new ser. v. 1-5, July 4, 1829-1834? Boston.

3 v. weekly.

Title varies: Nov. 1824- Masonic mirror: and mechanics' intelligencer.- July 4, 1829, Masonic mirror: science, literature and miscellany (running title: Boston masonic mirror) July 3, 1830- Boston masonic mirror.

The *Mirror* provided a variety of material on the Masons, including coverage of their meetings and articles opposing antimasonry. In addition, contents included biography, poetry, anecdotes, short tales, some politics, addresses to members, and articles and items on science, agriculture, manufacturing, and commerce.

Masonic Mirror: and Mechanics' Intelligencer
v1-2, no.1   Nov. 27, 1824-Dec. 31, 1825   APS II, Reel 73

v2, no.2-v3   Jan. 7, 1826-Dec. 22, 1827   APS II, Reel 589

Masonic Mirror: Science, Literature and Miscellany.
nsv1   July 4, 1829-June 26, 1830   APS II, Reel 590

Boston Masonic Mirror
nsv2-3   July 3, 1830-June 23, 1832   APS II, Reel 590
nsv4-5   June 30, 1832-Jan. 25, 1834   Reel 591

Many pages are stained and have faded print. New series vol.5: no. 13 is missing; pages 3-4 of no. 31 are missing; not available for photographing.

Microfilm edition was prepared from DLC, MH, and MWA copies.

BOSTON MECHANIC, AND JOURNAL OF THE USEFUL ARTS AND SCIENCES. v. 1-4; Jan. 1832-Feb. 1836. Boston, G.W. Light, 1832-

v. illus., plates. monthly.

Title varies: Jan. 1832-Dec. 1833: The Young mechanic. Jan.-Dec. 1834: The Mechanic.

Editors: T. Claston, G.W. Light, J.M. Wightman.

Conducted by "an association of practical mechanics," this magazine proposed to "diffuse general elementary knowledge," to discuss questions and queries sent by readers, and to publicize new inventions. It published about one page each of questions and answers; listings of new publications and American patents; short notes on inventions; and articles, with illustrations and diagrams, on scientific subjects—steam engines, the elements, minerals, and metals. Some non-scientific material appeared also.

Young Mechanic
v1-2   Jan. 1832-Dec. 1833   APS II, Reel 472

Mechanic
v3   Jan.-Dec. 1834   APS II, Reel 472

Boston Mechanic
v4   Jan. 1835-Feb. 1836   APS II, Reel 472

The index is bound and photographed at the end of each volume. Several pages are stained with some loss of text.

Microfilm edition was prepared from DLC and MB copies.

BOSTON MEDICAL AND SURGICAL JOURNAL. *SEE* Boston Medical Intelligencer; New-England Journal of Medicine, *and* New-England Medical Review and Journal.

BOSTON MEDICAL INTELLIGENCER. Devoted to the cause of physical education, and to the means of preventing and of curing diseases. v. 1-5; Apr. 29, 1823-Feb. 12, 1828. Boston, J. Cotton, 1823-28.

5 v. in 3. weekly.

Title-pages of v. 1-3 read: The Medical intelligencer; containing extracts from foreign and American journals; a variety of local intelligence on subjects connected with medicine ... (caption and running title: Boston medical intelligencer)

Editors: 1823-25, J.V.C. Smith.–1825-26, James Wilson.–1826-28, J.G. Coffin. United with the New England medical review and journal to form the Boston medical and surgical journal.

The *Boston Medical Intelligencer* began as a journal primarily for those in the medical field, but eventually came to be directed to the public as well, its chief object being to promote health by pointing out causes of disease and means of prevention and cure. It contained accounts of cases and articles on health, on various diseases and cures, and on improvements and discoveries in medical science. In addition, a wide variety of medical miscellany—local news, biographical sketches, information on hospitals, society proceedings, critical notices—and some nonmedical material were included.

v1-3, no.33   Apr. 29, 1823-Dec. 27, 1825   APS II, Reel 73
v3, no.34-v5   Jan. 31, 1826-Feb. 12, 1828   Reel 763

Many pages are stained; Vol.4: Issue 1 is repeated in number only; pages 405-12 are bound out of order.

Microfilm edition was prepared from CSt-L copy.

SEE ALSO: New-England Medical Review and Journal.

THE BOSTON MISCELLANY OF LITERATURE AND FASHION. v. 1-3, no.2; Jan. 1842-Feb. 1843. Boston and New York, Bradbury, Soden [1842-

v. plates (part col.) monthly.

Editors: 1842, Nathan Hale. 1843-H. T. Tuckerman. Vol. 3 has title: The Boston miscellany and lady's monthly magazine. cf. Sabin, Bibl. Amer. Subtitle varies.

Edited by Nathan Hale, Jr., this monthly magazine published sentimental prose and poetry, literary notices, essays, and illustrations, and also contained colored fashion plates and a piece of music in each issue. James Russell Lowell was a contributor throughout the year and did a series on Old English dramatists. Nathaniel Hawthorne contributed "A Virtuoso's Collection" and N.P. Willis, T.W. Parsons, W.A. Jones, Alexander H. Everett, and Edward Everett Hale were also writers for the magazine. Mrs. Sarah Hale's translations of German tales were a feature, and Poe's review of Griswold's *Poets and Poetry of America* appeared in the November number. The *Arcturus,* of New York, was combined with the *Miscellany* in June, 1842, bringing to it such writers as E.A. Duyckinck, Charles Fenno Hoffman, and Mrs. Kirkland. At the end of 1842, Hale resigned the editorship to Henry Tuckerman, who produced only two issues in 1843.

v1-3   Jan. 1842-Feb. 1843   APS II, Reel 310

Microfilm edition was prepared from MiU copy.

* **BOSTON MONTHLY MAGAZINE.** v. 1-2, no.2; June 1825-July 1826. [Boston]

2 v. in 1. plates, ports.

S.L. Knapp, editor.

This creditable but undistinguished monthly, begun in June 1825 by Samuel L. Knapp, resembled a review in its contents, but the articles were shorter than those of the reviews of that time. It contained memoirs of eminent persons, brief items on inventions and improvements in science and medicine, historical and travel articles, book reviews, and notices of new publications. It also provided foreign news, some poetry, and paragraphs on music; and was illustrated with lithographs by John Pendleton.

v1, nos. 1-7   June-Dec. 1825   APS II, Reel 74

v1-2   June 1825-July 1826   Reel 591

Microfilm edition was prepared from DLC copy.

BOSTON MUSICAL GAZETTE; a semimonthly journal, devoted to the science of music. v. 1-2, no.2; May 2, 1838-May 15, 1839. Boston [Otis, Broaders]

2 v.

Includes music.

Edited by B. Brown.

Published every other Wednesday in quarto form, this journal was devoted to the "science of music." It contained musical history, biographical sketches of eminent composers and performers, reviews of musical works, accounts of oratorios and concerts, musical societies, academies and schools. Most of the poetry included featured musical themes.

v1-2   May 2, 1838-May 15, 1839   APS II, Reel 408

Microfilm edition was prepared from PPi copy.

THE BOSTON MUSICAL REVIEW. Ed. by G.W. Peck, esq. v. 1 (no.1-4); Sept. 1-Nov. 1, 1845. Boston, Otis, Broaders [1845]

82 p. illus. (music) semimonthly.

A Boston musical magazine edited by G.W. Peck which printed four or five numbers in 1845. Each number was to contain one or more brief essays contributing to the general understanding of music, as well as articles of a lighter sort, notices of important concerts and new publications, a variety of miscellany, and two or three pages of music.

v1   Sept. 1-Nov. 1, 1845   APS II, Reel 770

Microfilm edition was prepared from DLC copy.

BOSTON MUSICAL VISITOR. *SEE* American Journal of Music and Musical Visitor.

BOSTON NEWS-LETTER, AND CITY RECORD. *SEE* Bowen's Boston News-Letter.

THE BOSTON PEARL, A GAZETTE OF POLITE LITERATURE. Devoted to original tales, legends, essays, translations, travelling, literary and historical sketches, biography, poetry, criticisms, music, etc. ... v. 1-6, no. 16; June 11, 1831-Sept. 14, 1836, Boston, Printed by John Emmes Dill [etc., etc.]

6 v. music, ports. Semimonthly, June 11, 1831-Aug. 2, 1834; weekly Aug. 20, 1834-Sept. 14, 1836. Vol. 3, July 6-Aug. 3, 1833 called no. 1-3 (caption title: The Bouquet: flowers of polite literature); v. 3, Aug. 17-Sept. 28, 1833 also called no. 1-3 (caption title: The Pearl and literary gazette) See also The Bouquet: Flowers of polite literature, Aug. 3, 1833, p. 24. Joseph Hurlbut's [notice]

Title varies: June 11, 1831-June 1, 1833, The Bouquet: flowers of polite literature ... — (caption title, July 6-Aug. 3, 1833: The Bouquet: flowers of polite literature)—Aug. 17, 1833-Aug. 2, 1834, The Pearl and literary gazette ... —Aug. 20, 1834-Sept. 5, 1835. The Boston pearl, and literary gazette ... (caption title, Aug. 20-Oct. 8, 1834: The Hartford pearl and literary gazette; Sept. 19, 1835-Sept. 14, 1836: The Boston pearl, a gazette devoted to polite literature)

Editors: June 11, 1831-Feb. 23, 1833, Melzar Gardner.—Mar. 9, 1833-July 20, 1833, Joseph Hurlbut.—Aug. 3, 1833-Sept. 14, 1836, Isaac C. Pray, Jr. (Dec. 13, 1834-Feb. 28, 1835, with Isaac McLellan, Jr.; (v.6, no.1) Sept. 14, 1836, H. Hastings Weld.) Imprint varies: June 11, 1831-Nov. 1833, Hartford, Conn., William A. Hawley [etc.]—Dec. 7, 1833-Jan. 18, 1834, Boston, Hartford, Conn.; [Isaac C. Pray, Jr.]—Feb. 1-Oct. 8, 1834, Hartford, Conn.; printed by Justin Jones.—Nov. 8, 1834-Sept. 14, 1836, Boston printed by John Emmes Dill [etc.]

A literary miscellany edited by Isaac Pray which pirated a good deal of its material. It published original and selected tales and poems, many of them of a sentimental nature, moral and humorous essays, legends, literary notices, and historical, biographical, and travel sketches. In addition, it contained much miscellaneous material and music for piano.

Bouquet: Flowers of Polite Literature
v1-2   June 11, 1831-June 1, 1833   APS II, Reel 788
v3, no. 1-3   July 6, 1833-Aug. 3, 1833   Reel 788

Pearl and Literary Gazette
v3   Aug. 17, 1833-Aug. 2, 1834   APS II, Reel 788

Hartford Pearl and LIterary Gazette
v4, no. 1-8   Aug. 20, 1834-Oct. 8, 1834   APS II, Reel 788

Boston Pearl and Literary Gazette
v4, no. 9-52   Nov. 8, 1834-Sept. 5, 1835   APS II, Reel 788

Boston Pearl, A Gazette of Polite Literature
v5-6   Sept. 19, 1835-Sept. 14, 1836   APS II, Reel 788

Several pages are tightly bound. Volume 2: Issue 26 is stained, with some loss of print. Volume 3: Lacks a table of contents. Issue 8 is not available for photographing. Volume 6: Contains only issues 6, 14-15. Best copy available for photographing.

Microfilm edition was prepared from CtY and MWA copies.

BOSTON PEARL AND LITERARY GAZETTE. *SEE* Boston Pearl, A Gazette of Polite Literature.

* **THE BOSTON QUARTERLY REVIEW.** v. 1-5; Jan. 1838-Oct. 1842. Boston, B.H. Green, 1838-42.

5 v.

O.A. Brownson, editor. Merged into the United States magazine and democratic review. In 1844 Brownson began the publication of a new periodical under title: Brownson's quarterly review.

Begun by Orestes A. Brownson, this quarterly review dealt mainly with philosophy, literature, sociology, and theology. Brownson wrote most of his review himself, discussing, among other things, the labor question and advocating the abolition of hereditary descent of property and of the Christian priesthood. He occasionally printed articles by Alexander H. Everett, George Bancroft, George Ripley, Bronson Alcott, Margaret Fuller, Anne C. Lynch, Elizabeth Peabody, and Albert Brisbane.

v1-5   Jan. 1838-Oct. 1842   APS II, Reel 380

Pagination is irregular

Microfilm edition was prepared from DLC copy.

SEE ALSO: Brownson's Quarterly Review.

BOSTON RECORDER. SEE Congregationalist and Herald of Gospel Liberty.

BOSTON RECORDER AND RELIGIOUS TELEGRAPH. SEE Congregationalist and Herald of Gospel Liberty.

BOSTON SATIRIST. SEE Satirist.

THE BOSTON SPECTATOR; devoted to politicks and belles-lettres. Ed. by John Park. v. 1 (no. 1-61); Jan. 1, 1814-Feb. 25, 1815.

1 v.

Includes many articles relative to the war of 1812.

This four-page politico-literary weekly edited by John Park published a "Political" section which featured many articles concerning the War of 1812. There was a weekly summary of events, a section of poetry, and a "Miscellaneous and Literary" department which included, among other items, series on "The Writer," "Tully," and "Horace."

v1, no.1-61   Jan. 1, 1814-Feb. 25, 1815   APS II, Reel 74

THE BOSTON WEEKLY-MAGAZINE. no. 1-3; Mar. 2-16, 1743. [Boston] Rogers and Fowle.

23 p.

"No other numbers have been found and probably no others were printed."–Richardson, L.A., A history of early American magazines, 1931, p. 364.

A pamphlet which published periodical essays from English magazines along with verse and news.

no. 1-3   Mar. 2-16, 1743   APS I, Reel 8

Microfilm edition was prepared from MH copy.

THE BOSTON WEEKLY MAGAZINE. Devoted to moral and entertaining literature, science, and the fine arts: containing original and selected tales, moral and humorous essays, sketches of nature and of society, elegant extracts, poetry, criticism, and selections from works of history and adventure: embellished with music. v.1-3; Sept. 8, 1838-Sept. 11, 1841. Boston, D.H. Ela and J.B. Hall, 1838-41.

3 v. illus. (incl. music)

This eight-page weekly was to be instructive and amusing, presenting a rich variety and including selections from the most valuable American and European works. It published poetry and tales, moral and humorous essays, reviews of new publications, selections from works of history and adventure, biographical and travel sketches, and short news items. The writings of Washington Irving, Nathaniel Hawthorne, and Mrs. Lydia Huntley Sigourney were included; and the text was embellished with illustrations and music for piano and flute.

v1-3   Sept. 8, 1838-Sept. 11, 1841   APS II, Reel 326
v1-3   Sept. 8, 1838-Sept. 11, 1841   Reel 784

Many pages are stained, with some loss of print.

Microfilm edition was prepared from MH and MiU copies.

THE BOSTON WEEKLY MAGAZINE, devoted to polite literature, useful science, biography, and dramatic criticism. v. 1-3, 1816-1819; new ser., no. 1-41, Mar. 20-Dec. 25, 1824. Boston [Tileston & Parmenter, etc.]

Vol. 2, no. 27-52, v. 3, no. 1, 24, 27-52; new ser., v. 1, no. 41 missing.

Caption title varies: -Oct. 4, 1817, Boston weekly magazine. Oct. 11-Dec. 27, 1817, Weekly magazine and ladies' miscellany. Jan. 3, 1818, Semiweekly magazine and merchantile advertiser. Jan. 10, 1818- Boston weekly magazine and ladies' miscellany. Vol. 2 lacks t.-p. and index. Title-page of v. 3 reads: The Boston weekly magazine, devoted to polite literature.

Original bound with miscellaneous material. Merged into Boston spectator.

This 4-page literary miscellany provided its readers with reviews of the latest plays performed at Boston theaters, along with reviews of new books, news summaries, moral essays, biographical sketches, poetry, humorous anecdotes, and much miscellaneous material. Science and agriculture also received some attention. Beginning with the second volume, serialized tales were added, and when the new series was begun in 1824, there was less on science and agriculture and more material of interest to women.

v1-ns.v1, no.40   Oct. 12, 1816-Dec. 18, 1824   APS II, Reel 74

BOUQUET: FLOWERS OF POLITE LITERATURE. SEE Boston Pearl, A Gazette of Polite Literature.

BOWEN'S BOSTON NEWS-LETTER, and city record. Jerome V.C. Smith, editor. v. 1-2; Nov. 5, 1825-Dec. 30, 1826. Boston, A. Bowen, 1826

2 v. illus. weekly.

Caption title: The Boston news-letter, and city record. (Vol. 1, no. 1, has title: The City record, and Boston news-letter)

Published by Abel Bowen, this weekly was established to preserve Boston's past and record its present. In addition to publishing historical events, it recorded current local events—news, proceedings of City Council, reports of trials, lists of laws and ordinances, and obituary notices, as well as providing national and international news. There was also a section for legal papers, such as court orders, sales of real estate, census statistics, copy right notices, etc., and occasional articles on the theater.

City Record, and Boston News-Letter
v1, no.1   Nov. 5, 1825   APS II, Reel 74

v1, no.1   Nov. 5, 1825   APS II, Reel 914

[Bowen's] Boston News-Letter and City Record
v1, no.2   Dec. 31, 1825   APS II, Reel 74

v1, no.2-v2   Dec. 31, 1825-Dec. 30, 1826   APS II, Reel 914

Reel 914: Volume 1: pages 105-112 stained, Pages 265-266 and 285, print missing. Contains Supplement, "The City Record", November 5, 1825-June 17, 1826 following the index. Volume 2: September 30, page 2, print faded.

Microfilm edition was prepared from DLC, NPV, CtHT, and CtHT-W copies.

BOYS' AND GIRLS' MAGAZINE AND FIRESIDE COMPANION. *SEE* Forrester's Boys' and Girls' Magazine, and Fireside Companion.

BROADWAY JOURNAL. v. 1-2; Jan. 4, 1845-Jan. 3, 1846. New York, 1845-1846.

2 v.

A literary periodical edited by Charles Briggs, ambitious young litterateur who had written for the *Knickerbocker;* contributors included Edgar Allan Poe and other well-known writers. Literary reviews were the chief subject, but art criticism, comment on theater and music, political articles, and poetry were also included. Serialized material included an extensive review of the exhibition of the National Academy of Art, and articles on the use of color in painting. Political comment opposed the Mexican War and was occasionally illustrated by cartoons engraved on wood.

v1-2   Jan. 4, 1845-Jan. 3, 1846   APS II, Reel 649

Microfilm edition was prepared from CtY copy.

BROTHER JONATHAN. A weekly compend of belles lettres and the fine arts, standard literature, and general intelligence. v.1-6; Jan. 1, 1842-Dec. 23, 1843. New York, Wilson [1842-43]

6 v. illus.

Forms the quarto library edition of the Brother Jonathan newspaper. A notice in the last number of v.6 states that it will hereafter be published in a folio form as it was when it first appeared. Edited by H.H. Weld, John Neal, G.M. Snow, Edward Stephens.

Since the early editors, Park Benjamin and Rev. Rufus Wilmot Griswold, of this quarto, were trained by Horace Greeley, they produced a periodical sensational in nature and featuring serial fiction. *Brother Jonathan* contained current news items, both foreign and domestic, articles on foreign travel, architecture and music, critical notes on books and drama and vital statistics. An ornate cover page introduced each issue. Original fashion plates decorated many issues, as well as wooducts "conveyed" from other periodicals. Advertisements were found on the back pages. Poems by Walt Whitman were a regular feature along with serials and fiction by such writers as Dickens, Mrs. Gore, Mrs. Moberly and Paul de Kock. Editors

included H. Hastings and John Neal. Later the periodical issued complete novels brought from Europe by boat and printed within twenty-four hours of arrival as extras.

v1-4   Jan. 1842-Apr. 29, 1843   APS II, Reel 409
v5-6   May 6, 1843-Dec. 23, 1843   Reel 410

Microfilm edition was prepared from DLC, MiU, and MiU-C copies.

BROWN'S LITERARY OMNIBUS; news, books entire, sketches, reviews, tales, miscellaneous intelligence. v. 1-2; Jan. 6, 1837-July 20, 1838. Philadelphia, Brown.

2 v. weekly.

Title varies: 1837, Waldie's literary omnibus ...

Imprint varies' 1837, A. Waldie. Absorbed by Saturday evening post.

The primary purpose of *Brown's Literary Omnibus* was to publish, in serialized form, the "newest and best books from London," including novels, travels, and memoirs. About 80 percent of each issue was devoted to printing a segment of a single novel, and the rest consisted of literary reviews, tales, poetry, sketches, information from the "world of letters," and European and American news.

Waldie's Literary Omnibus.
v 1   1837   APS II, Reel 1368

Brown's Literary Omnibus.
v 2   1838   APS II, Reel 1368

Several pages are stained, creased, and have print faded and show-through. Best copy available for photographing. Vol.1: Issue 2, Pgs. 3-4 are torn with some loss of text. Issue 3 and Pgs. 3-6 of issue 35 are missing; not available for photographing. Vol. 2: Issue 3 is missing.

Microfilm edition was prepared from WHi copy.

* **BROWNSON'S QUARTERLY REVIEW.** v. 1-3, 1844-46; new ser. v. 1-6, 1847-52; 3d ser. v. 1-3, 1853-55; New York ser. v. 1-4, 1856-59; 2d-3d New York ser. V. 1-4, 1860-63; National ser. v. 1, 1864; last ser. v. 1-3, 1873-75. Boston, B.H. Greene, 1844-55; New York, E. Dunigan, 1856-75.

24 v.

O.A. Brownson, editor. The Boston quarterly review, issued by Brownson from 1838 to 1842, was in 1843 merged into the United States magazine and democratic review. In 1844 Brownson severed his connection with the latter periodical and resumed publication of an independent organ under title: Brownson's quarterly review. This work was suspended from 1865 to 1872, inclusive, and ceased with Oct. 1875.

Orestes A. Brownson, considered by many to have been one of the most brilliant men of his time, edited this powerful, if sometimes quarrelsome, journal, and made it a strong voice of the Catholic Church shortly after its beginning. Brownson engaged in controversies within the Catholic Church, warring on "radicalism," "despotism," and to some extent, upon the Jesuits, and quarrelled with the Bishop of Philadelphia in 1861, a controversy that nearly ruined him. Other Catholic journals regularly attacked him. In 1864, though remaining a Catholic, he withdrew his journal from the ranks of religious publications, and started a new "National Series," which was intended to be a political rather than a religious paper, but was suspended after one year. Nine years later, he resumed his review, hoping with the "Last Series" to rehabilitate himself among

Catholics. Brownson was both editor and author, and his review was not open to contributions from others. He had little regard for pure literature, but gave attention to history, politics and sociology, as well as philosophy and religion. His work is marred by his over-readiness for a fight, by his indifference to tact, and by an often-careless style. Nevertheless, his reviews were remarkable journals, and were undoubtedly followed by many thinking minds on both sides of the Atlantic.

v1-3	Jan. 1844-Oct. 1846	APS II, Reel 507
nsv1-6	Jan. 1847-Oct. 1852	Reel 508
s3v1-2	Jan. 1853-1854	APS II, Reel 884
s3v3 (New York Series)-		
3 New York Series v3	1855-1862	Reel 885
3 New York Series v4-		
(National Series)-		
Last Series v1-3	1863-1875	Reel 886

New series vol. 4: pages 399-408 are stained with some loss of text. Series 3, vol. 3: content pages have been repaired.

Microfilm edition was prepared from C, CMenSP, DLC, IC, MChB, MdBE, Mi, MiD, MiDU, NhD, and NN copies.

BUCKEYE AND CINCINNATI MIRROR. *SEE* Cincinnati Mirror, and Western Gazette of Literature, Science, and the Arts.

BULLETIN (FORMERLY JOURNAL) OF THE AMERICAN GEOGRAPHICAL SOCIETY OF NEW YORK. *SEE* American Geographical Society of New York.

BURTON'S GENTLEMAN'S MAGAZINE AND AMERICAN MONTHLY REVIEW. v. 1-7; July 1837-Dec. 1840. Philadelphia, C. Alexander.

7 v. in 6. illus. (part col.) ports.

Title varies: July 1837-Feb. 1839, The Gentleman's magazine (varies slightly)–Dec. 1840, Graham's magazine. Other slight variations in title.

Edited by W.E. Burton (with E.A. Poe, 1839-40) United with the Casket in Jan. 1841 to form Graham's American monthly magazine.

Edited by William E. Burton, *Burton's Gentleman's Magazine* consisted mainly of stories and poems, but also presented some book reviews, pieces of music and illustrations, and a monthly calendar of American chronology, giving dates of important historical events.

Gentleman's Magazine

v1-v4, no.2	July 1837-Feb. 1839	APS II, Reel 311

Burton's Gentleman's Magazine and American Monthly Review

v4, no.3-v7, no.5	Mar. 1839-Nov. 1840	APS II, Reel 311

Graham's Magazine

v7, no.6	Dec. 1840	APS II, Reel 311

Microfilm edition was prepared from MiU copy.

CABINET. *SEE* National Magazine, or, Cabinet of the United States.

THE CABINET; a repository of polite literature. no.1-10; Jan. 5-Mar. 23, 1811. Boston, 1811.

160 p. front. (port.) weekly.

Manuscript index (3 p.) at end.

A magazine of polite literature including biographies, essays, anecdotes, tales and poetry whose early issues emphasized drama and the Boston theater but later expanded to include essays on various topics such as literary criticism, marriage, wit, female education and heroism.

no. 1-10	Jan. 5-Mar. 23, 1811	APS II, Reel 75

CALIFORNIAN. *SEE* Californian and Overland Monthly.

CALIFORNIAN; A WESTERN MONTHLY MAGAZINE. *SEE* Overland Monthly and Out West Magazine.

CALIFORNIAN AND OVERLAND MONTHLY. v. 1-6, nos. 1-36; Jan. 1880-1882. San Francisco.

6 v. monthly.

Vols. 1-6, no. 34 as Californian. Supersedes and is superseded by Overland monthly.

Four years after the suspension of the first series of *Overland Monthly,* the original founder, Anton Roman, again began publishing a magazine for Californians. The *Californian* resembled the old *Overland,* and soon gave way to its second series.

Californian

v 1-2	Jan.-Dec. 1880	APS III, Reel 172
v 3-6, no. 33	Jan. 1881-Sept. 1882	Reel 173

Californian and Overland Monthly

v 6, no. 34-36	Oct. 1882-Dec. 1882	APS III, Reel 173

Microfilm edition was prepared from MiU copy.

CALIFORNIAN ILLUSTRATED MAGAZINE. v.1-5, no.5, Oct. 1891-April 1894. San Francisco, 1891-1894.

5 v.

No numbers issued November-December 1891.

The *Californian Illustrated Magazine* began publication under the editorship of Charles Frederick Holder. It contained many good illustrations and the articles were written by the best of the western writers and some of those from the East. Charles F. Lumis, David Starr Jordan, Gertrude Atherton, and Joaquin Miller were frequently seen in the *Californian* pages. In 1894, Edward J. Livernash purchased the magazine and it was discontinued soon afterward.

v1-5	Oct. 1891-April 1894	APS III, Reel 6

Microfilm edition was prepared from MiU copy.

CAMPBELL'S FOREIGN MONTHLY MAGAZINE ... *SEE* Campbell's Foreign Semi-Monthly Magazine.

CAMPBELL'S FOREIGN SEMI-MONTHLY MAGAZINE, or Select miscellany of European literature and art. v. 1-6; Sept. 1842-Aug. 16, 1844. Philadelphia, J.M. Campbell [1842-44]

6 v. illus., plates, ports.

Vol. 1-3 have title: Campbell's foreign monthly magazine; or, Select miscellany of the periodical literature of Great Britain.

Begun in Philadelphia as a monthly by James M. Campbell, this mainly eclectic magazine was sold after the first year to John Sartain, the engraver, who made it a semimonthly and furnished it with handsome mezzotint plates. Most of its material was selected from British periodicals, and included poetry, serialized tales, letters, essays, sketches, narratives, and articles on science and the arts.

Campbell's Foreign Monthly Magazine ...
v1-3 Sept. 1842-Aug. 1843 APS II, Reel 381

Campbell's Foreign Semi-Monthly Magazine
v4-6 Sept. 1, 1843-Aug. 16, 1844 APS II, Reel 381

Pagination is irregular.

Microfilm edition was prepared from DLC copy.

THE CANDID EXAMINER. v. 1-2; June 19, 1825-June 18, 1827. Montrose, Pa.

2 v. biweekly.

Film incomplete; v. 1 wanting.

The *Candid Examiner* was a religious magazine which mainly promoted the Universalist doctrine. In addition to articles on religion and on the activities of Universalist societies, it included sermons, Bible studies, poetry, anecdotes, and a good deal of selected material, especially from Universalist magazines.

v2 June 19, 1826-June 18, 1827 APS II, Reel 546

Vol.2: Title page and index are missing. Issue 18 is misnumbered. Best copy available for photographing.

Microfilm edition was prepared from MWA copy.

CAREY'S LIBRARY OF CHOICE LITERATURE. Containing the best works of the day in biography, history, travels, novels, poetry, & c., & c. v. 1-2; Oct. 1, 1835-Mar. 26, 1836. Philadelphia, E.L. Carey & A. Hart, 1836-

2 v. weekly.

In October of 1835, E.L. Carey and A. Hart jointly began publishing *Carey's Library*. Plays, tales, and travel articles were included. There also appeared serially "The Life of Right Honorable Sir James MacKintosh" in Volume 1. Although few articles were signed, the names of Joanne Baillie, Leitch Ritchie, Esq., and C. Henningsen were found.

v1-2 Oct. 1, 1835-Mar. 26, 1836 APS II, Reel 916

Vols. 1-2 lack Indexes. Please refer to the Tables of Contents.

Microfilm edition was prepared from DLC, TNJ-P, and PCaD copies.

THE CAROLINA JOURNAL OF MEDICINE, SCIENCE AND AGRICULTURE. v. 1, no. 1-3; Jan.-July 1825, new series v.1, no.1-2, 1826. Charleston, S.C., Gray & Ellis.

quarterly.

Edited by T.Y. Simons and W. Michel.

Conducted by two physicians, Thomas Y. Simons and William Michel this quarterly journal published interesting extracts from foreign magazines as well as original papers on medicine, science, and agriculture. The papers, some written by the editors themselves, dealt with various diseases—yellow fever, smallpox, and epilepsy, and discussed soils and the culture of rice and the sweet potato, as well as horticulture, and various other science topics. In addition, there was a section of medical and philosophical news, some biographical sketches, and the proceedings of the Agricultural Society.

v1 Jan.-July 1825 APS II, Reel 75
v1-nsv1 Jan. 1825-May 1826 Reel 362

THE CAROLINA LAW JOURNAL. Edited by A. Blanding & D.J. McCord. v.1 (nos. 1-4); [July] 1830-Apr. 1831. Columbia, S.C., Printed at the Times and Gazette Office, 1831.

664 p. quarterly.

Edited by A. Blanding and D.J. McCord, this southern law magazine devoted most of its space to descriptions of legal cases, but also contained book reviews, biographical sketches, and articles on various laws and points of law, including much on marriage laws.

v1, nos. 1-4 July 1830-Apr. 1831 APS II, Reel 382

Microfilm edition was prepared from DLC copy.

THE CAROLINA LAW REPOSITORY. Containing biographical sketches of eminent judges; opinions of American and foreign jurists; and reports of cases adjudged in the Supreme court of North Carolina. v. 1-2; [March 1813-Sept. 1816] Raleigh: Printed by Joseph Gales, 1814-16.

2 v. semiannual.

This journal contained biographical sketches of eminent judges, opinions of American and foreign jurists on contemporary cases, and reports of cases adjudged in the Supreme Court of North Carolina.

v1-2 Mar. 1813-Sept. 1816 APS II, Reel 75

THE CASKET. v.1, no.1-26; Dec. 7, 1811-May 30, 1812. [Hudson, N.Y., C.N. Bement]

312 p. illus. weekly.

Edited by Charles Candid, pseud.

A magazine of popular literature that weekly featured stories, essays on morals or nature, amusing anecdotes, history, poetry and letters to the editor. Generally written to be amusing and instructive for the general public, the magazine's topics ranged from a poem on the subject of old maids to a moralizing essay on the maxim "Honesty is the best policy."

v1, no.1-26 Dec. 7, 1811-May 30, 1812 APS II, Reel 75

Vol.1, no.1: pgs. 3-10 are missing.

CASKET (PHILADELPHIA). *SEE* Graham's American Monthly Magazine of Literature, Art, and Fashion.

THE CASKET. Devoted to literature, science, the arts, news, &c. Ed. by Emerson Bennett. v. 1 (nos. 1-26); Apr. 15-Oct. 7, 1846. Cincinnati, O., 1846.

208 p. weekly.

This literary miscellany gave attention mainly to literature, science, and the arts, including in its contents sentimental prose and poetry, serialized tales, anecdotes, moral essays, literary notices, geographical sketches, historical items, and some science articles, in addition to short news items. Well-known writers whose work appeared in the *Casket* include Emerson Bennett, Mrs. Sophia H. Oliver, Caroline Orne, and Phoebe and Alice Cary.

v1, no.1-26   Apr. 15-Oct. 7, 1846   APS II, Reel 382

Microfilm edition was prepared from DLC copy.

CATHOLIC HISTORICAL RESEARCHES. *SEE* American Catholic Historical Researches.

CATHOLIC MIRROR. *SEE* United States Catholic Magazine.

THE CATHOLIC TELEGRAPH. v. 1- ; Oct. 22, 1831- . Cincinnati, 1831-.

weekly.

On film: v. 1-7, no. 1-22, 24-52; v. 8, no. 1-7, 9-52; v. 9, no. 2-33, 36-38, 40-52; v. 10-11, no. 1-30, 32-52; v. 12-15; Oct. 1831-Dec. 1846.

Begun in Cincinnati in 1831, this weekly religious periodical was "devoted to religion, literature and general intelligence." During its long life, its pages provided an explanation and defense of the Roman Catholic faith with discussions of church doctrine and the doctrines of other religions, along with church-related news from the U.S. and Europe. In addition, the *Telegraph* included biographies, poetry, and reviews of books and magazines, and also published a weekly news summary which included foreign and domestic news and market reports. Variety was afforded by selected literary, scientific, and miscellaneous articles.

v1-5	Oct. 22, 1831-Nov. 24, 1836	APS II, Reel 1717
v6-9	Dec. 8, 1836-Dec. 26, 1840	Reel 1718
v10-14	Jan. 2, 1841-Dec. 25, 1845	Reel 1719
v15	Jan. 1-Dec. 31, 1846	Reel 1720

Microfilm edition was prepared from DLC and OMtsjC copies.

* **THE CATHOLIC WORLD**, a monthly magazine of general literature and science. v.1- ; Apr. 1865- . New York, 1865.

83 v. illus.

Published by the Paulist Fathers. On film: v. 1-83, Apr. 1865-Sept. 1906

The Catholic World: A Monthly Magazine of General Literature and Science was begun in April of 1865 as a general magazine for Catholics by Father Isaac T. Hecker, founder of the Community of Paulist Fathers and of the Catholic Publication Society. At first, it

contained mostly selected articles from English and Italian periodicals with brief departments of science, art and books and few original articles. The contribution of original articles increased so greatly that the magazine soon became completely original and the word Eclectic was dropped from its title.

The editorial and literary aspects of the magazine were of high quality. Journalist J.R.G. Hassard was a member of the editorial staff, and Father A.F. Hewit was the most frequent contributor of the many Church dignitaries whose work regularly appeared in its pages. One of the magazine's continuous strengths was its high literary quality. Among the distinguished writers who regularly contributed were Agnes Repplier, Louise Imogen Guiney, Alice Meynell, Katharine Tynan, John Gilmary Shea, Aubrey DeVere, Rose H. Lathrop, Joyce Kilmer, Hilaire Belloc, G. K. Chesterton, Padraic Colum, and Theodore Maynard.

Though it has been a popular rather than a theological magazine, *Catholic World* has dealt with educational, social, literary and artistic matters from a Catholic point of view and has supported Church doctrines.

v1-3	Apr. 1865-Sept. 1866	APS III, Reel 729
v4-7	Oct. 1866-Sept. 1868	Reel 730
v8-11	Oct. 1868-Sept. 1870	Reel 731
v12-15	Oct. 1870-Sept. 1872	Reel 732
v16-19	Oct. 1872-Sept. 1874	Reel 733
v20-23	Oct. 1874-Sept. 1876	Reel 734
v24-27	Oct. 1876-Sept. 1878	Reel 735
v28-31	Oct. 1878-Sept. 1880	Reel 736
v32-35	Oct. 1880-Sept. 1882	Reel 737
v36-39	Oct. 1882-Sept. 1884	Reel 738
v40-43	Oct. 1884-Sept. 1886	Reel 739
v44-47	Oct. 1886-Sept. 1888	Reel 740
v48-51	Oct. 1888-Sept. 1890	Reel 741
v52-55	Oct. 1890-Sept. 1892	Reel 742
v56-59	Oct. 1892-Sept. 1894	Reel 743
v60-63	Oct. 1894-Sept. 1896	Reel 744
v64-67	Oct. 1896-Sept. 1898	Reel 745
v68-71	Oct. 1898-Sept. 1900	Reel 746
v72-75	Oct. 1900-Sept. 1902	Reel 747
v76-79	Oct. 1902-Sept. 1904	Reel 748
v80-83	Oct. 1904-Sept. 1906	Reel 749

Several pages are stained with some loss of text. Many pages are misnumbered. Vol. 11 and 48 contain supplements. Vol.44 and 45 have pages missing.

Microfilm edition was prepared from DCU, MdBPS, and OT copies.

THE CENSOR. v. 1-2; Nov. 23, 1771-May 2, 1772. Boston, E. Russell.

2 v. weekly.

A political paper.

v1-2   Nov. 23, 1771-May 2, 1772   APS I, Reel 8

Microfilm edition was prepared from MB copy.

THE CENTRAL LAW JOURNAL. v.1-100, no.12; Jan. 1, 1874-Mar. 25, 1927. St. Louis.

100 v. Weekly, 1874-1922, Jan.-Mar. 1927; semimonthly, 1923-26. Vol. 99, 1926, has only one no. for Dec. Issues for Feb.-Mar. 1927 have subtitle The lawyers' national weekly.

Editors: 1874, J.F. Dillon.–1875-77, 1885, S.D. Thompson.–1878-80, J.D. Lawson.–1881-83, W.L. Murfree, Jr.–1884, E. Greenhood. –1886-88, W.L. Murfree, Sr.–1889-June 1901, L.S. Metcalfe, Jr.–July 1901-Dec. 1905, July 1908-June 1909, July 1918-Dec. 1921, A.H. Robbins.–1906-June 1908, W.A. Gardner.–July 1909-June 1918, N.C. Collier.–1922-27, C.P. Berry. Imprint varies: 1874-75, Soule, Thomas & Wentworth.—1876, G.I. Jones.—Jan.-June 1877, S.D. Thompson.—July-Dec. 1877, Thompson & Stevenson.—1878-June 1888, W.H. Stevenson. Merged into the Lawyer and banker. On film: v. 1-100 and a separately published index to v. 1-54, 1874-July 1902.

This weekly journal devoted to the principles and problems of law was founded in St. Louis in 1874. It contained articles and essays on various phases of law as well as editorials, legal cases and opinions, notes on recent decisions, book reviews, and legal miscellany.

Although its main focus was decisions from midwestern courts, it also included major decisions and cases from other states, summaries of Supreme Court decisions, and news of the English court.

Index, v1-54	1874-1902	
v1-3	Jan. 1874-Dec. 1876	APS III, Reel 548
v4-8	Jan. 1877-June 1879	Reel 549
v9-13	July 1879-Dec. 1881	Reel 550
v14-18	Jan. 1882-June 1884	Reel 551
v19-23	July 1884-Dec. 1886	Reel 552
v24-27	Jan. 1887-Dec. 1888	Reel 553
v28-32	Jan. 1889-June 1891	Reel 554
v33-37	July 1891-Dec. 1893	Reel 555
v38-42	Jan. 1894-June 1896	Reel 556
v43-47	July 1896-Dec. 1898	Reel 557
v48-53	Jan. 1899-Dec. 1901	Reel 558
v54-59	Jan. 1902-Dec. 1904	Reel 559
v60-65	Jan. 1905-Dec. 1907	Reel 560
v66-71	Jan. 1908-Dec. 1910	Reel 561
v72-76	Jan. 1911-June 1913	Reel 562
v77-81	July 1913-Dec. 1915	Reel 563
v82-87	Jan. 1916-Dec. 1918	Reel 564
v88-93	Jan. 1919-Dec. 1921	Reel 565
v94-100	Jan. 1922-Mar. 1927	Reel 566

Index for volume 55-72 is lacking. Some pages are stained, marked, and have print faded. Pagination is irregular. Vol. 35: Pgs. 225-26 are creased. Vol. 70: Pgs. 253-54 are torn. Vol. 75: Several pages are tightly bound. Vol. 99: December issue is lacking.

Microfilm edition was prepared from C, InU, MiD, MoS, NcD, and NjP copies.

* **CENTURY, A POPULAR QUARTERLY.** v. 1-120, No. 2, Nov. 1870-May 1930. New York, 1870-1930.

120 v.

Vols. 1-22, 1870-Oct. 1881 as Scribner's monthly; 23-110, Nov. 1881-Oct. 1925 as Century illustrated magazine; 111-18, no. 4, Nov. 1925-Aug. 1929 Century monthly magazine. United with Forum to form Forum and Century.

On film: issues for Nov. 1870-Apr. 1906.

Dr. Josiah Gilbert Holland, the founding editor, contributed serial fiction and essays on morals, manners, politics, religion, and current events to the early issues. Henry James, Bret Harte, George W. Cable, Edward Eggleston, Edward Everett Hale, Joel Chandler Harris, Hans Christian Andersen, and Helen Hunt were among other famous contributors. The engravings, woodcuts, and other illustrations were abundant and of the highest quality. A long series on the South, one on the Civil War, and another on Lincoln were very popular and profitable for the magazine. Series and articles of historic and current interest rounded out the content of one of the most important magazines of the period.

Scribner's Monthly

v1-4	Nov. 1870-Oct. 1872	APS III, Reel 345
v5-8	Nov. 1872-Oct. 1874	Reel 346
v9-12	Nov. 1874-Oct. 1876	Reel 347
v13-16	Nov. 1876-Oct. 1878	Reel 348
v17-19	Nov. 1878-April 1880	Reel 349
v20-22	May 1880-Oct. 1881	Reel 350

Century Illustrated Magazine

v23-25	Nov. 1881-April 1883	APS III, Reel 351
v26-28	May 1883-Oct. 1884	Reel 352
v29-31	Nov. 1884-April 1886	Reel 353
v32-34	May 1886-Oct. 1887	Reel 354
v35-37	Nov. 1887-April 1889	Reel 355
v38-40	May 1889-Oct. 1890	Reel 356
v41-43	Nov. 1890-April 1892	Reel 357
v44-46	May 1892-Oct 1893	Reel 358
v47-49	Nov. 1893-April 1895	Reel 359
v50-52	May 1895-Oct. 1896	Reel 360
v53-55	Nov. 1896-April 1898	Reel 361
v56-58	May 1898-Oct. 1899	Reel 362
v59-61	Nov. 1899-April 1901	Reel 363
v62-64	May 1901-Oct. 1902	Reel 364
v65-67	Nov. 1902-April 1904	Reel 365
v68-70	May 1904-Oct. 1905	Reel 366
v71	Nov. 1905-April 1906	Reel 367

Vol.1: Cumulative Index for vols. 1-10. Vol. 21: Cumulative Index for vols. 21-30. Some pages are torn or stained, or have faded or missing print. The following volumes contain advertisement supplements following text: Vol. 21, Vol. 48, Vol. 55, Vol. 56, Vol. 61, Vol. 68.

Microfilm edition was prepared from InGrD, K, KPT, KyBB, and MiDU copies.

SEE ALSO: Forum and Century.

CENTURY ILLUSTRATED MAGAZINE. *SEE* Century, A Popular Quarterly *and* Forum and Century.

CENTURY MONTHLY MAGAZINE. *SEE* Century, A Popular Quarterly.

THE CHAP-BOOK; semi-monthly. A miscellany & review of belles lettres. v. 1-9, no. 4; May 15, 1894-July 1, 1898. Chicago, Stone & Kimball.

9 v. illus., plates (part col.) ports.

Subtitle varies.

H.S. Stone, editor. Merged into the Dial.

Meant to function only as an advertising device for a new publishing house, the *Chap-Book* began its brief but impressive life. The magazine was published at first in Cambridge, but moved to Chicago when interest in it became apparent.

Excellent short fiction and poetry appeared. Stephen Crane, Paul Lawrence Dunbar, Thomas B. Aldrich, and many others were among the contributors.

v1-9	May 15, 1894-July 1, 1898	APS III, Reel 61

Vol. 9: Index lacking. Please refer to the Table of Contents.

Microfilm edition was prepared from IC, InNU, and MiD copies.

CHARLESTON GOSPEL MESSENGER AND PROTESTANT EPISCOPAL REGISTER. v1-29, 1824-53. Charleston.

29 v. monthly.

Title varies: v1-2 as Gospel messenger and southern Christian register; v 3-11 as Gospel messenger and southern Episcopal register; v 12-18 as Gospel messenger and Protestant Episcopal register.

On film are volumes 1-16, 18-29.

A religious periodical published by members of the Episcopal Church and containing sermons, selected essays, poetry, local and international church news, doctrinal and Bible studies, and listings of new publications.

Gospel Messenger and Southern Christian Register
v1-2   1824-1825   APS II, Reel 76

Gospel Messenger and Southern Episcopal Register
v3-9   1826-1832   APS II, Reel 650
v10-11   1833-Dec. 1834   Reel 651

Gospel Messenger and Protestant Episcopal Register
v12-16, 18   Jan. 1835-Mar. 1842   APS II, Reel 651

Charleston Gospel Messenger and Protestant Episcopal Register
v19-23   Apr. 1842-Mar. 1847   APS II, Reel 652
v24-29   Apr. 1847-Mar. 1853   Reel 653

Best copy available for photographing. Pages are misnumbered throughout. Vol. 15: pages 313-14 are missing; pages 315-16 are partially torn. Vol. 16: pages 97-100 are missing; pages 121-22 are torn out. Vol. 21: Index is filmed preceding vol. 20.

Microfilm edition was prepared from CtHT, NNG, RPB and WHi copies.

THE CHARLESTON MEDICAL REGISTER FOR THE YEAR 1802, by David Ramsay. v. 1; 1803. Charleston, S.C., Printed by W.P. Young.

22 p.

Edited by David Ramsey, M.D., this was to be an annual statement by physicians of the principal health related events occurring in various cities. The entire volume consists of one article describing the various epidemics—smallpox, measles, influenza, and yellow fever—which occurred in Charleston in 1802, and their effects. It also lists the number of deaths and includes meteorological information.

v1   1803   APS II, Reel 546

Title page reads for the year 1802.

Microfilm edition was prepared from MBAt copy.

THE CHARLESTON SPECTATOR AND LADIES' LITERARY PORT FOLIO. v. 1, no. 1-25. Charleston, 1806.

200 p. weekly.

Copy filmed incomplete: part of no. 8 and all of no. 10-18 and 22 wanting.

Conducted by "Goggle, Spectacles, and Co.," this eight page literary miscellany devoted one page to poetry and the other seven pages were filled with tales, essays, anecdotes, and news of deaths and marriages and new publications.

v1, no.1-9, 19-21, 23-25   1806   APS II, Reel 6

Microfilm edition was prepared from MWA.

THE CHAUTAUQUAN; a weekly newsmagazine. [Official publication of Chautauqua instituion, a system of popular education.] v. 1-72; Oct. 1880-May 23, 1914. Meadville, Pa., Chautauqua Press [1880]-1914.

72 v. in 73. illus., plates, ports. 20-33 cm. Monthly except Aug. and Sept. 1880-89; monthly, 1890-May 1913; weekly, June 1913-May 1914. Includes a preliminary number, issued in Sept. 1880 (1 v.) Vols. 10-29 called also "New ser., v. 1-20".

Subtitle varies. From Oct. 1880 to July 1889: Organ of the Chautauqua literary and scientific circle.

Editors: Sept. 1880-Sept. 1899, T.L. Flood.–Oct. 1889-May 1914, F.C. Bray. Published in Meadville, Pa. 1880-99; Cleveland, O., 1899-1902; Springfield, O., 1902-04; Chautauqua, N.Y., 1904-14. Merged into the Independent.

As the title suggests, the *Chautauquan* was created to be the official paper of the Chautauqua movement. The movement's adult education classes were supplemented by required reading in *Chautauquan*, while the printed lectures and society's news enabled students to participate in correspondence courses.

The remarkable effect chautauquas had in spreading education drew a distinguished list of contributors. Arthur Gilman, Edward E. Hale, Theodore Roosevelt, and Sarah Orne Jewett were but a few of the many who filled the columns with travel, art, history, science, and literary criticism. Theology played a continuing role throughout the file. Social reform found place in the later issues.

The decline of the society brought about the *Chautauquan's* merger with *The Independent*.

v1-2   Sept. 1880-July 1882   APS III, Reel 173
v3-6   Oct. 1882-July 1886   Reel 174
v7-10   Oct. 1886-Mar. 1890   Reel 175
v11-14   Apr. 1890-Mar. 1892   Reel 176
v15-18   Apr. 1892-Mar. 1894   Reel 177
v19-22   Apr. 1894-Mar. 1896   Reel 178
v23-27   Apr. 1896-Sept. 1898   Reel 179
v28-32   Oct. 1898-Mar. 1901   Reel 180
v33-37   Apr. 1901-Aug. 1903   Reel 181
v38-42   Sept. 1903-Feb. 1906   Reel 182
v43-51   Mar. 1906-Aug. 1908   Reel 183
v52-60   Sept. 1908-Nov. 1910   Reel 184
v61-70   Dec. 1910-May 1913   Reel 185
v71-72   June 7, 1913-May 23, 1914 Reel 186

Some pages are stained, or have faded or missing print. A preliminary issue, dated September 1880, precedes Vol. 1, which begins in October. Vols. 1, 4, 10, 43, 71-72: lack some advertising pages. Vol. 27: contains a Supplement, "The Oldest Paper in America", bound following the September issue. Vol. 58: pages i-iv not available for photographing. Vol. 60: Book reviews advertised to precede Vol. 60 (see page 464) not available for photographing. Vols. 61-62: pages i-ix not available for photographing. Vol. 72: Following page 644 is a special issue entitled "Accomodations Number", pages 1-40.

Microfilm edition was prepared from C, CL, LNHT, MiD, MiKW, MiU, MoS, NjP, NbU, and OOxM copies.

SEE ALSO: Independent.

CHEAP REPOSITORY. no. 1-42. Philadelphia, Printed by B. & J. Johnson, 1800.

42 no. in 2 v. weekly.

Edited by H. More and others.

Primarily a religious magazine, the *Cheap Repository* undoubtedly "borrowed" much of its material from British publications. Its contents included a "History of the Plague in London in 1665," histories of martyrs, serialized moral tales, such as "The Two

Wealthy Farmers," and occasional poetry.

nos. 1-42	1800	APS II, Reel 207

Many pages are stained.

CHICAGO MEDICAL EXAMINER. *SEE* Medical Examiner.

CHICAGO MEDICAL JOURNAL AND EXAMINER. *SEE* Medical Examiner.

CHILD OF PALLAS: devoted mostly to the belles-lettres. By Charles Prentiss. v. 1 (no. 1-8); Nov. 1800-Jan. 1801. Baltimore, Warner & Hanna, 1800.

288 p. weekly.

The *Child of Pallas* was a weekly literary miscellany by Charles Prentiss. It contained some poetry and summaries of news but most of its space was filled with moral essays, anecdotes, and a great deal of miscellaneous material.

v1, no. 1-8	Nov. 1800-Jan. 1801	APS II, Reel 7

Microfilm edition was prepared from DLC copy.

CHILDREN'S HOUR. *SEE* St. Nicholas; An Illustrated Magazine for Young Folks.

THE CHILDREN'S MAGAZINE; calculated for the use of families and schools. Jan.- Apr. 1789. Hartford, Printed by Hudson and Goodwin.

192 p. monthly.

Film incomplete: Feb. 1789 (p. 49-96) wanting.

The first juvenile periodical.

Jan.-Apr. 1789	APS I, Reel 8

Microfilm edition was prepared from MBC, RPJCB and DLC copies.

THE CHILD'S FRIEND AND FAMILY MAGAZINE. v. 1-31, no. 6; 1843-Dec. 1858. Boston, L.C. Bowles.

31 v. plates, monthly.

Title varies: The Child's friend, designed for families and Sunday schools. The Child's friend and youth's magazine. The Child's friend and family magazine. V. 17-31 also as series 2, v.1-5, series 3, v1-8, series 4, v1-8.

Editors: Eliza L.C. Follen.—Anne W. Abbot.

Edited by Eliza L. Follen, this Boston children's magazine had a longer life than most of its kind. It was mainly an instructive and religiously-oriented magazine, providing short sermons, essays, moralistic stories, and informative articles on geography, history, natural science and other topics. Some illustrations and poetry also appeared.

v1-8	Oct. 1843-Sept. 1847	APS II, Reel 509
v9-17	Oct. 1847-1851	Reel 510
v18-25	1852-1855	Reel 511

v26-31	1856-1858	Reel 512

Several pages are missing; not available for photographing. Several pages have stains and print show-through with some loss of text. Vols. 3, 19, and 27: Pagination is irregular. Vol. 6: Pg. 97 has blurred print. Vol. 15: is bound together with Vol. 14.

Microfilm edition was prepared from MH and RPB copies.

CHILD'S FRIEND AND YOUTH'S MAGAZINE. *SEE* Child's Friend and Family Magazine.

THE CHILD'S NEWSPAPER. Published semi-monthly by Corey and Fairbank, Edited by Rev. Thomas Brainerd, assisted by Rev. B.P. Aydelotte, under the patronage of the Cincinnati Sunday School Union. v. 1, nos. 1-19, Jan. 7- Sept. 2, 1834. Cincinnati, 1834.

71 p.

Film covers: v. 1, no. 1-5, 7-11, 13-19.

Edited by Rev. Thomas Brainerd, this semimonthly children's magazine was published under the patronage of the Cincinnati Sunday School Union. It was a religiously-oriented instructional magazine and although it claimed to offer "pleasant" stories, it actually published a large number of sober and morbid articles on the deaths of children, funerals, murders, etc. It also contained prayers, moralistic and instructive stories, news items, and articles on plants and animals and on the children, dress, and customs of foreign lands.

v1, no.1-5, 7-11, 13-19	Jan. 7-Sept. 2, 1834	APS II, Reel 400

No. 12: Pgs. 41-44 missing.

Microfilm edition was prepared from OCIWHi copy.

THE CHRISTIAN ADVOCATE. v. 1-12; Jan. 1823-Dec. 1834. Philadelphia, A. Finley.

12 v. in 1. monthly.

Supersedes Presbyterian magazine. Edited by A. Green.

Although claiming to be largely non-sectarian and eclectic, the *Christian Advocate* was definitely Presbyterian; its creator, Ashbel Green, was strongly opposed to the union with the Congregational churches in the West, as well as to certain abuses in revivalism, and he made his magazine a power in the church. Much of the material, especially in the early volumes, was taken from other publications. Biography, essays, and religious and secular news are prominent in the file, and some literary reviews also appear. In 1830-31, it carried departments devoted to missions and education. With the founding of the *Presbyterian* in 1831 and Green's growing opposition to certain church policies, the *Advocate* lost subscribers, and it continued to decline until its suspension in 1834.

v1-3	Jan. 1823-1825	APS II, Reel 76
v4-8	Jan. 1826-Dec. 1830	APS II, Reel 592
v9-12	Jan. 1831-Dec. 1834	Reel 593

Microfilm edition was prepared from DLC copy.

SEE ALSO: Presbyterian Magazine.

CHRISTIAN ADVOCATE. v. 1-131, no. 37; Sept. 9, 1826-Sept. 27, 1956. [Chicago, Methodist Pub. House, etc.]

131 v. in 136. illus. weekly. Organ of the Methodist Episcopal Church, Sept. 2, 1826-May 11, 1939; of the Methodist Church, May 18, 1939-Sept. 27, 1956.

Title varies: Mar. 17, 1827-Aug. 29, 1828; Aug. 30, 1833-Dec. 28, 1865; Christian advocate and journal.—Sept. 5, 1828-Aug. 23, 1833, Christian advocate and journal and Zion's herald.

Published in New York, Sept. 9, 1826-Mar. 10, 1938; in Cincinnati (called "New York edition") Mar. 17, 1938-Dec. 26, 1940. Absorbed Zion's herald (founded 1823) and Religious messenger of the Philadelphia Conference in 1828. Absorbed the Methodist (New York) in Oct. 1882 and the Washington Christian advocate in Aug. 1926. Following the merger of Methodist churches (1939) absorbed on Jan. 2, 1941 the Methodist recorder and several regional editions of the Christian advocate. e.g., Christian advocate (Nashville) and Christian advocate. Northwestern edition (Chicago), etc. Superseded by the New Christian advocate and Together.

The *Christian Advocate* of New York was the leading weekly of the many published by the Methodist Episcopal Church. Founded in 1826 by Nathan Bangs, the *Advocate* was at first a religious newspaper, but later became more like a magazine. It reached a circulation of 70,000 in 1879. This well-illustrated magazine provided departments both for young people and for children, as well as sections offering Sunday school lessons, announcements, editorials, new book lists, and articles on health and the household, along with church news and general news summaries. James Monroe Buckley, who served as editor from 1800 to 1912, was the *Advocate's* most well-known editor; other notable editors included Dr. Thomas E. Bond, Abel Stevens, and C.H. Fowler.

Christian Advocate.
v1, no. 1-27   Sept. 9, 1826-Mar. 10, 1827   APS II, Reel 1749

Christian Advocate and Journal
v1, no.28-
v2, no.52   Mar. 17, 1827-Aug. 29, 1828   APS II, Reel 1749

Christian Advocate and Journal and Zion's Herald.
v3-4   Sept. 5, 1828-Aug. 27, 1830   APS II, Reel 1749
v5-7   Sept. 3, 1830-Aug. 23, 1833   Reel 1750

Christian Advocate and Journal.
v8   Aug. 30, 1833-Aug. 22, 1834   APS II, Reel 1750
v9-18   Aug. 29, 1834-Aug. 7, 1844   Reel 1751
v19-22   Aug. 14, 1844-Dec. 29, 1847   Reel 1752
v23-25   Jan. 5, 1848-Dec. 26, 1850   Reel 1753
v26-28   Jan. 2, 1851-Dec. 29, 1853   Reel 1754
v29-36   Jan. 5, 1854-Dec. 26, 1861   Reel 1755
v37-38   Jan. 2, 1862-Dec. 31, 1863   Reel 1756
v39-40   Jan. 7, 1864-Dec. 28, 1865   Reel 1757

Christian Advocate.
v41-42   Jan. 4, 1866-Dec. 26, 1867   APS II, Reel 1758
v43-44   Jan. 2, 1868-Dec. 30, 1869   Reel 1759
v45-46   Jan. 6, 1870-Dec. 28, 1871   Reel 1760
v47-48   Jan. 4, 1872-Dec. 25, 1873   Reel 1761
v49-50   Jan. 1, 1874-Dec. 30, 1875   Reel 1762
v51   Jan. 6-Dec. 28, 1876   Reel 1763
v52   Jan. 4-Dec. 27, 1877   Reel 1764
v53   Jan. 3-Dec. 26, 1878   Reel 1765
v54   Jan. 2-Dec. 25, 1879   Reel 1766
v55   Jan. 1-Dec. 30, 1880   Reel 1767
v56   Jan. 6-Dec. 29, 1881   Reel 1768
v57   Jan. 5-Dec. 28, 1882   Reel 1769
v58   Jan. 4-Dec. 27, 1883   Reel 1770
v59   Jan. 3-Dec. 25, 1884   Reel 1771
v60-61   Jan. 1, 1885-Dec. 30, 1886   Reel 1772
v62-63   Jan. 6, 1887-Dec. 27, 1888   Reel 1773

v64   Jan. 3-Dec. 26, 1889   Reel 1774
v65   Jan. 2-Dec. 25, 1890   Reel 1775
v66   Jan. 1-Dec. 31, 1891   Reel 1776
v67   Jan. 7-Dec. 29, 1892   Reel 1777
v68   Jan. 5-Dec. 28, 1893   Reel 1778
v69   Jan. 4-Dec. 27, 1894   Reel 1779
v70   Jan. 3-Dec. 26, 1895   Reel 1780
v73   Jan. 6-Dec. 29, 1898   Reel 1781
v74   Jan. 5-Dec. 28, 1899   Reel 1782
v75   Jan. 4-Dec. 27, 1900   Reel 1783
v76   Jan. 3-Dec. 26, 1901   Reel 1784
v77   Jan. 2-Dec. 25, 1902   Reel 1785
v78   Jan. 1-Dec. 31, 1903   Reel 1786
v79   Jan. 7-Dec. 29, 1904   Reel 1787
v80   Jan. 5-Dec. 28, 1905   Reel 1788

Microfilm edition was prepared from the DLC, GEU, ICU, IU, MoS, NBu, NjPT, NN, TNJ-R, UM, ViU, and WHi copies.

CHRISTIAN ADVOCATE AND JOURNAL. *SEE* Christian Advocate (Chicago).

CHRISTIAN ADVOCATE AND JOURNAL AND ZION'S HERALD. *SEE* Christian Advocate (Chicago).

THE CHRISTIAN BAPTIST. v. 1-7; Aug. 3, 1823-July 5, 1830? Bethany, Brooke Co. Va., A. Campbell.

7 v. monthly.

Edited by Alexander Campbell. Imprint varies slightly; Buffaloe, (Bethany) Brooke Co. Va. Superseded by Millennial Harbinger.

Cumulative index precedes v.4.

This periodical was a revitalized version of one previously published under the same name. The religious foundation of the magazine was based on a strict belief in the teachings of the New Testament and the rejection of all other sects, creeds and beliefs. Contents consisted of long didactic or critical essays on aspects of religion, letters to the editor, and some announcements of church functions.

v1-3   Aug. 3, 1823-June 1825   APS II, Reel 77

v4-7   Aug. 7, 1826-July 5, 1830?   APS II, Reel 1158

Microfilm edition was prepared from InU copy.

THE CHRISTIAN CABINET: or, Treasury of divine knowledge. v.1, no.1-5. Philadelphia, D. Brown, 1802.

170 p.

Only five numbers of this religious magazine were published. Contents included articles describing conversions, and the lives and deaths of Christians, as well as poetry and essays on various religious topics.

v1, no.1-5   1802   APS II, Reel 7

Microfilm edition was prepared from PHuJ copy.

CHRISTIAN CHRONICLE. v. 1, no. 1-26; Feb. 7-Dec. 26, 1818. Bennington, Vt., A.J. Haswell.

416 p. biweekly.

Copy filmed incomplete: no. 17 wanting.

This publication included religious essays, anecdotes, lessons, poems and obituaries. It also contained many interesting items on early missionary, religious and other societies in Vermont and New England.

v.1, nos.1-16, 18-26   Feb. 7-Dec. 26, 1818   APS II, Reel 77

CHRISTIAN DISCIPLE. *SEE* Christian Disciple and Theological Review.

* THE CHRISTIAN DISCIPLE AND THEOLOGICAL REVIEW. v. 1-6, May 1813-Dec. 1818; new ser., v. 1-5, 1819-23. Boston, Cummings and Hilliard, 1818-23.

11 v. Monthly, 1813-18; bimonthly, 1819-23.

Title varies: 1813-18, The Christian disciple.–1819-23, The Christian disciple and theological review.

Editors: 1813-18, Noah Worcester.–1819-23 Henry Ware, Jr. Superseded by the Christian examiner.

Established by a group of Unitarians, the monthly *Christian Disciple* was written in large part by its editor, Noah Worcester, and promoted the causes of Unitarianism and peace. Its purpose was "the promotion of spiritual and moral improvement" and its contents consisted of essays on various religious topics, religious news, biographical sketches, book reviews, and poetry. Worcester had become an advocate of international peace during the War of 1812, and was prominent in the foundation of the Massachusetts Peace Society in 1815, when he also began the quarterly *Friend of Peace*. At the end of 1818 he turned the *Disciple* over to Henry Ware, Jr., in order to give his full attention to the advocacy of peace. After five years, Ware resigned the editorship of the *Disciple* to John Gorham Palfrey, who renamed it the *Christian Examiner*.

Christian Disciple
v1-5   May 1813-Dec. 1817   APS II, Reel 77
v6   Jan. 1818-Dec. 1818   Reel 78

Christian Disciple and Theological Review
nsv1-nvs4   Jan./Feb. 1819-Nov./Dec. 1822   APS II, Reel 78
nsv5   Jan./Feb. 1823-Nov./Dec. 1823   Reel 79

SEE ALSO: Christian Examiner.

* THE CHRISTIAN EXAMINER. v. 1-5, v. 6-18 (new ser., v. 1-13), v. 19-35 (3d ser., v. 1-17), v. 36-62 (4th ser., v. 1-27), v. 63-79 (5th ser., v. 1-17), v. 80-87 (6th ser., v. 1-8); Jan. 1824-Nov. 1869. Boston, O. Everett; New York, C.S. Francis, 1824-69.

87 v. bimonthly.

Title varies: Jan. 1824-Dec. 1828, The Christian examiner and theological review.–Mar. 1829-Jan. 1844, The Christian examiner and general review. (Absorbed the Monthly miscellany in Jan. 1844) Jan. 1844-May 1857, The Christian examiner and religious miscellany.–July 1857-Nov. 1869, The Christian examiner.

The Christian disciple was established in 1813, under the auspices of Rev. W.E. Channing. Rev. Noah Worcester edited the work until 1818 and then surrendered it to Rev. Henry Ware, Jr. Mr. Ware was editor for 5 years, when the work passed into the hands of John Gorham Palfrey, who changed the title to the Christian examiner. In 1826 Mr. Palfrey transferred the Examiner to Francis Jenks, who was editor for nearly 6 years. In 1831 the work came under the charge of Rev. James Walker and Rev. F.W.P. Greenwood. Dr. Walker was succeeded in 1839 by Rev. William Ware, and the latter, after a few years, by A. Lamson and E.S. Gannett. From them the magazine passed into the hands of George Putnam and G.E. Ellis. In July 1857 Dr. Hedge and Rev. E.E. Hale assumed charge, and they were followed in time by Dr. Bellows, and the Rev. Messrs. Fox, Alger and Allen. In 1870 the Christian examiner was merged into "Old and new".

The *Christian Examiner* was founded as the *Christian Disciple* in Boston in 1813, changing to the name by which it became well-known in 1824. Like the *Disciple,* the *Examiner* promoted "spiritual and moral improvement," focused mainly on religious topics, and included some book reviews, religious news, and poetry. In 1857 Frederick H. Hedge and Edward Everett Hale took charge; this was a turning-point in the magazine's history, representing a triumph of more liberal ideas in New England Unitarianism, and the complete surrender of the *Examiner* to transcendentalism. The *Examiner* is one of the most important of the American religious reviews for several reasons: it was a tower of strength for Unitarians, defending the Unitarian point of view for more than half a century and waging war against the *Spirit of the Pilgrims,* an anti-Unitarian magazine; it did distinctive work in literary criticism; and it commented on social, philosophical, and educational problems. Its scope was broad; history, biography, theology, and even political discussions were given space in it. It had an impressive list of contributors–F.W.P. Greenwood, William Channing, Andrews Norton, Theodore Parker, Emerson, Joseph Henry Allen, George Ripley, and N.L. Frothingham.

Christian Examiner and Theological Review
v1-2   Jan. 1824-1825   APS II, Reel 79

Christian Examiner and Theological Review
v3-5   Jan. 1826-Dec. 1828   APS II, Reel 449

Christian Examiner and General Review
v6   Mar. 1829-July 1829   APS II, Reel 449
v7-13   Sept. 1829-Jan. 1833   Reel 450
v14-19   Mar. 1833-Jan. 1836   Reel 451
v20-25   Mar. 1836-Jan. 1839   Reel 452
v26-31   Mar. 1839-Jan. 1842   Reel 453
v32-35   Mar. 1842-Jan. 1844   Reel 454

Christian Examiner and Religious Miscellany
v36-37   Jan.-Nov. 1844   APS II, Reel 454
v38-43   Jan. 1845-Nov. 1847   Reel 455
v44-48   Jan. 1848-May 1850   Reel 456
v49-53   July 1850-Nov. 1852   Reel 457
v54-58   Jan. 1853-May 1855   Reel 458
v59-62   July 1855-May 1857   Reel 459

Christian Examiner
v63   July-Nov. 1857   APS II, Reel 459
v64-69   Jan. 1858-Nov. 1860   Reel 460
v70-75   Jan. 1861-Nov. 1863   Reel 461
v76-81   Jan. 1864-Nov. 1866   Reel 462
v82-87   Jan. 1867-Nov. 1869   Reel 463

The index is bound and photographed at the end of each volume. Several pages have print show-through and are stained with some loss of text. Pagination is irregular.

Microfilm edition was prepared from the CtY, DLC, MiU, and RPB copies.

SEE ALSO: Christian Disciple and Theological Review; *and* Monthly Miscellany of Religion and Letters.

**CHRISTIAN EXAMINER AND RELIGIOUS MISCEL-
LANY.** *SEE* Christian examiner.

CHRISTIAN EXAMINER AND THEOLOGICAL REVIEW.
SEE Christian examiner.

THE CHRISTIAN HERALD. v. 1-17; May 1818-1835.
Portsmouth, N.H.

Bimonthly, May 1818-July 1819; monthly Sept. 1819-Dec. 1825.

Edited by R. Foster. Film covers: v.1-7 (no. 1-8) v.8 (no.1-10); May
1818-Dec. 1825.

A religious periodical containing biographies, anecdotes, poetry,
essays, literary notices, extracts of articles from other magazines,
records of conversions and revivals, and missionary efforts in
Europe, Asia, Africa and Russia as well as among the North American Indians. The *Herald* advocated religious freedom and announced
the meetings and conferences of different faiths in New England
such as Baptist, Jewish, Methodist and Mahometan.

v1-5	May 1818-Mar. 27, 1823	APS II, Reel 79
v6-8	May 8, 1823-Dec. 1825	Reel 80

CHRISTIAN HERALD (NEW YORK). *SEE* Christian
Herald and Seaman's Magazine.

**THE CHRISTIAN HERALD AND SEAMAN'S MAGA-
ZINE.** v.1-11; Mar. 30, 1816-Nov. 1824. New York.

11 v. Weekly, Mar. 1816- semimonthly.

Title varies: Mar. 1816- The Christian herald. The Christian herald
and seaman's magazine.

Editor: 1816- J.E. Caldwell.

Edited and published in New York by John E. Caldwell, one of
the founders of the American Bible Society, this weekly religious
periodical attempted to provide religious reading, especially for
sailors, and added "And Seaman's Magazine" to its title in 1820. It
gave extensive coverage to Bible societies, particularly the American
Bible Society, and presented a variety of material on religion—
letters, poetry, speeches, essays, Sunday school reports, news on
missions, and anecdotes and narratives on religious topics.

Christian Herald.
v1-5	Mar. 1816-Mar. 1819	APS II, Reel 493
v6-7	April 1819-April 1821	Reel 494

Christian Herald and Seaman's Magazine.
v8	May 1821-May 1822	APS II, Reel 494
v9-11	May 1822-Nov. 1824	Reel 495

Several pages are misnumbered, stained and have print show-through
with some loss of text. Vols. 1, 5, & 9 have some missing pages. Vol.
1: Issue 17, Pg. 271 has blurred print. Pg. 326 is cropped with loss
of text.

Microfilm edition was prepared from PPPrHi, CtY, CtHT, MiU, DLC
and MH-AH copies.

THE CHRISTIAN HISTORY, containing accounts of the
revival and propagation of religion in Great-Britain &
America. no. 1-104; Mar. 5, 1743-Feb. 23, 1745. Boston T.
Prince 1744-45.

2 v. weekly.

Thomas Prince, jr., editor. One of the earliest of American magazines ... It was regularly published in weekly numbers ... from March
5, 1743, to February 23, 1745, making 104 numbers in all.—Sabin's
Dict. of books, relating to America. v. 15.

A chronicle of the "Great Awakening."

no. 1-104	Mar. 5, 1743-Feb. 23, 1745	APS I, Reel 10

Microfilm edition was prepared from MWA copy.

CHRISTIAN INDEX. v.1- ; July 4, 1829- . Philadelphia,
Washington, Atlanta, Ga.

v. weekly. Vol. 9+ also numbered as series 2 v. 1+ Supersedes
Columbia star.

Title varies: v. 1-3, 1829-30, Columbia star and Christian index.

On film: v. 1-8, July 4, 1829-June 29, 1833; s2v. 5, 1837; v. 60-61,
Mar. 23, 1882-Dec. 20, 1883; v. 63-65, 1885-1887; v. 79, 1899.
Many vols. have scattered issues missing.

The *Christian Index* was a Southern Baptist weekly publication
that began as the *Columbian Star,* was published in five cities in
three states, and achieved success at Atlanta, Georgia. It covered
missionary and temperance societies, and religious news; but dealt
more with the philosophical and spiritual topics of religion such as
"On Drawing Near to God," "The Way of Man is Not in Himself,"
"Love of Christ," and "Horrors of Atheism." The later editions
contain many advertisements for "wonder" drugs.

Columbian Star and Christian Index.
v1-3	July 4, 1829-Dec. 25, 1830	APS II, Reel 1826

Christian Index.
v4-8	Jan. 1, 1831-June 29, 1833	APS II, Reel 1826
[s2 v5], 60-61, 63	Jan. 5, 1837-Dec. 28, 1837;	
	Mar. 23, 1882-Dec. 20, 1883;	
	Jan. 1, 1885-Dec. 24, 1885	Reel 1827
v64-65, 79	Jan. 7, 1886-Dec. 24, 1887;	
	Jan. 5, 1889-Dec. 28, 1899	Reel 1828

Microfilm edition was prepared from the GMiW, NcD, and NRAB
copies.

CHRISTIAN INQUIRER. v. 1-21; Oct. 17, 1846-Nov. 29,
1866. New York, Unitarian Association of the state of New
York.

21 v. weekly.

Absorbed by Liberal Christian Dec. 22, 1866..

The *Christian Inquirer,* one of the leading Unitarian weeklies of
its time period, expressed evidence and proof for the "liberal Christian" sect with articles on "Scripture Proofs of Unitarianism" and
"The Position of Unitarianism Defined." Unitarian news, religious
instruction, stories, poems, notices of books and new publications
appear. Topics include "A Juvenile Department," "Mahomet and
the Koran," travel stories, and rights of women.

v1-5	Oct. 17 1846-Dec. 28, 1850	APS II, Reel 1885
v6-12	Oct. 11, 1851-Sept. 18, 1858	Reel 1886
v13-19	Oct. 2, 1858-Dec. 10, 1864	Reel 1887

Microfilm edition contains volumes 1-17, 19. Some issues are missing; not available for photographing.

Microfilm edition was prepared from the ICMe, IU, and MWA copies.

CHRISTIAN INQUIRER AND THE CHRISTIAN SECRETARY. *SEE* Watchman—examiner.

CHRISTIAN INTELLIGENCER. *SEE* Christian Intelligencer and Eastern Chronicle.

THE CHRISTIAN INTELLIGENCER AND EASTERN CHRONICLE. v. 1-16; Sept. 1821-Dec. 30, 1836. Portland, Me., Printed by Todd & Smith.

16 v. Frequency varies.

Vol. 1, no. 1-3 in Miscellaneous pamphlets, v. 839 (AC 901.M5) Title varies: Sept. 1821-Jan. 13, 1827, The Christian intelligencer.

Edited by R. Streeter.

The varied material published in this religious periodical included articles on the Universalists, proceedings of temperance societies, religious and secular news, sermons, poetry, and tales.

Christian Intelligencer.

v1-5	Sept. 1821-1825	APS II, Reel 80
v6	June 3, 1826-Jan. 13, 1827	APS II, Reel 593

Christian Intelligencer and Eastern Chronicle.

v7	Jan. 12-Dec. 28, 1827	APS II, Reel 593
v8-14	Jan. 4, 1828-Dec. 26, 1834	Reel 594
v15-16	Jan. 2, 1835-Dec. 30, 1836	Reel 595

Reels 593-595: Best copy available for photographing. Many pages are tightly bound with some loss of text. Vol. 7: Issue 1 and p. 208 are missing; Vol. 9: Issue 47 is misdated and bound out of order. Vol. 12: Issue 30 is missing. Vol. 14: Issue 11 is missing. Vol. 16: Issues 1, 4, 7, 16, 20-21, 27, 31-32, 39, 43, 45, and 49 are missing.

Microfilm edition was prepared from MeP copy.

THE CHRISTIAN JOURNAL, AND LITERARY REGISTER. v.1-14; Jan. 22, 1817-Dec. 1830. New York, T. & J. Swords.

Semimonthly, 1817-18; monthly, 1819-30.

v. 1, no. 4-5 missing.

A leading Episcopal magazine which furnished appropriate Sunday reading (eclectic in part) and religious news and reports. It was edited for the first two years by Bishop John Henry Hobard and the Reverend Benjamin T. Onderdonk, and editorship was carried on after that by the publishers, J. and T. Swords. The journal was never profitable and publication ceased in December of 1830.

v1-3	Jan. 22, 1817-1819	APS II, Reel 80
v4-9	1820-Dec. 1825	Reel 81
v10-14	Jan. 1826-Dec. 1830	APS II, Reel 763

Some stained pages throughout.

Microfilm edition was prepared from IaU copy.

CHRISTIAN LEADER. *SEE* Universalist.

THE CHRISTIAN MAGAZINE, conducted by members of Mendon association. v. 1-4; Jan. 1824-Dec. 1827. Providence, R.I., Printed by B. Field, 1824-25; Boston, T.R. Marvin, Printer, 1826-27.

4 v. monthly.

Conducted by members of the Mendon Association, this religious periodical contained religious news, including news of missions and of ordinations and installations, sermons, Bible studies, memoirs, and poetry.

v1-2	Jan. 1824-1825	APS II, Reel 81
v3-4	Jan. 1826-Dec. 1827	Reel 595

Microfilm edition was prepared from DLC copy.

THE CHRISTIAN MESSENGER. v. 1-4, no. 26; May 10, 1817-May 1, 1819. Baltimore, J.T. Russell.

4 v. weekly.

Editor: May 10, 1817-J.T. Russell. Ceased publication with v. 4, no. 26 (May 1, 1819) cf. Union list of serials.

A religious magazine which gave much coverage to missions and missionaries, as well as to reports of Bible societies and other societies. In addition, it published religious news, letters, anecdotes, and speeches.

v1-3	May 10, 1817-Oct. 31, 1818	APS II, Reel 595
v4	Nov. 7, 1818-May 1, 1819	Reel 82

Microfilm edition was prepared from PPPrHi copy.

THE CHRISTIAN MESSENGER. Being a miscellaneous work; directed to the improvement of the human mind; in prose and verse. v. 1, no. 1-5; Nov. 1815-Mar. 1816. Pittsford, N.Y., Printed by L. Knap.

120 p. monthly.

Edited by L. Knap.

This miscellany encouraged religious piety, morality and happiness primarily through articles about and explications of the Bible and Biblical teachings. Though poetry and general articles were included, most of the text dealt with explications of Biblical passages and commentary on New Testament parables.

v1, no. 1-5	Nov. 1815-Mar. 1816	APS II, Reel 82

THE CHRISTIAN MESSENGER, devoted to doctrine, religion, and morality. v. 1-2, no. 1-51, Aug. 7, 1819-July 21, 1821. Philadelphia.

2 v. in 1. weekly.

Edited by A. Kneeland. Merged into Philadelphia Universalist magazine and Christian messenger. Cf. Union list of serials.

The purpose of this weekly was to promote an acquaintance of different religious denominations. It included many articles and poems from other religious magazines such as *The Universalist* and *The Presbyterian Magazine* as well as letters, sermons and obituaries.

v1-2   Aug. 7, 1819-July 21, 1821   APS II, Reel 82

SEE ALSO: Philadelphia Universalist Magazine and Christian Messenger.

THE CHRISTIAN MIRROR. v. 1, no. 1-13; Jan. 22-Apr. 16, 1814. Charleston, S.C.

207 p. weekly.

Short-lived weekly that published personal essays on Christianity, anecdotes, biographies and poetry including some by Joseph Addison.

v1, no. 1-13   Jan. 22-Apr. 16, 1814   APS II, Reel 82

THE CHRISTIAN MONITOR. v. 1-7; Jan.-Mar. 1814-Oct.-Dec. 1818. Hallowell, Me.

7 v. quarterly.

The Christian Monitor was the first religious publication of its kind in Maine. It contained original essays and extracts from other publications on the doctrines and duties of Christianity. It also included expositions of particular passages of scripture, poetry, biographical sketches, anecdotes and reports of missionary efforts throughout the world. Also included were extracts of reports of various U.S. and foreign Bible Societies.

v1-7   Jan.-Mar. 1814-Oct.-Dec. 1818   APS II, Reel 83

CHRISTIAN MONITOR. v. 1-2; July 8, 1815-1817. Richmond, Va., 1815-1817.

2 v.

This religious periodical published information on the work of missionaries, proceedings of Bible and missionary societies, accounts of religious revivals, memoirs, anecdotes, poetry, and extracts from sermons.

v1-2   July 8, 1815-Aug. 30, 1817   APS II, Reel 596

Several pages are stained.

Microfilm edition was prepared from ViRUT copy.

THE CHRISTIAN MONITOR; a religious periodical work. v. 1-10 (no. 1-20); 1806-11. Boston, Munroe & Francis [etc.]

10 v. Quarterly?

Issued by Society for Promoting Christian Knowledge, Piety and Charity. Superseded by the Society's Religious tracts. Cf. Union list of serials. Lacking on film: v.3-4 (no.5-8).

Conducted by "a society for promoting Christian knowledge, piety, and charity," the *Christian Monitor* was intended for study or instruction in leading a Christian life. Each number was devoted to

one item or a series of similar items on the same subjects; for instance, the ninth number consisted of seven sermons "addressed to young persons," and other numbers contained sermons, prayers, meditations, or occasionally just one article.

v1-2, 5-6 (nos.1-4, 9-12)   1806-09   APS II, Reel 7

v7-10 (nos. 13-20)   1810-11   APS II, Reel 82

Microfilm edition was prepared from MB copy.

THE CHRISTIAN MONITOR, and religious intelligencer. v 1-2, June 1812-Aug. 28, 1813. New York, Paul & Thomas.

weekly.

Lacking on film: vol. 2

A weekly religious magazine which offered moral support and encouragement to its New England readers through essays, poetry, biographical sketches and descriptions of conversions and revivals. It also reported missionary progress abroad. In addition, it advertized religious meetings of all kinds and all denominations throughout New York City.

v1, no. 1-52   June 1812-June 26, 1813   APS II, Reel 83

THE CHRISTIAN OBSERVATORY: a religious and literary magazine. v.1-4, no.4; Jan. 1847-Apr. 1850. Boston, J.V. Beane.

4 v. in 2. monthly.

Edited 1847-48 and 1850 by A.W. McClure.

Edited by A.W. McClure, the *Christian Observatory* supported New England orthodoxy and presented a great variety of articles and reviews concerning religion and moral reform, as well as many sermons and studies on the Bible, sketches of some distinguished Puritans, and a series on the history of Unitarianism in New England. It also included listings of ordinations and installations.

v1-4   Jan. 1847-Apr. 1850   APS II, Reel 312

Microfilm edition was prepared from MH copy.

CHRISTIAN OBSERVER. v.1- ; Sept. 4, 1813- . Louisville, Ky., etc.

v. weekly. 1839-60? numbered as v. 18-39 continuing the numbering of Southern religious telegraph.

Title varies: v.1-10, 1813-Aug. 16, 1823, Religious remembrancer.

Early volumes published in Philadelphia. Lacking: v.[11]-18, Aug. 1823-Dec. 1839; v.40-82, Jan. 1861-Aug. 1895.

The *Christian Observer,* the oldest religious weekly with a record of continuous publication, was founded at the Presbyterian publishing center of Philadelphia in 1813 as the *Religious Remembrancer,* "A Presbyterian Family Newspaper." Among its variety of religious articles were biographical sketches, revivals of religion, theological essays, missionary information, discourses on the preciousness of Christ and the denying of Christ, and essays on bible verses.

The paper changed names several times, and in 1869 joined with the *Free Christian Commonwealth* in Louisville, Kentucky. Several of its contemporaries were swallowed up by its growth. In the early 1900's it was still a leading Presbyterian paper and contained stories and anecdotes, articles on such topics as "The Alcoholic problem," "Practical Suggestions for Church Work," "Saving Faith," "The

Anti-opium Campaign in China," "Work Among the Negroes," and "The Pioneer Woman Physician."

Religious Remembrancer.

v1-3	Sept. 4, 1813-Aug. 24, 1816	APS II, Reel 1887
v4-10	Aug. 31, 1816-Aug. 16, 1823	Reel 1888

Christian Observer.

v19 (nsv1)	Jan. 2, 1840-Dec. 24, 1840	APS II, Reel 1888
v20-23	Jan. 1, 1841-Dec. 27, 1844	Reel 1889
v24-27	Jan. 3, 1845-Dec. 30, 1848	Reel 1890
v28-31	Jan. 6, 1849-Dec. 25, 1852	Reel 1891
v32-35	Jan. 1, 1853-Dec. 25, 1856	Reel 1892
v36-39	Jan. 1, 1857-Dec. 27, 1860	Reel 1893
v83-84	Sept. 4, 1895-Dec. 30, 1896	Reel 1894
v85	Jan. 6-Dec. 29, 1897	Reel 1895
v86	Jan. 5-Dec. 28, 1898	Reel 1896
v87	Jan. 4-Dec. 27, 1899	Reel 1897
v88	Jan. 3-Dec. 26, 1900	Reel 1898
v89	Jan. 2-Dec. 25, 1901	Reel 1899
v90	Jan. 1-Dec. 31, 1902	Reel 1900
v91	Jan. 7-Dec. 30, 1903	Reel 1901
v92	Jan. 6-Dec. 28, 1904	Reel 1902
v93	Jan 4-Dec. 27, 1905	Reel 1903
v94	Jan. 3-Dec. 26, 1906	Reel 1904
v95	Jan. 2-Dec. 25, 1907	Reel 1905
v96	Jan. 1-Dec. 23, 1908	Reel 1906
v97	Jan. 6-Dec. 29, 1909	Reel 1907
v98	Jan. 5-Dec. 28, 1910	Reel 1908

Microfilm edition contains volumes 1-10, 19-39 and 83-98. Some issues are missing, not available for photographing.

Microfilm edition was prepared from the DLC, KyLoS, NjR, NN and PPPrHi copies.

CHRISTIAN OBSERVER AND ADVOCATE. *SEE* Christian Observer, Conducted by Members of the Established Church.

CHRISTIAN OBSERVER, CONDUCTED BY MEMBERS OF THE ESTABLISHED CHURCH. From the London ed. v.1-66; 1802-1866? Boston, New York [etc.]

66 v. monthly. Vol. 4-11, 13-18, 28-29, 31, 42 are the London edition. Vol. 22-25, London printed. Reprinted and published by Samuel Whiting, New York. Vol. 21 planned as general index; never published.

American ed. ceased publication with v. 66, 1866? London ed. ceased with v. 77, 1877. Title changed to Christian observer and advocate with v. 75. cf. Union list of serials.

On film: vols. 1-8 (reels 8-11) vols. 9-11, 13-18 (reels 83-86) vols. 19-25 (reels 208- 209) vols. 12, 26, 28, 29, 31, 42 (reel 1909) Imperfect: American ed. for some volumes unavailable for photographing.

Originally printed in London, this religious magazine was then reprinted and published in Boston and New York. Its pages were filled with sermons; religious news, including the activities of missionary and tract societies; foreign and domestic news; and lists and reviews of new publications, along with other literary news.

v1-3	Jan. 1802-Dec. 1804	APS II, Reel 8
v4-5	Jan. 1805-Dec. 1806	Reel 9
v6-7	Jan. 1807-Dec. 1808	Reel 10
v8	Jan.-Dec. 1809	Reel 11
v9	Jan.-Dec. 1810	APS II, Reel 83
v10-11, 13	Jan. 1811-Dec. 1814	Reel 84

v14-15	Jan. 1815-Dec. 1816	Reel 85
v16-18	Jan. 1817-Dec. 1819	Reel 86
v19-20, 22	Jan. 1820-Dec. 1822	APS II, Reel 208
v23-25	Jan. 1823-Dec. 1825	Reel 209
v12-42	Jan. 1813-Dec. 1842	Reel 1909

Vol. 3: title page and contents are missing.

Microfilm edition was prepared from the DLC, IaU, MdBE, MiU, and the NBu copy.

CHRISTIAN PARLOR MAGAZINE. v. 1-11, no.12, May 1844-Dec. 1854; new ser., v. 1, 1855. New York, 1844-1855.

12 v.

Merged into Happy home and parlor magazine.

Founded by the Rev. Darius Mead and later edited by the Rev. Joel T. Headley, this monthly was didactic in nature. It attempted to compete with ladies' magazines by using plates and woodcuts. Among contributors were Mrs. Sigourney, Lyman Beecher, and T.S. Arthur.

v1-7	May 1844-April 1851	APS II, Reel 1230
v8-nsv1	1852-1855	Reel 1231

Vols. 3 and 5: Title page reads, Gems for the Fireside. Vols. 4 and 9: Index and title page are missing. Vols. 8: Pgs. 141-42 are torn. Vols. 11: Pgs. 49 and 211 stained with some loss of text.

Microfilm edition was prepared from ICN, IaU, N, NN, Nh, NhD, OO, RPB, and WHi copies.

CHRISTIAN PHILANTHROPIST, devoted to literature and religion. V. 1, no.1-50; May 14, 1822-May 13, 1823. New Bedford [Mass.] D.K. Whitaker.

200 p. weekly.

Edited by D.K. Whitaker.

Edited by Daniel K. Whitaker, this weekly was mainly concerned with literature and religion and presented many articles on these subjects, along with religious and literary departments, and poetry. But there was also a variety of news—political news summaries, foreign news, news of Congress, marriage and death notices, and arrivals of ships.

v1, no.1-50	May 14, 1822-1823	APS II, Reel 87

CHRISTIAN REFLECTOR. v. 1-11, no. 19; May 10, 1838-May 11, 1848. Boston, Worchester.

11 v. weekly.

May 18, 1848 merged with Christian Watchman, later to become Watchman-examiner. Editors: 1838-1841, Cyrus P. Grosvenor.—1842-1858, Hiram A. Graves.

Lacking issue for Mar. 16, 1848.

Begun in 1838, the *Christian Reflector* was a religious paper for the Baptists of Massachusetts. Intended as a paper for the layman, the *Reflector* was outspoken in its advocation of temperance and morality, and of abolition. Cyrus P. Grosvenor edited the first four volumes. Although the paper was theological in nature, during his editorship, at least two or more articles concerning the slave and the abolitionary movement appeared each week. Beginning in 1842, the paper was edited by the Reverend Hiram A. Graves and the anti-slavery articles diminished. Baptist missionary news and colonization efforts were regularly featured throughout the file. In 1848, the *Reflector* merged with *Christian Watchman.* It was hoped that a combined newspaper from Boston would command the confidence and respect of the other states.

v1-2	May 1838-Dec. 1839	APS II, Reel 886
v3-6	Jan. 1840-Dec. 1843	Reel 887
v7-10	Jan. 1844-Dec. 1847	Reel 888
v11	Jan. 1848-May 1848	Reel 889

Vols. 5, 6, and 11 lack indexes and tables of contents. Vol. 11, March 16, 1848 issue lacking. Best copy available for photographing. Some pages are creased or stained.

Microfilm edition was prepared from MWA and NRAB copies.

CHRISTIAN REFLECTOR AND CHRISTIAN WATCHMAN. *SEE* Watchman-Examiner.

CHRISTIAN REFLECTOR AND WATCHMAN. *SEE* Christian Reflector.

CHRISTIAN REFORMER; or evangelical miscellany. v. 1, nos. 1-9, July 1, 1828- July 1829. Harrisburg, Pa., 1828-1829.

216 p.

The purpose of this monthly religious magazine was to spread religious knowledge, to promote inquiry into the Scriptures, and to evoke serious thought on the part of the reader. It was non-sectarian, and contents included poetry, news on missions, and discussions on doctrine.

v1, no.1-9	July 1, 1828-July 1829	APS II, Reel 382

Microfilm edition was prepared from MWA copy.

CHRISTIAN REGISTER. v. 1- Apr. 20, 1821- Boston.

Title varies: 1821-June 1835; Oct. 21, 1843-June 1957 as Christian register; July 1835-Oct. 14, 1843, Christian register and Boston observer; July 1957-Apr. 1961, Unitarian register, Current title, Unitarian register and the Universalist leader.

Film covers: v. 1-29; Apr. 20, 1821-Dec. 28, 1850.

This leading Unitarian weekly, published by the American Unitarian Association, included William Ellery Channing, Henry Ware, Jr., Andrews Norton, George Bancroft, Jared Sparks, and Edward Everett as some of its prominent contributors. In addition to articles on religion and news of the religious world, it presented foreign, domestic, and local news, activities of the Massachusetts state legislature and local courts, proceedings of Congress, book reviews, biography, and poetry of a religious nature.

Christian Register.

v1, no. 1-v3, no.42 v3, no.43-	Apr. 20, 1821-May 28, 1824	APS II, Reel 87
v4, no.52	June 4, 1824-Dec. 31, 1825	Reel 88
v5-7	Jan. 7, 1826-Dec. 27, 1828	APS II, Reel 596
v8-10	Jan. 3, 1827-Dec. 31, 1831	Reel 597

v11-14, no. 46	Jan. 7, 1832-June 27, 1835	Reel 598

Christian Register and Boston Observer.

v14, no. 47-52	July 4, 1835-Dec. 26, 1835	APS II, Reel 598
v15-17	Jan. 1, 1836-Dec. 29, 1838	Reel 599
v18-20	Jan. 5, 1839-Dec. 25, 1841	Reel 600
v21-22, no. 41	Jan. 1, 1842-Oct. 14, 1843	Reel 601

Christian Register.

v22, no. 42-v23	Oct. 21, 1843-Dec. 28, 1844	APS II, Reel 601
v24-26	Jan. 4, 1845-Dec. 25, 1847	Reel 602
v27-29	Jan. 1, 1848-Dec. 28, 1850	Reel 603

Many pages are stained and have faded print.

Microfilm edition was prepared from DLC and ICMe copies.

CHRISTIAN REGISTER. v.1, nos. 1-12; June 1822-May 1823. Lexington, Ky., 1822-1823.

763 p.

This polemical religious periodical was edited in Lexington by Thomas T. Skillman.

v1	June 1822-May 1823	APS II, Reel 1093

Vol.1: Badly stained, readable. Print missing P. 216, readable. P. 413 missing. Pgs. 457-465 misnumbered.

Microfilm edition was prepared from KyLxCB copy.

CHRISTIAN REGISTER AND BOSTON OBSERVER. *SEE* Christian Register (Boston).

THE CHRISTIAN REGISTER, AND MORAL AND THEOLOGICAL REVIEW. Edited by Thomas Y. How. v. 1-2, no. 1; July 1816-July 1817. New York, T. & J. Swords.

Edited by the Rev. Thomas Y. How, assistant rector of Trinity Church in New York, this religious magazine consisted largely of book reviews, both of religious and sectarian books. The remaining space was devoted to biographical sketches, religious articles, poetry and anecdotes, and a variety of religious news, including foreign and domestic news, news of the Episcopal Church, and coverage of the activities of various Bible and missionary societies.

v1-2, no. 1	July 1816-July 1817	APS II, Reel 88

CHRISTIAN REPOSITORY. *SEE* Circular.

* THE CHRISTIAN REVIEW. v. 1-28; Mar. 1836-Oct. 1863. Boston, Gould, Kendall & Lincoln: 1836-63.

28 v. quarterly.

Imprint varies: 1836-49, Boston, Gould, Kendall & Lincoln: [etc., etc.,] –1850-56, New-York, L. Colby and J. Ballard [etc.] –1857-58, Baltimore [35c.] –1859-60, New-York, Sheldon & co.– 1861-63, Rochester, N.Y., Benton & Andrews. Merged into Bibliotheca sacra.

Editors: 1836-37, J.D. Knowles.–1838, J.D. Knowles, Barnas Sears.–1839-41, Barnas Sears.– 1842-48, S.F. Smith.–1849. E.G. Sears.-1850-52, S.S. Cutting.-1853-55, Robert Turnbull, J.N. Murdock.–1856, J.J. Woolsey, W.C. Ulyat.–1857-58, Franklin

Wilson, G.B. Taylor.– 1859, E.G. Robinson, V.R. Hotchkiss.– 1860-63, E.G. Robinson.

Considered the best of the Baptist quarterlies, the *Christian Review* was founded to provide the sect with an organ. Some articles dealt with literary and educational topics but most were theological in nature, written by clergymen. When the periodical moved to New York in 1849, the scope of material became broader, with articles on human improvement, biographies, notices of recent publications and occasionally such diverse articles as a description of the glaciers of the Alps. Avoiding all political issues, the journal nonetheless did not survive the war.

v1-3	Mar. 1836-Dec. 1838	APS II, Reel 410
v4-8	Mar. 1839-Dec. 1843	Reel 411
v9-13	Mar. 1844-Dec. 1848	Reel 412
v14-17	Jan. 1849-Oct. 1852	Reel 413
v18-21	Jan. 1853-Oct. 1856	Reel 414
v22-25	Jan. 1857-Oct. 1860	Reel 415
v26-28	Jan. 1861-Oct. 1863	Reel 416

Pagination is irregular.

Microfilm edition was prepared from CtY and DLC copy.

CHRISTIAN SECRETARY. v.1-75, no. 15; Feb. 2, 1822-Mar. 25, 1896. Hartford, Conn.

weekly.

Issues for Feb. 1824-Dec. 1825 also called v. 1-2. v. 17-53, Mar. 23, 1838-Dec. 30, 1874, also called n.s.v. 1-37, no. 25. Superseded by Watchman-examiner. Early vols. published for the Connecticut Baptist Convention. On film: vols. 1-2, 1822-1825 (reels 88-89) vols. 2-29, 1826-1851 (reels 495-502) vols. 30, 35, 55-56, 68 (reels 1910)

Published for the Connecticut Baptist Convention and edited throughout the war and later by Elisha Cushman, the *Christian Secretary* was one of the more important Baptist weeklies. In its pages could be found, in addition to religious news and articles on religion, foreign and domestic news, biography, poetry, letters, and some advertising.

v1-2, no.103	Feb. 2, 1822-Jan. 17, 1824	APS II, Reel 88
s2v1-2, no. 48	Feb. 3, 1824-Dec. 26, 1825	Reel 89
s2v2, no. 49-s2v3	Jan. 1826-Jan. 1827	Reel 495
s2v4-s2v8	Jan. 1827-Jan. 1830	Reel 496
s2v9-s2v12	Jan. 1830-Jan. 1834	Reel 497
s2v13-s2v16	Jan. 1834-July 1837	Reel 498
s3v1-4 (17-20)	Mar. 1838-Mar. 1842	Reel 499
s3v5-7 (21-23)	Mar. 1842-Mar. 1845	Reel 500
s3v8-10 (24-26)	Mar. 1845-Mar. 1848	Reel 501
s3v11-13 (27-29)	Mar. 1848-Feb. 1851	Reel 502
v30-68	Mar. 7, 1851-Dec. 25, 1889	APS II, Reel 1910

Several pages are misnumbered, creased, stained, faded and tightly bound with some loss of text. Series 2, vol. 4: page 5 is cropped with some loss of text. Series 2 vol. vol. 14: issue 35 is missing. Series 2 Vol. 16: issue 1 is misdated. New series Vol. 12: issue 25 is missing. Vol. 35 (i.e. vol. 19) has nos. 5, 7, 12, 44 only. Have scattered issues for 1856.

Microfilm edition was prepared from Ct, CtY, DLC, and KyLoS copies.

CHRISTIAN SPECTATOR. *SEE* Quarterly Christian Spectator.

CHRISTIAN TELESCOPE. *SEE* Christian Telescope and Universalist Miscellany.

THE CHRISTIAN TELESCOPE AND UNIVERSALIST MISCELLANY.. v. 1-4; Aug. 7, 1824-Oct. 2, 1828. Providence, R.I., B. Cranston, 1824–

v. weekly.

Title varies: v. 1-2, The Christian Telescope.

Editor: Aug. 1824- David Pickering.

Edited by Rev. David Pickering, this weekly Universalist magazine was intended to disseminate and defend the Universalist doctrine. It consisted of sermons, religious articles, moral essays, poetry, and local news; and although some of the material was selected from other sources, most of its contents were original.

v1-2, no.22	Aug. 7, 1824-Dec. 31, 1825	APS II, Reel 89
v2, no.23-v4	Jan. 1826-Oct. 1828	Reel 1197

Many pages have faded print: some pages are stained. Vol. 4: no. 13, Pgs. 97-98 are missing in number only. No. 16, Pgs. 130-31 are missing; no. 20, Pgs. 164-65 are missing; No. 24, Pgs. 198-99 are missing in number only.

Microfilm edition was prepared from ICMe, MMeT, MMeT-Hi and NCaS copies.

CHRISTIAN UNION. *SEE* New Outlook.

THE CHRISTIAN VISITANT. v. 1 (no. 1-52); June 3, 1815-May 25, 1816. Albany, Pub. for the editor, by H.C. Southwick [1815-16]

1 p.l., 416 p., 1 l. weekly.

Includes "Valedictory. From the Albany register ... May 31, 1816" (1 leaf) Edited by Solomon Southwick.

This religious weekly was to be non-sectarian, and published news of the establishment and progress of various churches and of the activities of Bible and missionary societies. Along with religious news, it presented biographical sketches of eminent religious men, religious essays, prayers, letters, and a section of religious poetry.

v1, no.1-52	June 3, 1815-May 25, 1816	APS II, Reel 89

CHRISTIAN VISITOR. v.1; Jan.-Dec. 1823. Providence, Printed and published by B. Field.

450 p. monthly (irregular)

"Constant love of God the duty of Christians" proclaimed this religious monthly. All material included was religious in nature, such as articles on interpretation of the Bible, duties of Christians, the life of Christ and advice to the "rising generation." Poetry, anecdotes and meeting notes of the Domestic Missionary Society of Rhode Island filled the pages.

v1	Jan-Dec. 1823	APS II, Reel 401

Microfilm edition was prepared from MBC copy.

CHRISTIAN WATCHMAN. *SEE* Christian Reflector *and* Watchman-Examiner.

CHRISTIAN WATCHMAN AND CHRISTIAN REFLEC-TOR. *SEE* Watchman-Examiner.

CHRISTIAN WATCHMAN AND REFLECTOR. *SEE* Watchman-Examiner.

CHRISTIAN WORK. *SEE* Arena *and* New York Observer.

CHRISTIAN WORK AND THE EVANGELIST. *SEE* Evangelist and Religious Review.

THE CHRISTIAN'S MAGAZINE: designed to promote knowledge and influence of evangelical truth and order. v.1-4; 1806-11. New York, 1806-11.

4 v.

Vol. 1-2; printed by Hopkins and Seymour; v. 3, pub. by Williams and Whiting; v. 4, pub. by S. Whiting & co.

The *Christian's Magazine* offered a variety of religious news, both domestic and foreign—missionary news, news of installations and ordinations, and on various societies, including Bible societies, along with essays on doctrine and on the Presbyterian Church, the Reformed Church in Holland, and other Churches. In addition, it offered literary news, reviews, poetry and biography.

v1-2	1806-1807	APS II, Reel 11
v3-4	Jan. 1810-Dec. 1811	APS II, Reel 90

Microfilm edition was prepared from DLC copy.

THE CHRISTIAN'S MAGAZINE, REVIEWER, AND RELIGIOUS INTELLIGENCER. v. 1, no. 1-8; [May] 1805-[Jan.] 1808. Portsmouth, N.H.

300 p. Quarterly.

Edited by E. Smith.

This religious magazine by Elias Smith provided religious news, including accounts of revivals and conversions; reviewed sermons, books, and magazines; and also included a series on the history of the clergy.

v1, no. 1-8	May 1805-Jan. 1808	APS II, Reel 11

Microfilm edition was prepared from MB copy.

THE CHRISTIAN'S MONITOR, &c. no. 1-14; Dec. 8, 1798 June 8, 1799. Portland, Me., Rand & Burdick.

biweekly.

no. 1-12 not available for filming.

A religious magazine which included poetry, essays, letters, and articles on religious subjects.

no.13-14	May 25-June 8, 1799	APS I, Reel 10

Microfilm edition was prepared from MWA copy.

THE CHRISTIAN'S, SCHOLAR'S, AND FARMER'S MAGAZINE; calculated in an eminent degree, to promote religion; to disseminate useful knowledge; to afford literary pleasures and amuseument, and to advance the interest of agriculture. By a number of gentlemen. v. 1-2; Apr./May 1789-Feb./Mar. 1791. Elizabeth-town [N.J.] Printed by S. Kollock, 1789-[91]

2 v. bimonthly.

An encyclopedic repository specializing in serial treatises on rhetoric, farming, theology, Greek history, music, painting, etc. Poetry and current events were included.

v1-2	Apr./May 1789-Feb./Mar. 1791	APS I, Reel 10

Microfilm edition was prepared from MWA copy.

THE CHRISTIAN'S WEEKLY MONITOR; or, Sabbath morning repast. v. 1-4, no. 10; 1814-May 1818. [Sangerfield, N.Y.]

Issued in Civil and religious intelligencer, published Nov. 18, 1816-Sept 13, 1817; both titles have been combined for this series both photographed as they appear in the American Antiquarian Society's Library and the New York Public Library. Film incomplete: scattered issues wanting.

This religious weekly published news of Sabbath schools, missions and missionary societies, and the activities of Bible societies, and described revivals and conversions. In addition to news, there were occasional sermons, biographical sketches, and poetry.

v1-4	1814-May 1818	APS II, Reel 90

CHRONICLES OF THE NORTH AMERICAN SAVAGES. no. 1-5; May-Sept. 1835. [Cincinnati. T.H. Shreve]

5 no. monthly.

Contains an account of the dealings of the first English colonists with the Indians of Virginia; also of the Black-Hawk war. Includes vocabulariea of the "Saw-kee and Mus-quaw-ke Indian tongue," and an "Essay on the Chippewa Language."

Conducted by Isaac Galland.

This publication was devoted to the study of the American Indian. The five numbers published contained articles on the religion, history, and language of the American Indian, and included vocabulary lists for several different tribes.

no.1-5	May-Sept. 1835	APS II, Reel 382

Microfilm edition was prepared from WHi copy.

CHURCH RECORD. v. 1, no. 1-29; June 22, 1822-Mar. 22, 1823. Philadelphia, E. Littell.

312 p. weekly.

Superseded by Philadelphia recorder (later Episcopal recorder) Cf. Union list of serials.

Lacking on film: no. 29, Mar. 22, 1823.

Conducted by seven ministers, this Episcopal weekly focused much attention on missionary news, including news from various missionary publications and proceedings of the Domestic and Foreign Missionary Society, and also published short essays and local church news.

v1, no. 1-28   June 22, 1822-Mar. 8, 1823   APS II, Reel 90

SEE ALSO: Episcopal Recorder.

* **THE CHURCH REVIEW.** v̇. 1-60, 63; Apr. 1848-Oct. 1891, New Haven, Conn., Bassett & Bradley, 1848-61. New York, N.S. Richardson, 1862-91.

61 v. illus., plates, ports. Quarterly, 1848- ; bimonthly,; quarterly, 1881-82; monthly, 1883-Mar. 1884; quarterly, Oct. 1884-Apr. 1886; monthly, July 1886- ; quarterly, -Oct. 1891.

Title varies: Apr. 1848-Jan. 1858, The Church review, and ecclesiastical register. Apr. 1858-Jan. 1870, The American quarterly church review, and ecclesiastical register. Apr. 1870-Oct. 1871, The American quarterly church review. Jan. 1872-Apr. 1885, The American church review. July 1885-The Church review. Oct. 1889, The Church review and ecclesiastical register. Jan. 1890-Oct. 1891, The Church review.

Editors: Apr. 1848-Jan. 1868, N.S. Richardson.–Apr. 1868-Oct. 1871, Nov. 1874-Apr. 1875, J.M. Leavitt.–July 1875-Nov. 1880, E.B. Boggs.–Jan. 1881-Oct. 1891, H.M. Baum. Suspended Oct. 1861, Apr. 1862-Jan. 1863; Feb.-June, Aug., Sept., Nov.-Dec. 1888. Vols. 1-29 contain 4 nos. each; v. 32, 41-42, 48-50, 6 nos. each; v. 33-40, 44, 53-60, 63, 1 no. each; v. 43, 3 nos.; v. 45-46, 2 nos. each; v. 47, 2 nos. in 1; v 61-62 (Apr.-July 1891) appear never to have been published.

Founded and edited by Nathaniel S. Richardson, the *Church Review* became one of the leading papers of the Protestant Episcopal Church. Contributors such as Arthur Cleveland Coxe, Bishop Doane, Bishop Whittingham, and Clement C. Moore gave the *Review* a largely religious and theological nature. Space was also afforded education, literature, and social problems.

John McDowell Leavitt, M.H. Mallory, and Edward B. Boggs successively edited the *Review* after Richardson. However, the *Review* fell greatly out of respect during this period, and it was not until its last editor, Henry M. Baum, that it regained the prominence it once held.

Church Review, and Ecclesiastical Register.
v1-4   Apr. 1848-Jan. 1852   APS II, Reel 916
v5-10   Apr. 1852-Jan. 1858   Reel 917

American Quarterly Church Review, and Ecclesiastical Register.
v11   Apr. 1858-Jan. 1859   APS II, Reel 917
v12-18   Apr. 1859-Jan. 1867   Reel 918
v19-21   Apr. 1867-Jan. 1870   Reel 919

American Quarterly Church Review.
v22-23   Apr. 1870-Oct. 1871   APS II, Reel 919

American Church Review.
v24-26   Jan. 1872-Oct. 1874   APS II, Reel 919
v27-35   Jan. 1875-July 1881   Reel 920
v36-45   Oct. 1881-Apr. 1885   Reel 921

Church Review.
v46-50   July 1885-Dec. 1887   APS II, Reel 922
v51-63   Jan. 1888-Oct. 1891   Reel 923

Some pages are torn, stained, or have print missing. Pagination is irregular. Vols. 1-45, 47, and 56-63 lack indexes. Please refer to the

Tables of Contents. Vol. 26: Supplement, "Report on Life Insurance" bound between pages 320-321. Vol. 30: Supplement, "Ordinations for the Year Ending Advent 1877" bound between pages 160-161. Vol. 31: Supplement, "Home" bound between pages 80-81. Vol. 33: page 2 of Contents bound and photographed at the beginning of Volume 34. Vols. 35-37 are unnumbered.

Microfilm edition was prepared from MiD, OCI, and Nh copies.

CHURCH REVIEW, AND ECCLESIASTICAL REGISTER. *SEE* Church Review.

THE CHURCHMAN'S MAGAZINE. v.1-8, Jan. 1804-Nov./Dec. 1811; new ser., v.1-3, no.1, Jan./Feb. 1813-May/June 1815; new ser., v.1-5, Jan. 1821-Mar. 1827. New-Haven, Comstock, Griswold, etc.

Monthly, 1804-08?; bimonthly, 1809-15; monthly, 1821-27. Publication appears to have been suspended during 1812, 1816-20, 1824.

Vols. 1-2 have title: The Churchman's monthly magazine; or, Treasury of divine and useful knowledge ... By a committee appointed by the convocation of the Episcopal church of Connecticut.

Superseded by the Episcopal watchman. L.C. set incomplete: v.5 (1808) wanting.

This prominent Connecticut magazine proposed to communicate religious information and instruction, and to defend and explain the doctrines and principles of the Episcopal Church. It contained extracts from foreign and American religious works, sketches relating to the church and its history; biographical sketches, book reviews, and missionary news. Columns included "The Commentator" and "The Watchman," and there were occasional anecdotes and poems.

Churchman's Monthly Magazine.
v1-2   Jan. 1804-Dec. 1805   APS II, Reel 12

Churchman's Magazine.
v3-6   Jan. 1806-Dec. 1809   APS II, Reel 12

v7-nsv3   Jan./Dec. 1810-May/June 1815   APS II, Reel 91

s3v1-5   Jan. 1821-Mar. 1827   APS II, Reel 210

Microfilm edition was prepared from DLC, MiD copy.

SEE ALSO: Episcopal Watchman.

CHURCHMAN'S MONTHLY MAGAZINE; OR, TREASURY OF DIVINE AND USEFUL KNOWLEDGE. *SEE* Churchman's Magazine.

THE CHURCHMAN'S REPOSITORY FOR THE EASTERN DIOCESE. v.1, no. 1-6; July 1-Dec. 1, 1820. Newburyport, H.R. Stickney.

162 p. monthly.

Copy filmed incomplete: all after p. 1 of no. 6 wanting.

This monthly Episcopal magazine contained sermons, poetry, religious and missionary news, news on the state of the church, essays, on doctrine and morals, and reviews of new religious publications.

v1, no.1-6   July 1-Dec. 1, 1820   APS II, Reel 127

THE CINCINNATI LITERARY GAZETTE. v. 1-4; Jan. 1, 1824-Oct. 29, 1825. Cincinnati, J. P. Foote.

4 v. in 2. weekly.

No numbers issued Aug. 20-Sept. 3, 1825.

Published by John P. Foote, this literary weekly contained poetry, tales, biography, book reviews, and literary notices, but also included articles on history and natural history, sections of music, mathematics, and politics, a news summary, and scientific notices.

v1-4   Jan. 1, 1824-Oct. 29, 1825   APS II, Reel 127

CINCINNATI MIRROR, AND WESTERN GAZETTE OF LITERATURE, SCIENCE, AND THE ARTS. v. 1-5, no. 34; Oct. 1, 1831-Sept. 17, 1836. Cincinnati, 1831-1836.

5 v.

V. 5, nos. 1-13 repeated in numbering.

Oct. 31, 1835-Jan. 23, 1836 as Buckeye and Cincinnati Mirror.

A weekly miscellany, devoted mainly to literary and scientific subjects, which published a fair amount of original material as well as selections from popular magazines. It contained moral and humorous tales, poetry, essays, literary notices, biographical sketches, foreign and domestic news, occasional music, and a variety of miscellaneous items. Volume 3 included articles on "early times in the West," presenting sketches of scenery, people, history, and customs.

v1-5   Oct. 1, 1831-Sept. 17, 1836   APS II, Reel 789

Several pages are stained or have faded print. Many pages are creased, with some loss of print. Vol. 3: Issues 40-41 are badly stained. Best copy available for photographing.

Microfilm edition was prepared from OCHP copy.

THE CINCINNATI WEEKLY HERALD AND PHILANTHROPIST. v. 1-11; Jan. 1, 1836-Dec. 1, 1846. New Richmond, Cincinnati.

11 v. Vol. 3-4 also called new ser., v. 1-2. Issues also assigned consecutive "whole numbers" 1-532.

Title varies: Jan. 1, 1836-Oct. 11, 1843, the Philanthropist.

"Published by the Executive Committee of the Ohio Anti-slavery Society." Editors: 1836-1837, Birney, James Gillespie (with G. Bailey, Jr., 1837).—1838-1846, Bailey, Gamaliel, Jr.

The *Cincinnati Weekly Herald,* which began as the *Philanthropist,* an antislavery magazine published by the Ohio Sate Anti-Slavery Society, was at first devoted solely to opposing slavery, but was later expanded to include other material as well. This weekly published antislavery articles and speeches, news of the activities of antislavery societies, and Congressional proceedings and foreign news related to the slavery problem, in addition to commercial and political news, occasional poetry, and advertising.

Philanthropist.
v1-3   Jan. 1, 1836-Jan. 15, 1839   APS II, Reel 1409
v4-6   Jan. 22, 1839-July 16, 1842   Reel 1410
v7-8 no.4   July 23, 1842-Oct. 11, 1843   Reel 1411

Cincinnati Weekly Herald and Philanthropist
v8 no. 5-9   Oct. 18, 1843-Aug. 6, 1845   APS II, Reel 1411
v10-11   Sept. 17, 1845-Dec. 1, 1846   Reel 1412

All volumes lack indexes. Several issues are missing and not available for photographing. Many pages are stained, creased, torn, and tightly bound with some loss of text.

Microfilm edition was prepared from CtY, ICRL, MdBJ, and WHi copies.

THE CIRCULAR. v. 1-3; Apr. 14, 1821-Apr. 29, 1825. Wilmington, Del., Printed by R. Porter.

3 v. weekly.

Title varies: Apr. 14, 1821-Apr. 2, 1824, The Christian repository.

Superseded by the Philadelphian.

Published by Robert Porter, this religious magazine published much on missions, particularly the missions to the American Indians, to Palestine, and to the Sandwich Islands; and also gave attention to the subject of colonization, and to the activities of Bible societies. Each issue devoted sections to poetry, to summaries of religious news, and to biography, and included a youth's and a ladies' department.

Christian Repository.
v1-2   Apr. 14, 1821-Apr. 2, 1824   APS II, Reel 210a

Circular.
v3   Apr. 9, 1824-Apr. 29, 1825   APS II, Reel 210a

Some pages are stained.

SEE ALSO: Oneida Circular.

CITIZEN. *SEE* Round Table.

CITY RECORD, AND BOSTON NEWS-LETTER. *SEE* Bowen's Boston News-Letter and City Record.

CIVIL AND RELIGIOUS INTELLIGENCER. *SEE* Christian's Weekly Monitor.

THE CLUB-ROOM. no.1-4; Feb.-July, 1820. Boston, T. Swan [1820]

179 p.

This short-lived essay periodical was conducted by a philosophers' club which met once a week; contents were comprised of a variety of essays written by the club members and occasionally a contribution from a reader. Essay titles included: "Ennui," "Happiness," "The Village Grave-Yard," and "Ruins of Rome."

no.1-4   Feb.-July 1820   APS II, Reel 92

COBBETT'S POLITICAL REGISTER. v. 1-3, no. 7, American or v. 30, 33-34, no. 7, English. Jan. 6; 1816-Jan. 1818. New York, 1816-1818.

3 v.

William Cobbett, editor.

Cobbett's American Political Register was the American edition of several volumes of the *Political Register,* which had been published in London since 1802 by the British journalist and reformer, William Cobbett. This weekly magazine was arranged as letters or essays written by Cobbett and addressed to the people of America; it mainly concerned the political affairs and government, as well as the social problems, of Great Britain. The *Political Register* was considered one of the greatest reform journals of the period, but because of his views Cobbett had to flee England several times. In 1817 he fled to the U.S., returning to England in 1819; thus his magazine was written in the U.S. during this period.

v1-3, no.7 (American)	May 21, 1816-Jan. 10, 1818	APS II, Reel 92
v30, 33, 34, no.7 (English)	Jan. 6, 1816-Jan. 10, 1818	Reel 92

COHEN'S GAZETTE & LOTTERY REGISTER. v. 1-9, no. 29; May 2, 1814-Sept., 1830. Baltimore [J.I. Cohen]

9 v. weekly (irregular)

Title varies: v. 1, no. 3-v. 8 as Cohen's lottery gazette and register. Publication suspended June 16, 1819-Sept. 4, 1820.

Film covers: (on Reels 92-93): v.1, no. 1-67, May 2, 1814-Dec. 28, 1815; v. 4-5, no. 155-218, Nov. 20, 1817-June 9, 1819; n.s.v.l, no. 219-270, Sept. 11, 1820,-June 23, 1822; v.6-8, no. 32, no. 271-392, June 30, 1822-Dec. 8, 1825; and (on Reel 362): v.8, no.33-v.9, Feb. 16, 1826-Sept. 1, 1830

This four-page weekly magazine published by Cohen's Lottery and Exchange office devoted most of its attention to the state lottery, providing information on it and lists of winning numbers. It also published foreign and domestic news, current stock and food prices, and miscellaneous material.

Cohen's Gazette and Lottery Register.
v1, nos. 1-2	May 2-May 9, 1814	APS II, Reel 92

Cohen's Lottery Gazette and Register.
v1, no. 3-v5, no. 15	May 16, 1814-June 9, 1819	APS II, Reel 92
nsv1-v8, no. 23	Sept. 11, 1820-May 26, 1825	Reel 93

Cohen's Gazette and Lottery Register
v8, no. 24-32	June 9-Dec. 8, 1825	APS II, Reel 93
v8, no. 33-v9	Feb. 16, 1826-Sept. 1, 1830	Reel 362

COHEN'S LOTTERY GAZETTE AND REGISTER. *SEE* Cohen's Gazette and Lottery Register.

COLLECTIONS, historical and miscellaneous, and monthly literary journal. v. 1-3; Apr. 1822-Nov./Dec. 1824. Concord, N.H., Hill and Moore.

3 v.

Bimonthly (irregular) 1822; monthly, 1823-24. Title varies: v. 1, Collections, topographical, historical & biographical, relating principally to New Hampshire. Edited by J. Farmer and J.B. Moore.

The first volume was mainly historical in nature, containing much on the history of New Hampshire—sketches on Indian wars, descriptions of towns and places, biographical memoirs of eminent people, statistical tables, a monthly register of vital statistics, and weather information. The second volume, however, was expanded to include more literary material—essays, sketches of scenery, reviews of new publications, poetry and anecdotes. An appendix containing a record of political events, proceedings of the legislature, and articles on agriculture, inventions, and curiosities was included.

Collections, Topographical, Historical & Biographical ...
v1	Apr.-Dec. 1, 1822	APS II, Reel 93

Collections, Historical and Miscellaneous, and Monthly Literary Journal
v2, no. 1-8	Jan. 1823-Aug. 1823	APS II, Reel 93
v2 no. 9-v3	Sept. 1823-Nov./Dec. 1824	Reel 94

COLLECTIONS, TOPOGRAPHICAL, HISTORICAL & BIOGRAPHICAL ... *SEE* Collections, Historical and Miscellaneous, and Monthly Literary Journal.

COLLEGE DIRECTORY. *SEE* Old and New

THE COLLEGIAN; or, American students' magazine. v. 1, no. 1-2; Jan.-Feb. 1819. [New York]

48 p. monthly.

The *Collegian* was to be both instructive and entertaining, and was to consist mainly of contributions from readers. Contents included biographical sketches of philosophers, men of letters, and others, reviews of recent American publications, interesting anecdotes, poetry, speeches given at various college commencements, and a department of "Musa Americana," which consisted of pieces not previously published.

v1, no. 1-2	Jan.-Feb. 1819	APS II, Reel 94

COLMAN'S RURAL WORLD. v. 1-69, no. 10; 1849-May 1916. St. Louis, Mo., 1849-1916.

69 v. illus., plates. Frequency varies.

Title varies: 1849-64 as Valley farmer. Merged into Journal of agriculture.

On film: v. 1-6, Sept.; v. 6, Nov.; v. 7, Feb., Apr.-Nov.; v. 8-9, Jan.-June, Aug.-Dec.; v. 12-17, Nov., Dec. 22 & 29; v. 18-19; v. 22-23; v. 34; v. 36, Jan., Mar.-v. 37; v. 53; v. 55-56; v. 66-69, Jan. 5, 1916.

Devoted to the interests of "the cultivators of the soil in the Mississippi Valley," *Colman's Rural World* was published for the farmer and his family. Articles included treatment of stock, barn and home architecture (plans for a 19' x 25' house for under $300), butter-making, notices of agricultural societies, designs of various farm implements and tools, homemaking hints and recipes, poetry, advertisements, grain and stock prices, and fiction for children.

Valley Farmer
v1, no.1	Jan. 1849	APS II, Reel 416
v2-3	Jan. 1850-Dec. 1851	Reel 416
v1-8	Jan. 1849-Dec. 1856	APS III, Reel 750
v9-16	Jan. 1857-Dec. 1864	Reel 751

Colman's Rural World
v17-23	Jan. 1, 1865-Dec. 25, 1869	APS III, Reel 752
v34-36	Jan. 18, 1881-Dec. 27, 1883	Reel 753
v37	Jan. 3-Dec. 25, 1884	Reel 754
v53-55	Jan. 4, 1900-Dec. 31, 1902	Reel 754
v56	Jan. 7-Dec. 30, 1903	Reel 755
v66-67	Jan. 2, 1913-Dec. 31, 1914	Reel 755
v68-69	Jan. 7, 1915-Jan. 5, 1916	Reel 756

Best copy available for photographing. Several volumes lack title pages, indexes, text and advertisement pages. Several pages are tightly bound, torn, stained, creased, and have print faded with some loss of text. Pagination is irregular. Vols.2-21, 24-33, 35, 38-52, 54, and 57-65 are missing; not available for photographing. Vol. 1 microfilm edition contains issue number 1, January 1849. Vol. 6: October and December issues are missing. Vol.7: January, March and December issues are missing. Vol. 9: July issue is missing. Vol. 11: January, February and December issues are missing. Vol. 15 contains a supplement. Vol. 17: December 1 and December 15 issues are missing. Vol. 36: February issue is missing.

Microfilm edition was prepared from DLC, DNAL, ICJ, IU, MH, MoS, N,T, and TxU copies.

COLONIZATIONIST AND JOURNAL OF FREEDOM.
April 1833-April 1834. Boston, Geo. W. Light, 1834.

384 p.

July 1833 issue never published.

Concerned mainly with the colonization movement, which was attempting to resettle freed American Negroes in Africa, the *Colonizationist* presented the pros and cons of the movement, reported on the progress of the colonies in Africa, and provided coverage of the American Colonization Society and other colonization societies. Contents also included articles on slavery and the slave trade, poetry, letters, and news.

April 1833-April 1834   APS II, Reel 603

Microfilm edition was prepared from DLC copy.

THE COLUMBIA MAGAZINE.
Designed to promote evangelical knowledge and morality. To oppose the prevailing licentiousness of manners, particularly the violation of the Sabbath, intemperance, and profanity; and also to diffuse missionary and religious intelligence. Conducted by several friends of religion. v. 1; Sept. 1814-Aug. 1815. Hudson, A. Stoddard [1814-15]

384 p. monthly.

This religious magazine promised to oppose intemperance, profanity, and the disregard of the Sabbath, and to publish missionary and religious news. It gave information on missions and missionary societies and on moral and Bible societies, accounts of revivals, poetry, and notices of new publications.

v1   Sept. 1814-Aug. 1815   APS II, Reel 94

COLUMBIAN CHEMICAL SOCIETY OF PHILADELPHIA. MEMOIRS OF THE COLUMBIAN CHEMICAL SOCIETY OF PHILADELPHIA.
SEE Memoirs of the Columbian Chemical Society of Philadelphia.

COLUMBIAN HISTORIAN.
v. 1, no. 1-26; May 13, 1824-Mar. 11, 1825. New Richmond, Ohio, A.C. & J. Herron.

206 p. weekly (irregular)

This weekly historical magazine was to give an "impartial and faithful history" of North America. It included articles on "The Peopling of America," on the Indians, their wars, chiefs, language, customs, and archaeology, and accounts of the first English settle-

ments in Virginia and Pennsylvania. Some poetry was included.

v1, nos. 1-26   May 13, 1824-Mar. 11, 1825   APS II, Reel 95

THE COLUMBIAN LADY'S AND GENTLEMAN'S MAGAZINE,
embracing literature in every department: embellished with the finest steel and mezzotint engravings, music, and colored fashions. v. 1-9, v. 10, no. 1-[2]; Jan. 1844-Feb. 1849. New York, I. Post, 1844- [49]

10 v. plates (part col.) ports. monthly.

Caption title: The Columbian magazine.

Editors: 1844, John Inman.–1845-Apr. 1848, John Inman, R.A. West.–May-Dec. 1848, S.M. Chester.–Jan.-Feb. 1849, Darius Mead.

Edited by John Inman, the *Columbian Lady's and Gentleman's Magazine* was designed as a competitor for *Graham's* and was modeled after it in format. Its contents were made up mainly of poetry, book reviews and sentimental prose. In addition, it published a piece of music in each number and, for the first two years, two mezzotints and a colored fashion plate in each number, but beginning with 1848 fashion plates appeared less frequently. Inman wrote much for the magazine, as did Robert A. West, who became associate editor in 1845. Contributors, many the same as for *Graham's,* Included H.T. Tuckerman, James K. Paulding, Park Benjamin, John Neal, T.S. Arthur, Thomas Buchanan Read, Charles Fenno Hoffman, Alfred B. Street, and also the leading women writers of the times: Mrs. E.F. Ellet, Lydia Maria Child, "Fanny Forrester," Elizabeth Oakes Smith, Catherine M. Sedgwick, Mrs. Osgood, Mrs. Kirkland, and Mrs. Sigourney. Inman and West withdrew in 1848, to be succeeded by Stephen M. Chester for a few months, and then by the Rev. Darius Read, founder of the *Christian Parlor Magazine*. The *Columbian* was discontinued in 1849.

v1-10   Jan. 1844-Feb. 1849   APS II, Reel 313

Microfilm edition was prepared from MiU copy.

THE COLUMBIAN MAGAZINE;
comprehending ecclesiastical history, morality, religion, and other useful and interesting matter. v. 1, no. 1-5; Jan.-Aug. 1806. Danbury, Conn., J.C. Gray, 1806.

Vol. 1, no. 1-4? has title: Monthly magazine; comprehending ecclesiastical history, morality, religion ...

Original in the Connecticut state library. Film has v. 1, no. 1-3, 5.

This religious monthly promised to provide its readers with church history, studies of various religions, extracts from the writings of both modern and ancient authors, and religious news. Poetry and anecdotes and a few biographical sketches were also included in the contents.

Monthly Magazine; Comprehending Ecclesiastical History, ...
v1, no. 1-3   Jan.-Mar. 1806   APS II, Reel 32

Columbian Magazine; Comprehending Ecclesiastical History.
v1, no. 5   July & Aug. 1806   APS II, Reel 32

Microfilm edition was prepared from Ct copy.

COLUMBIAN MAGAZINE; OR, MONTHLY MISCELLANY.
SEE Universal Asylum and Columbian Magazine.

THE COLUMBIAN MUSEUM; or, universal asylum Jan.-June, 1793. Philadelphia, John Parker.

60, 8 Continues the Universal asylum and Columbian magazine.

Contains number for Jan., 1793 only; no more published.

A post-Revolution periodical offering a wide variety of material—articles on agricultural methods, commerce, politics, manners and morals, and law; poetry; biography; and vital statistics.

Jan.-June 1793   APS I, Reel 10

Microfilm edition was prepared from NN copy.

SEE ALSO: Universal Asylum and Columbian Magazine.

THE COLUMBIAN PHENIX AND BOSTON REVIEW. Containing useful information on literature, religion, morality, politics and philosophy; with many interesting particulars in history and biography. Forming a compendium of the present state of society. v. 1 (no. 1-7); Jan.-July 1800. Boston, Manning & Loring, [1800]

452 p. front., plates monthly.

Joseph Hawkins, editor.

Edited by Joseph Hawkins, the *Columbian Phenix and Boston Review* published an assortment of literary material—poetry, humorous anecdotes, biographical sketches, a few tales, and book reviews—as well as proceedings of the state legislature, national news, and news from Europe.

v1, no. 1-7   Jan.-July 1800   APS II, Reel 13

Microfilm edition was prepared from MiU-C copy.

THE COLUMBIAN STAR. v. 1-8, no. 18; Feb. 2, 1822-May 2, 1829. Washington, Anderson & Meehan.

8 v. weekly.

Issued Jan. 4, 1823-by the American Baptist Foreign Mission Society (called 1823-24, General Convention of the Baptist Denomination in the United States; 1825-Baptist General Convention) Edited by J.D. Knowles. Superseded by Columbian star and Christian index (later Christian index) Cf. Union list of serials.

This religious weekly contained sections for theology and religion, and for literary and political news. There were summaries of domestic and foreign affairs, Congressional proceedings, and weather information in addition to news of missionary efforts, both at home and abroad, reports of Bible societies, and poetry. Much of the material was selected.

v1-2	Feb. 2, 1822-Dec. 27, 1823	APS II, Reel 95
v3-4	Jan. 3, 1824-Dec. 31, 1825	Reel 96
v5-8	Jan. 7, 1826-May 2, 1829	APS II, Reel 1271

Vol. 4, no. 47 is lacking. Best copy available for photographing. Vol. 5: Several pages are tightly bound and creased. Issue 31, pages 121-22 are torn with some loss of text. Issues 13-30, 33-39, and 41 to end of volume are missing; not available for photographing. Vols. 6-8: Complete volumes are not available for photographing. The microfilm edition contains issues 17, 21, and 22 of volume 6 and issues 16 and 18 of volume 8. Vol. 7 is not available for photographing.

Microfilm edition was prepared from DLC and MWA copies.

COLUMBIAN STAR AND CHRISTIAN INDEX. *SEE* Christian Index *and* Columbian Star.

COLVIN'S WEEKLY REGISTER. v. 1 (no. 1-16); Jan. 16-Apr. 30, 1808. Washington [J.B. Colvin] 1808.

259 p.

Caption title. Three numbers of this work were issued before 1808. A notice in the number for Jan. 16, 1808 states that as some time had elapsed since the publication of these numbers the editor "preferred, therefore, a commencement of his work de novo."

Continued as the Monitor. cf. Bryan's Bibliography of the District of Columbia. John B. Colvin, editor.

This weekly was concerned with the affairs of government, and published a wide variety of material relevant to this topic—letters, extracts, speeches, reports of conventions, reports of the Secretary of the Treasury and other departments, foreign and domestic news, information on the economy and population and other statistical information.

v1, no. 1-16   Jan. 16-Apr. 30, 1808   APS II, Reel 382

Microfilm edition was prepared from DLC and N copies.

THE COMET [by Walter Wildfire, pseud.] No. 1-13; Oct. 19, 1811-Jan. 11, 1812. Boston, J.T. Buckingham.

Caption title, no. 2-6, 13, "By Walter Wildfire."

This miscellany edited by "Walter Wildfire" contained articles on literature, including some dealing with Russian literature, Frederick Schiller, and William Congreve, along with book reviews, lists of new publications, biographical sketches, much poetry, selections from foreign magazines, and many short items, such as anecdotes and maxims. The drama was given a good deal of attention; a section titled "Theatrical Recorder" discussed performances at The Boston Theatre and at foreign theaters, and there were notices of new plays and performers.

no.1-13   Oct. 19, 1811-Jan. 11, 1812   APS II, Reel 97

COMING AGE. *SEE* Arena.

COMMERCIAL AND FINANCIAL CHRONICLE. *SEE* Merchants' Magazine and Commercial Review.

COMMON SCHOOL ADVOCATE. v. 1-5; 1837-1841. Madison, Indiana [and] Cincinnati, 1837-1841.

5v.

Begun at Madison, Indiana, but later moved to Cincinnati, the *Common School Advocate* was the first western educational journal to last longer than 12 months. Its object was to promote primary schools in the southern and western states, and it was published under the supervision of Edward D. Mansfield and Lyman Harding, professors at Cincinnati College and by Alexander McGuffey, a professor in Woodward College. Many eminent teachers furnished articles: Professor Calvin E. Stowe contributed information on the educational systems of Prussia, Switzerland, and Germany, and William H. McGuffey contributed a good deal of material. Contents included book reviews, extracts, and articles on education, teachers, teaching methods, schools, and textbooks.

v1-5   1837-1841   APS II, Reel 383

Microfilm edition was prepared from OCHP copy.

COMMON SCHOOL ASSISTANT; a monthly paper, for the improvement of common school education. v. 1-5; Jan. 1836-Apr. 1840. Albany.

5 v. illus.

Subtitle varies.

Editor: Jan. 1836, J.O. Taylor.

The *Common School Assistant* was edited by J. Orville Taylor of New York. According to the "Prospectus" in issue one, only one student of every twenty furthered his studies. This monthly was devoted to assisting the remaining nineteen during their short period education.

| v1-5 | Jan. 1836-April 1840 | APS II, Reel 889 |

Volume 4, pages 35-36 and 79-80 are stained. Volumes 1-5 lack indexes or tables of contents.

Microfilm edition was prepared from DHEW, N, and NcD copies.

THE COMMON SCHOOL JOURNAL. v. 1-14, Nov. 1838-Dec. 1852. Boston, Marsh, Capen, Lyon and Webb.

14 v. plates. semimonthly.

Editors: 1838-48, Horace Mann.—1849-W. B. Fowle. Vols. 11-14 also called new ser., v. 1-4.

Begun by Horace Mann, secretary of the Massachusetts Board of Education, this semimonthly was one of the most important education journals of its time. Devoted to the cause of education, it proposed to improve the "common" schools and other means of education, to report on laws relating to schools and on the proceedings of the Massachusetts Board of Education as well as to explain the duties of parents and teachers, and address children on good behavior. Contents included essays and articles on Boston schools, children, teaching, books, and other education-related subjects and it also published letters, biographical material, anecdotes, lessons in grammar and other subjects, and extracts from various sources.

v1-2	Nov. 1838-Dec. 1840	APS II, Reel 512
v3-8	Jan. 1841-Dec. 1846	Reel 513
v9-14	Jan. 1847-Dec. 1852	Reel 514

Several pages have faded print and show-through with some loss of text. Vols. 6 and 10: Pagination is irregular.

Microfilm edition was prepared from CtY and MB copies.

COMPANION. *SEE* Observer.

THE COMPANION AND WEEKLY MISCELLANY. By Edward Easy, esquire [pseud.] v. 1-2 (no. 1-52); Nov. 3, 1804-Oct. 25, 1806.

2 v.

Continued as "The Observer. By Beatrice Ironside."

This weekly by "Edward Easy" was devoted mainly to criticism and satirical attacks on manners, morals, and "vice," but political and religious controversies were excluded. There was also some literary news, anecdotes, and poetry.

| v1-2 | Nov. 3, 1804-Oct. 25, 1806 | APS II, Reel 13 |

Microfilm edition was prepared from DLC copy.

CONGREGATIONAL REVIEW (CHICAGO). *SEE* New Englander and Yale Review.

CONGREGATIONALIST. *SEE* Congregationalist and Herald of Gospel Liberty.

CONGREGATIONALIST AND CHRISTIAN WORLD. *SEE* Congregationalist and Herald of Gospel Liberty.

CONGREGATIONALIST AND HERALD OF GOSPEL LIBERTY. v. 1-119, no. 13, 1816-March 29, 1934.

119 v. weekly.

Title varies: 1816, Recorder; 1817-1824, Boston recorder; 1825, Recorder and telegraph; 1826-June 30, 1830, Boston recorder and religious telegraph; July 7, 1830-May 11, 1849, Boston recorder; May 17, 1849-May 13, 1858, Puritan recorder; Also: Nov. 3, 1870-May 18, 1901, Congregationalist; May 25, 1901-Nov. 15, 1917, Congregationalist and Christian world.

On film: vols. 1-10; 1816-1825 (reels 97-99) vols. 1-35; 1816-1850 (reels 539-546) vols. 76-91; 1891-1906 (reels 1911-1924) Imperfect copy: vol. 76 has scattered issues; vol. 77 has issue no. 52 only.

Founded by Nathaniel Willis and Sidney E. Morse as the *Recorder* in 1816, this Congregationalist magazine presented religious news, including accounts of the proceedings of Bible societies, missionary societies, tract societies, and moral societies, and extensive coverage of missionary work. In addition to religious matter, it published American and foreign state papers, a journal of Congress, news, geographical and statistical material on foreign countries, new book notices, agricultural reports, anecdotes, and articles on education, intemperance, and other topics. Poetry included Nathaniel Parker Willis's biblical poems. The *Recorder* was merged with the *Congregationalist* in 1867 to form the *Congregationalist and Boston Recorder*, later the *Congregationalist and Herald of Gospel Liberty*.

Recorder

| v1 | Jan. 3-Dec. 24, 1816 | APS II, Reel 97 |
| v1 | Jan. 3-Dec. 24, 1816 | APS II, Reel 539 |

Boston Recorder

v2-3	Jan. 7, 1817-Dec. 26, 1818	APS II, Reel 97
v4-7, no. 30	Jan. 2, 1818-July 27, 1822	Reel 98
v7, no. 31-v9	Aug. 3, 1822-Dec. 25, 1824	Reel 99
v2-4	Jan. 1, 1817-Dec. 1819	APS II, Reel 539
v5-8	Jan. 1820-Dec. 1823	Reel 540
v9	Jan.-Dec. 1824	Reel 541

Recorder and Telegraph

| v10 | Jan. 1-Dec. 30, 1825 | APS II, Reel 99 |
| v10 | Jan. 1-Dec. 30, 1825 | APS II, Reel 541 |

Boston Recorder and Religious Telegraph

| v11-14 | July 14, 1826-Dec. 1829 | APS II, Reel 541 |
| v15, no. 1-26 | Jan.-June 30, 1830 | Reel 542 |

Boston Recorder

v15, no. 27-v19	July 7, 1830-Dec. 1834	APS II, Reel 542
v20-24	Jan. 1835-Dec. 1839	Reel 543
v25-29	Jan. 1840-Dec. 1844	Reel 544

v30-33	Jan. 1845-Dec. 1848	Reel 545
v34, no. 1-19	Jan.-May 11, 1849	Reel 546

Puritan Recorder

v34, no. 20-v35	May 17, 1849-Dec. 1850	APS II, Reel 546

Congregationalist

v76-78	Jan. 6, 1891-Dec. 28, 1893	APS II, Reel 1911
v79	Jan. 4-Dec. 27, 1894	Reel 1912
v80	Jan. 3-Dec. 26, 1895	Reel 1913
v81	Jan. 2-Dec. 31, 1896	Reel 1914
v82	Jan. 7-Dec. 30, 1897	Reel 1915
v83	Jan. 6-Dec. 29, 1898	Reel 1916
v84	Jan. 5-Dec. 28, 1899	Reel 1917
v85	Jan. 4-Dec. 29, 1900	Reel 1918
v86, nos. 1-20	Jan. 5-May 18, 1901	Reel 1919

Congregationalist and Christian World

v86	May 25, 1901-Dec. 28, 1901	APS II, Reel 1919
v87	Jan. 4-Dec. 27, 1902	Reel 1920
v88	Jan. 3-Dec. 26, 1903	Reel 1921
v89	Jan. 2-Dec. 31, 1904	Reel 1922
v90	Jan. 7-Dec. 30, 1905	Reel 1923
v91	Jan. 6-Dec. 29, 1906	Reel 1924

Reels 539-546: Indexes follow each volume. Many pages are creased, tightly bound, and torn with loss of text. Pagination is irregular. Vols. 1-4 and 33 are repeated in microfilm edition. Best copy available for photographing.

Microfilm edition was prepared from CtY, DLC and ICU NNuT copies.

SEE ALSO: Herald of Gospel Liberty.

CONNECTICUT ACADEMY OF ARTS AND SCIENCES, NEW HAVEN. MEMOIRS. v. 1, pt. 1-4, 1810-1816; v. 2, July 1910- New Haven, 1810-

illus., plates (part col.) map, tables.

Vols 2-published under the auspices of Yale university. Vol. 1 comprises 4 parts (412 p.) 8, published 1810-16. Papers read before the Academy appeared chiefly in the American journal of science from 1818 until the commencement of the series of Transactions in 1866. (cf. Handbook of learned societies and institutions, American. 1908. p. 173) The publications of the Memoirs was resumed in July, 1910, in 4. On film: issues for 1810-1816.

The Connecticut Academy of Arts and Sciences was formed to combine the efforts of literary men in Connecticut "for the promotion of useful knowledge." This periodical was made up of papers presented to the academy. Most were on scientific topics— meteorology, mathematics, chemistry, and medicine.

v1	1810-1816	APS II, Reel 770

Microfilm edition was prepared from KMK copy.

THE CONNECTICUT COMMON SCHOOL JOURNAL AND ANNALS OF EDUCATION, pub. monthly under the direction of the Conn. state teachers' association. v. 1-21; Aug. 1838-Dec. 1866. Hartford, Printed by Case, Tiffany & Burnham.

v. illus., pl., port.

Vol. 1-4 have title: The Connecticut common school journal, pub. under the direction of the Board of Commissioners of common schools.

Edited by Henry Barnard and others. Vols. 9-21 called also new ser., v. 1-13. Superseded by Connecticut school journal.

Published irregularly and edited by Henry Barnard (who later became United States Commissioner of Education), the *Connecticut Common School Journal* was established as an organ of the Connecticut Board of Commissioners of Common Schools and was one of the most famous school periodicals of the time. It contained valuable articles, studies of education in England, annual reports, documents, and other entries devoted to professional pedagogy.

Cumulative Index 1-4	1838-1842	APS II, Reel 789

Connecticut Common School Journal.

v1-4	Aug. 1838-Sept. 1, 1842	APS II, Reel 789

Connecticut Common School Journal and Annals of Education

v5-nsv3	Sept. 1851-Dec. 1856	APS II, Reel 790
nsv4-13	Jan. 1857-Dec. 1866	Reel 791

Publication was suspended from September 1842 to September 1851 Vol. 5: Microfilm edition includes essays titled "Normal Schools in the United States" and "Normal Schools in Europe." Vol. 8 and New Series Vol. 11: Title pages are lacking. Pagination is irregular and some pages appear to be missing. Best copy available for photographing.

Microfilm edition was prepared from CtHT, CtHi, CtY, DHEW, Ia-T, MH, MiU and N copies.

CONNECTICUT EVANGELICAL MAGAZINE. *SEE* Connecticut Evangelical Magazine and Religious Intelligencer.

THE CONNECTICUT EVANGELICAL MAGAZINE AND RELIGIOUS INTELLIGENCER. v. 1-7; July 1800-June 1807; [new ser.] v. 1-8, Jan. 1808-Dec. 1815. Hartford, Printed by Hudson and Goodwin [etc.]

15 v. ports. Monthly.

Title varies: v. 1-7, The Connecticut evangelical magazine.

Superseded by Religious intelligencer. Cf. Union list of serials.

Begun at Hartford in 1800, this monthly ran, with only one interruption, for 15 years. Among the religious news it offered was news of missions and missionary and Bible societies, and on revivals and ordinations of ministers. Essays on doctrine and other moral and religious subjects were plentiful, and there were Bible studies, sermons, poetry, anecdotes, and biographical sketches.

Connecticut Evangelical Magazine

v1-7	July 1800-June 1807	APS II, Reel 14

Connecticut Evangelical Magazine and Religious Intelligencer

nsv1	Jan.-Dec. 1808	APS II, Reel 127
nsv2-6	Jan. 1809-Dec. 1813	Reel 128
nsv7-8	Jan. 1814-Dec. 1815	Reel 129

Microfilm edition was prepared from CtY copy.

SEE ALSO: Religious Intelligencer ... Containing the Principal Transactions ...

THE CONNECTICUT MAGAZINE; or, Gentleman's and Lady's monthly museum of knowledge & rational entertainment. v. 1, no. 1-6; Jan.-June 1801. Bridgeport, L. Beach & S. Thompson.

336 (i.e. 378) p. illus., ports.

This monthly miscellany was both entertaining and informative. It published foreign and domestic news and marriage and death notices, and recorded the proceedings of Congress. Literary material such as poetry, biographical and historical sketches, extracts from travel books, and miscellaneous essays were also included and several issues contained portraits.

v1, no.1-6   Jan.-June 1801   APS II, Reel 15

Microfilm edition was prepared from CtY copy.

CONNECTICUT SCHOOL JOURNAL. *SEE* Connecticut Common School Journal and Annals of Education.

CONNECTICUT REPUBLICAN MAGAZINE. v. 1, no.1-4; July 1802-[1803]. Suffield.

160 p.

Edited by L. Pratt.

The contents of this political magazine by Luther Pratt included discussions of the political controversies of the time, as well as biographical sketches of Thomas Jefferson and other statesmen, and some poetry. The Constitution and an extract from Thomas Paine's "Common Sense" were also included.

v1, no. 1-4   July 1802-[1803]   APS II, Reel 15

Microfilm edition was prepared from MBat and OCiW copies.

THE CONTINENT; an illustrated weekly magazine, conducted by Albion W. Tourgee. v. 1-6; Feb. 15, 1882-Aug. 20, 1884. Philadelphia, New York, Our Continent Pub. Co.

6 v. illus.

Vols. 1-2 have title: Our continent.

Absorbed Potter's American monthly in Oct. 1882.

Founded and financed by Judge Albion W. Tourgee and Robert S. Davis, the *Continent* was well printed and illustrated. The journal, designed after the popular monthlies of miscellany and opinion, was fully expected to become the leading journal of its kind.

An able staff was employed and contributions from prominent writers were published. Unfortunately, the magazine's expense was greater than anticipated and subcriptions did not meet the editor's expectations. Less than three years after its first issue, the *Continent* ceased publication at a tremendous loss to its backers.

Our Continent.
v1-2   Feb.-Dec. 1882   APS III, Reel 99

The Continent; an Illustrated Weekly Magazine.
v3-6   Jan. 1883-Dec. 1884   APS III, Reel 100

Vols. 1, 5, 6: Index and Table of Contents lacking. Best copy available for photographing.

Microfilm edition was prepared from OMC, NPV, NjP, Nh, N, MBAt, Ia, and TxU copies.

SEE ALSO: Potter's American Monthly.

* **THE CONTINENTAL MONTHLY**; devoted to literature and national policy. v. 1-6; Jan. 1862-Dec. 1864. New York and Boston, J. R. Gilmore, 1862; New York, J.F. Trow, 1862-64.

6 v.

The *Continental Monthly* was founded shortly after the start of the Civil War, and strongly favored Lincoln and the Republican Party.

Political in nature, the monthly provided a considerable amount of wit and humor, German writing, and fiction. Contributors included Charles Godfrey Leland (editor until April 1863), James Gilmore (the publisher), Henry Carey Lea, George H. Boker, N.L. Frothingham, Richard B. Kimball, and Martha Walker Cook (subsequent editor to Leland).

v1-6   Jan. 1862-Dec. 1864   APS III, Reel 140

Microfilm edition was prepared from MiU and MiGr copies.

THE CORRECTOR. By Toby Tickler. no. 1-10; Mar. 28-Apr. 26, 1804. New York [S. Gould] 1804.

40 p.

This comic magazine by "Toby Tickler, Esq." was devoted to political satire.

no. 1-10   Mar. 28-Apr. 26, 1804   APS II, Reel 15

Microfilm edition was prepared from MBat copy.

THE CORRESPONDENT. v. 1-5; Jan. 20, 1827-July 18, 1829. New York, 1827-29.

5 v. weekly.

G. Houston, editor.

This religious magazine offered a wide variety of material on the subject of religion. Its articles, some of them serialized, discussed the different religions, and dealt with the various aspects of religion, as well as covering a variety of philosophical and moral problems. In addition, it included Bible studies and published both proceedings and lectures of the Free Press Association.

v1-5   Jan. 20, 1827-July 18, 1829   APS II, Reel 384

Microfilm edition was prepared from DLC copy.

THE CORSAIR. A gazette of literature, art, dramatic criticism, fashion and novelty. v. 1; Mar. 16, 1839-Mar. 7, 1840. New York, 1839-40.

831 p. weekly.

N.P. Willis, T.O. Porter, editors.

Published by Nathaniel Parker Willis and his friend Dr. T.O. Porter, this weekly publication pirated its material from various sources, mainly European. Willis contributed some writings on art and drama, and then went to Europe, leaving Dr. Porter in charge, sending back Thackeray's travel letters as well as letters of his own, to stimulate the *Corsair's* failing fortunes. But despite good writing, the *Corsair* declined and ended publication in March of 1840.

v1   Mar. 16, 1839-Mar. 7, 1840   APS II, Reel 384

Microfilm edition was prepared from DLC copy.

THE COSMOPOLITAN; a monthly illustrated magazine. v. 1-78, no. 3; Mar. 1886-Mar. 1925. New York [etc.] Schlicht & Field [etc.]

78 v. illus., plates, ports.

No numbers issued for July and Aug. 1888; Feb. 1920. Title varies slightly. Subtitle omitted after Apr. 1905. Edited by J.B. Walker, 1886(?)-June(?) 1905. Published by International Magazine Co., May 1905 on. Merged into Hearsts' international, later Hearst's international combined with cosmopolitan. On film: v. 1-42, Mar. 1886-Apr. 1907.

Published by the firm of Schlicht and Field of Rochester, this general literary magazine was moved to New York after a year and enlarged to 80 pages, but nevertheless the firm failed and the magazine passed through several hands before being bought in 1889 by John Brisben Walker, who edited it for 16 years. During Walker's first years of editorship, fiction and poetry were good and there were travel articles, book reviews, and a "Social Problems" department. By the end of 1892, *Cosmopolitan* had become one of the country's leading illustrated magazines. Walker was particularly interested in transportation; *Cosmopolitan's* consistent interest in aeronautics was unmatched by any other magazine of the period, and railroads, sailing ships, subways, and balloons were also given attention. The short story became important in the late nineties, with three or four in each issue, including writings by Rudyard Kipling, Mark Twain, Jack London, and Edith Wharton. By 1905, however, Walker had become too involved in automobile manufacturing to devote time to his magazine, and therefore he sold it to W.R. Hearst.

Under Hearst, the *Cosmopolitan* was more sensational than before. Fiction continued to be plentiful; some of Jack London's best stories were printed, and other writers included Ellis Parker Butler, E. Phillips Oppenheim, Bruno Lessing, and P.G. Wodehouse. Muckraking articles became important during the early years of Hearst's ownership, but in 1912 the interest in muckraking declined, and fiction became dominant. Stories such as Robert W. Chambers' "The Common Law" became standard fare, and sex was the dominant subject from 1912 until 1918. During the editorship of Ray Long, which began in 1918, fiction by H.G. Wells, Somerset Maugham, Edna Ferber, Sinclair Lewis, and Theodore Dreiser appeared. In 1925 Hearst consolidated his two general illustrated magazines under the title *Hearst's International Combined with Cosmopolitan.*

v1-2	Mar. 1886-Feb. 1887	APS III, Reel 660
v3-7	Mar. 1887-Oct. 1889	Reel 661
v8-12	Nov. 1889-Apr. 1892	Reel 662
v13-16	May 1892-Apr. 1894	Reel 663
v17-21	May 1894-Oct. 1896	Reel 664
v22-26	Nov. 1896-Oct. 1899	Reel 665
v27-31	May 1899-Oct. 1901	Reel 666
v32-36	Nov. 1901-Apr. 1904	Reel 667
v37-41	May 1904-Oct. 1906	Reel 668
v42	Nov. 1906-Apr. 1907	Reel 669

Some pages are stained or torn. Vol. 9: title page, table of contents, and index are missing; not available for photographing. Vol. 11 contains a supplement.

Microfilm edition was prepared from IC, InU, MiU, NBuG, and NjP copies.

THE COUNTRY COURIER. v. 1-2, no. 32; June 3, 1816-Mar. 24, 1817. New York.

2 v. semiweekly (irregular)

Supersedes the Examiner, New York, 1813-16. Edited by B. Gardenier.

Film covers: v. 1, no. 1-39, v. 2, no. 1-32; June 3, 1816-Oct. 21, 1816, Dec. 5, 1816- Mar. 24, 1817.

This semi-weekly magazine superseded the *Examiner* and was also edited by Barent Gardenier. While the *Examiner* was mainly a political magazine, the *Courier* focused on all kinds of news— foreign, domestic, local, and political, as well as the proceedings of Congress and the state legislature. Much of the material was selected from other papers, particularly the *New-York Courier,* a daily paper. There was also a column on literature called "The Critic," and some poetry and anecdotes.

v1-2   June 3, 1816-Mar. 24, 1817   APS II, Reel 100

SEE ALSO: Examiner; Containing Political Essays on the Most Important Events of the Time ... *and* Independent.

COURIER DE BOSTON; affiches, annonces, et avis. no. 1-26; 23 avril-15 oct. 1789. [Boston, S. Hall]

208 p. Weekly.

Printed in the French language, its chief functions were to further understanding and friendship between the French and American people and to print a digest of domestic and foreign news.

no. 1-26   Apr. 23-Oct. 15, 1789   APS I, Reel 10

Microfilm edition was prepared from MWA copy.

THE CRISIS. Devoted to the support of the democratic principles of Jefferson. v. 1 (no. 1-35); Mar. 7-Oct. 28, 1840, Richmond, Va., 1840.

280 p. weekly.

Caption title.

This weekly political sheet contained mostly political material, short news items, coverage of elections, Congressional debates, and proceedings of Congress.

v1, no. 1-35   Mar. 7-Oct. 28, 1840   APS II, Reel 385

Microfilm edition was prepared from DLC copy.

THE CRITIC. By Geoffrey Juvenal, esq. [pseud.] no. 1-20; Jan. 29-May 10, 1820. [Philadelphia] 1820.

177 p. Semiweekly, Jan. 29-Mar. 22, 1820; irregular, Mar. 29-May 10, 1820.

The *Critic* was a weekly satirical publication conducted by Geoffrey Juvenal; each number contained one or two essays and occasionally the satire was in the form of a letter or poem.

no. 1-20   Jan. 29-May 10, 1820   APS II, Reel 100

THE CRITIC. A weekly review of literature, fine arts, and the drama. v. 1-2, no. 7; Nov. 1, 1828-June 20, 1829. New York.

2 v.

Merged into New York mirror: a weekly gazette of literature and the fine arts.

Editor: 1828-William Leggett.

This literary weekly, begun in November, 1828 by William Leggett, met with so little encouragement that after six months its editor combined it with the *Mirror*. Leggett had had wide experience on the sea and on the western frontier, and these settings were reflected in the stilted but sometimes racy tales which he printed in his magazine. His longer story, "The Squatters," ran as a serial and he also wrote essays, poetry, and dramatic criticism and reviews; some of the best theatrical criticism of the times is contained in the *Critic*.

v1-2, no.7   Nov. 1, 1828-June 20, 1829   APS II, Reel 385

Microfilm edition was prepared from CSmH and NN copies.

THE CRITIC; an illustrated monthly review of literature, art, and life. v. 1-49, no. 3; Jan. 15, 1881-Sept. 1906. New York, Critic Printing and Pub Co.

49 v. illus., plates (part col.) ports., facsims. Biweekly 1881-82; weekly, 1883-June 1898; monthly, July 1898-Sept. 1906. Vols. 4-20 are called "New ser., v. 1-17", v. 21-34, "New ser., v. 18-31, old ser., v. 21-34". Absorbed Good literature in Jan. 1884, the Literary world in Jan. 1905.

Title varies: Jan. 1881-Dec. 1883, The Critic; a fortnightly review (1883, "a weekly review") of literature, the fine arts, music, and the drama. Jan.-June 1884, The Critic and good literature. July 1884-Dec. 1885, The Critic: a literary weekly, critical and eclectic. Jan. 1886-June 1898, The Critic: a weekly review of literature and the arts. July 1898- Sept. 1906, The Critic (Jan-Dec. 1905, "The Critic and literary world") an illustrated monthly review of literature, art, and life.

Editors: 1881-1901, Jeannette L. Gilder, J.B. Gilder.–1902-06, Jeannette L. Gilder. Merged into Putnam's monthly.

Throughout the early file of the *Critic*, the book review section was the outstanding feature. These reviews were written at first by the editors, Jeanette and Joseph Gilder, sister and brother, with the help of James Herbert Morse. Later contributions by James A. Harrison, W.J. Rolfe, J.Ranken Towse, Thomas Bailey Aldrich, Richard W. Gilder, and Edward Everett Hale also appeared.

In addition to the review section, departments of drama, fine arts, news notices, literature and poetry were well written and edited. Walter Whitman and Joel Chandler Harris were important correspondents. Discussions of popular fads found their way into the pages of the *Critic*; a few campaigns were actively supported, such as the construction of the Washington Memorial Arch in marble; and English literature was closely followed with an overly critical eye.

Putnam's purchased the weekly in 1898 turning it into a monthly. The book review section was shortened although it was still written by Jeanette Gilder. Illustrations were added; articles and poetry increased.

Critic
v1-3   Jan. 15, 1881-Dec. 1883   APS III, Reel 101

Critic and Good Literature
v4   Jan. 1884-June 1884   APS III, Reel 101

Critic.
v5-7	July 1884-Dec. 26, 1885	APS III, Reel 101
v8-15	Jan. 2, 1886-Dec. 28, 1889	Reel 102
v16-21	Jan. 4, 1890-Dec. 31, 1892	Reel 103
v22-26	Jan. 7, 1893-June 29, 1895	Reel 104
v27-31	July 6, 1895-Dec. 25, 1897	Reel 105
v32-37	Jan. 1, 1898-Dec. 1900	Reel 106
v38-43	Jan. 1901-Dec. 1903	Reel 107
v44-49	Jan. 1904-Sept. 1906	Reel 108

The following volumes have missing advertising pages: Vols. 2-5, 8, 11, 35, and 48. The following volumes have some torn pages: Vol. 13. (pgs. 143-44), vol. 15)pgs. 127-28), vol. 16 (pgs. 89-92), vol. 38 (pgs. 425-432).Additional notes: Pagination is irregular. Vol. 3: Index and Table of Contents are lacking. Best copy available for photographing. Vol. 4: title page is missing. Vol. 15: Advertising pages are bound out of order. Vol. 42: title page missing. Pg. 151 stained. Vol. 44: pgs. 567-68 missing in number only. Pg. 576 does not appear to exist. Index lists "Books Received" as being on pg. 576; actually found on pgs. 28-32 of advertising pages. Vol. 46-47: pgs. 1, 97, 193, 289 and 385 were not available for photographing. Vol. 46: Table of Contents lists "Books received" which is found on pgs. 27-30 of advertising pages.

Microfilm edition was prepared from NcD, C, NPV, MiEM, and CCC copies.

SEE ALSO: Literary World; A Monthly Review of Current Literature.

CRITIC AND GOOD LITERATURE. *SEE* Critic; An Illustrated Monthly Review of Literature, Art, And Life.

THE CULTIVATOR. v. 1-10; Mar. 1834-43; new ser., v. 1-9, 1844-52; 3d ser., v. 1-13, 1853-65. Albany, L. Tucker.

32 v. in 27. illus. monthly.

Published 1834-37 by the New York State Agricultural Society. Absorbed Genesee farmer and gardener's journal, Jan. 1840. Absorbed by Cultivator and country gentleman (later Country gentleman) Vols. 1-3 are 2d ed.

This monthly magazine was conducted by J. Buel until it was bought in 1839 by Luther Tucker who remained editor until he merged it with the *Country Gentleman* in 1865. Devoted to agriculture and horticulture, the periodical featured articles on a wide variety of topics—crops, livestock, and flowers, diseases of plants and animals and their treatments, improved agricultural methods, illustrated descriptions of farm machinery and implements, and information on silk culture and butter-making. In addition, space was given to coverage of agricultural societies, extracts from various journals, letters from readers, listings of new books, and some ads.

v1-4	Mar. 1834-Feb. 1838	APS II, Reel 514
v5-nsv4	Mar. 1838-Dec. 1847	Reel 515
nsv5-s3v2	Jan. 1848-Dec. 1854	Reel 516
s3v3-9	Jan. 1855-Dec. 1861	Reel 517
s3v10-13	Jan. 1862-Dec. 1865	Reel 518

Several pages have faded print and stains with some loss of text. nsv9: Pagination is irregular.

Microfilm edition was prepared from DLC, IU and OU copies.

SEE ALSO: Genesee Farmer and Gardener's Journal.

CULTIVATOR AND COUNTRY GENTLEMAN. *SEE* Cultivator.

CUMBERLAND PRESBYTERIAN QUARTERLY. *SEE* Cumberland Presbyterian Review.

CUMBERLAND PRESBYTERIAN QUARTERLY RE-VIEW. *SEE* Cumberland Presbyterian Review.

THE CUMBERLAND PRESBYTERIAN REVIEW. v. 1-20, 1845-1884. St. Louis, Mo., W.C. Logan.

20 v. Monthly, 1845-18; quarterly, 1870(?)-1884. "Suspended during the war." cf. Mott's history of American magazines, 1938. Volumes 6(?)-20, also called new ser. (2d ser.) v. 1(?)-15. v. 16-20, also numbered v. 1-5.

Title varies: 1845-18, The Theological medium; a monthly journal. devoted to doctrinal discussion, experimental and practical religion, education, benevolent enterprise, and church polity.—1870(?)-79, The Theological medium; a Cumberland Presbyterian quarterly.—1880, The Cumberland Presbyterian quarterly.—1881-83, The Cumberland Presbyterian quarterly review.

Imprint varies: 1845-18, Uniontown, Pa. and Louisville, Ky., Milton Bird. —1870(?)-72(?), Nashville, T.C. Blake.—1873(?)79, Nashville, M.B. DeWitt.—1880-83, Lebanon, Tenn., the Theological faculty of Cumberland University. No more published?

This review began as the *Theological Medium* in 1845 at Uniontown, Pennsylvania, with Milton Bird as editor and publisher. In 1848 Bird took the publication to Louisville. Although suspended during the war, the review was revived at Nashville in 1871, with T.C. Blake as editor. In 1880 J.D. Kirkpatrick took it to Lebanon, Tennessee, where it was edited by the faculty of Cumberland University under the title *Cumberland Presbyterian Quarterly*. W.C. Logan took it to St. Louis in 1884 where it expired as the *Cumberland Presbyterian Review.*

Theological Medium

v2-9	Nov. 1846-Oct. 1873	APS II, Reel 1368
v11-15	Jan. 1875-Oct. 1879	Reel 1369

Cumberland Presbyterian Quarterly.

v16	Jan. 1880-Oct. 1880	APS II, Reel 1369

Cumberland Presbyterian Quarterly Review.

v17-18	Jan. 1881-Oct. 1882	APS II, Reel 1369
v19	Jan. 1883-Oct. 1883	Reel 1370

Cumberland Presbyterian Review.

v20	Jan. 1884-Oct. 1884	APS II, Reel 1370

Vols. 1, 3, 5, 6, 8, 10 and 14 are not available for photographing. Several pages are stained and have print faded. Best copy available for photographing. Pagination is irregular. Vol. 2: Title pages and tables of contents for issues 1 and 2 are torn, Issue 2, title page is misdated. Issue 12, title page is missing. Pgs. 335-36 and 551-72 are torn with loss of text. Vol. 4: Some pages are cropped. Title page for issue 2 is missing. Vol. 7: Issue 1, table of contents is taped with some print covered. Vol. 12: Cover and content pages are bound and photographed at the end of the volume. Vol. 13 and 15: Pgs. are torn with some loss of text. Title page and contents are missing for issue 2.

Microfilm edition was prepared from DLC, MiD and WHi copies.

CURRENT HISTORY. *SEE* Forum and Century.

CURRENT LITERATURE. *SEE* Current Opinion.

CURRENT OPINION. v.1-78, no.4; July 1888-Apr. 1925. New York, Current Literature.

78 v. illus., ports. monthly.

Title varies: July 1888-Dec. 1912, Current literature. Absorbed Democracy, May 1920. Editors: July 1905-Aug. 1922, E.J. Wheeler (with F. Crane, May 1920-Aug. 1922).—Sept. 1922-Aug. 1925, F. Crane. Merged into Literary digest.—Union list of serials.

Current Opinion was, especially in its early years, one of the most attractive and entertaining eclectic journals ever published in English. Founded in 1888 by Frederick M. Somers, former editor of the San Francisco *Argonaut,* under the name of *Current literature,* this magazine's attractions were its great variety, short well-edited pieces and quality paper and printing. Its original emphasis was literary and included as regular features literary gossip and news, poetry, wit and humor, short stories and sketches, and some historical and scientific matter. These early issues are an excellent source of information about U.S. social history because they are full of sidelights on the American scene.

The selling of the magazine in 1891 by Somers began a series of changing editorships and changing formats. It went from quarto form to octavo form and back again several times. It also became more departmentalized with as many as 25 or more departments per issue. They ranged greatly and included "Current Literary Comment and Criticism," "Verse from Books and Magazines," "Random Reading: Current Topics," "Vanity Fair: Fads and Fashions," and "Historical, Statistical, General."

Difficulties began to develop around 1895 due to the increasing reluctance of magazines and newspapers to have their best articles reprinted by a competitor and also due to a decline in readership.

With the absorption of *Current History,* in March 1903, *Current Literature* increased its current affairs coverage by including a record of the month's great events, current newspaper cartoons, and "Books on Vital Issues."

Beginning in 1905, a former editor of *Literary Digest,* Edward J. Wheeler, became editor and revitalized *Current Literature* by adding a review of world events, a monthly "best" short story, and condensation and review of a play with illustration. In 1910, it absorbed *Van Norden's Magazine,* another current affairs magazine, in 1913 changed its name to *Current Opinion,* and in 1920 absorbed *Democracy.* Throughout these and other editorial changes, the content stayed very much the same.

In 1925, it merged with its long-time contemporary publication, the *Literary Digest.*

Current Literature

v1	July-Dec. 1888	APS III, Reel 689
v2-6	Jan. 1889-Apr. 1891	Reel 690
v7-11	May 1891-Dec. 1892	Reel 691
v12-15	Jan. 1893-June 1894	Reel 692
v16-19	July 1894-June 1896	Reel 693
v20-23	July 1896-June 1898	Reel 694
v24-28	July 1898-June 1900	Reel 695
v29-32	July 1900-June 1902	Reel 696
v33-36	July 1902-June 1904	Reel 697
v37-40	July 1904-June 1906	Reel 698
v41-44	July 1906-June 1908	Reel 699
v45-48	July 1908-June 1910	Reel 700
v49-52	July 1910-June 1912	Reel 701
v53	July 1912-Dec. 1912	Reel 702

Current Opinion

v54-56	Jan. 1913-June 1914	APS III, Reel 702
v57-61	July 1914-Dec. 1916	Reel 703
v62-66	Jan. 1917-June 1919	Reel 704
v67-70	July 1919-June 1921	Reel 705
v71-74	July 1921-June 1923	Reel 706
v75-78	July 1923-Apr. 1925	Reel 707

Vol. 13: P. 392 is stained. Vol. 78 lacks title page and index.

Microfilm edition was prepared from C, CS, Co, ICham, IU, MdBE, Mi, MiU, MnU, N, NdU, Nh, and OU copies.

THE CYNICK. By Growler Gruff, esquire [pseud.] Aided by a confederacy of lettered dogs. v. 1; Sept. 21-Dec. 12, 1811. Philadelphia, 1812.

1 p.l., iv, 210 p. weekly.

"The principal purpose of the little paper was to censure ... the theatrical magazines," p. 241.

This short-lived satirical magazine by "Growler Gruff" attacked the theater, local government, politics, and other aspects of life. A series titled "The Groans of the Town" presented satirical poetry.

v1, nos. 1-12   Sept. 21-Dec. 1811   APS II, Reel 100

DAEDELUS. *SEE* American Academy of Arts and Sciences, Boston. Proceedings.

THE DAGUERREOTYPE: a magazine of foreign literature and science: comp. chiefly from the periodical publications of England, France, and Germany. v. 1-3; Aug. 7, 1847-Apr. 14, 1849. Boston, J.M. Whittemore.

3 v. semimonthly (irregular)

Compiled chiefly from European periodicals, this eclectic magazine published choice articles from the best English reviews and magazines, and translations of selected articles from German and French publications. Its varied contents included stories and anecdotes, travel sketches, biography, literary and scientific news, and articles on history, geography, and on various countries and people. In addition, short reviews, listings of the more important new or forthcoming books, and some original articles appeared in its pages.

v1-3   Aug. 1847-Apr. 1849   APS II, Reel 473

Indexes are bound and photographed at the end of each volume.

Microfilm edition was prepared from MiU and NN copies.

* THE DANVILLE QUARTERLY REVIEW. Ed. by an association of ministers. v. 1-4; Mar. 1861-Dec. 1864. Danville, Ky., and Cincinnati, R.H. Collins, 1861-64.

4 v.

R.J. Breckinridge, F.P. Humphrey, and others, editors. v. 2-4 have cover-title Danville review.

The *Danville Quarterly Review* was founded to provide a more regional Presbyterian magazine than the eastern publications. Its chief editor was Robert J. Breckinridge. He embraced the ideals of the Union and of the Constitution, but rejected the idea of emancipation. Many of the associate editors sympathized with the South, quarreled with Breckinridge, and finally resigned.

Although the review's purpose was primarily theological, it became better known as a vehicle for editor Breckinridge's political views.

v1-4   Mar. 1861-Dec. 1864   APS III, Reel 186

Vols. 1-4: lack indexes. Please refer to the Table of Contents.

Microfilm edition was prepared from MiU copy.

THE DAWN, a semi-monthly magazine: containing original and selected essays, anecdotes, &c. in prose and poetry. Devoted to the instruction and amusement of the rising generation. v. 1, no. 1-12; May 1-Nov. 1, 1822. Wilmington, Del.

98 p.

Conducted by Lewis Wilson, this semi-monthly was intended for the instruction and amusement of youth and contained selections from other youth magazines as well as contributions from readers. Its varied contents also included poetry and anecdotes, letters to the editor, and essays on conduct, morals, love, and marriage..

v1, no. 1-12   May 1-Nov. 1, 1822   APS II, Reel 100

* DEBOW'S COMMERCIAL REVIEW OF THE SOUTH & WEST. *SEE* Debow's Review.

* DEBOW'S REVIEW. Agricultural, commercial, industrial progress & resources. v. 1-34, Jan. 1846-July/Aug. 1864; after the war series, v. 1-8, Jan. 1866-Oct. 1870; new ser., v. 1, no. 1-4, Oct. 1879-June 1880. New Orleans, J.D.B. DeBow, 1846-80.

48 v. illus., plates, ports., maps. monthly.

Beginning with v. 7 (July-Dec. 1849) new series are started at frequent intervals, and the numbering on the title-pages and captions is more or less irregular. Publication suspended Jan.-June 1849, inclusive; Sept. 1862-June 1864; Sept. 1864-Dec. 1865; Nov. 1870-Sept. 1879; Jan.-May 1880. Ceased publication June 1880? Title varies: Jan. 1846-June 1850, The Commercial review of the South and West; a monthly journal of trade, commerce, commercial polity, agriculture, manufactures, internal improvements and general literature (cover-title, Feb. 1847-June 1850: DeBow's commercial review of the South & West) July 1850-Dec. 1852, DeBow's review of the southern and western states. Devoted to commerce, agriculture, manufactures. Jan. 1853-July/Aug. 1864, DeBow's review and industrial resources, statistics, etc. Devoted to commerce, agriculture, manufactures. (Volumes from July 1861 to Aug. 1864 want title-pages; cover-title: DeBow's review. Industrial resources, etc.) Jan. 1866-Dec. 1867, DeBow's review, devoted to the restoration of the southern states. Jan. 1868-June 1880, DeBow's review ... Agricultural, commercial, industrial progress & resources (cover-title, Apr. 1869-Oct. 1870; DeBow's New Orleans monthly review).

Editors: Jan. 1846-Feb. 1867, J.D.B. DeBow.–Apr. 1867-Feb. 1868, R.G. Barnwell, E.Q. Bell.–Mar. 1868-Dec. 1879, W.M. Burwell. Published in New Orleans, 1846-52; New Orleans and Washington, 1853-60; New Orleans and Charleston, S.C., 1861-62; Columbia, S.C. 1864; New Orleans, etc., 1866-80. The Agricultural review of New York (established 1881) absorbed DeBow's review in Jan. 1884.

In establishing his famous journal of commerce, James De Bow committed himself to the principle that the South, lagging behind the North in the development of transportation, manufacturing, and agriculture, could best realize its potential by united effort with the North. The first number was filled with useful information about southern and western commerce and resources and the last 20 pages gave "Southern and Western Statistics," figures on foreign trade, market news, and brief notes on publication. Agricultural material is abundant in the file: cotton was a prominent topic, and cotton mills for the South were advocated. Rice growing, soils, forestry and plantation management were also discussed. Education was a common topic and railways, canals, river control, and plank roads also received much attention. The various southern commercial conventions were reported in detail. *De Bow's* was never distinguished in literature, which was originally relegated to a very humble place, but in 1850 a literary department was introduced and thereafter some stories, poems, occasional literary criticism, and some travel articles appeared. Politics entered the *Review* after the suspension of 1849. By this time, the unrest in the South could not be ignored and the slavery question finally became De Bow's major interest. He strongly advocated slavery and called for a greater independence of the Southern states. From month to month the *Review* discussed secession and slavery with eloquence and often with passion. However, following a suspension in 1864 and 1865 *De Bow's* returned urging acceptance of the reconstruction program of the Union and President Johnson. Publication ceased in 1880 due to the increased publishing expenses.

Commercial Review of the South and West
v1-4	Jan. 1846-Dec. 1847	APS II, Reel 382
v5-8	Jan. 1848-June 1850	Reel 383

De Bow's Review of the Southern and Western States
v9	July-Dec. 1850	APS II, Reel 383
v10-13	Jan. 1851-Dec. 1852	APS II, Reel 855

De Bow's Review and Industrial Resources, Statistics, etc.
v14	Jan.-June 1853	APS II, Reel 855
v15-19	July 1853-Dec. 1855	Reel 856
v20-24	Jan. 1856-June 1858	Reel 857
v25-28	July 1858-June 1860	Reel 858
v29-31	July 1860-Dec. 1861	Reel 859
v32-34	Jan. 1862-July/Aug. 1864	Reel 860

De Bow's Review, Devoted to the Restoration of the Southern States
After the war series 1-3 Jan. 1866-June 1867		APS II, Reel 860
After the war series 4 July-Dec. 1867		Reel 861

De Bow's Review
After the war series 5-6 Jan. 1868-Dec. 1869		APS II, Reel 861
After the war series 7-8 Jan. 1870-June 1880		Reel 862

Microfilm edition includes: Index to the second series of ten volumes. From July 1851 to June 1856. Pagination is irregular. Some advertisement pages are missing. Volume numbering for Vols. 10-34 is irregular. For the convenience of the reader we have used the Old Series numbering. Preceding Vol. 20 is an index to vols. 11-20. Vol. 29 and Vols. 31-34 lack indexes. Please refer to the tables of contents at the beginning of each issue. After the War Series Vols. 5-8 and the June 1880 issue lack indexes. Please refer to the cumulative Index on reel 855. Vols. 7-8 are combined. October 1879 and June 1880 are Volumes of one issue only.

Microfilm edition was prepared from MiD, RPB, KyL and Ms-Ar copies.

THE DEBTORS' JOURNAL. v. 1, no. 1-6; Sept. 23, 1820-Feb. 24, 1821. Boston.

1 v. Monthly.

Vol. 1, no. 1 is in Thorndike pamphlets, v. 61, no. 17; v. 1, no. 4 is in Moore pamphlets (AC901.M7), v. 126, no. 11; v. 1, no. 6 is in Thorndike pamphlets, v. 58, no.22. On film: no.1, 4, and 6.

The "association of gentlemen" who conducted this 16-page monthly believed that the debtors' laws of that time were extremely oppressive to the debtors and of little help to creditors, and they substantiated their claims by publishing articles on the bad effects of debtors' laws, on bankruptcy law, and on imprisonment. Some poetry was also included.

v1, nos.1, 4, and 6 Sept. 23, 1820-Feb. 24, 1821 APS II, Reel 100

DELINEATOR. *SEE* Pictorial Review.

DEMOCRACY. *SEE* Current Opinion.

* **DEMOCRATIC REVIEW.** *SEE* United States Democratic Review.

THE DESSERT TO THE TRUE AMERICAN. v. 1-2, no. 7; July 14, 1798-Aug. 19, 1799. [Philadelphia, S.F. Bradford]

2 v. weekly.

Supersedes the Philadelphia Minerva. Cf. Evans. American bibliography. Title varies: July 14-21, 1798, The Desert to the true American. Supplement to the True American. Cf. Evans. American bibliography.

Film incomplete: v. 2, no. 6 wanting.

A weekly literary magazine which presented much fiction, including serialized romances, fragments, tales, anecdotes, and poetry as well as essays and articles mainly addressed to women and concerned with manners and morals.

v1-2, no 7 July 14, 1798-Aug. 19, 1799 APS I, Reel 12

Some pages are missing.

Microfilm edition was prepared from MWA copy.

SEE ALSO: Philadelphia Minerva.

*THE DIAL: a magazine for literature, philosophy, and religion. v. 1-4; July 1840-Apr. 1844. Boston, James Munroe [etc.] London, John Chapman [etc.]

4 v. quarterly.

Editors: Margaret Fuller, R.W. Emerson, George Ripley.

The *Dial* has probably received more attention from the literary historian than any other periodical published in this country, and this is because for four years this quarterly journal of opinion and belles-lettres served as spokesman for New England transcendentalism. Margaret Fuller was editor of the *Dial* for the first half of its four years; and Ralph Waldo Emerson took over the editorship for the second half of its lifetime. The first number contained essays and poems by Miss Fuller, Emerson, Christopher Pearce Cranch, John Sullivan Dwight, Amos Bronson Alcott, W.H. Channing, and others; most of these people became chief writers during Miss Fuller's editorship. Under Emerson the *Dial* had somewhat more unity. The leading contributors were William Ellery Channing and Thoreau; Miss Fuller, Theodore Parker and Charles Lane were also prominent. Included in the contents were extracts from oriental religious writings, Emerson's "Lectures on the Times," and Channing's poetry.

v1-4 July 1840-Apr. 1844 APS II, Reel 546

Microfilm edition was prepared from MiU copy.

THE DIAL: a monthly magazine for literature, philosophy and religion. v.1; Jan.-Dec. 1860. Cincinnati, 1860.

778 p.

Editor: M.D. Conway.

Moncure D. Conway edited and wrote most of the articles for the *Dial*. In addition, O. B. Frothingham contributed to it, and poetry by Ralph Waldo Emerson, Frank Sanborn, and Myron Benton appeared. Although the magazine lasted only one year, it is remembered for its controversial articles on spiritualism and emancipation, including one article on the well-known John Brown. It ceased publication because of the labor required by the editor, and a lack of subscribers.

v1   Jan.-Dec. 1860   APS III, Reel 7

Vol. 1: pagination begins on page 9.

Microfilm edition was prepared from MiU copy.

* **THE DIAL**; a semi-monthly journal of literary criticism, discussion, and information. vol. 1-86 no. 7; May 1880-July 1929. Chicago, Dial Co.

86 v.

Subtitle varies.

Francis F. Browne established the *Dial* in Chicago in 1880, serving as editor until his death in 1913. Consistently conservative in its literary criticism, the *Dial* left European literature virtually untouched, but managed to give a good deal of attention to the British writers. Joseph Kirkland, William M. Payne, and many others contributed reviews.

Waldo R. Browne assumed editorship after his father. During a reorganization in 1916, the responsiblity passed to Clinton J. Massock. Under his editorship, the *Dial* little resembled the former volumes. The liberal minded editor included foreign literature and gave special attention to public issues. World reconstruction became a cause.

Three years later, Scofield Taylor purchased the *Dial*. The contents, again overhauled, resembled a magazine of arts and letters penned by scores of modernistic authors. The magazine failed to gain a wide circulation and publication ceased with the July 1929 issue.

v1-9	May 1880-Apr. 1889	APS III, Reel 187
v10-17	May 1889-Dec. 16, 1894	Reel 188
v18-24	Jan. 1, 1895-June 16, 1898	Reel 189
v25-30	July 1, 1898-June 16, 1901	Reel 190
v31-37	July 1, 1901-Dec. 16, 1904	Reel 191
v38-44	Jan. 1, 1905-June 16, 1908	Reel 192
v45-51	July 1, 1908-Dec. 16, 1911	Reel 193
v52-58	Jan. 1, 1912-June 10, 1915	Reel 194
v59-64	June 24, 21915-June 6, 1918	Reel 195
v65-69	July 18, 1918-Dec. 1920	Reel 196
v70-73	Jan. 1921-Dec. 1922	Reel 197
v74-78	Jan. 1923-June 1925	Reel 198
v79-84	July 1925-June 1928	Reel 199
v85-86	July 1928-July 1929	Reel 200

Some pages are stained or have print missing; some pages are missing or torn. Vols. 11, 12, 29, 31, 37, 44, 45, 49-55, 60-63: advertising pages not available for photographing. Vol. 74: April portrait "Lucreta" not available for photographing. Vol. 76: April portrait "Enfant an Cheval" not available for photographing. Vol. 82: April illustration, "Landscape" not available for photographing.

SEE ALSO: Chap-Book; Semi-Monthly.

DIANA, and ladies' spectator. v. 1, no. 1-4, 1822. Boston, 1822.

1 v. (unpaged)

Only four numbers of this small ladies' magazine were published.

Edited by M.L. Rainsford, this eight-page weekly proposed to amuse and instruct ladies, and included occasional musical pieces, poetry and tales, correspondence, and departments of science, religion, biography, and miscellany.

v1, nos. 1-4   1822   APS II, Reel 101

DIETETIC GAZETTE. *SEE* Medical Times and Register.

THE DISTRICT SCHOOL JOURNAL OF THE STATE OF NEW YORK. v. 1-12; Mar. 1840-Apr. 1852. Albany, Press of C. Van Benthuysen.

12 v. monthly.

Editors: 1840-45, Francis Dwight.—1846-47, S.S. Randall.—1848-49, W.H. Campbell.—1850, S.S. Randall.—1851-52, Edward Cooper.

This journal was subsidized by the state and was one of the more important periodicals concerned with education during the mid-1800s. It was devoted to the district schools, and was intended to publish decisions of the Superintendent of Common Schools, and make known all valuable improvements in means and methods of instruction.

v1-12   Mar. 25, 1840-Apr. 1852   APS II, Reel 770

Pagination is irregular. Vol. 1: Pages are stained and creased. Lacks title page and index. Vols. 3, 10-12: Lack index and table of contents. Vols. 5, 7: index appears at the end of the volumes. Vol. 9 is tightly bound.

Microfilm edition was prepared from ICRL and N copies.

DIXIE FARMER. *SEE* Southern Cultivator.

THE DOLLAR MAGAZINE. v. 1-8; Jan. 1848-Dec. 1851. New York, 1848-51.

8 v. in 4. illus., plates, ports. monthly.

Title varies: v. 1-6 (1848-50) Holdens dollar magazine of criticisms, biographies, sketches, essays, tales, reviews, poetry, etc., etc. (Subtitle varies slightly) v. 7-8 (1851) The Dollar magazine. (Added t.-p. for v. 7-8 retains earlier title)

C.F. Briggs, editor, Jan. 1848-June 1850. Published by C.W. Holden, 1848-Oct. 1849; W.H. Dietz (later Fowler & Dietz) Nov. 1849-Mar. 1851; E.A. & G.L. Duyckinck, Apr.-Dec. 1851. Merged into the North American miscellany.

Founded by Charles W. Holden, the *Dollar Magazine* was a cheap miscellany and was part of the movement for cheap literature which was most noticeable in the weekly field. It contained poetry and tales, sketches, essays, reviews, and illustrated biographies.

Holdens Dollar Magazine of Criticisms, Biographies, Sketches, Essays, Tales ...
v1-6   Jan. 1848-Dec. 1850   APS II, Reel 604

Dollar Magazine
v7-8   Jan.-Dec. 1851   APS II, Reel 604

Microfilm edition was prepared from DLC copy.

SEE ALSO: North American Miscellany and Dollar Magazine.

THE DOLLAR MAGAZINE; a literary, political, advertising, and miscellaneous newspaper. v. 1 (no. 1-11); Jan.-Dec. 1833. Philadelphia, E. Littell, 1833.

220 p. monthly (irregular)

Various paging. No. 10 bears date, Dec. 8, 1833; no. 11 (last number) undated.

This monthly magazine featured many long tales by the English author Harriet Martineau and contained poetry, humorous articles, a religious department, news, and ads for new books.

v1, no. 1-11   Jan.-Dec. 1833   APS II, Reel 385

Microfilm edition was prepared from DLC copy.

DOLLAR MAGAZINE; A monthly gazette of current literature, music and art. v. 1-2; 1841-42. New York, Wilson, 1841-42.

2 v. illus. (incl. ports.) plates.

Title varies: 1841, The Dollar magazine. A monthly gazette of current American and foreign literature, fashion, music, and novelty. 1842, Dollar magazine. A monthly gazette of current literature.

Editors: Jan.-Oct. 1841, N.P. Willis and H.H. Weld. Published in order to present the most valuable part of the contents of "Brother Jonathan" in octavo form. Replaced by the library edition of "Brother Jonathan."

Edited by Nathaniel Parker Willis and H. Hastings Weld, the *Dollar Magazine* was a mainly eclectic magazine which printed much of the material published in *Brother Jonathan*. It claimed to select the choicest current periodical literature from both Europe and America, and also contained fashion plates, musical pieces, poetry, tales, novellettes, essays, and anecdotes.

v1-2   1841-1842   APS II, Reel 385

Microfilm edition was prepared from DLC copy.

DOLLAR MONTHLY MAGAZINE. *SEE* Ballou's Monthly Magazine.

THE DRAMATIC MIRROR, AND LITERARY COMPANION. Devoted to the stage and the fine arts. v. 1, v. 2, no. 1-11; Aug. 14, 1841-May 7, 1842. New York and Philadelphia, Turner & Fisher, 1842.

2 v. in 1. illus. weekly.

James Rees, editor.

This weekly, which lasted only nine months, attempted to keep readers abreast of events in the world of the theater. It listed plays currently being performed, and presented illustrated biographies of actors and actresses and articles on drama and the fine arts, as well as poetry, essays, foreign news items, and selections from plays.

v1-2   Aug. 14, 1841-May 7, 1842   APS II, Reel 605

Microfilm edition was prepared from DLC copy.

DWIGHTS AMERICAN MAGAZINE, AND FAMILY NEWSPAPER, for the diffusion of useful knowledge and moral and religious principles. v. 1-6, no. 2, Feb. 1845-Feb. 1850; new ser. v. 1, no. 1, July 1851. New York.

7 v. illus. Weekly, 1845-Dec. 1848; monthly, Jan. 1, 1849-

Vols. 1-2 have caption and running title: American penny magazine. Editor: 1845-Theodore Dwight. Film incomplete: contains issue 3 only of v. 4, issues 1-2 only of v. 5. Vol. 6 lacking.

Originally called the *American Penny Magazine,* this monthly miscellany was a major rival for Sears's *New Pictorial Family Magazine* and sold for three cents. Its contents included a juvenile department, poetry, literary notices, recipes, biography, news and articles on geography and travel, archaeology, botany, and zoology. Wood engravings served for illustration.

v1-nsv1   Feb. 8, 1845-July 1, 1851   APS II, Reel 733

Vols. 4-5: Complete volumes are not available for photographing. The microfilm edition contains issue 3 only of vol. 4 and issues 1-2 only of vol. 5.

Microfilm edition was prepared from DLC copy.

EASTERN MAGAZINE. v. 1, nos. 1-12; July 1835-June 1836. Bangor, Maine, 1835-1836.

384 p.

United with Portland magazine to form Maine monthly magazine.

Published in Bangor, Maine, this monthly was edited by Matilda P. Carter for the first five months, and then by Charles Gilman. It published prose and poetry, including some poetry by Mrs. Jane R. Locke and Mrs. Lydia H. Sigourney, literary notices, and articles and news concerning both American and foreign literature, as well as material on the early history of the country.

v1, nos. 1-12   July 1835-June 1836   APS II, Reel 385

Microfilm edition was prepared from MWA copy.

SEE ALSO: Portland Magazine.

ECCENTRICITIES OF LITERATURE AND LIFE. *SEE* Recreative Magazine.

ECLECTIC MAGAZINE, AND MONTHLY EDITION OF THE LIVING AGE. *SEE* Eclectic Magazine of Foreign Literature.

*****THE ECLECTIC MAGAZINE OF FOREIGN LITERATURE.** v. 1-63, 1844-64; [v. 64-131] (new ser. v. 1-68), 1865-98; v. 132-145 (3d ser. v. 1-14), 1899-1905; v. 146-147, v. 148, no. 1-6, 1906-June 1907. New York and Philadelphia, Leavitt, Trow, 1844-1907.

148 v. plates, ports. monthly.

Jan. 1899-Dec. 1900, title reads: The Eclectic magazine, and monthly edition of the Living age. Editors: Jan. 1844-Apr. 1846, J.H. Agnew.—Sept. 1846-Oct. 1881, W.H. Bidwell. Imprint varies. Supersedes the Eclectic museum of foreign literature. Includes Index to the engravings: 1844-84.

The *Eclectic Magazine* was created when Leavitt, Trow and Company purchased the *Eclectic Museum* from Eliakim Littell in 1844, and gave it the new name. John Holmes Agnew of the Presbyterian clergy was the first editor, followed by Walter A. Bidwell, who edited the magazine until his death in 1881.

A vast amount of periodical literature is stored in the file of the *Eclectic Magazine*. It reprinted articles from the best of the English magazines, spanning the entire reign of Queen Victoria. In addition to printing "the cream of foreign periodical literature," it published some brief extracts from new books and some original articles and fiction in the later years. The finest feature was the engraving—John Sartain made about 225 portraits, chiefly mezzotints, for the *Eclectic*.

At the end of 1898, the magazine was sold to its weekly rival, the *Living Age,* of Boston, but rather than being discontinued or absorbed, it was handled as a monthly in conjunction with the *Living Age.* This union was unsuccessful, however, and in 1905 the two parted company and the *Eclectic* returned to New York, where it survived less than two years.

Eclectic Magazine of Foreign Literature

v1-5	Jan. 1844-Aug. 1845	APS II, Reel 519
v6-10	Sept. 1845-Apr. 1847	Reel 520
v11-15	May 1847-Dec. 1848	Reel 521
v16-20	Dec. 1848-Apr. 1849	Reel 522
v21	Sept.-Dec. 1850	Reel 523
Cumulative Index 1-96		Reel 945
Index to the Engravings (1844-1884)		Reel 945
v22-27	Jan. 1851-Dec. 1852	Reel 945
v28-33	Jan. 1853-Dec. 1854	Reel 946
v34-39	Jan. 1855-Dec. 1856	Reel 947
v40-45	Jan. 1857-Dec. 1858	Reel 948
v46-51	Jan. 1859-Dec. 1860	Reel 949
v52-57	Jan. 1861-Dec. 1862	Reel 950
v58-63	Jan. 1863-Dec. 1864	Reel 951
nsv1-4	Jan. 1865-Dec. 1866	Reel 952
nsv5-8	Jan. 1867-Dec. 1868	Reel 953
nsv9-12	Jan. 1869-Dec. 1870	Reel 954
nsv13-16	Jan. 1871-Dec. 1872	Reel 955
nsv17-20	Jan. 1873-Dec. 1874	Reel 956
nsv21-24	Jan. 1875-Dec. 1876	Reel 957
nsv25-28	Jan. 1877-Dec. 1878	Reel 958
nsv29-32	Jan. 1879-Dec. 1880	Reel 959
nsv33-35	Jan. 1881-June 1882	Reel 960
nsv36-38	July 1882-Dec. 1883	Reel 961
nsv39-41	Jan. 1884-June 1885	Reel 962
nsv42-44	July 1885-Dec. 1886	Reel 963
nsv45-47	Jan. 1887-June 1888	Reel 964
nsv48-50	July 1888-Dec. 1889	Reel 965
nsv51-54	Jan. 1890-Dec. 1891	Reel 966
nsv55-58	Jan. 1892-Dec. 1893	Reel 967
nsv59-62	Jan. 1894-Dec. 1895	Reel 968
nsv63-67	Jan. 1896-May 1898; Dec. 1898	Reel 969
nsv68	July 1898-Nov. 1898; June 1898	Reel 970

Eclectic Magazine, and Monthly Edition of the Living Age.

3sv1-4	Jan. 1899-Dec. 1900	APS II, Reel 970

Eclectic Magazine of Foreign Literature.

3sv5-8	Jan. 1901-Dec. 1902	APS II, Reel 971
3sv9-13	Jan. 1903-June 1905	Reel 972
3sv14-osv148	July 1905-June 1907	Reel 973

Some pages are torn, stained, have print missing, or have print show-through. Some pages are missing. Pagination is irregular. New series Vols. 13-54: have supplements for each issue. New series vol.38: Some advertising pages are missing. New series Vol.67: the December issue of Vol. 67 and the July issue of Vol. 68 were bound and photographed out of order. Series 3 Vol. 1-8: have supplements for each issue.

Microfilm edition prepared from DLC, IC, ICU KMK, NcGU; PSC, NjP, FJ, CoGRS, C, IaDmD, TxU, MiEM, ScU, NjMD, NbO, TxWB, InCW, VtMiM, and N & RPB copies.

*ECLECTIC MUSEUM. *SEE* Museum of Foreign Literature, Science, and Art.

* **THE ECLECTIC MUSEUM OF FOREIGN LITERATURE, SCIENCE AND ART.** Ed. by John Holmes Agnew. United ser., v. 1-3, v. 4, no. 1: Jan. 1843-Jan. 1844. New York and Philadelphia, E. Littell, 1843-44.

4 v. plates. monthly.

Vol. 1 has caption title: American eclectic and museum of literature, science, and art. Vol. 4, no. 1 edited by E. Littell.

Formed by the union of the American eclectic and the Museum of foreign literature, science and art. Owing to a dissolution of partnership, the Eclectic museum was superseded by the "Eclectic magazine of foreign literature, science, and art. Ed. by J.H. Agnes" and "Littell's living age. Conducted by E. Littell."

Edited by John Holmes Agnew, a Presbyterian clergyman, the *Eclectic Museum* promised to present to American readers an "extended view of the literature of Europe" by selecting its material from British reviews, magazines, and literary and scientific weekly papers and from the best continental publications. It contained articles on science, art, history, travel, and invention; and gave much information on life in Europe. Poetry, biography, news, and bibliographical notices were also included; illustration was provided by John Sartain's mezzotint portraits.

v1-4	Jan. 1843-Jan. 1844	APS II, Reel 605

Vol. 1: Pgs. 306-21 are misdated.

Microfilm edition was prepared from DLC copy.

SEE ALSO: Eclectic Magazine of Foreign Literature.

ECLECTIC REPERTORY AND ANALYTICAL REVIEW. *SEE* Journal of Foreign Medical Science and Literature.

ECONOMIC BULLETIN. *SEE* American Economic Association, Publications.

EDUCATION REPORTER. *SEE* American Annals of Education.

ELEPHANT. v. 1, no. 1-5; Jan. 22-Feb. 19, 1848. New York, 1848.

40 p. illus.

A comic periodical published for a few months by Cornelius Mathews, and rival to the *John-Donkey.* It contained miscellaneous news, wit, jokes, and satire, and many cartoons and pictures intended to illustrate the "follies of public men and public institutions."

v1	Jan. 22-Feb. 19, 1848	APS II, Reel 771

Lacks index and table of contents.

Microfilm edition was prepared from CtY copy.

THE EMERALD. v. 1, no. 1-18; Nov. 3, 1810-Mar. 2, 1811. Baltimore, B. Edes.

222 p. weekly.

Edited by Peter Pleasant, pseud.

Copy filmed incomplete: p. 91-94 wanting.

Most of the items in this literary miscellany by "Peter Pleasant and Co." were short; the contents included sentimental prose and poetry, biographical sketches, letters from readers, extracts from other publications, and news of deaths and marriages.

v1, no. 1-18   Nov. 3, 1810-Mar. 2, 1811   APS II, Reel 101

EMERALD AND BALTIMORE LITERARY GAZETTE. v. 1-2, nos. 1-52; March 29, 1828- April 11, 1829. Baltimore, 1828-1829.

2 v.

A weekly miscellany, edited by poet Rufus Dawes, which began in 1828 and was merged the following year with the new *Baltimore Minerva.* It contained material selected from American and European periodicals—moral, humorous, and scientific essays, poetry and tales, biographical sketches, anecdotes, news, fashion, music, and critical reviews.

v1-2   Mar. 29, 1828-Apr. 11, 1829   APS II, Reel 605

Best copy available for photographing. Many pages are stained, tightly bound and misnumbered. Issues 2, 9, 11-13, 27, 34, 36, 38, 40, 43, and 47 are missing, not available for photographing.

Microfilm edition was prepared from CtY copy.

THE EMERALD, OR, MISCELLANY OF LITERATURE, containing sketches of the manners, principles and amusements of the age. v. 1-2, May 3, 1806-Oct. 17, 1807; new establishment, v. 1, Oct. 24, 1807-Oct. 15, 1808. Boston, Belcher & Armstrong, 1806-08.

3 v. weekly. Title varies slightly. Vol. 1, new establishment, has imprint: Boston, Pub. for the proprietor [O.C. Greenleaf] by E.G. House, 1808.

Supersedes Boston magazine.

This 12-page eclectic miscellany was a continuation of the *Boston Magazine,* and printed the same type of material; that is, serial novels and attention to the theater. It contained a theatrical review called "The Ordeal," as well as literary news, biography, and poetry. In October of 1807 it was sold to Oliver C. Greenleaf, who ran it during its last year.

v1-2, nsv1   May 3, 1806-Oct. 15, 1808   APS II, Reel 15

Microfilm edition was prepared from DLC copy.

SEE ALSO: Boston Magazine.

EMERSON'S MAGAZINE AND PUTNAM'S MONTHLY. v.1-7 (no.1-54); May 1854-Nov. 1858. New York, J. M. Emerson.

7 v. illus (incl. ports.) plates. monthly. No numbers issued for May 1855, May-June 1856. Vol. 3-4 called "New ser."

Title varies: May 1854-Mar. 1856, The United States magazine of science, art, manufactures, agriculture, commerce and trade. July 1856-June 1857, The United States magazine. July-Sept. 1857, Emerson's United States magazine. Oct. 1857-Nov. 1858, Emerson's magazine and Putnam's monthly.

Absorbed Putnam's monthly in Oct. 1857. Superseded by the Great republic monthly.

This monthly was founded by Alexander Jones and edited by Seba Smith who had earlier created the Yankee comic character, Major Jack Downing. Smith contributed a great deal of the content as did his wife, Elizabeth Oakes Smith, who wrote poetry and drama criticism. Little fiction was included, but there were many woodcuts and much humor on various subjects.

United States Magazine of Science, Art, Manufactures, Agriculture, Commerce and Trade
v1-2   May 15, 1854-Apr. 1856   APS III, Reel 264

United States Magazine
v3-4   July 1856-June 1857   APS III, Reel 265

Emerson's United States Magazine
v5, nos. 37-39   July-Sept. 1857   APS III, Reel 265

Emerson's Magazine and Putnam's Monthly
v5, nos. 40-v7   Oct. 1857-Nov. 1858   APS III, Reel 265

Some pages are creased, torn, or have print missing. Vol. 7: pagination is irregular.

Microfilm edition was prepared from CtHT MiU, MnM, NhD copies.

SEE ALSO: Putnam's Magazine.

EMERSON'S UNITED STATES MAGAZINE. *SEE* Putnam's Magazine *and* Emerson's Magazine and Putnam's Monthly.

EMERY'S JOURNAL OF AGRICULTURE. *SEE* Prairie Farmer.

THE EMPORIUM OF ARTS & SCIENCES. v. 1-2, May 1812-Apr. 1813; new ser., v. 1-3, June 1813-Oct. 1814. Philadelphia, J. Delaplaine, 1812; Kimber & Richardson, 1813-14.

5 v. plates, ports. Monthly, 1812-Apr. 1813; bimonthly, June 1813-1814.

Editors: v. 1-2, J.R. Coxe.—new ser., Thomas Cooper.

Conducted by John Redman Coxe, professor at the University of Pennsylvania, the *Emporium* was mainly concerned with the state of science in Europe and was to provide practical information on scientific research, particularly information contained in foreign papers on chemistry, mineralogy, and other science topics. Lists of patents and some diagrams and pictures were included. The new series was edited by Thomas Cooper, a well-known American scientist of that time, and dealt mainly with applied science— manufacturing, machinery, engines, and geology.

v1-nsv3   May 1812-Oct. 1814   APS II, Reel 101

EPISCOPAL MAGAZINE. v. 1-2; Jan. 1820-Dec. 1821. Philadelphia, S. Potter.

2 v. monthly.

Religious articles, news of missions and the activities of missionary societies and other religious news, Bible studies, biography, and addresses made up the contents of this Episcopal magazine.

v1-2   Jan. 1820-Dec. 1821   APS II, Reel 129

EPISCOPAL RECORDER. v.1-46; 1822-Nov. 27, 1919; new series v.1-   ; Dec. 1919-   . Philadelphia.

v. weekly.

Supersedes Church record (Philadelphia). Title varies: v. 1-8, Philadelphia recorder.

On film: v. 1-28, lacking v. 1, no. 7, 10-11, 19, 25, 30, 34; v. 2, no. 72, 84-85, 88; v. 3, no. 41-52; v. 5, no. 4-5, 8-11, 13, 18, 20, 22-23, 25, 27, 29, 33-38, 40-51; v. 6, no. 2, 4-7, 11-41, 48; v. 7, no. 1-11; v. 8, no. 16, 19, 27, 35, 46; v. 16. no. 20; v. 17, no. 25; v. 18, no. 51; v. 20, no. 51; v. 21, no. 9, 17; v. 27, no. 39, 46, 52.

Founded in 1822 by Bishop B.B. Smith and surviving well into the twentieth century, this Philadelphia magazine was the chief organ of the Reformed Episcopal church. This weekly religious paper had a newspaper-type format, publishing many short items—essays and articles on religious topics, sermons, domestic and foreign news, and religious intelligence, including church announcements, and news of missions, Sunday schools, and Bible societies. There was a section for children, as well as some poetry, book reviews, and biographical sketches.

Philadelphia Recorder
v1-3   Apr. 5, 1823-Dec. 31, 1825   APS II, Reel 1684
v4-8   Apr. 1, 1826-Mar. 26, 1831   Reel 1685

Episcopal Recorder
v9-11   Apr. 2, 1831-Mar. 29, 1834   APS II, Reel 1686
v12-14   Apr. 5, 1834-Mar. 25, 1837   Reel 1687
v15-17   Apr. 1, 1837-Mar. 21, 1840   Reel 1688
v18-20   Mar. 28, 1840-Mar. 18, 1843   Reel 1689
v21-23   Mar. 25, 1843-Mar. 14, 1846   Reel 1690
v24-26   Mar. 21, 1846-Mar. 10, 1849   Reel 1691
v27-28   Mar. 17, 1849-Mar. 22, 1851   Reel 1692

Microfilm edition was prepared from CtHt, DLC, MWA, NcD, and PBL copies.

THE EPISCOPAL WATCHMAN. v. 1-7, no. 26; Mar. 26, 1827-Nov. 2, 1833. Hartford, H.&F. J. Huntington.

7 v. weekly. No numbers were pub. in April 1830.

Supersedes the Churchman's magazine and the Gospel advocate. Editors: Mar. 1827-Mar. 1829, G.W. Doane, William Croswell,—Apr. 1829-Mar. 1830, Palmer Dyer.

The *Episcopal Watchman* was established to fill the void left by the *Churchman's Magazine* and the disappearing *Gospel Advocate*. Although it was largely theological in nature, portions were devoted to miscellaneous literary and scientific articles.

v1-5   Mar. 1827-May 1832   APS II, Reel 889
v6-7   May 1832-Nov. 1833   Reel 890

Volumes 6-7, lack indexes or tables of contents. Volume 7, *Union List of Serials* indicates there may have been more issues after November 2, 1833. However, we have been unable to locate any.

Microfilm edition prepared from Ct, CtHT, MiU, and NNG copies.

SEE ALSO: Churchman's Magazine *and* Gospel Advocate.

THE ESCRITOIR; or, Masonic and miscellaneous album. Being a periodical journal, devoted to masonry, science and arts, popular tales, miscellany current news &c., &c. v. 1; Jan. 28, 1826-Jan. 20, 1827. Albany, E.B. Child.

416 p. weekly.

Superseded by the American masonick record.

Concerned mainly with the masonic order in New York, it listed meeting dates and members and gave coverage to elections and activities of the various chapters. It also contained poetry and short stories.

v1   Jan. 28, 1826-Jan. 20, 1827   APS II, Reel 792

Some stained pages throughout.

Microfilm edition was prepared from DLC and MWA copies.

THE EUTERPEIAD; an album of music, poetry & prose. v. 1-2, no. 13; Apr. 15, 1830-Nov. 1, 1831. New York, G.W. Bleecker.

2 v. pl., ports. semimonthly. Contains music. Engraved t.-p., with vignette.

From Oct. 15, 1830 to Apr. 15, 1831 called "New ser." Editors: Apr.-Oct. 1, 1830, Charles Dingley.—Oct. 15-Dec. 1830, John Thomas.—Jan.-Apr. 1831, James Boardman.

Edited by C. Dingley, *Euterpeiad* was intended to be a magazine "devoted to the interests of music"; included were essays on music and style, biographical sketches and anecdotes of eminent musicians, reviews of musical publications, critiques on musical performances, and new and original music in each number. It also contained a variety of miscellaneous prose and poetry and lectures on morals, manners, and dress.

v1-2   Apr. 15, 1830-Nov. 1, 1831   APS II, Reel 771

vol. 2: Tightly bound. Best copy available for photographing.

Microfilm edition was prepared from MiD-B, NIC and RPB copies.

THE EUTERPEIAD; or, Musical intelligencer, and ladies gazette. Devoted to the diffusion of musical information, polite literature, and belles lettres. v.1-3, no.19, 1820-Mar. 1823; new ser. v.1, no.1-2, May-June 1823. Boston, T. Badger Jr., 1821-

3 v. Weekly, Apr. 1820-Mar. 1821: biweekly. Apr. 1821-Aug. 1822; monthly, Sept. 1822-Mar. 16, 1823.

Includes music. Title varies.

Film includes: Minerviad: devoted to Literature and Amusement for the Ladies. (Mar. 30-Sept. 7, 1822).

Edited by John R. Parker and later by Charles Dingley, this musical periodical began as a four-page weekly but later became a semimonthly and finally a monthly. It included a brief history of music, recorded the progress of the art and proceedings of musical societies, and reviewed new musical works and musical performances. Contents also included musical pieces, biographical sketches of musicians, articles on inventions and improvements in musical instruments, and anecdotes. The second volume added a ladies' department "Ladies' Gazette," but this was later discontinued.

v1-nsv1, no.2   Apr. 1820-June 1823   APS II, Reel 102

EVANGELICAL AND LITERARY MAGAZINE. *SEE* Literary and Evangelical Magazine.

EVANGELICAL AND LITERARY MAGAZINE AND MISSIONARY CHRONICLE. *SEE* Literary and Evangelical Magazine.

THE EVANGELICAL GUARDIAN AND REVIEW. By an association of clergymen in New York. v. 1-2; May 1817-Apr. 1819. New York, J. Eastburn, 1817-18.

2 v. monthly.

This religious periodical by "an association" of New York clergymen provided news of missionary activities, including the proceedings of the Baptist Missionary Society and the London Missionary Society, and coverage of the activities of various Bible societies, including the American Bible Society and the British and Foreign Bible Society, along with Sunday school news. Contents also included some biographical sketches, extracts from sermons, book reviews, poetry, and literary news.

v1-2   May 1817-Apr. 1819   APS II, Reel 102

THE EVANGELICAL INTELLIGENCER. v. 1-3, Jan. 1805-June 1807; new ser., v. 1-3, July 1807-Dec. 1809. Philadelphia, W.P. Farrand.

6 v. ports. monthly.

Title varies: 1805-June 1807, The General Assembly's missionary magazine; or, Evangelical intelligencer (caption title: The Assembly's missionary magazine; or, Evangelical intelligencer)

Issued by the General Assembly of the Presbyterian Church in the U.S.A. Edited by W. P. Farrand.

William P. Farrand was editor of this missionary magazine throughout its five years of publication. Published under the patronage of the General Assembly of the Presbyterian Church, the *Intelligencer* featured biographical sketches of Presbyterian ministers, many of them accompanied by portraits. In addition to the biographies, it presented accounts of missions and missionary societies, along with other religious news, moral and religious essays and anecdotes, studies of Bible passages, lists of new religious publications, and some poetry.

General Assembly's Missionary Magazine.
v1-3   Jan. 1805-June 1807   APS II, Reel 16

Evangelical Intelligencer.
nsv1-3   July 1807-Dec. 1809   APS II, Reel 17

Microfilm edition was prepared from MB and MBaT copies.

EVANGELICAL LUMINARY. v. 1; Jan.-Dec. 1824. Schoharie, N.Y.

96 p. monthly.

The *Evangelical Luminary's* object was to refute Calvinism, and to this end it published articles on Calvinism and quotations from Calvin's works, as well as articles on religion in general and extracts from sermons.

v1, no. 1-12   Jan.-Dec. 1824   APS II, Reel 103

EVANGELICAL MAGAZINE. *SEE* Evangelical Magazine and Gospel Advocate.

EVANGELICAL MAGAZINE AND GOSPEL ADVOCATE. Devoted to theoretical and practical religion, free inquiry, religious liberty, and intelligence. v. 1-3, Apr. 21, 1827-Dec. 26, 1829; new ser. v. 1-19, 1830-48. Utica, N.Y., Printed by Dauby & Maynard, 1829-

22 v. Biweekly, Apr. 1828-Oct. 1829; weekly, Nov. 1829-

Absorbed the Gospel advocate of Auburn in Jan. 1830. Formed by the union of the Utica magazine and the Evangelical repository of Troy. The volume numbering of the latter is continued. Title varies: Apr. 1827-Mar. 1828, Evangelical repository. Apr. 1828-Mar. 1829, Utica evangelical magazine: devoted to theoretical and practical religion, free inquiry, religious liberty and intelligence. Apr.-Dec. 1829, The Evangelical magazine: devoted to theoretical and practical religion, free inquiry. Jan. 1830-   The Evangelical magazine and gospel advocate.

Editors: Apr. 1828-   Dolphus Skinner (with Lemuel Willis, Apr. 1828-Feb. 1829). Absorbed Herald of truth in 1838.

A biweekly religious periodical edited and published by Dolphus Skinner which was to be a journal of important events in the "Christian community," particularly of the Universalist Church. It contained sermons, religious essays, scriptural expositions, and poetry.

Evangelical Repository
v1   Apr. 21, 1827-Mar. 15, 1828   APS II, Reel 792

Utica Evangelical Magazine
v2   Apr. 5, 1828-Mar. 21, 1829   APS II, Reel 792

Evangelical Magazine
v3   Apr.-Dec. 1929   APS II, Reel 792

Evangelical Magazine and Gospel Advocate
nsv1-5   Jan. 1830-Dec. 27, 1834   APS II, Reel 792
nsv6-12   Jan. 3, 1835-Dec. 24, 1841   Reel 793
nsv13-19   Jan. 7, 1842-Dec. 29, 1848   Reel 794

Some pages are stained, torn, tightly bound or creased, with some loss of print. Best copy available for photographing. New series vol. 4: Issue for Sept. 7, 1833 is not available for photographing.

Microfilm edition was prepared from Ia-T, NCaS and OO copies.

SEE ALSO: Gospel Advocate and Impartial Investigator.

EVANGELICAL MAGAZINE AND MISSIONARY CHRONICLE. *SEE* Beauties of the Evangelical Magazine.

EVANGELICAL MONITOR. v. 1-3, no. 26; Apr. 14, 1821-Apr. 17, 1824. Woodstock, Vt., W. Chapin.

3 v. semimonthly.

Published every other Saturday, this periodical stated that its "prime object shall be to record the works of the Lord." Excluding all advertisements and politics, the *Monitor* contained history and progress of the Foreign Missionary Society and letters and reports from missions. Moral and religious essays were frequent. The second volume included more foreign and domestic news items, poetry, vital statistics, ordinations and installations..

v1-3   Apr. 14, 1821-Apr. 17, 1824   APS II, Reel 401

vol. 3: Tightly bound.

Microfilm edition was prepared from MBC copy.

THE EVANGELICAL RECORD, AND WESTERN REVIEW. v. 1-2; Jan. 1812-Dec. 1813. Lexington, Ky., Printed by T.T. Skillman.

2 v. monthly.

J.P. Campbell, editor.

This Presbyterian magazine gave much attention to the activities of missionary societies in London and elsewhere, to news of foreign missions and to the reports of the British and Foreign Bible Society and other societies. In addition, contents included other religious news, book reviews, and articles dealing with Sunday schools, church history, the life of Calvin, and ways of converting Jews to Christianity.

v1   Jan.-Dec. 1812   APS II, Reel 129
v2   Jan.-Dec. 1813   Reel 130

EVANGELICAL RECORDER. v. 1-2 (no. 1-52); Jan. 31, 1818-Sept. 8, 1821. Auburn, etc., N.Y., C. Davis, etc.

2 v.

Weekly, Jan. 31-Sept. 5, 1818; irregular, June 5, 1819-Sept. 8, 1921. Edited by D.C. Lansing.

This weekly religious periodical was concerned with the state of religion in various parts of the world, and thus devoted a large share of its space to news of missions, reports of missionary and Bible societies, accounts of religious sects, and news of revivals, with the remainder of its space given over to reviews of religious publications, biographical sketches, sermons, and poetry.

v1-2   Jan. 31, 1818-Sept. 8, 1821   APS II, Reel 103

no. 23-37 duplicated.

THE EVANGELICAL REPERTORY. v. 1; July 15, 1823-June 15, 1824. Boston.

192 p. monthly.

Edited by E. Turner.

Edited by Edward Turner, this Universalist magazine published material discussing and defending Universalism, as well as articles on general religious topics, church news, and poetry.

v1, no. 1-12   July 15, 1823-June 15, 1824   APS II, Reel 103

EVANGELICAL REPOSITORY. v. 1; Jan.-Dec. 1816. Philadelphia, E.H. Cummins.

12 no. monthly.

Edited by E.H. Cummins.

This religious monthly published by Ebenezer Harlow Cummins presented a biographical sketch at the beginning of each issue, and contained a variety of religious and literary news, including news of missions and revivals, and reports of Bible societies.

v1, nos. 1-12   Jan.-Dec. 1816   APS II, Reel 130

SEE ALSO: Evangelical Magazine and Gospel Advocate *and* Religious Monitor and Evangelical Repository.

THE EVANGELICAL WITNESS. v. 1-4; Aug. 1822-1826. Newburgh, N.Y., Printed by W.M. Gazlay, etc.

4 v. monthly.

Edited by J.R. Willson.

This monthly religious magazine, edited by James R. Willson, was published under the patronage of the American Evangelical Tract Society. Contents included essays and articles on religious subjects, news items and statistics concerning the churches, book reviews, poetry, Bible studies, and some non-religious material.

v1-2   Aug. 1822-July 1824   APS II, Reel 103
v3   Jan.-Dec. 1825   Reel 104

v4   Jan.-Dec. 1826   APS II, Reel 606

Microfilm edition was prepared from N copy.

EVANGELISCHES MAGAZIN, unter der Aufsicht der deutschen evangelischlutherischen Synode. v. 1-4, Oct. 1811-1817. Philadelphia, 1811-1817.

4 v.

Published under the supervision of the German Evangelical Lutheran synod, this German-language magazine included a variety of religious material, such as poetry, anecdotes, and articles on Martin Luther and his beliefs.

v1-4   Oct. 1811-Sept. 1817   APS II, Reel 104

EVANGELIST. v. 1-2, no. 12; Jan. 1824-Dec. 1825. Hartford, Conn., 1824-1825.

2 v.

This Congregational newspaper was founded in 1824 to promote revivals, temperance, and other reforms.

v1-2   Jan. 1824-Dec. 1825   APS II, Reel 1271

Vol. 1: Several pages are stained. Cover page for issue 7 is torn. Pgs. 247-48 are misnumbered.

Microfilm edition was prepared from MiD, NcD, and WHi copies.

EVANGELIST AND RELIGIOUS REVIEW. v. 1-73; Mar. 6, 1830-July 24, 1902. New York.

68 v. weekly.

Title varies: 1830-Mar. 1902, New York evangelist. Subtitle also varies.
Includes quarto ed. for v. 13-14, 1842-43. Vol. 33-34, 1862-63 misnumbered as v. 32-33. Merged into Christian work and the evangelist, later Christian work.

A Presbyterian weekly newspaper founded in 1832 to promote revivals, temperance and other reforms. Joshua Leavitt, anti-slavery advocate, was editor from 1832 to 1837. He later edited the *Emancipator,* of the Anti-Slavery Society. During the Civil War period, *The Evangelist* was a strong anti-slavery publication. A wide variety of magazines and books are reviewed, including *Atlantic Monthly* and *Harper's Magazine.* News for farmers, scientific news, bills in Congress, foreign religious news, progress of the gospel, and occupations for women are a few of the topics included. From 1865 to 1885, the *New York Evangelist* spoke for the New School Presbyterians. In its later years, *The Evangelist and Religious Review* became a monthly magazine designed to uplift and develop a spiritual nature in its readers. It reported church activities and expressions of spiritual enlightenment.

New York Evangelist

v1-7	Mar. 6, 1830-Dec. 24, 1836	APS II, Reel 1829
v8-12	Jan. 2, 1837-Dec. 25, 1841	Reel 1830
v13-15	Jan. 6, 1842-Dec. 26, 1844	Reel 1831
v16-19	Jan. 6, 1845-Dec. 28, 1848	Reel 1832
v20-23	Jan. 4, 1849-Dec. 30, 1852	Reel 1833
v24-27	Jan. 6, 1853-Dec. 25, 1856	Reel 1834
v28-30	Jan. 1, 1857-Dec. 29, 1859	Reel 1835
v31-32	Jan. 5, 1860-Dec. 26, 1861	Reel 1836
v33-34	Jan. 2, 1862-Dec. 31, 1863	Reel 1837
v35-36	Jan. 7, 1864-Dec. 23, 1865	Reel 1838
v39-40	Jan. 2, 1868-Dec. 30, 1869	Reel 1839
v41-42	Jan. 6, 1870-Dec. 28, 1871	Reel 1840
v43-44	Jan. 4, 1872-Dec. 25, 1873	Reel 1841
v45-46	Jan. 1, 1874-Dec. 30, 1875	Reel 1842
v47-48	Jan. 6, 1876-Dec. 27, 1877	Reel 1843
v50-51	Jan. 2, 1879-Dec. 30, 1880	Reel 1844
v52-53	Jan. 6, 1881-Dec. 28, 1882	Reel 1845
v54-55	Jan. 4, 1883-Dec. 25, 1884	Reel 1846
v56-57	Jan. 1, 1885-Dec. 30, 1886	Reel 1847
v58-59	Jan. 6, 1887-Dec. 27, 1888	Reel 1848
v60-63	Sept. 19, 1889-Aug. 25, 1892	Reel 1849
v65	Jan. 4-Dec. 27, 1894	Reel 1850
v66	Jan. 3-Dec. 26, 1895	Reel 1851
v67	Jan. 2-Dec. 31, 1896	Reel 1852
v68-69	Jan. 7, 1897-Dec. 29, 1898	Reel 1853
v70-71	Jan. 5, 1899-Dec. 27, 1900	Reel 1854
v72-73, no. 10	Jan. 3, 1901-Mar. 6, 1902	Reel 1855

Evangelist and Religious Review.

v73, no. 11-30	Mar. 13, 1902-July 24, 1902	APS II, Reel 1855

Volumes 3-4, 37-38, 49 and 64 are missing; not available for photographing. Several volumes lack some issues.

Microfilm edition was prepared from the DLC, NN, and NNUT copies.

THE EVENING FIRE-SIDE; or, Literary miscellany. v. 1-2; Dec. 15, 1804-Dec. 27, 1806. Philadelphia, J. Rakestraw, 1805-06.

2 v. weekly.

Vol. 1 has title: The Evening fire-side; or, Weekly intelligence in the civil, natural, moral, literary and religious worlds ... Supersedes the Weekly monitor.

On film: Weekly monitor, v. 1, no. 1-26; June 6-Dec. 8, 1804, filmed between volumes 1 and 2 of the Evening fire-side.

This weekly miscellany devoted most of its space to articles on science and agriculture, moral essays, poetry, and summaries of foreign and domestic news.

v1-2	Dec. 15, 1804-Dec. 27, 1806	APS II, Reel 18

Microfilm edition was prepared from DLC copy.

EVENING MIRROR. *SEE* New York Mirror: A Weekly Gazette of Literature and the Fine Arts.

THE EVERGREEN: a monthly magazine of new and popular tales and poetry. v. 1-2; Jan. 1840-June 1841. New York, J. Winchester, 1840-41.

2 v. plates, port.

This monthly periodical featured writings by Longfellow, Oliver Wendell Holmes, Washington Irving, Charles Dickens, Mrs. Catherine Gore, Audubon and Mrs. Lydia Sigourney. The pages were filled with short stories, poetry, plays, music, essays, sermons and contemporary fiction. Engravings, usually illustrating the articles, were frequently used.

v1-2	Jan. 1840-June 1841	APS II, Reel 448

Microfilm edition was prepared from MiU and VW copies.

THE EVERY BODY'S ALBUM; a humorous collection of tales, quips, quirks, anecdotes, and facetiae. v. 1-[2; July 1836-June 1837?] Philadelphia, C. Alexander, 1836-[37]

2 v. illus. monthly.

Every Body's Album was a short-lived whimsical paper published in Philadelphia by Charles Alexander. Some comic illustrations were included.

v1-2	July 1836-June 1837	APS II, Reel 924

Microfilm edition was prepared from MH, MnU, CtHT, and DLC copies.

* **EVERY SATURDAY**: a journal of choice reading. v. 1-8, Jan. 1866-69; new ser., v. 1-3, 1870-71; new ser., v. 1-4, 1872-73; new ser., v. 1-2, Jan.-Oct. 1874. Boston, Ticknor and Fields.

17 v. illus. (incl. ports.) plates. weekly.

Title varies: 1866-69, Every Saturday: a journal of choice reading selected from foreign current literature. 1870-71, Every Saturday: an illustrated weekly journal. 1872-74, Every Saturday: a journal of choice reading. Merged into Littells living age, Nov. 1874.

Every Saturday was an eclectic magazine borrowing chiefly from English journals. Reade, Yates, Dickens, and Thackeray were among the English authors. Few original American contributions appeared, although Bret Harte furnished two short pieces for publication.

v1-5	Jan. 1866-June 1868	APS III, Reel 148
v6-nsv1	July 1869-Dec. 1870	Reel 149
nsv2-3sv2	Jan. 1871-Dec. 1872	Reel 150
3sv3-4sv2	Jan. 1873-Oct. 1874	Reel 151

Vol. 4: contains special Christmas issue. Series Four Vol. 2: Supplement at end entitled "His Two Wives."

Microfilm edition was prepared from MiU, MiEM, IC, OT, NjP, CL, C, C-S, Nh, and N copies.

SEE ALSO: Living Age.

EVERY YOUTH'S GAZETTE, a semi-monthly journal devoted to the amusement, instruction, and moral culture of the young. v. 1, nos. 1-28; Jan. 22-Dec. 31, 1842. New York, 1842.

414 p.

The editor of this children's magazine promised that "a pure moral tone" would pervade its columns, and certainly much of the material was instructive and serious in tone. Illustrated articles about animals, trees, and nature in general were plentiful; science, adventure, and travel were also popular topics. In addition, contents included poetry, letters to readers, and short anecdotes.

v1   Jan. 22-Dec. 31, 1842 APS II, Reel 606

Several pages are stained and torn.

Microfilm edition was prepared from MWA and OClWHi copies.

THE EVIDENCE; or, Religious and moral gazette. v. 1, no. 1-52; Jan. 14, 1807-Mar. 5, 1808. [Catskill, N.Y., M. Croswell]

416 p. Weekly (irregular)

This religious magazine featured a series of sermons addressed to young people and included a variety of other religious material—moral essays, Bible studies, biographical sketches, poetry, and anecdotes.

v1, no. 1-52 Jan. 14, 1807-Mar. 5, 1808 APS II, Reel 18

Microfilm edition was prepared from N copy.

EXAMINER. *SEE* Watchman-Examiner.

EXAMINER AND HESPERIAN. v. 1-2; May 1839-1840. Pittsburgh, 1839-1840.

2 v.

Title varies: v. 1 as Literary examiner and western monthly review.

Edited by E. Burke Fisher and W.H. Burleigh, this Pittsburgh literary magazine published poetry and tales, literary reviews, biographical sketches, and articles on geography.

Literary Examiner and Western Monthly Review.
v1   1839   APS II, Reel 386

Examiner and Hesperian.
v2   1840   APS II, Reel 386

Microfilm edition was prepared from OClWHi copy.

EXAMINER; containing political essays on the most important events of the time; public laws and official documents. v. 1-5, no. 21, Oct. 25, 1813-May 27, 1816. New York, 1813-1816.

5 v.

Superseded by Country courier.

Edited by Barent Gardenier, the *Examiner* was mainly political, advocating peace and the republican point of view. It published speeches and addresses, important state-papers, Congressional proceedings, and political essays.

v1, no.1-6 Oct. 25, 1813-Dec. 5, 1813 APS II, Reel 104
v1, no 7-v5, no 2 Jan. 1, 1814-Dec. 25, 1815 Reel 105
v5, no 3-21 Jan. 1, 1816-May 27, 1816 Reel 106

SEE ALSO: Country Courier.

THE EXPERIENCED CHRISTIAN'S MAGAZINE: consisting chiefly of original narrations, showing the increase of Christ's kingdom in America. v.1-2; May 1796-Apr. 1806. New-York, J. C. Totten.

2 v. Monthly.

Publication suspended May 1797-Apr. 1805. Subtitle varies.

Edited by W. Phoebus.

Edited by Rev. William Phoebus, the *Experienced Christian's Magazine* was founded primarily to publish accounts of the lives and deaths of Christians; sermons, poetry, and anecdotes rounded out the contents.

v1   May 1796-Apr. 1797 APS I, Reel 12

v2   May 1805-Apr. 1806 APS II, Reel 18

Microfilm edition was prepared from PHi and RPB copy.

THE EXPOSITOR. A weekly journal of foreign and domestic intelligence, literature, science, and the fine arts. v.1 (no.1-31); Dec. 8, 1838-July 20, 1839. New York, 1838-39. 1838-39.

312 p.

L.F. Tasistro, editor.

According to the Prospectus of the *Expositor,* arrangements had been made "with several European correspondents for obtaining early critical notices ... local gossip ... and ... translations from German, Spanish, and Italian" writings. However, the publication lasted for only a brief time because of delinquent accounts.

v1   Dec. 8, 1838-July 20, 1839 APS II, Reel 924

Vol. 1 lacks Index and Table of Contents. Page 85 is stained.

Microfilm edition was prepared from NN copy.

THE EXPOSITOR AND UNIVERSALIST REVIEW. v.1-2, 1831-1832; new ser. v.1-4, 1833-1840. Boston, G. W. Bazin, 1831-40.

v. bimonthly. Vol. 1, new ser., is called also "v. 3, old ser." Publication suspended from 1834 to 1837 inclusive.

Title varies: 1830-32, Universalist expositor. 1833-40, The Expositor and Universalist review.

Edited by Hosea Ballou and Hosea Ballou 2d. Superseded by Universalist quarterly and general review.

This scholarly religious magazine explored in depth various religious topics from the Universalist point of view. Contents included dissertations on points of Biblical literature, explanations of scriptural phrases and subjects, doctrinal discussions, sermons, occasional reviews of religious books, and some poetry.

Universalist Expositor.
v1-2   July 1830-May 1832   APS II, Reel 473

Expositor and Universalist Review.
nsv1-4   Jan. 1833-Nov. 1840   APS II, Reel 474

New Series Vol. 2: Pgs. 410-411 are missing. Pagination is irregular.

Microfilm edition was prepared from MB and MWA copies.

SEE ALSO: Universalist Quarterly and General Review.

THE EYE: by Obadiah Optic. v. 1-2; Jan.-Dec. 1808. Philadelphia, J.W. Scott, 1808.

2 v. weekly.

This essay periodical by "Obadiah Optic" presented essays on morals and "vices" and occasionally on other topics. In addition, poetry, occasional tales, and some material on agriculture and history were included.

v1-2   Jan. 7-Dec. 29, 1808   APS II, Reel 19

Microfilm edition was prepared from DLC copy.

FAMILY FAVORITE AND TEMPERANCE JOURNAL. v. 1, nos. 1-9; Dec. 1849-Sept. 1850. Adrian, Mich., 1849-1850.

48 p.

While primarily a religious and temperance magazine, the *Family Favorite* offered a variety of other reading matter as well. It published sermons, sentimental and religious poetry, travel sketches, notices of new publications, and articles on temperance, morals, and education, as well as anecdotes, short miscellaneous items, ads, and some illustrations. Much of the material was selected from other sources.

v1, no.1-9   Dec. 1849-Sept. 1850   APS II, Reel 386

Microfilm edition was prepared from MiD-B copy.

THE FAMILY LYCEUM. Designed for instruction and entertainment, and adapted to families, schools and lyceums. v. 1-2, no. 5; July 28, 1832-Dec. 7, 1833. Boston, G.W. Light.

2 v. illus. weekly.

Merged into scientific tracts.

Josiah Holbrook, editor. On film: issues for July 28, 1832-Aug. 10, 1833 and 2 unnumbered undated issues called "Family lyceum: Extra."

Established by Josiah Holbrook, the *Family Lyceum* was an organ for the lyceum movement, and was devoted to the popularization of science. The object of this weekly was to furnish material that would be entertaining, instructive, and useful to the family, school, and village lyceum. It included reports of the various lyceums and schools, and attempted to present science in simple terms. Questions on the contents of the previous issue were provided at the end of each number.

v1   July 28, 1832-Aug. 10, 1833   APS II, Reel 771

Vol.1: Index appears on page 208. Pages 57-58 are wrinkled, with some loss of print.

Microfilm edition was prepared from DLC copy.

THE FAMILY MAGAZINE; or, Monthly abstract of general knowledge. v. 1-8; Apr. 20, 1833-1840-41. New York, Redfield & Lindsay, 1834-40.

8 v. illus., plates, ports., maps. No more published.

Vols. 2-8. reprints (v. 2-3 have title: The Family magazine or General abstract of useful knowledge) Vol. 1 has title: The Family magazine, or Weekly abstract of general knowledge. Edited by Origen Bacheler.

Founded as a weekly by Origen Bacheler in 1833, the *Family Magazine* was one of the "knowledge" magazines and was an imitation of Knight's *Penny Magazine* of London. Written in a popular style, it was filled with "systematic courses of general knowledge" in many branches and was rather copiously illustrated with woodcuts. It was made a monthly in June, 1834. At first it focused mainly on astronomy, mythology, natural science, biography, and "wonders of the world," such as unusual buildings, towers, and mountains, but later expanded its range of topics to include articles on famous people and places, on New York City and state, and on geology, botany, history, and literature. A farmer's department was added and poetry and literary notices were also included. The *Family Magazine* is especially valuable for its many woodcuts of towns, cities, and buildings, which give a good picture of how they looked in the early 1800's.

v1   Apr. 20, 1833-Apr. 12, 1834   APS II, Reel 474
v2-5   1834-1838   Reel 475
v6-8   1839-1841   Reel 476

Several pages are stained with some loss of text. Vol. 2: Pages 138-45, 226-33 are bound and photographed out of order.

Microfilm edition was prepared from DLC and NN copies.

THE FAMILY MINSTREL: a musical and literary journal. v. 1, nos. 1-24, Jan. 15, 1835-Jan. 15, 1836. New York, 1835-1836.

188 p.

The *Family Minstrel* was comprised of original and selected literature, poetry, and musical pieces. The magazine was managed by Charles Dingley.

v1   Jan. 1835-Jan. 1836   APS II, Reel 973

Mass No. 13 was not available for photography. Best copy available.

Microfilm edition was prepared from CtY, DLC, MH, NPV, and RPB copies.

FARMER AND GARDENER. *SEE* American Farmer.

THE FARMER'S AND PLANTER'S FRIEND. no. 1-7; Mar. 26-Apr. 24, 1821. Philadelphia.

7 no. irregular.

The seven numbers of this magazine published contained essays discussing the harmful economic effects on farmers and planters caused by too many farmers and too little manufacturing and explored the reasons for the decline in cotton prices. It advocated such solutions as reducing the number of farmers and planters and imposing duties on the products of foreign countries.

no. 1-7   1821   APS II, Reel 106

THE FARMERS CABINET AND AMERICAN HERD BOOK, devoted to agriculture, horticulture, and rural and domestic affairs. v. 1-12; July 1, 1836-July 15, 1848. Philadelphia, Moore & Waterhouse, 1837-48.

12 v. illus. Semimonthly, July 1836-Jan. 1838; monthly, Feb. 1838-July 1848.

From July 1836 to July 1840 title reads: The Farmers cabinet; devoted to agriculture, horticulture, and rural economy.

Editors: July 1836-Dec. 1839, F.S. Wiggins.–May 1840-July 1843, James Pedder (with Josiah Tatum, Aug. 1842-July 1843).–Aug. 1843-July 1848, Josiah Tatum. Merged into the American Agriculturist.

This Philadelphia magazine presented information on all areas of agriculture and horticulture–descriptions and diagrams of implements, articles on various methods of caring for farm buildings, equipment, and livestock, and advice on blights and diseases of crops and plants. The various breeds of horses and cattle are described in a series of articles, many of which are accompanied by pictures. Current prices and poetry are also included in the contents.

v 1-6   July 1, 1836-July 15, 1842   APS II, Reel 314
v7-12   Aug. 15, 1842-July 15, 1848   Reel 315

Microfilm edition was prepared from N copy.

FARMER'S GUIDE. *SEE* Indiana Farmer's Guide.

FARMER'S REGISTER; a monthly publication. v. 1-10, June 1833-Dec. 1842; new ser., v. 1, nos. 1-3, Jan. 31-Mar. 31, 1843. Shellbanks, Va. [and] Petersburgh, Va., 1833-1843.

11 v.

Edited first by Edmund Ruffin and later by Thomas S. Pleasants, this monthly farming magazine was devoted to the improvement of agriculture and was almost exclusively concerned with agricultural topics, including articles on breeding stock, on diseases of crops and animals, and on improved methods of planting and harvesting. In addition, there was information on fruit trees, geology, soils, beekeeping, and silkworm culture, and numerous selections from British agricultural magazines. Diagrams or pictures accompanied many articles.

v1-2   June 1833-May 1835   APS II, Reel 334
v3-5   May 1835-Mar. 1838   Reel 335
v6-7   Apr. 1838-Dec. 1839   Reel 336

v8-9   Jan. 1840-Dec. 1841   Reel 337
v10-nsv1, no. 3   Jan. 1842-Mar. 1843   Reel 338

Pagination is irregular. New series vol. 1 contains some torn pages.

Microfilm edition was prepared from ViU copy.

FARMING. *SEE* Southern Cultivator.

FARRIER'S MAGAZINE. v. 1-2, 1818. Philadelphia, 1818.

2 v.

Compiled by James Carver from the lectures and practices of various European veterinary colleges, this quarterly magazine attempted to provide the farmer or gentleman with all the information needed to care for the diseases of his own horses. Contents included descriptions of the horse's anatomy, physiology, and pathology, along with surgical procedures, cures for ailments, and medicines. Information on lameness and the shoeing of horses was also provided. Plates accompanied many of the articles, and a history of the Royal Veterinary College of London was included.

v1-2   1818   APS II, Reel 106

FESSENDEN'S SILK MANUAL AND PRACTICAL FARMER. v. 1-2, no. 9; May 1835-April 1837. Boston, 1835-1837.

2 v.

Title varies.

Agricultural magazine edited by Thomas Green Fessenden, editor of the *New England Farmer,* from which much of the material was selected. In addition to coverage of farming and agricultural methods, it attempted to provide the latest information and developments on the growing of mulberry trees and the manufacture of silk.

v1-2   May 1835-Feb. 1837   APS II, Reel 734

Microfilm edition ends with volume 2 no. 9, February 1837.

Microfilm edition was prepared from IU and MH-BA copies.

FLAG OF OUR UNION. v. 1-26, 1846-Oct. 29, 1870. Boston, Mass., Elliott, Thomas & Talbot.

26 v. illus. weekly.

Caption title.

Film incomplete: v. 1-8, 26 wanting.

This story weekly published writings of Poe, Park Benjamin, Sylvanus Cobb, Horatio Alger, Mrs. Osgood, and Mrs. Sigourney. Founded by Frederick Gleason, it was later sold to Maturin M. Ballou.

v9-10   Jan. 7, 1854-Dec. 29, 1855   APS II, Reel 1158
v11-122   Jan. 5, 1856-Dec. 26, 1857   Reel 1159
v13-15   Jan. 2, 1858-Dec. 29, 1860   Reel 1160
v16-19   Jan. 5, 1861-Oct. 29, 1864   Reel 1161
v20   Jan. 7, 1865-Dec. 30, 1865   Reel 1162
v21   Jan. 6, 1866-Dec. 29, 1866   Reel 1163
v22   Jan. 5, 1867-Dec. 28, 1867   Reel 1164
v23   Jan. 4, 1868-Dec. 26, 1868   Reel 1165

v24-25   Jan. 2, 1869-May 14, 1870   Reel 1166

Some pages stained, creased, and torn with some loss of text. Some print faded. Vols. 9, 10, 11, and 13-23 lack indexes. Vol. 14: January-March 12, and March 26-July 2 issues are missing. Vol. 15: March 3, April 7, August 11-18, September 8, and October 6 issues are missing. Vol. 16: November 30 issue is missing. Vol. 17: January 18-February issues are missing. Vol. 18: July 18, pages 3-6 are missing. Vol. 20, 23, and 25 have several pages missing; not available for photographing. Vol. 21: January 6 issue, pages 1-2 are missing.

Microfilm edition was prepared from DLC, InU, and RPB copies.

THE FLORIAD. v. 1 (no. 1-15); May 24-Dec. 6, 1811. Schenectady [W.S. Buell]

1 v. semimonthly.

Published by the literary societies of Union college.

Published by the two principal literary societies of Union College of Schenectady, New York, this semi-monthly was devoted solely to literature, and contained literary news, original essays on education, morals, and other topics, a column called "The Rambler," some religious and historical material, biographical sketches, and poetry.

v1, no. 1-15   May 24-Dec. 6, 1811   APS II, Reel 106

THE FLY; or, Juvenile miscellany. v. 1, no. 1-13; Oct. 16, 1805-Apr. 2, 1806. [Boston, Printed by J. Ball]

52 p. semimonthly.

Edited by S. Scribble, pseud.

Edited by "Simon Scribble and Co.," this miscellany for children contained both literary and humorous material—poetry, anecdotes, tales, essays, and historical and biographical sketches.

v1, no. 1-13   Oct. 16, 1805-Apr. 2, 1806   APS II, Reel 19

Microfilm edition was prepared from MWA copy.

FLY LEAF. *SEE* Philistine; A Periodical of Protest.

FOEDERAL AMERICAN MONTHLY. *SEE* Knickerbocker.

THE FOOL. no. 1-3; Feb.-Apr. 1, 1807. [Salem, Mass.]

12 p. monthly.

Edited by T. Brainless, pseud.

Only three numbers of this satirical magazine were published. Edited by "Thomas Brainless," it appears to have been a satire on the miscellaneous magazines of its day; it had the standard format, with such items as the weather, fashions, marriage notices, literary news, and anecdotes, but all were humorous.

no. 1-3   Feb.-Apr. 1807   APS II, Reel 19

Microfilm edition was prepared from MH copy.

FOREST AND STREAM; a journal of outdoor life, travel, nature study, shooting, fishing, yachting. v. 1-100; Aug. 14, 1873-July 1930. New York, Forest and Stream Pub. Co.

100 v. illus. Weekly, 1873-1914; monthly, 1915-30. "Forest and stream" bird notes. An index and summary of all the ornithological matter contained in "Forest and stream." Vols. I-XII. Compiled by H.B. Bailey. New York, Forest and Stream Pub. Co., 1881.

Volume numbers irregular: Jan.-Mar. 1929 called v. 99, no. 1-3; Apr.-Dec. 1929 called 62d year, no. 4-12; Jan.-July 1930, 63d year, no. 1-7. Subtitle varies. Vols. 1-12 were edited by Charles Hallock, v. 87-[100] by W.A. Bruette. Absorbed Rod and gun in May 1877. Merged into Field and Stream.

Forest and Stream's subject matter was that of hunting, fishing, natural history, and conservation. It was influential in bringing about conservation reforms.

v1-4	Aug. 14, 1873-Aug. 5, 1875	APS III, Reel 208
v5-8	Aug. 12, 1875-Aug. 2, 1877	Reel 209
v9-13	Aug. 9, 1877-Jan. 1880	Reel 210
v14-17	Feb. 1880-Jan. 1882	Reel 211
v18-20	Feb. 1882-July 1883	Reel 212
v21-24	Aug. 1883-July 1885	Reel 213
v25-28	July 30, 1885-July 1887	Reel 214
v29-32	July 28, 1887-July 18, 1889	Reel 215
v33-36	July 25, 1889-July 16, 1891	Reel 216
v37-39	July 23, 1891-Dec. 28, 1892	Reel 217
v40-42	Jan. 5, 1893-June 30, 1894	Reel 218
v43-45	July 7, 1894-Dec. 28, 1895	Reel 219
v 46-50	Jan. 4, 1896-June 25, 1898	Reel 220
v51-54	July 2, 1898-June 30, 1900	Reel 221
v55-57	July 7, 1900-Dec. 28, 1901	Reel 222
v58-60	Jan. 4, 1902-June 27, 1903	Reel 223
v61-63	July 1903-Dec. 1904	Reel 224
v64-66	Jan. 7, 1905-June 30, 1906	Reel 225
v67-68	July 7, 1906-June 29, 1907	Reel 226
v69-71	July 6, 1907-Dec. 26, 1908	Reel 227
v72-74	Jan. 2, 1909-June 25, 1910	Reel 228
v75-77	July 2, 1910-Dec. 30, 1911	Reel 229
v78-80	Jan. 6, 19122-June 28, 1913	Reel 230
v81-85	July 5, 1913-Dec. 1915	Reel 231
v86-89	Jan. 1916-Dec. 1919	Reel 232
v90-93	Jan. 1920-Dec. 1923	Reel 233
v94-97	Jan. 1924-Dec. 1927	Reel 234
v98-100	Jan. 1928-July 1930	Reel 235

Pagination is irregular. Some pages are torn, stained, or have faded or missing print. Some advertising pages are lacking. Several pages are tightly bound. Vol. 32: Contains Supplements number 1: "Duck Shooting," number 2: "New York Dog Show," number 3: "Salmon and Trout," and numbers 4, 5 and 6: "Trap Tournaments." Vol.33: Contains Supplement number 7: "In Foreign Lands," and number 8: "Fish of Florida Waters." Vol. 34: Pages 491 and 492 bound and filmed between pages 506 and 507. Vol. 35: Contains Supplement number 9: "The Basses and Their Allies." Vol. 38: May 12 issue contains Supplement on "Trap Shooting." Vol. 40: Picture for February 2 issue is at beginning of book. Vol. 67: Contains November 24 Supplement, "Federal Protection of Wildfowl." Vol. 84: Title page reads Volume 84 Part 1. Vol. 85: Title page reads Volume 84 Part 2. Vol. 86: Title page and first page of index printed as Vol. 85 instead of 86. Vols. 98, 99 and 100: lack indexes; please refer to contents.

Microfilm edition was prepared from C, CoCrS, CtHT-W, DeWI, DNAL, DSI, MdBE, MoS, NhD and NNM copies.

FORRESTER'S BOYS' AND GIRLS' MAGAZINE, AND FIRESIDE COMPANION. v. 1-20, no. 6; Jan. 1848-Dec. 1857. [Boston, F. & G.C. Rand]

20 v. illus., ports. monthly.

Title varies: vol. 1-6 as Boys' and girls' magazine and fireside companion.

Editor: Francis Forrester, pseud. of Daniel Wise. Merged into the Student and schoolmate.

Founded by "Mark Forrester" this children's magazine was intended to be both amusing and instructive. It contained stories of adventure and of travel in strange lands; and described inventions and the habits of animals. Science articles gave simplified explanations of such scientific equipment and phenomena as the barometer, the microscope, magnetism, and volcanoes. Essays gave instructions on behavior, and musical pieces, fables, riddles, and poetry provided entertainment. Many pictures, some of them in color, illustrated the articles.

Boys' and Girls' Magazine and Fireside Companion.

v1-6	Jan. 1848-Dec. 1850	APS II, Reel 606

Forrester's Boys' and Girls' Magazine, and Fireside Companion.

v7-8	Jan.-Dec. 1851	APS II, Reel 606
v9-20	Jan. 1852-Dec. 1857	Reel 607

Microfilm edition was prepared from DLC and MB copies.

FORUM. *SEE* Century, A Popular Quarterly *and* Forum and Century.

FORUM AND CENTURY. v.1-103, no.6; Mar. 1886-June 1940. New York, Forum Pub. Co. [1886]-1940.

103 v. illus., maps, ports. Monthly, Mar. 1886-June 1902; quarterly, July 1902- June 1908; monthly, July 1906-June 1940. Index, volumes I to XXXII [Mar. 1886-Feb. 1902] Compiled by Anna Lorraine Guthrie. Minneapolis, H.W. Wilson, 1902.

Founded by Isaac L. Rice. Title varies: Mar. 1886-June 1930, The Forum. July 1930-June 1940, Forum and Century.

Editors: 1886-91, L.S. Metcalf.–1891-95, W.H. Page.–1897-June 1907, J.M. Rice.–July 1907-Dec. 1909, F.T. Cooper.–1910-15, Arthur Hooley.–1916-20, Mitchell Kennerley, Edwin Wildman and others.–Nov. 1920-June 1923. G.H. Payne.–July 1923-June 1940, H.G. Leach. Published in New York and London by M. Kennerley from 1910-1916. Absorbed the Century illustrated monthly magazine in 1930. Merged into Current history.

Current political, social, scientific, education, and literary news was written about by many famous authors, and reform movements in particular were treated extensively in *Forum and Century*. Isaac Leopold Rice provided financial backing for many years, first for Lorettus Sutton Metcalf as editor. Metcalf exercised extreme editorial control but set the tone for later years by publishing symposia and debates on controversial issues. He was succeeded after five years by Walter Hines Page who also published famous authors, but later under the editorial direction of Alfred E. Keet and Joseph Rice, most of the content was contributed by the editorial staff. Fiction and poetry were added in 1908 under Frederick T. Cooper and an emphasis on literature and art was held for many years.

Forum

v1-5	Mar. 1886-Aug. 1888	APS III, Reel 272
Cumulative index 1-32	1886-1902	Reel 272
v6-10	Sept. 1888-Feb. 1891	Reel 273
v11-15	Mar. 1891-Aug. 1893	Reel 274
v16-19	Sept. 1893-Aug. 1895	Reel 275
v20-24	Mar. 1896-Feb. 1898	Reel 276
v25-29	Mar. 1898-Aug. 1900	Reel 277
v30-34	Sept. 1900-June 1903	Reel 278
v35-40	July 1903-Dec. 1908	Reel 279
v41-45	Jan. 1909-June 1911	Reel 280
v46-50	July 1911-Dec. 1913	Reel 281
v51-54	Jan. 1914-Dec. 1915	Reel 282
v55-58	Jan. 1916-Dec. 1917	Reel 283
v59-63	Jan. 1918-June 1920	Reel 284
v64-69	July 1920-June 1924	Reel 285
v70-73	July 1924-June 1925	Reel 286
v74-76	July 1925-Dec. 1926	Reel 287
v77-79	Jan. 1927-June 1928	Reel 288
v80-83	July 1928-June 1930	Reel 289

Forum and Century

v84-88	July 1930-Dec. 1932	APS III, Reel 290
v89-94	Jan. 1933-Dec. 1935	Reel 291
v95-101	Jan. 1936-June 1939	Reel 292
v102-103	July 1939-June 1940	Reel 293

Some pages are stained or have print missing. Vol. 12: Pgs. 15-16 are bound out of order. Vol. 65: Pgs. 116-128 are missing.

Microfilm edition was prepared from DLC, InS, MiD, MiU, MoS, and OU copies.

SEE ALSO: Century, A Popular Quarterly.

FRANK LESLIE'S POPULAR MONTHLY. *SEE* American Magazine.

* FRANKLIN INSTITUTE, PHILADELPHIA. JOURNAL ... devoted to science and the mechanic arts. v.1- , Jan. 1826- . Philadelphia.

v. illus. (part col.) ports., maps (part fold.) Monthly, forming 2 v. a year.

Vol. numbers irregular: v. [5-30] 1828-40, numbered new ser., v. 1-26; v. [31]-130, 1841-90, numbered also ser. 3, v. 1-100 (v. [31-41] have ser. 3 numbering only.) Supersedes the American mechanics' magazine. Title varies: v. 1-4, 1826-27, The Franklin journal, and American mechanics' magazine; devoted to the useful arts, internal improvements and general science ... v. 5-82, 1828-66, Journal of the Franklin Institute, of the State of Pennsylvania, for the Promotion of the Mechanic Arts; devoted to mechanical and physical science, civil engineering, the arts and manufactures, and the recording of American and other patent inventions (subtitle varies; individual nos. in 1828 have title: The Franklin journal ...)

vols. 1-69 include more or less complete patent reports of the U.S. Patent Office for the years 1825-59. cf. Index to v. 1-120 of the Journal, p. [415] Vols. 119-121, 124-133, 135-140 accompanied by supplements; those with v. 124-132, 135-140 comprise summaries of meteorological reports of the Pennsylvania State Weather Service for Sept. 1887-May 1895. Vol. 101 accompanied by an atlas of tables (31 cm.). Indexes: Vols. 1-120, 1826-85. 1 v. Vols. 121-140, 1886-95. 1 v. Vols. 141-160, 1896-1905. 1 v. Vols. 161-180, 1906-15. 1 v. Vols. 181-200, 1916-25. 1 v. On film: v. 1-52; Jan. 1826-Dec. 1851.

Thomas P. Jones founded the *American Mechanics' Magazine* In 1825, but merged it into the Franklin Institute Journal the next year. Jones continued as editor for 20 years. The *Journal* became a most valuable repository of information concerning scientific subjects. For many years lists of patents from the United States, England and France were printed. Transactions of the Franklin Institute, meteorological reports, essays on various scientific disciplines and articles on such diverse subjects as the origin and history of glass and porcelain were included. Illustrations in the form of plates, plus diagrams, charts and maps were frequently printed.

Franklin Journal, and American Mechanics' Magazine.
v1-4   Jan. 1826-Dec. 1827   APS II, Reel 282

Journal of the Franklin Institute ...
v5-9	Jan. 1828-June 1830	APS II, Reel 282
v10-18	July 1830-Dec. 1834	Reel 283
v19-26	Jan. 1835-Dec. 1838	Reel 284
v27-35	Jan. 1839-June 1843	Reel 285
v36-44	July 1843-Dec. 1847	Reel 286
v45-52	Jan. 1848-Dec. 1851	Reel 287

FRANKLIN JOURNAL AND AMERICAN MECHANICS' MAGAZINE. *SEE* American Mechanics' Magazine *and* Franklin Institute, Philadelphia. Journal ... Devoted to Science ...

THE FRANKLIN MINERVA. v. 1 (no. 1-26); Feb. 2, 1799-Jan. 18, 1800. Chambersburg, Pa., Printed by G.K. Harper, 1799-1800.

1 v. biweekly.

Caption title.

The first two pages of this four-page magazine were devoted to sentimental stories and moral essays, page three listed deaths and marriages and included miscellaneous items, and the last page consisted entirely of poems, anecdotes, and epigrams.

v1   Feb. 2, 1799-Jan. 4, 1800   APS II, Reel 546

Several issues and pages are missing. Many pages are torn, with loss of text. Best copy available for photographing.

Microfilm edition was prepared from DLC copy.

THE FREE ENQUIRER. v. 1-3, Oct. 1, 1825-Oct. 22, 1828; 2d ser., v. 1-5, Oct. 29, 1928-Oct. 19, 1933; 3d ser., v. 1-2, Oct. 27, 1833-June 28, 1835. New York, H.D. Robinson, Printer.

10 v. in 9. illus. weekly.

Vols. 1-3 (1st. ser.) have title: The New-Harmony gazette.

Editors: Oct-Dec. 14, 1825, William Owen, R.L. Jennings.–Dec. 21, 1825-Feb. 1826, R.L. Jennings.–Mar.-Aug.? 1826, William Pelham.–Oct. 1826-May 9, 1827, R.D. Owen.–May 16, 1827-Mar. 5, 1828, William Owen.–Mar. 19-June 11, 1828, R.D. Owen, William Owen.–June 18- July 16, 1828, Frances Wright, William Owen.–July 23, 1828-Oct. 1832, Frances Wright, R.D. Owen and others.–Dec. 1832-June 1835, H.D. Robinson. Published in New Harmony, Ind. until March 1829.

The *New-Harmony Gazette* was created to interpret the experimental socialistic community established at New-Harmony, Indiana by the Welsh manufacturer and philanthropist, Robert Owen. Edited chiefly by Robert L. Jennings, Frances Wright, and two of Robert Owen's sons, this eight-page weekly was devoted to the exposition of Robert Owen's theories on the social system, to articles on social and religious topics by other members of the Community, and to a record of the progress of the experiment and the life at New-Harmony, and is an excellent source for study of this trial of communistic theory. By fall of 1828, the Community had disintegrated and in October a new series of the paper was begun. Its new title, the *New-Harmony and Nashoba Gazette, or the Free Enquirer*, reflected a new interest-an educational experiment with freed

Negroes on a tract in western Tennessee called Nashoba. The new paper, a socialist and agnostic journal, was somewhat broader in scope than its predecessor. Soon the Nashoba experiment failed also and early in 1829 Miss Wright and Robert Dale Owen took the periodical to New York, where it was conducted for six years. The editors were the chief contributors. Controversy was its main forte; it discussed religion, politics, sociology, and education, and advocated feminism, socialism, agnosticism, and other "isms." The advocacy of these doctrines, generally disapproved of by the American public, probably accounts for its failure to achieve success.

New-Harmony Gazette.
v1-3   Oct. 1, 1825-Oct. 22, 1828   APS II, Reel 1498

Free Inquirer.
| s2 v1-3 | Oct. 29, 1828-Oct. 22, 1831 | APS II, Reel 1498 |
| s2 v4-s3v2 | Oct. 29, 1831-June 28, 1835 | Reel 1499 |

Several pages are stained, creased, tightly bound, misnumbered, or have print faded with some loss of text. Pagination is irregular. Series Two Vol. 4: Pgs. 135-36 and 155-58 are missing; not available for photographing.

Microfilm edition was prepared from C, IU, N, NBuG, NPV, and PU copies.

FREE TRADE ADVOCATE AND JOURNAL OF POLITICAL ECONOMY. *SEE* Banner of the Constitution.

THE FREE UNIVERSAL MAGAZINE. v. 1 (no. 1-4); Apr./June 1793-Jan./Mar. 1794. New York, Printed by L. Jones for the Rev. A. Sarjent.

4 no. quarterly.

On film: v. 1, no. 2; no. 1, 3 and 4 wanting.

The first magazine south of Philadelphia, this religious quarterly presented hymns, anecdotes, queries and answers, and articles on varied religious topics.

v1, no. 2   Sept. 6, 1793   APS I, Reel 12

Microfilm edition was prepared from NN copy.

THE FREEMASONS MAGAZINE AND GENERAL MISCELLANY. v. 1-2; Apr. 1811-Mar. 1812. Philadelphia, Levis & Weaver, 1811-12.

2 v. illus., front., plates, port. monthly.

George Richards, editor.

This 80-page magazine devoted one-third of its space to the masons, one-third to women, and one-third to miscellaneous material. Masonic material included a history of masonry, news of the activities of various lodges, addresses and orations, and poetry. The ladies' department contained tales, essays, and much advice on love and marriage, while the miscellaneous section was comprised of biographical sketches, criticism, and articles on history and travel, science, philosophy, agriculture, and manufacturing, as well as some anecdotes and stories.

v1-2   Apr. 1811-Mar. 1812   APS II, Reel 106

THE FRIEND; a periodical work devoted to religion, literature, and useful miscellany. v. 1 (no. 1-12); July 1815-June 1816. Albany, D. & S. A. Abbey.

300 p. monthly.

This periodical contained religious news, essays on religious and literary subjects, biographical and historical sketches, accounts of new inventions, and a section on agriculture. In addition, it presented literary news, poetry, and book reviews.

v1, no. 1-12   July 1815-June 1816   APS II, Reel 107

THE FRIEND; a religious and literary journal. v.1-128, no.26; Oct. 13, 1827-July 1955. Philadelphia.

128 v. Weekly 1827-June 29, 1933; biweekly July 6, 1933-1955.

Superseded by Friend's journal.

On film: v. 1-24, reels 523-26; v. 25-79, reels 1412-1419. Bound with v. 21: Friends, Society of. Philadelphia Yearly Meeting. An appeal for the ancient doctrines of the religious Society of Friends. Philadelphia, 1848.

The oldest of the various periodicals fostered by the Society of Friends, *Friend* proposed to "furnish the Society of Friends an agreeable and instructive miscellany," and its eight pages were filled with brief literary and scientific articles, travel items, original and selected poetry, biography, and current events, as well as doctrinal reading and articles dealing with the various "concerns" of the Friends—peace, temperance, antimasonry, antislavery and colonization, and Indian education. Although politics played no part in the *Friend,* the last page was devoted to a "Summary of Events" during the fifties and throughout the war, and the testimony against war was maintained during the conflict. The first few volumes are more literary than the later volumes, which include much more science and more memoirs of distinguished Friends. Addison, Johnson, and other eighteenth century essayists are reprinted, and famous poets represented include Cowper, Whittier, Bryant, and Mrs. Lydia H. Sigourney.

v1-5	Oct. 13, 1827-Oct. 6, 1832	APS II, Reel 523
v6-10	Oct. 13, 1832-Sept. 30, 1837	Reel 524
v11-17	Oct. 7, 1837-Sept. 21, 1844	Reel 525
v18-24	Sept. 28, 1844-Dec. 28, 1850	Reel 526
v25-30	Sept. 20, 1851-Sept. 5, 1857	APS II, Reel 1412
v31-37	Sept. 12, 1857-Aug. 27, 1864	Reel 1413
v38-44	Sept. 3, 1864-Aug. 19, 1871	Reel 1414
v45-50	Aug. 26, 1871-Aug. 11, 1877	Reel 1415
v51-57	Aug. 18, 1877-Aug. 2, 1884	Reel 1416
v58-64	Aug. 9, 1884-July 25, 1891	Reel 1417
v65-71	Aug. 1, 1891-July 16, 1898	Reel 1418
v72-79	July 23, 1898-July 7, 1906	Reel 1419

Several pages are stained, creased and have faded print with some loss of text. Pagination is irregular. Vol. 7: Issue No. 29, Apr. 26, 1834 is missing. Vol. 24: nos. 16-52 are missing.

Microfilm edition was prepared from DLC, ICU, MH, NBuG, NcD, and RPB copies.

THE FRIEND OF PEACE: by Philo Pacificus [pseud.] (Worcester, Noah, 1758-1837.) v. 1-4; [1815-1827] Boston, J.T. Buckingham [1819?]; Cambridge, Printed by Hilliard and Metcalf, 1821-27.

4 v.

Issued in quarterly numbers, written almost entirely by Worcester himself. Bound and photographed at beginning of vol. 1: A solemn review of the custom of war; showing that war is the effect of popular delusion, and proposing a remedy. By Philo Pacificas [pseud]. Bound and photographed at end of v. 3: Supplements, "National dangers and means of escape" and "Annual report of the Massachusetts Peace Society" [1822]

The Reverend Noah Worcester, a Unitarian, became an advocate of international peace during the War of 1812. In 1813 he began his *Christian Disciple,* and in 1815 was prominent in the foundation of the Massachusetts Peace Society, and also founded in the *Friend of Peace.* This quarterly expressed the sentiments of the anti-war movement which developed following the War of 1812 and included articles on Napoleon's campaign in Russia as well as other material opposing war and the annual reports of the Massachusetts Peace Society. In 1818 Worcester resigned his editorship of the *Christian Disciple* in order to devote his full attention to the advocacy of peace.

v1, nos. 1-7	1815-?	APS II, Reel 211
v1-4	1815-1827	APS II, Reel 1072

Microfilm edition was prepared from ICMe copy.

THE FRIENDLY VISITOR, being a collection of select and original pieces, instructive and entertaining, suitable to be read in all families. v.1; Jan. 1, 1825-Dec. 28, 1825. New York, 1825.

2 p.l., 408 p., 21. weekly.

No. 51 not published. Edited by W. M. Stilwell.

Both original and selected material made up the contents of this eight-page family magazine. Although the *Friendly Visitor* focused mainly on religious subjects, such as Bible studies, it also included a summary of foreign and domestic news events, poetry, and biographical sketches.

v1, no.1-52   Jan. 1-Dec. 28, 1825   APS II, Reel 107

FRIENDS' INTELLIGENCER. v. 1-112, no. 26; Mar. 30, 1844-June 25, 1955. Philadelphia, J. Richards.

112 v.

Title varies: Friends' weekly intelligencer. Ed. by the association of Friends.

On film: v.1-6 appears in reels 735-736; v.7-67 in reels 1167-91.

A religious magazine which was the organ of the Society of Friends and one of several periodicals published by the society.

Friends' Weekly Intelligencer

v1-4	Mar. 30, 1844-Mar. 25, 1848	APS II, Reel 735
v5-6	Apr. 1, 1848-Mar. 23, 1850	Reel 736
v7-9	Mar. 30, 1850-Mar. 19, 1853	Reel 1167

Friends' Intelligencer

v10	Mar. 26, 1853-Mar. 18, 1854	APS II, Reel 1167
v11-13	Mar. 25, 1854-Mar. 14, 1857	Reel 1168
v14-16	Mar. 21, 1857-Mar. 10, 1860	Reel 1169
v17-19	Mar. 17, 1860-Mar. 7, 1863	Reel 1170
v20-22	Mar. 14, 1863-Mar. 3, 1866	Reel 1171
v23-25	Mar. 10, 1866-Feb. 27, 1869	Reel 1172
v26-28	Mar. 6, 1869-Feb. 24, 1872	Reel 1173
v29-31	Mar. 2, 1872-Feb. 20, 1875	Reel 1174
v32-33	Feb. 27, 1875-Feb. 17, 1877	Reel 1175
v34-36	Feb. 24, 1877-Feb. 14, 1880	Reel 1176

v37-39	Feb. 21, 1880-Feb. 10, 1883	Reel 1177
v40-42	Feb. 17, 1893-Dec. 26, 1885	Reel 1178
v43-44	Jan. 2, 1886-Dec. 31, 1887	Reel 1179
v45-46	Jan. 7, 1888-Dec. 28, 1889	Reel 1180
v47-48	Jan. 4, 1890-Dec. 26, 1891	Reel 1181
v49-50	Jan. 2, 1892-Dec. 30, 1893	Reel 1182
v51-52	Jan. 6, 1894-Dec. 28, 1895	Reel 1183
v53-54	Jan. 4, 1896-Dec. 25, 1897	Reel 1184
v55-56	Jan. 1, 1898-Dec. 30, 1899	Reel 1185
v57-58	Jan. 6, 1900-Dec. 28, 1901	Reel 1186
v59-60	Jan. 4, 1902-Dec. 26, 1903	Reel 1187
v61-62	Jan. 2, 1904-Dec. 30, 1905	Reel 1188
v63-64	Jan. 6, 1906-Dec. 28, 1907	Reel 1189
v65-66	Jan. 4, 1908-Dec. 25, 1909	Reel 1190
v67	Jan. 1, 1910-Dec. 31, 1910	Reel 1191

Several pages are stained and tightly bound; some pages have print faded and show-through with some loss of text. Some pages are misnumbered. Volume 42: Index is photographed following page 216. Volume 47: Pages 3-4 of Index are photographed following page 8. Volume 50: Page 146 is missing. Volume 51: Pages 418 and 567-68 are repeated in number only. Volumes 53, 65, and 67 contain supplements.

Microfilm edition was prepared from DLC, IC, MH, PHC, and PP copies.

FRIEND'S JOURNAL. *SEE* Friend; A Religious and Literary Journal.

FRIENDS' REVIEW; a religious, literary and miscellaneous journal. v.1-48, Sept. 4, 1847-July 5, 1894. Philadelphia, J. Tatum, 1848-

48 v. weekly.

United with Christian worker to form American friend.

Editors: Sept. 1847-Enoch Lewis.—Samuel Rhoads.

Founded and edited by Enoch Lewis, the *Friends' Review* represented the more tolerant and progressive elements of the Society of Friends. Samuel Rhoads succeeded to the editorship in 1856 and conducted the journal through the Civil War. This Philadelphia weekly consistently maintained its testimony against both slavery and war throughout these years. When emancipation came in 1863, it turned to projects for aiding the freedmen. Successive editors to Lewis and Rhoads were William J. Allinson, Henry Hartshorne, James E. Rhoads, and Rufus M. Jones. The *Review,* which was a well-printed small quarto of sixteen pages, gave much space to reports of activities of Friends in various sections of the country and published biographical accounts, journals, poems, and a summary of foreign and domestic news. In 1894 the *Friends' Review* was superseded by *American Friend.*

v1-2	Sept. 4, 1847-Sept. 15, 1849	APS II, Reel 386
v3-4	Sept. 22, 1849-Sept. 13, 1851	Reel 387
v5-7	Sept. 20, 1851-Sept. 9, 1854	Reel 924
v8-11	Sept. 16, 1854-Sept. 4, 1858	Reel 925
v12-16	Sept. 11, 1858-Aug. 29, 1862	Reel 926
v17-20	Sept. 5, 1863-Aug. 24, 1867	Reel 927
v21-24	Aug. 31, 1867-Aug. 19, 1871	Reel 928
v25-27	Aug. 26, 1871-Aug. 15, 1874	Reel 929
v28-31	Aug. 22, 1874-Aug. 10, 1878	Reel 930
v32-35	Aug. 17, 1878-Aug. 5, 1882	Reel 931
v36-40	Aug. 12, 1882-July 28, 1887	Reel 932
v41-44	Aug. 4, 1887-July 23, 1891	Reel 933
v45-48	July 30, 1891-July 5, 1894	Reel 934

Some pages are stained, torn, tightly bound, or have faded print.

Pagination is irregular. Vol. 9: Contains a Supplement entitled "Stephen Grellet." Vol. 31: Contains Supplement "Biennial Bible-School Conference," with January 12 issue. Vols. 47-48 lack indexes. Please refer to the Tables of Contents.

Microfilm edition was prepared from DLC, NcGuG, NcD, PHC, InRE, PBm, IaU, and MWA copies.

FRIENDS' WEEKLY INTELLIGENCER. *SEE* Friends' Intelligencer.

*THE GALAXY. A magazine of entertaining reading. v. 1-24, v. 25, no. 1; May 1866-Jan. 1878. New York, W.C. & F. P. Church, 1866-68; Sheldon, 1868-78.

25 v. in 24. illus., plates, ports., map. Semi-monthly, 1866-Apr. 1867; monthly, May 1867-1878.

W.C. Church, editor. Short story, The Claverings, by Anthony Trollope, complete in serial form in vol. 1. Merged into Atlantic monthly, Feb. 1878.

The *Galaxy* was best known for the pages it devoted to fiction in each and every issue. At least one serial, sometimes two or three, and a number of short stories and poems were included. Richard Grant White, Justin McCarthy, Rebecca Harding Davis, Jane G. Austin, and Paul Hamilton Hayne (to name only a few) contributed often. However, the most popular section was entitled "Memoranda." This was written and edited by Mark Twain. Although this department appeared for only a year, it was then that the magazine reached its highest circulation.

By 1878, circulation had declined greatly and the *Galaxy* was absorbed by the *Atlantic Monthly.*

v1-4	May 1866-Dec. 1867	APS III, Reel 7
v5-8	Jan. 1868-Dec. 1869	Reel 8
v9-12	Jan. 1870-Dec. 1871	Reel 9
v13-16	Jan. 1872-Dec. 1873	Reel 10
v17-20	Jan. 1874-Dec. 1875	Reel 11
v21-25	Jan. 1876-Jan. 1878	Reel 12

Vol. 1: pages 566-596 are misnumbered as 666-696. Vol. 25 lacks index. Please refer to the table of contents.

Microfilm edition was prepared from MiD and MiU copies.

GARDENER'S MONTHLY AND HORTICULTURAL ADVERTISER. *SEE* Horticulturist and Journal of Rural Art and Rural Taste.

GARDENER'S MONTHLY AND HORTICULTURIST. *SEE* Horticulturist and Journal of Rural Art and Rural Taste.

THE GARLAND; or, New general repository of fugitive poetry. v. 1, no. 1-3; June-Aug. 1825. Auburn, N.Y., T.M. Skinner.

48 p. monthly.

Edited by G.A. Gamage.

The *Garland* published only three numbers. This monthly magazine consisted almost entirely of sentimental poetry, most of which was selected from both American and foreign magazines.

| v1, no. 1-3 | June-Aug. 1825 | APS II, Reel 107 |

THE GAZETTEER. v. 1; Jan. 7-Dec. 29, 1824. Philadelphia.

1 v. weekly.

Supersedes the Philadelphia Universalist magazine and Christian messenger.

Edited by A. Kneeland.

Edited by the Rev. Abner Kneeland, this Universalist periodical was devoted to religion, science, and morality and also published foreign and domestic news and vital statistics. Poetry and selections from the *Boston Universalist Magazine* appeared frequently.

v1, no. 1-52   Jan. 7-Dec. 29, 1824   APS II, Reel 107

SEE ALSO: Philadelphia Universalist Magazine and Christian Messenger.

GEISTLICHES MAGAZIEN. num. 1-50 [1764]-[2. folge] num. 1-15 [1770-72?] Germantown.

Caption title. Preface signed: Christoph Sauer.

Seidensticker's First century of German printing in America gives title: Ein Geistliches magazien, oder: Aus den schatzen der schrifftgelehrten zum himmelreich gelehrt, dargereichtes altes und neues, and adds note "The numbers of this religious magazine were not dated; they appeared between 1764 and 1770 and were given away, not sold. It is the first religious periodical printed in America. In one of the early numbers the publisher states that the type used was made in Germantown." Film covers num. 1-15.

A German religious magazine containing religious observations, essays, sermons, poetry, simple catechisms, and narratives designed for family reading. Selections from many writers, usually German devouts, were included, and articles on the religious education of children were emphasized.

nos. 1-15   1770-1772?   APS I, Reel 12

Microfilm edition was prepared from PHi copy.

GENERAL ASSEMBLY'S MISSIONARY MAGAZINE. *SEE* Evangelical Intelligencer.

GENERAL CONVENTION OF THE BAPTIST DENOMINATION IN THE UNITED STATES. *SEE* Latter Day Luminary.

THE GENERAL MAGAZINE, AND HISTORICAL CHRONICLE, FOR ALL THE BRITISH plantations in America. v. 1 (no. 1-6); Jan.-June 1741. Philadelphia, B. Franklin.

1 v. monthly.

The second American periodical published articles on parliament, state assemblies, the currency question, and religion. Edited and published by Benjamin Franklin.

v1, no. 1-6   Jan.-June 1741   APS I, Reel 12

Some pages are missing.

Microfilm edition was prepared from NN copy.

GENERAL MAGAZINE AND IMPARTIAL REVIEW OF KNOWLEDGE & ENTERTAINMENT. v. 1; June-Aug. 1798. Baltimore 1798.

1 v. monthly.

No. for Aug., 1798 wanting.

Included much sentimental fiction and also poetry, plays, anecdotes, and essays on religion and marriage.

v1   June-July, 1798   APS I, Reel 13

Microfilm edition was prepared from MWA and MdBE copy.

*THE GENERAL REPOSITORY AND REVIEW. v. 1-4; Jan. 1812-Oct. 1813. Cambridge, Mass., W. Hilliard, 1812-13.

4 v. quarterly.

Supersedes Monthly anthology and Boston review.

Andrews Norton, editor.

Founded in 1812 by Andrews Norton, a tutor at Harvard, this review superseded the *Monthly Anthology* and was considered by some to be a forerunner of the *North American Review,* begun in 1815. It was designed to promote the new liberal theology of Unitarianism—contributors included Edward Everett and John Pickering—but it also published news on Harvard. There were departments of theology, review, and foreign literary news, as well as a literary department containing poetry, biography, and selected material. In the middle of its second year, the *Repository* was turned over to "A Society of Gentlemen."

v1   Jan. 1812-Apr. 1812   APS II, Reel 107
v2-4   July 1812-Oct. 1813   Reel 108

Note: v2, Oct. 1812 appears before v2, July 1812 on film.

SEE ALSO: Monthly Anthology, and Boston Review.

GENESEE FARMER. v.1-26; 1840-1865. Rochester, N.Y., 1840-1865.

v15-26, 1854-65 as s2 v. 1-5, 1840-44 as New Genessee farmer and gardeners' journal. Merged into American agriculturist.

The *Genesee Farmer* was founded in 1840 by John J. Thomas and M.B. Bateham, claiming descent from the original *Genesee Farmer* founded by Luther Tucker, and eventually united with the *Cultivator* and moved to Albany. Thomas and Bateham's magazine was devoted to agriculture and horticulture, and after 1842 was edited by such famous agricultural writers as Henry Colman and Joseph Harris.

New Genesee Farmer and Gardeners' Journal
v1-5   Jan. 1840-Dec. 1844   APS II, Reel 795

Genesee Farmer
v6-13   Jan. 1845-Dec. 1852   APS II, Reel 795
v14-s2 v 22   Jan. 1853-Dec. 1861   Reel 796
s2 v 23-26   Jan. 1862-Dec. 1865   Reel 797

Vol. 1: Pages 106-12 are bound out of order. Vol. 6: Pages 183-86 are not available for photographing.

Microfilm edition was prepared from CU, DNAL, MiU, N and ViBlbV copies.

THE GENESEE FARMER AND GARDENER'S JOURNAL. v.1-9; Jan. 1, 1831-Nov. 30, 1839. Rochester, N.Y., L. Tucker.

9 v. illus. weekly.

Editors: Jan. 1, 1831-Feb. 16, 1833, N. Goodsell.—Feb. 23, 1833-Nov. 30, 1839, L. Tucker and others. Merged into the Cultivator.

Begun by Luther Tucker in 1831, the *Genesee Farmer* was one of the most prominent agricultural magazines. This weekly was dignified, pious, and in a stilted way, literary. It was devoted to agriculture and horticulture and published much useful information on agricultural methods, various fruits and vegetables, breeding, and farm machinery, and also included coverage of agricultural and horticultural societies, meteorological tables, and some diagrams and illustrations. Special features included a dictionary of agricultural terms, "Hints to Farmers," and information on bees, maple sugar, soapmaking, and silk culture. There was also some nonagricultural material, such as miscellaneous essays and letters, poetry, anecdotes, recipes, current prices, and articles on education and New York canals.

v1-4	Jan. 1, 1831-Dec. 27, 1834	APS II, Reel 316
v5-8	Jan. 3, 1835-Dec. 29, 1838	Reel 317
v9	Jan. 5-Nov. 30, 1839	Reel 318

Microfilm edition was prepared from NIC copy.

SEE ALSO: Cultivator.

GENIUS OF LIBERTY. *SEE* Genius of Universal Emancipation.

GENIUS OF UNIVERSAL EMANCIPATION. v. 1-16; 1821-39. Mount Pleasant, Ohio; Philadelphia; Baltimore, etc., 1821-339.

16 v.

Title varies. Numbering irregular. Superseded by Genius of liberty.

Edited by B. Lundy.

Benjamin Lundy, a crusader against slavery, began his antislavery magazine without capital and with only six subscribers. Founded in Mount Pleasant, Ohio, in 1821, it was moved to several different cities including Philadelphia and Baltimore and finally to Lowell, Illinois. The *Genius,* which favored gradual abolition and colonization, published plans for abolition of slavery, reports of important law cases, proceedings of various abolition and other societies, biographical and historical sketches, poetry and anecdotes, and a summary of foreign and domestic news.

v1-4 and v1 [i.e. v5], nos. 1-18	July 1821-Dec. 1825	APS II, Reel 108

v1, no. 19- nsv2 [i.e. 5-8]	Jan. 7, 1826-Aug. 30, 1828	Reel 1272
nsv3-16 [i.e. 9-16]	Sept. 6, 1828-Mar 8, 1839	Reel 1273

Best copy available for photographing. Several volumes have stained or torn pages. Pagination is irregular. Third Series Vols. 1-3 [i.e. Vols. 11-13]: include supplements photographed at end of volumes. Third Series Vol. 3 [i.e. Vol. 13]: Pages 177-80 and 193-200 appear to be missing. Fourth Series Vol. 1 [i.e. Vol. 14]: Foldout is photographed at end of volume. Fifth Series Vol. 1 [i.e. Vol. 15]: Index, title page, and issue 4 are missing. Vol. 16: Title page and index are missing. Microfilm edition includes only no. 3; other issues not available for photographing.

Microfilm edition was prepared from DHU, NHC, and NIC copies.

THE GENTLEMAN AND LADY'S TOWN AND COUNTRY MAGAZINE; or, Repository of instruction and entertainment. v. 1 (no. 1-9); May 1784-Jan. 1785. Boston, Printed and sold by Weeden and Barrett.

1 v. Monthly.

Film incomplete: no. 9 wanting.

The first magazine to give special attention to women through fiction and advice.

v1, no. 1-8	May-Dec. 1784	APS I, Reel 13

Microfilm edition was prepared from MWA copy.

GENTLEMAN'S MAGAZINE. *SEE* Burton's Gentleman's Magazine and American Monthly Review.

THE GENTLEMEN AND LADIES' TOWN AND COUNTRY MAGAZINE: consisting of literature, history, politics, arts, manners, and amusements, with various other matter. v. 1-2, no. 7; Feb. 1789-Aug. 1790. Boston, Nathaniel Coverly.

2 v. 1 illus., plates. monthly.

Film incomplete: v. 2 wanting.

This monthly magazine contained an assortment of prose and poetry which emphasized the popular reign of sentiment and sensibility; many of these were contributed by a local following of women. Also included were foreign and domestic news, odd biographical and historical anecdotes, and other miscellaneous items.

v1	Feb. 1789-Jan. 1790	APS I, Reel 13

Microfilm edition was prepared from MB copy.

GEOGRAPHICAL AND MILITARY MUSEUM. *SEE* Military Monitor, and American Register.

GEOGRAPHICAL, HISTORICAL, AND STATISTICAL REPOSITORY. By William Darby. v. 1, no. 1-2; Sept.-Oct. 1824. Philadelphia.

1 v. fold. front., fold. pl., fold. map.

No. 1 consists principally of a geographical view and history of Pennsylvania.

Caption title: Darby's repository.

Edited by William Darby, this publication was divided into three sections: geography, history, and statistics. The only two numbers published dealt mainly with the geography of Pennsylvania, the history of North America and Pennsylvania, and statistics on various proposed canals and other topics. Diagrams and maps are included.

v1, no. 1	Sept. 1824	APS II, Reel 100
v1, no. 1-2	Sept.-Oct. 1824	Reel 130

GEOGRAPHICAL REVIEW. *SEE* American Geographical Society of New York.

THE GEORGIA ANALYTICAL REPOSITORY. v. 1, no. 1-6; May/June 1802-Mar./Apr. 1803. Savannah, Seymour, Woolhopter & Stebbins.

228 p. Bimonthly.

Edited by H. Holcombe.

Henry Holcombe, pastor of the Baptist Church in Savannah, conducted this religious magazine, which focused mainly on religious news, missionary news, and church history. It also offered sermons, biographical sketches, and poetry.

v1, no. 1-6   May/June 1802-Mar./Apr. 1803   APS II, Reel 19

THE GERMAN CORRESPONDENT. v. 1, no. 1-6; Jan. 1820-Jan. 1821. New York, P. Schmidt.

96 p. monthly.

Publication suspended June-Dec. 1820. Vol. 1, no. 6 also called new ser., no. 1. Edited by Hermann, pseud.

This short-lived New York paper, which was designed "to make German literature known to our countrymen," was started shortly after the second war with England in an attempt to divert attention from British literature. It published a variety of news about Germany, as well as political news and coverage of inventions and discoveries, and progress in the arts. It listed new publications, and included German reviews of some American publications, biographical sketches of eminent men, and poetry.

v1, no. 1-6   Jan. 1820-Jan. 1821   APS II, Reel 130

GERMAN REFORMED MESSENGER. *SEE* Reformed Church Messenger.

THE GLEANER; or, Monthly magazine. v. 1-2, no. 3; Sept. 1808-Nov. 1809. Lancaster, Pa., W. Greer.

2 v.

Title varies: Sept.-Nov. 1809, The Monthly magazine.

This Lancaster monthly conducted by Stacy Potts was divided into three sections. First there was a general section of moral essays, speeches and addresses, and miscellaneous articles, followed by a section of poetry, and ending with the "Register and Gazette," a section which published news on the government and on laws, and the proceedings of the legislature.

Gleaner; or, Monthly Magazine.
v1   Sept. 1808-Aug. 1809   APS II, Reel 32

Monthly Magazine.
v2   Sept.-Nov. 1809   APS II, Reel 32

v1; no. 1, 6, and 9 are incomplete.

Microfilm edition was prepared from WHi copy.

GLEASON'S PICTORIAL DRAWING-ROOM COMPANION. *SEE* Ballou's Pictorial Drawing-Room Companion.

THE GLOBE. By T. O'Connor. v. 1; Jan.-June 1819. New York, Printed by J. Oram, 1819.

384 p. monthly.

This monthly by T. O'Connor focused mainly on news, both domestic and foreign, devoting about half its space to news from abroad, particularly events in Ireland, England, Spain, and France. There was also a great deal of miscellaneous material such as cures for various ailments, interesting and unusual occurrences, and anecdotes.

v1, no. 1-6   Jan.-June 1819   APS II, Reel 109

GODEY'S BOOK AND MAGAZINE. *SEE* Godey's Magazine.

GODEY'S LADY'S BOOK. *SEE* American Ladies' Magazine; Arthur's Magazine; *and* Godey's Magazine.

⁎GODEY'S LADY'S BOOK, AND LADIES' AMERICAN MAGAZINE. *SEE* Godey's Magazine.

⁎GODEY'S MAGAZINE. v. 1-137; July 1830-Aug. 1898. New York, Godey Co., [1830-98]

137 v. in illus., plates (part fold.) ports., plans. monthly. Part of the illustrative material is colored. Includes music.

Title varies: 1830-39, The Lady's book (varies) 1840-43, Godey's lady's book, and ladies' American magazine. Jan. 1844-June 1848, Godey's magazine and lady's book (caption title: Godey's lady's book) July 1848-June 1854, Godey's lady's book. July 1854-Dec. 1882, Godey's book and magazine. Jan. 1883-Sept. 1892. Godey's lady's book. Oct. 1892-Aug. 1898, Godey's magazine (cover-title, Oct. 1892-Jan. 1894: Godey's America's first magazine)

Founded, and for many years edited by L.A. Godey (with Mrs. Sarah J. Hale, 1873-77). Vols. 1-125, no. 747 were published in Philadelphia. Absorbed the American ladies' magazine in Jan. 1837. Absorbed by the Puritan in Oct. 1

Godey's Magazine, begun in 1830 by Louis A. Godey, was by far the most popular women's periodical of its day. Achieving a circulation of 150,000 before the war, it was anxiously awaited by its many fans, who read and re-read the sentimental stories and poems, studied and copied the fashions, and even cut out and framed the engravings. The key to its success was the section of fashion plates, which were hand-colored by more than 100 women employed by Godey. In 1837, Godey bought Mrs. Sarah J. Hale's *Ladies' Magazine* and obtained Mrs. Hale as editor; this marked the beginning of the magazine's best literary period. In the years between 1837 and 1850 all the popular writers of the time appeared in its pages; contributors included Emerson, Longfellow, Holmes, Hawthorne, Harriet Beecher Stowe, and Edgar Allan Poe, in addition to tales and poetry, contents included light essays, biography, sketches, humor, book reviews, recipes, and articles on music, art, fashions, health, and beauty. Sentiment was abundant, and politics were excluded, but much on the education of women appeared. S. Annie Frost took over as editor in 1877, and in 1883 the magazine was purchased and edited by J.H. Haulenbeek. Unfortunately, *Godey's* was now in a serious decline which could not be halted, and in 1898 it was absorbed by the *Puritan.*

Lady's Book
v1-6   July 1830-June 1833   APS II, Reel 772

Monthly Magazine of Belles-Lettres and the Arts, the Lady's Book
v7-9	July 1833-Dec. 1834	APS II, Reel 772

Lady's Book
v10	Jan-June 1835	APS II, Reel 772
v11-19	July 1835-Dec. 1839	Reel 773

Godey's Lady's Book, and Ladies' American Magazine
v20	Jan-June 1840	APS II, Reel 773
v21-27	July 1840-Dec. 1843	Reel 774

Godey's Magazine and Lady's Book
v28-29	Jan.-Dec. 1844	APS II, Reel 774
v30-36	Jan. 1845-June 1848	Reel 775

Godey's Lady's Book
v37	July-Dec. 1848	APS II, Reel 775
v38-41	Jan. 1849-Dec. 1850	Reel 776
v42-44	Jan. 1851-June 1852	Reel 862
v45-48	July 1852-June 1854	Reel 863

Godey's Lady's Book and Magazine
v49-53	July 1854-Dec. 1856	APS II, Reel 864
v54-58	Jan. 1857-June 1859	Reel 865
v59-64	July 1859-June 1862	Reel 866
v65-70	July 1862-June 1865	Reel 867
v71-76	July 1865-June 1868	Reel 868
v77-81	July 1868-Dec. 1870	Reel 869
v82-86	Jan. 1871-June 1873	Reel 870
v87-91	July 1873-Dec. 1875	Reel 871
v92-96	Jan. 1876-June 1878	Reel 872
v97-102	July 1878-June 1881	Reel 873
v103-105	July 1881-Dec. 1882	Reel 874

Godey's Lady's Book
v106-108	Jan. 1883-June 1884	APS II, Reel 874
v109-114	July 1884-June 1887	Reel 875
v115-119	July 1887-Dec. 1889	Reel 876
v120-124	Jan. 1890-June 1892	Reel 877
v125, no. 745-747	July-Sept. 1892	Reel 878

Godey's Magazine
v125, no. 748-v128	Oct. 1892-June 1894	APS II, Reel 878
v129-132	July 1894-June 1896	Reel 879
v133-137	July 1896-Aug. 1898	Reel 880

Reels 772-776: Pagination is irregular. Best copy available for photographing. Several volumes lack many of the plates. Vol. 1: Pgs. 283-88 are bound out of order. Vol. 38: Pgs. 157-58, 229-30, 301-02, 371-74 are missing. Reels 867-880: Pagination is irregular. Vol. 50, Vol. 64 and Vols. 65-114, several plates were not available for photographing. Vol. 60, pages 361-62, Vol. 116, pages 46-47 and Vol. 131, pages i-ii of index were not available for photographing. Vol. 107 cover page should read July 1883-December 1883. Vol. 109 cover page should read July 1884-December 1884.

Microfilm edition was prepared from CL, CtY, DLC, KMK, KU, MiD, MiU, Mi, CLCO, RP, MoS, NcD, IC, NB, NPV, TU and WHi copies.

GODEY'S MAGAZINE AND LADY'S BOOK. *SEE* Godey's Magazine.

GOOD LITERATURE. *SEE* Critic; An Illustrated Monthly Review of Literature, Art, and Life.

GOOD WORK. *SEE* Baptist Missionary Magazine.

THE GOSPEL ADVOCATE; conducted by a society of gentlemen. v. 1-6; 1821-26. Boston, J.W. Ingraham.

6 v. monthly.

Published in Newburyport, Mass., from Jan-April 1821. United with the Episcopal watchman in 1827.

Film covers: v. 1-5; 1821-1825.

This Episcopal magazine contained a theology department and published sermons and missionary news, along with some literary and political news and poetry.

v1-5	1821-1825	APS II, Reel 109

SEE ALSO: Episcopal Watchman and Gospel Advocate and Impartial Investigator.

GOSPEL ADVOCATE AND IMPARTIAL INVESTI-GATOR. v. 1-7, 1823-29. Buffalo [and] Auburn, 1823-29

7 v.

Vols. 1-4 as Gospel advocate. Merged into Evangelical magazine and gospel advocate.

Thomas Gross was the first editor of this weekly Universalist paper, which was begun in Buffalo in 1823; he was succeeded by L.S. Everett in the fall of 1825. The *Advocate* was moved to Auburn at the beginning of 1827, with Everett remaining as editor unitl the end of 1828, when he was replaced by Orestes A. Brownson. Contents included proceedings of Universalist society meetings, articles on religion, doctrine, and Bible studies, and some poetry and anecdotes.

v1-3	1823-1825	APS II, Reel 110
v4-7	Jan. 13, 1826-Dec. 26, 1829	Reel 1072

Vol. 7: Pages 144-145 missing in number only.

Microfilm edition was prepared from MMeT, NRCR, N, and NRU copies.

GOSPEL ADVOCATE OF AUBURN. *SEE* Evangelical Magazine and Gospel Advocate.

THE GOSPEL HERALD. v. 1-7, no. 26; Apr. 22, 1820-May 5, 1827; new ser., v. 1, no. 26; Jan. 3-Dec. 19, 1829. New York, 1821-

7 v. Biweekly.

Henry Fitz, editor.

Edited by Henry Fitz, this weekly religious paper was "open to all religious sects" and gave broad coverage to a discussion of various religions, dealing with many controversial issues and providing articles on doctrine, as well as sermons, essays, poetry, biography, and anecdotes.

v1-7	Apr. 22, 1820-May 5, 1827	APS II, Reel 503
nsv1	Jan. 3, 1829-Dec. 19, 1829	Reel 503

Several pages are tightly bound, stained and faded with some loss of text.

Microfilm edition was prepared from DLC and MMeT copies.

THE GOSPEL INQUIRER. v. 1; June 21, 1823-June 5, 1824. Little Falls, N.Y., C. Nichols.

208 p. biweekly.

Edited by G.B. Lisher.

This Universalist magazine published information on Universalist meetings, associations, and new churches, and selections from the *Universalist Magazine,* as well as sermons, biographical sketches, and occasional poetry and anecdotes.

v1, no. 1-26   June 21, 1823-June 5, 1824   APS II, Reel 110

GOSPEL PALLADIUM. v.1-2, no.1; 1823-July 16, 1824. Warren, R.I., etc.

2 v.

On film: v.1, no. 6 and v. 2, no. 1 only.

Edited by Reuben Potter, Jr., the *Gospel Palladium* was devoted not only to religion and morality but to literature and scientific news as well. It presented sermons, general news, poetry and anecdotes, departments for ladies and for parents, and much miscellaneous material.

v1, no. 6   Aug. 22, 1823   APS II, Reel 110
v2, no. 1   July 16, 1824   Reel 110

GOSPEL TRUMPET. v. 1-2, 1822-Dec. 1823. Dayton, Ohio, S. & M. M. Henkle.

2 v. monthly.

Vol. 1 wanting.

This short-lived religious magazine reported on Sunday schools and on the American Colonization Society in addition to publishing missionary news, articles on doctrine and on Unitarianism, and biography and poetry.

v2, no. 1-12   Jan.-Dec. 1823   APS II, Reel 130

THE GOSPEL VISITANT, Being principally original tracts on moral and religious subjects. v. 1-3, no. 2; June 1811-July 1818. Haverhill, etc. Printed by P.N. Green, etc.

3 v. quarterly.

Editors: Thomas Jones, Hosea Ballou, Abner Kneeland, Edward Turner, etc.

The first volume of this quarterly Universalist magazine was conducted by several Universalist ministers—Thomas Jones, Hosea Ballou, Abner Kneeland, and Edward Turner, but after four numbers was suspended for five years. When it began publishing again in 1817, it was edited by Edward Turner and Hosea Ballou. Most of the material was original, consisting of essays on questions of doctrine and religion, but contents also included extracts from other publications, poetry, sermons, letters, and news of ordinations and installations.

v1-3   June 1811-July 1818   APS II, Reel 110

THE GRAHAM JOURNAL OF HEALTH AND LONGEVITY. Devoted to the practical illustration of the science of human life, as taught by Sylvester Graham and others. David Campbell, editor. v. 1-3; April 1837-Dec. 1839. Boston and New York, 1837-39.

3 v. weekly, 1837; bi-weekly, 1838-39.

Title varies slightly. United with the Library of health.

Edited by David Campbell, this periodical promoted Grahamism; that is, the crusade begun by Sylvester Graham which advocated the use of unbolted flour for the making of bread.

v1-3   Apr. 4, 1837-Dec. 14, 1839   APS II, Reel 777

Volume 3: Lacks index.

Microfilm edition was prepared from Ia-T copy.

GRAHAM'S AMERICAN MONTHLY MAGAZINE OF LITERATURE, ART, AND FASHION. v. 1-53; Jan. 1826-Dec. 1858. Philadelphia, G.R. Graham, 1841-

53 v. illus., plates (part col.) ports.

Formed by the union of the Casket and the Gentleman's magazine. Continues the volume numbering of the Casket. Title varies: Jan. 1826-Dec. 1830 and May 1839-Nov. 1840, Casket. Jan. 1831-Apr. 1839, Atkinson's casket. Jan. 1841-Dec. 1842, Graham's lady's and gentleman's magazine. Jan.-June 1843, Graham's magazine of literature and art ... July 1843-June 1844, Graham's lady's and gentleman's magazine ... July 1844- Graham's American monthly magazine of literature and art (later "of literature, art, and fashion"). Caption title: 1841- Graham's magazine.

Editors: Jan. 1841- G.R. Graham; with E.A. Poe, Jan. 1841-May 1842.–C.J. Peterson, Mrs. Ann S. Stephens, 1842,–R.W. Griswold, July 1842-June 1843.–R.T. Conrad, Jan.-June 1848.–J.R. Chandler, J.C. Taylor, Oct. 1848-Dec. 1849. Continued as the American monthly, Jan. 1859. cf. Smyth, Phila. magazines, p. 224.

Graham's American Magazine began as the *Casket,* a miscellany of tales and articles taken chiefly from other periodicals, with puzzles, jokes, music, and poetry. Illustrations consisted of engraved plates and some woodcuts of flowers and of American scenery. Although it is important chiefly as the earlier series of *Graham's,* in its heyday the *Casket* achieved a wide popularity. When George R. Graham purchased the magazine in May, 1839, he modelled it after the *Gentleman's Magazine,* publishing rather sensational tales dealing with love, American adventure, and the Orient, along with poetry, a little travel, and book reviews. But *Graham's* forged far ahead of its model in both literary value and illustration. James Russell Lowell, Edgar Allan Poe, Mrs. Lydia H. Sigourney, George Pope Morris, Alfred B. Street, and Thomas Buchanan Read were among its writers for the first year, and in the following years, other well-known writers were added—William Cullen Bryant, James Fenimore Cooper, Richard Henry Dana, Henry Wadsworth Longfellow, Mrs. Emma C. Embury, Mrs. Seba Smith, and Nathaniel Parker Willis. One of its chief distinctions was its light essays; poetry, too, was important, both because of the fame of the contributors and the space devoted to it. Another feature was its illustrations, which included mezzotints by John Sartain, colored fashion plates, and many plates of sentimental and domestic scenes and landscapes. After 1850, however, it became difficult to compete with *Harper's* and the magazine began to languish, finally being suspended in 1858. But during its lifetime, it had published some important work by the best American writers of the time.

Casket

v1-4	Feb. 1826-Dec. 1829	APS II, Reel 547
v5	Jan.-Dec. 1830	Reel 548

Atkinson's Casket

v6-8	Jan. 1831-Dec. 1833	APS II, Reel 548
v9-11	Jan. 1834-Dec. 1836	Reel 549
v12-14, no. 4	Jan. 1837-Apr. 1839	Reel 550

Casket

v14, no.5-v15	May-Dec. 1839	APS II, Reel 550
v16-17	Jan.-Nov. 1840	Reel 551

Graham's Lady's and Gentleman's Magazine

v18-21	Jan. 1841-Dec. 1842	APS II, Reel 551

Graham's Magazine of Literature and Art

v22	Jan.-June 1843	APS II, Reel 552

Graham's Lady's and Gentleman's Magazine

v23-24	July 1843-June 1844	APS II, Reel 552

Graham's American Monthly Magazine of Literature, Art, and Fashion

v25-27	July 1844-Dec. 1845	APS II, Reel 552
v28-32	Jan. 1846-June 1848	Reel 553
v33-35	July 1848-Dec. 1849	Reel 554
v36-38	Jan. 1850-June 1851	Reel 555
v39-41	July 1851-Dec. 1852	Reel 556
v42-44	Jan. 1853-June 1854	Reel 557
v45-47	July 1854-Dec. 1855	Reel 558
v48-50	Jan. 1856-June 1857	Reel 559
v51-53	July 1857-Dec. 1858	Reel 560

Many pages are creased, tightly bound, stained, or torn with some loss of text. Several pages are misnumbered. The microfilm edition begins with vol.1, issue 2. Vols. 8, 13, 14, 17, and 25: Title page and indexes are missing. Vols. 14-15 are bound and photographed together. Vol. 17: Issue 6 is missing. Vols. 23-27 are misnumbered. Vol. 47: Issue 6 title page and plates are bound in vol. 53.

Microfilm edition was prepared from Ia-T, IaU, MB, N, OCI and PPiU copies.

SEE ALSO: Burton's Gentleman's Magazine and American Monthly Review.

GRAHAMS LADY'S AND GENTLEMAN'S MAGAZINE. *SEE* Graham's American Monthly Magazine of Literature, Art, and Fashion.

GRAHAM'S MAGAZINE. *SEE* Burton's Gentleman's Magazine and American Monthly Review.

GRAHAM'S MAGAZINE OF LITERATURE AND ART. *SEE* Graham's American Monthly Magazine of Literature, Art, and Fashion.

GREAT REPUBLIC MONTHLY. *SEE* Emerson's Magazine and Putnam's Monthly.

THE GREEN MOUNTAIN GEM; a monthly journal of literature, science and the arts. v. 1-7; 1843-49. Bradford, Vt.

7 v.

Editor: A.B.F. Hildreth. Title varies.

This monthly journal was to contain moral and entertaining literature and news of the literary world. It published sentimental prose and poetry, music, moral essays, biography, critical notices of books and other new publications, an agricultural report, and articles on history, travel, and geography. Also included were science and art columns and foreign and domestic news.

v1-7	1843-1849	APS II, Reel 654

Microfilm edition was prepared from DLC, IU and VtU copies.

THE GREEN MOUNTAIN REPOSITORY; for the year 1832. Ed. by Z. Thompson. Burlington, Printed by E. Smith.

284 p. monthly.

The *Green Mountain Repository* focused mainly on science and local and state history, including no fiction and very little poetry. Most of the articles, short essays, and biographies dealt with the history of the state and with the early settlers, or with botany, zoology, mathematics, or other scientific subjects. Each issue contained a math question, a review of new school books, and a miscellaneous section of short anecdotes and interesting facts.

no. 1-12	1832	APS II, Reel 654

Microfilm edition was prepared from DLC copy.

GREENBANK'S PERIODICAL LIBRARY. *SEE* Periodical Library.

THE GRIDIRON. v.1, no.1-26; Aug. 29, 1822-May 8, 1823. Dayton, Ohio, J. Anderson.

208 p. biweekly.

This weekly *Gridiron* is chiefly interesting as an example of partisan journalism of the day, and is thought to be the earliest humorous publication west of the Ohio river. Focusing strongly on local affairs, it promised to be "the unceasing and indefatigable advocate and friend of virtuous and moral citizens ... and the continued and determined tormenter of all 'evil doers'." Although largely made up of abusive political satire, it also contained some literature, poetry and humor, including puns, anecdotes, and riddles. It appears to have been the product of a campaign for election to Congress between Judge Joseph H. Crane and Dr. William Blodget, and although Blodget is the main target, many prominent Daytonians are also attacked and thus the *Gridiron* is important as a source on the history of the Miami area.

v1, no. 1-26	Aug. 29, 1822-May 8, 1823	APS II, Reel 111

GRIFFIN'S JOURNAL. *SEE* American Catholic Historical Researches.

THE GUARDIAN. v. 1, no. 1-52; 1807-Nov. 12, 1808. Albany.

200 p. Weekly.

No. 23 and 49 omitted in numbering. Film incomplete: no. 1, 25, 35, 43, 52 wanting.

Poetry, tales, anecdotes, and biographical sketches made up the contents of the *Guardian* of Albany. A few ads also appeared in its pages.

v1, no.1-14, 26-34,
36-42, 44-51   1807-1808   APS II, Reel 19

Microfilm edition was prepared from MiU-C copy.

SEE ALSO: Monitor

THE GUARDIAN AND MONITOR. A monthly publication, devoted to the moral improvement of the rising generation. v. 1-10, no. 12; 1819-Dec. 1828. New Haven, N. Whiting, etc.

illus., plates.

Vol. 7 called "New series." Vols. 1-6 have title: The Guardian, or Youth's religious instructor. Editor: E.B. Coleman.

According to its subtitle, this children's magazine was "devoted to the moral improvement of the rising generation," and to this end it published sermons, essays on behavior, hints to children, and news on Sunday schools, revivals, and missions, as well as some poetry.

Guardian, or Youth's Religious Instructor
v1-5   Jan. 1819-Dec. 1823   APS II, Reel 111
v6   Jan.-Dec. 1824   Reel 112

Guardian and Monitor
v7   Jan.-Dec. 1825   APS II, Reel 112
v8-10   Jan. 1826-Dec. 1828   Reel 881

Vol. 9: pages 241-252 are stained. Vol. 10: pages are stained throughout.

Microfilm edition was prepared from DLC and CtHT-W copies.

SEE ALSO: Monitor, Designed to Improve the Taste ...

GUARDIAN, OR YOUTH'S RELIGIOUS INSTRUCTOR. *SEE* Guardian and Monitor.

GUNTON'S MAGAZINE. v. 1-27; Mar. 1891-Dec. 1904. New York.

27 v. illus., facsims., ports. monthly. No numbers were published for Aug. 1891 and June 1892.

Title varies: Mar. 1891-Dec. 1895, The Social economist.–Jan. 1896-Apr. 1898, Gunton's magazine of American economics (later "of practical economics" and "of social economics") and political science.

Edited by G. Gunton. Published by The School of Social Economics (etc.) Mar. 1891-June 1897(?) Filmed copy imperfect: wanting t.p. for most numbers and t.p. for many vols.

Called *Social Economist* during its first five years, this Republian monthly was subsidized by Standard Oil Company and became the spokesman of trusts, a high protective tariff, and what the Democrats termed "special privilege." Book reviews, an news chronicle, and some miscellany made it less a series of propaganda tracts and more a magazine. Although most of its contributors were obscure writers, Senator George F. Hoar, President J.G. Schurman, Carroll D. Wright, and Horace White wrote for it in its early years.

Social Economist.
v1-9   Mar. 1891-Dec. 1895   APS III, Reel 473

Gunton's Magazine of American Economics and Political Science.
v10-14, no. 4   Jan. 1896-Apr. 1898   APS III, Reel 474

Gunton's Magazine.
v14, no. 5-16   May 1898-June 1899   APS III, Reel 474
v17-22   July 1899-June 1902   Reel 475
v23-27   July 1902-Dec. 1904   Reel 476

Vol. 6: Tables of contents for January-May 1894 are not available for photographing. Vol. 15: Title page is torn. Vol. 27: Table of contents for July 1904 is not available for photographing.

Microfilm edition was prepared from C, CL, MiU, and NBuG copies.

GUNTON'S MAGAZINE OF AMERICAN ECONOMICS AND POLITICAL SCIENCE. *SEE* Gunton's Magazine.

THE HALCYON ITINERARY; and true millennium messenger. no. 1-6; Aug. 1807-Jan. 1808. Marietta [Ohio] Printed by S. Fairlamb.

211 p. Monthly.

This religious monthly published a variety of material, including studies of doctrine and Scriptures, and extracts from Josephus's writings on Jewish history.

no. 1-6   Aug. 1807-Jan. 1808   APS II, Reel 19

Microfilm edition was prepared from DLC copy.

THE HALCYON LUMINARY, AND THEOLOGICAL REPOSITORY, a monthly magazine, devoted to religion and polite literature. Conducted by a society of gentlemen. v. 1-2; Jan. 1812-Dec. 1813. New York, S. Woodworth.

2 v. plates. monthly.

This monthly miscellany contained both religious and non-religious material. Contents included Bible studies and articles on doctrine, letters from readers and replies to these letters, biographical sketches, poetry, musical pieces, and some illustrated articles on science and on health and cures for disease.

v1   Jan.-Dec. 1812   APS II, Reel 112

v2   Jan.-Dec. 1813   Reel 464

Reel 464: Several pages are stained with some loss of text. Pages 244-245 are missing.

Microfilm edition was prepared from DLC copy.

HANGMAN. *SEE* Prisoner's Friend.

THE HAPPY HOME AND PARLOR MAGAZINE. v. 1-10; Jan. 1855-Jan. 1860. Boston, C. Stone.

10 v. illus., plates. monthly.

Editors: Jan. 1855-Dec. 1857, A.R. Baker.–Jan. 1858-Jan. 1860, William Thayer. No more published?

The Rev. Abijah R. Baker, pastor of the Congregational Church at Wellesley, Massachusetts, edited this family-oriented religious magazine until 1858 with the assistance of his wife, Harriette Newell Woods Baker, herself an author. Baker was succeeded in the editorship by the Rev. William M. Thayer. The *Happy Home* did not advocate any particular doctrine, and was concerned mainly with improving family life and relations between parents and children and between husbands and wives, and thus it offered much instructive material—moral tales, essays by ministers, including some on Christian integrity in business, Bible stories, Biblical notes, prayers, biographical sketches, and poetry. Musical pieces appeared in most issues. Not all the material was religious, however; there was much on fashion, sentimental prose and poetry, household hints and recipes, foreign and domestic news, book notices, some humor, and numerous illustrations. A children's department was added during the later years.

| v1-6 | 1855-1857 | APS III, Reel 756 |
| v7-10 | 1858-1860 | Reel 757 |

Several pages and plates are missing. Pagination is irregular.

Microfilm edition was prepared from CoCC, N, and RPB copies.

SEE ALSO: Christian Parlor Magazine.

HARBINGER, devoted to social and political progress. v. 1-8, no. 15; June 14, 1845-Feb. 10, 1849. New York, 1845-1849.

8 v.

Published first at Brook Farm and then in New York, *Harbinger* was an organ of American Fourierism, but also gave attention to literary and musical criticism as well as social reform. As a vehicle for the writings of transcendentalists, it was a successor of the *Dial*, also the heritor of the Brook Farm *Phalanx,* which it superseded in 1845, and of Albert Brisbane's *Future*. It was an interesting, vigorous, and lively periodical and valuable as a source for the study of New England transcendentalism. Contents were varied: included were translations of George Sands's *Consuelo* and Fourier's *Cosmogony,* reports from other phalanges, articles on music and on the hard conditions of laborers, and political material opposing slavery and the war with Mexico.

| v1-8 | June 14, 1845-Feb. 10, 1849 | APS II, Reel 674 |

Vol. 8: Index is lacking.

Microfilm edition was prepared from MH, NHi and NNC copies.

THE HARBINGER OF THE MISSISSIPPI VALLEY. v. 1, no. 1-2; Mar.-Apr. 1832. [Frankfort?, Ky.]

32 p. monthly.

This religious magazine covered activities of the Kentucky Temperance Society, and of Sunday schools, and contained poetry and articles on temperance and on the colonization movement, including news of the progress of colonization in Africa.

| v1 | Mar-Apr. 1832 | APS II, Reel 560 |

Microfilm edition was prepared from CSmH and WHi copies.

HARPER'S BAZAAR. v. 1- Nov. 1867- . New York, Harper, 1868- 19-

v. illus., plates, ports., patterns. Weekly, Nov. 1867-Apr. 1901;

monthly, May 1901-

Title varies slightly.

On film: issues for Nov. 1867-Nov. 1912.

Wilkie Collins, William Black, William Dean Howells, Justin McCarthy, and John Kendrick Bangs were among the contributors to this highly successful women's magazine. Serial fiction, verse, styles, patterns, cartoons by Nast, and articles on interior design and house and garden were featured. In the early years, it was patterned after *Der Bazar* of Berlin, and the title was *Harper's Bazar* until 1929.

v1-2	Nov. 1867-Dec. 1869	APS III, Reel 430
v3-4	Jan. 1870-Dec. 1871	Reel 431
v5-6	Jan. 1872-Dec. 1873	Reel 432
v7-9	Jan. 1874-Dec. 1876	Reel 433
v10-12	Jan. 1877-Dec. 1879	Reel 434
v13-15	Jan. 1880-Dec. 1882	Reel 435
v16-18	Jan. 1883-Dec. 1885	Reel 436
v19-20	Jan. 1886-Dec. 1887	Reel 437
v21-22	Jan. 1888-Dec. 1889	Reel 438
v23-24	Jan. 1890-Dec. 1891	Reel 439
v25-26	Jan. 1892-Dec. 1893	Reel 440
v27-28	Jan. 1894-Dec. 1895	Reel 441
v29-30	Jan. 1896-Dec. 1897	Reel 442
v31-32	Jan. 1898-Dec. 1899	Reel 443
v33	Jan. 1900-Dec. 1900	Reel 444
v34-35	Jan. 1901-Dec. 1901	Reel 445
v36-37	Jan. 1902-Dec. 1903	Reel 446
v38-39	Jan. 1904-Dec. 1905	Reel 447
v40-41	Jan. 1906-Dec. 1907	Reel 448
v42-43	Jan. 1908-Dec. 1909	Reel 449
v44-46	Jan. 1910-Nov 1912	Reel 450

Pagination is irregular. Some pages are stained, torn, or have print missing. Many volumes have pages repeated. Several volumes lack indexes. Supplements follow several volumes. Vol. 32: pgs. 581-85 are missing.

Microfilm edition was prepared from CL copy.

HARPER'S NEW MONTHLY MAGAZINE. *SEE* International Monthly Magazine of Literature, Science and Art.

HARPER'S WEEKLY. *SEE* Independent.

HARTFORD PEARL AND LITERARY GAZETTE. *SEE* Boston Pearl, A Gazette of Polite Literature.

THE HARVARD LYCEUM. v. 1; July 14, 1810-March 9, 1811. Cambridge, Published, semi-monthly, by Hilliard and Metcalf, 1811.

1 p.l., 432 p. biweekly.

Edited by Edward Everett, Samuel Gilman, N.L. Frothingham, and other members of the senior class in Harvard college. "This is the first paper that ever was attempted by the students of Harvard."

Conducted by members of the senior class at Harvard, this semi-monthly literary journal was the first Harvard periodical. Edward Everett and John Chipman Gray were among its editors. The *Lyceum* dealt with American and classical literature, math, and natural history and included some original poetry, moral and religious essays, and miscellany.

| v1, no. 1-18 | July 14, 1810-Mar. 9, 1811 | APS II, Reel 112 |

THE HARVARD REGISTER. no. I-XII; March, 1827-Feb. 1828. Cambridge, Hilliard and Brown, 1828.

384 p. monthly.

A literary periodical conducted by members of Harvard. Harvard undergraduates wrote most of the material—poetry, historical sketches and writings on Harvard and the life there, and essays and articles on literature, drama, and the classics.

no. 1-12   Mar. 1827-Feb. 1828   APS II, Reel 777

Index is lacking.

Microfilm edition was prepared from NN copy.

THE HARVARD REGISTER; an illustrated monthly. Ed. and pub. at Harvard college by Moses King. v. 1-3; Jan. 1880-July, 1881. Cambridge, Mass. [1880-81]

3 v. in 2. illus.

Title varies: 1880, The Harvard register. A monthly periodical devoted to the interests of higher education. 1881, The Harvard register; an illustrated monthly.

The *Harvard Register* stands as a salute to Harvard College by Moses King. Articles such as "The Money Value of a College Education" by Andrew Preston Peabody appeared in the first issue, and "Education in Nova Scotia" by Arthur Wentworth Eaton in the fourth issue of the second volume. Similar essays were afforded by John Trowbridge, Thomas Hill, Cazneau Palfrey, Arthur Gilman, William Dean Howells, Charles C. Everett, Edward Everett Hale, and Charles William Eliot.

The Harvard buildings and adjacent lands, societies, regulations, notices, graduating classes, biographies and obituary notices filled the remaining columns.

v1-3   Jan. 1880-July 1881   APS III, Reel 109

Microfilm edition was prepared from MiU copy.

HARVARDIANA. v. 1-4; [Sept.?] 1834-July 1838. Cambridge and Boston, J. Munroe, 1835-38.

4 v. monthly.

1837-38, monthly during the college year.

A literary journal conducted by Harvard undergraduates which contained poetry, essays, reviews of new books, and excerpts from recent publications along with other literary material. James Russell Lowell was one of the editors in 1838.

v1-4   1834-1838   APS II, Reel 655

Microfilm edition was prepared from CSmH and MH copies.

HAZARD'S REGISTER OF PENNSYLVANIA, devoted to the preservation of facts and documents, and every kind of useful information respecting the state of Pennsylvania. Ed. by Samuel Hazard. Vol. I-XVI. January, 1828-December, 1835. Philadelphia, Printed by W.F. Geddes [1828-35]

16 v. illus. weekly.

Vols. I-VII (1828-31) have title: The Register of Pennsylvania.

Edited by Samuel Hazard, the *Register* was devoted to the preservation of material and information relating to Pennsylvania. It published facts, documents, and anecdotes concerning the state's early history, Indian history and treaties, the Revolution, and natural history; state papers and public documents; and a chronicle of events; as well as information on finances, commerce, manufactures, and agriculture. In addition, it contained descriptions of cities, towns, and counties, biographies of distinguished men; reports of various societies; and proceedings of Congress, the state legislature and city councils. Much statistical material was included.

Register of Pennsylvania.
v1-2	Jan. 5-Dec. 27, 1828	APS II, Reel 476
v3-7	Jan. 3, 1829-June 25, 1831	Reel 477

Hazard's Register of Pennsylvania.
v8	July 2-Dec. 31, 1831	APS II, Reel 477
v9-13	Jan. 7, 1832-June 28, 1834	Reel 478
v14-16	July 5, 1834-Dec. 26, 1835	Reel 479

Pagination is irregular. Several pages are stained with some loss of text.

Vol. 7: Page 258 is cropped with some loss of text.

Microfilm edition was prepared from DLC and MiU copies.

HEALTH. v. 1-77; Dec. 1, 1845-Dec. 1892; 2nd ser. v. 43-64, no. 1; Jan. 1893-Jan. 1914. New York.

99 v. Semimonthly, 1845-1847; monthly, 1848-1914. Vol. numbers are irregular.

Title varies: 1845-1861, Water-cure journal.—1862, Hygienic teacher and Water-cure journal.—1863-92, Herald of health.—1893-1897, Journal of hygiene and Herald of health.— 1898-1900, Omega. Subtitle varies.

Merged into Physical culture. On film: v. 1-34, v. 36-40; v. 42, no. 1-3; v. 43-44; v. 48-49; v. 51; 2nd ser. v. 50, no. 9-63.

During the mid-1800's, there was great interest in the "water cure," a means of curing and preventing disease without the use of drugs of any kind. The *Water-Cure Journal,* as it was originally titled, was one of the most successful of the periodicals dealing with this subject. In addition to articles on various water treatments and the uses of water, it was concerned with physiology, pathology, and physical, moral, and intellectual development and gave information on cleanliness, clothing, ventilation, diet, pregnancy and prevention of disease.

When it became the *Herald of Health* in 1863, the space previously devoted to the "water cure" began to be filled by more varied contents, while the emphasis on physical, moral, and intellectual development was maintained. Articles dealt with hygiene, the rearing of children, care of the sick and various cures for illness, and the evils of alcohol; in addition there were recipes, poetry, notices of new publications, and answers to readers' questions. The magazine became still more varied in 1900 when its title was changed to *Health.* During this period it emphasized physical culture and recreation, as well as providing information on health care and diet. Its pages now contained many illustrations and advertisements, as well as occasional travel and adventure articles.

Water-Cure Journal
v1-6	Dec. 1845-Dec. 1848	APS II, Reel 576
v7-24	Jan. 1849-Dec. 1857	Reel 577
v25-33	Jan. 1858-Dec. 1861	Reel 578

Hygienic Teacher and Water-Cure Journal
v34	Jan.-Dec. 1862	APS II, Reel 578

Herald of Health

v36-44	Jan. 1864-Dec. 1867	APS II, Reel 1692
v48-49, 51	July 1869-Dec. 1892	Reel 1693

Health

nsv50-53	Sept. 1900-Dec. 1903	APS II, Reel 1693
nsv55-56	Jan. 1905-Dec. 1906	Reel 1694
nsv57-59	Jan. 1907-Dec. 1909	Reel 1695
nsv60-63	Jan. 1910-Dec. 1913	Reel 1696

Reels 576-578: Several pages are stained, faded, and tightly bound with some loss of text. Pagination is irregular. Reels 1692-1696: Volume numbers are irregular. Microfilm edition ends December, 1913.

Microfilm edition was prepared from DLC, DNLM, MH, MiU, and OCU copies.

HEALTH JOURNAL AND INDEPENDENT MAGAZINE. *SEE* Phalanx: Organ of the Doctrine of Association.

HEARST'S INTERNATIONAL. *SEE* Cosmopolitan; A Monthly Illustrated Magazine.

HEBREW STUDENT: A MONTHLY JOURNAL IN THE INTERESTS OF OLD TESTAMENT LITERATURE AND INTERPRETATION. *SEE* Biblical World.

L'HEMISPHERE, JOURNAL FRANCAIS; contenant des varietes litteraires et politiques, dedie aux Americains amateurs de la langue francaise. v. 1-2 (no. 1-52); Oct. 7, 1809-Sept. 28, 1811. Philadelphie.

2 v. Weekly.

Edited by J.J. Negrin.

This French-language literary and political journal included some sections written in both French and English. It published poetry, biographical sketches and political news.

v1, nos. 1-9	Oct. 7-Dec. 30, 1809	APS II, Reel 19
v1-2, nos. 10-52	Jan. 13, 1810-Sept. 28, 1811	Reel 113

Microfilm edition was prepared from PHi copy.

HERALD OF GOSPEL LIBERTY. v. 1-122, no. 9; Sept. 1, 1808-Feb. 27, 1930. Dayton, Ohio, Portsmouth, N.H., Christian Pub. Association [etc.]

49 v. illus. biweekly; weekly.

Official organ of the Christian Church. Founded and for some time edited by E. Smith. Absorbed the Journal of Christian education in 1928. Merged with the Congregationalist to form the Congregationalist and herald of gospel liberty.

On film: v. 1, no. 1-35 (reel 19) v. 75-84, 95-99, 102-110, 113-122 (reels 1925-1934)

Founded by Elias Smith in Portsmouth, New Hampshire in 1808, the *Herald of Gospel Liberty* was the first religious weekly. It published sermons, religious news and a series of essays on liberty, along with poetry and anecdotes. During its long lifetime, it underwent a number of changes of location and name, finally ending publication in Dayton, Ohio in 1930.

v1, no. 1-35	Sept. 1, 1808-1809	APS II, Reel 19
v75-78	Jan. 4, 1883-Dec. 23, 1886	Reel 1925
v79-82	Jan. 6, 1887-Dec. 25, 1890	Reel 1926
v83-96	Jan. 1, 1891-Dec. 29, 1904	Reel 1927
v97-103	Jan. 5, 1905-Mar. 30, 1911	Reel 1928
v104-106	Jan. 18, 1912-Dec. 31, 1914	Reel 1929
v107-108	Jan. 7, 1915-Dec. 28, 1916	Reel 1930
v109-114	Jan. 4, 1917-Dec. 28, 1922	Reel 1931
v115-117	Jan. 4, 1923-DEc. 31, 1925	Reel 1932
v118-120	Jan. 7, 1926-Jan. 1929	Reel 1933
v121-122	Jan. 3, 1929-Feb. 27, 1930	Reel 1934

Some volumes and issues are missing; not available for photographing.

Microfilm edition was prepared from the CtW, ICT, NNuT and WHi copies.

SEE ALSO: Congregationalist and Herald of Gospel Liberty

HERALD OF HEALTH. *SEE* Health.

THE HERALD OF LIFE AND IMMORTALITY. v.1, no.1-8; Jan. 1819-Oct. 1820. Boston.

144 p. quarterly.

Edited by E. Smith.

This religious magazine, which proclaimed the doctrines of Universalism, was edited by Elias Smith, who had earlier founded what was probably the first religious magazine, the *Herald of Gospel Liberty,* at Portsmouth, New Hampshire, in 1808. The *Herald of Life* published articles on Universalist and other doctrines, minutes of Universalist association meetings, news of Bible societies, sermons, and poetry.

v1, no. 1-8	Jan. 1819-Oct. 1820	APS II, Reel 113

HERALD OF SALVATION. v. 1-2, no. 25; Nov. 30, 1822-Feb. 26, 1825. Watertown, N.Y., 1822-1825.

2 v.

Edited by the Rev. Pittmorse, this semimonthly promoted the doctrine of Universalism, including in its contents religious news, poetry, and some selected material.

v1-2, no. 25	Nov. 30, 1822-Feb. 26, 1825	APS II, Reel 113

HERALD OF SALVATION. (PHILADELPHIA) *SEE* Universalist.

THE HERALD OF TRUTH, a monthly periodical, devoted to the interests of religion, philosophy, literature, science and art. L.A. Hine, editor, v. 1-4, no. 1; Jan. 1847-July 1848. Cincinnati, J. White, Printer, 1847-48.

3 v.

Published by a company.

Edited by Lucius A. Hine, the *Herald of Truth* was a well-printed review which focused mainly on religion, philosophy, literature, science, and the arts, and engaged vigorously in the reforms of the day but claimed to be non-sectarian and nonpartisan. It published a good deal of poetry, including some by the Cary sisters, Phoebe and Alice, and reviews of new publications.

v1-4, no.1   Jan. 1847-July 1848   APS II, Reel 388

Microfilm edition was prepared from WHi copy.

THE HERALD OF TRUTH; a periodical work, consisting of essays and arguments, original and selected, the design of which is to illustrate and confirm the heavenly truths of New Jerusalem. Edited by Nathaniel Holley. v. 1, no. 1-26; Mar. 17, 1825-May 18, 1826. Cincinnati, Morgan, Lodge and Fisher, Printers, 1826.

400 p.

Irregular.

This Swedenborgian publication conducted by Nathaniel Holley published extracts from the writings of Emanuel Swedenborg, articles on doctrine, and poetry.

v1, 1-26   Mar. 17, 1825-May 18, 1826   APS II, Reel 113

SEE ALSO: Evangelical Magazine and Gospel Advocate.

*THE HESPERIAN; a monthly miscellany of general literature, original and select. Ed. by William D. Gallagher, v.1-3; May 1838-Nov. 1839. Columbus, O., J.D. Nichols, 1838-39.

3 v.

Title of v. 1: The Hesperian; or, Western monthly magazine. Edited by William D. Gallagher and Otway Curry. Vol. 3 published in Cincinnati.

A lengthy publication of 80 or 90 pages which lasted only one-and-a-half years, this magazine depended on material from other sources. Poetry, fiction, book reviews, travelogues, and biographies filled the many pages along with articles on the history, buildings and roads of Ohio. Noted authors whose writings were included were James Fenimore Cooper, Rousseau and William Henry Harrison. The periodical also made use of the slender output of literature of "the frontier."

v1-3   May 1838-Nov. 1839   APS II, Reel 417

v2: p. 489-92 missing in number only. V3: May number not issued.

Microfilm edition was prepared from DLC and MH copy.

THE HIEROPHANT; or, Monthly journal of sacred symbols and prophecy. Conducted by George Bush. v. 1 (no. 1-12); June 1842-May 1843. New York, M.H. Newman.

288 p.

Conducted by George Bush, this monthly religious magazine was mainly devoted to a discussion and explication of Bible prophecy, but it also published occasional essays and dissertations of a more general nature, studies of Bible passages, and brief book notices.

v1, no. 1-12   June 1842-May 1843   APS II, Reel 388

THE HISTORICAL FAMILY LIBRARY, devoted to the republication of standard history. v. 1-[4]; June 20, 1835-[1841] Cadiz, O., D. Christy.

4 v. irregular.

Included on film: new ed. of both History of the war in the Peninsula, by F.W.P. Napier, Part 1; and History of the decline and fall of the Roman Empire, by E. Gibbon (called v. 1-2). These three vols. appear to comprise v. [2-4] of The Historical family library.

The *Library's* purpose was to present a full and complete outline of history down to modern times, and was an attempt to place a library of standard history within reach of almost everyone. It presented complete works; some of these were Hallam's *History of the State of Europe during the Middle Ages,* Chambers' *Rebellion in Scotland,* Ramsay's *History of the American Revolution,* Guizot's revision of Gibbon's *History of the Decline and Fall of the Roman Empire,* and Napier's *History of the War in the Peninsula.* Usually one work would take several numbers to complete, and it comprised the entire contents of those several numbers.

June 20, 1835-1841   APS II, Reel 737

Several pages are stained. Microfilm edition includes June 20, 1835-1841.

Microfilm edition was prepared from DLC and OMidU copies.

*THE HISTORICAL MAGAZINE, and notes and queries concerning the antiquities, history, and biography of America. v. 1-23; Jan. 1857-Apr. 1875. Boston, C.B. Richardson.

23 v. facsims., maps. pl., ports. monthly.

Editors: 1857, J.W. Dean.-1858, George Folsom.-1859-65, J.G. Shea.-Jan.-June 1866, H.R. Stiles.-July 1866-Apr. 1875, H.B. Dawson. Imprint varies: 1857, Boston, C.B. Richardson; London, J.R. Smith-1858-63, New York, C.B. Richardson; London, Trubner & co.-1864-65, New York, J.G. Shea.-1866-75, Morrisania, N.Y., H.B. Dawson. v. 11-20 also called 2d ser., v. 1-10; v. 21-23 also called 3d ser., v.1-3. Suspended Sept.-Oct. 1871, Apr. 1872-Mar. 1873. No regular no. published Apr. 1874-Mar. 1875; extra no. published Mar. and Dec. 1874, Jan., Mar. and May 1875.

Devoted to recording the antiquities of America, the *Historical Magazine* began publication in 1857. The magazine was successively edited by John Ward Dean, George Folsom, J.G. Shea, and H.R. Stiles until 1866 when Henry B. Dawson assumed the responsibilities of editor, publisher, and proprietor. Due to the last editor's ailing health, the magazine was sometimes published irregularly or suspended. Finally, in 1875, the publication ceased with the exception of a few extra numbers that appeared. However, the monthly left behind a volume of original papers, collections of original letters, correspondence, and diaries, historical society proceedings, biographies, book reviews and reprints of archaic tracts and poems.

v1-6   Jan. 1857-Dec. 1862   APS III, Reel 26
v7-2sv6   Jan. 1863-Dec. 1869   Reel 27
v2s7-3sv3   Jan. 1870-Apr. 1875   Reel 28

Some pages are stained, torn, or have faded print or print show-through. Pagination is irregular. Vol. 5, articles entitled "Shakespeare's in Folio" follows page 380. Vol. 7: An article entitled "Order of Lieut. Gov. Liesler" follows page 384. Second Series Vol. 10 lacks index. Lacks extra numbers for March and May, 1875. Best copy available for photographing.

Microfilm edition was prepared from C, MiU, NPV and NR copies.

THE HISTORICAL REGISTER OF THE UNITED STATES ... v. 1-4 [1812-14] Philadelphia, G. Palmer [etc.] 1814-16.

4 v. Vols. 1-2, published in Washington by T.H. Palmer.

Edited by T.H. Palmer.

Contents: v. 1-2. From the description of war in 1812 to Jan. 1, 1814.-v. 3-4. For 1814.

Edited by T.H. Palmer, this periodical was devoted to preserving an authentic and complete collection of American state papers and official records. It published two volumes each year; the first was devoted to legislative proceedings and news of inventions and progress made in the arts and manufacturing, while the second recorded historical events. Contents included "Annals of America," official documents and state papers, "Review of the political institutions of the U.S.," a history of the proceedings of Congress, and a history of important events from the declaration of the war to 1814.

v1-4   1812-1814   APS II, Reel 113
                                                        Reel 114

HISTORICAL RESEARCHS IN WESTERN PENNSYL-VANIA, PRINCIPALLY CATHOLIC. *SEE* American Catholic Historical Researches.

HIVE. v. 1, nos. 1-26; May 19-Dec. 11, 1810. Lancaster, Pa., 1810.

268 p.

Nos. 21-24 wanting.

The editor of this weekly miscellany, William Hamilton, or "Will Honeycomb," states in the prospectus that his magazine will be devoted to literature, science and the arts as well as to religion, morality, and education. Much of the material was contributed by readers; contents consisted mainly of miscellaneous essays, biographical sketches, a good deal of poetry, and a "Variety" section of sayings, anecdotes, and maxims.

v1, nos. 1-20, 25-26   May 19-Dec. 11, 1810   APS II, Reel 114

SEE ALSO: Lancaster Hive.

HOLDENS DOLLAR MAGAZINE OF CRITICISMS, BIOGRAPHIES, SKETCHES, ESSAYS, TALES, RE-VIEWS, POETRY. *SEE* Dollar Magazine.

HOLSTON CONFERENCE MESSENGER. *SEE* Messenger. (Methodist Episcopal Church. Conference. Holston).

HOLSTON MESSENGER. *SEE* Messenger (Methodist Episcopal Church. Conference. Holston).

HOME JOURNAL. *SEE* Town and Country.

HOME MAGAZINE. *SEE* Arthur's Home Magazine.

HOPKINSIAN MAGAZINE. v. 1-4; 1824-Dec. 1832. Providence, R.I., 1824-1832.

4 v.

Suspended during 1830.

Hopkinsian Magazine was published for the benefit of the religious followers of Samuel Hopkins. The editor was the Reverend Otis Thompson. However, the magazine met with little support, being suspended in 1830, and finally ceasing in 1832.

v1-4   Jan. 1824-Dec. 31, 1832   APS II, Reel 914

Some pages are stained or have print missing or faded. Pagination is irregular.

Microfilm edition was prepared from DLC, NNUT, and ICT copies.

HORTICULTURAL REGISTER, AND GARDENER'S MAGAZINE. v. 1-4; Jan. 1835-Dec. 1838. Boston. G.C. Barrett, 1835-39.

4 v. monthly.

Editors: 1835, T.G. Fessenden, J.E. Teschemacher.—1836-37, T.G. Fessenden, Joseph Breck.—1838, Joseph Breck.

Edited by Thomas Green Fessenden and J.E. Teschemacher, this magazine was devoted to gardening, orchards, and the cultivation of flowers. It provided articles on the growing and protecting of plants, including various kinds of flowers, fruits, vegetables, vines, and trees, and hints for destroying insects and preserving fruits and vegetables. Colored plates accompanied many of the articles. The activities of the Massachusetts Horticultural Society and other societies were given space as were letters from readers, extracts from European magazines, and listings of foreign publications.

v1-4   Jan. 1, 1835-Dec. 1838   APS II, Reel 527

Pagination is irregular.

Microfilm edition was prepared from DLC and N copies.

HORTICULTURIST AND JOURNAL OF RURAL ART AND RURAL TASTE. v. 1-30, no. 12 (nos. 1-354) July 1846-Dec. 1875. Albany, New York; etc., 1846-1875.

30 v.

Vols. 8-30 also as Series 2 vols. 1-23, United with Gardener's monthly and Horticultural advertiser to form Gardener's monthly and horticulturist.

A weekly horticultural magazine which was founded in Albany by Luther Tucker but changed homes and ownership several times before merging with its rival, the *Gardener's Monthly, in 1875. It* was notable during Tucker's ownership (1846-53) for articles on architecture (with engravings) and for imaginative writing, and during Vick's ownership (1853-55) for its handsome appearance and hand-colored plates of fruits and flowers.

v1-5   July 1846-Dec. 1850   APS II, Reel 656

v6-10   Jan. 1851-Dec. 1855   APS II, Reel 890
v11-17   Jan. 1856-Dec. 1862   Reel 891
v18-27   Jan. 1863-Dec. 1871   Reel 892
v28-30   Jan. 1872-Dec. 1875   Reel 893

Vol. 15, some advertising pages are lacking. Some pages are stained or torn. Pagination is irregular.

Microfilm edition was prepared from MiU, N, NNC, OrCS, and TU copies.

* **HOURS AT HOME**; a popular monthly of instruction and recreation. v. 1-11; May 1865-Oct. 1870. New York, C. Scribner [1865-70]

11 v. illus., maps, plates, port.

Title varies: May 1865-May 1867. Hours at home: a popular monthly, devoted to religious and useful literature. June 1867-Oct. 1870. Hours at home: a popular monthly of instruction and recreation.

J.M. Sherwood, editor, 1865-1869. Merged into Scribner's monthly in Nov. 1870.

Edited by James Manning Sherwood, *Hours at Home* provided religious instruction and entertainment. The theological (Presbyterian) aspect encompassed the literary articles, poetry, travel sketches, historical articles, and biographies comprising the monthly. Articles by Helen M. Brown, Rufus Anderson, Frances Eastwood, William Gilmore Simms, George B. Bacon, Mary E. Atkinson, Horace Bushnell, James O. Noyes, Joseph T. Headley, Julia (Ward) Howe, Lorenzo Dow, and George M. Towle were but a few of the many found on the pages.

v1-2	May 1865-Apr. 1866	APS III, Reel 28
v3-9	May 1866-Oct. 1869	Reel 29
v10-11	Nov. 1869-Oct. 1870	Reel 30

Microfilm edition was prepared from MiU and NjPT copies.

SEE ALSO: Century *and* Scribner's Monthly.

THE HUMMING BIRD; or, Herald of taste. v. 1, no. 1-5. Apr. 14, June 9, 1798. Newfield [Conn.] L. Beach.

5 no.

Lacking on film: no. 2-4.

Poetry, anecdotes, and sentimental fiction make up the contents of this periodical.

| v1, no.1, 5 | Apr. 14-June 9, 1798 | APS I, Reel 13 |

Microfilm edition was prepared from MWA copy.

THE HUNTINGDON LITERARY MUSEUM, AND MONTHLY MISCELLANY. v. 1, no. 1-12; Jan.-Dec. 1810. Huntingdon, Penn., J. M'Cahan, Printer.

1 v.

Caption title.

Editors: 1810- W.R. Smith, M. Canan.

Edited by William R. Smith and Moses Canan, this miscellany contained geographical sketches of areas of the U.S.; a variety of information on Pennsylvania; essays on science, literature, and history; and some criticism and biographical sketches, as well as occasional poetry, humor, and miscellany.

| v1, no. 1-12 | Jan.-Dec. 1810 | APS II, Reel 114 |

THE HUNTRESS. v. 1-16, v. 17, no. 1-[18], Dec. 2, 1836-May 27, 1854; new ser., v. 1, no. 1-3, June 24-July 24, 1854. Washington, D.C., 1836-54.

18 v. in 8. weekly.

Caption title. Anne Royall, editor.

Supersedes Paul Pry (Dec. 3, 1831-Nov. 19, 1836. 5 v.) Vol. 7, no. 44-v 16, no. 11 (Dec. 9, 1843-May 27, 1854) called new series.

In 1836, Mrs. Anne Royall replaced *Paul Pry* with the *Huntress.* Like its predecessor, the *Huntress* was best known for the highly personal commentary by the editor concerning Washington personalities.

v1-8	Dec. 2, 1836-Feb. 8, 1845	APS II, Reel 935
v9-14	Feb. 15, 1845-Feb. 7, 1852	Reel 936
v15-New Series	Feb. 14, 1852-July 24, 1854	Reel 937

Vol. 1-New Series Vol. 1 lack Indexes. Many pages are creased, repaired, stained, or have print missing. Best copy available for photographing. Beginning with Vol. 12, many issues are misnumbered. The following issues are lacking from this film. Vol. 9: February 29, March 1, July 5, August 23-30, September 6, November 1, 1845; and January 1, 1846 Vol. 10: June 20, 1846 Vol. 11: March 6, August 28, October 23, December 11, 1847 Vol. 12: January 22, July 15, December 2, 1848; January 20, 1849 Vol. 13: March 10, June 30, October 13, November 17, 1849 Vol. 14: May 11, June 15, July 13, November 9, 1850; May 17, June 1851 Vol. 15: June 5, September 4, 1852 Vol. 16: March 19, October 1, 1853 Vol. 17: March 11, 1854

Microfilm edition was prepared from DLC copy.

* **HUNT'S MERCHANTS' MAGAZINE.** *SEE* Merchants' Magazine and Commercial review.

HYGIENIC TEACHER AND WATER–CURE JOURNAL. *SEE* Water-cure Journal.

THE IDLE MAN. v. 1-2, no. 1; 1821-22. New York, Wiley & Halsted.

2 v.

Edited by R. H. Dana.

Each issue of this essay periodical by Richard Henry Dana presented an essay or two on various topics, and one or more poems. Some essay titles are "Domestic Life," "Men and Books," "The Hypochondriac," and "Musings."

| v1-2 | 1821-1822 | APS II, Reel 115 |

* **THE ILLINOIS MONTHLY MAGAZINE.** Conducted by James Hall. v. 1-2 (no. 1-24); Oct. 1830-Sept. 1832. Vandalia, Printed by R. Blackwell, 1831; Cincinnati, Corey and Fairbank, 1832.

2 v.

Continued as the Western monthly magazine (1833-37)

One of the most interesting magazine files of a pioneer region is that of the *Illinois Monthly Magazine* and its continuation, the *Western Monthly Magazine.* The founder, editor, and chief contributor was Judge James Hall, who wrote about two-thirds of the material, including some good indigenous western tales and sketches, some articles, fictional and otherwise, based on his naval experiences, and much information designed to attract settlers. The rest of the contents was made up of selected material and contributions by Morris Birkbeck, John M. Peck, Governor Edward Coles, and Dr. Asa Fitch. The serial "Notes on Illinois" was an important section of the magazine.

v1-2   Oct. 1830-Sept. 1832   APS II, Reel 389

Microfilm edition was prepared from DLC copy.

THE ILLUSTRATED FAMILY MAGAZINE; for the diffusion of useful knowledge. v. 1-3, v. 4, no. 1-3; Feb. 1845-Sept. 1846. Boston, Bradbury, Soden. 1845-46.

4 v. in 2. illus. monthly.

Title varies: 1845, The New England family magazine.

R.L. Wade, editor. A note in the number for Sept., 1846, states that the magazine will be superseded by a new weekly newspaper.

This informational periodical, edited by Robert L. Wade, printed very little fiction and intentionally omitted sentimental tales. Most of the material was descriptive-biographies of famous people; and articles telling of famous battles, great adventures, American scenery, and the people and sights of foreign lands. Some science articles, essays, and poetry appeared also; rather badly printed woodcuts illustrated the text.

New England Family Magazine.
v1-2   Feb. 1-Dec. 1845   APS II, Reel 777

Illustrated Family Magazine.
v3-4   Jan.-Sept. 1846   APS II, Reel 777

Vols. 2-4: Indexes and tables of contents are lacking. Vols. 2 and 4: Title pages are lacking.

Microfilm edition was prepared from CtY and MnU copies.

IMPARTIAL GAZETTEER, AND SATURDAY EVENING POST. *SEE* Ladies' Weekly Museum.

THE INDEPENDENT ... v. 1-121 (no. 4089); Dec. 7, 1848-Oct. 13, 1928. New York, S.W. Benedict [etc., 1848-1924]; Boston, Independent publications.

121 v. in 139. illus. weekly (May 1922-Sept. 1924; biweekly)

Vols. 1-106 (Dec. 1848-Sept. 1921) have title: The Independent. Inv. 107-121 (Oct. 1921- Oct. 1928) title pages read: The Independent ... devoted to the consideration of politics, social and economic tendencies, history, literature, and the arts (title varies slightly) individual numbers have titles: Oct. 1921-Apr.1922, The Independent and the weekly review; May 1922-Aug. 16, 1924, The Independent, a fortnightly journal of information and discussion; Aug. 30, 1924-Oct. 1928, The Independent, a ... journal of free opinion.

Editors: 1848-61, Leonard Bacon, J.P. Thompson, R.S. Storrs (Joshua Leavitt, assistant editor).—1861-64, H.W. Beecher.—1864-70, Theodore Tilton. —1870-96, H.C. Bowen.—1896-1913, W.H. Ward.—1914-Sept. 1921, Hamilton Holt.—Oct. 1921-Feb. 1924, H. de W. Fuller (with Fabian Franklin, Oct. 1921-Apr. 1922).—Mar. 1924-Oct. 1928, R.E. Danielson, C.A. Herter. Absorbed the Chautauquan in June 1914, Harper's weekly in May 1916, the Countryside and suburban life in Aug. 1917, the Weekly review in Oct. 1921. Merged into the Outlook in Oct. 1928.

Established by a group of New York businessmen and Congregational ministers, this weekly "religious newspaper" filled its four pages with foreign and domestic news, musical selections, missionary news, advertising, vital statistics, and articles by correspondents. The *Independent* was greatly concerned with slavery and its extreme position on the fugitive slave law almost destroyed it in its second year. But it survived to publish *Uncle Tom's Cabin,* and made Harriet Beecher Stowe a leading contributor. Another contributor, Henry Ward Beecher, became editor in 1861 but after only two years was succeeded by Theodore Tilton, who replaced the dead slavery issue with the women's suffrage issue. During the next 65 years, the *Independent* underwent a number of changes in size, ownership, and editorship, reaching its greatest circulation in 1870, but although circulation decreased in the 1870's and 1880's it maintained an important position among American magazines. Its departments of religious news were strong, and it also gave attention to general events and to questions of the day. There were sections devoted to science, the fine arts, music, education, Sunday schools, farm and garden, and literature. Poetry contributors included Bryant, Longfellow, Holmes, and Emily Dickinson.

v1-2	Dec. 7, 1848-Dec. 1850	APS II, Reel 418
v3-5	Jan. 2, 1851-Dec. 29, 1853	Reel 1420
v6-7	Jan. 5, 1854-Dec. 27, 1855	Reel 1421
v8-9	Jan. 3, 1856-Dec. 31, 1857	Reel 1422
v10-11	Jan. 7, 1858-Dec. 29, 1859	Reel 1423
v12-13	Jan. 5, 1860-Dec. 26, 1861	Reel 1424
v14-15	Jan. 2, 1862-Dec. 31, 1863	Reel 1425
v16-17	Jan. 7, 1864-Dec. 28, 1865	Reel 1426
v18-19	Jan. 4, 1866-Dec. 26, 1867	Reel 1427
v20-21	Jan. 2, 1868-Dec. 30, 1869	Reel 1428
v22	Jan. 6-Dec. 29, 1870	Reel 1429
v23	Jan. 5-Dec. 28, 1871	Reel 1430
v24	Jan. 4-Dec. 26, 1872	Reel 1431
v25	Jan. 2-Dec. 25, 1873	Reel 1432
v26	Jan. 1-Dec. 31, 1874	Reel 1433
v27	Jan. 7-Dec. 30, 1875	Reel 1434
v28	Jan. 6-Dec. 28, 1876	Reel 1435
v29	Jan. 4-Dec. 27, 1877	Reel 1436
v30	Jan. 3-Dec. 26, 1878	Reel 1437
v31	Jan. 2-Dec. 25, 1879	Reel 1438
v32	Jan. 1-Dec. 30, 1880	Reel 1439
v33	Jan. 6-Dec. 29, 1881	Reel 1440
v34	Jan. 5-Dec. 28, 1882	Reel 1441
v35	Jan. 4-Dec. 27, 1883	Reel 1442
v36	Jan. 3-Dec. 25, 1884	Reel 1443
v37	Jan. 1-Dec. 31, 1885	Reel 1444
v38	Jan. 7-Dec. 30, 1886	Reel 1445
v39	Jan. 20-Dec. 29, 1887	Reel 1446
v40	Jan. 5-Dec. 27, 1888	Reel 1447
v41	Jan. 3-Dec. 26, 1889	Reel 1448
v42	Jan. 2-Dec. 25, 1890	Reel 1449
v43	Jan. 1-Dec. 31, 1891	Reel 1450
v44	Jan. 7-Dec. 29, 1892	Reel 1451
v45	Jan. 5-Dec. 28, 1893	Reel 1452
v46	Jan. 4-Dec. 27, 1894	Reel 1453
v47	Jan. 3-Dec. 26, 1895	Reel 1454
v48	Jan. 2-Dec. 31, 1896	Reel 1455
v49	Jan. 7-Dec. 30, 1897	Reel 1456
v50	Jan. 6-Dec. 29, 1898	Reel 1457
v51	Jan. 5-Dec. 28, 1899	Reel 1458
v52	Jan. 4-Dec. 27, 1900	Reel 1459
v53	Jan. 3-Dec. 26, 1901	Reel 1460
v54	Jan. 2-Dec. 25, 1902	Reel 1461
v55	Jan. 1-Dec. 31, 1903	Reel 1462
v56-57	Jan. 7-Dec. 29, 1904	Reel 1463
v58-59	Jan. 5-Dec. 28, 1905	Reel 1464
v60-61	Jan. 4-Dec. 27, 1906	Reel 1465
v62-63	Jan. 3-Dec. 26, 1907	Reel 1466
v64-65	Jan. 2-Dec. 31, 1908	Reel 1467
v66-67	Jan. 7-Dec. 30, 1909	Reel 1468
v68-69	Jan. 6-Dec. 29, 1910	Reel 1469
v70-71	Jan. 5-Dec. 28, 1911	Reel 1470

v72-73	Jan. 4-Dec. 26, 1912	Reel 1471
v74-76	Jan. 2-Dec. 25, 1913	Reel 1472
v77-80	Jan. 5-Dec. 28, 1914	Reel 1473
v81-86	Jan. 4, 1915-June 26, 1916	Reel 1474
v87-90	July 3, 1916-June 30, 1917	Reel 1475
v91-93	July 7, 1917-Mar. 30, 1918	Reel 1476
v94-100	Apr. 6, 1918-Dec. 27, 1919	Reel 1477
v101-107	Jan. 3, 1920-Dec. 31, 1921	Reel 1478
v108-113	Jan. 7, 1922-Dec. 27, 1924	Reel 1479
v114-117	Jan. 3, 1925-Dec. 25, 1926	Reel 1480
v118-121	Jan. 1, 1927-Oct. 13, 1928	Reel 1481

Reel 418: Pagination is irregular. Reels 1420-1481: Several pages are stained, creased, torn, tightly bound, or have print blurred and faded with some loss of text. Vol. 39: nos. 1988-89 are missing, not available for photographing. Some volumes contain supplements.

Microfilm edition was prepared from C, CtHT, DLC, IC, InU, Ia-T, MB, Mi, MiD, MiU, NB, NBuG, NIC, NcD, NcGU, NhD, NjP, ODW, OrU, and WHi copies.

INDEPENDENT AND THE WEEKLY REVIEW. *SEE* Independent.

THE INDEPENDENT REFLECTOR. no. 1-52; Nov. 30, 1752-Nov. 22, 1753. [New York, J. Parker]

212 p. Weekly.

Edited by W. Livingston.

A political paper.

no. 1-52	Nov. 30, 1752-Nov. 22, 1753	APS I, Reel 13

Microfilm edition was prepared from MiU-C copy.

INDEPENDENT REFLECTOR–SUPPLEMENT. *SEE* Occasional Reverberator.

THE INDEPENDENT REPUBLICAN; and miscellaneous magazine. v. 1, no. 1; Aug. 1805. Newburyport [Mass] W. & J. Gilman.

24 p.

This political magazine proposed to support and defend Federalism, but only one number was published. Among its contents were national news items, poetry and a "Miscellany" section.

v1, no.1	Aug. 1, 1805	APS II, Reel 19

Microfilm edition was prepared from MWA copy.

INDIANA FARMER. *SEE* Western Farmer and Gardener.

INDIANA FARMER'S GUIDE. v. 1-72, no. 48, Feb. 1, 1845-Dec. 1, 1917; (2d series) v. 29, no. 49-v. 35, Dec. 8, 1917-Dec. 29, 1923; (3d series) v. 80- , 1924- Huntington, Ind., Guide Pub. Co. [etc.]

v. illus. Frequency varies. (1st series) v. 33, no. 37-v, 53, no. 36 omitted in numbering.

Continues Farmer's guide (Dec. 8, 1917-1923) Title varies:

1845-Dec. 1917 as Indiana farmer; Feb. 5, 1927-Feb. 4, 1928, and Sept. 9, 1934-Jan. 11, 1941 as Farmer's guide.

Another periodical started at same time and with similar title was edited by Henry Ward Beecher; this merged in 1846 with Western Farmer & Gardener. cf. Mott. Hist. of Amer. Magazines, vol. 1. On film: v. 2, Sept. 1852-Aug. 15, 1853; v. 7, Apr. 1858-Mar. 1859; v. 30-34, Jan. 5, 1918-Dec. 30, 1922.

The *Indian Farmer's Guide* devoted much of its space to information important to farmers, such as articles on marketing farm products, on farmers' problems and farmers' organization affairs, as well as items on crops, livestock, fertilizers, and farm equipment. But there was also a "Home and Family" section and, for the kids, a "Weekly Sunday School Lesson" and "Sleepy Time Tales."

Indiana Farmer

v2, 7	Sept. 1, 1852-Aug. 15, 1853	APS II, Reel 1797
	Apr. 18, 1858-Mar. 1859	

Indiana Farmer's Guide

s2 v30	Jan. 5-Dec. 28, 1918	APS II, Reel 1797
s2 v 31	Jan. 4-Dec. 27, 1919	Reel 1798
s2 v 32	Jan. 3-Dec. 25, 1920	Reel 1799
s2 v33	Jan. 1-Dec. 31, 1921	Reel 1800
s2 v 34	Jan. 7-Dec. 30, 1922	Reel 1801

Several volumes are missing; not available for photographing.

Microfilm edition was prepared from DNAL and ICJ copies.

INLAND ARCHITECT. *SEE* American Architect and Architecture.

THE INQUISTOR. v. 1-2, no. 4; Dec. 30, 1818-Jan. 19, 1820. Philadelphia, J. M'Minn.

2 v. weekly.

Copy filmed incomplete: v. 1, no. 51-52 and v. 2, no. 1-3 wanting.

Mainly for women, this four-page magazine lasted only a little over a year. It presented poetry, anecdotes, advice on love and marriage, much sentimental prose, and a serialized tale, "Sophia," which ran through almost all of the first volume.

v1, no.1-v.2, no.4	Dec. 30, 1818-Jan. 19, 1820	APS II, Reel 211

THE INSTRUCTOR. v. 1, no. 1-10; Mar. 6-May 8, 1755. [New York, Printed by J. Parker and W. Weyman] 1755.

40 p. weekly.

A diminutive four-page weekly which fought the territorial claims of France and Spain in the New World with rational essays and encyclopedic articles. Five numbers were largely concerned with the international conflict in America. Other material included fables, historical summaries, moral essays, social banter, and an occasional poem.

v1, no. 1-10	Mar. 6-May 8, 1755	APS I, Reel 13

Microfilm edition was prepared from DLC copy.

THE INTELLECTUAL REGALE; or, Ladies' tea tray. v. 1-2, no. 33; Nov. 19, 1814-Dec. 30, 1815. Philadelphia.

2 v. weekly.

This literary miscellany for women featured a serialized tale, "Clermont Herbert; or, Presentiment," which ran through all but the last issue, and also presented poetry, essays, vital statistics and short items on geography, biography, and morality.

v1-2   Nov. 19, 1814-Dec. 30, 1815   APS II, Reel 115

* **INTERNATIONAL MAGAZINE OF LITERATURE, ART AND SCIENCE.** *SEE* International Monthly Magazine of Literature, Science and Art.

INTERNATIONAL MISCELLANY OF LITERATURE, ART AND SCIENCE. *SEE* International Monthly Magazine of Literature, Science and Art.

* **THE INTERNATIONAL MONTHLY MAGAZINE OF LITERATURE, SCIENCE AND ART.** v. 1-5; July 1850-Apr. 1852. New York, Stringer & Townsend [1850-52]

5 v. illus., port.

Titles of single numbers vary: July-Aug. 1850, International weekly miscellany of literature, art, and science. Oct-Nov. 1850, The International miscellany of literature, art, and science. Dec. 1850-Apr. 1852, The International magazine of literature, art and science.

Merged into Harper's new monthly magazine.

The *International Monthly Magazine* devoted space to fiction, poetry, biographical articles, travel, and took a special interest in literary criticism. It was ably edited by Rufus Wilmot Griswold assisted by Charles G. Leland. Many of the English serials were reprinted and a fashion department with illustrations was added in November of 1850. On the whole, it resembled its greatest rival, *Harper's Magazine.*

v1-5   July 1850-Apr. 1852   APS III, Reel 109

Vol. 1: page 426 has print missing. Pages 424-443 and 428 have print show-through.

Microfilm edition was prepared from MiU copy.

* **THE INTERNATIONAL REVIEW.** v. 1-14, no. 4/5; Jan. 1874-June 1883. New York, A.S. Barnes [1874-83]

14 v. plates, port.

Bimonthly, 1874-78; monthly, 1879-83. Editors: July 1880-July 1881, J.T. Morse, Jr., H. C. Lodge.—Jan.-Aug. 1882, R.P. Porter, Henry Gannett.—Sept 1882-Jan. 1883, R.P. Porter.—Feb.-June 1883, W.R. Balch.

Issues covered by the *International Review* were largely social or economic, extending into history, politics, the military, and graphic arts. Agriculture, travel, and education were included to a lesser degree. Edited successively by John T. Morse and Henry Cabot Lodge, Robert Percival Porter and Henry Gannett, and William Ralston Balch, contributors to the early volumes included well-known American and British writers. Some European contributions appeared.During the last half of the file, the American contributions came to dominate the pages.

Cumulative Index, 1-9   1874-80   APS III, Reel 152
v1-4   Jan. 1874-Dec. 1877   Reel 152
v5-9   Jan. 1878-Dec. 1880   Reel 153
v10-14   Jan. 1881-June 1883   Reel 154

Microfilm edition was prepared from MiU and MiD copies.

INTERNATIONAL WEEKLY MISCELLANY OF LITERATURE, ART AND SCIENCE. *SEE* International Monthly Magazine of Literature, Science and Art.

INVESTIGATOR. *SEE* Investigator and Advocate of Independence.

THE INVESTIGATOR AND ADVOCATE OF INDEPENDENCE. Science, religion, literature, etc. v. 1-2; Jan. 1845-Dec. 1846. [Washington, C. Drew, 1845-46]

2 v. monthly.

Title varies: Jan-1845, The Investigator: religious, moral, scientific, etc. (Subtitle varies slightly) -Dec. 1846, The Investigator and advocate of independence. Science, religion, literature, etc.

J.F. Polk, editor.

Primarily a religious publication, this title was edited by Josiah F. Polk. It included sermons and scientific papers.

Investigator
v1   Jan.-Dec. 1845   APS II, Reel 1197

Investigator and Advocate of Independence
v2   Jan.-Dec. 1846   APS II, Reel 1197

Vol. 1: Title page is missing. Page 63 is missing in number only. All pages in May issues are stained. August-December issues are missing. Vol. 2: Index is not available for photographing.

Microfilm edition was prepared from DLC copy.

INVESTIGATOR AND EXPOSITOR. v. 1, nos. 1-16; July 4, 1839-Oct. 1840. Troy, Ohio, 1839-1840.

240 p.

Published by Richard C. Langdon and edited by the Whig Executive Committee of Miami County, Ohio, this monthly published political news and transcripts of U.S. Treasury Department statements.

v1   July 4, 1839-Oct. 1840   APS II, Reel 1231

Index is missing; not available for photographing. Some pages are stained, creased, or have faded print. No. 5: December issue not published.

Microfilm edition was prepared from OCA copy.

INVESTIGATOR AND GENERAL INTELLIGENCER. v. 1-2; 1827-1828. Providence, 1827-1828.

Merged into National philanthropist, later Genius of temperance.

Edited by William Goodell, this magazine advocated various social reforms and published poetry, some news, miscellany, and ads.

v2, no. 8   Dec. 4, 1828   APS II, Reel 389

Microfilm includes vol. 2, no. 8 only.

Microfilm edition was prepared from DLC copy.

THE IRIS; or, Literary messenger. v. 1; Nov. 1840-Oct. 1841. New York, 1840-41.

1 p.1., 578 p. monthly.

The numbers for Sept. and Oct. 1841 were issued together (called on cover "nos. XI & XII, Sept. and Oct., 1841;" called in caption title "no. 11, Sept., 1841")

A monthly literary periodical which was devoted mainly to science and literature, including popular tales, poetry, translations of foreign literature, philosophical and literary essays, reviews of recent publications, historical and biographical sketches, and a number of articles on science. It featured accounts of various literary institutions in the country and "The Editor's Table," which contained miscellaneous notices, reviews, and general remarks.

v1   Nov. 1840-Oct. 1841   APS II, Reel 656

Index appears at the end of the volume. Pages 232-43 are missing in number only.

Microfilm edition was prepared from DLC copy.

THE IRISH SHIELD. A historical and literary weekly paper. v. 1-4; 1829-31. Philadelphia, [n.d.]

4 v.

Editor: George Pepper. Vol. 3 has title: The Irish shield and literary panorama.

The Irish Shield, edited by George Pepper, was published for the Irishmen in the United States. Serially, there appeared the "History of Ireland" with additional miscellaneous news from the "emerald isle." Some original poetry also appeared. With Volume 4, the format changed to newspaper size. Soon afterward, publication ceased.

v1-4   Jan. 1829-Aug. 31, 1831   APS II, Reel 937

Vol. 1: May issue is misdated as April. Vols. 2 and 4: The microfilm edition contains only June 1830 of Vol. 2 and Aug. 26, 1831 of Vol. 4. Best copy available for photographing. Vol. 3: Some pages are stained, creased, or tightly bound. Pgs. 349-350 are repeated in number only.

Microfilm edition was prepared from DLC, DCU, ICHi, ICU, and NCH copies.

ISRAEL'S ADVOCATE; or, The restoration of the Jews contemplated and urged. v. 1-5, 1823-1827. [New York, J.P. Haven]

5 v. monthly.

Includes the proceedings of the American Society for Meliorating the Condition of the Jews.

This 16-page monthly was devoted to the conversion of Jews to Christianity in the United States and abroad. Many of the articles and letters contained firsthand accounts of Jewish conversion, and the reports of the American Society for Meliorating the Condition of the Jews were also published.

v1-3   Jan. 1823-Dec. 1825   APS II, Reel 130

v4-5   Jan. 1826-Dec. 1827   APS II, Reel 401

Microfilm edition was prepared from MWA copy.

THE JEFFERSONIAN.. v. 1; Feb. 17, 1838-Feb. 9, 1839. Albany, N.Y., [J. Henry] 1838-39.

416 p. weekly.

Caption title. Edited by Horace Greeley.

A weekly political magazine edited by Horace Greeley which, according to him, would furnish the counties and neighborhood with "correct and reliable information on political subjects." It dealt mainly with elections and activities of Congress and other legislative bodies, publishing speeches made in Congress, debates on bills, reports of Congressional committees, and coverage of the activities of the New York legislature, in addition to small political items, and a summary of news. Material on education and agriculture and some poetry were included as well.

v1   Feb. 17, 1838-Feb. 9, 1839   APS II, Reel 797

Many pages are misnumbered.

Microfilm edition was prepared from MWA and MiU copies.

THE JESUIT; or, Catholic sentinel. v. 1-5; Sept. 5, 1829-Dec. 27, 1834. Boston, H.L. Devereaux [etc.]

5 v. illus. weekly.

Title varies: Oct. 1, 1831-Sept. 21, 1832, United States Catholic sentinel.

Superseded by Literary and Catholic sentinel.

Founded in Boston in 1829 by Bishop B.J. Fenwick, the *Jesuit* became one of the best known of the Catholic papers.

Jesuit; or, Catholic Sentinel.
v1-2   Sept. 1829-Aug. 1831   APS II, Reel 1370

United States Catholic Sentinel
v3   Oct. 1, 1831-Sept. 21, 1832   Reel 1371

Jesuit; or, Catholic Sentinel
v4-5   Oct. 1833-Dec. 1834   Reel 1371

Several pages are stained and torn with some loss of text. Pagination is irregular. Vol. 3: Pgs. 97-98, 121-22, 193-94, 209-10 and 377-78 are missing. Vols. 4 and 5 lack indexes.

Microfilm edition was prepared from LNL, MBtS and NN copies.

THE JEW; being a defence of Judaism against all adversaries, and particularly against the insidious attacks of Israel's advocate v. 1-2; Mar. 5583 [1823]-Mar. 5585 [1825] New York, [L. Emanuel]

481 p; monthly.

Edited by S.H. Jackson.

This monthly magazine was concerned with defending Judaism against attack by its various adversaries and particularly against attacks by *Israel's Advocate,* a magazine which was devoted to the conversion of Jews to Christianity.

v1-2   Mar. 1823-Mar. 1825   APS II, Reel 131

JOHN ENGLISHMAN, IN DEFENCE OF THE ENGLISH CONSTITUTION. no. 1-10; Apr. 9-July 5. 1755. [New York, Printed by J. Parker and W. Weyman]

1 v. weekly.

Title varies: Apr. 9, 1755, John Englishman's true notion of sister churches.

A political folio.

no 1-10   Apr. 9-July 5, 1755   APS I, Reel 13

Some pages are lacking.

Microfilm edition was prepared from NN and CtY copy.

JOHN ENGLISHMAN'S TRUE NOTION OF SISTER CHURCHES. *SEE* John Englishman, In Defence of the English Constitution.

THE JOHN–DONKEY. v. 1-2; Jan. 1-Oct. 21, 1848. New York, G. Dexter [1848]

2 v. illus., plates weekly.

A weekly satirical publication which was considered the best humorous periodical attempted to that date. Most articles satirized contemporary events and fads, organizations, movements, or persons, and politics figured prominently in them. The satire was often scurrilous, attacking such people as Greeley and Poe. Each issue contained a series of pictures of John Donkey himself in various attitudes, a political cartoon, and several smaller cuts. Although it attained a circulation of 12,000, it was ruined by libel suits in 1848.

v1-2   Jan. 1-Oct. 21, 1848   APS II, Reel 657

Volume 2: Issues 8-12 are missing in number only.

Microfilm edition was prepared from CtY and MWA copies.

JOURNAL AND REVIEW. *SEE* Quarterly Journal and Review.

JOURNAL DES DAMES; ou, Les souvenirs d'un viellard. Dedie aux dames des Etats Unis, redige et imprime au benefice d' un etablissement public, par un hermite des rives du Pasaic. v. 1-2; jan.-dec. 1810. New York, 1810.

2 v. in 1. monthly.

Printed by the children of the Economical school. Caption title: Ladies' journal. Running title: Varietes litteraires: ou, Les souvenirs d' un viellard.

Written in French, this ladies' journal published historical items, poetry, literary varieties, extracts from new European literary publications, reviews of new books, and a section of literature. Political material was excluded.

v1-2   Jan.-Dec. 1810   APS II, Reel 115

JOURNAL INUTILE; ou, Melanges politiques et litteraires. v. 1-2 (no. 1-26); 1824-19 mai 1825. New York.

2 v. weekly.

Film covers: no. 9-26, Jan. 20-May 19, 1825.

Written in French, this political and literary miscellany published travel articles, biography, poetry and anecdotes, a variety of essays, and other literary material.

v1-2 (no. 9-20, 22-26) Jan. 20-May 19, 1825   APS II, Reel 131

JOURNAL OF AGRICULTURE. *SEE* American farmer's Magazine; Colman's Rural World; and Monthly Journal of Agriculture.

JOURNAL OF THE AMERICAN GEOGRAPHICAL AND STATISTICAL SOCIETY. *SEE* American Geographical Society of New York.

JOURNAL OF THE AMERICAN GEOGRAPHICAL SOCIETY OF NEW YORK. *SEE* American Geographical Society of New York.

THE JOURNAL OF BELLES LETTRES. (In Select circulating library, v. 1-17, no. 16; June 1832 [i.e., 1833]-Apr. 1842. Philadelphia.)

Weekly, v. 1-14; v. 15-16, 5 no. a month.

Issued with Waldie's select circulating library as a supplement. Vol. 15-17, no. 6, caption (Journal of belles lettres) dropped. The new series, covering dates Jan. 15, 1833-Jan. 7, 1834, is in 2 vols. identical with the issues of the same dates of the original series. New ser., v. 1, no. 1-26 corresponds to the original series, v. 1, no. 14-v. 2, no. 13; new ser., v. 2, no. 1-26 to v. 2, no. 14-39. Publication was suspended in 1840, after 6 numbers had been issued. It was resumed in 1841. The numbers are disregarded in the volume numbering. pt. 2 of 1839 forming v. 14; pt. 1 of 1841, v. 15. John Jay Smith, editor.

Published by Adam Waldie as an accompaniment to his *Select Circulating Library,* the *Journal* contained reprints of reviews and notices of new books from the London Press. Also included were literary anecdotes, miscellany, lists of new books published or in process in London and America, and occasional extracts from new publications.

v1-17   June 25, 1832-Apr. 1842   APS II, Reel 1314

Vol. 4: Nos. 2, 9, and 10 have pages 3-4 missing Vol. 5 is not available for photographing. Vol. 11: No. 6 is bound and filmed out of order.

Microfilm edition was prepared from MWA, MiD, and N copies.

JOURNAL OF BELLES–LETTRES. v. 1, no. 1-5; Nov. 20, 1819-Feb. 26, 1820. Lexington [Ky.] T. Smith.

80 p. biweekly.

Copy filmed incomplete: no. 2 and 4 wanting.

Published by Thomas Smith and edited by Mariano and Everett, this semimonthly literary journal began November 20, 1819 but was suspended after only five numbers "for want of sufficient patronage." It was devoted mainly to Italian and French literature but also included some German and Scandinavian works. In addition to translated works, there were essays on both ancient and modern literature, literary news, poetry, and some political articles.

v1, no. 1, 3, 5   Nov. 20, 1819-Feb. 26, 1820   APS II, Reel 116

JOURNAL OF CHRISTIAN EDUCATION. *SEE* Herald of Gospel Liberty.

JOURNAL OF EDUCATION. v. 1-2; March 1838-Feb. 1840. Detroit [and] Marshall, Mich., 1838-1840.

2 v.

This monthly, for parents, teachers, and friends of education, was one of several state education journals of the time.

v1-2   Mar. 1838-Feb. 1840   APS II, Reel 1231

Vol. 1: Pages 11-14 have print faded. Supplement follows June issue.

Microfilm edition was prepared from DHEW and MiYEM copies.

THE JOURNAL OF FOREIGN MEDICAL SCIENCE AND LITERATURE. v. 1-10, Oct. 1810-Oct. 1820; [new ser.] v. 1-4, Jan. 1821-Oct. 1824. Philadelphia, A. Finley, 1811-[24]

14 v. illus., plates (part fold.) fold. tab. quarterly.

New ser., v.1, no.1-2 called v.11, no.1-2. Title varies: v.1-10, Eclectic repertory and analytical review, medical and philosophical. New ser., v.1-4, The Journal of foreign medical science and literature. New ser., v.1-2, no.[1] have caption title: Eclectic repertory and analytical review.

Vols. 1-10 edited by a Society of physicians; new ser., v.1-3, by Samuel Emlen (with William Price, new ser., v.1-2); new ser., v.4, by J.D. Godman. Imprint varies: v.1, Philadelphia, A. Finley.—v.2-10, Philadelphia, T. Dobson (later T. Dobson and son).—new ser., v.1-2, Philadelphia, E. Littell, and New York, R.N. Henry.—new ser., v.3-4, Philadelphia, E. Littell. Merged into American medical recorder. Book-plate of J. Wilson Moore.

Begun in October, 1810 as the *Eclectic Repertory*, this quarterly medical journal was conducted for ten years by an association of Philadelphia physicians and was then taken over by Eliakim Littell and renamed *Journal of Foreign Medical Science and Literature.* Edited by S. Emlen, Jr., and William Price, the *Journal's* contents were largely made up of selections from foreign medical magazines, journals, and reviews, but it also offered some original contributions, along with reviews, medical news, and notices of new publications, both American and foreign.

Eclectic Repertory and Analytical Review
v1-5   Oct. 1810-Oct. 1815   APS II, Reel 116
v6-9   Jan. 1816-Oct. 1819   Reel 117
v10-   Jan.-Oct. 1820   Reel 118
Journal of Foreign Medical Science and Literature
nsv1-3   Jan. 1821-Oct. 1823   APS II, Reel 118
nsv4   Jan.-Oct. 1824   Reel 119

✳ **JOURNAL OF THE FRANKLIN INSTITUTE.** *SEE* American Mechanics' Magazine. and Franklin Institute, Philadelphia. Journal ... Devoted to Science ...

THE JOURNAL OF HEALTH. Conducted by an association of physicians. v. 1-4; Sept. 9, 1829-Aug. 1833. Philadelphia, S.C. Atkinson, 1830-33.

4 v. illus., pl., port.

Semimonthly, 1829-Aug. 1832; monthly, Sept. 1832-1833. Caption title of v. 4 reads: The Journal of health, and recreation.

This popular health magazine was published first by Henry H. Porter and, after his financial failure, by Samuel C. Atkinson, publisher of the *Saturday Evening Post.* It attempted to present, in simple language, the rules for maintaining good health. Explicitly opposing empiricism, and the use of tobacco and alcohol, it emphasized the necessity of fresh air, good food, exercise, healthful clothing, and the proper correlation of mind and body. In addition, it explored the causes and prevention of disease, gave information on quarantine regulations and sanitary laws, and discussed hygiene.

v1-4   Sept. 1829-Aug. 1833   APS II, Reel 479

Several pages are stained with some loss of text. Pagination is irregular. Vol. 4: Title page is missing.

Microfilm edition was prepared from DLC and MiU copies.

JOURNAL OF HUMANITY. *SEE* Spirit of the Age and Journal of Humanity.

JOURNAL OF HYGIENE AND HERALD OF HEALTH. *SEE* Health.

THE JOURNAL OF JURISPRUDENCE, a new series of the American law journal. v. 1; 1821. Philadelphia, M. Carey.

8, 541 p.

Four no. a year. Edited by J.E. Hall. Supersedes American law Journal.

This law journal's purpose was to point out the difficulties caused by differences in state laws. It published statutes of various state legislatures and the most important judicial decisions of the federal and state courts and also gave attention to law outside the U.S., providing translations of foreign works on law and "An Analytical Digest of the Reports of Cases Decided in the English Courts of Common Law."

v1   1821   APS II, Reel 119

SEE ALSO: American Law Journal (Hall).

JOURNAL OF THE LAW-SCHOOL, and of the moot-court attached to it, at Needham, in Virginia. Needham, Va. Law School. With an appendix, comprising a variety of precedents adapted to the proceedings of the courts, agreeably to the revised code of 1819, and of the pleadings in law and equity, with complete records thereof. v. 1; 1822. Richmond, Printed by J. & G. Cochran.

371 p. fold. tables.

Edited by C. Taylor.

The only volume of this journal published was concerned mainly with the mock court which was set up so that students in the law school at Needham, Virginia could practice arguing cases. Its contents included the proceedings of the moot-court—the opening address, organization, and rules of the moot-court, appointment of officers, calender, and accounts of cases. An appendix contained special cases and situations.

v1   1822   APS II, Reel 121

JOURNAL OF MUSICK. no. 1-24; 1810. Baltimore, Madame Le Pelletier.

169 p. music. semimonthly.

Published by Madame Le Pelletier, this Baltimore music magazine consisted entirely of musical pieces, many with lyrics, for the piano and for voice. Italian and French pieces were included as well as English.

v1, no. 1-24   1810   APS II, Reel 119

JOURNAL OF THE NATIONAL INSTITUTE OF SOCIAL SCIENCES. *SEE* Journal of Social Science, Containing the Proceedings of the American Association.

JOURNAL OF THE PHILADELPHIA COLLEGE OF PHARMACY. *SEE* American Journal of Pharmacy.

JOURNAL OF PRACTICAL METAPHYSICS. *SEE* Arena.

JOURNAL OF PRISON DISCIPLINE AND PHILAN-THROPY. v. 1-16, new series v. 1-58; 1845-1919. Philadelphia, Pennsylvania Prison Society [etc.]

74 v. quarterly; annually. Suspended July 1847-July 1848.

Title varies: 1845-1856, Pennsylvania journal of prison discipline and philanthropy.

Issued under the direction of the Pennsylvania prison society instituted in 1787 as the Philadelphia society for alleviating the miseries of public prisons. Superseded by Prison journal. Vol. 10 contains index for v. 1-10. A prologue to no. 59 of the Journal ... entitled Review of the county jails in Pennsylvania, official report, by Albert H. Votaw, was published in May 1920 by the Pennsylvania Prison Society. On film: v. 1-10 (reels 480-481), v. 11-n.s.v. 58, prologue (reels 1934-1935)

Published by the Pennsylvania Prison Society in Philadelphia, this magazine explored prison conditions and promoted prison reform. Its articles and reports dealt with conditions and discipline in prisons, and with the best methods of conducting prisons and treating prisoners. It included descriptions, many accompanied by pictures and diagrams, of penitentiaries and other institutions, as well as surveys of the prisons in various states and foreign countries. Other social problems—juvenile delinquency, pauperism, insanity, and drunkenness—were also given coverage.

Pennsylvania Journal of Prison Discipline and Philanthropy
v1-5   Jan. 1845-Oct. 1850   APS II Reel 480
v6-10   Jan. 1851-Oct. 1855   Reel 481

v11   Jan.-Dec. 1856   APS II, Reel 1934

Journal of Prison Discipline and Philanthropy
v12-nsv12   Jan. 1857-Jan. 1873   APS II, Reel 1934
nsv13-59   Jan. 1874-May 1920   Reel 1935

Vols. 5 and 8: Title page is missing.

Microfilm edition was prepared from DLC, MH, MiU, MoS, and PU copies.

THE JOURNAL OF SCIENCE AND THE ARTS. Edited at the Royal institution of Great Britain. v. 1-5; 1817-1818. New York, J. Eastburn.

illus., plates, quarterly.

Seal of the Royal institution of Great Britain on title-pages. Caption title: The Quarterly journal of science and the arts. Includes proceedings of the Royal society of London, Royal society of Edinburgh, etc. Includes section "Select list of new publications".

Edited at the Royal Institution of Great Britain, the *Journal of Science and the Arts* was an American reprint of the *Quarterly Journal of Science,* and was to be a collection of useful scientific information. Contributions were made by members of the Royal Institution and others of scientific and literary eminence. The *Journal* published papers on all fields of science, proceedings of the Royal Society of London and the Royal Society of Edinburgh, reviews of foreign journals, lists of new publications, and weather information. Diagrams and illustrations accompanied many of the papers.

v1-5   1817-1818   APS II, Reel 120

* **JOURNAL OF SOCIAL SCIENCE,** containing the proceedings of the American association. no. 1-46; June 1869-Dec. 1909. New York, Boston [1869]-1909.

46 v. in 45. illus., tables, diagr.

Nos. 1-35, 1869-97, have title, Journal of social science: containing the transactions of the American association. Nos. 12-22, 24-37 have subtitle: Saratoga papers of 1880-99; nos. 38-40, Washington papers of 1900-02; nos. 41-43, Boston papers of 1903-05; no. 44, New York papers of 1906; no 45, Buffalo papers of 1907; no. 46, New York papers of 1909. Nos. 6-7 paged continuously. No. 10 erroneously numbered 9. Editors: 1874-96, F.B. Sanborn.—1897-1904, F.S. Root.—1905, F.B. Sanborn.—1906-09, I.F. Russell. Superseded by the Journal of the National institute of social sciences.

The *Journal of Social Science* was published by the American Association for the Promotion of Social Sciences. There were many distinguished contributors and articles on the single-tax debate, free silver, and other political and economic topics.

v1-17   June 1869-May 1883   APS III, Reel 266
v18-34   May 1884-Nov. 1896   Reel 267
v35-46   Dec. 1897-Dec. 1909   Reel 268

Microfilm edition was prepared from Mi, MiU, NbU, NhD copies.

* **THE JOURNAL OF SPECULATIVE PHILOSOPHY.** Ed. by Wm. T. Harris. v. 1-22; 1867- Dec. 1893. St. Louis, G. Knapp Printers, 1867-80; New York, D. Appleton, 1880-93.

22 v.

1867-87 published quarterly; v. 22, nos. 1-2 published Jan.-Apr. 1888, no. 3, Sept. 1892, no. 4, Dec. 1893. Index ... vol. I-XV: v. 15, p. 433-444.

The *Journal of Speculative Philosophy,* founded and edited by William T. Harris, distinguished itself for publishing the early writings of many of our great American thinkers. Among these are William Ellery Channing, John Weiss, J. Elliot Cabot, G. Stanley Hall and A. P. Peabody. In addition, numerous translations of European writings are found in the early volumes. The most important of these deal with German philosophy.

Cumulative Index, v1-15   1867-1881   APS III, Reel 13
v1-10   1867-Oct. 1876   Reel 13
v11-18   Jan. 1877-Oct. 1884   Reel 14
v19-22   Jan. 1885-Dec. 1893   Reel 15

Vol. 9, pgs. 163-320 have irregular pagination. Vol. 22, issues 1 and 2, January and April 1888, are combined. The table of contents for the September 1892 and December 1893 issues were bound and photographed at the end of the volumes.

Microfilm edition was prepared from MiU copy.

JOURNAL (RHODE ISLAND INSTITUTE OF INSTRUCTION). *SEE* Rhode Island Institute of Instruction Journal.

JUDY. v. 1, no. 1-13; Nov. 28, 1846-Feb. 20, 1847. New York, H. Long & Bros. [etc.]

1 v. illus. weekly.

Henry Grattan Plunkett was editor of this short-lived humorous paper, which modeled itself after the London *Punch.* It contained much satire on government, and poked fun at many aspects of American life, particularly life in New York City, through the use of jokes, anecdotes, poetry, and articles, and a great many cartoons and pictures. But in April, 1847, the *Democratic Review* wrote its obituary: "A sister has departed from among us; Judy is no more. Her short career was closed by a surfeit of indigestible pleasantries ..."

v1, nos. 1-13   Nov. 1846-Feb. 1847   APS II, Reel 481

Microfilm edition was prepared from CtY copy.

JUVENILE GAZETTE. v. 1, no. 1-3; Nov. 1819-Jan. 1820. Providence.

3 no. monthly.

The four pages of this short-lived children's magazine contained essays on behavior, manners, and dress, and also included some short news items, poetry, and for amusement, jokes and riddles.

v1, no. 1-3   Nov. 1819-Jan. 1820   APS II, Reel 121

THE JUVENILE MAGAZINE. no, 1-4; May 1811-Aug. 1813. Philadelphia.

Lacking on film: no. 2.

Conducted by Arthur Donaldson, who established a school for Blacks in Philadelphia in 1809, the *Juvenile Magazine* was designed for the use and entertainment of Blacks and particularly for use in schools. Among the contents were an account of Donaldson's school, miscellaneous material on Blacks and slavery, a history of Africa, an arithmetic section, biographical sketches, religious material and a good deal of poetry.

no. 1, 3, 4   May 1811-Aug. 1813   APS II, Reel 121

THE JUVENILE MAGAZINE; or, Miscellaneous repository of useful information. v. 1-4; 1802-1803. Philadelphia, Printed for Benjamin Johnson.

4 v. illus., plates.

The *Juvenile Magazine* was the second children's magazine to be published in the U.S.; the first was *Children's Magazine,* published in 1789. Contents included essays, articles on natural science, biographical sketches, poetry, some illustrations, and reviews of school books and other juvenile publications.

v1-4   1802-1803   APS II, Reel 19

Microfilm edition was prepared from DLC, MWA and NN.

THE JUVENILE MIRROR; or, Educational magazine. v. 1, no. 4; Mar. 1812. New York, Smith & Forman.

217-288 p.

Directed to both teachers and pupils, the *Juvenile Mirror* was concerned with education and morality. Its articles dealt with such topics as behavior, the requisition of teachers, the education of young ladies, the inadequacy of instruction methods, and the "folly and misery" of idleness.

v1, no.4   Mar. 1812   APS II, Reel 121

THE JUVENILE MISCELLANY. v. 1-4, Sept. 1826-July 1828; new ser., v. 1-6, Sept. 1828-Aug. 1831; 3d ser., v. 1-6 [Sept.] 1831-Aug. 1834. Boston, J. Putnam, 1826-34.

16 v. illus., plates (part col.) bimonthly.

Superseded by Juvenile Miscellany (Hale).

Mrs. D.L. Child, editor.

Edited by Mrs. D.L. Child, this small children's periodical was designed "for the instruction and amusement of youth." The majority of articles were for the purpose of instructing, either morally or otherwise and many were in the form of conversations. Among the contents were poetry, stories, dramas, biography, book reviews, and articles on geography, botany, birds, animals, and other science topics. Illustrations and riddles provided entertainment for the reader.

v1-3   Sept. 1826-Jan. 1828   APS II, Reel 389
v4-s3v6   Mar. 1828-Aug. 1834   Reel 390

Microfilm edition was prepared from DLC copy.

JUVENILE MISCELLANY (HALE). *SEE* Juvenile Miscellany.

THE JUVENILE PORT-FOLIO, and literary miscellany; devoted to the instruction and amusement of youth. Conducted by Thomas G. Condie. v. 1-4; Oct. 17, 1812-Dec. 7, 1816. Philadelphia, Printed by J. Bioren for the editor, 1813-16.

4 v. in 2. weekly.

Superseded by the Parlour companion.

Edited and published by thirteen-year-old Thomas G. Condie, Jr., the *Juvenile Port-Folio* was one of the most interesting of the juvenile periodicals. Although supposedly devoted to the instruction and amusement of youth, it was not at all childish and actually offered more for women than for children. This four-page weekly magazine included articles on literature, manners, dress, and customs, as well as poetry, anecdotes, romantic tales, biography, and a variety of other material.

v1-4   Oct. 17, 1812-Dec. 1816   APS II, Reel 212

SEE ALSO: Parlour Companion.

THE JUVENILE REPOSITORY. v. 1, no. 1; July 1811. [Boston]

36 p.

This mainly eclectic children's magazine presented, in the sole number published, a piece on George Washington, some poetry, Bible studies, religious articles, and question and answer sections on theology and philosophy.

v1, no.1   July 1811   APS II, Reel 121

KENNEBEC FARMER AND JOURNAL OF THE USEFUL ARTS. *SEE* Maine Farmer.

THE KEY. v. 1, no. 1-27; Jan. 13-July 14, 1798. Frederick Town [Md.] D. Cary, 1798.

213 p. weekly.

Caption title. John D. Carey, editor. "The earliest periodical issued to Maryland. Twenty-seven numbers published."–Sabin. cf. also the Historical magazine, v. 1, p. 317.

A miscellany which emphasized romantic and sentimental fiction and articles giving advice to women on love and marriage. Also included were sketches, essays, poetry, and anecdotes on a variety of topics.

v1, no. 1-27   Jan. 13-July 14, 1798   APS I, Reel 13

Microfilm edition was prepared from DLC copy.

KNICKERBOCKER MONTHLY. *SEE* Knickerbocker.

* THE KNICKERBOCKER; or, New York monthly magazine. v. 1-65, v. 66, no. 1-1: Jan. 1833-Oct. 1865. New York, 1833-65.

66 v. plates, ports.

Title varies: 1833-62, The Knickerbocker: or, New York monthly magazine (Jan.-June, 1833: The Knickerbocker) 1863-Feb. 1864, The Knickerbocker monthly: a national magazine. Mar.-Dec. 1864, The American monthly knickerbocker. Jan.-June, 1865, The American monthly. July-Oct. 1865, Foederal American monthly. (Caption title: The Foederal American. Cover title: Foederal American monthly)

Editors: 1833, C.F. Hoffman.–Oct. 1833-34, Timothy Flint.–1834-61 L.G. Clark.–Oct.1862-Feb. 1864, Kinahan Cornwallis.–Mar. 1864-Oct. 1865, J.H. Agnew.

Originally called the *Knickerbocker,* this magazine's first editor, Charles Fenno Hoffman, was succeeded after three months by S.D. Langtree. In May, 1834, it waas purchased by Lewis Gaylord Clark and Clement M. Edson, who raised the circulation to 5,000 in less than three years. Willis Gaylord Clark, the editor's twin brother, and an associate editor until 1841, was a chief contributor, and other contributors included Washington Irving, John T. Irving, Cooper, Bryant, and other prominent New Yorkers like Paulding, Hoffman, Verplanck, Halleck, Willis, Sands, Fay, and George William Curtis.

New England was represented by Longfellow, Hawthorne, Whittier, and Holmes. Much attention was also paid to the West; James Hall, Mrs. Kirkland, and Albert Pike were frequent contributors, along with "Ned Buntline." H.R. Schoolcraft had a series on the Lake Superior region and there was much on western travel. Humor was very important in the *Knickerbocker* and the "Editor's Table" contributed much to humor. Travel, both foreign and domestic, is given some coverage, as well as some discussion of science in the thirties and some mention of politics. By 1850 it had plainly deteriorated. Clark retired from the editorship in 1861 and after this the magazine underwent several changes: Charles Godfrey Leland made it a republican monthly in 1861, in 1862 it again became nonpartisan; then John Holmes Agnew made it into an organ of the Democratic party. In July 1865 its name was changed to the *Foederal American Monthly* and after the October 1865 issue publication was suspended.

Knickerbocker: or, New York Monthly Magazine.

v1-6	Jan. 1833-Dec. 1835	APS II, Reel 349
v7-11	Jan. 1836-June 1838	Reel 350
v12-17	Jul. 1838-June 1841	Reel 351
v18-22	Jul. 1841-Dec. 1843	Reel 352
v23-27	Jan. 1844-June 1846	Reel 353
v28-33	Jul. 1846-June 1849	Reel 354
v34-39	Jul. 1849-June 1852	Reel 355
v40-44	Jul. 1852-Dec. 1854	Reel 356
v45-48	Jan. 1855-Dec. 1856	Reel 357
v49-53	Jan. 1857-June 1859	Reel 358
v54-57	Jul. 1859-June 1861	Reel 359
v58-60	Jul. 1861-Dec. 1862	Reel 360

Knickerbocker Monthly: a National Magazine.

v61	Jan.-June 1863	APS II, Reel 360
v62	Jul.-Dec. 1863	Reel 361

American Monthly Knickerbocker.

v63-64	Jan.-Dec. 1864	APS II, Reel 361

American Monthly.

v65	Jan.-June 1865	APS II, Reel 361

Foederal American Monthly.

v66	Jul.-Oct. 1865	APS II, Reel 361

Pagination is irregular. Some pages are missing.

Microfilm edition was prepared from DLC copy.

LADIES AFTERNOON VISITOR. v. 1 (no. 1-13); Dec. 4, 1806-Feb. 28, 1807. Boston, E. French.

52 p. weekly.

Vol. 1, no. 1, called Ladies visitor.

This short-lived literary periodical conducted by Ebenezer French provided biographical and historical pieces, humor in the form of anecdotes, vital statistics, and poetry, but political material was excluded.

Ladies Visitor.

v1, no. 1	Dec. 4, 1806	APS II, Reel 20

Ladies Afternoon Visitor.

v1, no. 2-13	Dec. 11, 1806-Feb. 28, 1807	APS II, Reel 20

Microfilm edition was prepared from DLC copy.

LADIES' COMPANION, A MONTHLY MAGAZINE. *SEE* Ladies' Companion, and Literary Expositor.

THE LADIES' COMPANION, AND LITERARY EXPOSITOR; a monthly magazine embracing every department of literature. v. 1-20, May 1834-Apr. 1844; new ser., v. 1, May-Oct. 1844. New York, W.W. Snowden,

21 v. includes music. vol. 21 also as nsv1.

Vols. 1-18 have title: The Ladies' companion, a monthly magazine; devoted to literature and the fine arts (subtitle varies)

W.W. Snowden, editor, assisted by Mrs. Lydia H. Sigourney, Mrs. Emma C. Embury and others.

A New York imitator of the Philadelphia *Godey's* and *Graham's*, edited and published by William W. Snowden. Its list of contributors (including Poe and Longfellow) was similar to that of its rivals, though it ran more to fiction and made much of its engravings. It included original and selected material, music and fashion, some reviews, and a theatrical department, but sentimental poetry and tales held the chief place. From the first, a plate appeared in each issue; later this was increased to two steel or copper engravings in addition to the fashion plate. A.B. Durand contributed many landscapes to the early volumes.

Ladies' Companion, a Monthly Magazine.

v1-8	May 1834-Apr. 1838	APS II, Reel 738
v9-16	May 1838-Apr. 1842	Reel 739
v17-18	May 1842-Apr. 1843	Reel 740

Ladies' Companion, and Literary Expositor.

v19-21	May 1843-Oct. 1844	APS II, Reel 740

Microfilm edition was prepared from DLC, ICN and IaU copies.

THE LADIES' GARLAND. v. 1-4; Feb. 14, 1824-June 7, 1828. Harpers Ferry, Va., J.S. Gallaher.

4 v. weekly.

Publication suspended Feb. 10-May 12, 1827.

This magazine was "designed for the edification and improvement of females" and presented the usual fare of women's periodicals of that day—poetry, fragments, and tales, most of a sentimental and moral tone, travel sketches, biography, anecdotes, and articles on history—but it also provided information on fashions and gave some attention to education for women. Much of the material was selected from other sources.

v1-4	Feb. 14, 1824-June 7, 1828	APS II, Reel 561

Several pages are stained or have faded print with some loss of text. Vol. 1: Issues 3 and 7 are misdated.

Microfilm edition was prepared from DLC, MiU, Vi and WvU copies.

LADIES' GARLAND AND FAMILY WREATH embracing tales, sketches, incidents, history, poetry, music, etc. v 1-16, no. 3, April 15, 1837-September 1849; new ser. (ser. 3), v. 3, no. 10-v. 4, no. 12, Oct. 1849-Dec. 1850. Philadelphia, 1837-1850.

18 v.

The *Garland* is an example of the cheap periodical for women which flourished in the forties. It began as a 16-page paper, illustrated with inferior woodcuts, but was later expanded to 24 pages, and included hand-colored woodcuts of flowers and fashions. Lydia Jane Pierson was the magazine's chief writer, and Lydia H. Sigourney and T.S. Arthur were also contributors, but a considerable proportion of its material was "selected" from other magazines

and from books. Poems and tales, advice to women, occasional musical pieces, essays, biography, historical narratives, and anecdotes made up the contents, and education for women was advocated.

v1-11	Apr. 15, 1837-June 1847	APS II, Reel 608
v12-(s3)v4	Jul. 1847-Dec. 1850	Reel 609

Several pages are stained with some loss of text. Microfilm edition includes: vols. 1-15, April 15, 1837-June 1849; new series (series 3) vol. 3, January 1849-December 1849; and new series (series 3) vol. 4, Jan. 1850-Dec. 1850.

Microfilm edition was prepared from MBAt, MH, NN, and PHi copies.

THE LADIES' HOME JOURNAL. v. 1- Dec. 1883- Philadelphia [Curtis]

v. illus. monthly.

Title varies: Dec. 1883-May 1889, The Ladies' home journal and practical housekeeper.

Editors: Dec. 1883-Dec. 1889, Louisa Knapp.–Jan. 1890-Oct. 1919, E. W. Bok. On film: v. 1, Jan. 1884-v. 24, Nov. 1907, except for v. 22, Dec. 1904.

In 1879 Cyrus Hermann Kotzschmar Curtis founded a paper called *Tribune and Farmer* which featured a women's department edited by the publisher's wife. Within a few years this "Woman and the Home" section was issued as a monthly supplement called *Ladies' Home Journal and Practical Housekeeper*, and thus was begun one of the most famous of all women's magazines. Though a cheaply printed little paper, it had variety and appealed to middle-class women, and was a success from the beginning, claiming a circulation of 25,000 at the end of a year. Curtis continued to try to increase circulation, however, by attracting new writers, and by 1886 the list of famous contributors included Elizabeth Stuart Phelps, Harriet Prescott Spofford, Rose Terry Cooke, Mary Jane Holmes, and Will Carleton. Edward William Bok succeeded Mrs. Curtis in 1889 and during his thirty years as editor, the *Journal* continued to improve. Its keynote became intimacy; there were a number of intimate personality sketches of famous people, in addition to Ruth Ashmore's "Side Talks with Girls" and Mrs. Margaret Bottome's "Heart to Heart Talks." Around the turn of the century the *Journal* was publishing the writings of such famous American writers as Mark Twain, Bret Harte, Conan Doyle, Hamlin Garland, Joel Chandler Harris, and Sarah Orne Jewett, and during the first decade of the new century writings by Jane Addams, Helen Keller and Rudyard Kipling appeared.

During the years following Bok's resignation in 1920, there were several editors, but Bok's policies were continued in general. New features included a department for teenage girls called "The Sub-Deb," and favorite writers included Galsworthy, Tarkington, Willa Cather, Edna Ferber and Bess Streeter Aldrich. Intimacy continued to be the *Journal's* trademark when a husband and wife team, Bruce and Beatrice Blackmar Gould took over the editorship in 1935. One of the most popular features was "How America Lives," a series of articles describing the lives of typical American families, and another was Gladys Taber's "Diary of Domesticity," an intimate account of a family's life. There were both fiction and nonfiction serials, including John Gunther's "Death Be Not Proud," Margaret Mead's "Male and Female," and Pearl Buck's "The Child Who Never Grew."

Ladies' Home Journal and Practical Housekeeper.

v1-4	Jan. 1884-Nov. 1887	APS III, Reel 757
v5-6, no. 6	Dec. 1887-May 1889	Reel 758

Ladies' Home Journal.

v6, no.7-v7	June 1889-Nov. 1890	APS III, Reel 758

v8-10	Dec. 1890-Nov. 1893	Reel 759
v11-13	Dec. 1893-Nov. 1896	Reel 760
v14-16	Dec. 1896-Nov. 1899	Reel 761
v17-18	Dec. 1899-Nov. 1901	Reel 762
v19-20	Dec. 1901-Nov. 1903	Reel 763
v21-22	Dec. 1903-Nov. 1905	Reel 764
v23	Dec. 1905-Nov. 1906	Reel 765
v24	Dec. 1906-Nov. 1907	Reel 766

Several pages are torn and taped with some loss of text. Some title pages are lacking. Some volumes contain supplements. Vol. 22: December issue is missing. Vol. 24: Title page and index are lacking.

Microfilm edition was prepared from DLC and MB copies.

LADIES' HOME JOURNAL AND PRACTICAL HOUSE-KEEPER. *SEE* Ladies' Home Journal.

LADIES' JOURNAL. *SEE* Journal Des Dames.

THE LADIES' LITERARY CABINET, being a repository of miscellaneous literary productions, both original and selected, in prose and verse. v. 1, May 15-Nov. 6, 1819; new ser., v. 1-7, Nov. 13, 1819-Dec. 21, 1822. New York, N. Smith, etc.

7 v. in 3. pl. weekly.

Publication was suspended from Oct. 12 to Nov. 18, 1822, inclusive. Samuel Woodworth, editor, May 1819-Aug. 1820. "This was the harbinger of the New York mirror."– Sabin, Dictionary of books relating to America. v. 10.

Edited throughout most of its life by Samuel Woodworth, this weekly periodical for women published much miscellany; in addition to the usual magazine fare such as tales and poetry, anecdotes, essays, and fashions, the *Literary Cabinet* featured "The Housewife's Manual," which contained recipes and household hints; a rhyming dictionary; biographies of women; a chronology of world history; and some musical pieces. It also published news items, articles on drama, and reviews.

v1-nsv4	May 15, 1819-Nov. 3, 1821	APS II, Reel 121
nsv5-7	Nov. 10, 1821-Dec. 21, 1822	Reel 122

LADIES LITERARY MUSEUM. *SEE* Literary and Musical Magazine.

LADIES' LITERARY PORTFOLIO: a general miscellany devoted to the fine arts and sciences. v. 1, nos. 1-52; Dec. 10, 1828-Dec. 9, 1829. Philadelphia, 1828-1829.

415 p.

Superseded by Literary portfolio.

The *Ladies Literary Portfolio,* edited by Thomas Cottrell Clarke, was a general miscellany devoted to the woman. Articles from many other periodicals were liberally used, although a great amount of original material appeared. The writing of Mrs. Hermans and Mrs. Harriet Muzzy was most frequently seen. Pieces by T.C. Clarke, The Reverend George Colby, and Hannah F. Gould are also included.

v1	Dec. 10, 1828-Dec. 9, 1829	APS II, Reel 893

Some pages are stained or have print missing. Page 400 is mis-numbered.

Microfilm edition was prepared from PHi copy.

LADIES' MAGAZINE. *SEE* American Ladies' Magazine.

LADIES' MAGAZINE AND LITERARY GAZETTE. *SEE* American Ladies' Magazine.

THE LADIES MAGAZINE; intended to aid in the cause of piety, religion and morality. Ed. by a lady. v.1; Mar. 1823-June 1824. Providence, J. Miller, printer, 1823-24.

cover-title, 384 p. monthly.

Paging irregular: no. 297-312 omitted, no. 317-332 repeated. No numbers issued for the months of May-Aug. 1823.

This religious monthly contains discussions of various religious topics, extracts from religious works, accounts of conversions, poetry, sermons, and biography.

v1, no.1-12	Mar. 1823-June 1824	APS II, Reel 122

LADIES' MAGAZINE OF LITERATURE, FASHION AND FINE ARTS. *SEE* Arthur's Magazine.

LADIES' MONITOR. *SEE* Lady's Monitor.

THE LADIES MUSEUM. v.1, no.1-14; Mar. 8-June 7, 1800. [Philadelphia, I. Ralston]

1 v. weekly.

Vol. 1 no. 1 preceded by an introductory issue dated Feb. 25, 1800. Film incomplete: no.7, 13 and parts of no.10, 12 wanting.

Isaac Ralston was the editor of this literary magazine for women. One of its four pages was devoted to poetry and anecdotes and the rest were filled with moral essays and serialized tales.

v1,no.1-14	Feb. 25-June 7, 1800	APS II, Reel 20

Microfilm edition was prepared from PPL copy.

LADIES MUSEUM. v.1; July 16, 1825-July 22, 1826. Providence, R.I.

208 p. weekly.

Edited and published by E. W. Maxcy. Film covers: v1, no.1-23; July 16-Dec. 31, 1825.

This four-page literary miscellany for women published a good deal of sentimental prose and poetry, along with essays and book reviews, and much miscellaneous material.

v1, no.1-23	July 16-Dec. 31, 1825	APS II, Reel 122

LADIES' NATIONAL MAGAZINE. *SEE* Peterson Magazine.

LADIES' PEARL. *SEE* Lady's Pearl.

LADIES PORT FOLIO. v.1-2, no.3; Jan. 1, 1820-July 8, 1820. Boston, S. T. Goss, 1820-.

v. weekly.

Film covers: v.1, no.1-25; Jan. 1-June 17, 1820 and v.2, no.3; July 8, 1820.

This literary miscellany devoted one of its eight pages to poetry, while the other seven were filled with tales, anecdotes, a few reviews, some biography and theater news, local news items and miscellany.

| v1 (no.1-25) | Jan. 1-June 17, 1820 | APS II, Reel 122 |
| nsv2, no.3 | July 8, 1820 | Reel 122 |

THE LADIES' REPOSITORY; a monthly periodical, devoted to literature, art, and religion. v.1-27, 1841-67; v.28-34 (new ser., v.1-14) 1868-74; v.35-36 (3d ser., v.1-4) 1875-76. Cincinnati, J.F. Wright and L. Swormstedt, for the Methodist Episcopal Church; New York, G. Lane and C.B. Tippett, 1841-76.

36 v. in 38. illus., plates, ports. Vols. 10-27, 32-33, 35-36 have added t.-p., engraved.

Title varies: 1841-48, The Ladies repository, and gatherings of the West: a monthly periodical devoted to literature and religion. 1849-72, The Ladies' repository; a monthly periodical devoted to literature and religion. 1873-76, The Ladies' repository: a monthly periodical devoted to literature, art, and religion.

Editors: 1841-July 1844, B.F. Tefft.—1852, W.C. Larrabee.—1853-63, D.W. Clark.—1864-June 1872, I.W. Wiley.—July 1872-June 1876, E. Wentworth.—July-Dec. 1876, Daniel Curry. Continued as the National repository.

The idea of this women's magazine originated with Samuel Williams, a Cincinnati Methodist, who thought that Christian women needed a magazine less worldly than *Godey's Lady's Book* and Snowden's *Lady's Companion*. Written largely by ministers, this exceptionally well-printed little magazine contained well-written essays of a moral character, plenty of poetry, articles on historical and scientific matters, and book reviews. Among western writers were Alice Cary, who contributed over a hundred sketches and poems, her sister Phoebe Cary, Otway Curry, Moncure D. Conway, and Joshua R. Giddings; and New England contributors included Mrs. Lydia Sigourney, Hannah F. Gould, and Julia C. R. Dorr. By 1851, each issue published a piece of music and two steel plates, usually landscapes or portraits.

When Davis E. Clark took over the editorship in 1853, the magazine became brighter and attained a circulation of 40,000. Unlike his predecessors, Clark included fictional pieces and made the *Repository* a magazine for the whole family. After the war it began to decline and in 1876 was replaced by the *National Repository*. The *Ladies' Repository* was an excellent representative of the Methodistic mind and heart. Its essays, sketches, and poems, its good steel engravings, and its moral tone gave it a charm all its own.

Ladies Repository, and Gatherings of the West.
| v1-6 | Jan. 1841-Dec. 1846 | APS II, Reel 482 |
| v7-8 | Jan. 1847-Dec. 1848 | Reel 483 |

Ladies' Repository; a monthly periodical ...
| v9-10 | Jan. 1849-Dec. 1850 | APS II, Reel 483 |

v10-13	Jan. 1850-Dec. 1853	Reel 893
v14-18	Jan. 1854-Dec. 1858	Reel 894
v19-22	Jan. 1859-Dec. 1862	Reel 895
v23-26	Jan. 1863-Dec. 1866	Reel 896
v27-30	Jan. 1867-Dec. 1870	Reel 897
v31-34	Jan. 1871-Dec. 1874	Reel 898

| v35-36 | Jan. 1875-Dec. 1876 | Reel 899 |

Several pages have print show-through and stains with some loss of text.

Microfilm edition was prepared from DLC, MiD, MiU, and RPB copies.

SEE ALSO: National Repository, Devoted to General and Religious Literature, Criticism and Art.

LADIES' REPOSITORY, AND GATHERINGS OF THE WEST. *SEE* Ladies' Repository.

LADIES' VISITOR. v.1, no.1-13; May 24, 1819-Apr. 18, 1820. [Marietta, Pa., W. Peirce]

205 p. monthly (irregular)

Published by William Peirce, this monthly women's magazine contained sentimental tales and poetry, moral essays, biographies of royalty, and anecdotes. "Grasmere," a serialized tale, ran through many issues.

| v1, no1-13 | May 24, 1819-Apr. 18, 1820 | APS II, Reel 212 |

LADIES VISITOR. (Boston). *SEE* Ladies Afternoon Visitor. (Boston).

THE LADIES' WEEKLY MUSEUM; or, Polite repository of amusement and instruction; being an assemblage of whatever can interest the mind, or exalt the character of the American fair. v.1-24, no.13, May 17, 1788-May 2, 1812; new ser., v.1-2, May 9, 1812-Apr. 30, 1814; new ser. [i.e. 3d] v.1-6, May 1814-Oct. 25, 1817. New York, J. Oram.

Title varies: -Sept. 13, 1788, Impartial gazetteer, and Saturday evening post. Sept. 20, 1788-May 7, 1791, The New-York weekly musuem. May 14, 1791-The Weekly museum. -Apr. 1817, New-York weekly museum. May 1817- The Ladies' weekly museum.

This four-page women's magazine presented much material of a sentimental and moral nature—romantic stories, some in serialized form, poetry, anecdotes, a morality column, brief reviews of plays, local and foreign news, and advertisements.

Impartial Gazetteer, and Saturday Evening Post.
| v1, no.7-18 | June 28-Sept. 13, 1788 | APS II, Reel 561 |

New-York Weekly Museum.
| v1, no.19-v3 | Sept. 20, 1788-May 7, 1791 | APS II, Reel 561 |

Weekly Museum.
v4-7	May 14, 1791-May 2, 1795	APS II, Reel 561
v8-15	May 9, 1795-Dec. 31, 1803	Reel 562
v16-17, no.32	Jan. 7, 1804-Aug. 10, 1805	Reel 563

New-York Weekly Museum.
v17, no.33-v23	Aug. 17, 1805-Dec. 28, 1811	APS II, Reel 563
nsv1-s3v3	May 9, 1812-Apr. 27, 1816	Reel 564
s3v4-5	May 4, 1816-Apr. 26, 1817	Reel 565

Ladies' Weekly Museum.
| s3v6 | May 3-Oct. 25, 1817 | APS II, Reel 565 |

Best copy available for photographing: many issues and pages are missing from the microfilm edition. Several pages are stained, torn, or tightly bound with some loss of text.

Microfilm edition was prepared from CtHT, CtY, DLC, MH, MiU, MWA, N, NNNPsI, PPHi, and RPB copies.

SEE ALSO: Weekly Visitor and Ladies' Museum.

LADIES' WREATH, a magazine devoted to literature, industry and religion. v.1-23, no.3 (no.1-177) May 1846-January 1861; new ser. v.1, no.1-6 (no.184-89) August 1861-January 1862. New York, 1846-1862.

24 v. Vols. 15, 18-23 and new ser. vol. 1 are not available.

Edited by Helen Irving, this monthly featured music, etchings, fiction, and poetry. Like some other women's magazines, this was bound into yearly volumes to be used as gift books.

v1-7	May 1846-1853	APS II, Reel 1232
v8-17	1854-1859	Reel 1233

Pagination is irregular. Some pages are stained. Vol. 13: Index and April issue are missing. Vol. 14: Index and July issue are missing. Vol. 16: Index is missing. Vol. 17: Index is missing.

Microfilm edition was prepared from CtHT, DLC, KyLo, MiU, NBuG, NjP, RPB, and WHi copies.

THE LADY & GENTLEMAN'S POCKET MAGAZINE OF LITERARY AND POLITE AMUSEMENT ... v.1; Aug. 15-Nov. 1796. New York, Printed by J. Tiebout.

245 p. illus. monthly.

Primarily contains literary works, poetry, and articles on mythology, manners, and morals, much of it selected from European sources.

v1	Aug.-Nov. 1796	APS I, Reel 14

Microfilm edition was prepared from NHi copy.

LADYS AND GENTLEMANS WEEKLY LITERARY MUSEUM AND MUSICAL MAGAZINE. *SEE* Literary and Musical Magazine.

LADYS AND GENTLEMANS WEEKLY MUSEUM AND PHILADELPHIA REPORTER. *SEE* Literary and Musical Magazine.

LADY'S BOOK. *SEE* Godey's Magazine.

LADY'S FRIEND. *SEE* Arthur's Home Magazine.

LADY'S HOME MAGAZINE. *SEE* Arthur's Home Magazine.

THE LADY'S MAGAZINE AND MUSICAL REPOSITORY. v.1-3; Jan. 1801-June 1802. New York, Printed by G. & R. Waite for N. Bell.

3 v. monthly.

The *Lady's Magazine* provided its readers with both entertainment and information. There was a good deal of poetry, some anecdotes, and occasional musical pieces, along with local news, vital statistics, and national and international news.

v1-3	Jan. 1801-June 1802	APS II, Reel 20

Microfilm edition was prepared from DLC copy.

THE LADY'S MAGAZINE, and repository of entertaining knowledge. By a literary society. v.1-2; June 1792-May 1793. Philadelphia, W. Gibbons [1792-93]

2 v. pl. monthly.

Caption title: The Ladies magazine.

An early women's magazine.

v1-2	June 1792-May 1793	APS I, Reel 14

Microfilm edition was prepared from MWA copy.

THE LADY'S MISCELLANY: or, weekly visitor, and entertaining companion for the use and amusement of both sexes. v.1-15; Oct. 9, 1802-Oct. 17, 1812. New York, Samuel B. White [etc.]

15 v.

Title varies: v. 1-4, The Weekly visitor, or, ladies' miscellany ... v. 5-9, The Lady's weekly miscellany (caption title, v. 5, no. 1-v. 11, no. 2: The Lady's weekly miscellany; v. 11, no. 3-v. 15, no. 26: The Lady's miscellany; or the weekly visitor for the use and amusement of both sexes.

Copy filmed imperfect: v. 4, no. 1-6, and v. 8, issue 13 missing.

This women's magazine was intended "to improve the minds and amuse the leisure hours of women"; it offered serialized tales and romances, articles on fashion, and much humorous material in the form of jokes, anecdotes, poetry, and satire. In addition, it provided reviews of local theater performances, biography, extracts from European publications, and brief news items.

Weekly Visitor, or Ladies' Miscellany
v1-4	Oct. 9, 1802-Oct. 25, 1806	APS II, Reel 20

Lady's Weekly Miscellany
v5-10, no.10	Nov. 1, 1806-Dec. 30, 1809	APS II, Reel 21
v10, no.11-v11, no.2	Jan. 6-May 5, 1810	Reel 212

Lady's Miscellany; or the Weekly Visitor ...
v11, no.3-v12, no.10	May 12-Dec. 29, 1810	APS II, Reel 212
v12, no.11-v15, no.26	Jan. 5, 1811-Oct. 17, 1813	Reel 213

Microfilm edition was prepared from NHi copy.

THE LADY'S MONITOR. v.1, no.1-41; Aug. 8, 1801-May 29, 1802. New York [P. Heard, etc.]

328 p. weekly.

Title varies: Aug. 8-Oct. 3, 1801, Ladies' monitor.

Film incomplete: no. 1-2 and part of no. 3 (p.1-18) wanting. Superseded by New York journal and weekly monitor. Cf. Union list of serials.

This women's magazine kept its readers up to date on the latest London fashions, new country dances, and literary news, as well as providing reviews of recent plays, travel sketches, and biography. For amusement there were sentimental tales, poetry, and puzzles.

Ladies' Monitor
v1, no.3-9   Aug. 22-Oct. 3, 1801   APS II, Reel 20

Lady's Monitor
v1, no.10-41   Oct. 10, 1801-May 29, 1802   APS II, Reel 20

Microfilm edition was prepared from MWA copy.

LADY'S PEARL. v.1-4, no.1; June 1840-July, 1843. Lowell, Mass., 1840-1843.

4 v.

Vols. 1-2 as Ladies' pearl.

A monthly magazine intended primarily for women and "devoted to moral, entertaining and instructive literature." It published much sentimental fiction as well as poetry, biographies of famous women, moral essays, historical incidents, sketches, and anecdotes. Marriage, love, and motherhood were favorite topics. The text was embellished with many illustrations and original musical pieces.

Ladies' Pearl
v1-2   June 1840-June 1842   APS II, Reel 657

Lady's Pearl
v3-4   July 1842-July 1843   APS II, Reel 657

Volume 4: Issue 1, pages 3-10 are not available for photographing.

Microfilm edition was prepared from DLC, MWA and MiU copies.

LADY'S WEEKLY MISCELLANY. *SEE* Lady's Miscellany.

LADY'S WESTERN MAGAZINE AND GARLAND OF THE VALLEY. v.1, nos.1-6; Jan.-June 1849. Cincinnati, 1849.

192 p.

Lady's Western Magazine and Garland of the Valley was published by Charles L. Wilson and edited by Benjamin F. Taylor, Chicago's first man of letters, and J. E. Hurlbut.

v1   Jan.-June 1849   APS II, Reel 1093

Many pages are stained. Vol. 1: No Index is available.

Microfilm edition was prepared from NcD copy.

LADY'S WORLD. *SEE* Peterson Magazine.

THE LANCASTER HIVE; devoted to morality, literature, biography, history, poetry, agriculture, &c. &c. v.1-2; June 22, 1803-June 12, 1805. Lancaster [Pa.] McDowell & Greear.

2v. weekly.

Caption title and running title: The Hive.

This 4-page miscellany by Charles McDowell published essays on morals and other topics, along with some tales, biographical sketches, poetry, and humorous anecdotes. Some of the material was satirical.

v1-2   June 22, 1803-June 12, 1805   APS II, Reel 22

Microfilm edition was prepared from MWA and PHi copy.

THE LANCET. no.1; [June 1803. Newark, N.J., Newark Gazette]

4 p.

Edited by Dr. Sangrado, jun. [pseud.]

This satirical magazine by "Dr. Sangrado" was designed to "draw off fever and arrest disease," and consisted mainly of satire on Newark government and politicians.

no.1   June 1803   APS II, Reel 22

Microfilm edition was prepared from MWA copy.

THE LATTER DAY LUMINARY. v.1-6; Feb. 1818-Dec. 1825. Philadelphia, Anderson and Meehan.

6 v. Quarterly, Feb. 1818-Nov. 1821; monthly, Jan. 1822-Dec. 1825. Two issues published each May, 1818-21, one containing the annual report of the American Baptist Foreign Mission Society issued under earlier names. Vols. 1-2 (Feb. 1818-Nov. 1821) also called no. 1-20.

Issued by the American Baptist Foreign Mission Society under earlier names: 1818-May 1820, Baptist Board of Foreign Missions for the United States.—May 1820-Dec. 1825, General Convention of the Baptist Denomination in the United States (varies slightly)

Conducted by a committee of the Baptist Board of Foreign Missions for the United States, the *Latter Day Luminary* was designed to keep readers up to date on the state and progress of missions, both in the U.S. and abroad; it published missionary news and reports of the Board. In addition to a "Miscellaneous" section of church news, news of Bible societies and revivals, and obituaries, it also included poetry, reviews, biographical sketches, and occasional essays.

v1   Feb. 1818-Nov. 1819   APS II, Reel 122
v2-6   Feb. 1820-Dec. 1825   Reel 123

LAW INTELLIGENCER. *SEE* United States Law Intelligencer and Review.

LAW REPORTER. *SEE* Monthly Law Reporter.

LAWYER AND BANKER. *SEE* Central Law Journal.

THE LAY-MAN'S MAGAZINE. v.1, no.1-51; Nov. 16, 1815-Nov. 7, 1816. Martinsburgh [Va.]

408 p. weekly.

Copy filmed incomplete: no. 24, 30-31, 40, 47-50 wanting.

This Episcopal magazine published information on Bible societies, a variety of church news, including obituaries, and occasional poetry and hymns.

v1, no.1-51   Nov. 16, 1815-Nov. 7, 1816   APS II, Reel 123

LESLIE'S MONTHLY MAGAZINE. *SEE* American Magazine.

THE LIBERAL CHRISTIAN. v.1; Jan. 11, 1823-Mar. 6, 1824. Brooklyn, Conn., 1823-24.

200 p. biweekly (irregular)

This Unitarian magazine contained articles on religion in general as well as articles on the Unitarian doctrine, and presented comparisons of the Unitarian religion with others. Extracts from books and sermons, and occasional prayers and hymns rounded out the contents.

v1   Jan. 11, 1823-Mar. 6, 1824   APS II, Reel 123

LIBERAL CHRISTIAN (New York) *SEE* Christian Inquirer.

LIBERATOR. v.1-35; Jan. 1, 1831-Dec. 29, 1865. Boston, 1831-1865.

35 v.

Edited by William Lloyd Garrison.

Founded by William Lloyd Garrison in 1831, the *Liberator* was the greatest of all the antislavery magazines and aroused much bitter antagonism. This Boston weekly has immense historical importance and no small literary value. It was to be an immediate-abolition paper, to support peace and temperance, and to contain a fair proportion of literary miscellany and news. Opposition to colonization occupied many pages; however, Garrison did approve of boycotting the products of slavery and also advocated disunion. He promised his support to women's rights as early as 1837. A department called "The Refuge of Oppression" quoted from the worst of the fire-eating southern editorials, and small woodcuts illustrating slavery scenes appeared occasionally. John Rankin's "Letters on American Slavery" were printed serially in the second volume. After the thirteenth amendment to the Constitution was adopted, the *Liberator* was felt to have served its purpose and was discontinued.

v1-4   Jan. 1, 1831-Dec. 27, 1834   APS II, Reel 391
v5-8   Jan. 3, 1835-Dec. 28, 1838   Reel 392
v9-12   Jan. 4, 1839-Dec. 30, 1842   Reel 393
v13-16   Jan. 6, 1843-Dec. 25, 1846   Reel 394
v17-20   Jan. 1, 1847-Dec. 27, 1850   Reel 395
v21-24   Jan. 3, 1851-Dec. 29, 1854   Reel 396
25-28   Jan. 5, 1855-Dec. 31, 1858   Reel 397
v29-32   Jan. 7, 1859-Dec. 26, 1862   Reel 398
v33-35   Jan. 2, 1863-Dec. 29, 1865   Reel 399

LIBERTY (not the daughter but the mother of order). v.1-17, no.1; Aug. 6, 1881-Apr. 1908. New York [etc.] B. R. Tucker.

17 v. irregular.

Suspended Dec. 1900-Dec. 1902. Vols. 1-17 also called whole no. 1-403. Subtitle omitted, v. 16-17. Edited by B.R. Tucker.

Benjamin R. Tucker was one of several magazine editors who supported the doctrines of anarchy; he published the *Radical Review* at New Bedford, Massachusetts from 1877-78, and in 1881 he established his *Liberty*, a biweekly which for twenty-five years advocated anarchy, free love, and other radical doctrines. *Liberty* began as a 4-page paper, and during its first volume its front page was devoted to sections entitled "On Picket Duty" and "About Progressive People." The back page features poetry, and "Liberty's Library," which listed books on anarchy and free love, while the remaining space was devoted to various articles and essays on anarchy, liberty, and other doctrines. In later volumes, *Liberty* increased in size and added longer poems, serialized prose, including a serial romance by N.G. Tchernychewsky, book advertisements, and a section titled "The Beauties of Government." Some material on women's suffrage also appeared.

v1-10   Aug. 6, 1881-May 4, 1895   APS III, Reel 669
v11-17   May 18, 1895-April 1908   Reel 670

Several volumes lack title pages and indexes. Several pages are stained, creased, tightly bound, torn and taped with some loss of text.

Microfilm edition was prepared from IU and MiU copies.

THE LIBERTY BELL. By friends of freedom. v.1-15; 1839-1858. Boston, Massachusetts anti-slavery fair, 1839-46; (National Anti-Slavery Bazaar), 1847-58.

15 v. plates, ports.

"Edited and published annually in Boston, by Maria Weston Chapman, 1843 to 1858 (one or two years being omitted)"–Samuel May, Catalogue of anti-slavery publications in America. No volumes issued for 1840, 1850, 1854-55, 1857. cf. Faxon, Literary annuals and gift books.

Published by the National Anti-Slavery Fair, the *Liberty Bell* was mainly concerned with freedom for slaves, but touched on other kinds of freedoms as well. Its contents were made up mainly of prose and poetry—essays, short articles, and a good deal of poetry, as well as a few speeches. Articles dealt with various aspects of slavery—its evils, the slave trade, conditions in the West Indies, the life of a slave, slave prisons, etc. Famous people whose writings appeared in the *Liberty Bell* include Lydia Maria Child, James Russell Lowell, Eliza Lee Follen, Lucretia Mott, William Lloyd Garrison, Henry Longfellow, Frederick Douglass, Elizabeth Barrett Browning, and Ralph Waldo Emerson.

no.1-12   1839-1852   APS II, Reel 491
no.13-15   1853-1858   Reel 492

1843: Pages 44-45 are missing. 1851: Pages 145-47 are missing. vail-

Microfilm edition was prepared from the RPB copy.

LIBRARY OF HEALTH. *SEE* Graham Journal of Health and Longevity.

LIFE. v.1-103 (no.1-2620); Jan. 4, 1883-Nov. 1936. New York, Pub. at the Life Office [etc.]

103 v. illus.

Weekly, Jan. 4, 1883-Nov. 27, 1931; monthly, Dec. 1931-Nov. 1936. Founded and edited until his death, by J.A. Mitchell. Superseded by Life (Chicago)

John Ames Mitchell founded *Life* on January 4, 1883 with the idea of creating a satirical weekly of high artistic and literary merit to rival existing comic magazines such as *Puck* and *Judge*. *Life* presented a satire which was biting, a genteel humor which was clever and fresh.

With the literary side being ably handled by Edward S. Martin, and later by John Kendrick Bangs, Mitchell was able to lavish his care on illustrations. It was as a picture paper that *Life* was started and it appeared at first as though Mitchell would have to do most of the illustrations himself. Soon other artists were being drawn to *Life,* including F.W. Attwood, E.W. Kemble, and Charles Dana Gibson, creator of the famous "Gibson girl" who graced *Life's* pages for nearly twenty years. The art work in *Life* developed to a very high point in the nineties. In addition to line drawings, halftones and wash drawings became common to its pages.

It was a wedding of delicacy and force that made *Life* of the eighties and nineties the distinctive magazine that it was. The paper kept abreast of current events, of developments in manners and morals, of politics, of drama, literature, and the arts. It refused partisan allegiance in political contests, though it had its favorite leaders and its principles. It waged crusades against the protective tariff, against the cruelties of vivisection, and against sabbatarianism.

Life was one of the magazines whose prosperity was securely based on circulation. It easily weathered the panic of 1907. Circulation rose in the second decade reaching 150,000 in 1916. It reached the height of its success just before the United States entered the First World War. It had then completed two full decades of very general acceptance by the more discriminating classes of American readers. It had become one of the two or three greatest satirical weeklies ever published in this country.

Mitchell died in July 1918 and his death was a crushing blow to *Life,* so fully had he been its guiding spirit. Charles Dana Gibson became chief owner in 1920. The magazine began to include new features, motion picture coverage, a "Neighborhood News" department, and a gossip page. *Life* had more variety and broader geographical coverage than in earlier years, but it had lost the more or less insulated distinctiveness which had been characteristic of it.

Life might well have ended its fine career in 1928. It was no longer the subtle *Life* of old. In its last decade it was a strayed rebeler, having lost its way in a confused world, and was unable to keep apace with new magazines, such as *The New Yorker*. *Life* was not bankrupt however, when in October 1936, with its November issue off the presses, it decided to give up the battle and accept an offer from Time, Inc. Its subscription list, features, and humor went to *Judge,* long its competitor. Its name was reserved for the new picture magazine to be launched in November.

v1-4	Jan. 1883-Dec. 1884	APS III, Reel 500
5-10	Jan. 1885-Dec. 1887	Reel 501
v11-16	Jan. 1888-Dec. 1890	Reel 502
v17-22	Jan. 1891-Dec. 1893	Reel 503
v23-28	Jan. 1894-Dec. 1896	Reel 504
v29-33	Jan. 1897-June 1899	Reel 505
v34-38	July 1899-Dec. 1901	Reel 506
v39-42	Jan. 1902-Dec. 1903	Reel 507
v43-46	Jan. 1904-Dec. 1905	Reel 508
v47-49	Jan. 1906-June 1907	Reel 509
v50-52	July 1907-Dec. 1908	Reel 510
v53-55	Jan. 1909-June 1910	Reel 511
v56-57	July 1910-June 1911	Reel 512
v58-59	July 1911-June 1912	Reel 513
v60-61	July 1912-June 1913	Reel 514
v62-63	July 1913-June 1914	Reel 515
v64-65	July 1914-June 1915	Reel 516
v66-67	July 1915-June 1916	Reel 517
v68-69	July 1916-June 1917	Reel 518
v70-71	July 1917-June 1918	Reel 519
v72-73	July 1918-June 1919	Reel 520
v74-75	July 1919-June 1920	Reel 521
v76-78	July 1920-Dec. 1921	Reel 522
v79-81	Jan. 1922-June 1923	Reel 523
v82-84	July 1923-Dec. 1924	Reel 524
v85-86	Jan. 1925-Dec. 1925	Reel 525
v87-88	Jan. 1926-Dec. 1926	Reel 526
v89-90	Jan. 1927-Dec. 1927	Reel 527
v91-92	Jan. 1928-Dec. 1928	Reel 528
v93-94	Jan. 1929-Dec. 1929	Reel 529
v95-97	Jan. 1930-June 1931	Reel 530
v98-100	July 1931-Dec. 1933	Reel 531
v101-103	Jan. 1934-Nov. 1936	Reel 532

Tables of contents for several volumes are not available for photographing. Several volumes have stained, torn, taped, and tightly bound pages with some loss of text. Some advertisement pages are missing from page count. Vols. 9, 16, 18, and 28-29: Pagination is irregular. Vol. 22: Cover page is misdated. Vol. 48: Cover page and page 1 of table of contents are not available for photographing. Issue 1236 is misnumbered.

Microfilm edition was prepared from IC, MiD, MnU, MoS, N, NBu, NPV, NhD, NjP, and TxH copies.

LIFE (Chicago). *SEE* Life.

LIFE AND LIGHT FOR WOMAN. *SEE* Missionary Herald at Home and Abroad.

LIFE ILLUSTRATED. *SEE* Phrenological Journal and Science of Health.

* LIPPINCOTT'S MAGAZINE OF LITERATURE, SCIENCE AND EDUCATION. *SEE* McBride's Magazine.

*LIPPINCOTT'S MAGAZINE OF POPULAR LITERATURE AND SCIENCE. *SEE* McBride's Magazine.

LIPPINCOTT'S MONTHLY MAGAZINE. *SEE* McBride's Magazine.

LITERARY AND CATHOLIC SENTINEL. *SEE* Jesuit.

THE LITERARY AND EVANGELICAL MAGAZINE. v.1-11; Jan. 1818-Dec. 1828. Richmond, Va., N. Pollard, etc.

11 v. monthly.

Title varies: 1818-1820 (v.1-3) The Virginia evangelical and literary magazine. 1821 (v.4) The Evangelical and literary magazine and missionary chronice conducted by John H. Rice ... 1822-23 (v.5-6) The Evangelical and literary magazine. 1824-28 (v.7-11) The Literary and evangelical magazine.

Although primarily a religious magazine, this periodical also published nonreligious material, such as literary and philosophical news, book reviews, poetry, and articles on history and on foreign countries. Religious material included sermons, articles on doctrine, discussions on the Bible, biographies, coverage of missions and missionary and Bible societies, and listings of new religious publications.

Virginia Evangelical and Literary Magazine

v1-3	Jan. 1818-Dec. 1820	APS II, Reel 124

Evangelical and Literary Magazine and Missionary Chronicle

v4	Jan.-Dec. 1821	Reel 124

Evangelical and Literary Magazine
v5-6   Jan. 1822-Dec. 1823   Reel 125

Literary and Evangelical Magazine
v7-8   Jan. 1824-Dec. 1825   APS II, Reel 125

v9-11   Jan. 1826-Dec. 1828   Reel 464

Several pages are stained with some loss of text.

Microfilm edition was prepared from DLC copy.

LITERARY AND MUSICAL MAGAZINE. v.1-4, no.14; July 5, 1817-Sept. 13, 1819; new ser. v.1 (no.1-24) Aug. 24, 1819-June 9, 1820. Philadelphia, H.C. Lewis, ed.

4 v. in 1. weekly.

Title varies: July 5, 1817-July 13, 1818, Ladies literary museum; or, Weekly repository. July 27-Sept. 30, 1818, Ladys and gentlemans weekly museum and Philadelphia reporter. Jan. 1-Mar. 1, 1819, Ladys and gentlemans weekly literary museum and musical magazine.

Suspended Oct.-Dec., 1818. New ser. v.1 called also v.4, no.15-38.

This weekly literary miscellany began as the *Ladies' Literary Museum,* and was mainly for the purpose of amusement, containing sentimental tales, fashions, poetry, biographical sketches, and humorous items and anecdotes. When it was renamed the *Lady's and Gentleman's Weekly Museum and Philadelphia Reporter* in 1818, it added instructive material, such as moral essays, literary notices, news of political events, and other domestic and foreign news. In 1819 it again changed its title, becoming the *Lady's and Gentleman's Weekly Literary Museum and Musical Magazine,* and added musical pieces, with the rest of the contents remaining essentially the same as before.

Ladies Literary Museum; or, Weekly Repository
v1-2   -July 5, 1817-July 13, 1818   APS II, Reel 213

Ladys and Gentlemans Weekly Museum and Philadelphia Reporter
v3, no.1-10   July 27-Sept. 30, 1818   Reel 213

Ladys and Gentlemans Weekly Literary Museum and Musical Magazine
v3, no.11-19   Jan. 1-Mar. 1, 1819   Reel 213

Literary and Musical Magazine
v3, no.20-v4, no.38
(i.e. no.24)   Mar. 8, 1819-June 9, 1820   Reel 213

Pagination is irregular. Some torn pages.

THE LITERARY AND PHILOSOPHICAL REPERTORY: embracing discoveries and improvements in the physical sciences; the liberal and fine arts; essays moral and religious; occasional notices and reviews of new publications; and articles of miscellaneous intelligence. Ed. by a number of gentlemen. v.1-2; Apr. 1812-May 1817. Middlebury, Vt., Printed for S. Swift by T.C. Strong [1812-17]

2 v.

Vol. 2 has imprint: Middlebury, Vt., Printed and published by T.C. Strong.

Edited by "a number of gentlemen," this magazine proposed to include news of discoveries, inventions, and improvements in the sciences and the fine arts, moral and religious essays, notices and reviews of new publications, and articles of miscellaneous news. There was a department of poetry, "The Medley," letters on "Modern Paris," sermons, and selected papers.

v1-2   Apr. 1812-May 1817   APS II, Reel 126

LITERARY AND PHILOSOPHICAL SOCIETY OF NEW-YORK. *SEE* Transactions of the Literary and Philosophical Society of New-York.

THE LITERARY AND SCIENTIFIC REPOSITORY, and critical review. v.[1]-4 (no.1-8); June 1820-May 1822. New York, Wiley and Halsted, 1820-22.

4v. pl., port. quarterly.

Superseded by United States magazine and literary and political repository.

No. 1 dated June 1820 on caption, July 1820 on t.-p. and cover; no.8 dated May 1822 on caption, June 1822 on cover.

This quarterly review was edited by Col. Charles K. Gardner, who was at that time adjutant general of the northern division of the army. Being mainly eclectic at first, this journal borrowed much of its contents from British magazines, but by the third volume about half the material was original. Biography, science, economics, and agriculture were given attention and there were comments on books, lists of new publications, and some poetry. Gardner lent his pages to the paper war with England, reprinting in the second number the *Edinburgh's* review of Robert Walsh's *An Appeal from the Judgments of Great Britain Respecting the United States.* Fitz-Greene Halleck's elegy on the death of Joseph Rodman Drake was an outstanding literary contribution.

v1-4   June 1820-May 1822   APS II, Reel 126

SEE ALSO: United States Magazine and Literary and Political Repository.

* **THE LITERARY AND THEOLOGICAL REVIEW.** v.1-6; Jan. 1834-Dec. 1839. New York, D. Appleton; Boston, W. Pierce, 1834-39.

6 v. quarterly.

Editors: 1834-37, L. Woods, jun.–1838-39, C.D. Pigeon.

Founded and edited by Leonard Woods, this periodical was the organ of the Congregational and Presbyterian denominations. It contained articles written by clergy and teachers, and although orthodox theology was the chief material, it also included some literary criticism and articles on education, social questions, and science.

v1-6   Jan. 1834-Dec. 1839   APS II, Reel 798

Microfilm edition was prepared from MiD copy.

LITERARY CABINET. v.1, no.1-20; Nov. 15, 1806-Oct. 31, 1807. [New-Haven, O. Steele]

160 p. Biweekly (irregular)

Edited by members of the senior class, Yale University. Film incomplete: no.19 p.145-152 wanting.

Published at Yale in 1806 and 1807, the *Literary Cabinet* was the first American college magazine. It was intended to help students practice the art of writing, and was edited by members of the senior class. The contents were made up mainly of essays and poetry.

nos.1-18, 20   1806-1807   APS II, Reel 22

Microfilm edition was prepared from CSmH copy.

THE LITERARY CABINET AND WESTERN OLIVE BRANCH. v.1 (no.1-8) 1832-33; new ser., v.1 (no.1-26) (no.9-34); Feb. 16, 1833-Feb. 8, 1834. St. Clairsville, Ohio, Printed for the editor by H.J. Howard.

2 v. illus. semimonthly.

Superseded by the Western gem and cabinet of literature, science and news.

Edited by T. Gregg. Began publication in 1832. cf. Union list of serials.

This periodical, edited by Thomas Gregg, emphasized literature and presented original and selected tales and poetry, literary notices and reviews, biography, sketches, and a good deal of miscellaneous material. In addition, science and art columns and articles on the history of Ohio were included.

nsv1   Feb. 16, 1833-Feb. 8, 1834   APS II, Reel 565

Microfilm edition includes only new series volume 1.

Microfilm edition was prepared from NNHi and OCIWHi copies.

LITERARY CASKET. (Pittsburgh) *SEE* Western Literary Magazine.

THE LITERARY CASKET: devoted to literature, the arts, and sciences. v.1; Mar. 4, 1826-Feb. 3, 1827. Hartford, Norton & Russell, 1827.

1 p.l., 208 p. biweekly.

This semimonthly published by Benjamin H. Norton and John Russell was intended to amuse and instruct. Its widely varied material included original and selected moral tales; biographical sketches of distinguished persons; religious, moral, and philosophical essays; poetry; and listings of new and choice publications, as well as articles on travel and history. There were departments for the ladies and for scientific instruction; jokes and anecdotes provided amusement.

v1   Mar. 4, 1826-Feb. 3, 1827   APS II, Reel 777

Microfilm edition was prepared from DLC and WHi copies.

THE LITERARY COMPANION. v.1, no.1-13; June 16-Sept. 8, 1821. New York, G. & J. Huntley.

208 p. weekly.

This short-lived literary miscellany presented some tales and poetry, literary news, occasional biographical sketches, information on the weather, and some foreign news.

v1, nos.1-13   June 16-Sept. 8, 1821   APS II, Reel 131

LITERARY DIGEST. *SEE* Current Opinion.

THE LITERARY EMPORIUM; a compendium of religious, literary, and philosophical knowledge. v.1-5, no.1; Jan. 1845-Jan. 1847. New York, J. K. Wellman.

5 v. plates (part col.) port. monthly.

A monthly publication of poetry, fiction, plates, and articles on philosophy, literature, and religion.

v1-5   Jan. 1845-Jan. 1847   APS II, Reel 1233

Vol. 5 is incomplete; best copy available for photographing.

Microfilm edition was prepared from DLC and MiU copies.

LITERARY EXAMINER AND WESTERN MONTHLY REVIEW. *SEE* Examiner and Hesperian.

LITERARY FOCUS. v.1, no.1-12; June 1827-May 1828. Oxford, Ohio, Miami University, 1827-1828.

240 p.

Literary monthly edited and published by the Erodelphian and Union Literary Societies of Miami University. It contained tales, poetry, biography, essays on intemperance, slavery and similar topics, listings of new publications, a humor section, and some science articles and math problems.

v1   June 1827-May 1828   APS II, Reel 777

Microfilm edition was prepared from OOxM and RPB copies.

THE LITERARY GAZETTE. v.1-2 (no.1-32); Aug. 1, 1834-June 26, 1835. Concord, N.H., D. D. Fisk, 1834-35.

2 v. in 1. 1 illus. Weekly, Aug. 1834-Mar. 1835; semimonthly, Apr.?-June 1835.

Caption title. Edited by Asa Fowler and others.

This literary miscellany featured musical pieces, writings by Nathaniel Parker Willis and Mrs. Lydia H. Sigourney, and a number of articles on education and on teeth, in addition to biographical and travel sketches, poetry and tales, literary notices, and news.

v1-2, no.1-32   Aug. 1, 1834-June 26, 1835   APS II, Reel 400

Microfilm edition was prepared from WhM copy.

THE LITERARY GAZETTE AND AMERICAN ATHENAEUM. v.1-3, no.26; Sept. 10, 1825-Mar. 3, 1827. New York [J. G. Brooks & G. Bond]

3 v. weekly.

Title varies: Sept. 10, 1825-Mar. 4, 1826, The New York literary gazette and Phi beta kappa repository. Mar. 11, 1826- The New York literary gazette, and American athenaeum.

Editors: Sept. 1825- J. G. Brooks (with George Bond, Mar.-Apr. 1826) Preceded by the Minerva. Absorbed the American athenaeum, Mar. 1826.

This partially eclectic weekly superseded *Minerva,* and was edited by James G. Brooks. It printed many popular tales, criticism, poetry, and reviews of books and plays.

New York Literary Gazette and Phi Beta Kappa Repository
v1   Sept. 10, 1825-Mar. 4, 1826   APS II, Reel 741

New York Literary Gazette and American Athenaeum
v2   Mar. 11, 1826-Sept. 2, 1826   Reel 741

Literary Gazette and American Athenaeum
v3   Sept. 9, 1826-Mar. 3, 1827   Reel 741

Microfilm edition was prepared from CtY and NjP copies.

THE LITERARY GAZETTE: or, Journal of criticism, science, and the arts. Being a collection of original and selected essays. v.1, no.1-52; Jan. 6-Dec. 29, 1821. Philadelphia [J. Maxwell]

829 p. illus. weekly.

Forms a third series of the Analectic magazine.

James Maxwell, a Philadelphia printer, bought the *Analectic Magazine* in 1819, began a new series in 1820, and in 1821 made it a weekly and changed its name to *The Literary Gazette.* Modeled after the London *Literary Gazette,* this 16-page magazine proposed "to give an account of every new American book to which access can be had," and was filled with book reviews. It also contained selections from the literary and scientific journals of Great Britain, as well as biographies of distinguished men, proceedings of scientific societies in Europe and the U.S., and notices of discoveries and inventions, with lists of new patents. In addition there was some poetry, occasional items on the fine arts, and essays on society and manners and on the history and laws of the U.S. The *Gazette* was abandoned at the end of the year.

v1, no.1-52   Jan. 6-Dec. 29, 1821   APS II, Reel 131

SEE ALSO: Analectic Magazine.

THE LITERARY GEMINAE, a monthly magazine in English and French. v.1; June 1839-May 1840. Worcester, Mass., E. Burritt [1839-40]

cover-title, 288 p.

Each number contains an English and a French section, each section having separate paging. Elihu Burritt, editor.

A monthly literary magazine which published simultaneously an English and a French issue. The French issue, titled *Les Gemeaux Litteraires,* was similar but not identical in content to the English one. Both contained poetry, tales, essays, and much translated material, in addition to original and selected articles.

v1   June 1839-May 1840   APS II, Reel 657

Microfilm edition was prepared from MiU copy.

LITERARY GEMS. v.1, nos.1-28; April 10-July 1833. New York, 1833.

112 p.

This four-page literary magazine was to present choice selections from the best American and European writings, and extracts from well-known works, as well as poetry, anecdotes, and miscellaneous

information. Articles generally dealt with biography, geography and travel, literature, and the American Indian.

v1   April 10-July 1833   APS II, Reel 799

Best copy available for photographing. Page 99: Some loss of print.

Microfilm edition was prepared from NHi copy.

LITERARY INQUIRER. v.1-3, no.13; Jan. 1, 1833-Oct. 15, 1834. Buffalo, N.Y., 1833-1834.

3 v. semimonthly.

A semimonthly journal published under the patronage of the Buffalo Lyceum and devoted exclusively to literature, science, and "general intelligence." In the literary department were tales, poetry, essays, anecdotes, humorous sketches, a series on British literature, and notices and reviews of new works. Occasional scientific articles dealt with botany and geology; and general intelligence included such material as domestic and foreign news, proceedings of state and national legislatures, proceedings of the Buffalo Lyceum, biographical memoirs of eminent persons, and articles on history and the arts.

v1-3   Jan. 1, 1833-Oct. 15, 1834   APS II, Reel 799

Some pages are stained. Vol. 3: Index is lacking.

Microfilm edition was prepared from MWA, MiD and NBu copies.

LITERARY JOURNAL; a repository of polite literature and fine arts. v.1, nos.1-13; Nov. 1834-June 1835. Schenectady, N.Y., 1834-1835.

104 p.

Vol. 1, nos. 1-6 as Wreath; devoted to polite literature.

A literary magazine which emphasized original material, with sections devoted to tales, poetry, essays, literary criticism, and miscellany. Also included were jokes and anecdotes and some selected material.

Wreath; Devoted to Polite Literature
v1, no.1-6   Nov. 1834-Feb. 1835   APS II, Reel 657

Literary Journal
v1, no.7-13   Mar.-June 1835   Reel 657

Microfilm edition was prepared from RPB copy.

THE LITERARY JOURNAL, AND WEEKLY REGISTER OF SCIENCE AND THE ARTS. Ed. by Albert G. Greene. v.1; June 8, 1833-May 31, 1834. Providence, J. Knowles, 1833-34.

412 p.

Edited by Albert G. Greene, this journal was devoted mainly to literature and science, poetry, tales, essays, literary reviews, selections from the best American and foreign periodicals, and articles concerning education, morality, science, literature, and the fine arts. Much space was allotted to the early history of the county and to biographies of many authors, including Burns, Southey, and Shelley.

v1   June 8, 1833-May 31, 1834   APS II, Reel 799

Many pages are stained.

Microfilm edition was prepared from CtY and IaU copies.

LITERARY MAGAZINE. v.1, no.1; Jan. 1, 1835. Boston, 1835.

48 p.

This short-lived literary periodical published poetry and tales, music, essays, publication notices, sketches of scenery, and some satirical material.

v1, no.1   Jan. 1, 1835   APS II, Reel 400

Microfilm edition was prepared from MWA copy.

THE LITERARY MAGAZINE, AND AMERICAN REGISTER. v.1-8; Oct. 1803-Dec. 1807. Philadelphia, J. Conrad, 1804-08.

8 v. monthly.

Charles Brockden Brown, editor.

This monthly, begun by Charles Brockden Brown in Philadelphia in October, 1803, was similar to his New York *Monthly,* but gave more attention to political chronicles and general intelligence and contained less fiction than the *Monthly* had. The contents were varied; most pieces were brief, and about half were original. Agriculture, travel, feminism, and literature were among the topics, and there was also much medical information, especially concerning yellow fever and smallpox. Brown claimed that inoculation for smallpox had done more harm than good.

v1-2   Oct. 1803-Dec. 1804   APS II, Reel 22
v3-8   Jan. 1805-Dec. 1807   Reel 23

Microfilm edition was prepared from DLC copy.

LITERARY MESSENGER. *SEE* Western Literary Messenger.

THE LITERARY MIRROR. v.1; Feb. 20, 1808-Feb. 11, 1809. [Portsmouth, N.H., S. Sewall]

208 p. weekly.

Edited by S. Sewall. No. 1, 43 incomplete.

Published weekly by Stephen Sewall, this 4-page literary miscellany was made up of tales, poetry and anecdotes, short moral essays, local news items, biographical sketches, and much miscellaneous material. There were a few advertisements.

v1   Feb. 20, 1808-Feb. 11, 1809   APS II, Reel 24

Microfilm edition was prepared from MB and Nh copy.

THE LITERARY MISCELLANY, containing elegant selections of the most admired fugitive pieces, and extracts from works of the greatest merit, with originals. Prose and poetry. v.1-2 (no.1-16); 1795. Philadelphia, T. Stephens, 1795.

[256] p.

Various pagings. Lacking on film: no. 9-16 and scattered pages.

A periodical focusing mainly on literary material. Each issue includes several fiction pieces and several poems, some by well-known authors such as Goldsmith, Thomas Gray, and Andrew Marvell.

v1, no.1-8   1795   APS I, Reel 14

Microfilm edition was prepared from DLC copy.

THE LITERARY MISCELLANY, including dissertations and essays on subjects of literature, science, and morals; biographical and historical sketches; critical remarks on language; with occasional reviews. v.1-2; 1805-06. Cambridge [Mass.] W. Hilliard, 1805-06.

2 v. port. quarterly.

"By the Phi beta kappa society of Harvard college."—Sabin, Dict. of books relating to America, v.10.

Published quarterly by the Harvard Phi Beta Kappa Society in 1805 and 1805, the *Literary Miscellany* presented, in serial form, a "Retrospect of the Eighteenth Century," "Primitive History," memoirs of Count Rumford, and articles on ethics and early German literature. In addition, there were other articles on languages and literature, translations of classical poetry, biographical sketches, literary news, book reviews, and poetry.

v1-2   1805-1806   APS II, Reel 24

Microfilm edition was prepared from MiU-C copy.

THE LITERARY MISCELLANY; or, Monthly review, a periodical work. By Charles N. Baldwin. v.1, no.1-4; May-Aug. 1811. New York, Riley & Adams, 1811.

338 p.

Vol. 1 includes supplement.

Edited by Charles N. Baldwin, this short-lived magazine contained tales, poetry, biographical sketches, literary news items, miscellaneous essays, and occasional reviews. A serialized tale, "Netley Abbey," ran through all four numbers, as did a series on drama.

v1, nos.1-4   May-Aug. 1811   APS II, Reel 131

THE LITERARY MUSEUM, or, Monthly magazine. Jan.-June, 1797. West-Chester [Pa.] Derrick & Sharples, [1797]

336 p. pl.

Articles on a variety of subjects, including travel, agriculture, and remedies for illness, as well as biography and fiction, appear on the first pages. In separate sections following this are original and selected poetry, the "Monthly Chronicle," including foreign and domestic news, and a listing of deaths and marriages. Some engravings embellish the text.

Jan.-June 1797   APS I, Reel 14

Microfilm edition was prepared from MWA copy.

THE LITERARY PAMPHLETEER, containing some observations on the best mode of promoting the cause of literature in the State of Kentucky; and a review of the late administration of the Transylvania University. no.1-6. Paris, Ky., Lyle & Keenon, 1823.

6 no.

Edited by J. M'Farland.

This short-lived periodical was concerned with education and with promoting an interest in literature in Kentucky. "Brief Essays on Education" appear in several numbers, and there are a number of articles on Transylvania University.

no.1-6   1823   APS II, Reel 132

LITERARY PORTFOLIO. *SEE* Ladies' Literary Portfolio.

LITERARY REGISTER; a weekly paper. Edited by the professors of Miami University. v.1-2, no.26; June 2, 1828-June 27, 1829. Oxford, Ohio, 1828-1829.

2 v.

Vol. 1: pages 24-31 are repeated; some pages are torn. Vol. 2: pages 207-08 and index are missing.

Horticulture, mathematics, and political economy were also discussed in this literary paper.

v1-2   June 2, 1828-June 27, 1829   APS II, Reel 1234

Microfilm edition was prepared from OOxM and RPB copies.

LITERARY TABLET. v.1-2; 1833-Mar. 29, 1834. New Haven, Conn., 1833-1834.

2 v. Vol. 1, nos. 1-20, 25-26 wanting.

A literary periodical which contained much original material—moral and sentimental tales, poetry, reviews of books and magazines, biography, essays, and other literary items. It also featured an editorial column, occasional woodcuts with descriptions, and jokes and anecdotes.

v1-2   1833-Mar. 29, 1834   APS II, Reel 657

Microfilm edition was prepared from CtY copy.

THE LITERARY TABLET; or, A general repository of useful entertainment; consisting of essays original and selected, in poetry and prose. v.1-4; Aug. 6, 1803-Aug. 5, 1807. Hanover, N.H., M. Davis.

4v. Biweekly.

Edited by N. Orlando [pseud.]

This biweekly miscellany devoted one of its four pages to poetry and the other three to original and selected essays on religion and morality; a variety of articles on history, the fine arts, literature, and agriculture; biographical sketches, and anecdotes.

v1-4   Aug. 6, 1803-Aug. 5, 1807   APS II, Reel 24

Microfilm edition was prepared from MWA copy.

THE LITERARY UNION: a journal of progress, in literature and education, religion and politics, science and agriculture. v.1-2, no.13, Apr. 7-Dec. 29, 1849; new ser., v.1-2, no.1, Jan.-Jul. 1850. Syracuse [N.Y.] W. W. Newman.

4 v. weekly.

J. M. Winchell, James Johonnot, editors.

This periodical proposed to encourage the development of American literature and to raise its standards; therefore, it avoided sentimental fiction and material from foreign sources. Its publishers promised to promote education, expose corruption, advocate moral reform, and afford intellectual improvement to farmers, mechanics, and laborers. Among its contents were poetry, tales, foreign and domestic news, literary notices and reviews, biographical sketches, and articles on education, science, agriculture, history, travel, religion, and politics.

v1-nsv2   Apr. 7, 1849-July 1850   APS II, Reel 742

Microfilm edition was prepared from DLC copy.

THE LITERARY WORLD. v.1-13; Feb. 6, 1847-Dec. 31, 1853. New York, Osgood, 1847-53.

13 v. in 12. illus. weekly.

Vols. 1-2 have title: The Literary world. A gazette for authors, readers, and publishers. v. 3-10, The Literary world: a journal of society (later "of science") literature, and art. (Caption title, v. 3-11, The Literary world. A journal of American and foreign literature, science, and art)

Editors: Feb.-Apr. 1847, E. A. Duyckinck.–May 1847-Sept. 1848, C. F. Hoffman.–Oct. 1848-Dec. 1853, E. A. Duyckinck, G. L. Duyckinck.

Begun in 1847 by Osgood and Company, the *Literary World* was the first important American weekly to be devoted chiefly to the discussion of current books. Evert A. Duyckinck was editor for the first few months, followed by Charles Fenno Hoffman, who remained for a year and a half. Book reviews were the chief staple, and there were departments of fine arts, drama, music, and "literary intelligence." When the Duyckinck brothers became editors in October, 1848, they introduced greater variety, adding travel sketches, portrayals of manners and amusements in New York, discussions of political and social matters in "The Colonel's Club," a few woodcuts, and some translations. Copious quotations from the more attractive books were included. In 1852 a disastrous fire brought the magazine to an end, but the thirteen volumes published contain much valuable material on the development of American literature from 1847 to 1852.

v1	Feb. 1847-July 1847	APS II, Reel 483
v2-5	Aug. 1847-Dec. 1849	Reel 484
v6-10	Jan. 1850-June 1852	Reel 485
v11-13	July 1852-Dec. 1853	Reel 486

Several volumes have pages that are bound and photographed out of order. Several pages have print show-through and are stained or torn with some loss of text. Vol. 10: Lacks title page and index.

Microfilm edition was prepared from CtY, DLC and MiU copies.

THE LITERARY WORLD; a monthly review of current literature. v.1-35; June 1870-Dec. 1904. Boston, S.R. Crocker.

35 v. illus. Monthly, June 1870-biweekly, Jan. 1879-Mar. 1900; monthly, Apr. 1900-Dec. 1904.

Subtitle varies slightly. 1870-79, separate numbers have title: The Literary world: choice readings from the best new books, and critical reviews. Published by E. H. Hames & co. Apr. 1877-Dec. 1902; L. C. Page & company, Jan. 1903-Dec. 1904. Absorbed Robinson's epitome of literature in Sept. 1879. Merged into the Critic.

Editors: Sept. 1870-Mar. 1877, S. R. Crocker.–1878-87, Edward Abbott.–1888-95, N. P. Gilman.–1895-1902, Edward Abbott (with Madeline V. Abbott, Oct. 1898-Dec. 1899)–1903-1904, Bliss Carman (with Herbert Copeland, May-July 1903)

S. R. Crocker founded the *Literary World* as a help to book buyers. His reviews of literary works were sound, although they lacked the liveliness to give the *World* popular appeal. In 1877, the ailing Crocker was replaced by the Reverend Edward Abbot. He edited the remaining file with the exception of 1889-95, when N. P. Gilman was in charge. Under Abbot's guidance, Arthur Gilman, Henry C. Lodge, Charles Thwing, and others became correspondents. In the 1880's, French and German contributions were added. The finances of the *Literary World* failed to gain solvency. It was finally merged into the *Critic* in 1904.

v1-10	June 1870-Dec. 1879	APS III, Reel 155
v11-16	Jan. 1880-Dec. 1885	Reel 156
v17-22	Jan. 1886-Dec. 1891	Reel 157
v23-28	Jan. 1892-Dec. 1897	Reel 158
v29-35	Jan. 1898-Dec. 1904	Reel 159

Vols. 1-2: Index not available. Vol. 35: Index not available. Please refer to the letter at beginning of Volume.

Microfilm edition was prepared from MiU, OrU, TxDN and MA copies.

SEE ALSO: Critic; An Illustrated Monthly Review of Literature, Art, and Life.

* **LITTELL'S LIVING AGE.** *SEE* Every Saturday: A Journal of Choice Reading, *and* Living Age.

LITTLE CORPORAL AND SCHOOLDAY MAGAZINE. *SEE* St. Nicholas; An Illustrated Magazine for Young Folks.

* **THE LIVING AGE.** v.1-360, no.6; May 11, 1844-Aug. 1941. Boston, Littell.

v. plates, 4,499 no. weekly.

Vols. 37-56 called also "2d ser., v.1-20"; v.57-88, "3d ser., v.1-32"; v.89-115, "4th ser., v.1-27"; v.116-199, "5th ser., v.1-84"; v.200-218, "6th ser., v.1-19"; v.219-287, "7th ser., v.1-69"; v.288- "8th ser., v.1- " Title varies: 1844-96, Littell's living age. 1897-19 The Living age.

Editors: 1844-70, E. Littell.–1870-96, R.S. Littell. Published by T.H. Carter & company [etc.] 1844-46; Littell, son & company [etc.] 1846-96; The Living age company, 1896-19 . Absorbed Every Saturday: a journal of choice reading, in November 1874.

In 1808 the Living age and the Eclectic magazine were consolidated. This involved no change in the Living age. The Eclectic magazine was increased in size and issued (1899-1900) as the Eclectic magazine and monthly edition of the Living age.

Begun by Eliakim Littell in 1844, *Living Age* was an eclectic magazine, publishing varied material taken chiefly from British periodicals. Though it had a small circulation, it was important in bringing foreign literature to the American public. A special effort was made to select material which would interest American readers, and nearly all the comment of British periodicals on American affairs appeared in it. There was some poetry, and a liberal amount of fiction. Although it was the more serious material from the *Edinburgh,* the *Quarterly,* the *Westminster, Blackwood's, Fraser,* and later the *Cornhill* that was responsible for its great appeal, the lighter weeklies such as Dickens' *Household Words* were also drawn upon. When Littell died in 1870, his son Robert took over, remaining as editor until his death in 1896, at which time the "Littell's" was dropped from the title and the subject matter broadened somewhat. In 1898 it absorbed its rival, the *Eclectic Magazine,* and in 1919 the Atlantic Monthly Company bought the magazine, changing it to a monthly in 1927. In 1928 it was taken over by World Topics Corporation, and finally expired in 1941 under the editorship of Joseph Hilton Smyth.

Littell's Living Age

v1-5	May 11, 1844-June 28, 1845	APS II, Reel 319
v6-10	July 5, 1845-Sept. 26, 1846	Reel 320
v11-16	Oct. 3, 1846-Mar. 25, 1848	Reel 321
v17-22	Apr. 1, 1848-Sept. 29, 1849	Reel 322
v23-27	Oct. 6, 1849-Dec. 28, 1850	Reel 323
Cumulative Index 1-100	1844-1869	Reel 974
v28-31	Jan.-Dec. 1851	Reel 974
v32-36	Jan. 1852-Mar. 1853	Reel 975
v37-42	April 1853-Sept. 1854	Reel 976
v43-47	Oct. 1854-Dec. 1855	Reel 977
v48-51	Jan.-Dec. 1856	Reel 978
v52-56	Jan. 1857-Mar. 1858	Reel 979
v57-59	April-Dec. 1858	Reel 980
v60-64	Jan. 1859-Mar. 1860	Reel 981
v65-69	April 1860-June 1861	Reel 982
v70-74	July 1861-Sept. 1862	Reel 983
v75-80	Oct. 1862-Mar. 1864	Reel 984
v81-86	April 1864-Sept. 1865	Reel 985
v87-92	Oct. 1865-Mar. 1867	Reel 986
v93-96	April 1867-Mar. 1868	Reel 987
v97-101	April 1868-June 1869	Reel 988
v102-106	July 1869-Sept. 1870	Reel 989
v107-111	Oct. 1870-Dec. 1871	Reel 990
v112-115	Jan. 1872-Dec. 1872	Reel 991
v116-119	Jan. 1873-Dec. 1873	Reel 992
v120-123	Jan. 1874-Dec. 1874	Reel 993
v124-127	Jan. 1875-Dec. 1875	Reel 994
v128-132	Jan. 1876-Mar. 1877	Reel 995
v133-136	April 1877-Mar. 1878	Reel 996
v137-140	April 1878-Mar. 1879	Reel 997
v141-144	April 1879-Mar. 1880	Reel 998
v145-149	April 1880-June 1881	Reel 999
v150-154	July 1881-Sept. 1882	Reel 1000
v155	Oct. 1882-Dec. 1882	Reel 1001
v156-159	Jan. 1883-Dec. 1883	Reel 1002
v160-163	Jan. 1884-Dec. 1884	Reel 1003
v164-167	Jan. 1885-Dec. 1885	Reel 1004
v168-172	Jan. 1886-Mar. 1887	Reel 1005
v173-176	April 1887-Mar. 1888	Reel 1006
v177-180	April 1888-Mar. 1889	Reel 1007
v181-183	April 1889-Dec. 1889	Reel 1008
v184-187	Jan. 1890-Dec. 1890	Reel 1009
v188-191	Jan. 1891-Dec. 1891	Reel 1010
v192-195	Jan. 1892-Dec. 1892	Reel 1011
v196-199	Jan. 1893-Dec. 1893	Reel 1012
v200-203	Jan. 1894-Dec. 1894	Reel 1013
v204-207	Jan. 1895-Dec. 1895	Reel 1014
v208-211	Jan. 1896-Dec. 1896	Reel 1015

Living Age

v212-215	Jan. 1897-Dec. 1897	Reel 1016
v216-219	Jan. 1898-Dec. 1898	Reel 1017
v220-223	Jan. 1899-Dec. 1899	Reel 1018

v224-227	Jan. 1900-Dec. 1900	Reel 1019
v228-230	Jan. 1901-Sept. 1901	Reel 1020
v231-234	Oct. 1901-Sept. 1902	Reel 1021
v235-238	Oct. 1902-Sept. 1903	Reel 1022
v239-242	Oct. 1903-Sept. 1904	Reel 1023
v243-246	Oct. 1904-Sept. 1905	Reel 1024
v247-250	Oct. 1905-Sept. 1906	Reel 1025
v251-254	Oct. 1906-Sept. 1907	Reel 1026
v255-258	Oct. 1907-Sept. 1908	Reel 1027
v259-262	Oct. 1908-Sept. 1909	Reel 1028
v263-266	Oct. 1909-Sept. 1910	Reel 1029
v267-270	Oct. 1910-Sept. 1911	Reel 1030
v271-274	Oct. 1911-Sept. 1912	Reel 1031
v275-278	Oct. 1912-Sept. 1913	Reel 1032
v279-282	Oct. 1913-Sept. 1914	Reel 1033
v283-286	Oct. 1914-Sept. 1915	Reel 1034
v287-290	Oct. 1915-Sept. 1916	Reel 1035
v291-294	Oct. 1916-Sept. 1917	Reel 1036
v295-298	Oct. 1917-Sept. 1918	Reel 1037
v299-302	Oct. 1918-Sept. 1919	Reel 1038
v303-306	Oct. 1919-Sept. 1920	Reel 1039
v307-310	Oct. 1920-Sept. 1921	Reel 1040
v311-314	Oct. 1921-Sept. 1922	Reel 1041
v315-318	Oct. 1922-Sept. 1923	Reel 1042
v319-323	Oct. 1923-Dec. 1924	Reel 1043
v324-327	Jan. 1925-Dec. 1925	Reel 1044
v328-332	Jan. 1926-June 1927	Reel 1045
v333-335	July 1927-Feb. 1929	Reel 1046
v336-339	Mar. 1929-Feb. 1931	Reel 1047
v340-343	Mar. 1931-Feb. 1933	Reel 1048
v344-348	Mar. 1933-Aug. 1935	Reel 1049
v349-354	Sept. 1935-Aug. 1938	Reel 1050
v355-359	Sept. 1938-Feb. 1941	Reel 1051
v360	Mar. 1941-Aug. 1941	Reel 1052

Many pages are stained or torn or have missing or faded print. Pagination is irregular. Vol. 40: Plate missing for page 97. Vol. 41: Plates for pages 193, 385 and 433 are missing. Vol. 42: Plates for pages 289 and 433 are bound on opposite pages. Vol. 43: Plates for 49, 193, 337 and 577 are missing. Vol. 62: Plate missing for page 1. Vol. 109: Index photographed at beginning and end of Volume. Vol. 311: Index is contained within Contents pages.

Microfilm edition was prepared from C, CCC, DLC, FDS, GDS, GU, IaDL, IaDm, IdU, InGrD, Mi, MiD, MiEM, MiU, and Nh copies.

SEE ALSO: Eclectic Magazine of Foreign Literature.

LOUISVILLE JOURNAL OF MEDICINE AND SURGERY. v.1, nos.1-2; Jan.-April, 1838. Louisville, Ky., 1838.

504 p.

A medical journal which proposed to be a full and faithful record of the improvements in the medical profession. It published original papers, reports of cases at Louisville Marine Hospital and in private practice, reviews of new works in all branches of medicine, and medical news. After a short life, it was merged with the *Western Journal of the Medical and Physical Sciences* to form the *Western Journal of Medicine and Surgery.*

v1	Jan.-April 1838	APS II, Reel 657

Issue 1: Pages 80-89 are bound out of order.

Microfilm edition was prepared from CtY copy.

SEE ALSO: Western Journal of the Medical and Physical Sciences *and* Western Journal of Medicine and Surgery.

LOUISVILLE REVIEW. *SEE* Western Journal of Medicine and Surgery.

THE LOWELL OFFERING. Written, edited and published by female operatives employed in the mills. No.1-4, Oct. 1840-Mar. 1841; [new ser.] v.1-5, [Apr. 1841]-Dec. 1845. Lowell, Powers & Bagley, 1840-45.

6 v. illus., plates. Bimonthly, Oct.-Dec. 1840; monthly, Feb. 1841-Dec. 1845.

Title varies: 1840-42, The Lowell offering; a repository of original articles, written exclusively by females actively employed in the mills (title varies slightly) Oct. 1842-Sept. 1843, The Lowell offering and magazine. Written and edited by female operatives. Nov. 1843-Dec. 1845, The Lowell offering. Absorbed the Operatives' magazine, Oct. 1842?

Editors: 1840-42, A. C. Thomas.—Oct. 1842-Dec. 1845, Harriet Farley. Nos. 1-4 (1840-41) were printed by A. Watson; published by Powers & Bagley, 1841-42; W. Schouler, 1843; Misses Curtis and Farley, 1844-45. Publication ceased with Dec. 1845. "In September, 1847, Miss Farley resumed the publication and issued one copy under the title the New England offering. This magazine was re-issued in 1848, from April to December, continued through 1849, and until March, 1850"—Robinson, Harriet R., Loom and spindle.

The most prominent of several magazines produced by New England factory employees. This small literary magazine, which was written, edited, and published by the female operatives of the Lowell, Massachusetts, woolen mills, was concerned with labor conditions, and attracted international attention among students of social and economic problems.

no.1-nsv5	Oct. 1840-Dec. 1845	APS II, Reel 675

Microfilm edition was prepared from MH copy.

LOWELL OFFERING AND MAGAZINE. *SEE* Lowell Offering.

LYRE; or, New York musical journal. v.1; June 1, 1824-May 1, 1825. New York, 1824-25.

188 p.

Edited by James H. Swindells, this monthly presented a variety of music-related material, including essays on music and style, reviews of musical works, critiques of performances, news of musical societies, and biographical sketches of eminent musicians, both American and foreign. In addition, there were two pages of music in each issue, a ladies' department, and some poetry and anecdotes.

v1	June 1, 1824-May 1, 1825	APS II, Reel 132

*✱ **McBRIDE'S MAGAZINE.** v.1-97, Jan. 1868-April 1916. Philadelphia, 1868-1916.

97 v.

Vols. 1-7, 1868-71 as Lippincott's magazine of literature, science and education, 8-36, July 1871-85 Lippincott's magazine of popular literature and science, 37-96, 1886-Aug. 1915 Lippincott's monthly magazine. Merged into Scribner's magazine.

Edited in Philadelphia for the first seventeen years by John Foster Kirk, *Lippincott's Magazine* published many notable English and American writers including Henry James, Oscar Wilde, Amelie Rive, Conan Doyle, and Rudyard Kipling. In addition to long and short fiction, there was much literary criticism and many book reviews and illustrated travel articles. Although the contents were of high quality, competition with popular New York magazines eventually caused *Lippincott's* to be sold in 1914 to McBride, Nast and Company who moved it to New York and changed the name to *McBride's Magazine*. After a short time, however, it was merged with *Scribner's*.

Lippincott's Magazine of Literature, Science and Education

| v1-3 | Jan. 1868-June 1869 | APS III, Reel 316 |
| v4-7 | July 1869-June 1871 | Reel 317 |

Lippincott's Magazine of Popular Literature and Science

v8	July-Dec. 1871	Reel 317
v9-13	Jan. 1872-June 1874	Reel 318
v14-17	July 1874-June 1876	Reel 319
v18-21	July 1876-June 1878	Reel 320
v22-25	July 1878-June 1880	Reel 321
v26-30	July 1880-Dec. 1882	Reel 322
v31-35	Jan. 1883-June 1885	Reel 323
v36	July-Dec. 1885	Reel 324

Lippincott's Monthly Magazine

v37-39	Jan. 1886-July 1887	Reel 324
v40-42	July 1887-Dec. 1888	Reel 325
v43-45	Jan. 1889-June 1890	Reel 326
v46-49	July 1890-June 1892	Reel 327
v50-53	July 1892-June 1894	Reel 328
v54-57	July 1894-June 1896	Reel 329
v58-60	July 1896-Dec. 1897	Reel 330
v61-63	Jan. 1898-June 1899	Reel 331
v64-66	July 1899-Dec. 1900	Reel 332
v67-70	Jan. 1901-Dec. 1902	Reel 333
v71-74	Jan. 1903-Dec. 1904	Reel 334
v75-77	Jan. 1905-June 1906	Reel 335
v78-80	July 1906-June 1907	Reel 336
v81-83	Jan. 1908-June 1909	Reel 337
v84-86	July 1909-Dec. 1910	Reel 338
v87-89	Jan. 1911-June 1912	Reel 339
v90-93	July 1912-June 1914	Reel 340
v94-96	July 1914-Aug. 1915	Reel 341

McBride's Magazine

| v97 | Sept. 1915-Apr. 1916 | Reel 341 |

Some pages are torn or stained; best copy available for photographing. Vol. 1: Title page is missing.

Microfilm edition was prepared from C, CCC, CL, IaDm, MH, MWiW, MiD, MnU, MoS, MoU, N, NbO, NjP, OT, PPi, and WaS copies.

McCLURE'S MAGAZINE. v.1-57, June 1893-Aug. 1924; new ser., v.1-2, May 1925-Jan. 1926; [new ser.] v.56, no.6, June 1926; [new ser.] v.57-62, July 1926-Mar. 1929. New York, S. S. McClure.

66 v. illus., facsims., plates, ports. monthly. Suspended Oct. 1921-Feb. 1922; Sept. 1924-Apr. 1925; Feb.-May 1926.

Title varies: June 1926-Sept. 1927, Mc'Clures, the magazine of romance.—Oct. 1927-June 1928, McClure's.—July 1928-Mar. 1929, The New McClure's.

Founded and edited for many years by S. S. McClure. Imprint varies: June 1926-June 1928, International publications.—July 1928-Mar. 1929, Magnus. Merged into Smart Set. Microfilm edition includes v.1-62 and an index to v.1-18. New ser. v.56-57 wanting.

Samuel S. McClure and John S. Phillip began their famous magazine in 1893 as an appendage to their business of syndicating fiction. *McClure's* soon gained popular approval and success, largely through its publication of Ida M. Tarbell's illustrated series on Napoleon and Lincoln. Other factors contributing to its success were scientific articles highlighting new discoveries, features on wild animals, trains, and exploration, and substantial contributions in fiction. These features helped to put *McClure's* in the forefront of American magazines in circulation, advertising patronage, and prestige.

McClure's exerted a tremendous influence on the thinking of the American people, particularly during the muckraking period. Tarbell's "History of the Standard Oil Company" spearheaded the movement. It was followed by Lincoln Steffens' expose "The Shame of Cities," which was perhaps the chief series of the whole muckraking movement.

By the end of this period, *McClure's* was beginning its decline. It changed hands several times and was suspended and revived three times between 1921 and 1927. In 1928 it was again revived, this time as *New McClure's Magazine*, and survived another year before merging into *New Smart Set* in 1929.

McClure's Magazine

Cumulative Index, v1-18	1893-1902	APS III, Reel 477
v1-6	June 1893-May 1896	Reel 477
v7-9	June 1896-Oct. 1897	Reel 478
v10-13	Nov. 1897-Oct. 1899	Reel 479
v14-18	Nov. 1899-April 1902	Reel 480
v19-23	May 1902-Oct. 1904	Reel 481
v24-28	Nov. 1904-April 1907	Reel 482
v29-31	May 1907-Oct. 1908	Reel 483
v32-34	Nov. 1908-April 1910	Reel 484
v35-38	May 1910-April 1912	Reel 485
v39-41	May 1912-Oct. 1913	Reel 486
v42-43	Nov. 1913-Oct. 1914	Reel 487
v44-47	Nov. 1914-Oct. 1916	Reel 488
v48-51-A	Nov. 1916-Dec. 1919	Reel 489
v52-54	Jan. 1920-Feb. 1923	Reel 490
v55-57	Mar. 1923-Aug. 1924	Reel 491
nsv1-2	May 1925-Jan. 1926	Reel 492

Mc'Clures, the Magazine of Romance

| v58-59, no.3 | June 1926-Sept. 1927 | Reel 492 |

McClure's

| v59, no.4-6 | Oct.-Dec. 1927 | Reel 492 |
| v60 | Jan.-June 1928 | Reel 493 |

New McClure's

| v61-62 | July 1928-Mar. 1929 | Reel 493 |

Several volumes contain supplements. Some advertisement pages are missing from page count. Many volumes have stained or torn pages. Some pages are tightly bound with some loss of text. Vols. 16, 44, and New Series Vol. 1: Pagination is irregular. Vol. 32: Page 79 has faded print. Vol. 53: Issue 3, pages 8-9 have print missing. Vol. 57A is lacking.

Microfilm edition was prepared from C, CCC, DLC, ICU, KyLo, Mi, MiD, MiU, MnNC, MnS, MoS, MtBC, NhD, NjP, and ODa copies.

Mc'CLURES, THE MAGAZINE OF ROMANCE. *SEE* McClure's Magazine.

MAGAZINE FOR THE MILLION. v.1, no.1-11; Feb. 17-Apr. 27, 1844. New York.

264 p.

A literary magazine professing to cater to the taste of "the million," and offering serialized tales, poetry, biography, travel articles, an editorial column, and a weekly review of current literature. It also contained readers' correspondence, some humor and interesting anecdotes, and illustrations.

v1   Feb. 17-Apr. 27, 1844   APS II, Reel 742

Index and title page are lacking.

Microfilm edition was prepared from NN copy.

THE MAGAZINE OF USEFUL AND ENTERTAINING KNOWLEDGE. v.1-2, no.5; June 15, 1830-May 1831. New York.

2 v. front., illus.

Caption title.

Vol. 1, nos. 1-2, have title: Mechanics' & farmers' magazine of useful knowledge.

Edited by two members of the New York Lyceum of Natural History, this magazine was to be both useful and entertaining. It dealt mainly with science, agriculture, and horticulture, providing information and advice on agricultural and horticultural methods, as well as much practical advice for domestic problems—recipes, household hints, and health care. Articles kept the reader abreast of the latest inventions and the most recent developments in the areas of mechanics, engineering, meteorology, chemistry, astronomy, and mathematics. In addition, space was given to biography, society proceedings, reviews of new publications, and articles covering fine arts, travel, and education. Occasional woodcuts and engravings embellished the text.

Mechanics' & Farmers' Magazine of Useful Knowledge
v1, no.1-2   June 15-July 15, 1830   APS II, Reel 742

Magazine of Useful and Entertaining Knowledge
v1, no.3-v2, no.5   Aug. 1830-May 1831   Reel 742

Several pages are stained. Pagination is irregular. Index is lacking. Vols. 1 and 2 are bound and photographed together.

Microfilm edition was prepared from DLC copy.

MAGAZINE OF WESTERN HISTORY. SEE National Magazine; A Monthly Journal of American History.

MAGNOLIA; or, Literary tablet. v.1, no.1-26; Oct. 5, 1833-Sept. 20, 1834. Hudson, N.Y., 1833-1834.

498 p.

This semimonthly literary journal was "devoted to literature, moral and sentimental tales, poetry, etc.," and was to provide instruction and amusement, but no political or religious controversy. It contained selections from the best writers of the day, historical and statistical sketches, notices of new publications, letters to the editor, and tales, poetry, anecdotes and biography. A section called "The Magnolia" contained notes from the editor, magazine reviews, and local news. Selected material was taken from a number of British magazines—London Metropolitan, London Monthly Magazine, and Tait's Edinburgh Magazine, as well as from a number of American publications.

v1   Oct. 5, 1833-Sept. 20, 1834   APS II, Reel 777

Some pages are stained.

Microfilm edition was prepared from WHi copy.

THE MAGNOLIA; or, Southern Apalachian. A literary magazine and monthly review. v.1-4, Jan. 1840-June 1842; new ser., v.1-2, July 1842-June 1843. Charleston, S.C., P. C. Pendleton, 1840-43.

6 v. plates.

Title varies: Jan.-Dec.? 1840, The Southern ladies' book: a magazine of literature, science and arts. Jan. 1841-June 1842, The Magnolia; or Southern monthly. July 1842-June 1843, The Magnolia; or, Southern Apalachian.

Editors: Jan. 1840-June 1842, P. C. Pendleton (with G. F. Pierce, 1840).—July 1842-June 1843, W. G. Simms. Published in Macon, Ga., 1840; Savannah, 1841-June 1842; Charleston, S.C., July 1842-June 1843.

The Magnolia was begun in 1840 in Macon, Georgia, as the Southern Ladies' Book, a Methodist miscellany and parlor magazine. Abandoned in this form after ten months, it was taken to Savannah, and its name changed in 1841 to Magnolia; or, Southern Monthly. It was little more successful in Savannah, lasting only eighteen months, and in July, 1842 was moved to Charleston, where it immediately achieved a position of some importance under the editorship of William Gilmore Simms. It was then called the Magnolia; or, Southern Apalachian, and contained fiction, poetry, and criticism written by Simms himself, with contributions by Judge Augustus B. Longstreet, Dr. William A. Carruthers, A. B. Meek, and Mary E. Lee. In its last phase it was a comparatively entertaining periodical, though its criticisms of both art and literature were inclined to be more vigorous than trustworthy. It carried an insert of "advertising miscellany," but had no illustrations.

Southern Ladies' Book: a Magazine of Literature, Science and Arts
v1-2   Jan.-Dec. 1840   APS II, Reel 676

Magnolia; or Southern Monthly
v3-4   Jan. 1841-June 1842   Reel 676

Magnolia; or, Southern Apalachian
nsv1-2   July 1842-June 1843   Reel 676

Best copy available for photographing. Many pages are tightly bound, torn, or stained. Vol. 1: Lacks index. Vol. 2: Issue 4 (October 1840) has several torn pages, with some loss of print.

Microfilm edition was prepared from DLC, GU, NcD and T copies.

MAINE FARMER. v.1-92; 1833-June 8, 1924. Augusta.

92 v. weekly.

Title varies: Jan. 21-Mar. 11, 1833, Kennebec farmer and journal of the useful arts.—Mar. 18, 1833-Jan. 1, 1842, Maine farmer and journal of the useful arts (varies slightly)—Jan. 15, 1842-Dec. 30, 1843, Maine farmer and mechanics advocate. Founded and edited for many years by E. Holmes.

Issues for Jan. 15, 1842-Dec. 30, 1843 called "new series," v.1-2 (no.470-572) On film: v.1-18, 20-68.

The earlier issues of this weekly were concerned entirely with news by or for farmers. Such material as articles on stock raising, farm machinery, stock and plant diseases, committee reports from fairs, legislative issues of particular interest to farmers, addresses to New England argicultural societies, letters to the editor on various farming techniques and problems filled the pages.

A "ladies department" which later became "miscellany" featured poetry and homemaking hints. Early advertisements were small and for a variety of products ranging from a "tooth key" to grave stones. The few illustrations were of fruit or plants. Material from other farm journals was reprinted. Meeting notices of the Anti-Slavery Society, the Temperance Society, cattle shows and fairs were printed.

In 1843 the weekly expanded in size and variety of news items including more advertising and fiction. The format changed back to that of earlier issues in 1844 with mostly agricultural news on the front page and national and international news, fiction, advertisements and market prices on inside pages. More illustrations were used in the later issues.

Kennebec Farmer and Journal of the Useful Arts
v1, no.1-8	Jan. 21-Mar. 11, 1833	APS II, Reel 422

Maine Farmer and Journal of the Useful Arts
v1, no.9-v4	Mar. 18, 1833-Jan. 27, 1837	Reel 422
v5-7	Feb. 14, 1837-Jan. 4, 1840	Reel 423
v8-9	Jan. 11, 1840-Jan. 1, 1842	Reel 424

Maine Farmer and Mechanics Advocate
nsv1 (v10)	Jan. 15-Dec. 31, 1842	Reel 424
nsv2 (v11)	Jan. 7-Dec. 30, 1843	Reel 425

Maine Farmer
v12-13	Jan. 4, 1844-Dec. 25, 1845	Reel 425
v14-16	Jan. 1, 1846-Dec. 28, 1848	Reel 426
v17-18	Jan. 4, 1849-Dec. 26, 1850	Reel 427
v20-21	Jan. 1852-Dec. 1853	Reel 1371
v22-24	Dec. 29, 1853-Dec. 18, 1856	Reel 1372
v25-27	Dec. 25, 1856-Dec. 15, 1859	Reel 1373
v28-30	Dec. 22, 1859-Dec. 11, 1862	Reel 1374
v31-33	Dec. 18, 1862-Dec. 7, 1865	Reel 1375
v34-36	Dec. 14, 1865-Dec. 5, 1868	Reel 1376
v37-39	Dec. 12, 1868-Dec. 2, 1871	Reel 1377
v40-42	Dec. 9, 1871-Nov. 28, 1874	Reel 1378
v43-45	Dec. 5, 1874-Nov. 24, 1877	Reel 1379
v46-48	Dec. 1, 1877-Nov. 20, 1880	Reel 1380
v49-51	Nov. 25, 1880-Nov. 15, 1883	Reel 1381
v52-55	Nov. 22, 1883-Nov. 10, 1887	Reel 1382
v56-59	Nov. 17, 1887-Nov. 5, 1891	Reel 1383
v60-61	Nov. 12, 1891-Nov. 2, 1893	Reel 1384
v62-63	Nov. 9, 1893-Oct. 31, 1895	Reel 1385
v64-65	Nov. 7, 1895-Oct. 28, 1897	Reel 1386
v66-67	Nov. 4, 1897-Oct. 26, 1899	Reel 1387
v68	Nov. 2, 1899-Oct. 25, 1900	Reel 1388

Several volumes lack indexes. Many pages are torn, stained, creased, tightly bound, and have print faded with some loss of text. Pagination is irregular. Best copy available for photographing. Vol. 19 is not available for photographing. Vol. 23: Issue 1 is photographed with vol. 22; issue 2 is missing. Vol. 29 contains a supplement. Vol. 35: Issue 15 is misdated. Vol. 65: Issue 36, page 8 and issue 37, page 1 are missing. Vol. 67: Issues 34 and 47, pages 6 and 7 are photographed out of order.

Microfilm edition was prepared from Me, MeBa, MeU and NN copies.

MAINE FARMER AND JOURNAL OF THE USEFUL ARTS. *SEE* Maine Farmer.

MAINE FARMER AND MECHANICS ADVOCATE. *SEE* Maine Farmer.

THE MAINE MONTHLY MAGAZINE. Ed. by Charles Gilman. v.1; July 1836-June 1837. Bangor, Duren & Thatcher; Portland, E. Stephens, 1837.

vi, 568 p. pl.

Formed by the union of the Portland magazine and the Eastern magazine.

Edited by Charles Gilman, the *Maine Monthly Magazine* was formed by the union of the *Portland Magazine* and the *Eastern Magazine* of Bangor. Included in its contents were travel sketches; reviews; poetry, including some by Mrs. Ann S. Stephens, who had been editor of the *Portland Magazine;* a series on Old English prose writers; and studies on philosophy, geology, botany, and literature.

v1, no.1-12	July 1836-June 1837	APS II, Reel 486

Several pages are stained with some print missing.

Microfilm edition was prepared from DLC and MB copies.

SEE ALSO: Eastern Magazine *and* Portland Magazine.

THE MAN. v.1-3, no.98; Feb. 18-Dec. 22, 1834. New York, G. H. Evans.

3 v. Daily except Sunday.

Man was the second labor paper to be published in the U.S. Devoted to the working man and noted for its opposition to the Bank of the United States, it contained much on trade unions, banking, currency, and elections and also included poetry, news items, Presidential messages, and proceedings of Congress and of the New York legislature.

v1	Feb. 18-May 16, 1834	APS II, Reel 565
v2-3	May 17-Dec. 22, 1834	Reel 566

Several issues are missing. Many pages are stained, creased, tightly bound, and have print show-through with some loss of text. Best copy available for photographing.

Microfilm edition was prepared from N and NNC copies.

THE MANHATTAN. An illustrated literary magazine. v.1-3, v.4, no.1-3; Jan. 1883-Sept. 1884. New York, J. W. Orr [1883]; Manhattan Magazine Co. [1883-84]

4 v. illus., plates, ports. monthly.

W. H. Forman, editor.

Financed and published by John W. Orr, the *Manhattan* began as an organ of the Odd Fellows' Society. However, this affiliation was dropped after the first few numbers. The travel articles, book reviews, poetry and serials as well as the illustrations (by means of process engraving) found in the later issues established the *Manhattan* as an excellent magazine.

v1-3	Jan. 1883-June 1884	APS III, Reel 30
v4	July-Sept. 1884	Reel 31

Vol. 1: pages 160-62 are repeated in number only. Vol. 2: tightly bound. Vol. 4: Index not available for photographing. Please refer to the Table of Contents.

Microfilm edition was prepared from MiU, MoS, and MnU copies.

THE MANIFESTO. Published by the United societies. v.1-29; Jan. 1871-Dec. 1899. Shakers, N.Y., 1871-99.

29 v. in 17. plates, port. monthly.

Vol. 1-2, 6-7 as Shaker; v. 3-5 Shaker and Shakeress monthly; v. 8-13 Shaker manifesto.

Editors: 1871-72, G. A. Lomas.–1873-75, F. W. Evans.–1876-81,

G. A. Lomas.–1882-90, H. C. Blinn. Published in Shakers, N.Y., 1871-72; Mt. Lebanon, N.Y., 1873-75; Shaker Village, N.H., 1876-77; Shakers, N.Y., etc., 1878-89; East Canterbury, N.H., 1890-99.

The purpose of the *Manifesto* was to state simply the religious views held by the Shakers. G. Albert Lomas, F. W. Evans, and Henry Clay Blinn served as editors.

Shaker
| v1-2 | 1871-1872 | APS III, Reel 62 |
| Cum. Index, v3-5 | 1873-1875 | Reel 62 |

Shaker and Shakeress Monthly
| v3-5 | 1873-1875 | Reel 62 |

Shaker
| v6-7 | 1876-1877 | Reel 62 |

Shaker Manifesto
| v8-13 | 1878-1883 | Reel 62 |

Manifesto
| v14-16 | 1884-1886 | Reel 62 |
| v17-29 | 1887-1899 | Reel 63 |

Vols. 1-2: Indexes lacking. Please refer to the Tables of Contents.

Microfilm edition was prepared from MiU, NhD, NjMD, NjPT, and WHi copies.

THE MANUSCRIPT. v.1-2 (no.1-12); 1827-28. New York, G. & C. Carvill, and E. Bliss, 1828.

2 v.

Vol. 1: 2d edition. Ascribed to Rev. Mr. Griggs in Sabin's Biblioteca americana.

This literary magazine promised to amuse and increase knowledge, and to censure vice through satire; contents included stories, essays, poetry, occasional biography and criticism, and articles on history.

| v1-2 | 1828 | APS II, Reel 609 |

Microfilm edition was prepared from DLC copy.

THE MASONIC CASKET, designed for the benefit of free and accepted masons, and for the information of such as wish to know the order and proceedings of the fraternity. By Ebenezer Chase. v.1-3; Jan./Feb. A.L. 5823 [i.e. 1823]-June A.L. 5826 [i.e. 1826] Enfield, N.H.

2 v. in 1.

Film covers: v.2, no.1-12; July, A.L. 5824 [i.e. 1824]-Nov., A.L. 5825 [i.e. 1825]

The *Masonic Casket* contained a variety of news on the masons– on the activities of various lodges in New England, Ohio, and elsewhere, orations, sermons, and extracts of addresses. In addition, some essays, poetry, anecdotes, and musical pieces appeared.

| v2 | July 1824-Nov. 1825 | APS II, Reel 132 |

MASONIC MIRROR. *SEE* Boston Masonic Mirror.

THE MASONIC MISCELLANY AND LADIES LITERARY MAGAZINE. v.1-2; July 1821-June 1823. Lexington, Ky., W. G. Hunt.

2 v. monthly.

Copy filmed incomplete: v. 1, no. 8-9, 11 wanting.

As its title implies, this magazine was composed of two parts; the first section was devoted to masonry, including masonic news and material on the history of masonry. The second section, "Ladies' Literary Magazine," contained sentimental prose and poetry, anecdotes, a series of "Letters from Tennessee," and a variety of articles concerning women, including such topics as education for women.

| v1-2 | 1821-1823 | APS II, Reel 214 |

THE MASSACHUSETTS AGRICULTURAL REPOSITORY AND JOURNAL. v.1-10; 1798-Apr. 1832. Boston.

10 v. illus.

Frequency varies. Other slight variations in title. Issues for 1798-1810 consist of unnumbered papers with title, Papers on agriculture (1809, Georgik papers). Issued by the Massachusetts Society for Promoting Agriculture (sometimes called Massachusetts Agricultural Society). Copy filmed incomplete: scattered issues of v.1-2 wanting.

Conducted by the trustees of the Massachusetts Agricultural Society, this magazine published reports of the society's committees and a variety of information on various aspects of farming, such as silk production, crops and animals, and horticulture. Diagrams and illustrations of animals, insects, and farm equipment were included.

[v1-2]	1801-1810	APS II, Reel 214
v3-5	1813-1819	Reel 214
v6-8	1820-1825	Reel 215
v9-10	Jan. 1826-Apr. 1832	APS II, Reel 566

Microfilm edition was prepared from DLC and N copies.

THE MASSACHUSETTS BAPTIST MISSIONARY MAGAZINE. v.1-4; Sept. 1803-Dec. 1816. Boston, Printed by Manning & Loring, and Lincoln & Edmands.

4 v. Irregular.

Edited by T. Baldwin and others. Superseded by the American Baptist magazine and missionary intelligencer (later Baptist missionary magazine) Issued by Massachusetts Baptist Convention (called 1803-07, Massachusetts Baptist Missionary Society; 1808-16, Baptist Missionary Society in Massachusetts)

Founded as a semiannual in 1803 by Rev. Thomas Baldwin, the *Massachusetts Baptist Missionary Magazine* became a quarterly after a few years. It ministered to the great interest of the times in missionary activity, giving extensive coverage to missions, particularly to missions in India. British and other foreign Bible societies also received attention, and biographical sketches, poetry, anecdotes, and religious news added variety to the contents.

| v1-2, no.8 | Sept. 1803-1809 | APS II, Reel 25 |
| v2, no.9-v4, no.12 | Mar. 1810-Dec. 1816 | APS II, Reel 216 |

Microfilm edition was prepared from DLC and ICU copy.

SEE ALSO: Baptist Missionary Magazine.

THE MASSACHUSETTS MAGAZINE; or, Monthly museum. Containing the literature, history, politics, arts, manners & amusements of the age. v.1-8; Jan. 1789-Dec. 1796. Boston, Printed by Isaiah Thomas and Ebenezer T. Andrews, 1789-96.

8 v. fronts., plates, ports., maps.

Vol. 1 has title: The Massachusetts magazine: or, Monthly museum of knowledge and rational entertainment. Containing, poetry, musick, biography, history, physick, geography, morality, criticism ... &c. &c.

No numbers were issued for Jan.-Mar., 1796. Editors: Apr. 1795-June 1796, T. M. Harris.–July-Dec. 1796, William Bigelow.

Serial essays, fiction, poetry, music, engravings, current events, and reprints made up the content of this important publication.

v1-4	Jan. 1789-Dec. 1792	APS I, Reel 15
v5-8	Jan. 1793-Dec. 1796	Reel 16

Some pages are lacking.

Microfilm edition was prepared from MiU-C copy.

MASSACHUSETTS MEDICAL SOCIETY. MEDICAL COMMUNICATIONS. v.1-24; 1790-1913. Boston.

24 v. illus., maps, plates. Vol. 5-16 also called 2d. ser., v. 1-12.

Title varies: v.1, Medical papers ...–v.2, Medical communications and dissertations.–v.3, Medical papers ... (cover title, Medical dissertations ...)–v.4, Medical dissertations ...

Each volume includes an appendix (separately paged) containing the proceedings of the Society. Two supplements follow v. 24: "Proceedings of the Council Oct. 2, 1912-June 10, 1913" (72 p.); and "Supplement to Bulletin 3, Nov. 1, 1913" (39 p.).

Published by the Massachusetts Medical Society, this medical journal contained papers written by members of the society on cases and treatments, as well as articles on the state of the medical profession and on other medical subjects; these were often illustrated with diagrams. Also included were society proceedings and biographical sketches of important medical figures.

v1-4	1790-1829	APS II, Reel 677
v5-8	1830-1854	Reel 678
v9-11	1854-1880	APS II, Reel 1314
v12-16	1881-1895	Reel 1315
v17-19	1896-1904	Reel 1316
v20-24	1905-1913	Reel 1317

Vol. 11: Pgs. 47-48 of the Proceedings are missing in number only. Vol. 24: Supplements follow volume.

Microfilm edition was prepared from ICRL, MH and MiU copies.

THE MASSACHUSETTS MISSIONARY MAGAZINE, containing religious and interesting communications, calculated to edify Christians, and inform the rising generation. v.1-5; May 1803-May 1808. Salem, J. Cushing [1803]; Boston, E. Lincoln, 1804-07.

5 v. monthly.

Vol. 2, p. 33-40 missing in number only. Edited by Nathanael Emmons and others. Merged into the Panoplist, later Missionary herald. Bound with v. 2: Emmons, Nathanael. A sermon, delivered before the Massachusetts missionary society, at their annual meeting in Boston, May 27, 1800, Charlestown, 1800.

Published by the Massachusetts Missionary Society and edited by a group of thirteen editors appointed by the Society, the *Massachusetts Missionary Magazine* was begun in Salem in 1803 and moved to Boston in 1804. It published narratives on conversions and revivals of religion, studies on doctrine and passages of Scripture, biographical sketches, poetry, and a variety of religious news. After five years it was absorbed by the *Panoplist,* which later became the *Missionary Herald.*

v1-5	May 1803-May 1808	APS II, Reel 25

Microfilm edition was prepared from DLC copy.

SEE ALSO: Missionary Herald at Home and Abroad.

MASSACHUSETTS PLOUGHMAN AND NEW ENGLAND JOURNAL OF AGRICULTURE. v.1-65; 1840-Nov. 17, 1906. Boston, New England Agricultural Society.

65 v.

An important agricultural journal founded in Boston in 1840 by the New England Agricultural Society.

v1-5	Jan. 15, 1842-Sept. 26, 1846	APS II, Reel 1274
v6-8	Oct. 3, 1846-Sept. 29, 1849	Reel 1275
v9-29	Oct. 6, 1849-Sept. 17, 1870	Reel 1276
v30-32	Oct. 1, 1870-Sept. 27, 1873	Reel 1277
v33-37	Oct. 4, 1873-Sept. 28, 1878	Reel 1278
v38-41	Oct. 5, 1878-Sept. 30, 1882	Reel 1279
v42-44	Oct. 14, 1882-Sept. 26, 1885	Reel 1280
v45-48	Oct. 3, 1885-Dec. 29, 1888	Reel 1281
v56-57	Oct. 10, 1896-Sept. 24, 1898	Reel 1282
v58-59	Oct. 1, 1898-Sept. 22, 1900	Reel 1283
v60-61	Sept. 29, 1900-Sept. 20, 1902	Reel 1284
v62	Sept. 27, 1902-Sept. 19, 1903	Reel 1285
v63-64	Sept. 26, 1903-Dec. 30, 1905	Reel 1286
v65	Jan. 6-Nov. 17, 1906	Reel 1287

Best copy available for photographing. Many volumes have creased, torn, or stained pages with some loss of print. Several volumes are tightly bound with some loss of text. Some pages are missing. Pagination is irregular. Scattered issues are missing from vols. 1-3, 7, 10, 27-36, 38-47, 56, 64. Vols. 11-26 and 49-55 are missing.

Microfilm edition was prepared from DLC, DNAL, MWA, and MiU-C copies.

*THE MASSACHUSETTS QUARTERLY REVIEW. v.1-3; Dec. 1847-Sept. 1850. Boston, Coolidge & Wiley, 1848-50.

3 v.

Ralph Waldo Emerson, Theodore Parker, and J. Elliot Cabot were the editors of this quarterly magazine. To an extent, it was a successor to the *Dial,* but was more practical, more reformatory, and more political. Slavery was a major topic. Parker was responsible for many of the political articles, brief reviews and literary criticism, and translations of German poetry which made up the contents of the magazine. Contributors included Samuel G. Howe, Henry James the elder, Francis Lieber, and James Russell Lowell.

v1-3	Dec. 1847-Sept. 1850	APS II, Reel 658

Microfilm edition was prepared from MiU copy.

MASSACHUSETTS SPY. *SEE* Worcester Magazine.

THE MASSACHUSETTS TEACHER: a journal of school and home education. v.1-27; 1848-1874. Boston, S. Coolidge; Mass. Teachers' Association [1857]-74.

v. illus. (incl. plans) plates, ports. monthly.

From 18   to 1855 title reads: The Massachusetts teacher. Edited by a committee of the Massachusetts teachers' association. 1872, The Teacher. In Jan. 1875 the Massachusetts teacher, the Connecticut school journal and other publications were united to form the New England journal of education. Vols. 9-18 also called new ser., v. 1-10; v. 19-26, ser. 3, v. 1-8.

This educational journal was the first monthly edited by a board appointed by a state teachers' association. It contained articles on education, schools, teaching methods, and school-related problems as well as news of appointments and reports of the NEA and other teachers' associations. In addition, it published poetry, notices of new books and magazines, and a number of papers on non-education subjects.

Massachusetts Teacher
v1-8   Jan. 1, 1848-Dec. 1855   APS II, Reel 610

Massachusetts Teacher and Journal of Home and School Education
v9   Jan.-Dec. 1856   Reel 610
v10-16   Jan. 1857-Dec. 1863   Reel 611
v17-22   Jan. 1864-Dec. 1869   Reel 612
v23-24   Jan. 1870-Dec. 1871   Reel 613

Teacher
v25   Jan.-Dec. 1872   Reel 613

Massachusetts Teacher
v26-27   Jan. 1873-Dec. 1874   Reel 613

Microfilm edition was prepared from DLC copy.

THE MASSACHUSETTS WATCHMAN, and periodical journal. v.1, no.1-12; June 1809-May 1810. Palmer [Mass.] E. Terry.

143 p. Monthly.

This monthly gave much attention to religion, publishing religious news, Bible studies, and short moral essays, but also included general news items, some biography, and poetry and anecdotes.

v1, no.1-7   June-Dec. 1809   APS II, Reel 26

v1, no.8-12   Jan.-May 1810   APS II, Reel 216

Microfilm edition was prepared from NHi copy.

THE MATHEMATICAL CORRESPONDENT. v.1-2, no.1; 1804-1807. New-York, Sage and Clough, 1804-06.

248 p. diagrs.

v. 2 published Reading, Pa. for R. Adrain, 1807.

Conducted by R. Adrain, this math magazine is very similar to another edited by Adrain, *The Analyst; or Mathematical Museum,* which began publication in Philadelphia in 1808. Like the Philadelphia magazine, this one was to contain "new elucidations, discoveries and improvements, in various branches of the mathe-

matics," and contained several articles on mathematics theory, and sections of problems and solutions.

v1-2, no.1   1804-1807   APS II, Reel 26

Microfilm edition was prepared from NN and PPAmP copy.

✻ THE MATHEMATICAL MONTHLY. Ed. by J. D. Runkle. v.1-3; Oct. 1858-Sept. 1861. Cambridge [Mass.] J. Bartlett, 1858-61.

3 v. illus., plates, ports., diagrs.

Vol. 1 published in Cambridge and London; v.2, in New York and London; v.3, in Cambridge, New York and London. "A complete catalogue of the writings of Sir John Herschel": v.3, p.220-227.

Mathematical Monthly was edited in Cambridge by John D. Runkle. Among the contributors were Simon Newcomb, O. T. Root, and Benjamin Peirce.

v1-3   Oct. 1858-Sept. 1861   APS III, Reel 269

Index and Contents at beginning of each volume.

Microfilm edition was prepared from MiD copy.

MECHANIC. *SEE* Boston Mechanic, and Journal of the Useful Arts and Sciences.

MECHANIC APPRENTICE. v.1 (no.1-12); May 1845-April 1846. Boston [Mechanic Apprentices' Library Association, 1846]

96 p. monthly.

Walter Murray, J. M. W. Yerrington and others, editors.

A literary miscellany written and published by members of the Mechanic Apprentices' Association of Boston and intended to be its official organ. In addition to coverage of the association's activities, it presented serialized tales, biographical pieces, reviews of current magazines, moral essays, and poetry, as well as articles on science, travel, literature, and history.

v1   May 1845-April 1846.   APS II, Reel 742

Index and title page are lacking. Pages 65-68 are stained, with some loss of print.

Microfilm edition was prepared from DLC copy.

MECHANIC'S ADVOCATE. v.1-2; Dec. 3, 1846-1848. Albany, N.Y., 1846-1848.

2 v.

Edited by John Tanner, this weekly mechanic's magazine succeeded the *New York State Mechanic* and was much like it in form and content, but was more literary. It published some fiction, politics, and miscellany and contained serial stories by J. N. T. Tucker, T. S. Arthur, and others. It contained contributions by the most distinguished mechanics in the U.S., lists of patents and inventions, some diagrams, poetry, tales, and selections from other sources.

v1-2   Dec. 3, 1846-1848   APS II, Reel 400

Pagination is irregular. Vol. 2: some pages are missing.

Microfilm edition was prepared from MH-BA and WW copies.

MECHANICS' AND FARMERS' MAGAZINE OF USEFUL KNOWLEDGE. *SEE* Magazine of Useful and Entertaining Knowledge.

MECHANICS' MAGAZINE, and journal of the Mechanics' institute. v.1-10 (no.1-244); Jan. 1833-Aug. 1837. New York, D. K. Minor and J. E. Challis.

10 v. illus., plates, ports., diagrs. monthly.

John Knight, editor, 1834. From Jan. 1833-Feb. 1836 title reads: Mechanics' magazine, and register of invention and improvements.

"Appendix ... On the economy of manufactures [by Charles Babbage]": v.1, 84p. at end. (Also issued separately under title: On the economy of machinery and manufactures). Vols. 5-6 include supplement: "The Apprentice's companion," v.1, no.1-4; Apr.-July 1835. (Separately paged). In July, 1838, merged into American railroad journal.

This abundantly illustrated scientific magazine published material on a variety of science topics, focusing mainly on recent inventions and methods. Many articles dealt with the steam engine, shipbuilding, railroads, machinery, and manufacturing processes; and most were accompanied by diagrams. A good deal of the material was selected from European scientific works. Contents also included a meteorological record, analysis of scientific periodicals, and memoirs.

v1-2	Jan.-Dec. 1833	APS II, Reel 613
v3-10	Jan. 1834-May 26, 1837	Reel 614

Vol. 10: Microfilm edition ends with May 26, 1837.

Microfilm edition was prepared from DLC and MH copies.

MECHANICS' MAGAZINE, and journal of public internal improvement; devoted to the useful arts, and the recording of projects, inventions, and discoveries of the age. v.1-7, Feb. 1830-Jan. 1836. Boston, 1830-1836.

7 v. monthly.

Mechanics' Magazine was published for a short time in Boston, one of the early centers of mechanics magazines.

v1	Feb. 1830-Jan. 1831	APS II, Reel 1093

Although Union List of Serials indicates *Mechanics' Magazine* was published from February 1830-1836 in 7 volumes, the National Union Catalog indicates only 12 issues between February 1830 and January 1831 were published. Further research of this periodical does not disclose the existence of volumes 2-7. Vol. 1: Pages 2-5, 280, 288 are missing.

Microfilm edition was prepared from MnU copy.

MECHANICS' MAGAZINE, AND REGISTER OF INVENTIONS AND IMPROVEMENTS. *SEE* Mechanics' Magazine, and Journal of the Mechanics' Institute.

LE MEDIATEUR; journal politique et litteraire. v.1, no.1-21, 2 avril-8 aout, 1814. Philadelphia, etc.

348 p. weekly.

This French-language weekly focused mainly on political and literary topics. There was a great deal of news, both American and foreign, material on the history of France, book reviews, poetry, and miscellaneous essays.

v1, no.1-21	Apr. 2-Aug. 8, 1814	APS II, Reel 132

THE MEDICAL AND AGRICULTURAL REGISTER, for the years 1806 and 1807. v.1; Jan. 1806-Dec. 1807. Boston, Manning & Loring.

1 v. monthly.

At head of title: Useful family book. Edited by Daniel Adams, M.B.

Edited by Daniel Adams, this magazine was designed for family use, and contained much practical information on caring for the sick, animal husbandry, and on the raising of crops, as well as a variety of household hints, information on the weather, and statistics on deaths and causes of deaths in Boston.

v1, no.1-24	Jan. 1806-Dec. 1807	APS II, Reel 26

Microfilm edition was prepared from MiU copy.

THE MEDICAL & SURGICAL REGISTER; consisting chiefly of cases in the New York Hospital. v.1, pts.1-2. New York, Collins, 1818-20.

x, 406 p. illus.

Edited by J. Watts, V. Mott and A.H. Stevens.

This medical journal consisted chiefly of descriptions of cases handled in the New York Hospital during the years 1818 to 1820. Most of the material was written by the journals' three editors, John Watts, Valentine Mott, and Alexander H. Stevens, who were all physicians; and some articles were accompanied by plates. A special feature was a long article on the yellow fever epidemic of 1819.

v1, pts.1-2	1818-1820	APS II, Reel 216

MEDICAL AND SURGICAL REPORTER. v.1-11; Oct. 1847-Sept. 1858. Burlington, N.J. [and] Philadelphia, 1847-1858.

11 v.

Vols. 1-7, 1847-54 as New Jersey medical reporter and Transactions of the New Jersey Medical Society; Vol. 8, 1855 New Jersey medical reporter. Superseded by Medical and surgical reporter. Philadelphia.

A journal of medical science containing news of recent discoveries and of recently-developed methods.

New Jersey Medical Reporter and Transactions of the New Jersey Medical Society

v1-4	Oct. 1847-Sept. 1851	APS II, Reel 1287
v5-7	Oct. 1851-Dec. 1854	Reel 1288

New Jersey Medical Reporter

v8	Jan.-Dec. 1855	Reel 1288

Medical and Surgical Reporter
v9-11   Jan. 1856-Sept. 1858   Reel 1288

Best copy available for photographing. Some pages are stained or have irregular pagination. Vol. 6: Issue 7, pages 241-72 are missing; not available for photographing.

Microfilm edition was prepared from ICJ and MiU copies.

SEE ALSO: Medical and Surgical Reporter (Philadelphia).

MEDICAL AND SURGICAL REPORTER. v.1-78, no.5; Oct. 1, 1858-May 16, 1898. Philadelphia, 1858-1898.

78 v.

Supersedes Medical and surgical reporter. Burlington, New Jersey. Suspended Nov.-Dec. 1864.

A weekly publication containing scientific and medical news of discoveries and recently-developed methods.

v1-2	Oct. 1858-Sept. 1859	APS II, Reel 1197
v3-7	Oct. 1859-Mar. 1862	Reel 1198
v8-13	April 1862-Dec. 1865	Reel 1199
v14-18	Jan. 1866-June 1868	Reel 1200
v19-23	July 1868-Dec. 1870	Reel 1201
v24-28	Jan. 1871-June 1873	Reel 1202
v29-34	July 1873-June 1876	Reel 1203
v35-40	July 1876-June 1879	Reel 1204
v41-45	July 1879-Dec. 1881	Reel 1205
v46-49	Jan. 1882-Dec. 1883	Reel 1206
v50-53	Jan. 1884-Dec. 1885	Reel 1207
v54-56	Jan. 1886-June 1887	Reel 1208
v57-59	July 1887-Dec. 1888	Reel 1209
v60-63	Jan. 1889-Dec. 1890	Reel 1210
v64-66	Jan. 1891-June 1892	Reel 1211
v67-69	July 1892-Dec. 1893	Reel 1212
v70-72	Jan. 1894-June 1895	Reel 1213
v73-76	July 1895-June 1897	Reel 1214
v77-78	July 1897-May 1898	Reel 1215

Several pages are stained, torn, and tightly bound with some loss of text. Some pages have faded print and show-through. Pagination is irregular. Vol. 4: Pages 195-96 are missing. Vols. 12-14: Title pages are misdated. Vol. 71: Pages 415-18 and 584-88 are missing; not available for photographing.

Microfilm edition was prepared from C, CLM, ICRM, ICS, MiU, MnSRM, N, and NBuU copies.

SEE ALSO: Medical and Surgical Reporter (Burlington, New Jersey).

MEDICAL COMMUNICATIONS AND DISSERTATIONS. *SEE* Massachusetts Medical Society. Medical Communications.

MEDICAL DISSERTATIONS. *SEE* Massachusetts Medical Society. Medical Communications.

THE MEDICAL EXAMINER. v.1-7, Jan. 3, 1838-Dec. 26, 1844; New ser., v.1-12 (no.1-144), Jan. 1845-Dec. 1856. Philadelphia, Lindsay & Blakiston.

19 v. illus. Frequency varies.

Title varies: 1843, The Medical examiner and retrospect of the medical sciences.—1844-53, The Medical examiner and record of medical science. United with the Louisville review to form the North American medico-chirurgical review.

Case histories of various diseases and operations, lectures, bibliographies of medical books, foreign news, biographies and lists of accidents and cases at Pennsylvania hospitals were the subject matter of most articles in this periodical. Drawings and charts of reported cases were printed occasionally. Frequent attacks were made on homoeopathy. In later issues long statistical lists of population, twin births, weather and results of surveys were printed. Accounts of annual meetings of the AMA and the Medical Society of Pennsylvania were given. Although the magazine remained the same size over the years of publication, the format varied from one to two columns.

Medical Examiner
v1-2	Jan. 3, 1838-Dec. 28, 1839	APS II, Reel 428
v3-4	Jan. 4 [1840]-Dec. 25, 1841	Reel 429
nsv1 (i.e.v5)	Jan. 1-Dec. 24, 1842	Reel 430

Medical Examiner and Retrospect of the Medical Sciences
v6	Jan. 21-Dec. 30, 1843	Reel 430

Medical Examiner and Record of Medical Science
v7-nsv1 (v8)	Jan. 13, 1844-Dec. 1845	Reel 431
nsv2-3 (v9-10)	Jan. 1846-Dec. 1847	Reel 432
nsv4-5 (v11-12)	Jan. 1848-Dec. 1849	Reel 433
nsv6-7 (v13-14)	Jan. 1850-Dec. 1851	Reel 434
nsv8-9 (v15-16)	Jan. 1852-Dec. 1853	Reel 435

Medical Examiner
nsv10-11 (v17-18)	Jan. 1854-Dec. 1855	Reel 436
nsv12 (v19)	Jan.-Dec. 1856	Reel 437

Pagination is irregular. Some pages are tightly bound.

Microfilm edition was prepared from MiU, PP, and PU copies.

MEDICAL EXAMINER; a semi-monthly journal of medical sciences. v.1-16, no.13; Jan. 1860-July 1, 1875. Chicago, 1860-1875.

16 v.

Vols. 1-12, 1860-71 as Chicago medical examiner. United with Chicago medical journal to form Chicago medical journal and examiner.

Original articles, clinical reports, case studies, and editorials made up the content of this scientific journal.

Chicago Medical Examiner
v1-4	Jan. 1860-Dec. 1863	APS II, Reel 1234
v5-9	Jan. 1864-Dec. 1868	Reel 1235
v10-12	Jan. 1869-Nov./Dec. 1871	Reel 1236

Medical Examiner
v13-14	Jan. 1, 1872-Dec. 1873	Reel 1236
v15-16	Jan. 1874-July 1875	Reel 1237

Pagination is irregular. Some pages are stained, torn, or have faded print. Vols. 6-9: several advertisement pages are missing.

Microfilm edition was prepared from CSt-Law, ICRL, IU-M, MnSRM, and N copies.

MEDICAL EXAMINER AND RECORD OF MEDICAL SCIENCE. *SEE* Medical Examiner.

MEDICAL EXAMINER AND RETROSPECT OF THE MEDICAL SCIENCES. *SEE* Medical Examiner.

MEDICAL INTELLIGENCER. *SEE* Boston Medical Intelligencer.

THE MEDICAL NEWS. v.1-87; 1843-Dec. 30, 1905. New York, Lea Brothers.

v. in. illus. Monthly, 18 -81; weekly, 1882-1905.

Supersedes American medical intelligencer. Publication began in 1843. cf. Union list of serials.

Title varies: 1843-79, The Medical news (caption title: The Medical news and library) 1880-81, The Medical news and abstract.

Editors: 1880-81, I. M. Hays.–Nov. 16, 1889-May 1891, H. A. Hare.–June 1891-1895, G. M. Gould.–1896-Aug. 1900, J. R. Goffe.–Sept. 1900-1905, S. E. Jelliffe. Vols. 18-67 were published in Philadelphia. Absorbed the Monthly abstract of medical science in Jan. 1880. Merged into New York medical journal (later Medical record)

Begun by Dr. Isaac Hays, the *Medical News* became one of the leading medical journals of its day. It published miscellaneous medical news, including foreign news, reports of clinical lectures, accounts of cases and operations in the various medical schools and hospitals, articles exposing quackery, ads for new medical books, and many illustrations. A section titled "The Library" contained a series of lectures on the principal branches of medical science.

Medical News
v1-8	1843-1850	APS II, Reel 658
v9-24	Jan. 1851-Dec. 1866	Reel 1073
v25-34	Jan. 1867-Dec. 1876	Reel 1074
v35-37	Jan. 1877-Dec. 1879	Reel 1075

Medical News and Abstract
v38-39	Jan. 1880-Dec. 1881	Reel 1075

Medical News
v40	Jan.-June 24, 1882	Reel 1075
v41-45	July 1, 1882-Dec. 27, 1884	Reel 1076
v46-50	Jan. 3, 1885-June 25, 1887	Reel 1077
v51-55	July 2, 1887-Dec. 28, 1889	Reel 1078
v56-60	Jan. 4, 1890-June 25, 1892	Reel 1079
v61-64	July 2, 1892-June 30, 1894	Reel 1080
v65-68	July 7, 1894-June 27, 1896	Reel 1081
v69-72	July 4, 1896-June 25, 1898	Reel 1082
v73-76	July 2, 1898-June 30, 1900	Reel 1083
v77-79	July 7, 1900-Dec. 28, 1901	Reel 1084
v80-82	Jan. 4, 1902-June 27, 1903	Reel 1085
v83-85	July 4, 1903-Dec. 31, 1904	Reel 1086
v86-87	Jan. 7-Dec. 30, 1905	Reel 1087

Reel 658: Indexes appear at the end of each volume. Reels 1073-1087: Some pages are torn or stained. Vols. 9-26, 29-30, and 32 lack Supplements. Best copy available for photographing. Vols. 27-28 and 31: Supplements photographed at end. Vols. 33-34: Supplements photographed following Volume 34. Vols. 35-36: Supplements photographed following Volume 36. Vol. 37: Supplement photographed at end.

Microfilm edition was prepared from CtY, DLC, ICRL, MiU, NbU-M, NBuU, PPJ, and ScCM copies.

MEDICAL NEWS AND ABSTRACT. *SEE* Medical News.

MEDICAL NEWS AND LIBRARY. *SEE* American Medical Intelligencer.

MEDICAL NEWS-PAPER; or, The doctor and the physician. v.1, no.1-26; Jan. 1, 1822-Feb. 15, 1824. Boston.

103 p.

Edited by Elias Smith, the *Medical News-Paper* was directed to the general public and took a stand against quack medicine and against the practice of bleeding. It gave much information on medicines, herbs, and cures for ailments, featured a series on the history of medicine, and included general articles on the state of medicine, and on doctors and quacks, as well as information on the effects of poison on the human system.

v1, nos.1-26	Jan. 1, 1822-Feb. 15, 1824	APS II, Reel 217

Microfilm edition ends Feb. 15, 1824. Some torn pages.

MEDICAL PAPERS. *SEE* Massachusetts Medical Society. Medical Communications.

THE MEDICAL REFORMER. v1, no.1-6; Jan. 1-June 1, 1823. New York, a.d.

140 p. monthly.

The *Medical Reformer* was conducted by a physician who was concerned with the "unhappy and deplorable state of medicine" of that time. Its articles condemned the practice of bleeding, discussed doctors' lack of knowledge in treating various ailments, and warned against the harmful effects of mercury and arsenic when used as medicines.

v1, no.1-6	Jan. 1-June 1, 1823	APS II, Reel 132

MEDICAL REGISTER. *SEE* Medical Times and Register.

THE MEDICAL REPOSITORY OF ORIGINAL ESSAYS AND INTELLIGENCE, relative to physic, surgery, chemistry, and natural history. v.1-23; 1797-1824. New-York, T. & J. Swords [etc.]

23 v. Quarterly. Vols. 7-12 also called 2d hexade, v.1-6; v.13-15 also called 3d hexade, v.1-3; v.16-23 also called new ser., v.1-8.

Title varies slightly.

Edited by S. L. Mitchill and others, 1797-1821.·

Founded in the midst of the yellow fever epidemic by three physicians, Samuel Latham Mitchill, Elihu Hubbard Smith, and Edward Miller, the quarterly *Medical Repository* was the first medical journal in America to enjoy a high reputation at home and abroad. The editors promised to give special attention to the study of epidemics, to the connection between climate and health, and to diet, and devoted much space in the early volumes to the yellow fever epidemic, while later volumes gave attention to the winter, or spotted, fever. In addition, there were abundant case histories, American and foreign medical news, reviews of American medical books, and information on non-medical branches of sciences, such as natural history, geography, chemistry, and mineralogy.

v1-3, no.4	1797-1800	APS I, Reel 14
v3-6	1800-1803	APS II, Reel 26
v7-12	1804-1809	Reel 27
v13-15	1809-1812	APS II, Reel 132
v16-20	1813-1820	Reel 133
v21-23	1821-1824	Reel 134

Some pages are stained.

Microfilm edition was prepared from DLC and MWA copies.

MEDICAL REVIEW, AND ANALECTIC JOURNAL. *SEE* American Medical Review and Journal of Original and Selected Papers in Medicine and Surgery.

MEDICAL TIMES. *SEE* Medical Times and Register.

THE MEDICAL TIMES AND REGISTER. v.1-41, no.8; Oct. 1, 1870-Aug. 1903. Philadelphia, Boston, Medical pub. co.

41 v. Frequency varies. Vols. 1-41 also as whole no. 1-1032.

Title varies: 1870-Sept. 15, 1871, Medical times.–1871-89, Philadelphia medical times.–1889-95, Times and register. Absorbed the following, 1889: American medical digest, Medical register, Dietetic gazette. Subtitle varies.

Imprint varies: 1870-89, Philadelphia, J. B. Lippincott.–1889-93, Philadelphia and New York, Medical Press Co.

This semimonthly journal of medicine and surgery devoted sections to orthopedics, ophthalmology, clinical medicine, current medical and surgical literature, book reviews, reports of medical societies, selections from other periodicals, and papers on various treatments and case studies.

Medical Times

| v1 | Oct. 1, 1870-Sept. 15, 1871 | APS II, Reel 1388 |

Philadelphia Medical Times

v2-3	Oct. 1871-Sept. 27, 1873	Reel 1388
v4-8	Oct. 4, 1873-Sept. 28, 1878	Reel 1389
v9-13	Oct. 12, 1878-Sept. 22, 1883	Reel 1390
v14-17	Oct. 6, 1883-Sept. 17, 1887	Reel 1391
v18-19	Oct. 1, 1887-Apr. 15, 1889	Reel 1392

Times and Register

v20	May 4, 1889-June 28, 1890	Reel 1392
v21-23	July 5, 1890-Dec. 26, 1891	Reel 1393
v24-27	Jan. 2, 1892-June 30, 1894	Reel 1394
v28-30	July 7, 1894-Dec. 28, 1895	Reel 1395

Medical Times and Register

| v31-33 | Jan. 4, 1896-June 26, 1897 | Reel 1395 |
| v34-41 | July 10, 1897-Aug. 1903 | Reel 1396 |

Several pages are misnumbered, tightly bound, creased, torn, or have print faded. Some volumes lack advertisement pages. Vol. 16: Pages 2-3 are missing; not available for photographing. Vol. 20 (Part I): July 13 issue and pages 793-98 are missing. Vol. 20 (Part II): Mar. 15 and 22 issues are missing. Vol. 21: Pages 495-96 are missing. Vol. 40: Title page and table of contents are missing.

Microfilm edition was prepared from ICRL, ICS, MB, MdBM, MiU, N and NBuU copies.

MEDICATIO LOCALIS. *SEE* Physician's Magazine.

THE MEDLEY; or, Monthly miscellany. v.1; Jan.-Dec. 1803. Lexington, Ky., D. Bradford.

Collation of the original: 286 p.

Film incomplete: t.p. and p. 285-286 wanting.

The *Medley,* published in Lexington, Kentucky in 1803, was apparently the first general magazine west of Pittsburgh. Its contents consisted largely of selected material; there was a section of poetry, moral essays, descriptions of fashion, hints to women, articles on commerce, geography, and agriculture, and much miscellaneous material.

| v1 | Jan.-Dec. 1803 | APS II, Reel 28 |

Microfilm edition was prepared from DLC copy.

MEMOIRS OF THE COLUMBIAN CHEMICAL SOCIETY OF PHILADELPHIA. v.1. [Philadelphia] I. Peirce, 1813.

xv, 231 p.

This periodical published the Constitution and papers of the Columbian Chemical Society; papers dealt with experiments and observations concerning a wide range of scientific areas, including chemistry, botany, meteorology, and mineralogy.

| v1 | 1813 | APS II, Reel 95 |

MERCERSBURG QUARTERLY REVIEW. *SEE* Reformed Church Review.

*✶**MERCERSBURG REVIEW.*** *SEE* Reformed Church Review.

✶ **THE MERCHANTS' MAGAZINE AND COMMERCIAL REVIEW.** v.1-63; July 1839-Dec. 1870. New York, F. Hunt, 1840-70.

63 v. plates, ports., maps, tables. monthly.

Caption of v.1-43 and t.-p. of v.16, 23-43 read: Hunt's merchants' magazine. Editors: 1839-Mar. 1858, Feeeman Hunt.–June 1858-1860, T. P. Kettell.–1861, I. S. Homans, W. B. Dana.–1862-1870, W. B. Dana. Merged into the Commercial and financial chronicle, Jan. 1871.

Established by Freeman Hunt, this well-known general commerce magazine was an encyclopedia of commercial subjects, remarkable for its orderly arrangement of masses of material. It promised to discuss every subject interesting or useful to the merchant. The chief subjects were commercial statistics, commercial regulations and treaties, statistics of population, railroads, canals, and roads, mercantile law, and mercantile libraries and associations, the currency, insurance, banking, navigation, U.S. and foreign commerce, and biographies of successful merchants. Francis Wharton, George Tucker, James H. Lanman, J. W. Scott, and George S. Boutwell were among the most valued contributors to the earlier volumes. The troubles of the United States Bank occupied some space in the early volumes and a series on "The Morals of Trade" by J. N. Bellows ran through the years 1842-43.

| v1-7 | July 1839-Dec. 1842 | APS II, Reel 339 |

v8-14	Jan. 1843-June 1846	Reel 340
v15-21	July 1846-Dec. 1849	Reel 341
v22-27	Jan. 1850-June 1852	Reel 342
v28-33	Jan. 1853-Dec. 1855	Reel 343
v34-39	Jan. 1856-Dec. 1858	Reel 344
v40-44	Jan. 1859-June 1861	Reel 345
v45-51	July 1861-Dec. 1864	Reel 346
v52-57	Jan. 1865-Dec. 1867	Reel 347
v58-63	Jan. 1868-Dec. 1870	Reel 348

Pagination is irregular. Some pages are torn, stained, or have faded print.

Microfilm edition was prepared from MiU copy.

MERRIMACK MAGAZINE AND LADIES' LITERARY CABINET. v.1, no.1-52; Aug. 17, 1805-Aug. 9, 1806. Newburyport, Mass., Whittingham and J. Gilman.

208 p. weekly.

Supersedes Merrimack weekly. Cf. Union list of serials. Absorbed Merrimack miscellany in Oct. 1805.

This four-page literary miscellany offered its readers a good deal of sentimental prose and poetry, along with historical sketches, literary notices, vital statistics, and news items. In addition, there were some advertisements and miscellaneous selections.

v1, no.1-52	Aug. 17, 1805-Aug. 9, 1806	APS II, Reel 28

Microfilm edition was prepared from MWA copy.

SEE ALSO: Merrimack Miscellany.

THE MERRIMACK MAGAZINE, and monthly register, of politics, agriculture, literature, and religion. v.1, no.1-7; Jan. 1-July 1825. Haverhill, Mass. [E. W. Reinhart, Printer] 1825.

112 p.

Caption title.

Jeremiah Spofford, editor.

This varied monthly magazine offered something for almost everyone; literary material included poetry, book reviews, and biographies; and there was an agriculture department, and a religious department which published religious news including news of missions and tract societies. In addition, there were news summaries, census statistics, and much miscellaneous material.

v1, nos. 1-7	Jan. 1-July 1825	APS II, Reel 217

MERRIMACK MISCELLANY. v.1, no.1-18; June 8-Oct. 5, 1805 [Newburyport, Mass.] W. B. Allen.

72 p. Weekly.

Edited by A. Allworthy. Merged into Merrimack magazine and ladies' literary cabinet. Cf. Union list of serials.

This weekly literary miscellany, begun in June 1805 by Aaron Allworth and Co., published essays, historical and biographical sketches, poetry, literary notices, and letters from the correspondence of well-known writers, along with much miscellaneous material. After only four months it was merged into the *Merrimack Magazine and Ladies' Literary Cabinet,* a similar magazine which

had begun publication in August of 1805.

v1, no.1-18	June 8-Oct. 5, 1805	APS II, Reel 28

Microfilm edition was prepared from MWA copy.

SEE ALSO: Merrimack Magazine and Ladies' Literary Cabinet.

MERRIMACK WEEKLY. *SEE* Merrimack Magazine and Ladies' Literary Cabinet.

MERRY'S MUSEUM AND PARLEY'S MAGAZINE. *SEE* Merry's Museum for Boys and Girls.

MERRY'S MUSEUM AND WOODWORTH'S CABINET. *SEE* Merry's Museum for Boys and Girls.

MERRY'S MUSEUM FOR BOYS AND GIRLS. v.1-65; Feb. 1841-Nov. 1872. Boston, H. B. Fuller [etc.]

65 v. illus., plates. monthly. Vols. 31-50 also called new series, v.1-20; v.55-58 also called new ser. v.1-4.

Title varies: 1841-1851, Robert Merry's Museum.—1851-1857, Merry's museum and Parley's magazine.—1858-1866, Merry's museum, Parley's magazine, Woodworth's cabinet, and the Schoolfellow.—1867, Merry's museum and Woodworth's cabinet.

Absorbed Parley's magazine, Aug. 1845; Playmate, July 1848; Woodworth's youth's cabinet, May 1857; Schoolfellow, Oct. 1857. Editors: 1841-1854, Samuel G. Goodrich; 1858-1866, John Newton Sterns; 1867-1872, Lousia May Alcott. Merged into Youth's companion. Film includes v.1-42, 51-60; except for v.56, no.4 and 6.

Established by Samuel G. Goodrich in 1841, this very popular children's periodical claimed a circulation of 13,000 in 1852. The *Museum* was similar in many ways to *Parley's Magazine,* which was merged with it in 1844, but contained more adventure and thrills than *Parley's.* The most important part of the sixteen-page magazine during Goodrich's editorship was that devoted to the tales of the famous "Parley"; these were moral and didactic but nevertheless very popular. "Parley" used stories of travels by balloon to teach geography, as well as historical lore, painlessly. Another prominent feature was a series of natural history articles illustrated with pictures of wild animals. Woodcuts, musical pieces, puzzles, and poems were plentiful. Goodrich was succeeded in the editorship in 1855 by Stephen T. Allen, who was followed by John N. Sterns. Louisa May Alcott edited the *Museum* from 1867 to 1870; during her editorship contents included articles on French history, stories of adventure, and excerpts from "An Old-Fashioned Girl."

Robert Merry's Museum

v1-20	Feb. 1841-Dec. 1850	APS II, Reel 743
v21-22	Jan.-Dec. 1851	Reel 1499

Merry's Museum and Parley's Magazine

v23-26	Jan. 1852-Dec. 1853	Reel 1499
v27-34 (nsv4)	Jan. 1854-Dec. 1857	Reel 1500

Merry's Museum, Parley's Magazine, Woodworth's Cabinet and the Schoolfellow

v35 (nsv5)-v42 (nsv12)	Jan. 1858-Dec. 1861	Reel 1500
v51 (nsv21)-v52 (nsv22)	Jan.-Dec. 1866	Reel 1500

Merry's Museum and Woodworth's Cabinet

v53 (nsv23)-v54 (nsv24)	Jan.-Dec. 1867	Reel 1501

Merry's Museum for Boys and Girls
v55-60   Jan. 1868-Dec. 1871   Reel 1501

Vols. 2 and 4: Lack title pages and table of contents. Best copy available for photographing. Some pages are torn or stained with some loss of text. Vol. 30: Pages 181-84 are missing. New Series Vols. 9-10: title page and index are lacking. New Series Vol. 11: title page is bound and photographed with volume 41. Vols. 43-50 are missing; not available for photographing. Vols. 51-52; 53-54; 55-56; 57-58; and 59-60 are bound and photographed together. Vol. 56: issues 4 and 6 are missing.

Microfilm edition was prepared from CtY, DLC, MiD, MnU, N, NJQ, and NjP copies.

MERRY'S MUSEUM, PARLEY'S MAGAZINE, WOODWORTH'S CABINET, AND THE SCHOOLFELLOW. *SEE* Merry's Museum for Boys and Girls.

MESSENGER. (Chambersburg, Pa.) *SEE* Reformed Church Messenger.

THE MESSENGER. (Methodist Episcopal Church. Conference. Holston.) v.1-4, no.11; Jan. 6, 1826-Dec. 29, 1827. Knoxville, Tenn.

4 v. weekly.

Supersedes the Western Arminiam and Christian instructor. Title varies: Jan. 6, 1826-May 5, 1827, The Holston Conference messenger.–May 13, 1827-? The Messenger for the Holston Conference.–18 -18 , The Holston messenger. Edited by T. Stringfield.

On film: v.1-2.

This religious paper, which concerned itself mainly with the Methodist Episcopal church, contained accounts of missionary activities and revivals; coverage of various Bible, Sunday School, and benevolent societies; essays on theology, church government, and temperance; poetry; some pieces on science; and selections from other magazines.

Holston Conference Messenger
v1, no.1-18   Jan. 6, 1826-May 5, 1827   APS II, Reel 1370

Messenger for the Holston Conference
v1, no.19-26;
v2, no.27-52   May 13-Dec. 29, 1827   Reel 1370

Several pages are stained. Pagination is irregular. Vol. 1: Index is lacking. Issues 1 and 2 are misdated. Page 307 is tightly bound.

Microfilm edition was prepared from TxDaM copy.

MESSENGER FOR THE HOLSTON CONFERENCE. *SEE* Messenger. (Methodist Episcopal Church. Conference. Holston.)

MESSENGER OF THE EVANGELICAL AND REFORMED CHURCH. *SEE* Reformed Church Messenger.

MESSENGER OF THE GERMAN REFORMED CHURCH. *SEE* Reformed Church Messenger.

THE MESSENGER OF PEACE, devoted to doctrine, religion, and morality. v.1, no.1-26; Mar. 13, 1824-Feb. 26, 1825. Hudson, N.Y., Printed by A. Stoddard.

204 p. biweekly.

Edited by R. Carrique.

Edited by Richard Carrique, the *Messenger of Peace* was devoted to "doctrine, religion, and morality." It contained sermons, Bible studies, poetry and anecdotes, and news of new churches and of activities of missionary and Bible societies.

v1, no.1-26   Mar. 13, 1824-Feb. 26, 1825   APS II, Reel 217

METHODIST CHURCHMAN. *SEE* Zion's Herald.

METHODIST EPISCOPAL CHURCH. CONFERENCE. HOLSTON. MESSENGER. *SEE* Messenger (Methodist Episcopal Church. Conference. Holston).

* **METHODIST MAGAZINE AND QUARTERLY REVIEW.** *SEE* Methodist Review.

THE METHODIST MAGAZINE, containing original sermons, experiences, letters, and other religious pieces ... v.1-2; Jan. 1797-Dec. 1798. Philadelphia, Printed by H. Tuckniss.

2 v. Monthly.

Film incomplete: Sept.-Dec. 1798 wanting.

Published by Rev. John Dickins, this religious periodical printed sermons, letters from readers, biographical sketches, anecdotes, serialized articles, and poetry intended to communicate religious knowledge and provide instructive entertainment.

v1-2   Jan. 1797-Aug. 1798   APS I, Reel 17

Microfilm edition was prepared from MWA copy.

SEE ALSO: Methodist Review.

METHODIST PROTESTANT RECORDER. *SEE* Methodist Recorder.

* **METHODIST QUARTERLY REVIEW.** *SEE* Methodist Review.

METHODIST RECORDER. v.1-4, (no.1-48), 1824-July 1828; new ser. v.1, Jan. 7, 1831- Baltimore, 1824-

Title varies: 1824-July 1929 as Mutual rights and Methodist Protestant.–Aug. 1929-July 1940 as Methodist Protestant Recorder.

On film: v.1.

Published monthly by a committee of ministers and laymen, this Methodist magazine contained sermons and poetry.

Mutual Rights and Methodist Protestant
v1   Aug. 1824-July 1825   APS II, Reel 217

* THE METHODIST REVIEW. v.1-11, Jan. 1818-Dec. 1828; v.12-22 (new ser., v.1-11), Jan. 1830-Oct. 1840; v.23-30 (3rd ser., v.1-8), Jan. 1841-Oct. 1848; v.31-66 (4th ser., v.1-36), Jan. 1849-Oct. 1884; v.67-114, no.3 (5th ser., v.1-47), Jan. 1885-May/June 1931. New York, J. Soule and T. Mason, 1818-[1912]; New York, Methodist Book Concern [1912-31]

113 v. ports. Monthly, 1818-28; quarterly, 1830-84; bimonthly, 1885-1931.

Index to the Methodist quarterly review. Including the Methodist magazine, and the Methodist magazine and quarterly review, 1818-1881. By Elijah H. Pilcher, D.D. New York, Phillips & Hunt; Cincinnati, Walden & Stowe, 1884. Volume numbers irregular: no.100 omitted. Publication suspended, Nov.-Dec. 1827, Jan.-Dec. 1829, inclusive. Title varies: Jan. 1818-Dec. 1828, The Methodist magazine (later "The Methodist magazine, designed as a compend of useful knowledge and of religious and missionary intelligence").—Jan. 1830-Oct. 1840, The Methodist magazine and quarterly review.—Jan. 1841-Oct. 1884, The Methodist quarterly review.—Jan. 1885-June 1931, The Methodist review.

Editors: 1818-24, Thomas Mason (with Jushua Soule, 1818-20; Nathan Bangs, 1820-24).—1824-31, John Emory (with Nathan Bangs, 1824-28; Beverly Waugh, 1830-31).—1832-36, Nathan Bangs.—1836-40, Samuel Luckey.—1840-48, George Peck.—1848-56, John M'Clintock.—1856-84, D. D. Whedon.—1884-87, Daniel Curry.—1888-92, J. W. Mendenhall.—1893-June 1920, W. V. Kelley.—July 1920-Nov. 1930, George Elliott.

One of America's oldest religious reviews, the *Methodist Review* was in general modeled after the *Arminian Magazine* of the English Methodists, and published extracts from that magazine and others. It proposed to defend Arminianism and to "circulate religious knowledge" and to that end included material under such headings as Divinity, Biography, Scripture Illustrated, Miscellany, Religious and Missionary Intelligence, Obituaries, and Poetry. An outstanding feature of the first series was the accounts of religious revivals in Ohio, Kentucky, and Tennessee. The second series, 1830-40 was a compromise between the review and the magazine miscellany. It was not until 1841, when a new series under the name of the *Methodist Quarterly Review* was begun, that the magazine took its place among the best church publications, but it was under Daniel D. Whedon, its editor from 1856 to 1884, that it achieved its highest point of general influence. Whedon wrote vigorously, giving attention to general literature, public affairs, education, and science as well as to theology and church polity. Anti-slavery articles by Whedon and by Abel Stevens were published and throughout the war the *Review* was loyal to Lincoln. In later years the content and emphases varied as the editorial duties changed hands.

Methodist Magazine

v1-5	Jan. 1818-Dec. 1822	APS II, Reel 135
v6-8	Jan. 1823-Dec. 1825	Reel 136
v9-11	Jan. 1826-Dec. 1828	APS II, Reel 327

Methodist Magazine and Quarterly Review

v12	Jan.-Oct. 1830	Reel 327
v13-17	Jan. 1831-Oct. 1835	Reel 328
v18-22	Jan. 1836-Oct. 1840	Reel 329

Methodist Quarterly Review

v23-26	Jan. 1841-Oct. 1844	Reel 330
v27-29	Jan. 1845-Oct. 1847	Reel 331
v30-32	Jan. 1848-Oct. 1850	Reel 332
v33-35	Jan. 1851-Oct. 1853	APS II, Reel 1093
v36-40	Jan. 1854-Oct. 1858	Reel 1094
v41-45	Jan. 1859-Oct. 1863	Reel 1095
v46-50	Jan. 1864-Oct. 1868	Reel 1096
v51-55	Jan. 1869-Oct. 1873	Reel 1097
v56-59	Jan. 1874-Oct. 1877	Reel 1098
v60-63	Jan. 1878-Oct. 1881	Reel 1099
v64-66	Jan. 1882-Oct. 1884	Reel 1100

Methodist Review

v67	Jan.-Nov. 1885	Reel 1100
v68-71	Jan. 1886-Nov. 1889	Reel 1101
v72-74	Jan. 1890-Nov. 1892	Reel 1102
v75-77	Jan. 1893-Dec. 1895	Reel 1103
v78-80	Jan. 1896-Nov. 1898	Reel 1104
v81-83	Jan. 1899-Nov. 1901	Reel 1105
v84-86	Jan. 1902-Nov. 1904	Reel 1106
v87-89	Jan. 1905-Dec. 1907	Reel 1107
v90-93	Jan. 1908-Dec. 1911	Reel 1108
v94-97	Jan. 1912-Dec. 1915	Reel 1109
v98-102	Jan. 1916-Dec. 1919	Reel 1110
v103-106	Jan. 1920-Dec. 1923	Reel 1111
v107-110	Jan. 1924-Dec. 1927	Reel 1112
v111-114	Jan. 1928-June 1931	Reel 1113

Pagination is irregular.

Microfilm edition was prepared from DLC and MiU copies.

MICHIGAN BUSINESS FARMER. *SEE* Michigan Farmer.

MICHIGAN FARMER. v.1- , Feb. 15, 1843- Lansing, Mi. [etc.]

v. illus. Frequency varies.

Issues for Jan. 1, 1859-Mar. 22, 1862 called new ser. v.1-4, no.6; July 1862-June 20, 1908 called new ser. [ser.3] v.1-53, no.25; June 27, 1908- called old ser. v.130, no.26- . Supersedes Western farmer. Subtitle varies. Absorbed the Michigan business farmer in 1928.

On film: v.1-16; new ser. v.1-4, no.6; new ser. [ser. 3] v.2; v.12; v.13, no.2-45, 47-52; v.14-21; v.31, no.2-52; v.32-38; v.44, no.8; v.45-53, no.25; old ser. v.130, no.26-131.

Begun as a semi-monthly, the *Michigan Farmer* later became a monthly and for the second half of its life was a weekly. It had many different editors. For the first few years it was devoted exclusively to agriculture, horticulture, and the household, but in 1853 an education section was added. Contents included articles on caring for livestock and crops, and illustrated articles on farm machinery. Particular attention was given to Michigan farmers and to state fairs; and the "Rambles" series described various cities and towns in Michigan. The *Michigan Farmer* of the 1880's was an eight-page weekly containing sections on agriculture and horticulture, a veterinary department, and a "household" department, as well as news summaries, pictures of prize-winning stock, poetry, and many ads. Later it was expanded to about 20 pages per issue, and added building plans for houses and farm buildings, grange news, and a "Magazine Section" containing stories for children, a women's department, stock prices, and ads.

v1-8	Feb. 15, 1843-Dec. 1850	APS II, Reel 324
v9-15	Jan. 1851-Dec. 1857	APS II, Reel 1502
v16-nsv4	Jan. 1858-Mar. 22, 1862	Reel 1503
s3v2	July 1863-June 1864	Reel 1504
s3v12	Jan. 4-Dec. 27, 1881	Reel 1504
s3v13	Jan. 10-Dec. 26, 1882	Reel 1505
s3v14	Jan. 2-Dec. 25, 1883	Reel 1506
s3v15	Jan. 1-Dec. 30, 1884	Reel 1507

s3v16	Jan. 6-Dec. 29, 1885	Reel 1508
s3v17	Jan. 5-Dec. 28, 1886	Reel 1509
s3v18	Jan. 4-Dec. 26, 1887	Reel 1510
s3v19	Jan. 2-Dec. 29, 1888	Reel 1511
s3v20	Jan. 5-Dec. 28, 1889	Reel 1512
s3v21	Jan. 4-Dec. 27, 1890	Reel 1513
s3v31-34	Jan. 9, 1897-Dec. 31, 1898	Reel 1514
s3v35-38	Jan. 7, 1899-Dec. 29, 1900	Reel 1515
s3v44-47	Aug. 22, 1903-June 24, 1905	Reel 1516
s3v48-50	July 1, 1905-Dec. 29, 1906	Reel 1517
s3v51-osv130	Jan. 5, 1907-June 27, 1908	Reel 1518
osv131	July 4-Dec. 26, 1908	Reel 1519

Reels 1502-1519: Best copy available for photographing. Pagination is irregular. Several pages are stained, torn, and have print faded with some loss of text. Some issues are misnumbered and contain supplements. Several volumes have title page and index lacking. Old Series Vol. 130, no.26, June 27, 1908 is bound and photographed following Series Three Vol. 53. Old Series Vol. 131: pages 524-31 appear to be missing.

Microfilm edition was prepared from DLC, MiU, MU, and MiEM copies.

MICROSCOPE. v.1-7, no.21 (nos.1-337) 1821-Dec. 29, 1827. Albany, N.Y., 1821-1827.

7 v.

1821-1823 as Microscope and independent examiner.

Film incomplete: vols. 1, 6, and 7 missing; scattered issues missing.

This miscellany consisted mainly of satirical articles on politics and government, book reviews, poetry, and letters to the editor.

Microscope, and Independent Examiner
v2	Mar. 1, 1823	APS II, Reel 217
v3, no.27, 42	Oct. 11, 1823; Jan. 24, 1824	Reel 217

Microscope
v4, no.1, 28,		
33, 48	Mar. 13, 1824-Feb. 5, 1825	Reel 217
v5, no.10	May 14, 1825	Reel 217

SEE ALSO: Microscope and General Advertiser.

THE MICROSCOPE, ed. by a fraternity of gentlemen. v.1-2 (no.1-50); Mar. 21-Sept. 8, 1820. New Haven, A. H. Maltby, 1820.

2 v. in 1. plates. semiweekly.

This literary magazine edited by "a fraternity of gentlemen" contained much satire and published poetry, stories, letters from readers, and articles on literature, writing, and conversation.

v1-2, nos.1-50	Mar. 21-Sept. 8, 1820	APS II, Reel 217

THE MICROSCOPE AND GENERAL ADVERTISER. v.1-2, no.20; Apr. 17, 1824-Sept. 10, 1825. Louisville, Ky. [etc.]

2 v. weekly (irregular)

Title varies: Apr. 17-Oct. 23, 1824, The Microscope.

Established April 17, 1824 in Louisville, Kentucky by "Tim Tickler, Jr., Esq.," this 4-page weekly proposed to suppress vice and

"to shoot folly as it flies." As a result of its activities, the office was raided and destroyed and the *Microscope* was then moved to New Albany, Indiana. In October of 1824 the title was enlarged to *The Microscope and General Advertiser* and the contents were expanded to include foreign and domestic news, legal notices, election results, miscellaneous items, and advertising.

Microscope
v1, nos1-26	Apr. 17-Oct. 23, 1824	APS II, Reel 136

Microscope and General Advertiser
v1, nos.27-52,		
v2, nos.1-20	Oct. 30, 1824-Sept. 10, 1825	Reel 136

THE MILITARY AND NAVAL MAGAZINE OF THE UNITED STATES. Ed. by Benjamin Homans. v.1-6; Mar. 1833-Feb. 1836. Washington, Thompson and Homans, 1833-36.

6 v. monthly.

Merged into Army and navy chronicle.

This magazine, edited by Benjamin Homans, published a wide assortment of materials on both the army and the navy—appointments, biographical items on officers, U.S. laws concerning the military, information on the marine corps and the militia, on military posts, and firearms, and descriptions of battles. Naval material included a meteorological journal and information on navigation, descriptions of ships, and improvements and inventions concerning ships, sailing, and sea life in general. Officers' reminiscences on their lives at sea provided variety and entertainment.

v1-6	Mar. 1833-Feb. 1836	APS II, Reel 615

Pagination is irregular. Vol. 6: Index and table of contents are missing; not available for photographing.

Microfilm edition was prepared from DLC and NN copies.

SEE ALSO: Army and Navy Chronicle.

THE MILITARY MAGAZINE AND RECORD OF THE VOLUNTEERS OF THE CITY AND COUNTY OF PHILADELPHIA. Comprising authentic data of their institution, organization, and matters generally pertaining thereto. Ed. by William M. Huddy. v.1-3; Mar. 1839-June 1842. Philadelphia, W. M. Huddy.

3 v. plates, ports.

This volume contains nos. 1-12; Mar. 1839-Feb. 1840, extra illustrated with numerous autographs, letters, documents, facsimiles, newspaper clippings, plates, etc. It belonged to Col. William H. Elsegood from whom many of the autographs originate. The t.-p. and preface were apparently printed in advance; the terms of subscriptions for 2 vols., to be issued in monthly numbers, are announced in the preface.

This military pictorial magazine was originally conceived as a local publication containing illustrations and records of the Volunteer Corps of Philadelphia, but was expanded to include the regiments of several states, including some Southern states, as well as the Navy and Marines. It mainly covers Philadelphia and other Pennsylvania cities, New York, Washington, D.C., and Boston. Elegant full-page illustrations depict the uniforms of the various regiments, various encampments, and famous officers. Accompanying textual material further describes the regiments and their uniforms, and layouts of camps and forts, and gives biographical sketches of the officers. Poetry, anecdotes, literary notices, and occasional tales of war are also included, but descriptions of various battles, mainly those of the Revolutionary War and the War of 1812, are given the most attention.

v1-3   Mar. 1839-June 1842   APS II, Reel 744

Microfilm edition was prepared from PHi copy.

THE MILITARY MONITOR, AND AMERICAN REGISTER. Containing a correct record of the events of the war between the United States of America and their territories, and the United Kingdom of Great Britain and Ireland, and the dependencies thereof. Declared on the 18th day of June, 1812, v. 1-2, no. 32; Aug. 17, 1812-Apr. 2, [1814] New York, J. Desnoues, 1813-.

2v. weekly.

Lacking on film: several issues of vol. 2.
Included on film: Geographical and military museum nos. 5 and 8-13; Mar. 26-May 23, 1814.

This weekly military magazine promised to present a faithful record of the events of the war with England; it described battles and listed enemy vessels captured, and also published reviews of military publications and items on military instruction. In addition to the military material, it printed public state papers and proceedings of Congress and provided a weekly summary of foreign and domestic news, extracts from foreign and American journals and newspapers, occasional political essays, and poetry.

Military Monitor
v1, nos.1-52   Aug. 17, 1812-Aug. 23, 1813   APS II, Reel 136
v2, nos.1-2, 4, 26, 31-32   Aug. 28, 1813-Apr. 2, 1814   Reel 136

Geographical and Military Museum
v1, nos. 5 and 8-13   Mar. 26-May 23, 1814   Reel 136

THE MILITIA REPORTER. Containing the trials of Capt. Jos. Loring, Capt. Amos Binney, Capt. Thomas Howe, taken from authentic documents for the information of the officers of the militia. v. 1; 1810. Boston, Printed by T. Kennard.

299 p.

The only volume of the *Militia Reporter* published was devoted entirely to accounts of the trials of three militia captains: Joseph Loring, Amos Binney, and Thomas Howe. Related material is appended at the end of each account.

v1   1810   APS II, Reel 137

MILLENNIAL HARBINGER. *SEE* Christian Baptist.

THE MINERVA; or, Literary, entertaining, and scientific journal: containing a variety of original and select articles, arranged under the following heads: popular tales, the gleaner, the traveller, the drama, biography, arts and sciences, literature, poetry, etc. v. 1-2, Apr. 6, 1822-Apr. 3, 1824; new ser., v. 1-3, Apr. 10, 1824-Sept. 3, 1825. New York [G.L. Birch] 1822-25.

5 v.

Superseded by the New York literary gazette.
George Houston and J.G. Brooks, editors.

Edited by George Houston and James G. Brooks, this weekly miscellany offered a variety of both original and selected material. In addition to articles on literature, the arts, and science, its readers could find popular tales, travel sketches, biographical sketches, reviews of books and plays, and notices of new publications, as well as some anecdotes and riddles, and about two pages of poetry.

v1-nsv3   Apr. 6, 1822-Sept. 3, 1825   APS II, Reel 137

Vol. 2, no.51 missing.

SEE ALSO: Literary Gazette and American Athenaeum.

MINERVIAD: DEVOTED TO LITERATURE AND AMUSEMENT... *SEE* Euterpeiad.

MINING AMERICAN. *SEE* Utahnian.

MINING INDUSTRY AND REVIEW. *SEE* Utahnian.

MIRROR OF LITERATURE, AMUSEMENT AND INSTRUCTION. v1-10; 1825. Boston, 1825.

10 v.

Film covers vols.5-6, 10, 1823-25.

The varied contents of this literary miscellany included a series on "British Galleries of Art" and a number of biographical and travel sketches, as well as poetry and anecdotes, and articles on music, literature, and manners and customs.

v5-6, 10   1823-25   APS II, Reel 138

THE MIRROR OF TASTE AND DRAMATIC CENSOR. v1-4; Jan. 1810-Dec. 1811. Philadelphia, Bradford and Inskeep, 1810-11.

4 v. plates, ports. monthly.

A drama is appended to each number of v.1-2.
S.C. Carpenter, editor.
Imprint varies: v.1-2 (1810) Philadelphia, Bradford and Inskeep; New York, Inskeep and Bradford; [etc., etc.]-v.3-4 (1811) Philadelphia, T.B. Zantzinger and co.

One of the most important magazines of its time which was devoted chiefly to the drama (and the only one which outlasted a single theatrical season) was Stephen Cullen Carpenter's monthly theatrical review, the *Mirror of Taste.* The *Mirror,* which contained interesting and valuable criticisms of the stage and of theatrical life, was divided into four sections: "The Domestic Dramatic Censor" contained a journal of theater activities in Philadelphia and in most major cities; the "Foreign Dramatic Censor" gave accounts of theaters in Great Britain; "Stage Biography" gave biographies of actors and actresses; and "Miscellany" contained book reviews, poetry, and plays.

v1-4   Jan. 1810-Dec. 1811   APS II, Reel 218

MISCELLANEOUS CABINET. v.1, no. 1-26; July 12, 1823-Jan. 3, 1824. [Schenectady, N.Y.]

208 p. weekly.

Copy filmed incomplete: scattered p. wanting.

The *Miscellaneous Cabinet* offered a variety of information—news on missions, on education for women, and on science and the arts, as well as a weekly summary of foreign and domestic news and a "masonic calendar." Essays, humorous material, and a poetry department rounded out the contents.

v1, nos.1-26   July 12, 1823-Jan. 3, 1824   APS II, Reel 218

THE MISCELLANEOUS MAGAZINE. v. 1; Jan.-Dec.1824. Trenton, N.J., P.S. Wiggins, 1824.

1 p.1., 284p.   monthly.

This monthly miscellany devoted about half its space to religious material—coverage of events in the religious world, news on missions and missionaries, moral essays, and an "Essays on Faith" series. The other half of the magazine contained essays on a variety of topics, literary and scientific news, poetry, a monthly register of foreign and domestic news, and articles on the American Colonization Society and on peace societies.

v1   Jan.-Dec. 1824   APS II, Reel 139

MISCELLANIES. *SEE* Talisman.

MISCELLANIES ON HOMEOPATHY. *SEE* American Journal of Homeopathy.

THE MISCELLANY. v. 1, no.1-26; June 10-Dec. 2, 1805. [Trenton, N.J., J. Oram]

104 p.   Weekly.

This miscellany edited by James Oram survived for only six months. Among its offerings were moral essays, occasional tales, a series on classical literature, some articles on education, poetry, and anecdotes. It also provided short news items and vital statistics.

v1, no.1-20, 22-26   June 10-Dec. 2, 1805   APS II, Reel 28

Film incomplete: Vol. 1, no.21 wanting.

Microfilm edition was prepared from PPL copy.

MISS LESLIE'S MAGAZINE. *SEE* Arthur's Magazine.

MISSION STUDIES AND MONTHLY BULLETINS. *SEE* Missionary Herald at Home and Abroad.

MISSIONARY HERALD. *SEE* Massachusetts Missionary Magazine, *and* Missionary Herald at Home and Abroad.

THE MISSIONARY HERALD AT HOME AND ABROAD. v. 1-147, no. 3; June 1805-Mar. 1951. Boston.

illus., plates, ports., maps (part fold.)
Film covers: v1-102; June 1805-Dec. 1906.
Monthly (except July and Aug., 1940-).

Vols. 4-8 called new ser. v.1-5.
From 1818-20, v. 14-16, the Missionary herald was published in two editions; one issued separately and the other as part of the Panoplist. Published by the Missions council of the Congregational and Christian churches for the American board of commissioners for foreign missions and the Board of home missions, Sept. 1939-.

Title varies: 1805-May 1808, The Panoplist; [or, The Christian's armory]; June 1808-1817, The Panoplist, and missionary magazine (varies slightly); 1818-20, The Panoplist, and missionary herald. 1821-27, The Missionary herald. 1828-Mar. 1934, The Missionary herald, containing the proceedings of the American board of commissioners for foreign missions (subtitle varies). Apr. 1934- The Missionary Herald at home and abroad.

Vols. 1-61 published in Boston; v. 62-78, in Cambridge, Mass.; v. 79-136, no. 1, in Boston. Absorbed the Massachusetts missionary magazine in June 1808; Life and light for woman, Mission studies and Monthly bulletins in Jan. 1923; the American missionary in Apr. 1934.

Founded in 1805 by Rev. Jedediah Morse to repudiate the new doctrines of Unitarianism, the *Panoplist* made doctrinal propaganda its chief business, and essays and sermons on theological principles were staple fare. It also published reviews of both religious and secular works, biography, and religious poetry. After the *Massachusetts Missionary Magazine* was merged with it in 1808, information and news of missionary activity increased greatly, and in 1821 it was converted to a missionary organ and renamed the *Missionary Herald*. Edited by Jeremiah Evarts, who had succeeded Morse as editor of the *Panoplist* in 1810, it became an important Congregationalist missionary monthly, surviving until 1951.

Panoplist
v1-3   June 1805-May 1808   APS II, Reel 29

Panoplist and Missionary Magazine
v4-5, no.7   June 1808-Dec. 1809   Reel 29

v2[i.e. v5], no.8-v5[i.e. v8]   Jan. 1810-May 1813   Reel 139
v9-12, no.9   June 1813-Sept. 1816   Reel 140
v12, no.10-v13   Oct. 1816-Dec. 1817   Reel 141

Panoplist and Missionary Herald
v14-15   Jan. 1818-Dec. 1819   Reel 141
v16   1820   Reel 142

Missionary Herald
v17-21   1821-1825   Reel 142

v22-30   Jan. 1826-Dec. 1834   Reel 764
v31-37   Jan. 1835-Dec. 1841   Reel 765
v38-46   Jan. 1842-Dec. 1850   Reel 766

v47-51   Jan. 1851-Dec. 1855   Reel 1237
v52-60   Jan. 1856-Dec. 1864   Reel 1238
v61-68   Jan. 1865-Dec. 1872   Reel 1239
v69-76   Jan. 1873-Dec. 1880   Reel 1240
v77-82   Jan. 1881-Dec. 1886   Reel 1241
v83-88   Jan. 1887-Dec. 1892   Reel 1242
v89-94   Jan. 1893-Dec. 1898   Reel 1243
v95-99   Jan. 1899-Dec. 1903   Reel 1244
v100-102   Jan. 1904-Dec. 1906   Reel 1245

Reels 764-766: Pagination is irregular.
Reels 1237-1245: Several pages are stained, creased, or torn with some faded print. Vol. 50: Supplement follows volume. Vol. 74: Pg. 432 is misnumbered. Vol. 94: Supplement follows June issue. Vol. 101: Supplement follows July issue.

Microfilm edition was prepared from CCC, MiU, MNUT, NRCR, NjP, NjPT, and WHi copies.

MISSIONARY MAGAZINE. *SEE* Baptist Missionary Magazine.

MISSIONS. *SEE* Baptist Missionary Magazine.

MISTLETOE. v.1, nos. 1-3; Jan.-Mar. 1849. Athens, Ga., 1849.

64 p.

Superseded by Wheler's southern monthly magazine.

Mistletoe was a temperance magazine which devoted all of its space to the temperance movement. It gave coverage to the activities of the Sons of Temperance, and published articles, stories, and poetry warning against the evils of alcohol.

v1, no.1-3   Jan.-Mar. 1849   APS II, Reel 400

Microfilm edition was prepared from NN copy.

THE MONIST, a quarterly magazine devoted to the philosophy of science. v. 1-46, no. 2; Oct. 1890-July 1936. Chicago, Open Court Pub. Co.

46 v. illus., plates, facsims.

Founded by Edward C. Hegeler.

Subtitle varies.
Editor: Oct. 1890- Paul Carus.
Volumes 2, 4, and 5 include appendices. Index: v.1-30, 1890-1920.
On film: issues for Oct. 1890-Oct. 1905.

Monist was published in Chicago by Edward Carl Hegeler and edited by Paul Carus, a German scholar who had earlier edited *Open Court.*

v1-5	Oct. 1890-July 1895	APS III, Reel 342
v6-10	Oct. 1895-July 1900	Reel 343
v11-15	Oct. 1900-Oct. 1905	Reel 344

Some pages are stained or torn. Vol. 2: Appendix entitled "Kant and Spencer" follows after volume. Vol. 4: Appendix entitled "The Dawn of New Religious Era" follows after April issue. Vol. 5: Appendix entitled "De Rerum Natura" follows after the January issue. Appendix entitled "The Soul" follows after the April issue.

Microfilm edition was prepared from MiU copy.

MONITOR. *SEE* Colvin's Weekly Register.

THE MONITOR, designed to improve the taste, the understanding, and the heart. v. 1-2, no. 12; Jan. 1823-Dec. 1824. Boston, R. Bannister.

2 v. illus. monthly.

Edited by H. Wilbur.
Merged into the Guardian to form the Guardian and monitor, Jan. 1825.

Film also contains vol. 7 of Guardian and monitor.

Intended for young people 15 and up, this religious monthly was both to entertain and instruct. Contents included religious and moral essays, poetry and tales, literary notices, biographical sketches of martyrs and Bible characters, and some simple science articles, as well as instructive articles giving hints to parents on moral training for children and advice and sermons on the Christian life. In addition the *Monitor* reported on the activities of education and benevolent societies, and on missions and Bible classes.

v1-2   Jan. 1823-Dec. 1824   APS II, Reel 143

MONTHLY ABSTRACT OF MEDICAL SCIENCE. *SEE* Medical News.

MONTHLY AMERICAN JOURNAL OF GEOLOGY AND NATURAL SCIENCE. v. 1, nos. 1-12; July 1831-June 1832. Philadelphia, 1831-32.

576 p.

The main purpose of this scientific magazine was to expand the public's knowledge of American geology and archaeology, about which relatively little was published at that time, and to keep readers abreast of the latest scientific developments. It also provided information on the state of natural science in Europe and included articles on the structure of Indian languages, critical reviews of recent scientific works, and illustrations.

v1   July 1831-June 1832   APS II, Reel 659

Title pages and table of contents for all issues are bound and filmed at the end of the volume.

Microfilm edition was prepared from CtY copy.

THE MONTHLY ANTHOLOGY, AND BOSTON REVIEW. Containing sketches and reports of philosophy, religion, history, arts, and manners. v. 1-10; Nov. 1803-June 1811. Boston, Munroe & Francis, 1804-11.

10 v.

Cover-title reads, Nov. 1803-Apr. 1804: The Monthly anthology; or, Magazine of polite literature ... Ed. by Sylvanus Per-se [pseud.] Boston, Printed by E. Lincoln.–May-July 1804: The Monthly Anthology: or, Massachusetts magazine ... Boston, Munroe & Francis.

Edited by D.P. Adams (Sylvanus Per-se, pseud.) Nov. 1803-Apr. 1804; from May 1804 by William Emerson, later by S.C. Thacher and other members of the Anthology club. cf. Mass. hist. soc., Proc., v. 2, p. 387-389. Vols. 3-4 include appendix: "The Political cabinet."

Superseded by General repository and review.

Edited at first by a Boston schoolmaster, Phineas Adams, the *Monthly Anthology* published material from European magazines along with some original book reviews, sermons, and verse. Original material increased when Rev. William Emerson became editor; there was a poetry department, some tales, a "periodical essays" series, and a number of other series, including "The Botanist," "Biographia Americana," and "The Theologist," in addition to popular medicinal information, extracts from many books, state papers, news, and a catalog of new publications. In 1805 the Anthology Society took over the magazine, but it changed very little. It gave much attention to classical literature, and published letters from Europe by John Lowell and Alexander H. Everett.

v1-3	Nov. 1803-Dec. 1806	APS II, Reel 30
v4-6	Jan. 1807-June 1809	Reel 31
v7	July-Dec. 1809	Reel 32
v8	Jan.-June 1810	Reel 143
v9-10	July 1810-June 1811	Reel 144

Microfilm edition was prepared from MiU copy.

SEE ALSO: General repository and review.

THE MONTHLY CHRONICLE OF EVENTS, DISCOVERIES, IMPROVEMENTS, AND OPINIONS. Intended for the popular diffusion of useful knowledge, and an authentic record of facts for future reference. v. 1-3; Apr. 1840-Dec. 1842.Boston, S.N. Dickinson, 1840-42.

3 v. maps.

Nathan Hale, editor.

Intended to be chiefly an authentic record of facts and events. The most popular subject areas were: geography, education, history and economics of foreign countries, exploration and recent discoveries, the state of domestic and international railroads, and banks. The "Chronology" section listed important events by date, so that each volume contained a complete listing of one year's events. Some humorous sketches appeared, and articles were illustrated with many maps and pictures.

v1-3   Apr. 1840-Dec. 1842   APS II, Reel 745

Vol. 2: No issue published for October 1841.

Microfilm edition was prepared from DLC copy.

THE MONTHLY JOURNAL OF AGRICULTURE, containing the best current productions in promotion of agricultural improvement, including the choicest prize essays issued in Europe and America. With original contributions from eminent farmers and statesmen. v. 1-3; July 1845-June 1848. New York, Greeley & McElrath, 1846-48.

3 v. illus., fronts, (part col.) plates (part col.) ports., facsim. (The Farmers' library and monthly journal of agriculture.)

Caption title: Monthly journal of agriculture. Title-page of v. 1 reads: The monthly journal of agriculture; v. 2-3: The Journal of agriculture ...
J.S. Skinner, editor.

Superseded by the Plough, the loom, and the anvil (later American farmer's magazine)

Using essays on agriculture previously published in the United States and Europe combined with original contributions of eminent farmers and statesmen, the Journal of Agriculture promoted agricultural improvements.
Eclectic in nature, the magazine featured articles on farming in foreign countries and the U.S., biographies, farm management, plant and stock diseases, agricultural machines, insects and botany and geology as applied to farming. One of the featured accounts was by George Washington to Sir John Sinclair describing the agricultural advantages of the United States in 1796.

v1-3   July 1845-June 1848   APS II, Reel 419

Pagination is irregular.

Microfilm edition was prepared from DLC copy.

MONTHLY JOURNAL OF FOREIGN MEDICINE. v. 1-3, Jan. 1828-June 1829. Philadelphia, 1828-1829.

3 v.

Also with title: Spirit of the European medical journals.

This medical journal provided a review of the latest developments in the medical field outside the U.S.; it was composed entirely of material from European and other foreign sources—selections from journals, and a few original papers written by European doctors. The articles covered a variety of topics, usually presenting case studies and descriptions of treatments for disease and injury. A listing of new European publications was also given.

v1-3   Jan. 1828-June 1829   APS II, Reel 659

Microfilm edition was prepared from DLC and MiU copies.

THE MONTHLY JOURNAL OF MEDICINE, containing selections from European journals, the transactions of learned societies, & c. and embracing a concise analysis of the physicians. v. 1-6 (no. 1-36); Jan. 1823-Dec. 1825. Hartford, Huntington and Hopkins.

6 v.

Numbering is irregular. Feb., Dec. 1824 incorrectly as Feb. 1823, Dec. 1825.

Conducted by an association of physicians, this medical journal proposed to give a comprehensive view of medical science. It included a monthly summary of cases, and descriptions of selected cases, selections from European journals, transactions of medical societies, reviews of medical books, and an analysis of American medical journals.

v1-3, no.4   Jan. 1823-Apr. 1824   APS II, Reel 144
v3, no.1-v6   Jan. 1824-Dec. 1825   Reel 145

vol. 3: Some pages are torn.

THE MONTHLY LAW REPORTER. v.1-27, no.7; Mar. 10, 1838-May 1866. Boston, W. Guild.

27 v.

Publication suspended Sept. 1861-Feb. 1862 and Aug. 1865-Mar. 1866. Issues for May 1848-May 1858 (v. 11-21, no. 1) also called new ser. v. 1-11, no. 1. Title varies: Mar. 10, 1838-Apr. 1848, The law reporter.

Founded and for some years edited by P.W. Chandler.

Reviews of circuit, district and supreme court cases in the United States and England, digests of late court decisions, and biographies of leading jurists were among the articles printed by this monthly. Also included were obituary notices, lectures, reviews, of new publications, lists of bankruptcies in several states and legislative action.

Law Reporter
v1-7   Mar. 10, 1838-Apr. 1845   APS II, Reel 288
v8-10   May 1845-Apr. 1848   Reel 289

Monthly Law Reporter
v11-13   May 1848-Apr. 1851   Reel 289
v14-18   May 1851-Apr. 1856   Reel 290
v19-22   May 1856-Apr. 1860   Reel 291
v23-27   May 1860-May 1866   Reel 292

MONTHLY LITERARY MISCELLANY. *SEE* Wellman's Miscellany.

MONTHLY MAGAZINE (Lancaster, Pa.) *SEE* Gleaner.

THE MONTHLY MAGAZINE, AND AMERICAN RE-VIEW. v. 1-3; Apr. 1799-Dec. 1800. New-York, T. & J. Swords, 1800.

3 v.

Continued as the American review, and literary journal.
Charles Brockden Brown, editor.

Poetry, fiction, current events, scientific and literary articles, and book reviews were printed along with writings by Charles Brockden Brown.

v1-3   Apr. 1799-Dec. 1800   APS I, Reel 17

Microfilm edition was prepared from DLC copy.

SEE ALSO: American Review, and Literary Journal for 1801-02.

THE MONTHLY MAGAZINE AND LITERARY JOUR-NAL. v. 1-2; May 1812-Apr. 1813. Winchester, Va., J. Heiskell, 1812-13.

2 v. plates.

Edited by John Heiskell.

This monthly miscellany published articles on agriculture, and papers and documents concerning population, commerce, and manufacturing, both of Virginia and of the U.S.; and also included a four-page poetry department, biographical sketches, much on love and marriage, some engravings, anecdotes, and miscellaneous articles and essays.

v1-2   May 1812-Apr. 1813   APS II, Reel 145

MONTHLY MAGAZINE; COMPREHENDING ECCLE-SIASTICAL HISTORY, MORALITY, RELIGION ... *SEE* Columbian Magazine.

MONTHLY MAGAZINE OF BELLES-LETTRES AND THE LADY'S BOOK. *SEE* Godey's Magazine.

THE MONTHLY MILITARY REPOSITORY. Respect-fully inscribed to the military of the United States of America. By Charles Smith. v. 1-2, 1796-1797. New York, 1796-97.

2 v. front. (port.) pl., fold, maps.

A military periodical covering most aspects of the subject. In-cluded are: extracts from histories of European wars and descrip-tions of American Revolution battles, with military plans extracts from military works and from some European military periodicals; instruction on military strategy, conduct, and clothing; along with anecdotes, poetry, memoirs, and maxims.

v1-2   1796-1797   APS I, Reel 18

Microfilm edition was prepared from MWA copy.

MONTHLY MISCELLANY. *SEE* Christian Examiner *and* Monthly Miscellany of Religion and Letters.

THE MONTHLY MISCELLANY OF RELIGION AND LETTERS. v. 1-9; Apr. 1839-Dec. 1843. Boston, W. Crosby, 1839-43.

9 v.

Caption title: The Monthly miscellany.
Editors: 1839, C. Palfrey.–1840-43, E.S.Gannett. Vol. 1 wants t.-p. Vol. 8 includes supplement. Merged into the Christian examiner.

This miscellany was intended to furnish religious reading, dis-cussing subjects of religion and morals, as well as literature in its religious aspects; and also to convey religious news, particularly in relation to the history of the Unitarian church in both the U.S. and Britain. Though founded on Unitarian views, it was not contro-versial. Contents included sermons, religious news, book reviews, essays, poetry, and listings of ordinations and dedications.

v1-9   Apr. 1839-Dec. 1843   APS II, Reel 778

Vol. 1: Lacks index and title page. October-December 1839 issues are numbered as vol. 2, issues 1-3.

Microfilm edition was prepared from MiD copy.

THE MONTHLY MISCELLANY; or, Vermont magazine. v. 1, no. 1-6; Apr.-Sept. 1794. Bennington, A. Haswell.

336 p.

Except for the "Congressional Register" section, most material was of a sentimental nature–tales, anecdotes, fragments, and articles on love, marriage, and related topics. Included were reprints from French and other magazines, and some original poetry.

v1, no.1-6   Apr.-Sept. 1794   APS I, Reel 18

Microfilm edition was prepared from NHi copy.

THE MONTHLY OFFERING. By John A. Collins. v. 1-2; July 1840-Nov./Dec. 1842. Boston, Anti-Slavery Office, 1841-42.

2 v.

Includes songs with music.
No numbers published Mar.-Aug., 1841, inclusive.

Monthly Offering was a publication devoted to anti-slavery articles, stories, poems, and songs. William Lloyd Garrison and Maria Weston Chapman were among the contributors.

v1-2   July 1840-Oct. 1842   APS II, Reel 1245

Vol. 2: Pages 129-48 are missing in number only. Issue for Sept.-Oct. lacks table of contents. Issue for Nov.-Dec. is missing. Best copy available for photographing.

Microfilm edition was prepared from DLC copy.

THE MONTHLY RECORDER, a magazine. v. 1, no. 5; Apr.-Aug. 1813. New York, Pub. by D. Longworth, for the editor [1813]

[5]-68 p.

Cover title.

With its "Congressional Record," "Dramatic Record" of the New York theater, and "Monthly Record of Public Events," the

Monthly Recorder kept the reader up to date on what was happening in Congress, the theater, and in national and world affairs. In addition, it reviewed new publications, gave coverage to the fine arts, and included biographical sketches, some accompanied by portraits.

v1, no.1-5   Apr.-Aug. 1813   APS II, Reel 146

THE MONTHLY REGISTER, MAGAZINE, AND REVIEW OF THE UNITED STATES. v. 1-4, no. 1; [Jan.] 1805-Dec. 1807. Charleston, S.C., Printed by G.M. Bounetheau, 1806; New York, W.P. Farrand and E. Sargeant [etc., etc.] 1807.

4 v.

Publication suspended Sept. 1805-Mar., Sept.-Nov. 1806. Cf. Union list of serials.
Vol. 1 issued in 2 pts.
Title varies: v. 1 [pt. 1] The history of the American Revolution, including an impartial examination of the causes which produced that important event; and monthly register of the United States, from the date of their independence to the present time (caption title: The Monthly register, and review of the United States)— v. 1 [pt. 2] The Monthly review and literary miscellany of the United States. Running title, v. 1: The Monthly register and review.

Edited by S.C. Carpenter and J. Bristed.

On film: following this title; v. 1 pt. 2 appears as a separate entry, APS II, no. 441, called the Monthly review and literary miscellany of the United States.

Founded in 1805 in Charleston, South Carolina, by Stephen C. Carpenter, who was also editor of the Charleston *Courier*, the *Monthly Register* was divided into two separately paged sections. The first consisted of a "Retrospective History" of the American Revolution, and a "History of the Passing Times," and the second, titled "Monthly Review and Literary Miscellany" contained an essay series called "The Wanderer," a serialized "moral tale" called "Men and Women," reviews of American publications, and poetry. French literature also received attention. The division into two sections was abandoned in later volumes. Carpenter took his magazine to New York in late 1806 and John Bristed, his associate editor, succeeded him as editor in June, 1807. The magazine was suspended in December of 1807.

v1-4, no.1   [Jan.?] 1805-Dec. 1807   APS II, Reel 33

SEE ALSO: Monthly Review and Literary Miscellany of the United States.

MONTHLY RELIGIOUS MAGAZINE. *SEE* Monthly Religious Magazine and Theological Review *and* Unitarian Review.

MONTHLY RELIGIOUS MAGAZINE AND INDEPENDENT JOURNAL. *SEE* Monthly Religious Magazine and Theological Review.

* THE MONTHLY RELIGIOUS MAGAZINE AND THEOLOGICAL REVIEW. v. 1-50, v. 51, no. 1-2; Jan. 1844-Feb. 1874. Boston, L.C. Bowles, 1844-74.

51 v. in 49.

Title varies: 1844-55, The Monthly religious magazine. 1856-60, The Monthly religious magazine and independent journal. 1861-69;

The Monthly religious magazine. Jan.-July 1870, The Monthly review and religious magazine. Aug. 1870-1873, The Religious magazine and monthly review. Jan.-Feb. 1874, The Monthly religious magazine and theological review.

Editors: 1844-58, F.D. Huntington.—1859-June 1870, E.H. Sears and R. Ellis—July-Dec. 1870, E.H. Sears and J.W. Thompson.—1871-74, J.H. Morison.

Superseded by the Unitarian review.

The *Monthly Religious Magazine and Theological Review* began with Unitarian affiliations and its contributors were chiefly great Unitarian writers, but the content was substantially undenominational. It was first a pamphlet of religious miscellany for family reading, but in 1858 it became more general and more denominational and theological.

Monthly Religious Magazine
v1-7   Jan. 1844-Dec. 1850   APS II, Reel 1114
v8-15, no.1   Jan. 1851-Jan. 1856   Reel 1115

Monthly Religious Magazine and Independent Journal
v15, no.2-6   Feb.-June 1856   Reel 1115
v16-23   July 1856-June 1860   Reel 1116
v24-v25, no.1   July 1860-Jan. 1861   Reel 1117

Monthly Religious Magazine
v25, no.2-v32   Feb. 1861-Dec. 1864   Reel 1117
v33-40   Jan. 1865-Dec. 1868   Reel 1118
v41-42   Jan.-Dec. 1869   Reel 1119

Monthly Review and Religious Magazine
v43-44, no.1   Jan.-July 1870   Reel 1119

Religious Magazine and Monthly Review
v44, no.2-v46   Aug. 1870-Dec. 1871   Reel 1119
v47-50   Jan. 1872-Dec. 1873   Reel 1120

Monthly Religious Magazine and Theological Review
v51   Jan.-Dec. 1874   Reel 1120

Some pages are torn, stained, or have print missing. Vol. 7: pgs. 266, 528, and 561 are missing. Vol. 32: July issue is misnumbered and misdated as Vol. 31, no. 7. Vol. 48: pg. 452 is misnumbered.

Microfilm edition was prepared from MoS, NBu and NNUT copies.

THE MONTHLY REPOSITORY AND LIBRARY OF ENTERTAINING KNOWLEDGE. v. 1-5; June 1830-Sept. 1834. New York, F.S. Wiggins.

5 v. illus., plates.

Editor: June 1830- F.S. Wiggins.
Film incomplete: v. 5 wanting.

Poetry, moral essays, popular literary history, essays based on the classics, and articles on natural history made up the bulk of this miscellany.

v1-4   June 1830-May 1834   APS II, Reel 1215

Vol. 3: Pages 326-27 are missing in number only; Vol. 5 is missing; not available for photographing.

Microfilm edition was prepared from MiD and NPV copies.

MONTHLY REVIEW AND LITERARY MISCELLANY OF THE UNITED STATES. v. 1, Jan. 1805-Aug. 1806. Charleston, S.C.

Caption title: Monthly register and review.

Edited by Stephen C. Carpenter, who was also editor of the Charleston *Courier,* the *Monthly Review and Literary Miscellany* contained an essay series called "The Wanderer," a serialized "moral tale" called "Men and Women," reviews of American publications, and poetry. French literature also received attention.

v1   [1805]-1806   APS II, Reel 33

Also photoed with APS 440 (Monthly Register, Magazine, and Review of the United States).

Microfilm edition was prepared from the N copy.

SEE ALSO: Monthly Register, Magazine, and Review of the United States.

MONTHLY REVIEW AND RELIGIOUS MAGAZINE. *SEE* Monthly Religious Magazine and Theological Review.

THE MONTHLY SCIENTIFIC JOURNAL, containing disquisitions in natural philosophy, chemistry, and the arts. v. 1, no. 1-6; Feb.-July 1818. New York, W. Marrat.

152 p.

Edited by W. Marrat.

This science magazine presented a variety of science articles, a section of science questions and answers, chemistry experiments, and a mathematics section with problems, as well as occasional biographical sketches and literary notices.

v1, no.1-6   Feb.-July 1818   APS II, Reel 146

THE MONTHLY VISITANT; or, Something old. v.1, no.6; July-Dec. 1816. Alexandria, Printed by S. Snowden.

6 no.

Revivals, Sunday schools, Bible societies, and peace societies are some of the topics covered by the articles in the *Monthly Visitant;* this religious magazine also published Bible studies, sermons, poetry and anecdotes, letters, and extracts from various religious publications.

v1, no.1-6   July-Dec. 1816   APS II, Reel 146

MOONSHINE. no. 1-5; June 20-July 23, 1807. Baltimore, S. Jefferis.

56 p.

Weekly (irregular).
Edited by the Lunarian Society.
Bound with The Portfolio, new ser., v. 5, 1808.

Published by the Lunarian Society, this literary magazine consisted of poetry and essays; some of the material was satirical in nature. In order to add more variety, the editors added an issue of the *Baltimore Magazine* to the fifth number of *Moonshine.*

no.1-5   June 20-July 23, 1807   APS II, Reel 33

THE MORAL ADVOCATE, a monthly publication on war, duelling, capital punishment, and prison discipline. v. 1-3, no. 12; Mar. 1821-[Oct.?] 1824. Mt. Pleasant, Ohio.

3 v. in 2.

Publication suspended Apr.-May, July, Oct. 1821 and Sept.-Dec. 1823.
Edited by E. Bates.

This pacifist magazine was conducted by Elisha Bates, a Quaker who also published an antislavery magazine called the *Philanthropist* from 1818 to 1822. The *Moral Advocate,* which condemned war, slavery, duelling, and capital punishment, published reports of peace societies, information on prisons, including penitentiaries in Ohio, and a variety of speeches, addresses, and reports.

v1-3   Mar. 1821-1824   APS II, Reel 146

THE MORAL AND RELIGIOUS CABINET, containing short accounts of Christian experience, together with instructive and useful extracts, intended to promote the happiness of pious minds. v. 1, no. 1-26; Jan. 2-June 25, 1808. New-York.

404 p. Weekly.

Edited by J.C. Totten.

Poetry, moral essays, and accounts of "pious lives and happy deaths" occupied the bulk of the contents of this religious magazine edited by John C. Totten.

v1, no.1-26   Jan. 2-June 25, 1808   APS II, Reel 34

Microfilm edition was prepared from NN copy.

THE MORALIST. v. 1, no. 1-11; May 27-Nov. 7, 1814. New York, Tunison & Snowden.

153 p.

(Miscellaneous pamphlets, v. 524, no. 1)
Irregular.

Each issue of the *Moralist* consisted of an essay written by one or more of its seven editors. The essays generally dealt with personal observations and experiences, and contained some satire on New York society and fashions.

v1, no.1-11   May 27-Nov. 7, 1814   APS II, Reel 146

MORNING STAR. *SEE* Watchman-Examiner.

MORRIS'S NATIONAL PRESS, A JOURNAL FOR HOME. *SEE* Town and Country.

MUSEUM OF FOREIGN LITERATURE. *SEE* American Eclectic.

* **THE MUSEUM OF FOREIGN LITERATURE, SCIENCE, AND ART.** v. 1-45; July 1822-Dec. 1842. Philadelphia, E. Littel [1822-42]

45 v. plates, ports., facsims. monthly.

Vols. 29-45 are called also "new ser., v. 1-17".
Mar.-Sept. 1837 in one no.; June-Nov. 1842 in one no.
From July 1822, to Dec. 1832, title reads: The Museum of foreign literature and science.

Editors: July 1822-June 1823, Robert Walsh.–July 1823-Dec. 1834, Ellakim Littel.–Jan.-Dec. 1835, J.J. Smith.–Jan. 1836-Dec. 1842, Ellakim Littell.

Supersedes the Saturday magazine.
United with the American eclectic in January 1843, to form the Eclectic museum.

Edited at first by Robert Walsh, Jr. and then by Eliakim and Squier Littell, the monthly *Museum of Foreign Literature, Science, and Art* was the leading American eclectic for twenty years. Much of its contents were selected from British magazines; included were reviews, poetry, literary and scientific news, biographical sketches of British authors, lists of new British publications, and articles on literature. The engraved portraits in each number were a popular feature. After 1830, plates were published regularly, and the magazine began to devote a large proportion of its space to serial fiction by Dickens, Reade, Bulwer, Thackeray and other popular English novelists.

v1	July-Dec. 1822	APS II, Reel 146
v2-4	Jan. 1823-June 1824	Reel 147
v5-7	July 1824-Dec. 1825	Reel 148
v1	July-Dec. 1822	Reel 1245
v2-7	Jan. 1823-Dec. 1825	Reel 1246
v8-12	Jan. 1826-Apr. 1828	Reel 1247
v13-18	May 1828-June 1831	Reel 1248
v19-22	July 1831-June 1833	Reel 1249
v23-26	July 1833-June 1835	Reel 1250
v27-31	July 1835-Dec. 1837	Reel 1251
v32-36	Jan. 1838-Aug. 1839	Reel 1252
v37-42	Sept. 1839-Aug. 1841	Reel 1253
v43-45	Sept. 1841-Dec. 1842	Reel 1254

Several pages are stained, torn, and tightly bound with some loss of text; some have faded print and show-through. Many volumes have misnumbered pages.

Vols. 39-43: Pages are missing from the indexes; Vol. 43: Supplement follows volume.

Microfilm edition was prepared from C, DLC, GEU, InGrD, MWelC, and MiD copies.

SEE ALSO: Eclectic Museum of Foreign Literature, Science, and Art *and* Saturday Magazine.

MUSEUM OF FOREIGN LITERATURE AND SCIENCE.
SEE Museum of Foreign Literature, Science, and Art *and* Saturday Magazine.

THE MUSICAL CABINET; a monthly collection of vocal and instrumental music, and musical literature. pt. 1 (no. 1-12); July 1841-June 1842. Boston, Bradbury, Soden, 1842.

v. port.

Editors: July 1841-G.J. Webb, T.B. Hayward.

Musical Cabinet was edited by T.B. Hayward (who had previously edited *Musical Magazine*) and George J. Webb. Its short life was similar to other musical magazines of the time.

v1	July 1841-June 1842	APS II, Reel 1120

Microfilm edition was prepared from CtHT-W copy.

MUSICAL MAGAZINE. v. 1-2; May 1835-Apr. 1837. New York, 1835-1837.

2 v.

Published by Ezra Collier and edited by Thomas Hastings, the *Musical Magazine* was to be devoted to both the theoretical and practical aspects of music.

v1-2	May 1835-Apr. 1837	APS II, Reel 840

The music pages for volume 1 will be found after volume 2.

Microfilm edition was prepared from NNU-H copy.

THE MUSICAL MAGAZINE; containing a variety of favorite pieces. no. 1-6; 1792-[1801?] Cheshire [Conn.] W. Law.

6 no. music.

Issued in 6 no., 1792-1801. Cf. Union list of serials.
Edited by A. Law.

One of two eighteenth-century music magazines.

no.1-6	1792-[1801?]	APS I, Reel 18

Microfilm edition was prepared from CtY copy.

THE MUSICAL MAGAZINE; or, Repository of musical science, literature and intelligence. v. 1-3; Jan. 5, 1839-Apr. 24, 1842. Boston, Otis, Broaders, 1839-42.

3 v. biweekly.

No numbers issued Dec. 4, 1841-Apr. 10, 1842, inclusive. Editors: 1839, H.T. Hach, T.B. Hayward.–1840-42, H.T. Hach.

Edited by H. Theodor Hach and T.B. Hayward, this early magazine began publication at the time that music was introduced in the public schools of Boston. Articles from English sources were reprinted along with translations of German articles.

v1-3	Jan. 5, 1839-Apr. 24, 1842	APS II, Reel 1216

Vol. 1: Pages 134-37 and 145-48 are stained; Vol. 3: Pages 57-64 are stained; 411-14 are torn and taped.

Microfilm edition was prepared from DLC, Ia-T, and MH copies.

MUSICAL REPORTER. v. 1, no. 1-9; Jan.-Sept. 1841. Boston, 1841.

432 p.

After a rather scathing editorial on how the first issue was accepted, the line was drawn and the purpose defined: "We shall therefore act independently, fearless of consequences, always regarding the contributions and advice of our friends as a favor, which we will endeavor to repay in good and ample measure." Another editorial called "Ourselves" appeared. They were being persecuted for being associated with the ill-fated *Musical Visitor.* Suddenly, without explanation, publication ceased.

v1	Jan.-Sept. 1841	APS II, Reel 840

Best copy available: some pages are stained; index is missing.

Microfilm edition was prepared from NRU copy.

THE MUSICAL VISITOR, a magazine of musical literature and music. v.1-26; Oct. 1871-Dec. 1897. Cincinnati, J. Church, 1897.

26 v. illus., ports. monthly.
Includes musical supplements.

v1-12, no.1 as Church's musical visitor.

Editor: -Dec. 1897, J.R. Murphy.

Devoted to music and the fine arts, this journal included serial installments, verse, biographical sketches, correspondence, and reviews, as well as music.

Church's Musical Visitor
v1-12, no.1	Oct. 1871-Jan. 1883	APS II, Reel 1289

Musical Visitor
v12, no.2-v13	Feb. 1883-Dec. 1884	Reel 1289
v14-21	Jan. 1885-Dec. 1892	Reel 1290
v22-26	Jan. 1893-Dec. 1897	Reel 1291

Best copy available for photographing. Pagination is irregular. All indexes and some pages are missing. The following issues are missing: v.3, no.1; v.10, nos.1-3; v.14, no.12; v.22, no.8; v.23, no.9. The following volumes are missing: vols.4-9 and 15-16. Vols.24-26: Music supplements are included at the end of several issues.

Microfilm edition was prepared from DLC and KAS copies.

SEE ALSO: American Journal of Music and Musical Visitor.

MUTUAL RIGHTS AND METHODIST PROTESTANT. *SEE* Methodist Recorder.

THE NASSAU LITERARY MAGAZINE. v.1- Feb. 1842- Princeton, N.J., 1842-

v. map.
On film: v. 1-63, 1842-1908; v.7 and 52 are missing.
Monthly during the college year.

Conducted by the senior class of Princeton university.
Title varies: Feb. 1842-Sept. 1848, The Nassau monthly.

Bound and filmed at end of v.18: "Supplement to the Nassau Literary Magazine" and "A Vindication of Lady Macbeth." The "Supplement" actually an independently printed essay "written for the Apr. no. ... but prohibited by the faculty of the college."

This long-lived college literary periodical was conducted by the senior class at Princeton and published poetry, biographical sketches, stories, and many short essays and articles on a wide variety of topics, including history, literature, mythology, philosophy, and fine arts. Around the turn of the century it increased its advertising and added a section called "Book Talk" which included reviews and notices of new books.

Nassau Monthly
v1-6	Feb. 1842-May 1847	APS II, Reel 1482

Nassau Literary Magazine
v8-20	Sept. 1848-May 1860	Reel 1482
v21-33	Sept. 1860-May 1878	Reel 1483
v34-43	June 1878-Apr. 1888	Reel 1484
v44-50	May 1888-Apr. 1895	Reel 1485
v51-63	May 1895-Mar. 1908	Reel 1486

Many volumes lack title page, index, some issues, and advertisement pages. Some pages are stained, misnumbered or have print faded. Best copy available for photographing.

Vol. 18: contains a supplement.
Vol. 27: June issue is misnumbered as vol. 28.

Microfilm edition was prepared from NjP copy.

NASSAU MONTHLY. *SEE* Nassau Literary Magazine.

NATIONAL BAPTIST. *SEE* Watchman-Examiner.

NATIONAL ERA. v.1-14; Jan. 1847-Mar. 1860. Washington, 1847-1860.

14 v.

One of the most famous of the abolitionary papers was the *National Era*. Begun and edited by Dr. Gamaliel Bailey in 1847, the *Era* was wholly committed to the cause of freedom for the slave. Its fiery articles did much to incite furor among the Northern sympathizers. The outstanding example of this was the first publication of Harriet Beecher Stowe's *Uncle Tom's Cabin,* which ran serially in 1851-52. This story is claimed to have contributed more to the War than any other writing on slavery. And it certainly contributed immensely to the *Era's* fame. Articles on the Compromise of 1850 and on John Brown's raid are also included in the columns. In addition, some excellent poetry will be found.

v1	Jan.-Dec. 1847	APS II, Reel 899
v2-4	Jan. 6, 1848-Dec. 26, 1850	Reel 900
v5-7	Jan. 2, 1851-Dec. 29, 1853	Reel 901
v8-10	Jan. 1854-Dec. 1856	Reel 902
v11-14	Jan. 1857-Mar. 1860	Reel 903

Some pages are stained, torn or are tightly bound. Pagination is irregular. Vols. 13-14 lack indexes and tables of contents.

Microfilm edition was prepared from CtHT-W, InU, NIC, NhD, RP, and RPB copies.

NATIONAL GOVERNMENT JOURNAL, AND REGISTER OF OFFICIAL PAPERS. v.1-2, no.22; Dec. 3, 1823-Nov. 29, 1825. [Washington, P. Force, 1823-24]

2 p. 1., 874 (i.e. 880) col. weekly.

Title varies: Dec. 3, 1823-June 5, 1824, (extra). Peter Force, editor.

This journal published proceedings of Congress, foreign and domestic state papers and documents, statistical information and tables, tariff lists, and letters. It also listed new laws and appointments.

National Journal (extra)
v1, nos.1-30	Dec. 3, 1823-June 5, 1824	APS II, Reel 149

National Government Journal and Register of Official Papers
v1, nos.31-55; v2, nos.1-22	June 9-Nov. 29, 1825	Reel 149

NATIONAL JOURNAL. *SEE* National Government Journal, and Register of Official Papers.

THE NATIONAL MAGAZINE; a monthly journal of American history. v.1-18, v.19, no.1-8/9; Nov. 1884-Sept./Oct. 1894. Cleveland [1884-88]; New York, Magazine of Western History Pub. Co. [1888-94]

19 v. illus., plates, ports.

Vols. 1-14 as Magazine of Western History.

Editors: Nov. 1884-Apr. 1887, W.W. Williams.–Nov. 1887-Oct. 1891, J.H. Kennedy. "Copies of this magazine exist in 1895, '96 and '97, but were probably never sold."–Boston book company, Check list of American and English ... periodicals.

The *National Magazine* was founded by William W. Williams in Cleveland under the title of *Magazine of Western History*. As the latter title indicated, the western states were the primary interest of the articles on the history and lives of pioneers. The exclusiveness of the "West" was dropped after moving the magazine to New York in 1888. Owing to the press of work, the publisher killed the journal in 1894. Henry J. Seymour, C.W. Butterfield, and W.H. Venable were contributors to the early volumes.

Magazine of Western History

v1-4	Nov. 1884-Oct. 1886	APS III, Reel 160
v5-8	Nov. 1886-Oct. 1888	Reel 161
v9-13	Nov. 1888-Apr. 1891	Reel 162
v14	May-Oct. 1891	Reel 163

National Magazine; A Monthly Journal of American History

v15-19	Nov. 1891-Oct. 1894	Reel 163

Microfilm edition was prepared from MiU, OMC, and OT copies.

THE NATIONAL MAGAZINE AND REPUBLICAN REVIEW. v.1-2, no.2; Jan.-June 1839. Washington, D.C., Fulton & Smith.

2v. monthly.

Editor: Jan.-Mar. 1839, H.J. Brent.

A literary and political journal which defended and maintained the Whig party viewpoint–that of opposing the existing administration. Political material included coverage of elections and the activities of Parliament and Congress, and in addition, the journal published poetry and tales; book reviews; and articles on history, drama, and literature.

v1-2	Jan.-June 1839	APS II, Reel 799

Microfilm edition was prepared from CtY copy.

* THE NATIONAL MAGAZINE; devoted to literature, art, and religion. v.1-13; July 1852-Dec. 1858. New York, Carlton & Phillips, 1852-[58]

13 v. illus., ports. monthly.

Editors: 1852-June 1856, Abel Stevens.–July 1856-1858, James Floy.

An eclectic monthly begun in New York in 1852 by the Methodist Church with the aim of presenting the attractions of *Harper's* without those "morbid appeals to the passions" to be found in fiction. It included departments of religious and literary news and was illustrated by woodcuts.

v1-7	July 1852-Dec. 1855	APS II, Reel 814
v8-13	Jan. 1856-Dec. 1858	Reel 815

Microfilm edition was prepared from MiU copy.

NATIONAL MAGAZINE; or, Cabinet of the United States. no. [1]-8; [Oct.?] 1801-Jan. 11, 1802. Washington, Washington Printing and Bookselling Co., 1801-02.

1 p.l., 64, 64, 64, [20] p. Weekly (irregular).

Richard Dinsmore, editor.
Formed by the union of the National magazine (Richmond, etc., 1799-1800) and the Cabinet.
Lacking on film: no.7.

Edited by Richard Dinsmore, this weekly was a continuation of the *National Magazine* of Richmond. It was comprised of three departments: the first was devoted to politics; the second to science, agriculture, manufacturing, and commerce; and the third to literature, including poetry and anecdotes, biographical and historical sketches, and literary notices.

no.1-6, 8	Oct. 1801-Jan. 1802	APS II, Reel 34

Microfilm edition was prepared from DLC copy.

NATIONAL MAGAZINE; or, lady's emporium. v.1-2; Nov. 1830-July 1831. Baltimore, 1830-1831.

2 v.

Edited and published by Mrs. Mary Barney, the *National Magazine* was directed to ladies and was to be generally literary and occasionally political. In addition to short stories and poetry, it published play reviews, biography, and original and selected pieces on a variety of topics–science, history, education, novel writing, railroads, travel, and people and customs of foreign lands.

v1-2	Nov. 1830-July 1831	APS II, Reel 799

Vol. 2: Title page, table of contents, and index are lacking. Pages 159-60 are missing in number only.

Microfilm edition was prepared from MWA and MdBP copies.

NATIONAL MAGAZINE; or, A political, historical, biographical, and literary repository. v.1-2 (no.1-8) v.3, no.1, sec.1-4; June 1, 1799-Dec. 22, 1800. By James Lyon. Richmond, Va. [etc.] the editor, 1799-[1800]

3 v. semiquarterly.

No. 7 has imprint: District of Columbia, Printed by the editor, 1800. The National magazine and the Cabinet were united in 1801 to form the National magazine, or Cabinet of the United States.

Vol. 2, no.9-vol.3, no.1 are lacking.

First magazine in Richmond.

v1-2, no.8	1799	APS I, Reel 18

Microfilm edition was prepared from MWA and DLC copy.

THE NATIONAL MUSEUM AND WEEKLY GAZETTE OF DISCOVERIES, NATURAL SCIENCES, AND THE ARTS. v.1, no.1-16; Nov. 13, 1813-Nov. 12, 1814. Baltimore, C.M. Mann.

128 p.

Title varies slightly.
Lacking on film: nos.2, 5-6.

The *National Museum* contained a variety of news, but focused mainly on the progress made in agriculture, manufacturing, and the arts. The first nine numbers contained political news but with the tenth number this was replaced with news of discoveries, inventions, and improvements, and accounts of the latest scientific research. The remainder of the *Museum's* space was devoted to news summaries, notices of new publications, and a "Miscellaneous" department containing anecdotes, stories, and humorous items.

v1, nos.1, 3-4, 7-16 Nov. 13, 1813-Nov. 12, 1814 APS II, Reel 149

NATIONAL PHILANTHROPIST. *SEE* Investigator and General Intelligencer.

NATIONAL PILOT. *SEE* Pilot.

THE NATIONAL POLICE GAZETTE ... v.1- Sept. 1845-19 . New York, Camp & Wilkes [etc.]

v. illus., plates, ports. weekly.

Editors: Oct. 1845-1857, George Wilkes and Enoch E. Camp.–1857-1872, George W. Matsell.–1872-1877, Herbert R. Mooney.–1877-? Richard Kyle Fox.

On film: v.1-89, 1845-1906.

Modeled on English papers of a similar nature, the *National Police Gazette* made its appearance on September 13, 1845, with the ostensible purpose of exposing criminals and vice. Crime news was its main feature and its bold procedures placed the *Gazette* and its first editor, George Wilkes, under attack by the crime bosses on the one hand and the police department on the other. In 1850 the *Gazette* plant was demolished during an assault which resulted in six deaths.

The paper was going full blast within a short time, but the pace was too much to keep up. The *Gazette* declined throughout the Civil War and in 1866, Wilkes sold it—to his erstwhile enemy, Chief of Police Matsell. Sensationalism to the tune of sex followed with illustrated stories of scandal. The weekly *Gazette* however, could not compete with dailies already satisfying the appetites for scandal and the *Gazette* once more declined.

After several very rough years, an Irishman named Richard K. Fox became publisher and aided the *Gazette's* recovery. Early in 1878 the *Gazette* became the familiar sixteen-page quarto printed on pale pink stock. The paper plunged deeper into sex—sex scandals, sex crimes, sex pictures, sex advertising. Sports also became a feature, with reports of prize fights remaining a regular fare.

By 1890 the paper was carrying two full pages of advertising, mostly of a disreputable kind. It still featured crime, as well as scandals, hangings, weird "news," along with pictures of burlesque queens in tights, ring news, racing, and so on. It was not offered for sale at most reputable newsstands, but it was to be found in practically every barroom and barber shop in America.

Several blows in the early 1900's brought the *Gazette* to its knees: the eighteenth amendment knocked out its barroom circulation; bobbed hairstyles and the opening of barber shops to women resulted in the lost of most barber shop subscriptions. After a temporary boom of circulation during the war, subscriptions again fell off and in February 1932, the *Gazette* was sold out as bankrupt for $545. It was revived the next year with its familiar pink cover, this time featuring confession stories.

v1-22	Oct. 1845-Aug. 31, 1867	APS II, Reel 1318
v23-24	Sept. 7, 1867-Sept. 20, 1879	Reel 1319
v35-36	Sept. 27, 1879-Sept. 18, 1880	Reel 1320
v37-38	Sept. 25, 1880-Oct. 1, 1881	Reel 1321
v39-40	Oct. 8, 1881-Oct. 14, 1882	Reel 1322
v41-42	Oct. 21, 1882-Oct. 13, 1883	Reel 1323
v43-44	Oct. 20, 1883-Sept. 27, 1884	Reel 1324
v45-46	Oct. 4, 1884-Sept. 19, 1885	Reel 1325
v47-48	Sept. 26, 1885-Sept. 25, 1886	Reel 1326
v49-50	Oct. 2, 1886-Sept. 24, 1887	Reel 1327
v51-52	Oct. 1, 1887-Sept. 22, 1888	Reel 1328
v53-54	Sept. 29, 1888-Sept. 21, 1889	Reel 1329
v55-57	Sept. 28, 1889-Mar. 14, 1891	Reel 1330
v59-62	Sept. 26, 1891-May 20, 1893	Reel 1331
v63	Sept. 2, 1893-Sept. 8, 1894	Reel 1332
v65-67	Sept. 15, 1894-Feb. 29, 1896	Reel 1333
v69-75	Sept. 5, 1896-Feb. 10, 1900	Reel 1334
v76-78	Feb. 17, 1900-June 29, 1901	Reel 1335
v79-80	July 6, 1901-June 28, 1902	Reel 1336
v81-82	July 5, 1902-June 27, 1903	Reel 1337
v83-84	July 4, 1903-June 25, 1904	Reel 1338
v85-86	July 2, 1904-June 24, 1905	Reel 1339
v87-89	July 1, 1905-Dec. 29, 1906	Reel 1340

Best copy available for photographing. Vols. 3, 5, 7-20, 24-27, 29-31, 58, and 70-73 are missing. Scattered issues are missing throughout. Vols. 4, 6, 21, and 28 contain only one issue each. Some issues have pages missing. Pagination is irregular. Many pages are stained, creased, torn, taped or tightly bound or have faded print. Several volumes include supplements. Vol. 1: Issues 1-4 are the reprint edition dated Oct. 16, 1845.

Microfilm edition was prepared from DLC copy.

NATIONAL PREACHER AND THE PRAYER-MEETING. *SEE* National Preacher and Village Pulpit.

THE NATIONAL PREACHER AND VILLAGE PULPIT. Original—monthly. From living ministers of the United States. v.1-40, June 1826-1866. [v.32- new ser. v.1-Jan. 1858-] New York, Printed by J & J. Harper 1826-

10 v. ports.

Title varies: June 1826-May 1828, The national preacher; or, Original monthly sermons from living ministers ... June 1828-Dec. 1857, The American national preacher. (Caption title, June 1828-Aug. 1831: The National preacher) Jan. 1858- The National preacher and village pulpit. Original—monthly. From living ministers of the United States. The National preacher and the prayer-meeting.

Editors: 1826-38, Austin Dickinson.–1839-40, Darius Mead.–1841-47, W. H. Bidwell.–1848-49, J.M. Sherwood.–1850, F.C. Woodworth.–1851-52, J.M. Sherwood.–1853-56, Eber Carpenter.–1857- W.H. Bidwell.

v. 32-40 called also new ser. v.1-9.

The *National Preacher and Village Pulpit* was begun to provide a simple method of spreading the gospel and introducing ministers to different sections of the country. It was a well organized, monthly publication edited in succession by the Reverends Austin Dickinson, Darius Mead, W.H. Bidwell, J. Manning Sherwood, F.C. Woodworth, and Eber Carpenter. Among the many ministers contributing to the file were Jacob Abbott, Thomas H. Skinner, William B. Sprague, Edward Hitchcock, Edward Beecher, John Hubbard Church, Horace Bushnell, Robert Baird, Theodore D. Woolsey, Henry Ward Beecher, and Enoch Pond.

Cumulative Index, 1-38	1826-1864	APS II, Reel 1087

National Preacher; or, Original Monthly Sermons from Living Ministers

v1-2	June 1826-May 1828	Reel 1087

American National Preacher

v3-5	June 1828-May 1831	Reel 1087
v6-21	June 1831-Dec. 1847	Reel 1088
v22-31	Jan. 1848-Dec. 1857	Reel 1089

National Preacher and Village Pulpit

nsv1-2	Jan. 1858-Dec. 1859	Reel 1089
nsv3-9	Jan. 1860-Dec. 1866	Reel 1090

Pagination is irregular. Some pages are stained. Vol. 4: Numbering continues from Vol. 3.

Microfilm edition was prepared from C, GEU, IaU, MeLB, MNF, NCH, and NIC copies.

NATIONAL RECORDER. *SEE* Saturday Magazine.

THE NATIONAL REGISTER, a weekly paper, containing a series of the important public documents, and the proceedings of Congress; statistical tables, reports and essays, original and selected, upon agriculture, manufactures, commerce, and finance; science, literature and the arts; and biographical sketches; with summary statements of the current news and political events; making two volumes yearly. v.1-10, Mar. 2, 1816-Oct. 7, 1820. Washington, J.K. Mead, 1816-20.

9 v. in 7.

Published documents concerned with the federal government—presidential messages and appointments, Congressional proceedings and documents, and various reports, as well as documents on foreign affairs and miscellaneous material. Also included summaries of domestic and foreign news.

v1-8	Mar. 2, 1816-Dec. 25, 1819	APS II, Reel 800
v9-10	Jan. 1-Oct. 7, 1820	Reel 801

Vol. 8: Index is lacking.
Vol. 9: Issues for June 10, 17, 24, 1820, are lacking.
Vol. 10: Issue for September 9, 1820, is lacking.

Microfilm edition was prepared from MWA, Mi, VtNN and WHi copies.

NATIONAL REPOSITORY, devoted to general and religious literature, criticism, and art. Daniel Curry, editor. v.1-8; Jan. 1877-Dec. 1880. Cincinnati, Hitchcock and Walden; New York, Nelson and Phillips, 1877-80.

8 v. in 5. illus., ports. monthly.

Preceded by the Ladies' repository.

The *National Repository* was a vain attempt to save the dying women's magazine, *Ladies Repository,* which had been centered around Cincinnati. It had been hoped that greater geographical circulation would revive the monthly. Religion, travel, art, foreign affairs, and fiction were included. Selections from English journals were occasionally printed. Mary Lowe Dickenson, Mrs. A.C. Hall, Daniel Wise, and Mary S. Robinson were among the contributors.

v1-6	Jan. 1877-Dec. 1879	APS III, Reel 110
v7-8	Jan.-Dec. 1880	Reel 111

Vols. 1-8: Indexes lacking. Please refer to the Tables of Contents.

Microfilm edition was prepared from MiU and WHi copies.

SEE ALSO: Ladies' Repository.

THE NATURALIST, containing treatises on natural history, chemistry, domestic and rural economy, manufactures, and arts. Edited by D.J. Browne, v.1-2; Dec. 1830-Dec. 1832. Boston, Peirce and Parker, 1831-32.

2 v. illus., plates (part col.) monthly.

No number was issued for Jan. 1831.

By using plain language and adding numerous illustrations to the text, this science magazine presented both older and more recent scientific material in simplified terms for the average reader. Contents included many short articles on plants, trees, and animals; information on silk manufacture; serialized articles on man and ornithology; book reviews; and a "meteorological journal."

v1-2	Dec. 1830-Dec. 1832	APS II, Reel 801

Microfilm edition was prepared from Ia-T copy.

*THE NAVAL MAGAZINE.** Ed. by the Rev. C.S. Stewart. v.1-2; Jan. 1836-Nov. 1837. New York, United States Naval Lyceum, J.S. Taylor, 1836-37.

2 v. map, plan. bimonthly.

This well-printed bimonthly magazine offered much on nautical science in addition to some general science and literary material. Nautical articles covered such areas as astrology; navigation; and construction, storage, and equipment of ships. Naval intelligence, meteorological tables, maps, and diagrams were also included. Other articles dealt with natural history, geography, and statistics. Tales and poetry, sketches of cruises, reviews, and biography made up the literary portion of the magazine.

v1-2	Jan. 1836-Nov. 1837	APS II, Reel 816

Vol. 1: Lacks index and table of contents.
Vol. 2: The Naval Register was bound and photographed with volume 2.

Microfilm edition was prepared from IU and MiD copies.

NEEDHAM, VA. LAW SCHOOL. JOURNAL... *SEE* Journal of the Law-School...

THE NEW AMERICAN MAGAZINE. no.1-27; Jan. 1758-Mar. 1760. Woodbridge, N.J., Printed and sold by J. Parker.

27 no. monthly.

Supersedes the American magazine and monthly chronicle for the British colonies. Cf. Evans. American bibliography.

Edited by S. Americanus (pseud. of Samuel Nevill).

Current political events and serial essays were published.

no.1-27	Jan. 1758-Mar. 1760	APS I, Reel 19

Microfilm edition was prepared from PPL copy.

SEE ALSO: American Magazine and Monthly Chronicle for the British Colonies.

NEW CHRISTIAN ADVOCATE. *SEE* Christian Advocate. (Chicago).

NEW ENGLAND CHRISTIAN HERALD. *SEE* Zion's Herald.

NEW ENGLAND FAMILY MAGAZINE. *SEE* Illustrated Family Magazine.

THE NEW ENGLAND FARMER; a monthly journal. v.1-16; Dec. 9, 1848-Dec. 1864; new ser., v.1-5, Jan. 1867-Dec. 1871. Boston, Nourse, Eaton.

21 v. illus.

Biweekly, Dec. 9, 1848-Dec. 20, 1851; monthly, Jan. 1852-Dec. 1871.
Supersedes the New England farmer and horticultural register.

A semimonthly publication (until 1871) dealing with agriculture.

v1-4	Dec. 1848-Dec. 1852	APS II, Reel 1191
v5-9	Jan. 1853-Dec. 1857	Reel 1192
v10-15	Jan. 1858-Dec. 1863	Reel 1193
v16-nsv1-5	Jan. 1864-Dec. 1871	Reel 1194

Several pages are stained, creased and torn with some loss of text. Some print faded and show-through. Pagination is irregular.

Vol. 3: Pgs. 334-35 are missing; not available for photographing.
Vol. 9: Pg. 558 is misnumbered.
Vol. 16 contains 8 issues; index is missing.

Microfilm edition was prepared from ICRL, MiD, and N copies.

THE NEW ENGLAND FARMER, and horticultural register. v.1-24, Aug. 3, 1822-June 24, 1846; v.47-93, no.12, Jan. 1, 1868-Mar. 22, 1913. Boston, J. Breck [etc.]

70 v. illus. weekly.

Vols. 10-24 also called new ser., v.1-15.
Organ of the Horticultural Society of Massachusetts, 1822-1846.
Title varies slightly.
Caption title: The New England farmer.
Edited for first 15 years by T.G. Fessenden.
Sometimes confused with an unrelated Boston periodical by the same name (1848-64).

Film incomplete: v.52-56, 65, 67, 70-93, and miscellaneous numbers wanting. v.69 includes only issue 16, Apr. 19, 1890.

Edited until his death in 1837 by the brilliant Thomas Green Fessenden, the *New England Farmer and Horticultural Register* was one of the most interesting and long-lived of the early agricultural journals, surviving until 1913. Fessenden made a good editor, attracting the contributions of leading farmers. He printed some of his own "Moral Lessons in Rhyme" and other pieces; he kept a poetry corner, and spiced his columns with jokes and anecdotes. Agricultural societies furnished their reports and proceedings and there were regular news summaries and produce market reports. Among the more famous contributors were Daniel Webster, Timothy Pickering, and John Lowell. Fessenden was succeeded by a number of editors, and in later years, stories, grange news, more and bigger ads, and a women's column were added, but the contents remained essentially the same as when Fessenden was editor.

v1-4, no.20	Aug. 1822-Dec. 1825	APS II, Reel 149
v4-10	July 29, 1825-July 11, 1832	Reel 1397
v11-17	July 18, 1832-July 3, 1839	Reel 1398
v18-24	July 10, 1839-June 24, 1846	Reel 1399
v47-51	Nov. 21, 1868-Dec. 28, 1872	Reel 1400
v57-59	Jan. 5, 1878-Dec. 25, 1880	Reel 1401
v60-63	Jan. 15, 1881-Dec. 27, 1884	Reel 1402
v64-66	Jan. 3, 1885-Dec. 31, 1887	Reel 1403
v68-69	Jan. 5, 1889-Apr. 19, 1890	Reel 1404

Several pages are stained, torn, creased, or have print faded with some loss of text; several pages are misnumbered. Pagination is irregular. Best copy available for photographing.

Vol. 47: Issues 1-46 and 48 are missing; not available for photographing.
Vol. 48: Issues, 1, 4, 19, 21 and 32 are missing.
Vol. 49: Issues 16 and 49 are missing.
Vol. 50: Issues 18 and 26 are missing.
Vol. 51: Issue 22 is missing.
Vol. 60: Issues 1, 2, 4, 14, 16, 20, 31, 32, 36, 38, 49, 51 and 52 are missing.
Vol. 61: Issues 1, 8, 9, 13, 23, 31, 35, 36, 39-43, 45, 48 and 50-52 are missing.
Vol. 64: Issues 28, 33 and 48 are missing.
Vol. 66: Issue 1 pages 1-2 are missing. Issues 2, 17, 21, 26, 28, 32, 35, 38, 41, 43, 48 and 52 are missing.
Vol. 68: Issues 13, 17, 18, 20, 25, 27-29, 31, 34, 39, 42-44, 47-49 and 52 are missing.

Microfilm edition was prepared from DLC, ICRL, InLP, InU, MU, MWA, MiU-C and NN copies.

SEE ALSO: New England Farmer, A Monthly Journal (Boston.)

NEW-ENGLAND GALAXY. v1-21, no.44, Oct. 1817-Nov. 1838; new ser., v.1 no.1-14, Dec. 28, 1838-Mar. 29, 1839. Boston, J. T. Buckingham.

22 v. weekly.

From Oct. 10, 1817, to Oct. 6, 1820 title reads: New-England galaxy & masonic magazine.
Editor: J.T. Buckingham.

On film: vol. 1-20.

Joseph T. Buckingham founded the weekly *New England Galaxy* and was its editor until 1828, when he sold it to Willard Phillips and Theophilus Parsons. This literary miscellany consisted mainly of biographies, poetry, political and literary material, and masonic and agricultural news; and it gave special attention to the Boston theater. In 1824 it published William Austin's "Peter Rugg, the Missing Man."

New England Galaxy and Masonic Magazine

v1-3 (nos.1-116)	Oct. 10, 1817-Dec. 31, 1819	APS II, Reel 150
v3 (no.117-156)	Jan. 7, 1820-Oct. 6, 1820	Reel 151

New England Galaxy and United States Literary Advertiser

v4-5	Oct. 13, 1820-Dec. 27, 1822	Reel 151
v6-8	Jan. 3, 1823-Dec. 30, 1825	Reel 152
v9	Jan. 6, 1826-Dec. 29, 1826	Reel 1120
v10-13	Jan. 5, 1827-Dec. 31, 1830	Reel 1121
v14-17	Jan. 7, 1831-Dec. 27, 1834	Reel 1122
v18-20	Jan. 3, 1835-Dec. 31, 1836	Reel 1123

Vols. 9-20: No Index or Contents available.
Vol. 9: January 20, 1826 two pages missing.
Vol. 11: August 15, 1828 bound before August 8, 1828. Volume numbers misprinted.
Vol. 13: April 29, 1830 missing. April 23, 30, 1830 missing. May 27, June 4, 11, 1830 missing. June 25, July 16, 23, 30, August 6, 1830 missing. August 27, September 3, 17, 24, October 1, 8, 29, November 5, December 24, 1830 missing.
Vol. 15: Apr. 21-28 pages missing.
Vol. 19: January, March 26, missing. May 28 missing. November 12 missing. Volume ends with December 24.
Vol. 20: Starts with December 31.

Microfilm edition was prepared from MeBa, MWA, WHi copies.

SEE ALSO: Yankee and Boston Literary Gazette.

NEW-ENGLAND GALAXY & MASONIC MAGAZINE. *SEE* New-England Galaxy.

* THE NEW-ENGLAND HISTORICAL AND GENEALOGICAL REGISTER. v.1-Jan. 1847- Boston, S.G. Drake.

v. plates, ports., maps, facsims., tables.
Published quarterly by the New England historic genealogical society.

Vols. 23-27 have title: The New-England historical & genealogical register and antiquarian journal.

Editors: 1847, William Coswell.—1848-61, S.G. Drake and others.—1862-64, J.W. Dean.—1864-65, W.B. Trask.—1866-67, Elias Nason.—1868-75, A.H. Hoyt.—1876-Jan. 1901, J.W. Dean.—Apr. 1901-Oct. 1907, H.E. Woods.—1908-12, F.A. Foster.—1913- H.E. Scott.

Imprint varies: v.1-15, Boston, S.G. Drake [etc.] 1847-61 (v.6 pub. by T. Prince, v.11 by C.B. Richardson).—v.16-18, Albany, J. Munsell, 1863-64.—v.19- Boston, The Society, 1865-.

Indexes: Cumulative indexes. Vols. 1-41, 1847-1887; v.1-50 Jan. 1847-1896; v.1-10, 1847-1856, precede v.1. Place index. Vols. 1-41, 1847-1888, in v. 42.

Beginning with v.54 there is issued an annual supplement to the April number consisting of "Proceedings of the New-England historical genealogical society at the annual meeting ... 1900-".

On film: v.1-59; Jan. 1847-Oct. 1905.

Started by the New-England Historic-Genealogical Society, the *New-England Historical and Genealogical Register* published portraits, biographies, and genealogies of early Americans, historical documents, and book notices. Among the editors were William Cogswell, Samuel Drake, John W. Dean, William B. Trask, Elias Nason, Albert Hoyt, and Henry E. Woods.

New-England Historical and Genealogical Register

Cumulative Index 1-41	1847-1887	APS II, Reel 1053
Cumulative index 1-50	Jan. 1847-Oct. 1896	Reel 1053
Cumulative index 1-10	1847-1856	Reel 1053
v1-8	Jan. 1847-Oct. 1854	Reel 1053
v9-10	Jan. 1855-Oct. 1856	Reel 1054
Cumulative index 11-15	1857-1861	Reel 1054
v11-16	Jan. 1857-Oct. 1862	Reel 1054
v17-22	Jan. 1863-Oct. 1868	Reel 1055

New-England Historical and Genealogical Register and Antiquarian Journal

v23-24	Jan. 1869-Oct. 1870	Reel 1055
v25-27	Jan. 1871-Oct. 1873	Reel 1056

New-England Historical and Genealogical Register

v28-31	Jan. 1874-Oct. 1. 1877	Reel 1056
v32-39	Jan. 1878-Oct. 1885	Reel 1057
v40-45	Jan. 1886-Oct. 1891	Reel 1058
v46-50	Jan. 1892-Oct. 1896	Reel 1059
v51-55	Jan. 1897-Oct. 1901	Reel 1060
v56-59	Jan. 1902-Oct. 1905	Reel 1061

Pagination is irregular. Some pages are stained, torn, or have print missing.

Cumulative Index for Vols. 1-41 is entitled "Place Index to the Register. Cumulative Index for Vols. 1-50 is entitled "Index to Genealogies and Pedigrees." Cumulative Index for Vols. 1-10 is entitled "General Index." Following the October issue of Vol. 1, is a circular entitled "Circular Number Three of the New England Historic Genealogical Society." Vol. 42: Following the October issue, there is a Place Index to the Register for Vol. 1-41. Vol. 45: Following the index, there is an index of names and places in the Rolls of Membership for the years 1844-1890. The Rolls of Membership is at the end of the Volume.

Vol. 52: There is an Index to Testators in Water's Genealogical Gleanings for Vols. 37-42. Vols. 54-55: Following the October issues, there is a supplement entitled "Proceedings of the New-England Historic Genealogical Society." Vols. 56-59: Following the October issues, there is a supplement entitled "Proceedings of the New-England Historic Genealogical Society."

Microfilm edition was prepared from MiD, MiU, and NjP copies.

SEE ALSO: New Hampshire Repository.

NEW ENGLAND JOURNAL OF DENTISTRY AND ALLIED SCIENCES. v.1-3, no.12, Jan. 1882-Dec. 1884. Springfield, Mass., 1882-1884.

3 v.

v.3, nos.11-12 are reprints of Archives of dentistry v.1, nos.11-12.

New England Journal of Dentistry and Allied Sciences was a regional journal of current research and practice in dentistry and related sciences.

v1-3	Jan. 1882-Dec. 1884	APS III, Reel 269

Pages 301-304 are repeated in number only.

Microfilm edition was prepared from IaU, PU copies.

NEW ENGLAND JOURNAL OF EDUCATION. *SEE* Massachusetts Teacher.

THE NEW ENGLAND JOURNAL OF MEDICINE. v.1- ; Feb. 19, 1928- Boston.

illus., ports. weekly.

Formed by the union of the New England medical review and journal and the Boston medical intelligencer. Vols. 78-87 called also "new ser., v.1-10." Official organ of the Massachusetts Medical Society, July 2, 1914- of the New England Surgical Society, Oct. 19, 1916- and of other state medical societies.

Title varies: Feb. 19, 1828-Feb. 16, 1928, The Boston medical and surgical journal.
On film: issues for Feb. 19, 1828-Jan. 29, 1851.

In addition to the usual case studies and articles on medical methods and treatments, this medical periodical published selections from foreign medical journals, transactions of medical societies, biographical sketches, hospital reports, and reports of deaths in Boston. It was well illustrated and contained a number of advertisements.

Boston Medical and Surgical Journal

v1-8	Feb. 19, 1828-Aug. 1833	APS II, Reel 660
v9-18	Aug. 14, 1833-Aug. 1, 1838	Reel 661
v19-28	Aug. 8, 1838-Aug. 2, 1843	Reel 662
v29-36	Aug. 9, 1843-July 28, 1847	Reel 663
v37-43	Aug. 4, 1847-Jan. 29, 1851	Reel 664

Microfilm edition was prepared from IU, MiU and N copies.

THE NEW-ENGLAND JOURNAL OF MEDICINE AND SURGERY, and collateral branches of science. v.1-15, Jan. 1812-Oct. 1826. Boston, Bradford and Read.

15 v. plates, quarterly.

Superseded by the New-England medical review and journal. From 18-- to 1824, "conducted by a number of physicians"; from 1825 to 1826 by Walter Channing and John Ware.

Conducted by Dr. Walter Channing, Jr. and Dr. John Ware, this medical journal, which survived for fifteen years, included articles on the history and treatment of diseases in New England, descriptions of important cases and treatments, a medical news section, a meteorological journal, book reviews, and lists of new medical publications.

v1-3	Jan. 1812-Oct. 1814	Reel 153
v4-6	Jan. 1815-Oct. 1817	Reel 154
v7-9	Jan. 1818-Oct. 1820	Reel 155
v10-12	Jan. 1821-Oct. 1823	Reel 156
v13-14	Jan. 1824-Oct. 1825	Reel 157
v15	Jan.-Oct. 1826	Reel 944

Microfilm edition was prepared from ICRL, N, and Nh copies.

SEE ALSO: New England Medical Review and Journal.

NEW ENGLAND LITERARY HERALD. no.1-2; Sept. 1809-Jan. 1810. Boston, Farrand, Mallory.

2 no.

Published by Farrand, Mallory and Co., a book publishing firm, the sole purpose of the *New England Literary Herald* was to list and describe new and forthcoming books and periodicals, both their own and those of other publishers. Only two numbers were published.

no.1	Sept. 1809	APS II, Reel 34
no.2	Jan. 1810	Reel 218

Microfilm edition was prepared from DLC copy.

* NEW-ENGLAND MAGAZINE. v.1-9; July 1831-Dec. 1835. Boston, 1831-1835.

9 v.

Merged into American monthly magazine.

Perhaps the most important general magazine published in New England before the birth of the *Atlantic Monthly* was Buckingham's *New-England Magazine*. While its list of contributors was distinguished, the remuneration was small; one dollar per page of prose and two dollars for poetry. Longfellow, Hawthorne, Holmes, Whittier, Everett, George Hillard, Noah Webster and Samuel Kittell were but some of the people who wrote for the *Magazine*. In October 1834, Joseph Buckingham sold it to Samuel Howe and John O. Sargent. In March of 1835, Park Benjamin became editor and proprietor. In the ten issues he edited, the *New-England Magazine* reached its highest literary importance. In the June 1835 issue appeared the opening of Hawthorne's "The Ambitious Guest."

v1-7	July 1831-Dec. 1834	APS II, Reel 841
v8-9	Jan.-Dec. 1835	Reel 842

Microfilm edition was prepared from MiD, LN and NhD copies.

SEE ALSO: American Monthly Magazine *and* American Monthly Review.

THE NEW ENGLAND MAGAZINE OF KNOWLEDGE AND PLEASURE. no.1-3; Aug., Oct. 1758, Mar. 1759. Boston, Printed by B. Mecom [etc.]

3 no.

Title varies slightly.

Edited by U. Filter, pseud. of B. Mecom.

An eclectic collection of essays, extracts, and news.

no.1-3	Aug. 1758-Oct. 1758, Mar. 1759	APS I, Reel 19

Microfilm edition was prepared from MB and DLC copy.

THE NEW-ENGLAND MEDICAL REVIEW AND JOURNAL. Conducted by Walter Channing, and John Ware. v.1; Jan.-Oct. 1827. Boston, Wells and Lilly, 1827.

iv, 444p. plates. quarterly.

Supersedes the New England journal of medicine and surgery.
United with the Boston medical intelligencer to form the Boston Medical and surgical journal.

A medical journal conducted by Walter Channing and John Ware, which contained case descriptions, original papers, and treatises dealing with the medical profession. Diagrams illustrated these and other miscellaneous articles. Also included were reviews and reports of medical societies.

v1	Jan.-Oct. 1827	APS II, Reel 802

Microfilm edition was prepared from Ia-T copy.

SEE ALSO: Boston Medical Intelligencer *and* New England Journal of Medicine.

THE NEW ENGLAND MISSIONARY INTELLIGENCER, and general repository for the promotion of useful knowledge and evangelical doctrine. v.1, no.1-3; Jan.-Oct. 1819. Concord, N.Y., Printed by Hill and Moore.

84 p.

This short-lived Methodist periodical was mainly concerned with the activities of the Methodist Missionary Society, but also presented poetry and occasional biographical sketches.

v1, no1-3	Jan.-Oct. 1819	APS II, Reel 157

THE NEW-ENGLAND MISSIONARY MAGAZINE, for promoting useful knowledge and evangelical doctrine. [no.] 1-4; 1815-16. Concord [N.H.] Printed by I. Hill, 1815-16.

iv, 144 p.

Among the varied contents of this Methodist magazine were accounts of conversions, of the plague in London, and of the Inquisition, a history of persecution of Christians, and biographical sketches of several ministers, in addition to news of revivals, essays on religious subjects, and poetry.

no.1-4	1815-1816	APS II, Reel 157

NEW ENGLAND OFFERING. *SEE* Lowell Offering.

NEW ENGLAND QUARTERLY JOURNAL OF MEDICINE AND SURGERY. v.1, nos.1-4; July 1842-Apr. 1843. Boston, D. Clapp, 1843.

595 p.

A medical journal containing the standard material–original papers on recent cases and medical methods, reviews and bibliographic notices of recent medical publications, extracts from foreign and American medical journals, and a summary of the most recent medical news.

| v1 | July 1842-Apr. 1843 | APS II, Reel 816 |

Microfilm edition was prepared from MiU copy.

THE NEW ENGLAND QUARTERLY MAGAZINE; comprehending literature, morals and amusement. no.1-3; Apr.-Dec. 1802. Bost⌣⌣, H. Sprague, 1802.

3 v.

Only three numbers of this quarterly miscellany were published. Among the topics discussed in its pages were literature, philosophy, morals, education, science, agriculture, and manufacturing, and its contents also included book reviews, travel sketches, poetry, and biographical sketches, many of them about women.

| no.1-3 | Apr.-Dec. 1802 | APS II, Reel 34 |

Microfilm edition was prepared from DLC copy.

THE NEW-ENGLAND TELEGRAPH, AND ECLECTIC REVIEW. v.1-2; Jan. 1835-Dec. 1836. North Wrentham, Mass., 1835-36.

2 v. in 1. monthly.

Vol. 1 called also "new ser."
Moses Thacher, editor.

Edited by Moses Thacher, this was primarily a religious magazine, containing sermons, missionary news, religious and moral poetry, anecdotes, reviews of new publications, articles on slavery, and coverage of societies opposing slander, gambling, slavery, and smoking. Illustrations were included.

| v1-2 | Jan. 1835-Dec. 1836 | APS II, Reel 802 |

Vol. 1: Page 118 is misnumbered.

Microfilm edition was prepared from MBC and MWiW copies.

* NEW ENGLANDER. *SEE* New Englander and Yale Review.

* NEW ENGLANDER AND YALE REVIEW. v.1-36; 1843-77; v.37-[56] (new ser., v.1-20) 1878-Mar 1892. New Haven, W.L. Kingsley [1843-92]

56 v. plates, ports., map, plan.
Quarterly, 1843-77; bimonthly, 1878-85; monthly, 1886-92.
Vol. 9 has imprint: New York, S.W. Benedict, 1851.
Vol. 20 is an index to v.1-19.

Title varies: 1843-85, The New Englander. 1886-92, New Englander and Yale review.

Editors: 1843-46, E.R. Tyler.–1857?-65, W.L. Kingsley.–1866-75, W.L. Kingsley, G.P. Fisher, Timothy Dwight. Absorbed the

Congregational review, of Chicago, in 1872. Ceased publication in 1892, being replaced by the Yale review.

Begun by Edward Royall Tyler, the *New Englander* was one of the best religious quarterlies of the period. It was strongly Congregationalistic and an advocate of abolition. Although the greatest amount of space was allotted to theology, much attention was also given to controversy and nonreligious material. Politics, education, temperance, literary criticism, and history were dealt with regularly; scientific articles appeared occasionally. Fiction and poetry, and discussions of economics, philosophy, and social problems were also included. Many distinguished men were associated with the journal as editors; among these were Horace Bushnell, William T. Bacon, Noah Porter, and Theodor Woolsey. In 1892 the *New Englander* was sold, and shortly afterwards the *Yale Review* appeared in its place.

New Englander
| v1-4 | 1843-1846 | APS II, Reel 679 |
| v5-8 | 1847-1850 | Reel 680 |

Cumulative Index 1-19	Mar. 1843-Oct. 1861	Reel 904
v9-14	Feb. 1851-Nov. 1856	Reel 904
v15-18	Feb. 1857-Nov. 1860	Reel 905
v19-24	Jan. 1861-Oct. 1865	Reel 906
v25-29	Jan. 1866-Oct. 1870	Reel 907
v30-34	Jan. 1871-Oct. 1875	Reel 908
v35-39	Jan. 1876-Nov. 1880	Reel 909
v40-44	Jan. 1881-Nov. 1885	Reel 910

New Englander and Yale Review
| v45-51 | Jan. 1886-Dec. 1889 | Reel 911 |
| v52-56 | Jan. 1890-Mar. 1892 | Reel 912 |

Reels 904-912: Pagination is irregular. Some pages are stained. Vol. 9 also known as New Series Vol. 3. Vols. 15-16 lack indexes. Please refer to table of contents in each individual volume. Vol. 43, pages 479-486 missing; not available for photographing.

Microfilm edition was prepared from ICT, MiU, MnNC, NjP, and OCX copies.

NEW GENESEE FARMER AND GARDENERS' JOURNAL. *SEE* Genesee Farmer.

THE NEW HAMPSHIRE & VERMONT MAGAZINE, AND GENERAL REPOSITORY. v.1, no.[1]-4; July-Oct. 1797. Haverhill, N.H., J.M. Dunham.

184 p. monthly.

Film incomplete: no.2-3 (Aug.-Sept. 1797) wanting.

Mainly oriented toward government and politics, this monthly published the Declaration of Independence, the Constitution, reports of legislative bodies, treaties, and European news as well as biography, poetry, and anecdotes.

| v1, no.1, 4 | July, Oct. 1797 | APS I, Reel 20 |

Microfilm edition was prepared from DLC copy.

THE NEWHAMPSHIRE MAGAZINE; The Monthly repository of useful information. v.1, no.1-6; June-Nov. 1793. Concord, E. Russell.

384 p. monthly.

Contained much sentimental and romantic literature–novels, fragments, poetry, and pieces on love, manners and morals.

v1, no.1-6   June-Nov. 1793   APS I, Reel 19

Microfilm edition was prepared from WHi copy.

THE NEW-HAMPSHIRE NEW JERUSALEM MAGAZINE AND PRIMITIVE RELIGIOUS INTELLIGENCER. [no.1] Feb. 5, 1805. Portsmouth, N.H., J. Leigh.

22 p.

Contains selections from the writings of Emanuel Swedenborg.

This religious periodical proposed to publish selections from the writings of Emanuel Swedenborg and other members of the New Jerusalem Church, but it did not survive past its first number. The issue dated February 5, 1805 published a copy of the constitution of the New Jerusalem Church of Baltimore, prayers, and a hymn.

no.1   Feb. 5, 1805   APS II, Reel 34

Microfilm edition was prepared from DLC copy.

THE NEW HAMPSHIRE REPOSITORY; devoted to education, literature and religion. Conducted by Rev. William Cogswell. v.1, v.2, no.1-2; Oct. 1845-Jan. 1847. Gilmanton, Printed by A. Prescott, 1846-47.

2 v. in 1. ports. quarterly.

Merged into the New England historical and genealogical register.

In the words of the editor, the Reverend William Cogswell, this periodical is a "New Hampshire work" directed to ministers, officers of courts, attorneys, physicians and graduates of Dartmouth College. Volume 1, number 1 was issued under the auspices of the Gilmanton Theological Seminary. Shortly, the Reverend announced that he had been asked to become editor of the *New England Historical and Genealogical Register* and the two were merged.

v1-2   Oct. 1845-Jan. 1847   APS II, Reel 842

Microfilm edition was prepared from MiU copy.

NEW-HARMONY GAZETTE. *SEE* Free Enquirer.

THE NEW-HAVEN GAZETTE, AND THE CONNECTICUT MAGAZINE. v.1-4; Feb. 16, 1786-June 18, 1789. New Haven, J. Meigs.

4 v. weekly.

Issues for Sept. 18, 1788 and Dec. 11, 1788-June 18, 1789 lacking on film. Edited by J. Meigs.

Exhibited the tense political atmosphere of 1786-88 and advocated the adoption of a strong federal constitution. In addition to news, it contained essays, poetry, reprints, and much original material.

v1-3   Feb. 16, 1786-Dec. 4, 1788   APS I, Reel 20

Microfilm edition was prepared from MWA and WHi copy.

THE NEW JERSEY AND PENNSYLVANIA AGRICULTURAL MONTHLY INTELLIGENCER AND FARMER'S MAGAZINE. v.1; nos.1-10; May 2, 1825-Oct. 26, 1826.

1 v.

Issues for 1825 have caption title: The Agricultural Magazine.

Edited by Samuel Ellis, this monthly agricultural magazine provided information on methods for raising crops and livestock, on current prices, and on the activities of agricultural societies along with other regional farming news.

v1   May, Oct. and Nov. 1825   APS II, Reel 158

v1   May 2, 1825-Oct. 26, 1826   Reel 1123

Some pages have faded print. Reel 1123: Introduction page states there are 12 issues and 400 pages. We have only 10 issues and 432 pages. Vol. 1: No Index available.

Microfilm edition was prepared from NjR copy.

THE NEW-JERSEY MAGAZINE AND MONTHLY ADVERTISER. Dec. 1786-Feb. 1787. New Brunswick, Printed by F. Quequelle and J. Prange.

3 no. monthly.

Patterned after earlier magazines, it contained mostly reprinted material, general essays on morals and manners, sentimental essays and melancholy love stories, poetry, and articles on diversified subjects—medicine, social morality, religion, and literary criticism.

Dec. 1786-Feb. 1787   APS I, Reel 21

Microfilm edition was prepared from DLC and NN copies.

NEW JERSEY MEDICAL REPORTER. *SEE* Medical and Surgical Reporter. (Burlington, N.J.)

NEW JERSEY MEDICAL REPORTER AND TRANSACTIONS OF THE NEW JERSEY MEDICAL SOCIETY. *SEE* Medical and Surgical Reporter. (Burlington, N.J.)

THE NEW JERSEY MONTHLY MAGAZINE. v.1, no.1; Apr. 1825. [Newark]

32 p.

The only number of this literary miscellany published contained poetry, biography, and essays on literature, travel, and other topics.

v1, no.1   Apr. 1825   APS II, Reel 158

THE NEW JERUSALEM CHURCH REPOSITORY. v.1, no.1-8; Jan. 1817-Dec. 1818. Philadelphia, Printed by L.R. Bailey.

540 p. quarterly.

Issued by the American Society for the Dissemination of the Doctrines of the New Jerusalem Church.
Superseded by the New Jerusalem record.

The purpose of this religious quarterly was to disseminate the doctrines of Emanuel Swedenborg. It published extracts from Swedenborg's writings and biographical material, news of churches and church societies, book reviews and notices of new publications, Bible studies, and poetry.

v1, no.1-8   Jan. 1817-Dec. 1818   APS II, Reel 157

SEE ALSO: New Jerusalem Record.

THE NEW JERUSALEM MISSIONARY AND INTELLECTUAL REPOSITORY. v.1; May 1823-Apr. 1824. New York.

384 p. monthly.

Edited by S. Woodworth.

Published by the "New-York Society for Dissemination of the Heavenly Doctrines of the New-Jerusalem," this monthly Swedenborgian magazine was devoted to theological subjects and particularly to the writings and ideas of Emanuel Swedenborg.

v1   May 1823-Apr. 1824   APS II, Reel 158

THE NEW JERUSALEM RECORD. v.1, no.1; July 1820. [Philadelphia]

16 p.

Supersedes the New Jerusalem Church repository.

This short-lived Swedenborgian magazine was a successor to the *New Jerusalem Church Repository,* and like the *Repository,* the *Record* promoted the doctrines of Emanuel Swedenborg. It contained church-related news and the proceedings of a convention held in Philadelphia in May, 1820.

v1, no.1   July 1820   APS II, Reel 158

SEE ALSO: New Jerusalem Church Repository.

NEW MCCLURE'S. *SEE* McClure's Magazine.

THE NEW MIRROR; edited by G.P. Morris and N.P. Willis. v.1-3; Apr. 8, 1843-Sept. 28, 1844. New York, Morris, Willis, 1843-44.

3 v. illus., plates ports. weekly.

Vol. 1, no.1 has title: The New mirror, of literature, amusement, and instruction. Edited by George P. Morris, illustrated by J.G. Chapman.

Supersedes the New York mirror (1823-42)
Superseded by the Weekly mirror (called later New York mirror).
Extra numbers were published with the New mirror. These numbers and others issued in the same form compose the "Mirror library" edited by Morris and Willis.

The *New Mirror* was edited by Nathaniel Parker Willis and managed by George Pope Morris who had formerly edited the *New York Mirror.* The *New Mirror* is described well by its subhead:

"Containing Original Papers, Tales of Romance, Sketches of Society, Manners, and Everyday Life; Domestic and Foreign Correspondence; Wit and Humor; Fashion and Gossip; the Fine Arts, and Literary, Musical, and Dramatic Criticism; Extracts from New Works; Poetry, Original and Selected; the Spirit of the Public Journals, etc., etc."

After about a year, it was discontinued in favor of a daily newspaper, the *Evening Mirror* and its adjunct, the *Weekly Mirror.*

v1-3   Apr. 8, 1843-Sept. 28, 1844   APS II, Reel 1124

Vols. 1-3: no indexes are available. Some pages are stained, taped, or damaged..

Microfilm edition was prepared from NB copy.

SEE ALSO: New York Mirror: A Weekly Gazette of Literature and the Fine Arts.

THE NEW MONTHLY MAGAZINE AND LITERARY JOURNAL. American ed. v.1-10, 1821-1825; new ser., v.1-3, 1833-1834. Boston, Allen and Ticknor.

10 v.

"Republished" from the English copy, the *New Monthly Magazine* gave Americans insight into British literary writings. The earlier volumes contained miscellaneous essays, occasional poetry, and some literary criticism, while the later years were expanded to include book reviews and Parliamentary and foreign news. Contributors included Thomas Bayly, William Godwin, Mrs. Hermans, and "Sylvanus Swanquill, Esq."

v1-2	Jan.-Dec. 1821	APS II, Reel 158
v3-5	Jan. 1822-June 1823	Reel 159
v6-8	July 1823-Dec. 1824	Reel 160
v9-10	Jan.-Dec. 1825	Reel 161
nsv1-3	Jan. 1833-June 1834	Reel 881

Reel 881: Pagination is irregular. Some pages are stained.

Microfilm edition was prepared from IMunS copy.

NEW ORLEANS MISCELLANY; a monthly periodical, devoted to the interests of popular science, and to the advancement of southern literature. v.1, no.1-3; Dec. 1847-Feb. 1848. New Orleans, 1847-1848.

1 v. (various pagings)

Edited by D. Macaulay.

Edited by D. Macaulay, the *New Orleans Miscellany* was a magazine of science and literature dedicated to the "Southern Public."

v1   Dec. 1847-Feb. 1848   APS II, Reel 973

Index lacking; please refer to the Table of Contents. Pages 9-16 are missing. The Jan. (no2) issue ends page 178; Feb. issue begins with page 105. Pages 143-158 are missing. Best copy available for photographing.

Microfilm edition was prepared from LU copy.

NEW OUTLOOK. v.1-165, no.6; Jan. 1870-June 1935. New York, Outlook Pub. Co.

165 v. in 164. illus., plates, ports.
Weekly, Jan. 1870-Jan. 1932; monthly, Feb. 1932-June 1935.
Publication suspended, May-Sept. 1932, inclusive.

Title varies: Jan. 1870-June 1893, The Christian union. July 1893-Oct. 17, 1928, The Outlook. Oct. 24, 1928-Feb. 1932, Outlook and Independent. Mar.-Apr. 1932, Outlook. Oct. 1932-June 1935, New Outlook.

Editors: Oct. 1932-Mar. 1934, Alfred E. Smith.—Apr. 1934-June 1935, Francis Walton.

First edited by Henry Ward Beecher, this religious weekly was very successful. Sermons, Sunday School lessons, and fiction were emphasized until the change in name to *Outlook* when current events, autobiographies of famous people, travel writings, and art and literary criticism gained importance. Among the contributors were Harriet Beecher Stowe, Helen Hunt Jackson, Edward Eggleston, Louisa May Alcott, E.E. Hale, and Theodor Roosevelt. Lyman Abbott, editor for 47 years, was assisted by H.W. Mabie.

Christian Union

v1	Jan. 1870-June 1870	APS III, Reel 367
v2-3	July 1870-June 1871	Reel 368
v4-6	July 1871-Dec. 1872	Reel 369
v7-9	Jan. 1873-July 1874	Reel 370
v10-12	July 1874-Dec. 1875	Reel 371
v13-15	Jan. 1876-June 1877	Reel 372
v16-18	July 1877-Dec. 1878	Reel 373
v19-21	Jan. 1879-June 1880	Reel 374
v22-24	July 1880-Dec. 1881	Reel 375
v25-27	Jan. 1882-June 1883	Reel 376
v28-30	July 1883-Dec. 1884	Reel 377
v31-32	Jan. 1885-Dec. 1885	Reel 378
v33-34	Jan. 1886-Dec. 1886	Reel 379
v35-36	Jan. 1887-Dec. 1887	Reel 380
v37-38	Jan. 1888-Dec. 1888	Reel 381
v39-40	Jan. 1889-Dec. 1889	Reel 382
v41-42	Jan. 1890-Dec. 1890	Reel 383
v43-44	Jan. 1891-Dec. 1891	Reel 384
v45-46	Jan. 1892-Dec. 1892	Reel 385
v47	Jan.-June 1893	Reel 386

Outlook

v48	July-Dec. 1893	Reel 386
v49-50	Jan. 1894-Dec. 1894	Reel 387
v51-52	Jan. 1895-Dec. 1895	Reel 388
v53-54	Jan. 1896-Dec. 1896	Reel 389
v55-57	Jan. 1897-Dec. 1897	Reel 390
v58-60	Jan. 1898-Dec. 1898	Reel 391
v61-63	Jan. 1899-Dec. 1899	Reel 392
v64-66	Jan. 1900-Dec. 1900	Reel 393
v67-69	Jan. 1901-Dec. 1901	Reel 394
v70-72	Jan. 1902-Dec. 1902	Reel 395
v73-75	Jan. 1903-Dec. 1903	Reel 396
v76-78	Jan. 1904-Dec. 1904	Reel 397
v79-81	Jan. 1905-Dec. 1905	Reel 398
v82-83	Jan. 1906-Aug. 1906	Reel 399
v84-85	Sept. 1906-Apr. 1907	Reel 400
v86-88	May 1907-Apr. 1908	Reel 401
v89-91	May 1908-Apr. 1909	Reel 402
v92-94	May 1909-Apr. 1910	Reel 403
v95-97	May 1910-Apr. 1911	Reel 404
v98-100	May 1911-Apr. 1912	Reel 405
v101-103	May 1912-Apr. 1913	Reel 406
v104-106	May 1913-Apr. 1914	Reel 407
v107-109	May 1914-Apr. 1915	Reel 408
v110-112	May 1915-Apr. 1916	Reel 409
v113-115	May 1916-Apr. 1917	Reel 410
v116-118	May 1917-Apr. 1918	Reel 411
v119-121	May 1918-Apr. 1919	Reel 412
v122-125	May 1919-Aug. 1920	Reel 413
v126-129	Sept. 1920-Dec. 1921	Reel 414
v130-132	Jan. 1922-Dec. 1922	Reel 415
v133-135	Jan. 1923-Dec. 1923	Reel 416
v136-138	Jan. 1924-Dec. 1924	Reel 417
v139-142	Jan. 1925-Apr. 1926	Reel 418
v143-147	May 1926-Dec. 1927	Reel 419
v148-150	Jan.-Oct. 17, 1928	Reel 420

Outlook and Independent

v150-151	Oct. 24, 1928-Apr. 1929	Reel 420
v152-155	May 1929-Aug. 1930	Reel 421
v156-159	Sept. 1930-Dec. 1931	Reel 422
v160	Jan.-Feb. 1932	Reel 423

Outlook

v160	Mar.-Apr. 1932	Reel 423

New Outlook

v161-165	Oct. 1932-June 1935	Reel 423

Some pages are stained, torn, tightly bound, or have print missing. Pagination is irregular. Many pages are missing and Table of Contents is missing for many issues. Vol. 1, No. 1: Contains hand written Index. Vol. 5: No Index for issues 1-26. Vol. 6: No Index for issues 1-26. Vol. 7: Advertisement supplement follows end of text. Vol. 19, No.10: Advertisement supplement appears on pages 1-4. No.23: Advertisement supplement appears on pages 545-48. Vol. 35, No.11: Advertisement supplement appears at end of text. Vol. 36, No.17: Advertisement supplement appears at end of text.

Microfilm was prepared from C,CCC, DLC, Ia-T, Mi, MiEM, NBuG, NIC, NSyU, and WHi copies.

NEW PETERSON MAGAZINE. *SEE* Peterson Magazine.

NEW PRINCETON REVIEW. *SEE* Princeton Review.

THE NEW STAR. Feb. 2, 1796. Hartford, A. Kinsley.

2 p.

Intended as a weekly, but existing in a unique number.

The only issue published dealt with emigration to Kentucky and with activities of the House of Representatives.

Feb. 2, 1796	APS I, Reel 23

Microfilm edition was prepared from MWA copy.

THE NEW STAR; a Republican miscellaneous, literary paper. no.1-26; Apr. 11-Oct. 3, 1797. Concord, Russel & Davis.

208 p. Weekly.

Two editions were simultaneously issued with the same title, number, date and paging: one a Republican paper, devoted to general news; the other, A Republican miscellaneous and literary paper, devoted wholly to literature. Cf. Evans. American bibliography. This film includes both editions.

"A Republican paper" was devoted to foreign and domestic events, political articles, affairs of legislative bodies, and general news; "A Republican miscellaneous and literary paper" contained poetry, humorous anecdotes, essays on morals and marriage, advice on conduct, and other literary material.

no.1-26	Apr. 11-Oct. 3, 1797	APS I, Reel 23

Nos. 1 and 11 are missing.

Microfilm edition was prepared from NhHi copy.

NEW TIME. *SEE* Arena.

THE NEW WORLD; a quarterly review of religion, ethics and theology. v.1-9 (no. 1-36); Mar. 1892-Dec. 1900. Boston and New York, Houghton, Mifflin; London, Gay and Bird [1892-1900]

9 v.

Supersedes Unitarian review.
Includes section "Book reviews".

C.C. Everett, C.H. Toy, Orello Cone, N.P. Gilman, editors.

Edited by Orello Cone, the Professors Charles C. Everett and Crawford H. Toy, and the Reverend Nicholas P. Gilman, the *New World* provided a well-written theological review. John White Chadwick, Joseph Henry Allen, Charles B. Upton, Josiah Royce, George A. Barton, William H. Lyon, and many others contributed the reviews and essays.

v1-4	Mar. 1892-Dec. 1895	APS III, Reel 31
v5-9	Mar. 1896-Dec. 1900	Reel 32

Microfilm edition was prepared from MiU copy.

SEE ALSO: Unitarian Review.

THE NEW WORLD; a weekly family journal of popular literature, science, art and news. v.1-10, June 6, 1840-May 10, 1845. New York, J. Winchester [etc.]

10 v. illus.
"Quarto edition."

Subtitle varies.
––– Extra series: no.1-104/105; Apr. 16, 1842-Jan. 1844. New York, J. Winchester.

v. illus.

No. 1-22 called Extra numbers.
Included at the end are, "Books for the people": Modern Chivalry, Loiterings of Arthur O'Leary, S.D., or, Accounts of Irish heirs, and the life and adventures of Martin Chuzzlewit. New York, 1844. Folio edition: v.1-2 (no.1-62), Oct. 26, 1839-Dec. 26, 1840. 2 v. illus. "No more published?"

The *New World* was one of the "mammoth" weeklies of the 1840's, so called because its pages were sometimes more than four feet long and eleven columns wide. A quarto edition was also published. Editors Park Benjamin and Rufus Wilmot Griswold, who had previously served as editors of a rival paper, the *Brother Jonathan,* set out to beat the book publishers by reprinting complete novels as "extras." Their messengers would meet the incoming steamships, thus receiving the earliest copies of the new English novels, which were then quickly set into type. The regular issue featured tales, poetry, and articles on literature, science, music, and the arts. After Benjamin and his colleague James Aldrich were succeeded in Mar. 1844 by Henry C. Deming and the Rev. James McKay, the *New World* became somewhat tamer; political, naval, military, and foreign news were given coverage, more illustrations appeared, and serialized tales, such as "The Wandering Jew" were featured in many issues.

v1-2	June 6, 1840-June 26, 1841	APS II, Reel 1696
v3-5	July 3, 1841-Dec. 31, 1842	Reel 1697
v6-8	Jan. 7, 1843-June 29, 1844	Reel 1698
v9-10	July 6, 1844-May 10, 1845	Reel 1699
Extra series no. 1-38	Oct.-Dec. 1842	Reel 1700
Extra series no.39-105	Dec. 1842-Jan. 1844	Reel 1700
Folio edition 1-2	Oct. 26, 1839-Dec. 26, 1840	Reel 1700

Extra series numbers 9-10, 23-24 and 78 are lacking; not available for photographing.

Microfilm edition was prepared from DLC, IU, NjP and PU copies.

NEW YORK BAPTIST REGISTER. *SEE* Western New York Baptist Magazine.

NEW YORK CITIZEN AND ROUND TABLE. *SEE* Round Table.

THE NEW YORK CITY HALL RECORDER, containing reports of the most interesting trials and decisions which have arisen in the various Courts of judicature, for the trial of jury causes in the hall, particularly in the Court of Sessions. v.1-6; Jan. 1817-Jan. 1822. New York, Printed by C.N. Baldwin.

6 v. monthly.

Edited by D. Rogers.

Edited by Daniel Rogers, an attorney, this publication consisted entirely of brief descriptions of various legal cases which were tried in the New York City Hall. Critical and explanatory notes and remarks were included and summaries and an index appear at the end.

v1-6	Jan. 1817-Jan. 1822	APS II, Reel 211

Pagination is irregular in Vol. 2 and Vol. 4; Vol. 5 contains 13 issues.

NEW YORK DISTRICT SCHOOL JOURNAL. *SEE* District School Journal of the State of New York.

NEW YORK EVANGELIST. *SEE* Evangelist and Religious Review.

NEW YORK FARMER. v.1-10, Jan. 1828-Dec. 1837. New York, New York Horticultural Society, 1828-1837.

10 v.

Subtitle varies; vols.6-10 also as new ser. vol.1-5.

Regional agricultural journal edited in the early 1830's by Samuel Fleet.

v1-7	Jan. 1828-Dec. 1834	APS II, Reel 1195
v8-10	Jan. 1835-Oct. 1837	Reel 1196

Several pages are stained, creased, torn, or tightly bound with some loss of text. Some print faded. Vol. 1: Pages 117-20 are missing; pagination is irregular. Vol. 5: June 21 issue lacks title page. Vol. 10: Index is missing.

Microfilm edition was prepared from ICRL, InLP, N, NIC, NjP, and WHi copies.

THE NEW YORK GENEALOGICAL AND BIOGRAPHICAL RECORD. Devoted to the interests of American genealogy and biography. v.1- Jan. 1870- New York, New York Genealogical and Biographical Society [1870-19

v. illus., plates (incl. coats of arms) ports., maps. plans, facsims. quarterly.

Supersedes Bulletin of the New York genealogical and biographical Society (v.1, no.1; Dec. 1869)
Editors: 1895-Jan. 1900, R.H. Greene.-Apr. 1900-Jan. 1902, H.R. Stiles.-Apr. 1902-Apr. 1907, M.E. Dwight.-July 1907-Jan. 1910, G.A. Morrison.-Apr. 1910-Jan. 1911, H.S. Mott.-Apr. 1911-Jan. 1912, J.R. Totten.-Apr. 1912-H.S. Motto. On p. 3 of cover this

work is listed as v.5 of the Collections of the society; no volume number appears on t.-p. In 1913 another work was published as v.5 of the Collections with volume number on t.-p. Cumulative index for v.1-38 appears at beginning of v.1. On film: issues for 1870-1910.

This quarterly continuation of the Society's *Bulletin* contained biographies of literary, political, and military personalities, genealogical records, portraits, and church and probate data.

v1-10	1870-1879	APS III, reel 451
v11-20	1880-1889	Reel 452
v21-30	1890-1899	Reel 453
v31-37	1900-1906	Reel 454
v38-41	1907-1910	Reel 455

Vol. 1: No Subject Index. Vol. 17: Pages 117-96 are missing in number only. Vol. 22 and 25: Table of Contents for issue number 1 is torn.

Microfilm edition was prepared from CSmH and DLC copies.

SEE ALSO: New York Genealogical and Biographical Society. Bulletin ...

NEW YORK GENEALOGICAL AND BIOGRAPHICAL SOCIETY. Bulletin of the New York genealogical and biographical society. v.1, no.1; Dec. 1869. [New York, 1869]

8 p.

Caption title.
Superseded by the New York genealogical and biographical record.

Only one issue of this predecessor to the *New York Genealogical and Biographical Record* was published.

| v1 | Dec. 1869 | APS III, Reel 451 |

Microfilm edition was prepared from DLC copy.

SEE ALSO: New York Genealogical and Biographical Record.

NEW YORK ILLUSTRATED MAGAZINE OF LITERATURE AND ART. Edited by Lawrence Labree. v.1-3; Sept. 20, 1845-[June?] 1847. New York, W. Taylor, 1846-47.

3 v. illus., plates.
Added title-pages, engraved.

Weekly, Sept.-Dec.? 1845; monthly, 1846-47.
Vol. 1 has imprint on added t.-p.: New York, Robinson & co., 1845.
Supersedes Rover.

Included in this periodical are numerous elegantly-finished steel engravings. For the most part, however, there are stories and poems to delight the ladies.

| v1-3 | Sept. 20, 1845-June 1847 | APS II, Reel 842 |

Microfilm edition was prepared from MiD and CtY copies.

SEE ALSO: Rover.

NEW YORK ILLUSTRATED NEWS. *SEE* Ballou's Pictorial Drawing-Room Companion.

NEW YORK JOURNAL AND WEEKLY MONITOR. *SEE* Lady's Monitor.

NEW YORK JOURNAL OF MEDICINE. v.1-10, July 1843-May 1848; ser. 2, v.1-16, July 1848-May 1856; ser. 3, v.1-8, July 1856-May 1860. New York, 1848-1860.

34 v.

Ser. 1-2 as New York journal of medicine and collateral science. Superseded by American medical times.

Although this medical journal with its continuation did not quite outlast the war, it was an important periodical. It covered anatomy, physiology, pathology, surgery, obstetrics, and toxicology, among other areas, and included sections which presented original papers describing new methods of treatment for various illnesses, American and foreign medical news, reviews of new publications, and a "meteorological register."

v1-10	July 1843-May 1848	APS II, Reel 665
nsv1-8	July 1848-May 1852	Reel 666
nsv9-16	July 1852-May 1856	Reel 667
s3v1-8	July 1856-May 1860	Reel 668

Microfilm edition was prepared from MiU copy.

NEW YORK JOURNAL OF MEDICINE AND COLLATERAL SCIENCES. *SEE* New York Journal of Medicine.

NEW YORK LAW REVIEW. *SEE* American Law Review.

THE NEW-YORK LEGAL OBSERVER, containing reports of cases decided in the courts of equity and common law, and important decisions in the English courts; also, articles on legal subjects, with a table of cases, a general index, and a digest of the reports. Edited by Samuel Owen. v.1-12; Oct. 1, 1842-Nov./Dec. 1854. New York, S. Owen, 1843-54.

12 v.
Weekly (irregular) Oct. 1842-May 1843; semimonthly (irregular) June 1843-May 1844; monthly, Mar. 1845-Nov./Dec. 1854. Publication suspended June 1844-Feb. 1845, inclusive.

This legal magazine, edited by Samuel Owen and lasting 13 years, was intended mainly for those in the legal profession. It reported on cases in the U.S. and on important decisions in the English courts, gave accounts of remarkable trials, reviewed new works, and included articles on legal subjects, news of legal appointments, and digests of cases. On the lighter side, it provided epigrams, anecdotes, and some legal fiction.

| v1-4 | Oct. 1, 1842-Dec. 1846 | APS II, Reel 802 |
| v5-12 | Jan. 1847-Dec. 1854 | Reel 803 |

Several volumes have duplicate page numbers. Vol. 5: Pgs. 467-68 are not available for photographing. Vol. 6: Pgs. 161-68 are missing in number only.

Microfilm edition was prepared from Ia-T, MiU and NBu copies.

NEW YORK LITERARY GAZETTE. nos. 1-24; Feb. 2-July 13, 1839. New York, 1839.

24 no.

The *New York Literary Gazette,* edited by James Aldrich, gave reviews of art and of literary works. In addition, notes on the theater, some poetry, and original correspondence appeared.

no.1-24   Feb. 2-July 13, 1839   APS II, Reel 973

Several pages are lacking. Best copy available for photographing.

Microfilm edition was prepared from NN, NHi, and MWA copies.

SEE ALSO: American Athenaeum, A Repository of Belles Lettres, Science and the Arts *and* Minerva.

NEW YORK LITERARY GAZETTE AND JOURNAL OF BELLES LETTRES, ARTS, SCIENCE, &c. nos.1-19; Sept. 1, 1834-Mar. 14, 1835. New York, 1834-1835.

19 no.

Reviews of new publications, and art and drama criticism were the main subjects treated in this journal edited by A.D. Paterson.

Nov. 15, 1834-Feb. 14, 1835   APS II, Reel 1292

Best copy available for photographing. Complete numbers are not available for photographing. The microfilm edition contains nos. 6-7, 10, 12, and 15. Some pages are stained, creased, tightly bound, and have print missing.

Microfilm edition was prepared from DLC copy.

NEW YORK LITERARY GAZETTE AND PHI BETA KAPPA REPOSITORY. *SEE* Literary Gazette and American Athenaeum.

THE NEW-YORK LITERARY JOURNAL, and belles-lettres repository. v.1-4; May 1819-Apr. 1821. New York, A.T. Goodrich & co. [etc.] 1819-21.

4 v. monthly.

Title varies: May 1819-Apr. 1820, The Belles-lettres repository, and monthly magazine. (Title varies slightly) May 1820-Apr. 1821, The New-York literary journal and belles-lettres repository.

Begun as a monthly, this literary magazine presented a wide assortment of material on literature and the arts. Included were notices of new publications, both American and foreign, biographical sketches of literary figures, and a variety of news on the fine arts, such as notices of art exhibitions and musical events. Some poetry and light readings were also provided, along with items on manners and morals.

Belles-Lettres Repository, and Monthly Magazine
v1   May 1819-Oct. 1819   APS II, Reel 161
v2   Nov. 1819-Apr. 1820   Reel 162

New-York Literary Journal, and Belles-Lettres Repository
v3-4   May 1820-Apr. 1821   Reel 162

THE NEW-YORK MAGAZINE AND GENERAL REPOSITORY OF USEFUL KNOWLEDGE. v.1 (no.1-3); May 1-July 1, 1814. New York, 1814.

128 p.

Caption title
James Hardie, editor.

Edited by James Hardie, this monthly miscellany was concerned with promoting literature, education, morality, and religion, and also gave coverage to improvements in agriculture, manufacturing, mechanics, and in various arts and sciences. Some biography and poetry, mainly by American poets, were also included, and news summaries appeared at the end.

v1, nos1-3   May 1-July 1, 1814   APS II, Reel 162

THE NEW-YORK MAGAZINE, OR LITERARY REPOSITORY. v.1-6, Jan. 1790-Dec. 1795; new ser., v.1-2, Jan. 1796-Dec. 1797. New York, T. and J. Swords, 1790-97.

8 v. plates, maps. monthly.

One of the longest-lived magazines of the eighteenth century, the *New York Magazine,* included accounts of the theatre and travel along with current events and extracts.

v1-3   Jan. 1790-Dec. 1792   APS I, Reel 21
v4-6   Jan. 1793-Dec. 1795   Reel 22
nsv1-2   Jan. 1796-Dec. 1797   Reel 22

Some pages are lacking.

Microfilm edition was prepared from MiU-C and NN copies.

THE NEW-YORK MEDICAL AND PHILOSOPHICAL JOURNAL AND REVIEW. v.1-3. New-York, T. & J. Swords, 1809-11.

3 v. Two no. a year.

This varied medical journal published papers by physicians describing cases and treatments, reviewed medical books, and gave statistics on deaths in New York, including cause of death, and also included foreign and domestic news items and articles on science and chemistry.

v1   1809   APS II, Reel 34

v2-3   1810-1811   Reel 162

Microfilm edition was prepared from MB copy.

THE NEW YORK MEDICAL AND PHYSICAL JOURNAL. v.1-9; Jan. 1822-Dec. 1830. New York, E. Bliss and E. White.

9 v. illus; quarterly.

v.8-9 also called new ser. v.1-2.

This medical journal described recent advances in the medical field, both in the U.S. and abroad, and contained articles on diseases and treatments, reviews of recent medical publications, bibliographical notices, and a section of medical news, which reported on medical legislation and the activities of medical societies and colleges.

v1-3   Jan. 1822-Dec. 1824   APS II, Reel 163
v4   Jan.-Dec. 1825   Reel 164

v5-6   Jan. 1826-Dec. 1827   Reel 718
v7-9   Jan. 1828-Dec. 1830   Reel 719

Microfilm edition was prepared from CSt-L copy.

NEW YORK MEDICAL JOURNAL. *SEE* Medical News.

THE NEW YORK MEDICAL MAGAZINE. v.1 no.1-2; Jan. 1814-Jan. 1815. New York, Printed by N. van Riper.

364 p. annual.

Edited by V. Motto and H.U. Onderdonk.

This medical journal was edited by Valentine Mott, a professor at the University of New York, and Henry Onderdonk, a member of the Royal College of Surgeons in London. It published papers on medical theory, and on various diseases and treatments, descriptions of cases, book reviews, and foreign and domestic medical news items.

v1, nos.1-2   Jan. 1814-Jan. 1815   APS II, Reel 164

THE NEW-YORK MIRROR: a weekly gazette of literature and the fine arts. v.1-20; Aug. 2, 1823-Dec. 31, 1842. New York, G. P. Morris, 1824-42.

20 v. in 19. illus., plates, ports.

Absorbed the American monthly magazine in Sept. 1831.
Title varies: v.107, The New-york mirror, and ladies' literary gazette. v.8, Caption: The New-York mirror, a repository of polite literature and the arts. (Title-page: The New-York mirror, and ladies' literary gazette) v.9-18, The New-York mirror: a weekly journal, devoted to literature and the fine arts. v.19-20, Caption title: The New-York mirror: a weekly gazette of literature and the fine arts. (Title-page of v.20: The New-York mirror: a weekly gazette of the belles lettres and the fine arts ...)

Founded by Samuel Woodworth and George P. Morris. Woodworth withdrew from the editorship at the close of the first volume. T.S. Fay and N.P. Willis were later associated with Morris as editors. Continued as the New mirror (3 v. Apr. 8, 1843-Sept. 28, 1844) which was succeeded by the Weekly mirror (1 v. Oct. 12, 1844-Apr. 5, 1845) and the Evening mirror. In 1845 Morris founded the National press and changed the title in Nov. 1846 to the Home journal (continued in Mar. 1901 as Town and country).

Founded in 1823 by the poets George Pope Morris and Samuel Woodworth, the *Mirror* was a well-printed and illustrated eight-page quarto of miscellaneous character. It played a very important part in the rise of the Knickerbocker literary school, and was a fashionable journal of New York society. Its great forte was its comment on the passing interests of the day—fads and foibles, the enthusiasms of the people, the great popular interests—and thus for the social historian is an invaluable record. Literary reviews; original tales, usually sentimental; notes on music; a weekly record of New York theater; biography; verse; familiar essays; and "Desultory Selections"—these came to make up the *Mirror's* bill of fare. Politics were ignored, and dramatic and art criticism were important elements. Attention was given to women's interests as well, including a monthly fashion section. The *Mirror* was one of the earliest papers to use woodcuts extensively; in 1827 a few engravings on copper, chiefly of public buildings, appeared, and thereafter there were about four a year. In the late thirties it was transferred to Daniel Fanshaw, and cheaper eclectic material appeared. In spite of an improvement just before the suspension, it was abandoned at the end of 1842.

v1-2, no.22   Aug. 2, 1823-Dec. 25, 1824   APS II, Reel 164
v2, no.23-v3, no.23   Jan. 1-Dec. 31, 1825   Reel 165

v3, no.24-v10   Jan. 7, 1826-June 29, 1833   Reel 785
v11-17   July 6, 1833-June 20, 1840   Reel 786
v18-20   June 27, 1840-Dec. 31, 1842   Reel 787

Some pages are stained throughout. Vol. 8: Issue 51 repeats page numbering of issue 50.

Microfilm edition was prepared from MWA, MiD, MiU and N copies.

SEE ALSO: American Monthly Magazine; Critic. A Weekly Review of Literature, Fine Arts, and the Drama; New Mirror.

NEW-YORK MIRROR, AND LADIES' LITERARY GAZETTE. *SEE* New-York Mirror.

THE NEW-YORK MISSIONARY MAGAZINE, and repository of religious intelligence. v.1-4; [Jan.] 1800-Dec. 1803. New York, Printed by T. & J. Swords for C. Davis.

4 v.
Bimonthly, 1800-01; monthly, 1802-03.

The *New York Missionary Magazine* was an organ of the interdenominational New York Missionary Society and was the first of its kind. Content material, much of it selected, was made up of proceedings of missionary societies, stories of missionary experiences, accounts of revivals, religious news, and some biography and miscellany.

v1-4   Jan. 1800-Dec. 1803   APS II, Reel 35

Vol. 1: p. 1 missing.

Microfilm edition was prepared from MiU and DLC copy.

THE NEW YORK MONTHLY CHRONICLE OF MEDICINE AND SURGERY. v.1; July 1824-June 1825. New York, E. Bliss & E. White.

380 p. monthly.

This medical journal consisted of original papers by physicians on medical theory, on various cases and treatments, and on the progress of medical science, as well as selections from other magazine and lists and reviews of new medical books.

v1, nos.1-12   July 1824-June 1825   APS II, Reel 165

THE NEW-YORK MONTHLY MAGAZINE. Jan. 1-Mar. 1, 1824. New York [James Oram]

3 no.

The contents of James Oram's *New York Monthly Magazine* were of a very miscellaneous nature, and it did not survive past its third number. Among the varied contents are tales, fragments, poetry, anecdotes, travel sketches, reviews, news of deaths and marriages, a column called "The Moralist," and articles on orphan homes and mental institutions.

Jan. 1-Mar. 1, 1824   APS II, Reel 165

NEW YORK OBSERVER. v.1-91; May 17, 1823-May 30, 1912. New York.

61 v. illus., ports., maps. weekly.
Vol. 90-91 misnumbered as v. 89-90.

Absorbed the New York religious chronicle Nov. 4, 1826.
Title varies: Nov. 4, 1826- New York observer and chronicle.
Merged into Christian work.

Established by S.E. Morse and R.C. Morse.
From 1851 to Dec. 6, 1888, issued in 2 parts: Religious department and Secular department. On film: v.11-13, 1833-1835; v.18-25, 1840-1847; v.29-47, 1851-1869; v.50-57, 1872-Oct. 16, 1879; v.66, Dec. 27, 1888; v.67, Jan. 24, 1889; v.72-91, 1894-May 30, 1912. May vols. have scattered issues or pages missing.

This orthodox Presbyterian publication was begun in 1823 by Sidney E. and Richard Morse, brothers of the inventor Samuel Morse. Religious topics and viewpoints were the main focus of the newspaper, representing the conservative part of the Presbyterian church. Topics covered in the early part of the nineteenth century include "Religion the Only Safe Basis of Popular Education," "On the Idolatry and Superstition of Popery," "Danger of Reading Infidel Writings," and "Why Is There a Hell?" War topics–"The Union Must Be Saved," "Progress of the War," and "Rebuilding the Ruins,"–were covered during the 1860's.

The *New York Observer* was one of the important New York journals in the period after the Civil War and Editors and Proprietors, Sidney E. Morse Jr. & Co., claimed the newspaper's independence from the Presbyterian church. Religious news and topics were still the main focus, but events of the Congregationalists, Episcopalians, Baptists, and Unitarians were covered. By the 1880's the publication was practically undenominational.

The *New York Observer* switched to a smaller size publication in the 1890's and lost its newspaper character. Coverage included international topics such as "Latest News from South Africa," "Woman's Place in India," and "The Only Hope for China–Christian Youth," and an expansion of news coverage in addition to religious news.

New York Observer and Chronicle

v11-23	Jan. 5, 1833-Dec. 27, 1845	APS II, Reel 1856
v24-31	Jan. 3, 1846-Dec. 29, 1853	Reel 1857
v32-35	Jan. 5, 1854-Dec. 31, 1857	Reel 1858
v36-38	Jan. 28, 1858-Dec. 27, 1860	Reel 1859
v39-43	Jan. 3, 1861-Dec. 28, 1865	Reel 1860
v44-46	Jan. 4, 1866-Dec. 31, 1868	Reel 1861
v47-53	Jan. 7, 1869-Dec. 30, 1875	Reel 1862
v54-72	Jan. 6, 1876-Dec. 27, 1894	Reel 1863
v73	Jan. 3-Dec. 26, 1895	Reel 1864
v74	Jan. 2-Dec. 31, 1896	Reel 1865
v75	Jan. 7-Dec. 30, 1897	Reel 1866
v76-77	Jan. 6, 1898-Dec. 28, 1899	Reel 1867
v78-79	Jan. 4, 1900-Dec. 26, 1901	Reel 1868
v80-81	Jan. 2, 1902-Dec. 31, 1903	Reel 1869
v82-83	Jan. 7, 1904-Dec. 28, 1905	Reel 1870
v84-85	Jan. 4, 1906-Dec. 26, 1907	Reel 1871
v86-87	Jan. 2, 1908-Dec. 30, 1909	Reel 1872
v88-90	Jan. 6, 1910-Dec. 28, 1911	Reel 1873
v91	Jan. 4-May 30, 1912	Reel 1874

Microfilm edition begins Jan. 5, 1833.

Microfilm edition was prepared from IU, MiU, NNUT, NRCR, and WHi copies.

SEE ALSO: New York Religious Chronicle.

NEW YORK OBSERVER AND CHRONICLE. *SEE* New York Observer.

NEW YORK REGISTER AND ANTIMASONIC REVIEW. *SEE* Anti-Masonic Review, and Magazine.

NEW YORK RELIGIOUS CHRONICLE. v.1-4; 1823-26. New York, J. Gray.

4 v. weekly.

Merged into New York observer. Cf. Union list of serials.
Lacking on film: Vols. 1 and 4.

This religious weekly resembled a newspaper; it had a science column, a literary section, and many miscellaneous items; and contained poetry, a news summary, and much news on missions, including missions to the American Indians, to South Africa, and to Palestine.

v2-3	1824-1825	APS II, Reel 166

SEE ALSO: New York Observer.

* **THE NEW YORK REVIEW.** v.1-10; Mar. 1837-Apr. 1842. New York, G. Dearborn, 1838-42.

10 v. map. quarterly.

Editors: 1837, F.L. Hawks.–1837-40, C.S. Henry.–1840-42, J.G. Cogswell.
Index: 1-10 in 10.

The *New York Review* was founded by the Reverend Caleb S. Henry, an Episcopal priest and professor of philosophy. It was a scholarly journal and its reputation was outstanding. In spite of the fact that many well-known scholars contributed to the *Review,* the articles were never signed. After a succession of editors some of whom brought extensive talents to the position, the periodical ceased publication . . . probably because of its rather high price of a dollar and a quarter a number.

v1-7	Mar. 1837-Oct. 1840	APS III, Reel 843
v8-10	Jan. 1841-Apr. 1842	Reel 844

Microfilm edition was prepared from MiU copy.

THE NEW YORK REVIEW AND ATHENEUM MAGAZINE. v.1-2; June 1825-May 1826. New York, E. Bliss & E. White, 1825-26.

2 v. monthly.

Each number is in 2 parts: The New York review, The Atheneum magazine.
R.C. Sands, W.C. Bryant, editors.

Preceded by the Atlantic magazine.
In July 1826 merged into the United States literary gazette, which continued in October 1826 as the United States review and literary gazette.

Begun as a successor to the *Atlantic Magazine,* this literary magazine was made up of two parts: the "New-York Review" was devoted mainly to book reviews; and the "Atheneum Magazine" emphasized literature, science, and art, and included poetry, new book notices, letters, essays, and brief news items. Its three editors, William Cullen Bryant, Robert C. Sands, and Henry J. Anderson, wrote much of the material, and its impressive list of contributors included Fitz-Greene Halleck, Nathaniel P. Willis, George Bancroft, Caleb Cushing, Richard Henry Dana, and Henry Wadsworth Longfellow.

v1-2	June-Dec. 1825	APS II, Reel 166
v2	Jan.-May 1826	Reel 615

Reel 615: Several pages are stained.

Microfilm edition was prepared from DLC copy.

SEE ALSO: Atlantic Magazine *and* United States Literary Gazette.

NEW YORK SENTINEL AND WORKING MAN'S ADVOCATE. *SEE* Working Man's Advocate.

THE NEW YORK STATE MECHANIC, a journal of the manual arts, trades, and manufactures. v.1-2, no.28; Nov. 20, 1841-June 17, 1843. Albany, Printed by Joel Munsell, 1842.

2 v. illus. (incl. ports.) weekly.

"Under the direction of the New York State Mechanic Association," Nov. 1841-Nov. 1842.

The *New York State Mechanic* was an eight-page quarto published weekly. Occasionally, a wood-cut illustration appeared.

v1-2   Nov. 20, 1841-June 17, 1843   APS II, Reel 938

Vol. 1, Part 2: pgs. 3-6 misnumbered. Pgs. 74-77 missing in number only. Vol. 2: Index lacking. Best copy available for photographing.

Microfilm edition was prepared from N and MWA copies.

NEW YORK TEACHER. *SEE* American Educational Monthly; A Magazine of Popular Instruction and Literature.

NEW YORK TEACHER AND AMERICAN EDUCATIONAL MONTHLY. *SEE* American Educational Monthly; A Magazine of Popular Instruction and Literature.

NEW YORK TELESCOPE. v.1-7, no.13; June 5, 1824-Aug. 28, 1830. New York, 1824-1830.

7 v.

Vols. 1-6, no.26 as Telescope.
Vols. 5-7 wanting.

Published by William Burnett and Company, this weekly was primarily devoted to religious and moral principles, but also published some poetry and news.

Telescope
v1-4   June 5, 1824-May 24, 1828   APS II, Reel 1254

Some pages are torn and stained; some have print faded. Pagination is irregular. Vol. 3: Index and issues for Aug. 26 and Apr. 21 are missing. Supplement follows issue for May 12. Vol. 4: Index is missing.

Microfilm edition was prepared from MnU and WHi copies.

THE NEW YORK TRACT MAGAZINE AND CHRISTIAN MISCELLANY. v.1-3; 1824-1828. Albany, New York State Tract Society.

[241]-264 p.

Issued in 3 v., 1824-28. Cf. Union list of serials.
Film covers issue for Nov. 1824 (No other issues available)

Published by the New York State Tract Society, this religious magazine reported on the activities of various tract societies, and listed their publications and also gave attention to missionary news. A children's department, occasional poetry, and miscellaneous articles on religious topics rounded out the contents.

v1, no.11   Nov. 1824   APS II, Reel 166

THE NEW-YORK WEEKLY MAGAZINE; or, Miscellaneous repository: forming an interesting collection of original and select literary productions in prose and verse: calculated for instruction and rational entertainment-the promotion of moral and useful knowledge-and to enlarge and correct the understandings of youth. v.1-3 (no.1-112); July 1, 1795-Aug. 23, 1797. New-York. J. Bull [etc.] 1796-97.

3 v. in 2 plates.

Vol. 3, no.105-112 called also 1-8.
From July 5, to Aug. 23, 1797, title reads: Sentimental & literary magazine.

One of the earliest magazines to place emphasis on fiction, it included much trite advice to young women, poems, meteorological tables, "elegant extracts," and many tales and fragments.

New York Weekly Magazine
v1-2   July 1, 1795-June 28, 1797   APS I, Reel 23

Sentimental and Literary Magazine
v3   July 5-Aug. 23, 1797   Reel 27

Some pages are missing.

Microfilm edition was prepared from DLC copy.

NEW-YORK WEEKLY MUSEUM. *SEE* Ladies' Weekly Museum.

NEW YORK WEEKLY TRIBUNE. *SEE* New-Yorker.

THE NEW-YORKER. v.1-11; Mar. 26, 1836-Sept. 11, 1841. New York, H. Greeley.

11 v. weekly.

A quarto ed. was issued from Mar. 26, 1836, to Sept. 11, 1841. Superseded by the New York weekly tribune.

Horace Greeley, Editor.

Selecting much of the literature from other magazines, Horace Greeley founded the *New-Yorker*. Two editions of the Whiggish paper were circulated. One was a folio which began in 1834 and the second was a quarto edition begun in 1836. Greeley was assisted for a time by R. Griswold, Park Benjamin, and Henry Ware. In the last weekly issue, September 11, 1841, the subscribers were advised that the *New-Yorker* would be replaced by the *New York Weekly Tribune*. Since the *Tribune* was to be a Whig political paper, subscribers could choose between it, the *New World* which was another literary weekly, or have their money refunded.

v1-2   Mar. 26, 1836-Mar. 18, 1837   APS II, Reel 1090
v3-8   Mar. 25, 1837-Mar. 14, 1840   Reel 1091
v9-11   Mar. 21, 1840-Sept. 11, 1841   Reel 1092

Vols. 1-11: Pages are stained and print is faded throughout. Vol. 8: Pages 302-303 and 341-344 are lacking. Best copy available for photographing.

Microfilm edition was prepared from CSt copy.

THE NIGHTINGALE; or, A melange de litterature; a periodical publication. Edited by John Lathrop, vol. 1 (no.1-36): May 10-July 30, 1796. Boston; Printed for the proprietors, at their office, Quaker-Lane. 1796.

432 p.

Triweekly.

A collection of novels, fragments, anecdotes, poetry, biography, and essays on classical literature, art, and a variety of other subjects.

v1, no.1-36   May 10-July 30, 1796   APS I, Reel 23

Microfilm edition was prepared from MWA copy.

* **NILES' NATIONAL REGISTER**, containing political, historical, geographical, scientific, statistical, economical, and biographical documents, essay and facts; together with notices of the arts and manufactures, and a record of the events of the time. v.1-12, 13-24 (new ser., v.1-12), 25-36 (3d ser., v.1-12), 37-50 (4th ser., v.1-14), 51-73 (5th ser., v.1-23), 74-76, no.13; Sept. 7, 1811-Sept. 28, 1849. Baltimore.

76 v. weekly.

Title varies: 1811-Aug. 1814 (v.1-6) The Weekly register ... (Running title of v.6; Niles' weekly register) Sept. 1814-Aug. 1837, Niles' weekly register.

Editors: 1811-Aug.1836-(W.O. Niles, assistant editor from Jan. 1827-Oct. 1830).—Sept. 1836-Oct. 1839, W.O. Niles.—Oct. 1839-Feb. 1848, J. Hughes.—July 1848-Sept. 1949, G. Beatty. Published in Baltimore, 1811-37; Washington, 1837-39; Baltimore, 1839-48; Philadelphia, 1848-49. Publication was suspended from Mar. to June 1848, July-Aug. 1849. Vols. 5, 7-9, 15-16 contain supplements. Index: vol. 1-12, 1811-17. The American register and international journal, ed. by John Hancock (New York, 1861) was designed as the continuation of Niles' register.

Founded and edited for 25 years by Hezekiah Niles, this weekly contained "political, historical, geographical, scientific, statistical, economical, and biographical documents, essays and facts together with notices of the arts and manufactures and a record of the events of the times." Described by a contemporary as "precise in everything," Niles was non-partisan and reliable in reporting facts although he did have some editorial expression in the early volumes. Because of its presentation of factual material, the *Register* performed an invaluable service to newspaper editors, the public and historians by providing statistics about the first half of the 19th century. A great deal of print was devoted to reports of Congressional sessions, news of Indian tribes and settlements and wars and upheavals in Europe.

Weekly Register
v1-3	Sept. 7, 1811-Feb. 27, 1813	APS II, Reel 167
v4-6	Mar. 6, 1813-Aug. 27, 1814	Reel 168

Niles' Weekly Register
v7-8	Sept. 10, 1814-Aug. 26, 1815	Reel 169
v9-11	Sept. 2, 1815-Feb. 22, 1817	Reel 170
v12-14	Mar. 1, 1817-Aug. 22, 1818	Reel 171
v15-16	Aug. 29, 1818-Aug. 21, 1819	Reel 172
v17-19	Sept. 4, 1819-Feb. 24, 1821	Reel 173
v20-22	Mar. 3, 1821-Aug. 24, 1822	Reel 174
v23-25	Sept. 7, 1822-Feb. 24, 1824	Reel 175
v26-28	Mar. 6, 1824-Aug. 27, 1825	Reel 176
v29	Sept. 2-Dec. 31, 1825	Reel 177
v30-33	Mar. 4, 1826-Feb. 23, 1828	Reel 254
v34-37	Mar. 1, 1828-Feb. 20, 1830	Reel 255
v38-40	Feb. 27, 1830-Aug. 27, 1831	Reel 256
v41-43	Sept. 3, 1831-Feb. 23, 1833	Reel 257
v44-47	Mar. 2, 1833-Feb. 28, 1835	Reel 258
v48-50	Mar. 7, 1835-Aug. 27, 1836	Reel 259
v51-52	Sept. 3, 1836-Aug. 26, 1837	Reel 260

Niles' National Register
v53-54	Sept. 2, 1837-Aug. 25, 1838	Reel 261
v55-56	Sept. 1, 1838-Aug. 24, 1839	Reel 262
v57-58	Aug. 31, 1839-Aug. 29, 1840	Reel 263
v59-60	Sept. 5, 1840-Aug. 28, 1841	Reel 264
v61-64	Sept. 4, 1841-Aug. 20, 1843	Reel 265
v65-68	Sept. 2, 1843-Aug. 30, 1845	Reel 266
v69-70	Sept. 6, 1845-Aug. 29, 1846	Reel 267
v71-73	Sept. 5, 1846-Feb. 26, 1848	Reel 268
v74-76	July 5, 1848-Sept. 28, 1849	Reel 269

NILES' WEEKLY REGISTER. *SEE* Niles' National Register.

NORTH AMERICAN. Or, Weekly journal of politics, science and literature. v.1; May 19-Nov. 24, 1827. Baltimore [S. Sands] 1827.

224 p.

The *North American* was comprised of political, scientific, and literary pieces selected from numerous other papers. After only one volume, Samuel Sands, the printer and publisher, ended his short-term venture to further pursue his job-printing business.

v1   May 19-Nov. 24, 1827   APS II, Reel 973

Vol. 1: many pages are stained. Sept. 8 issue: page 163 is taped.

Microfilm edition was prepared from MdBE and MWA copies.

NORTH AMERICAN ARCHIVES OF MEDICAL AND SURGICAL SCIENCE. Edited by E. Geddings. v.1-2; Oct. 1834-Sept. 1835. Baltimore, Carey, Hart, 1835.

2 v. illus., fold. pl. monthly.

Supersedes Baltimore medical and surgical journal and review.

Originally the *Baltimore Medical and Surgical Journal and Review*, this medical periodical, edited by E. Geddings, was intended to inform its readers of recent improvements made in the medical profession at home and abroad. Contents included articles and selected papers on cases, book reviews, lists of books and periodicals received, activities of medical societies, obituaries, and miscellanea.

v1-2   Oct. 1834-Sept. 1835   APS II, Reel 804

Vol. 1: Pgs. 344-61 are misnumbered.

Microfilm edition was prepared from NcD copy.

SEE ALSO: Baltimore Medical and Surgical Journal and Review.

NORTH AMERICAN MAGAZINE. *SEE* North American Quarterly Magazine.

THE NORTH AMERICAN MEDICAL AND SURGICAL JOURNAL. v.1-12; Jan. 1826- Oct 1831. Philadelphia, J. Dobson, 1826-31.

12 v. illus., plates (part col., part fold.) quarterly.

Vols. 1-7 edited by H.L. Hodge, Franklin Bache, C. D. Meigs. B.H. Coates, Rene La Roche. Vols. 5-12 published by the Kappa lambda association of the United States.

In addition to papers on various medical subjects, this journal provided a summary of progress in medicine, a quarterly list of American medical publications, a review of medical literature, reviews of selected publications, and biography.

v1-4   Jan. 1826-Aug. 1827   APS II, Reel 804
v5-12   Jan. 1828-Oct. 1831   Reel 805

Many pages are stained. Pagination is irregular.

Microfilm edition was prepared from CtW, ICRM, N and NcD copies.

NORTH AMERICAN MEDICOCHIRURGICAL REVIEW.
SEE Medical Examiner.

NORTH AMERICAN MISCELLANY. *SEE* Dollar Magazine *and* North American Miscellany and Dollar Magazine.

THE NORTH AMERICAN MISCELLANY AND DOLLAR MAGAZINE. v1-4; Feb. 1, 1851-[Aug.?] 1852, New York, Angell, Engel & Hewitt, 1852.

4 v. in 3. illus., pl.
Vol. 3, no1-4 (Sept.-Dec. 1851) called in caption new ser., no.1-4.
Later issues are neither numbered nor dated.
Weekly, Feb. 1-July 26, 1851; monthly, Sept. 1851-Aug. 1852.

Title varies: v.1-2 (Feb. 1-July 26, 1851) The North American miscellany; a weekly magazine of choice selections from the current literature of this country and Europe. v.3-4 (Sept. 1851-Aug. 1852) The North American miscellany and Dollar magazine.

Caption title, Feb. 1-Dec. 1851, The North American miscellany. Absorbed the Dollar magazine Jan. 1852.

The *North American Miscellany* was a neatly-printed magazine featuring selections from other journals. Some illustrations were included.

North American Miscellany; a Weekly Magazine of Choice Selections from the Current Literature of this Country and Europe
v1-2   Feb.-July 1851   APS II, Reel 939

North American Miscellany and Dollar Magazine
v3-4   Sept. 1851-Aug. 1852   Reel 940

Vol. 2: pg. 276 repaired. Vol. 4: pgs. 281-288 are missing in number only.

Microfilm edition was prepared from CL, DLC, NPV, and TxU copies.

SEE ALSO: Dollar Magazine.

THE NORTH AMERICAN QUARTERLY MAGAZINE.
By Sumner Lincoln Fairfield. v.1-9; Nov. 1832-June 1838. Philadelphia, C. Sherman, 1833-38.

9 v. in 8.
Published in Philadelphia, 1832-36; Washington, 1836; Baltimore, 1838.

From Nov. 1832 to Apr. 1835 title reads: The North American magazine.

Monthly, Nov. 1832-Apr. 1835; quarterly, 1835-June 1838. Suspended during 1837.

The *North American Quarterly* was founded by Sumner Lincoln Fairfield, the poet. Although it contained some well-written criticism, by 1837, the publication had been suspended. Only two subsequent issues, edited by Nathan C. Brooks, appeared in 1838.

North American Magazine
v1-4   Nov. 1832-Oct. 1834   APS II, Reel 938
v5   Nov. 1834-Apr. 1835   Reel 939

North American Quarterly Magazine
v6-9   July 1835-June 1838   Reel 939

Some pages are stained, torn, or have faded or missing print.

Vols. 1-9 lack Indexes. Please refer to the Tables of Contents. Vol. 8: pages 337-52 are missing. Best copy available for photographing.

Microfilm edition was prepared from CtY, DLC, N, and TxU copies.

* THE NORTH AMERICAN REVIEW. v.1-248; May 1815-Winter 1939/40. Boston, Wells and Lilly, 1815-77 [etc., etc.]

248 v. plates, ports., maps, facsims.
Bimonthly, May 1815-Sept. 1818; quarterly, Dec. 1818-Oct. 1876; bimonthly, Jan. 1877-Dec. 1878; monthly, Jan. 1879-Aug. 1906; semi-monthly, Sept. 1906-Aug. 1907; monthly, Sept. 1907-

Vols. 10-30 called also "new ser., v.1-21."
From May 1815 to Apr. 1821 title reads: The North-American review and miscellaneous journal.

Editors: 1815-17, William Tudor.–1817-18, Jared Sparks (with Willard Phillips and others)–1818-19, E.T. Channing (with R.H. Dana and others)–1820-23, Edward Everett.–1824-30, Jared Sparks.–1830-35, A.H. Everett.–1836-42, J.G. Palfrey.–1843-53, Francis Bowen.–1853-63, A.P. Peabody.–1863-72, J.R. Lowell (with C.E. Norton, 1863-68; E.W. Gurney, 1868-70; Henry Adams, 1870-72.–1872-76, Henry Adams (with H.C. Lodge, 1873-76.–1877, J.H. Ward.–1878-89. A.T. Rice.–1889-96, Lloyd Bryce.–1896-99, D.A. Munro.–1899-1921, G.H. McHarvey.

During its first sixty years, the *North American Review* was dignified, respected, and rather dull; contents were mostly long essays on law, religion, education, classical writings, travel, philosophy, and history. When Andrew P. Peabody became editor in 1853, the range of material was broadened to include articles on slavery, science, nature, and landscape art. French literature was given special attention, as was literary criticism. Beginning in 1864, James Russell Lowell and Charles Eliot Norton built up a staff of contributors which included Edwin L. Godkin, Charles Francis Adams, Jr., James Parton, and George William Curtis, editor of *Harper's Weekly*. During the early 70's the *Review* emphasized history and in addition to political articles in nearly every issue, it offered articles on evolution and philology. Well-known writers of literary criticism included Francis A. Palgrave, William Dean Howells, and Henry James.

The *Review* underwent a radical change in 1877 when Allen Thorndike Rice took over as editor; it became an open forum for opinion and controversy became the policy. Politics, economics, and religion were the most prominent topics, but drama was also given some attention. Articles on women and their position, and on science, education, foreign affairs, and art appeared as well.

Under George Harvey's editorship, which began in 1899, the *Review* put much emphasis on international affairs; the Philippine question and the Boer War were given attention and a "World Politics" department was begun. Mark Twain was a leading contributor. Contents became more varied when Walter Butler Mahony became editor in 1926. In addition to articles on social problems, economics, politics, and art, there were book reviews, a few short stories, and sections on "The Literary Landscape" and "The Financial Outlook."

North American Review and Miscellaneous Journal

v1-2	May 1815-Mar. 1816	APS II, Reel 177
v3-5	May 1816-Sept. 1817	Reel 178
v6-9	Nov. 1817-Sept. 1819	Reel 179
v10-12	Jan. 1820-Apr. 1821	Reel 180

North American Review

v13-15	July 1821-Oct. 18, 1822	Reel 181
v16-18	Jan. 1823-Apr. 1824	Reel 182
v19-21	July 1824-Oct. 1825	Reel 183
v22-25	Jan. 1826-Oct. 1827	Reel 270
v26-29	Jan. 1828-Oct. 1829	Reel 271
v30-33	Jan. 1830-Oct. 1831	Reel 272
v34-37	Jan. 1832-Oct. 1833	Reel 273
v38-41	Jan. 1834-Oct. 1835	Reel 274
v42-45	Jan. 1836-Oct. 1837	Reel 275
v46-49	Jan. 1838-Oct. 1839	Reel 276
v50-53	Jan. 1840-Oct. 1841	Reel 277
v54-57	Jan. 1842-Oct. 1843	Reel 278
v58-61	Jan. 1844-Oct. 1845	Reel 279
v62-66	Jan. 1846-Apr. 1848	Reel 280
v67-71	July 1848-Oct. 1850	Reel 281
v72-79	Jan. 1851-Oct. 1854	Reel 1613
v80-86	Jan. 1855-Apr. 1858	Reel 1614
v87-93	July 1858-Oct. 1861	Reel 1615
v94-99	Jan. 1862-Oct. 1864	Reel 1616
v100-105	Jan. 1865-Oct. 1867	Reel 1617
v106-112	Jan. 1868-Apr. 1871	Reel 1618
v113-120	July 1871-Apr. 1875	Reel 1619
v121-127	July 1875-Dec. 1878	Reel 1620
v128-133	Jan. 1879-Dec. 1881	Reel 1621
v134-139	Jan. 1882-Dec. 1884	Reel 1622
v140-145	Jan. 1885-Dec. 1887	Reel 1623
v146-150	Jan. 1888-June 1890	Reel 1624
v151-155	July 1890-Dec. 1892	Reel 1625
v156-160	Jan. 1893-June 1895	Reel 1626
v161-165	July 1895-Dec. 1897	Reel 1627
v166-170	Jan. 1898-June 1900	Reel 1628
v171-174	July 1900-June 1902	Reel 1629
v175-178	July 1902-June 1904	Reel 1630
v179-181	July 1904-Dec. 1905	Reel 1631
v182-184	Jan. 1906-Apr. 1907	Reel 1632
v185-188	May 1907-Dec. 1908	Reel 1633
v189-192	Jan. 1909-Dec. 1910	Reel 1634
v193-196	Jan. 1911-Dec. 1912	Reel 1635
v197-200	Jan. 1913-Dec. 1914	Reel 1636
v201-203	Jan. 1915-June 1916	Reel 1637
v204-206	July 1916-Dec. 1917	Reel 1638
v207-209	Jan. 1918-June 1919	Reel 1639
v210-213	July 1919-June 1921	Reel 1640
v214-217	July 192-June 1923	Reel 1641
v218-222	July 1923-Feb. 1926	Reel 1642
v223-226	Mar. 1926-Dec. 1928	Reel 1643
v227-230	Jan. 1929-Dec. 1930	Reel 1644
v231-235	Jan. 1931-June 1933	Reel 1645
v236-241	July 1933-June 1936	Reel 1646
v242-248	Autumn 1936-Winter 1939/40	Reel 1647

Reels 177-183 include Index 1-125, 1815-17.

Microfilm edition was prepared from MiD and NcD copies.

NORTH-AMERICAN REVIEW AND MISCELLANEOUS JOURNAL. *SEE* North American Review.

THE NORTH-CAROLINA MAGAZINE; or, Universal intelligencer. v.1-2 (no.1-33); June 1/8, 1764-Jan. 11/18, 1765. [Newbern, Printed by J. Davis]

33 no. weekly.

Film incomplete: v.1, no1-4, no.19, no.28 wanting.

A newspaper which somewhat resembled a magazine. The first two pages contained essays and texts of important legislative acts while the remainder dealt with news and advertisements.

v12, no.1-33	June1/8, 1764-Jan. 11/18, 1765	APS I, Reel 23

Microfilm edition was prepared from DLC copy.

NORTH-CAROLINA MAGAZINE, POLITICAL, HISTORICAL, AND MISCELLANEOUS. v.1, no.1, Aug. 1813. [n.p.] 1813.

32 p.

Evidently only one number of this miscellany was published. Its contents included much on the navy, summaries of foreign and domestic news, proceedings of Congress, tales and poetry, a biographical sketch, some historical sketches, and miscellaneous articles.

v1, no.1	Aug. 1813	Reel 400

NORTHERN LIGHT: devoted to free discussion, and to the diffusion of useful knowledge, miscellaneous literature, and general intelligence. v.1-4, no.5; Apr. 1841-Sept. 1844. Albany, N.Y., 1841-1844.

4 v.

To embrace knowledge on the political economy, agriculture, literary and scientific miscellany and general intelligence was the purpose of this periodical. It includes statistics of the day on many areas of these subjects.

v1-4	Apr. 1841-Sept. 1844	APS II, Reel 844

In the Library of Congress copy, the Sept. 1844 issue of vol. 4 was bound before the August issue. (Photographed as bound) Retake from Boston Public Library for pages 29-30, 49-64 of vol. 4 may be found after vol. 4.

Microfilm edition was prepared from MB, N, and TxU copies.

NORTON'S LITERARY ADVERTISER. *SEE* American Literary Gazette and Publishers' Circular.

NORTON'S LITERARY GAZETTE AND PUBLISHER'S CIRCULAR. *SEE* American Literary Gazette and Publisher's Circular.

OASIS; a monthly magazine devoted to literature, science and the arts. v.1; Aug. 1837-July 1838. Oswego, N.Y., 1837-1838.

189 p.

A monthly miscellany edited by Joseph Neilson and John S. Randall which published selected material of both American and European authors. Among its varied contents were: essays and poetry, news, biographical sketches, musical pieces, reviews of new publications, and articles on Indians, literature, geology, and education.

v1	Aug. 12, 1837-July 28, 1838	APS II, Reel 806

Microfilm edition was prepared from MWA copy.

THE OBSERVER. By Beatrice Ironside. v.1-2; Nov. 29, 1806-Dec. 26, 1807. Baltimore, J. Robinson, 1806-07.

2 v. weekly.

Caption title, v.1, no.1: The Observer, and repertory of original and selected essays, in verse & prose, on topics of polite literature, &c. ...
Preceded by the Companion.

Edited by "Beatric Ironside," the *Observer* was a successor to the *Companion* and was one of several literary weeklies published in Baltimore in the early 1800's. This miscellany presented varied literary material, such as essays, brief novels and tales, biographical sketches, travel sketches, poetry, and literary news, but also provided some articles on the fine arts, agricultural news, and reports of judicial decisions made in the courts.

v1-2   Nov. 29, 1806-Dec. 26, 1807   APS II, Reel 36

Microfilm edition was prepared from DLC copy.

SEE ALSO: Companion and Weekly Miscellany.

THE OBSERVER. no.[1]-25; Feb. 19-Aug. 6, 1809. [New-York, W. Elliot, 1809]

196 (i.e. 200) p.

Pub. every Sunday morning.
Caption title.
Paging irregular: no.110-112 repeated

A moral and religious section, some poetry, brief news items, and marriage and death notices made up the contents of the weekly *Observer.*

no.1-25   Feb. 19-Aug. 6, 1809   APS II, Reel 36

Microfilm edition was prepared from DLC copy.

THE OBSERVER. no.1-28; Oct. 14, 1810-Apr. 21, 1811. New York.

28 no.

This instructive and informative magazine kept abreast of the latest foreign and domestic news and advances in the arts, sciences, and in manufacturing. It also included moral and religious essays, poetry, some book advertisements, and vital statistics.

no.1-28   Oct. 14, 1810-Apr. 21, 1811   APS II, Reel 218

THE OCCASIONAL REVERBERATOR. no.1-4; Sept. 7-Oct. 5, 1753. [New York]

4 no.
Weekly, Sept. 7-21, 1753.

Issued as a Supplement to the Independent reflector.

One of several magazines which helped American essay writing for periodicals attain new heights in cogent exposition and argument. It was established by friends of William Livingston, editor of *The Independent reflector,* to enable him to reply to his adversaries in the religious and political controversy raging in New York at that time.

no.1-4   Sept. 7-Oct. 5, 1753   APS I, Reel 24

Microfilm edition was prepared from MiU-C copy.

THE ODD FELLOWS' MAGAZINE. v.1, no.1-2; Oct. 1, 1825-Jan. 1, 1826. Baltimore, J. Roach.

2 no. ports quarterly.

Includes the Odd Fellows magazine, Manchester, Eng., new ser., Mar.-June 1828 (72p.) and an oration by Dr. F.D. Yates, D.G. dated Feb. 22, 1826.

The Society of Odd Fellows published both American and British editions of this quarterly magazine. The Manchester edition was to contain material of interest to members of the Society, proceedings of various lodges, and biographical sketches of officers, while the Baltimore edition was to contain everything of interest in the Manchester edition with additions from the American society. Contents also included letters to the editor, news of deaths, and information on the weather, as well as some tales, poetry, and anecdotes.

v1, no.1-2	Oct. 1, 1825-Jan. 1, 1826	APS II, Reel 218
new series (Manchester, Eng.)	Mar.-June, 1828	Reel 218

v1, no1-2	Oct. 1, 1825-Jan. 1, 1826	Reel 839
new series	Mar.-June 1828	Reel 839
Oration by Yates	Feb. 22, 1826	Reel 839

Microfilm edition was prepared from KyL and N copies.

OHIO COMMON SCHOOL DIRECTOR. v.1, nos.1-6; Mar.-Nov. 1838. Columbus, 1838.

96 p.

The *Ohio Common School Director* was one of the earliest of the state journals designed especially for public school teachers.

v1   Mar.-Nov. 1838   APS II, Reel 940

Vol. 1: Photostatic copy. Best copy available for photographing.

Microfilm edition was prepared from MnU, OU, and OCHP copies.

OHIO CULTIVATOR. v.1-22, Jan. 1845-Dec. 1866. Columbus, 1845-66.

22 v.

Merged into Ohio farmer.

Agriculture, horticulture, domestic and rural economy, and practical advice were the subjects of this regional semi-monthly.

v1-2	Jan. 1, 1845-Dec. 15, 1846	APS II, Reel 1254
v3-9	Jan. 1, 1847-Dec. 15, 1853	Reel 1255
v10-16	Jan. 1, 1854-Dec. 15, 1860	Reel 1256
v17-22	Jan. 1, 1861-Dec. 1866	Reel 1257

Several pages are torn, creased, stained, or have faded print with some loss of text. Pagination is irregular. Vol. 13: Pgs. 370-71 are missing. Vol. 14: Pgs. 369-70 are missing. Vol. 17: Issues are published monthly. Vol. 18: Index and issues for Nov. and Dec. are missing. Vols. 19-21 are missing; not available for photographing. Vol. 22: Index is missing.

Microfilm edition was prepared from DLC, KMK, and OOxM copies.

OHIO FARMER. v.1- , June 1, 1852- . Cleveland.

v. weekly.

Vols.23-43 missing in number only.
Subtitle varies.

On film: v.5-6, 8, 14-49, 51-52, 55-64, 67-69, 83-110; Jan. 5, 1856-Dec. 29, 1906 (Some vols have scattered issues missing)

Established by Thomas Brown at Cleveland, the *Ohio Farmer* was one of the important farm papers of the midwest. This weekly provided the farmer and his family with a variety of information and entertainment: for the farmer there were articles on agriculture, gardening, dairy products, poultry, and fruit-growing, as well as grange news. For the women there were recipes, household items and a women's department, and, for the children, a "Youth's Department."

v5	Jan. 5-Dec. 27, 1856	APS II, Reel 1801
v6-14	Jan. 3, 1857-Dec. 30, 1865	Reel 1802
v15-16	Jan. 6, 1866-Dec. 28, 1867	Reel 1803
v17-19	Jan. 4, 1868-Dec. 24, 1870	Reel 1804
v20-44	Jan. 7, 1871-Dec. 27, 1873	Reel 1805
v45-51	Jan. 3, 1874-June 30, 1877	Reel 1806
v52-60	July 7, 1877-Dec. 31, 1881	Reel 1807
v61-68	Jan. 7, 1882-Dec. 26, 1885	Reel 1808
v69-86	Jan. 2, 1886-Dec. 27, 1894	Reel 1809
v87-91	Jan. 3, 1895-June 24, 1897	Reel 1810
v92-96	July 1, 1897-Dec. 28, 1899	Reel 1811
v97-101	Jan. 4, 1900-June 26, 1902	Reel 1812
v102-105	July 3, 1902-June 25, 1904	Reel 1813
v106-109	July 2, 1904-June 30, 1906	Reel 1814
v110	July 7-Dec. 29, 1906	Reel 1815

Microfilm edition was prepared from DNAL, IU, KMK, MoU, NIC, OOxM, OU, and WvU copies.

SEE ALSO: Ohio Cultivator.

THE OHIO MEDICAL AND SURGICAL JOURNAL. v.1-16, no.6 Sept. 1848-Nov. 1864; new ser. v.1-3, no.6, June 1876-Dec. 1878. Columbus, J.H. Riley [etc.]

19 v. bimonthly.

Film incomplete: new ser. v.3, no.4-6 wanting.

This medical journal included articles on medicine in general, as well as descriptions of specific cases and treatments for a variety of medical problems. It attempted to keep abreast of the latest developments in medicine in the U.S. and abroad, and published proceedings of the American Medical Association and some book reviews.

v1-4	Sept. 1, 1848-July 1, 1852	APS II, Reel 1404
v5-11	Sept. 1, 1852-July 1, 1859	Reel 1405
v12-nsv3	Sept. 1, 1859-June 1878	Reel 1406

Some pages are stained and tightly bound. Pagination is irregular. Vols. 2 and 6-9 lack title pages. Vol. 9 contains "Catalogue of Drugs" supplement. Vol. 16: Title page and index are missing.

Microfilm edition was prepared from ICU, MiU, NSySU-M and OU copies.

OHIO MEDICAL REPOSITORY OF ORIGINAL AND SELECTED INTELLIGENCE. v.1; Apr. 1, 1826-Apr. 18, 1827. Cincinnati, 1826-1827.

94 p.

Edited by Guy W. Wright and James M. Mason.

The principal design of the *Ohio Medical Repository* was "to promote and extend the knowledge of Medicine and Surgery" westward from the Alleghenies. It appeared semi-monthly.

v1	Apr. 1, 1826-Apr. 18, 1827	APS II, Reel 973

Vol. 1: many pages throughout are stained.

Microfilm edition was prepared from DNLM copy.

THE OHIO MISCELLANEOUS MUSEUM. v.1, no.1-5; Jan.-May 1822. Lebanon.

232 p. illus. monthly.

This miscellany, which proposed to publish news of politics, science, trade, commerce, literature, and fine and useful arts, did not survive past its fifth number. Among its literary contents were tales, poetry, and anecdotes, book reviews, lists of new publications, and extracts from biographical sketches and other books; and articles on archaeology, history, and travel appeared frequently. Religious news and national affairs were given coverage, as were agricultural and manufacturing improvements and inventions.

v1, nos.1-5	Jan.-May 1822	APS II, Reel 218

*OLD AND NEW. v.1-11, no.5; Jan. 1870-May 1875. Boston, H.O. Houghton; New York, Hurd and Houghton, 1870-75.

11 v. monthly.

E.E. Hale, editor.
Merged into Scribner's monthly.
Supersedes Christian examiner.

Includes: College directory [giving the name, locality, course of study, faculty, and number of students, of 175 or more of the Principal collegiate institutions of the United States]. [Boston, Robert Bros. 1872-74].

Versatile and well-informed, Edward Everett Hale plunged into the editorship of *Old and New*. He managed quite well to display his personality throughout the file, but five years later, he reported that the strain was too much. Perhaps it was not the strain of editing, but of trying to mesh the literary and political review with the theological magazine. In his attempt to please everyone, he managed to disgust the Unitarian Association (who had backed the new venture) and bore the serial readers with purity. There were some outstanding contributions by Harriet Beecher Stowe, George Trollope, Christina Rossetti and others in addition to those of the editor.

v1-4	Jan. 1870-Dec. 1871	APS III, Reel 130
v5-10	Jan. 1872-Dec. 1874	Reel 131
v11	Jan.-May 1875	Reel 132

Several volumes contain supplements. Some pages are torn, stained, or have print missing. Vol. 2: title is misdated July 1870-Jan. 1871. Vol. 11: Index is lacking; please refer to the Table of Contents.

Microfilm edition was prepared from MiU and NjP copies.

SEE ALSO: Christian Examiner.

OLD AND NEW TESTAMENT STUDENT. *SEE* Biblical World.

THE OLD GUARD. v.1-8; June 1862-Dec. 1870. New York, C.C. Burr.

8 v. col. plates, ports. monthly.

Subtitle varies.
Editors: 1863-69, C.C. Burr.–T.D. English.

The projector and first editor of *Old Guard,* Reverend C.C. Burr, staunchly supported the Southern view on slavery. His journal, published in New York, was in short a "Copperhead." The articles were consistently anti-Lincoln, anti-Republican, bitter, and very violent. Little, if any, sympathy for the Southern cause was gained through its efforts.

v1-6	Jan. 1863-Dec. 1868	APS III, Reel 64
v7-8	Jan. 1869-Dec. 1870	Reel 65

Best copy available for photographing. Some pages are torn or stained. Issues for June-Dec. 1862 are lacking. Vol. 1: pgs. 169-192 are missing in number only. Vol. 6: July and Nov. issues lack portrait.

Microfilm edition was prepared from MiU, and OMC copies.

OLD TESTAMENT STUDENT. *SEE* Biblical World.

THE OLDEN TIME; a monthly publication, devoted to the preservation of documents and other authentic information in relation to the early explorations, and the settlement and improvement of the country around the head of the Ohio. v.1-2 [Jan. 1846-Dec. 1848] Ed. by Neville B. Craig. Pittsburgh, J.W. Cook, 1846-48.

2 v. map, facsim.

According to its subtitle, the *Olden Time* was "devoted to the preservation of documents and other authentic information in relation to the early explorations, and the settlement and improvement of the country around the head of Ohio."

v1-2	Jan. 1846-Dec. 1847	APS II, Reel 844

Microfilm edition was prepared from the IGK copy.

THE OLIO, A LITERARY AND MISCELLANEOUS PAPER. Containing, biographical sketches of the most eminent naval and military characters in the United States; extracts from history, travels, geography and novels; poetry, anecdotes, bon-mots, & c. & c. together with a brief account of the passing events of the day. v1-2, no.1; Jan. 27, 1813-Feb. 5, 1814. New York, S. Marks.

426 p. weekly.

This miscellany published foreign and domestic news, recorded local marriages and deaths, and offered anecdotes, poetry and tales, and extracts from works of history, travel, and geography. In addition, it included biographical sketches of naval and military people, as well as others.

v1-2, no.1	Jan. 27, 1813-Feb. 5, 1814	APS II, Reel 219

OLIVER OPTIC'S MAGAZINE. Our boys and girls. Oliver Optic [pseud.] editor. v.1-18 (no.1-269); Jan. 1867-Dec. 1875. Boston, Lee and Shepard [1867]-75.

18 v. in 9. illus., plates, ports. weekly, 1867-70; monthly, 1871-75.

Vols. 1-14 have caption title: Our boys and girls.

Oliver Optic's Magazine contained poems, music, amusements, and most of all, fiction, for young people. It was edited and in part written by Oliver Optic, known in private life as William T. Adams.

v1-8	Jan. 5, 1867-Dec. 31, 1870	APS III, Reel 236
v9-14	Jan. 1871-Dec. 1873	Reel 237
v15-18	Jan. 1874-Dec. 1875	Reel 238

Some pages are stained, torn, or have print show-through or print missing. Vols. 1-18: Lack indexes; please refer to contents. Vols. 3-4: July 4 issue has a 4-page Supplement at the end.

Microfilm edition was prepared from DLC and MiU copies.

OLIVER'S MAGAZINE. By Benjamin L. Oliver. no.1; Oct. 1841. Boston, M.A. Dow, 1841.

54, [2] p.

According to the Prospectus, *Oliver's Magazine,* by "Benjamin Oliver," was to give "useful information and innocent entertainment." The editor announced a second number for Jan. 1842 and requested subscription fees in advance. This number failed to materialize.

no.1	Oct. 1841	APS II, Reel 940

No.1: Index not available for photographing.

Microfilm edition was prepared from DLC copy.

OMEGA. *SEE* Health.

OMNIUM GATHERUM, a monthly magazine, recording authentick accounts of the most remarkable productions, events, and occurrences, in providence, nature, and art. v.1; Nov. 1809-Oct. 1810. Boston: Printed by T. Kennard, 1810.

560 p. illus. (facsim.) plates, ports.

This miscellany included biography, news items, poetry and anecdotes, and listed deaths and marriages. A section called "London Paragraphs" presented short items of British news and much miscellaneous material.

v1, no1-2	Nov.-Dec. 1809	APS II, Reel 36
v1, no2-13	Jan.-Oct. 1810	Reel 219

Microfilm edition was prepared from DLC copy.

ONEIDA CIRCULAR. A weekly journal of home, science and general intelligence. Pub. by the Oneida & Wallingford communities. v1-12, Nov. 6, 1851-Feb. 22, 1864; new ser., v.1-13, no.10, Mar. 21, 1864-Mar. 9, 1876. Brooklyn, N.Y. [etc.]

25 v.
Issued semiweekly, Nov. 1852-Nov. 1853; 3 times a week, Dec. 1853-Dec. 1854.

"The continuation of the Free church circular, published till recently at Oneida; the Spiritual magazine [i.e. Spiritual moralist?] Perfectionist, and Witness, published through a succession of years at Putney, Vt.; and the Perfectionist, published in 1834, at New Haven Conn."

Title varies: 1851-70, The Circular—1871-76, Oneida circular ... Editors: 1851-Oct. 1852, J.H. Noyes.—Nov. 1852-Nov. 1853, J.H. & G.W. Noyes.—Dec. 1853-1854, "Ed. by a community".—1855-Feb. 1864, "By the Oneida community".—Mar. 1864-Apr. 1865, T.L. Pitt.—May 1865-July 1866, G.W. Noyes.—Aug. 1866-Sept. 1867, Alfred Barron.—1871-72, W.A. Hinds.—Jan.-Sept. 8, 1873, Tirzah C. Miller.—Sept. 15, 1873-Mar. 1876, Harriet M. Worden.

Published in Brooklyn, 1851-54; Oneida, N.Y., 1855-Feb. 1864; Mount Tom (Wallingford, Conn.) Mar. 1864-Mar. 9, 1868; Oneida community, Mar. 23, 1868-1876. Superseded by the American socialist (1876-79).

The weekly *Oneida Circular* was the organ of the perfectionist communities founded by John Hymphrey Noyes, and was preceded by three or four other periodicals edited by him and published by these communities. After the perfectionist community was driven out of Putney, Vermont, colonies were established at Oneida, New York and at Wallingford, Connecticut. The *Free Church Circular* was published at Oneida from 1847 until 1851, when its plant was destroyed by fire, and a new series under the title *Circular* was begun at Brooklyn. After two annual volumes, it was moved to Oneida and after 10 years was moved to Wallingford, and then back to Oneida. In his *Circular* Noyes expounded his doctrines of spiritualism, communism, and free love. The early volumes dealt mainly with religion and its relationship to communism, and featured sections of "Home-Talks" and "Table-Talks." In later years the contents were broadened to include more on science, as well as poetry, U.S. and foreign news, lists of new publications, and miscellaneous items. Articles dealt with the beliefs of the perfectionist community, and the "Community Journal" kept the reader informed of the latest activities in the community.

Circular

v1-2	Nov. 6, 1851-Nov. 12, 1853	APS III, Reel 670
v3-7	Dec. 6, 1853-Jan. 20, 1859	Reel 671
v8-nsv2	Jan. 27, 1859-Mar. 12, 1866	Reel 672
nsv3-7	Mar. 19, 1866-Dec. 26, 1870	Reel 673

Oneida Circular

nsv8-13	Jan. 2, 1871-Mar. 9, 1876	Reel 674

Several vols. lack title pages. Several pages are stained, creased, or torn, and have print show-through with some loss of text. Vol. 6: issue 51 is missing. Vol. 12: issue 29 is missing; not available for photographing. Page 63 is repeated in number only; page 64 is misnumbered.

Microfilm edition was prepared from DLC, IU, NhD, NIC, and WHi copies.

SEE ALSO: American Socialist.

THE OPEN COURT, a quarterly magazine. [Devoted to the science of religion, the religion of science, and the extension of the religious parliament idea] v.1-50 (no.1-939); Feb. 17, 1887-Oct. 1936. Chicago, Open Court Pub. Co.

50 v. illus., plates, ports.
Biweekly, Feb. 1887-Feb. 1888; weekly, Mar. 1888-Dec. 1896; monthly, Jan. 1897-1933; quarterly, 1934-1936.

Subtitle varies.
Editor: Feb. 1887-1919, Paul Carus.
Twenty years of the Open court, an index of contributed and editorial articles including authors and titles alphabetically arranged in one. Dictionary catalogue. Vols. i-xx, 1887-1906. Chicago, Open Court Pub. C., 1907. On film: issues for Feb. 17, 1887-Dec. 1905.

Open Court published poetry, fiction, literary essays, travel accounts, and articles on German philosophy, Greek drama, and the American Indian. It was, however, primarily dedicated to discussion of religious reform and was the successor to *Index,* the organ of the Free Religious Association.

v1-3	Feb. 17, 1887-Feb. 20, 1890	APS III, Reel 293
v4-8	Feb. 27, 1890-Dec. 27, 1894	Reel 294
v9-13	Jan. 3, 1895-Dec. 1899	Reel 295
v14-17	Jan. 1900-Dec. 1903	Reel 296
v18-19	Jan. 1904-Dec. 1905	Reel 297

Some pages are stained. Vol. 2: Contents photographed at the end of the volume. Vols. 4-8: Contents for issue nos. 164-383 are photographed at the end of the issues. Vol. 7: Includes a supplement entitled "Supplement to the *Open Court*". Vols. 9-10: Contents for issue nos. 384-487 were photographed at the end of the issues. Vols. 11-13: Contents for the Dec. issue were photographed at the end of the volume.

Microfilm edition was prepared from CL, InTI, TNJ, and TxDaM copies.

OPERA GLASS, devoted to the fine arts, literature and the drama. v.1; Sept. 8, 1828-Nov. 3, 1828. New York, 1828.

1 v.

Edited by John S. Wallace.

Opera Glass was a short-lived theatrical journal edited by John S. Wallace.

v1	Sept. 8,-Nov. 3, 1828	APS II, Reel 1124

Vol. 1: No Index available.

Microfilm edition was prepared from MnU copy.

OPERATIVES' MAGAZINE. *SEE* Lowell Offering.

THE ORDEAL: a critical journal of politicks and literature. v.1; Jan. 7-July 1, 1809. Boston, J.T. Buckingham, 1809.

iv, 412 p. weekly.

J.T. Buckingham, editor.

This short-lived magazine was concerned both with politics and literature; it devoted several sections to politics, and also gave attention to reviews of recent publications, poetry, and the theater.

v1	Jan. 7-July 1, 1809	APS II, Reel 36

ORIENTAL AND BIBLICAL JOURNAL. *SEE* American Antiquarian and Oriental Journal.

THE ORION, a monthly magazine of literature and art. Ed. by William C. Richards. v.1-4, no.6; Mar. 1842-Aug. 1844. Penfield, Ga., W. Richards.

4 v. plates (part col.)

No numbers issued Oct. 1842, May-Aug. 1843.
Subtitle varies.
Vol. 4 includes supplement, "Il Capannetto."

Serial fiction and poetry made up most of the content of this short-lived magazine which was edited by William C. Richards.

v1-4   Mar. 1842-Aug. 1844   APS II, Reel 1216

Vol. 4: Many pages are stained throughout.

Microfilm edition was prepared from GEU, MnU, TxU, and WHi copies.

OUR CONTINENT. *SEE* Continent *and* Potter's American Monthly.

OUR YOUNG FOLKS. An illustrated magazine for boys and girls. v.1-9; Jan. 1865-Dec. 1873. Boston, Ticknor and Fields, 1865-73.

9 v. illus. plates (part col.) port. monthly.

Vol. 2 has added t.-p., in colors.
Merged into St. Nicholas, Jan. 1874.

Editors: 1865-67, J.T. Trowbridge, Gail Hamilton (Pseud. of Mary A. Dodge) Lucy Larcom.–1868-73, J.T. Trowbridge, Lucy Larcom.

The juvenile miscellany, *Our Young Folks,* was ably edited by J.T. Trowbridge, Lucy Larcom, and Gail Hamilton. The magazine contained the usual music, enigmas, and charades, as well as some very well-written stories, articles, and serials contributed by Harriet Beecher Stowe, John G. Whittier, and Louisa May Alcott.

v1-3   Jan. 1865-Dec. 1867   APS III, Reel 65
v4-9   Jan. 1868-Dec. 1873   Reel 66

Microfilm edition was prepared from MiU, NPV, OOxM, and PR copies.

SEE ALSO: St. Nicholas; an Illustrated Magazine for Young Folks.

OUT WEST. *SEE* Overland Monthly and Out West Magazine.

OUTING AND THE WHEELMAN. *SEE* Outing; Sport, Adventure, Travel, Fiction.

OUTING MAGAZINE, THE OUTDOOR MAGAZINE OF HUMAN INTEREST. *SEE* Outing; Sport, Adventure, Travel, Fiction.

OUTING; sport, adventure, travel, fiction. v.1-82, no.1; May 1882-Apr. 1923. New York, Outing Pub. Co., 1882-1923.

v. illus., plates (part col.) monthly.

Title varies: May 1882-Dec. 1883 (v.1-2) Outing, a journal of recreation. Jan. 1884-Mar. 1885, Outing and the Wheelman. Apr. 1885-Mar. 1906, Outing, an illustrated monthly magazine of recreation (subtitle varies). Apr. 1906-Apr. 1913, The Outing magazine, the outdoor magazine of human interest. May 1913-Apr. 1923, Outing: sport, adventure, travel, fiction (cover-title: Outing).

Editors: Feb. 1886-Aug. 1887, Poultney Bigelow.–Apr. 1888-Mar. 1900, J.H. Worman (with B.J. Worman, 1897-1900).–Apr. 1900-Feb. 1909, Caspar Whitney.–1909?-Apr. 1923, Albert Britt.
Imprint varies: 1882, Albany, W.B. Howland–1882-83, Albany, Outing Publishing and Printing Co., Limited.–1884-85, Boston, The Wheelman Company.–1886-1923, New York [etc.] Outing Publishing Company.

Absorbed the Wheelman in Jan. 1884; v.3, no.1-3 of the Wheelman (issued Oct.-Dec. 1883) were counted as the first 3 numbers of v.3 of the consolidated magazine, Jan. 1884 bearing the number v.3, no. 4. Absorbed All outdoors in Mar. 1922. On film: issues for Oct. 1882-Mar. 1911.

Outing was a gentleman's outdoor magazine which included articles on all amateur sports. Contributions by well-known sportsmen were about hunting, fishing, college athletics, rowing, cricket, yachting, travel, exploration, and photography. Cycling was emphasized in some long serial publications. Ownership changed hands many times, and throughout most of its life, *Outing* was on insecure financial footing.

Outing, a Journal of Recreation
v1-2   Oct. 1882-Dec. 1883   APS III, Reel 297

Outing and the Wheelman
v.3   Jan.-Mar. 1884   Reel 297
v.4-5   Apr. 1884-Mar. 1885   Reel 298

Outing, an Illustrated Monthly Magazine of Recreation
v6-8   Apr. 1885- Sept. 1886   Reel 298
v9-14   Oct. 1886-Sept. 1889   Reel 299
v15-19   Oct. 1889-Mar. 1892   Reel 300
v20-25   Apr. 1892-Sept. 1895   Reel 301
v26-30   Oct. 1895-Sept. 1897   Reel 302
v31-34   Oct. 1897-Sept. 1899   Reel 303
v35-39   Oct. 1899-Mar. 1902   Reel 304
v40-43   Apr. 1902-Mar. 1904   Reel 305
v44-47   Apr. 1904-Mar. 1906   Reel 306

Outing Magazine
v48-51   Apr. 1906-Mar. 1908   Reel 307
v52-55   Apr. 1908-Mar. 1910   Reel 308
v56-57   Apr. 1910-Mar. 1911   Reel 309

Microfilm edition was prepared from C, CCC, CLSM, FJ, FU, InS, MoS, MWiW, NbO, NjP, and ScU copies.

OUTLOOK. *SEE* Independent; *and* New Outlook.

OUTLOOK AND INDEPENDENT. *SEE* New Outlook.

*** OVERLAND MONTHLY.** *SEE* Californian and Overland Monthly; *and* Overland Monthly and Out West Magazine.

*** OVERLAND MONTHLY AND OUT WEST MAGAZINE.** v.1-15, July 1868-Dec. 1875; 2d ser., v.1-93, no.4; Jan. 1883-1935. San Francisco, A. Roman, 1868-75; San Francisco, Overland Pub. Co.

108 v. illus., plates (part col.) ports., maps.

Title varies: July 1868-Dec. 1875, Jan. 1883-Dec. 1886, The Overland monthly, devoted to the development of the country. Jan. 1887-July 1923, The Overland monthly. Aug. 1923- Overland monthly and Out West magazine.

Publication suspended from 1876 to 1882, inclusive. The second series (begun Jan. 1883 by the California publishing company) was formed by the union of the old Overland monthly and the Californian; a western monthly magazine (published Jan. 1880-Dec. 1882. 6 v. Absorbed Out West in May 1923.

Bret Harte, editor, 1868-1870.

Anton Roman founded the *Overland Monthly* with one eye on promoting California and the other on offering western writers a medium for their work. By far, the most prosperous volumes belong to the early years when Francis Bret Harte was an editor and contributor. His first tale published in the second number and entitled "The Luck of Roaring Camp" brought instant acclaim from the East. For two years, until 1870, Harte's active editing and occasional pieces made *Overland* a smash success. When Harte resigned to take a post back East, the magazine promptly retrogressed, losing money for its new proprietor, John H. Carmany. After struggling for five years, the monthly was suspended in 1875. Readers will find this First Series affords a valuable insight into California history—in particular, its Indians, gold mining, and Chinese population. W.C. Bartlett, Ina Coobrith, Benjamin P. Avery, J. Ross Brown, Prentice Mulford, Edward Rowland Sill, and Daniel Coit Gilman are but a few in the long list of contributors.

In 1883, a Second Series emerged. Many of the former contributors as well as many new authors offered their literary talent. Josiah Royce, Albert S. Cook, Maria Louise Pool, Sara Halstead, and John V. Cheney name only a few. Although the *Overland* remained a source of Californian intelligence, the scope was broadened to include national news. Some political articles also appeared from time to time.

v1-7	July 1868-Dec. 1871	APS III, Reel 33
v8-14	Jan. 1872-June 1875	Reel 34
v15-2sv5	July 1875-June 1885	Reel 35
2sv6-10	July 1885-Dec. 1887	Reel 36
2sv11-15	Jan. 1888-June 1890	Reel 37
2sv16-20	July 1890-Dec. 1892	Reel 38
2sv21-24	Jan. 1893-Dec. 1894	Reel 39
2sv25-28	Jan. 1895-Dec. 1896	Reel 40
2sv29-33	Jan. 1897-June 1899	Reel 41
2sv34-39	July 1899-June 1902	Reel 42
2sv40-44	July 1902-Dec. 1904	Reel 43
2sv45-49	Jan. 1905-June 1907	Reel 44
2sv50-54	July 1907-Dec. 1909	Reel 45
2sv55-59	Jan. 1910-June 1912	Reel 46
2sv60-64	July 1912-Dec. 1914	Reel 47
2sv65-69	Jan. 1915-June 1917	Reel 48
2sv70-75	July 1917-June 1920	Reel 49
2sv76-82	July 1920-Dec. 1924	Reel 50
2sv83-88	Jan. 1925-Dec. 1930	Reel 51
2sv89-93	Jan. 1931-June 1935	Reel 52

Pagination is irregular. Some pages are stained, torn, or have faded or missing print. Some volumes are tightly bound. Many advertising pages throughout Volumes are missing. First Series Vols. 1-15: pages 5-8 are missing. Second Series Vol. 1: pages 111-12 are lacking. Second Series Vol. 8: "History of Overland Monthly" follows at end of Volume. Second Series Vol. 20: advertising pages follow page 360. Bound and photographed out of order. Appear to be complete. Second Series Vol. 22: lacks the agricultural issue I-VIII for Sept. "Announcements" for 1894 in November issue. Second Series Vols. 38-39: Please note that pagination is continued from Vol. 38 to 39. Second Series Vol. 49: six pages appear to be missing between 468-85. Second Series Vol. 52: Two pages between 394-402 appear to be missing. Second Series Vol. 57: lacking pages 91-124 and 219-250; not available for photographing. Second Series Vol. 66: lacking pages 179-187, 549-558. Second Series Vol. 72: lacking pages 91-92, 275-280, 367-371, 455-460 and 643-644. Second Series Vol. 74: pages 89-90 missing. Second Series Vol. 78: July-August issues combined. Second Series Vol. 83: Index dated incorrectly. Second Series Vol. 84: Index numbered incorrectly. Second Series Vol. 90: pages 23-26 not photographed, contained the Index for Vol. 89; were not replaced in Vol. 90. Second Series Vol. 93: Index not available. Please refer to the Table of Contents.

Microfilm edition was prepared from MiU, MiD, InI, CL, C, NjP, NcD, OOxM, Mi, MiGr, TxWB, K, ScU, LNHT, OAU, KyL, and OkT copies.

OVERLAND MONTHLY, DEVOTED TO THE DEVELOPMENT OF THE COUNTRY. *SEE* Overland Monthly and Out West Magazine.

PACKARD'S MONTHLY. *SEE* Phrenological Journal and Science of Health.

PANOPLIST. *SEE* Massachusetts Missionary Magazine *and* Missionary Herald at Home and Abroad.

PANOPLIST AND MISSIONARY MAGAZINE. *SEE* Missionary Herald at Home and Abroad.

PARLEY'S MAGAZINE. v.1-12; Mar. 16, 1833-Dec. 1844. New York, C.S. Francis.

12 v. illus., plates.

A juvenile miscellany founded in 1833 by Samuel G. Goodrich. It was instructive and moral, and featured a large number of woodcuts—12,000 in the first nine volumes. These woodcuts decorated the cover and illustrated the stories; pictures of wild animals and travel scenes appeared throughout. A great variety of material was included: Bible stories, little moralized tales, fables, dialogues, poems, letters, puzzles, and games. Articles dealt with geography, travel, natural history and with various industries and arts; also included were bits of curious information and directions for physical exercises. A page of music appeared in many issues, and serials included *Travels in Canada* with "Peter Parley," published in 1841. In 1844 it merged with *Merry's Museum for Boys and Girls,* which Goodrich had begun in 1841.

v1-6	Mar. 16, 1833-Dec. 1838	APS II, Reel 669
v7-12	Jan. 1839-Dec. 1844	Reel 670

Microfilm edition was prepared from ICU copy.

SEE ALSO: Merry's Museum for Boy's and Girls.

THE PARLOUR COMPANION. v.1-3, no.34; 1817-Aug. 21, 1819. Philadelphia.

3 v. weekly.

Superseded the Juvenile port-folio and literary miscellany.

Published by Thomas G. Condie, Jr., the *Parlour Companion* was a successor to the *Juvenile Port-Folio,* also edited by Condie. Like the *Port-Folio,* the *Parlour Companion* was a four-page weekly and was similar to it in content, but contained less variety and, in general, the first two pages contained installments of serialized tales, the third page contained anecdotes and miscellany, and the back page was devoted to poetry.

v1-3, no.34	1817-Aug. 21, 1819	APS II, Reel 219

SEE ALSO: Juvenile Port-Folio.

PARLOUR REVIEW, AND JOURNAL OF MUSIC, LITERATURE, AND THE FINE ARTS. nos.1-10, 1838. Philadelphia, 1838.

10 no.

In two editions: French and English.

v1	Jan. 6-Mar. 10, 1838	APS II, Reel 845

Index and table of contents are lacking. In the music section, a page from a composition called "The Funeral March" by L. Van Beethoven is torn. Best copy available.

Microfilm edition was prepared from RPB copy.

THE PARTERRE, a weekly magazine, conducted by a trio. v.1-2; June 15, 1816-June 28, 1817. Philadelphia, Printed by Probasco & Justice [1816]-17.

2 v. in 1.

Edited by Nathaniel Chapman (with W.P. Dewees, J.D. Godman, 1825-27)

Conducted by "a trio," this weekly miscellany was to disseminate "useful knowledge" for both young and old and was to amuse as well as instruct. In addition to serialized tales, it featured the "Chamber of Fashion," a column in which fashion was satirized, and a series called "The Escritoire" by "Simon Scribble." It also included sentimental prose and poetry, essays on faults and self-improvement, biographical sketches, and anecdotes.

v1-2   June 15, 1816-June 28, 1817   APS II, Reel 184

THE PARTHENON; or, Literary and scientific museum. v.1, no.1-16; Aug. 22-Dec. 8, 1827. New York [Woodworth, Webb]

1 v. weekly.

Editor: Aug. 1827-Samuel Woodworth.
Film incomplete: no.5 and 13-16 wanting.

Among the subjects treated in this departmentalized weekly were antiquities, mythology, history, biography, geology, natural philosophy, and rural economy. Published by S. Woodworth.

v1   Aug. 22, 1827-Nov. 7, 1827   APS II, Reel 1257

Several pages have faded print. Pgs. 35-38 are missing. Pgs. 45-46 are bound out of order.

Microfilm edition was prepared from CSmH copy.

THE PASTIME; a literary paper. v.1-2, no.7; Feb. 21, 1807-June 25, 1808. [Schenectady, N.Y., R. Schermerhorn etc.]

2 v. weekly (irregular)
Edited by J.H. Payne.

This Schenectady literary magazine published original poetry and essays, literary news, some biographical sketches and anecdotes, and articles on the fine arts and the history of literature.

v1-2, no.7   Feb. 21, 1807-June 25, 1808   APS II, Reel 36

THE PATHFINDER. no.1-15; Feb. 25-June 3, 1843. New York.

15 no. weekly.
Seventh issue numbered incorrectly as no.6. Continuous paging, p. 1-240.

The *Pathfinder* was basically divided into three sections: "The Political Pathfinder" contained discussions of current political and social questions; "The Literary Pathfinder" included criticisms of new publications, extracts from new books and magazines, short tales, and the latest literary news; and "The Commercial Pathfinder" published a weekly review of the stock market, current prices in New York and other commerce news. Later, sections devoted to music and theater were added. In addition, it published foreign and domestic news, proceedings of Congress and the state legislature, poetry, and some ads.

no.2-15   Mar. 4-June 3, 1843   APS II, Reel 1407

Several pages are stained and have print faded. Title page, index and nos. 1, 6 and 11 are lacking. Best copy available for photographing. No. 7 is misnumbered.

Microfilm edition was prepared from NBuG copy.

THE PATRIOT, or, Scourge of aristocracy. v.1. Stonington-port, Conn., S. Trumbull, 1801-02.

416 p.

The *Patriot* was a weekly political magazine which published essays, articles, and speeches to support its viewpoint, which was republican, anti-federalist, and in favor of Thomas Jefferson. Proceedings of Congress and some poetry were also included.

v1   1801-1802   APS II, Reel 36

PAUL PRY. *SEE* Huntress.

PEARL AND LITERARY GAZETTE. *SEE* Boston Pearl, A Gazette of Polite Literature.

PENNSYLVANIA JOURNAL OF PRISON DISCIPLINE AND PHILANTHROPY. *SEE* Journal of Prison Discipline and Philanthropy.

PENNSYLVANIA LAW JOURNAL. *SEE* American Law Journal.

* **THE PENNSYLVANIA MAGAZINE OF HISTORY AND BIOGRAPHY**. v.1-, 1877- Philadelphia, Historical Society of Pennsylvania.

illus. quarterly.

Issues for 1877-Jan. 1935 called also no. 1-233.
Indexes: Vols. 1-75, 1877-1951. 1 v.
On film: issues for 1877-Oct. 1906.

This famous biographical and historical quarterly also published writings of Mark Twain, Constance Fenimore Woolson, Thomas Wentworth Higginson, and Benjamin Silliman.

v1-7	1877-1883	APS III, Reel 456
v8-13	1884-1889	Reel 457
v14-18	1890-1894	Reel 458
v19-23	1895-1899	Reel 459
v24-29	1900-1905	Reel 460
v30	Mar. 1906-Oct. 1906	Reel 461

Microfilm edition was prepared from C, CSmH, and NjP copies.

THE PENNSYLVANIA MAGAZINE; or, American monthly museum. v.1-2; Jan. 1775-July 1776. Philadelphia, R. Aitken [1775-76]

2 v. illus., plates, port., maps, plans.
Thomas Paine, editor.

Edited by Thomas Paine, it printed a running account of the war and a good variety of material from British and American sources as well as original contributions. In addition to political material, it presented biography, scientific articles, and comment on marriage and education.

| v1-2 | Jan. 1775-July 1776 | APS I, Reel 24 |

Some pages are missing.

Microfilm edition was prepared from MiU-C copy.

THE PENNY POST, containing fresh news, advertisements, useful hints, &c. no.1-9; Jan. 9-27, 1769. [Philadelphia, Printed and sold by B. Mecom]

32 p.
Three no. a week.

A magazine-like newspaper which adhered to the British political point of view, it focused mainly on foreign and domestic news but also included short pieces, epigrams, poems, and brief essays on general subjects.

| no.1-9 | Jan. 9-27, 1769 | APS I, Reel 24 |

Microfilm edition was prepared from PPL copy.

PEOPLE'S ILLUSTRATED WEEKLY AND PRAIRIE FARMER. *SEE* Prairie Farmer.

PEOPLE'S RIGHTS. *SEE* Working Man's Advocate.

PERIODICAL LIBRARY. v.1-3; 1833. Philadelphia, 1833.

3 v.
Running title: Greenbank's periodical library.

Intended to supply in the cheapest possible form publication of new and standard works of poetry, biography, and memoirs, and works on travel, history, science, and adventure. Each issue usually consisted of one or more complete works, though sometimes one work filled several numbers. Contents included *The Life and Trials of Henry Pestalozzi,* the *History of Peter the Great,* the essays of Charles Lamb, the travels of Hazlitt, as well as writings on Sir Walter Scott, Lord Byron, William Wordsworth, and Sir Walter Raleigh, and many other subjects—the West Indies, Italian art, the voyages of Captain Parry, the Ottoman Empire.

| v1-3 | 1833 | APS II, Reel 736 |

Microfilm edition was prepared from MiU and NjP copies.

PERIODICAL SKETCHES. no.1; 1820. New York, A.T. Goodrich.

35 p.

Edited by an American patriot, pseud.

Only one number of this magazine was published and it was entirely devoted to an article describing an Indian attack, which was titled "Sketch of an Indian Irruption into the Town of Shawangunk, in the year 1780."

| no.1 | 1820 | APS II, Reel 184 |

THE PETERSON MAGAZINE. v.1-113; Jan. 1842-Apr. 1898. Philadelphia, C.J. Peterson. New York, Penfield Pub. Co., 1894-98.

113 v. illus., plates (part col.) monthly.

Title varies: -May 1843, The Lady's world. June 1843 The Artist and lady's world. (Engraved t.-p. for Jan.-June 1843 reads: Ladies national magazine) July 1843- The Ladies' national magazine (Caption title, Jan. 1848- : Peterson's magazine, t.-p. reads: The Ladies' national magazine) Peterson's magazine (t.-p. reads: Peterson's ladies national magazine; caption title: Peterson's magazine) Dec. 1892-1894, The New Peterson magazine, 1894-1898, The Peterson magazine.

Editors: Ann S. Stephens, C.J. Peterson.–C.J. Peterson.
Absorbed the Artist in June 1843. Merged into the Argosy.

Founded in Jan. 1842, by Charles J. Peterson, this women's magazine included serial installments, short stories, poems, patterns, publisher's notes, and book reviews. Among its contributors were Mrs. Ann S. Stephens and Emily H. May.

Lady's World of Fashion
| v1-2 | Jan.-Dec. 1842 | APS II, Reel 1292 |

Lady's World
| v3 | Jan.-May 1843 | Reel 1292 |

Artist and Lady's World
| v3 | June 1843 | Reel 1292 |

Ladies' National Magazine
| v4-11 | July 1843-June 1847 | Reel 1292 |
| v12-14 | July 1847-Dec. 1848 | Reel 1293 |

Peterson's Magazine
v15-21	Jan. 1849-June 1852	Reel 1293
v22-29	July 1852-June 1856	Reel 1294
v30-36	July 1856-Dec. 1859	Reel 1295
v37-42	Jn. 1860-Dec. 1862	Reel 1296
v43-48	Jan. 1863-Dec. 1865	Reel 1297
v49-55	Jan. 1866-Dec. 1869	Reel 1298
v56-61	July 1869-June 1872	Reel 1299
v62-68	July 1872-Dec. 1875	Reel 1300
v69-74	Jan. 1876-Dec. 1878	Reel 1301
v75-80	Jan. 1879-Dec. 1881	Reel 1302
v81-87	Jan. 1882-June 1885	Reel 1303
v88-93	July 1885-June 1888	Reel 1304
v94-99	July 1888-June 1891	Reel 1305
v100-102	July 1891-Nov. 1892	Reel 1306

New Peterson Magazine
| nsv1-2(103-104) | Dec. 1892-Dec. 1893 | Reel 1306 |
| nsv3-4, no2 | Jan.-Aug. 1894 | Reel 1307 |

Peterson Magazine
| nsv4, no3-v6 | Sept. 1894-Dec. 1896 | Reel 1307 |
| nsv7(113) | Jan.-Dec. 1897 | Reel 1308 |

Best copy available for photographing. Some pages have print show-through or are stained or torn. Several volumes have pages missing. Vols. 40-101: blank pages opposite plates were not filmed in some issues and are missing from page count. Some advertisement pages are missing. New series vol. 5: issue 7 is misnumbered as new series vol. 6. New series vol. 8 is lacking; not available for photographing.

Microfilm edition was prepared from CoGrS, CU, DLC, GA, IC, InU, KyLo, MiU, MnU, MoS, NBuG, NPV, NR, NhD, NjP, OrU, PLeB, PPi, RPB, TKL, TxHR, TxU, and WHi copies.

PETERSON'S LADIES NATIONAL MAGAZINE. *SEE* Peterson Magazine.

LE PETIT CENSEUR. Semaine critique & litteraire, francaise & anglaise. no.1-12; 19 sept.-5 dec. 1805. [Philadelphia]

284 p.

This Philadelphia literary weekly was written in French, with some parts in English. It provided news from the U.S., from France, and from other countries, a section of politics, and historical, literary, and religious material, as well as some memoirs, features on fashions, and occasional poetry.

no.1-12   Sept. 19-Dec. 5, 1805   APS II, Reel 37

LE PETIT CENSEUR, CRITIQUE ET LITTERAIRE; journal francais a New-York. no.1-17; 4 juil-13 aout 1805. New-York.

136 p. Three no. a week.

Edited by Alexis Daudet, this French-language magazine published two issues per week. It gave attention to political news, foreign news, women's fashions, new books, and literature and the fine arts, including the theater. Some poetry and anecdotes were included.

no.1-17   July 4-Aug. 13, 1805   APS II, Reel 37

THE PHALANX: organ of the doctrine of association. v.1 (no.1-23); Oct. 5, 1843-May 28, 1845. New York, Pub. for the proprietors by J. Winchester [1843-45]

355, [1] p.

Absorbed the Health journal and independent magazine in Oct. 1843.
Title varies: Oct. 1843-Apr. 1844, The Phalanx: or, Journal of social science. Devoted to the cause of association, or a social reform, and the elevation of the human race ... May 1844-May 1845, The Phalanx: organ of the doctrine of association.

Albert Brisbane and Osborne Macdaniel, editors.

Albert Brisbane, the messiah of Fourierism in America, established the monthly *Phalanx* in 1843 for the purpose of propagating the newly discovered movement. It was soon made a weekly and in 1845 was moved to Brook Farm, where it was succeeded by the *Harbinger* in 1845.

v1   Oct. 5, 1843-May 28, 1845   APS II, Reel 671

Microfilm edition was prepared from DLC copy.

PHILADELPHIA ALBUM AND LADIES' LITERARY GAZETTE. *SEE* Philadelphia Album and Ladies' Literary Port Folio.

THE PHILADELPHIA ALBUM AND LADIES' LITERARY PORT FOLIO. v.1-8; Apr., 1826-Dec. 27, 1834. Philadelphia, T.C. Clarke.

8 v. plates. weekly.
Volume numbering irregular. On Jan. 2, 1830, v.4 was recommenced on account of irregularity in previous issues of the 4th vol. 9 numbers had already been issued.

Title varies: June 7, 1826-May 30, 1827, The Album and ladies' weekly gazette. June 6, 1827-July 3, 1830, Philadelphia album and ladies' literary gazette. July 10, 1830-Philadelphia album and ladies' literary portfolio.

Editor: Robert Morris.
Ceased publication from May 27, 1829-Jan. 2, 1830.
Merged into Pennsylvania inquirer, later Philadelphia inquirer.

Begun by Thomas Cottrell Clarke in 1826, this women's weekly was a newspaper-like magazine intended to be a moral, amusing, and valuable miscellany. It dealt with matters particularly of interest to women—manners, conversation, dress, and beauty, as well as providing sentimental fiction, moral stories, biographical sketches, a weekly summary of domestic and foreign news, extracts from new publications, and essays on a variety of topics. Also included were recipes, anecdotes, book reviews, and listings of plays. Much space was occupied by selected material.

Album and Ladies' Weekly Gazette
v1   June 7, 1826-May 30, 1827   APS II, Reel 721

Philadelphia Album and Ladies Literary Gazette
v2   June 6, 1827-May 28, 1828   Reel 721
v3   June 4, 1828-May 27, 1829   Reel 722
v4, no1-27   Jan. 2-July 3, 1830   Reel 723

Philadelphia Album and Ladies' Literary Portfolio
v4, no.28-v5   July 10, 1830-Dec. 31, 1831   Reel 723
v6-7   Jan. 7, 1832-Dec. 28, 1833   Reel 724
v8   Jan. 4-Dec. 27, 1834   Reel 725

Microfilm edition begins with June 7, 1826. Several volumes lack indexes and title pages. Vols. 4 and 5 are bound and photographed together.

Microfilm edition was prepared from DLC, PHi and WHi copies.

THE PHILADELPHIA JOURNAL OF THE MEDICAL AND PHYSICAL SCIENCES. v.1-9, 1820-24; v.[10]-14 (new ser., v.1-5) 1825-27. Philadelphia, M. Carey, 1820-27.

14 v. illus., plates, quarterly.

Superseded by American Journal of the Medical Sciences.

Dr. Nathaniel Chapman, a professor of medicine at the University of Pennsylvania, founded this medical journal in 1820 in reply to Sydney Smith's attack on American culture which appeared in the *Edinburgh Review*. Smith's question "What does the world yet owe to American physicians and surgeons?" was adopted as the motto of this quarterly journal, which traced the progress of medicine in the U.S. It contained articles on medical theory and experimentation, case descriptions written by the editors and by other physicians, medical news, and biography, along with criticism of medical literature, including foreign journals.

v1-5   Jan. 1820-1822   APS II, Reel 184
v6-14   1823-Dec. 1827   Reel 185

SEE ALSO: American Journal of the Medical Sciences.

THE PHILADELPHIA MAGAZINE AND REVIEW; or, Monthly Repository of information and amusement. v.1 (no. 1-6); Jan.-June 1799. Philadelphia, Benjamin Davies.

vi [7]-415 (i.e. 420), [3] p. front.

Paging irregular: nos. 308-312 repeated.

Printed selections on various subjects from European publications, especially from Great Britain, reviews of new British and domestic publications, summaries of foreign and domestic news and politics, records of deaths and marriages, and poetry.

v1, no1-6   Jan.-June 1799   APS I, Reel 24

Microfilm edition was prepared from DLC copy.

PHILADELPHIA MAGAZINE, and weekly repertory. v.1, nos.1-36; Jan.-Nov. 7, 1818. Philadelphia, 1818.

1 v. (various pagings)

Subtitle varies.

This weekly literary miscellany proposed to devote a large portion of its space to original prose and verse, but much of its sentimental fiction and poetry were selected from other publications. Special features were its biographical sketches of eminent women and its criticism of the theater. Geography and history were given some attention; and anecdotes, some of them humorous, and a summary of weekly news, rounded out the contents.

v1, nos. 1-36   Jan.-Nov. 7, 1818   APS II, Reel 186

THE PHILADELPHIA MEDICAL AND PHYSICAL JOURNAL. Collected and arranged by Benjamin Smith Barton, M.D. v.1-3; [Nov. 1804]-1808. Philadelphia, J. Conrad.

3 v. plates, tables.

Includes 1st-3rd supplement, Mar. 1806-May, 1809.

Dr. Benjamin Smith Barton, a professor at the University of Pennsylvania, conducted his medical and scientific journal for four years. The first section contained original papers on medicine and on various scientific subjects—natural science, geography, agriculture, and archaeology. The medical papers dealt with yellow fever epidemics, and other types of fevers, as well as with other medical problems and treatments. Other sections of the magazine provided biographical sketches of physicians, reviews of new medical and scientific publications, and miscellaneous items of interest.

v1-3   Nov. 1804-1808   APS II, Reel 37

Supplement
v1-3   Mar. 1806-May 1809   Reel 37

THE PHILADELPHIA MEDICAL MUSEUM, conducted by John Redman Coxe, M.D. v.1-6, 1805-1809; new ser., v.1, 1810. Philadelphia, T. Dobson, etc.

7 v. plates, ports, facsim.

Conducted by John Redman Coxe of the University of Pennsylvania medical school, this medical journal described various medical cases, diseases, and cures. Original papers were contained in the first section, called "Medical Museum," while a second section, the "Medical and Philosophical Register" contained all other material, which included selected papers, lists of new publications, book reviews, some biography, and much miscellaneous medical information.

v1-6   1805-1809   APS II, Reel 38

nsv1   1810   Reel 186

PHILADELPHIA MEDICAL TIMES. *SEE* Medical Times and Register.

THE PHILADELPHIA MINERVA, containing a variety of fugitive pieces in prose and poetry, original and selected. v.1-4, no.23 (no.1-179); Feb. 7, 1795-July 7, 1798. Philadelphia, Woodruff & Turner [etc.]

4 v. weekly.

Superseded by the Dessert to the true American. Cf. Evans. American bibliography. Film incomplete: v.1, no.1-2, 29 (Feb. 7-14, Aug. 22, 1795) wanting.

A literary miscellany notable chiefly because it reached the comparatively great age of three and a half years.

v1-4 (no.1-179)   Feb. 7, 1795-July 7, 1798   APS I, Reel 25

Microfilm edition was prepared from MWA and WHi copies.

SEE ALSO: Dessert to the True American.

THE PHILADELPHIA MONTHLY MAGAZINE. Devoted to general literature and the fine arts. v.1-2, Oct. 1827-Sept. 1828 [new ser.] v.1-6, Nov. 1828-1830. Philadelphia, J. Dobson.

8 v. monthly.

Editors: Oct. 1827-July 1828, I.C. Snowden.—Sept. 1828- B.R. Evans. Film incomplete: new ser. v.2-6 wanting.

The *Philadelphia Monthly Magazine,* "devoted to general literature and the fine arts", was conducted by Dr. Isaac Clarkson Snowden. Following his death in July of 1828, B.R. Evans assumed the editorship.

v1-nsv1   Oct. 1827-Oct. 1829   APS II, Reel 1092

Vol. 1-New Series Vol. 1: Indexes are not available; please refer to the Tables of Contents for each issue.

Microfilm edition was prepared from CtW and WHi copies.

THE PHILADELHPIA MONTHLY MAGAZINE; or, Universal repository of knowledge and entertainment. v.1-2 (no.1-9); Jan.-Sept. 1798. Philadelphia, T. Condie.

2 v. illus., ports.

Includes History of the pestilence, commonly called yellow fever, by Thomas Condie and Richard Folwell.
Edited by T. Condie.

In addition to the usual material—fiction and poetry, foreign and domestic news, and miscellaneous articles—it published weather reports, current prices and rates of exchange, occasional articles on the theater, and a serial biography of Washington. Several ads and illustrations appeared in each issue.

v1-2 (no.1-9)   Jan.-Sept. 1798   APS I, Reel 25

Microfilm edition was prepared from MiU-C copy.

THE PHILADELPHIA MUSEUM; or, Register of natural history and the arts. v.1, no.1; Jan. 1824. Philadelphia, Printed at the Museum Press.

16 p.

The object of the *Philadelphia Museum* was to promote interest in the study of science, but only one number was published. Its contents included a sketch of the history of the Philadelphia Museum, articles on the fine arts, on the bat and opposum, and on magnetism and other science topics, as well as poetry and some news.

v1, no.1   Jan. 1824   APS II, Reel 186

PHILADELPHIA RECORDER. *SEE* Church Record *and* Episcopal Recorder.

PHILADELPHIA REGISTER, AND NATIONAL RE-CORDER. *SEE* Saturday Magazine.

THE PHILADELPHIA REPERTORY. Devoted to literature and useful intelligence. v.1-2; May 5, 1810-May 16, 1812. Philadelphia, D. Heartt, 1811-[12]

2 v. in 1. weekly.

This weekly literary magazine published prose and poetry, biography, literary notices, domestic and foreign news, religious and moral essays, science articles, and proceedings of the state legislature. There were some humorous anecdotes, occasional fashion news, and listings of marriages and deaths.

v1-2   May 5, 1810-May 16, 1812   APS II, Reel 186

PHILADELPHIA REPOSITORY AND WEEKLY REGISTER. *SEE* Repository and Ladies' Weekly Museum.

THE PHILADELPHIA UNIVERSALIST MAGAZINE AND CHRISTIAN MESSENGER, devoted to doctrine, religion, and morality. v.1-2; Aug. 1821-July 1823. Philadelphia, J. Young, Printer.

2 v. monthly.

Supersedes the Christian messenger.
Edited by A. Kneeland.
Superseded by the Gazetteer.

Edited by Rev. Abner Kneeland, this Universalist periodical was a continuation of the *Christian Messenger* and was devoted to "doctrine, religion, and morality." It offered moral and religious essays, poetry, and sermons, as well as news of church activities.

v1-2   Aug. 1821-July 1823   APS II, Reel 187

SEE ALSO: Christian Messenger *and* Gazetteer.

PHILADELPHIAN. *SEE* Circular.

PHILADELPHIER MAGAZIN FUR FREUNDE DER DEUTSCHEN LITERATUR IN AMERIKA. no.1-12, Jan.-Dec. 1824; n.F., Nr. 1-10; (alte Nr. 13-22) Jan.-Okt. 1825. Reading und Philadelphia, etc.

22 v.

Title varies: Jan.-Dec. 1824, Readinger magazin fur freunde der deutschen literatur in Amerika. Jan. 1825- Philadelphier magazin fur freunde der deutschen literatur in Amerika.

Editor: Jan. 1824- J.C. Gossler.
Pub. in Reading, Pa., Jan.-Oct. 1824; in Philadelphia, Nov. 1824-

Readinger Magazin fur Freunde der Deutschen Literatur in Amerika
v1, no.1-12   Jan.-Dec. 1824   APS II, Reel 1196

Philadelphier Magazine fur Freunde der Deutschen Literatur in Amerika
nsv1, no.1-10   Jan.-Oct. 1825   Reel 1196

Microfilm edition was prepared from NCaS copy.

PHILADELPHISCHES MAGAZIN; oder, Unterhaltender Gesellschafter, fur die Deutschen in America. 1 Bd., Stuck 1; 1. May 1798. Philadelphia, Gedruckt bey H. und J.R. Kammerer, jun.

48 p.

A German-language miscellany which was intended mainly for entertainment, and featured articles emphasizing the unusual and extraordinary—strange occurrences, escapes from danger, curious narratives, and adventure. It included a wide variety of material, however, including biography, history, anecdotes, poetry, reports and descriptions of noteworthy persons in Europe and America, some politics, and selections from the writings of well-known historians, travelers, philosophers, and natural scientists.

v1, no.1   May 1, 1798   APS I, Reel 25

Microfilm edition was prepared from PHi copy.

PHILANTHROPIST. *SEE* Cincinnati Weekly Herald and Philanthropist.

PHILANTHROPIST, a weekly journal containing essays, on moral and religious subjects. v.1; Aug. 29, 1817-Dec. 26, 1817; [n.s.] v.1-7, no.26, Dec. 11, 1818-May 15, 1822. Mt. Pleasant, Ohio.

9 v.

Established Aug. 29, 1817 by Charles Osborn and purchased by Elisha Bates on Oct. 8, 1818. Bates adopted a new series volume numbering, cf. Brigham. History and bibliography of American newspapers 1690-1820. Imperfect copy: scattered pages, issues lacking.

Edited by Elisha Bates, the *Philanthropist* was an antislavery paper which was chiefly notable for Benjamin Lundy's antislavery writings. Agriculture and mechanics were given some attention, and the proceedings of the state and national legislatures, brief news items, and poetry were also published.

v1, no.7, 13-16   Oct. 24, Dec. 5-26, 1817   APS II, Reel 187
[n.s.] v1-3   Dec. 11, 1818- Apr. 26, 1820   Reel 187
[n.s.] v4-7   Apr. 29, 1820-Apr. 27, 1822   Reel 188

Many pages have faded print.

THE PHILISTINE; a periodical of protest. v.1-41, no.2; June 1895-July 1915. [East Aurora, N.Y., Roycrofters (etc.)]

41 v. illus. monthly.

Subtitle varies.
Absorbed the Fly leaf, May 1896.

"Printed ... for the Society of Philistines and published by them ..."
Founded and edited for many years by Elbert Hubbard.
On film: v.1-23, 1895-Nov. 1906 and an index to v.1-20, compiled by Julia Ditto Young.

Founded in 1895 by Elbert Hubbard, the *Philistine* was one of the first of the popular pocket magazines. Professing socialism and colorfully criticizing literary editors, magazines, and publishing houses, Hubbard's little magazine became a surprising success. As Hubbard's personal and financial success became secure, the philosophy of the *Philistine* gradually changed toward big business. Hubbard's "Message to Garcia," which applied the lessons of a soldier's loyalty and faithfulness to employer-employee relations, met with immediate acclaim from businss and industry and produced a large demand for reprints. In 1915 Hubbard went down with the *Lusitania.* With his death the *Philistine,* which had largely been Hubbard's work, was discontinued.

Index 1-20	1895-May 1905	APS III, Reel 589
v1-10	June 1895-May 1900	Reel 589
v11-23	June 1900-Nov. 1906	Reel 590

The microfilm edition concludes with Nov. issue of 1906. Vol. 5: Lacks title page. Vol. 6: Lacks title page and issue numbering. Vol. 21: Pages 164-65, 172-73, and 177 have faded print.

Microfilm edition was prepared from C, MnU, and OU copies.

THE PHILOBIBLION; a monthly bibliographical journal. Containing critical notices of, and extracts from, rare, curious, and valuable old books. v.1-2; Dec. 1861-Dec. 1863. New York, G.P. Philes, 1861-63.

2 v.

Edited by George Philip Philes. Nos.1-12 and 24 have cover-title The Philobiblion; a monthly catalogue and literary journal. The catalog appended to each number forms a supplement, separately paged.

Philobiblion was edited by G.P. Philes. It included "critical notices of, and extracts from, rare, curious, and valuable old books."

| v1-2 | Dec. 1861-Dec. 1863 | APS III, Reel 270 |

Vol. 1: Pgs. 271-272 have print missing.

Microfilm edition was prepared from NBuG and NjP copies.

THE PHRENOLOGICAL JOURNAL AND SCIENCE OF HEALTH. v.1-124, no.1; Oct. 1838-Jan. 1911. Philadelphia; New York.

124 v. illus., plates, ports. monthly.
Vol. numbering irregular; v.87 repeated in numbering. v.50-123 also called new ser. v.1-76.

Editors: 1838-41, Nathan Allen.–1841-44, O.S. Fowler, L.N. Fowler.–1844-54, O.S. Fowler, L.N. Fowler, S.R. Wells.–1854-63, L.N. Fowler, S.R. Wells.–1863-75, S.R. Wells.–1875-96, H.S. Drayton, N. Sizer.–1897- H.S. Drayton, N. Sizer, J. A. Fowler.
Absorbed Life illustrated in May 1861; Packard's monthly in Apr. 1870; Science of health in July 1876; the Phrenological magazine (London) in Jan. 1897.

America's first journal of phrenology was founded in 1838 by Nathan Allen, a young medical student. The journal was sold in 1841 to O.S. and L.N. Fowler, who were joined in 1852 by Dr. Samuel R. Wells. The *Phrenological Journal* carried on its cover the familiar drawing of the human head divided into compartments designating various traits. It made a specialty of analyses of

mental characteristics of famous persons, illustrating its articles with portraits. Other features included were physiognomy, ethnology, and articles of miscellany. In later years it was largely a health journal.

American Phrenological Journal
Cumulative Index, v1-3		APS II, Reel 1341
v1-7	Oct. 1838-Dec. 1845	Reel 1341
v8-18	Jan. 1846-Dec. 1853	Reel 1342
v19-37	Jan. 1854-June 1863	Reel 1343
v38-49	July 1863-Dec. 1869	Reel 1344

Phrenological Journal and Science of Health
v50-57	Jan. 1870-Dec. 1873	Reel 1345
v58-64	Jan. 1874-June 1877	Reel 1346
v65-74	July 1877-June 1882	Reel 1347
v75-83	July 1882-Dec. 1886	Reel 1348
v84-92	Jan. 1887-Dec. 1891	Reel 1349
v93-102	Jan. 1892-Dec. 1896	Reel 1350
v103-112	Jan. 1897-Dec. 1901	Reel 1351
v113-119	Jan. 1902-Dec. 1906	Reel 1352
v120-124	Jan. 1907-Jan. 1911	Reel 1353

Several volumes have irregular numbering. Some volumes have stained or faded print, or creased pages. Vol. 6: Issues 1, 4-5, 7-9, and 12 are not available for photographing. Vol. 59: Supplement follows volume. Vol. 76: Supplement follows no. 2.

Microfilm edition was prepared from GEU, IaU, InNhW, MH, MU, MnM, MoS, N, Nh, NjMD, OC, OCLoyd, PHuJ, PSt, and RPB copies.

PHRENOLOGICAL MAGAZINE. *SEE* Phrenological Journal and Science of Health.

PHYSICAL CULTURE. *SEE* Health.

THE PHYSICIANS' AND SURGEONS' INVESTIGATOR; a monthly journal devoted to the best interests of the profession. v.1-10; 1880-89. Buffalo, N.Y., Physicians and Surgeons Association.

10 v. monthly.

Subtitle varies.
Founded and edited by the faculty of the College of Physicians and Surgeons of Buffalo, N.Y. The editor in chief position was held by various members of the faculty. Published by the Investigator Publ. Co., 1886-89. Issues for July-Sept. 1880 and Jan.-Feb. 1883 include "Annual annoucement of the College of Physicians and Surgeons." Microfilm edition wanting v.3; v4, no.3, 5, 10, 12; v8, no. 9, 12. Vol. 10 ends with no. 9.

The *Physicians' and Surgeons' Investigator* was founded and edited by the faculty of the Homeopathic College of Physicians and Surgeons of Buffalo. Published as an exponent of rational homeopathy, it included articles on diagnosis and treatment, medical news and miscellany, book reviews and book notices.

| v1-8 | Jan. 1880-Nov. 1887 | APS III, Reel 567 |
| v9-10 | Jan. 1888-Sept. 1889 | Reel 568 |

Vol. 8: Several pages are tightly bound. No. 5 lacks table of contents. Vol. 9: Pages 289-300 are missing in number only.

Microfilm edition was prepared from CSt-Law, DNLM, L, MiU, and NBuU copies.

THE PHYSICIAN'S MAGAZINE. v.1 (no.1-3); Aug. 1885-Mar. 1886. Philadelphia, Foote & Swift, 1885-86.

242 p. illus. quarterly (irregular)

Caption title.
Supersedes Medicatio localis.
"Prospectus"; p. [1]-54.

The *Physician's Magazine* was a short-lived quarterly published by Foote and Swift in Philadelphia for those of the medical profession.

v1	Aug. 1885-Mar. 1886	APS III, Reel 67

Vol. 1: Index is bound and photographed at the end of the volume.

Microfilm edition was prepared from DLC copy.

PICTORIAL REVIEW ... v.1-40, no.6; Sept. 1899-Mar. 1939. New York, American fashion co.; [etc., etc.] 1899-19 .

40 v. illus. (incl. ports.) monthly.

Editors: Dec. 1899-Dec. 1901. William McDowell.—Mar. 1909-A.T. Vance. Merged with Delineator May 1937; title changed to Pictorial review combined with Delineator. On film: issues for Sept. 15, 1889-Dec. 1906.

This famous women's magazine, which began as a house organ of Albert McDowell's System of Dressmaking and Tailoring, was at first concerned only with women's fashions, but was later expanded to encompass a variety of material of interest to women. This abundantly illustrated monthly included sections titled "Fashion Chat," "The Housewife," "In Motherland," and "Women of All Nations," and offered instructions and patterns for making clothes, information on fashion, advice for housewives and mothers, recipes and luncheon plans, stories, music, some theater news, and much advertising. In 1903 and the years that followed, it added book reviews, poetry, home medical guides, articles on gardening and needlework, some material for children, including children's fashions, and miscellaneous essays. In May, 1937, *Delineator*, another successful women's magazine, was combined with the *Pictorial Review* and the title was changed to *Pictorial Review combined with Delineator*.

v1-5	Sept. 15, 1899-Sept. 1904	APS II, Reel 1487
v6-8	Oct. 1904-Dec. 1906	Reel 1488

Vols. 1-5 lack indexes. Vols. 1 and 6 have torn or missing pages. Vol. 1: issue 5 is missing; not available for photographing.

Microfilm edition was prepared from DLC copy.

PICTORIAL REVIEW COMBINED WITH DELINEATOR. *SEE* Pictorial Review.

THE PILGRIM, or monthly visitor. v.1, no.1-12; May 8, 1822-Apr. 8, 1823. New Haven, 1822-23.

478 p. plates. monthly.

Caption title: The Pilgrim.

Included in the *Pilgrim's* varied contents were articles on the Christian life, accounts of revivals, a summary of religious news, including news on missions and Sunday schools, sermons, poetry, anecdotes, and literary notices.

v1	May 8, 1822-Apr. 8, 1823	APS II, Reel 188

THE PILOT. v1-3 (no.1-156); Sept. 6, 1821-Sept. 11, 1824. New Haven, S.M. Dutton.

3 v. weekly.

Title varies: Sept. 6, 1821-Mar. 13, 1823, The national pilot.

The *Pilot* was concerned with improving agriculture and encouraging trade and industry. It resembled a newspaper, having much miscellaneous material, and had sections for poetry, news, moral items, anecdotes, literature, religion, and miscellany. Also included in the contents were articles of foreign countries, agricultural items, and listings of current prices.

National Pilot

v1-2, no.78	Sept. 6, 1821-Mar. 13, 1823	APS II, Reel 189

Pilot

v2, no.79-v3	Mar. 20, 1823-Sept. 11, 1824	Reel 189

THE PIONEER. A literary and critical magazine. J.R. Lowell and R. Carter, editors and proprietors. v.1, no.1-3; Jan.-Mar. 1843. Boston, Leland and Whiting [1843]

1 v. plates, monthly.

This literary magazine, a joint endeavor of James Russell Lowell and Robert Carter, was intended to provide a substitute for the sentimental fiction so popular at that time. It was to contain original material and articles from the best American authors; however, only three numbers were published. It included poetry, art criticism, musical comment, book reviews, and writings by Lowell and Poe, and was illustrated with wood and steel engravings.

v1	Jan.-Mar. 1843	APS II, Reel 745

Title page is lacking.

Microfilm edition was prepared from MiU copy.

THE PIONEER, consisting of essays, literary, moral and theological. Graham, David. v.1, no.1-7; Feb. 28-Oct. 8, 1812. Pittsburgh, Printed by S. Engels.

301 p. monthly (irregular)

Although its editor, David Graham, was a pastor of the United Congregational Church, the *Pioneer* did not emphasize theological subjects. Its essays also gave attention to Grecian literature and the ancient classics, education, the origins of language, the art of reading and periodical essay-writing. Poetry and biographical sketches were also among its contents.

v1, nos.1-7	Feb. 28-Oct. 8, 1812	APS II, Reel 189

✻ THE PIONEER; or, California monthly magazine. Ed. by F.C. Ewer. v1-4; Jan. 1854-Dec. 1855. San Francisco, Cal., Le Count and Strong, 1854-55.

4 v.

Vol. 1 published by W. H. Brooks & company.
"The first California magazine."—Sabin's Dictionary of books relating to America.

The *Pioneer* was founded by Ferdinand C. Ewer and claimed in issue one to be the first "periodical of purely literary type." The contributors included "John Pheonix," Edward A. Pollock, and Mrs. S.A. Donner.

v1-4   Jan. 1854-Dec. 1855   APS III, Reel 15

Microfilm edition was prepared from CSt and MiD copies.

THE PISCATAQUA EVANGELICAL MAGAZINE. v.1-4, no.2; Jan./Feb. 1805-Mar./Apr. 1808. Amherst, N.H., J. Cushing.

4 v. Bimonthly.

Issued by the Piscataqua Missionary Society.

Essays on moral and religious topics, Bible studies, religious news, poetry, and biographical sketches made up the contents of this bimonthly religious magazine published by the Piscataqua Association of Ministers.

v1-4, no.2   Jan./Feb. 1805-Mar./Apr. 1808   APS II, Reel 39

THE PITTSBURGH RECORDER, containing religious literary and political information. v.1-6, no.45; Jan. 25, 1822-Dec. 1827. Pittsburgh, J. Andrews.

6 v.
(Moore pamphlets, v.28, no.17; v.86, no.1; v.87, no.1)
weekly.

Title varies slightly.
Published by the Synod of Pittsburgh, Presbyterian Church of the U.S.A. Superseded by Spectator (Pittsburgh) Cf. Union list of serials.

Published under the patronage of the members of the synod of Pittsburgh, this Presbyterian weekly was devoted to religious information such as missionary news, Sunday school news, and news of Bible societies; but also provided other useful information, including accounts of new inventions, discoveries, and improvements. A small portion was devoted to political news, both domestic and foreign, especially news relating to state and national governments.

v1   Jan. 25, 1822-Jan. 17, 1823   APS II, Reel 219
v2   Jan. 24, 1823-Jan. 23, 1824   Reel 220

v3-6   Feb. 3, 1824-Dec. 25, 1827   Reel 1052

Microfilm edition was prepared from PPi and PPPrHi.

PLAYMATE. *SEE* Merry's Museum for Boys and Girls.

PLOUGHBOY. *SEE* Ploughboy, and Journal of the Board of Agriculture.

THE PLOUGH BOY, AND JOURNAL OF THE BOARD OF AGRICULTURE. v.1-4, no.51; June 5, 1819-July 15, 1823. Albany, Printed by J.O. Cole.

4 v. illus. weekly.

Title varies: June 5, 1819-Jan. 15, 1820, The Plough boy. By Henry Homespun, jr. [pseud. of Solomon Southwick]

The *Plough Boy* was established by Solomon Southwick, who edited it under the name of "Henry Homespun." It published articles on gardening and agricultural methods, veterinary medicine, and entomology, as well as proceedings of agricultural societies, book reviews, poetry, biography, and foreign and domestic news.

Plough Boy
v1, no.1-33   June 5, 1819-Jan. 15, 1820   APS II, Reel 190

Plough Boy, and Journal of the Board of Agriculture
v1, no.34-v3, no.31   Jan. 22, 1820-Dec. 29, 1821   Reel 190
v3, no.32-v4, no.51   Jan. 5, 1822-July 15, 1823   Reel 191

PLOUGH, THE LOOM AND THE ANVIL. *SEE* American Farmer's Magazine, *and* Monthly Journal of Agriculture.

POCKET MAGAZINE. *SEE* American Magazine (New York, Frank Leslie).

POLICE GAZETTE. *SEE* National Police Gazette.

POLITICAL CENSOR. *SEE* Porcupine's Political Censor.

THE POLITICAL ECONOMIST. no.1-13; Jan. 24-May 1, 1824. Philadelphia, J.R.S. Skerett.

208 p. weekly.

Edited by the author of the Olive branch (i.e. M. Carey)

Devoted to the U.S. economy and trade, the *Political Economist* was particularly concerned with resuscitating national industry through tariffs on foreign goods. To support this viewpoint, the *Economist* published articles, letters, statistics, extracts from speeches and various publications, and articles on the tariffs of various countries.

no.1-13   Jan. 24-May 1, 1824   APS II, Reel 191

POLITICAL ECONOMIST; an emporium of statistical philosophy. v.1, no.1; Oct. 1824. Baltimore, 1824.

208 p.

Edited by "A Society of Gentlemen," this magazine was evidently intended to deal with various national problems, particularly economics and politics, but only one number was published. This issue dealt with the regulation of currency and with domestic industry and commerce in various states.

v1, no.1   Oct. 1824   APS II, Reel 191

THE POLITICAL MAGAZINE AND MISCELLANEOUS REPOSITORY. Containing ancient and modern political and miscellaneous pieces, prose and poetical. v.1, no.1-2; Oct.-Nov. 1800. Ballston [N.Y.] Printed and sold by W. Child.

96 p.

This short-lived political magazine by William Child was republican and thus supported Jefferson and opposed the federalists. Contents included a variety of articles supporting the republican viewpoint, assorted material on Jefferson, including extracts from some of his writings, and the Constitution. In addition to the political content, there was some miscellaneous material, including poetry and articles on Niagara Falls and the caverns of Virginia.

v1, no.1-2   Oct.-Nov. 1800   APS II, Reel 39

POLITICAL SCIENCE QUARTERLY. v.1- , Mar. 1886- .
New York, Ginn [etc.]

v. charts.

Vols. 1-23 (1886-1908) edited by the Faculty of political science of Columbia University; v.24- (1909-) edited for the Academy of political science in the city of New York by the Faculty of political science of Columbia University.

Managing editors: 1886-93, Munroe Smith.–1894-1903, W.A. Dunning,–1904-13, Munroe Smith.–1914- T.R. Powell.

–––Index to vols. I-XXX: 1886-1930. Lancaster, New York, Ginn, 1916. 184 p.

On film: v.1-20 with index for v.1-30.

The *Political Science Quarterly* began in Mar. 1886 under the editorship of the political science faculty of Columbia University. Its managing editor during most of its first quarter-century was Munroe Smith. Most of its articles were contributed by its editors, the most frequent early contributors being Edwin R.A. Seligman, John Bassett Moore, Franklin H. Giddings, James Harvey Robinson, Samuel McCune Lindsay, and Charles A. Beard. It also published papers by Woodrow Wilson, Arthur T. Hadley, Albert Shaw, Horace White, and others. It was nonpartisan and covered topics in politics, economics, sociology and history. The book review department was important and a "Record of Political Events" was included semiannually beginning in 1888. The *New Princeton Review,* a shortlived bimonthly containing literary and art criticism and political and religious articles, merged with the *Political Science Quarterly* at the end of 1888.

Index: 1-30	1886-1915	APS III, Reel 767
v1-4	Mar. 1886-Dec. 1889	Reel 767
v5-8	Mar. 1890-Dec. 1893	Reel 768
v9-12	Mar. 1894-Dec. 1897	Reel 769
v13-16	Mar. 1898-Dec. 1901	Reel 770
v17-20	Mar. 1902-Dec. 1905	Reel 771

Several pages are stained with some loss of text.

Microfilm edition was prepared from MiU copy.

THE POLYANTHOS. v.1-5, Dec. 1805-July 1807; new ser. v.1-2, Feb.-Sept. 1812; (series 3) v.1-4, Oct. 1812-Sept. 1814. Boston, J.T. Buckingham, 1806-14.

plates, ports. monthly.

Vols. 1-4 of the 3d series have engraved t.-p. bearing title: The Polyanthos enlarged; caption title reads: The Polyanthos.

Discontinued with July 1807; resumed publication in a new ser., Feb. 1812, cf. Sabin, Bibl. amer.

Joseph T. Buckingham's monthly *Polyanthos* was a well-illustrated miscellany which included interesting theater reviews. Royall Tyler, Buckingham, several clerical contributors, and other magazines supplied the contents, which were miscellaneous collections of poetry and romances, literary and theatrical news, book reviews, historical sketches, short items and anecdotes, and articles on mythology, fashions, and morals. A portrait appeared in each number; most were by Samuel Harris, and many were accompanied by biographical sketches.

Polyanthos
| v1-5 | Dec. 1805-July 1807 | APS II, Reel 39 |
| nsv1-2 | Feb. -Sept. 1812 | Reel 191 |

Polyanthos Enlarged
| s3v1 | Oct. 1812-Mar. 1813 | Reel 191 |
| s3v2-4 | Apr. 1813-Sept. 1814 | Reel 192 |

PORCUPINE'S POLITICAL CENSOR ... v.1-2; Mar. 1796-Mar. 1797. Philadelphia, W. Cobbett.

2v. in 1. pl. monthly.

June-Aug., 1796, Feb., 1797, no issues were published.

Individual t.p. reads: Mar.-Sept., 1796, the Political Censor, or Monthly Review (later 'or review') of the most interesting political occurrences, relative to the United States of America. By Peter Porcupine. (Nov. 1796-Mar. 1797, subtitle varies.)

A political monthly edited by William Cobbett, alias Peter Porcupine, in which sessions of Congress were reported and freely commented upon.

| Mar. 1796-Mar. 1797 | APS I, Reel 26 |

Microfilm edition was prepared from MWA copy.

* THE PORT FOLIO. By Oliver Oldschool, v.1-5, 1801-05; new ser., v.1-6, 1806-08; new [3d] ser., v.1-8, 1809-12; 3d [i.e. 4th] ser., v.1-6, 1813-15; 4th [i.e. 5th] ser., v.1-20, 1816-25; Hall's 2d ser., v.1-2, July 1826-Dec. 1827. Philadelphia, Printed by H. Maxwell, [etc., etc.]

47 v. plates (part col.) ports., maps, plans, facsims.
Publication suspended Jan.-June 1826 and Jan.-June 1827. [3d] ser., v.1, t.-p. reads: The Port folio, a monthly magazine, devoted to useful science [etc] ...
Caption title, Jan.-May 1822: The Portfolio, and New York monthly magazine.

Founded by Joseph Dennie in connection with Asbury Dickins and edited by Dennie until 1812. "The editors ... from the death of Dennie until 1827, when the magazine finally ceased, were Paul Allen, Nicholas Biddle, Dr. Charles Caldwell, Thomas Cooper, Judge Workman, John Elihu Hall, and his three brothers."–Smyth's Philadelphia magazines. The Port folio was published by Harrison Hall, beginning with 1816.

Weekly, 1801-08; monthly 1809-19, 1822-27; quarterly, 1820-21.
On film: issues for 1801-Dec. 1827.

The *Port Folio* was from the beginning a magazine of literary and political ambitions. Joseph Dennie, the first owner and editor, was by far the most flamboyant and successful; he strongly favored England's system over the newly formed American democratic government and hence his pen name "Oliver Oldschool." Dennie's sharp wit greatly contributed to the magazine's approval by the more sophisticated class in Philadelphia. The sections of poetry, biography, manners, fashion, and travel were more or less pointed criticisms of American character. Dennie sold his publication after 1807 but did not relinquish editorship until 1809. Under his successor, Nicholas Biddle, the *Port Folio* became more of a review and less partisan in nature. After Dennie's death in 1812, political material was excluded altogether. The next editor, Dr. Charles Caldwell, was perhaps most noted for the amount of material devoted to the War of 1812. In 1816 Harrison Hall purchased the magazine and named his brother, John E. Hall, as editor. Hall attempted to bring back the *Port Folio's* old sparkle, but was not very successful. Throughout the life of the magazine it was plagued by monetary problems and finally ceased publication in Dec. 1827. But it is valuable for its excellent store of writings on political and social movements by such writers as John Quincy Adams, Thomas Campbell, Leigh Hunt, Charles Brockden Brown, Thomas Fessenden, William Dunlap, and Royall Tyler.

v1-4	Jan. 3, 1801-Dec. 29, 1804	Reel 40
v5-nsv4	Jan. 12, 1805-Dec. 26, 1807	Reel 41
nsv5-s3v2	Jan. 2, 1808-Dec. 1809	Reel 42
s3v3-4	Jan.-Dec. 1810	Reel 220
s3v5-7	Jan. 1811-June 1812	Reel 221
s3v8-s4v2	July 1812-Dec. 1813	Reel 222
s4v3-5	Jan. 1814-June 1815	Reel 223
s4v6-s5v3	July 1815-June 1817	Reel 224
s5v4-7	July 1817-June 1819	Reel 225
s5v8-11	July 1819-1821	Reel 226
s5v12-15	1821-1823	Reel 227
s5v16-20	1823-1825	Reel 228
s6, v1-2	July 1826-Dec. 1827	Reel 915

Reel 221: Series 3, vol. 6: pages 595-596 are torn. Reel 222: Series 4 starts with vol. 1, Jan.-June, 1813; film title indicates this is series 3.

Microfilm edition was prepared from DLC, NjP and Vi copies.

THE PORTICO, a repository of science & literature. v.1-5, no.4/6; 1816-Apr./June 1818. Baltimore, Md., Neale Wills & Cole.

5 v. plates. monthly.

Vol. 1 has engraved t.-p. by George Fairman.
Vols. 3-4 have title: The Portico. Editor: 1816-Stephen Simpson.

Founded by Dr. Tobias Watkins and his brother-in-law Stephen Simpson, the monthly *Portico* was a well-conducted literary miscellany. The editors wrote much of the material, and there were contributions of poetry, criticism, science, and miscellany by others: John Neal, John Pierpont, and Paul Allen all contributed extensively, and other contributors included H.M. Brackenridge, William Gwynn, E. Denison, and John H.B. Latrobe. Literary criticism received the most attention in the *Portico;* Byron, Scott, Southey, Moore, Fielding, Cowper, and Cumberland were discussed at length, and American books were also given some attention. Travel and biography, poetry, and some science and mathematics also appeared, along with some religion, but no politics. Most of the wit and humor was supplied in the essay series and the "Delphian Evenings."

v1-2	Jan.-Dec. 1816	APS II, Reel 192
v3-5	Jan. 1817-Apr./June 1818	Reel 193

PORTLAND MAGAZINE. v.1, no.1-5; May 11-June 8, 1805. [Portland, Me., W. Jenks]

20 p. Weekly.

Only five numbers of this 4-page weekly miscellany were published. Intended chiefly for women, it contained summaries of foreign and domestic news, notices of deaths and marriages, a department of moral essays, literary notices, and about a page of poetry, along with some material on agriculture and history, and much miscellany.

v1, no.1-5	May 11-June 8, 1805	APS II, Reel 42

THE PORTLAND MAGAZINE; devoted to literature. v.1-2; Oct. 1834-June 1836. Portland [Me.] E. Stephens, 1835-36.

2 v. monthly.

United with the Eastern magazine to form the Maine monthly magazine. Edited by Mrs. Ann S. Stephens.

A women's magazine edited by Mrs. Ann Stephens, who wrote most of the material. It contained poetry, tales, moral essays, magazine reviews, biographies, extracts from other magazines, such as the *Knickerbocker,* and articles on such topics as nature, phrenology, botany, and travel. Eventually it was merged with *Eastern Magazine* to form the *Maine Monthly Magazine.*

v1-2	Oct. 1, 1834-June 1, 1836	APS II, Reel 746

Microfilm edition was prepared from DLC copy.

THE PORTSMOUTH WEEKLY MAGAZINE; a repository of miscellaneous literary matters in prose and verse. v.1, no.1-54; July 1, 1824-June 30, 1825. Portsmouth, N.H., J.T. Gibbs.

1 v.

Film incomplete: no. 47 and 51 wanting.

Published by John T. Gibbs, this weekly literary miscellany featured a department for ladies, a "Moralist" column, and a "Novelist" column, which included serialized tales. Jokes and anecdotes appeared in the "Amusement" column, and poetry, book reviews, biographies, and news summaries were also included, among the contents.

v1, nos.1-46, 48-50, 52-54	July 1, 1824-June 30, 1825	APS II, Reel 193

*** POTTER'S AMERICAN MONTHLY:** an illustrated magazine of history, literature, science and art. v.1-19; 1872-Sept. 1882. Philadelphia, J.E. Potter.

16 v. in 8. illus., port., maps, facsim, music.

Title varies: v.1-3 as American historical record.
Merged, Oct. 1882, into Our continent.

Devoted to history and biography, *Potter's American Monthly* was excellently illustrated under the first editor, Benson J. Lossing. John E. Potter took over the monthly in 1875 adding literature, science, and art to its contents. Near the end of the file, the historical aspect was deleted and circulation dropped.

American Historical Record

v1-3	Jan. 1872-Dec. 1874	APS III, Reel 67

Potter's American Monthly

v4-7	Jan. 1875-Dec. 1876	Reel 67
v8-15	Jan. 1877-Dec. 1880	Reel 68
v16-19	Jan. 1881-Sept. 1882	Reel 69

Several pages are creased, torn or stained. Vols. 4-19: Index lacking; please refer to the Tables of Contents.

Microfilm edition was prepared from MiD, Nh, and NjP copies.

THE POUGHKEEPSIE CASKET: a semi-monthly literary journal, devoted exclusively to the different branches of polite literature. v.1-4; Jan. 2, 1836-Apr. 3, 1841. Poughkeepsie, Killey & Lossing.

4 v. illus.

Editors: E.B. Killey, B.J. Lossing.

A semimonthly literary journal which contained original and serialized tales, poetry, fashion, historical sketches, reviews of new works, news, humor, and articles on archaeology, ornithology, fine arts, plus a variety of miscellaneous material. It also featured occasional illustrations, which increased in number in the later issues.

v1-4	Jan. 2, 1836-Apr. 3, 1841	APS II, Reel 746

Several pages are stained, marked, creased, and have light print with some loss of text. Publication was suspended from Jan. 1837-Apr. 1839. Vol. 2: Page 104 is misnumbered.

Microfilm edition was prepared from N and NHi copies.

PRAIRIE FARMER. v.1- ; 1841- . Chicago.

v. illus. monthly; weekly.

Supersedes Union agriculturist.
Absorbed Emery's journal of agriculture, July, 1858.
Vol. 18, no.41-v.37, no.26, Oct. 7, 1858-1868 also numbered v.2, no.15-v.21; v.38 omitted in numbering. cf. Union list of serials.

Title varies: 1841-42, v.1-2, Union agriculturist and western prairie farmer; 1882, v.54, no.1-6 (Sept. 2-Oct. 5) People's illustrated weekly and prairie farmer.

On film: whole no.v.1-10 (reels 747-748) whole no. v.11-15, 18-19, 21-23 [29-36] 43-48 (reels 1720-1726) v.39, 41-42 (reel 1936) Imperfect copy: Lacking whole no. v.14, no.1; v. 30, no.27; v.48, no.5, 7.

A leading agricultural magazine founded by the Union Agricultural Society of Chicago and a champion of farmers' rights. It supported the grange movement and in 1873 created a department devoted to the grange. Besides articles on agriculture, horticulture, and stock raising, it provided general and market news, a children's column, and departments dealing with health, household problems, and veterinary medicine.

Union Agriculturist and Western Prairie Farmer

v1-2	Jan. 1841-Dec. 1842	APS II, Reel 747

Prairie Farmer

v3-8	Jan. 1843-Oct. 1848	Reel 747
v9-10	Jan. 1849-Dec. 1850	Reel 748
v11-15	Jan. 1851-Dec. 1855	Reel 1720
v18-23 (nsv2-7)	July 1, 1858-June 27, 1861	Reel 1721
v29-34 (nsv13-18)	Jan. 2, 1864-Dec. 29, 1866	Reel 1722
v35-36 (nsv19-20)	Jan. 5-Dec. 28, 1867	Reel 1723
v39, 41-42	July 4, 1868-Dec. 30, 1871	Reel 1936
v43	Jan. 6-Dec. 28, 1872	Reel 1723
v44-45	Jan. 4, 1873-Dec. 26, 1874	Reel 1724
v46-47	Jan. 2, 1875-Dec. 30, 1876	Reel 1725
v48	Jan. 6,-Dec. 29, 1877	Reel 1726

Reels 747-748: Some advertising pages are missing. Reels 1720-1726: Pagination is irregular.

Microfilm edition was prepared from CSmH, DLC, DNAL, ICJ, MH, and MnU copies.

THE PRESBYTERIAN MAGAZINE. v.1-2; Jan. 1821-Dec. 1822. Philadelphia, 1821-1822.

2 v. monthly.

Superseded by Christian advocate.

This monthly was founded in Philadelphia by William Neill, a leading Presbyterian clergyman who later became president of Dickinson College. Among its contents were essays on doctrine and church history and government, biography, religious poetry,

biblical studies, and religious news. In addition, it listed new publications, and reviewed both old and new books.

v1	Jan.-Dec. 1821	Reel 193
v2	Jan.-Dec. 1822	Reel 194

SEE ALSO: Christian Advocate (Philadelphia).

PRESBYTERIAN QUARTERLY AND PRINCETON REVIEW. *SEE* Princeton Review.

PRESBYTERIAN QUARTERLY REVIEW. *SEE* American Presbyterian Review.

THE PRESENT. v.1; Sept. 1843-Apr. 1844. [New York]

432 p. monthly.

W.H. Channing, editor.

Edited by William Henry Channing, this periodical advocated social reform in general and the association movement in particular. In addition to providing coverage of the various reform movements, it included original articles, translations, and selections dealing with religion, philosophy, and social science; extracts from Pierre Leroux's *L'Humanite;* and poetry, prayers, essays, stories, and biography.

v1	Sept. 1843-Apr. 1, 1844	APS II, Reel 748

Issue 4 appears to be missing in number only.

Microfilm edition was prepared from MiU copy.

THE PRINCETON MAGAZINE. Ed. by William C. Alexander. v.1; Mar. 1850-Feb. 1851. [Princeton, N.J.] J.T. Robinson.

1 v.

An intellectual and philosophical magazine which contained little fiction, but was made up of poetry, book reviews, moral essays, biographies, studies of ancient people and their customs, articles on famous writers and their works and on history and travel. Much material on classical works also appeared.

v1	Mar. 1850-Feb. 1851	APS II, Reel 748

Microfilm edition was prepared from NjP copy.

* **THE PRINCETON REVIEW.** v.1-4, 1825-28; new ser., v.1-43, 1829-71; new ser., v.1-6, 1872-77; 54th-60th year, 1878-84; 61st-63d year, v.1-6, 1886-88. New York, G. & C. Carvill, 1825-[88]

73 v.
Quarterly, 1825?-77; bimonthly, 1878-88.
Publication suspended during 1885.

Title varies: 1825-28, Biblical repertory. A collection of tracts in Biblical literature.—1829, Biblical repertory. A journal of Biblical literature and theological science, conducted by an association of gentlemen.—1830-36, The Biblical repertory and theological review. Conducted by an association of gentlemen in Princeton (subtitle varies slightly) 1837-71, The Biblical repertory and Princeton review.—1872-77, The Presbyterian quarterly and Princeton review.—1878-84, The Princeton review.—1885-88, The New Princeton review.

Editors: 1825-71, Charles Hodge (with L.H. Atwater, 1869-71).– 1872-76, L.H. Atwater, H.B. Smith.–1877, L.H. Atwater, J.M. Sherwood.–1883-84, J.M. Libbey.

Imprint varies: 1825, Princeton press, Printed by D.A. Borrenstein.–1826-28? New-York, G. & C. Carvill.–1829, Princeton, N.J., H. Madden, printer.–1830, Philadelphia, J. Kay, jun. & co.; [etc., etc]–1831-68, Philadelphia, Russell & Martien [etc.]– 1869-84, New York, C. Scribner & co. [etc.]–1886-88, New York, A.C. Armstrong & son; London, Hodder & Stoughton. Absorbed the American Presbyterian review in 1872.

The *Princeton Review* is best remembered as having developed what is known as the "Princeton theology," mainly through the efforts of its great editor, Charles Hodge. The *Review* was a distinctly professional quarterly for the clergy and as Hodge was a follower of Archibald Alexander, it related purely Calvinistic thought. Because of the *Review's* stand, it was strongly opposed by *Bibliotheca Sacra,* then published at Andover, New Jersey. This controversey between the two schools of thought raged for over forty years, until Hodge retired his editorship in 1871. From 1871 until it merged with *Political Science Quarterly* in 1888, the *Review* was less theological in nature, which probably accounts for its decline. Although Hodge was the largest contributor, articles by James W. Alexander, Joseph Addison, Samuel Tyler, J. W. Youmans, and William H. Green appeared. In addition, Charles D. Warner, James McCosh, and Woodrow Wilson contributed to the final volumes.

Biblical Repertory (subtitle varies)

v1	1825	APS II, Reel 229
v2-3	1826-1827	Reel 566
v4-(s2)v3	1828-1831	Reel 567
(s2)v4-7	1832-1835	Reel 568
(s2) v8-11	1836-1839	Reel 569
(s2)v12-15	1840-1843	Reel 570
(s2) v16-19	1844-1847	Reel 571
(s2)v20-22	1848-1850	Reel 572
(s2)v23-27	Jan. 1851-Oct. 1855	Reel 846
(s2)v28-31	Jan. 1856-Oct. 1859	Reel 847
(s2)v32-36	Jan. 1860-Oct. 1864	Reel 848
(s2)v37-41	Jan. 1865-Oct. 1869	Reel 849
(s2)v42-43	Jan. 1870-Oct. 1871	Reel 850

Presbyterian Quarterly and Princeton Review

(s3)v1-3	Jan. 1872-Oct. 1874	Reel 850
(3)v4-6	Jan. 1875-Oct. 1877	Reel 851

Princeton Review

(s4)v1	Jan.-May 1878	Reel 851
(s4)v2-6	July 1878-Nov. 1880	Reel 852
(s4)v7-14	Jan. 1881-Nov. 1884	Reel 853

New Princeton Review

(s5)v1-6	Jan. 1886-Nov. 1888	Reel 854

Pagination is irregular. Several pages are stained or torn and some have faded print with loss of text. Second series Vols. 23–29, 31, 43: the Oct. issue table of contents was photographed at the end of the volume. Fifth series Vols. 1 and 3: the May issue tables of contents were photographed at the end of the volumes. Fifth series Vol. 2, the Sept. issue table of contents was photographed at the end of the volume. Fifth series Vol. 4: the July issue table of contents was photographed at the end of the volume. Fifth series Vol. 6, the Nov. issue table of contents was photographed at the end of the issue.

Microfilm edition was prepared from CtY, MiU, and N copies.

PRISON JOURNAL. *SEE* Journal of Prison Discipline and Philanthropy.

PRISONER'S FRIEND: a monthly magazine devoted to criminal reform, philosophy, science, literature, and art. v1-4, 1845-48; new ser., v.1-13, no.12, Sept. 1848-June 1861. [New ser.] v.1-184. Boston.

17 v. plates, ports., plan. weekly.

Title varies slightly.
Preceded by the Hangman.

Editor: Charles Spear (with J.M. Spear.)
Film incomplete: new ser. v.10-13 wanting.

A Boston weekly which dealt with prison reform. It had originally been titled the *Hangman,* and contributors included Charles Sumner, Dr. S.G. Howe, and Dr. Walter Channing.

v1-nsv3	Jan. 1, 1845-Aug. 1851	APS II, Reel 749
nsv4-9	Sept. 1851-Aug. 1857	Reel 750

Best copy available for photographing. Many pages are stained with loss of text. Several volumes have irregular pagination. Vol. 1: Pages 36-37 are missing. Vol. 2: Pages 170-71 are missing. Vols. 3-4: Indexes are lacking. Vol. 3: Pages 81-88 and 153-56 are missing. Vol. 4: Microfilm edition includes issues 11-12, 21, and 33, 1848.

Microfilm edition was prepared from DLC and MWA copies.

PROSPECT: or, View of the moral world. v.1-2, no.13, 1803-Mar. 30, 1805. [New-York, E. Palmer, 1805]

v. weekly.

Edited by Elihu Palmer, the *Prospect* was devoted to religion and philosophy. It appears to have been opposed to the Christian religion and devoted most of its space to articles exploring Christian beliefs and the stories, events, and miracles described in the Bible. In addition, there were a few articles on Persian and Indian philosophy, and occasional biographical sketches.

v1-2, no.13	1803-Mar. 30, 1805	APS II, Reel 42

THE PROVIDENCE THEOLOGICAL MAGAZINE. v.1, no.1; Sept. 1821. Providence, Miller and Hutchens.

32 p.

In addition to anecdotes, this short-lived religious periodical included such articles as: "Evidence of God's Existence," "Divine Perfections," "The Goodness of God," and "Relations of Religious Experience."

v1, no.1	Sept. 1821	APS II, Reel 194

PUBLISHERS' AND STATIONERS' WEEKLY TRADE CIRCULAR. *SEE* American Literary Gazette and Publishers' Circular.

PUBLISHERS' WEEKLY. *SEE* American Literary Gazette and Publishers' Circular.

PUCK. v1-83 (no.1-2121); Mar. 1877-Sept. 1918. New York, Keppler & Schwarzmann.

83 v. illus. (part col.) plates (part col.) col. ports. weekly.

Puck was one of the brightest and most original of the 19th century American comic ventures. The brainstorm of a German immigrant, Joseph Keppler, *Puck* wielded a swift sword against public abuse. From the first, the dominant feature was the brash, colored caricatures drawn by Keppler which carried *Puck* to a position of political power. Less noticeable, but just as important was the editing of Henry Bunner.

Puck vigorously attacked Tammany Hall, the Standard Oil Company, Western Union, and presidential hopefuls such as Blaine and Bryan. The suffrage movement and religious figures were no less spared, and no stone was unturned in blasting ballot abuses, high tariffs, and "free silver." Labor received more sympathetic gestures although its practices were far from exonerated. On a lighter side, puns remained a chief staple throughout the file, society and the theater were mentioned, and short stories were featured. *Puck* lost some of its soul in the mid-nineties with the deaths of Keppler and Bunner. For a time, it was ineptly edited by Harry Wilson, followed by John Kendrick Bangs who restored some of *Puck's* humor. The magazine became militant prior to World War I under the editorship of Arthur Hamilton Folwell. In 1916, *Puck* was purchased by Hearst's International and became enmeshed in unimportant accounts of the theater and newsy miscellanea.

v1-3	Mar. 1877-Sept. 4, 1878	APS III, Reel 69
v4-9	Sept. 11, 1878-Sept. 7, 1881	Reel 70
v10-15	Sept. 7, 1881-Aug. 27, 1884	Reel 71
v16-21	Sept. 3, 1884-Aug. 24, 1887	Reel 72
v22-26	Aug. 31, 1857-Feb. 19, 1890	Reel 73
v27-31	Feb. 26, 1890-Aug. 17, 1892	Reel 74
v32-37	Aug. 24, 1892-Aug. 14, 1895	Reel 75
v38-42	Aug. 21, 1895-Feb. 9, 1898	Reel 76
v43-48	Feb. 16, 1898-Feb. 6, 1901	Reel 77
v49-54	Feb. 13, 1901-Jan. 27, 1904	Reel 78
v55-59	Feb. 3, 1904-July 25, 1906	Reel 79
v60-65	Aug. 1, 1906-July 21, 1909	Reel 80
v66-71	July 28, 1909-July 17, 1912	Reel 81
v72-76	July 24, 1912-Jan. 16, 1915	Reel 82
v77-80	Jan. 23, 1915-Jan. 13, 1917	Reel 83
v81-83	Jan. 20, 1917-Sept. 5, 1918	Reel 84

Best copy available for photographing. Many volumes are missing Indexes and Tables of Contents. Pagination is irregular. Several volumes have torn or missing pages. Several volumes contain supplements. Vols. 10 and 11 have some duplicate issues.

Microfilm edition was prepared from DLC, GEU, IC, MBAt, MdBE, MeB, MiD, MoK, N, NBP, NhD, TNJ, and WaS copies.

PUNCHINELLO. v.1-2; Apr. 2-Dec. 24, 1870. New York, Punchinello Pub. Co., 1870

2 v. illus., plates. weekly.

A short-lived comic paper of 1870 was *Punchinello,* an imitation of London's *Punch.* It carried a number of woodcuts in each issue, usually satirizing social or political problems. It failed to be very funny and ceased in December after losing the money of its backers, the Erie Railway heads, Jay Gould and Jim Fisk, and the Tammany kingpins, William M. Tweed and P.B. Sweeney.

v1-2	Apr.-Dec. 1870	APS III, Reel 164

Vol. 2: Index not available for photographing.

Microfilm edition was prepared from MiU copy.

PURITAN. *SEE* Godey's Magazine.

PURITAN RECORDER. *SEE* Congregationalist and Herald of Gospel Liberty.

* **PUTNAM'S MAGAZINE.** Original papers on literature, science, art, and national interests. v.1-10; Jan. 1853-Dec. 1857; new ser., v.1-6; Jan. 1868-Nov. 1870. New York, G.P. Putnam.

16 v. illus., plates, port. monthly.

Title varies: 1853-57, Putnam's monthly magazine of American literature, science, and art. 1868-70, Putnam's magazine. Original papers on literature, science, art, and national interests.

Established by Geo. P. Putnam, with the assistance of Geo. Wm. Curtis and others. Mr. Putnam's connection with the first series ceased in 1855. In Oct. 1857 this series was merged into "Emerson's United States magazine," which was continued as "Emerson's magazine and Putnam's monthly," and ceased publication with Nov. 1858. (Through June 1858 there were some numbers of "Emerson's magazine" issued with cover-title: "Putnam's magazine," v.11) The new series of "Putnam's magazine," published by G.P. Putnam and sons, was merged into "Scribner's monthly" Dec. 1870.

Fashioned after *Blackwood's, Putnam's Magazine* was the lively endeavor of Charles Briggs and George William Curtis. The contributions, although unsigned, came from the best American pens. Horace Greeley, Parke Goodwin, James Fenimore Cooper, Henry Thoreau, Richard Henry Stoddard, and a great number of others filled the columns with political spice and literary excellence. Always in financial difficulty, the magazine was suspended for a decade. It finally succumbed in 1870.

Putnam's Monthly Magazine of American Literature, Science, and Art

v1-4	Jan. 1853-Dec. 1854	APS III, Reel 164
v5-9	Jan. 1855-June 1857	Reel 165
v10	July-Dec. 1857	Reel 166

Putnam's Magazine. Original Papers on Literature, Science, Art, and National Interests

nsv1-3	Jan. 1868-June 1869	Reel 166
nsv4-6	July 1869-Nov. 1870	Reel 167

Vol. 9: title page reads July rather than June. New Series Vol. 6: Supplement photographed at the end of the Volume entitled "Eirene, or a Woman's Right."

Microfilm edition was prepared from MiDU, MiU, NhD, NPV, NR, and TxHR copies.

SEE ALSO: Emerson's Magazine and Putnam's Monthly.

* **PUTNAM'S MONTHLY.** *SEE* Emerson's Magazine and Putnam's Monthly; *and* Putnam's Magazine.

* **PUTNAM'S MONTHLY MAGAZINE OF AMERICAN LITERATURE, SCIENCE, AND ART.** *SEE* Putnam's Magazine.

THE QUARTERLY CHRISTIAN SPECTATOR. v.1-[8], 1819-26; new ser. v.1-2, 1827-28; [3d ser.] v.1-10, 1829-38. New Haven [1819-38]

20 v.

Title varies: 1819-28, The Christian spectator [monthly] 1829-38, The Quarterly Christian spectator. Merged into the American Biblical repository.

"Conducted by an Association of Gentlemen," this orthodox journal of the New England theology began as a monthly and became a quarterly in 1829. Contributors included many of the prominent clerical writers of New England. Much attention is given to the missionary activities of the Presbyterian and Congregational churches and also among its contents are theological articles, a few literary reviews, a public affairs section, religious news, listings of new publications, sermons, biographical sketches, and obituaries. The *Spectator* favored colonization rather than abolition as a solution to the problem of slavery.

Christian Spectator

v1-2	1819-Dec. 1820	APS II, Reel 194
v3-4	Jan. 1821-Dec. 1822	Reel 195
v5-7	Jan. 1, 1823-Dec. 1, 1825	Reel 196
v8-nsv2	Jan. 1826-Dec. 1828	Reel 229

Quarterly Christian Spectator

s3v1-4	Mar. 1829-Dec. 1832	Reel 230
s3v5-7	Mar. 1833-Dec. 1835	Reel 231
s3v8-10	Mar. 1836-Dec. 1838	Reel 232

SEE ALSO: Biblical Repository and Classical Review.

THE QUARTERLY JOURNAL AND REVIEW. v.1 (no.1-4); Jan./Mar.-Oct./Dec. 1846. Cincinnati, L.A. Hine.

1 v. illus.

Caption title: Journal and review.
L.A. Hine, editor.

The *Quarterly Journal and Review* was a well-printed magazine consisting of short stories, poetry, literary reviews, science, and political essays. Emerson Bennett, Albert Pike, and Alice Carey were among the contributors to the short-lived quarterly. It was merged into the *Herald of Truth* after the fourth issue.

v1	Jan.-Oct. 1846	APS II, Reel 1092

Although *Union List of Serials* reports issue 4 dated Oct./Dec., we find no mention of the December date in the issue.

Microfilm edition was prepared from DLC copy.

QUARTERLY JOURNAL OF THE AMERICAN EDUCATION SOCIETY. *SEE* American Quarterly Register.

THE QUARTERLY JOURNAL OF ECONOMICS. Pub. for Harvard University. v.1- Oct. 1886- . Boston, G.H. Ellis, 1887-1909, [etc., etc.]

v. charts, tables.

Editors: Oct. 1886-Oct. 1896, C.F. Dunbar and others.—Jan. 1897-F.W. Taussig and others. Vols. 1-22 include the section "Recent publications upon economics."
On film: issues for 1886-Aug. 1906. Includes Index, vols.1-10, 1886-1896.

Among the contributors to the *Quarterly Journal of Economics* were the leading economists of our country. Charles Dunbar and F.W. Taussig, editors in succession, were prominent correspondents along with Charles C. Beardsley, W.J. Ashley, Frank L. Olmstead, Edward Cummings, N.P. Gilman, Arthur T. Hadley, F.E. Haynes, William B. Shaw, Charles Conant, Edward S. Meade, and John Bascom. Currency, banking, foreign trade, taxes, labor, and the silver question were but a few of the controversial issues found on the pages.

Cumulative Index, 1-10	1886-1896	APS III, Reel 167
v1-3	Oct. 1886-July 1889	Reel 167
v4-10	Oct. 1889-July 1896	Reel 168
v11-16	Oct. 1896-Aug. 1902	Reel 169
v17-20	Nov. 1902-Aug. 1906	Reel 170

Microfilm edition was prepared from MiU copy.

QUARTERLY JOURNAL OF SCIENCE AND THE ARTS. *SEE* Journal of Science and the Arts.

QUARTERLY REGISTER. *SEE* American Quarterly Register.

QUARTERLY REGISTER AND JOURNAL OF THE AMERICAN EDUCATION SOCIETY. *SEE* American Quarterly Register.

QUARTERLY REGISTER OF THE AMERICAN EDUCATION SOCIETY. *SEE* American Quarterly Register.

QUARTERLY SUNDAY SCHOOL MAGAZINE. *SEE* American Sunday School Magazine *and* American Sunday-school Teachers' Magazine and Journal of Education.

THE RADICAL. no.1-2; 1821. New York, Printed by W. Grattan.

2 no.

Bound with Clark, Aaron. Manual, compiled and prepared for the use of the Assembly, 1816.

This short-lived magazine printed by William Grattan was concerned with government and the appointment of judges.

no1-2	1821	APS II, Reel 197

* **THE RADICAL.** v.1-10; Sept. 1865-June 1872. Boston [etc., Samuel H. Morse, etc.]

10 v. monthly.
Suspended July 1870-Jan. 1871.

Supersedes the Radical: A journal for science and religious culture (June-July, 1865)
Title varies: Sept. 1865-June 1868, The Radical: a monthly magazine, devoted to religion.

Edited by Samuel H. Morse (Sept. 1867-June 1869, with Joseph B. Marvin); v.1-2 published in London by Trubner & Co.
Religion and Social Science. Delivered at the second annual meeting of the free religious association, May 28, 1869. By D.H. Wasson, with v.6.

The three main contributors to the *Radical* were John Weiss, Samuel Johnson, and David A. Wasson. All of these men were followers of Theodore Parker and the *Radical* reflects many of his views toward religion.

v1	Sept. 1865-Aug. 1866	APS III, Reel 15
v2-8	Sept. 1866-July 1871	Reel 16
v9-10	Aug. 1871-June 1872	Reel 17

Vol. 1: the article listed on page 449 is on page 494. Vol. 6, pages 39-56 of the May 28, 1869 issue entitled "Religion and Social Science" are bound and photographed at the end.

Microfilm edition was prepared from MiU, PSC, and TxU copies.

RADICAL, IN CONTINUATION OF WORKING MAN'S ADVOCATE. *SEE* Working Man's Advocate.

RAILWAY TIMES. v.1-24; 1849-72. Boston.

24 v. weekly.

Title varies: 1849-1859, American railway times.
Film lacks: v.1 except nos. 64, 66, 72, 75; v.14, no.43.

Except for a few general science articles and the stock market report, the weekly *Railway Times* was devoted almost exclusively to railroading. All aspects of railroads were covered, from the construction of the railroad cars to the economics of the railroad business—articles dealt with iron and steel processing, new equipment and methods, railroad safety, construction of rails, bridges, and tunnels, and the problems of various railroads. In addition, timetables of various railways were published.

American Railway Times

v1-2	Dec. 1, 1849-Dec. 26, 1850	APS II, Reel 1726
v3-5	Jan. 2, 1851-Dec. 29, 1853	Reel 1727
v6-8	Jan. 5, 1854-Dec. 25, 1856	Reel 1728
v9-11	Jan. 1, 1857-Dec. 24, 1859	Reel 1729

Railway Times

v12-14	Jan. 7, 1860-Dec. 27, 1862	Reel 1730
v15-18	Jan. 3, 1863-Dec. 29, 1866	Reel 1731
v19-21	Jan. 5, 1867-Dec. 25, 1869	Reel 1732
v22-24	Jan. 1, 1870-Nov. 2, 1872	Reel 1733

Microfilm edition was prepared from CSt, DBRA, MH and MiU copies.

THE RAMBLERS' MAGAZINE, and New-York theatrical register: for the season of 1809-10. v.1. v.2. [n.1?] New-York, D. Longworth [1809-10?]

2 v. in 1. port.

Vol. 2 has no t.-p.

This New York literary miscellany devoted a large potion of its space to the theater, providing reviews of plays performed in New York and biographical sketches of various performers. A section called "The Perambulator" contained the writer's observations while taking walks around New York. Fashion news, poetry, and some satirical and miscellaneous material were also included.

v1-2, no.1	1809-1810	APS II, Reel 43

READINGER MAGAZIN FUR FREUNDE DER DEUTSCHEN LITERATUR IN AMERIKA. *SEE* Philadelphier Magazin fur Freunde der Deutschen Literatur in Amerika.

RECORDER. *SEE* Congregationalist and Herald of Gospel Liberty.

RECORDER AND TELEGRAPH. *SEE* Congregationalist and Herald of Gospel Liberty.

RECORDS OF THE AMERICAN CATHOLIC HISTORICAL SOCIETY. *SEE* American Catholic Historical Researches.

THE RECREATIVE MAGAZINE, or Eccentricities of literature and life. v.1, no.6; 1822. Boston, London, Munroe and Francis.

6 v.
Added t.-p. bears title: Eccentricities of literature and life; or the recreative magazine. American ed. of the Recreative review; London, Wallis and co., 1821-22.

This unusual magazine contained light reading, much trivia, and whimsical humor. It dealt with almost every imaginable topic, emphasizing odd and interesting facts. Some areas covered were famous people, both ancient and modern, including authors, language and dialects, and many trivial topics such as personal habits, hair, beards, eating, and drinking.

v1	1822	APS II, Reel 197

THE REFLECTOR. no.1; Sept. 1821. Boston, Printed by Wells and Lilly.

64 p.

The only number of this magazine ever published presented essays on widely varying topics; among these were "Pride and Vanity," "Excitement," and "Thoughts on Eloquence in Composition and Speaking."

no.1	Sept. 1821	APS II, Reel 197

REFORMED CHURCH MESSENGER. v.1-109, no.10; July 18, 1835-Ja. 30, 1936. Chambersburg, Pa., 1835-64; Philadelphia, 1864-1936.

v. illus. weekly.
Supersedes Messenger of the German Reformed Church.
Vols. 42-44, 70, 97-100 omitted in numbering.

Title varies: July-Aug. 1835, Weekly messenger of the Reformed Church; Sept. 2, 1835-Aug. 15, 1838, Weekly messenger of the German Reformed Church; Aug. 22, 1838-Nov. 1848, Weekly messenger; Dec. 1848-Aug. 1867, German reformed messenger; Sept. 1867-Dec. 1875, Reformed church messenger; Jan. 1876-Dec. 1887, Messenger.

United with Evangelical herald and Christian world to form Messenger of the Evangelical and Reformed Church.
On film: v.7-9, 17-40, 45-47, 58-59, 74-75; 1841-43, 1851-74, 1876-78, 1890-91, 1905-06. (Scattered issues missing)

Published by the Reformed Church of the United States, this weekly magazine provided its readers with church news, news of foreign missions, Sunday school lessons, sermons, book reviews, a "Home and Young Folks" section and a summary of weekly general news. Special numbers dealing with specific topics such as education, foreign missions, home missions and homes for orphans were issued periodically.

Weekly Messenger

v7-8	Sept. 22, 1841-Sept. 13, 1843	APS II, Reel 1815
v9	Sept. 27, 1843-Sept. 11, 1844	Reel 1816

German Reformed Messenger

v17-18	Sept. 10, 1851-Aug. 31, 1853	Reel 1816
v19-21	Sept. 7, 1853-Aug. 27, 1856	Reel 1817

v22-24	Sept. 3, 1856-Aug. 24, 1859	Reel 1818
v25-28	Aug. 31, 1859-Sept. 16, 1863	Reel 1819
v29-32	Sept. 23, 1863-Aug. 28, 1867	Reel 1820

Reformed Church Messenger

v33-36	Sept. 4, 1867-Dec. 28, 1870	Reel 1821
v37-39	Jan. 4, 1871-Dec. 24, 1873	Reel 1822
v40	Jan. 7-Dec. 30, 1874	Reel 1823

Messenger

v45-46	Jan. 5, 1876-Dec. 26, 1877	Reel 1823
v47	Jan. 3-Dec. 25, 1978	Reel 1824

Reformed Church Messenger

v58-59, 74	July 3, 1890-Dec. 28, 1905	Reel 1824
v75	Jan. 4-Dec. 27, 1906	Reel 1825

Microfilm edition was prepared from DLC and NNUT copies.

---

* **REFORMED CHURCH REVIEW.** v.1-73; 1849-Oct. 1926. Lancaster, Pa., etc., 1849-1926.

73 v.

Vols. 1-4, 1849-52 and 9-25, 1857-78 as Mercersburg review; vols. 5-8, 1853-56 Mercersburg quarterly review; vols. 26-43, 1879-96 Reformed quarterly review. Suspended 1862-66.

Also numbered as v1-13, 1849-61; s2v1-12, 1867-78; ns(s3) v1-18, 1879-96; s4 v1-25, 1897-1921; s5v1-5 no4, 1922-O 1926. Index: 1-17 in 18.

Founded in 1849 by the alumni of Marshall College at Mercersburg, Pennsylvania, this periodical emphasized the historical basis of Christianity. Originally called the *Mercersburg Review*, it was first edited by John W. Nevin, and influenced by Philip Schaff, later a leading church historian. It was filled with controversy, and during its early years included some poetry and essays and some political comment. Forced to suspend during the war, the *Review* was resumed in 1867 by T.G. Apple, and moved to Lancaster, changing its name to the *Reformed Quarterly Review* in 1879. It was less fresh and attractive than before, but more conciliatory. In the fourth series, started in 1897, more sociological and economic writing appeared and circulation increased.

Mercersburg Review

v1-2	1849-1850	APS II, Reel 671
v3-4	Jan. 1851-Oct. 1852	Reel 1217

Mercersburg Quarterly Review

v5-7	Jan. 1853-Oct. 1855	Reel 1217
v8	Jan.-Oct. 1856	Reel 1218

Mercersburg Review

v9-13	Jan. 1857-Oct. 1861	Reel 1218
s2v1-5 (14-18)	Jan. 1867-Oct. 1871	Reel 1219
s2v6-10 (19-23)	Jan. 1872-Oct. 1876	Reel 1220
s2v11-12 (24-25)	Jan. 1877-Oct. 1878	Reel 1221

Reformed Quarterly Review

s3v1-3 (26-28)	Jan. 1879-Oct. 1891	Reel 1221
s3v4-9 (29-34)	Jan. 1882-Oct. 1887	Reel 1222
s3v10-15 (35-40)	Jan. 1888-Oct. 1893	Reel 1223
s3v16-18 (41-43)	Jan. 1894-Oct. 1896	Reel 1224

Reformed Church Review

s4v1-3 (44-46)	Jan. 1897-Oct. 1899	Reel 1224
s4v4-8 (47-51)	Jan. 1900-Oct. 1904	Reel 1225
s4v9-13 (52-56)	Jan. 1905-Oct. 1909	Reel 1226
s4v14-19 (57-62)	Jan. 1910-Oct. 1915	Reel 1227
s4v20-25 (63-68)	Jan. 1916-Oct. 1921	Reel 1228
s5 v1-5 (69-73)	Jan. 1922-Oct. 1926	Reel 1229

Pagination is irregular. Vol. 2: Title pages and preliminary pages for the individual issues are bound and photographed at the end of the volume. Vol. 3: Contains a cumulative Table of Contents, 1849-1871. Cumulative Index of Authors of Articles, 1912-1926, found at the end of Series 5, Vol. 5.

Microfilm edition was prepared from DLC, IC, ICT, ICU, NjMD, NjPT, PCC, PLF, and PPi copies.

---

* **REFORMED QUARTERLY REVIEW.** *SEE* Reformed Church Review.

REFORMER. *SEE* Reformer and Christian.

THE REFORMER AND CHRISTIAN; a religious work ... v.1-14, no.6; Jan. 1, 1820-Nov. 1835. Philadelphia, Printed by J. Rakestraw.

v. in. monthly.

Title varies: vol. 1-12 as Reformer.

A religious periodical which provided extensive coverage of national and international religious controversy and events as well as much discussion of the various religions. The editor's purpose was to expose "clerical schemes and undertakings" and "fashionable religion." He also opposed missionary operations and theological seminaries. Some poetry and much selected material was included.

Reformer

v1-6	Jan. 1, 1820-Dec. 1, 1825	APS II, Reel 233
v7-12, no.7	Jan. 1826-Dec. 1831	Reel 720

Reformer and Christian

v12, no8-v14	Feb. 1832-Nov. 1835	Reel 720

Microfilm edition was prepared from MiU and NjR copies.

THE RELIGIOUS AND LITERARY REPOSITORY. v.1, no.1-24; Jan. 15-Dec. 23, 1820. Annapolis.

384 p. biweekly.

Edited by a society of laymen, members of the Protestant Episcopal Church.

Edited by laymen of the Episcopal Church, this religious periodical published sermons, hymns, addresses, religious news, and articles on various phases of religion, including doctrine.

v1, nos.1-24	Jan. 15-Dec. 23, 1820	APS II, Reel 197

---

* **RELIGIOUS CABINET: A MONTHLY PERIODICAL.** *SEE* United States Catholic Magazine.

THE RELIGIOUS ENQUIRER. v.1, no.1; Oct. 1811. Cooperstown [N.Y.] Printed by J.H. & H. Prentiss.

30 p.

The only number of this Universalist magazine published included two poems, an article on Calvinism, and a letter to the Methodist Conference.

v1, no.1	Oct. 1811	APS II, Reel 197

THE RELIGIOUS INFORMER. v.1-6; July 20, 1819-Dec. 1825. Enfield, N.H., E. Chase.

6 v. music. Biweekly, July 20-Dec. 25, 1819; monthly, Jan. 1820-Dec. 1825.

Issues for Jan.-Dec. 1820 called new ser., v. 1 but constitute v.2. Title varies: Jan.-Dec. 1822, Religious informer, and Free-Will Baptist register.

Edited by E. Chase.

This religious magazine published accounts of revivals of many denominations, giving particular attention to the Freewill Baptists. It also devoted a good portion of its space to religious news, both foreign and domestic, treatises on religious subjects, hymns, poetry, obituary notices, and a news summary. Letters, anecdotes, and selections from other magazines rounded out the contents of the *Religious Informer*.

Religious Informer
v1-2	July 20, 1819-Dec. 1821	APS II, Reel 197

Religious Informer, and Free-Will Baptist Register
v3	Jan.-Dec. 1822	Reel 197

Religious Informer
v4-6	Jan. 1823-Dec. 1825	Reel 198

RELIGIOUS INFORMER, AND FREE-WILL BAPTIST REGISTER. *SEE* Religious Informer.

THE RELIGIOUS INQUIRER. Published by an association of gentlemen, containing doctrinal, controversial, historical, and practical matter, and articles of religious intelligence and miscellany. v.1-15; Nov. 10, 1821-Nov. 1836. Hartford, Conn., J. Russell, Printer.

15 v. biweekly.

Editor: Nov. 1821- Richard Carrique.
Film incomplete: v.6-15 wanting.

In addition to printing material on the Universalist doctrine and news about Universalist societies, this Universalist magazine, which was published by "an association of gentlemen," covered the activities of missionary societies and published news about missions in India and elsewhere and concerning new churches and meeting-houses. Extracts from the Boston *Universalist Magazine* were included, as well as biography, poetry, sermons, and letters.

v1-5	Nov. 10, 1821-Dec. 24, 1825	APS II, Reel 234

Pagination is irregular. Vol. 2: Some pages are torn.

THE RELIGIOUS INSTRUCTOR; designed to promote useful knowledge, sound morality and vital piety. v.1; Sept. 1810-Aug. 1811. Carlisle [Pa.] A. Loudon.

482 p. monthly.

Edited by ministers of the Presbyterian Church.

Published under the superintendence of several ministers of the Presbyterian Church, this Presbyterian monthly provided sermons, biographical sketches, poetry, Bible studies, and essays on doctrine, religious duty, and the religious education of children. In addition, it reported on various Bible and tract societies and on the activities of missions.

v1	Sept. 1810-Aug. 1811	APS II, Reel 198

THE RELIGIOUS INTELLIGENCER ... containing the principal transactions of the various Bible and missionary societies, with particular accounts of revivals of religion. v.1-22; June 1, 1816-Oct. 7, 1837. New-Haven [N. Whiting]

22 v. illus. weekly.

Subtitle varies.
Supersedes the Connecticut evangelical magazine and religious intelligencer.

Conducted by Nathan Whiting, the *Religious Intelligencer* published the transactions of the various Bible and missionary societies, accounts of revivals, and progress reports of missions to the American Indians, to Hawaii, to Palestine, and elsewhere, with the space being divided equally between foreign and domestic news. In addition, it contained Sunday school news, obituaries and ordinations, religious biography, literary news, short news summaries, and some poetry. Essays on temperance and a variety of other moral and religious topics were increased in later volumes.

v1, no.1-24	June 1-Nov. 9, 1816	APS II, Reel 198
v1, no.25-v4, no.30	Nov. 1816-Dec. 25, 1819	Reel 199
v4, no.31-v6	Jan. 1, 1820-May 25, 1822	Reel 200
v7-8	June 1, 1822-May 29, 1824	Reel 201
v9-10, no.31	June 5, 1824-Dec. 31, 1825	Reel 202
v10, no.32-v11	Jan. 1826-May 1827	Reel 234
v12-14	June 1827-May 1830	Reel 235
v15-16	June 5, 1830-May 26, 1832	Reel 1488
v17-20	June 2, 1832-May 28, 1836	Reel 1489
v21-22	June 4, 1836-Oct. 7, 1837	Reel 1490

Several pages are stained, creased, tightly-bound or have print faded and show-through with some loss of text. Pagination is irregular. Vol. 16: nos. 27-29 are missing. Vol. 18: nos. 38-39 and 46 are missing. Vols. 21 and 22 lack title page and index.

Microfilm edition was prepared from MoS and OOxM copies.

SEE ALSO: Connecticut Evangelical Magazine and Religious Intelligencer.

A RELIGIOUS MAGAZINE; containing an account of the united churches of Christ, commonly called Free-Will Baptist. v.1-2; Jan. 1811-Sept. 1822. Kennebunk [etc., Me.] Printed by J.K. Remich [etc.]

2 v.
Quarterly, Jan. 1811-Oct. 1812; 3 no. a year, Aug. 1820-Sept. 1822.

Publication suspended Nov. 1812-July 1820.
Subtitle varies slightly.
Edited by J. Buzzell.

During its eleven years, this Freewill Baptist magazine provided a variety of material on both the Baptists and other religious groups. It published a series on church history and another series titled "An account of late reformations and revivals of religion." Religious news, such as proceedings of meetings and accounts of revivals in Rhode Island, was given space, as were addresses, articles on doctrine, and poetry.

v1-2	Jan. 1811-Sept. 22, 1822	APS II, Reel 202

RELIGIOUS MAGAZINE AND MONTHLY REVIEW. *SEE* Monthly Religious Magazine and Theological Review.

RELIGIOUS MESSENGER OF THE PHILADELPHIA CONFERENCE. *SEE* Christian Advocate. (Chicago)

THE RELIGIOUS MISCELLANY, containing information relative to the church of Christ; together with interesting literary, scientific and political intelligence. v.1-3; Jan. 17, 1823-July 2, 1824. Carlisle, Fleming and Geddes, 1823-24.

3 v. weekly.

Title varies slightly.

Missionary news occupied a large portion of this religious periodical–included were accounts of missions among the American Indians, and in Ceylon, India, and Africa. Other news of interest to the Christian community included news of Sunday schools, accounts of revivals, and coverage of the American Colonization Society and various Bible and missionary societies. In addition, there were brief news summaries, poetry, anecdotes, and book reviews.

v1-3   Jan. 17, 1823-July 2, 1824   APS II, Reel 203

RELIGIOUS MONITOR AND EVANGELICAL REPOSITORY. v.1-18; May 1824-May 1842. Philadelphia [etc.] Printed by W.S. Young.

18 v. monthly.

Title varies slightly.
Superseded by Evangelical repository (Philadelphia)

Established to "aid the cause of religion and morality," the *Religious Monitor* was devoted to the principles of the reformation as set forth in the "formularies of the Westminster divines and of the churches of Holland." Later volumes, however, were edited by a minister of the Associated Presbyterian Church. A great deal of the material was from European magazines and included explanations of difficult Scripture passages, biographical sketches, religious anecdotes, and excerpts from sermons and speeches. In later issues long essays on marriage, Christian education of children, temperance, the dangers of novel reading and warnings against Popery and Masons often filled most of an entire issue. Some poetry was published.

v1-4   May 1824-May 1828   APS II, Reel 401
v5-11   June 1828-May 1835   Reel 402
v12-18   June 1835-May 1842   Reel 403

Some pages are torn or stained. Pagination is irregular.

Microfilm edition was prepared from DLC, NN and PP copies.

THE RELIGIOUS MONITOR; or, Theological scales. v.1, no.1-13; Apr. 7-Sept. 22, 1798. Danbury [Conn.] Douglas & Nichols.

102 p. Biweekly.

A religious bi-weekly which published a variety of original and selected material on religious and moral subjects, including biographical sketches, anecdotes, poetry, and a number of hymns.

no.1-13   Apr. 7-Sept. 22, 1798   APS I, Reel 26

A few pages are lacking.

Microfilm edition was prepared from NN copy.

THE RELIGIOUS MUSEUM. v.1 (no.1-52); July 15, 1818-July 21, 1819. Northumberland, Pa., H. Frick.

208 p. weekly;

Edited by R.F.N. Smith.

This religious magazine contained a variety of news on revivals, on Sunday schools, on various societies, and on missions. Societies covered included missionary societies, American and foreign Bible societies, education societies, and the Philadelphia Tract Society; and articles covered missions in India, Ceylon, Burma and the South Sea Islands. Some material was selected from British magazines and contents included poetry, anecdotes, and obituaries.

v1   July 15, 1818-July 21, 1819   APS II, Reel 203

RELIGIOUS REMEMBRANCER. *SEE* Christian Observer.

THE RELIGIOUS REPOSITORY. v.1-2; Sept./Oct. 1807-July/Aug. 1809. Concord, N.H., Printed by G. Hough.

2 v. bimonthly.

Published by the New Hampshire Missionary Society.

Published under the patronage of the New-Hampshire Missionary Society, the *Religious Repository* offered accounts of the experiences of "pious" people, short essays on doctrine and on the duties of the Christian, biographical sketches, and poetry, as well as news of the activities of missionary societies and other religious news.

v1-2   Sept./Oct. 1807-July/Aug. 1809   APS II, Reel 43

RELIGIOUS TRACTS (SOCIETY FOR PROMOTING CHRISTIAN KNOWLEDGE, PIETY, AND CHARITY). *SEE* Christian Monitor. A Religious Periodical Work.

THE REMEMBRANCER, FOR LORD'S DAY EVENINGS. no.1-2; Jan. 1-8, 1797. Exeter, Mass., H. Ranlet.

14 p. Weekly.

Joseph Brown, editor.

Each issue of this weekly religious octavo consisted of an essay on "the being of God."

no.1-2   Jan. 1-8, 1797   APS I, Reel 26

Microfilm edition was prepared from MBat copy.

THE REMEMBRANCER; or, Debtors prison recorder. v.1, no.1-6; Apr. 8-May 15, 1820. New York, J.B. Jansen.

48 p. weekly.

Copy filmed incomplete: no. 5 (p. 33-40) wanting.

This weekly journal was concerned with the problem of imprisonment for debt; it described incidents which occurred in the prisons and listed prisoners received and discharged. In addition, it published poetry, criticism on the drama, listings of marriages and deaths and information on the Humane Society of New York and on a variety of other topics, including the arts and sciences.

v1, no.1-4, 6   Apr. 8-May 15, 1820   APS II, Reel 204

THE REPOSITORY AND LADIES' WEEKLY MUSEUM.
v.1-6; no.16; Nov. 15, 1800-Apr. 5, 1806. Philadelphia,
Printed by D. Hogan.

6 v. illus.
Publication suspended Aug. 14-Sept. 25, 1802.

Title varies: v.1-5 (Nov. 15, 1800-June 29, 1805) The Philadelphia
repository, and weekly register.

Edited by D. Hogan and others.
Some issues are missing.

During its five-and-a-half-year existence, this 8-page weekly miscellany was edited successively by David Hogan, John W. Scott,
and Thomas Irwin. Among its contents were original essays, serialized tales, extracts from both new and older publications, biographical sketches, and some material on the theater. Most issues contained pieces of music, and for the first four volumes the last page
was devoted to poetry.

Philadelphia Repository and Weekly Register
v1-5   Nov. 15, 1800-June 29, 1805   APS II, Reel 43

Repository and Ladies' Weekly Museum
v6   Dec. 14, 1805-Apr. 5, 1806   Reel 43

THE REPOSITORY OF KNOWLEDGE, historical, literary,
miscellaneous, and theological. [v.1 (no.1-2); Apr. 15-May,
1801] Philadelphia [Hugh Maxwell]

1 v. biweekly.

This short-lived Philadelphia religious magazine featured lectures
on doctrine, material on the history of the church, miscellaneous
pieces on Christianity, biographical sketches and poetry.

v1, no.1-2   Apr. 15-May 1801   APS II, Reel 44

**THE REPOSITORY OF KNOWLEDGE, HISTORICAL,
LITERARY, MISCELLANEOUS,** and theological. v.1
(no.1-2); Jan. 1802-Feb. 1802. Philadelphia, John Adams,
1802.

123 p. monthly.

No. 2 printed by H. Maxwell.
Reprint: originally published Apr. 15-May 1801.

This short-lived Philadelphia religious magazine featured lectures
on doctrine, material on the history of the church, miscellaneous
pieces on Christianity, biographical sketches and poetry.

v1, no.1-2   Jan.-Feb. 1802   APS II, Reel 44

THE REPUBLIC OF LETTERS; a republication of standard literature. v.1-6; 1834-36. New York, G. Dearborn,
1834-

6 v.

Vols. 1-2 have title; The republic of letters; a republication of standard literature.
Editor: 1835- Mrs. A.H. Nicholas.

Works of Pope and Milton and standard histories were reprinted
in this short-lived periodical. Mrs. A.H. Nicholas was the editor.

v1-4   1834-1835   APS II, Reel 1257
v5-6   1836   Reel 1258

Some pages have faded print or print missing.

Microfilm edition was prepared from NjP copy.

A REPUBLICAN MAGAZINE; or, Repository of political truths. v.1, no.1-4; Oct. 1-Dec. 15, 1798. Fairhaven,
Vt.

192 p.

Caption title: The scourge of aristocracy, and repository of important political truths.

Edited by J. Lyon.

A political magazine designed to strengthen the cause of Re-
publicanism against the aristocracy. It published proceedings of
patriotic meetings, dialogues, extracts from speeches. Livingston's
speech on the sedition bid, articles on domestic and foreign events,
particularly French, and some poetry.

v1, no.1-4   Oct. 1-Dec. 15, 1798   APS I, Reel 26

Some pages are missing.

Microfilm edition was prepared from NN copy.

REPUBLICAN RUSH-LIGHT. *SEE* Rush-Light.

THE RHODE ISLAND BAPTIST. v.1; Oct. 1823-Sept.
1824. Providence, J. Miller, printer.

290 p. monthly.

Edited by A. Brown.

Edited by Allen Brown, this Baptist magazine published articles
on Baptists and other religious groups and on doctrine, Bible studies, poetry, anecdotes, extracts from various religious publications
and many short miscellaneous items.

v1, nos.1-12   Oct. 1823-Sept. 1824   APS II, Reel 204

RHODE ISLAND INSTITUTE OF INSTRUCTION. Journal. v.1-3; Nov. 1845-1848. Providence.

3 v. ilus. (plans) semimonthly (irreg.)

Editor: Henry Barnard.
Contains extra no. for Nov. 6, 1845-July 1, 1846.

This educational journal was devoted to improving the public
schools and other means of education in Rhode Island. It was comprised of three sections: The regular semimonthly number contained articles and documents relating to the history, condition,
and improvement of schools in the state and on laws of the state
concerning schools. The *Extras* published all official circulars,
notices for school meetings, with their proceedings, and information on individual schools and on improvements in education in
other states and countries. The "Education Tracts" contained
lengthy discussions of important educational topics.

v1-3   Nov. 1845-1848   APS II, Reel 389

Vol. 2: Pagination is irregular. Vol. 3: Contains index to Vols. 1-3.

Microfilm edition was prepared from MiU copy.

THE RHODE ISLAND LITERARY REPOSITORY, a monthly magazine. Containing biographical sketches, reviews, dissertations, literary researches, poetry, anecdotes, &c. v.1; Apr. 1814-Mar. 1815. Providence, R.I., Robinson and Howland [1814-15]

2 p. l., 672 p. illus., ports.

Isaac Bailey, editor.

Dates on title page incorrectly as Apr. 1814-Apr. 1915.

This monthly literary miscellany published much poetry, as well as a variety of other literary material—biographical sketches, book reviews, anecdotes, and maxims—and articles on politics, math, chemistry, botany, and general science.

v1, nos.1-12   Apr. 1814-Mar. 1815   APS II, Reel 204

THE RIVERSIDE MAGAZINE FOR YOUNG PEOPLE. An illustrated monthly. v.1-4; Jan. 1867-Dec. 1870. New York, Hurd and Houghton, 1868-70.

4 v. illus., pl., music.

H.E. Scudder, editor.
Merged into Scribner's monthly.

The *Riverside Monthly* was a miscellany devoted to the entertainment of the young. Horace E. Scudder edited the monthly during its short-lived career.

v1-4   Jan. 1867-Dec. 1870   APS III, Reel 52

Vol. 4: pages 541-42 are torn.

Microfilm edition was prepared from FJ, MiU, and Nh copies.

THE ROANOKE RELIGIOUS CORRESPONDENT; or, Monthly evangelical visitant. v.1-2; Aug. 1821-Dec. 1823. Danville, Va.

2 v.

Publication suspended Aug.-Dec. 1822.

Published at Danville, Virginia, this monthly religious magazine published a "Letter to a young minister" in each number; together they made up a comprehensive sketch of church history. Another series was "The Virginia Baptist Chronicle." Missions were given coverage, including those in Burma, Palestine, and those of the Cherokee nation; and contents also included a variety of religious articles, foreign news, letters, essays, poetry, and anecdotes.

v1-2   Aug. 1821-Dec. 1823   APS II, Reel 204

ROBERT MERRY'S MUSEUM. *SEE* Merry's Museum for Boys and Girls.

ROBERT'S SEMI-MONTHLY MAGAZINE FOR TOWN AND COUNTRY. v.1-2; Jan. 15, 1841-Jan. 1, 1842. Boston, G. Roberts, 1841-42.

2 v. illus., plates.
Paged continuously.

Vol. 1 has half-title: Semi-monthly magazine.

"There are two editions of no. I, the first containing 40 pages, the second 16 pages. Merged in the Quarto notion."–Sabin's Dict. of books relating to America.

Robert's Semi-Monthly Magazine, for Town and Country was the *Reader's Digest* of its day. It included the literature of the day in a convenient form for those who wished to "keep up with the current." It stated in the preface to volume 1 that a large portion of the literature was useless and that it was the object of the editor to "winnow the wheat and throw the chaff away."

v1-2   Jan. 15, 1841-Jan. 1, 1842   APS II, Reel 845

The index which was found in volume 2 does not correspond to the editions of numbers 1-4 contained therein.

Microfilm edition was prepared from N and WHi copies.

ROBINSON'S EPITOME OF LITERATURE. *SEE* Literary World; A Monthly Review of Current Literature.

ROBINSON'S MAGAZINE, a weekly repository of original papers; and selections from the English magazines. v.1-2; July 18, 1818-1819. Baltimore, Joseph Robinson, 1818-

2 v.

This weekly magazine borrowed a good deal of its material from British publications, including the *Edinburgh Magazine,* though there was original material as well. A series of "Letters from Italy" ran through many issues and there was some attention to fashion and a good deal of writing on travel and people of foreign countries. Literary material included tales and poetry, biography, anecdotes, articles on literature, and notices of new books.

v1   July 18-Dec. 30, 1818   APS II, Reel 204
v2   Jan. 2-June 26, 1819   Reel 205

THE ROCHESTER MAGAZINE, AND THEOLOGICAL REVIEW, consisting of essays, extracts, reviews, and biblical criticisms. v.1 (no.1-12); Jan.-Dec. 1824. Rochester, N.Y., L.W. Sibley, 1824-

1 v. monthly.

Editor: 1824- J.S. Thompson.

Edited by John Samuel Thompson, this Universalist magazine covered the activities of the Western Association of Universalists in New York and published articles on doctrine and on the Bible, essays, religious poetry, lectures, and letters.

v1, nos.1-12   Jan.-Dec. 1824   APS II, Reel 205

ROSE BUD, OR YOUTH'S GAZETTE. *SEE* Southern Rose.

ROSE OF THE VALLEY. v.1-2, no.6; Jan. 1839-July 1840. Cincinnati, 1839-1840.

2 v.
V. 2 wanting.

Subtitle varies.

This short-lived journal published by G.G. Moore was devoted to literature, instruction, and amusement, containing essays, poetry, biographical sketches, and miscellaneous notes.

v1   1839   APS II, Reel 1308

Best copy available. Vol. 1: Many pages are stained.

Microfilm edition was prepared from DLC and MnU copies.

THE ROUGH AND READY. v.1, no.1-13; Dec. 12, 1846-Mar. 13, 1847. Concord [N.H.] 1846-47.

[52] p. weekly.

True Osgood, editor.

v1   Dec. 12, 1846-Mar. 13, 1847   APS II, Reel 845

Microfilm edition was prepared from DLC copy.

THE ROUND TABLE. A Saturday review of politics, finance, literature, society, and art. v.1-9, v.10, no. [1]; Dec. 19, 1863-July 3, 1869. New York, H.E. & C.H. Sweetser, 1863-69.

10 v. in 9.

Vol. 1 has title: The Round table; a weekly record of the notable, the useful and the tasteful.

Publication was suspended from July 30, 1864, to Sept. 2, 1865, inclusive. Sept. 9 to Dec. 30, 1865, are called "New ser., no. 1-17." In July 1869, the Round table was merged into the Citizen, which continued as the New York citizen and round table.

An informal staff of correspondents in various large cities, along with the editors, Charles H. Sweetser and Henry E. Sweetser, wrote for this controversial weekly journal. Political comment, literary and art criticism, and attacks on religious periodicals made up most of the content.

v1-4   Dec. 1863-Dec. 1866   APS III, Reel 461
v5-10   Jan. 1867-July 1869   Reel 462

Vols. 1, 3, and 10 have no indexes. Some pages are torn, creased, or stained. Vols. 7 and 8 have pages missing.

Microfilm edition was prepared from MH, MiU, MoS, NPV, and NjP copies.

THE ROVER: a weekly magazine of tales, poetry, and engravings, also sketches of travel, history and biography. v.1-5; Mar. 1843-Sept. 13, 1845. New York, Labree, Dean, 1843-

5 v. plates.

Editors: v.1. Seba Smith, Lawrence Labree.–v. 2- Seba Smith.–v. Lawrence Labree.
Superseded by New York illustrated magazine.

The first volume of the *Rover* was comprised of short stories, poetry and engravings, edited by Seba Smith and Lawrence Labree. Later volumes expanded when historical, biographical, and travel articles were added. Seba Smith, C.J. Hoffman, and Mrs. Elizabeth Oakes Smith were frequent contributors although Caroline Lee Hentz, Thomas Buchanan Read, Thomas Haynes Bayly, and John Greenleaf Whittier were also represented. However, the general public greatly disliked the periodical's name. In September, 1845, the *New York Illustrated Magazine* superseded the *Rover*.

v1-2   1843-1844   APS II, Reel 912
v3-5   1844-Sept. 1845   Reel 913

Some pages are stained or creased.

Microfilm edition was prepared from MeB, N, and NjP copies.

SEE ALSO: New York Illustrated Magazine of Literature and Art.

THE ROYAL AMERICAN MAGAZINE, OR UNIVERSAL REPOSITORY OF INSTRUCTION AND AMUSEMENT. v1-2, no.3; Jan. 1774-Mar. 1775. Boston, I. Thomas [etc.]

2 v. in 1. plates. monthly.

Editors: Jan.-June 1774, Isaiah Thomas.–July 1774-Mar. 1775, Joseph Greenleaf. Contains series of engravings by Paul Revere. Reprint of pt. of Hutchinson's history of Massachusetts appended.

An illustrated miscellany of original material together with selections from English magazines, books, and documents, including essays, fiction, advice to the lovelorn, and articles on politics and current events. It was the first magazine in the Colonies to adequately use illustrations; these included a series of engravings by Paul Revere.

v1-2   Jan. 1774-Mar. 1775   APS I, Reel 26

Microfilm edition was prepared from MWA copy.

ROYAL SPIRITUAL MAGAZINE; or, The Christian's grand treasure. v.1; Jan.-Dec. 1771. Philadelphia, J.M'Gibbons.

vi, 72 p.

A religious magazine which defended the doctrines of Calvin.

v1   Jan.-Dec. 1771   APS I, Reel 26

Microfilm edition was prepared from MWA copy.

THE ROYCROFT QUARTERLY. no.1-3; May 1896-Nov. 1896. East Aurora, N.Y., Roycroft Printing Shop, 1896-

The first issue of this handsomely-printed journal contained seven poems by Stephen Crane and a sketch about him. G.B. Shaw's "On Going to Church" and "Foreign Ideas in the Catholic Church in America" by the Reverend Father George Zurcher made up the remainder of the content.

no.1-3   May-Nov. 1896   APS III, Reel 462

Microfilm edition was prepared from DLC and MH copies.

THE RURAL CASKET. v.1, no.1-15; June 5-Sept. 11, 1798. [Poughkeepsie, Printed by Power and Southwick]

1 v. weekly.

Basically moralistic in nature, this weekly was directed toward self-improvement; this is reflected in its poetry, anecdotes, "moral tales," and essays on virtues and vices. Also included were foreign and domestic news, medical remedies, advice on marriage, and humorous anecdotes as well as miscellaneous articles.

v1., no.1-15   June 5-Sept. 11, 1798   APS I, Reel 33

Microfilm edition was prepared from NN copy.

THE RURAL MAGAZINE ... v.1, no.1-52; Feb. 17, 1798-Feb. 9, 1799. [Newark: Printed by J.H. Williams for the proprietors] 1798-99.

Weekly.

Contents included poetry, tales, essays, anecdotes, and maxims as well as articles generally concerned with agriculture, religion, history, art, literature, and morality.

v1, no.1-52   Feb. 17, 1798-Feb. 9, 1799   APS I, Reel 27

Microfilm edition was prepared from DLC copy.

THE RURAL MAGAZINE AND FARMER'S MONTHLY MUSEUM, devoted to history, biography, agriculture, manufacture, miscellany, poetry, and foreign and domestic intelligence. Ed. by S. Putnam Waldo. v.1, no.1-6; Feb. to July 1819. Hartford, J. & W. Russell, 1819.

208 p.

Edited by S. Putnam Waldo, this magazine for farmers devoted much space to agriculture but also gave attention to manufacturing, history, and biography. Agricultural material included general articles and coverage of cattle shows, fairs, and agricultural societies, and other material consisted of a series on the history of Connecticut, biographies of important state people, state papers, coverage of manufacturing improvements, foreign and domestic news, notices of new publications, and poetry.

v1, nos.1-6   Feb.-July 1819   APS II, Reel 205

THE RURAL MAGAZINE AND LITERARY EVENING FIRE-SIDE. v.1; Jan.-Dec. 1820. Philadelphia, R. & C. Johnson.

480 p. monthly.

The *Rural Magazine* combined the features of a farming magazine and a literary miscellany. It proposed to furnish information on the science of agriculture and on recent improvements in farming by publishing pieces written by local farmers and articles selected from European works and from American newspapers. Information on agricultural societies was also included. Among the non-agricultural material were extracts from new publications, especially biography and travel; information on scientific subjects; essays and articles on history, geography, social conditions, religion, government, and literature; and poetry.

v1, nos. 1-12   Jan.-Dec. 1820   APS II, Reel 205

THE RURAL MAGAZINE; or, Vermont repository. Devoted to literary, moral, historical, and political improvement. v.1-2; Jan. 1795-Dec. 1796. Rutland, S. Williams [1795-96]

2 v. monthly.

Samuel Williams, editor.

Contents included historical and political documents, medical papers, a serial history of the American Revolution, biographical sketches, articles on natural science and travel, weather information, and poetry.

v1-2   Jan. 1795-Dec. 1796   APS I, Reel 27

Several pages are lacking.

Microfilm edition was prepared from DLC copy.

RURAL REGISTER. *SEE* American Farmer.

THE RURAL REPOSITORY DEVOTED TO POLITE LITERATURE, such as moral and sentimental tales, original communications, biography, traveling sketches, poetry, amusing miscellany, humorous and historical anecdotes, &c. v.1-27; June 12, 1824-Oct. 4, 1851. Hudson [N.Y.] W.B. Stoddard.

27 v. plates. biweekly.

Title varies: The Rural repository; or, Bower of literature; a semi-monthly literary and entertaining journal: containing a variety of original and select articles. The Rural repository devoted to polite literature.

A literary miscellany containing a variety of original and selected material, including popular tales, biography, travel articles, poetry, anecdotes, epigrams, riddles, letters to the editor, and some local news.

v1-10   June 12, 1824-May 24, 1834   APS II, Reel 681
v11-19   June 17, 1834-June 3, 1843   Reel 682
v20-27   Aug. 26, 1843-Oct. 4, 1851   Reel 683

Vols. 5-9 also called new series vols. 1-5; 10-15 also called new series vols. 1-6; 16 and 17 also called new series vol. 7.

Microfilm edition was prepared from DLC, ICN, MWA, NN, NjR and RPB copies.

RURAL REPOSITORY; OR, BOWER OF LITERATURE; A SEMI-MONTHLY LITERARY AND ENTERTAINING JOURNAL. *SEE* Rural Repository Devoted to Polite Literature, Such as Moral and Sentimental Tales ....

THE RUSH-LIGHT. (Cobbett, William, 1763-1835). [v.1, no.1-6; v.2, no.1] 15th Feb.-30th Aug. 1800. By Peter Porcupine [pseud.] New York; Published by William Cobbett, [1800]

7 no. in 1 v.

Nos. 1 and 2 have cover-title, with contents and imprint (in no. 1 "New Yokk[!]"), the remainder caption titles only. No. 1, 15th Feb.; no.2, 28th Feb. (p. 112: End of no.II.–Mar.10, 1800); no.3, 15th Mar (p. 160: End of no. III–Mar. 24); no. 4, 31st Mar. (p. 208: End of no. iv–Apr. 14); no. 5, 30th Apr; no. 6, 30th Aug.; "no. VII–being the first number of volume II" undated, has caption title "The Republican Rush-light". No. 6 dated at end (p. 309) London, August 30, 1800. At end of no. 7 (p. 48) "Finis".

The *Rush-Light* was the third of three similar periodicals edited by William Cobbett, alias Peter Porcupine. The first was a political monthly called *Porcupine's Political Censor,* after which he began a daily paper, *Porcupine's Gazette and United States Advertiser.* In the *Gazette* he continued to make war on the French, and the democrats, and during the Philadelphia yellow fever epidemic of 1797 he attacked the city administration and, in particular, a Philadelphia physician, Dr. Rush. The attacks on Rush and the resulting libel suit put an end to Cobbett's Philadelphia career, but he continued his attack on Rush from New York, where he published his *Rush-Light,* later called *Republican Rush-Light.* Earlier issues devoted most of their space to the "noted blood-letting physician of Philadelphia" and his supporters, while later issues were more concerned with political issues from the Republican point of view.

Rush-light
v1, no.1-6   Feb. 15-Aug. 30, 1800   APS II, Reel 44

Republican Rush-light
v2, no.1   undated   Reel 44

RUSSELL'S MAGAZINE. v.1-6; Apr. 1857-Mar. 1860. Charleston [S.C.] Walker, Evans, 1857-60.

6 v. monthly.

P.H. Hayne, editor.

Russell's Magazine was founded by William Gilmore Simms and co-edited by Paul Hamilton Hayne. The magazine, intended to be a local paper, contained a great deal of poetry and aspired to be a literary work. It failed in this attempt, however, and became an ardent defender of the Southern position prior to the War.

v1-6   Apr. 1857-Mar. 1860   APS III, Reel 17

Microfilm edition was prepared from WHi copy.

RUTGERS LITERARY MISCELLANY. A monthly periodical. v.1; Jan.-Dec. 1842. New Brunswick, N.J., Rutgers College [1842]

2 p.1., 192 p.

B.F. Romaine, editor.

The *Miscellany* is comprised of original prose and poetry, and was published at Rutgers University. Unfortunately many of the articles are unsigned.

v1   Jan.-Dec. 1842   APS II, Reel 880

Microfilm edition was prepared from DLC copy.

THE SABBATH SCHOOL REPOSITORY AND TEACHER'S ASSISTANT: devoted to the interests of Sabbath schools ... v.1 (no.1-12); Jan.-Dec. 1823. New Haven.

288 p. monthly.

Edited by E.B. Coleman.

This religious magazine was concerned mainly with Sunday schools and published information on the history of Sunday schools, on Sunday-school unions, and on the activities of various Sunday schools in the area, in addition to providing addresses, poetry and anecdotes, and much material for children.

v1, nos. 1-12   Jan.-Dec. 1823   APS II, Reel 205

SABBATH SCHOOL VISITANT. v.1-2, no.12; June 1824-Feb. 1826. Utica, N.Y., 1824-1826.

2 v.

Sabbath School Visitant was one of many religious periodicals of an inspirational nature.

v1-2   June 7, 1824-Feb. 1826   APS II, Reel 1124

Vol. 2: No Index or Contents available.

Microfilm edition was prepared from NCH copy.

ST. NICHOLAS; an illustrated magazine for young folks. v.1-67, no.4, Nov. 1873-Feb. 1940; v.70, no.1-4, Mar.-June 1943. New York, Century.

68 v. illus., plates, ports, monthly.

Absorbed Our young folks, Jan. 1874; Children's hour, July 1874; Little corporal and Schoolday magazine, May 1875; Wide awake; Sept. 1893. Subtitle varies.

Editor: 1873-Aug. 1905, M.M. Dodge.
Published by Scribner, 1873-July 1881.
On film: v.1-34, 1873-Oct. 1907.

Founded by Roswell Smith in 1873, *St. Nicholas* was a monthly magazine for children. Its editor, Mrs. Mary Mapes Dodge, was convinced that it should not "be a milk-and-water variety of the periodicals for adults." A handsome magazine from the first, *St. Nicholas* was beautifully printed and copiously illustrated by artists and wood engravers. *St. Nicholas* was distinguished by the high quality of its fiction. All of the leading writers for children appeared among its contributors including Trowbridge, Louisa Alcott, Kipling, Harte, Clemens, Stevenson, and numerous others. As *St. Nick* entered the twentieth century it showed a certain flagging in vitality and a slow but steady decline in circulation. The magazine became more departmentalized and placed less emphasis on stories and articles. In 1905, Mrs. Dodge died and was succeeded as editor by William Clarke.

v1-5	Nov. 1873-Oct. 1878	APS III, Reel 591
v6-9	Nov. 1878-Oct. 1882	Reel 592
v10-13	Nov. 1882-Oct. 1886	Reel 593
v14-17	Nov. 1886-Oct. 1890	Reel 594
v18-21	Nov. 1890-Oct. 1894	Reel 595
v22-24	Nov. 1894-Oct. 1897	Reel 596
v25-28	Nov. 1897-Oct. 1901	Reel 597
v29-31	Nov. 1901-Oct. 1904	Reel 598
v32-34	Nov. 1904-Oct. 1907	Reel 599

Volumes lack indexes. Some pages are torn.

Microfilm edition was prepared from the MnU copy.

SEE ALSO: Our Young Folks.

ST. TAMMANYS MAGAZINE. v.1, no.1-5; Nov. 9-Dec. 17, 1821. New York, C.S. Van Winkle.

80 p.

A short-lived literary miscellany which contained stories and many short tales, poetry, literary notices and book reviews, obituaries, and a good deal of miscellaneous material.

v1, nos.1-5   Nov. 9-Dec. 17, 1821   APS II, Reel 205

SALMAGUNDI; or, The whim-whams and opinions of Launcelot Langstaff, esq., and others. no.1-20, Jan. 24, 1807-Jan. 25, 1808. New York, D. Longworth.

2 v.

Paged continuously.
By Washington Irving, William Irving and James K. Paulding. No. 1, 3, 5, 3d ed.; no. 2, 4th ed.; no.4, 6-8, 2nd ed.; the remaining numbers presumably the 1st ed. A second series in 3 vols (15 nos.) entirely by Paulding, was issued May, 1819 to Sept. 1820. cf. His Literary life, by his son, p. 116.

Written by Washington Irving, his brother William, and his brother-in-law, James Kirk Paulding, *Salmagundi* was one of the early satirical publications and the model for many of them. It poked fun at the fads and follies of New York, including women's fashions, commented on the theater, and satirized a number of well-known personalities, including Joseph Dennie. William Irving wrote the poetry.

no.1-20   Jan. 24, 1807-Jan. 25, 1808   APS II, Reel 44

SALMAGUNDI (Paulding) Ser. 2 (no.1-13); May 30, 1819-Aug. 19, 1820. Second series. By Launcelot Langstaff [pseud.] 1st ed. Philadelphia, M. Thomas; New York, J. Maxwell, Printer, 1819-20.

3 v. in 2.

Contains papers, no. I-XV; no. III is first dated paper, Saturday, July 13, 1819; the last paper has date, Saturday, Sept. 2d, 1820. Called ser. 2 in continuation of Salmagundi (Irving)

James Kirke Paulding, a contributor to Washington Irving's *Salmagundi,* initiated a second series of this satirical journal in Philadelphia, writing it all himself. The second series met with much less success than the original.

s2v2-3   Oct. 2, 1819-Aug. 19, 1820   APS II, Reel 1308

Best copy available. Issues 1-6 are missing; not available for photographing. Issues 7-14: Indexes and tables of contents are missing; not available for photographing.

Microfilm edition was prepared from CSmH and MH copies.

SEE ALSO: Salmagundi (Irving).

SARGENT'S NEW MONTHLY MAGAZINE, OF LITERATURE, FASHION, AND THE FINE ARTS. Ed. by Epes Sargent. v.1 (no.1-6); Jan.-June 1843. New York, Sargent; New Orleans, Norman, Steele, 1843.

284 p. plates (part col.)

Nathaniel Hawthorne, Helen Berkeley, John Quincy Adams, Oliver Wendell Holmes and John Greenleaf Whittier were among the famous contributors. Engravings, music, poetry, fiction, and announcements of new books made up the content.

v1   Jan.-June 1843   APS II, Reel 1258

Microfilm edition was prepared from MnU copy.

SARTAIN'S UNION MAGAZINE OF LITERATURE AND ART. v.1-10, v.11, no.1-2; July 1847-Aug. 1852. New York, 1847-48; Philadelphia, 1849-52.

11 v. illus., plates (part col.) monthly.

Title varies: 1847-48, The Union magazine of literature and art. 1849-52, Sartain's union magazine of literature and art.

Editors: 1847-48, Mrs. C.M. Kirkland.–1849-51, Mr. C.M. Kirkland, J.S. Hart.–1851-52, John Sartain.

Founded in New York by Mrs. Caroline M. Kirkland under the title *Union Magazine of Literature and Art,* this general monthly magazine was gay and gossipy, with a certain amount of information. Mrs. Kirkland wrote western stories for her magazine and it also contained the usual sentimental and very moral tales, light sketches, poetry, essays on literary subjects, and short book reviews. Contributors included T.S. Arthur, John Neal, H.T. Tuckerman,

W.G. Simms, W.A. Jones, Park Benjamin, and C.F. Hoffman, besides the contingent of women writers–Mrs. Lydia H. Sigourney, Mrs. Frances S. Osgood, Mrs. Emma Embury, Mrs. Elizabeth F. Ellet, Mrs. Lydia Marie Child, and the Misses Catherine Sedgwick, Hannah Gould, and "Grace Greenwood." Copiously illustrated with steel, mezzotint, and wood engravings, music, and colored fashions, it appeared to be a strong competitor for such magazines as *Graham's, Godey's,* and *Peterson's,* but it did not prosper. At the end of 1848 John Sartain and William Sloanaker bought the magazine, moving it to Philadelphia and changing the name to *Sartain's Union Magazine.* It bore a strong resemblance to *Graham's.* Among its contributors were Henry Wadsworth Longfellow, James Russell Lowell, Edgar Allan Poe, William Cullen Bryant, Nathaniel Parker Willis, and Thomas Buchanan Read. Poe's "The Bells" and "The Poetic Principle" were among the most important publications, and book reviews, musical criticism, and art exhibitions were also included. In illustration the *Union Magazine* was especially brilliant; at least three plates were furnished with each number, and some colored lithographs of flowers and other subjects appeared.

Union Magazine of Literature and Art
v1	July-Dec. 1847	APS II, Reel 572
v2-3	Jan.-Dec. 1848	Reel 573

Sartain's Union Magazine of Literature and Art
v4-7	Jan. 1849-Dec. 1850	Reel 573
v8-11	Jan. 1851-Aug. 1852	Reel 574

Vols. 4-5: Indexes are photographed at end of volume. Vol. 11: Lacks index.

Microfilm edition was prepared from the DLC copy.

THE SATIRIST. By Lodowick Lash'em [pseud.] no.1-13; Jan. 16-May 9, 1812. Boston [J.L. Edwards], [1812]

1 v. illus. weekly (irregular)

Caption title.
Nos. 11-13 have title: The Boston satirist, or Weekly museum.

Established by James L. Edwards in 1812, this comic periodical was edited by "Lodowick Lash'em" and was a lampoon paper whose object was to "lash vice and folly." Some poetry was included.

Satirist
no.1-10	Jan. 16-Apr. 11, 1812	APS II, Reel 205

Boston Satirist, or Weekly Museum
no.11-13	Apr. 20-May 9, 1812	Reel 205

SATURDAY BULLETIN. *SEE* Saturday Evening Post.

SATURDAY EVENING POST, an illustrated weekly magazine. v1- Aug. 18, 1821- Philadelphia.

v. illus.

Absorbed the Saturday bulletin in Jan. 1833; Saturday news in Jan. 1839.
Title varies: 1831-Jan. 1839, Atkinson's Saturday evening post. Subtitle varies.

On film: v.1-4, no.53 (reels 236-237) v.5, no.27-v64 (reels 1936-1947)
Imperfect copy: Scattered issues missing for years 1821-22, 1824-25. Entire issues missing for years 1858-59.

Once called "the great American nickelodean," the *Saturday Evening Post* has, with its great diversity of offerings, amused and informed Americans longer than any other general magazine. Begun Aug. 4, 1821, with Thomas Cottrell Clarke as editor, this weekly 4-page paper had five columns per page, and contained news, short articles by the editor, and literary miscellany, much of it selected. All political controversy was avoided. In the fall of 1822 a "Dramatic Summary," which reviews plays mainly at Philadelphia theaters, was begun. The content of the paper gradually improved, and its five columns increased to six. The front page of a typical number of the *Post* in 1825 contained a column and a half of poetry, some tales, a section of household hints, and a department of periodical essays. On the second page were domestic and foreign news items and miscellaneous feature material, while the third and fourth pages contained nonpolitical editorials, news, advertisements, death and marriage notices, and more poetry. In 1826 Clarke was replaced by Morton McMichael. In 1828 Samuel C. Atkinson became the sole publisher, with Benjamin Mathias as his editor, and thus began the second phase of the *Post's* history.

During its first twenty-five years the *Post* was not particularly outstanding, but during its second twenty-five years it became a well-known Saturday miscellany, publishing the works of both famous and lesser-known contributors. Its third quarter-century was spent obscurely. This was followed by the Curtis-Lorimer era, which lasted for forty-five years, including the Stout editorship; it was in this period that the *Post* became an American institution. The modern period began in 1942, when Ben Hibbs became editor.

Saturday Evening Post

v1, no.3-v3, no.51	Aug. 18, 1821-Dec. 18, 1824	APS II, Reel 236
v4, no.1-53	Jan.-Dec. 1825	Reel 237
	July 8, 1826-Dec. 27, 1828	Reel 1936
	Jan. 3, 1829-Dec. 25, 1830	Reel 1937

Atkinson's Saturday Evening Post

	Feb. 5, 1831-Dec. 19, 1835	Reel 1937
	Jan. 2, 1836-Nov. 2, 1839	Reel 1938

Saturday Evening Post

	Nov. 9, 1839-Dec. 29, 1849	Reel 1938
	Jan. 5, 1850-Dec. 26, 1857	Reel 1939
	Jan. 7, 1860-Dec. 28, 1861	Reel 1940
	Jan. 4, 1862-Aug. 26, 1865	Reel 1941
	Jan. 6, 1866-Dec. 25, 1869	Reel 1942
	Jan. 1, 1870-Dec. 27, 1873	Reel 1943
	Jan. 3, 1874-Dec. 29, 1877	Reel 1944
	Jan. 5, 1878-Dec. 31, 1881	Reel 1945
	Jan. 2, 1882-Dec. 29, 1883	Reel 1946
	Jan. 5, 1884-July 11, 1885	Reel 1947

Microfilm edition was prepared from the DLC and DSI copies.

SEE ALSO: Brown's Literary Omnibus.

THE SATURDAY MAGAZINE: being in great part a compilation from the British reviews, magazines, and scientific journals. v.1-5, Jan. 2, 1819-June 30, 1821; new ser. v.1-2, July 7, 1821-July 29, 1822. Philadelphia, Littell & Henry, 1819-22.

7 v. illus. weekly.

Title varies: Jan.-June 1819, The Philadelphia register, and national recorder. July 1819-June 1821, The National recorder. July 1821-July 1822, The Saturday magazine.

Eliakim Littell, editor.
Superseded by the Museum of foreign literature and science, later the Museum of foreign literature, science, and art. Film ends with issue for June 29, 1822.

The *Saturday Magazine* began as the *Philadelphia Register,* a weekly paper established in 1819 by Eliakim Littell and R. Norris Henry. It dealt with agriculture, manufacturing, politics, slavery, and Congress and the legislature, and also published poetry and foreign and domestic news. In July of that year, it became a literary eclectic under the name of *National Recorder* and although it was renamed the *Saturday Magazine* in July 1821 its character remained essentially the same. Much of its contents were taken from British reviews, magazines, and scientific journals. It contained material on agriculture, including papers read before the Agricultural Society of Philadelphia, scientific and literary news, biography, poetry, travel articles and miscellaneous short pieces and anecdotes. In addition, the *Saturday Magazine* introduced Charles Lamb's "Essays of Elia" and Thomas De Quincey's "The Confessions of an English Opium Eater" to the American public.

Philadelphia Register and National Recorder

v1	Jan. 2-June 26, 1819	APS II, Reel 237

National Recorder

v2-4	July 3, 1819-Dec. 30, 1820	Reel 237
v5	Jan. 6-June 30, 1821	Reel 238

Saturday Magazine

nsv1-2	July 7, 1821-June 29, 1822	Reel 238

SEE ALSO: Museum of Foreign Literature, Science, and Art.

SATURDAY NEWS. *SEE* Saturday Evening Post.

SCHOOLFELLOW. *SEE* Merry's Museum for Boys and Girls.

SCIENCE OF HEALTH. *SEE* Phrenological Journal and Science of Health.

SCIENTIFIC AMERICAN. v1- ; Aug. 28, 1845- . New York, Munn, 1845-

v. illus. weekly.

On film: v.1-14, Aug. 28, 1845-June 25, 1859; new series v.1-59, July 2, 1859-Dec. 29, 1888; v.60-99, Jan. 5, 1889-Dec. 26, 1908. Film lacks: v.51, no.26, Dec. 27, 1884?

Founded by Rufus Porter, the *Scientific American* was a leading popular exponent of mechanical development and invention in the country, achieving a circulation of 14,000 by 1850. It was devoted primarily to new inventions, which were discussed and explained in illustrated articles, and even obscure and unsuccessful inventions were given at least a few lines of attention. One of the most important departments was the weekly publication of the official list of patents. Contents also included a variety of information of a mechanical and scientific nature, and news and commentary on the patent law. Astronomy, chemistry, medicine, and agriculture were given some attention, and transportation and manufacturing occupied much space. The Civil War brought an increase in articles about arms and naval devices. During the '90's, the World's Fair at Chicago, electrical and aeronautical developments, and especially the automobile, were given a great deal of attention. Its columns of queries and answers, its willingness to answer correspondents by letter, its lucidity, and its appeal to the ambitious youth of a machine age all help to explain why *Scientific American* endeared itself to several generations of readers.

v1-7	Aug. 28, 1845-Sept. 11, 1852	APS II, Reel 616
v8-14	Sept. 18, 1852-June 25, 1859	Reel 617
nsv1-7	July 2, 1859-Dec. 27, 1862	Reel 618
nsv8-14	Jan. 3, 1863-June 23, 1866	Reel 619

nsv15-20	June 30, 1866-June 26, 1869	Reel 1734
nsv21-26	July 18, 1869-June 22, 1872	Reel 1735
nsv27-32	July 6, 1872-June 25, 1875	Reel 1736
nsv33-38	July 3, 1875-June 29, 1878	Reel 1737
nsv39-44	July 6, 1878-June 25, 1881	Reel 1738
nsv45-50	July 2, 1881-June 28, 1884	Reel 1739
nsv51-56	July 5, 1884-June 25, 1887	Reel 1740
nsv57-62	July 2, 1887-June 28, 1890	Reel 1741
v63-68	July 5, 1890-June 24, 1893	Reel 1742
v69-73	July 1, 1893-Dec. 28, 1895	Reel 1743
v74-78	Jan. 4, 1896-June 25, 1898	Reel 1744
v79-83	July 2, 1898-Dec. 29, 1900	Reel 1745
v84-89	Jan. 5, 1901-Dec. 26, 1903	Reel 1746
v90-94	Jan. 2, 1904-June 30, 1906	Reel 1747
v95-99	July 7, 1906-Dec. 26, 1908	Reel 1748

Several pages are stained, torn, and have faded print with some loss of text.

Microfilm edition was prepared from DLC, ICJ, MiU and MU copies.

THE SCIENTIFIC JOURNAL. v.1, no.1-10; Feb. 1818-Jan. 1820. Perth Amboy, N.J.

ii, 192 p.

Publication suspended Sept. 1818-June 1819.

Edited by W. Marrat.

This magazine was almost entirely devoted to science and related topics; it contained much material on electricity, gravitation, chemistry, biology, and math, and provided math and science questions and answers. It also dealt with science-related problems, such as preventing rust and cleaning books and stains. Literary notices and some biography were also included.

v1, nos.1-10   Feb. 1818-Jan. 1820   APS II, Reel 239

SCIENTIFIC TRACTS. SEE Family Lyceum.

THE SCOURGE. v.1, no.1-16; Aug. 10-Dec. 28, 1811. Boston, M. Butler.

1 v. weekly (irregular)

Edited by Tim Touchstone, pseud.

This comic periodical was edited by Merrill Butler, alias "Tim Touchstone," who was later sent to jail for libel. It was an offspring of several British comic magazines of similar purpose and contained satire on politics and government, as well as biographical sketches, poetry, and literary notices.

v1, no.1-16   Aug. 10-Dec. 28, 1811   APS II, Reel 239

* SCRIBNER'S MONTHLY. SEE Century, A Popular Quarterly; Hours at Home, A Popular Monthly of Instruction and Recreation; McBride's Magazine; Old and New; Putnam's Magazine; and Riverside Magazine for Young People.

SCRIPTURAL INTERPRETER. v.1-7; 1831-1836. Boston, 1831-1836.

7 v.

A religious periodical founded and edited by Ezra Gannett. It was called "a little in advance of the Unitarianism of the time."

v1-7   Jan. 1831-Dec. 1836   APS II, Reel 751

Vols. 2 and 3: some pages are stained.

Microfilm edition was prepared from MH copy.

SELECT CIRCULATING LIBRARY. SEE Journal of Belles Lettres and Waldie's Select Circulating Library.

* THE SELECT JOURNAL OF FOREIGN PERIODICAL LITERATURE. v.1-4; Jan. 1833-Oct. 1834. Boston, C. Bowen, 1833-34.

4 v. quarterly.

Editors: Andrews Norton, Charles Folsom.

One of the superior American eclectic magazines was the Select Journal. Although it derived almost all of its literature from the best of the British writers, the editing of Charles Folsom and Andrews Norton was its outstanding achievement. Readers will find liberal space in the magazine afforded the editor's comments.

v1-2	1833	APS II, Reel 913
v3-4	1834	Reel 913

Microfilm edition was prepared from the MiU copy.

SELECT REVIEWS, AND SPIRIT OF THE FOREIGN MAGAZINES. SEE Select Reviews of Literature, and Spirit of Foreign Magazines.

SELECT REVIEWS OF LITERATURE, AND SPIRIT OF FOREIGN MAGAZINES. v.1-8 (no.1-48); Jan. 1809-Dec. 1812. Philadelphia, J.F. Watson [etc.]

8 v. pl., ports. monthly.

Vols. 6-8 have added t.-p., engraved.
Title varies: Jan. 1809-June 1811, Select reviews, and spirit of the foreign magazines. By E. Bronson, and others.

"Ed. by Samuel Ewing."—A.H. Smyth, Philadelphia magazines. Continued as the Analectic magazine.

Select Reviews was a purely eclectic monthly magazine which was conducted until July 1811 by Enos Bronson and then purchased by J.F. Watson, who changed the title slightly. Its 72 pages were filled with material which was chiefly British in origin, including book reviews, memoirs, biography, poetry and anecdotes, and articles on literature and travel. It also listed recent and proposed British and American publications.

Select Reviews, and Spirit of the Foreign Magazines
v1-2	Jan.-Dec. 1809	APS II, Reel 44
v3-5	Jan. 1810-June 1811	Reel 239

Select Reviews of Literature, and Spirit of Foreign Magazines
v6	July-Dec. 1811	Reel 239
v7-8	Jan.-Dec. 1812	Reel 240

SEE ALSO: Analectic Magazine.

SENTIMENTAL & LITERARY MAGAZINE. SEE New-York Weekly Magazine; or, Miscellaneous Repository ...

SHAKER AND SHAKERESS MONTHLY. *SEE* Manifesto.

SHAKER MANIFESTO. *SEE* Manifesto.

SHAKERS. *SEE* Manifesto.

SHAKESPEARIANA; a critical and contemporary review of Shakespearian literature. v.1-10 (no.1-90); Nov. 1883-1893. Philadelphia, L. Scott Pub. Co.

10 v. illus., plates, ports, facsims., tables. Monthly, 1883-89; quarterly, 1890-93.

Title varies: 1883-89, Shakespeariana. (Conducted, 1886-88, by Charlotte Porter, 1889, by the Shakespeare society of New York.) 1890-93, Shakespeariana; a critical and contemporary review of Shakespearian literature conducted by the Shakespeare society of New York.

Vols. 6-10 published in New York.
With v.3-5 were issued "Selected reprints. A series of Shakespeare illustrations forming supplements to Shakespeariana."
With v.6 was issued "The Teachers' supplement. Conducted by W.S. Allis," no1-2, May-Oct. 1889.

Shakespeariana was edited by Appleton Morgan and sponsored by the New York Shakespeare Society. It contained notes on editors of Shakespeare, portraits of Shakespeare, reports from Shakespeare clubs, and articles on topics such as the Bacon controversy.

v1-6	Nov. 1883-Dec. 1889	APS III, Reel 270
v7-10	Jan. 1890-1893	Reel 271

Vol. 8: Pagination is irregular.

Microfilm edition was prepared from C, MnU copies.

SIMMS'S MAGAZINE. *SEE* Southern and Western Monthly Magazine and Review.

SMART SET. *SEE* McClure's Magazine.

SMITH'S WEEKLY. *SEE* Anglo American.

SOCIAL ECONOMIST. *SEE* Gunton's Magazine.

SOMETHING. Ed. by Nemo Nobody, esq. v.1; Nov. 18, 1809-May 12, 1810. Boston, 1809-10.

416 p. weekly.

Caption title.
James Fennell, editor. Cf. Cushing, Initials and pseudonyms.

A satirical periodical edited by "Nemo Nobody, Esq." of Boston which lasted for six months in 1809-10. Not all of the material was satirical; much was of a serious nature, but in general it censured vices and presented a moralistic viewpoint, covering such topics as manners, morals, religion, and marriage. Contents included poetry, essays, reviews of plays, and a section which answered readers' questions on a variety of topics.

v1, no.1-7	Nov. 18-Dec. 30, 1809	APS II, Reel 44

v1, no.8-26	Jan. 6-May 12, 1810	Reel 671

Microfilm edition was prepared from DLC copy.

SOUTH-CAROLINA WEEKLY MUSEUM AND COMPLETE MAGAZINE OF ENTERTAINMENT AND INTELLIGENCE. v.1-3; Jan. 1, 1797-July 1, 1798. Charleston, Printed by W.P. Harrison.

836 p.

On film: v.1, Jan. 1-July 1, 1797.

The only magazine south of Baltimore in the 18th century. Contents of this miscellany included state papers of the home and foreign governments, tales, "fragments," verses, and essays.

v1	Jan. 1-July 1, 1797	APS I, Reel 28

Microfilm edition was prepared from DLC copy.

SOUTHERN AGRICULTURIST, HORTICULTURIST, AND REGISTER OF RURAL AFFAIRS. v.1-12, 1828-1839; 1840; new ser. v.1-6, 1841-Dec. 1846. Charleston, 1828-1846.

16 v.

v1-12 as Southern agriculturist and register of rural affairs; 1840 Southern cabinet of agriculture, horticulture, rural and domestic economy.

An important agricultural magazine established in 1828 and edited by J.D. Legare. It published original papers on agriculture, horticulture, botany, rural affairs, and domestic economy; and also proceedings of agricultural societies of the U.S. and Europe, reviews of works on farming, miscellaneous agricultural items, and some light reading.

Southern Agriculturist and Register of Rural Affairs

v1-5	Jan. 1828-Dec. 1832	APS II, Reel 806
v6-9	Jan. 1833-Dec. 1836	Reel 807
v10-12	Jan. 1837-Dec. 1839	Reel 808

Southern Cabinet of Agriculture, Horticulture, Rural and Domestic Economy

v1	Jan.-Dec. 1840	Reel 808

Southern Agriculturist, Horticulturist, and Register of Rural Affairs

nsv1	Jan.-Dec. 1841	Reel 808
nsv2-6	Jan.-1842-Dec. 1846	Reel 809

Vol. for 1840: Stained throughout.

Microfilm edition was prepared from AU, NIC, NcD, NjP, ScU and T copies.

SOUTHERN AND WESTERN LITERARY MESSENGER AND REVIEW. *SEE* Southern Literary Messenger.

THE SOUTHERN AND WESTERN MONTHLY MAGAZINE AND REVIEW. v.1-2; Jan.-Dec. 1845. Charleston [S.C.] Burges & James.

2 v.

Intended to supersede Magnolia.
Caption title: Southern and western magazine review.

Commonly called "Simms's Magazine". cf. Mott, A hist. of Amer. magazines, v.1.

Edited by W.G. Simms.
Merged into the Southern literary messenger.
On film: v.1-2 and partial index for v.1.

One of the more important Charleston magazines of the period, the *Southern and Western Monthly Magazine and Review* was commonly called "Simms's Monthly Magazine" after its editor, William Gilmore Simms, who wrote most of it. Not only did he write the "Editorial Bureau" at the end of each issue, in which a dozen or more books are reviewed, but he supplied most of the articles, stories and poems. The tales included some of Simms' best–"Those Old Lunes!" and "The Snake of the Cabin." A good sketch of Daniel Boone, and one of Chevalier Bayard ran through two or three issues each. Mrs. E.F. Ellet, Mrs. Caroline Lee Hentz, Evert A. Duyckinck, Albert Pike, J.M. Legare, Dr. T. H. Chivers, and several others contributed from time to time, though none of them consistently.

| v1-2 | Jan.-Dec. 1845 | APS II, Reel 1407 |

Many pages are stained. Volume 2 lacks index.

Microfilm edition was prepared from NcD copy.

SOUTHERN CULTIVATOR. v.1-93; Mar. 1843-July 1935. Atlanta, Ga.

93 v. illus.
Frequency varies.

Absorbed Dixie Farmer, 1882; Farming, 1926.
Subtitle varies.
Imprint varies: 1843-1860, Augusta, W.S. Jones.–1861-1866, Augusta, D. Redmond.
Merged into Southern Farmer.

On film: v.1-21; v.22, no.1-3, v.23, no.1-2; v.24, no.1, 3, 5, 10-12; v.25-36; v.38, no.1-7, 9-10, 12; v.39; v.40, no.11-12; v.41, no.1-2, 4-9; v.43, no.1-3, 5; v.44, no.11; v.45-53; v.54, no.1-8; v.56, no.20; v.57; v.59, no.1-12; v.60-64.

Founded as a semi-monthly by J.W. and W.S. Jones in Augusta in 1843, the *Southern Cultivator* was "devoted to southern agriculture, designed to improve the mind and elevate the character of the tillers of the soil, and to introduce a more enlightened system of culture." It moved to Athens after the war, and then to Atlanta, changing its frequency of issue, absorbing a number of other farm journals, and adding the title of one of them, the *Dixie Farmer*, to its own in 1886. A typical 32-page issue of the *Southern Cultivator* in the early 1900's consisted of articles on crops, such as cotton, peanuts, and silk, and on planting, fertilizers, labor problems, and blacks, with sections on "The Dairy," "Poultry," and "Gardening and Live Stock." "The Farm Home" offered hints for the sick room, recipes, and advice on canning. In addition, there were occasional fashion items, letters from readers, Atlanta market reports, and several pages of advertising.

v1-9	Mar. 1, 1843-Dec. 1851	APS II, Reel 1519
v10-16	Jan. 1852-Dec. 1858	Reel 1520
v17-24	Jan. 1859-Dec. 1866	Reel 1521
v25-28	Jan. 1867-Dec. 1870	Reel 1522
v29-33	Jan. 1871-Dec. 1875	Reel 1523
v34-41	Jan. 1876-Sept. 1883	Reel 1524
v43-48	Jan. 1885-Dec. 1890	Reel 1525
v49-52	Jan. 1891-Dec. 1894	Reel 1526
v53-60	Jan. 1895-Dec. 15, 1902	Reel 1527
v61-63	Jan. 1, 1903-Dec. 15, 1905	Reel 1528
v64	Jan. 1-Dec. 15, 1906	Reel 1529

Best copy available for photographing. Several pages are stained, misnumbered, missing or repeated in number only, creased, torn; or, have print faded with some loss of text. Some indexes are missing; not available for photographing. Vol. 9: pgs. 177-178 are missing. Vol. 24: Issue 5, pgs. 121-122 are missing. Vol. 43: issue 1 is misdated. Vol. 57: issue 13, pgs. 1-2 are missing. Issue 17, pgs. 17-18 are mising. Vol. 59: issue 12 is incomplete.

Microfilm edition was prepared from DNAL, GA, GMiW, MU, NN, NcD, NjP, OFH, PPi, ScCleU, and TxU copies.

SOUTHERN FARMER. *SEE* Southern Cultivator.

*SOUTHERN HISTORICAL SOCIETY. Southern historical society papers. v.1-38, 1876-1910; new ser., no.1-14 (whole no. 39-52) 1914-1959. Richmond, Va. [1876]-1959.

v. illus., plates, ports.

An author and subject index to the Southern historical society papers, vols. 1-38, comp. by Mrs. Kate Pleasants Minor, reference librarian, under the direction of Earl G. Swem, assistant librarian. Richmond, D. Bottom; Superintendent of Public Printing, 1913.

Vols. 1-6 monthly, forming 2 vols. a year; v.7-12 monthly, forming 1 vol. a year; v. 13- annual.
Editor: 1887-1910, R.A. Brock.

Publication committee, 1914-19: W.G. McCabe, G.L. Christian, Archer Anderson. Vol. 15 has subtitle: Paroles of the Army of northern Virginia, R.E. Lee, gen., C.S. A., commanding, surrendered at Appomattox C.H., Va., Apr. 9, 1865, to Lieutenant-General U.S. Grant, commanding armies of the U.S. Now first printed from the duplicate originals in the archives of the Southern historical society, ed., with introduction, by R.A. Brock. "General index of first ten volumes Southern historical society papers": 20 p. at end of v.10. "A roster of general offices ... &c., in Confederate service ... By Charles C. Jones, Jr.", issued as supplement to v.1-3, with separate pagination. Vol. 7 wants t.p. JSU. On film: vols. 1-33.

This, like several other journals of the time, was devoted to the description of the "causes, progress, and results" of the Civil War from the southern point of view. Edited by J. William Jones, the monthly became a quarterly and then an annual.

v1-4	Jan. 1876-Dec. 1877	APS III, Reel 309
Cumulative Index 1-10	1876-1882	Reel 309
v5-11	Jan. 1878-Dec. 1883	Reel 310
v12-19	Jan. 1884-Dec. 1891	Reel 311
v20-28	Jan. 1892-Dec. 1900	Reel 312
v29-33	Jan. 1901-Dec. 1905	Reel 313

Some advertising pages are missing. Vols. 1-3: "Confederate Roster" follows the last issue of each volume. "Annual Report of the Executive Committee" follows vol. 1. Vol. 4: Pg. 266 is misnumbered. Vol. 5: Pg. 237 has print missing. Vol. 15: Contains the list of "Paroles of the Army of Northern Virginia." Vols. 15-33: Indexes precede each volume.

Microfilm edition was prepared from NcD copy.

SOUTHERN LADIES' BOOK. *SEE* Magnolia; Or, Southern Apalachian.

THE SOUTHERN LITERARY GAZETTE. v.1, Sept. 1828-Mar. 1829; new ser., v.1, no.1-11, May 15-Oct. 15, 1829. Charleston, P.M.S. Neufville, Printer, 1828-[29]

2 v. in 1. plates.

Monthly, Sept. 1828-Mar. 1829; semimonthly, May-Oct. 1829.
Editors: Sept. 1828-Mar. 1829, W.G. Simms, J.W. Simmons.–May-Oct. 1829, W.G. Simms.

One of numerous literary magazines published in Charleston, this was the first of several done by William Gilmore Simms.

v1-nsv1	Sept. 1828-Oct. 1829	APS II, Reel 1258

Vol. 1: Pagination is irregular. Pgs. 187-90 are missing. New Series Vol. 1: Issue no. 8 and pages 47-48 and 169-92 are missing; not available for photographing.

Microfilm edition was prepared from DLC copy.

* THE SOUTHERN LITERARY JOURNAL AND MAGAZINE OF ARTS. v.1-3; new ser. v.1, 3-4; Sept. 1835-Dec. 1838. Charleston, S.C., J.S. Burges, 1836-38.

6 v. monthly.

Title varies slightly.
Editors: 1835-37, D.K. Whitaker.–1838, B.R. Carroll.
New series, v. 2, Sept.-Dec. 1837, not issued.
Ceased publication with Dec. 1838.

Founded and edited by Daniel K. Whitaker, the *Southern Literary Journal* was regional in its appeal. It recorded the progress and achievement of southern culture, defended slavery, and encouraged southern authors. The leading contributor was William Gilmore Simms, who was already the foremost literary figure in the South; he wrote sketches, criticisms, and verse in abundance. The *Journal's* tone was that of a review rather than of a popular magazine; essays on fine arts and literary notices were of some importance. After the magazine was taken over by Bartholomew Rivers Carroll in 1838, it became somewhat livelier, publishing dramatic reviews and fiction by Mrs. Elizabeth F. Ellet and others, but it lasted only a year.

v1	Sept. 1835-Feb. 1836	APS II, Reel 574
v2-nsv3	Mar. 1836-June 1838	Reel 575
v4	July-Dec. 1838	Reel 576

Pagination is irregular.

Microfilm edition was prepared from the DLC and NcU copies.

*THE SOUTHERN LITERARY MESSENGER; devoted to every department of literature, and the fine arts ... v.1-38; Aug. 1834-June 1864. Richmond, T.W. White [etc.] 1835-64.

38 v in 36. illus., plates, maps. monthly.

No numbers issued Sept. 1834, Oct., Nov. 1835, Dec. 1836. Vol. 22-23 called also "new ser., v.1-12." Numbering irregular during 1862-63. From Jan. 1846 to Dec. 1847 title reads: The Southern and western literary messenger and review.

Editors: Aug. 1834-May 1835, J.E. Heath.–June-Sept. 1835, T.W. White and others.– Dec. 1835-Nov. 1836, E.A. Poe.–Jan. 1837–Jan. 1843, T.W. Whit eand others.–Aug. 1843-Oct. 1847, B.B. Minor.–Nov. 1847- May 1860, J.R. Thompson.–June 1860-Jan. 1864, G.W. Bagby.–Jan.-June 1864, F.H. Alfriend.

Absorbed the Southern and western monthly magazine and review in Jan. 1846. No more published.

As the "literary repository for the Virginia Historical and Philosophical Society," the *Messenger* printed travelogues, biography, translations of famous works, poetry, addresses, book reviews, sentimental fiction, law cases, "extracts of a novel that will never be published," history and geological reports of Virginia and meeting notices of the Society.

Among its more well-known contributors were Edgar Allan Poe, Mrs. Lydia Sigourney, James Fenimore Cooper, Oliver Oldschool and W. Gilmore Simms. Most of the articles and poetry were signed only with initials.

A history of the Civil War ran for several years in the magazine. Often continued stories and articles filled most of the pages of an issue. Long critical essays on well-known books or issues of the time were quite common. Illustrations were infrequent.

Southern Literary Messenger

v1-3	Aug. 1834-Dec. 1837	APS II, Reel 438
v4-6	Jan. 1838-Dec. 1840	Reel 439
v7-9	Jan. 1841-Dec. 1843	Reel 440
v10-11	Jan. 1844-Dec. 1845	Reel 441

Southern and Western Literary Messenger and Review

v12-13	Jan. 1846-Dec. 1847	Reel 441

Southern Literary Messenger

v14-16	Jan. 1848-Dec. 1850	Reel 442
v17-19	Jan. 1851-Dec. 1853	Reel 443
v20-23	Jan. 1854-Dec. 1856	Reel 444
v24-29	Jan. 1857-Dec. 1859	Reel 445
v30-33	Jan. 1860-Dec. 1861	Reel 446
v34-38	Jan. 1862-June 1864	Reel 447

Pagination is irregular.

Microfilm edition was prepared from DLC, MiU and NW copy.

SEE ALSO: Southern and Western Monthly Magazine and Review.

SOUTHERN PLANTER. v.1- Jan. 1841- Richmond [Va.] P.D. Bernard [etc.]

v. illus.

Monthly, except for Jan. 1882-June 1882 when semimonthly. Vols. for 1867-1875 (v. 28-36) also called new ser., v. 1-9.

Title varies: 1867-1881, Southern planter and farmer.
Film includes v.1-67, except for v.22-27; v.41, no.4-6; v.43, no.4, 7-11.

One of the most successful of the Virginia farm papers was the *Southern Planter* of Richmond, which was established in 1841, but was suspended between 1862 and 1867 because of the war. This monthly was devoted mianly to agriculture, horticulture, and the household arts. Its first editor, C.T. Botts, was succeeded by several others during the magazine's long lifetime. At first it mainly published extracts from both foreign and domestic agricultural publications, along with news concerning the South, but later expanded its contents to include a greater variety of material. It presented information on fertilizers and soil improvement, on crops, such as tobacco and cotton, and on diseases of crops and animals, along with an outline of "Work for the Month." A "Home" department contained household hints, features, and poetry, while other departments were concerned with granges, livestock and the dairy, the garden and orchard, poultry, and horses. In addition, the *Southern Planter* published economic news, prices, news of agricultural societieis, as ection of ads, occasional fiction, and magazine reviews.

Southern Planter

v1-7	Jan. 1841-Dec. 1847	APS II, Reel 1529
v8-15	Jan. 1848-Dec. 1855	Reel 1530
v16-19	Jan. 1856-Dec. 1859	Reel 1531
v20-27	Jan. 1860-Dec. 1866	Reel 1532

Southern Planter and Farmer

nsv1-2 (v28-29)	Jan. 1867-Dec. 1868	Reel 1532
nsv3-5 (v30-32)	Jan. 1869-Dec. 1871	Reel 1533
nsv6-8 (v33-35)	Jan. 1872-Dec. 1874	Reel 1534
nsv9 (v36)-38	Jan. 1875-Dec. 1877	Reel 1535
v39-42	Jan. 1878-Dec. 1881	Reel 1536

Southern Planter

v43-47	Jan. 15, 1882-Dec. 1886	Reel 1537
v48-51	Jan. 1887-Dec. 1890	Reel 1538
v52-56	Jan. 1891-Dec. 1895	Reel 1539
v57-61	Jan. 1896-Dec. 1900	Reel 1540
v62-65	Jan. 1901-Dec. 1904	Reel 1541
v66-67	Jan. 1905-Dec. 1906	Reel 1542

Several volumes lack title page and index. Some pages are stained, torn, or tightly bound; or, have print faded with some loss of text. Pagination is irregular. Some issues contain supplements. Vol. 11: pages 200-201 are missing. Vol. 17: issue 3 is misdated and misnumbered. Vol. 42: page 254 is missing. Vol. 58: pages 529-30 are missing.

Microfilm edition was prepared from CSmH, DLC, DNAL, IU, MU, MiU, NcD, NjP, TxU, VBP, VRU, and WvU copies.

SOUTHERN PLANTER AND FARMER. *SEE* Southern Planter.

* THE SOUTHERN QUARTERLY REVIEW. v.1-16, Jan. 1842-Jan. 1850; v.17-28 (new ser., v.1-12), Apr. 1850-Oct.? 1855; v.29-30 (new ser., v.1-2), Apr. 1856-Feb. 1857. New Orleans, 1842-57.

30 v. maps.

Editors: 1842-47, D.K. Whitaker.—1847-49, Milton Clapp.—1849-55, W.G. Simms.—1856-57? J.H. Thornwell. Published in New Orleans, 1842; Charleston, S.C., 1842-55; Columbia, S.C., 1856-57?

The *Southern Quarterly Review,* though perhaps not equal to its predecessor, the *Southern Review,* was one of the best southern reviews before the war and one of the great American quarterlies. It was committed to the defense of slavery, opposed British aggression, an advocated states' rights and free trade. Although many of its articles were dull and very long, it wielded some influence and strikingly and faithfully reflected the thought and feeling of the South from 1842 to 1857. Articles generally dealt with the slavery debate, discussion of the tariff, and other political questions; attention was also given to education, science, and philosophy.

v1-8	Jan. 1842-Oct. 1845	APS II, Reel 684
v9-15	Jan. 1846-July 1849	Reel 685
v16-22	Oct. 1849-Oct. 1852	Reel 686
v23-30	Jan. 1853-Feb. 1857	Reel 687

Vols. 14-15 and 21-23 lack indexes.

Microfilm edition was prepared from MiU and NcU copies.

* THE SOUTHERN REVIEW. v.1-8; Feb. 1828-Feb. 1832. Charleston, A.E. Miller, 1828-32.

8 v. pl., tables. quarterly.

No number issued for Feb. 1831.

The *Southern Review* represents one of the earliest attempts to express the culture and learning of the South in periodical literature, and was considered the classic southern review by many. It consisted mainly of reviews of poetry and books, including many biographies and some books on Greek literature. Editor Stephen Elliott wrote chiefly on science and history, and his associate Hugh Swinton Legare, wrote on the classics, contemporary literature, law, and other subjects. Besides Elliott and Legare, chief contributors included Thomas Cooper, president of the College of South Carolina, who wrote on scientific subjects; Robert Henry, a professor at the same college, who did literary articles; Senator Robert Y. Hayne, who wrote on the navy; Professor T.C. Wallace, who wrote on mathematics and Hebrew; Josiah C. Nott; the ethnologist, Thomas S. Grimke and D.J. McCord, both members of the South Carolina legislature, and other prominent people. The *Review* was discontinued when Legare went abroad in 1832.

v1-8	Feb. 1828-Feb. 1832	APS II, Reel 325

Microfilm edition was prepared from MiU copy.

* THE SOUTHERN REVIEW. v.1-26, no.51; Jan. 1867-July 1879. Baltimore, Bledsoe and Browne.

26 v. quarterly.

Published under the auspices of the M.E. church, South, 1871-
Editors: Jan. 1867-Oct. 1877, A.T. Bledsoe (with Mrs. S.B. Herrick, Jan. 1875-Oct. 1877)—Jan.-Oct. 1787, Mrs. S.B. Herrick.
Imprint varies: Baltimore, Bledsoe and Browne [etc.] 1867-71.—St. Louis, Southwestern book and pub. co.; [etc., etc.] 1871-75.—Baltimore, Bledsoe & Herrick; [etc., etc.] 1875-78.)

Albert Taylor Bledsoe was zealously pro-South and his *Southern Review* gives an excellent interpretation of Southern thinking following the Civil War. Although much of his quarterly contains controversial material, the literary sections are very well written. Readers will note a greater religious content after 1871 when the Methodist Church South adopted the *Review.*

v1-8	Jan. 1867-Oct. 1870	APS III, Reel 18
v9-17	Jan. 1871-Apr. 1875	Reel 19
v18-26	July 1875-July 1879	Reel 20

Vols. 1-26 lack indexes. Please refer to the monthly table of contents. Vol. 12: page 496 is misprinted as 466.

Microfilm edition was prepared from NB, NcD, LU, OU and ViU copies.

SOUTHERN ROSE. v.1-7; Aug. 11, 1832-Aug. 17, 1839. Charleston, S.C., W. Estill for the editor, 1832-39.

7 v. in 5. illus., pl. Weekly, Aug. 1832-Aug. 1834; biweekly, Sept. 1834-Aug. 1839.

Title varies: Aug. 1832-Aug. 24, 1833, The Rose bud, or Youth's gazette. Aug. 31, 1833-Aug. 1835, Southern rose bud ... Sept. 1835-Aug. 1839, The Southern rose.

Caroline H. Gilman, editor.
Published by W. Estill, Aug. 1832-Feb. 1833; by J.S. Burges and others, Mar. 1833-Aug. 1838; by B.B. Hussey, Sept. 1838-Aug. 1839. Vol. 1, no.1, reprint, by J.S. Burges.

An extremely sentimental Southern periodical which began as a children's magazine, but gradually directed itself more to the mature reader. In addition to the juvenile department, it had a moral and religious department, and published sentimental fiction and poetry, reviews of recent books, original sketches, and other miscellaneous material.

Rose Bud, or Youth's Gazette

v1	Aug. 11, 1832-Aug. 24, 1833	APS II, Reel 688

Southern Rose Bud
v2-3   Aug. 31, 1833-Aug. 1835   Reel 688

Southern Rose
v4-7   Sept. 1835-Aug. 17, 1839   Reel 688

SOUTHERN ROSE BUD. *SEE* Southern Rose.

SOUTHWESTERN LITERARY JOURNAL AND MONTH-LY REVIEW. *SEE* Western Literary Journal and Monthly Review.

THE SOUVENIR. v.1-2; July 4, 1827-June 20, 1829. Philadelphia, P. Price, Jr.

2 v. plates. weekly.

This ladies' magazine featured fashion plates, with descriptions of the latest fashions, along with sentimental fiction and poetry, essays on women and their behavior, biographical sketches, a humor column, a synopsis of news, and some illustrations. It also reviewed plays and listed recent publications.

v1-2   July 4, 1827-June 20, 1829   APS II, Reel 1407

Several pages are stained, torn and taped with some loss of text. Pagination is irregular. Vol. 1: Issues 32 and 43 are missing; not available for photographing. Vol. 2: Issues 3-11, 45, and 50 are missing.

Microfilm edition was prepared from N copy.

SPECTACLES. v.1, no.5-6, 11; June 6-13, July 18, 1807. Baltimore [J. Harmer]

3 no. Weekly.

This four-page comic periodical published satirical articles on fads and fashions of the day, along with poetry and news of recent marriages.

v1, no.5-6, 11   June 6-July 18, 1807   APS II, Reel 44

SPECTATOR. *SEE* Pittsburgh Recorder.

SPIRIT OF THE AGE AND JOURNAL OF HUMANITY. v.1, nos. 1-44; May 23, 1833-Mar. 20, 1834. Boston, 1833-1834.

Superseded by Journal of humanity.

This weekly edited by B.B. Thatcher resembled a newspaper in having four pages of six columns each, small print, many small items, and most advertising on the back page. Although it contained much miscellaneous information, it emphasized social problems, devoting a special section to temperance, which it supported, and much space to abolition and other social movements, and to the activities of various societies. In addition, it provided book reviews, poetry, anecdotes, items of local and foreign news, and a special section on Boston.

v1   May 23, 1833-Mar. 20, 1834   APS II, Reel 753

Best copy available for photographing. Index and table of contents are lacking. Issue 14 is lacking.

Microfilm edition was prepared from CtY copy.

SPIRIT OF THE EUROPEAN MEDICAL JOURNALS. *SEE* Monthly Journal of Foreign Medicine.

SPIRIT OF THE FORUM, and Hudson remarker. no.1; Apr. 16, 1817. Hudson, N.Y.

16 p. (Miscellaneous pamphlets, v. 1073, no. 2)

Conducted by an "association of gentlemen," the *Spirit of the Forum* was to publish addresses to a society called "Forum of the City of Hudson" and was concerned with city transactions, institutions, and problems. Only one number was published; its contents included an essay on the education of the poor, coverage of the Forum's activities, and a poem.

no.1   Apr. 16, 1817   APS II, Reel 240

SPIRIT OF THE XIX CENTURY. By Robert J. Breckinridge. v.1-2; 1842-43. Baltimore, Printed by R.J. Matchett, 1842-43.

2 v. monthly.

Succeeded the Baltimore literary and religious magazine.

This religious periodical, edited by Robert J. Breckinridge, superseded the *Baltimore Literary and Religious Magazine*. It gave broad coverage to the religious controversies of the day, including both domestic and international events and problems. Included in its pages were sermons; notices of new books and pamphlets; and articles on religious history, on the various religions, and on slavery and related topics.

v1-2   Jan. 1842-Dec. 1843   APS II, Reel 779

Microfilm edition was prepared from ICU, MB, OOxM and PU copies.

SEE ALSO: Baltimore Literary and Religious Magazine.

***THE SPIRIT OF THE PILGRIMS.** v.1-6; 1828-33. Boston, Peirce and Williams.

6 v. monthly.

After the *Panoplist* was converted into a missionary organ in 1821, orthodox Congregationalism was without a controversial magazine until some of the leaders of Calvinistic theology in Boston got together in 1827 and determined to issue a magazine to war against Unitarianism. Thus the *Spirit of the Pilgrims,* a magazine of religious controversy, was created in 1828. In addition to much controversial material, it contained a serial history of Unitarianism, and other serials on various religious topics.

v1-6   Jan. 1828-Dec. 1833   APS II, Reel 752

Microfilm edition was prepared from MiU copy.

THE SPIRIT OF THE PUBLIC JOURNALS; or, Beauties of the American newspapers. 1805. Baltimore, G. Dobbin & Murphy.

300 p.

Edited by G. Bourne.

This eclectic magazine was made up entirely of selections from about 100 American newspapers. Most selections were essays or poems; all political material was excluded.

1805   APS II, Reel 44

SPIRIT OF THE TIMES; a chronicle of the turf, agriculture, field sports, literature and the stage. v.1-31, no.20; Dec. 10, 1831-June 22, 1861. New York, 1831-1861.

31 v.

United with Traveller, 1832?-1834, as Traveller and Spirit of the times.

Spirit of the Times is said to have been the first all-around sporting journal in the U.S. In addition to racing, its specialty, it dealt with field sports, hunting and fishing, agriculture, literature, fashion, and the theater; and also published news, court proceedings, poetry, and advertisements.

Spirit of the Times
v1, no.1-50	Dec. 10, 1831-Nov. 24, 1832	APS II, Reel 620

Traveller and Spirit of the Times
v1, no.51-v2	Dec. 1, 1832-Oct. 6, 1833	Reel 620

Spirit of the Times
v5-6	Jan. 3, 1835-Feb. 11, 1837	Reel 620
v7-8	Feb. 18, 1837-Feb. 23, 1839	Reel 621
v9	Mar. 9, 1839-Feb. 29, 1840	Reel 622
v10	Mar. 7, 1840-Feb. 27, 1841	Reel 623
v11	Mar. 6, 1841-Feb. 26, 1842	Reel 624
v12	Mar. 5, 1842-Feb. 25, 1843	Reel 625
v13	Mar. 4, 1843-Feb. 24, 1844	Reel 626
v14	Mar. 2, 1844-Feb. 22, 1845	Reel 627
v15	Mar. 1, 1845-Feb. 21, 1846	Reel 628
v16	Feb. 28, 1846-Feb. 20, 1847	Reel 629
v17-18	Feb. 27, 1847-Feb. 17, 1849	Reel 630
v19	Feb. 24, 1849-Feb. 16, 1850	Reel 631
v20	Feb. 23, 1850-Feb. 15, 1851	Reel 632
v21	Feb. 22, 1851-Feb. 14, 1852	Reel 633
v22	Feb. 21, 1852-Feb. 12, 1853	Reel 634
v23	Feb. 19, 1853-Feb. 11, 1854	Reel 635
v24-25	Feb. 18, 1854-Feb. 9, 1856	Reel 636
v26	Feb. 16, 1856-Feb. 7, 1857	Reel 637
v27	Feb. 14, 1857-Feb. 6, 1858	Reel 638
v28	Feb. 13, 1858-Feb. 5, 1859	Reel 639
v29-31	Feb. 12, 1859-June 22, 1861	Reel 640

Best copy available for photographing. Several pages are stained, torn, taped, tightly bound and have faded print and show-through with loss of text. Some issues are misnumbered. Vol. 1: Nos. 2-7, 11, 13-14, and 42 are missing. Vol. 2: Nos. 55-56, 123-25, 131, 140, 142, 145, and 147 are missing. Vols. 3-4 are missing. Vol. 5: Nos. 3-15, 17-18, 20-49, and 51 are missing.

Microfilm edition was prepared from CtY, DLC, KyU, MWA, N, NR, OU, and PPiU copies.

THE SPIRITUAL MAGAZINE; or, Gospel treasury. v.1, no.1-2; Jan. 1813-May 1814. n.p.

1 v. (Moore pamphlets, v.5, no.7)

Edited by George S. White, this religious magazine was intended to expose the errors of Hopkinsianism and to promote the doctrines of Luther. The two numbers published contained poetry, letters, an extract from the writings of Calvin, and articles on the doctrine of the Church of Scotland.

v1, no.1-2	Jan. 1813-May 1814	APS II, Reel 240

STAND; by a society of young men. no.1-7; Dec. 21, 1819-1820. Hartford, Conn., 1820.

7 no.

No. for Dec. 21, 1819 reads "Second Edition"
Lacking on film: no.6.

The *Stand* was published by a society called the "invincibles," who considered women to have too great an advantage over men, and it proposed to take a stand against chivalry and the domination of the "fair sex." It ridiculed the follies of both sexes, and contained essays, poetry, and much satirical material.

no.1-5, 7	Dec 21, 1819-Aug. 14, 1820	APS II, Reel 333

Microfilm edition was prepared from MBAt copy.

THE STRANGER, a literary paper. v.1; July 3, 1813-June 25, 1814. Albany: Published by John Cook, at his reading-room. E. & E. Hosford, Printers, 1814.

8, 416 p. Weekly, July 1813; semimonthly, Aug. 1813-June 1814.

Caption title: The Stranger.

A literary magazine which offered book reviews, poetry, biographical sketches, a meteorological journal, and articles on travel, literature, the theater, and other topics.

v1	July 3, 1813-June 25, 1814	APS II, Reel 810

Microfilm edition was prepared from MiU copy.

STRYKER'S AMERICAN REGISTER AND MAGAZINE. Conducted by James Stryker. v.1-6; May 1848-1851. Philadelphia [1848-53]

6 v. illus.

Vol. 1-3 have title and imprint: The American quarterly register and magazine ... Philadelphia, E.C. and J. Biddle [etc., 1848]-49.

Vol.4-6 consist of one number each; v.4 and 5 (bearing dates July 1850 and Jan. 1851 respectively) contain "Historical register of 1850," v.6 (copyrighted 1853) contains "Historical register of 1851." Imprint: v.4-5, Washington, W.M. Morrison; New York, C.S. Francis & Co.; [etc., etc.] v.6, New York, Published for the proprietors.

Although this quarterly review was a rather naively selected miscellany with emphasis on elegiac verse, some of its contents—historical reviews, chronology, statistics, and documents—have real value for the historian.

American Quarterly Register and Magazine
v1-3	May 1848-Dec. 1849	APS II, Reel 672

Stryker's American Register and Magazine
v4-6	July 1850-1851	Reel 672

Indexes appear at the end of each volume.

Microfilm edition was prepared from MiU copy.

STUDENT AND SCHOOLMATE. *SEE* Forrester's Boys' and Girls' Magazine, and Fireside Companion.

THE SUBTERRANEAN. v.1-4; [1843?]-May 22, 1847. New York, L. N. Carr [etc.]

4 v. weekly.

Copy filmed incomplete: v.1-2 and v.4, no. 46 wanting.
Vols. 3-4, edited by M. Walsh.
Began publication in 1843. Cf. Dict. Amer. biog.

Edited by Mike Walsh, this magazine was dedicated to the needs of the working man, and proposed to advocate the "cause of the poor and oppressed," and fight "tyranny, injustice and corruption." It contained articles on politics and history, a fair amount of poetry and tales, selections from other magazines, and much miscellaneous material.

v3-4   May 24, 1845-May 22, 1847   APS II, Reel 576

Several pages are stained or faded with some loss of text. Best copy available for photographing.

Microfilm edition was prepared from the NN copy.

SUBTERRANEAN, UNITED WITH THE WORKING MAN'S ADVOCATE. *SEE* Working Man's Advocate.

SUNDAY SCHOOL REPOSITORY. v.1-2, nos. 1-18; 1816-Feb. 1819. New York, 1816-1819.

2 v.

Lacking on film; nos. 1-8, 12.

This magazine contained a variety of material on Sunday schools, including histories of Sunday schools and methods of conducting them, reports of various Sunday school societies, and Sunday schools in the U.S. and foreign countries.

nos. 9-11, 13-18   June, 1817-Feb. 1819   APS II, Reel 333

Microfilm edition was prepared from MH-AH copy.

THE SUNDAY VISITANT; or, Weekly repository of Christian knowledge. Ed. by A. Fowler, A.M. v.1-2; Jan. 3, 1818-Dec. 25, 1819. Charleston (S.C.) [T.B. Stephens, Printer] 1818-19.

2 v. in 1.

This weekly Episcopal magazine was intended to be instructive to everyone, but particularly to young people, concerning the duties of Christians, and was to explain the Scriptures, and the rites and ceremonies of the church. Contents included many short pieces on theological and other topics, biographical sketches of the clergy of the Episcopal Church, poetry, and obituary notices.

v1-2   Jan. 3, 1818-Dec. 25, 1819   APS II, Reel 240

Vol. 2: some pages are stained.

THE TABLET. A miscellaneous paper, devoted to the belles lettres. v.1, no. 1-13; May 19-Aug. 11, 1795. [Boston, W. Spotswood] 1795.

52 p. weekly.

A Boston essay periodical which was Joseph Dennie's first adventure in the magazine field.

v1, no.1-13   May 19-Aug. 11, 1795   APS I, Reel 28

Microfilm edition was prepared from MWA copy.

THE TALISMAN. v.1-3; 1828-1830. New York, E. Bliss.

3 v. fronts., plates.

Preface signed Francis Herbert. This was the joint pseudonym of W.C. Bryant, R.C. Sands and G.C. Verplanck under which they edited the Talisman from 1828 to 1830.

Reissued in 1833 as the Miscellanies, by G.C. Verplanck, W.C. Bryant and R.C. Sands.

All of the material in this miscellany was written by Francis Herbert, its editor. Contents included much poetry, tales, travel sketches and descriptions of scenery, essays, historical sketches, and illustrations.

v1-3   1828-1830   APS II, Reel 400

Microfilm edition was prepared from MiU copy.

TEACHER. *SEE* Massachusetts Teacher.

TEACHER'S GUIDE AND PARENT'S ASSISTANT. v.1 (no.1-24); Nov. 1, 1826-Dec. 1, 1827. Portland, Shirley & Hyde, printers.

382 p.

Monthly, Nov. 1-Dec. 1, 1826; semimonthly, 1827.
Edited by J.L. Parkhurst.

This educational journal proposed to deal with the physical, moral, and religious, as well as literary and intellectual education of the young, and to help parents in the discharge of their duties. It published information on teaching, considering each of the various branches of study and offering suggestions as to teaching modes for each, and discussed various schools, textbooks, children's books, and methods used by the most distinguished and successful instructors.

v1-24   Nov. 1826-Dec. 1827   APS II, Reel 1407

Best copy available for photographing. Some pages are torn, tightly bound or misnumbered.

Microfilm edition was prepared from NN copy.

TELESCOPE. *SEE* New York Telescope.

TEMPLE. *SEE* Arena.

TENNESSEE FARMER, a monthly publication devoted to agriculture, horticulture, and the useful arts. v.1-5, Dec. 1834-Dec. 1840. Jonesborough.

5 v. in 4.

Merged into Agriculturist, and journal of the state and county societies. Subtitle varies.

Film incomplete: v.5 wanting.

This monthly agricultural magazine edited by Thomas Emerson was concerned with imparting information on soils and fertilizers, on cultivating crops and on rearing livestock. There were articles on new farm machinery, on diseases of animals, and on care of fruit trees, and a good deal on silk culture and beet sugar production, in addition to proceedings of agricultural conventions, and a series on the education of farmers. Poetry, moral essays and recipes provided variety.

v1-4   Dec. 1834-Dec. 1839   APS II, Reel 1490

Some pages are stained, creased, and have faded print. Vol. 3: pages 232-33 are missing. Vol. 4: title page, nos. 3, 6, and 8 are missing.

Microfilm edition was prepared from DNAL and T copies.

THEATRICAL BUDGET. v.1-11, 1823; new ser. no. 1-13, 1828. New York, 1823-1828.

11 v.

Vols. 1-11 and new ser. nos. 7-13 are lacking.

Short poems and "comic recitations" made up the content of this short-lived periodical.

ns, nos.1-6   1828   APS II, Reel 1258

Pgs. 41-42 are missing.

Microfilm edition was prepared from NIC copy.

THE THEATRICAL CENSOR. no.1-17; Dec. 9, 1805-Mar. 3, 1806. Philadelphia [J. Watts]

134 p. irregular.

No. 15 and 16 are dated Mar. 15-17, 1806.

This theatrical magazine conducted by "a citizen" consisted almost entirely of reviews of the various plays presented in Philadelphia during the month of December, 1805 and in January, February, and March of 1805.

no.1-17   Dec. 9, 1805-Mar. 3, 1806   APS II, Reel 44

* **THE THEOLOGICAL AND LITERARY JOURNAL.** Ed. by David N. Lord. v.1-13; July 1848-Apr. 1861. New York, F. Knight, 1849-61.

13 v. quarterly.

The *Theological and Literary Journal* provided a great amount of space in its columns to prophetic Scriptures and the condemnation of contemporary geology. Its largest contributor and editor was David N. Lord, although George Duffield, R. W. Dickinson and others wrote for the journal.

v1-3   July 1848-Apr. 1851   APS II, Reel 940
v4-8   July 1851-Apr. 1856   Reel 941
v9-12   July 1856-Apr. 1860   Reel 942
v13   July 1860-Apr. 1861   Reel 943

Some pages are stained, torn, or have print missing.

Microfilm edition was prepared from ICT, NcD, and OOxM copies.

THE THEOLOGICAL MAGAZINE, or Synopsis of modern religious sentiment. On a new plan ... v.1-3; July/Aug. 1795-Dec. 1798/Jan./Feb. 1799. New-York: Printed by T. and J. Swords for C. Davis [etc.] 1796-99.

3 v. bimonthly (irregular)

A religious magazine containing dissertations on religious subjects, narratives of conversions, religious news, reviews, and poetry. Contributors were chiefly Congregational and Presbyterian.

v1-3   July/Aug. 1795-Dec. 1798/Jan./Feb. 1799   APS I, Reel 28

Microfilm edition was prepared from MiU-C copy.

THEOLOGICAL MEDIUM. *SEE* Cumberland Presbyterian Review.

THEOLOGICAL REPERTORY, AND CHURCHMAN'S GUIDE. v.1-8, new ser. v.1-3; Aug. 1819-Dec. 1830. Washington, D.C.

11 v. in 8. monthly.

Title varies: Aug. 1819-Dec. 1828, Washington theological repertory ...

On film: v.1-7 (reel 241) v.8, n.s.v. 1-3 (reel 1948)

Conducted by clergymen of the Episcopal Church, this Episcopal magazine contained a theological department, as well as essays on the history and policy of the church, book reviews, biographies, and Bible studies, and published a variety of religious news, including information on the American Colonization Society, news on missions, and miscellaneous foreign and domestic news items.

Washington Theological Repertory
v1-7   Aug. 1819-July 1826   APS II, Reel 241
v8-nsv1   Aug. 1826-Dec. 1828   Reel 1948

Theological Repertory, and Churchman's Guide
nsv2-3   Jan. 1829-Dec. 1830   Reel 1948

Reel 1948: Some issues are missing; not available for photographing.

Microfilm edition was prepared from CSmH and DLC copies.

THE THEOLOGICAL REVIEW AND GENERAL REPOSITORY OF RELIGIOUS AND MORAL INFORMATION. v.1; Jan.-Oct. 1822. Baltimore, Printed by J.D. Toy.

600 p. quarterly.

Edited by J. Gray.

This quarterly religious magazine published articles on Bible studies and various religious topics as well as biographies, book reviews, anecdotes, and obituaries.

v1, nos.1-4   Jan.-Oct. 1822   APS II, Reel 206

THE THEOPHILANTHROPIST: containing critical, moral, theological, and literary essays, in monthly numbers. By a society. no.1-9. New York, 1810.

384 p.

This deist magazine was evidently published by the Society of Philanthropy and was to contain critical, moral, theological, and literary essays as well as works of little-known philosophers, biographical sketches, political essays, and news of advances in agriculture and manufactures. There is much on Thomas Paine, who had died in the preceding year, and much railing against the Calvinists and Methodists.

no.1-9   1810   APS II, Reel 333

Microfilm edition was prepared from MiU copy.

THE THESPIAN MIRROR; a periodical comprising a collection of dramatic biography, theatrical criticism, miscellaneous literature, poetry, &c. &c. v.1, no.1-14; Dec. 28, 1805-May 31, 1806. New York, Printed by Southwick & Hardcastle.

120 p. weekly.

Edited by J.H. Payne.

This short-lived theatrical review was conducted by thirteen-year old John Howard Payne, who later became a famous actor and also wrote the song "Home Sweet Home." His magazine brought him into prominence although he at first tried to hide his activities from his father, who was opposed to his son's artistic ambitions. The *Mirror* contained theatrical criticism and biographical sketches of actors, along with some miscellaneous literary material, including poetry.

v1, no.1-14   Dec. 28, 1805-May 31, 1806   APS II, Reel 44

THE THESPIAN MONITOR, and dramatick miscellany. By Barnaby Bangbar, esq. [pseud.] v.1 (no.1-4); Nov. 25-Dec. 16, 1809. Philadelphia: Mathew Carey, 1809.

cover-title, 72 p.

This short-lived theatrical review by "Barnaby Bangbar, Esq." devoted most of its attention to reviewing plays presented at the New-Theatre in Philadelphia, but it also provided news about various actors, and biographical sketches of some of them.

v1, no.1-4   Nov. 25-Dec. 16, 1809   APS II, Reel 44

THESPIAN ORACLE; or, Monthly mirror, consisting of original pieces and selections from performances of merit, relating chiefly to the most admired dramatic compositions. v.1, no.1; Jan. 1798. Philadelphia, T.B. Freeman.

24 p.

The first theatrical review. Included in the only number published were articles on the theater selected from both foreign and domestic sources, biographical sketches of performers, a review of a play, poetry, and anecdotes.

v1, no.1   Jan. 1798   APS I, Reel 29

Microfilm edition was prepared from MH copy.

THE THISTLE. v.1, no.1-3; Aug. 4-Sept. 1, 1807. Boston, Etheridge & Bliss.

72 p. Weekly (irregular)

Edited by R. Rover, pseud., and others.

This short-lived comic periodical by "Roderic Rover" was made up of humorous articles and poetry written by the editor and his brother "Joe." Much of the material was concerned with other members of the "Rover" family.

v1, no.1-3   Aug. 4-Sept. 1, 1807   APS II, Reel 44

THE TICKLER. v.1-6; Sept. 16, 1807-Nov. 17, 1813. Philadelphia, G. Helmbold.

6 v.

Edited by Toby Scratch'em, pseud.
Film covers: v.1, no.1, 37, 52; v.2, 1-26, 28, 43-46.

Begun in Philadelphia in 1807 by George Helmbold and edited by "Toby Scratch'em," the *Tickler* was one of the earliest of the true comic papers. It kept up its flow of satire for six years, attacking local and national politicians and government. It also contained some advertising and poetry.

v1-2   1807-1809   APS II, Reel 45

THE TIME PIECE; and literary companion. v.1-3 (no.1-150); Mar. 13, 1797-Aug. 28, 1798. [New York] P. Freneau, & A. Menut.

Philip Freneau, editor.
Imperfect: issues for v.3, no.148 and 150 lacking on film.

A four-page tri-weekly which published domestic and foreign news, proceedings of legislative bodies, serialized articles on politics and other subjects, as well as poetry, anecdotes, and a number of ads.

v1-3, no.1-150   Mar. 13, 1797-Aug. 28, 1798   APS I, Reel 29

Microfilm edition was prepared from DLC copy.

TIMES AND REGISTER. *SEE* Medical Times and Register.

TOGETHER. *SEE* Christian Advocate. (Chicago)

THE TOILET; a weekly collection of literary pieces, principally designed for the amusement of ladies. v.1, no.1-8; Jan. 17-Mar. 7, 1801. Charlestown, S. Etheridge.

62 p.

This weekly literary miscellany was mainly for the entertainment of women. Its contents included essays about women, moral essays, poetry, and a series of sketches on varied topics.

v1, no.1-8   Jan. 17-Mar. 17, 1801   APS II, Reel 45

TOKEN OF REMEMBRANCE. *SEE* Amaranth, or, Token of Remembrance.

THE TOWN. v.1, no.1-5; Jan. 1-12, 1807. New-York [J. Osborn]

1 v. Issued several times a week.

This four-page paper was concerned mainly with the theater; it reviewed New York plays, and also published news of London fashions, lists of new British publications, and miscellaneous literary pieces, including some poetry.

v1, no.1-5   Jan. 1-12, 1807   APS II, Reel 45

TOWN AND COUNTRY. v.1- ; Feb. 14, 1846- . New York.

v. illus. weekly.

Title varies: 1846-Nov. 14, 1846 Morris's national press, a journal for home, Nov. 21, 1846-Mar. 23, 1901, The home journal.

Nathaniel Parker Willis and George Pope Morris founded the *National Press: A Home Journal* in 1846. Willis was a poet and essayist with an established reputation; an entertaining writer with a light and musical style, wit, and a love for gossip. General Morris was the most popular song writer of his time. The name of the periodical was soon changed to the *Home Journal*. Willis, the chief attraction, wrote for the paper regularly and voluminously, although he sometimes did not visit the office for weeks at a time. Personal sketches of public characters and stirring scenes of New York appeared. The operas and theatres, the shops, the omnibuses, Broadway, the museum, the art galleries, the cafes, the hotels, the balls and receptions, and the changes in customs and dress were chronicled. Fiction was included—original tales and novelettes, new novels, romance and reality, stories translated from Chinese, German and French. Entertaining miscellany appeared—"Gossip and News of Parisian Journals," and "Returned Love Letters." Many selections were borrowed from other journals; and, except in a few instances, contributors were paid nothing. Occasionally a pirated English novel was issued in monthly supplements.

The *Home Journal* lost its distinctive literary style after the deaths of Morris and Willis in the 1860's. It became one of a class of urban papers that appealed to a small number of rather wealthy subscribers. Society news, art and letters, styles, gossip about amusements, and light essays and verse were presented.

In 1901 the Stuyvesant Company was organized to take over the publication of the *Home Journal,* the name was changed to *Town and Country,* and articles and pictures of fine homes and gardens in the city and country were the main emphasis. Theatre, fashion, and men's and women's golf coverage were other topics.

Morris's National Press, a Journal for Home

Feb. 14-Nov. 14, 1846		APS II, Reel 1948

Home Journal

	Nov. 21, 1846-Dec. 18, 1847	Reel 1948
	May 6, 1848-Dec. 28, 1850	Reel 1949
	Feb. 8, 1851-Dec. 27, 1856	Reel 1950

Town and Country

v57	Mar. 15, 1902-Mar. 7, 1903	Reel 1951
v58	Mar. 14, 1903-Mar. 5, 1904	Reel 1952
v59	Mar. 12, 1904-Mar. 4, 1905	Reel 1953
v60	Mar. 11, 1905-Mar. 3, 1906	Reel 1954
v61	Mar. 10, 1906-Mar. 16, 1907	Reel 1955
v62	Mar. 23, 1907-Mar. 14, 1908	Reel 1956
v65	Mar. 19, 1910-Mar. 11, 1911	Reel 1957
v66	Mar. 18, 1911-Mar. 9, 1912	Reel 1958
v67	Mar. 16, 1912-Mar. 8, 1913	Reel 1959

Microfilm edition includes 1846-51, 1854-56, 1902-08, and 1910-13. Some issues and pages are missing; not available for photographing.

Microfilm edition was prepared from DLC, ICU, and NN copies.

TRANSACTIONS OF THE LITERARY AND PHILOSO-PHICAL SOCIETY OF NEW-YORK. Instituted in the year MDCCCXIV. v.1-2, pt. 1; 1815-1825. New York, Pub. for the Society, by Van Winkle and Wiley.

2 v. plates.
Vol. 2, pt. 1, half-title.

De Witt Clinton was among the charter members of the Literary and Philosophical Society of New York, and was also its first president. Included is the act of Incorporation, the Laws and Regula-tions, the list of officers and members and the first discourse . . . written by Clinton.

v1-2	1815-1825	APS II, Reel 840

Vol. 2: lacks table of contents and index. Text begins with page 25. Several newspaper clippings and handwritten notes are included in the microfilm edition. Best copy available. Some pages are stained.

Microfilm edition was prepared from DI-GS and NNM copies.

TRANSYLVANIA JOURNAL OF MEDICINE AND THE ASSOCIATE SCIENCES. v.1-12; Feb. 1828-Mar. 1839. Lexington, Ky.

12 v. quarterly.
Vol. 9 also numbered new series no. 1.

The medical profession was making great progress in the 1830's and 1840's. Every major population center had its medical reviews, journals, or intelligencers. Physicians and surgeons presented articles and accounts of cases to fellow practitioners. The *Transylvania Journal of Medicine and the Associate Sciences* included such topics as causes of fever, bandaging gun-shot wounds, winter epidemics, poisoning by opium, skull fractures and depressions, mania cured by counter-irritation, changes in matter and their causes, accounts of lunatic asylums, the cultivation of medicinal plants, the plague, and the use of trephine in epilepsy.

v1-3	Feb. 1828-Nov. 1830	APS II, Reel 1960
v4-5	Feb. 1831-Nov./Dec. 1832	Reel 1961
v9	Jan.-Dec. 1836	Reel 1961

Microfilm edition contains 1828-32 and 1836.

Microfilm edition was prepared from CSmH and GU copies.

TRAVELLER. *SEE* Spirit of the Times.

TRAVELLER AND SPIRIT OF THE TIMES. *SEE* Spirit of the Times.

TRUE AMERICAN (Philadelphia) SUPPLEMENT. *SEE* Dessert to the True American.

TRUMPET AND CHRISTIAN FREEMAN. *SEE* Universalist (Boston).

TRUMPET AND FREEMAN. *SEE* Universalist (Boston).

TRUMPET AND UNIVERSALIST MAGAZINE. *SEE* Universalist (Boston).

THE TRUTH. no.1-2; Sept.-Oct. 1819. New Haven.

2 no. monthly.

Edited by J. Ironside, pseud.

Only two numbers of *The Truth* were published, and among their miscellaneous contents were poetry, satire on fashions of the day, an article on tariffs, a letter on a civic problem, and essays including "Meditations on Life and Death."

no.1-2	Sept.-Oct. 1819	APS II, Reel 242

UNCLE SAM'S MAGAZINE. *SEE* United Service.

UNION AGRICULTURIST. *SEE* Prairie Farmer.

UNION AGRICULTURIST AND WESTERN PRAIRIE FARMER. *SEE* Prairie Farmer.

UNION MAGAZINE OF LITERATURE AND ART. *SEE* Sartain's Union Magazine of Literature and Art.

THE UNITARIAN DEFENDANT. no; 1-11; June 22-Nov. 16, 1822. Charleston, S.C.

44 p. biweekly (irregular)

Defending Unitarian beliefs was the purpose of the *Unitarian Defendant*. It consisted mainly of essays, some serialized, including "On the Attempt to Deprive Unitarians of the Name of Christians," which ran through the second, third, and fourth numbers, and "Unitarians Defended by Their Opponents," which ran through numbers 5, 6, 10, and 11. Only eleven numbers were published.

no.1-11   June 22-Nov. 16, 1822   APS II, Reel 242

UNITARIAN; devoted to the statement, explanation, and defence of the principles of Unitarian Christianity. v.1, nos. 1-4; Nov. 18, 1827-Feb. 15, 1828. New York, 1827-1828.

224 p.

A quarterly publication edited by William Ware who later edited the *Examiner*.

v1   Nov. 18, 1827-Feb. 15, 1828   APS II, Reel 1196

Vol. 1: Pages 58, 61, and 108 are missing; not available for photographing.

Microfilm edition was prepared from ICMe copy.

THE UNITARIAN MISCELLANY AND CHRISTIAN MONITOR. v.1-6 (no.1-48); Jan. 1821-Dec. 1824. Baltimore, Baltimore Unitarian Book Society, 1821-24.

6 v. monthly.

Editors: Jan. 1821-Dec. 1822, Jared Sparks.—Jan. 1823-Dec. 1824. F.W. Greenwood.

The *Miscellany* was edited by Jared Sparks until 1823 and was continued through December 1824 by F.W. P. Greenwood. It published articles on doctrine, discussions of Calvinism, and much on Unitarianism, including the history of Unitarianism, as well as sermons, memoirs, letters, essays, poetry, obituary notices, and ordinations.

v1-6   Jan. 1821-Dec. 1824   APS II, Reel 206

UNITARIAN REGISTER. *SEE* Christian Register (Boston).

UNITARIAN REGISTER AND THE UNIVERSALIST LEADER. *SEE* Christian Register (Boston).

*THE UNITARIAN REVIEW.** v.1-36; Mar. 1874-Dec. 1891. Boston, L.C. Bowles, 1874-[91]

36 v. monthly.

Preceded by the Monthly religious magazine.
Title varies: 1874-86, The Unitarian review and religious magazine. 1877-91, The Unitarian review. (Cover-title, Jan.-Dec. 1891: The Unitarian review; a liberal monthly journal of religion and letters)

Editors: Mar.-June 1874, Charles Lowe.—Aug.-Dec. 1874, H.W. Foote.—1875-79, J.H. Morison, H.H. Barber.—1880-84, H.H. Barber, James De Normandie.—1885-86, James De Normandie.—1887-91, J.H. Allen.

When *Christian Examiner* ceased publication, the *Unitarian Review* was projected as a replacement. Although the *Review* listed an outstanding file of contributors, the editing was rather dismal. The file contains a great deal of interesting material dealing with theology and literature. Articles of art, music, and economics are also included.

Unitarian Review and Religious Magazine

v1-6	Mar. 1874-Dec. 1876	APS III, Reel 21
v7-12	Jan. 1877-Dec. 1879	Reel 22
v13-19	Jan. 1880-June 1883	Reel 23
v20-26	July 1883-Dec. 1886	Reel 24

Unitarian Review

v27	Jan.-June 1887	Reel 24
Cum Index, v27-34	1887-1890	Reel 25
v28-36	July 1887-Dec. 1891	Reel 25

Microfilm edition was prepared from MiU and MiEM copies.

SEE ALSO: Monthly Religious Magazine and Theological Review *and* New World.

UNITARIAN REVIEW AND RELIGIOUS MAGAZINE. *SEE* Unitarian Review.

THE UNITED BRETHREN'S MISSIONARY INTELLIGENCER, and religious miscellany; containing the most recent accounts relating to the United Brethren's missions among the heathen; with other interesting communications from the records of that church. v. 1-10, no.4; 1822-1849. Philadelphia, For the Protestant Episcopal Church of the United Brethren [1822-30]; New York, For the missionary fund of the Church of the United Brethren at New York Protestant Episcopal Press [1831]-

v. quarterly.

Contains quarterly reports on the efforts of the Protestant Episcopal Church of the United Brethren to convert the heathens of all the world.

v1-3	1822-1830	APS II, Reel 1258
v4-9	1831-1848	Reel 1259

Best copy available. Pagination is irregular. Vol. 2: Issue no. 2 is missing. Vol. 8: Pgs. 449 and 456 have faded print. Vol. 10 is missing; not available for photographing.

Microfilm edition was prepared from MH-AN, NNG, and NRCR copies.

UNITED SERVICE; a quarterly review of military and naval affairs. v.1-14, Jan. 1879-Mar. 1886; ser. 2, v.1-17, no.4, Jan. 1889- Apr. 1897; ser. 3, v.1-8, no.6, Jan. 1902-

Dec. 1905. Philadelphia [and] New York, 1879-1905.

39 v.

Subtitle varies. Superseded May 1886-Dec. 1888; May 1897-Dec. 1901. Merged into Uncle Sam's magazine.

United Service was a military journal devoted to the Army and Navy. Lewis R. Hamersly was in charge of the naval department and George A. Woodward presided over the military section. Entertaining pieces were also offered. The magazine erratically moved back and forth from Philadelphia to New York, suspended publication, and finally merged into *Uncle Sam's Magazine*.

v1-5	Jan. 1879-Dec. 1881	APS III, Reel 132
v6-10	Jan. 1882-June 1884	Reel 133
v11-nsv1	July 1884-June 1889	Reel 134
nsv2-6	July 1889-Dec. 1891	Reel 135
nsv7-11	Jan. 1892-June 1894	Reel 136
nsv12-17	July 1894-Apr. 1897	Reel 137
3sv1-5	Jan. 1902-June 1904	Reel 138
3sv6-8	July 1904-Dec. 1905	Reel 139

Vols. 1-13, n.s. vols. 1-16 and third series vols. 1-8: lack indexes; please refer to table of contents. Vol. 11 and new series vol. 11: some advertising pages are missing. Vols. 14 and new series vol. 17: index and table of contents are missing.

Microfilm edition was prepared from CL, MiD, MiU, NBu, Nh, PPi, and ViNeM copies.

* THE UNITED STATES CATHOLIC MAGAZINE. Edited by Charles I. White. v.1-8; Jan. 1842-Dec. 29, 1849. Baltimore, J. Murphy, 1842-49.

8 v. plates (part fold.) ports.
Monthly, 1842-48; weekly, 1849.

Title varies: 1842, The Religious cabinet: a monthly periodical ... 1843, The United States Catholic magazine: a monthly periodical ... 1844-48, The United States Catholic magazine and monthly review. 1849, The United States Catholic magazine. Superseded by the Catholic mirror.

The *United States Catholic Magazine* began as the *Religious Cabinet,* a sixty-four page eclectic containing selections from religious writings. After it changed its name in 1843, it became less eclectic and published some fiction, devotional poetry, and a considerable amount of "ecclesiastical intelligence." It was illustrated by several plates each year. As the official organ of the archbishop of Baltimore, it became important as an interpreter of the news; and some articles, such as those on the anti-Catholic riots of Philadelphia and New York, are of permanent value.

Religious Cabinet: a Monthly Periodical
v1	1842	APS II, Reel 689

United States Catholic Magazine: a Monthly Periodical
v2	1843	Reel 689

United States Catholic Magazine and Monthly Review
v3-4	1844-1845	Reel 689
v5-7	1846-1848	Reel 690

United States Catholic Magazine
v8	1849	Reel 690

Vols. 1-3 and 8: Indexes are missing.

Microfilm edition was prepared from DLC, ICN and MiU copies.

UNITED STATES CATHOLIC MAGAZINE AND MONTHLY REVIEW. *SEE* United States Catholic Magazine.

UNITED STATES CATHOLIC MISCELLANY. v.1-39, Je. 5, 1822-1861. Charleston, S.C.

39 v. weekly.
Suspended Je. 1823-May 1824; Jan.-Je. 1826.

On film: v.1; v.4-6, Jan. 5, 1825-Je. 30. 1827; v.7, Sept. 1827-Je. 1828 (Scattered issues only) v.8-14; Jl. 5, 1828-Je. 20, 1835 (Scattered pages missing)

The *United States Catholic Miscellany* was the first strictly religious journal established in this country in defense of the Catholic doctrine. Poetry, pastoral letters, Irish Catholic Association news, and religious articles appear. "The Pope's Supremacy," "Civil Rights and Religious Privileges," "The Religion of the Sun," "The Difficulties of Protestantism," and "Thoughts on death," are representative topics.

v1-5	June 5, 1822-Dec. 28, 1825	APS II, Reel 1961
v6-14	July 22, 1826-June 20, 1835	Reel 1962

Microfilm edition was prepared from NcD and Txu copies.

UNITED STATES CATHOLIC SENTINEL. *SEE* Jesuit.

THE UNITED STATES CHRISTIAN MAGAZINE. v.1, no.1-3; 1796. New-York, T. and J. Swords.

235 p.

A religious periodical which presented biography, letters, reviews of new publications, essays on doctrine, Bible interpretation, and foreign and domestic religious news.

v1, no.1-3	1796	APS I, Reel 30

Microfilm edition was prepared from CtY copy.

* THE UNITED STATES DEMOCRATIC REVIEW. v.1-29, Oct. 1837-Dec. 1851; v.30-31 (new ser., v.1-2) 1852; [v.32-38] (new ser., v. 1-7) 1853-56; v.39-43, Jan. 1857-Oct. 1859. Washington, Langtree and O'Sullivan, 1838-40; New York, J. & H.G. Langley, 1841-59.

43 v. illus., plates, ports, maps, facsim. monthly.

Vols. 1-3, 5-8 contain the political and literary portions; v.4 the historical register department, of the numbers published from Oct. 1837 to Dec. 1840. Publication suspended Nov.-Dec. 1837, Aug. 1838, Jan.-June 1841, Oct. 1853-May 1854, May-Sept. 1859, inclusive.

Title varies: Oct. 1837-Dec. 1851, The United States magazine and democratic review,. 1852, Democratic review 1853-Jan. 1856, The United States review. Feb. 1856-Oct. 1859, The United States Democratic review.

Editors: 1846-51, T.P. Kettell.-1853-55, D.W. Holly.-1856, S.W. Cone.-1857-58, Conrad Swackhamer.-1859, Conrad Swackhamer, Isaac Lawrence. Film incomplete: v. 39 lacking.

This general magazine was most famous under the editorship of John O'Sullivan (1837-46), when the combination of literature of real excellence with vigorous articles on political, economic and social questions made it an important periodical. Contributors included Bryant, Hawthorne, Whittier, Lowell, and Longfellow, and these writers continued for 10 years to enrich the *Democrat's* pages, doing much to give it the good literary standing it enjoyed in the years 1837-46. It also contained good comparatively lively tales, poetry, and book reviews. But less literary articles on questions of national policy afforded the piece de resistance of each issue. Portraits of famous statesmen appeared throughout the years, and taken altogether, the file furnishes an interesting portrait gallery. In 1846 financial disaster overtook Sullivan and the *Democratic Review* passed into other hands. Although by that time most of the famous writers had left, some good material still appeared. In 1853 it disappeared from sight and it was not until the *United States Review* was united with it in 1856 that it recovered any of its former prominence. Nevertheless, it ended in 1859.

United States Magazine, and Democratic Review

v1-8	Oct. 1837-Dec. 1840	APS II, Reel 691
v9-15	July 1841-Dec. 1844	Reel 692
v16-22	Jan. 1845-June 1848	Reel 693
v23-29	July 1848-Dec. 1851	Reel 694

Democrat's Review

v30-31	Jan. 1852-Dec. 1852	Reel 695

United States Review

v32-37, no.1	Jan. 1853-Jan. 1856	Reel 695

United States Democratic Review

v37, no.2-6	Feb.-July 1856	Reel 695
v38, 40-43	Aug. 1856-Oct. 1859	Reel 696

Microfilm edition was prepared from MiU and NjR copies.

THE UNITED STATES INTELLIGENCER AND REVIEW. v.1-3; Jan. 1829-Dec. 1831. Providence, 1829-30; Philadelphia, P.N. Nicklin and T. Johnson, 1830-31.

3 v. monthly.

Caption title of individual numbers of v.1: Law intelligencer.
Edited by J.K. Angell.

Founded at Providence in 1829, this legal magazine was intended to be a synopsis of changes and progress in the field of law. Articles discussed recent and interesting cases and pointed out differences between states in decisions. Also included were listings of cases in the Supreme Court and in the states; reviews of new treatises, digests, and books; changes in the judiciary, with biographical sketches; and miscellaneous news of interesting events in the legal world.

v1-3	Jan. 1829-Dec. 1831	APS II, Reel 741

Vol. 2: Pagination is irregular.

Microfilm edition was prepared from DLC copy.

UNITED STATES LAW JOURNAL. v.1-2 (no.1-6); June 1822-Apr. 1826. New Haven. (Conn.) Gray & Hewit, 1822-23. New York, Printed by G.F. Hopkins, 1826

2 v.
Vol. 1 consists of no.1-4 (June 1822-Apr. 1823); v.2, no.5-6 (Jan.-Apr. 1826) suspended in 1823; resumed in Jan. 1826.

Vol. 1 has title: United States law journal, and civilian's magazine. Edited by several members of the bar.

United States Law Journal, and Civilian's Magazine

v1, no.1-4	June 1822-Apr. 1823	APS II, Reel 944

United States Law Journal

v2, no.5-6	Jan.-Apr. 1826	Reel 944

Vol. 1: Index for volume is found at the end. Vol. 2: Lacks index; please refer to the Contents at the beginning of each issue.

Microfilm edition was prepared from MiU and WaU copies.

UNITED STATES LAW JOURNAL, AND CIVILIAN'S MAGAZINE. *SEE* United States Law Journal.

UNITED STATES LAW REVIEW. *SEE* American Law Review.

* THE UNITED STATES LITERARY GAZETTE. v.1-4; Apr. 1824-Sept. 1826. Boston, Cummings, Hilliard, 1825-26.

4 v.
Semimonthly, Apr. 1824-June1826; monthly, July-Sept. 1826.

Vols. 3-4 published by H. Gray.
Absorbed the New York review and Atheneum magazine in July 1826. Continued in Oct. 1826 as the United States review and literary gazette.

Begun in 1824, this literary miscellany was first edited by a brilliant young educator, James G. Carter. In less than a year, he was succeeded by Theophilus Parsons, who enlarged the magazine and added an eight-page "Literary Advertiser." Devoted primarily to literary news, the semimonthly *Gazette* contained book reviews, publishers' announcements, current news, and miscellany, but it is most interesting now because of its excellent poetry, including some by Henry Wadsworth Longfellow, and William Cullen Bryant. Longfellow, who was then a student at Bowdoin, contributed some of his early verse, as well as four prose sketches under the title of "The Lay Monastery," and Bryant contributed more of his poetry to the *Gazette* than to any other magazine, including his "Rizpah," which appeared in the first number. Other contributors included J.G. Percival, R.H. Dana, Rufus Dawes, Grenville Mellen, and John A. Jones.

v1-4	Apr. 1824-Sept. 1826	APS II, Reel 242

SEE ALSO: New York Review and Atheneum Magazine.

THE UNITED STATES MAGAZINE; a repository of history, politics and literature. v.1; Jan.-Dec. 1779. Philadelphia, F. Bailey [1779]

504, [2] p. monthly.

H.H. Brackenridge, editor.

Literary magazine which followed the progress of the war and the problems facing the new nation. Included articles of many writers, including Philip Freneau, Charles Lee, William Livingston, and the editor, H.H. Brackenridge.

v1	Jan.-Dec. 1779	APS I, Reel 30

Some pages are missing.

Microfilm edition was prepared from MiU-C copy.

UNITED STATES MAGAZINE AND DEMOCRATIC REVIEW. *SEE* Boston Quarterly Review; Brownson's Quarterly Review; *and* United States Democratic Review.

THE UNITED STATES MAGAZINE AND LITERARY AND POLITICAL REPOSITORY. new ser. v.1, no.1; Jan. 1823. New York, C. Wiley.

106 p.

Supersedes Literary and scientific repository, and critical review.

This literary miscellany, which did not survive past its first number, published reviews of books, plays, and pamphlets, listed periodical publications, and contained a summary of political events, and a variety of literary and scientific news.

nsv1, no.1   Jan. 1823   APS II, Reel 243

SEE ALSO: Literary and Scientific Repository, and Critical Review.

UNITED STATES MAGAZINE OF SCIENCE, ART, MANUFACTURES, AGRICULTURE, COMMERCE AND TRADE. *SEE* Emerson's Magazine and Putnam's Monthly.

UNITED STATES MAGAZINE, or, General repository of useful instruction and rational amusement. v.1, no.1-[5], Apr.-Aug. 1794. Newark, N.-J., J. Woods, 1794.

284 p. Monthly.

A miscellany containing foreign and domestic news, addresses, essays and articles on politics, agriculture, history, natural history, and medicine, in addition to poetry and humorous anecdotes.

v1, no.1-5   Apr.-Aug. 1794   APS I, Reel 30

Microfilm edition was prepared from MWA copy.

UNITED STATES MILITARY PHILOSOPHICAL SOCIETY. Extracts from the minutes of the United States military philosophical society at a meeting[s] held October 6, 1806, January 30, 1808 [and] December 28, 1809. [n.p., 1807?-10?]

3 no. in 1 v.

List of members in the issues for 1808 and 1809.
Concerning this society there is the following notice in the Annual report of the U.S. National museum, 1896/97, pt. II (A memorial of George Brown Goode) p. 277: "1802, a United States Corps of engineers and military academy was organized by law and established at West Point ... and the United States military philosophical society was established with the whole Engineer corps of the army for a nucleus. This society had for its object 'the collecting and disseminating of military science'. Its membership during the ten years of its existence included most of the leading men in the country, civilians as well as officers in the army and navy. Meetings were held in New York and Washington, as well as in West Point, and it seems to have been the first national scientific society ... At least three fascicles of Extracts from the minutes of the United States military society were printed: one for the stated meeting, October 6, 1806 [4 ≠ , 14 pp.]; one for an occasional meeting at Washington, January 30, 1808 [4 ≠ , pp. 1-23 (1)]; and one for an occasional meeting at New York, December 28, 1809 [4 ≠ , pp. 1-22]. The manuscript records, in four volumes, are said to be in the possession of the New York historical society."

Shortly after the United States Military Academy and the U.S. Corps of Engineers were established at West Point in 1802, the U.S. Military Philosophical Society was begun, with the Engineer Corps of the Army as a nucleus. Its object was "the collecting and disseminating of military science," and its membership included

most of the leading men in the country, both civilians and officers in the army and navy. It appears to have been the first national scientific society. The extracts from the minutes of meetings include member lists, proceedings of meetings, and addresses given at meetings.

1806-1809   APS II, Reel 45

THE UNITED STATES' NAVAL CHRONICLE. By Charles W. Goldsborough. vol. 1. Washington, J. Wilson, 1824.

395, xii p.

"All published."–Sabin.

Edited by Charles W. Goldsborough, the *Naval Chronicle* was devoted exclusively to the navy. Included in the wide variety of information it offered was a history of the navy and of legislation affecting it, biographies of many officers, statistics on the budget and many statistical tables, and articles concerning navy yards, the navy hospital, the Revolutionary navy, equipment, ships, and crews.

v1   1824   APS II, Reel 243

UNITED STATES REVIEW (Washington). *SEE* United States Democratic Review.

THE UNITED STATES REVIEW AND LITERARY GAZETTE. v.1-2; Oct. 1826-Sept. 1827. Boston, Bowles and Dearborn; New York, G. and C. Carvill, 1827.

2 v. monthly.

Editors: W.C. Bryant, Charles Folsom.
Formed by the union of the United States literary gazette (Apr. 1824-Sept. 1826) and the New York review and Atheneum magazine (June 1825-May 1826)

Edited by William Cullen Bryant in New York and Charles Folsom in Boston, this monthly was issued simultaneously in both cities and was especially noted for its poetry. During its short life, the *United States Review and Literary Gazette* published some of the best poetry of William Cullen Bryant and Fitz-Greene Halleck.

v1-2   Oct. 1826-Sept. 1827   APS II, Reel 1124

Vol. 2: Index not photographed at end.

Microfilm edition was prepared from OU copy.

SEE ALSO: New York Review and Atheneum Magazine *and* United States Literary Gazette.

* **THE UNITED STATES SERVICE MAGAZINE.** v.1-5; Jan. 1864-June 1866. New York, C.B. Richardson, 1864-66.

5 v. ports. monthly.

Henry Coppee, editor.

One of the best periodicals arising from the Civil War was the *United States Service Magazine,* edited by Professor Henry Coppee. Unlike its competitors, the *Magazine* added poetry, literature, art, and fiction to the usual naval and military reports. Publication ceased because it was felt that the journal was no longer needed following the War.

v1-5   Jan. 1864-June 1866   APS III, Reel 53

Microfilm edition was prepared from MiU copy.

THE UNIVERSAL ASYLUM AND COLUMBIAN MAGAZINE. v.1-[9] Sept. 1786-Dec. 1792. Philadelphia, Printed by W. Young [etc.]

9 v. illus., ports., maps.

Title varies: v.1-4, The Columbian magazine; or, Monthly miscellany ... (caption title, Mar.-June 1790: The Universal Asylum and monthly miscellany) Continued as the Columbian museum; or, Universal asylum. Vol. [7] called v.1; v.[8-9] called v.1-2.

The handsomest magazine of its century. Noted for its fiction, engravings, essay series, and articles on agriculture, mechanics, travel, etc. in its first four years. The later years were devoted to recording the history of the Revolutionary War.

Columbian Magazine
v1-4   Sept. 1786-Feb. 1790   APS I, Reel 11

Universal Asylum and Columbian Magazine
v4-9   Mar. 1790-Dec. 1792   Reel 30

Some pages are lacking.

Microfilm edition was prepared from DLC, MiU-C and MWA copies.

SEE ALSO: Columbian Museum; or, Universal Asylum.

UNIVERSAL ASYLUM AND MONTHLY MISCELLANY. *SEE* Universal Asylum and Columbian Magazine.

UNIVERSALIST. v1-60, no. 35; July 3, 1819-Dec. 28, 1878. Boston, 1819-1878.

60 v.

Vols. 10-42 also as new series v.1-33.
Title varies: 1819-June 1828 as Universalist magazine; July 1828-Apr. 1862 as Trumpet and Universalist magazine; Apr. 1862-Jan. 1863 as Trumpet and Christian freeman; Jan.-Dec. 1863 as Trumpet and freeman.

Edited by H. Ballou.
Merged into the Christian leader (later the Universalist leader) in 1878. Film covers: v.1-15 and v.18-32, July 1819-June 1851.

Originally called *Universalist Magazine* and later the *Trumpet and Universalist Magazine,* this periodical was the leading weekly of the Universalist denomination. Edited by Hosea Ballou, and later by Hosea Ballou, 2nd and by Thomas Whittemore, this magazine was, during its early years, devoted mainly to doctrine, religion, and morality, publishing sermons, poetry, and articles on Universalist doctrine and on the progress of Universalism, along with news on missions and the activities of Universalist societies. During the 1830's and 1840's, however, contents were broadened to include more secular material such as general news items, articles on literature and education and a "Miscellany" column.

Universalist Magazine
v1-4, no.1   July 3, 1819-June 29, 1822   APS II, Reel 243
v4, no.1-v7   June 29, 1822-June 17, 1826   Reel 244

v8-9   June 24, 1826-June 28, 1828   Reel 1701

Trumpet and Universalist Magazine
v10-12   July 5, 1828-June 25, 1831   Reel 1701

v13-18   July 2, 1831-June 17, 1838   Reel 1702
v19-22   June 24, 1837-June 19, 1841   Reel 1703
v23-26   June 26, 1841-June 14, 1845   Reel 1704
v27-29   June 21, 1845-June 10, 1848   Reel 1705
v30-32   June 17, 1848-June 7, 1851   Reel 1706

Reels 1701-1706: Pagination is irregular.

Microfilm edition was prepared from ICMe, MWA, and NCaS copies.

THE UNIVERSALIST, consisting of essays, lectures, extracts and miscellaneous pieces; tending to explain and defend the doctrine of modern universalism. v.1, no.1-24; Apr. 1, 1825-Mar. 15, 1826. Utica, N.Y., A.G. Dauby, 1825-

1 v. semimonthly.

Editor: Apr. 1825- J.S. Thompson. Superseded by Herald of salvation (Philadelphia).

Reverend John S. Thompson was the first editor of this periodical founded to promote and defend the doctrines of universalism.

v1   Apr. 1, 1825-Mar. 15, 1826   APS II, Reel 1308

Best copy available for photographing. Vol. 1: Many pages are stained. Pgs. 157-58 are bound between pgs. 160-61. Pgs. 172-73 are missing; not available for photographing. Supplement entitled "The Christian Guide" follows pg. 200.

Microfilm edition was prepared from DLC copy.

UNIVERSALIST EXPOSITOR. *SEE* Expositor and Universalist Review.

UNIVERSALIST MAGAZINE. *SEE* Universalist.

* THE UNIVERSALIST QUARTERLY AND GENERAL REVIEW. v.1-20, Jan. 1844-Oct. 1863; v.[21]-48 (new ser., v.1-28) Jan. 1864-Oct. 1891. Boston, A. Tompkins, 1844-64; N.E. Universalist Pub. House, 1865-91.

48 v.

"General index": v.48 p.[1]-22 at end.
Supersedes the Expositor and Universalist review.
Editors: Jan. 1844-Oct. 1855? Hosea Ballou.-Jan. 1856?-Oct. 1863? G.H. Emerson.-Jan. 1864-Apr. 1886, T.B. Thayer.-July 1886-Oct. 1891, Richard Eddy.

Hosea Ballou II, backed by Abel Tompkins as publisher, started this review in January 1844 "to represent the scholarship and literary culture of the Universalist Church, as well as its theology." Thus it was somewhat more literary than many of its class. Ballou's own blasts against slavery were a feature and an index of the *Review's* continuing interest in politics. Taken over by the Universalist Publishing House in 1865, the *Review* continually lost money, in spite of the effort to boost circulation in 1883 by reduction of the subscription price. It was discontinued after October 1891 for financial reasons.

v1-7   Jan. 1844-Oct. 1850   APS II, Reel 697

General Index, v1-48   Reel 1357
v8-11   Jan. 1851-Oct. 1854   Reel 1357
v12-18   Jan. 1855-Oct. 1861   Reel 1358

v19-24	Jan. 1862-Oct. 1867	Reel 1359
v25-30	Jan. 1868-Oct. 1873	Reel 1360
v31-36	Jan. 1874-Oct. 1879	Reel 1361
v37-42	Jan. 1880-Oct. 1885	Reel 1362
v43-48	Jan. 1886-Oct. 1891	Reel 1363

Vol. 9 and New Series Vols. 4, 13, 16, 26, and 28: Pagination is irregular. New Series Vol. 26: Article XXVI is misnumbered.

Microfilm edition was prepared from DLC, MiD and MnU copies.

UNIVERSALIST WATCHMAN, REPOSITORY AND CHRONICLE. v.1-9, 1820-29; new ser. v.1-49, May 1829-Woodstock, Vt., W. Bell.

58 v. weekly.
v1-9, 1820-24 as Christian repository.

Editor: William Bell.
Lacking on film: v.7-9; new series v.1-2, 5-9, 11-15, and 19-49.

Founded by Samuel S. Loveland as *Christian Repository,* this journal included sermons, essays regarding doctrine and morality, and biblical commentary.

Christian Repository
v1-6	July 1820-Dec. 1825	APS II, Reel 1309

Universalist Watchman
nsv3-4	Apr. 30, 1831-Apr. 20, 1833	Reel 1309
nsv10-18	June 30, 1838-July 9, 1847	Reel 1310

Best copy available for photographing. Some volumes have torn, stained, or missing pages. Pagination is irregular. Vol. 1: cover pages for vol. 2, issue 1 are bound between pgs. 36 and 37. Vol. 4: issue 4 is repeated Vol. 5: General index for vols. 1-5 is bound and filmed at end of volume. Vol. 6: issues following Dec. 1825 to end of volume are missing; not available for photographing.

Microfilm edition was prepared from DLC, MMeT, MWA, N, and NhD copies.

THE USEFUL CABINET, published in monthly numbers for the Newengland Association of Inventors and Patrons of Useful Arts. v.1, no.1-6; Jan.-June 1808. Boston, E.C. Beals.

144 p. illus.

This monthly was published by the Newengland Association of Inventors and Patrons of Useful Arts, and was concerned with the progress of all the arts and sciences, but gave most attention to new inventions and discoveries, and particularly to labor-saving machines. Among the topics discussed in its pages were construction of fireplaces, new methods of extracting teeth, and mathematical theories.

v1, no.1-6	Jan.-June 1808	APS II, Reel 45

UTAHNIAN. v.1, nos. 1-32, June 20, 1896-Apr. 1897. Salt Lake City.

1 v. (various pagings) illus.

Merged into Mining industry and review, later Mining American.

The *Utahnian* was a short-lived journal which eventually merged with *Mining Industry and Review.*

v1	June 20, 1896-Apr. 1897	APS III, Reel 271

No index or contents available.

Microfilm edition was prepared from KHi, NN copies.

THE UTICA CHRISTIAN MAGAZINE, designed to prompt the spirit of research, and diffuse religious information. v.1-3; July 1813-June 1816. Utica, N.Y., Printed by Merrell & Camp for Cornelius Davis, 1814-

3 v. monthly.

"Published under the inspection of a committee of Congregational and Presbyterian clergymen."

Conducted with the help of a committee of Congregational and Presbyterian clergymen, the *Utica Christian Magazine* published religious news from all parts of the world. Included were accounts of revivals, activities of missionaries, reports of the London Missionary Society and of various Bible societies, as well as news of New York churches. In addition, there were sermons, Bible studies, articles on doctrine, biographies, book reviews, and poetry and anecdotes.

v1-3	July 1813-June 1816	APS II, Reel 244

THE UTICA CHRISTIAN REPOSITORY, containing various pieces on doctrinal & practical subjects of religion, mostly original. Also, a summary of religious intelligence. v.1-5; Jan. 1822-Dec. 1826. Utica, N.Y., Merrell & Hastings, 1822-26.

5 v. monthly.

The *Christian Repository* provided sermons and Bible studies, news of missions to the American Indians, and coverage of revivals and the activities of various societies, such as the American Bible Society, American Jew Society, and American Educational Society. A serialized article on "The Pilgrim's Progress in the Nineteenth Century" was a special feature.

v1-5	Jan. 1822-Dec. 1826	APS II, Reel 245

UTICA EVANGELICAL MAGAZINE. *SEE* Evangelical Magazine and Gospel Advocate.

UTICA MAGAZINE. *SEE* Evangelical Magazine and Gospel Advocate.

THE VACCINE INQUIRER; or, Miscellaneous collections relative to vaccination. no.1-6; Feb. 1822-[June?] 1824. [Baltimore]

286 p.

This magazine, which was conducted by a group of physicians, dealt exclusively with the topic of vaccination, which was still a relatively new concept at that time. Contents included a history of vaccination, including descriptions of the first cases; many general articles on vaccination and descriptions of recent cases; and coverage of various epidemics. Only six numbers were published.

no.1-6	Feb. 1822-June 1824	APS II, Reel 246

VALLEY FARMER. *SEE* Colman's Rural World.

VANITY FAIR. v.1-7 (no.1-169); Dec. 31, 1859; July 4, 1863. New York, L.H. Stephens.

7 v. illus., plates.

Weekly, 1859-62, May-July 4, 1863; monthly, Jan.-Feb. 1863. No issues for Mar. and Apr. 1863.

Edited by W.A. Stephens.

With financial backing from Frank J. Thompson and an editorial staff provided by the Stephenses, the comic paper *Vanity Fair* came into being on December 31, 1859. Illustration was a main feature in this satirical weekly with wooducts by Henry Louis Stephens, Frank Bellew, Ned Miller, and others. Frequent objects of caricature were political figures such as Buchanan, Douglas, and Greeley.

Vanity Fair was unsympathetic with the Negro's situation and was critical of the war and policies of the government at Washington. The paper was full of war features: a humorous treatise on military tacts, a series of "Humors of the War," and elegies of the famous dead. George Arnold's series of "McArone" papers burlesquing war correspondence was a chief attraction after December 1860.

Politics and war were not the only subjects in *Vanity Fair.* Poetry, drama, book reviews, and treatises also found their way into its pages. A major attraction was the series of contributions by Charles Farrar Browne, writing under the name of "Artemus Ward."

Vanity Fair never attained widespread popularity. Its attacks on abolitionists and the Negro during the war brought it many enemies. Mounting prices of materials and a reduced subscription rate also contributed to the paper's demise. At the beginning of 1863 it resorted to monthly publication and seemed to expire after the second monthly number. On May 2 it was resurrected for what proved to be a final series of ten weekly numbers.

v1-4	Dec. 31, 1859-Dec. 28, 1861	APS III, Reel 568
v5-7	Jan. 4, 1862-July 4, 1863	Reel 569

Vol. 2: Pgs. 97-98 are missing. Vols. 3 and 5: Pagination is irregular. Vol. 7: Index and table of contents are missing.

Microfilm edition was prepared from CSmH and TxU copies.

VARIETES LITTERAIRES. *SEE* Journal des Dames.

VEHICLE. *SEE* Western New York Baptist Magazine.

THE VERMONT BAPTIST MISSIONARY MAGAZINE. v.1, no.1-6; Jan. 1811-Apr. 1812. Rutland, Printed by W. Fay.

192 p. Four no. a year.

Issued by the Vermont Baptist Association.

The six numbers of this Baptist periodical focused mainly on missionary news, and included histories of the missionaries in India. Other material included coverage of ordinations and revivals, poetry, and anecdotes, essays, biographical sketches, and extracts from sermons.

v1, no.1-6	Jan. 1811-Apr. 1812	APS II, Reel 246

THE VIGIL. no.1-6; Feb. 27-Apr. 3, 1798. Charleston [S.C.] W.P. Young.

48 p. Weekly.

Edited by R. Beresford. Cf. Evans, American bibliography.

Each number of this diminutive weekly consisted of an essay, usually dealing with human faults or vices—selfishness, idleness, etc.

no.1-6	Feb. 27-Apr. 3, 1798	APS I, Reel 31

Microfilm edition was prepared from ScC copy.

VILLAGE MUSEUM. Cortland Village, v.1, nos.1-6; Oct. 9-Nov. 20, 1820. New York, 1820.

1 v. (unpaged)

Edited by "Genius and Co.," this short-lived 4-page magazine proposed "to promote literature and give amusement to the youthful mind." Among its varied contents were tales and poetry, jokes and anecdotes, and essays on science and morality.

v1, nos. 1-6	Oct. 9-Nov. 20, 1820	APS II, Reel 246

THE VILLAGER, a literary paper. v.1, no.1-6; Apr.-June 1819. [Greenwich Village, N.Y., 1819]

96 p. semimonthly.

During its brief three-month existence, this literary miscellany published poetry, occasional reviews, anecdotes, religious and scientific materials, and articles on philosophy and economy, and also gave some coverage to foreign and domestic news.

v1, no.1-6	Apr.-June 1819	APS II, Reel2 46

VIRGINIA EVANGELICAL AND LITERARY MAGAZINE. *SEE* Literary and Evangelical Magazine.

VIRGINIA HISTORICAL REGISTER, AND LITERARY ADVERTISER. *SEE* Virginia Historical Register, and Literary Companion.

THE VIRGINIA HISTORICAL REGISTER, AND LITERARY COMPANION. Ed. by William Maxwell. v.1-6; Jan. 1848-Oct. 1853. Richmond, Macfarlane & Ferguson, 1848-53.

6 v. in 3. quarterly.

Title varies: 1848-49, The Virginia historical register, and literary advertiser. 1850-51, The Virginia historical register, and literary note book. 1852-53, The Virginia historical register, and literary companion.

Edited by William Maxwell, the *Register* was an organ of the Virginia Historical Society. In addition to local histories, some biographies and original letters appeared.

Virginia Historical Register, and Literary Advertiser
v1-2	Jan. 1848-Oct. 1849	APS II, Reel 943

Virginia Historical Register, and Literary Note book
v3-4	Jan. 1850-Oct. 1851	Reel 943

Virginia Historical Register, and Literary Companion
v5-6	Jan. 1852-Oct. 1853	Reel 943

Some pages are stained, or have faded or missing print. Vols. 1-6 lack indexes; please refer to the Tables of Contents.

Microfilm edition was prepared from MBAt, NcD, and Nh copies.

VIRGINIA HISTORICAL REGISTER, AND LITERARY NOTE BOOK. *SEE* Virginia Historical Register, and Literary Companion.

THE VIRGINIA LITERARY MUSEUM AND JOURNAL OF BELLES LETTRES, ARTS, SCIENCES &c. v.1; June 17, 1829-June 9, 1830. Charlottesville, F. Carr.

830 p. weekly.

Title varies slightly.
Edited at the University of Virginia.
Includes index.

This weekly college publication was the first periodical issued by the University of Virginia students. Relying mainly on professors for contributions, it was to be a literary and scientific journal, treating science in a popular style. Although principally devoted to science, philology, and literature, it also dealt with the history of Virginia and other states, university news, religion and politics and also contained some poetry and biography.

v1, nos.1-52   June 17, 1829-June 9, 1830   APS II, Reel 1407

Some pages are tightly bound. Pages 176 and 201 are misnumbered.

Microfilm edition was prepared from NjP copy.

THE VIRGINIA RELIGIOUS MAGAZINE. v.1-3; Oct. 1804-Nov./Dec. 1807. Lexington [Va.] S. Walkup.

3 v. Bimonthly.

Issued by the Synod of Virginia, Presbyterian Church in the U.S.A.

Published under the patronage of the Synod of Virginia, this religious periodical included missionary news, news of revivals, Bible studies, sermons, essays, poetry, and biographical sketches.

v1-3   Oct. 1804-Nov./Dec. 1807   APS II, Reel 45

THE VISITOR. v.1-2; Feb. 11, 1809-Aug. 18, 1810. Richmond [Lynch & Southgate]

2 v. in 1.
Biweekly, Feb. 11, 1809-Jan. 27, 1810; weekly, Feb. 10-Aug. 18, 1810.
Vol. 2, no. 20, p. 83-84 wanting.

This literary miscellany published news summaries, both foreign and domestic, local marriage and death notices, and a variety of literary material, which included poetry and tales, biography, short essays, fragments, and anecdotes. Occasional musical pieces appeared also.

v1, no.1-24   1809   APS II, Reel 46

v1, no.25-v2   Jan. 13-Aug. 18, 1810   Reel 246

WALDIE'S LIBRARY. *SEE* Waldie's Select Circulating Library.

WALDIE'S LITERARY OMNIBUS. *SEE* Brown's Literary Omnibus.

WALDIE'S SELECT CIRCULATING LIBRARY. v.1-[17]; Oct. 1, 1832-Apr. 1842. Philadelphia, A. Waldie [etc.] 1833-42.

17 v. weekly.

Caption title.
Title-pages read: The Select circulating library. Containing the best popular literature, including memoirs, biography, novels, tales, travels, voyages, &c. In v.15-[17] caption title reads: Waldie's library. Title-page of v.[17] wanting; covers have title: Waldie's select circulating library, and journal of polite literature.

A notice in v.1, no.16, states that "the first thirteen numbers are entirely exhausted, but a new series, no.1, was commenced with Sarrans' Memoirs." The new series, covering dates Jan. 15, 1833-Jan. 7, 1834, is in 2 vols. identical with the issues of the same dates of the original series. New ser., v.1, no.1-26 corresponds to the original series, v.1, no.14-v.2, no.13; new ser., v.2, no.1-26 to v.2, no.14-39. Publication was suspended in 1840, after six numbers had been issued. It was resumed in 1841. The numbers are disregarded in the volume numbering, pt. 2 of 1839 forming v.14; pt. 1 of 1841, v.15. John Jay Smith, editor.

Founded by Adam Waldie in 1832, the *Library* was designed as an inexpensive means of disseminating new literature to its subscribers. It included memoirs, biography, novels, tales, travels, and voyages issued in installments.

v1-5   Oct. 1, 1832-June 30, 1835   APS II, Reel 1354
v6-10   July 7, 1835-Dec. 26, 1837   Reel 1355
v11-15   Jan. 2, 1838-June 1841   Reel 1356
v16-17   July 1841-Apr. 1842   Reel 1357

Several pages are torn, stained, or tightly bound with faded print. Pagination is irregular. Vol. 2: Issues 4 and 9-11 are not available for photographing. Vol. 3: title page is missing. Vol. 17: title page and table of contents are missing.

Microfilm edition was prepared from DLC, MiD, MnU, N, PPi, TNJ, and TxHR copies.

WALDIE'S SELECT CIRCULATING LIBRARY, AND JOURNAL OF POLITE LITERATURE. *SEE* Waldie's Select Circulating Library.

WALHALLA. Bd. 1-4; Juli 1845-Juni 1847. Philadelphia.

4 v. monthly.

Band 4 also called Bd. 2. Some issues misnumbered.

Published in Philadelphia, this German-language magazine attempted to provide both information and amusement. It consisted mainly of prose and poetry, with some serialized fiction and a section of miscellany which included fables and myths, biographical sketches, and items on places of interest. A few illustrations embellished the text.

v1-4   July 1845-June 1847   APS II, Reel 1408

Several pages are stained and have print faded. Pagination is irregular. Vols. 1 and 3 have torn or missing pages. Vols. 1-4 lack title pages and indexes. Vol. 4: issue no. 1 is missing.

Microfilm edition was prepared from OU copy.

THE WASHINGTON QUARTERLY MAGAZINE OF ARTS, SCIENCE AND LITERATURE. With illustrative engravings. Robert Little, editor. v.1, no.1-2; July 1823-Apr. 1824. Washington, P. Thompson, 1823.

156 p.

Edited by Robert Little, this quarterly was mainly concerned with trade and manufacturing. It offered articles relating to trade, agriculture, and canals, and published specifications of patents of recent inventions and improvements of machinery and methods. Many articles were accompanied by diagrams and drawings. Contents also included selections from British scientific publications, meteorological reports, and poetry.

v1, no.1-2   July 1823-Apr. 1824   APS II, Reel 246

WASHINGTON THEOLOGICAL REPERTORY. *SEE* Theological Repertory, and Churchman's Guide.

THE WASP. v.1, no.1-12; July 7, 1802-Jan. 26, 1803. Hudson [N.Y., H. Croswell]

1 v. irregular.

Edited by Robert Rusticoat, pseud.

Edited by "Robert Rusticoat, Esq.," the *Wasp* was devoted to political satire. It supported the Republican viewpoint, and most of its material was intended to oppose the statements made in Charles Holt's *Bee,* another local paper, which was Democratic in its political leanings.

v1, no.1-12   July 7, 1802-Jan. 26, 1803   APS II, Reel 46

THE WATCHMAN. [no. 1; 1819, New Haven, Conn.]

24 p.

Only one number of the *Watchman* was published. Its purpose was to defend the Episcopal Church from attack by other magazines, particularly the *Christian Spectator,* an orthodox journal of New England theology. In addition to letters concerning the *Christian Spectator,* its contents consisted of essays, religious news, and reviews of magazines.

no.1   1819   APS II, Reel 246

SEE ALSO: Watchman-Examiner.

WATCHMAN AND REFLECTOR. *SEE* Watchman-Examiner.

WATCHMAN-EXAMINER, a national Baptist paper. v.1-Boston, True and Weston, 1819- .

v. illus. (incl. ports.) weekly.

"Continuing the Watchman, established 1819, the Examiner, established 1823, the Morning star, established 1826, also the National Baptist, the Christian inquirer and the Christian secretary." Title varies: June 1819-May 1848, The Christian watchman.–May 18-Oct. 19, 1848, Christian reflector and Christian watchman.–Oct. 26, 1848-Dec. 1850, Christian watchman and Christian reflector.–Jan. 1851-Dec. 18, 1866, The Christian watchman and reflector.–Jan. 1867?-Dec. 1875, The Watchman and reflector.–Jan. 1876-Aug. 1913, The Watchman ...–Sept. 1913- The Watch-

man-examiner. Absorbed the Reflector in 1848, the Morning star in Oct. 1911, the Examiner in Sept. 1913, the Baptist commonwealth in July 1917.

On film: v.1-42, 1819-1861; v.75-88, 1894-1906. Scattered issues missing.

Founded in 1819 as the *Christian Watchman,* this Baptist magazine later became the *Watchman-Examiner,* the greatest of the Baptist journals, representing a union of 23 papers. This weekly resembled a newspaper and its object was to present important religious news of every kind, as well as some non-religious material. Religious news included reports of Bible, missionary, and tract societies, both in the U.S. and abroad; accounts of revivals; and news on missions, on various churches, and on ordinations. Non-religious material included general news, poetry, book reviews, biography, and articles on history, education, and agriculture.

Christian Watchman
v1-nsv2, no.3   May 1819-Dec. 1820   APS II, Reel 246
nsv2, no.4-v5, no.20   Jan. 1821-Apr. 1824   Reel 247
v5, no.21-v7   May 1824-Dec. 1826   Reel 248

v8-11   Dec. 8, 1826-Dec. 31, 1830   Reel 1491
v12-15   Jan. 7, 1831-Dec. 26, 1834   Reel 1492
v16-19   Jan. 2, 1835-Dec. 28, 1838   Reel 1493
v20-23   Jan. 5, 1839-Dec. 30, 1842   Reel 1494
v24-27   Jan. 6, 1843-Dec. 25, 1846   Reel 1495
v28-29, no.19   Jan. 1, 1847-May 11, 1848   Reel 1496

Christian Reflector and Christian Watchman
v29, no.20-no.42   May 18-Oct. 19, 1848   Reel 1496

Christian Watchman and Christian Reflector
v29, no.43-v31   Oct. 26, 1848-Dec. 26, 1850   Reel 1496

Christian Watchman and Reflector
v32-35   Jan. 2, 1851-Dec. 28, 1854   Reel 1497

v36-39   Jan. 4, 1855-Dec. 30, 1858   Reel 1874
v40-42   Jan. 6, 1859-Dec. 26, 1861   Reel 1875

Watchman
v75   Sept. 20-Dec. 27, 1894   Reel 1875
v76   Jan. 3-Dec. 19, 1895   Reel 1876
v77-78   Jan. 2, 1896-Nov. 11, 1897   Reel 1877
v79-81   Sept. 29, 1898-Dec. 27, 1900   Reel 1878
v82-83   Jan. 3-Dec. 26, 1901   Reel 1879
v84   Jan. 2-Dec. 25, 1902   Reel 1880
v85   Jan. 1-Dec. 31, 1903   Reel 1881
v86   Jan. 7-Dec. 29, 1904   Reel 1882
v87-88   Jan. 5, 1905-Dec. 20, 1906   Reel 1883

Vols. 10 and 32-35 lack indexes. Several pages are creased, stained, torn, and tightly-bound with some loss of text. Some pages are misnumbered. Vol. 24: no. 1 is misdated. Vol. 32: no. 38 is missing; not available for photographing. Vols. for 1862-1893 are missing; not available for photographing.

Microfilm edition was prepared from C, ICU, MB, NHC, NN, NWA and RPB copies.

SEE ALSO: Christian Reflector *and* Christian Secretary.

WATER-CURE JOURNAL. *SEE* Health.

THE WEEKLY INSPECTOR. v.1-2; Aug. 30, 1806-Aug. 22, 1807. New York, printed by Hopkins and Seymour.

2 v.

Edited by T.G. Fessenden.

This little eight-page magazine was devoted principally to politics and promoted the Federalist viewpoint. It published editorials, abstracts of foreign and domestic news, miscellaneous sketches of a literary and scientific nature, brief book reviews, and some poetry.

v1-2   Aug. 30, 1806-Aug. 22, 1807   APS II, Reel 1408

Some pages are stained and tightly bound. Vols. 1-2 lack indexes. Vol. 1: Title page is misdated. Pages 1-2 are torn.

Microfilm edition was prepared from DLC, MnU and NjP copies.

THE WEEKLY MAGAZINE OF ORIGINAL ESSAYS, FUGITIVE PIECES, AND INTERESTING INTELLIGENCE. v.1-4 (no.1-47); Feb. 3, 1798-June 1, 1799. Philadelphia, J. Watters.

4 v.

Publication suspended from Sept. 1798 to Jan. 1799.

James Watters, editor, Feb.-Aug., 1798.
Vols. 1-2 include appendix of state papers.
Film incomplete: v. 4, no. 47 wanting.

A weekly which emphasized fiction, included serial articles on art, and published a number of contributions by Charles Brockden Brown. It was suspended in August 1798, following the death of the editor in the yellow fever epidemic.

v1-2   Feb. 3-July 28, 1798   APS I, Reel 31
v3-4   Aug. 4, 1798-May 25, 1799   Reel 32

Microfilm is in reverse order.

Microfilm edition was prepared from NHi and MWA copies.

WEEKLY MESSENGER. SEE Reformed Church Messenger.

WEEKLY MESSENGER OF THE GERMAN REFORMED CHURCH. SEE Reformed Church Messenger.

WEEKLY MESSENGER OF THE REFORMED CHURCH. SEE Reformed Church Messenger.

WEEKLY MIRROR. SEE New Mirror and New York Mirror: A Weekly Gazette of Literature and the Fine Arts.

WEEKLY MONITOR (Philadelphia). SEE Evening Fireside.

THE WEEKLY MONITOR, entertaining and instructive, designed to be interesting to all, but particularly intended as a guide to youth in the way of morality and religion. v.1, no.1-13; June 4-Sept. 20, 1817. Boston, Farnham and Badger.

214 p.

Although its contents included jokes and anecdotes, the *Weekly Monitor* was mainly concerned with promoting morality among youth. To achieve this it offered religious and moral departments,

many short moral items, and a series called "The Friend to Youth." Some poetry appeared and deaths and marriages were listed.

v1, no.1-3   June 4-Sept. 20, 1817   APS II, Reel 248

THE WEEKLY MUSEUM. v.1, no.1-21; Jan. 8-May 28, 1797. Baltimore, J. Smith and C. Jackson.

2 no.

On film: nos. 5-6 only.

A Sunday miscellany published foreign and local news, reports on legislatures, and articles on agriculture and government, along with poetry and humorous anecdotes.

v1, no.5-6   Feb. 5-12, 1797   APS I, Reel 33

Microfilm edition was prepared from MH copy.

SEE ALSO: Ladies' Weekly Museum.

THE WEEKLY RECORDER; a newspaper conveying important intelligence and other useful matter under the three general heads of theology, literature, and national affairs. v.1-7, no. 52; July 5, 1814-Oct. 6, 1821. Chillicothe, O., J. Andrews, 1814-

7 v.

The *Weekly Recorder* was concerned primarily with theology, literature, and national affairs. Theological material included a variety of religious news, Bible studies, essays on doctrine, and biographies; and attention was also given to literary news, articles on education and history, news of recent inventions, and geographical sketches. The area of national affairs was given comprehensive coverage, and foreign and naval news were also included. There was occasional religious, moral, and humorous poetry.

v1   July 5, 1814-June 1815   APS II, Reel 248
v2-4   July 1815-July 1818   Reel 249
v5-7   Aug. 1818-Oct. 6, 1821   Reel 250

WEEKLY REGISTER. SEE Niles' National Register.

WEEKLY REVIEW. SEE Independent.

THE WEEKLY VISITANT; moral, poetical, humorous, &c., v.1, no.1-52; Jan. 1-Dec. 27, 1806. Salem [Mass.] H. Pool.

416 p.

The *Weekly Visitant* was a literary miscellany which published moral and scientific essays, tales, biographical sketches, news items, and a poetry department. Politics were excluded.

v1, no.1-52   Jan. 1-Dec. 27, 1806   APS II, Reel 46

THE WEEKLY VISITOR. v1-3, no.3; May 12, 1810-May 25, 1811. New York, A.C. Morton.

3 v.

Copy filmed incomplete: v.1, p. 1-2 wanting.

This small weekly magazine was a literary miscellany; its pages included serialized tales, fragments, anecdotes, local news, including marriages and death notices, moral essays, and many short miscellaneous items. The last two pages were usually devoted to sentimental poetry. Some satire on fashion appeared and an editorial column, "The Gleaner," was a regular feature.

v1-3, no.3   May 12, 1810-May 25, 1811   APS II, Reel 251

WEEKLY VISITOR AND LADIES' MUSEUM. v.1-5, Nov. 1817-Apr.? 1820; n.s.v.1-7, May 1820?-Oct. 18, 1823. New York, A.Ming.

6 v.

Formed by the union of Weekly visitor; or Ladies miscellany, and Ladies weekly museum.

On film: v.1-4, Nov. 1817-Oct. 30, 1819; n.s.v.5-6, May 1822-Apr. 1823. Scattered pages missing.

A women's literary magazine published by Alexander Ming with the purpose "To Wake the Soul by Tender Strokes of Art; To Raise the Genius, and to Mend the Heart." Persian tales, Old English tales, and Russian literature are a sampling of the short story literature. Poems, anecdotes, fashion, and biographies of women and famous composers such as Haydn and Mozart are included. Articles appear on female education, love and marriage, jealousy, seduction, morals, customs, children, and respect due to husbands.

v1-4   Nov. 1, 1817-Oct. 30, 1819   APS II, Reel 1884
nsv5-6   May 4, 1822-Apr. 19, 1823   Reel 1884

Microfilm edition was prepared from the DLC and IU copies.

WEEKLY VISITOR; OR LADIES MISCELLANY. SEE Lady's Miscellany and Weekly Visitor and Ladies' Museum.

WELCOME GUEST. SEE Ballou's Pictorial Drawing-Room Companion.

WELLMAN'S LITERARY MISCELLANY. SEE Wellman's Miscellany.

WELLMAN'S MISCELLANY. v.1-10, July 1849-Aug. 1854; ser. 2, v.1-7, Jan. 1870-Feb. 1873. Detroit [and] Adrian, Mich.

17 v.

1849-51 as Wellman's literary miscellany; Mar. 1851-Feb. 1853 Monthly literary miscellany; Mar. 1853-Aug. 1854 Western literary cabinet. Suspended Sept. 1854-Dec. 1869.

Film incomplete: issues for July-Aug. 1854, Apr.-June 1870, and Oct.-Dec. 1872 were not available for photographing.

The western literary magazines were begun for the most part to bring gracious living into the harsh environment, and *Wellman's Miscellany* was one of the first of these to be successful. Its stated purpose was "to furnish in a cheap form a literature calculated to develop the mind, and advance it in knowledge and virtue." Because there was little or no advertising, the magazine depended on the sale of subscriptions, and in almost every issue, the publishers pleaded for their money from subscribers who had neglected to pay.

Wellman's Literary Miscellany
v1-4, no.2   July 1849-Feb. 1851   APS II, Reel 779

Monthly Literary Miscellany
v4, no.3-v8, no.2   Mar. 1851-Feb. 1853   Reel 779

Western Literary Miscellany
v8, no.3-v9, no.1   Mar.-July 1853   Reel 779

Western Literary Cabinet
v9, no.2-v10   Aug. 1853-June 1854   Reel 779

Wellman's Miscellany
s2v1-7   Jan. 1870-Feb. 1873   Reel 780

Most volumes have table of contents and/or title page lacking. Several volumes have tightly bound pages. Pagination is irregular. Series 2, Vol. 5: No issues published for May and June 1872.

Microfilm edition was prepared from MH, MiU and MnU copies.

THE WESLEYAN REPOSITORY. v.1-3; Apr. 12, 1821-Apr. 1824. Philadelphia, W.S. Stockton, 1821/2-24.

3 v.

Vol. 1 (published biweekly in Trenton, N.J.) has title: The Wesleyan repository, and religious intelligencer; v.2 wanting in L.C. set; v.3 (published monthly in Philadelphia) has title: The Wesleyan repository.

Edited by W.S. Stockton.

This Methodist magazine offered much on the Methodist Church—articles on the General Conference and on church government, and a series on the history of the church. A summary of religious news, including news of missions, book reviews, biographical notices, and poetry appeared regularly.

v1-3   Apr. 12, 1821-Apr. 1824   APS II, Reel 251

Vol. 1: title page is missing.

THE WESTERN ACADEMICIAN AND JOURNAL OF EDUCATION AND SCIENCE. Ed. by J.W. Picket. v.1; Mar. 1837-Feb. 1838. Cincinnati, J.R. Allbach, 1837-38.

iv, 704 p. monthly.

Includes the Proceedings and the Constitution of the Western literary institute and college of professional teachers, 7th annual meeting, p. 481-700.

Published by the Western Literary Institute and edited by John W. Pickett, a pioneer in educational journalism, this educational magazine proposed to "support broad, radical, and liberal education" and to "embrace departments of general literature and physical sciences." Among its contributors were William H. McGuffey, Alexander Kinmont, and other western educational leaders. Contents included meteorological observations, literary notices, essays and articles on history, math, classical literature, geology, electricity, language, and natural science, and most importantly, on education—books, teaching, schools, academies and colleges, and the philosophy and history of education. The last few volumes contained the proceedings of the College of Professional Teachers, and many reports and addresses.

v1, nos.1-12   Mar. 1837-Feb. 1838   APS II, Reel 486

Microfilm edition was prepared from the CtY copy.

WESTERN ARMINIAN AND CHRISTIAN INSTRUCTOR. *SEE* Messenger (Methodist Episcopal Church Conference. Holston.)

WESTERN CHRISTIAN ADVOCATE. v.1- May 2, 1834- Cincinnati, Walden & Stowe, Western Methodist Book Concern [etc.]

v. weekly.
Western edition of the Christian Advocate. cf. Union List of serials.

On film: v.1-9, 35-36 (Scattered issues only); v.41, 47-50 (Scattered issues missing); 1834-43, 1868-69, 1874, 1880-83.

This Methodist weekly established in 1834 in Cincinnati published articles on literature, agriculture and the home, as well as poetry, Bible lessons, religious news items and articles on varied religious topics.

v1-3	May 2, 1834-Apr. 21, 1837	APS II, Reel 1789
v4-6	Apr. 28, 1837-Apr. 17, 1840	Reel 1790
v7-35	Apr. 24, 1840-Dec. 9, 1868	Reel 1791
v36-41	Feb. 3, 1869-Dec. 30, 1874	Reel 1792
v47	Jan. 14-Dec. 29, 1880	Reel 1793
v48	Jan. 5-Dec. 28, 1881	Reel 1794
v49	Jan. 4-Dec. 27, 1882	Reel 1795
v50	Jan. 3-Dec. 26, 1883	Reel 1796

Microfilm edition was prepared from the DLC, IEG, IU, TxDaM, and WHi copies.

THE WESTERN CHRISTIAN MONITOR. v.1 (no. 1-12); Jan.-Dec., 1816- Chillicothe [O.], Fredonian Press [1816]-

1 v. monthly.

Editor: Jan. 1816- William Beauchamp.

This Methodist periodical provided sermons, accounts of religious experiences, narratives on the lives and deaths of religious persons, and a variety of moral and religious pieces, including poetry, and extracts from the best writers on theology.

v1, no.1-12	Jan.-Dec. 1816	APS II, Reel 252

Some pages have faded print and print show-through.

THE WESTERN EXAMINER, a journal embodying a full and impartial enquiry into the truth or falsity of the Christian religion; whether philosophically or historically viewed. v.1-2, no.46; 1834-Dec. 10, 1835. St. Louis [J. Bobb, 1834]-36.

2 v. weekly.

"Edited by an association."

Although this weekly claimed to be a "full and impartial enquiry into the truth or falsity of the Christian religion," in general its articles and essays were openly opposed to Christianity, and much of the material was satirical. Contents also included poetry, anecdotes, travel sketches, biography, and some articles on history.

v1-2	Nov. 1833-Dec. 1835	APS II, Reel 487

Several pages are stained with some print missing. Microfilm edition includes specimen number, dated November 19, 1833.

Microfilm edition was prepared from DLC, IU, and NN copies.

WESTERN FARMER AND GARDENER. v.1-3, no.12; Feb. 1, 1845-Jan. 1, 1848. Indianapolis, J.D. Defrees.

3 v.
Semimonthly, v.1-2; monthly, v.3.

Title varies: 1845, The Indiana farmer; Jan. 1, 1846, absorbed Western farmer and gardener and adopted its title.

Edited by Henry Ward Beecher.
Published by S.V.B. Noel, 1845-46.

Edited by Henry Ward Beecher, this journal's chief object was the improvement of farming. It provided articles on farming methods, cultivation of crops, raising of livestock, gardening and care of fruit trees, and solutions to such problems as blights and insect pests, curing meat, and preserving food in winter. In addition, it published information on prices and the weather, reviews of other magazines, and proceedings of the legislature.

Indiana Farmer and Gardener

v1	Feb.-Dec. 1845	APS II, Reel 1408

Western Farmer and Gardener

v2-3	Jan. 1846-Jan. 1848	Reel 1408

Many pages are stained, tightly bound, or have print faded with some loss of text. Best copy available for photographing. Vol. 1: pgs. 350-51 are missing; not available for photographing. Vol. 3: Pgs. 89, 93 and 98 are misnumbered. Issue 11 is missing.

Microfilm edition was prepared from In copy.

THE WESTERN FARMER AND GARDENER; devoted to agriculture, horticulture, and rural economy. v.1-5; Sept. 1839-July 1845. Cincinnati, E.J. Hooper.

5 v. illus., plates. monthly.

Vol. 1 has title: The Western farmer, devoted to agriculture, horticulture, and rural economy.
Editors: 1839-40, E.J. Hooper.—1840-41, Thomas Affleck.

An attractive and useful magazine which provided much information for farmers on a wide variety of subjects—discussions of agricultural and horticultural methods, agricultural products, animals and their diseases, as well as recipes, cures for illness, and household hints for farmers' wives. In addition, it published Miami Valley Agricultural Society Reports, answered letters, reported on fairs, and included biography, moral essays, and short pieces on history. Full-page illustrations embellished the text.

Western Farmer, devoted to Agriculture, Horticulture, and Rural Economy

v1	Sept. 1839-Aug.1840	APS II, Reel 698

Western Farmer and Gardener

v2-5	Oct. 1840-July 1845	Reel 698

Vol. 1: Index is lacking.

Microfilm edition was prepared from DLC and ICU copies.

WESTERN FARMER, AND RECORD OF GENERAL INTELLIGENCE (Detroit). *SEE* Michigan Farmer.

WESTERN FARMER, DEVOTED TO AGRICULTURE, HORTICULTURE, AND RURAL ECONOMY. *SEE* Western Farmer and Gardener; Devoted to Agriculture, Horticulture and Rural Economy (Cincinnati).

WESTERN GEM AND CABINET OF LITERATURE, SCIENCE AND NEWS. *SEE* Literary Cabinet and Western Olive Branch.

THE WESTERN GLEANER; or, Repository for arts, sciences, and literature. v.1-2, no.4; Dec. 1813-Sept. 1814. Pittsburgh, Cramer, Spear and Eichbaum.

2 v. monthly.

This literary and scientific miscellany was "devoted to the advancement of science." It recorded discoveries in zoology, botany, mineralogy and in many areas of applied science, and included articles on coal and salt and on bleaching and dyeing processes. In the literary area it published book reviews, poetry, biography, and translations from French, German, Italian and Spanish sources.

v1-2, no.4   Dec. 1813-Sept. 1814   APS II, Reel 252

* THE WESTERN JOURNAL AND CIVILIAN; devoted to agriculture, manufactures, mechanic arts, internal improvement, commerce, public policy, and polite literature. v.1-15, no.5; Jan. 1848-Apr. 1856. St. Louis, Charles & Hammond, Printers.

15 v. plates, ports., maps. monthly.

Vols. 10-13 called also "new ser., v.4-7".
Title varies: 1848-Sept. 1851, The Western journal of agriculture, manufactures, mechanic arts, internal improvement, commerce, and general literature. M. Tarver & T.F. Risk, editors and proprietors. Oct. 1851-Mar. 1856, The Western journal and civilian, devoted to agriculture manufactures, mechanic arts, internal improvement, commerce, public policy, and polite literature ... M. Tarver & H. Cobb, editors & proprietors.

An informative though amateurish miscellany of eight years' duration which was begun in St. Louis by T.F. Risk. After Risk retired in August. 1851, his partner, Micajah Tarver, continued the magazine with the help of H. Cobb, who introduced some literary features, using translations especially, in order to vary the monotony of informative material. Chateaubriand's *Atala* was printed serially. The file is valuable for articles on early railroad projects and for material on the development of the upper Mississippi Valley. A few steel plates and woodcuts and several lithographs serve for illustration.

Western Journal of Agriculture, Manufactures, Mechanic Arts, Internal Improvement, Commerce, and General Literature
v1-6   Jan. 1848-Sept. 1851   APS II, Reel 699

Western Journal and Civilian
v7   Oct. 1851-Mar 1852   Reel 699
v8-15   Apr. 1852-Apr. 1856   Reel 700

Microfilm edition was prepared from CSmH, CtY, DLC and ICU copies.

WESTERN JOURNAL OF AGRICULTURE, MANUFACTURES, MECHANIC ARTS, INTERNAL IMPROVEMENT, COMMERCE AND GENERAL LITERATURE. *SEE* Western Journal and Civilian.

THE WESTERN JOURNAL OF THE MEDICAL AND PHYSICAL SCIENCES. v.1-12 (no.1-45); Apr. 1827-July 1838. Cincinnati.

12 v.
Frequency varies.

Vols. 7-12 called also 2d hexade, v.1-6 (no.25-45)
Title varies: v.1-2, no.1, The Western medical and physical journal. Issues numbered v.2, no.1 published for both titles.
Vols. for Apr.-June 1837-Apr.-June 1838 published by the Medical Faculty of the Cincinnati College.

Founded and edited by D.Drake.
United with the Louisville journal of medicine and surgery to form the Western journal of medicine and surgery. Cf. Union list of serials. A separately paged supplement accompanies v.9.

This quarterly medical periodical, edited by Daniel Drake, published papers on diseases and injuries, case studies, and reports on the cholera epidemic. It also included articles on geology, botany, and other scientific topics, news concerning the Medical College of Ohio, medical societies, and hospitals, and a meteorological register.

Western Medical and Physical Journal
v1-2, no.1   Apr. 1827-May 1828   APS II, Reel 578

Western Journal of the Medical and Physical Sciences
v2, no.2-v3   May 1828-Mar. 1830   Reel 578
v4-8   Apr. 1830-Mar. 1835   Reel 579
v9-12   Apr. 1835-July 1838   Reel 580

Several pages are stained, faded, and tightly bound with some loss of text. Pagination is irregular. Vol. 2: Issues 1-2 are dated May.

Microfilm edition was prepared from the InU, LNT-M, MiU, and NN copies.
SEE ALSO: Western Journal of Medicine and Surgery.

THE WESTERN JOURNAL OF MEDICINE AND SURGERY. v.1-32; 1840-1855. Louisville, Prentice & Weissinger.

32 v. monthly.

Formed by the union of the Western journal of the medical and physical sciences and the Louisville journal of medicine and surgery. Editors: L.P. Yandell.–L.P. Yandell, T.S. Bell. Continued as the Louisville review. Vols. 29-32 lack indexes.

A Louisville medical journal which, with predecessors and successors, covered a span of 35 years and contained original papers on cases and treatments, notices and reviews of recent publications, selected material from American and foreign journals, and the latest medical news.

v1-8   Jan. 1840-Dec. 1843   APS II, Reel 701
v9-15   Jan. 1844-June 1847   Reel 702
v16-22   July 1847-Dec. 1850   Reel 703
v23-28   Jan. 1851-Dec. 1853   Reel 704
v29-32   Jan. 1854-Dec. 1855   Reel 705

Vols. 29-32: Indexes are lacking.

Microfilm edition was prepared from DNLM, MiU, NNNAM and PPC copies.

SEE ALSO: Western Journal of the Medical and Physical Sciences.

THE WESTERN LADIES' CASKET. v.1, no.1-5; Jan.-Feb. 1, 1824. [Connersville, Ind.]

This short-lived ladies' miscellany published only five numbers. Among the varied contents of the last number were an article on the principles of dyeing and a tale entitled "The Rose in January."

v1, no.5   Feb. 1, 1824   APS II, Reel 252

Microfilm edition includes no.5 only.

* **THE WESTERN LAW JOURNAL.** v.1-10, Oct. 1843-Oct. 1853. Cincinnati, Desilver and Burr, 1843-53.

10 v. monthly.

Edited by T. Walker (with C.D. Coffin, Aug. 1846-Sept. 1848; C. Gilman, Oct. 1847-Sept. 1848; M.E. Curwen, Oct. 1850-Sept. 1853); v.6-10 also called new ser. v.1-5.

This monthly legal periodical, edited by Judge Timothy Walker, a professor of law in Cincinnati College, was to be devoted to law, and its object was to gather from and diffuse among the lawyers of the "West" whatever was most noteworthy in their profession. Contents included notes on recent decisions, reports of recent and interesting cases, notices of new law books, biographical sketches of lawyers, letters, some poetry and anecdotes, and items on laws, law schools, and miscellaneous law-related information.

v1-3	Oct. 1843-Sept. 1846	APS II, Reel 487
v4-7	Oct. 1846-Sept. 1850	Reel 488
v8-10	Oct. 1850-Sept. 1853	Reel 489

Microfilm edition ends with the Sept. 1853 issue. Several pages are stained with some print missing.

Microfilm edition was prepared from DLC copy.

WESTERN LITERARY CABINET. *SEE* Wellman's Miscellany.

WESTERN LITERARY CASKET. *SEE* Western Literary Magazine.

* **THE WESTERN LITERARY JOURNAL, AND MONTHLY REVIEW.** Edited by William D. Gallagher. v.1 (no.1-6); June-Nov. 1836. Cincinnati, Smith and Day.

iv, 440 p.

Merged into Western monthly magazine.

Edited by William D. Gallagher, this literary magazine offered the usual fare—poetry and tales, biographical sketches, essays, literary notices, and reviews.

| v1, nos.1-6 | June-Nov. 1836 | APS II, Reel 527 |

Microfilm edition was prepared from the DLC copy.

SEE ALSO: Western Monthly Magazine, and Literary Journal

WESTERN LITERARY JOURNAL AND MONTHLY REVIEW. E.Z.C. Judson and L.A. Hine, editors. v.1, no.1-6; Nov. 1844-Apr. 1845. Cincinnati, Robinson & Jones.

iv, 372 p.

Issued simultaneously in Nashville, Tenn. as the Southwestern literary journal and monthly review.

Edited by Lucius A. Hine, this literary periodical published a good deal of poetry and fiction, including sentimental tales, and reviews of recent books and periodicals. Essays on education and other topics, coverage of local events and "sketches of the Florida war" were also included. Although a promising journal, financial difficulties prevented it from surviving past six issues.

| v1, nos.1-6 | Nov. 1844-Apr. 1845 | APS II, Reel 527 |

Microfilm edition was prepared from the IU copy.

WESTERN LITERARY MAGAZINE. v.1-4, no.7; June 1840-June 1844. Pittsburgh, Pa., 1840-1844.

4 v.

Vols. 1-2, 1840-May 1842 as Literary messenger; Vol. 3, Nos. 1-8, July 1842-April 1843 Literary casket; vol. 3, nos. 9-12, May-Aug. 1843 Western literary casket. None published June 1842, Mar.-Apr. 1844.

Instruction and entertainment were the goals of this monthly. It published unsigned original poetry and short fiction in the early issues; later it included longer fiction and some material selected from other publications.

Literary Messenger
| v1-2 | June 1840-May 1842 | APS II, Reel 1260 |

Literary Casket
| v3, nos.1-8 | July 1842-Apr. 1843 | Reel 1260 |

Western Literary Casket
| v3, nos. 9-12 | May-Aug. 1843 | Reel 1260 |

Western Literary Magazine
| v4, no.1-7 | Sept. 1843-Feb. 1844 | Reel 1260 |

Several pages are stained or torn. Some issues have faded or missing print. Vol. 1: pgs. 73-74 are missing. Vol. 4: issue no. 1 lacks table of contents; issue nos. 6-7 are missing.

Microfilm edition was prepared from PPi copy.

WESTERN LITERARY MISCELLANY. *SEE* Wellman's Miscellany.

WESTERN LUMINARY. v.1-11; July 14, 1824-Oct. 21, 1835. Lexington, Ky., 1824-1835.

11 v.

United with Cincinnati journal to form Cincinnati journal and Western luminary, later Cincinnati journal.

An interdenominational journal founded by Thomas T. Skillman in 1824 and published by him for more than ten years before being sold to Eli Taylor of Cincinnati.

v1-4	July 14, 1824-June 25, 1828	APS II, Reel 1311
v5-8	July 2, 1828-June 27, 1832	Reel 1312
v9-11	Jan. 9, 1833-Dec. 31, 1834	Reel 1313

Best copy available for photographing. Several volumes have stained, creased, or torn pages. Some issues have irregular pagination. Vols. 1-11: Indexes, tables of contents, and title pages are missing. Vol. 6: Issues, 7, 14, 16, 25, 27, 34, 47, and 52 are missing; not available for photographing. Dec. 2, 1829, issue is misdated. Vol. 8: Issues 2-3, 22, 41, 43-44, 46, and 48-49 are missing; not available for photographing. Jan. 4, 1832, issue is misdated. Vol. 9: Issues 1-26 and 49-50 are missing; not available for photographing. Vol. 10: Issues 17, 29, 34-35, 38, 40, 43, and 47 are missing; not available for photographing. Vol. 11: Issue 26 to end of volume is lacking; not available for photographing. Microfilm edition ends with issue 25, Dec. 31, 1834.

Microfilm edition was prepared from MH, NcMHi, and WHi copies.

WESTERN MAGAZINE AND REVIEW. *SEE* Western Monthly Review.

TITLE INDEX

WESTERN MEDICAL AND PHYSICAL JOURNAL. *SEE* Western Journal of the Medical and Physical Sciences.

THE WESTERN MESSENGER; devoted to religion, life, and literature. v.1-8; June 1835-Apr. 1841. Cincinnati, T.H. Shreve, 1835-41.

8 v. in 5. monthly (irregular)

Title varies slightly.
Published in Louisville by the Western Unitarian association [etc.] Apr. 1836-Apr. 1839.
Publication suspended from Nov. 1839-Apr. 1840.
Nov. 1837-Oct. 1839, J.F. Clarke, editor; May-Oct. 1839, W.H. Channing and J.H. Perkins, assistant editors.

The *Western Messenger* was considered one of the most important magazines published in the West during the years when "West" meant the region between the Appalachians and the Mississippi. Though usually regarded as a literary periodical because of its poetry and criticism, it was begun primarily as the organ of the Unitarian religion. The editors were chiefly clergymen, and sermons and doctrinal essays were prominent. But after the first two years, it became less and less sectarian.

As a regional magazine, the *Messenger* felt the obligation to interpret the Western country; it published much on religion, literature, and culture of the West, sketches of Western preachers, and a series on "Western poetry." But the group who founded it derived their chief inspiration from New England. The Unitarian sermons were by such famous New England preachers as N.L. Frothingham, George W. Hosmer, and Francis Parkman; some of the poetry and criticism was by New England transcendentalists, such as Emerson, Margaret Fuller, and Jones Very, and the editors were all transplanted New Englanders.

v1	June 1835-July 1836	APS II, Reel 489
v2-8	Aug. 1836-Apr. 1841	Reel 490

Several pages have faded print with some loss of text. Pagination is irregular. Vols. 6-7 are bound and photographed together; title page and index are missing.

Microfilm edition was prepared from the CtY copy.

WESTERN MINERVA; or, American annals of knowledge and literature. v.1, no.1; Jan. 1820. Lexington, Ky., Pub. for the editors by T. Smith, 1821.

88 p.

"Projected as a quarterly magazine, but only the first number was printed, and this was suppressed before there was any distribution."

Edited by C.S. Rafinesque.

This literary and scientific journal did not survive past its first number. In the sole issue published can be found scientific news, poetry, and articles on literature, agriculture, manufacturing, medicine, ethics, and on a wide variety of science fields, including archaeology and mineralogy. There is also much statistical material.

v1, no.1   Jan. 1820   APS II, Reel 252

THE WESTERN MISCELLANY. Ed. by B.F. Ells. v.1; July 1848-June 1849. Dayton, O., B.F. Ells, 1848-49.

384 p. illus., ports. monthly.

Edited and published by B.F. Ells, this family magazine published biographies, recipes, anecdotes, and statistics along with articles on Shakerism, medicine, and travels.

v1   July 1848-June 1849   APS II, Reel 1260

Pages 160 and 374 have faded print.

Microfilm edition was prepared from OOxM copy.

THE WESTERN MISSIONARY MAGAZINE, and repository of religious intelligence. v.1-2; Feb. 1803-Apr. 1805. Washington, Pa., J. Colerick.

2 v. Monthly.

Issued by the Synod of Pittsburgh, Presbyterian Church in the U.S.A.

This religious monthly, published under the patronage of the Synod of Pittsburgh, contained original and selected pieces on a variety of religious subjects, biographical sketches, church history, missionary news and news of revivals, sermons and studies on prophecy and on the Scriptures, and a few hymns and poems.

v1-2   Feb. 1803-Apr. 1805   APS II, Reel 46

WESTERN MONTHLY MAGAZINE. *SEE* Illinois Monthly Magazine; Western Literary Journal and Monthly Review; *and* Western Monthly Magazine, and Literary Journal.

✻**THE WESTERN MONTHLY MAGAZINE, AND LITERARY JOURNAL.** v.1-5, Jan. 1833-Dec. 1836; new ser., v.1, Feb.-June 1837. Cincinnati, Corey & Fairbank, 1833-37.

6 v. in 5. pl., ports.

Absorbed the Western literary journal and monthly review in 1837.
Vol. 1 covers year 1833; v.2, 1834; v.3, Jan.-June 1835 (t.-p. reads: Jan.-Dec. 1835); v.4, July-Dec. 1835 (t.-p. reads: Jan.-June 1835); v.5, 1836; new ser., v.1 has no t.-p.
Title varies: 1833-35, The Western monthly magazine, a continuation of the Illinois monthly magazine. 1836, The Western monthly magazine. 1837, The Western monthly magazine and literary journal.

Editors: Jan. 1833-June 1836, James Hall.—July-Dec. 1836, J.R. Fry.

A continuation of James Hall's *Illinois Monthly Magazine* published at Vandalia, Illinois, the *Western Monthly* was the most successful of the early western magazines, claiming a circulation of about three thousand in its ninth month. It was more dignified than its predecessor, reflecting less of the freedom and ease of the frontier and offering better literary reviews and a good deal of science material. Western travel, letters from Cuba, and a serial history of Ohio added variety; and contributors, who were recruited largely from the country west of the Appalachians, included such famous names as William D. Gallagher, Otway Curry, Hannah Gould, Caroline Lee Hentz, E.D. Mansfield, and Harriet Beecher.

Following a quarrel between Hall and his publisher, Hall withdrew from the editorship in 1836 and Joseph Reese Fry conducted the magazine for six months. It then merged with William D. Gallagher's *Western Literary Journal and Monthly Review* to form the *Western Monthly Magazine and Literary Journal* but after only five numbers, it was suspended in June, 1837.

v1-5, nsv1, nos.1-5   Jan. 1833-June 1837   APS II, Reel 528

Pagination is irregular. Vol. 4: Title page is misdated.

Microfilm edition was prepared from CtY and IGK copies.

* **THE WESTERN MONTHLY REVIEW.** By Timothy Flint. v.1-3; May 1827-June 1830. Cincinnati, E.H. Flint, 1828-30.

3 v.

Vol. 1, no.1-2 have cover-title: The Western quarterly review; no.1-3 have caption title: The Western magazine and review. Title-page reads: The Western monthly review.

An attempt to combine the solid, weighty review and the entertaining and miscellaneous magazine, it served as an interpreter of the "West" to the East and as a recorder of the culture of the new region. The magazine championed morals, and presented a good deal of religious material, poetry, and critical reviews, but very little on politics. Three-fourths of all material was supplied by the editor, and at the beginning all of it was written by him, including the occasional romantic and sentimental tales which made up the magazine's only fiction. Selected material appeared increasingly toward the latter part of the publication's existence.

v1-3   May 1827-June 1830   APS II, Reel 673

Vol. 2: Pagination is irregular.

Microfilm edition was prepared from DLC copy.

THE WESTERN NEW YORK BAPTIST MAGAZINE. v.1-4; May 1814-Nov. 1825. Morrisville [N.Y.] Printed for the Hamilton Baptist Missionary Society by J.B. Johnson.

4 v. quarterly (irregular)

Title varies: May 1814-Nov. 1816, The Vehicle; or, New-York northwestern Christian magazine (subtitle varies)
Merged into the New York Baptist register (later the Examiner) Cf. Union list of serials.

This Baptist magazine was begun as the *Vehicle, or Madison and Cayuga Christian Magazine,* in Hamilton, New York, but later moved to Morrisville, New York. Published by the Hamilton Baptist Missionary Society, it contained much on missions and on missionary and Bible societies, and also offered occasional biographical sketches and memoirs, some Bible studies, and sermons, poetry, and anecdotes.

Vehicle
v1   May 1814-Nov. 1816   APS II, Reel 252

Western New York Baptist Magazine
v2   Feb. 1817-Nov. 1819   Reel 252
v3-4   Feb. 1820-Aug. 1825   Reel 253

Pagination is irregular. Some issues and scattered pages missing; not available for photographing.

THE WESTERN QUARTERLY REPORTER OF MEDICAL, SURGICAL, AND NATURAL SCIENCE. v.1-2, no. 2; 1822-23. Cincinnati, J.P. Foote [etc., etc.]

2 v.

Edited by Dr. John D. Godman, this Cincinnati medical journal offered general medical articles and articles on education, anatomy, and medical jurisprudence, as well as American medical news, selections from foreign journals, and book reviews. Zoology, geology and other natural science topics received some attention and diagrams and tables accompanied some of the articles.

v1-2   Jan. 1822-1823   APS II, Reel 1497

Several pages are stained. Vol. 1: pgs. 303, 311, 343, and 360 are misnumbered. Vol. 2: Index and pgs. 26-27 are missing; not available for photographing.

Microfilm edition was prepared from MiU and OU copies.

THE WESTERN QUARTERLY REVIEW. v.1, no.1-2; Jan.-Apr. 1849. Cincinnati, J.S. Hitchcock.

408 p.

This short-lived Cincinnati review published poetry, reviews, biography, and bibliographical notices, as well as articles on history, science, and other subjects.

v1, nos.1-2   Jan.-Apr. 1849   APS II, Reel 529

Microfilm edition was prepared from CtY copy.

WESTERN RECORDER. v.1-10; 1824-1833. Utica, N.Y., 1824-1833.

10 v.

The *Western Recorder* was a religious newspaper which was sponsored by the Western Education Society and the Auburn Theological Seminary. In addition to religious and missionary news, it included some poetry and music.

v1-2   Jan. 1824-Dec. 1825   APS II, Reel 1260
v3-6   Jan. 1826-Dec. 1829   Reel 1261
v7-10   Jan. 1830-Oct. 1833   Reel 1262

Vols. 1 and 3-8 lack indexes. Several pages are stained, creased and torn with some loss of text; some have print faded. Pagination is irregular. Vols. 3 and 10 have pages missing. Vol. 9 is missing; not available for photographing.

Microfilm edition was prepared from N and NCH copies.

THE WESTERN REVIEW. v.1, no.1; Apr. 1846. Columbus, O., C. C. & G.R. Hazewell, 1846-

1 v.

Only one issue of this magazine was published and it focused mainly on history, government, and politics, featuring such material as: reports of the Secretary of the Treasury, and the Secretary of the Navy, reports and speeches to the House and Senate, proceedings of the State Convention of the Democracy of Ohio, and articles dealing with English history, the history of Rome, and the history of war in France and Belgium.

v1, no.1   Apr. 1846   APS II, Reel 529

Microfilm edition was prepared from the CtY copy.

* **THE WESTERN REVIEW AND MISCELLANEOUS MAGAZINE,** a monthly publication, devoted to literature and science. v.1-4, no.6; Aug. 1819-July 1821. Lexington, Ky., W.G. Hunt, 1820-

4 v.

Paging erroneous; v.3, p. 217-218, 263-264, v.4, p. 281-282 are omitted; v.3, p. 241-242, 255-256, v.4, p. 289-290 are duplicated.

Founded in August, 1819, by William Gibbes Hunt, this monthly was one of the most interesting of the early western periodicals, a fact which was due in large part to such leading contributors as Horace Holley, president of Transylvania University at Lexington and some of the scholars he had brought with him. President Holley furnished verse and a variety of articles, and Constantine S. Rafinesque, a professor of botany and natural history, wrote a series on the botany of Kentucky and on the fish of the Ohio River, as well as some poetry, John D. Clifford supplied a series on Indian antiquities, and a series of stories of Indian fighting—"Heroic and Sanguinary Conflicts with the Indians" also appeared. A typical issue began with several book reviews, followed by a section of "Miscellany" and ending with several pages of poetry, both in English and in foreign languages. In 1820 the *Review* suffered several misfortunes and was suspended in July, 1821.

v1-4, no.6   Aug. 1819-July 1821   APS II, Reel 253

WHEELMAN. *SEE* Outing; Sport, Adventure, Travel, Fiction.

WHELER'S SOUTHERN MONTHLY MAGAZINE. *SEE* Mistletoe.

WIDE AWAKE. *SEE* St. Nicholas; an Illustrated Magazine for Young Folks.

THE WITNESS; a collection of original and selected pieces on various religious subjects. v.1, no.1-6; Jan.-June 1809. Boston, Manning and Loring.

288 p. Monthly.

This religious magazine published an assortment of original and selected material—sermons, Bible studies, articles on doctrine, religious news, biographical sketches, and poetry and anecdotes.

v1, no.1-6   Jan.-June 1809   APS II, Reel 46

WOODWORTH'S YOUTH CABINET. *SEE* Merry's Museum for Boys and Girls.

WORCESTER MAGAZINE ... Containing, politicks, miscellanies, poetry, and news. v.1-4; Apr. 1786-Mar. 1788. Worcester, Mass., I. Thomas.

4 v. weekly.

Published as a substitute for the *Massachusetts spy* during its suspension, its most interesting and valuable features were politics and "intelligence," and its most important literary contribution was an essay series—"The Worcester speculator." It also included agricultural articles, medical notes, anecdotes, recipes, and miscellaneous articles.

v1-4   Apr. 1786-Mar. 1788   APS I, Reel 33

Some pages are missing.

Microfilm edition was prepared from MWA copy.

* **THE WORCESTER MAGAZINE AND HISTORICAL JOURNAL.** v.1-2; Oct. 1825-Oct. 1826. Worcester, [Mass.] Rodgers & Griffin, 1826.

2 v. port. monthly.

Vol. 2 printed by C. Griffin.
Edited and published by William Lincoln and C.C. Baldwyn.

Proposed to include both original and selected material from the latest European and American periodicals and from new books and works not accessible to most readers. It emphasized historical material, particularly of Worcester County; in fact, the second volume was almost entirely devoted to a detailed history of the county. Also included short moral and literary essays, notices of improvements in the arts and advances in science, poetry, biography, travel articles, amusing anecdotes, and general news.

v1-2   Oct. 1825-Oct. 1826   APS II, Reel 720

Vol. 1: Pgs. 64-65 are bound out of order. Vol. 2: Index appears at the end of the volume.

Microfilm edition was prepared from DLC and MiU copies.

THE WORKING MAN'S ADVOCATE (National reform association) v.1-7, Oct. 31, 1829-36; new ser. v.1-6, 1844-49. New York [J. Windt and G.H. Evans]

13 v. illus. (incl. port.) weekly.

Title varies: June 9-Aug. 14, 1830 as New York sentinel and working man's advocate; July 24-27, 1844 as People's rights; Oct. 12-Dec. 21, 1844 as Subterranean united with the Workingman's advocate; Mar. 29, 1845-1849 as Young America.

Editor: G.H. Evans.
Also included on film: Radical, in continuation of Workingman's advocate (1841-1843).

Founded by G.H. Evans, this magazine was an organ of the National Reform Association and was one of the more important of the magazines devoted to the interests of the working man. Contents included foreign and domestic news, news of elections, poetry, and advertisements.

Workingman's Advocate
v1, no.1-32   Oct. 31, 1829-June 5, 1830   APS II, Reel 581

New York Sentinel and Working Man's Advocate
v1, no.33-52   June 9-Aug. 14, 1830   Reel 581

Workingman's Advocate
v2-4   Aug. 21, 1830-Aug. 10, 1833   Reel 581
v2-7 (rep. vols)   1830-1836   Reel 582

Radical, in Continuation of Working Man's Advocate
v1-2, no.4   Jan. 1841-Apr. 1843   Reel 582

Workingman's Advocate
nsv1, no.1-17   Mar. 16, 1844-July 20, 1844   Reel 583

People's Rights
nsv1, no.18-19   July 24-27, 1844   Reel 583

Workingman's Advocate
nsv1, no.19-28   Aug. 3-Oct. 5, 1844   Reel 583

Subterranean, United with the Workingman's Advocate
nsv1, no.29-39   Oct. 12-Dec. 21, 1844   Reel 583

Workingman's Advocate
nsv1, no.40-52   Dec. 28, 1844-Mar. 22, 1845   Reel 583

Young America
nsv2-5 Mar. 29, 1845-Sept. 23, 1848 Reel 583

Microfilm edition is incomplete, lacking some volumes and issues. Several pages are creased, faded, stained, and have print show-though, with some loss of text. Best copy available for photographing.

Microfilm edition was prepared from DLC, KHi, NN, NNC, and NHi copies.

WORLD AFFAIRS. v.1- June 1837- Washington, American Peace Society [etc.]

v. illus., ports.
Quarterly, 1837-Mar. 1838; monthly (irregular) June 1838-Apr. 1929; quarterly, Aug. 1929-
Irregularities in volume numbering; 1869-June 1884 also called new ser. v.1-15; v.34-46 omitted in numbering.

Supersedes the American advocate of peace (Hartford).
Title varies: 1837-45, The advocate of peace.—1846, The Advocate of peace and universal brotherhood.—1847-Mar. 1932, The American advocate of peace and arbitration, American advocate of peace, Advocate of peace (cover-title, Mar. 1920-Mar. 1932: Advocate of peace through justice)
Includes the Annual report of the American Peace Society.

Film includes: v.1-18; new ser. v1-5; v.6, no.2-10, 12; v.7-11; v.12, no.1, 3-12; v.13-15; v.54, no.3, 7-9; v.55-68.

Published by the American Peace Society, the *Advocate of Peace,* as it was originally known, was a new series of the *American Advocate of Peace* of Hartford, Connecticut. It was at various times a monthly, a bimonthly, and a quarterly publication. George Beckwith, the Society's secretary, was editor for many years, and Holmes, Whittier, and Bryant were contributors. In 1910 it was moved to Washington, and later renamed *World Affairs.* The *Advocate of Peace* published much material relating to the American Peace Society, including proceedings of meetings, annual reports, and addresses to the Society, and reported on the progress being made in the peace movement, both in the U.S. and abroad. Articles on the causes of war and its evils, war in relation to religion, and remedies for war were plentiful; in addition, there were sketches of various wars, some poetry, and miscellaneous items. During the Civil War, the *Advocate* concentrated its efforts on opposing international conflict. Around the turn of the century book reviews, short news items on the peace movement, and a few advertisements were added. There was much discussion of international disputes and methods of solving them; international arbitration, reduction of armaments, and a "congress of nations" were advocated.

Advocate of Peace
v1-6 June 1837-Dec. 1845 APS II, Reel 584

Advocate of Peace and Universal Brotherhood
v7 (nsv1) Jan.-Dec. 1846 Reel 584

Advocate of Peace
v8 (nsv2) Jan. 1847-Nov./Dec. 1850 Reel 584
v9-18 Jan./Feb. 1851-Nov./Dec. 1868 Reel 1543
nsv1-15 Jan. 1869-June 1884 Reel 1544
v54-57 June 1892-Dec. 1895 Reel 1544
v58-68 Jan. 1896-Dec. 1906 Reel 1545

Best copy available for photographing. Several pages have print faded with some loss of text. Some issues are misnumbered; pagination is irregular. New Series Vol. 1: some issues are bound and photographed out of order. New Series Vol. 3 contains a supplement. New Series Vol. 6: Issue 3 is bound and photographed before issue 2. Issue 9, second part, is bound and photographed after issue 10. New Series Vol. 14: issue 2, pages 11-12 are missing.

Microfilm edition was prepared from DLC, MH, MH-AH, and MiU copies.

THE YALE LITERARY MAGAZINE. Conducted by the students of Yale university. v.1- Feb. 1836- New Haven, Herrick & Noyes, 1836-

plates, ports.

Previously published monthly during the college year; now irregular. The regular issue for Feb. 1864 was suppressed. The editorial board then divided into two sections and each section published a magazine for Feb., Mar., and Apr., 1864.

Conducted by the students of Yale College, the *Yale Literary Magazine* was the earliest of the long-lived college monthlies and one of the most successful of all college magazines. It was not intended to be instructive, and contained much prose and poetry, and a good deal of humorous and satirical material, in addition to literary notices, essays on literature and history, travel sketches, and biographical pieces on authors and other famous people. William M. Evarts, Sylvester Judd, C.J. Stille, J.P. Thompson, and George H. Colton were among the contributors to the early volumes.

v1-5 Feb. 1836-Aug. 1840 APS II, Reel 529
v6-11 Nov. 1840-Aug. 1846 Reel 530
v12-16 Nov. 1846-July 1851 Reel 531

Microfilm edition includes vols. 1-16, 1836-51. Several pages are stained and spotted with some loss of text. Pagination is irregular. Volume 4: Pages 241-45 are missing; not available for photographing.

Microfilm edition was prepared from CtY and DLC copies.

YALE REVIEW. *SEE* New Englander and Yale Review.

THE YANKEE AND BOSTON LITERARY GAZETTE. v1-2, Jan. 1, 1828-June 25, 1829; new ser., no.1-6, July-Dec. 1829. Portland [J. Adams Jr.] 1828-29.

3 v. front.
Weekly, Jan. 1828-June 1829; monthly, July-Dec. 1829.
Volume numbering irregular; new ser., no.1-6 called v.2, no.79-82.
Jan. 1-Aug. 13, 1828, title reads: The Yankee.

John Neal, editor (with J.W. Miller, Aug. 1828-June 1829)
Published in Boston, Oct. 1828-Dec. 1829.
Absorbed the Boston literary gazette, Aug. 13, 1828; the Bachelor's journal, Sept. 24, 1828.
Merged into the New England galaxy. cf. Duyckinck, v.1, p. 875.

Founded in 1828 by John Neal, this periodical included essays, extracts, reviews, verse, and sermons. Subjects such as philosophy, literature, and education were treated from a utilitarian viewpoint.

v1-nsno6 Jan. 1, 1828-Dec. 1829 APS II, Reel 131

Vol. 1: Index is torn and stained. New Series nos. 1-6: Indexes are missing. Dec. 1829 number is misdated.

Microfilm edition was prepared from DLC, L, MnU, and NPV copies.

YANKEE DOODLE. v1-2 (no.1-52); Oct. 10, 1846-Oct. 2, 1847. New York, William H. Graham.

2 v. illus., plates. weekly.

From the 5th no. of v.2 until its cessation, published by J.A. Fraetas. Microfilm edition appears to be lacking title pages for the 1847 issues.

Edited by the satirist Cornelius Mathews, and assisted by Richard Grant White and George G. Foster, this short-lived humorous paper lasted only about a year. Nathaniel Willis and Horace Greeley also contributed, and Charles Martin drew pictures. In addition to pictures and cartoons, *Yankee Doodle* published news, poetry, jokes, and much material satirizing local, national, and international issues and government.

v1-2   1846-1847   APS II, Reel 1408

Pagination is irregular. Pgs. 255-56 are missing; not available for photographing.

Microfilm edition was prepared from MH and VtU copies.

YOUNG AMERICA. *SEE* Working Man's Advocate.

YOUNG MECHANIC. *SEE* Boston Mechanic, and Journal of Useful Arts and Sciences.

YOUTH'S CABINET. v.1, nos.1-4; Mar. 31-Apr. 21, 1815. Utica, N.Y., 1815.

1 v. (unpaged)

Chiefly designed "for the improvement of youth," this little four-page magazine contained instructive essays and moralistic stories, as well as poetry, essays, and anecdotes.

v1, no.1-4   Mar. 31-Apr. 21, 1815   APS II, Reel 333

Microfilm edition was prepared from MB copy.

THE YOUTH'S COMPANION. v.1-103, no.9; Apr. 1827-Sept. 1929. Boston, Perry Mason Co. [etc.]

103 v. illus.

Weekly, 1827-1927; monthly, 1928-1928.
Volume number irregular: v.37 repeated; v.69 omitted in numbering. Title varies slightly.
Editors: 1827-57, Nathaniel Willis.—1857-99, D.S. Ford. Continued by American Boy. Cf. Mott, F.L., A history of American magazines, v.2.

On film: v.1-103, no.9, except for v.2, no.43; v.34, no.29; v.36; v.52, no.44; v.54, no.43; v.55, no.43.

Edited by Nathaniel Willis for thirty years, the *Youth's Companion* was one of the most important of the American juvenile magazines. Begun as the children's section of the *Recorder,* a Boston Congregational paper, it became a separate 4-page weekly in 1827. It was to be instructive as well as entertaining, and early volumes included many morbid pieces on dead or dying children. Though some original material appeared, much of the contents were selected. Offerings became more varied in the 1840's: there were departments of moral tales, religion, morality, biography, natural history, and education, Willis's successor, Daniel S. Ford, continued the moral emphasis of the magazine but decreased its image as a Sunday school paper, including more fiction and original material. In the sixties, the "Premium List," which displayed pages of gifts to those obtaining subscriptions, was begun. These premiums were a major reason for the *Companion's* popularity; another reason was that it attempted to interest the entire family and not only the children. Famous names such as Harriet Beecher Stowe and Elizabeth Stuart Phelps began appearing in the 60's, and during the eighties and nineties Theodore Roosevelt, Grover Cleveland, and Booker T. Washington contributed articles. There was poetry by Tennyson, Longfellow, Whittier, Whitman, Aldrich and Stedman, as well as a column of current events and articles on medicine and history. From the sixties on, illustrations were plentiful and well done. During the first decade of the new century, the *Companion's* circulation began a gradual decline, and in the fall of 1929 it was merged with the *American Boy.*

v1-12	Apr. 16, 1827-May 10, 1839	APS II, Reel 1546
v13-24	May 17, 1839-Apr. 24, 1851	Reel 1547
v25-35	May 1, 1851-Dec. 26, 1861	Reel 1548
v37-43	Jan. 1, 1863-Dec. 29, 1870	Reel 1549
v44-48	Jan. 5, 1871-Dec. 30, 1875	Reel 1550
v49-53	Jan. 6, 1876-Dec. 30, 1880	Reel 1551
v54-57	Jan. 6, 1881-Dec. 25, 1884	Reel 1552
v58-60	Jan. 1, 1885-Dec. 29, 1887	Reel 1553
v61-63	Jan. 5, 1888-Dec. 25, 1890	Reel 1554
v64-65	Jan. 1, 1891-Dec. 29, 1892	Reel 1555
v66-67	Jan. 5, 1893-Dec. 27, 1894	Reel 1556
v68-70	Jan. 3, 1895-Dec. 31, 1896	Reel 1557
v71-72	Jan. 7, 1897-Dec. 29, 1898	Reel 1558
v73-74	Jan. 5, 1899-Dec. 27, 1900	Reel 1559
v75-76	Jan. 3, 1901-Dec. 25, 1902	Reel 1560
v77-78	Jan. 1, 1903-Dec. 29, 1904	Reel 1561
v79-80	Jan. 5, 1905-Dec. 27, 1906	Reel 1562
v81-82	Jan. 3, 1907-Dec. 31, 1908	Reel 1563
v83-84	Jan. 7, 1909-Dec. 29, 1910	Reel 1564
v85-86	Jan. 5, 1911-Dec. 26, 1912	Reel 1565
v87-88	Jan. 2, 1913-Dec. 31, 1914	Reel 1566
v89-90	Jan. 7, 1915-Dec. 28, 1916	Reel 1567
v91-92	Jan. 4, 1917-Dec. 26, 1918	Reel 1568
v93-95	Jan. 2, 1919-Dec. 29, 1921	Reel 1569
v96-98	Jan. 5, 1922-Dec. 25, 1924	Reel 1570
v99-101	Jan. 1, 1925-Dec.1927	Reel 1571
v102-103	Jan. 1928-Sept. 1929	Reel 1572

Some volumes lack title page, index and some advertisement pages. Several pages are stained, torn, creased; or have print blurred and faded with some loss of text. Some volumes contain supplements. Pagination is irregular. Vol. 2: pgs. 195-96 are missing. Vol. 13: pgs. 26-27 are missing. Vol. 64: cover page is missing.

Microfilm edition was prepared from DLC, IC, IU, MH, MWA, Mi, MiD, MiU, NBu, NBuG, and NjP copies.

SEE ALSO: Merry's Museum for Boys and Girls.

YOUTH'S REPOSITORY OF CHRISTIAN KNOWLEDGE. nos.1-2; Mar.-Sept. 1813. New Haven, Conn., 1813.

2 no.

Edited by Henry Whitlock, this magazine's main purpose was to give religious instruction to children. It contained a series of lessons, many with questions following, short addresses and sermons, and biographical sketches.

nos.1-2   Mar.-Sept. 1813   APS II, Reel 333

Microfilm edition was prepared from MWA copy.

ZION'S HERALD. v.1- 1823- Boston.

v. illus. weekly.
Issues for 1829-1867 (v.7-44) also called new ser. v.1-38.

Superseded by Methodist churchman.
Title varies: 1829-1833, New England Christian herald; 1842-1867, Zion's herald and Wesleyan journal.

On film: vols. 1-84 (reels 1572-1612) vols. 85-88 (reels 1963-1966) Imperfect: Have only scattered issues for some vols. Lacking complete v.6, nsv1-5, nsv23-26.

Begun in Boston in 1823, *Zion's Herald* is one of the oldest and greatest of the Methodist weekly magazines. Noted for its independence and spirit, the *Herald* devoted much space in its early years to religious controversies with Calvinism and Universalism, while also giving attention to news of Methodist missions and churches and to Methodist church history. It was strongly opposed to slavery and in 1835 took up the cause of abolitionist William Lloyd Garrison when he was attacked by a mob in Boston. The *Herald* also advocated temperance and women's rights. There were departments for women and for children, and in later years, a family department was added, and children's stories, book reviews, illustrations and advertisements became more plentiful. Contents also included short sermons, poetry, biography, and political, literary, and scientific news items.

Zion's Herald
v1-2	Jan. 9, 1823-Dec. 29, 1824	APS II, Reel 1572
v3-5	Jan. 5, 1825-Dec. 26, 1827	Reel 1573
nsv6	Jan. 7-Dec. 30, 1835	Reel 1574
nsv7-9	Jan. 6, 1836-Dec. 26, 1838	Reel 1574
nsv10-12	Oct. 9, 1839-Dec. 26, 1841	Reel 1575

Zion's Herald and Wesleyan Journal
nsv13-17	Jan. 1842-Dec. 26, 1846	Reel 1575
nsv18-21	Jan. 6, 1847-Dec. 25, 1850	Reel 1576
nsv22-30	Jan. 1, 1851-Dec. 28, 1859	Reel 1577
nsv31-35	Jan. 4, 1860-Dec. 28, 1864	Reel 1578
nsv36-38	Jan. 4, 1865-Dec. 26, 1867	Reel 1579

Zion's Herald
v45-47	Jan. 2, 1868-Dec. 29, 1870	Reel 1580
v48-49	Jan. 5, 1871-Dec. 26, 1872	Reel 1581
v50	Jan. 2-Dec. 25, 1873	Reel 1582
v51	Jan. 1-Dec. 31, 1874	Reel 1583
v52	Jan. 7-Dec. 30, 1875	Reel 1584
v53	Jan. 6-Dec. 28, 1876	Reel 1585
v54	Jan. 4-Dec. 27, 1877	Reel 1586
v55	Jan. 3-Dec. 26, 1878	Reel 1587
v56	Jan. 2-Dec. 25, 1879	Reel 1588
v57	Jan. 1-Dec. 30, 1880	Reel 1589
v58	Jan. 6-Dec. 29, 1881	Reel 1590
v59	Jan. 4-Dec. 27, 1882	Reel 1591
v60	Jan. 3-Dec. 26, 1883	Reel 1592
v61	Jan. 2-Dec. 31, 1884	Reel 1593
v62	Jan. 7-Dec. 30, 1885	Reel 1594
v63	Jan. 6-Dec. 29, 1886	Reel 1595
v64	Jan. 5-Dec. 28, 1887	Reel 1596
v65-66	Jan. 4-Dec. 26, 1888	Reel 1597
v67	Jan. 2-Dec. 25, 1889	Reel 1598
v68	Jan. 1-Dec. 31, 1890	Reel 1599
v69	Jan. 7-Dec. 30, 1891	Reel 1600
v70	Jan. 6-Dec. 28, 1892	Reel 1601
v71-72	Jan. 4, 1893-Dec. 26, 1894	Reel 1602
v73-74	Jan. 2, 1895-Dec. 30, 1896	Reel 1603
v75-76	Jan. 6, 1897-Dec. 28, 1898	Reel 1604
v77	Jan. 4-Dec. 27, 1899	Reel 1605
v78	Jan. 3-Dec. 26, 1900	Reel 1606
v79	Jan. 2-Dec. 25, 1901	Reel 1607
v80	Jan. 1-Dec. 31, 1902	Reel 1608
v81	Jan. 7-Dec. 30, 1903	Reel 1609
v82	Jan. 6-Dec. 28, 1904	Reel 1610
v83	Jan. 4-Dec. 27, 1905	Reel 1611
v84	Jan. 3-Dec. 26, 1906	Reel 1612
v85	Jan. 2-Dec. 25, 1907	Reel 1963
v86	Jan. 1-Dec. 30, 1908	Reel 1964
v87	Jan. 6-Dec. 29, 1909	Reel 1965
v88	Jan. 5-Dec. 28, 1910	Reel 1966

Best copy available for photographing. Several pages are misnumbered, stained, torn, taped, tightly bound; or have print blurred and faded with some loss of text. New Series Vol. 30: page 16 is missing; pages 183-84 are bound and photographed in New Series Vol. 29. Vol. 45: issue 3 and pages 315-16 and 319-20 are bound and photographed out of order. Vol. 46: issue 2 is bound and photographed out of order. Vol. 50: page 307 is missing. Vol. 59: page 322 is missing. Vol. 75: pages 595-96 are missing. Vol. 77: page 517 is missing.

Microfilm edition was prepared from CtW, DLC, MWA, and MiU copies.

SEE ALSO: Christian Advocate (Chicago).

ZION'S HERALD AND WESLEYAN JOURNAL. *SEE* Zion's Herald.

THE ZODIAC, a monthly periodical, devoted to science, literature and the arts. Pub. by E. Perry. v.1-2, no.7; July 1835-Jan. 1837. Albany, Press of Packard and Van Benthuvsen.

A monthly miscellany published by E. Perry of Albany and intended to be a literary companion to both young and old. It published many selections from *Blackwood's Magazine, Chambers' Edinburgh Journal,* and other British periodicals, as well as poetry and tales, foreign news, meteorological tables and reports, and some translations. Serialized material included "Letters from India," a poem on India, and lectures on American literature.

v1-2	July 1835-Jan. 1837	APS II, Reel 753

Vol. 2: Title page is lacking.

Microfilm edition was prepared from ICU copy.

SUBJECT INDEX

Godey's Magazine: Vol. 126, Jan. 1826 issue

SUBJECT INDEX

ABOLITIONISTS
Abolition intelligencer and missionary magazine. APS II, Reel 47.
Abolitionist. APS II, Reel 362.
Evangelist and religious review. APS II, Reels 1829-1855.
Liberator. APS II, Reels 391-399.
National era. APS II, Reels 899-903.
New Englander and Yale review. APS II, Reels 679-680, 904-912.

ACTORS—Biography
Dramatic mirror, and literary companion. APS II, Reel 605.
Mirror of taste and dramatic censor. APS II, Reel 218.
Ramblers' magazine. APS II, Reel 43.
Thespian oracle. APS I, Reel 29.

ACTRESSES—Biography
Dramatic mirror, and literary companion. APS II, Reel 605.

AESTHETICS
Literary inquirer. APS II, Reel 799.
Magnolia; or, Literary tablet. APS II, Reel 777.
Mirror of literature, amusement and instruction. APS II, Reel 138.
Pioneer, consisting of essays, literary, moral and theological. APS II, Reel 189.

AFRICA—History
African intelligencer. APS II, Reel 49.

AGRICULTURE
Agricultural museum. APS II, Reel 49.
American farmer. APS II, Reels 51-52, 1062-1071.
Archives of useful knowledge. APS II, Reel 65.
Carolina journal of medicine. APS II, Reels 75, 362.
Christian's, scholar's, and farmer's magazine. APS I, Reel 10.
Colman's rural world. APS III, Reels 750-756.
Cultivator. APS II, Reels 514-518.
Farmers cabinet and American herd book. APS II, Reels 314-315.
Fessenden's silk manual and practical farmer. APS II, Reel 734.
Genesee farmer and gardener's journal. APS II, Reels 316-318.
Magazine of useful and entertaining knowledge. APS II, Reel 742.
Massachusetts agricultural repository and journal. APS II, Reels 214-215, 566.
Medical and agricultural register, for the years 1806 and 1807. APS II, Reel 26.
Monthly journal of agriculture. APS II, Reel 419.
New England farmer. APS II, Reels 1191-1194.
New Jersey and Pennsylvania agricultural monthly intelligencer. APS II, Reels 158, 1123.
Northern light. APS II, Reel 844.
Plough boy. APS II, Reels 190, 191.
Rural magazine. APS I, Reel 27.
Rural magazine and farmer's monthly museum. APS II, Reel 205.
Rural magazine and literary evening fire-side. APS II, Reel 205.
Southern cultivator. APS II, Reels 1519-1529.
Southern planter. APS II, Reels 1529-1542.
Tennessee farmer. APS II, Reel 1490.
Theophilanthropist. APS II, Reel 333.
Universal asylum and Columbian magazine. APS I, Reels 11, 30.
Washington quarterly magazine. APS II, Reel 246.
Western farmer and gardener. APS II, Reel 1408.
Western farmer and gardener; devoted to agriculture. APS II, Reel 698.

Economic Aspects
Farmer's and planter's friend. APS II, Reel 106.

Indiana
Indiana farmer's guide. APS II, Reels 1797-1801

Maine
Maine farmer. APS II, Reels 422-427, 1371-88.

Massachusetts
Massachusetts ploughman and New England journal of agriculture. APS II, Reels 1274-1287.

New England
New England farmer, and horticultural register. APS II, Reels 149, 1397-1404.
Massachusetts ploughman and New England journal of agriculture. APS II, Reels 1274-1287.

New York (City)
New York farmer. APS II, Reels 1195-1196.

New York (State)—Genesee County
Genesee farmer. APS II, Reels 795-797.

Ohio
Ohio cultivator. APS II, Reels 1254-1257.
Ohio farmer. APS II, Reels 1801-1815.

United States
American agriculturist. APS II, Reels 364-365.
American cultivator. APS II, Reels 465-467.
American farmer's magazine. APS II, Reels 503-507.
Farmers cabinet and American herd book. APS II, Reels 314-315.
Farmer's register. APS II, Reels 334-338.
Plough boy. APS II, Reels 190, 191.

United States—Southern States
Southern agriculturist, horticulturist, and register of rural affairs. APS II, Reels 806-809.
Southern cultivator. APS II, Reels 1519-1529.
Southern planter. APS II, Reels 1529-1542.

ALIEN AND SEDITION LAWS, 1798.
Republican magazine. APS I, Reel 26.

ALMANACS, AMERICAN
American almanac. APS II, Reels 810-812.

AMERICA—Antiquities
American antiquarian and oriental journal. APS III, Reels 54-57.

History
Columbian historian. APS II, Reel 95.

AMERICAN DRAMA
Thespian oracle. APS I, Reel 29.

AMERICAN FICTION—18th Century
American museum, or, Universal magazine. APS I, Reels 4-5.
Humming bird. APS I, Reel 13.

Weekly magazine of original essays. APS I, Reels 31-32.

19th Century
Ballou's monthly magazine. APS III, Reels 716-729.
Baltimore literary monument. APS II, Reel 379.
Chap-book. APS III, Reel 61.
Cosmopolitan. APS III, Reels 660-669.
Every Saturday. APS III, Reels 148-151.
Flag of our Union. APS II, Reels 1158-1166.
Magnolia. APS II, Reel 676.
New-England magazine.. APS II, Reels 841-842.
Sargent's new monthly magazine. APS II, Reel 1258.
Southern and western monthly magazine and review. APS II, Reel 1407.
Western literary magazine. APS II, Reel 1260.

AMERICAN LITERATURE—18th Century
Cabinet. APS II, Reel 75.
Censor. APS I, Reel 8.

19th Century
American gleaner and Virginia magazine. APS II, Reel 1.
American metropolitan magazine. APS II, Reel 333.
American monthly magazine. Boston. APS II, Reel 468.
American monthly magazine. Philadelphia. APS II, Reel 57.
American quarterly observer. APS II, Reel 297.
Atlantic souvenir. APS II, Reel 1367.
Balance, and state journal. APS II, Reels 3-5, 70.
Ballou's pictorial drawing-room companion. APS III, Reels 249-252.
Baltimore literary and religious magazine. APS II, Reels 585-586.
Baltimore magazine. APS II, Reel 6.
Baltimore monthly visiter. APS II, Reel 408.
Baltimore monument. APS II, Reel 769.
Boston quarterly review. APS II, Reel 380.
Burton's gentleman's magazine and American monthly review. APS II, Reel 311.
Californian and overland monthly. APS III, Reels 172-173.
Charleston spectator and ladies' literary portfolio. APS II, Reel 6.
Collections, historical and miscellaneous, and monthly literary journal. APS II, Reels 93-94.
Critic. Weekly review of literature, fine arts, and the drama. APS II, Reel 385.
Current opinion. APS III, Reels 689-707.
Dial: a magazine for literature, philosophy, and religion. APS II, Reel 546.
Eastern magazine. APS II, Reel 385.
Emerson's magazine and Putnam's monthly. APS III, Reels 264-265.
Graham's American monthly magazine of literature, art, and fashion. APS II, Reels 547-560.
Green Mountain gem. APS II, Reel 654.
Ladies afternoon visitor. APS II, Reel 20.
Literary magazine, and American register. APS II, Reels 22-23.
Literary union. APS II, Reel 742.
Literary world. APS II, Reel 483-486.
Magnolia. APS II, Reel 676.
National magazine; or, Cabinet of the United States. APS II, Reel 34.
New-England magazine. APS II, Reels 841-842.
New York review and Atheneum. APS II, Reels 166, 615.
Pioneer. APS II, Reel 745.
Putnam's magazine. APS III, Reels 164-167.
Sartain's union magazine of literature and art. APS II, Reels 572-574.
Southern literary gazette. APS II, Reel 1258.
Southern literary journal and magazine of arts. APS II, Reels 574-576.
United States Democratic review. APS II, Reels 691-696.
Western Minerva. APS II, Reel 252.
Western messenger. APS II, Reels 489-490.
Western monthly magazine, and literary journal. APS II, Reel 528.
Youth's companion. APS II, Reels 1546-1572.

Bibliography
American literary gazette and publishers' circular. APS II, Reels 780-783.

Southern States
New Orleans miscellany. APS II, Reel 973.

AMERICAN POETRY—1783-1850.
American moral & sentimental magazine. APS I, Reel 3.
American museum, or, Universal magazine. APS I, Reels 4-5.
Columbian lady's and gentleman's magazine. APS II, Reel 313.
Humming bird. APS I, Reel 13.

19th Century
American monthly magazine. APS II, Reel 57.
Ballou's monthly magazine. APS III, Reels 716-729.
Baltimore literary monument. APS II, Reel 379.
Belford's monthly. APS III, Reels 586-589.
Chap-book. APS III, Reel 61.
Emerson's magazine and Putnam's monthly. APS III, Reels 264-265.
Dial: a magazine for literature, philosophy, and religion. APS II, Reel 546.
Franklin Minerva. APS II, Reel 546.
Garland. APS II, Reel 107.
Graham's American monthly magazine of literature, art, and fashion. APS II, Reels 547-560.
Hive. APS II, Reel 114.
Literary union. APS II, Reel 742.
New-England magazine. APS II, Reels 841-842.
New-York magazine and general repository. APS II, Reel 162.
Pioneer. APS II, Reel 745.
Roycroft quarterly. APS III, Reel 462.
Sargent's new monthly magazine. APS II, Reel 1258.
Sartain's union magazine of literature and art. APS II, Reels 572-574.
Southern and western monthly magazine and review. APS II, Reel 1407.
Spirit of the public journals. APS II, Reel 44.
United States Democratic review. APS II, Reels 691-696.
United States Literary gazette. APS II, Reel 242.
United States review and literary gazette. APS II, Reel 1124.
Western literary magazine. APS II, Reel 1260.

AMERICAN PROSE LITERATURE
American moral & sentimental magazine. APS I, Reel 3.
Century, a popular quarterly. APS III, Reels 345-367.
Columbian lady's and gentleman's magazine. APS II, Reel 313.

ANARCHISM AND ANARCHISTS
Liberty (not the daughter but the mother of order). APS III, Reels 669-670.

ANECDOTES
Literary tablet. APS II, Reel 24.

ANTIMASONIC PARTY
Anti-masonic review, and magazine. APS II, Reel 769.

ANTIQUITIES
Parthenon. APS II, Reel 1257.

ARBITRATION, INTERNATIONAL
World affairs. APS II, Reels 584, 1543-1545.

ARCHAEOLOGY
American antiquarian and oriental journal. APS III, Reel 54-57.
Monthly American journal of geology and natural science. APS II, Reel 659.

ARCHITECTURE
American architect and architecture. APS III, Reels 600-649.
Iris. APS II, Reel 656.

ART
Aldine, the art journal of America. APS III, Reels 239-240.
Art amateur. APS III, Reels 580-585.
Ladies' literary portfolio. APS II, Reel 893.
Literary and philosophical repertory. APS II, Reel 126.
Literary casket. APS II, Reel 777.
Nassau literary magazine. APS II, Reels 1482-1486.
National magazine: devoted to literature, art, and religion. APS II, Reels 814-815.
New York literary gazette and journal of belles lettres, arts, science, &c. APS II, Reel 1292.
Opera glass. APS II, Reel 1124.
Parlour review, and journal of music, literature, and the fine arts. APS II, Reel 845.
Philadelphia museum. APS II, Reel 186.
Weekly magazine of original essays. APS I, Reels 31-32.

American
American metropolitan magazine. APS II, Reel 333.

British
Eclectic museum of foreign literature, science and art. APS II, Reel 605.

Modern-19th Century
American people's journal of science, literature, and art. APS II, Reel 333.

ART CRITICISM
Magnolia; or, Southern Apalachian. APS II, Reel 676.
New York literary gazette. APS II, Reel 973.
Pioneer. APS II, Reel 745.
Round table. APS III, Reels 461-462.

ARTISTS—UNITED STATES
Atlantic souvenir. APS II, Reel 1367.

ARTS
American monthly magazine. APS II, Reel 377.
Anglo American, a journal. APS II, Reels 647-649.
Appletons' journal. APS III, Reels 244-249.
Arcturus. APS II, Reel 734.
Boston journal of philosophy and the arts. APS II, Reel 73.
Boston magazine. APS II, Reel 6.
Broadway journal. APS II, Reel 649.
Christian's, scholar's, and farmer's magazine. APS I, Reel 10.
Critic. APS III, Reels 101-108.
Herald of truth. APS II, Reel 388.
International monthly magazine of literature, science and art. APS III, Reel 109.
Literary tablet. APS II, Reel 24.
National repository. APS III, Reels 110-111.
Pastime. APS II, Reel 36.
Philadelphia monthly magazine. APS II, Reel 1092.
Putnam's magazine. APS III, Reels 164-167.
Sartain's union magazine of literature and art. APS II, Reels 572-574.

New York
American Whig review. APS II, Reels 302-304.

ASTRONOMY
American magazine, and repository of useful literature. APS II, Reel 376.

AUTHORS, ENGLISH—BIOGRAPHY
Museum of foreign literature, science, and art. APS II, Reels 146-148, 1245-1254.

BANKS AND BANKING
Bankers' magazine. APS II, Reels 587-588, 1648-1683.
Man. APS II, Reels 565-566.

United States
Bankers magazine. APS II, Reels 587-588, 1648-1683.

BAPTISTS
Baptist quarterly. APS III, Reels 4-5.
Baptist quarterly review. APS III, Reels 59-60.
Christian baptist. APS II, Reels 77, 1158.
Christian index. APS II, Reels 1826-1828.
Christian reflector. APS II, Reels 886-889.
Christian review. APS II, Reels 410-416.
Christian secretary. APS II, Reels 88-89, 495-502, 1910.
Columbian star. APS II, Reels 95-96, 1271.
Rhode Island Baptist. APS II, Reel 204.
Vermont Baptist missionary magazine. APS II, Reel 246.
Watchman-examiner. APS II, Reels 246-248, 1491-1497, 1874-1883.
Western New York Baptist magazine. APS II, Reels 252-253.

Doctrinal and Controversial Works
Christian baptist. APS II, Reels 77, 1158.

Missions
Baptist missionary magazine. APS II, Reels 71-72, 535-539, 830-838.
Christian reflector. APS II, Reels 886-889.
Latter day luminary. APS II, Reels 122-123.
Massachusetts Baptist missionary magazine. APS II, Reels 25, 216.
Vermont Baptist missionary magazine. APS II, Reel 246.

BIBLE
Gospel advocate and impartial investigator. APS II, Reels 110, 1072.

Commentaries
Theological and literary journal. APS II, Reels 940-943.

Criticism, Interpretation, Etc.
Biblical world. APS III, Reels 254-264.
Scriptural interpreter. APS II, Reel 751.

Interpretation
Scriptural interpreter. APS II, Reel 751.

Prophecies
Hierophant. APS II, Reel 388.

Societies, Etc.
Circular. APS II, Reel 210 a.
Evangelical guardian and review. APS II, Reel 102.
New York telescope. APS II, Reel 1254.

Study
Advocate for the testimony of God. APS II, Reel 767.
Berean; or Scripture-searcher. APS II, Reel 6, 72.
Biblical world. APS III, Reels 254-264.
Christian messenger, Baltimore. APS II, Reels 82, 595.
Christian messenger. Being a miscellaneous work. APS II, Reel 82.
Christian reformer. APS II, Reel 382.
Evidence. APS II, Reel 18.
Friendly visitor. APS II, Reel 107.
Halcyon itinerary. APS II, Reel 19.
Hierophant. APS II, Reel 388.
Lay-man's magazine. APS II, Reel 123.
Religious monitor and evangelical repository. APS II, Reels 401-403.

Utica Christian repository. APS II, Reel 245.

BIBLIOGRAPHY
New England literary herald. APS II, Reels 34, 218.

Rare Books
Philobiblion. APS III, Reel 270.

BIOGRAPHY
Nightingale. APS I, Reel 23.
Periodical library. APS II, Reel 736.
Weekly visitant. APS II, Reel 46.

19th Century—Portraits
Polyanthos. APS II, Reels 39, 191-192.

BLACK HAWK WAR, 1832
Chronicles of the North American savages. APS II, Reel 382.

BOOKS, REVIEWS
American annals of education. APS II, Reels 293-294.
American magazine, and repository of useful literature. APS II, Reel 376.
American magazine, containing a miscellaneous collection. APS I, Reel 2.
American monthly magazine and critical review. APS II, Reel 58.
American quarterly review. APS II, Reels 298-301.
American review, and literary journal, for 1801-1802. APS II, Reel 3.
Bookman. APS III, Reels 112-130.
Boston lyceum. APS II, Reel 379.
Broadway journal. APS II, Reel 649.
Christian register, and moral and theological review. APS II, Reel 88.
Columbian lady's and gentleman's magazine. APS II, Reel 313.
Critic. APS III, Reels 101-108.
Friend. APS II, Reel 107.
Journal of belles lettres. APS II, Reel 1314.
Literary and evangelical magazine. APS II, Reel 124-125, 464.
Literary gazette: or, Journal of criticism, science, and the arts. APS II, Reel 131.
Literary miscellany. APS II, Reel 24.
Literary union. APS II, Reel 742.
Literary world. APS II, Reels 483-486.
Manhattan. APS II, Reels 30-31.
Monthly magazine, and American review. APS I, Reel 17.
National magazine and republican review. APS II, Reel 799.
Pioneer. APS II, Reel 745.
Quarterly journal and review. APS II, Reel 1092.
Select reviews of literature, and spirit of foreign magazines. APS II, Reels 44, 239-240.
Southern and western monthly magazine and review. APS II, Reel 1407.
United States literary gazette. APS II, Reel 242.
United States magazine and literary and political repository. APS II Reel 243.
Western review and miscellaneous magazine. APS II, Reel 253.

BOSTON—History
Bowen's Boston news-letter. APS II, Reels 74, 914.

Politics and Government.
Bowen's Boston news-letter. APS II, Reels 74, 914.

Schools
Common school journal. APS II, Reels 512-514.

BOSTON. MECHANIC APPRENTICES' LIBRARY ASSOCIATION
Mechanic apprentice. APS II, Reel 742.

BOTANY
Maine monthly magazine. APS II, Reel 486.
Western gleaner. APS II, Reel 252.
Western review and miscellaneous magazine. APS II, Reel 253.

BROOK FARM
Harbinger, devoted to social and political progress. APS II, Reel 674.
Phalanx. APS II, Reel 671.

CALIFORNIA
Californian illustrated magazine. APS III, Reel 6.

History
Californian and overland monthly. APS III, Reels 172-173.
Overland monthly and Out West magazine. APS III, Reels 33-52.

History—Gold Discoveries
Overland monthly and Out West magazine. APS III, Reels 33-52.

CALVINISM
Bibliotheca sacra. APS II, Reel 379.
Evangelical luminary. APS II, Reel 103.
Princeton review. APS II, Reels 229, 566-572, 846-854.
Royal spiritual magazine. APS I, Reel 26.

CAMPAIGN LITERATURE, 1804-DEMOCRATIC—REPUBLICAN
Corrector. APS II, Reel 15.

CAMPAIGN LITERATURE, 1840—DEMOCRATIC
Crisis. APS II, Reel 385.

CAPITAL PUNISHMENT
Moral advocate. APS II, Reel 146.
Prisoner's friend. APS II, Reels 749-750.

CAPITALISM
Philistine. APS III, Reels 589-590.

CARICATURES AND CARTOONS
Yankee doodle. APS II, Reel 1408.

CATALOGS BOOKSELLER'S—UNITED STATES
New England literary herald. APS II, Reels 34, 218.

CATHOLIC CHURCH
Catholic telegraph. APS II, Reels 1717-1720.
Catholic world. APS III, Reels 729-749.
Jesuit. APS II, Reels 1370-1371.
United States Catholic magazine. APS II, Reels 689-690.
United States Catholic miscellany. APS II, Reels 1961-1962.

Doctrinal and Controversial works
Brownson's quarterly review. APS II, Reels 507-508, 884-886.

CATHOLIC CHURCH IN THE UNITED STATES
American Catholic quarterly review. APS III, Reels 650-660.
Roycroft quarterly. APS III, Reel 462.

CATHOLIC LITERATURE
Catholic world. APS III, Reels 729-749.

CATHOLICS IN THE UNITED STATES
American Catholic historical researches. APS III, Reels 201-202.

CHARITABLE BEQUESTS
Annals of beneficence. APS II, Reel 64.

CHARITIES
Journal of prison discipline and philanthropy. APS II, Reels 480-481, 1934-1935.

CHAUTAUQUAS
Chautauquan. APS III, Reels 173-186.

CHEMICAL ENGINEERING
American repertory of arts, sciences, and manufactures. APS II, Reel 646.

CHEMISTRY
American journal of science. APS II, Reels 53, 53A, 754-762, 817-830.

Societies, etc.
Memoirs of the Columbian chemical society of Philadelphia. APS II, Reel 95.

CHEROKEE INDIANS—MISSIONS
Roanoke religious correspondent. APS II, Reel 204.

CHILDREN—CONDUCT OF LIFE
Child's friend and family magazine. APS II, Reels 509-512.
Child's newspaper. APS II, Reel 400.
Juvenile mirror. APS II, Reel 121.

CHILDREN'S LITERATURE
Arthur's home magazine. APS III, Reels 533-547.
Child's friend and family magazine. APS II, Reels 509-512.
Child's newspaper. APS II, Reel 400.
Fly. APS II, Reel 19.
Forrester's boys' and girls' magazine, and fireside companion. APS II, Reels 606-607.
Juvenile gazette. APS II, Reel 121.
Juvenile magazine. APS II, Reel 19.
Juvenile miscellany. APS II, Reels 389-390.
Juvenile port-folio. APS II, Reel 212.
Juvenile repository. APS II, Reel 121.
Merry's museum for boys and girls. APS II, Reels 743, 1499-1501.
Oliver Optic's magazine. APS III, Reels 236-238.
Our young folks. APS III, Reels 65-66.
Parley's magazine. APS II, Reels 669-670.
Parlour companion. APS II, Reel 219.
Riverside magazine for young people. APS III, Reel 52.
St. Nicholas. APS III, Reels 591-599.
Southern rose. APS II, Reel 688.
Youth's companion. APS II, Reels 1546-1572.

CHINESE IN THE UNITED STATES
Overland monthly and Out West magazine. APS III, Reels 33-52.

CHIPPEWA LANGUAGE
Chronicles of the North American savages. APS II, Reel 382.

CHRISTIAN BIOGRAPHY
Christian mirror. APS II, Reel 82.
Evangelical repository. APS II, Reel 130.
Experienced Christian's magazine. APS I, Reel 12; APS II, Reel 18.

CHRISTIAN EDUCATION
Berean. A religious publication. APS II, Reels 72, 539.

CHRISTIAN LIFE
Advocate of peace and Christian patriot. APS II, Reel 584.
American expositor. APS II, Reel 365.
Christian reformer. APS II, Reel 382.
Christian visitor. APS II, Reel 401.
Family favorite and temperance journal. APS II, Reel 386.
Happy home and parlor magazine. APS III, Reels 756-757.
Moral and religious cabinet. APS II, Reel 34.
New-England telegraph, and eclectic review. APS II, Reel 802.
Pilgrim. APS II, Reel 188.
Religious instructor. APS II, Reel 198.
Western monthly review. APS II, Reel 673.
Youth's repository of Christian knowledge. APS II, Reel 333.

Biblical Teaching
Advocate for the testimony of God. APS II, Reel 767.

Study and Teaching
Christian monitor. APS II, Reel 83.
Christian monitor; a religious periodical work. APS II, Reels 7, 82.
Christian parlor magazine. APS II, Reels 1230-1231.

CHRISTIAN LITERATURE
Christian mirror. APS II, Reel 82.

CHRISTIANITY
Christian magazine. APS II, Reels 81, 595.

Controversial Literature
Prospect. APS II, Reel 42.
Western examiner. APS II, Reel 487.

New England
Christian observatory. APS II, Reel 312.

CHURCH HISTORY
Columbian magazine. APS II, Reel 32.
New-England missionary magazine. APS II, Reel 157.
Repository of knowledge, historical, literary, miscellaneous, and theological. Philadelphia, [Hugh Maxwell]. APS II, Reel 44.
Repository of knowledge, historical, literary, miscellaneous, and theological. Philadelphia, John Adams, 1802. APS II, Reel 44.

CHURCH OF ENGLAND
Christian observer, conducted by members of the established church. APS II, Reels 8-11, 83-86, 208-209, 1909.

CIVICS
American magazine of civics. APS III, Reels 203-204.

CLASSICAL LITERATURE
Western academician and journal of education and science.
APS II, Reel 486.

Appreciation
Princeton magazine. APS II, Reel 748.

CLASSICAL PHILOLOGY
American journal of philology. APS III, Reels 424-429.

CLERGY
Princeton review. APS II, Reels 229, 566-572, 846-854.

CLERGY, TRAINING OF
American quarterly register. APS II, Reels 532-534.

COLLECTIVE SETTLEMENTS—NEW HARMONY, INDIANA
Free enquirer. APS II, Reels 1498-1499.

COLLEGE AND SCHOOL JOURNALISM
Collegian. APS II, Reel 94.

COLLEGE AND SCHOOL PERIODICALS
Harvard lyceum. APS II, Reel 112.

COLONIZATION
Colonizationist and journal of freedom. APS II, Reel 603.

COMMERCE
Archives of useful knowledge. APS II, Reel 65.
Merchants' magazine and commercial review. APS II, Reels 339-348.
Pathfinder. APS II, Reel 1407.
Washington quarterly magazine. APS II, Reel 246.

COMMUNISM
Free enquirer. APS II, Reels 1498-1499.

COMPROMISE OF 1850
National era. APS II, Reels 899-903.

CONDUCT OF LIFE—EARLY WORKS TO 1900
Rural casket. APS I, Reel 33.

CONFEDERATE STATES OF AMERICA—HISTORY
Southern historical society. APS III, Reels 309-313.

CONGREGATIONAL CHURCHES
Christian observatory. APS II, Reel 312.
Congregationalist and herald of gospel liberty. APS II, Reels 97-99, 539-546, 1911-1924.
Spirit of the Pilgrims. APS II, Reel 752.

Missions
Missionary herald at home and abroad. APS II, Reels 29, 139-142, 764-766, 1237-1245.
Quarterly Christian spectator. APS II, Reels 194-196, 229-232.

CONGREGATIONALISM
Hopkinsian magazine. APS II, Reel 914.
Literary and theological review. APS II, Reel 798.
New Englander and Yale review. APS II, Reels 679-680, 904-912.

CONVERTS
Christian cabinet. APS II, Reel 7.
Christian monitor, and religious intelligencer. APS II, Reel 83.
Massachusetts missionary magazine. APS II, Reel 25.

COUNTRY LIFE—NEW YORK
Horticulturist and journal of rural art and rural taste. APS II, Reels 656, 890-893.

COURTS-MARTIAL AND COURTS OF INQUIRY— UNITED STATES—CASES
Militia reporter. APS II, Reel 137.

CRIME AND CRIMINALS
National police gazette. APS II, Reels 1318-1340.

CRIMINAL LAW—United States.
New York City hall recorder. APS II, Reel 211.

CRITICISM
American monthly magazine. APS II, Reel 468.

CURIOSITIES AND WONDERS—EARLY WORKS TO 1900
American magazine of wonders and marvellous chronicle. APS II, Reel 1.

DANCING
Lady's monitor. APS II, Reel 20.

DAYTON, OHIO—HISTORY
Gridiron. APS II, Reel 111.

DEATH—SERMONS
Experienced Christian's magazine. APS I, Reel 12; APS II, Reel 18.

DEBT, IMPRISONMENT FOR
Remembrancer. APS II, Reel 204.

DEBTOR AND CREDITOR
Debtors' journal. APS II, Reel 100.

DEMOCRATIC PARTY—UNITED STATES
Belford's monthly. APS III, Reels 586-589.
Crisis. APS II, Reel 385.
Knickerbocker. APS II, Reels 349-361.

DENTISTRY—New England
New England journal of dentistry and allied sciences. APS III, Reel 269.

Practice
New England journal of dentistry and allied sciences. APS III, Reel 269.

SUBJECT INDEX

DIDACTIC LITERATURE
American critic and general review. APS II, Reel 51.

DRAMA
Dramatic mirror, and literary companion. APS II, Reel 605.
Opera glass. APS II, Reel 1124.
Theatrical budget. APS II, Reel 1258.

History And Criticism
Critic. A weekly review of literature, fine arts, and the drama.
    APS II, Reel 385.

DRAMATIC CRITICISM
Emerson's magazine and Putnam's monthly. APS III, Reels 264-265.
Literary gazette and American athenaeum. APS II, Reel 741.
New York literary gazette and journal of belles lettres, arts,
    science, &c. APS II, Reel 1292.
Philadelphia magazine, and weekly repertory. APS II, Reel 186.
Thespian mirror. APS II, Reel 44.

DRESSMAKING
Arthur's home magazine. APS III, Reels 533-547.
Harper's bazaar. APS III, Reel 430-450.
Pictorial review. APS II, Reels 1487-1488.

ECONOMIC HISTORY
International review. APS III, Reels 152-154.

ECONOMICS
Journal of social science. APS III, Reels 266-268.
Literary and scientific repository. APS II, Reel 126.
Literary register. APS II, Reel 1234.
Monthly chronicle of events. APS II, Reel 745.
Political economist. APS II, Reel 191.
Quarterly journal of economics. APS III, Reels 167-170.

EDUCATION—Connecticut
Connecticut common school journal. APS II, Reels 789-791.

History
American journal of education. APS III, Reels 85-91.

Michigan
Journal of education. APS II, Reel 1231.

Philosophy
Academician. APS II, Reel 47.

United States
Academician. APS II, Reel 47.
American annals of education. APS II, Reels 293-294.
American educational monthly. APS III, Reels 171-172.
American journal of education. APS III, Reels 85-91.
American quarterly register. APS II, Reels 532-534.
Common school journal. APS II, Reels 512-514.
District school journal of the state of New York. APS II, Reel 770.
Journal of education. APS II, Reel 1231.
Literary pamphleteer. APS II, Reel 132.
Literary union. APS II, Reel 742.
McBride's magazine. APS III, Reels 316-341.
Massachusetts teacher. APS II, Reels 610-613.
New Hampshire repository. APS II, Reel 842.
Rhode Island Institute of Instruction. Journal. APS II, Reel 389.
Western academician and journal of education and science. APS II,
    Reel 486.

EDUCATION, ELEMENTARY
American annals of education. APS II, Reels 293-294.
Common school assistant. APS II, Reel 889.

Southern States
Common school advocate. APS II, Reel 383.

EDUCATION, HIGHER
Harvard register. APS III, Reel 109.

EDUCATION OF CHILDREN
Common school assistant. APS II, Reel 889.
Juvenile mirror. APS II, Reel 121.
Teacher's guide and parent's assistant. APS II, Reel 1407.

EDUCATION OF WOMEN
American journal of education. APS III, Reel 85-91.
Godey's magazine. APS II, Reels 772-776, 862-880.
Ladies' garland. APS II, Reel 561.
Ladies' garland and family wreath. APS II, Reels 608-609.
Miscellaneous cabinet. APS II, Reel 218.

ENCYCLOPEDIAS AND DICTIONARIES
American repertory of arts, sciences, and useful literature. APS II,
    Reel 734.

ENGLISH DRAMA
Baltimore repertory of papers on literary and other topics.
    APS II, Reel 71.

ENGLISH ESSAYS
Boston weekly-magazine. APS I, Reel 8.

ENGLISH FICTION-19th CENTURY
Living age. APS II, Reels 319-323, 974-1052.

ENGLISH LITERATURE
Atheneum; or, spirit of the English magazines. APS II, Reel 66-69,
    1365-1367.
Robinson's magazine. APS II, Reels 204-205.
Saturday magazine. APS II, Reels 237-238.

19th Century
Analectic magazine. APS II, Reels 61-64.
Anglo-American magazine. APS II, Reel 378.
Brown's literary omnibus. APS II, Reel 1368.
Campbell's foreign semi-monthly magazine. APS II, Reel 381.
Daguerreotype. APS II, Reel 473.
Eclectic museum of foreign literature, science and art. APS II,
    Reel 605.
Every Saturday. APS III, Reels 148-151.
Literary and scientific repository. APS II, Reel 126.
Living age. APS II, Reels 319-323, 974-1052.
Museum of foreign literature, science, and art. APS II, Reels 146-
    148, 1245-1254.
New monthly magazine and literary journal. APS II, Reels 158-161,
    881.
Select journal of foreign periodical literature. APS II, Reel 913.
Select reviews of literature, and spirit of foreign magazines. APS II,
    Reels 44, 239-240.
Zodiac. APS II, Reel 753.

ENGLISH POETRY—18th Century
Boston weekly-magazine. APS I, Reel 8.

19th Century
Eclectic museum of foreign literature, science and art. APS II, Reel 605.
Zodiac. APS II, Reel 753.

EPIDEMICS
Medical repository of original essays and intelligence. APS I, Reel 14; APS II, Reels 26-27, 132-134.
Vaccine inquirer. APS II, Reel 246.

Charleston, S.C., 1802
Charleston medical register for the year 1802. APS II, Reel 546.

ESSAYS
Aeronaut. APS II, Reels 48-49.
American monthly review. APS II, Reel 768.
Boston magazine, containing, a collection of instructive and entertaining essays. APS I, Reel 9.
Club-room. APS II, Reel 92.
Dial: a magazine for literature, philosophy, and religion. APS II, Reel 546.
Eastern magazine. APS II, Reel 385.
Examiner and hesperian. APS II, Reel 386.
Eye. APS II, Reel 19.
Franklin Minerva. APS II, Reel 546.
Gleaner; or, Monthly magazine. APS II, Reel 32.
Idle man. APS II, Reel 115.
Literary geminae. APS II, Reel 657.
Magazine for the million. APS II, Reel 742.
Miscellaneous magazine. APS II, Reel 139.
Monthly register, magazine, and review of the United States. APS II, Reel 33.
Moralist. APS II, Reel 146.
North American review. APS II, Reels 177-183, 270-281, 1613-1647.
Occasional reverberator. APS I, Reel 24.
Periodical library. APS II, Reel 736.
Pioneer, consisting of essays, literary, moral and theological. APS II, Reel 189.
Quarterly journal and review. APS II, Reel 1092.
Reflector. APS II, Reel 197.
Repository and ladies' weekly museum. APS II, Reel 43.
Spirit of the public journals. APS II, Reel 44.
Talisman. APS II, Reel 400.
Universal asylum and Columbian magazine. APS I, Reels 11, 30.
Weekly visitant. APS II, Reel 46.
Worcester magazine. APS I, Reel 33.
Yale literary magazine. APS II, Reels 529-531.

ETHICS
American moral & sentimental magazine. APS I, Reel 3.
Guardian and monitor. APS II, Reels 111-112, 881.
Messenger of peace. APS II, Reel 217.
New world. APS III, Reels 31-32.
Rural casket. APS I, Reel 33.
Weekly monitor. APS II, Reel 248.

EUROPE—History
Historical family library. APS II, Reel 737.

History—1789-1815
American register. APS II, Reels 2, 59.

History—1815-1848
American register; or, Summary review of history, politics, and literature. APS II, Reel 59.

History—Year-Books
American register; or general repository of history, politics and science. APS II, Reels 2, 59.

American register; or, Summary review of history, politics, and literature. APS II, Reel 59.

EVANGELICALISM
Beauties of the Evangelical magazine. APS II, Reel 6.
Christian history. APS I, Reel 10.
Christian reformer. APS II, Reel 382.
Columbia magazine. APS II, Reel 94.
Connecticut evangelical magazine and religious intelligencer. APS II, Reels 14, 127-129.

EVANGELISTIC WORK
Evangelical luminary. APS II, Reel 103.
Evangelical recorder. APS II, Reel 103.
Evangelical repertory. APS II, Reel 103.
Evangelical witness. APS II, Reels 103-104, 606.
Evangelist. APS II, Reel 1271.
Religious miscellany. APS II, Reel 203.
Roanoke religious correspondent. APS II, Reel 204.

FACTORY SYSTEM—UNITED STATES—LOWELL, MASSACHUSETTS
Lowell offering. APS II, Reel 675.

FARM LIFE
Indiana farmer's guide. APS II, Reels 1797-1801.
Prairie farmer. APS II, Reels 747-748, 1720-1726, 1936.

Ohio
Ohio cultivator. APS II, Reels 1254-1257.

United States
Maine farmer. APS II, Reels 422, 427, 1371-88.

FARM MANAGEMENT
Tennessee farmer. APS II, Reel 1490.

FARMERS
American farmer's magazine. APS II, Reels 503-507.
Farmer's register. APS II, Reels 334-338.

Michigan
Michigan farmer. APS II, Reels 324, 1502-1519.

New York (City)
New York farmer. APS II, Reels 1195-1196.

New York (State)—Genesee County
Genesee farmer. APS II, Reels 795-797.

United States
Colman's rural world. APS II, Reel 416.
Southern agriculturist, horticulturist, and register of rural affairs. APS II, Reels 806-809.

FASHION
American literary magazine. APS II, Reel 787.
Arthur's home magazine. APS III, Reels 533-547.
Artist. APS II, Reel 649.
Boston magazine. APS II, Reel 6.
Boston miscellany of literature and fashion. APS II, Reel 310.
Dollar magazine; A monthly gazette of current literature, music and art. APS II, Reel 385.
Godey's magazine. APS II, Reels 772-776, 862-880.
Ladies' garland. APS II, Reel 561.
Ladies' garland and family wreath. APS II, Reels 608-609.
Lady's monitor. APS II, Reel 20.

Peterson magazine. APS II, Reels 1292-1308.
Pictorial review. APS II, Reels 1487-1488.
Poughkeepsie casket. APS II, Reel 746.
Souvenir. APS II, Reel 1407.
Town. APS II, Reel 45.

FEDERAL GOVERNMENT
Independent republican. APS II, Reel 19.

FEDERAL PARTY
Weekly inspector. APS II, Reel 1408.

FICTION-18th Century
American magazine, containing a miscellaneous collection. APS I, Reel 2.
General magazine and impartial review of knowledge & entertainment. APS I, Reel 13.
Literary miscellany. APS I, Reel 14.
Monthly miscellany; or, Vermont magazine. APS I, Reel 18.
Newhampshire magazine. APS I, Reel 19.
New-York weekly magazine. APS I, Reels 23, 27.
Universal asylum and Columbian magazine. APS I, Reels 11, 30.

19th Century
American monthly magazine. APS II, Reel 377.
Atlantic magazine. APS II, Reel 70.
Beadle's monthly. APS III, Reel 26.
Boston magazine. APS II, Reel 6.
Boston weekly magazine. APS II, Reels 326, 784.
Brother Jonathan. APS II, Reels 409-410.
Emerald, or, Miscellany of literature. APS II, Reel 15.
Franklin Minerva. APS II, Reel 546.
Galaxy. APS III, Reels 7-12.
Ladies' companion, and literary expositor. APS II, Reels 738-740.
Literary emporium. APS II, Reel 1233.
Manhattan. APS III, Reels 30-31.
Mechanic's advocate. APS II, Reel 400.
Microscope. APS II, Reel 217.
National repository. APS II, Reels 110-111.
Open court. APS III, Reels 293-297.
Orion. APS II, reel 1216.
Quarterly journal and review. APS II, Reel 1092.
Repository and ladies' weekly museum. APS II, Reel 43.
St. Tammanys magazine. APS II, Reel 205.
Weekly visitant. APS II, Reel 46.

FISHING
Forest and stream. APS III, Reels 208-235.

FLORICULTURE
Horticultural register, and gardener's magazine. APS II, Reel 527.

FOOD—PRESERVATION
Western farmer and gardener. APS II, Reel 1408.

FOREIGN NEWS
Globe. APS II, Reel 109.
Philadelphia magazine and review. APS I, Reel 24.

FOX INDIANS
Chronicles of the North American savages. APS II, Reel 382.

FRANCE—HISTORY—19th Century
Mediateur. APS II, Reel 132.

Politics and Government
Mediateur. APS II, Reel 132.

FREE BAPTISTS
Religious informer. APS II, Reels 197-198.
Religious magazine; containing an account of the united churches of Christ. APS II, Reel 202.

FREE LOVE
Liberty (not the daughter but the mother of order). APS III, Reels 669-670.

FREE THOUGHT
Western examiner. APS II, Reel 487.

FREE TRADE AND PROTECTION
American laborer. APS II, Reel 644.
Gunton's magazine. APS III, Reels 473-476.
Southern quarterly review. APS II, Reels 684-687.

FREEDMEN IN INDIANA
Free enquirer. APS II, Reels 1498-1499.

FREEMASONS
Amaranth; or, Masonic garland. APS II, Reel 404.
American Masonic register, and ladies and gentlemen's magazine. APS II, Reel 54.
American masonic register and literary companion. APS II, Reels 915-916.
Anti-masonic review, and magazine. APS II, Reel 769.
Freemasons magazine and general miscellany. APS II, Reel 106.
Masonic casket. APS II, Reel 132.
Masonic miscellany and ladies literary magazine. APS II, Reel 214.
New-England galaxy. APS II, Reels 150-152, 1120-1123.

FREEMASONS. BOSTON
Boston masonic mirror. APS II, Reels 73, 589-591.

FREEMASONS. NEW YORK
Escritoir. APS II, Reel 792.

FRENCH IN THE UNITED STATES
Annales philosophiques. APS II, Reel 3.
Courier de Boston. APS I, Reel 10.

FRENCH LANGUAGE
Annales philosophiques. APS II, Reel 3.
Courier de Boston. APS I, Reel 10.
Hemisphere, journal francais. APS II, Reels 19, 113.
Journal des dames. APS II, Reel 115.
Journal inutile. APS II, Reel 131.
Petit censeur, critique et litteraire. APS II, Reel 37.

FRENCH LITERATURE
Daguerreotype. APS II, Reel 473.
Hemisphere, journal francais. APS II, Reels 19, 113.
Journal inutile. APS II, Reel 131.
Journal of belles-lettres. Lexington, Ky. APS II, Reel 116.
Mediateur. APS II, Reel 132.

Translation into English
Literary geminae. APS II, Reel 657.

FRENCH-AMERICAN LITERATURE
Petit censeur. APS II, Reel 37.

FRIENDS, SOCIETY OF
Friend; a religious and literary journal. APS II, Reels 523-526,
1412-1419.
Friends' intelligencer. APS II, Reels 735-736, 1167-1191.
Friends review. APS II, Reels 386-387, 924-934.

GARDENING
American farmer. APS II, Reels 51-52, 1062-1071.
Horticultural register, and gardener's magazine. APS II, Reel 527.
Western farmer and gardener. APS II, Reel 698.

GENEALOGY
American historical register and monthly gazette. APS III, Reel 58.

GENERAL CONVENTION OF THE CHRISTIAN CHURCH
Herald of gospel liberty. APS II, Reels 19, 1925-1934.

GEOGRAPHY
Geographical, historical, and statistical repository. APS II, Reels
100, 130.
Monthly chronicle of events. APS II, Reel 745.

Societies, etc.
American Geographical Society of New York. Bulletin. APS III,
Reel 708.

GEOLOGY
American journal of science. APS II, Reels 53, 53A, 754-762,
817-830.
Maine monthly magazine. APS II, Reel 486.
Monthly American journal of geology and natural science.
APS II, Reel 659.
Parthenon. APS II, Reel 1257.
Theological and literary journal. APS II, Reels 940-943.

United States
American mineralogical journal. APS II, Reel 57.

GERMAN EVANGELICAL SYNOD OF NORTH AMERICA
Evangelisches Magazin. APS II, Reel 104.

GERMAN LANGUAGE
Evangelisches Magazin. APS II, Reel 104.
Geistliches magazien. APS I, Reel 12.
Walhalla. APS II, Reel 1408.

GERMAN LITERATURE
Daguerreotype. APS II, Reel 473.
German correspondent. APS II, Reel 130.
Philadelphier magazin. APS II, Reel 1196.

Translations Into English
Expositor. APS II, Reel 924.

GERMAN POETRY—TRANSLATIONS INTO ENGLISH
Massachusetts quarterly review. APS II, Reel 658.

GERMANS IN THE UNITED STATES
German correspondent. APS II, Reel 130.

Philadelphisches Magazin. APS I, Reel 25.

GIFT-BOOKS (ANNUALS, ETC.)
Atlantic souvenir. APS II, Reel 1367.

GOD
Remembrancer, for Lord's Day evenings. APS I, Reel 26.

GRAHAM FLOUR
Graham journal of health and longevity. APS II, Reel 777.

GRAHAMITES
Graham journal of health and longevity. APS II, Reel 777.

GREAT AWAKENING
Christian history. APS I, Reel 10.

GREAT BRITAIN—History—18th Century
American magazine and historical chronicle. APS I, Reel 1.

Politics and Government
Cobbett's political register. APS II, Reel 92.
John Englishman, in defence of the English constitution.
APS I, Reel 13.

GREAT BRITAIN. CONSTITUTION
John Englishman, in defence of the English constitution.
APS I, Reel 13.

**HARPERS FERRY, WEST VIRGINIA—JOHN BROWNS
RAID**
National era. APS II, Reels 899-903.

HARVARD UNIVERSITY
General repository and review. APS II, Reels 107-108.
Harvard lyceum. APS II, Reel 112.
Harvard register. APS II, Reel 777.
Harvard register; an illustrated monthly. APS III, Reel 109.

HISTORICAL SOCIETIES—UNITED STATES
American historical register and monthly gazette. APS III,
Reel 58.

HISTORY
Christian's scholar's and farmer's magazine. APS I, Reel 10.
Nassau literary magazine. APS II, Reels 1482-1486.
Parthenon. APS II, Reel 1257.

19th Century
Monthly chronicle of events. APS II, Reel 745.
Periodical library. APS II, Reel 736.

HOMEOPATHY
American journal of homoeopathia. APS II, Reel 365.
American journal of homoeopathy. APS II, Reel 365.
American journal of homeopathy. Philadelphia. APS II, Reel 295.
Physicians' and surgeons' investigator. APS III, Reels 567-568.

HORSE-RACING
American turf register and sporting magazine. APS II, Reels 404-
407.

SUBJECT INDEX

Spirit of the times. APS II, Reels 620-640.

HORSES
American turf register and sporting magazine. APS II, Reel 404-407.

HORTICULTURE
Genesee farmer and gardeners journal. APS II, Reels 316-318.
Literary register. APS II, Reel 1234.
Magazine of useful and entertaining knowledge. APS II, Reel 742.
Tennessee farmer. APS II, Reel 1490.

New York
Horticulturist and journal of rural art and rural taste. APS II, Reels 656, 890-893.

HUDSON, NEW YORK—HISTORY
Spirit of the forum. APS II, Reel 240.

HUMAN BEHAVIOR—ADDRESSES, ESSAYS, LECTURES
Vigil. APS I, Reel 31.

HUNTING
Forest and stream. APS III, Reels 208-235.

HYDROTHERAPY
Health. APS II, Reels 516-576, 1692-1696.

HYGIENE
Health. APS II, Reels 516-576, 1692-1696.
Journal of health. APS II, Reel 479.

ILLINOIS—HISTORY—1778-1865
Illinois monthly magazine. APS II, Reel 389.

INDIANS—LANGUAGES
Atlantic journal, and friend of knowledge. APS II, Reel 839.

INDIANS, TREATMENT OF—UNITED STATES
American Society for Promoting the Civilization and General Improvement of the Indian Tribes in the United States. The first annual report. APS II, Reel 534.

INDIANS OF NORTH AMERICA
Chronicles of the North American savages. APS II, Reel 382.

Antiquities
Western review and miscellaneous magazine. APS II, Reel 253.

Education
American Society for Promoting the Civilization and General Improvement of the Indian Tribes in the United States. The first annual report. APS II, Reel 534.

Languages
American Society for Promoting the Civilization and General Improvement of the Indian Tribes in the United States. The first annual report. APS II, Reel 534.

Missions
Circular. APS II, Reel 210a.

Religious intelligencer. APS II, Reels 198-202, 234-235, 1488-1490.

Ohio Valley
American pioneer. APS II, Reel 297.

Social Life and Customs
Columbian historian. APS II, Reel 95.

Virginia
Chronicles of the North American savages. APS II, Reel 382.

Wars
Columbian historian. APS II, Reel 95.
Periodical sketches. APS II, Reel 184.

INDUSTRIAL ARTS
Agricultural museum. APS II, Reel 49.
American mechanics' magazine. APS II, Reels 54, 763.
American museum, and repository of arts and sciences. APS II, Reel 58.
American repertory of arts, sciences, and manufactures. APS II, Reel 646.
Boston mechanic, and journal of the useful arts and sciences. APS II, Reel 472.
Emporium of arts & sciences. APS II, Reel 101.
Mechanics' magazine, and journal of the Mechanics' institute. APS II, Reels 613-614.
Mechanics' magazine, and journal of public internal improvement. APS II, Reel 1093.

INSTRUMENTAL MUSIC—TO 1800
Musical magazine. APS I, Reel 18.

INTERNATIONAL RELATIONS
World affairs. APS II, Reels 584, 1543-1545.

INVENTIONS
American museum, and repository of arts and sciences. APS II, Reel 58.
American review, and literary journal, for 1801-1802. APS II, Reel 3.
Literary and philosophical repertory. APS II, Reel 126.
Magazine of useful and entertaining knowledge. APS II, Reel 742.
Mechanic's advocate. APS II, Reel 400.
National museum and weekly gazette. APS II, Reel 149.
Scientific American. APS II, Reels 616-619, 1734-1748.
Useful cabinet. APS II, Reel 45.

IRELAND—HISTORY—19TH CENTURY
Irish shield. APS II, Reel 937.

IRISH LITERATURE
Irish shield. APS II, Reel 937.

ISRAEL'S ADVOCATE
Jew. APS II, Reel 131.

ITALIAN LITERATURE—19th Century
Journal of belles-lettres. APS II, Reel 116.

Translations into English
Expositor. APS II, Reel 924.

JEWS—HISTORY
Halcyon itinerary. APS II, Reel 19.

JOURNALISM—UNITED STATES
American monitor. APS I, Reel 3.

Globe. APS II, Reel 109.
Penny post. APS I, Reel 24.
Time piece. APS I, Reel 29.
Weekly museum. APS I, Reel 33.

JOURNALISM, RELIGIOUS
Adviser. APS II, Reels 1, 47.
Almoner. APS II, Reel 51.
Christian register, and moral and theological review. APS II,
    Reel 88.
Christian visitant. APS II, Reel 89.
Christian's magazine: designed to promote the knowledge. APS II,
    Reels, 11, 90.
Christian's magazine, reviewer, and religious intelligencer. APS II,
    Reel 11.
Churchman's magazine. APS II, Reels 12, 91, 210.
Churchman's repository for the eastern diocese. APS II, Reel 127.
Columbia magazine. APS II, Reel 94.
Columbian star. APS II, Reels 95-96, 1271.
Congregationalist and herald of gospel liberty. APS II, Reels 97-
    99, 539-546, 1911-1924.
Connecticut evangelical magazine and religious intelligencer.
    APS II, Reels 14, 127-129.
Evangelical witness. APS II, Reels 103-104, 606.
Georgia analytical repository. APS II, Reel 19.
Lay-man's magazine. APS II, Reel 123.
Massachusetts watchman. APS II, Reels 26, 216.
Miscellaneous magazine. APS II, Reel 139.
Monthly visitant. APS II, Reel 146.
New York religious chronicle. APS II, Reel 166.
Religious informer. APS II, Reels 197-198.
Religious intelligencer. APS II, Reels 198-202, 234-235, 1488-
    1490.
Spirit of the XIX. century. APS II, Reel 779.
United States Christian magazine. APS I, Reel 30.
Utica Christian magazine. APS II, Reel 244.
Western recorder. APS II, Reels 1260-1262.

JUDAISM—APOLOGETIC WORKS
Jew. APS II, Reel 131.

JUDGES
Carolina law repository. APS II, Reel 75.

Biography
American law magazine. APS II, Reel 732.
Monthly law reporter. APS II, Reels 288-292.

KENTUCKY—EMIGRATION AND IMMIGRATION
New star. APS I, Reel 23.

LABOR AND LABORING CLASSES
American magazine of civics. APS III, Reels 203-204.
Mechanic apprentice. APS II, Reel 742.
Subterranean. APS II, Reel 576.
Working man's advocate. APS II, Reel 581-583.

Political Activity
Subterranean. APS II, Reel 576.

LAW
American quarterly observer. APS II, Reel 297.
Carolina law journal. APS II, Reel 382.
Carolina law repository. APS II, Reel 75.

Addresses, Essays, Lectures
American law journal. Philadelphia, Walker. APS II, Reels 730-731.

Interpretation and Construction
Journal of jurisprudence. APS II, Reel 119.

Maryland
American law journal. (Hall). APS II, Reels 1, 53.

New York (State)
New-York legal observer. APS II, Reels 802-803.

Ohio
Western law journal. APS II, Reels 487-489.

Study and Teaching
Journal of the Law-School, and of the moot-court attached to it,
    at Needham, in Virginia. APS II, Reel 121.

United States
Albany law journal. APS III, Reels 570-580.
American jurist and law magazine. APS II, Reels 726-729.
American law journal. (Hall). APS II, Reels 1, 53.
American law journal. Philadelphia, Walker. APS II, Reels 730-731.
American law magazine. APS II, Reel 732.
American law review. APS III, Reels 463-472.
American lawyer. APS III, Reels 240-243.
Annual law register of the United States. APS II, Reel 65.
Central law journal. APS III, Reels 548-566.
United States law intelligencer and review. APS II, Reel 741.
United States law journal. APS II, Reel 944.
Western law journal. APS II, Reels 487-489.

LAW REPORTS, DIGESTS, ETC.—UNITED STATES
American law journal. (Hall). APS II, Reels 1, 53.
American law journal. Philadelphia, Walker. APS II, Reels 730-731.
Carolina law repository. APS II, Reel 75.
Journal of jurisprudence. APS II, Reel 119.
Monthly law reporter. APS II, Reels 288-292.
New York City hall recorder. APS II, Reel 211.
New-York legal observer. APS II, Reels 802-803.
United States law intelligencer and review. APS II, Reel 741.
United States law journal. APS II, Reel 944.
Western law journal. APS II, Reel 487-489.

LAWYERS
Annual law register of the United States. APS II, Reel 65.

LIBERIA
African repository. APS II, Reels 49, 641-644, 881-884.

LITERARY RECREATIONS
Recreative magazine. APS II, Reel 197.

LITERATURE
Baltimore weekly magazine complete in one volume. APS II, Reel
    6.
Boston miscellany of literature and fashion. APS II, Reel 310.
Christian philanthropist. APS II, Reel 87.
Christian's, scholar's, and farmer's magazine. APS I, Reel 10.
Tablet. APS I, Reel 28.

Collections
Bibelot. APS III, Reels 252-253.

History and Criticism
Albany bouquet and literary spectator. APS II, Reel 767.
Bookman. APS III, Reels 112-130.
Dial; a semi-monthly journal of literary criticism, discussion,
    and information. APS III, Reels 187-200.

Literary journal; a repository of polite literature and fine arts.
APS II, Reel 657.
Literary miscellany. APS II, Reel 24.
Literary world. APS III, Reels 155-159.
New Outlook. APS III, Reels 367-423.
North American quarterly magazine. APS II, Reels 938-939.
Round table. APS III, Reels 461-462.
Pastime. APS II, Reel 36.

Miscellanea

Albany bouquet and literary spectator. APS II, Reel 767.
Amaranth. A semi-monthly publication. APS II, Reel 784.
American eagle magazine. APS II, Reel 365.
American expositor. APS II, Reel 365.
American magazine. APS III, Reels 675-689.
American universal magazine. APS I, Reels 6-7.
Ariel. APS II, Reel 839.
Boston magazine, containing, a collection of instructive
and entertaining essays. APS I, Reel 9.
Emerald. APS II, Reel 101.
Emerald and Baltimore literary gazette. APS II, Reel 605.
Evening fire-side. APS II, Reel 18.
Freemasons magazine and general miscellany. APS II, Reel 106.
Gospel palladium. APS II, Reel 110.
Guardian. APS II, Reel 19.
Huntingdon literary museum. APS II, Reel 114.
Key. APS I, Reel 13.
Ladies port folio. APS II, Reel 122.
Lady's miscellany. APS II, Reels 20-21, 212-213.
Lady's monitor. APS II, Reel 20.
Lancaster hive. APS II, Reel 22.
Literary companion. APS II, Reel 131.
Literary gems. APS II, Reel 799.
Literary journal; a repository of polite literature and fine arts.
APS II, Reel 657.
Literary mirror. APS II, Reel 24.
Literary miscellany. APS II, Reel 131.
Literary tablet. APS II, Reel 657.
Mechanic apprentice. APS II, Reel 742.
Merrimack magazine and ladies' literary cabinet. APS II, Reel 28.
Merrimack magazine, and monthly register. APS II, Reel 217.
Merrimack miscellany. APS II, Reel 28.
Microscope. APS II, Reel 217.
Mirror of literature, amusement and instruction. APS II, Reel 138.
Monthly magazine and literary journal. APS II, Reel 145.
Monthly repository and library of entertaining knowledge. APS II,
Reel 1215.
New Jersey monthly magazine. APS II, Reel 158.
New York literary gazette. APS II, Reel 973.
New-York magazine and general repository. APS II, Reel 162.
New-York monthly magazine. APS II, Reel 165.
Northern light. APS II, Reel 844.
Oasis. APS II, Reel 806.
Observer. By Beatrice Ironside. APS II, Reel 36.
Ohio miscellaneous museum. APS II, Reel 218.
Omnium gatherum. APS II, Reels 36, 219.
Philadelphia Minerva. APS I, Reel 25.
Polyanthos. APS II, Reels 39, 191-192.
Portico. APS II, Reels 192-193.
Portland magazine. APS II, Reel 42.
Portsmouth weekly magazine. APS II, Reel 193.
Poughkeepsie casket. APS II, Reel 746.
Royal American magazine. APS I, Reel 26.
Rural magazine. APS I, Reel 27.
Rural repository devoted to polite literature. APS II, Reels 681-
683.
Rutgers literary miscellany. APS II, Reel 880.
South-Carolina weekly museum. APS I, Reel 28.
Stand. APS II, Reel 333.
Universalist. APS II, Reels 243-246, 1701-1706.
Villager. APS II, Reel 246.
Visitor. APS II, Reels 46, 246.
Weekly visitor. APS II, Reel 251.

Wellman's miscellany. APS II, Reels 779-780.
Western literary magazine. APS II, Reel 1260.

Societies, etc.

Transactions of the Literary and philosophical society of
New-York. APS II, Reel 840.

LITERATURE, MODERN-18th Century

American Apollo. APS I, Reel 1.
American magazine, containing a miscellaneous collection. APS I,
Reel 2.
American monthly review. APS I, Reel 3.
Boston monthly magazine. APS II, Reels 74, 591.
Boston weekly magazine, devoted to polite literature, useful
science, biography, and dramatic criticism. APS II, Reel 74.
Columbian phenix and Boston review. APS II, Reel 13.
Comet. APS II, Reel 97.
Connecticut magazine. APS II, Reel 15.
Dessert to the true American. APS I, Reel 12.
Massachusetts magazine. APS I, Reels 15-16.
Monthly magazine, and American review. APS I, Reel 17.
Nightingale. APS I, Reel 23.

19th Century

Albion. APS II, Reels 50, 706-718, 1263-1270.
American athenaeum. APS II, Reel 51.
American eclectic. APS II, Reel 295.
American magazine, and repository of useful literature. APS II,
Reel 376.
American monthly review. APS II, Reel 768.
American museum of literature and the arts. APS II, Reel 646.
American people's journal of science, literature, and art. APS II,
Reel 333.
American Whig review. APS II, Reels 302-304.
Anglo American. APS II, Reels 647-649.
Appletons' journal. APS III, Reels 244-249.
Aristidean. APS II, Reel 378.
Atlantic magazine. APS II, Reel 70.
Baltimore repertory of papers on literary and other topics. APS II,
Reel 71.
Beadle's monthly. APS III, Reel 26.
Boston literary magazine. APS II, Reel 379.
Boston lyceum. APS II, Reel 379.
Boston pearl, a gazette of polite literature. APS II, Reel 788.
Boston weekly magazine. APS II, Reels 326, 784.
Brown's literary omnibus. APS II, Reel 1368.
Carey's library of choice literature. APS II, Reel 916.
Casket. Devoted to literature, science, the arts, news, &c.
APS II, Reel 382.
Child of Pallas: devoted mostly to the belles-lettres. APS II, Reel 7.
Christian register. APS II, Reels 87-88, 596-603.
Cincinnati literary gazette. APS II, Reel 127.
Cincinnati mirror, and Western gazette. APS II, Reel 789.
Continental monthly. APS III, Reel 140.
Corsair. APS II, Reel 384.
Critic. APS III, Reels 101-108.
Dawn. APS II, Reel 100.
Dial. APS III, Reel 7.
Dollar magazine; A monthly gazette. APS II, Reel 385.
Eclectic magazine of foreign literature. APS II, Reels 519-523.
945-973.
Emerald, or, Miscellany of literature. APS II, Reel 15.
Evergreen. APS II, Reel 448.
Examiner and hesperian. APS II, Reel 386.
Family minstrel. APS II, Reel 973.
Floriad. APS II, Reel 106.
Forum and Century. APS III, Reels 272-293.
Godey's magazine. APS II, Reels 772-776, 862-880.
Halcyon luminary. APS II, Reels 112, 464.
Harvardiana. APS II, Reel 655.
Hesperian. APS II, Reel 417.

International monthly magazine of literature, science and art. APS III, Reel 109.

Iris. APS II, Reel 656.

Journal of belles-lettres. Lexington. APS II, Reel 116.

Journal of belles lettres. Philadelphia. APS II, Reel 1314.

Lady & gentleman's pocket magazine. APS I, Reel 14.

Literary magazine. APS II, Reel 400.

Literary and evangelical magazine. APS II, Reels 124-125, 464.

Literary and philosophical repertory. APS II, Reel 126.

Literary cabinet and western olive branch. APS II, Reel 565.

Literary casket. APS II, Reel 777.

Literary focus. APS II, Reel 777.

Literary gazette and American athenaeum. APS II, Reel 741.

Literary inquirer. APS II, Reel 799.

Literary journal. APS II, Reel 799.

Literary magazine. APS II, Reel 400.

Literary register. APS II, Reel 1234.

McBride's magazine. APS III, Reels 316-341.

Magnolia; or, Literary tablet. APS II, Reel 777.

Maine monthly magazine. APS II, Reel 486.

Massachusetts quarterly review. APS II, Reel 658.

Miscellaneous cabinet. APS II, Reel 218.

Miscellany. APS II, Reel 28.

Monthly anthology, and Boston review. APS II, Reels 30-32, 143-144.

Nassau literary magazine. APS II, Reels 1482-1486.

National magazine. APS II, Reels 814-815.

New England quarterly magazine. APS II, Reel 34.

New York literary gazette and journal of belles lettres, arts, science, &c. APS II, Reel 1292.

New-York literary journal. APS II, Reels 161-162.

New York review. APS III, Reels 843-844.

New-Yorker. APS II, Reels 1090-1092.

New Hampshire repository. APS II, Reel 842.

North American. APS II, Reel 973.

North American review. APS II, Reels 177-183, 270-281, 1613-1647.

Old and new. APS III, Reels 130-132.

Opera glass. APS II, Reel 1124.

Ordeal. APS II, Reel 36.

Parlour review, and journal of music, literature, and the fine arts. APS II, Reel 845.

Pathfinder. APS II, Reel 1407.

Philadelphia magazine. APS II, Reel 186.

Philadelphia monthly magazine. APS II, Reel 1092.

Philadelphia repertory. APS II, Reel 186.

Pioneer. APS III, Reel 15.

Present. APS II, Reel 748.

Republic of letters. APS II, Reels 1257-1258.

Rhode Island literary repository. APS II, Reel 204.

Robinson's magazine. APS II, Reels 204-205.

Rural magazine and literary evening fire-side. APS II, Reel 205.

Southern literary messenger. APS II, Reels 438-447.

Southern review. Baltimore. APS III, Reels 18-20.

Southern review. Charleston. APS II, Reel 325.

Stranger. APS II, Reel 810.

United States review and literary gazette. APS II, Reel 1124.

Universalist quarterly and general review. APS II, Reels 697, 1357-1363.

Virginia literary museum and journal of belles lettres. APS II, Reel 1407.

Western gleaner. APS II, Reel 252.

Western literary journal, and monthly review. June-Nov. 1836. APS II, Reel 527.

Western literary journal and monthly review. Nov. 1844-Apr. 1845. APS II, Reel 527.

Western quarterly review. APS II, Reel 529.

Worcester magazine and historical journal. APS II, Reel 720.

LOTTERIES—MARYLAND

Cohen's gazette & lottery register. APS II, Reels 92-93, 362.

LUNARIAN SOCIETY

Moonshine. APS II, Reel 33.

LYON, MATTHEW, 1750-1822

Republican magazine; or, Repository of political truths. APS I, Reel 26.

MANNERS AND CUSTOMS

American literary magazine. APS II, Reel 787.

Companion and weekly miscellany. APS II, Reel 13.

Dessert to the true American. APS I, Reel 12.

Happy home and parlor magazine. APS III, Reels 756-757.

New star. APS I, Reel 23.

Newhampshire magazine. APS I, Reel 19.

MARRIAGE LAW

Carolina law journal. APS II, Reel 382.

MASSACHUSETTS—POLITICS AND GOVERNMENT

American cultivator. APS II, Reels 465-467.

MATHEMATICS

Analyst. APS II, Reels 3, 64.

Cincinnati literary gazette. APS II, Reel 127.

Literary register. APS II, Reel 1234.

Mathematical correspondent. APS II, Reel 26.

Mathematical monthly. APS III, Reel 269.

MEAT—PRESERVATION

Western farmer and gardener. APS II, Reel 1408.

MECHANICS

Mechanic's advocate. APS II, Reel 400.

MEDICAL ETHICS

AEsculapian register. APS II, Reel 49.

MEDICAL LITERATURE

American journal of the medical sciences. APS II, Reels 368-375, 1125-1157.

American medical and philosophical register. APS II, Reel 54.

American medical intelligencer. APS II, Reel 296.

American medical recorder. APS II, Reels 55-56, 645.

American medical review. APS II, Reels 57, 846, 954.

Baltimore medical and philosophical lycaeum. APS II, Reel 71.

Baltimore medical and physical recorder. APS II, Reel 6.

Baltimore medical and surgical journal and review. APS II, Reel 379.

Baltimore monthly journal of medicine and surgery. APS II, Reel 534.

Baltimore philosophical journal and review. APS II, Reel 71.

Journal of foreign medical science and literature. APS II, Reels 116-119.

Massachusetts Medical Society. Medical communications. APS II, Reels 677-678, 1314-1317.

Medical & surgical register. APS II, Reel 216.

Medical and surgical reporter. Burlington, N.J. [and] Philadelphia. APS II, Reels 1287-1288.

Medical and surgical reporter. Philadelphia. APS II, Reels 1197-1215.

Medical examiner. APS II, Reels 428-437.

Medical examiner; a semi-monthly journal. APS II, Reels 1234-1237.

Medical news. APS II, Reels 658, 1073-1087.

Medical times and Register. APS II, Reels 1388-1396.

Monthly journal of foreign medicine. APS II, Reel 659.

Monthly journal of medicine. APS II, Reels 144-145.

New-England journal of medicine and surgery. APS II, Reels 153-157, 944.

New-England medical review and journal. APS II, Reel 802.

New-York medical and philosophical journal and review. APS II, Reels 34, 162.

New York medical and physical journal. APS II, Reels 163-164, 718-719.

New York medical magazine. APS II, Reel 164.

New York monthly chronicle of medicine and surgery. APS II, Reel 165.

North American archives of medical and surgical science. APS II, Reel 804.

North American medical and surgical journal. APS II, Reels 804-805.

Ohio medical and surgical journal. APS II, Reels 1404-1406.

Ohio medical repository of original and selected intelligence. APS II, Reel 973.

Philadelphia journal of the medical and physical sciences. APS II, Reels 184-185.

Philadelphia medical museum. APS II, Reels 38, 186.

Transylvania journal of medicine and the associate sciences. APS II, Reels 1960-1961.

Western journal of the medical and physical sciences. APS II, Reels 578-580.

Western journal of medicine and surgery. APS II, Reels 701-705.

Western quarterly reporter of medical, surgical, and natural science. APS II, Reel 1497.

MEDICAL SOCIETIES—UNITED STATES

Massachusetts Medical Society. Medical communications. APS II, Reels 677-678, 1314-1317.

Medical examiner. APS II, Reels 428-437.

MEDICINE

American journal of the medical sciences. APS II, Reels 368-375. 1125-1157.

American medical and philosophical register. APS II, Reel 54.

American medical intelligencer. APS II, Reel 296.

American medical recorder. APS II, Reels 55-56, 645.

American medical review. APS II, Reels 57, 846, 944.

Baltimore medical and philosophical lycaeum. APS II, Reel 71.

Baltimore monthly journal of medicine and surgery. APS II, Reel 534.

Baltimore medical and physical recorder. APS II, Reel 6.

Baltimore medical and surgical journal and review. APS II, Reel 379.

Boston medical intelligencer. APS II, Reels 73, 763.

Carolina journal of medicine. APS II, Reels 75, 362.

Charleston medical register for the year 1802. APS II, Reel 546.

Journal of foreign medical science and literature. APS II, Reels 116-119.

Medical and agricultural register, for the years 1806 and 1807. APS II, Reel 26.

Medical & surgical register. APS II, Reel 216.

Medical and surgical reporter. Burlington, N.J. [and] Philadelphia. APS II, Reels 1287-1288.

Medical and surgical reporter. Philadelphia. APS II, Reels 1197-1215.

Medical examiner. APS II, Reels 428-437.

Medical examiner; a semi-monthly journal. APS II, Reels 1234-1237.

Medical news. APS II, Reels 658, 1073-1087.

Medical repository of original essays and intelligence. APS I, Reel 14. APS II, Reels 26-27, 132-134.

Medical Times and Register. APS II, Reels 1388-1396.

Monthly journal of foreign medicine. APS II, Reel 659.

Monthly journal of medicine. APS II, Reels 144-145.

New England journal of medicine. APS II, Reels 660-644.

New-England journal of medicine and surgery. APS II, Reels 153-157, 944.

New-England medical review and journal. APS II, Reel 802.

New-York medical and philosophical journal and review. APS II, Reels 34, 162.

New York medical and physical journal. APS II, Reels 163-164, 718-719.

New York medical magazine. APS II, Reel 164.

New York monthly chronicle of medicine and surgery. APS II, Reel 165.

North American archives of medical and surgical science. APS II, Reel 804.

North American medical and surgical journal. APS II, Reels 804-805.

Ohio medical and surgical journal. APS II, Reels 1404-1406.

Ohio medical repository of original and selected intelligence. APS II, Reel 973.

Philadelphia journal of the medical and physical sciences. APS II, Reels 184-185.

Philadelphia medical and physical journal. APS II, Reel 37.

Philadelphia medical museum. APS II, Reels 38, 186.

Physicians' and surgeons' investigator. APS III, Reels 567-568.

Physician's magazine. APS III, Reel 67.

Transylvania journal of medicine and the associate sciences. APS II, Reels 1960-1961.

Western journal of medicine and surgery. APS II, Reels 701-705.

Western journal of the medical and physical sciences. APS II, Reels 578-580.

Western quarterly reporter of medical, surgical, and natural science. APS II, Reel 1497.

History
AEsculapian register. APS II, Reel 49.

Kentucky--Louisville
Louisville journal of medicine and surgery. APS II, Reel 657.

Massachusetts
Massachusetts Medical Society. Medical communications. APS II, Reels 677-678, 1314-1317.

New England
New England quarterly journal of medicine and surgery. APS II, Reel 816.

New York (State)
New York journal of medicine. APS II, Reels 665-668.

Practice
Louisville journal of medicine and surgery. APS II, Reel 657.

Medical reformer. APS II, Reel 132.

New England quarterly journal of medicine and surgery. APS II, Reel 816.

New York journal of medicine. APS II, Reels 665-668.

MEDICINE, POPULAR

Health. APS II, Reels 576-578, 1692-1696.

Medical news-paper. APS II, Reel 217.

MEDICINE, PREVENTIVE

Medical news-paper. APS II, Reel 217.

MERCHANTS—BIOGRAPHY

Merchants' magazine and commercial review. APS II, Reels 339-348.

METALLURGY

American repertory of arts, sciences, and manufactures. APS II, Reel 646.

METEOROLOGY

American meteorological journal. APS III, Reels 314-316.

Pennsylvania
Franklin Institute, Philadelphia. Journal. APS II, Reels 282-287.

SUBJECT INDEX

METHODISM
Ladies' repository. APS II, Reels 482, 893-899.
Methodist recorder. APS II, Reel 217.
National magazine. APS II, Reels 814-815.
Western Christian monitor. APS II, Reel 252.

METHODIST CHURCH
Christian advocate. APS II, Reels 1749-1788.
Methodist magazine, containing original sermons. APS I, Reel 17.
New England missionary intelligencer. APS II, Reel 157.
New-England missionary magazine. APS II, Reel 157.
Western Christian Advocate. APS II, Reels 1789-1796.
Zion's herald. APS II, Reels 1572-1612, 1963-1966.

Publishing
Christian advocate. APS II, Reels 1749-1788.

METHODIST EPISCOPAL CHURCH
Methodist review. APS II, Reels 135-136, 327-332, 1093-1113.

METHODIST EPISCOPAL CHURCH IN TENN.
Messenger. APS II, Reel 1370.

METHODIST PROTESTANT CHURCH
Wesleyan repository. APS II, Reel 251.

METHODISTS
Methodist recorder. APS II, Reel 217.

MICHIGAN—FAIRS
Michigan farmer. APS II, Reels 324, 1502-1519.

MILITARY ART AND SCIENCE
Army and navy chronicle. APS II, Reels 469-471.
Army and navy chronicle, and scientific repository. APS II, Reel 472.
Military and naval magazine of the United States. APS II, Reel 615.
Military magazine and record of the volunteers of the city. APS II, Reel 744.
Monthly military repository. APS I, Reel 18.
United service. APS III, Reels 132-139.
United States military philosophical society. APS II, Reel 45.
United States service magazine. APS III, Reel 53.

MILLENNIALISM
Alethian critic. APS II, Reel 945.

MILLENNIUM
American millenarian. APS II, Reel 1093.
Halcyon itinerary. APS II, Reel 19.

MINERAL INDUSTRIES—UTAH
Utahnian. APS III, Reel 271.

MINERALOGY
American mineralogical journal. APS II, Reel 57.

MISSIONARIES
New York telescope. APS II, Reel 1254.

MISSIONS
Abolition intelligencer and missionary magazine. APS II, Reel 47.
Christian monitor. Richmond, VA. APS II, Reel 596.
Christian's weekly monitor. APS II, Reel 90.
Church record. APS II, Reel 90.
Congregationalist and herald of gospel liberty. APS II, Reels 97-99, 539-546, 1911-1924.
Evangelical guardian and review. APS II, Reel 102.
Evangelical intelligencer. APS II, Reel 16-17.
Evangelical monitor. APS II, Reel 401.
Evangelical recorder. APS II, Reel 103.
Miscellaneous cabinet. APS II, Reel 218.
New-York missionary magazine. APS II, Reel 35.
Religious inquirer. APS II, Reel 234.

British
Evangelical record, and western review. APS II, Reels 129-130.

Jews
Israel's advocate. APS II, Reels 130, 401.

New England
Christian chronicle. APS II, Reel 77.

MISSISSIPPI VALLEY—HISTORY—1803-1865
Western journal and civilian. APS II, Reels 699-700.

MISSOURI—ECONOMIC CONDITIONS
Western journal and civilian. APS II, Reels 699-700.

MORAL EDUCATION—JUVENILE LITERATURE
Guardian and monitor. A monthly publication. APS II, Reels 111-112, 881.

MORAVIANS—MISSIONS
United Brethren's missionary intelligencer. APS II, Reels 1258-1259.

MUSIC
American magazine of useful and entertaining knowledge. APS II, Reel 768.
American musical magazine. APS I, Reel 6.
Boston magazine, containing, a collection of instructive and entertaining essays. APS I, Reel 9.
Broadway journal. APS II, Reel 649.
Cincinnati literary gazette. APS II, Reel 127.
Dollar magazine; A monthly gazette of current literature, music and art. APS II, Reel 385.
Euterpeiad; an album of music, poetry & prose. APS II, Reel 771.
Euterpeiad; or, Musical intelligencer, and ladies gazette. APS II, Reel 102.
Evergreen. APS II, Reel 448.
Family minstrel. APS II, Reel 973.
Happy home and parlor magazine. APS III, Reels 756-757.
Journal of musick. APS II, Reel 119.
Lady's magazine and musical repository. APS II, Reel 20.
Literary and musical magazine. APS II, Reel 213.
Literary gazette. APS II, Reel 400.
Literary magazine. APS II, Reel 400.
Lyre. APS II, Reel 132.
Musical cabinet. APS II, Reel 1120.
Musical magazine. APS II, Reel 840.
Musical magazine; containing a variety of favorite pieces. APS I, Reel 18.
Musical magazine; or, Repository of musical science. APS II, Reel 1216.
Musical reporter. APS II, Reel 840.
Musical visitor. APS II, Reels 1289-1291.

Parlour review, and journal of music, literature, and the fine arts. APS II, Reel 845.
Sargent's new monthly magazine. APS II, Reel 1258.
Sartain's union magazine of literature and art. APS II, Reels 572-574.
Visitor. APS II, Reels 46, 246.

19th Century
Boston musical gazette. APS II, Reel 408.
Boston musical review. APS II, Reel 770.

History and Criticism
Boston musical gazette. APS II, Reel 408.

Philosophy and Aesthetics
American journal of music and musical visitor. APS II, Reel 725.
American musical journal. APS II, Reel 769.

Theory
Musical magazine. APS II, Reel 840.

United States
American journal of music and musical visitor. APS II, Reel 725.
American musical journal. APS II, Reel 769.

MUSIC, AMERICAN
American journal of music and musical visitor. APS II, Reel 725.
American musical journal. APS II, Reel 769.

MUSICAL CRITICISM
Lyre. APS II, Reel 132.

MUSICAL INSTRUMENTS
Musical cabinet. APS II, Reel 1120.

MUSICAL SOCIETIES
Euterpeiad; or, Musical intelligencer, and ladies gazette. APS II, Reel 102.

MUSICIANS—BIOGRAPHY
Euterpeiad; an album of music, poetry & prose. APS II, Reel 771.
Euterpeiad; or, Musical intelligencer, and ladies gazette. APS II, Reel 102.
Lyre. APS II, Reel 132.

MYTHOLOGY
Parthenon. APS II, Reel 1257.

NATIONAL REPUBLICAN PARTY
National magazine and republican review. APS II, Reel 799.

NATURAL HISTORY
Advocate of science, and annals of natural history. APS II, Reel 532.
Atlantic journal, and friend of knowledge. APS II, Reel 839.
Monthly American journal of geology and natural science. APS II, Reel 659.
Naturalist. APS II, Reel 801.
Philadelphia medical and physical journal. APS II, Reel 37.
Philadelphia museum. APS II, Reel 186.

North America
Annals of nature. APS II, Reel 64.

NAVAL ART AND SCIENCE
Army and navy chronicle. APS II, Reels 469-471.
Army and navy chronicle, and scientific repository. APS II, Reel 472.
Military and naval magazine of the United States. APS II, Reel 615.
Naval magazine. APS II, Reel 816.
United service. APS III, Reels 132-139.

NEEDHAM, VIRGINIA. LAW SCHOOL
Journal of the Law-School, and of the moot-court attached to it, at Needham, in Virginia. APS II, Reel 121.

NEEDLEWORK
Harper's bazaar. APS III, Reels 430-450.

NEGRO CHILDREN—JUVENILE LITERATURE
Juvenile magazine. APS II, Reel 121.

NEGROES—Colonization
Genius of universal emancipation. APS II, Reels 108, 1272-1273.

Colonization—Africa
African intelligencer. APS II, Reel 49.
African repository. APS II, Reels 49, 641-644, 881-884.
Colonizationist and journal of freedom. APS II, Reel 603.
Harbinger of the Mississippi Valley. APS II, Reel 560.

Education
Juvenile magazine. APS II, Reel 121.

NEW ENGLAND-Genealogy
New-England historical and genealogical register. APS II, Reels 1053-1061.

History
New-England historical and genealogical register. APS II, Reels 1053-1061.

NEW HAMPSHIRE
New Hampshire repository. APS II, Reel 842.

History
Collections, historical and miscellaneous, and monthly literary journal. APS II, Reels 93-94.

Politics and Government
Rough and ready. APS II, Reel 845.

NEW JERUSALEM CHURCH
Herald of truth. APS II, Reel 113.
New-Hampshire New Jerusalem magazine. APS II, Reel 34.
New Jerusalem Church repository. APS II, Reel 157.
New Jerusalem missionary and intellectual repository. APS II, Reel 158.
New Jerusalem record. APS II, Reel 158.

NEW YORK—Benevolent and Moral Institutions and Societies.
Remembrancer. APS II, Reel 204.

Statistics, Vital
New-York medical and philosophical journal and review. APS II, Reels 34, 162.

NEW YORK (STATE)—Genealogy
New York genealogical and biographical record. APS III, Reels 451-455.
New York Genealogical and Biographical Society. Bulletin. APS III, Reel 451.

History
New York genealogical and biographical record. APS III, Reels 451-455.
New York Genealogical and Biographical Society. Bulletin. APS III, Reel 451.

Politics and Government
Balance, and state journal. APS II, Reels 3-5, 70.
Jeffersonian. APS II, Reel 797.
Man. APS II, Reels 565-566.
Radical. APS II, Reel 197.

Public Schools
District school journal of the state of New York. APS II, Reel 770.

NEWARK, NEW JERSEY—POLITICS AND GOVERNMENT
Lancet. APS II, Reel 22.

ODD-FELLOWS, INDEPENDENT ORDER OF
Odd Fellows' magazine. APS II, Reels 218, 839.

OHIO—History
American pioneer. APS II, Reel 297.

1787-1865
Literary cabinet and western olive branch. APS II, Reel 565.
Western monthly magazine, and literary journal. APS II, Reel 528.

Politics And Government-1815-1861
Investigator and expositor. APS II, Reel 1231.

OHIO VALLEY—HISTORY
American pioneer. APS II, Reel 297.
Olden time. APS II, Reel 844.

ONEIDA COMMUNITY
American socialist. APS III, Reel 243.
Oneida circular. APS III, Reels 670-674.

OUTDOOR LIFE
Forest and stream. APS III, Reels 208-235.

PACIFISM
Friend. APS II, Reels 523-526, 1412-1419.
Friends review. APS II, Reels 386-387, 924-934.
Liberator. APS II, Reels 391-399.

PATENT LAWS AND LEGISLATION—UNITED STATES
Scientific American. APS II, Reels 616-619, 1734-1748.

PATENTS
American review, and literary journal, for 1801-1802. APS II, Reel 3.
Washington quarterly magazine. APS II, Reel 246.

United States
American museum, and repository of arts and sciences. APS II, Reel 58.

Franklin Institute, Philadelphia. Journal. APS II, Reels 282-287.
Mechanic's advocate. APS II, Reel 400.

PATRIOTIC SOCIETIES
American historical register and monthly gazette. APS III, Reel 58.

PATRONS OF HUSBANDRY
Prairie farmer. APS II, Reels 747-748, 1720-1726, 1936.

PEACE
Advocate of peace and Christian patriot. APS II, Reel 584.
Friend of peace. APS II, Reels 211, 1072.
World affairs. APS II, Reels 584, 1543-1545.

PEACE SOCIETIES
Christian disciple and theological review. APS II, Reels 77-79.

PENNSYLVANIA
Geographical, historical, and statistical repository. APS II, Reels 100, 130.

History
Hazard's register of Pennsylvania. APS II, Reels 476-479.
Huntingdon literary museum. APS II, Reel 114.
Olden time. APS II, Reel 844.
Pennsylvania magazine of history and biography. APS III, Reels 456-461.

Militia
Military magazine and record of the volunteers of the city. APS II, Reel 744.

Statistics
Hazard's register of Pennsylvania. APS II, Reels 476-479.

PHARMACY
American journal of pharmacy. APS II, Reels 366-368, 1707-1716.

PHILOLOGY
American journal of philology. APS III, Reels 424-429.

PHILOSOPHY
Baltimore philosophical journal and review. APS II, Reel 71.
Free enquirer. APS II, Reels 1498-1499.
Journal of speculative philosophy. APS III, Reels 13-15.
Pioneer, consisting of essays, literary, moral and theological. APS II, Reel 189.

German
Open court. APS III, Reels 293-297.

PHILOSOPHY AND RELIGION
Prospect. APS II, Reel 42.

PHRENOLOGY
Phrenological journal and science of health. APS II, Reels 1341-1353.

PHYSICIANS
Louisville journal of medicine and surgery. APS II, Reel 657.
New York journal of medicine. APS II, Reels 665-668.

Biography
Philadelphia medical and physical journal. APS II, Reel 37.

POETRY
Baltimore phoenix and budget. APS II, Reel 770.
Friend. APS II, Reel 107.
Literary miscellany. APS II, Reel 24.
Open court. APS III, Reels 293-297.
Pastime. APS II, Reel 36.
Repository and ladies' weekly museum. APS II, Reel 43.

Collections
Bibelot. APS III, Reels 252-253.

Early Works to 1800
American magazine and monthly chronicle for the British
    colonies. APS I, Reel 2.
American monthly review. APS I, Reel 3.
General magazine and impartial review of knowledge &
    entertainment. APS I, Reel 13.
Literary miscellany. APS I, Reel 14.
Monthly magazine, and American review. APS I, Reel 17.
New star. APS I, Reel 23.
New Hampshire & Vermont magazine. APS I, Reel 20.
Newhampshire magazine. APS I, Reel 19.
New-Haven gazette, and the Connecticut magazine. APS I, Reel 20.
Rural magazine. APS I, Reel 27.

POETRY, MODERN—19th CENTURY
American monthly review. APS II, Reel 768.
Anglo American. APS II, Reels 647-649.
Anglo-American magazine. APS II, Reel 378.
Aristidean. APS II, Reel 378.
Evergreen. APS II, Reel 448.
Herald of truth. APS II, Reel 388.
Idle man. APS II, Reel 115.
Ladies' repository. APS II, Reels 482, 893-899.
Lady's magazine and musical repository. APS II, Reel 20.
Literary emporium. APS II, Reel 1233.
Literary gazette and American athenaeum. APS II, Reel 741.
Literary geminae. APS II, Reel 657.
Literary gems. APS II, Reel 799.
Maine monthly magazine. APS II, Reel 486.
Manhattan. APS III, Reels 30-31.
Microscope. APS II, Reel 217.
National magazine and republican review. APS II, Reel 799.
Orion. APS II, Reel 1216.
Periodical library. APS II, Reel 736.
Quarterly journal and review. APS II, Reel 1092.
Rural magazine and farmer's monthly museum. APS II, Reel 205.
Russell's magazine. APS III, Reel 17.
St. Tammanys magazine. APS II, Reel 205.
Stranger. APS II, Reel 810.
Talisman. APS II, Reel 400.
Theatrical budget. APS II, Reel 1258.
Truth. APS II, Reel 242.
Western Minerva. APS II, Reel 252.
Western quarterly review. APS II, Reel 529.
Western review and miscellaneous magazine. APS II, Reel 253.
Yale literary magazine. APS II, Reel 529-531.

POETS, AMERICAN
Independent. APS II, Reels 418, 1420-1464.

19th Century
Brother Jonathan. APS II, Reels 409-410.
United States literary gazette. APS II, Reel 242.

POLITICAL SATIRE
The ————. APS II, Reel 333.
Continental monthly. APS III, Reel 140.
Corrector. APS II, Reel 15.
Elephant. APS II, Reel 771.
Gridiron. APS II, Reel 111.
John-donkey. APS II, Reel 657.
Judy. APS II, Reel 481.
Lancet. APS II, Reel 22.
Microscope and general advertiser. APS II, Reel 136.
Puck. APS III, Reels 69-84.
Scourge. APS II, Reel 239.
Tickler. APS II, Reel 45.
Wasp. APS II, Reel 46.
Yankee doodle. APS II, Reel 1408.

POLITICAL SCIENCE
American magazine of civics. APS III, Reels 203-204.
Aristidean. APS II, Reel 378.
Examiner. APS II, Reels 104-106.
Journal of social science. APS III, Reels 266-268.
Mediateur. APS II, Reel 132.
National register. APS II, Reels 800-801.
Old and new. APS III, Reels 130-132.
Political science quarterly. APS III, Reels 767-771.

Miscellanea
Political magazine and miscellaneous repository. APS II, Reel 39.

POLITICS AND GOVERNMENT
National magazine and republican review. APS II, Reel 799.

POPULAR CULTURE
Albany bouquet and literary spectator. APS II, Reel 767.
Oliver's magazine. APS II, Reel 940.
Southern rose. APS II, Reel 688.

POPULATION—STATISTICS
Merchants' magazine and commercial review. APS II, Reels 339-348.

PORTRAITS
American quarterly register. APS II, Reels 532-534.

PRESBYTERIAN CHURCH
Christian observer. APS II, Reels 1887-1908.
Evangelical intelligencer. APS II, Reels 16-17.
New York observer. APS II, Reels 1856-1874.
Pittsburgh recorder. APS II, Reels 219-220, 1052.

Missions
Quarterly Christian spectator. APS II, Reels 194-196, 229-232.

PRESBYTERIAN CHURCH IN THE UNITED STATES
Christian advocate. APS II, Reels 76, 592-593.
Cumberland Presbyterian review. APS II, Reels 1368-1370.
Danville quarterly review. APS III, Reel 186.
Presbyterian magazine. APS II, Reels 193-194.
Religious instructor. APS II, Reel 198.
Virginia religious magazine. APS II, Reel 45.
Western missionary magazine. APS II, Reel 46.

Synods. Virginia
Virginia religious magazine. APS II, Reel 45.

PRESBYTERIANISM
American Presbyterian review. APS III, Reels 205-207.
Christian observer. APS II, Reels 1887-1908.
Evangelical record, and western review. APS II, Reels 129-130.
Literary and theological review. APS II, Reel 798.

PRESS, BAPTIST
Baptist quarterly review. APS III, Reels 59-60.
Christian review. APS II, Reels 410-416.
Christian secretary. APS II, Reels 88-89, 495-502, 1910.
Watchman-examiner. APS II, Reels 246-248, 1491-1497, 1874-
1883.

PRESS, CATHOLIC
American Catholic quarterly review. APS III, Reels 650-660.
Brownson's quarterly review. APS II, Reels 507-508, 884-886.
Catholic telegraph. APS II, Reels 1717-1720.
Jesuit. APS II, Reels 1370-1371.
United States Catholic magazine. APS II, Reels 689-690.
United States Catholic miscellany. APS II, Reels 1961-1962.

PRESS, CHILDREN
Children's magazine. APS I, Reel 8.

PRESS, RELIGIOUS
Evangelist and religious review. APS II, Reels 1829-1855.

PRISON DISCIPLINE
Moral advocate. APS II, Reel 146.

PRISONS
Journal of prison discipline and philanthropy. APS II, Reels 480-
481, 1934-1935.
Prisoner's friend. APS II, Reels 749-750.

Pennsylvania
Journal of prison discipline and philanthropy. APS II, Reels 480-
481, 1934-1935.

PROSE LITERATURE
Baltimore phoenix and budget. APS II, Reel 770.

PROTESTANT EPISCOPAL CHURCH IN THE UNITED STATES
Christian journal, and literary register. APS II, Reel 80-81, 763.
Christian observer, conducted by members of the established
church. APS II, Reels 8-11, 83-86, 208-209, 1909.
Church record. APS II, Reel 90.
Church review. APS II, Reels 916-923.
Churchman's magazine. APS II, Reels 12, 91, 210.
Churchman's repository for the eastern diocese. APS II, Reel 127.
Episcopal magazine. APS II, Reel 129.
Episcopal recorder. APS II, Reels 1684-1692.
Episcopal watchman. APS II, Reels 889-890.
Gospel advocate. APS II, Reel 109.
Religious and literary repository. APS II, Reel 197.
Sunday visitant. APS II, Reel 240.
Theological repertory, and churchman's guide. APS II, Reels 241,
1948.
Watchman. APS II, Reel 246.

Charleston, South Carolina
Charleston gospel messenger and protestant episcopal register. APS
II, Reels 76, 650-653.

Missions
Episcopal magazine. APS II, Reel 129.

PROTESTANTISM
Baltimore literary and religious magazine. APS II, Reels 585-586.

PUBLIC HEALTH
Boston medical intelligencer. APS II, Reels 73, 763.
Health. APS II, Reels 576-578, 1692-1696.
Journal of health. APS II, Reel 479.
Medical and agricultural register, for the years 1806 and 1807.
APS II, Reel 26.

PUBLIC SCHOOLS
Common school advocate. APS II, Reel 383.

Connecticut
Connecticut common school journal. APS II, Reels 789-791.

Ohio
Ohio common school director. APS II, Reel 940.

Rhode Island
Rhode Island Institute of Instruction. Journal. APS II, Reel 389.

PUBLISHERS AND PUBLISHING—London, England
Journal of belles lettres. APS II, Reel 1314.

United States
Journal of belles lettres. APS II, Reel 1314.

RAILROADS
Railway times. APS II, Reels 1726-1733.
Western journal and civilian. APS II, Reels 699-700.

REDEMPTION—BIBLICAL TEACHING
Arminian magazine. APS I, Reel 8.

REFORMED CHURCH IN THE UNITED STATES
Reformed church messenger. APS II, Reels 1815-1825.
Reformed church review. APS II, Reels 671, 1217-1229.

RELIGION
Christian monitor. Hallowell, Me. APS II, Reel 83.
Christian monitor. Richmond, Va. APS II, Reel 596.
Christian monitor, and religious intelligencer. APS II, Reel 83.
Christian parlor magazine. APS II, Reels 1230-1231.
Christian philanthropist. APS II, Reel 87.
Christian register. APS II, Reel 1093.
Evangelical monitor. APS II, Reel 401.
Gospel herald. APS II, Reel 503.
Gospel inquirer. APS II, Reel 110.
Gospel palladium. APS II, Reel 110.
Halcyon luminary. APS II, Reels 112, 464.
Investigator and advocate of independence. APS II, Reel 1197.
Literary emporium. APS II, Reel 1233.
Messenger of peace. APS II, Reel 217.
National repository. APS III, Reels 110-111.
New Hampshire repository. APS II, Reel 842.
Open court. APS III, Reels 293-297.
Religious museum. APS II, Reel 203.

Controversial Literature
Andover review. APS III, Reels 1-4.
Christian register. APS II, Reel 1093.

Reformed church review. APS II, Reels 671, 1217-1229.
Reformer and Christian. APS II, Reels 233, 720.
Spirit of the Pilgrims. APS II, Reel 752.
Spiritual magazine. APS II, Reel 240.
Zion's herald. APS II, Reels 1572-1612, 1963-1966.

RELIGION AND ETHICS
New York telescope. APS II, Reel 1254.

RELIGIONS
Columbian magazine. APS II, Reel 32.
Correspondent. APS II, Reel 384.

Controversial Literature
Gospel herald. APS II, Reel 503.
Religious monitor and evangelical repository. APS II, Reels 401-403.
Spirit of the XIX. century. APS II, Reel 779.
Theophilanthropist. APS II, Reel 333.

Ethics
Christian messenger, devoted to doctrine, religion, and morality. APS II, Reel 82.

RELIGIOUS EDUCATION
American Sunday-school teachers' magazine and journal of education. APS II, Reel 1158.
Sabbath school visitant. APS II, Reel 1124.
Sunday school repository. APS II, Reel 333.

RELIGIOUS LIBERTY
Christian herald. APS II, Reels 79-80.

RELIGIOUS LITERATURE
Andover review. APS III, Reels 1-4.
Christian chronicle. APS II, Reel 77.
Christian herald. APS II, Reels 79-80.
Christian herald and seaman's magazine. APS II, Reels 493-495.
Cheap repository. APS II, Reel 207.
Christian's monitor. APS I, Reel 10.
Free universal magazine. APS I, Reel 12.
Friend; a periodical work devoted to religion. APS II, Reel 107.
Geistliches magazien. APS I, Reel 12.
Gospel trumpet. APS II, Reel 130.
Herald of truth. APS II, Reel 388.
Literary tablet. APS II, Reel 24.
Methodist magazine. APS I, Reel 17.
Monthly miscellany of religion and letters. APS II, Reel 778.
New world. APS III, Reels 31-32.
Observer. APS II, Reel 36.
Philadelphia Universalist magazine and Christian messenger. APS II, Reel 187.
Piscataqua evangelical magazine. APS II, Reel 39.
Presbyterian magazine. APS II, Reels 193-194.
Providence theological magazine. APS II, Reel 194.
Religious monitor. APS I, Reel 26.
Religious repository. APS II, Reel 43.
Remembrancer, for Lord's Day evenings. APS I, Reel 26.
Theological magazine, or Synopsis of modern religious sentiment. APS I, Reel 28.
Theological review and general repository of religious and moral information. APS II, Reel 206.
Witness. APS II, Reel 46.

RELIGIOUS THOUGHT
Hopkinsian magazine. APS II, Reel 914.

RELIGIOUS TOLERANCE
Christian examiner. APS II, Reels 79, 449-463.

REVIVALS
Christian monitor, and religious intelligencer. APS II, Reel 83.
Evangelist. APS II, Reel 1271.
Massachusetts missionary magazine. APS II, Reel 25.
Religious museum. APS II, Reel 203.
Utica Christian repository. APS II, Reel 245.

RUSH, BENJAMIN, 1745-1813
Rush-light. APS II, Reel 44.

SACRED VOCAL MUSIC—TO 1800
American musical magazine. APS I, Reel 6.

SALVATION
Herald of salvation. APS II, Reel 113.

SATIRE
Barber's shop. APS II, Reel 6.
Companion and weekly miscellany. APS II, Reel 13.
Critic. APS II, Reel 100.
Cynick. APS II, Reel 100.
Fool. APS II, Reel 19.
Gridiron. APS II, Reel 111.
John-donkey. APS II, Reel 657.
Judy. APS II, Reel 481.
Lancaster hive. APS II, Reel 22.
Life. APS III, Reels 500-532.
Literary magazine. APS II, Reel 400.
Manuscript. APS II, Reel 609.
Microscope. Albany, N.Y. APS II, Reel 217.
Microscope, New Haven. APS II, Reel 217.
Moralist. APS II, Reel 146.
Parterre. APS II, Reel 184.
Puck. APS III, Reels 69-84.
Punchinello. APS III, Reel 164.
Salmagundi. APS II, Reel 44.
Salmagundi (Paulding). APS II, Reel 1308.
Satirist. APS II, Reel 205.
Something. APS II, Reels 44, 671.
Spectacles. APS II, Reel 44.
Stand. APS II, Reel 333.
Truth. APS II, Reel 242.
Western examiner. APS II, Reel 487.
Yale literary magazine. APS II, Reels 529-531.
Yankee doodle. APS II, Reel 1408.

SATIRE, AMERICAN—NEW YORK
Salmagundi. APS II, Reel 44.

SAUK INDIANS
Chronicles of the North American savages. APS II, Reel 382.

SCHOOLS—UNITED STATES
Massachusetts teacher. APS II, Reels 610-613.

SCIENCE
Advocate of science. APS II, Reel 532.
American athenaeum. APS II, Reel 51.
American journal of science. APS II, Reel 53, 53A, 754-762, 817-830.

American magazine and monthly chronicle for the British colonies. APS I, Reel 2.

American magazine, and repository of useful literature. APS II, Reel 376.

American magazine; or, General repository. APS I, Reel 2.

American monthly review. APS I, Reel 3.

American people's journal of science, literature, and art. APS II, Reel 333.

Boston journal of philosophy and the arts. APS II, Reel 73.

Carolina journal of medicine, science and agriculture. APS II, Reels 75, 362.

Casket. Devoted to literature, science, the arts, news, &c. APS II, Reel 382.

Cincinnati mirror, and Western gazette. APS II, Reel 789.

Eclectic museum of foreign literature, science and art. APS II, Reel 605.

Family lyceum. APS II, Reel 771.

Franklin Institute, Philadelphia. Journal. APS II, Reels 282-287.

International monthly magazine of literature, science and art. APS III, Reel 109.

Iris. APS II, Reel 656.

Journal of science and the arts. APS II, Reel 120.

Ladies' literary portfolio. APS II, Reel 893.

Literary and scientific repository. APS II, Reel 126.

Literary casket. APS II, Reel 777.

Literary inquirer. APS II, Reel 799.

McBride's magazine. APS III, Reels 316-341.

Magazine of useful and entertaining knowledge. APS II, Reel 742.

Medical repository of original essays and intelligence. APS I, Reel 14; APS II, Reels 26-27, 132-134.

Monthly scientific journal. APS II, Reel 146.

National magazine. APS II, Reel 34.

National museum and weekly gazette. APS II, Reel 149.

Naturalist. APS II, Reel 801.

New Orleans miscellany. APS II, Reel 973.

North American. APS II, Reel 973.

Northern light. APS II, Reel 844.

Philadelphia museum. APS II, Reel 186.

Quarterly Journal and review. APS II, Reel 1092.

Scientific American. APS II, Reels 616-619, 1734-1748.

Scientific Journal. APS II, Reel 239.

Southern review. APS II, Reel 325.

Western gleaner. APS II, Reel 252.

Western Minerva. APS II, Reel 252.

Western monthly magazine, and literary journal. APS II, Reel 528.

Western quarterly review. APS II, Reel 529.

Philosophy

Monist. APS III, Reels 342-344.

Popular Works

Virginia literary museum and journal of belles lettres. APS II, Reel 1407.

Societies, etc.

American Academy of Arts and Sciences, Boston. Memoirs. APS II, Reels 363-364, 1364-1365.

American Academy of Arts and Sciences, Boston. Proceedings. APS III, Reels 141-147.

Connecticut Academy of Arts and Sciences, New Haven. Memoirs. APS II, Reel 770.

Transactions of the Literary and philosophical society of New-York. APS II, Reel 840.

SCIENTIFIC LITERATURE

American Academy of Arts and Sciences, Boston. Memoirs. APS II, Reels 363-364, 1364-1365.

SCIENTIFIC SOCIETIES—Great Britain

Literary gazette. APS II, Reel 131.

Pennsylvania—Philadelphia

Memoirs of the Columbian chemical society of Philadelphia. APS II, Reel 95.

United States

Literary gazette. APS II, Reel 131.

SEAMEN

Christian herald and seaman's magazine. APS II, Reels 493-495.

SECURITIES

Bankers' magazine. APS II, Reels 587-588, 1648-1683.

SERICULTURE

Fessenden's silk manual and practical farmer. APS II, Reel 734.

SERMONS

Investigator and advocate of independence. APS II, Reel 1197.

National preacher and village pulpit. APS II, Reels 1087-1090.

New Outlook. APS III, Reels 367-423.

Zion's herald. APS II, Reels 1572-1612, 1963-1966.

SEX CRIMES

National police gazette. APS II, Reels 1318-1340.

SHAKERS

Manifesto. APS III, Reels 62-63.

SHAKESPEARE, WILLIAM, 1564-1616—CRITICISM AND INTERPRETATION

Shakespeariana. APS III, Reels 270-271.

SLAVERY—JUSTIFICATION

DeBow's review. APS II, Reels 382, 383, 855-862.

Old guard. APS III, Reels 64-65.

Southern literary journal and magazine of arts. APS II, Reels 574-576.

Southern quarterly review. APS II, Reels 684-687.

SLAVERY IN THE UNITED STATES

Abolition intelligencer and missionary magazine. APS II, Reel 47.

Abolitionist. APS II, Reel 362.

African intelligencer. APS II, Reel 49.

African repository. APS II, Reels 49, 641-644, 881-884.

Anti-slavery record. APS II, Reel 408.

Anti-slavery reporter. APS II, Reel 378.

Cincinnati weekly herald and philanthropist. APS II, Reels 1409-1412.

DeBow's review. APS II, Reels 382, 383, 855-862.

Friend. APS II, Reels 523-526, 1412-1419.

Liberator. APS II, Reels 391-399.

Liberty bell. APS II, Reels 491-492.

Massachusetts quarterly review. APS II, Reel 658.

Monthly offering. APS II, Reel 1245.

National era. APS II, Reels 899-903.

New-England telegraph, and eclectic review. APS II, Reel 802.

Universalist quarterly and general review. APS II, Reels 697, 1357-1363.

Vanity Fair. APS III, Reels 568-569.

Anti-Slavery Movements

American anti-slavery reporter. APS II, Reel 725.

Anti-slavery examiner. APS II, Reel 408.

Friends review. APS II, Reels 386-387, 924-934.

Genius of universal emancipation. APS II, Reels 108, 1272-1273.
Philanthropist. APS II, Reels 187-188.

Conditions of Slaves
Anti-slavery record. APS II, Reel 408.
Liberty bell. APS II, Reels 491-492.

Controversial Literature
Monthly offering. APS II, Reel 1245.

Emancipation
Dial: a monthly magazine for literature, philosophy and religion. APS III, Reel 7.

Fugitive Slaves
Independent. APS II, Reels 418, 1420-1464.

SLAVE-TRADE
Liberty bell. APS II, Reels 491-492.

SMALLPOX—PREVENTION
Literary magazine, and American register. APS II, Reels 22-23.

SOCIAL CHANGE
Harbinger. APS II, Reel 674.
Phalanx. APS II, Reel 671.

SOCIAL HISTORY
Forum and Century. APS III, Reels 272-293.
McClure's magazine. APS III, Reels 477-493.

SOCIAL HISTORY—19th CENTURY
Arena. APS III, Reels 92-99.
International review. APS III, Reels 152-154.

SOCIAL MOVEMENTS
Spirit of the age and journal of humanity. APS II, Reel 753.

SOCIAL PROBLEMS
Arena. APS III, Reels 92-99.
Aurora. APS II, Reel 769.
Free enquirer. APS II, Reels 1498-1499.
Moral advocate. APS II, Reel 146.
Spirit of the age and journal of humanity. APS II, Reel 753.

SOCIAL REFORMERS
Arena. APS III, Reels 92-99.

United States
Present. APS II, Reel 748.

SOCIAL SCIENCES
Journal of social science. APS III, Reels 266-268.
Political science quarterly. APS III, Reels 767-771.

SOCIALISM
Philistine. APS III, Reels 589-590.

SOUTH CAROLINA—POLITICS AND GOVERNMENT
South-Carolina weekly museum. APS I, Reel 28.

SOUTHERN STATES
Southern and western monthly magazine and review. APS II, Reel 1407.

Commerce
DeBow's review. APS II, Reels 382, 383, 855-862.

History
Century, a popular quarterly. APS III, Reels 345-367.

History—1783-1865
Russell's magazine. APS III, Reel 17.
Southern literary journal and magazine of arts. APS II, Reels 574-576.
Southern quarterly review. APS II, Reels 684-687.
Southern review. APS II, Reel 325.

History—1865-1877
Southern review. APS III, Reels 18-20.

Industries
DeBow's review. APS II, Reels 382, 383, 855-862.

SPANISH LITERATURE—TRANSLATIONS INTO ENGLISH
Expositor. APS II, Reel 924.

SPIRITUALISM (PHILOSOPHY)
Dial: a monthly magazine for literature, philosophy and religion. APS III, Reel 7.

SPORTS
American turf register and sporting magazine. APS II, Reels 404-407.
Forest and stream. APS III, Reels 208-235.
National police gazette. APS II, Reels 1318-1340.
Outing. APS III, Reels 297-309.

United States
Spirit of the times. APS II, Reels 620-640.

STATE RIGHTS
Southern quarterly review. APS II, Reels 684-687.

STATESMEN—BIOGRAPHY
American Whig review. APS II, Reels 302-304.

STILWELLITES
Friendly visitor. APS II, Reel 107.

STOCK AND STOCKBREEDING
Farmers cabinet and American herd book. APS II, Reels 314-315.

SUNDAY-SCHOOLS
American Sunday school magazine. APS II, Reel 305.
American Sunday-school teachers' magazine and journal of education. APS II, Reel 1158.
Christian's weekly monitor. APS II, Reel 90.
Gospel trumpet. APS II, Reel 130.
Harbinger of the Mississippi Valley. APS II, Reel 560.
Sabbath school repository. APS II, Reel 205.
Sabbath school visitant. APS II, Reel 1124.
Sunday school repository. APS II, Reel 333.

SURGEONS
Louisville journal of medicine and surgery. APS II, Reel 657.

New England
New England quarterly journal of medicine and surgery. APS II, Reel 816.

SURGERY
American medical review. APS II, Reels 57, 846, 944.
Baltimore medical and surgical journal and review. APS II, Reel 379.
Baltimore monthly journal of medicine and surgery. APS II, Reel 534.
Medical and surgical reporter. Burlington, N.J. [and] Philadelphia, 1846-1858. APS II, Reels 1287-1288.
Medical and surgical reporter. Philadelphia, 1858-1898. APS II, Reels 1197-1215.
Medical Times and Register. APS II, Reels 1388-1396.
New England journal of medicine. APS II, Reels 660-664.
New-England medical review and journal. APS II, Reel 802.
New England quarterly journal of medicine and surgery. APS II, Reel 816.
North American archives of medical and surgical science. APS II, Reel 804.
North American medical and surgical journal. APS II, Reels 804-805.
Ohio medical and surgical journal. APS II, Reels 1404-1406.
Ohio medical repository of original and selected intelligence. APS II, Reel 973.
Western journal of the medical and physical sciences. APS II, Reels 578-580.
Western journal of medicine and surgery. APS II, Reels 701-705.
Western quarterly reporter of medical, surgical, and natural science. APS II, Reel 1497.

TALES
Anglo-American magazine. APS II, Reel 378.
Literary geminae. APS II, Reel 657.
New-York weekly magazine. APS I, Reels 23, 27.
St. Tammanys magazine. APS II, Reel 205.
Talisman. APS II, Reel 400.

TARIFF—UNITED STATES
American laborer. APS II, Reel 644.
Political economist. APS II, Reel 191.

TEACHERS—OHIO
Ohio common school director. APS II, Reel 940.

TEACHING
Massachusetts teacher. APS II, Reels 610-613.

TECHNOLOGY
American mechanics' magazine. APS II, Reels 54, 763.
American repertory of arts, sciences, and manufactures. APS II, Reel 646.
Archives of useful knowledge. APS II, Reel 65.
Boston mechanic, and journal of the useful arts and sciences. APS II, Reel 472.
Emporium of arts & sciences. APS II, Reel 101.
Franklin Institute, Philadelphia. Journal. APS II, Reels 282-287.
Mechanics' magazine, and journal of the Mechanics' institute. APS II, Reels 613-614.
Mechanics' magazine, and journal of public internal improvement. APS II, Reel 1093.
New York state mechanic. APS II, Reel 938.
Rural magazine and farmer's monthly museum. APS II, Reel 205.
Scientific American. APS II, Reels 616-619, 1734-1748.
Theophilanthropist. APS II, Reel 333.
Useful cabinet. APS II, Reel 45.

TEMPERANCE
Evangelist. APS II, Reel 1271.
Harbinger of the Mississippi Valley. APS II, Reel 560.
Mistletoe. APS II, Reel 400.

Poetry
Mistletoe. APS II, Reel 400.

Societies
Mistletoe. APS II, Reel 400.

TEMPERANCE AND RELIGION
Family favorite and temperance journal. APS II, Reel 386.

THEATER
American monthly magazine. APS II, Reel 377.
Appletons' journal. APS III, Reels 244-249.
Arcturus. APS II, Reel 734.
Broadway journal. APS II, Reel 649.
Cynick. APS II, Reel 100.
Dramatic mirror, and literary companion. APS II, Reel 605.
Mirror of taste and dramatic censor. APS II, Reel 218.
New York literary gazette. APS II, Reel 973.
New York magazine, or Literary repository. APS I, Reels 21-22.
Stranger. APS II, Reel 810.
Theatrical censor. APS II, Reel 44.
Thespian mirror. APS II, Reel 44.
Thespian monitor. APS II, Reel 44.
Thespian oracle. APS I, Reel 29.

Baltimore, Maryland—Reviews
Baltimore weekly magazine complete in one volume. APS II, Reel 6.

Biography
Thespian mirror. APS II, Reel 44.

New York
Monthly recorder. APS II, Reel 146.
Ramblers' magazine. APS II, Reel 43.

New York—Reviews
Town. APS II, Reel 45.

Philadelphia
Cynick. APS II, Reel 100.
Thespian monitor. APS II, Reel 44.

Philadelphia—Reviews
Theatrical censor. APS II, Reel 44.

Reviews
Comet. APS II, Reel 97.
Mirror of taste and dramatic censor. APS II, Reel 218.
Polyanthos. APS II, Reels 39, 191-192.
Ramblers' magazine. APS II, Reel 43.
United States magazine and literary and political repository. APS II, Reel 243.

THEOLOGY
Adviser. APS II, Reels 1, 47.
Baltimore literary and religious magazine. APS II, Reels 585-586.
Beauties of the Evangelical magazine. APS II, Reel 6.
Berean. A religious publication. APS II, Reels 72, 539.
Berean; or Scripture-searcher. APS II, Reels 6, 72.
Bibliotheca sacra. APS II, Reel 379.
Christian cabinet. APS II, Reel 7.
Christian messenger. APS II, Reels 82, 595.
Christian messenger. Being a miscellaneous work. APS II, Reel 82.
Christian monitor. APS II, Reels 7, 82.
Christian review. APS II, Reels 410-416.
Christian visitor. APS II, Reel 401.

Christian's, scholar's, and farmer's magazine. APS I, Reel 10.
Church review. APS II, Reels 916-923.
Circular. APS II, Reel 210a.
Correspondent. APS II, Reel 384.
Evangelical guardian and review. APS II, Reel 102.
Evangelical repository. APS II, Reel 130.
Evidence. APS II, Reel 18.
Experienced Christian's magazine. APS I, Reel 12, APS II, Reel 18.
Expositor and Universalist review. APS II, Reel 473.
Halcyon luminary. APS II, Reels 112, 464.
Literary and evangelical magazine. APS II, Reels 124-125, 464.
Literary and theological review. APS II, Reel 798.
New-England telegraph, and eclectic review. APS II, Reel 802.
Old and new. APS III, Reels 130-132.
Pilgrim. APS II, Reel 188.
Piscataqua evangelical magazine. APS II, Reel 39.
Providence theological magazine. APS II, Reel 194.
Radical. APS III, Reels 15-17.
Reformer and Christian. APS II, Reels 233, 720.
Religious monitor and evangelical repository. APS II, Reels 401-403.
Religious monitor; or, Theological scales. APS I, Reel 26.
Religious repository. APS II, Reel 43.
Repository of knowledge, historical, literary, miscellaneous, and theological. APS II, Reel 44.
Royal spiritual magazine. APS I, Reel 26.
Spiritual magazine. APS II, Reel 240.
Theological review and general repository of religious and moral information. APS II, Reel 206.
Utica Christian repository. APS II, Reel 245.
Witness. APS II, Reel 46.

Collected Works—18th Century
Biblical repository and classical review. APS II, Reels 306-310.

THEOLOGY, PRACTICAL
New-York missionary magazine. APS II, Reel 35.

TRACT SOCIETIES
New York tract magazine and Christian miscellany. APS II, Reel 166.

TRACTS
Cheap repository. APS II, Reel 207.

TRADE UNIONS
Man. APS II, Reels 565-566.

TRANSCENDENTALISM (NEW ENGLAND)
Dial: a magazine for literature, philosophy, and religion. APS II, Reel 546.
Harbinger. APS II, Reel 674.
Phalanx. APS II, Reel 671.

TRIALS—NEW YORK (CITY)
New York City hall recorder. APS II, Reel 211.

TRUSTS, INDUSTRIAL—UNITED STATES
Gunton's magazine. APS III, Reels 473-476.

UNITARIANISM
Christian disciple and theological review. APS II, Reels 77-79.
Christian examiner. APS II, Reels 79, 449-463.
Christian inquirer. APS II, Reels 1885-1887.

Christian observatory. APS II, Reel 312.
Christian register. APS II, Reels 87-88, 596-603.
General repository and review. APS II, Reels 107-108.
Liberal Christian. APS II, Reel 123.
Monthly religious magazine and theological review. APS II, Reels 1114-1120.
Radical. APS III, Reels 15-17.
Spirit of the Pilgrims. APS II, Reel 752.
Unitarian. APS II, Reel 1196.
Unitarian defendant. APS II, Reel 242.
Unitarian miscellany and Christian monitor. APS II, Reel 206.
Unitarian review. APS III, Reels 21-25.
Western messenger. APS II, Reels 489-490.

UNITED STATES—Army
United States service magazine. APS III, Reel 53.

Biography
Potter's American monthly. APS III, Reels 67-69.

Civilization—19th Century
American cultivator. APS II, Reels 465-467.
American magazine; a monthly miscellany. APS II, Reel 53.
Arcturus. APS II, Reel 734.
Christian's monitor. APS I, Reel 10.
Columbian Museum. APS I, Reel 10.
Country courier. APS II, Reel 100.
Gentlemen and ladies' town and country magazine. APS I, Reel 13.
Investigator and general intelligencer. APS II, Reel 389.
Olio, a literary and miscellaneous paper. APS II, Reel 219.
Philadelphia monthly magazine. APS I, Reel 25.
Weekly recorder. APS II, Reels 248-250.

Economic Conditions
Western journal and civilian. APS II, Reels 699-700.

Economic Conditions—1865-1918
American Economic Association. Publications. APS III, Reels 494-500.
Economic Policy
Gunton's magazine. APS III, Reels 473-476.

Foreign Relations
Instructor. APS I, Reel 13.

Historical Geography
Huntingdon literary museum. APS II, Reel 114.

History
American Catholic historical researches. APS III, Reels 201-202.
American historical magazine. APS II, Reel 767.
American historical register and monthly gazette. APS III, Reel 58.
American pioneer. APS II, Reel 297.
Historical family library. APS II, Reel 737.
Monthly register, magazine, and review of the United States. APS II, Reel 33.
National magazine; a monthly journal of American history. APS III, Reels 160-163.

Colonial Period, Ca. 1600-1775
American magazine and historical chronicle. APS I, Reel 1.
General magazine, and historical chronicle. APS I, Reel 12.
Instructor. APS I, Reel 13.

Seven Years War, 1756-1763
Monthly military repository. APS I, Reel 18.

Revolution, 1775-1783
American museum, or, Universal magazine. APS I, Reel 4-5.
Monthly military repository. APS I, Reel 18.
Pennsylvania magazine: or, American monthly museum. APS I, Reel 24.

Revolution, 1775-1783 (con't)

Rural magazine. APS I, Reel 27.
United States magazine. APS I, Reel 30.
Universal asylum and Columbian magazine. APS I, Reels 11, 30.

Revolution, 1775-1783—Campaigns and Battles

Military magazine and record of the volunteers of the city.
APS II, Reel 744.

1783-1815

American Apollo. APS I, Reel 1.
Monthly magazine, and American review. APS I, Reel 17.
New York magazine, or Literary repository. APS I, Reels 21-22.

Constitutional Period, 1789-1809

American register; or general repository of history, politics and
science. APS II, Reels 2, 59.
National magazine; or, A political, historical, biographical, and
literary repository. APS I, Reel 18.
New-Haven gazette, and the Connecticut magazine. APS I,
Reel 20.

19th Century

Eastern magazine. APS II, Reel 385.
Family magazine. APS II, Reels 474-476.
Literary journal, and weekly register of science and the arts.
APS II, Reel 799.
New Englander and Yale review. APS II, Reels 679-680, 904-
912.
Niles' national register. APS II, Reels 167-177, 254-269.
North-Carolina magazine, political, historical, and miscellaneous.
APS II, Reel 400.
Rover. APS II, Reels 912-913.
Stryker's American register and magazine. APS II, Reel 672.
Subterranean. APS II, Reel 576.
Western review. APS II, Reel 529.

1809-1817

American review of history and politics. APS II, Reel 60.

War of 1812

Boston spectator. APS II, Reel 74.
Historical register of the United States. APS II, Reels 113-114.
Military magazine and record of the volunteers of the city. APS
II, Reel 744.
Military monitor, and American register. APS II, Reel 136.

1815-1861

American register; or, Summary review of history, politics, and
literature. APS II, Reel 59.

1849-1877

Historical magazine. APS III, Reels 26-28.

Civil War, 1861-1865

Century, a popular quarterly. APS III, Reels 345-367.
Danville quarterly review. APS III, Reel 186.
New York observer. APS II, Reels 1856-1874.
Old guard. APS III, Reels 64-65.
Southern historical society. APS III, Reels 309-313.
Southern literary messenger. APS II, Reels 438-447.
Vanity Fair. APS III, Reels 568-569.

1865-1898

Potter's American monthly. APS III, Reels 67-69.

1898————

New Outlook. APS III, Reels 367-423.

Anecdotes, Facetiae, Satire, etc.

Hive. APS II, Reel 114.

Intellectual Life

Princeton magazine. APS II, Reel 748.

Navy—History

Analectic magazine. APS II, Reels 61-64.
North-Carolina magazine, political, historical, and miscellaneous.
APS II, Reel 400.
United States' naval chronicle. APS II, Reel 243.

Politics And Government

American magazine and historical chronicle. APS I, Reel 1.
American magazine; or, General repository. APS I, Reel 2.
American review of history and politics. APS II, Reel 60.
American Whig review. APS II, Reels 302-304.
Army and navy chronicle, and scientific repository. APS II, Reel
472.
Aurora. APS II, Reel 769.
Banner of the constitution. APS II, Reel 586.
Boston spectator. APS II, Reel 74.
Cincinnati weekly herald and philanthropist. APS II, Reels 1409-
1412.
Connecticut Republican magazine. APS II, Reel 15.
Corrector. APS II, Reel 15.
Examiner. APS II, Reels 104-106.
Forum and Century. APS II, Reels 272-293.
Independent reflector. APS I, Reel 13.
Jeffersonian. APS II, Reel 797.
Knickerbocker. APS II, Reels 349-361.
Literary union. APS II, Reel 742.
Man. APS II, Reels 565-566.
Massachusetts quarterly review. APS II, Reel 658.
Monthly recorder, a magazine. APS II, Reel 146.
National register. APS II, Reels 800-801.
New Englander and Yale review. APS II, Reels 679-680, 904-912.
New star. APS I, Reel 23.
New-Yorker. APS II, Reels 1090-1092.
North American. APS II, Reel 973.
North-Carolina magazine, political, historical, and miscellaneous.
APS II, Reel 400.
Northern light. APS II, Reel 844.
Pathfinder. APS II, Reel 1407.
Philanthropist. APS II, Reels 187-188.
Pittsburgh recorder. APS II, Reels 219-220, 1052.
Political economist. APS II, Reel 191.
Putnam's magazine. APS III, Reels 164-167.
Rough and ready. APS II, Reel 845.
Round table. APS III, Reels 461-462.
United States Democratic review. APS II, Reels 691-696.
United States magazine and literary and political repository. APS II,
Reel 243.
Western review. APS II, Reel 529.

Colonial Period, Ca. 1600-1775

American magazine; or, A monthly view of the political state
of the British colonies. APS I, Reel 2.
Censor. APS I, Reel 8.
New American magazine. APS I, Reel 19.

1775-1783

United States magazine; a repository of history, politics and
literature. APS I, Reel 30.

1783-1815

American Apollo. APS I, Reel 1.
New Hampshire & Vermont magazine. APS I, Reel 20.
Rural magazine; or, Vermont repository. APS I, Reel 27.
South-Carolina weekly museum. APS I, Reel 28.
Time piece. APS I, Reel 29.
Worcester magazine. APS I, Reel 33.

1789-1797

Porcupine's Political Censor. APS I, Reel 26.

Constitutional Period, 1789-1809

National magazine; or, A political, historical, biographical, and
literary repository. APS I, Reel 18.

1797-1801
Republican magazine. APS I, Reel 26.
Rush-light. APS II, Reel 44.

1801-1805
National magazine; or, Cabinet of the United States. APS II, Reel 34.

1801-1809
Colvin's weekly register. APS II, Reel 382.
Patriot. APS II, Reel 36.
Weekly inspector. APS II, Reel 1408.

1801-1827
Gleaner; or, Monthly magazine. APS II, Reel 32.
Port folio. APS II, Reels 40-42, 220-228, 915.

War of 1812
Historical register of the United States. APS II, Reels 113-114.
Military monitor, and American register. APS II, Reel 136.
Ordeal. APS II, Reel 36.

1815-1861
Investigator and expositor. APS II, Reel 1231.
National government journal. APS II, Reel 149.
National register. APS II, Reels 800-801.

Civil War, 1861-1865
Albion. APS II, Reels 50, 706-718, 1263-1270.
Old guard. APS III, Reels 64-65.

1865-1898
Old guard. APS III, Reels 64-65.

Caricature and Cartoons
Puck. APS III, Reels 69-84.

Popular Culture
Aeronaut. APS II, Reels 48-49.
American magazine. APS III, Reels 675-689.
American magazine of useful and entertaining knowledge. APS II, Reel 768.
Casket. APS II, Reel 75.
Continent. APS III, Reels 99-100.
Cosmopolitan. APS III, Reels 660-669.
Dollar magazine. APS II, Reel 604.
Dollar magazine; a literary, political, advertising, and miscellaneous newspaper. APS II, Reel 385.
Dwights American magazine, and family newspaper. APS II, Reel 733.
Family lyceum. APS II, Reel 771.
Family magazine. APS II, Reels 474-476.
Galaxy. APS III, Reels 7-12.
General magazine and impartial review of knowledge & entertainment. APS I, Reel 13.
Green Mountain gem. APS II, Reel 654.
Hours at home. APS III, Reels 28-30.
Illustrated family magazine. APS II, Reel 777.
Independent. APS II, Reels 418, 1420-1464.
Knickerbocker. APS II, Reels 349-361.
Ladies' home journal. APS III, Reels 757-766.
Life. APS III, Reels 500-532.
Literary and musical magazine. APS II, Reel 213.
Literary gazette. APS II, Reel 400.
Literary museum, or, Monthly magazine. APS I, Reel 14.
McClure's magazine. APS III, Reels 477-493.
Magazine for the million. APS II, Reel 742.
Massachusetts magazine. APS I, Reels 15-16.
Medley. APS II, Reel 28.
Minerva. APS II, Reel 137.
Monthly chronicle of events. APS II, Reel 745.
New England magazine of knowledge and pleasure. APS I, Reel 19.

New-Jersey magazine and monthly advertiser. APS I, Reel 21.
New mirror. APS II, Reel 1124.
New world. APS II, Reels 1696-1700.
New-York mirror. APS II, Reels 164-165, 785-787.
North American miscellany and dollar magazine. APS II, Reels 939-940.
North-Carolina magazine. APS I, Reel 23.
Observer. APS II, Reel 218.
Parterre. APS II, Reel 184.
Pilot. APS II, Reel 189.
Robert's semi-monthly magazine for town and country. APS II, 845.
Rose of the valley. APS II, Reel 1308.
Rover. APS II, Reel 912-913.
Rural magazine. APS I, Reel 27.
Saturday evening post. APS II, Reels 236-237, 1936-1947.
Town and country. APS II, Reels 1948-1959.
United States magazine, or, General repository. APS I, Reel 30.
Waldie's select circulating library. APS II, Reels 1354-1357.
Western miscellany. APS II, Reel 1260.
Yankee and Boston literary gazette. APS II, Reel 1313.

Rural Conditions
Colman's rural world. APS II, Reel 416.
Prairie farmer. APS II, Reels 747-748, 1720-1726, 1936.

Social Conditions
Port folio. APS II, Reels 40-42, 220-228, 915.

Social Conditions–To 1865
Columbian museum. APS I, Reel 10.
Investigator and general intelligencer. APS II, Reel 389.

Social Life and Customs
American magazine. APS III, Reels 675-689.

Social Life and Customs–19th Century
Current opinion. APS III, Reels 689-707.

Southern States–Rural Conditions
Southern agriculturist, horticulturist, and register of rural affairs. APS II, Reels 806-809.

Statistics–19th Century
Niles' national register. APS II, Reels 167-177, 254-269.

Statistics, Vital
Franklin Minerva. APS II, Reel 546.

UNIVERSALISM
Candid examiner. APS II, Reel 546.
Christian intelligencer and eastern chronicle. APS II, Reels 80, 593-595.
Christian telescope and Universalist Miscellany. APS II, Reels 89, 1197.
Evangelical magazine and gospel advocate. APS II, Reels 792-794.
Evangelical repertory. APS II, Reel 103.
Expositor and Universalist review. APS II, Reel 473.
Gazetteer. APS II, Reel 107.
Gospel advocate and impartial investigator. APS II, Reels 110, 1072.
Gospel inquirer. APS II, Reel 110.
Gospel visitant. APS II, Reel 110.
Herald of life and immortality. APS II, Reel 113.
Herald of salvation. APS II, Reel 113.
Religious enquirer. APS II, Reel 197.
Religious inquirer. APS II, Reel 234.
Rochester magazine. APS II, Reel 205.
Universalist. APS II, Reels 243-244, 1701-1706.
Universalist, consisting of essays. APS II, Reel 1308.

Universalist quarterly and general review. APS II, Reels 697, 1357-1363.

Universalist watchman, repository and chronicle. APS II, Reels 1309-1310.

UNIVERSALIST CHURCH
Christian messenger, devoted to doctrine, religion, and morality. APS II, Reel 82.

Philadelphia Universalist magazine and Christian messenger. APS II, Reel 187.

UTAH
Utahnian. APS III, Reel 271.

VACCINATION–COLLECTED WORKS
Vaccine inquirer. APS II, Reel 246.

VERMONT–Anecdotes, Facetiae, Satire, etc.
Green Mountain repository. APS II, Reel 654.

History
Green Mountain repository. APS II, Reel 654.

VETERINARY COLLEGES
Farrier's magazine. APS II, Reel 106.

VETERINARY MEDICINE
Farrier's magazine. APS II, Reel 106.

VIRGINIA–HISTORY
Virginia historical register. APS II, Reel 943.
Virginia literary museum and journal of belles lettres. APS II, Reel 1407.

VIRGINIA, UNIVERSITY
Virginia literary museum and journal of belles lettres. APS II, Reel 1407.

VOCAL MUSIC
American musical magazine. APS II, Reel 2.

WAR
Friend of peace. APS II, Reels 211, 1072.

WASHINGTON, D.C.
The————————. APS II, Reel 333.

Biography
Huntress. APS II, Reels 935-937.

THE WEST
Western luminary. APS II, Reels 1311-1313.
Western monthly review. APS II, Reel 673.

History
National magazine. APS III, Reels 160-163.

History–To 1848
Illinois monthly magazine. APS II, Reel 389.
Western messenger. APS II, Reels 489-490.

WESTERN STORIES
Hesperian. APS II, Reel 417.
Illinois monthly magazine. APS II, Reel 389.
Overland monthly and Out West magazine. APS III, Reels 33-52.

WHIG PARTY
National magazine and republican review. APS II, Reel 799.

Ohio
Investigator and expositor. APS II, Reel 1231.

WIT AND HUMOR
American magazine and monthly chronicle for the British colonies. APS I, Reel 2.
American monthly magazine. APS II, Reel 468.
Every body's album. APS II, Reel 924.
Forrester's boys' and girls' magazine, and fireside companion. APS II, Reels 606-607.
John-donkey. APS II, Reel 657.
Life. APS III, Reels 500-532.
Manuscript. APS II, Reel 609.
Recreative magazine. APS II, Reel 197.
Scourge. APS II, Reel 239.
Theatrical budget. APS II, Reel 1258.
Thistle. APS II, Reel 44.

WOMAN
Arthur's magazine. APS II, Reel 378.
Dessert to the true American. APS I, Reel 12.
Godey's magazine. APS II, Reels 772-776, 862-880.
Key. APS I, Reel 13.
National magazine. APS II, Reel 799.

Biography
Ariel. APS II, Reel 839.
Lady's pearl. APS II, Reel 657.
New England quarterly magazine. APS II, Reel 34.
Philadelphia magazine, and weekly repertory. APS II, Reel 186.
Weekly visitor and ladies' museum. APS II, Reel 1884.

Conduct Of Life
Ladies' weekly museum. APS II, Reels 561-565.

Employment–Lowell, Massachusetts
Lowell offering. APS II, Reel 675.

Rights Of Women
American magazine of civics. APS III, Reel 203-204.
Christian inquirer. APS II, Reels 1885-1887.
Stand. APS II, Reel 333.

Social And Moral Questions
Ladies magazine. APS II, Reel 122.

WOMEN'S PERIODICALS
Amaranth. APS II, Reel 813.
American ladies' magazine. APS II, Reels 420-421.
Arthur's home magazine. APS III, Reels 533-547.
Arthur's magazine. APS II, Reel 378.
Artist. APS II, Reel 649.
Diana. APS II, Reel 101.
Gentleman and lady's town and country magazine; or, repository of instruction and entertainment. APS I, Reel 13.
Harper's bazaar. APS III, Reels 430-450.
Inquisitor. APS II, Reel 211.
Intellectual regale. APS II, Reel 115.
Journal des dames. APS II, Reel 115.
Juvenile port-folio. APS II, Reel 212.

Ladies' companion, and literary expositor. APS II, Reels 738-740.
Ladies' garland. APS II, Reel 561.
Ladies' garland and family wreath. APS II, Reels 608-609.
Ladies' home journal. APS III, Reels 757-766.
Ladies' literary cabinet. APS II, Reels 121-122.
Ladies' literary portfolio. APS II, Reel 893.
Ladies magazine. APS II, Reel 122.
Ladies museum. Philadelphia, I. Ralston. APS II, Reel 20.
Ladies museum. Providence, R.I. APS II, Reel 122.
Ladies port folio. APS II, Reel 122.
Ladies' repository. APS II, Reels 482, 893-899.
Ladies' visitor. APS II, Reel 212.
Ladies' weekly museum. APS II, Reels 561-565.
Ladies' wreath. APS II, Reels 1232-1233.
Lady's magazine, and repository of entertaining knowledge. APS I, Reel 14.
Lady's miscellany. APS II, Reels 20-21, 212-213.
Lady's pearl. APS II, Reel 657.
Lady's western magazine and garland of the valley. APS II, Reel 1093.
Lowell offering. APS II, Reel 675.
Masonic miscellany and ladies literary magazine. APS II, Reel 214.
National magazine. APS II, Reel 799.
National repository. APS III, Reels 110-111.
New York illustrated magazine of literature and art. APS II, Reel 842.
Peterson magazine. APS II, Reels 1292-1308.
Philadelphia album and ladies' literary port folio. APS II, Reels 721-725.
Pictorial review. APS II, Reels 1487-1488.
Portland magazine. APS II, Reel 746.
Souvenir. APS II, Reel 1407.
Toilet. APS II, Reel 45.
Weekly visitor and ladies' museum. APS II, Reel 1884.
Western ladies' casket. APS II, Reel 252.

WORCESTER CO., MASS.–HISTORY

Worcester magazine and historical journal. APS II, Reel 720.

YALE UNIVERSITY

Athenaeum. APS II, Reel 65.

Literary cabinet. APS II, Reel 22.
Yale literary magazine. APS II, Reels 529-531.

YELLOW FEVER

Literary magazine, and American register. APS II, Reels 22-23.
Medical repository of original essays and intelligence. APS I, Reel 14; APS II, Reel 26-27, 132-134.
Philadelphia medical and physical journal. APS II, Reel 37.

New York, 1819

Medical & surgical register. APS II, Reel 216.

Philadelphia, 1798

Philadelphia monthly magazine. APS I, Reel 25.

YOUTH

Every youth's gazette. APS II, Reel 606.
Youth's cabinet. APS II, Reel 333.

Anecdotes, Facetiae, Satire, etc.

Village museum. APS II, Reel 246.

Conduct Of Life

Dawn. APS II, Reel 100.
Every youth's gazette. APS II, Reel 606.
Juvenile miscellany. APS II, Reels 389-390.
Monitor, designed to improve the taste, the understanding, and the heart. APS II, Reel 143.
Weekly monitor. APS II, Reel 248.

Religious Life

Weekly monitor, entertaining and instructive. APS II, Reel 248.
Youth's repository of Christian knowledge. APS II, Reel 333.

ZOOLOGY

Western gleaner. APS II, Reel 252.

North America

Annals of nature. APS II, Reel 64.

McClure's Magazine: Vol. 7, no. 5; Oct. 1896

EDITOR
INDEX

EDITOR INDEX

ABBOT, ANNE WALES
Child's friend and family magazine. APS II, Reels 509-512.

ABBOTT, EDWARD, 1841-1908
Literary world. APS III, Reels 155-159.

ACADEMY OF POLITICAL SCIENCE, NEW YORK
Political science quarterly. APS III, Reels 767-771.

ADAMS, DANIEL, 1773-1864
Medical and agricultural register, for the years 1806 and 1807. APS II, Reel 26.

ADAMS, DAVID PHINEAS
Monthly anthology, and Boston review. APS II, Reels 30-32, 143-144.

ADAMS, WILLIAM TAYLOR, 1822-1897
Oliver Optic's magazine. APS III, Reels 236-238.

ADRAIN, ROBERT 1775-1843
Analyst; or Mathematical museum. APS II, Reels 3, 64.

AFFLECK, THOMAS
Western farmer and gardener. APS II, Reel 698.

AGNEW, JOHN HOLMES, 1804-1865
American eclectic. APS II, Reel 295.
Biblical repository and classical review. APS II, Reels 306-310.
Eclectic magazine of foreign literature. APS II, Reels 519-523, 945-973.
Eclectic museum of foreign literature, science and art. APS II, Reel 605.
Knickerbocker. APS II, Reels 349-361.

ALCOTT, LOUISA MAY, 1832-1888
Merry's museum for boys and girls. APS II, Reels 743, 1499-1501.

ALCOTT, WILLIAM ALEXANDER, 1798-1859
American annals of education. APS II, Reels 293-294.

ALEXANDER, WILLIAM C.
Princeton magazine. APS II, Reel 748.

ALFRIEND, FRANK H.
Southern literary messenger. APS II, Reels 438-447.

ALLEN, JOSEPH HENRY, 1820-1898
Unitarian review. APS III, Reels 21-25.

ALLEN, NATHAN, 1813-1889
Phrenological journal and science of health. APS II, Reels 1341-1353.

ALLWORTHY, AARON
Merrimack miscellany. APS II, Reel 28.

AMERICAN ANTI-SLAVERY SOCIETY
American anti-slavery reporter. APS II, Reel 725.
Anti-slavery examiner. APS II, Reel 408.
Anti-slavery record. APS II, Reel 408.

AMERICAN BAPTIST FOREIGN MISSION SOCIETY
Baptist missionary magazine. APS II, Reels 71-72, 535-539, 830-838.
Columbian star. APS II, Reels 95-96, 1271.

Latter day luminary. APS II, Reels 122-123.

AMERICAN BAPTIST PUBLICATION SOCIETY
Baptist quarterly. APS III, Reels 4-5.

AMERICAN BOARD OF COMMISSIONERS FOR FOREIGN MISSIONS
Missionary herald at home and abroad. APS II, Reels 29, 139-142, 764-766, 1237-1245.

AMERICAN CATHOLIC HISTORICAL SOCIETY OF PHILADELPHIA
American Catholic historical researches. APS III, Reels 201-202.

AMERICAN COLONIZATION SOCIETY
African intelligencer. APS II, Reel 49.
African repository. APS II, Reels 49, 641-644, 881-884.

AMERICAN PEACE SOCIETY
World affairs. APS II, Reels 584, 1543-1545.

AMERICAN SOCIAL SCIENCE ASSOCIATION
Journal of social science. APS III, Reels 266-268.

AMERICAN SOCIETY FOR THE DISSEMINATION OF THE DOCTRINES OF THE NEW JERUSALEM CHURCH
New Jerusalem Church repository. APS II, Reel 157.

AMERICAN SOCIETY FOR MELIORATING THE CONDITION OF THE JEWS
Israel's advocate. APS II, Reels 130, 401.

AMERICAN SUNDAY-SCHOOL UNION
American Sunday school magazine. APS II, Reel 305.

ANGELL, JOSEPH KINNICUT, 1794-1857
United States law intelligencer and review. APS II, Reel 741.

ARTHUR, TIMOTHY SHAY, 1809-1885
Baltimore literary monument. APS II, Reel 379.

ASBURY, FRANCIS
Arminian magazine. APS I, Reel 8.

ATWATER, LYMAN HOTCHKISS, 1813-1883
Princeton review. APS II, Reels 229, 566-572, 846-854.

BACHE, FRANKLIN, 1792-1864
North American medical and surgical journal. APS II, Reel 804-805.

BACHELER, ORIGEN
Family magazine. APS II, Reels 474-476.

BACON, LEONARD, 1802-1881
Independent. APS II, Reels 418, 1420-1464.

BAGBY, GEORGE WILLIAM, 1828-1883
Southern literary messenger. APS II, Reels 438-447.

BAILEY, GAMALIEL, JR., 1807-1859
Cincinnati weekly herald and philanthropist. APS II, Reels 1409-1412.

BAILEY, HARRY B.
Forest and stream. APS III, Reels 208-235.

BAILEY, ISAAC
Rhode Island literary repository. APS II, Reel 204.

BAKER, ABIJAH RICHARDSON, 1805-1876
Happy home and parlor magazine. APS III, Reels 756-757.

BALCH, WILLIAM RALSTON, 1852-1917
International review. APS III, Reels 152-154.

BALDWIN, CHARLES N.
Literary miscellany; or, Monthly review, a periodical work. APS II, Reel 131.

BALDWIN, CHRISTOPHER COLUMBUS, 1800-1835
Worcester magazine and historical journal. APS II, Reel 720.

BALDWIN, THOMAS, 1753-1825
Massachusetts Baptist missionary magazine. APS II, Reels 25, 216.

BALLOU, HOSEA, 1771-1852
Expositor and Universalist review. APS II, Reel 473.
Gospel visitant. APS II, Reel 110.
Universalist. APS II, Reels 243-244, 1701-1706.

BALLOU, HOSEA, 1796-1861
Expositor and Universalist review. APS II, Reel 473.
Universalist quarterly and general review. APS II, Reels 697, 1357-1363.

BALLOU, MATURIN MURRAY, 1820-1895
Ballou's pictorial drawing-room companion. APS III, Reels 249-252.

BANGBAR, BARNABY, esq., pseud.
Thespian monitor. APS II, Reel 44.

BANGS, NATHAN, 1778-1862
Methodist review. APS II, Reels 135-136, 327-332, and 1093-1113.

BARBER, HENRY H.
Unitarian review. APS III, Reels 21-25.

BARNARD, HENRY, 1811-1900
American journal of education. APS III, Reels 85-91.
Connecticut common school journal. APS II, Reels 789-791.
Rhode Island Institute of Instruction. Journal. APS II, Reel 389.

BARNWELL, R. G.
DeBow's review. APS II, Reels 382, 383, 855-862.

BARRON, ALFRED
Oneida circular. APS III, Reels 670-674.

BARTLETT, JOHN SHERREN, 1790-1863
Albion. APS II, Reels 50, 706-718, 1263-1270.

BARTON, BENJAMIN SMITH, 1766-1815
Philadelphia medical and physical journal. APS II, Reel 37.

BATES, ELISHA, 1779 or 80-1861
Moral advocate, a monthly publication. APS II, Reel 146.
Philanthropist, a weekly journal containing essays. APS II, Reels 187-188.

BAUM, HENRY MASON, 1848-
Church review. APS II, Reels 916-923.

BAUMES, JOHN ROSS, 1833-
Baptist quarterly review. APS III, Reels 59-60.

BEATTY, GEORGE
Niles' national register. APS II, Reels 167-177, 254-269.

BEAUCHAMP, WILLIAM, 1772-1824
Western Christian monitor. APS II, Reel 252.

BECKWITH, GEORGE CONE, 1800-1870
World affairs. APS II, Reels 584, 1543-1545.

BEECHER, HENRY WARD, 1813-1887
Independent. APS II, Reels 418, 1420-1464.
Western farmer and gardener. APS II, Reel 1408.

BELL, EDWIN Q.
DeBow's review. APS II, Reels 382, 383, 855-862.

BELL, THEODORE STOUT, 1807-1884
Western journal of medicine and surgery. APS II, Reels 701-705.

BELL, WILLIAM, 1791-1871
Universalist watchman, repository and chronicle. APS II, Reels 1309-1310.

BENNETT, EMERSON, 1822-1905
Casket. APS II, Reel 382.

BERESFORD, RICHARD. d. 1804?
Vigil. APS I, Reel 31.

BERRY, CLAUDE P., 1877-
Central law journal. APS III, Reels 548-566.

BIDWELL, WALTER HILLIARD, 1798-1881
Biblical repository and classical review. APS II, Reels 306-310.
Eclectic magazine of foreign literature. APS II, Reels 519-523, 945-973.
National preacher and village pulpit. APS II, Reels 1087-1090.

BIGELOW, POULTNEY, 1855-
Outing; sport, adventure, travel, fiction. APS III, Reels 297-309.

BIGELOW, WILLIAM, 1773-1844
Massachusetts magazine; or, Monthly museum. APS I, Reels 15-16.

BIGLOW, H.
American monthly magazine and critical review. APS II, Reel 58.

BIRNEY, JAMES GILLESPIE, 1792-1857
Cincinnati weekly herald and philanthropist. APS II, Reels 1409-1412.

BLANDING, ABRAHAM, 1776-1839
Carolina law journal. APS II, Reel 382.

BLEDSOE, ALBERT TAYLOR, 1809-1877
Southern review. APS III, Reels 18-20.

BLINN, HENRY CLAY, 1834-1905
Manifesto. APS III, Reels 62-63.

BOARDMAN, JAMES,
Euterpeiad; an album of music, poetry & prose. APS II, Reel 771.

BOGGS, EDWARD BRENTON, 1821-1895
Church review. APS II, Reels 916-923.

BOK, EDWARD WILLIAM, 1863-1930
Ladies' home journal. APS III, Reels 757-766.

BOLLES, ALBERT SIDNEY, 1840-
Bankers magazine. APS II, Reels 587-588, 1648-1683.

BOND, GEORGE
Literary gazette and American athenaeum. APS II, Reel 741.

BOSTON ANTHOLOGY SOCIETY
Monthly anthology, and Boston review. APS II, Reels 30-32, 143-144.

BOURNE, GEORGE, 1780-1845
Spirit of the public journals. APS II, Reel 44.

BOURNE, H.
Boston literary magazine. APS II, Reel 379.

BOWEN, ABEL, 1790-1850
Bowen's Boston news-letter. APS II, Reels 74, 914.

BOWEN, FRANCIS, 1811-1890
American almanac and repository of useful knowledge. APS II, Reels 810-812.
North American review. APS II, Reels 177-183, 270-281, 1613-1647.

BOWEN, HENRY CHANDLER, 1813-1896
Independent. APS II, Reels 418, 1420-1464.

BRACKENRIDGE, HUGH HENRY, 1748-1816
United States magazine: a repository of history, politics and literature. APS I, Reel 30.

BRAINERD, THOMAS, 1804-1866
Child's newspaper. APS II, Reel 400.

BRAINLESS, THOMAS, pseud.
Fool. APS II, Reel 19.

BRAY, FRANK CHAPIN, 1866-
Chautauquan. APS III, Reels 173-186.

BRECK, JOSEPH, 1794-1873
Horticultural register, and gardener's magazine. APS II, Reel 527.

BRECKINRIDGE, ROBERT JEFFERSON, 1800-1871
Baltimore literary and religious magazine. APS II, Reels 585-586.
Danville quarterly review. APS III, Reel 186.

BRENT, HENRY JOHNSON, 1811-1880
National magazine and republican review. APS II, Reel 799.

BRIGGS, CHARLES FREDERICK, 1804-1877
Dollar magazine. APS II, Reel 604.

BRISBANE, ALBERT, 1809-1890
Phalanx. APS II, Reel 671.

BRISTED, JOHN, 1778-1855
Monthly register, magazine, and review of the United States. APS II, Reel 33.

BRITT, ALBERT, 1874-
Outing; sport, adventure, travel, fiction. APS III, Reels 297-309.

BROCK, ROBERT ALONZO, 1839-1914
Southern historical society. APS III, Reels 309-313.

BRONSON, ENOS, d. 1824?
Select reviews of literature, and spirit of foreign magazines. APS II, Reels 44, 239-240.

BRONSON, TILLOTSON, 1762-1826
Churchman's magazine. APS II, Reels 12, 91, 210.

BROOKS, ARTHUR ANDERSON, b. 1856
American Geographical Society of New York. Bulletin (formerly Journal). APS III, Reels 708-716.

BROOKS, JAMES GORDON, 1801-1841
Literary gazette and American athenaeum. APS II, Reel 741.
Minerva. APS II, Reel 137.

BROOKS, NATHAN COVINGTON, 1809-1898
American museum of literature and the arts. APS II, Reel 646.

BROWN, ALLEN, 1788-1870
Rhode Island Baptist. APS II, Reel 204.

BROWN, BARTHOLOMEW, 1772-1854
Boston musical gazette. APS II, Reel 408.

BROWN, CHARLES BROCKDEN, 1771-1810
American register; or general repository of history, politics and science. APS II, Reels 2, 59.
American review, and literary journal, for 1801-1802. APS II, Reel 3.
Literary magazine, and American register. APS II, Reels 22-23.

BROWNE, DANIEL JAY, b. 1804
Naturalist. APS II, Reel 801.

BROWNE, IRVING, 1835-1899
Albany law journal. APS III, Reels 570-580.

BROWNING, CHARLES HOARY
American historical register and monthly gazette. APS III, Reel 58.

BROWNSON, ORESTES AUGUSTUS, 1803-1876
Boston quarterly review. APS II, Reel 380.
Brownson's quarterly review. APS II, Reels 507-508, 884-886.

BRUCE, ARCHIBALD, 1777-1818
American mineralogical journal. APS II, Reel 57.

BRUETTE, WILLIAM ARTHUR, 1873-
Forest and stream. APS III, Reels 208-235.

BRYANT, WILLIAM CULLEN, 1794-1878
New York review and atheneum magazine. APS II, Reels 166, 615.
Talisman. APS II, Reel 400.
United States review and literary gazette. APS II, Reel 1124.

BUCKINGHAM, JOSEPH TINKER, 1779-1861
New-England galaxy. APS II, Reels 150-152, 1120-1123.
Ordeal. APS II, Reel 36.
Polyanthos. APS II, Reels 39, 191-192.

BURR, CHARLES CHAUNCEY, 1817-1883
Old guard. APS III, Reels 64-65.

BURRITT, ELIHU, 1810-1879
Literary geminae. APS II, Reel 657.
World affairs. APS II, Reels 584, 1543-1545.

BURTON, ASA, 1752-1836
Adviser: or, Vermont evangelical magazine. APS II, Reels 1, 47.

BURTON, WILLIAM EVANS, 1802-1860
Burton's gentleman's magazine and American monthly review. APS II, Reel 311.

BURWELL, WILLIAM MACCREARY, 1809-1888
DeBow's review. APS II, Reels 382-383, 855-862.

BUSH, GEORGE, 1796-1859
Hierophant. APS II, Reel 388.

BUSHNELL, MADELINE VAUGHAN ABBOTT, 1871-1904
Literary world. APS III, Reels 155-159.

BUTLER, MERRILL
Scourge. APS II, Reel 239.

BUTON, ERNEST DE WITT, 1856-1925
Biblical world. APS II, Reels 254-264.

BUZZELL, JOHN, 1798-1863
Religious magazine; containing an account of the united churches of Christ. APS II, Reel 202.

CALDWELL, JOHN E.
Christian herald and seaman's magazine. APS II, Reels 493-495.

CAMP, ENOCH E.
National police gazette. APS II, Reels 1318-1340.

CAMPBELL, ALEXANDER, 1788-1866
Christian baptist. APS II, Reels 77, 1158.

CAMPBELL, JOHN POAGE, 1767-1814
Evangelical record, and western review. APS II, Reels 129-130.

CANDID, CHARLES, pseud.
Casket. APS II, Reel 75.

CAREY, MATHEW, 1760-1839
American museum, or, Universal magazine. APS I, Reels 4-5.
Political economist. APS II, Reel 191.

CARMAN, BLISS, 1861-1929
Literary world. APS III, Reels 155-159.

CARPENTER, EBER
National preacher and village pulpit. APS II, Reels 1087-1090.

CARPENTER, STEPHEN CULLEN, d. ca. 1820
Mirror of taste and dramatic censor. APS II, Reel 218.
Monthly register, magazine, and review of the United States. APS II, Reel 33.

CARRIQUE, RICHARD
Messenger of peace. APS II, Reel 217.
Religious inquirer. APS II, Reel 234.

CARROLL, BARTHOLOMEW RIVERS
Southern literary journal and magazine of arts. APS II, Reels 574-576.

CARSON, JOSEPH, 1808-1876
American journal of pharmacy. APS II, Reels 366-368, 1707-1716.

CARTER, ROBERT, 1819-1879
Pioneer. APS II, Reel 745.

CARUS, PAUL, 1852-1919
Monist. APS III, Reels 342-344.
Open court. APS III, Reels 293-297.

CARY, JOHN D.
Key. APS I, Reel 13.

CATHOLIC CHURCH IN THE UNITED STATES
United States Catholic miscellany. APS II, Reels 1961-1962.

CHANDLER, JOSEPH RIPLEY, 1792-1880
Graham's American monthly magazine of literature. APS II, Reels 547-560.

CHANDLER, PELEG WHITMAN, 1816-1889
Monthly law reporter. APS II, Reels 288-292.

CHANNING, EDWARD TYRREL, 1790-1856
North American review. APS II, Reels 177-183, 270-281, 1613-1647.

CHANNING, WALTER, 1786-1876
New-England journal of medicine and surgery. APS II, Reels 153-157, 944.
New-England medical review and journal. APS II, Reel 802.

CHANNING, WILLIAM HENRY, 1810-1884
Present. APS II, Reel 748.
Western messenger. APS II, Reels 489-490.

CHAPMAN, MARIA WESTON, 1806-1885
Liberty bell. APS II, Reels 491-492.

CHAPMAN, NATHANIEL, 1780-1853
Philadelphia journal of the medical and physical sciences. APS II, Reels 184-185.

CHASE, EBENEZER
Masonic casket. APS II, Reel 132.
Religious informer. APS II, Reels 197-198.

CHAUTAUQUA INSTITUTION, CHAUTAUQUA, N.Y.
Chautauquan. APS III, Reels 173-186.

CHAUTAUQUA LITERARY AND SCIENTIFIC CIRCLE
Chautauquan. APS III, Reels 173-186.

CHESTER, STEPHEN M.
Columbian lady's and gentleman's magazine. APS II, Reel 313.

CHICAGO. UNIVERSITY
Biblical world. APS III, Reels 254-264.

CHILD, LYDIA MARIA FRANCIS, 1802-1880
Juvenile miscellany. APS II, Reels 389-390.

CHURCH, WILLIAM CONANT, 1836-1917
Galaxy. APS III, Reels 7-12.

CHURCHILL, JOHN WESLEY, 1839-1900
Andover review. APS III, Reels 1-4.

CINCINNATI COLLEGE
Western journal of the medical and physical sciences. APS II, Reels 578-580.

CLAPP, MILTON
Southern quarterly review. APS II, Reels 684-687.

CLARK, DAVIS WASGATT, 1812-1871
Ladies' repository. APS II, Reels 482, 893-899.

CLARK, LEWIS GAYLORD, 1808-1873
Knickerbocker. APS II, Reels 349-361.

CLARKE, JAMES FREEMAN, 1810-1888
Western messenger. APS II, Reel 489-490.

CLAXTON, TIMOTHY
Boston mechanic, and journal of the useful arts and sciences. APS II, reel 472.

COATES, BENJAMIN HORNOR, 1797-1881
North American medical and surgical journal. APS II, Reels 804-805.

COBB, H.
Western journal and civilian. APS II, Reels 699-700.

COBBETT, WILLIAM, 1763-1835
Cobbett's political register. APS II, Reel 92.
Porcupine's Political Censor. APS I, Reel 26.

COFFIN, JOHN GORHAM, 1770-1829
Boston medical intelligencer. APS II, Reels 73, 763.

COGSWELL, JOSEPH GREEN, 1786-1871
New York review. APS III, Reels 843-844.

COGSWELL, WILLIAM, 1787-1850
American quarterly register. APS II, Reels 532-534.
New-England historical and genealogical register. APS II, Reels 1053-1061.
New Hampshire repository. APS II, Reel 842.

COKE, THOMAS
Arminian magazine. APS I, Reel 8.

COLEMAN, E. B.
Guardian and monitor. APS II, Reels 111-112, 881.

COLEMAN, ELIPHALET BEECHER, d. 1856
Sabbath school repository and teacher's assistant. APS II, Reel 205.

COLHOUN, SAMUEL
American medical recorder. APS II, Reels 55-56, 645.

COLLEGE OF PHYSICIANS AND SURGEONS OF BUFFALO, N.Y.
Physicians' and surgeons' investigator. APS III, Reels 567-568.

COLLIER, NEEDHAM CALVIN, 1847-
Central law journal. APS III, Reels 548-566.

COLLINS, JOHN A.
Monthly offering. APS II, Reel 1245.

COLTON, GEORGE HOOKER, 1818-1847
American Whig review. APS II, Reels 302-304.

COLUMBIA UNIVERSITY. FACULTY OF POLITICAL SCIENCE
Political science quarterly. APS III, Reels 767-771.

COLVIN, JOHN B.
Baltimore weekly magazine complete in one volume. APS II, Reel 6.
Colvin's weekly register. APS II, Reel 382.

CONDIE, THOMAS G.
Juvenile port-folio. APS II, Reel 212.
Philadelphia monthly magazine. APS I, Reel 25.

CONE, ORELLO, 1835-1905
New world. APS III, Reels 31-32.

CONE, SPENCER WALLACE, 1819-1888
United States Democratic review. APS II, Reels 691-696.

CONGREGATIONAL EDUCATION SOCIETY, BOSTON
American quarterly register. APS II, Reels 532-534.

CONNECTICUT. BOARD OF COMMISSIONERS OF COMMON SCHOOLS
Connecticut common school journal. APS II, Reels 789-791.

CONRAD, ROBERT TAYLOR, 1810-1858
Graham's American monthly magazine of literature. APS II, Reels 547-560.

CONWAY, MONCURE DANIEL, 1832-1907
Dial: a monthly magazine for literature, philosophy and religion. APS III, Reel 7.

COOKE, PARSONS
Congregationalist and herald of gospel liberty. APS II, 97-99, 539-546, 1911-1924.

COOPER, EDWARD
District school journal of the state of New York. APS II, Reel 770.

COOPER, FREDERIC TABER, 1864-1937
Forum and Century. APS III, Reels 272-293.

COOPER, THOMAS, 1759-1839
Emporium of arts & sciences. APS II, Reel 101.

COPELAND, HERBERT
Literary world. APS III, Reels 155-159.

COPPEE, HENRY, 1821-1895
United States service magazine. APS III, Reel 53.

CORCORAN, JAMES ANDREW, 1820-1889
American Catholic quarterly review. APS III, Reels 650-660.

CORNELIUS, ELIAS, 1794-1832
American quarterly register. APS II, Reels 532-534.

CORNWALLIS, KINAHAN, 1839-1917
Knickerbocker. APS II, Reels 349-361.

COXE, JOHN REDMAN, 1773-1864
Philadelphia medical museum. APS II, Reels 38, 186.
Emporium of arts & sciences. APS II, Reel 101.

CRANE, FRANK, 1861-
Current opinion. APS III, Reels 689-707.

CREAMER, DAVID
Baltimore monument. APS II, Reel 769.

CROCKER, SAMUEL R., d. 1877?
Literary world. APS III, Reels 155-159.

CROSS, ANDREW BOYD, 1809 or 10-1889
Baltimore literary and religious magazine. APS II, Reels 585-586.

CROSWELL, HARRY, 1778-1858
Balance, and state journal. APS II, Reels 3-5, 70.

CROSWELL, WILLIAM, 1804-1851
Episcopal watchman. APS II, Reels 889-890.

CROW, JOHN FINLEY
Abolition intelligencer and missionary magazine. APS II, Reel 47.

CUMMINS, EBENEZER HARLOW
Evangelical repository. APS II, Reel 130.

CURRY, DANIEL, 1809-1887
Ladies' repository. APS II, Reels 482, 893-899.
Methodist review. APS II, Reels 135-136, 327-332, and 1093-1113.
National repository. APS III, Reels 110-111.

CURRY, OTWAY, 1804-1855
Hesperian. APS II, Reel 417.

DANA, EDWARD SALISBURY, 1849-1935
American journal of science. APS II, Reels 53, 53A, 754-762, 817-830.

DANA, JAMES DWIGHT, 1813-1895
American journal of science. APS II, Reels 53, 53A, 754-762, 817-830.

DANA, RICHARD HENRY, 1787-1879
Idle man. APS II, Reel 115.

DANA, WILLIAM B.
Merchants' magazine and commercial review. APS II, Reels 339-348.

DANIELSON, RICHARD ELY, 1885-
Independent. APS II, Reels 418, 1420-1464.

DARBY, WILLIAM, 1775-1854
Geographical, historical, and statistical repository. APS II, Reels 100, 130.

DARUSMONT, FRANCES WRIGHT, 1795-1852
Free enquirer. APS II, Reels 1498-1499.

DAVID, EDWARD W., 1810?-1868
American law journal. APS II, Reels 730-731.

DAVIDGE, JOHN BEALE, 1768-1829
Baltimore philosophical journal and review. APS II, Reel 71.

DAVIS, CORNELIUS
New-York missionary magazine. APS II, Reel 35.

DAVIS, MOSES, OF HANOVER, N.H.
Literary tablet. APS II, Reel 24.

DAWSON, HENRY BARTON, 1821-1889
Historical magazine. APS III, Reels 26-28.

DEAN, JOHN WARD, 1815-1902
Historical magazine. APS II, Reels 26-28.
New-England historical and genealogical register. APS III, Reels 1053-1061.

DEBOW, JAMES DUNWOODY BROWNSON, 1820-1867
DeBow's review. APS II, Reels 382, 383, 855-862.

DENNIE, JOSEPH, 1768-1812
Port folio. APS II, Reels 40-42, 220-228, 915.

DE NORMANDIE, JAMES, 1836-
Unitarian review. APS III, Reels 21-25.

DEWEES, WILLIAM POTTS, 1768-1841
Philadelphia journal of the medical and physical sciences. APS II, Reels 184-185.

DEWITT, CHARLES G.
Periodical sketches. APS II, Reel 184.

DICKINSON, AUSTIN, 1791-1849
National preacher and village pulpit. APS II, Reels 1087-1090.

DILLON, JOHN FORREST, 1831-1914
Central law journal. APS III, Reels 548-566.

DINGLEY, CHARLES
Euterpeiad; an album of music, poetry & prose. APS II, Reel 771.

DINSMORE, RICHARD, d. 1811
National magazine. APS II, Reel 34.

DOANE, GEORGE WASHINGTON, 1799-1859
Episcopal watchman. APS II, Reel 889-890.

DODGE, MARY ABIGAIL, 1833-1896
Our young folks. APS III, Reels 65-66.

DODGE, MRS. MARY (MAPES) 1838-1905
St. Nicholas; an illustrated magazine for young folks. APS III, Reels 591-599.

DRAKE, DANIEL, 1785-1852
Western journal of the medical and physical sciences. APS II, Reels 578-580.

DRAKE, SAMUEL GARDNER, 1798-1875
New-England historical and genealogical register. APS II, Reels 1053-1061.

DRAYTON, HENRY SHIPMAN, 1840-
Phrenological journal and science of health. APS II, Reels 1341-1353.

DUANE, WILLIAM, 1760-1835
Aurora. APS II, Reel 769.

DUNBAR, CHARLES FRANKLIN, 1830-1900
Quarterly journal of economics. APS III, Reels 167-170.

DUNGLISON, ROBLEY, 1796-1869
American medical intelligencer. APS II, Reel 296.

DUNNING, WILLIAM ARCHIBALD, 1857-1922
Political science quarterly. APS III, Reels 767-771.

DUYCKINCK, EVERT AUGUSTUS, 1816-1878
Arcturus. APS II, Reel 734.
Literary world. APS II, Reels 483-486.

DUYCKINCK, GEORGE LONG, 1823-1863
Literary world. APS II, Reels 483-486.

DWIGHT, FRANCIS, 1808-1845
District school journal of the state of New York. APS II, Reel 770.

DWIGHT, MELATIAH EVERETT
New York genealogical and biographical record. APS III, Reels 451-455.

DWIGHT, THEODORE, 1796-1866
Dwights American magazine, and family newspaper. APS II, Reel 733.

DWIGHT, TIMOTHY, 1828-1916
New Englander and Yale review. APS II, Reels 679-680, 904-912.

DYER, PALMER
Episcopal watchman. APS II, Reels 889-890.

EASY, EDWARD, pseud.
Companion and weekly miscellany. APS II, Reel 13.

EATON, LUCIEN, 1831-1890
American law review. APS III, Reels 463-472.

EBERLE, JOHN, 1787-1838
American medical recorder. APS II, Reels 55-56, 645.
American medical review. APS II, Reels 57, 846, 944.

ECONOMICAL SCHOOL, NEW YORK
Journal des dames. APS II, Reel 115.

EDDY, RICHARD, 1828-1906
Universalist quarterly and general review. APS II, Reels 697, 1357-1363.

EDWARDS, BELA BATES, 1802-1852
American quarterly observer. APS II, Reel 297.
American quarterly register. APS II, Reels 532-534.
Biblical repository and classical review. APS II, Reels 306-310.

ELLIS, BENJAMIN, 1798-1831
American journal of pharmacy. APS II, Reels 366-368, 1707-1716.

ELLIOT, SETH
American museum, and repository of arts and sciences. APS II, Reel 58.

ELLIOTT, GEORGE, 1851-1930
Methodist review. APS II, Reels 135-136, 327-332, and 1093-1113.

ELLIS, RUFUS, 1819-1885
Monthly religious magazine and theological review. APS II, Reels 1114-1120.

ELLS, B. F.
Western miscellany. APS II, Reel 1260.

EMBURY, EMMA CATHERINE MANLEY, 1806-1863
Ladies' companion, and literary expositor. APS II, Reels 738-740.

EMERSON, GEORGE HOMER, 1822-1898
Universalist quarterly and general review. APS II, Reels 697, 1357-1363.

EMERSON, RALPH WALDO, 1803-1882
Dial: a magazine for literature, philosophy, and religion. APS II, Reel 546.

EMERSON, WILLIAM, 1769-1811
Monthly anthology, and Boston review. APS II, Reels 30-32, 143-144.

EMLEN, SAMUEL, 1789-1828
Journal of foreign medical science and literature. APS II, Reels 116-119.

EMMONS, NATHANAEL, 1745-1840
Massachusetts missionary magazine. APS II, Reel 25.

EMORY, JOHN, bp., 1789-1835
Methodist review. APS II, Reels 135-136, 327-332, and 1093-1113.

ENGLISH, THOMAS DUNN, 1819-1902
Old guard. APS III, Reels 64-65.

EVANS, B. R.
Philadelphia monthly magazine. APS II, Reel 1092.

EVANS, FREDERICK WILLIAM, 1808-1896
Manifesto. APS III, Reels 62-63.

EVANS, GEORGE HENRY, 1805-1855
Working man's advocate. APS II, Reels 581-583.

EVERETT, ALEXANDER HILL, 1790-1847
North American review. APS II, Reels 177-183, 270-281, 1613-1647.

EVERETT, CHARLES CARROLL, 1829-1900
New world. APS III, Reels 31-32.

EVERETT, EDWARD, 1794-1865
Harvard lyceum. APS II, Reel 112.
North American review. APS II, Reels 177-183, 270-281, 1613-1647.

EWER, FERDINAND CARTWRIGHT, 1826-1883
Pioneer. APS III, Reel 15.

FAIRFIELD, SUMNER LINCOLN, 1803-1844
North American quarterly magazine. APS II, Reels 938-939.

FANNING, NEUVILLE O.
Arena. APS III, Reels 92-99.

FARLEY, HARRIET, 1817-1907
Lowell offering. APS II, Reel 675.

FARMER, JOHN, 1789-1838
Collections, historical and miscellaneous. APS II, Reels 93-94.

FARRAND MALLORY & CO., PUB.
New England literary herald. APS II, Reels 34, 218.

FARRAND, WILLIAM POWELL, d. 1839
Evangelical intelligencer. APS II, Reels 16-17.

FAY, THEODORE SEDGWICK, 1807-1898
New-York mirror. APS II, Reels 164-165, 785-787.

FENNELL, JAMES, 1766-1816
Something. APS II, Reels 44, 671.

FERGUSON, MILTON JAMES, 1879
Bibelot. APS III, Reels 252-253.

FESSENDEN, THOMAS GREEN, 1771-1837
Horticultural register, and gardeners' magazine. APS II, Reel 527.
New England farmer, and horticultural register. APS II, Reels 149, 1397-1404.
Weekly inspector. APS II, Reel 1408.

FISHER, GEORGE PARK, 1827-1909
New Englander and Yale review. APS II, Reels 679-680, 904-912.

FISHER, JOHN CHARLTON, d. 1849
Albion. APS II, Reels 50, 706-718, 1263-1270.

FITZ, HENRY
Gospel herald. APS II, Reel 503.

FLINT, TIMOTHY, 1780-1840
Knickerbocker. APS II, Reels 349-361.
Western monthly review. APS II, Reel 673.

FLOOD, THEODORE L., 1842-
Chautauquan. APS III, Reels 173-186.

FLOWER, BENJAMIN ORANGE, 1858-1918
Arena. APS III, Reels 92-99.

FLOY, JAMES, 1806-1863
National magazine: devoted to literature, art, and religion. APS II, Reels 814-815.

FLOYD, JOHN G.
Bankers magazine. APS II, Reels 587-588, 1648-1683.

FOLSOM, CHARLES, 1794-1872
Select journal of foreign periodical literature. APS II, Reel 913.
United States review and literary gazette. APS II, Reel 1124.

FOLSOM, GEORGE, 1802-1869
Historical magazine. APS III, Reels 26-28.

FOOTE, HENRY WILDER, 1838-1889
Unitarian review. APS III, Reels 21-25.

FORCE, PETER, 1790-1868
National government journal, and register of official papers. APS II, Reel 149.

FORCE, WILLIAM QUEREAU, 1820-1880
Army and navy chronicle, and scientific repository. APS II, Reel 472.

FORD, DANIEL SHARP, 1822-1899
Youth's companion. APS II, Reels 1546-1572.

FORMAN, WILLIAM HENRY
Manhattan. APS III, Reels 30-31.

FOSTER, FRANCIS APTHORP, 1872-
New-England historical and genealogical register. APS II, Reels 1053-1061.

FOSTER, ROBERT
Christian herald. APS II, Reels 79-80.

FOWLE, WILLIAM BENTLEY, 1795-1865
Common school journal. APS II, Reels 512-514.

FOWLER, ANDREW, 1760-1850
Sunday visitant. APS II, Reel 240.

FOWLER, ASA, 1811-1885
Literary gazette. APS II, Reel 400.

FOWLER, JESSIE ALLEN
Phrenological journal and science of health. APS II, Reels 1341-1353.

FOWLER, LORENZO NILES, 1811-1896
Phrenological journal and science of health. APS II, Reels 1341-1353.

FOWLER, ORSON SQUIRE, 1809-1887
Phrenological journal and science of health. APS II, Reels 1341-1353.

FOX, RICHARD KYLE, 1846
National police gazette. APS II, Reels 1318-1340.

FRANCIS, JOHN WAKEFIELD, 1789-1861
American medical and philosophical register. APS II, Reel 54.

FRANKLIN, BENJAMIN, 1706-1790
General magazine, and historical chronicle. APS I, Reel 12.

FRANKLIN, FABIAN, 1853-
Independent. APS II, Reels 418, 1420-1464.

FRASER, DONALD, fl. 1797
American magazine of wonders and marvellous chronicle. APS II, Reel 1.

FRENEAU, PHILIP MORIN, 1752-1832
Time piece. APS I, Reel 29.

FRY, JOSEPH REESE, 1811-1865
Western monthly magazine, and literary journal. APS II, Reel 528.

FULLER, HAROLD DE WOLF, 1874
Independent. APS II, Reels 418, 1420-1464.

GALLAGHER, WILLIAM DAVIS, 1808-1894
Hesperian. APS II, Reel 417.
Western literary journal, and monthly review. APS II, Reel 527

GALLAHER, JOHN S.
Ladies' garland. APS II, Reel 561.

GALLAND, ISAAC, 1790-1858
Chronicles of the North American savages. APS II, Reel 382.

GAMAGE, GILBERT ASH, d. 1832
Garland. APS II, Reel 107.

GANNETT, EZRA STILES, 1801-1871
Monthly miscellany of religion and letters. APS II, Reel 778.

GANNETT, HENRY, 1846-1914
International review. APS III, Reels 152-154.

GARDENIER, BARENT, d. 1822
Country courier. APS II, Reel 100.

GARDNER, CHARLES KITCHELL, 1787-1869
Literary and scientific repository, and critical review. APS II, Reel 126.

GARDNER, MELZAR
Boston pearl, a gazette of polite literature. APS II, Reel 788.

GARDNER, WILLIAM ARTHUR, 1855-1921
Central law journal. APS III, Reels 548-566.

GARRISON, WILLIAM LLOYD, 1805-1879
Abolitionist. APS II, Reel 362.
Liberator. APS II, Reels 391-399.

GEDDINGS, ELI, 1799-1878
Baltimore medical and surgical journal and review. APS II, Reel 379.
North American archives of medical and surgical science. APS II, Reel 804.

GENERAL COUNCIL OF THE CONGREGATIONAL AND CHRISTIAN CHURCHES OF THE UNITED STATES. BOARD OF HOME MISSIONS
Missionary herald at home and abroad. APS II, Reels 29, 139-142 764-766, 1237-1245.

GENERAL COUNCIL OF THE CONGREGATIONAL AND CHRISTIAN CHURCHES OF THE UNITED STATES. MISSIONS COUNCIL
Missionary herald at home and abroad. APS II, Reels 29, 139-142, 764-766, 1237-1245.

GIBBONS, WILLIAM PETERS, b. 1812
Advocate of science. APS II, Reel 532.
Advocate of science, and annals of natural history. APS II, Reel 532.

GILDER, JEANNETTE LEONARD, 1849-1916
Critic; an illustrated monthly review. APS III, Reels 101-108.

GILDER, JOSEPH BENSON, 1858-1936
Critic; an illustrated monthly review. APS III, Reels 101-108.

GILDERSLEEVE, BASIL LANNEAU, 1831-1924
American journal of philology. APS III, Reels 424-429.

GILMAN, CAROLINE HOWARD, 1794-1888
Southern rose. APS II, Reel 688.

GILMAN, CHARLES
Maine monthly magazine. APS II, Reel 486.

GILMAN, NICHOLAS PAINE, 1849-1912
Literary world. APS III, Reels 155-159.
New world. APS III, Reels 31-32.

GODEY, LOUIS ANTOINE, 1804-1878
Godey's magazine. APS II, Reels 772-776, 862-880.

GODMAN, JOHN DAVIDSON, 1794-1830
Journal of foreign medical science and literature. APS II, Reels 116-119.
Philadelphia journal of the medical and physical sciences. APS II, Reels 184-185.
Western quarterly reporter of medical. APS II, Reel 1497.

GOFFE, JAMES RIDDLE, 1851-1931
Medical news. APS II, Reels 658, 1073-1087.

GOLDSBOROUGH, CHARLES WASHINGTON, 1779-1843.
United States' naval chronicle. APS II, Reel 243.

GOODRICH, SAMUEL GRISWOLD, 1793-1860
Merry's museum for boys and girls. APS II, Reels 743, 1499-1501.

GOODSELL, N.
Genesee farmer and gardener's journal. APS II, Reels 316-318.

GOSSLER, J. C.
Philadelphier magazin. APS II, Reel 1196.

GOULD, GEORGE MILBRY, 1848-1922
Medical news. APS II, Reels 658, 1073-1087.

GOULD, MARCUS T. C., 1793-1860
American repertory of arts, sciences, and useful literature. APS II, Reel 734.

GRAHAM, DAVID
Pioneer, consisting of essays. APS II, Reel 189.

GRAHAM, GEORGE REX, 1813-1894
Graham's American monthly magazine of literature. APS II, Reels 547-560.

GRAVES, HIRAM A.
Christian reflector. APS II, Reels 886-889.

GRAY, JAMES, 1770-1824
Theological review and general repository of religious and moral information. APS II, Reel 206.

GRAY, JOHN CHIPMAN, 1839-1915
American law review. APS III, Reels 463-472.

GREELEY, HORACE, 1811-1872
Jeffersonian. APS II, Reel 797.
New-Yorker. APS II, Reels 1090-1092.

GREEN, ASHBEL, 1762-1848
Christian advocate. APS II, Reels 76, 592-593.

GREENE, ALBERT GORTON, 1802-1868
Literary journal, and weekly register of science and the arts. APS II, Reel 799.

GREENE, RICHARD HENRY, 1839-1926
New York genealogical and biographical record. APS III, Reels 451-455.

GREENHOOD, ELISHA
Central law journal. APS III, Reels 548-566.

GREENLEAF, JOSEPH 1720-1809
Royal American magazine. APS I, Reel 26.

GREENWOOD, FRANCIS WILLIAM PITT, 1797-1843
Unitarian miscellany and Christian monitor. APS II, Reel 206.

GREGG, THOMAS, b. 1808
Literary cabinet and western olive branch. APS II, Reel 565.

GRIFFIN, MARTIN IGNATIUS JOSEPH, 1842-1911
American Catholic historical researches. APS III, Reels 201-202.

GRIFFIN, WILLIAM LEO JOSEPH
American Catholic historical researches. APS III, Reels 201-202.

GRIFFITH, ROBERT EGLESFELD, 1798-1850
American journal of pharmacy. APS II, Reels 366-368, 1707-1716.

GRIFFITH, WILLIAM, 1766-1826
Annual law register of the United States. APS II, Reel 65.

GRINNELL, CHARLES EDWARD, 1841-1916
American law review. APS III, Reels 463-472.

GRISWOLD, RUFUS WILMOT, 1815-1857
Graham's American monthly magazine of literature. APS II, Reels 547-560.

GROSVENOR, CYRUS P.
Christian reflector. APS II, Reels 886-889.

GRUFF, GROWLER, pseud.
Cynick. APS II, Reel 100.

GUNTON, GEORGE, 1845-1919
Gunton's magazine. APS III, Reels 473-476.

GURLEY, RALPH RANDOLPH, 1797-1872
African repository. APS II, Reels 49, 641-644, 881-884.

GUTHRIE, ANNA LORRAINE
Forum and Century. APS III, Reels 272-293.

HACH, H. THEODOR
Musical magazine; or, Repository of musical science. APS II, Reel 1216.

HALE, EDWARD EVERETT, 1822-1909
Old and new. APS III, Reels 130-132.

HALE, NATHAN, 1784-1863
Monthly chronicle of events, discoveries, improvements. APS II, Reel 745.

HALE, NATHAN, 1818-1871
Boston miscellany of literature and fashion. APS II, Reel 310.

HALE, SARAH JOSEPHA BUELL, 1788-1879
American ladies' magazine. APS II, Reels 420-421.
Godey's magazine. APS II, Reels 772-776, 862-880.

HALL, JAMES, 1793-1868
Illinois monthly magazine. APS II, Reel 389.
Western monthly magazine, and literary journal. APS II, Reel 528.

HALL, JOHN ELIHU, 1783-1829
American law journal. APS II, Reels 1, 53.
Journal of jurisprudence. APS II, Reel 119.
Port folio. APS II, Reels 40-42, 220-228, 915.

HALLOCK, CHARLES, 1834-1917
Forest and stream. APS III, Reels 208-235.

HALLOCK, GERARD
Congregationalist and herald of gospel liberty. APS II, Reels 97-99, 539-546, 1911-1924.

HAMILTON BAPTIST MISSIONARY SOCIETY
Western New York Baptist magazine. APS II, Reels 252-253.

HAMLINE, LEONIDAS LENT, BP., 1797-1865
Ladies' repository. APS II, Reels 482, 893-899.

HANAFORD, WILLIAM G.
Boston literary magazine. APS II, Reel 379.

HARDIE, JAMES, 1750?-1826?
New-York magazine and general repository. APS II, Reel 162.

HARE, HOBART AMORY, 1862-1931
Medical news. APS II, Reels 658, 1073-1087.

HARPER, WILLIAM RAINEY, 1856-1906
Biblical world. APS III, Reels 254-264.

HARRIS, GEORGE, 1844-1922
Andover review. APS III, Reels 1-4.

HARRIS, THADDEUS MASON, 1768-1842
Massachusetts magazine; or, Monthly museum. APS I, Reels 15-16.

HARRIS, WILLIAM TORREY, 1835-1909
Journal of speculative philosophy. APS III, Reels 13-15.

HART, JOHN SEELY, 1810-1877
Sartain's union magazine of literature and art. APS II, Reels 572-574.

HARTE, BRET, 1839-1902
Overland monthly and Out West magazine. APS III, Reels 33-52.

HARTFORD SOCIETY FOR YOUNG MEN
Stand; by a society of young men. APS II, Reel 333.

HARVARD UNIVERSITY
Harvardiana. APS II, Reel 655.
Quarterly journal of economics. APS III, Reels 167-170.

HAWKINS, JOSEPH
Columbian phenix and Boston review. APS II, Reel 13.

HAWKS, FRANCIS LISTER, 1798-1866
New York review. APS III, Reels 843-844.

HAWTHORNE, ELIZABETH MANNING, 1802-1883
American magazine of useful and entertaining knowledge. APS II, Reel 768.

HAWTHORNE, NATHANIEL, 1804-1864
American magazine of useful and entertaining knowledge. APS II, Reel 768.

HAYNE, PAUL HAMILTON, 1830-1836
Russell's magazine. APS III, Reel 17.

HAYS, ISAAC, 1796-1879
Philadelphia journal of the medical and physical sciences. APS II, Reels 184-185.

HAYS, ISAAC MINIS, 1847-1925
Medical news. APS II, Reels 658, 1073-1087.

HAYWARD, T. B.
Musical cabinet. APS II, Reel 1120.
Musical magazine; or, Repository of musical science. APS II, Reel 1216.

HAZARD, SAMUEL, 1784-1870
Hazard's register of Pennsylvania. APS II, Reels 476-479.

HEATH, JAMES E.
Southern literary messenger. APS II, Reels 438-447.

HEGELER, EDWARD C. 1835-1910
Monist. APS III, Reels 342-344.

HEISKELL, JOHN
Monthly magazine and literary journal. APS II, Reel 145.

HELMBOLD, GEORGE
Tickler. APS II, Reel 45.

HENRY, CALEB SPRAGUE, 1804-1884
New York review. APS III, Reels 843-844.

HERMANN, pseud.
German correspondent. APS II, Reel 130.

HERRICK, SOPHIA M'ILVAINE BLEDSOE, 1837-1919
Southern review. APS III, Reels 18-20.

HERTER, CHRISTIAN ARCHIBALD, 1895-
Independent. APS II, Reels 418, 1420-1464.

HILDRETH, AZRO BENJAMIN FRANKLIN, 1816-
Green Mountain gem. APS II, Reel 654.

HINCKS, EDWARD YOUNG, 1844-
Andover review. APS III, Reels 1-4.

HINDS, WILLIAM A.
Oneida circular. APS III, Reels 670-674.

HINE, LUCIUS ALONZO, d. 1906
Herald of truth. APS II, Reel 388.
Quarterly journal and review. APS II, Reel 1092.
Western literary journal and monthly review. APS II, Reel 527.

HITCHCOCK, IRA IRVINE, b. 1793
American farmer; devoted to agriculture. APS II, Reels 51-52, 1062-1071.

HOAR, SAMUEL, 1845-1904
American law review. APS III, Reels 463-472.

HODGE, CHARLES, 1797-1878
Princeton review. APS II, Reels 229, 566-572, 846-854.

HODGE, HUGH LENOX, 1796-1873.
North American medical and surgical journal. APS II, Reels 804-805.

HOFFMAN, CHARLES FENNO, 1806-1884
Knickerbocker. APS II, Reels 349-361.
Literary world. APS II, Reels 483-486.

HOGAN, DAVID
Repository and ladies' weekly museum. APS II, Reel 43.

HOLBROOK, JOSIAH, 1788-1854
Family lyceum. APS II, Reel 771.

HOLCOMBE, HENRY, 1762-1824
Georgia analytical repository. APS II, Reel 19.

HOLLEY, NATHANIEL, 1771-1861
Herald of truth. APS II, Reel 113.

HOLLEY, ORVILLE LUTHER, 1791-1861
American monthly magazine and critical review. APS II, Reel 58.

HOLLY, D. W.
United States Democratic review. APS II, Reels 691-696.

HOLMES, EZEKIEL, 1801-1865
Maine farmer. APS II, Reels 422-427, 1371-1388.

HOLMES, OLIVER WENDELL, 1841-1935
American law review. APS III, Reels 463-472.

HOLT, HAMILTON, 1872-
Independent. APS II, Reels 418, 1420-1464.

HOMANS, BENJAMIN
Army and navy chronicle. APS II, Reels 469-471.
Military and naval magazine of the United States. APS II, Reel 615.

HOMANS, BENJAMIN, JR.
Bankers magazine. APS II, Reels 587-588, 1648-1683.

HOMANS, ISAAC SMITH, 1807-1874
Bankers magazine. APS II, Reels 587-588, 1648-1683.
Merchants' magazine and commercial review. APS II, Reels 339-348.

HOMANS, ISAAC SMITH, JR.
Bankers magazine. APS II, Reels 587-588, 1648-1683.

HOOLEY, ARTHUR, 1875-1928
Forum and Century. APS III, Reels 272-293.

HOOPER, EDWARD JAMES, b. 1803
Western farmer and gardener. APS II, Reel 698.

HOSACK, DAVID, 1769-1835
American medical and philosophical register. APS II, Reel 54.

HOUGH, JOHN, 1783-1861
Adviser; or, Vermont evangelical magazine. APS II, Reels 1, 47.

HOUSTON, GEORGE
Minerva. APS II, Reel 137.

HOW, THOMAS YARDLEY
Christian register, and moral and theological review. APS II, Reel 88.

HOYT, ALBERT HARRISON, 1826-1915
New-England historical and genealogical register. APS II, Reels 1053-1061.

HUBBARD, ELBERT, 1856-1915
Philistine; a periodical of protest. APS III, Reels 589-590.

HUDDY, WILLIAM
Military magazine and record of the volunteers. APS II, Reel 744.

HUGHES, JEREMIAH, 1783-1848
Niles' national register. APS II, Reels 167-177, 254-269.

HUMPHREY, EDWARD PORTER, 1809-1887
Danville quarterly review. APS III, Reel 186.

HUNT, FREEMAN, 1804-1858
Merchants' magazine and commercial review. APS II, Reels 339-348.

HUNTINGTON, FREDERIC DAN, BP., 1819-1904
Monthly religious magazine and theological review. APS II, Reels 1114-1120.

HURLBUT, JOSEPH
Boston pearl, a gazette of polite literature. APS II, Reel 788.

INMAN, JOHN, 1805-1850
Columbian lady's and gentleman's magazine. APS II, Reel 313.

IRONSIDE, BEATRICE, pseud.
Observer. APS II, Reel 36.

IRONSIDE, J., pseud.
Truth. APS II, Reel 242.

IRVING, WASHINGTON, 1783-1859
Analectic magazine. APS II, Reels 61-64.
Salmagundi. APS II, Reel 44.

IRVING, WILLIAM, 1766-1821
Salmagundi. APS II, Reel 44.

JACKSON, SOLOMON HENRY
Jew. APS II, Reel 131.

JELLIFFE, SMITH ELY, 1866-
Medical news. APS II, Reels 658, 1073-1087.

JENNINGS, ROBERT L.
Free enquirer. APS II, Reels 1498-1499.

JOHONNOT, JAMES, 1823-1888
Literary union. APS II, Reel 742.

JONES, LEONARD AUGUSTUS, 1832-1909
American law review. APS III, Reels 463-472.

JONES, THOMAS
Gospel visitant. APS II, Reel 110.

JUDSON, EDWARD ZANE CARROLL, 1823-1886
Western literary journal and monthly review. APS II, Reel 527.

JUVENAL, GEOFFREY, pseud.
Critic. APS II, Reel 100.

KAPPA LAMBDA ASSOCIATION OF THE UNITED STATES
North American medical and surgical journal. APS II, Reels 804-805.

KELLEY, WILLIAM VALENTINE, 1843-
Methodist review. APS II, Reels 135-136, 327-332, and 1093-1113.

KENNEDY, JAMES HENRY, 1849-
National magazine. APS III, Reels 160-163.

KENNEDY, ROBERT V.
Amaranth. APS II, Reel 784.

KETTELL, THOMAS PRENTICE
Merchants' magazine and commercial review. APS II, Reels 339-348.
United States Democratic review. APS II, Reels 691-696.

KILLEY, EGBERT B.
Poughkeepsie casket. APS II, Reel 746.

KINGSLEY, WILLIAM LATHROP, 1824-1896
New Englander and Yale review. APS II, Reels 679-680, 904-912.

KINNAMAN, J. O., 1877-
American antiquarian and oriental journal. APS III, Reels 54-57.

KIRBY, S. R.
American journal of homoeopathy. APS II, Reel 365.

KIRK, THOMAS
American moral & sentimental magazine. APS I, Reel 3.

KIRKLAND, CAROLINE MATILDA STANSBURY, 1801-1864
Sartain's union magazine of literature and art. APS II, Reels 572-574.

KNAP, LUSCOMB
Christian messenger. APS II, Reel 82.

KNAPP, LOUISA
Ladies' home journal. APS III, Reel 757-766.

KNAPP, SAMUEL LORENZO, 1784-1836
Boston monthly magazine. APS II, Reels 74, 591.

KNEELAND, ABNER, 1774-1844
Christian messenger. APS II, Reel 82.
Gazetteer. APS II, Reel 107.
Gospel visitant. APS II, Reel 110.
Philadelphia Universalist magazine and Christian messenger. APS II, Reel 187.

KNIGHT, JOHN, fl. 1833-1834
Mechanics' magazine, and journal of the Mechanics' institute. APS II, Reels 613-614.

KNOWLES, JAMES DAVIS, 1798-1838
Columbian star. APS II, Reels 95-96, 1271.

KRAEMER, HENRY, 1868-1924
American journal of pharmacy. APS II, Reels 366-368, 1707-1716.

LABAGH, ISAAC PETER, 1804-1879
American millenarian and prophetic review. APS II, Reel 1093.

LABREE, LAWRENCE
New York illustrated magazine of literature and art. APS II, Reel 842.
Rover. APS II, Reels 912-913.

LAMBING, ANDREW ARNOLD, 1842-1918
American Catholic historical researches. APS III, Reels 201-202.

LANDON, WILLIAM
American metropolitan magazine. APS II, Reel 333.

LANSING, DIRCK CORNELIUS, 1785-1857
Evangelical recorder. APS II, Reel 103.

LARCOM, LUCY, 1826-1893
Our young folks. APS III, Reels 65-66.

LA ROCHE, RENE, 1795-1872
North American medical and surgical journal. APS II, Reels 804-805.

LARRABEE, WILLIAM CLARK, 1802-1859
Ladies' repository. APS II, Reels 482, 893-899.

LATHROP, JOHN, 1772-1820
Nightingale. APS I, Reel 23.

LAW, ANDREW, 1748-1821
Musical magazine. APS I, Reel 18.

LAWRENCE, ISAAC, b. 1828
United States Democratic review. APS II, Reels 691-696.

LAWSON, JOHN DAVISON, 1852-1921
Central law journal. APS III, Reels 548-566.

LEACH, HENRY GODDARD, 1880-
Forum and Century. APS III, Reels 272-293.

LEAVITT, JOHN MCDOWELL, 1824-
Church review. APS II, Reels 916-923.

LEAVITT, JOSHUA, 1794-1873
Independent. APS II, Reels 418, 1420-1464.

LEGGETT, WILLIAM, 1802-1839
Critic. A weekly review of literature, fine arts, and the drama. APS II, Reel 385.

LESLIE, FRANK, 1821-1880
American magazine. APS III, Reels 675-689.

LESLIE, MIRIAM FLORENCE (FOLLINE) SQUIER, "MRS. FRANK LESLIE," d. 1914
American magazine. APS III, Reels 675-689.

LEWIS, ENOCH, 1776-1856
Friends review. APS II, Reels 386-387, 924-934.

LIBBEY, JONAS M.
Princeton review. APS II, Reels 229, 566-572, 846-854.

LIGHT, GEORGE WASHINGTON, 1809-1868
Boston mechanic, and journal of the useful arts and sciences. APS II, Reel 472.

LINCOLN, WILLIAM, 1801-1843
Worcester magazine and historical journal. APS II, Reel 720.

LISHER, G. B.
Gospel inquirer. APS II, Reel 110.

LITTELL, ELIAKIM, 1797-1870
Eclectic museum of foreign literature, science and art. APS II, Reel 605.
Living age. APS II, Reels 319-323, 974-1052.
Museum of foreign literature, science, and art. APS II, Reels 146-148, 1245-1254.
Saturday magazine: being in great part a compilation from the British reviews, magazines, and scientific journals. APS II, Reels 237-238.

LITTELL, ROBERT S., 1831-1896
Living age. APS II, Reels 319-323, 974-1052.

LITTLE, ROBERT, d. 1827
Washington quarterly magazine of arts, science and literature. APS II, Reel 246.

LIVINGSTON, WILLIAM, 1723-1790
Independent reflector. APS I, Reel 13.

LODGE, HENRY CABOT, 1850-1924
International review. APS III, Reels 152-154.

LOGAN HISTORICAL SOCIETY
American pioneer. APS II, Reel 297.

LOMAS, GEORGE ALBERT
Manifesto. APS III, Reels 62-63.

LORD, DAVID NEVINS, 1792-1880
Theological and literary journal. APS II, Reels 940-943.

LOSSING, BENSON JOHN, 1813-1891
Poughkeepsie casket. APS II, Reel 746.

LOWE, CHARLES, 1828-1874
Unitarian review. APS III, Reels 21-25.

LOWELL, JAMES RUSSELL, 1819-1891
Pioneer. APS II, Reel 745.

LUCKEY, SAMUEL, 1791-1869
Methodist review. APS II, Reels 135-136, 327-332, and 1093-1113.

LUNDY, BENJAMIN, 1789-1839
Genius of universal emancipation. APS II, Reels 108, 1272-1273.

LYON, JAMES
National magazine; or, A political, historical, biographical, and literary repository. APS I, Reel 18.

LYON, JAMES, OF FAIRHAVEN, VT.
Republican magazine. APS I, Reel 26.

MACARTHUR, ROBERT STUART, 1841-1923
Baptist quarterly review. APS III, Reels 59-60.

MACAULAY, D.
New Orleans miscellany. APS II, Reel 973.

MCCLELLAN, GEORGE, 1796-1847
American medical review. APS II, Reels 57, 846, 944.

MCCLINTOCK, JOHN, 1814-1870
Methodist review. APS II, Reels 135-136, 327-332, and 1093-1113.

MCCLURE, ALEXANDER WILSON, 1808-1865
Christian observatory. APS II, Reel 312.

MCCLURE, SAMUEL SIDNEY, 1857-1949
McClure's magazine. APS III, Reels 477-493.

MCCORD, DAVID JAMES, 1797-1855
Carolina law journal. APS II, Reel 382.

MACDANIEL, OSBORNE
Phalanx. APS II, Reel 671.

MCDOWELL, WILLIAM
Pictorial review. APS II, Reels 1487-1488.

M'FARLAND, JOHN
Literary pamphleteer. APS II, Reel 132.

MCHENRY, JAMES, 1785-1843
American monthly magazine. APS II, Reel 57.

MCJILTON, JOHN NELSON, 1805-1875
Baltimore literary monument. APS II, Reel 379.
Baltimore monument. APS II, Reel 769.

MCLEAN, JOHN EMERY, 1865-
Arena. APS III, Reels 92-99.

MCLELLAN, ISAAC, JR.
Boston pearl, a gazette of polite literature. APS II, Reel 788.

MALACH, JOHN MICHAEL, 1831-1893
American journal of pharmacy. APS II, Reels 366-368, 1707-1716.

MANN, HORACE, 1796-1859
Common school journal. APS II, Reels 512-514.

MAPES, JAMES JAY, 1806-1866
American repertory of arts, sciences, and manufactures. APS II, Reel 646.

MARKS, MONTAGUE
Art amateur. APS III, Reels 580-585.

MARRAT, WILLIAM, 1772-1852
Monthly scientific journal, containing disquisitions. APS II, Reel 146.
Scientific journal. ASP II, Reel 239.

MARVIN, JOSEPH B.
Radical. APS III, Reels 15-17.

MARYLAND. LAWS, STATUTES, ETC.
American law journal. APS II, Reels 1, 53.

MARYLAND STATE AGRICULTURAL SOCIETY
American farmer; devoted to agriculture. APS II, Reels 51-52, 1062-1071.

MASON, JAMES M.
Ohio medical repository of original and selected intelligence. APS II, Reel 973.

MASON, THOMAS, 1769-1851
Methodist review. APS II, Reels 135-136, 327-332, and 1093-1113.

MASSACHUSETTS ANTI-SLAVERY FAIR
Liberty bell. APS II, Reels 491-492.

MASSACHUSETTS ANTI-SLAVERY SOCIETY
Abolitionist. APS II, Reel 362.

MASSACHUSETTS BAPTIST CONVENTION
Baptist missionary magazine. APS II, Reels 71-72, 535-539, 830-838.
Massachusetts Baptist missionary magazine. APS II, Reels 25, 216.

MASSACHUSETTS MEDICAL SOCIETY
New England journal of medicine. APS II, Reels 660-664.

MASSACHUSETTS PEACE SOCIETY (FOUNDED 1815)
Friend of peace. APS II, Reels 211, 1072.

MASSACHUSETTS SOCIETY FOR PROMOTING AGRICULTURE
Massachusetts agricultural repository and journal. APS II, Reels 214-215, 566.

MASSACHUSETTS SOCIETY FOR PROMOTING AGRICULTURE. GEORGIK PAPERS
Massachusetts agricultural repository and journal. APS II, Reels 214-215, 566.

MASSACHUSETTS SOCIETY FOR PROMOTING AGRICULTURE. PAPERS ON AGRICULTURE
Massachusetts agricultural repository and journal. ASP II, Reels 214-215, 566.

MASSACHUSETTS TEACHERS' ASSOCIATION
Massachusetts teacher. APS II, Reels 610-613.

MATHEWS, CORNELIUS, 1817-1889
Arcturus. APS II, Reel 734.
Yankee doodle. APS II, Reel 1408.

MATHEWS, SHALLER, 1863-
Biblical world. APS III, Reels 254-264.

MATSELL, GEORGE W.
National police gazette. APS II, Reels 1318-1340.

MAXCY, EATON W.
Ladies museum. APS II, Reel 122.

MAXWELL, WILLIAM, 1784-1857
Virginia historical register, and literary companion. APS II, Reel 943.

MEAD, DARIUS
Columbian lady's and gentleman's magazine. APS II, Reel 313.
National preacher and village pulpit. APS II, Reels 1087-1090.

MEASE, JAMES, 1771-1846
Archives of useful knowledge. APS II, Reel 65.

MECOM, BENJAMIN, b. 1732
New England magazine of knowledge and pleasure. APS I, Reel 19.

MEIGS, CHARLES DELUCENA, 1792-1869
North American medical and surgical journal. APS II, Reels 804-805.

MEIGS, JOSIAH, 1757-1822
New-Haven gazette, and the Connecticut magazine. APS I, Reel 20.

MENDENHALL, JAMES WILLIAM, 1844-1892
Methodist review. APS II, Reels 135-136, 327-332, and 1093-1113.

MENDON ASSOCIATION, MENDON, MASS.
Christian magazine. APS II, Reels 81, 595.

METCALF, LORETTUS SUTTON, 1837-
Forum and Century. APS III, Reels 272-293.

METCALFE, LYNE SHACKELFORD, JR.
Central law journal. APS III, Reels 548-566.

METHODIST EPISCOPAL CHURCH
Christian advocate. APS II, Reels 1749-1788.
Western Christian advocate. APS II, Reels 1789-1796.

METHODIST EPISCOPAL CHURCH, SOUTH
Southern review. APS III, Reels 18-20.

MICHEL, WILLIAM
Carolina journal of medicine, science and agriculture. APS II, Reels 75, 362.

MILLER, CHARLES WILLIAM EMIL, 1863-1934
American journal of philology. APS III, Reels 424-429.

MILLER, JAMES WILLIAMS, d. 1829
Yankee and Boston literary gazette. APS II, Reel 1313.

MILLER, TIRZAH C.
Oneida circular. APS III, Reels 670-674.

MINOR, BENJAMIN BLAKE, 1818-1905
Southern literary messenger. APS II, Reels 438-447.

MINOR, KATE PLEASANTS
Southern historical society. APS III, Reels 309-313.

MITCHELL, JOHN AMES, 1845-1918
Life. APS III, Reels 500-532.

MITCHILL, SAMUEL LATHAM, 1764-1831
Medical repository of original essays and intelligence. APS II, Reels 26-27, 132-134.

MOONEY, HERBERT R.
National police gazette. APS II, Reels 1318-1340.

MOORE, CHARLES WHITLOCK, 1801-1873
Amaranth; or, Masonic garland. APS II, Reel 404.

MOORE, JACOB BAILEY, 1797-1853
Collections, historical and miscellaneous. APS II, Reels 93-94.

MOORE, MARTIN
Congregationalist and herald of gospel liberty. APS II, Reels 97-99, 539-546, 1911-1924.

MORE, HANNAH, 1745-1833
Cheap repository. APS II, Reel 207.

MORISON, JOHN HOPKINS, 1808-1896
Monthly religious magazine and theological review. APS II, Reels 1114-1120.
Unitarian review. APS III, Reels 21-25.

MORRIS, GEORGE POPE, 1802-1864
New mirror. APS II, Reel 1124.
New-York mirror. APS II, Reels 164-165, 785-787.

MORRIS, ROBERT
Philadelphia album and ladies' literary port folio. APS II, Reels 721-725.

MORRISON, GEORGE AUSTIN, 1864-1916
New York genealogical and biographical record. APS III, Reels 451-455.

MORSE, JEDIDIAH, 1761-1826
American Society for Promoting the Civilization and General Improvement of the Indian Tribes in the United States. The first annual report. APS II, Reel 534.

MORSE, JOHN TORREY, 1840-1937
International review. APS III, Reels 152-154.

MORSE, RICHARD CAREY, 1795-1868
New York observer. APS II, Reels 1856-1874.

MORSE, S. E.
Congregationalist and herald of gospel liberty. APS II, Reels 97-99, 539-546, 1911-1924.

MORSE, SAMUEL H.
Radical. APS III, Reels 15-17.

MORSE, SIDNEY EDWARDS, 1794-1871
New York observer. APS II, Reels 1856-1874.

MOSHER, THOMAS BIRD, 1852-1923
Bibelot. APS III, Reels 252-253.

MOTT, HOPPER STRIKER, 1854-1924
New York genealogical and biographical record. APS III, Reels 451-455.

MOTT, VALENTINE, 1785-1865
Medical & surgical register. APS II, Reel 216.
New York medical magazine. APS II, Reel 164.

MURFREE, WILLIAM LAW, JR.
Central law journal. APS III, Reels 548-566.

MURRAY, JAMES R.
Musical visitor. APS II, Reels 1289-1291.

MURRAY, WALTER
Mechanic apprentice. APS II, Reel 742.

MUSS-ARNOLT, WILLIAM, 1860-
American journal of philology. APS III, Reels 424-429.

NASON, ELIAS, 1811-1887
New-England historical and genealogical register. APS II, Reels 1053-1061.

NATIONAL ANTI-SLAVERY BAZAAR, BOSTON
Liberty bell. By friends of freedom. APS II, Reels 491-492.

NATIONAL REFORM ASSOCIATION
Working man's advocate. APS II, Reels 581-583.

NEAL, JOHN, 1793-1876
Brother Jonathan. APS II, Reels 409-410.
Yankee and Boston literary gazette. APS II, Reel 1313.

NEGRIN, J. J.
L'Hemisphere, journal francais. APS II, Reels 19, 113.

NEVILL, SAMUEL, 1697?-1764
New American magazine. APS I, Reel 19.

NEW ENGLAND AGRICULTURAL SOCIETY
Massachusetts ploughman and New England journal of agriculture. APS II, Reels 1274-1287.

NEW ENGLAND ASSOCIATION OF INVENTORS, AND PATRONS OF USEFUL ARTS
Useful cabinet. APS II, Reel 45.

NEW ENGLAND HISTORIC GENEALOGICAL SOCIETY
New-England historical and genealogical register. APS II, Reels 1053-1061.

NEW ENGLAND SURGICAL SOCIETY
New England journal of medicine. APS II, Reels 660-664.

NEW HAMPSHIRE MISSIONARY SOCIETY
Religious repository. APS II, Reel 43.

NEW YORK (CITY) COURTS
New York City hall recorder. APS II, Reel 211.

NEW YORK (COUNTY) COURT OF GENERAL SESSIONS
New York City hall recorder. APS II, Reel 211.

NEW YORK GENEALOGICAL AND BIOGRAPHICAL SOCIETY
New York genealogical and biographical record. APS III, Reels 451-455.

NEW YORK HOSPITAL
Medical & surgical register. APS II, Reel 216.

NEW YORK. MECHANICS' INSTITUTE
Mechanics' magazine. APS II, Reels 613-614.

NEW YORK STATE AGRICULTURAL SOCIETY
Cultivator. APS II, Reels 514-518.

NEW YORK STATE ASSOCIATION OF MECHANICS, ALBANY
New York state mechanic. APS II, Reel 938.

NEW YORK (STATE) BOARD OF AGRICULTURE
Plough boy, and journal of the Board of agriculture. APS II, Reels 190, 191.

NEW YORK STATE HORTICULTURAL SOCIETY (FOUNDED 1818)
New York farmer. APS II, Reels 1195-1196.

NEW YORK STATE TRACT SOCIETY
New York tract magazine and Christian miscellany. APS II, Reel 166.

NICHOLAS, A. H.
Republic of letters. APS II, Reels 1257-1258.

NICOLA, LEWIS, 1717-1807
American magazine: or, General repository. APS I, Reel 2.

NILES, HEZEKIAH, 1777-1839
Niles' national register. APS II, Reels 167-177, 254-269.

NILES, WILLIAM OGDEN
Niles' national register. APS II, Reels 167-177, 254-269.

NONDESCRIPT, NONIUS, ESQ., pseud.
The ————. APS II, Reel 333.

NORTH CAROLINA. SUPREME COURT
Carolina law repository. APS II, Reel 75.

NORTON, ANDREWS, 1786-1853
General repository and review. APS II, Reels 107-108.
Select journal of foreign periodical literature. APS II, Reel 913.

NOYES, GEORGE W.
Oneida circular. APS III, Reels 670-674.

NOYES, JOHN HUMPHREY, 1811-1886
American socialist. APS III, Reel 243.
Oneida circular. APS III, Reels 670-674.

O'CONNOR, THOMAS, 1770-1855
Globe. APS II, Reel 109.

OLIVER, BENJAMIN LYNDE, 1788-1843
Oliver's magazine. APS II, Reel 940.

ONEIDA COMMUNITY
Oneida circular. APS III, Reels 670-674.

OSBORN, CHARLES
Philanthropist, a weekly journal containing essays, on moral and religious subjects. APS II, Reels 187-188.

OSGOOD, TRUE
Rough and ready. APS II, Reel 845.

OSSOLI, SARAH MARGARET FULLER, MARCHESA D', 1810-1850
Dial: a magazine for literature, philosophy, and religion. APS II, Reel 546.

OWEN, ROBERT DALE, 1801-1877
Free enquirer. APS II, Reels 1498-1499.

OWEN, SAMUEL
New-York legal observer. APS II, Reels 802-803.

OWEN, WILLIAM, 1802-1842
Free enquirer. APS II, Reels 1498-1499.

PAGE, WALTER HINES, 1855-1918
Forum and Century. APS III, Reels 272-293.

PAINE, THOMAS, 1737-1809
Pennsylvania magazine. APS I, Reel 24.

PALFREY, C.
Monthly miscellany of religion and letters. APS II, Reel 778.

PALFREY, JOHN GORHAM, 1796-1881
North American review. APS II, Reels 177-183, 270-281, 1613-1647.

PALMER, ELIHU, 1764-1806
Prospect: or, View of the moral world. APS II, Reel 42.

PALMER, THOMAS H.
Historical register of the United States. APS II, Reels 113-114.

PARK, JOHN, 1775-1852
Boston spectator. APS II, Reel 74.

PARKER, JOHN R.
Euterpeiad; or, Musical intelligencer, and ladies gazette. APS II, Reel 102.

PATTERSON, ALEXANDER D., d. 1847
Anglo American. APS II, Reels 647-649.

PATTERSON, CHARLES BRODLE, 1854-1917
Arena. APS III, Reels 92-99.

PAULDING, JAMES KIRKE, 1778-1860
Salmagundi; (Joint Author). APS II, Reel 44.
Salmagundi (Paulding). APS II, Reel 1308.

PAYNE, GEORGE HENRY, 1876-
Forum and Century. APS III, Reels 272-293.

PAYNE, JOHN HOWARD, 1791-1852
Pastime. APS II, Reel 36.
Thespian mirror. APS II, Reel 44.

PECK, GEORGE, 1797-1876
Methodist review. APS II, Reels 135-136, 327-332, and 1093-1113.

PECK, GEORGE WASHINGTON, 1817-1859
Boston musical review. APS II, Reel 770.

PEDDER, JAMES, 1775-1859
Farmers cabinet and American herd book. APS II, Reels 314-315.

PEET, STEPHEN DENISON, 1831-1914
American antiquarian and oriental journal. APS III, Reels 54-57.

PELHAM, WILLIAM
Free enquirer. APS II, Reels 1498-1499.

PENDLETON, PHILIP C.
Magnolia; or, Southern Apalachian. APS II, Reel 676.

PENNSYLVANIA HISTORICAL SOCIETY
Pennsylvania magazine of history and biography. APS III, Reels 456-461.

PENNSYLVANIA PRISON SOCIETY
Journal of prison discipline and philanthropy. APS II, Reels 480-481, 1934-1935.

PEPPER, GEORGE, 1835
Irish shield. APS II, Reel 937.

PERKINS, JAMES HANDASYD, 1810-1849
Western messenger. APS II, Reels 489-490.

PETERS, ABSALOM, 1793-1869
American eclectic. APS II, Reel 295.
Biblical repository and classical review. APS II, Reels 306-310.

PETERSON, CHARLES JACOBS, 1819-1887
Graham's American monthly magazine of literature, art, and
    fashion. APS II, Reels 547-560.
Peterson magazine. APS II, Reels 1292-1308.

PHILADELPHIA COLLEGE OF PHARMACY
American journal of pharmacy. APS II, Reels 366-368, 1707-1716.

PHILBROOK, FREDERICK BACON
American historical register and monthly gazette. APS III, Reel 58.

PHILES, GEORGE PHILIP, 1828-1913
Philobiblion. APS III, Reel 270.

PHOEBUS, WILLIAM, 1754-1831
Experienced Christian's magazine. APS I, Reel 12; APS II, Reel 18.

PIATT, DON, 1819-1891
Belford's monthly. APS III, Reels 586-589.

PICKERING, DAVID, 1789?-1859
Christian telescope and Universalist Miscellany. APS II, Reels 89,
    1197.

PICKET, ALBERT, 1771-1850
Academician. APS II, Reel 47.

PICKET, JOHN, W.
Academician. APS II, Reel 47.
Western academician and journal of education and science. APS II,
    Reel 486.

PIERCE, GEORGE FOSTER, 1811-1884
Magnolia; or, Southern Apalachian. APS II, Reel 676.

PIGEON, CHARLES D.
Literary and theological review. APS II, Reel 798.

PILCHER, ELIJAH HOMES, 1810-1887
Methodist review. APS II, Reels 135-136, 327-332, and 1093-1113.

PISCATAQUA MISSIONARY SOCIETY
Piscataqua evangelical magazine. APS II, Reel 39.

PITT, THEODORE L.
Oneida circular. APS III, Reels 670-674.

PLEASANT, PETER, pseud.
Emerald. APS II, Reel 101.

POE, EDGAR ALLAN, 1809-1849
Burton's gentleman's magazine and American monthly review.
    APS II, Reel 311.
Graham's American monthly magazine of literature, art, and
    fashion. APS II, Reels 547-560.
Southern literary messenger. APS II, Reels 438-447.

POLK, JAMES F.
Investigator and advocate of independence. APS II, Reel 1197.

PORTER, CHARLOTTE ENDYMION, 1859-
Shakespeariana. APS III, Reels 270-271.

PORTER, ROBERT PERCIVAL, 1852-1917
International review. APS III, Reels 152-154.

POTTER, NATHANIEL, 1770-1843
Baltimore medical and philosophical lycaeum. APS II, Reel 71.

POTTER, TIMOTHY O.
Corsair. APS II, Reel 384.

POWELL, THOMAS REED, 1880-
Political science quarterly. APS III, Reels 767-771.

PRATT, LUTHER
American Masonic register. APS II, Reel 54.
Connecticut Republican magazine. APS II, Reel 15.

PRAY, ISAAC CLARK, 1813-1869
Boston pearl, a gazette of polite literature. APS II, Reel 788.

PRENDERGAST, EDMOND FRANCIS, abp., 1843-1918
American Catholic quarterly review. APS III, Reels 650-660.

PRENTISS, CHARLES, 1774-1820
Child of Pallas. APS II, Reel 7.
Thistle. APS II, Reel 44.

PRESBYTERIAN CHURCH IN THE U.S.A.
Religious instructor. APS II, Reel 198.

**PRESBYTERIAN CHURCH IN THE U.S.A. GENERAL
    ASSEMBLY**
Evangelical intelligencer. APS II, Reels 16-17.
Presbyterian magazine. APS II, Reels 193-194.

**PRESBYTERIAN CHURCH IN THE U.S.A. SYNODS.
    PITTSBURGH**
Pittsburgh recorder, containing religious literary and political
    information. APS II, Reels 219-220, 1052.
Western missionary magazine. APS II, Reel 46.

PRICE, WILLIAM
Journal of foreign medical science and literature. APS II, Reels
    116-119.

PRINCE, THOMAS, 1722-1748
Christian history. APS I, Reel 10.

PRINCETON UNIVERSITY
Nassau literary magazine. APS II, Reels 1482-1486.

PROCTOR, WILLIAM, 1817-1874
American journal of pharmacy. APS II, Reels 366-368, 1707-1716.

PROTESTANT EPISCOPAL CHURCH IN THE U.S.A.
Religious and literary repository. APS II, Reel 197.

RAFINESQUE, CONSTANTINE SAMUEL, 1783-1840
Atlantic journal, and friend of knowledge. APS II, Reel 839.
Western Minerva. APS II, Reel 252.

RAMSAY, DAVID, 1749-1815
Charleston medical register for the year 1802. APS II, Reel 546.

REES, JAMES, 1802-1885
Dramatic mirror, and literary companion. APS II, Reel 605.

RHOADS, SAMUEL
Friends review. APS II, Reels 386-387, 924-934.

RHODES, BRADFORD, 1845-1924
Bankers magazine. APS II, Reels 587-588, 1648-1683.

RICE, ISAAC LEOPOLD, 1850-1915
Forum and Century. APS III, Reels 272-293.

RICE, JOHN HOLT, 1777-1831
Literary and evangelical magazine. APS II, Reels 124-125, 464.

RICE, JOSEPH MAYER, 1857-1934
Forum and Century. APS III, Reels 272-293.

RICHARDS, GEORGE, d. 1814
Freemasons magazine and general miscellany. APS II, Reel 106.

RICHARDS, WILLIAM CAREY, 1818-1892
Orion. APS II, Reel 1216.

RICHARDSON, NATHANIEL SMITH, 1810-1883
Church review. APS II, Reels 916-923.

RIDDEL, SAMUEL HOPKINS, 1800-1876
American quarterly register. APS II, Reels 532-534.

RIDPATH, JOHN CLARK 1840-1900
Arena. APS III, Reels 92-99.

RIPLEY, GEORGE, 1802-1880
Dial: a magazine for literature, philosophy, and religion. APS II, Reel 546.

RISK, T. F.
Western journal and civilian. APS II, Reels 699-700.

ROBBINS, ALEXANDER HENRY, 1875-
Central law journal. APS III, Reels 548-566.

ROBBINS, JAMES J.
American law journal. APS II, Reels 730-731.

ROBERTS, EDWARD P.
American farmer. APS II, Reels 51-52, 1062-1071.

ROBINSON, EDWARD, 1794-1863
Biblical repository and classical review. APS II, Reels 306-310.

ROBINSON, JOSEPH
Robinson's magazine. APS II, Reels 204-205.

RODE, CHARLES R., 1825-1865
American literary gazette and publishers' circular. APS II, Reels 780-783.

ROGERS, DANIEL, 1780-1839
New York City hall recorder. APS II, Reel 211.

ROMAINE, BENJAMIN FRANKLIN, 1820-1874
Rutgers literary miscellany. APS II, Reel 880.

ROOT, FREDERICK STANLEY, 1853-1906
Journal of social science. APS III, Reels 266-268.

ROPES, JOHN CODMAN, 1836-1899
American law review. APS III, Reels 463-472.

ROYAL INSTITUTION OF GREAT BRITAIN, LONDON
Journal of science and the arts. APS II, Reel 120.

ROYALL, ANNE NEWPORT, 1769-1854
Huntress. APS II, Reels 935-937.

RUNKLE, JOHN DANIEL, 1822-1902
Mathematical monthly. APS III, Reel 269.

RUSSELL, JOSHUA T.
Christian messenger. APS II, Reels 82, 595.

RUSSELL, WILLIAM, 1798-1873
American annals of education. APS II, Reels 293-294.

RUSTICOAT, ROBERT, pseud.
Wasp. APS II, Reel 46.

RUTGERS UNIVERSITY, NEW BRUNSWICK, N.J.
Rutgers literary miscellany. APS II, Reel 880.

RYAN, PATRICK JOHN, 1831-1911
American Catholic quarterly review. APS III, Reels 650-660.

SANBORN, FRANKLIN BENJAMIN, 1831-1917
Journal of social science. APS III, Reels 266-268.

SANDS, ROBERT CHARLES, 1799-1832
Atlantic magazine. APS II, Reel 70.
New York review and Atheneum. APS II, Reels 166, 615.
Talisman. APS II, Reel 400.

SANDS, SAMUEL
American farmer; devoted to agriculture. APS II, Reels 51-52, 1062-1071.

SANDS, WILLIAM B.
American farmer; devoted to agriculture. APS II, Reels 51-52, 1062-1071.

SANGER, GEORGE PARTRIDGE, 1819-1890
American almanac and repository of useful knowledge. APS II, Reels 810-812.

SANGRADO, DR., pseud.
Lancet. APS II, Reel 22.

SARGENT, EPES, 1813-1880
Sargent's new monthly magazine, of literature, fashion, and the fine arts. APS II, Reel 1258.

SARTAIN, JOHN, 1808-1897
Sartain's union magazine of literature and art. APS II, Reels 572-574.

SCOTT, HENRY EDWARDS, 1859-
New-England historical and genealogical register. APS II, Reels 1053-1061.

SCRIBBLE, SIMON, pseud.
Fly. APS II, Reel 19.

SCUDDER, HORACE ELISHA, 1838-1902
Riverside magazine for young people. APS III, Reel 52.

SEARS, EDMUND HAMILTON, 1810-1876
Monthly religious magazine and theological review. APS II, Reels 1114-1120.

SEDGWICK, ARTHUR GEORGE, 1844-1915
American law review. APS III, Reels 463-472.

SEDGWICK, ELLERY, 1872-
American magazine. APS III, Reels 675-689.

SEWALL, STEPHEN
Literary mirror. APS II, Reel 24.

SHAKESPEARE SOCIETY OF NEW YORK
Shakespeariana. APS III, Reels 270-271.

SHEA, JOHN DAWSON GILMARY, 1824-1892
Historical magazine. APS III, Reels 26-28.

SHERWOOD, JAMES MANNING, 1814-1890
American presbyterian review. APS III, Reels 205-207.
Biblical repository and classical review. APS II, Reels 306-310.
Hours at home. APS III, Reels 28-30.

National preacher and village pulpit. APS II, Reels 1087-1090.
Princeton review. APS II, Reels 229, 566-572, 846-854.

SIGOURNEY, LYDIA HOWARD HUNTLEY, 1791-1865
Ladies' companion, and literary expositor. APS II, Reels 738-740.

SILLIMAN, BENJAMIN, 1779-1864
American journal of science. APS II, Reels 53, 53A, 754-762, 817-830.

SILLIMAN, BENJAMIN, 1816-1885
American journal of science. APS II, Reels 53, 53A, 754-762, 817-830.

SIMMONS, JAMES WRIGHT, b. 1790
Southern literary gazette. APS II, Reel 1258.

SIMMS, WILLIAM GILMORE, 1806-1870
Magnolia; or, Southern Apalachian. APS II, Reel 676.
Southern and western monthly magazine and review. APS II, Reel 1407.
Southern literary gazette. APS II, Reel 1258.
Southern quarterly review. APS II, Reels 684-687.

SIMONS, THOMAS YOUNG, 1798-1857
Carolina journal of medicine, science and agriculture. APS II, Reels 75, 362.

SIMPSON, STEPHEN, 1789-1854
Portico. APS II, Reels 192-193.

SIZER, NELSON, 1812-1897
Phrenological journal and science of health. APS II, Reels 1341-1353.

SKILLMAN, THOMAS T.
Christian register. APS II, Reel 1093.

SKINNER, DOLPHUS
Evangelical magazine and gospel advocate. APS II, Reels 792-794.

SKINNER, JOHN STUART, 1788-1851
American farmer; devoted to agriculture. APS II, Reels 51-52, 1062-1071.
Monthly journal of agriculture. APS II, Reel 419.

SMITH, ALFRED EMANUEL, 1873-
New Outlook. APS III, Reels 367-423.

SMITH, CHARLES, 1768-1808
Monthly military repository. APS I, Reel 18.

SMITH, ELIAS, 1769-1846
Christian's magazine, reviewer, and religious intelligencer. APS II, Reel 11.
Herald of gospel liberty. APS II, Reels 19, 1925-1934.
Herald of life and immortality. APS II, Reel 113.

SMITH, GIDEAN B.
American farmer; devoted to agriculture. APS II, Reels 51-52, 1062-1071.

SMITH, HENRY BOYNTON, 1815-1877
American Presbyterian review. APS III, Reels 205-207.
Princeton review. APS II, Reels 229, 566-572, 846-854.

SMITH, JEROME VAN CROWNINSHIELD, 1800-1879
Boston medical intelligencer. APS II, Reels 73, 763.
Bowen's Boston news-letter, and city record. APS II, Reels 74, 914.

SMITH, JOHN JAY, 1798-1881
Journal of belles lettres. APS II, Reel 1314.
Museum of foreign literature, science, and art. APS II, Reels 146-148, 1245-1254.

Waldie's select circulating library. APS II, Reels 1354-1357.

SMITH, LUCIUS EDWIN, 1822-
Baptist quarterly. APS III, Reels 4-5.

SMITH, MUNROE, 1854-1926
Political science quarterly. APS III, Reels 767-771.

SMITH, NATHAN, 1762-1828
American medical review. APS II, Reels 57, 846, 944.

SMITH, NATHAN RYNO, 1797-1877
American medical review. APS II, Reels 57, 846, 944.
Baltimore monthly journal of medicine and surgery. APS II, Reel 534.

SMITH, ROBERT F. N.
Religious museum. APS II, Reel 203.

SMITH, SEBA, 1792-1868
Rover. APS II, Reels 912-913.

SMITH, WILLIAM, 1727-1803
American magazine and monthly chronicle. APS I, Reel 2.

SMYTH, EGBERT COFFIN, 1829-1904
Andover review. APS III, Reels 1-4.

SNODGRASS, JOSEPH EVANS
American museum of literature and the arts. APS II, Reel 646.

SNOW, GEORGE M.
Brother Jonathan. APS II, Reels 409-410.

SNOW, R. A.
American Journal of homoeopathy. APS II, Reel 365.

SNOWDEN, ISAAC CLARKSON, 1791-1828
Philadelphia monthly magazine. APS II, Reel 1092.

SNOWDEN, WILLIAM W.
Ladies' companion, and literary expositor. APS II, Reels 738-740.

SOCIETY FOR PROMOTING CHRISTIAN KNOWLEDGE, PIETY AND CHARITY
Christian monitor; a religious periodical work. APS II, Reels 7, 82.

SOULE, JOSHUA, BP., 1781-1867
Methodist review. APS II, Reels 135-136, 327-332, and 1093-1113.

SOUTHWICK, SOLOMON, 1773-1839
Christian visitant. APS II, Reel 89.
Plough boy, and journal of the Board of agriculture. APS II, Reels 190, 191.

SOWER, CHRISTOPHER, BP., 1721-1784
Geistliches magazien. APS I, Reel 12.

SPARKS, JARED, 1789-1866
American almanac and repository of useful knowledge. APS II, Reels 810-812.
North American review. APS II, Reels 177-183, 270-281, 1613-1647.
Unitarian miscellany and Christian monitor. APS II, Reel 206.

SPEAR, CHARLES, 1801-1863
Prisoner's friend. APS II, Reels 749-750.

SPEAR, JOHN MURRAY
Prisoner's friend. APS II, Reels 749-750.

SPOFFORD, JEREMIAH, 1787-1880
Merrimack magazine. APS II, Reel 217.

SPRAGUE, TIMOTHY DWIGHT, 1819?-1849
American literary magazine. APS II, Reel 787.

STEARNS, JOHN NEWTON, 1820-1895
Merry's museum for boys and girls. APS II, Reels 743, 1499-1501.

STEVENS, ABEL, 1815-1897
National magazine. APS II, Reels 814-815.

STEVENS, ANN SOPHIA WINTERBOTHAM, 1813-1886
Graham's American monthly magazine of literature, art, and
fashion. APS II, Reels 547-560.
Peterson magazine. APS II, Reels 1292-1308.
Portland magazine. APS II, Reel 746.

STEPHENS, EDWARD
Brother Jonathan. APS II, Reels 409-410.

STEPHENS, WILLIAM ALLAN
Vanity Fair. APS III, Reels 568-569.

STEVENS, ALEXANDER HODGDON, 1789-1869
Medical & surgical register. APS II, Reel 216.

STEWART, CHARLES SAMUEL, 1795-1870
Naval magazine. APS II, Reel 816.

STILES, HENRY REED, 1832-1909
Historical magazine. APS III, Reels 26-28.
New York genealogical and biographical record. APS III, Reels
451-455.

STILWELL, WILLIAM M.
Friendly visitor. APS II, Reel 107.

STOCKTON, WILLIAM SMITH, 1785-1860
Wesleyan repository. APS II, Reel 251.

STONE, HERBERT STUART, 1871-
Chap-book. APS III, Reel 61.

STOREY, MOORFIELD, 1845-1929
American law review. APS III, Reels 463-472.

STORRS, R. S.
Congregationalist and herald of gospel liberty. APS II, Reels 97-
99, 539-546, 1911-1924.

STORRS, RICHARD SALTER, 1821-1900
Independent. APS II, Reels 418, 1420-1464.

STORY, ISAAC, 1774-1803
Barber's shop. APS II, Reel 6.

STREETER, RUSSELL
Christian intelligencer and eastern chronicle. APS II, Reels 80, 593-
595.

STRINGFIELD, T.
Messenger. APS II, Reel 1370.

STRYKER, JAMES, 1792-1864
Stryker's American register and magazine. APS II, Reel 672.

SWACKHAMER, CONRAD
United States Democratic review. APS II, Reels 691-696.

SWEDENBORG, EMANUEL, 1688-1722
New-Hampshire New Jerusalem magazine and primitive religious
intelligencer. APS II, Reel 34.

SWEM, EARL GREGG, 1870-
Southern historical society. APS III, Reels 309-313.

TARVER, MICAJAH
Western journal and civilian. APS II, Reels 699-700.

TASISTRO, LOUIS FITZGERALD
Expositor. APS II, Reel 924.

TAUSSIG, FRANK WILLIAM, 1859-
Quarterly journal of economics. APS III, Reels 167-170.

TAYLOR, BAYARD, 1825-1878
Graham's American monthly magazine of literature, art, and
fashion. APS II, Reels 547-560.

TAYLOR, CREED, 1766-1836
Journal of the Law-School, and of the moot-court attached to it,
at Needham, in Virginia. APS II, Reel 121.

TAYLOR, HANNIS, 1851-1922
American law review. APS III, Reels 463-472.

TAYLOR, JOHN ORVILLE, 1807-1890
Common school assistant. APS II, Reel 889.

**TEACHERS' ASSOCIATION OF THE STATE OF
CONNECTICUT**
Connecticut common school journal and annals of education.
APS II, Reels 789-791.

TEFFT, BENJAMIN FRANKLIN, 1813-1885
Ladies' repository; a monthly periodical. APS II, Reels 482, 893-
899.

TESCHEMACHER, JAMES ENGELBERT, 1790-1853
Horticultural register, and gardener's magazine. APS II, Reel 527.

THACHER, MOSES, 1795-1878
New-England telegraph, and eclectic review. APS II, Reel 802.

THACHER, SAMUEL COOPER, 1785-1818
Monthly anthology, and Boston review. APS II, Reels 30-32, 143-
144.

THAYER, THOMAS BALDWIN, 1812-1886
Universalist quarterly and general review. APS II, Reels 697, 1357-
1363.

THAYER, WILLIAM
Happy home and parlor magazine. APS III, Reels 756-757 .

THOMAS, ABEL CHARLES, 1807-1880
Lowell offering. APS II, Reel 675.

THOMAS, ISAIAH, 1749-1831
Royal American magazine. APS I, Reel 26.
Worcester magazine. APS I, Reel 33.

THOMAS, JOHN
Euterpeiad; an album of music, poetry & prose. APS II, Reel 771.

THOMAS, JOHN, 1805-1871
Advocate for the testimony of God. APS II, Reel 767.

THOMPSON, ISAAC GRANT, 1840-1879
Albany law journal. APS III, Reels 570-580.

THOMPSON, JAMES WILLIAM, 1805-1881
Monthly religious magazine and theological review. APS II, Reels
1114-1120.

THOMPSON, JOHN REUBEN, 1823-1873
Southern Literary Messenger. APS II, Reels 438-447.

THOMPSON, JOHN SAMUEL, b. 1787
Rochester magazine, and theological review. APS II, Reel 205.
Universalist. APS II, Reel 1308.

THOMPSON, JOSEPH PARRISH, 1819-1879
Independent. APS II, Reels 418, 1420-1464.

THOMPSON, SEYMOUR DWIGHT, 1842-1904
American law review. APS III, Reels 463-472.
Central law journal. APS III, Reels 548-566.

THOMSON, ZADOCK, 1796-1856
Green Mountain repository. APS II, Reel 654.

THOMSON, EDWARD, BP., 1810-1879
Ladies' repository; a monthly periodical. APS II, Reels 482, 893-899.

THORNWELL, JAMES HENLEY, 1812-1862
Southern quarterly review. APS II, Reels 684-687.

TILTON, THEODORE, 1835-1907
Independent. APS II, Reels 418, 1420-1464.

TOTTEN, JOHN C.
Moral and religious cabinet. APS II, Reel 34.

TOTTEN, JOHN REYNOLDS, 1856-
New York genealogical and biographical record. APS III, Reels 451-455.

TOURGEE, ALBION WINEGAR, 1838-1905
Continent. APS III, Reels 99-100.

TOY, CRAWFORD HOWELL, 1836-1919
New world. APS III, Reels 31-32.

TRANSYLVANIA UNIVERSITY, LEXINGTON, KY., 1788-1865
Literary pamphleteer. APS II, Reel 132.

TRASK, WILLIAM BLAKE, 1812-1906
New-England historical and genealogical register. APS II, Reels 1053-1061.

TREADWELL, DANIEL, 1791-1872
Boston journal of philosophy and the arts. APS II, Reel 73.

TREAT, SELAH B.
American eclectic. APS II, Reel 295.
Biblical repsitory and classical review. APS II, Reels 306-310.

TRIMBLE, HENRY, 1853-1898
American journal of pharmacy. APS II, Reels 366-368, 1707-1716.

TROWBRIDGE, JOHN TOWNSEND, 1827-1916
Our young folks. APS III, Reels 65-66.

TUCKER, BENJAMIN RICKETSON, 1854-
Liberty (not the daughter but the mother of order). APS III, Reels 669-670.

TUCKER, LUTHER, 1802-1873
Genesee farmer and gardener's journal. APS II, Reels 316-318.

TUCKER, WILLIAM JEWETT, 1839-1925
Andover review. APS III, Reels 1-4.

TUCKERMAN, HENRY THEODORE, 1813-1871
Boston miscellany of literature and fashion. APS II, Reel 310.

TUDOR, WILLIAM, 1779-1830
North American review. APS II, Reels 177-183, 270-281, 1613-1647.

TURNER, EDWARD
Evangelical repertory. APS II, Reel 103.
Gospel visitant. APS II, Reel 110.

TUTHILL, CORNELIUS, 1796?-1825
Microscope. APS II, Reel 217.

TYLER, EDWARD ROYALL, 1800-1848
New Englander and Yale review. APS II, Reels 679-680, 904-912.

TYNER, PAUL
Arena. APS III, Reels 92-99.

UNION UNIVERSITY. SCHENECTADY
Floriad. APS II, Reel 106.

UNITED STATES NAVAL LYCEUM
Naval magazine. APS II, Reel 816.

VANCE, ARTHUR TURNER, 1872-
Pictorial review. APS II, Reels 1487-1488.

VAN OOST, JOHN W.
Art amateur. APS III, Reels 580-585.

VEDDER, HENRY CLAY, 1853-1935
Baptist quarterly review. APS III, Reels 59-60.

VERMONT BAPTIST ASSOCIATION
Vermont Baptist missionary magazine. APS II, Reel 246.

VERPLANCK, GULIAN CROMMELIN, 1786-1870
Talisman. APS II, Reel 400.

WADE, ROBERT L.
Illustrated family magazine. APS II, Reel 777.

WALDIE, ADAM, 1792-1842
Journal of belles lettres. APS II, Reel 1314.
Waldie's select circulating library. APS II, Reels 1354-1357.

WALDO, SAMUEL PUTNAM, 1780-1826
Rural magazine and farmer's monthly museum. APS II, Reel 205.

WALKER, JOHN BRISBEN, 1847-1931
Cosmopolitan. APS III, Reels 660-669.

WALKER, TIMOTHY, 1808-1856
Western law journal. APS II, Reels 487-489.

WALLACE, HENRY EDWARD, 1814-1879
American law journal. APS II, Reels 730-731.

WALLACE, JOHN S.
Opera glass. APS II, Reel 1124.

WALLINGFORD COMMUNITY
Oneida circular. APS III, Reels 670-674.

WALSH, MICHAEL, 1810-1859
Subterranean. APS II, Reel 576.

WALSH, ROBERT, 1784-1859
American quarterly review. APS II, Reels 298-301.
American register; or general repository of history, politics and science. APS II, Reels 2, 59.
American register; or, Summary review of history, politics, and literature. APS II, Reel 59.
American review of history and politics. APS II, Reel 60.
Museum of foreign literature, science, and art. APS II, Reels 146-148, 1245-1254.

WALTON, FRANCIS
New Outlook. APS III, Reels 367-423.

WARD, HENRY DANA, d. 1884
Anti-masonic review, and magazine. APS II, Reel 769.

WARD, WILLIAM HAYES, 1835-1916
Independent. APS II, Reels 418, 1420-1464.

WARE, HENRY, 1794-1843
Christian disciple and theological review. APS II, Reels 77-79.

WARE, JOHN, 1795-1864
Boston journal of philosophy and the arts. APS II, Reel 73.
New-England journal of medicine and surgery. APS II, Reels 153-157, 944.
New-England medical review and journal. APS II, Reel 802.

WARE, WILLIAM, 1797-1852
Unitarian. APS II, Reel 1196.

WATKINS, TOBIAS, 1780-1855
Baltimore medical and physical recorder. APS II, Reel 6.

WATTERS, JAMES, d. 1798
Weekly magazine of original essays. APS I, Reels 31-32.

WATTS, JOHN, 1785-1831
Medical & surgical register. APS II, Reel 216.

WAUGH, BEVERLY, BP., 1789-1858
Methodist review. APS II, Reels 135-136, 327-332, and 1093-1113.

WEBB, GEORGE JAMES, 1803-1887
Musical cabinet. APS II, Reel 1120.

WEBBE, JOHN
American magazine; or, A monthly view of the political state of the British colonies. APS I, Reel 2.

WEBSTER, DAVID
American law journal. APS II, Reels 730-731.

WEBSTER, JAMES, 1803-1854
American medical recorder. APS II, Reels 55-56, 645.

WEBSTER, JOHN WHITE, 1793-1850
Boston journal of philosophy and the arts. APS II, Reel 73.

WEBSTER, NOAH, 1758-1843
American magazine, containing a miscellaneous collection. APS I, Reel 2.

WELD, H. HASTINGS
Boston pearl, a gazette of polite literature. APS II, Reel 788.

WELD, HORATIO HASTINGS, 1811-1888
Brother Jonathan. APS II, Reels 409-410.
Dollar magazine; A monthly gazette of current literature, music and art. APS II, Reel 385.

WELLS, SAMUEL ROBERT, 1820-1875
Phrenological journal and science of health. APS II, Reels 1341-1353.

WEST, ROBERT A.
Columbian lady's and gentleman's magazine. APS II, Reel 313.

WESTERN LITERARY INSTITUTE AND COLLEGE OF PROFESSIONAL TEACHERS
Western academician and journal of education and science. APS II, Reel 486.

WESTON, HENRY GRIGGS, 1820-1909
Baptist quarterly. APS III, Reels 4-5.

WHEDON, DANIEL DENISON, 1808-1885
Methodist review. APS II, Reels 135-136, 327-332, and 1093-1113.

WHEELER, EDWARD JEWITT, 1859-1922
Current opinion. APS III, Reels 689-707.

WHELPLEY, JAMES DAVENPORT, 1817-1872
American Whig review. APS II, Reels 302-304.

WHITAKER, DANIEL KIMBALL, 1801-1881
Christian philanthropist. APS II, Reel 87.
Southern literary journal and magazine of arts. APS II, Reels 574-576.
Southern quarterly review. APS II, Reels 684-687.

WHITE, CHARLES IGNATIUS, 1807-1878
United States Catholic magazine. APS II, Reels 689-690.

WHITE, THOMAS W., 1788?-1843
Southern literary messenger. APS II, Reels 438-447.

WHITNEY, CASPAR, 1862-1929
Outing; sport, adventure, travel, fiction. APS III, Reels 297-309.

WIGGINS, FRANCIS S., d. 1840
Farmers cabinet and American herd book. APS II, Reels 314-315.
Monthly repository and library of entertaining knowledge. APS II, Reel 1215.

WIGHTMAN, J. M.
Boston mechanic, and journal of the useful arts and sciences. APS II, Reel 472.

WILBUR, HERVEY, 1787-1852
Monitor, designed to improve the taste, the understanding, and the heart. APS II, Reel 143.

WILDFIRE, WALTER, pseud.
Comet. APS II, Reel 97.

WILKES, GEORGE
National police gazette. APS II, Reels 1318-1340.

WILLIAMS, JOHN S.
American pioneer. APS II, Reel 297.

WILLIAMS, SAMUEL, 1743-1817
Rural magazine; or, Vermont repository. APS I, Reel 27.

WILLIAMS, WILLIAM W.
National magazine. APS III, Reels 160-163.

WILLIS, LEMUEL
Evangelical magazine and gospel advocate. APS II, Reels 792-794.

WILLIS, NATHANIEL PARKER, 1780-1870
Congregationalist and herald of gospel liberty. APS II, Reels 97-99, 539-546, 1911-1924.
Youth's companion. APS II, Reels 1546-1572.

WILLIS, NATHANIEL PARKER, 1806-1867
American monthly magazine. APS II, Reel 468.
Corsair. APS II, Reel 384.
Dollar magazine; A monthly gazette of current literature, music and art. APS II, Reel 385.
New mirror. APS II, Reel 1124.
New-York mirror. APS II, Reels 164-165, 785-787.

WILLSON, JAMES RENWICK, 1780-1853
Evangelical witness. APS II, Reels 103-104, 606.

WILSON, JAMES
Boston medical intelligencer. APS II, Reels 73, 763.

WILSON, LEWIS
Dawn, a semi-monthly magazine. APS II, Reel 100.

WINCHELL, J. M.
Literary union. APS II, Reel 742.

WISE, DANIEL, 1813-1896
Forrester's boys' and girls' magazine. APS II, Reels 606-607.

WOODBRIDGE, J. E.
Congregationalist and herald of gospel liberty. APS II, Reels 97-99, 539-546, 1911-1924.

WOODBRIDGE, WILLIAM CHANNING, 1794-1845
American annals of education. APS II, Reels 293-294.

WOODS, HENRY ERNEST, 1857-1916
New-England historical and genealogical register. APS II, Reels 1053-1061.

WOODS, LEONARD, 1807-1878
Literary and theological review. APS II, Reel 798.

WOODWARD, WILLIAM WALLIS
Beauties of the Evangelical magazine. APS II, Reel 6.

WOODWORTH, FRANCIS CHANNING, 1812-1859
National preacher and village pulpit. APS II, Reels 1087-1090.

WOODWORTH, SAMUEL, 1785-1842
Ladies' literary cabinet. APS II, Reels 121-122.
New Jerusalem missionary and intellectual repository. APS II, Reel 158.
New-York mirror. APS II, Reels 164-165, 785-787.
Parthenon. APS II, Reel 1257.

WORCESTER, JOSEPH EMERSON, 1784-1865
American almanac and repository of useful knowledge. APS II, Reels 810-812.

WORCESTER, NOAH, 1758-1837
Christian disciple and theological review. APS II, Reels 77-79.
Friend of Peace. APS II, Reels 211, 1072.

WORDEN, HARRIET M.
Oneida circular. APS III, Reels 670-674.

WORMAN, BEN JAMES, 1870-
Outing. APS III, Reels 297-309.

WORMAN, JAMES HENRY, 1835-1930
Outing. APS III, Reels 297-309.

WORTHINGTON, N. B.
American farmer; devoted to agriculture. APS II, Reels 51-52, 1062-1071.

WRIGHT, GUY W.
Ohio medical repository. APS II, Reel 973.

YALE UNIVERSITY
Connecticut Academy of Arts and Sciences, New Haven. Memoirs. APS II, Reel 770.
Literary cabinet. APS II, Reel 22.
Yale literary magazine. APS II, Reels 529-531.

YANDELL, LUNSFORD PITTS, 1805-1878
Western journal of medicine and surgery. APS II, Reels 701-705.

YERRINGTON, JAMES M. W., d. 1893
Mechanic apprentice. APS II, Reel 742.

YOUNG, WILLIAM, 1809-1888
Albion, a journal of news, politics, and literature. APS II, Reels 50, 706-718, 1263-1270.

YOUNGMAN, ELMER HASKELL, 1861-
Bankers magazine. APS II, Reels 587-588, 1648-1683.

McClure's Magazine: Vol. 34, no. 6; Apr. 1910

REEL
NUMBER
INDEX

UNITS/REEL NUMBERS LIST

American Periodicals—18th Century (APS I)

Reels 1-33

American Periodicals—1800-1850 (APS II)

Unit 1, Reels 1-46
Unit 2, Reels 47-86
Unit 3, Reels 87-126
Unit 4, Reels 127-166
Unit 5, Reels 167-206
Unit 6, Reels 207-253
Unit 7, Reels 254-292
Unit 8, Reels 293-326
Unit 9, Reels 327-361
Unit 10, Reels 362-400
Unit 11, Reels 401-448
Unit 12, Reels 449-492
Unit 13, Reels 493-531
Unit 14, Reels 532-583
Unit 15, Reels 584-640

Unit 16, Reels 641-673
Unit 17, Reels 674-705
Unit 18, Reels 706-753
Unit 19, Reels 754-784
Unit 20, Reels 785-816
Unit 21, Reels 817-845
Unit 22, Reels 846-880
Unit 23, Reels 881-913
Unit 24, Reels 914-943
Unit 25, Reels 944-973
Unit 26, Reels 974-1001
Unit 27, Reels 1002-1030
Unit 28, Reels 1031-1061
Unit 29, Reels 1062-1092
Unit 30, Reels 1093-1124
Unit 31, Reels 1125-1151

Unit 32, Reels 1152-1196
Unit 33, Reels 1197-1229
Unit 34, Reels 1230-1262
Unit 35, Reels 1263-1313
Unit 36, Reels 1314-1363
Unit 37, Reels 1364-1408
Unit 38-39, Reels 1409-1497
Unit 40, Reels 1498-1545
Unit 41, Reels 1546-1612
Unit 42, Reels 1613-1647
Unit 43-44, Reels 1648-1706
Unit 45, Reels 1707-1748
Unit 46, Reels 1749-1825
Unit 47, Reels 1826-1884
Unit 48, Reels 1885-1966

American Periodicals—1850-1900, Civil War and Reconstruction (APS III)

Unit 1, Reels 1-25
Unit 2, Reels 26-53
Unit 3, Reels 54-84
Unit 4, Reels 85-111
Unit 5, Reels 112-139
Unit 6, Reels 140-170
Unit 7, Reels 171-200

Unit 8, Reels 201-238
Unit 9, Reels 239-271
Unit 10, Reels 272-313
Unit 11, Reels 314-344
Unit 12, Reels 345-386
Unit 13, Reels 387-423
Unit 14, Reels 424-462

Unit 15, Reels 463-493
Unit 16, Reels 494-532
Unit 17, Reels 533-569
Unit 18, Reels 570-599
Unit 19-20, Reels 600-674
Unit 21, Reels 675-707
Unit 22-23, Reels 708-771

REEL NUMBER INDEX

AMERICAN PERIODICALS—18th Century (APS I)

REEL

1   AMERICAN APOLLO. v1; Jan.6, 1792-Sept. 28, 1792

1   AMERICAN MAGAZINE AND HISTORICAL CHRONICLE. v1-3; Sept. 1743-Dec. 1746.

2   AMERICAN MAGAZINE. . . no[1]-12; Dec. 1787-Nov. 1788.

2   AMERICAN MAGAZINE; OR, A MONTHLY VIEW OF THE POLITICAL STATE OF THE BRITISH COLONIES. v1; Jan.-Mar. 1741.

2   AMERICAN MAGAZINE; OR, GENERAL REPOSITORY. Jan.-Sept. 1769.

2   AMERICAN MAGAZINE AND MONTHLY CHRONICLE FOR THE BRITISH COLONIES. v1; Oct. 1757-Oct. 1758.

3   AMERICAN MONTHLY REVIEW. v1-3; Jan.-Dec. 1795.

3   AMERICAN MONITOR. v1, no1; Oct. 1785.

3   AMERICAN MORAL & SENTIMENTAL MAGAZINE. v1-2; July 3, 1797-May 21, 1798.

4-5   AMERICAN MUSEUM, OR, UNIVERSAL MAGAZINE
         American Museum, Or, Repository of Ancient and Modern Fugitive Pieces, etc. Prose and Poetical
         Reel 4   v1-4; Jan. 1787-Dec. 1788
         American Museum, or, Universal Magazine
         Reel 4   v5; Jan. 1789-June 1789
         Reel 5   v6-12; July 1789-Dec. 1792

6   AMERICAN MUSICAL MAGAZINE. v1, no1-12; May 1786-Sept. 1787.

6-7   AMERICAN UNIVERSAL MAGAZINE
         Reel 6   v1-2; Jan. 2, 1797-June 13, 1797
         Reel 7   v3-4; July 10, 1797-Mar. 7, 1798

8   ARMINIAN MAGAZINE. v1-2; Jan. 1789-Dec. 1790.

8   BOSTON WEEKLY-MAGAZINE. no1-3; Mar 2-16, 1743.

8   CENSOR. v1-2; Nov. 23, 1771-May 2, 1772.

8   CHILDREN'S MAGAZINE. Jan.-Apr. 1789.

9   BOSTON MAGAZINE. v1-3; Oct. 1783-Nov./Dec. 1786.

10   CHRISTIAN HISTORY. no1-104; Mar. 5, 1743-Feb 23, 1745.

10   CHRISTIAN'S MONITOR. no13-14; May 25-June 8, 1799

10   CHRISTIAN'S, SCHOLAR'S, AND FARMER'S MAGAZINE. v1-2; Apr./May 1789-Feb./Mar. 1791.

REEL

10   COLUMBIAN MUSEUM. Jan-June, 1793

10   COURIER DE BOSTON. no1-26; Apr. 23-Oct. 15, 1789.

11   UNIVERSAL ASYLUM AND COLUMBIAN MAGAZINE
         Columbian Magazine
         Reel 11   v1-4; Sept. 1786-1790

12   DESSERT TO THE TRUE AMERICAN. v1-2, no7; July 14, 1798-Aug. 19, 1799.

12   EXPERIENCED CHRISTIAN'S MAGAZINE. v1; May 1796-Apr. 1797.

12   FREE UNIVERSAL MAGAZINE. v1, no2; Sept. 6, 1793.

12   GEISTLICHES MAGAZIEN. nos 1-15; 1770-1772?.

12   GENERAL MAGAZINE, AND HISTORICAL CHRONICLE, FOR ALL THE BRITISH PLANTATIONS IN AMERICA. v1, no1-6; Jan-June 1741.

13   GENERAL MAGAZINE AND IMPARTIAL REVIEW OF KNOWLEDGE & ENTERTAINMENT. v1; June-July, 1798.

13   GENTLEMAN AND LADY'S TOWN AND COUNTRY MAGAZINE. v1, no1-8; May-Dec. 1784.

13   GENTLEMEN AND LADIES' TOWN AND COUNTRY MAGAZINE: CONSISTING OF LITERATURE . . . v1; Feb. 1789-Jan. 1790.

13   HUMMING BIRD. v1, no1, 5; Apr. 14-June 9, 1798.

13   INDEPENDENT REFLECTOR. no1-52; Nov. 30, 1752-Nov. 22, 1753.

13   INSTRUCTOR. v1, no 1-10; Mar. 6-May 8, 1755.

13   JOHN ENGLISHMAN, IN DEFENCE OF THE ENGLISH CONSTITUTION. no1-10; Apr. 9-July 5, 1755.

13   KEY. v1, no1-27; Jan. 13-July 14, 1798.

14   LADY'S MAGAZINE, AND REPOSITORY OF ENTERTAINING KNOWLEDGE. v1-2; June 1792-May 1793.

14   LADY & GENTLEMAN'S POCKET MAGAZINE OF LITERARY AND POLITE AMUSEMENT . . . v1; Aug.-Nov. 1796.

14   LITERARY MISCELLANY. v1, no1-8; 1795.

14   LITERARY MUSEUM, OR, MONTHLY MAGAZINE. Jan.-June 1797.

REEL

14   **MEDICAL REPOSITORY OF ORIGINAL ESSAYS AND INTELLIGENCE.** v1-3; 1797-1800.

15-16   **MASSACHUSETTS MAGAZINE**
Reel 15   v1-4; Jan. 1789-Dec. 1792
Reel 16   v5-8; Jan. 1793-Dec. 1796

17   **METHODIST MAGAZINE.** v1-2; Jan. 1797-Aug. 1798.

17   **MONTHLY MAGAZINE, AND AMERICAN REVIEW.** v1-3; Apr. 1799-Dec. 1800.

18   **MONTHLY MILITARY REPOSITORY.** v1-2; 1796-1797.

18   **MONTHLY MISCELLANY.** v1, no1-6; Apr.-Sept. 1794.

18   **MUSICAL MAGAZINE.** no1-6; 1792-[1801?].

18   **NATIONAL MAGAZINE.** v1-2, no8; 1799.

19   **NEW AMERICAN MAGAZINE.** no1-27; Jan. 1758-Mar. 1760.

19   **NEW ENGLAND MAGAZINE OF KNOWLEDGE AND PLEASURE.** no1-3; Aug. 1758, Oct. 1758, Mar. 1759.

19   **NEWHAMPSHIRE MAGAZINE.** v1, no1-6; June-Nov. 1793.

20   **NEW HAMPSHIRE & VERMONT MAGAZINE.** v1, no1, 4; July, Oct. 1797.

20   **NEW-HAVEN GAZETTE, AND THE CONNECTICUT MAGAZINE.** v1-3; Feb. 16, 1786-Dec. 4, 1788.

21   **NEW-JERSEY MAGAZINE AND MONTHLY ADVERTISER.** Dec. 1786-Feb. 1787.

21-22   **NEW YORK MAGAZINE, OR LITERARY REPOSITORY**
Reel 21   v1-3; Jan, 1790-Dec. 1792
Reel 22   v4-6; Jan. 1793-Dec. 1795
Reel 22   ns v1-2; Jan. 1796-Dec. 1797

23   **NEW-YORK WEEKLY MAGAZINE.** v1-2; July 1, 1795-June 28, 1797.

23   **NEW STAR.** Feb 2, 1796.

23   **NEW STAR; A REPUBLICAN MISCELLANEOUS, LITERARY PAPER.** no1-26; Apr. 11-Oct. 3, 1797.

23   **NIGHTINGALE.** v1, no1-36; May 10-July 30, 1796.

23   **NORTH-CAROLINA MAGAZINE.** v1-2, no1-33; June 1/8, 1764-Jan. 11/18, 1765.

24   **OCCASIONAL REVERBERATOR.** no1-4; Sept. 7-Oct. 5, 1753.

24   **PENNSYLVANIA MAGAZINE.** v1-2; Jan. 1775-July 1776.

24   **PENNY POST.** no1-9; Jan. 9-27, 1769.

24   **PHILADELPHIA MAGAZINE AND REVIEW.** v1, no1-6; Jan-June 1799.

REEL

25   **PHILADELPHIA MINERVA.** v1-4 (no1-179); Feb. 7, 1795-July 7, 1798.

25   **PHILADELPHIA MONTHLY MAGAZINE.** v1-2 (no1-9); Jan.-Sept. 1798.

25   **PHILADELPHISCHES MAGAZIN.** v1, no1; May 1, 1798.

26   **PORCUPINE'S POLITICAL CENSOR.** Mar. 1796-Mar. 1797.

26   **RELIGIOUS MONITOR.** no1-13; Apr. 7-Sept. 22, 1798.

26   **REMEMBRANCER, FOR LORD'S DAY EVENINGS.** no1-2; Jan. 1-8, 1797.

26   **REPUBLICAN MAGAZINE.** v1, no1-4; Oct. 1-Dec. 15, 1798.

26   **ROYAL AMERICAN MAGAZINE.** v1-2; Jan. 1774-Mar. 1775.

26   **ROYAL SPIRITUAL MAGAZINE.** v1; Jan.-Dec. 1771.

27   **RURAL MAGAZINE; OR, VERMONT REPOSITORY.** v1-2; Jan. 1795-Dec. 1796.

27   **RURAL MAGAZINE.** v1, no1-52; Feb. 17, 1798-Feb. 9, 1799.

27   **NEW-YORK WEEKLY MAGAZINE**
Sentimental and Literary Magazine
Reel 27   v3; July 5-Aug. 23, 1797

28   **SOUTH-CAROLINA WEEKLY MUSEUM AND COMPLETE MAGAZINE OF ENTERTAINMENT AND INTELLIGENCE.** v1; Jan.1-July 1, 1797.

28   **TABLET.** v1, no1-13; May 19-Aug. 11, 1795.

28   **THEOLOGICAL MAGAZINE.** v1-3; July/Aug. 1795-Dec. 1798/Jan./Feb. 1799.

29   **THESPIAN ORACLE.** v1, no1; Jan. 1798.

29   **TIME PIECE.** v1-3, no1-150; Mar. 13, 1797-Aug. 28, 1798.

30   **UNITED STATES CHRISTIAN MAGAZINE.** v1, no1-3; 1796.

30   **UNITED STATES MAGAZINE: A REPOSITORY OF HISTORY, POLITICS AND LITERATURE.** v1; Jan.-Dec. 1779.

30   **UNITED STATES MAGAZINE, OR, GENERAL REPOSITORY OF USEFUL INSTRUCTION.** v1-, no1-5; Apr.-Aug. 1794.

30   **UNIVERSAL ASYLUM AND COLUMBIAN MAGAZINE.** v4-9; Mar. 1790-Dec. 1792.

31   **VIGIL.** no1-6; Feb. 27-Apr. 3, 1798.

31-32   **WEEKLY MAGAZINE OF ORIGINAL ESSAYS, FUGITIVE PIECES, AND INTERESTING INTELLIGENCE**
Reel 31   v1-2; Feb. 3-July 28, 1798
Reel 32   v3-4; Aug. 4, 1798-May 25, 1799

REEL

33   WEEKLY MUSEUM. v1, no5-6; Feb. 5-12, 1797.

33   WORCESTER MAGAZINE. v1-4; Apr. 1786-Mar. 1788.

33   RURAL CASKET. v1, no1-15; June 5-Sept. 11, 1798.

AMERICAN PERIODICALS—1800-1850 (APS II)

Unit 1

1   ADVISER; OR, VERMONT EVANGELICAL MAGA-ZINE. v1; Jan.-Dec. 1809.

1   AMERICAN GLEANER AND VIRGINIA MAGA-ZINE. v1, no1-18; Jan.-Dec. 1807.

1   AMERICAN LAW JOURNAL (Hall)
     American Law Journal and Miscellaneous Repertory
     Reel 1   v1-2; Jan. 1808-Aug. 1809.

1   AMERICAN MAGAZINE OF WONDERS AND MAR-VELLOUS CHRONICLE. v1-2; 1809.

2   AMERICAN MUSICAL MAGAZINE. v1, no2; Jan. 1801.

2   AMERICAN REGISTER. v1-5; 1806-09.

3   AMERICAN REVIEW, AND LITERARY JOURNAL, FOR 1801-1802. v1-2; 1801-1802.

3   ANALYST; OR MATHEMATICAL MUSEUM. v1; 1808.

3   ANNALES PHILOSOPHIQUES, POLITIQUES ET LITTERAIRES. no1, 1807.

3-5   BALANCE, AND STATE JOURNAL
      Balance and Columbian Repository
      Reel 3   v1-2, no52; Jan. 5, 1802-Dec. 27, 1803
      Reel 4   v3-6; Jan. 3, 1804-Dec. 29, 1807
      Balance
      Reel 5   v7; Jan. 5-Dec. 27, 1808
      Balance, and New-York State Journal
      Reel 5   nsv1; Jan. 4-Dec. 29, 1809

6   BALTIMORE MAGAZINE. July 1807.

6   BALTIMORE MEDICAL AND PHYSICAL RECORDER. v1-2, no1; Apr. 1808-Aug. 1809.

6   BALTIMORE WEEKLY MAGAZINE COMPLETE IN ONE VOLUME. v1; Apr. 26, 1800-May 27, 1801.

6   BARBER'S SHOP. no1-4; 1807-1808.

6   BEAUTIES OF THE EVANGELICAL MAGAZINE. v1-2; 1802-1803.

6   BEREAN; OR SCRIPTURE-SEARCHER. v1, no1-6; 1802-[1809].

6   BOSTON MAGAZINE
     Boston Weekly Magazine; devoted to . . .
     Reel 6   v1-3; Oct. 30, 1802-Oct. 19, 1805
     Boston Magazine
     Reel 6   nsv1; Oct. 26, 1805-Feb. 22, 1806

REEL

6   CHARLESTON SPECTATOR AND LADIES' LITER-ARY PORT FOLIO. v1, no1-9, 19-21, 23-25; 1806.

7   CHILD OF PALLAS. v1, no1-8; Nov. 1800-Jan. 1801.

7   CHRISTIAN CABINET. v1, no1-5; 1802.

7   CHRISTIAN MONITOR. v1-2, 5-6 (nos1-4, 9-12); 1806-09.

8-11 CHRISTIAN OBSERVER, CONDUCTED BY MEM-BERS OF THE ESTABLISHED CHURCH
      Christian Observer . . .
      Reel 8   v1-3; Jan. 1802-Dec. 1804
      Reel 9   v4-5; Jan. 1805-Dec. 1806
      Reel 10   v6-7; Jan. 1807-Dec. 1808
      Reel 11   v8; Jan.-Dec. 1809

11   CHRISTIAN'S MAGAZINE, REVIEWER, AND RELI-GIOUS INTELLIGENCER. v1, no1-8; May 1805-Jan. 1808.

11   CHRISTIAN'S MAGAZINE. v1-2; 1806-1807.

12   CHURCHMAN'S MAGAZINE
     Churchman's Monthly Magazine
     Reel 12   v1-2; Jan. 1804-Dec. 1805
     Churchman's Magazine
     Reel 12   v3-6; Jan. 1806-Dec. 1809

13   COLUMBIAN PHENIX AND BOSTON REVIEW. v1, no1-7; Jan.-July 1800.

13   COMPANION AND WEEKLY MISCELLANY. v1-2; Nov. 3, 1804-Oct. 25, 1806.

14   CONNECTICUT EVANGELICAL MAGAZINE AND RELIGIOUS INTELLIGENCER
     Connecticut Evangelical Magazine
     Reel 14   v1-7; July 1800-June 1807

15   CONNECTICUT MAGAZINE. v1, no1-6; Jan.-June 1801.

15   CONNECTICUT REPUBLICAN MAGAZINE. v1, no1-4; July 1802-[1803].

15   CORRECTOR. no1-10; Mar. 28-Apr. 26, 1804.

15   EMERALD, OR, MISCELLANY OF LITERATURE. v1-2, nsv1; May 3, 1806-Oct. 15, 1808.

16-17 EVANGELICAL INTELLIGENCER
       General Assembly's Missionary Magazine
       Reel 16   v1-3; Jan. 1805-June 1807
       Evangelical Intelligencer
       Reel 17   nsv1-3; July 1807-Dec. 1809

18   EVENING FIRE-SIDE. v1-2; Dec. 15, 1804-Dec. 27, 1806.

18   EVIDENCE. v1, no1-52; Jan. 14, 1807-Mar. 5, 1808.

18   EXPERIENCED CHRISTIAN'S MAGAZINE. v2; May 1805-Apr. 1806.

19   EYE. v1-2; Jan. 7-Dec. 29, 1808.

19   FLY. v1, no1-13; Oct. 16, 1805-Apr. 2, 1806

REEL

19   FOOL. no1-3; Feb.-Apr. 1807.

19   GEORGIA ANALYTICAL REPOSITORY. v1, no1-6; May/June 1802-Mar./Apr. 1803.

19   GUARDIAN. v1, no2-24, 26-34, 36-42, 44-51; 1807-1808.

19   HALCYON ITINERARY. no1-6; Aug. 1807-Jan. 1808.

19   L'HEMISPHERE, JOURNAL FRANCAIS. v1, nos. 1-9; Oct. 7-Dec. 30, 1809.

19   HERALD OF GOSPEL LIBERTY. v1, no1-35; Sept. 1, 1808-1809.

19   INDEPENDENT REPUBLICAN. v1, no1; Aug. 1, 1805.

19   JUVENILE MAGAZINE. v1-4; 1802-1803.

20   LADIES AFTERNOON VISITOR
      Ladies Visitor
         Reel 20   v1, no1; Dec. 4, 1806
      Ladies Afternoon Visitor
         Reel 20   v1, no2-13; Dec. 11, 1806-Feb. 28, 1807

20   LADIES MUSEUM. v1, no1-14; Feb. 25-June 7, 1800.

20   LADY'S MAGAZINE AND MUSICAL REPOSITORY. v1-3; Jan. 1801-June 1802.

20   LADY'S MONITOR
      Ladies' Monitor
         Reel 20   v1, no3-9; Aug.22-Oct. 3, 1801
      Lady's Monitor
         Reel 20   v1, no10-41; Oct.10, 1801-May 29, 1802

20-21 LADY'S MISCELLANY
      Weekly Visitor, Or, Ladies' Miscellany
         Reel 20   v1-4; Oct. 9, 1802-Oct. 25, 1806
      Lady's Weekly Miscellany
         Reel 21   v5-10, no10; Nov. 1, 1806-Dec. 30, 1809

22   LANCASTER HIVE. v1-2; June 22, 1803-June 12, 1805.

22   LANCET. no1; June 1803.

22   LITERARY CABINET. nos1-18, 20; 1806-1807.

22-23 LITERARY MAGAZINE, AND AMERICAN REGIS-TER
         Reel 22   v1-2; Oct. 1803-Dec. 1804
         Reel 23   v3-8; Jan. 1805-Dec. 1807

24   LITERARY MIRROR. v1; Feb. 20, 1808-Feb. 11, 1809.

24   LITERARY MISCELLANY. v1-2; 1805-1806.

24   LITERARY TABLET. v1-4; Aug. 6, 1803-Aug. 5, 1807.

25   MASSACHUSETTS BAPTIST MISSIONARY MAGA-ZINE. v1-2, no8; Sept. 1803-1809.

25   MASSACHUSETTS MISSIONARY MAGAZINE. v1-5; May 1803-May 1808.

26   MASSACHUSETTS WATCHMAN. v1, no1-7; June-Dec. 1809.

26   MATHEMATICAL CORRESPONDENT. v1-2, no1; 1804-1807.

26   MEDICAL AND AGRICULTURAL REGISTER, FOR THE YEARS 1806 AND 1807. v1, no1-24; Jan. 1806-Dec. 1807.

26-27 MEDICAL REPOSITORY OF ORIGINAL ESSAYS AND INTELLIGENCE, RELATIVE TO PHYSIC, SUR-GERY, CHEMISTRY, AND NATURAL HISTORY
         Reel 26   v3-6; 1800-1803
         Reel 27   v7-12; 1804-1809

28   MEDLEY; OR, MONTHLY MISCELLANY. v1; Jan.-Dec. 1803.

28   MERRIMACK MAGAZINE AND LADIES' LITERARY CABINET. v1, no1-52; Aug. 17, 1805-Aug. 9, 1806.

28   MERRIMACK MISCELLANY. v1, no1-18; June 8-Oct. 5, 1805.

28   MISCELLANY. v1, no1-20, 22-26; June 10-Dec. 2, 1805.

29   MISSIONARY HERALD AT HOME AND ABROAD
      Panoplist
         Reel 29   v1-3; June 1805-May 1808
      Panoplist and Missionary Magazine
         Reel 29   v4-5, no7; June 1808-Dec. 1809

30-32 MONTHLY ANTHOLOGY, AND BOSTON REVIEW
         Reel 30   v1-3; Nov. 1803-Dec. 1806
         Reel 31   v4-6; Jan. 1807-June 1809
         Reel 32   v7; July-Dec. 1809

32   COLUMBIAN MAGAZINE
      Monthly Magazine; Comprehending Ecclesiastical History, . . .
         Reel 32   v1, no1-3; Jan.-Mar. 1806
      Columbian Magazine; Comprehending Ecclesiastical History, . . .
         Reel 32   v1, no5; July-Aug. 1806

32   GLEANER; OR, MONTHLY MAGAZINE
      Gleaner; or, Monthly Magazine
         Reel 32   v1; Sept. 1808-Aug. 1809
      Monthly Magazine
         Reel 32   v2; Sept.-Nov. 1809

33   MONTHLY REGISTER, MAGAZINE, AND REVIEW OF THE UNITED STATES. v1-4, no1; [Jan.?] 1805-Dec. 1807.

33   MONTHLY REVIEW AND LITERARY MISCELLANY OF THE UNITED STATES. v1; [1805]-1806.

33   MOONSHINE. no1-5; June 20-July 23, 1807.

34   MORAL AND RELIGIOUS CABINET. v1, no1-26; Jan. 2-June 25, 1808.

34   NATIONAL MAGAZINE. no1-6, 8; Oct. 1801- Jan. 1802.

34   NEW ENGLAND LITERARY HERALD. no1; Sept. 1809.

REEL

34 NEW ENGLAND QUARTERLY MAGAZINE. no1-3; Apr.-Dec. 1802.

34 NEW-HAMPSHIRE NEW JERUSALEM MAGAZINE AND PRIMITIVE RELIGIOUS INTELLIGENCER. no1; Feb. 5, 1805.

34 NEW-YORK MEDICAL AND PHILOSOPHICAL JOURNAL AND REVIEW. v1; 1809.

35 NEW-YORK MISSIONARY MAGAZINE. v1-4; Jan. 1800-Dec. 1803.

36 OBSERVER. v1-2; Nov. 29, 1806-Dec. 26, 1807.

36 OBSERVER. no1-25; Feb. 11-Aug. 6, 1809.

36 OMNIUM GATHERUM. v1, nos1-2; Nov.-Dec. 1809.

36 ORDEAL. v1; Jan. 7-July 1, 1809.

36 PASTIME. v1-2, no7; Feb. 21, 1807-June 25, 1808.

36 PATRIOT. v1; 1801-1802.

37 PETIT CENSEUR. no1-12; Sept. 19-Dec. 5, 1805.

37 PETIT CENSEUR, CRITIQUE ET LITTERAIRE. no1-17; July 4-Aug. 13, 1805.

37 PHILADELPHIA MEDICAL AND PHYSICAL JOURNAL
    Reel 37   v1-3; Nov. 1804-1808
    Supplement
    Reel 37   v1-3; Mar. 1806-May 1809

38 PHILADELPHIA MEDICAL MUSEUM. v1-6; 1805-1809.

39 PISCATAQUA EVANGELICAL MAGAZINE. v1-4, no2; Jan./Feb. 1805-Mar./Apr. 1808.

39 POLITICAL MAGAZINE AND MISCELLANEOUS REPOSITORY. v1, no1-2; Oct.-Nov. 1800.

39 POLYANTHOS. v1-5; Dec. 1805-July 1807.

40-42 PORT FOLIO
    Reel 40   v1-4; Jan. 3, 1801-Dec. 29, 1804
    Reel 41   v5-nsv4; Jan. 12, 1805-Dec. 26, 1807
    Reel 42   nsv5-s3v2; Jan. 2, 1808-Dec. 1809

42 PORTLAND MAGAZINE. v1, no1-5; May 11-June 8, 1805.

42 PROSPECT: OR, VIEW OF THE MORAL WORLD. v1-2, no13; 1803-Mar. 30, 1805.

43 RAMBLERS' MAGAZINE. v1-2, no1; 1809-1810.

43 RELIGIOUS REPOSITORY. v1-2; Sept./Oct. 1807-July/Aug. 1809.

43 REPOSITORY AND LADIES' WEEKLY MUSEUM
    Philadelphia Repository and Weekly Register
    Reel 43   v1-5; Nov. 15, 1800-June 29, 1805
    Repository and Ladies' Weekly Museum
    Reel 43   v6; Dec. 14, 1805-Apr. 5, 1806

44 REPOSITORY OF KNOWLEDGE. v1, no1-2; Apr. 15-May 1801.

REEL

44 REPOSITORY OF KNOWLEDGE, HISTORICAL, LITERARY, MISCELLANEOUS, AND THEOLOGICAL. v1, no1-2; Jan.-Feb. 1802.

44 RUSH-LIGHT
    Rush-light
    Reel 44   v1, no1-6; Feb. 15-Aug. 30, 1800
    Republican Rush-light
    Reel 44   v2, no1; undated

44 SALMAGUNDI. no1-20; Jan. 24, 1807-Jan. 25, 1808.

44 SELECT REVIEWS OF LITERATURE AND SPIRIT OF FOREIGN MAGAZINES
    Select Reviews, and Spirit of the Foreign Magazines
    Reel 44   v1, no1-v2, no12; Jan.-Dec. 1809

44 SOMETHING. v1, no1-7; Nov. 18-Dec. 30, 1809.

44 SPECTACLES. v1, no5-6, 11; June 6-July 18, 1807.

44 SPIRIT OF THE PUBLIC JOURNALS. 1805.

44 THEATRICAL CENSOR. no1-17; Dec. 9, 1805-Mar. 3, 1806.

44 THESPIAN MIRROR. v1, no1-14; Dec. 28, 1805-May 31, 1806.

44 THESPIAN MONITOR, AND DRAMATICK MISCELLANY. v1, no1-4; Nov. 25-Dec. 16, 1809.

44 THISTLE. v1, no1-3; Aug. 4-Sept. 1, 1807.

45 TICKLER. v1-2; 1807-1809.

45 TOILET. v1, no1-8; Jan. 17-Mar. 7, 1801.

45 TOWN. v1, no1-5; Jan. 1-12, 1807.

45 UNITED STATES MILITARY PHILOSOPHICAL SOCIETY. EXTRACTS FROM THE MINUTES . . . 1806-1809.

45 USEFUL CABINET. v1, no1-6; Jan.-June 1808.

45 VIRGINIA RELIGIOUS MAGAZINE. v1-3; Oct. 1804-Nov./Dec. 1807.

46 VISITOR. v1, no1-24; 1809.

46 WASP. v1, no1-12; July 7, 1802-Jan. 26, 1803.

46 WEEKLY VISITANT. v1, no1-52; Jan. 1-Dec. 27, 1806.

46 WESTERN MISSIONARY MAGAZINE. v1-2; Feb. 1803-Apr. 1805.

46 WITNESS. v1, no1-6; Jan.-June 1809.

Unit 2

47 ABOLITION INTELLIGENCER AND MISSIONARY MAGAZINE. v1, no1-7, 10-11; May 7, 1822-Mar. 1823.

47 ACADEMICIAN. v1, nos1-25; Feb. 7, 1818-Jan. 29, 1820.

REEL

47   **ADVISER.** v2-7; Jan. 1810-Dec. 1815.

48-49   **AERONAUT**
     Reel 48   v1-6; May 18, 1816-Oct. 4, 1817
     Reel 49   v7-13; Oct. 6, 1817-1822

49   **AESCULAPIAN REGISTER.** v1; June 17-Dec. 9, 1824.

49   **AFRICAN INTELLIGENCER.** v1, no1; July 1820.

49   **AFRICAN REPOSITORY**
     African Repository and Colonial Journal
     Reel 49   v1, nos1-10; Mar.-Dec. 1825

49   **AGRICULTURAL MUSEUM.** v1-2, no11; July 4, 1810-May 1812.

50   **ALBION.** v1-4; 1822-1825.

51   **ALMONER.** v1, no1-6; Apr. 1814-May 1815.

51   **AMERICAN ATHENAEUM.** v1, nos1-36; Apr. 21-Dec. 29, 1825.

51   **AMERICAN CRITIC AND GENERAL REVIEW.** v1, no1-2; Apr. 1-29, 1820.

51-52   **AMERICAN FARMER; DEVOTED TO AGRICULTURE**
     American Farmer, Containing Original Essays . . .
     Reel 51   v1, no1-52; Apr. 2, 1819-Mar. 24, 1820
     Reel 52   v1-7, no41; Apr. 2, 1819-Dec. 30, 1825

53&53a   **AMERICAN JOURNAL OF SCIENCE**
     American Journal of Science
     Reel 53   v1; July 1818-1819
     American Journal of Science and Arts
     Reel 53   v2, v9; 1820, 1825
     Reel 53a   v3-8, v10; 1821-24, 1826

53   **AMERICAN LAW JOURNAL (Hall)**
     American Law Journal and Miscellaneous Repertory
     Reel 53   v3; 1810-11

53   **AMERICAN MAGAZINE.** v1, no1-12; June 1815-May 1816.

54   **AMERICAN MASONIC REGISTER.** v1-2, no7; Sept. 1820-June 1823.

54   **AMERICAN MECHANICS' MAGAZINE.** v1-2, no40; Feb. 5-Dec. 24, 1825.

54   **AMERICAN MEDICAL AND PHILOSOPHICAL REGISTER.** v1-2, 4; July 1810-Apr. 1814.

55-56   **AMERICAN MEDICAL RECORDER**
     Reel 55   v1-5; Jan. 1818-Oct. 1822
     Reel 56   v6-8; Jan. 1823-Oct. 1825

57   **AMERICAN MEDICAL REVIEW**
     Medical Review and Analectic Journal
     Reel 57   v1; June 1824-Apr. 1825
     American Medical Review, and Journal of . . .
     Reel 57   v2; Sept.-Dec. 1825

57   **AMERICAN MINERALOGICAL JOURNAL.** v1, no1-4; Jan. 1810-1814.

REEL

57   **AMERICAN MONTHLY MAGAZINE.** v1-2; Jan.-Dec. 1824.

58   **AMERICAN MONTHLY MAGAZINE AND CRITICAL REVIEW.** v1-4; May 1817-Apr. 1819.

58   **AMERICAN MUSEUM, AND REPOSITORY OF ARTS AND SCIENCES.** v1, pt1; 1822.

59   **AMERICAN REGISTER; OR GENERAL REPOSITORY OF HISTORY, POLITICS AND SCIENCE.** v6-7; 1810.

59   **AMERICAN REGISTER; OR, SUMMARY REVIEW OF HISTORY, POLITICS, AND LITERATURE.** v1-2; 1817.

60   **AMERICAN REVIEW OF HISTORY AND POLITICS.** v1-4; Jan. 1811-Oct. 1812.

61-64   **ANALECTIC MAGAZINE**
     Reel 61   v1-5; 1813-June 1815
     Reel 62   v6-9; July 1815-Feb. 1817
     Reel 63   v9-14; Mar. 1817-Dec. 1819
     Reel 64   nsv1-2; 1820

64   **ANALYST; OR MATHEMATICAL MUSEUM.** nsv1; 1814.

64   **ANNALS OF BENEFICENCE.** no1-2; Oct. 16-31, 1823.

64   **ANNALS OF NATURE.** v1; 1820.

65   **ANNUAL LAW REGISTER OF THE UNITED STATES.** v3-4; 1821-22.

65   **ARCHIVES OF USEFUL KNOWLEDGE.** v1-3; July 1810-Apr. 1813.

65   **ATHENAEUM.** v1, nos1-15; Feb. 12-Aug. 6, 1814.

66-69   **ATHENEUM; OR, SPIRIT OF THE ENGLISH MAGAZINES**
     Reel 66   v1-6, no6; Apr. 1, 1817-Dec. 15, 1819
     Reel 67   v6, no7-v10, no6; Jan. 1, 1820-Dec. 15, 1821
     Reel 68   v10, no7-v13; Jan. 1, 1822-Sept. 15, 1823
     Reel 69   v14-v18; Oct. 1, 1823-Dec. 15, 1825

70   **ATLANTIC MAGAZINE.** v1-2; May 1824-Apr. 1825

70   **BALANCE, AND STATE JOURNAL**
     Balance and New York State Journal; Balance and State Journal
     Reel 70   nsv2-s3v1; Jan. 2, 1810-Dec. 24, 1811

71   **BALTIMORE MEDICAL AND PHILOSOPHICAL LYCAEUM.** v1, no1-4; Jan./Mar.-Oct./Dec. 1811.

71   **BALTIMORE PHILOSOPHICAL JOURNAL AND REVIEW.** no1; July 1823.

71   **BALTIMORE REPERTORY OF PAPERS ON LITERARY AND OTHER TOPICS.** v1, nos1-6; Jan.-June 1811.

71-72   **BAPTIST MISSIONARY MAGAZINE**
     American Baptist Magazine and Missionary Intelligencer
     Reel 71   v1-2, no6; Jan. 1817-Nov. 1819
     Reel 72   v2, no7-v4; Jan. 1820-Nov. 1824

REEL

American Baptist Magazine
Reel 72   v5; Jan.-Dec. 1825

72   BEREAN; OR SCRIPTURE-SEARCHER. v2, no2; 1810.

72   BEREAN. A RELIGIOUS PUBLICATION. v1-2; Feb. 23, 1824-June 1826.

73   BOSTON JOURNAL OF PHILOSOPHY AND THE ARTS. v1-3; May 1823-Dec. 1826.

73   BOSTON MASONIC MIRROR
Masonic Mirror: and Mechanics' Intelligencer
Reel 73   v1-2, no1; Nov. 27, 1824-Dec. 31, 1825

73   BOSTON MEDICAL INTELLIGENCER
Medical Intelligencer; Containing Extracts . . .
Reel 73   v1-3, no33; Apr. 29, 1823-Dec. 27, 1825

74   BOSTON MONTHLY MAGAZINE. v1, nos1-7; June-Dec. 1825.

74   BOSTON SPECTATOR. v1, no1-61; Jan. 1, 1814-Feb. 25, 1815.

74   BOSTON WEEKLY MAGAZINE. v1-nsv1, no40; Oct. 12, 1816-Dec. 18, 1824.

74   BOWEN'S BOSTON NEWS-LETTER
City Record, and Boston News-Letter
Reel 74   v1, no1; Nov. 5, 1825
[Bowen's] Boston News-Letter and City Record
Reel 74   v1, no2; Dec. 31, 1825

75   CABINET. no1-10; Jan. 5-Mar. 23, 1811.

75   CAROLINA JOURNAL OF MEDICINE, SCIENCE AND AGRICULTURE. v1; Jan.-July 1825.

75   CAROLINA LAW REPOSITORY. v1-2; Mar. 1813-Sept. 1816.

75   CASKET. v1, no1-26; Dec. 7, 1811-May 30, 1812.

76   CHARLESTON GOSPEL MESSENGER AND PRO-TESTANT EPISCOPAL REGISTER
Gospel Messenger and Southern Christian Register
Reel 76   v1-2; 1824-1825

76   CHRISTIAN ADVOCATE. v1-3; Jan. 1823-1825.

77   CHRISTIAN BAPTIST. v1-3; Aug. 3, 1823-June 1825.

77   CHRISTIAN CHRONICLE. v1, nos1-16 and 18-26; Feb. 7-Dec. 26, 1818.

77-79   CHRISTIAN DISCIPLE AND THEOLOGICAL RE-VIEW
Christian Disciple
Reel 77   v1-5; May 1813-Dec. 1817
Reel 78   v6; Jan.-Dec. 1818
Christian Disciple and Theological Review
Reel 78   nsv1-4; Jan./Feb. 1819-Nov./Dec. 1822
Reel 79   nsv5; Jan./Feb.-Nov./Dec. 1823

79   CHRISTIAN EXAMINER
Christian Examiner and Theological Review
Reel 79   v1-2; Jan. 1824-1825

REEL

79-80   CHRISTIAN HERALD
Reel 79   v1-5; May 1818-Mar. 27, 1823
Reel 80   v6-8; May 8, 1823-Dec. 1825

80   CHRISTIAN INTELLIGENCER AND EASTERN CHRONICLE
Christian Intelligencer
Reel 80   v1-5; Sept. 1821-1825

80-81   CHRISTIAN JOURNAL, AND LITERARY REGISTER
Reel 80   v1-3; Jan. 22, 1817-1819
Reel 81   v4-9; 1820-Dec. 1825

81   CHRISTIAN MAGAZINE. v1-2; Jan. 1824-1825.

82   CHRISTIAN MESSENGER. v1, no1-5; Nov. 1815-Mar. 1816.

82   CHRISTIAN MESSENGER. v4; Nov. 7, 1818-May 1, 1819.

82   CHRISTIAN MESSENGER. v1-2; Aug. 7, 1819- July 21, 1821.

82   CHRISTIAN MIRROR. v1, no1-13; Jan. 22-Apr. 16, 1814.

82   CHRISTIAN MONITOR; A RELIGIOUS PERIODICAL WORK. v7-10; 1810-11.

83   CHRISTIAN MONITOR, AND RELIGIOUS INTELLI-GENCER. v1, no1-52; June 1812-June 26, 1813.

83   CHRISTIAN MONITOR. v1-7; Jan.-Mar. 1814-Oct.-Dec. 1818.

83-86   CHRISTIAN OBSERVER, CONDUCTED BY MEM-BERS OF THE ESTABLISHED CHURCH
Reel 83   v9; Jan.-Dec. 1810
Reel 84   v10-11, 13; Jan. 1811-Dec. 1814
Reel 85   v14-15; Jan.1815-Dec. 1816
Reel 86   v16-18; Jan. 1817-Dec. 1819

Unit 3

87   CHRISTIAN PHILANTHROPIST. v1, no1-50; May 14, 1822-1823.

87-88   CHRISTIAN REGISTER
Reel 87   v1, no1-v3, no42; Apr. 20, 1821-May 28, 1824
Reel 88   v3, no43-v4, no52; June 4, 1824-Dec. 31, 1825

88   CHRISTIAN REGISTER, AND MORAL AND THEO-LOGICAL REVIEW. v1-2, no1; July 1816-July 1817.

88-89   CHRISTIAN SECRETARY
Reel 88   v1-2, no103; Feb. 2, 1822-Jan. 17, 1824
Reel 89   s2, v1-2, no48; Feb. 3, 1824-Dec. 26, 1825

89   CHRISTIAN TELESCOPE AND UNIVERSALIST MISCELLANY. v1-2; Aug. 7, 1824-Dec. 31, 1825.

89   CHRISTIAN VISITANT. v1, no1-52; June 3, 1815-May 25, 1816.

REEL

90 CHRISTIANS MAGAZINE. v3-4; Jan. 1810-Dec. 1811.

90 CHRISTIAN'S WEEKLY MONITOR. v1-4; 1814-May 1818.

90 CHURCH RECORD. v1, no1-28; June 22, 1822-Mar. 8, 1823.

91 CHURCHMAN'S MAGAZINE. v7-nsv3; Jan./Dec. 1810-May/June 1815.

92 CLUB-ROOM. no1-4; Feb.-July 1820.

92 COBBETT'S POLITICAL REGISTER. v1-3, no7 (American) or v30, 33, 34, no7 (English); May 21, 1816 or Jan. 6, 1816-Jan. 10, 1818.

92-93 COHEN'S GAZETTE & LOTTERY REGISTER
    Cohen's Gazette and Lottery Register
    Reel 92   v1, no1-2; May 2-May 9, 1814
    Cohen's Lottery Gazette and Register
    Reel 92   v1, no3-v5, no15; May 16, 1814-June 9, 1819
    Reel 93   nsv1-v8, no23; Sept. 11, 1820-May 26, 1825
    Cohen's Gazette & Lottery Register
    Reel 93   v8, no24-32; June 9-Dec. 8, 1825

93-94 COLLECTIONS, HISTORICAL AND MISCELLANE-OUS, AND MONTHLY LITERARY JOURNAL
    Collections, Topographical, Historical & Biographical
    Reel 93   v1; Apr.-Dec. 1822
    Collections, Historical and Miscellaneous, and Monthly Literary Journal
    Reel 93   v2, no1-8; Jan.-Aug. 1823
    Reel 94   v2, no9-v3; Sept. 1823-Nov./Dec. 1824

94 COLLEGIAN. v1, no1-2; Jan.-Feb. 1819.

94 COLUMBIA MAGAZINE. v1; Sept. 1814-Aug. 1815.

95 MEMOIRS OF THE COLUMBIAN CHEMICAL SOCI-ETY OF PHILADELPHIA. v1; 1813.

95 COLUMBIAN HISTORIAN. v1, nos1-26; May 13, 1824-Mar. 11, 1825.

95-96 COLUMBIAN STAR
    Reel 95   v1-2; Feb. 2, 1822-Dec. 27, 1823
    Reel 96   v3-4; Jan. 3, 1824-Dec. 31, 1825

97 COMET. no1-13; Oct. 19, 1811-Jan. 11, 1812.

97-99 CONGREGATIONALIST AND HERALD OF GOSPEL LIBERTY
    Recorder
    Reel 97   v1; Jan. 3-Dec. 24, 1816
    Boston Recorder
    Reel 97   v2-3; Jan. 7, 1817-Dec. 26, 1818
    Reel 98   v4-7, no30; Jan. 2, 1818-July 27, 1822
    Reel 99   v7, no31-v9; Aug. 3, 1822-Dec. 25, 1824
    Recorder and Telegraph
    Reel 99   v10; Jan. 1-Dec. 30, 1825

100 COUNTRY COURIER. v1-2; June 3, 1816-Mar. 24, 1817.

REEL

100 CRITIC. no1-20; Jan. 29-May 10, 1820.

100 CYNICK. v1, nos1-12; Sept. 21-Dec. 1811.

100 GEOGRAPHICAL, HISTORICAL, AND STATISTICAL REPOSITORY. v1, no1; Sept. 1824.

100 DAWN. v1, no1-12; May 1-Nov.1, 1822.

100 DEBTORS' JOURNAL. v1, nos1, 4 & 6; Sept. 23, 1820-Feb. 24, 1821.

101 DIANA, AND LADIES' SPECTATOR. v1, nos1-4; 1822.

101 EMERALD. v1, no1-18; Nov. 3, 1810-Mar. 2, 1811.

101 EMPORIUM OF ARTS & SCIENCES. v1-nsv3; May 1812-Oct. 1814.

102 EUTERPEIAD. v1-nsv1, no2; Apr. 1820-June 1823.

102 EVANGELICAL GUARDIAN AND REVIEW. v1-2; May 1817-Apr. 1819.

103 EVANGELICAL LUMINARY. v1, no1-12; Jan.-Dec. 1824.

103 EVANGELICAL RECORDER. v1-2; Jan. 31, 1818-Sept. 8, 1821.

103 EVANGELICAL REPERTORY. v1, no1-12; July 15-1823-June 15, 1824.

103-104 EVANGELICAL WITNESS
    Reel 103   v1-2; Aug. 1822-July 1824
    Reel 104   v3; Jan. 1824-Dec. 1825

104 EVANGELISCHES MAGAZIN. v1-4; Oct. 1811-Sept. 1817.

104-106 EXAMINER
    Reel 104   v1, no1-6; Oct. 25-Dec. 5, 1813
    Reel 105   v1, no7-v5, no2; Jan. 1, 1814-Dec. 25, 1815
    Reel 106   v5, no3-21; Jan. 1-May 27, 1816

106 FARMER'S AND PLANTER'S FRIEND. no1-7; 1821.

106 FARRIER'S MAGAZINE. v1-2; 1818.

106 FLORIAD. v1, no1-15; May 24-Dec. 6, 1811.

106 FREEMASONS MAGAZINE AND GENERAL MIS-CELLANY. v1-2; Apr. 1811-Mar. 1812.

107 FRIEND. v1, no1-12; July 1815-June 1816.

107 FRIENDLY VISITOR. v1, no1-52; Jan. 1-Dec. 28, 1825.

107 GARLAND. v1, no1-3; June-Aug. 1825.

107 GAZETTEER. v1, no1-52; Jan. 7-Dec. 29, 1824.

107-108 GENERAL REPOSITORY AND REVIEW
    Reel 107   v1; Jan.-Apr. 1812
    Reel 108   v2-4; July 1812-Oct. 1813

108 GENIUS OF UNIVERSAL EMANCIPATION. v1-4 and v1 [i.e. v5], nos1-18; July 1821-Dec. 1825.

REEL

109   GLOBE. v1, no1-6; Jan.-June 1819.

109   GOSPEL ADVOCATE. v1-5; 1821-1825.

110   GOSPEL ADVOCATE AND IMPARTIAL INVESTI-GATOR. v1-3; 1823-1825.

110   GOSPEL INQUIRER. v1, no1-26; June 21, 1823-June 5, 1824.

110   GOSPEL PALLADIUM. v1, no6 and v2, no1; Aug. 22, 1823 and July 16, 1824.

110   GOSPEL VISITANT. v1-3; June 1811-July 1818.

111   GRIDIRON. v1, no1-26; Aug. 29, 1822-May 8, 1823.

111-112   GUARDIAN AND MONITOR
Guardian, or Youth's Religious Instructor
Reel 111   v1-5; Jan. 1819-Dec. 1823
Reel 112   v6; Jan.-Dec. 1824
Guardian and Monitor
Reel 112   v7; Jan.-Dec. 1825

112   HALCYON LUMINARY. v1; Jan.-Dec. 1812.

112   HARVARD LYCEUM. v1, no1-18; July 14, 1810-Mar. 9, 1811.

113   L'HEMISPHERE, JOURNAL FRANCAIS. v1-2, nos10-52; Jan. 13, 1810-Sept. 28, 1811.

113   HERALD OF LIFE AND IMMORTALITY. v1, no1-8; Jan. 1819-Oct. 1820.

113   HERALD OF SALVATION. v1-2, no25; Nov. 30, 1822-Feb. 26, 1825.

113   HERALD OF TRUTH. v1, no1-26; Mar. 17, 1825-May 18, 1826.

113-114   HISTORICAL REGISTER OF THE UNITED STATES. v1-4; 1812-1814.

114   HIVE. v1, nos1-20, 25-26; May 19-Dec. 11, 1810.

114   HUNTINGDON LITERARY MUSEUM, AND MONTH-LY MISCELLANY. v1, no1-12; Jan.-Dec. 1810.

115   IDLE MAN. v1-2; 1821-1822.

115   INTELLECTUAL REGALE. v1-2; Nov. 19, 1814-Dec. 30, 1815.

115   JOURNAL DES DAMES. v1-2; Jan.-Dec. 1810.

116   JOURNAL OF BELLES-LETTRES. v1, no1, 3, 5; Nov. 20, 1819-Feb. 26, 1820.

116-119   JOURNAL OF FOREIGN MEDICAL SCIENCE AND LITERATURE
Eclectic Repertory and Analytical Review
Reel 116   v1-5; Oct. 1810-Oct. 1815
Reel 117   v6-9; Jan. 1816-Oct. 1819
Reel 118   v10; Jan.-Oct. 1820
Journal of Foreign Medical Science and Literature
Reel 118   nsv1-3; Jan. 1821-Oct. 1823
Reel 119   nsv4; Jan.-Oct. 1824

119   JOURNAL OF JURISPRUDENCE. v1; 1821.

REEL

119   JOURNAL OF MUSICK. v1, no1-24; 1810.

120   JOURNAL OF SCIENCE AND THE ARTS. v1-5; 1817-1818.

121   JOURNAL OF THE LAW-SCHOOL, AND OF THE MOOT-COURT ATTACHED TO IT, AT NEEDHAM, IN VIRGINIA. v1; 1822.

121   JUVENILE GAZETTE. v1, no1-3; Nov. 1819-Jan. 1820.

121   JUVENILE MAGAZINE. no1, 3, 4; May 1811-Aug. 1813.

121   JUVENILE MIRROR. v1, no4; Mar. 1812.

121   JUVENILE REPOSITORY. v1, no1; July 1811.

121-122   LADIES' LITERARY CABINET
Reel 121   v1-nsv4; May 15, 1819-Nov. 3, 1821
Reel 122   nsv5-7; Nov. 10, 1821-Dec. 21, 1822

122   LADIES MAGAZINE. v1, no1-12; Mar. 1823-June 1824.

122   LADIES MUSEUM. v1, no1-23; July 16-Dec. 31, 1825.

122   LADIES PORT FOLIO. v1 (nos1-25); Jan. 1-June 17, 1820 and nsv2, no3; July 8, 1820.

122-123   LATTER DAY LUMINARY
Reel 122   v1; Feb. 1818-Nov. 1819
Reel 123   v2-6; Feb. 1820-Dec. 1825

123   LAY-MAN'S MAGAZINE. v1, no1-51; Nov. 16, 1815-Nov. 7, 1816.

123   LIBERAL CHRISTIAN. v1; Jan. 11, 1823-Mar. 6, 1824.

124-125   LITERARY AND EVANGELICAL MAGAZINE
Virginia Evangelical and Literary Magazine
Reel 124   v1-3; Jan. 1818-Dec. 1820
Evangelical and Literary Magazine and Missionary Chronicle
Reel 124   v4; Jan.-Dec. 1821
Evangelical and Literary Magazine
Reel 125   v5-6; Jan. 1822-Dec. 1823
Literary and Evangelical Magazine
Reel 125   v7-8; Jan. 1824-Dec. 1825

126   LITERARY AND PHILOSOPHICAL REPERTORY. v1-2; Apr. 1812-May 1817.

126   LITERARY AND SCIENTIFIC REPOSITORY. v1-4; June 1820-May 1822.

Unit 4

127   CHURCHMAN'S REPOSITORY FOR THE EASTERN DIOCESE. v1, no1-6; July 1-Dec. 1, 1820.

127   CINCINNATI LITERARY GAZETTE. v1-4; Jan. 1, 1824-Oct. 29, 1825.

REEL

127-129 CONNECTICUT EVANGELICAL MAGAZINE AND
RELIGIOUS INTELLIGENCER
Reel 127   nsv1; Jan.-Dec. 1808
Reel 128   nsv2-6; Jan. 1809-Dec. 1813
Reel 129   nsv7-8; Jan. 1814-Dec. 1815

129 EPISCOPAL MAGAZINE. v1-2; Jan. 1820-Dec. 1821.

129-130 EVANGELICAL RECORD, AND WESTERN REVIEW
Reel 129   v1; Jan.-Dec. 1812
Reel 130   v2; Jan.-Dec. 1813

130 EVANGELICAL REPOSITORY. v1, nos1-12; Jan.-
Dec. 1816.

130 GEOGRAPHICAL, HISTORICAL, AND STATISTICAL
REPOSITORY. v1, no1-2; Sept.-Oct. 1824.

130 GERMAN CORRESPONDENT. v1, no1-6; Jan. 1820-
Jan. 1821.

130 GOSPEL TRUMPET. v2, nos1-12; Jan.-Dec. 1823.

130 ISRAEL'S ADVOCATE. v1-3; Jan. 1823-Dec. 1825.

131 JEW. v1-2; Mar. 1823-Mar. 1825.

131 JOURNAL INUTILE. v1-2 (no. 9-20, 22-26); Jan. 20-
May 19, 1825.

131 LITERARY COMPANION. v1, nos1-13; June 16-
Sept. 8, 1821.

131 LITERARY GAZETTE. v1, no1-52; Jan. 6-Dec. 29,
1821.

131 LITERARY MISCELLANY. v1, nos1-4; May-Aug.
1811.

132 LITERARY PAMPHLETEER. no1-6; 1823.

132 LYRE; OR, NEW YORK MUSICAL JOURNAL. v1;
June 1, 1824-May 1, 1825.

132 MASONIC CASKET. v2; July 1824-Nov. 1825.

132 LE MEDIATEUR. v1, no1-21; Apr. 2-Aug. 8, 1814.

132 MEDICAL REFORMER. v1, no1-6; Jan. 1-June 1,
1823.

132-134 MEDICAL REPOSITORY OF ORIGINAL ESSAYS AND
INTELLIGENCE
Reel 132   v13-15; 1809-1812
Reel 133   v16-20; 1813-1820
Reel 134   v21-23; 1821-1824

135-136 METHODIST REVIEW
Methodist Magazine
Reel 135   v1-5; Jan. 1818-Dec. 1822
Reel 136   v6-8; Jan. 1823-Dec. 1825

136 MICROSCOPE AND GENERAL ADVERTISER
Microscope
Reel 136   v1, nos1-26; Apr. 17-Oct. 23, 1824
Microscope and General Advertiser
Reel 136   v1, nos27-52, v2, nos1-20; Oct 30,
1824-Sept. 10, 1825

REEL

136 MILITARY MONITOR, AND AMERICAN REGISTER
Military Monitor
Reel 136   v1, no1-52; Aug. 17, 1812-Aug. 23,
1813
Reel 136   v2, no1-2; 4, 26, 31-32; Aug. 28, 1813-
Apr. 2, 1814
Geographical and Military Museum
Reel 136   v1, no5 and 8-13; Mar. 26-May 23,
1814

137 MILITIA REPORTER. v1; 1810.

137 MINERVA. v1-nsv3; Apr. 6, 1822-Sept. 3, 1825.

138 MIRROR OF LITERATURE, AMUSEMENT AND
INSTRUCTION. v5-6, 10; 1823-25.

139 MISCELLANEOUS MAGAZINE. v1; Jan.-Dec. 1824.

139-142 MISSIONARY HERALD AT HOME AND ABROAD
Panoplist, and Missionary Magazine
Reel 139   v2 (i.e., v5), no8-v5 (i.e., v8); Jan.
1810-May 1813
Reel 140   v9-12, no9; June 1813-Sept. 1816
Reel 141   v12, no10-v13; Oct. 1816-Dec. 1817
Panoplist, and Missionary Herald
Reel 141   v14-15; Jan. 1818-Dec. 1819
Reel 142   v16; 1820
Missionary Herald
Reel 142   v17-21; 1821-1825

143 MONITOR. v1-2; Jan. 1823-Dec. 1824.

143-144 MONTHLY ANTHOLOGY, AND BOSTON REVIEW
Reel 143   v8; Jan.-June 1810
Reel 144   v9-10; July 1810-June 1811

144-145 MONTHLY JOURNAL OF MEDICINE
Reel 144   v1-3, no4; Jan. 1823-Apr. 1824
Reel 145   v3, no1-v6; Jan. 1824-Dec. 1825

145 MONTHLY MAGAZINE AND LITERARY JOURNAL.
v1-2; May 1812-Apr. 1813.

146 MONTHLY RECORDER. v1, no1-5; Apr.-Aug. 1813.

146 MONTHLY SCIENTIFIC JOURNAL. v1, no1-6; Feb.-
July 1818.

146 MONTHLY VISITANT. v1, no1-6; July-Dec. 1816.

146 MORAL ADVOCATE. v1-3; Mar. 1821-1824.

146 MORALIST. v1, no1-11; May 27-Nov. 7, 1814.

146-148 MUSEUM OF FOREIGN LITERATURE, SCIENCE,
AND ART
Reel 146   v1; July-Dec. 1822
Reel 147   v2-4; Jan. 1823-June 1824
Reel 148   v5-7; July 1824-Dec. 1825

149 NATIONAL GOVERNMENT JOURNAL, AND REGIS-
TER OF OFFICIAL PAPERS
National Journal (extra)
Reel 149   v1, nos1-30; Dec 3, 1823-June 5, 1824
National Government Journal and Register of Official
Papers
Reel 149   v1, nos31-55; v2, nos1-22; June 9-
Nov. 29, 1825

REEL

149   NATIONAL MUSEUM AND WEEKLY GAZETTE. v1, nos1, 3-4, 7-16; Nov. 13, 1813-Nov. 12, 1814.

149   NEW ENGLAND FARMER. v1-4, no20; Aug. 1822-Dec. 1825.

150-152   NEW-ENGLAND GALAXY
New England Galaxy and Masonic Magazine
Reel 150   v1-3 (no1-116); Oct. 10, 1817-Dec. 31, 1819
Reel 151   v3 (no117-156); Jan. 7-Oct. 6, 1820
New England Galaxy and United States Literary Advertiser
Reel 151   v4-5; Oct. 13, 1820-Dec. 27, 1822
Reel 152   v6-8; Jan. 3, 1823-Dec. 30, 1825

153-157   NEW-ENGLAND JOURNAL OF MEDICINE AND SURGERY
Reel 153   v1-3; Jan. 1812-Oct. 1814
Reel 154   v4-6; Jan. 1815-Oct. 1817
Reel 155   v7-9; Jan. 1818-Oct. 1820
Reel 156   v10-12; Jan. 1821-Oct. 1823
Reel 157   v13-14; Jan. 1824-Oct. 1825

157   NEW ENGLAND MISSIONARY INTELLIGENCER. v1, no1-3; Jan.-Oct. 1819.

157   NEW-ENGLAND MISSIONARY MAGAZINE. no1-4; 1815-1816.

157   NEW JERUSALEM CHURCH REPOSITORY. v1, no1-8; Jan. 1817-Dec. 1818.

158   NEW JERSEY AND PENNSYLVANIA AGRICULTURAL MONTHLY. v1; May, Oct. and Nov. 1825.

158   NEW JERSEY MONTHLY MAGAZINE. v1, no1; Apr. 1825.

158   NEW JERUSALEM MISSIONARY AND INTELLECTUAL REPOSITORY. v1; May 1823-Apr. 1824.

158   NEW JERUSALEM RECORD. v1, no1; July 1820.

158-161   NEW MONTHLY MAGAZINE AND LITERARY JOURNAL
Reel 158   v1-2; Jan.-Dec. 1821
Reel 159   v3-5; Jan. 1822-June 1823
Reel 160   v6-8; July 1823-Dec. 1824
Reel 161   v9-10; Jan.-Dec. 1825

161-162   NEW-YORK LITERARY JOURNAL
Belles-Lettres Repository and Monthly Magazine
Reel 161   v1; May-Oct. 1819
Reel 162   v2; Nov. 1819-Apr. 1820
New-York Literary Journal and Belles-Lettres Repository
Reel 162   v3-4; May 1820-Apr. 1821

162   NEW-YORK MAGAZINE AND GENERAL REPOSITORY. v1, nos1-3; May 1-July 1, 1814.

162   NEW-YORK MEDICAL AND PHILOSOPHICAL JOURNAL AND REVIEW. v2-3; 1810-1811.

163-164   NEW YORK MEDICAL AND PHYSICAL JOURNAL
Reel 163   v1-3; Jan. 1822-Dec. 1824
Reel 164   v4; Jan.-Dec. 1825

164   NEW YORK MEDICAL MAGAZINE. v1, nos1-2; Jan. 1814-Jan. 1815.

REEL

164-165   NEW-YORK MIRROR
Reel 164   v1-2, no22; Aug. 2, 1823-Dec. 25, 1824
Reel 165   v2, no23-v3, no23; Jan. 1-Dec. 31, 1825

165   NEW YORK MONTHLY CHRONICLE OF MEDICINE AND SURGERY. v1, nos1-12; July 1824-June 1825.

165   NEW-YORK MONTHLY MAGAZINE. Jan. 1-Mar. 1, 1824.

166   NEW YORK RELIGIOUS CHRONICLE. v2-3; 1824-1825.

166   NEW YORK REVIEW AND ATHENEUM MAGAZINE. v1-2; June-Dec. 1825.

166   NEW YORK TRACT MAGAZINE AND CHRISTIAN MISCELLANY. v1, no11; Nov. 1824.

Unit 5

167-177   NILES' NATIONAL REGISTER
Weekly Register
Reel 167   v1-3; Sept. 7, 1811-Feb. 27, 1813
Reel 168   v4-6; Mar. 6, 1813-Aug. 27, 1814
Niles Weekly Register
Reel 169   v7-8; Sept. 10, 1814-Aug. 26, 1815
Reel 170   v9-11; Sept. 2, 1815-Feb. 22, 1817
Reel 171   v12-14; Mar. 1, 1817-Aug. 22, 1818
Reel 172   v15-16; Aug. 29, 1818-Aug. 21, 1819
Reel 173   v17-19; Sept. 4, 1819-Feb. 24, 1821
Reel 174   v20-22; Mar. 3, 1821-Aug. 24, 1822
Reel 175   v23-25; Sept. 7, 1822-Feb. 24, 1824
Reel 176   v26-28; Mar. 6, 1824-Aug. 27, 1825
Reel 177   v29; Sept. 2-Dec. 31, 1825

177-183   NORTH AMERICAN REVIEW
North-American Review and Miscellaneous Journal
Reel 177   v1-2; May 1815-Mar. 1816
Reel 178   v3-5; May 1816-Sept. 1817
Reel 179   v6-9; Nov. 1817-Sept. 1819
Reel 180   v10-12; Jan. 1820-Apr. 1821
North American Review
Reel 181   v13-15; July 1821-Oct. 18, 1822
Reel 182   v16-18; Jan. 1823-Apr. 1824
Reel 183   v19-21; July 1824-Oct. 1825

184   PARTERRE. v1-2; June 15, 1816-June 28, 1817.

184   PERIODICAL SKETCHES. no1; 1820.

184-185   PHILADELPHIA JOURNAL OF THE MEDICAL AND PHYSICAL SCIENCES
Reel 184   v1-5; Jan. 1820-1822
Reel 185   v6-14; 1823-Dec. 1827

186   PHILADELPHIA MAGAZINE, AND WEEKLY REPERTORY. v1, nos1-36; Jan.-Nov. 7, 1818.

186   PHILADELPHIA MEDICAL MUSEUM. nsv1; 1810.

186   PHILADELPHIA MUSEUM. v1, no1; Jan. 1824.

186   PHILADELPHIA REPERTORY. v1-2; May 5, 1810-May 16, 1812.

REEL

187   PHILADELPHIA UNIVERSALIST MAGAZINE AND CHRISTIAN MESSENGER. v1-2; Aug. 1821-July 1823.

187-188   PHILANTHROPIST, A WEEKLY JOURNAL CONTAINING ESSAYS
Philanthropist
Reel 187   v1, no7, 13-16; Oct. 24, Dec. 5-26, 1817
Reel 187   [n.s.] v1-3, Dec. 11, 1818-Apr. 26, 1820
Reel 188   [n.s.] v4-7; Apr. 29, 1820-Apr. 27, 1822

188   PILGRIM, OR MONTHLY VISITOR. v1; May 8, 1822-Apr. 8, 1823.

189   PILOT
National Pilot
Reel 189   v1-2, no78; Sept. 6, 1821-Mar. 13, 1823
Pilot
Reel 189   v2, no79-v3; Mar. 20, 1823-Sept. 11, 1824

189   PIONEER, CONSISTING OF ESSAYS, LITERARY, MORAL AND THEOLOGICAL. v1, nos1-7; Feb. 28-Oct. 8, 1812.

190-191   PLOUGH BOY, AND JOURNAL OF THE BOARD OF AGRICULTURE
Plough Boy
Reel 190   v1, no1-33; June 5, 1819-Jan. 15, 1820
Plough Boy, and Journal of the Board of Agriculture
Reel 190   v1, no34-v3, no31; Jan. 22, 1820-Dec. 29, 1821
Reel 191   v3, no32-v4, no51; Jan. 5, 1822-July 15, 1823

191   POLITICAL ECONOMIST; AN EMPORIUM OF STATISTICAL PHILOSOPHY. v1, no1; Oct. 1824.

191   POLITICAL ECONOMIST. no1-13; Jan. 24-May 1, 1824.

191-192   POLYANTHOS
Polyanthos
Reel 191   nsv1-2; Feb.-Sept. 1812
Polyanthos Enlarged
Reel 191   s3v1; Oct. 1812-Mar. 1813
Reel 192   s3v2-4; Apr. 1813-Sept. 1814

192-193   PORTICO
Reel 192   v1-2; Jan.-Dec. 1816
Reel 193   v3-5; Jan. 1817-Apr./June 1818

193   PORTSMOUTH WEEKLY MAGAZINE. v1, nos1-46, 48-50, 52-54; July 1, 1824-June 30, 1825.

193-194   PRESBYTERIAN MAGAZINE
Reel 193   v1; Jan.-Dec. 1821
Reel 194   v2; Jan.-Dec. 1822

194   PROVIDENCE THEOLOGICAL MAGAZINE. v1, no1; Sept. 1821.

194-196   QUARTERLY CHRISTIAN SPECTATOR
Christian Spectator
Reel 194   v1-2; 1819-Dec. 1820

REEL

Reel 195   v3-4; Jan. 1821-Dec. 1822
Reel 196   v5-7, no12; Jan. 1, 1823-Dec. 1, 1825

197   RADICAL. no1-2; 1821.

197   RECREATIVE MAGAZINE. v1; 1822.

197   REFLECTOR. no1; Sept. 1821.

197   RELIGIOUS AND LITERARY REPOSITORY. v1, nos1-24; Jan. 15-Dec. 23, 1820.

197   RELIGIOUS ENQUIRER. v1, no1; Oct. 1811.

197-198   RELIGIOUS INFORMER
Religious Informer
Reel 197   v1-2; July 20, 1819-Dec. 1821
Religious Informer, and Free-Will Baptist Register
Reel 197   v3; Jan.-Dec. 1822
Religious Informer
Reel 198   v4-6; Jan. 1823-Dec. 1825

198   RELIGIOUS INSTRUCTOR. v1; Sept. 1810-Aug. 1811.

198-202   RELIGIOUS INTELLIGENCER
Reel 198   v1, nos1-24; June-Nov. 9, 1816
Reel 199   v1, no25-v4, no30; Nov. 1816-Dec. 25, 1819
Reel 200   v4, no31-v6; Jan. 1, 1820-May 25, 1822
Reel 201   v7-8; June 1, 1822-May 29, 1824
Reel 202   v9-10, no31; June 5, 1824-Dec. 31, 1825

202   RELIGIOUS MAGAZINE. v1-2; Jan. 1811-Sept. 22, 1822.

203   RELIGIOUS MISCELLANY. v1-3; Jan. 17, 1823-July 2, 1824.

203   RELIGIOUS MUSEUM. v1; July 15, 1818-July 21, 1819.

204   REMEMBRANCER. v1, no1-4, 6; Apr. 8-May 15, 1820.

204   RHODE ISLAND BAPTIST. v1, nos1-12; Oct. 1823-Sept. 1824.

204   RHODE ISLAND LITERARY REPOSITORY. v1, nos1-12; Apr. 1814-Mar. 1815.

204   ROANOKE RELIGIOUS CORRESPONDENT. v1-2; Aug. 1821-Dec. 1823.

204-205   ROBINSON'S MAGAZINE
Reel 204   v1; July 18-Dec. 30, 1818
Reel 205   v2; Jan. 2-June 26, 1819

205   ROCHESTER MAGAZINE, AND THEOLOGICAL REVIEW. v1, nos1-12; Jan.-Dec. 1824.

205   RURAL MAGAZINE AND FARMER'S MONTHLY MUSEUM. v1, nos1-6; Feb.-July 1819.

205   RURAL MAGAZINE AND LITERARY EVENING FIRE-SIDE. v1, nos1-12; Jan.-Dec. 1820.

205   SABBATH SCHOOL REPOSITORY AND TEACHER'S ASSISTANT. v1, nos1-12; Jan.-Dec. 1823.

REEL

205   ST. TAMMANYS MAGAZINE. v1, nos1-5; Nov. 9-Dec. 17, 1821.

205   SATIRIST
Satirist
    Reel 205   no1-10; Jan. 16-Apr. 11, 1812
Boston Satirist, or Weekly Museum
    Reel 205   no11-13; Apr. 20-May 9, 1812

206   THEOLOGICAL REVIEW AND GENERAL REPOSITORY OF RELIGIOUS AND MORAL INFORMATION. v1, nos1-4; Jan.-Oct. 1822.

206   UNITARIAN MISCELLANY AND CHRISTIAN MONITOR. v1-6; Jan. 1821-Dec. 1824.

Unit 6

207   CHEAP REPOSITORY. nos1-42; 1800.

208-209   CHRISTIAN OBSERVER, CONDUCTED BY MEMBERS OF THE ESTABLISHED CHURCH
    Reel 208   v19-20, 22; Jan. 1820-Dec. 1822
    Reel 209   v23-25; Jan. 1823-Dec. 1825

210   CHURCHMAN'S MAGAZINE. s3v1-5; Jan. 1821-Mar. 1827.

210a   CIRCULAR
Christian Repository
    Reel 210a   v1-2; Apr. 14, 1821-Apr. 2, 1824
Circular
    Reel 210a   v3; Apr. 9, 1824-Apr. 29, 1825

211   NEW YORK CITY HALL RECORDER. v1-6; Jan. 1817-Jan. 1822.

211   FRIEND OF PEACE. v1, nos1-7; 1815-?

211   INQUISITOR. v1, no1-v2, no4; Dec. 30, 1818-Jan. 19, 1820.

212   JUVENILE PORT-FOLIO. v1-4; Oct. 17, 1812-Dec. 1816.

212   LADIES' VISITOR. v1, no1-13; May 24, 1819-Apr. 18, 1820.

212-213   LADY'S MISCELLANY
Lady's Weekly Miscellany
    Reel 212   v10, no11-v11, no2; Jan. 6-May 5, 1810
Lady's Miscellany; or the Weekly Visitor...
    Reel 212   v11, no3-v12, no10; May 12-Dec. 29, 1810
    Reel 213   v12, no11-v15, no26; Jan. 5, 1811-Oct. 17, 1812

213   LITERARY AND MUSICAL MAGAZINE
Ladies Literary Museum; or, Weekly Repository
    Reel 213   v1-2; July 5, 1817-July 13, 1818
Lady's and Gentleman's Weekly Museum and Philadelphia Reporter
    Reel 213   v3, no1-10; July 27-Sept. 30, 1818
Ladys and Gentlemans Weekly Literary Museum and Musical Magazine
    Reel 213   v3, no11-19; Jan. 1-Mar. 1, 1819

REEL

Literary and Musical Magazine
    Reel 213   v3, no20-v4, no38 (i.e., no24); Mar. 8, 1819-June 9, 1820

214   MASONIC MISCELLANY AND LADIES LITERARY MAGAZINE. v1-2; 1821-1823.

214-215   MASSACHUSETTS AGRICULTURAL REPOSITORY AND JOURNAL
    Reel 214   v1-2; 1801-1810
    Reel 214   v3-5; 1813-1819
    Reel 215   v6-8; 1820-1825

216   MASSACHUSETTS BAPTIST MISSIONARY MAGAZINE. v2, no9-v4, no12; Mar. 1810-Dec. 1816.

216   MASSACHUSETTS WATCHMAN. v1, no8-12; Jan.-May 1810.

216   MEDICAL & SURGICAL REGISTER. v1, pts1-2; 1818-1820.

217   MEDICAL NEWS-PAPER. v1, nos1-26; Jan. 1, 1822-Feb 15, 1824.

217   MERRIMACK MAGAZINE. v1, nos1-7; Jan. 1-July 1825.

217   MESSENGER OF PEACE. v1, no1-26; Mar. 13, 1824-Feb. 26, 1825.

217   METHODIST RECORDER
Mutual Rights and Methodist Protestant
    Reel 217   v1; Aug. 1824-July 1825

217   MICROSCOPE. v1-2, nos1-50; Mar. 21-Sept. 8, 1820.

217   MICROSCOPE
Microscope, and Independent Examiner
    Reel 217   v2; Mar. 1, 1823
    Reel 217   v3, no27 & 42; Oct. 11, 1823 & Jan. 24, 1824
Microscope
    Reel 217   v4, no1, 28, 33, 48; Mar. 13, 1824-Feb. 5, 1825
    Reel 217   v5, no10; May 14, 1825

218   MIRROR OF TASTE AND DRAMATIC CENSOR. v1-4; Jan. 1810-Dec. 1811.

218   MISCELLANEOUS CABINET. v1, nos1-26; July 12, 1823-Jan. 3, 1824.

218   NEW ENGLAND LITERARY HERALD. no2, Jan. 1810.

218   OBSERVER. no1-28; Oct. 14, 1810-Apr. 21, 1811.

218   ODD FELLOWS' MAGAZINE
    Reel 218   v1, nos1-2; Oct. 1, 1825-Jan. 1, 1826
    Reel 218   new series (Manchester, Eng.); Mar.-June, 1828

218   OHIO MISCELLANEOUS MUSEUM. v1, nos1-5; Jan.-May 1822.

219   OLIO, A LITERARY AND MISCELLANEOUS PAPER. v1-2, no1; Jan. 27, 1813-Feb. 5, 1814.

219   OMNIUM GATHERUM. v1, nos3-12; Jan.-Oct. 1810.

REEL

219   PARLOUR COMPANION. v1-3, no34; 1817-Aug. 21,
         1819.

219-220 PITTSBURGH RECORDER
         Reel 219   v1; Jan. 25, 1822-Jan. 17, 1823
         Reel 220   v2; Jan. 24, 1823-Jan. 23, 1824

220-228 PORT FOLIO
         Reel 220   s3v3-4; Jan.-Dec. 1810
         Reel 221   s3v5-7; Jan. 1811-June 1812
         Reel 222   s3v8-s4v2; July 1812-Dec. 1813
         Reel 223   s4v3-5; Jan. 1814-June 1815
         Reel 224   s4v6-s5v3; July 1815-June 1817
         Reel 225   s5v4-7; July 1817-June 1819
         Reel 226   s5v8-11; July 1819-1821
         Reel 227   s5v12-15; 1821-1823
         Reel 228   s5v16-20; 1823-1825

229   PRINCETON REVIEW
         Biblical Repertory
         Reel 229   v1; 1825.

229-232 QUARTERLY CHRISTIAN SPECTATOR
         Christian Spectator
         Reel 229   v8-nsv2; Jan. 1826-Dec. 1828
         Quarterly Christian Spectator
         Reel 230   s3v1-4; Mar. 1829-Dec. 1832
         Reel 231   s3v5-7; Mar. 1833-Dec. 1835
         Reel 232   s3v8-10; Mar. 1836-Dec. 1838

233   REFORMER AND CHRISTIAN
         Reformer
         Reel 233   v1-6; Jan. 1, 1820-Dec. 1, 1825

234   RELIGIOUS INQUIRER. v1-5; Nov. 10, 1821-Dec. 24,
         1825.

234-235 RELIGIOUS INTELLIGENCER . . .
         Reel 234   v10, no32-v11; Jan. 1826-May 1827
         Reel 235   v12-14; June 1827-May 1830

236-237 SATURDAY EVENING POST
         Reel 236   v1, no3-v3, no51; Aug. 18, 1821-Dec.
                       18, 1824
         Reel 237   v4, no1-53; Jan.-Dec. 1825

237-238 SATURDAY MAGAZINE
         Philadelphia Register and National Recorder
         Reel 237   v1; Jan. 2-June 26, 1819
         National Recorder
         Reel 237   v2-4; July 3, 1819-Dec. 30, 1820
         Reel 238   v5; Jan. 6-June 30, 1821
         Saturday Magazine
         Reel 238   nsv1-2; July 7, 1821-June 29, 1822

239   SCIENTIFIC JOURNAL. v1, nos1-10; Feb. 1818-
         Jan. 1820.

239   SCOURGE. v1, no1-16; Aug. 10-Dec. 28, 1811.

239-240 SELECT REVIEWS OF LITERATURE
         Select Reviews, and Spirit of the Foreign Magazines
         Reel 239   v3-5; Jan. 1810-June 1811
         Select Reviews of Literature, and Spirit of Foreign
         Magazines
         Reel 239   v6; July-Dec. 1811
         Reel 240   v7-8; Jan.-Dec. 1812

240   SPIRIT OF THE FORUM. no1; Apr. 16,
         1817.

240   SPIRITUAL MAGAZINE. v1, no1-2; Jan. 1813-May
         1814.

240   SUNDAY VISITANT. v1-2; Jan. 3, 1818-Dec. 25, 1819.

241   THEOLOGICAL REPERTORY, AND CHURCHMAN'S
         GUIDE
         Washington Theological Repertory
         Reel 241   v1-7; Aug. 1819-July 1826

242   TRUTH. no1-2; Sept.-Oct. 1819.

242   UNITARIAN DEFENDANT. no1-11; June 22-Nov. 16,
         1822.

242   UNITED STATES LITERARY GAZETTE. v1-4; Apr.
         1824-Sept. 1826.

243   UNITED STATES MAGAZINE AND LITERARY AND
         POLITICAL REPOSITORY. nsv1, no1; Jan. 1823.

243   THE UNITED STATES' NAVAL CHRONICLE. v1;
         1824.

243-244 UNIVERSALIST
         Universalist Magazine
         Reel 243   v1-4, no1; July 3, 1819-June 29, 1822
         Reel 244   v4, no1-v7; June 29, 1822-June 17,
                       1826

244   UTICA CHRISTIAN MAGAZINE. v1-3; July 1813-
         June 1816.

245   UTICA CHRISTIAN REPOSITORY. v1-5; Jan. 1822-
         Dec. 1826.

246   VACCINE INQUIRER. no1-6; Feb. 1822-June 1824.

246   VERMONT BAPTIST MISSIONARY MAGAZINE. v1,
         no1-6; Jan. 1811-Apr. 1812.

246   VILLAGE MUSEUM. v1, nos1-6; Oct. 9-Nov. 20,
         1820.

246   VILLAGER. v1, no1-6; Apr.-June 1819.

246   VISITOR. v1, no25-26, v2, no1-23; Jan. 13-Aug. 18,
         1810.

246   WASHINGTON QUARTERLY MAGAZINE OF ARTS,
         SCIENCE AND LITERATURE. v1, no1-2; July 1823-
         Apr. 1824.

246   WATCHMAN. no1; 1819.

246-248 WATCHMAN-EXAMINER
         Christian Watchman
         Reel 246   v1-nsv2, no3; May 1819-Dec. 1820
         Reel 247   nsv2, no4-v5, no20; Jan. 1821-Apr.
                       1824
         Reel 248   v5, no21-v7; May 1824-Dec. 1826

248   WEEKLY MONITOR. v1, no1-3; June 4-Sept. 20, 1817.

248-250 WEEKLY RECORDER
         Reel 248   v1; July 5, 1814-June 1815
         Reel 249   v2-4; July 1815-July 1818
         Reel 250   v5-7; Aug. 1818-Oct. 6, 1821

251   WEEKLY VISITOR. v1-3, no3; May 12, 1810-May 25,
         1811.

REEL

251   WESLEYAN REPOSITORY. v1-3; Apr. 12, 1821-
Apr. 1824.

252   WESTERN CHRISTIAN MONITOR. v1, no1-12; Jan.-
Dec. 1816.

252   WESTERN GLEANER. v1-2, no4; Dec. 1813-Sept.
1814.

252   WESTERN LADIES' CASKET. v1, no5; Feb 1, 1824.

252   WESTERN MINERVA. v1, no1; Jan. 1820.

252-253   WESTERN NEW YORK BAPTIST MAGAZINE
    Vehicle
    Reel 252   v1; May 1814-Nov. 1816
    Western New York Baptist Magazine
    Reel 252   v2; Feb. 1817-Nov. 1819
    Reel 253   v3-4; Feb. 1820-Aug. 1825

253   WESTERN REVIEW AND MISCELLANEOUS MAGA-
ZINE. v1-4, no6; Aug. 1819-July 1821.

Unit 7

254-269   NILES' NATIONAL REGISTER
    Niles Weekly Register
    Reel 254   v30-33; Mar. 4, 1826-Feb. 23, 1828
    Reel 255   v34-37; Mar. 1, 1828-Feb. 20, 1830
    Reel 256   v38-40; Feb. 27, 1830-Aug. 27, 1831
    Reel 257   v41-43; Sept. 3, 1831-Feb. 23, 1833
    Reel 258   v44-47; Mar. 2, 1833-Feb. 28, 1835
    Reel 259   v48-50; Mar. 7, 1835-Aug. 27, 1836
    Reel 260   v51-52; Sept. 3, 1836-Aug. 26, 1837
    Reel 261   v53-54; Sept. 2, 1837-Aug. 25, 1838
    Reel 262   v55-56; Sept. 1, 1838-Aug. 24, 1839
    Reel 263   v57-58; Aug. 31, 1839-Aug. 29, 1840
    Reel 264   v59-60; Sept. 5, 1840-Aug. 28, 1841
    Reel 265   v61-64; Sept 4, 1841-Aug. 20, 1843
    Reel 266   v65-68; Sept. 2, 1843-Aug. 30, 1845
    Reel 267   v69-70; Sept. 6, 1845-Aug. 29, 1846
    Reel 268   v71-73; Sept. 5, 1846-Feb. 26, 1848
    Reel 269   v74-76; July 5, 1848-Sept. 28, 1849

270-281   NORTH AMERICAN REVIEW
    North American Review
    Reel 270   v22-25; Jan. 1826-Oct. 1827
    Reel 271   v26-29; Jan. 1828-Oct. 1829
    Reel 272   v30-33; Jan. 1830-Oct. 1831
    Reel 273   v34-37; Jan. 1832-Oct. 1833
    Reel 274   v38-41; Jan. 1834-Oct. 1835
    Reel 275   v42-45; Jan. 1836-Oct. 1837
    Reel 276   v46-49; Jan. 1838-Oct. 1839
    Reel 277   v50-53; Jan. 1840-Oct. 1841
    Reel 278   v54-57; Jan. 1842-Oct. 1843
    Reel 279   v58-61; Jan. 1844-Oct. 1845
    Reel 280   v62-66; Jan. 1846-Apr. 1848
    Reel 281   v67-71; July 1848-Oct. 1850

282-287   FRANKLIN INSTITUTE, PHILADELPHIA.
JOURNAL . . .
    Franklin Journal, and American Mechanics Magazine
    Reel 282   v1-4; Jan. 1826-Dec. 1827
    Journal of the Franklin Institute
    Reel 282   v5-9; Jan. 1828-June 1830
    Reel 283   v10-18; July 1830-Dec. 1834
    Reel 284   v19-26; Jan. 1835-Dec. 1838
    Reel 285   v27-35; Jan. 1839-June 1843

REEL

    Reel 286   v36-44; July 1843-Dec. 1847
    Reel 287   v45-52; Jan. 1848-Dec. 1851

288-292   MONTHLY LAW REPORTER
    Law Reporter
    Reel 288   v1-7; Mar. 10, 1838-Apr. 1845
    Reel 289   v8-10; May 1845-Apr. 1848
    Monthly Law Reporter
    Reel 289   v11-13; May 1848-Apr. 1851
    Reel 290   v14-18; May 1851-Apr. 1856
    Reel 291   v19-22; May 1856-Apr. 1860
    Reel 292   v23-27; May 1860-May 1866

Unit 8

293-294   AMERICAN ANNALS OF EDUCATION
    American Journal of Education
    Reel 293   v1-nsv1, no5; Jan. 1826-July 1830
    American Journal, and Annals of Education and Instruction
    Reel 293   nsv1, no6-9; Aug.-Dec. 1830
    American Annals of Education
    Reel 293   s3v1, no1-12; Aug. 1830-Dec. 1831
    Reel 294   s3v2-s3v9; Jan. 1832-Dec. 1839

295   AMERICAN ECLECTIC. v1-4; Jan. 1841-Nov. 1842.

295   AMERICAN JOURNAL OF HOMEOPATHY . . .
    Reel 295   v1, no1-6; Aug. 1838-July 1839
    Miscellanies on Homeopathy
    Reel 295   1 vol; 1839

296   AMERICAN MEDICAL INTELLIGENCER
    Reel 296   v1-4; Apr. 1, 1837-Mar. 15, 1841
    Reel 296   nsv1; July 1841-June 1842

297   AMERICAN PIONEER. v1-2; Jan. 1842-Oct. 1843.

297   AMERICAN QUARTERLY OBSERVER. v1-3; July
1833-Oct. 1834.

298-301   AMERICAN QUARTERLY REVIEW
    Reel 298   v1-6; Mar. 1827-Dec. 1829
    Reel 299   v7-12; Mar. 1830-Dec. 1832
    Reel 300   v13-18; Mar. 1833-Dec. 1835
    Reel 301   v19-22; Mar. 1836-Dec. 1837

302-304   AMERICAN WHIG REVIEW
    American Review: a Whig Journal . . .
    Reel 302   v1-6; Jan. 1845-Dec. 1847
    Reel 303   v7-11, no4(28); Jan. 1848-Apr. 1850
    American Whig Review
    Reel 303   v11, no5-6 (29-30); May-June 1850
    Reel 304   v12-16; July 1850-Dec. 1852

305   AMERICAN SUNDAY SCHOOL MAGAZINE
    American Sunday School Magazine
    Reel 305   v1-7; July 1824-Dec. 1830
    Quarterly Sunday School Magazine
    Reel 305   v8; Apr. 1831-Jan. 1832

306-310   BIBLICAL REPOSITORY AND CLASSICAL REVIEW
    Biblical Repository
    Reel 306   v1-4; Jan. 1831-Oct. 1834
    Biblical Repository and Quarterly Observer
    Reel 306   v5-6; Jan.-Oct. 1835
    Reel 307   v7-8; Jan.-Oct. 1836

REEL

American Biblical Repository
Reel 307　v9-12; Jan. 1837-Oct. 1838
American Biblical Repository, Devoted to Biblical and General Literature
Reel 307　s2v1-3; Jan. 1839-Apr. 1840
Reel 308　s2v4-10; July 1840-Oct. 1843
Reel 309　s2v11-12; Jan.-Oct. 1844
Biblical Repository and Classical Review
Reel 309　s3v1-4; Jan. 1845-Oct. 1848
Reel 310　s3v5-6; Jan. 1849-Oct. 1850

310　BOSTON MISCELLANY OF LITERATURE AND FASHION. v1-3; Jan. 1842-Feb. 1843.

311　BURTON'S GENTLEMAN'S MAGAZINE AND AMERICAN MONTHLY REVIEW
Gentleman's Magazine
Reel 311　v1-4, no2; July 1837-Feb. 1839
Burton's Gentleman's Magazine and American Monthly Review
Reel 311　v4, no3-v7, no5; Mar. 1839-Nov. 1840
Graham's Magazine
Reel 311　v7, no6; Dec. 1840

312　CHRISTIAN OBSERVATORY. v1-4; Jan. 1847-Apr. 1850.

313　COLUMBIAN LADY'S AND GENTLEMAN'S MAGAZINE. v1-10; Jan. 1844-Feb. 1849.

314-315　FARMERS CABINET AND AMERICAN HERD BOOK
Reel 314　v1-6; July 1, 1836-July 15, 1842
Reel 315　v7-12; Aug. 15, 1842-July 15, 1848

316-318　GENESEE FARMER AND GARDENERS JOURNAL
Reel 316　v1-4; Jan. 1, 1831-Dec. 27, 1834
Reel 317　v5-8; Jan. 3, 1835-Dec. 29, 1838
Reel 318　v9; Jan. 5-Nov. 30, 1839

319-323　LIVING AGE
Littell's Living Age
Reel 319　v1-5; May 11, 1844-June 28, 1845
Reel 320　v6-10; July 5, 1845-Sept. 26, 1846
Reel 321　v11-16; Oct. 3, 1846-Mar. 25, 1848
Reel 322　v17-22; Apr. 1848-Sept. 29, 1849
Reel 323　v23-27; Oct. 6, 1849-Dec. 28, 1850

324　MICHIGAN FARMER. v1-8; Feb. 15, 1843-Dec. 1850.

325　SOUTHERN REVIEW. v1-8; Feb. 1828-Feb. 1832.

326　BOSTON WEEKLY MAGAZINE. v1-3; Sept. 8, 1838-Sept. 11, 1841.

Unit 9

327-332　METHODIST REVIEW
Methodist Magazine
Reel 327　v9-11; Jan. 1826-Dec. 1828
Methodist Magazine and Quarterly Review
Reel 327　v12; Jan.-Oct. 1830
Reel 328　v13-17; Jan. 1831-Oct. 1835
Reel 329　v18-22; Jan. 1836-Oct. 1840
Methodist Quarterly Review
Reel 330　v23-26; Jan. 1841-Oct. 1844
Reel 331　v27-29; Jan. 1845-Oct. 1847
Reel 332　v30-32; Jan. 1848-Oct. 1850

REEL

333　STAND. no1-5, 7; Dec. 21, 1819-Aug. 14, 1820.

333　SUNDAY SCHOOL REPOSITORY. nos9-11, 13-18; June 1817-Feb. 1819.

333　THEOPHILANTHROPIST. no1-9; 1810.

333　YOUTH'S CABINET. v1, nos1-4; Mar. 31-Apr. 21, 1815.

333　YOUTH'S REPOSITORY OF CHRISTIAN KNOWLEDGE. nos1-2; Mar.-Sept. 1813.

333　————. v1, no1-8; Feb. 18-May 18, 1826.

333　AMERICAN METROPOLITAN MAGAZINE. v1, no1-2; Jan.-Feb. 1849.

333　AMERICAN PEOPLE'S JOURNAL OF SCIENCE, LITERATURE, AND ART. v1, nos1-2; Jan.-Feb. 1850.

334-338　FARMER'S REGISTER
Reel 334　v1-2; June 1833-May 1835
Reel 335　v3-5; May 1835-Mar. 1838
Reel 336　v6-7; Apr. 1838-Dec. 1839
Reel 337　v8-9; Jan. 1840-Dec. 1841
Reel 338　v10-nsv1, no3; Jan. 1842-Mar. 1843

339-348　MERCHANTS' MAGAZINE AND COMMERCIAL REVIEW
Reel 339　v1-7; July 1839-Dec. 1842
Reel 340　v8-14; Jan. 1843-June 1846
Reel 341　v15-21; July 1846-Dec. 1849
Reel 342　v22-27; Jan. 1850-June 1852
Reel 343　v28-33; Jan. 1853-Dec. 1855
Reel 344　v34-39; Jan. 1856-Dec. 1858
Reel 345　v40-44; Jan. 1859-June 1861
Reel 346　v45-51; July 1861-Dec. 1864
Reel 347　v52-57; Jan. 1865-Dec. 1867
Reel 348　v58-63; Jan. 1868-Dec. 1870

349-361　KNICKERBOCKER
Knickerbocker: or, New York Monthly Magazine
Reel 349　v1-6; Jan. 1833-Dec. 1835
Reel 350　v7-11; Jan. 1836-June 1838
Reel 351　v12-17; July 1838-June 1841
Reel 352　v18-22; July 1841-Dec. 1843
Reel 353　v23-27; Jan. 1844-June 1846
Reel 354　v28-33; July 1846-June 1849
Reel 355　v34-39; July 1849-June 1852
Reel 356　v40-44; July 1852-Dec. 1854
Reel 357　v45-48; Jan. 1855-Dec. 1856
Reel 358　v49-53; Jan. 1857-June 1859
Reel 359　v54-57; July 1859-June 1861
Reel 360　v58-60; July 1861-Dec. 1862
Knickerbocker Monthly: a National Magazine
Reel 360　v61; Jan. 1863-June 1863
Reel 361　v62; July 1863-Dec. 1863
American Monthly Knickerbocker
Reel 361　v63-64; Jan.-Dec. 1864
American Monthly
Reel 361　v65; Jan-June 1865
Foederal American Monthly
Reel 361　v66; July-Oct. 1865

REEL

Unit 10

362   CAROLINA JOURNAL OF MEDICINE, SCIENCE AND AGRICULTURE. v1-nsv1; Jan. 1825-May 1826.

362   COHEN'S GAZETTE & LOTTERY REGISTER. v8, no33-v9; Feb. 16, 1826-Sept. 1, 1830.

362   ABOLITIONIST; OR, RECORD OF THE NEW ENGLAND ANTI-SLAVERY SOCIETY. v1; Jan.-Dec. 1833.

363-364   MEMOIRS OF THE AMERICAN ACADEMY OF ARTS AND SCIENCES
     Reel 363   v1-nsv1; 1785-1833
     Reel 364   nsv2-4; 1846-1850

364-365   AMERICAN AGRICULTURIST
     Reel 364   v1-4; Apr. 1842-Dec. 1845
     Reel 365   v5-9; Jan. 1846-Dec. 1850

365   AMERICAN EAGLE MAGAZINE. v1, no1-2; June-July 1847.

365   AMERICAN EXPOSITOR. v1, no1; May 1850.

365   AMERICAN JOURNAL OF HOMOEOPATHIA. v1, no1-4; Feb.-Aug. 1835.

365   AMERICAN JOURNAL OF HOMOEOPATHY. v1-9; no4; Apr. 25, 1846-Aug. 1854.

366-368   AMERICAN JOURNAL OF PHARMACY
     Journal of the Philadelphia College of Pharmacy
     Reel 366   v1, nos1-4; Dec. 1825-Nov. 1827
     Reel 366   nsv1-6; Apr. 1829-Jan. 1835
     American Journal of Pharmacy
     Reel 366   nsv7-8 (nsv1-2); Apr. 1835-Jan. 1837
     Reel 367   nsv9-18 (nsv3-12); Apr. 1837-Jan. 1847
     Reel 368   nsv19-24 (nsv13-18); Apr. 1847-Oct. 1852

368-375   AMERICAN JOURNAL OF THE MEDICAL SCIENCES
     Reel 368   v1-2; Nov. 1827-Aug. 1828
     Reel 369   v3-9; Nov. 1828-Feb. 1832
     Reel 370   v10-15; May 1832-Feb. 1835
     Reel 371   v16-21; May 1835-Feb. 1838
     Reel 372   v22-nsv1; May 1838-Apr. 1841
     Reel 373   nsv2-8; July 1841-Oct. 1844
     Reel 374   nsv9-15; Jan. 1845-Apr. 1848
     Reel 375   nsv16-20; July 1848-Oct. 1850

376   AMERICAN MAGAZINE. v1-2, no3; July 1841-Mar./Apr. 1842.

377   AMERICAN MONTHLY MAGAZINE. v1-nsv6 (v1-12); Mar. 1833-Oct. 1838.

378   ANGLO-AMERICAN MAGAZINE. v1; Feb.-July 1843.

378   ANTI-SLAVERY REPORTER. v1, no1-6; June-Nov. 1833.

378   ARISTIDEAN. v1, no1-6; Mar.-Dec. 1845.

378   ARTHUR'S MAGAZINE
     Ladies' Magazine of Literature, Fashion and Fine Arts
     Reel 378   v1; Jan.-June 1844

REEL

     Arthur's Ladies' Magazine of Elegant Literature and the Fine Arts
     Reel 378   v2-4; July 1844-Dec. 1845
     Arthur's Magazine
     Reel 378   v5; Jan-Apr. 1846

379   BALTIMORE LITERARY MONUMENT. v1-2; Oct. 1838-Oct. 1839.

379   BALTIMORE MEDICAL AND SURGICAL JOURNAL AND REVIEW. v1-2; Oct. 1833-Sept. 1834.

379   BIBLIOTHECA SACRA. no1-3; Feb., May, Dec. 1843.

379   BOSTON LITERARY MAGAZINE. v1, no1-12; May 1, 1832-Apr. 1833.

379   BOSTON LYCEUM. v1-2, no1-11; Jan.-Nov. 1827.

380   BOSTON QUARTERLY REVIEW. v1-5; Jan. 1838-Oct. 1842.

381   CAMPBELL'S FOREIGN SEMI-MONTHLY MAGAZINE
     Campbell's Foreign Monthly Magazine . . .
     Reel 381   v1-3; Sept. 1842-Aug. 1843
     Campbell's Foreign Semi-Monthly Magazine
     Reel 381   v4-6; Sept. 1, 1843-Aug. 16, 1844

382   CAROLINA LAW JOURNAL. v1, nos1-4; July 1830-Apr. 1831.

382   CASKET. v1, no1-26; Apr. 15-Oct. 7, 1846.

382   CHRISTIAN REFORMER. v1, no1-9; July 1, 1828-July 1829.

382   CHRONICLES OF THE NORTH AMERICAN SAVAGES. no1-5; May-Sept. 1835.

382   COLVIN'S WEEKLY REGISTER. v1, no1-16; Jan. 16-Apr. 30, 1808.

382-383   DEBOW'S REVIEW
     Commercial Review of the South and West
     Reel 382   v1-4; Jan. 1846-Dec. 1847
     Reel 383   v5-8; Jan. 1848-June 1850
     DeBow's Review of the Southern and Western States
     Reel 383   v9; July-Dec. 1850

383   COMMON SCHOOL ADVOCATE. v1-5; 1837-1841.

384   CORRESPONDENT. v1-5; Jan. 20, 1827-July 18, 1829.

384   CORSAIR. v1; Mar. 16, 1839-Mar. 7, 1840.

385   CRISIS. v1, no1-35; Mar. 7-Oct. 28, 1840.

385   CRITIC. v1-2, no7; Nov. 1, 1828-June 20, 1829.

385   DOLLAR MAGAZINE. v1, no1-11; Jan.-Dec. 1833.

385   DOLLAR MAGAZINE. v1-2; 1841-1842.

385   EASTERN MAGAZINE. v1, nos1-12; July 1835-June 1836.

386   EXAMINER AND HESPERIAN
     Literary Examiner and Western Monthly Review
     Reel 386   v1; 1839

REEL

Examiner and Hesperian
Reel 386   v2; 1840

386   **FAMILY FAVORITE AND TEMPERANCE
JOURNAL.** v1, no1-9; Dec. 1849-Sept. 1850.

386-387   **FRIENDS' REVIEW**
Reel 386   v1-2; Sept. 4, 1847-Sept. 15, 1849
Reel 387   v3-4; Sept. 22, 1849-Sept. 13, 1851

388   **HERALD OF TRUTH.** v1-4, no1; Jan. 1847-July 1848.

388   **HIEROPHANT.** v1, no1-12; June 1842-May 1843.

389   **ILLINOIS MONTHLY MAGAZINE.** v1-2; Oct. 1830-
Sept. 1832.

389   **INVESTIGATOR AND GENERAL INTELLIGENCER.**
v2, no8; Dec. 4, 1828.

389   **RHODE ISLAND INSTITUTE OF INSTRUCTION.** v1-
3; Nov. 1845-1848.

389-390   **JUVENILE MISCELLANY**
Reel 389   v1-3; Sept. 1826-Jan. 1828
Reel 390   v4-s3v6; Mar. 1828-Aug. 1834

391-399   **LIBERATOR**
Reel 391   v1-4; Jan. 1, 1831-Dec. 27, 1834
Reel 392   v5-8; Jan. 3, 1835-Dec. 28, 1838
Reel 393   v9-12; Jan. 4, 1839-Dec. 30, 1842
Reel 394   v13-16; Jan. 6, 1843-Dec. 25, 1846
Reel 395   v17-20; Jan. 1, 1847-Dec. 27, 1850
Reel 396   v21-24; Jan. 3, 1851-Dec. 29, 1854
Reel 397   v25-28; Jan. 5, 1855-Dec. 31, 1858
Reel 398   v29-32; Jan 7, 1859-Dec. 26, 1862
Reel 399   v33-35; Jan. 2, 1863-Dec. 29, 1865

400   **LITERARY GAZETTE.** v1-2, no1-32; Aug. 1, 1834-
June 26, 1835.

400   **LITERARY MAGAZINE.** v1, no1; Jan. 1, 1835.

400   **MECHANIC'S ADVOCATE.** v1-2; Dec. 3, 1846-1848.

400   **TALISMAN.** v1-3; 1828-1830.

400   **MISTLETOE.** v1, no1-3; Jan.-Mar. 1849.

400   **CHILD'S NEWSPAPER.** v1, no1-5, 7-11, 13-19; Jan. 7-
Sept. 2, 1834.

400   **NORTH-CAROLINA MAGAZINE, POLITICAL,
HISTORICAL, AND MISCELLANEOUS.** v1, no1;
Aug. 1813.

Unit 11

401   **CHRISTIAN VISITOR.** v1; Jan-Dec. 1823.

401   **EVANGELICAL MONITOR.** v1-3; Apr. 14, 1821-
Apr. 17, 1824.

401   **ISRAEL'S ADVOCATE.** v4-5, no12; Jan. 1826-Dec.
1827.

401-403   **RELIGIOUS MONITOR AND EVANGELICAL
REPOSITORY**
Reel 401   v1-4; May 1824-May 1828

REEL

Reel 402   v5-11; June 1828-May 1835
Reel 403   v12-18; June 1835-May 1842

404   **AMARANTH.** v1-2; Apr. 1828-Oct. 1829.

404-407   **AMERICAN TURF REGISTER AND SPORTING
MAGAZINE**
Reel 404   v1-3; Sept. 1829-Aug. 1832
Reel 405   v4-8; Sept. 1832-Nov. 1837
Reel 406   v9-12; Jan. 1838-Dec. 1841
Reel 407   v13-15; Jan. 1842-Dec. 1844

408   **ANTI-SLAVERY EXAMINER.** nos1-14; 1836-45.

408   **ANTI-SLAVERY RECORD.** v1-3; Jan. 1835-Dec. 1837.

408   **BALTIMORE MONTHLY VISITER.** v1, no1; Apr.
1842.

408   **BOSTON MUSICAL GAZETTE.** v1-2; May 2, 1838-
May 15, 1839.

409-410   **BROTHER JONATHAN**
Reel 409   v1-4; Jan. 1842-Apr. 29, 1843
Reel 410   v5-6; May 6-Dec. 23, 1843

410-416   **CHRISTIAN REVIEW**
Reel 410   v1-3; Mar. 1836-Dec. 1838
Reel 411   v4-8; Mar. 1839-Dec. 1843
Reel 412   v9-13; Mar. 1844-Dec. 1848
Reel 413   v14-17; Jan. 1849-Oct. 1852
Reel 414   v18-21; Jan. 1853-Oct. 1856
Reel 415   v22-25; Jan. 1857-Oct. 1860
Reel 416   v26-28; Jan. 1861-Oct. 1863

416   **COLMAN'S RURAL WORLD**
Valley Farmer
Reel 416   v1, no1; Jan. 1849
Reel 416   v2-3; Jan. 1850-Dec. 1851

417   **HESPERIAN.** v1-3; May 1838-Nov. 1839.

418   **INDEPENDENT.** v1-2; Dec. 7, 1848-Dec. 1850.

419   **MONTHLY JOURNAL OF AGRICULTURE.** v1-3;
July 1845-June 1848.

420-421   **AMERICAN LADIES' MAGAZINE**
Ladies' Magazine
Reel 420   v1-2; Jan. 1828-Dec. 1829
Ladies Magazine and Literary Gazette
Reel 420   v3-5; Jan. 1830-Dec. 1832
Reel 421   v6; Jan.-Dec. 1833
Ladies' Magazine
Reel 421   v7, no1; Jan. 1834
American Ladies' Magazine
Reel 421   v7, no2-v9; Feb. 1834-Dec. 1836

422-427   **MAINE FARMER**
Kennebec Farmer and Journal of Useful Arts
Reel 422   v1, nos1-8; Jan. 21-Mar. 11, 1833
Maine Farmer and Journal of the Useful Arts
Reel 422   v1, no9-v4; Mar. 18, 1833-Jan. 27,
1837
Reel 423   v5-7; Feb. 14, 1837-Jan. 4, 1840
Reel 424   v8-9; Jan. 11, 1840-Jan. 1, 1842
Maine Farmer and Mechanics Advocate
Reel 424   nsv1 (v10); Jan. 15-Dec. 31, 1842
Reel 425   nsv2 (v11); Jan. 7-Dec. 30, 1843

REEL

Maine Farmer
Reel 425   v12-13; Jan. 4, 1844-Dec. 25, 1845
Reel 426   v14-16; Jan. 1, 1846-Dec. 28, 1848
Reel 427   v17-18; Jan. 4, 1849-Dec. 26, 1850

428-437   MEDICAL EXAMINER
Medical Examiner
Reel 428   v1-2; Jan. 3, 1838-Dec. 28, 1839
Reel 429   v3-4; Jan. 4 [1840]-Dec. 25, 1841
Reel 430   nsv1(i.e., v5); Jan. 1, 1842-Dec. 24, 1842
Medical Examiner and Retrospect of the Medical Sciences
Reel 430   v6; Jan. 21, 1843-Dec. 30, 1843
Medical Examiner and Record of Medical Science
Reel 431   v7-nsv1 (v8); Jan. 13, 1844-Dec. 1845
Reel 432   nsv2-3 (v9-10); Jan. 1846-Dec. 1847
Reel 433   nsv4-5 (v11-12); Jan.-1848-Dec. 1849
Reel 434   nsv6-7 (v13-14); Jan. 1850-Dec. 1851
Reel 435   nsv8-9 (v15-16); Jan. 1852-Dec. 1853
Medical Examiner
Reel 436   nsv10-11(v17-18); Jan. 1854-Dec. 1855
Reel 437   nsv12 (v19); Jan. 1856-Dec. 1856

438-447   SOUTHERN LITERARY MESSENGER
Southern Literary Messenger
Reel 438   v1-3; Aug. 1834-Dec. 1837
Reel 439   v4-6; Jan. 1838-Dec. 1840
Reel 440   v7-9; Jan. 1841-Dec. 1843
Reel 441   v10-11; Jan. 1844-Dec. 1845
Southern and Western Literary Messenger and Review
Reel 441   v12-13; Jan. 1846-Dec. 1847
Southern Literary Messenger
Reel 442   v14-16; Jan. 1848-Dec. 1850
Reel 443   v17-19; Jan. 1851-Dec. 1853
Reel 444   v20-23; Jan. 1854-Dec. 1856
Reel 445   v24-29; Jan. 1857-Dec. 1859
Reel 446   v30-33; Jan. 1860-Dec. 1861
Reel 447   v34-38; Jan. 1862-June 1864

448   EVERGREEN. v1-2; Jan. 1840-June 1841.

Unit 12

449-463   CHRISTIAN EXAMINER
Christian Examiner and Theological Review
Reel 449   v3-5; Jan. 1826-Dec. 1828
Christian Examiner and General Review
Reel 449   v6; Mar. 1829-July 1829
Reel 450   v7-13; Sept. 1829-Jan. 1833
Reel 451   v14-19; Mar. 1833-Jan. 1836
Reel 452   v20-25; Mar. 1836-Jan. 1839
Reel 453   v26-31; Mar. 1839-Jan. 1842
Reel 454   v32-35; Mar. 1842-Jan. 1844
Christian Examiner and Religious Miscellany
Reel 454   v36-37; Jan.-Nov. 1844
Reel 455   v38-43; Jan. 1845-Nov. 1847
Reel 456   v44-48; Jan. 1848-May 1850
Reel 457   v49-53; July 1850-Nov. 1852
Reel 458   v54-58; Jan. 1853-May 1855
Reel 459   v59-62; July 1855-May 1857
Christian Examiner
Reel 459   v63; July-Nov. 1857
Reel 460   v64-69; Jan. 1858-Nov. 1860
Reel 461   v70-75; Jan. 1861-Nov. 1863
Reel 462   v76-81; Jan. 1864-Nov. 1866
Reel 463   v82-87; Jan. 1867-Nov. 1869

REEL

464   HALCYON LUMINARY, AND THEOLOGICAL REPOSITORY. v2; Jan-Dec. 1813.

464   LITERARY AND EVANGELICAL MAGAZINE. v9-11; Jan. 1826-Dec. 1828.

465-467   AMERICAN CULTIVATOR
Boston Cultivator
Reel 465   v1-6; Jan. 1839-Dec. 1844
Reel 466   v7-10; Jan. 1845-Dec. 1848
Reel 467   v11-12; Jan. 1849-Dec. 1850

468-469   AMERICAN MONTHLY MAGAZINE
Reel 468   v1; Apr. 1829-Mar. 1830
Reel 469   v2-3; Apr. 1830-July 1831

469-471   ARMY AND NAVY CHRONICLE
Reel 469   v1-2; Jan. 1835-July 1836
Reel 470   v3-8; July 1836-June 1839
Reel 471   v9-13; July 1839-May 1842

472   ARMY AND NAVY CHRONICLE, AND SCIENTIFIC REPOSITORY. v1-3; Jan. 1843-June 1844.

472   BOSTON MECHANIC, AND JOURNAL OF THE USEFUL ARTS AND SCIENCES
Young Mechanic
Reel 472   v1-2; Jan. 1832-Dec. 1833
Mechanic
Reel 472   v3; Jan.-Dec. 1834
Boston Mechanic
Reel 472   v4; Jan. 1835-Feb. 1836

473   DAGUERREOTYPE. v1-3; Aug. 1847-Apr. 1849.

473-474   EXPOSITOR AND UNIVERSALIST REVIEW
Universalist Expositor
Reel 473   v1-2; July 1830-May 1832
Expositor and Universalist Review
Reel 474   [nsv1-4]; Jan. 1833-Nov. 1840

474-476   FAMILY MAGAZINE
Reel 474   v1; Apr. 20, 1833-Apr. 12, 1834
Reel 475   v2-5; 1834-1838
Reel 476   v6-8; 1839-1841

476-479   HAZARD'S REGISTER OF PENNSYLVANIA
Register of Pennsylvania
Reel 476   v1-2; Jan. 5-Dec. 27, 1828
Reel 477   v3-7; Jan. 3, 1829-June 25, 1831
Hazard's Register of Pennsylvania
Reel 477   v8; July 2-Dec. 31, 1831
Reel 478   v9-13; Jan. 7, 1832-June 28, 1834
Reel 479   v14-16; July 5, 1834-Dec. 26, 1835

479   JOURNAL OF HEALTH. v1-4; Sept. 1829-Aug. 1833.

480-481   JOURNAL OF PRISON DISCIPLINE AND PHILANTHROPY
Pennsylvania Journal of Prison Discipline and Philanthropy
Reel 480   v1-5; Jan. 1845-Oct. 1850
Reel 481   v6-10; Jan. 1851-Oct. 1855

481   JUDY. v1, nos1-13; Nov. 1846-Feb. 1847.

482-483   LADIES' REPOSITORY; A MONTHLY PERIODICAL
Ladies Repository, and Gatherings of the West
Reel 482   v1-6; Jan. 1841-Dec. 1846
Reel 483   v7-8; Jan. 1847-Dec. 1848

REEL

Ladies Repository; a Monthly Periodical Devoted
to Literature and Religion
Reel 483   v9-10; Jan. 1849-Dec. 1850

483-486   LITERARY WORLD
Reel 483   v1; Feb.-July 1847
Reel 484   v2-5; Aug. 1847-Dec. 1849
Reel 485   v6-10; Jan. 1850-June 1852
Reel 486   v11-13; July 1852-Dec. 1853

486   MAINE MONTHLY MAGAZINE. v1, nos1-12; July
1836-June 1837.

486   WESTERN ACADEMICIAN AND JOURNAL OF
EDUCATION AND SCIENCE. v1, nos1-12; Mar.
1837-Feb. 1838.

487   WESTERN EXAMINER. v1-2; Nov. 1833-Dec. 1835.

487-489   WESTERN LAW JOURNAL
Reel 487   v1-3; Oct. 1843-Sept. 1846
Reel 488   v4-7; Oct. 1846-Sept. 1850
Reel 489   v8-10; Oct. 1850-Sept. 1853

489-490   WESTERN MESSENGER
Reel 489   v1; June 1835-July 1836
Reel 490   v2-8; Aug. 1836-Apr. 1841

491-492   LIBERTY BELL
Reel 491   v1-12; 1839-1852
Reel 492   v13-15; 1853-1858

Unit 13

493-495   CHRISTIAN HERALD AND SEAMAN'S MAGAZINE
Christian Herald
Reel 493   v1-5; Mar. 1816-Mar. 1819
Reel 494   v6-7; Apr. 1819-Apr. 1821
Christian Herald and Seaman's Magazine
Reel 494   v8; May 1821-May 1822
Reel 495   v9-11; May 1822-Nov. 1824

495-502   CHRISTIAN SECRETARY
Reel 495   s2v2, no49-s2v3; Jan. 1826-Jan. 1827
Reel 496   s2v4-s2v8; Jan. 1827-Jan. 1830
Reel 497   s2v9-s2v12; Jan. 1830-Jan. 1834
Reel 498   s2v13-s2v16; Jan. 1834-July 1837
Reel 499   s3v1-4 (17-20); Mar. 1838-Mar. 1842
Reel 500   s3v5-7 (21-23); Mar. 1842-Mar. 1845
Reel 501   s3v8-10 (24-26); Mar. 1845-Mar 1848
Reel 502   s3v11-13 (27-29); Mar. 1848-Feb.
1851

503   GOSPEL HERALD
Reel 503   v1-7; Apr. 22, 1820-May 5, 1827
Reel 503   nsv1; Jan. 3-Dec. 19, 1829

503-507   AMERICAN FARMER'S MAGAZINE
Plough, The Loom and the Anvil
Reel 503   v1; July 1848-June 1849
Reel 504   v2-4; July 1849-June 1852
Reel 505   v5-7; July 1852-June 1855
Reel 506   v8-10; July 1855-Dec. 1857
American Farmer's Magazine
Reel 507   v11-12; Jan. 1858-June 1859

507-508   BROWNSON'S QUARTERLY REVIEW
Reel 507   v1-3; Jan. 1844-Oct. 1846
Reel 508   nsv1-6; Jan. 1847-Oct. 1852

REEL

509-512   CHILD'S FRIEND AND FAMILY MAGAZINE
Reel 509   v1-8; Oct. 1843-Sept. 1847
Reel 510   v9-17; Oct. 1847-1851
Reel 511   v18-25; 1852-1855
Reel 512   v26-31; 1856-1858

512-514   COMMON SCHOOL JOURNAL
Reel 512   v1-2; Nov. 1838-Dec. 1840
Reel 513   v3-8; Jan. 1841-Dec. 1846
Reel 514   v9-14; Jan. 1847-Dec. 1852

514-518   CULTIVATOR
Reel 514   v1-4; Mar. 1834-Feb. 1838
Reel 515   v5-nsv4; Mar. 1838-Dec. 1847
Reel 516   nsv5-s3v2; Jan. 1848-Dec. 1854
Reel 517   s3v3-9; Jan. 1855-Dec. 1861
Reel 518   s3v10-13; Jan. 1862-Dec. 1865

519-523   ECLECTIC MAGAZINE OF FOREIGN LITERATURE
Reel 519   v1-5; Jan. 1844-Aug. 1845
Reel 520   v6-10; Sept. 1845-Apr. 1847
Reel 521   v11-15; May 1847-Dec. 1848
Reel 522   v16-20; Dec. 1848-Apr. 1849
Reel 523   v21; Sept.-Dec. 1850

523-526   FRIEND
Reel 523   v1-5; Oct. 13, 1827-Oct. 6, 1832
Reel 524   v6-10; Oct. 13, 1832-Sept. 30, 1837
Reel 525   v11-17; Oct. 7, 1837-Sept. 21, 1844
Reel 526   v18-24; Sept. 28, 1844-Dec. 28, 1850

527   HORTICULTURAL REGISTER, AND GARDENER'S
MAGAZINE. v1-4; Jan. 1, 1835-Dec. 1838.

527   WESTERN LITERARY JOURNAL AND MONTHLY
REVIEW. v1, nos1-6; Nov. 1844-Apr. 1845.

527   WESTERN LITERARY JOURNAL, AND MONTHLY
REVIEW. v1, nos1-6; June-Nov. 1836.

528   WESTERN MONTHLY MAGAZINE, AND LITERARY
JOURNAL. v1-5, nsv1, nos1-5; Jan. 1833-June 1837.

529   WESTERN QUARTERLY REVIEW. v1, nos1-2; Jan.-
Apr. 1849.

529   WESTERN REVIEW. v1, no1; Apr. 1846.

529-531   YALE LITERARY MAGAZINE
Reel 529   v1-5; Feb. 1836-Aug. 1840
Reel 530   v6-11; Nov. 1840-Aug. 1846
Reel 531   v12-16; Nov. 1846-July 1851

Unit 14

532   ADVOCATE OF SCIENCE. v1; Feb 18, 1833-Feb. 20,
1834.

532   ADVOCATE OF SCIENCE, AND ANNALS OF
NATURAL HISTORY. v1; Aug. 1834-Apr. 1835.

532-534   AMERICAN QUARTERLY REGISTER
Quarterly Journal of the American Education Society
Reel 532   v1, no1-6; July 1827-Oct. 1828
Quarterly Register and Journal of the American Edu-
cation Society
Reel 532   v1, no7-v2; Jan. 1829-May 1830

REEL

Quarterly Register of the American Education Society
Reel 532   v3; Aug. 1830-May 1831
American Quarterly Register
Reel 532   v4-6; Aug. 1831-May 1834
Reel 533   v7-12; Aug. 1834-May 1840
Reel 534   v13-15; Aug. 1840-May 1843
Quarterly Journal of the American Education Society
Reel 534   v16-18; Aug. 1843-May 1846

534   AMERICAN SOCIETY FOR PROMOTING THE
CIVILIZATION AND GENERAL IMPROVEMENT OF
THE INDIAN TRIBES IN THE UNITED STATES. no1;
1824.

534   BALTIMORE MONTHLY JOURNAL OF MEDICINE
AND SURGERY. v1, no1-12; Feb. 1830-Jan. 1831.

535-539   BAPTIST MISSIONARY MAGAZINE
American Baptist Magazine
Reel 535   v6-11; 1826-1831
Reel 536   v12-15; Jan. 1832-Dec. 1835
Baptist Missionary Magazine
Reel 536   v16-17; Jan. 1836-Dec. 1837
Reel 537   v18-23; 1838-1843
Reel 538   v24-28; 1844-1848
Reel 539   v29; Jan.-Dec. 1849
Missionary Magazine
Reel 539   v30; Jan.-Dec. 1850

539   BEREAN. v3-nsv1; July 1826-Sept. 1828.

539-546   CONGREGATIONALIST AND HERALD OF GOSPEL
LIBERTY
Recorder
Reel 539   v1; Jan. 3-Dec. 24, 1816
Boston Recorder
Reel 539   v2-4; Jan. 1, 1817-Dec. 1819
Reel 540   v5-8; Jan. 1820-Dec. 1823
Reel 541   v9; Jan.-Dec. 1824
Recorder and Telegraph
Reel 541   v10; Jan. 1-Dec. 30, 1825
Boston Recorder and Religious Telegraph
Reel 541   v11-14; July 14, 1826-Dec. 1829
Reel 542   v15, no1-26; Jan.-June 30, 1830
Boston Recorder
Reel 542   v15, no27-v19; July 7, 1830-Dec. 1834
Reel 543   v20-24; Jan. 1835-Dec. 1839
Reel 544   v25-29; Jan. 1840-Dec. 1844
Reel 545   v30-33; Jan. 1845-Dec. 1848
Reel 546   v34, no1-19; Jan.-May 11, 1849
Puritan Recorder
Reel 546   v34, no20-v35; May 17, 1849-Dec.
1850

546   CANDID EXAMINER. v2; June 19, 1826-June 18,
1827.

546   CHARLESTON MEDICAL REGISTER FOR THE
YEAR 1802. v1; 1803.

546   DIAL. v1-4; July 1840-Apr. 1844.

546   FRANKLIN MINERVA. v1; Feb. 2, 1799-Jan. 4, 1800.

547-560   GRAHAM'S AMERICAN MONTHLY MAGAZINE OF
LITERATURE, ART, AND FASHION
Casket
Reel 547   v1-4; Feb. 1826-Dec. 1829
Reel 548   v5; Jan.-Dec. 1830
Atkinson's Casket
Reel 548   v6-8; Jan. 1831-Dec. 1833

REEL

Reel 549   v9-11; Jan. 1834-Dec. 1836
Reel 550   v12-14, no4; Jan. 1837-Apr. 1839
Casket
Reel 550   v14, no5-v15; May-Dec. 1839
Reel 551   v16-17; Jan.-Nov. 1840
Graham's Lady's and Gentleman's Magazine
Reel 551   v18-21; Jan. 1841-Dec. 1842
Graham's Magazine of Literature and Art
Reel 552   v22; Jan.-June 1843
Graham's Lady's and Gentleman's Magazine
Reel 552   v23-24; July 1843-June 1844
**Graham's American Monthly Magazine of Literature,
Art, and Fashion**
Reel 552   v25-27; July 1844-Dec. 1845
Reel 553   v28-32; Jan. 1846-June 1848
Reel 554   v33-35; July 1848-Dec. 1849
Reel 555   v36-38; Jan. 1850-June 1851
Reel 556   v39-41; July 1851-Dec. 1852
Reel 557   v42-44; Jan. 1853-June 1854
Reel 558   v45-47; July 1854-Dec. 1855
Reel 559   v48-50; Jan. 1856-June 1857
Reel 560   v51-53; July 1857-Dec. 1858

560   HARBINGER OF THE MISSISSIPPI VALLEY. v1;
Mar.-Apr. 1832.

561   LADIES' GARLAND. v1-4; Feb. 14, 1824-June 7,
1828.

561-565   LADIES' WEEKLY MUSEUM
Impartial Gazetteer, and Saturday Evening Post
Reel 561   v1, no.7-18; June 28-Sept. 13, 1788
New-York Weekly Museum
Reel 561   v1, no19-v3; Sept. 20, 1788-May 7,
1791
Weekly Museum
Reel 561   v4-7; May 14, 1791-May 2, 1795
Reel 562   v8-15; May 9, 1795-Dec. 31, 1803
Reel 563   v16-17, no32; Jan. 7, 1804-Aug. 10,
1805
New-York Weekly Museum
Reel 563   v17, no33-v23; Aug. 17, 1805-Dec. 28,
1811
Reel 564   nsv1-s3v3; May 9, 1812-Apr. 27, 1816
Reel 565   s3v4-5; May 4, 1816-Apr. 26, 1817
Ladies' Weekly Museum
Reel 565   s3v6; May 3-Oct. 25, 1817

565   LITERARY CABINET AND WESTERN OLIVE
BRANCH. nsv1; Feb. 16, 1833-Feb. 8, 1834.

565-566   MAN
Reel 565   v1; Feb. 18-May 16, 1834
Reel 566   v2-3; May 17-Dec. 22, 1834

566   MASSACHUSETTS AGRICULTURAL REPOSITORY
AND JOURNAL. v9-10; Jan. 1826-Apr. 1832.

566-572   PRINCETON REVIEW
Biblical Repertory (subtitle varies)
Reel 566   v2-3; 1826-1827
Reel 567   v4-(s2) v3; 1828-1831
Reel 568   (s2) v4-7; 1832-1835
Reel 569   (s2) v8-11; 1836-1839
Reel 570   (s2) v12-15; 1840-1843
Reel 571   (s2) v16-19; 1844-1847
Reel 572   (s2) v20-22; 1848-1850

REEL

572-574 SARTAIN'S UNION MAGAZINE OF LITERATURE AND ART
Union Magazine of Literature and Art
Reel 572   v1; July-Dec. 1847
Reel 573   v2-3; Jan.-Dec. 1848
Sartain's Union Magazine of Literature and Art
Reel 573   v4-7; Jan. 1849-Dec. 1850
Reel 574   v8-11; Jan. 1851-Aug. 1852

574-576 SOUTHERN LITERARY JOURNAL AND MAGAZINE OF ARTS
Reel 574   v1; Sept. 1835-Feb. 1836
Reel 575   v2-nsv3; Mar. 1836-June 1838
Reel 576   v4; July-Dec. 1838

576 SUBTERRANEAN. v3-4; May 24, 1845-May 22, 1847.

576-578 HEALTH
Water-Cure Journal
Reel 576   v1-6; Dec. 1845-Dec. 1848
Reel 577   v7-24; Jan. 1849-Dec. 1857
Reel 578   v25-33; Jan. 1858-Dec. 1861
Hygienic Teacher and Water-Cure Journal
Reel 578   v34; Jan.-Dec. 1862

578-580 WESTERN JOURNAL OF THE MEDICAL AND PHYSICAL SCIENCES
Western Medical and Physical Journal
Reel 578   v1-2, no1; Apr. 1827-May 1828
Western Journal of the Medical and Physical Sciences
Reel 578   v2, no2-v3; May 1828-Mar. 1830
Reel 579   v4-8; Apr. 1830-Mar. 1835
Reel 580   v9-12; Apr. 1835-July 1838

581-583 WORKING MAN'S ADVOCATE
Workingman's Advocate
Reel 581   v1, no1-32; Oct. 31, 1829-June 5, 1830
New York Sentinel and Workingman's Advocate
Reel 581   v1, no33-52; June 9-Aug. 14, 1830
Workingman's Advocate
Reel 581   v2-4; Aug. 21, 1830-Aug. 10, 1833
Reel 582   v2-7 (rep. vols); 1830-1836
Radical, in Continuation of Workingman's Advocate
Reel 582   v1-2, no4; Jan. 1841-Apr. 1843
Workingman's Advocate
Reel 583   nsv1, no1-17; Mar. 16, 1844-July 20, 1844
People's Rights
Reel 583   nsv1, no18-19; July 24-27, 1844
Workingman's Advocate
Reel 583   nsv1, no19-28; Aug. 3-Oct. 5, 1844
Subterranean, United with the Workingman's Advocate
Reel 583   nsv1, no29-39; Oct. 12-Dec. 21, 1844
Workingman's Advocate
Reel 583   nsv1, no40-52; Dec. 28, 1844-Mar. 22, 1845
Young America
Reel 583   nsv2-5; Mar. 29, 1845-Sept. 23, 1848

Unit 15

584 ADVOCATE OF PEACE AND CHRISTIAN PATRIOT. no1-12; Sept. 1828-June 1829.

584 WORLD AFFAIRS
Advocate of Peace
Reel 584   v1-6; June 1837-Dec. 1845

REEL

Advocate of Peace and Universal Brotherhood
Reel 584   v7 (nsv1); Jan.-Dec. 1846
Advocate of Peace
Reel 584   v8 (nsv2); Jan. 1847-Nov./Dec. 1850

585-586 BALTIMORE LITERARY AND RELIGIOUS MAGAZINE
Reel 585   v1-5; Jan. 1835-Dec. 1839
Reel 586   v6-7; Jan. 1840-Dec. 1841

586 BANNER OF THE CONSTITUTION. v1-3; Dec. 5, 1829-Dec. 31, 1832.

587-588 BANKERS' MAGAZINE
Bankers' Magazine and State Financial Register
Reel 587   v1-3; July 1846-June 1849
Bankers' Magazine and Statistical Register
Reel 588   v4-5; July 1849-June 1851

589-591 BOSTON MASONIC MIRROR
Masonic Mirror: and Mechanics Intelligencer
Reel 589   v2, no2-v3; Jan. 7, 1826-Dec. 27, 1827
Masonic Mirror: Science, Literature and Miscellany
Reel 590   nsv1; July 4, 1829-June 26, 1830
Boston Masonic Mirror
Reel 590   nsv2-3; July 3, 1830-June 23, 1832
Reel 591   nsv4-5; June 30, 1832-Jan. 25, 1834

591 BOSTON MONTHLY MAGAZINE. v1-2; June 1825-July 1826.

592-593 CHRISTIAN ADVOCATE
Reel 592   v4-8; Jan. 1826-Dec. 1830
Reel 593   v9-12; Jan. 1831-Dec. 1834

593-595 CHRISTIAN INTELLIGENCER AND EASTERN CHRONICLE
Christian Intelligencer
Reel 593   v6; June 3, 1826-Jan. 13, 1827
Christian Intelligencer and Eastern Chronicle
Reel 593   v7; Jan. 12-Dec. 28, 1827
Reel 594   v8-14; Jan. 4, 1828-Dec. 26, 1834
Reel 595   v15-16; Jan. 2, 1835-Dec. 30, 1836

595 CHRISTIAN MAGAZINE. v3-4; Jan.- 1826-Dec. 1827.

595 CHRISTIAN MESSENGER. v1-3; May 10, 1817-Oct. 31, 1818.

596 CHRISTIAN MONITOR. v1-2; July 8, 1815-Aug. 30, 1817.

596-603 CHRISTIAN REGISTER
Christian Register
Reel 596   v5-7; Jan. 7, 1826-Dec. 27, 1828
Reel 597   v8-10; Jan. 3, 1829-Dec 31, 1831
Reel 598   v11-14, no46; Jan. 7, 1832-June 27, 1835
Christian Register and Boston Observer
Reel 598   v14, no47-72; July 4-Dec. 26, 1835
Reel 599   v15-17; Jan. 2, 1836-Dec. 29, 1838
Reel 600   v18-20; Jan. 5, 1839-Dec. 25, 1841
Reel 601   v21-22, no41; Jan. 1, 1842-Oct. 14, 1843
Christian Register
Reel 601   v22, no42-v23; Oct. 21, 1843-Dec. 28, 1844
Reel 602   v24-26; Jan. 4, 1845-Dec. 25, 1847
Reel 603   v27-29; Jan. 1, 1848-Dec. 28, 1850

<u>REEL</u>

603   COLONIZATIONIST AND JOURNAL OF FREEDOM.
      Apr. 1833-Apr. 1834.

604   DOLLAR MAGAZINE
      Holdens Dollar Magazine of Criticisms, Biographies,
      Sketches, Essays, Tales . . .
        Reel 604   v1-6; Jan. 1848-Dec. 1850
      Dollar Magazine
        Reel 604   v7-8; Jan.-Dec. 1851

605   DRAMATIC MIRROR AND LITERARY COM-
      PANION. v1-2; Aug. 14, 1841-May 7, 1842.

605   ECLECTIC MUSEUM OF FOREIGN LITERATURE,
      SCIENCE AND ART. v1-4; Jan. 1843-Jan. 1844.

605   EMERALD AND BALTIMORE LITERARY
      GAZETTE. v1-2; Mar. 29, 1828-Apr. 11, 1829.

606   EVANGELICAL WITNESS. v4; Jan.-Dec. 1826.

606   EVERY YOUTH'S GAZETTE. v1; Jan. 22-Dec. 31,
      1842.

606-607   FORRESTER'S BOYS' AND GIRLS' MAGAZINE,
          AND FIRESIDE COMPANION
          Boys' and Girls' Magazine and Fireside Companion
            Reel 606   v1-6; Jan. 1848-Dec. 1850
          Forrester's Boys' and Girls' Magazine, and Fireside
          Companion
            Reel 606   v7-8; Jan.-Dec. 1851
            Reel 607   v9-20; Jan. 1852-Dec. 1857

608-609   LADIES' GARLAND AND FAMILY WREATH
            Reel 608   v1-11; Apr. 15, 1837-June 1847
            Reel 609   v12-(s3) v4; July 1847-Dec. 1850

609   MANUSCRIPT. v1-2; 1828.

610-613   MASSACHUSETTS TEACHER
          Massachusetts Teacher
            Reel 610   v1-8; Jan. 1, 1848-Dec. 1855
          Massachusetts Teacher and Journal of Home and
          School Education
            Reel 610   v9; Jan.-Dec. 1856
            Reel 611   v10-16; Jan. 1857-Dec. 1863
            Reel 612   v17-22; Jan. 1864-Dec. 1869
            Reel 613   v23-24; Jan. 1870-Dec. 1871
          Teacher
            Reel 613   v25; Jan.-Dec. 1872
          Massachusetts Teacher
            Reel 613   v26-27; Jan. 1873-Dec. 1874

613-614   MECHANICS' MAGAZINE, AND JOURNAL OF THE
          MECHANICS' INSTITUTE
            Reel 613   v1-2; Jan.-Dec. 1833
            Reel 614   v3-10; Jan. 1834-May 26, 1837

615   MILITARY AND NAVAL MAGAZINE OF THE
      UNITED STATES. v1-6; Mar. 1833-Feb. 1836.

615   NEW YORK REVIEW AND ATHENEUM MAGAZINE.
      v2; Jan.-May 1826.

616-619   SCIENTIFIC AMERICAN
            Reel 616   v1-7; Aug. 28, 1845-Sept. 11, 1852
            Reel 617   v8-14; Sept. 18, 1852-June 25, 1859
            Reel 618   nsv1-7; July 2, 1859-Dec. 27, 1862
            Reel 619   nsv8-14; Jan. 3, 1863-June 23, 1866

<u>REEL</u>

620-640   SPIRIT OF THE TIMES
          Spirit of the Times
            Reel 620   v1, no1-50; Dec. 10, 1831-Nov. 24,
                        1832
          Traveller and Spirit of the Times
            Reel 620   v1, no51-v2; Dec. 1, 1832-Oct. 6, 1833
          Spirit of the Times
            Reel 620   v5-6; Jan. 3, 1835-Feb. 11, 1837
            Reel 621   v7-8; Feb. 18, 1837-Feb. 23, 1839
            Reel 622   v9; Mar. 9, 1839-Feb. 29, 1840
            Reel 623   v10; Mar. 7, 1840-Feb. 27, 1841
            Reel 624   v11; Mar. 6, 1841-Feb. 26, 1842
            Reel 625   v12; Mar. 5, 1842-Feb. 25, 1843
            Reel 626   v13; Mar 4, 1843-Feb. 24, 1844
            Reel 627   v14; Mar. 2, 1844-Feb. 22, 1845
            Reel 628   v15; Mar. 1, 1845-Feb. 21, 1846
            Reel 629   v16; Feb. 28, 1846-Feb. 20, 1847
            Reel 630   v17-18; Feb. 27, 1847-Feb. 17, 1849
            Reel 631   v19; Feb. 24, 1849-Feb. 16, 1850
            Reel 632   v20; Feb. 23, 1850-Feb. 15, 1851
            Reel 633   v21; Feb. 22, 1851-Feb. 14, 1852
            Reel 634   v22; Feb. 21, 1852-Feb. 12, 1853
            Reel 635   v23; Feb. 19, 1853-Feb. 11, 1854
            Reel 636   v24-25; Feb. 18, 1854-Feb. 9, 1856
            Reel 637   v26; Feb. 16, 1856-Feb. 7, 1857
            Reel 638   v27; Feb. 14, 1857-Feb. 6, 1858
            Reel 639   v28; Feb. 13, 1858-Feb. 5, 1859
            Reel 640   v29-31; Feb. 12, 1859-June 22, 1861

Unit 16

641-644   AFRICAN REPOSITORY
          African Repository and Colonial Journal
            Reel 641   v1-8; 1825-1832
            Reel 642   v9-15; 1833-1839
            Reel 643   v16-22; 1840-1846
            Reel 644   v23-25; 1847-1849
          African Repository
            Reel 644   v26; 1850

644   AMERICAN LABORER. v1; Apr. 1842-Mar. 1843.

645   AMERICAN MEDICAL RECORDER. v9-16; Jan.
      1826-Apr. 1829.

646   AMERICAN MUSEUM OF LITERATURE AND THE
      ARTS
      American Museum of Science, Literature, and the Arts
        Reel 646   v1; Sept.-Dec. 1838
      American Museum of Literature and the Arts
        Reel 646   v2; Jan.-June 1839

646   AMERICAN REPERTORY OF ARTS, SCIENCES,
      AND MANUFACTURES. v1-4; Jan. 1840-Jan. 1842.

647-649   ANGLO AMERICAN
            Reel 647   v1-4; Apr. 29, 1843-Apr. 19, 1845
            Reel 648   v5-8; Apr. 26, 1845-Apr. 17, 1847
            Reel 649   v9-10; Apr. 24-Nov. 13, 1847

649   ARTIST; A MONTHLY LADY'S BOOK. Sept. 1842-
      May 1843.

649   BROADWAY JOURNAL. v1-2; Jan. 4, 1845-Jan. 3,
      1846.

REEL

650-653   **CHARLESTON GOSPEL MESSENGER AND PRO-TESTANT EPISCOPAL REGISTER**

     Gospel Messenger and Southern Episcopal Register
        Reel 650   v3-9; 1826-1832
        Reel 651   v10-11; 1833-Dec. 1834
     Gospel Messenger and Protestant Episcopal Register
        Reel 651   v12-16, 18; Jan. 1835-Mar. 1842
     Charleston Gospel Messenger and Protestant Epis-copal Register
        Reel 652   v19-23; Apr. 1842-Mar. 1847
        Reel 653   v24-29; Apr. 1847-Mar. 1853

654   **GREEN MOUNTAIN GEM.** v1-7; 1843-1849.

654   **GREEN MOUNTAIN REPOSITORY.** no1-12; 1832.

655   **HARVARDIANA.** v1-4; 1834-1838.

656   **HORTICULTURIST AND JOURNAL OF RURAL ART AND RURAL TASTE.** v1-5; July 1846-Dec. 1850.

656   **IRIS; OR, LITERARY MESSENGER.** v1; Nov. 1840-Oct. 1841.

657   **JOHN-DONKEY.** v1-2; Jan. 1-Oct. 21, 1848.

657   **LADY'S PEARL**
     Ladies' Pearl
        Reel 657   v1-2; June 1840-June 1842
     Lady's Pearl
        Reel 657   v3-4; July 1842-July 1843

657   **LITERARY GEMINAE.** v1; June 1839-May 1840.

657   **LITERARY JOURNAL**
     Wreath; Devoted to Polite Literature
        Reel 657   v1, no1-6; Nov. 1834-Feb. 1835
     Literary Journal
        Reel 657   v1, no7-13; Mar.-June 1835

657   **LITERARY TABLET.** v1-2; 1833-Mar. 29, 1834.

657   **LOUISVILLE JOURNAL OF MEDICINE AND SUR-GERY.** v1; Jan.-Apr. 1838.

658   **MASSACHUSETTS QUARTERLY REVIEW.** v1-3; Dec. 1847-Sept. 1850.

658   **MEDICAL NEWS.** v1-8; 1843-1850.

659   **MONTHLY AMERICAN JOURNAL OF GEOLOGY AND NATURAL SCIENCE.** v1; July 1831-June 1832.

659   **MONTHLY JOURNAL OF FOREIGN MEDICINE.** v1-3; Jan. 1828-June 1829.

660-664   **NEW ENGLAND JOURNAL OF MEDICINE**
     Boston Medical and Surgical Journal
        Reel 660   v1-8; Feb. 19, 1828-Aug. 7, 1833
        Reel 661   v9-18; Aug. 14, 1833-Aug. 1, 1838
        Reel 662   v19-28; Aug. 8, 1838-Aug. 2, 1843
        Reel 663   v29-36; Aug. 9, 1843-July 28, 1847
        Reel 664   v37-43; Aug. 4, 1847-Jan. 29, 1851

665-668   **NEW YORK JOURNAL OF MEDICINE**
        Reel 665   v1-10; July 1843-May 1848
        Reel 666   nsv1-8; July 1848-May 1852
        Reel 667   nsv9-16; July 1852-May 1856
        Reel 668   s3v1-8; July 1856-May 1860

669-670   **PARLEY'S MAGAZINE**
        Reel 669   v1-6; Mar. 16, 1833-Dec. 1838
        Reel 670   v7-12; Jan. 1839-Dec. 1844

REEL

671   **PHALANX.** v1; Oct. 5, 1843-May 28, 1845.

671   **REFORMED CHURCH REVIEW**
     Mercersburg Review
        Reel 671   v1-2; 1849-1850

671   **SOMETHING.** v1; Jan. 6-May 12, 1810.

672   **STRYKER'S AMERICAN REGISTER AND MAGA-ZINE**
     American Quarterly Register and Magazine
        Reel 672   v1-3; May 1848-Dec. 1849
     Stryker's American Register and Magazine
        Reel 672   v4-6; July 1850-1851

673   **WESTERN MONTHLY REVIEW.** v1-3; May 1827-June 1830.

Unit 17

674   **HARBINGER, DEVOTED TO SOCIAL AND POLITI-CAL PROGRESS.** v1-8; June 14, 1845-Feb. 10, 1849.

675   **LOWELL OFFERING.** no1-nsv5; Oct. 1840-Dec. 1845.

676   **MAGNOLIA**
     Southern Ladies' Book: a Magazine of Literature, Science and Arts
        Reel 676   v1-2; Jan.-Dec. 1840
     Magnolia; or Southern Monthly
        Reel 676   v3-4; Jan. 1841-June 1842
     Magnolia; or, Southern Apalachian
        Reel 676   nsv1-2; July 1842-June 1843

677-678   **MASSACHUSETTS MEDICAL SOCIETY. MEDICAL COMMUNICATIONS**
        Reel 677   v1-4; 1790-1829
        Reel 678   v5-8; 1830-1854

679-680   **NEW ENGLANDER AND YALE REVIEW**
     New Englander
        Reel 679   v1-4; 1843-1846
        Reel 680   v5-8; 1847-1850

681-683   **RURAL REPOSITORY DEVOTED TO POLITE LITERATURE**
        Reel 681   v1-10; June 12, 1824-May 24, 1834
        Reel 682   v11-19; June 17, 1834-June 3, 1843
        Reel 683   v20-27; Aug. 26, 1843-Oct. 4, 1851

684-687   **SOUTHERN QUARTERLY REVIEW**
        Reel 684   v1-8; Jan. 1842-Oct. 1845
        Reel 685   v9-15; Jan. 1846-July 1849
        Reel 686   v16-22; Oct. 1849-Oct. 1852
        Reel 687   v23-30; Jan. 1853-Feb. 1857

688   **SOUTHERN ROSE**
     Rose Bud, or Youth's Gazette
        Reel 688   v1; Aug. 1832-Aug. 24, 1833
     Southern Rose Bud
        Reel 688   v2-3; Aug. 31, 1833-Aug. 1835
     Southern Rose
        Reel 688   v4-7; Sept. 1835-Aug. 1839

689-690   **UNITED STATES CATHOLIC MAGAZINE**
     Religious Cabinet: a Monthly Periodical
        Reel 689   v1; 1842
     United States Catholic Magazine: a Monthly Periodical
        Reel 689   v2; 1843

United States Catholic Magazine and Monthly Review
Reel 689   v3-4; 1844-1845
Reel 690   v5-7; 1846-1848
United States Catholic Magazine
Reel 690   v8; 1849

691-696 UNITED STATES DEMOCRATIC REVIEW
United States Magazine, and Democratic Review
Reel 691   v1-8; Oct. 1837-Dec. 1840
Reel 692   v9-15; July 1841-Dec. 1844
Reel 693   v16-22; Jan. 1845-June 1848
Reel 694   v23-29; July 1848-Dec. 1851
Democratic Review
Reel 695   v30-31; Jan.-Dec. 1852
United States Review
Reel 695   v32-37, no1; Jan. 1853-Jan. 1856
United States Democratic Review
Reel 695   v37, no2-6; Feb.-July 1856
Reel 696   v38, 40-43; Aug. 1856-Oct. 1859

697 UNIVERSALIST QUARTERLY AND GENERAL REVIEW. v1-7; Jan. 1844-Oct. 1850.

698 WESTERN FARMER AND GARDENER
Western Farmer; Devoted to Agriculture, Horticulture, and Rural Economy
Reel 698   v1; Sept. 1839-Aug. 1840
Western Farmer and Gardener
Reel 698   v2-5; Oct. 1840-July 1845

699-700 WESTERN JOURNAL AND CIVILIAN
Western Journal of Agriculture, Manufactures, Mechanic Arts, Internal Improvement, Commerce, and General Literature
Reel 699   v1-6; Jan. 1848-Sept. 1851
Western Journal and Civilian
Reel 699   v7; Oct. 1851-Mar. 1852
Reel 700   v8-15; Apr. 1852-Apr. 1856

701-705 WESTERN JOURNAL OF MEDICINE AND SURGERY
Reel 701   v1-8; Jan. 1840-Dec. 1843
Reel 702   v9-15; Jan. 1844-June 1847
Reel 703   v16-22; July 1847-Dec. 1850
Reel 704   v23-28; Jan. 1851-Dec. 1853
Reel 705   v29-32; Jan. 1854-Dec. 1855

Unit 18

706-718 ALBION
Reel 706   v5-7; June 17, 1826-June 6, 1829
Reel 707   v8-11; June 13, 1829-Dec. 29, 1832
Reel 708   nsv1-3; Jan. 5, 1833-Dec. 26, 1835
Reel 709   nsv4-6; Jan. 2, 1836-Dec. 29, 1838
Reel 710   nsv1-3; Jan. 5, 1839-Dec. 25, 1841
Reel 711   nsv1-2; Jan. 1, 1842-Dec. 30, 1843
Reel 712   nsv3-4; Jan. 6, 1844-Dec. 27, 1845
Reel 713   nsv5-6; Jan. 3, 1846-Dec. 25, 1847
Reel 714   nsv7-8; Jan. 1, 1848-Dec. 29, 1849
Reel 715   nsv9-10; Jan. 5, 1850-Dec. 27, 1851
Reel 716   nsv11-12; Jan. 3, 1852-Dec. 31, 1853
Reel 717   nsv13-14; Jan. 1, 1854-Dec. 29, 1855
Reel 718   nsv15; Jan. 5-Dec. 27, 1856

718-719 NEW YORK MEDICAL AND PHYSICAL JOURNAL
Reel 718   v5-6; Jan. 1826-Dec. 1827
Reel 719   v7-9; Jan. 1828-Dec. 1830

720 REFORMER AND CHRISTIAN
Reformer
Reel 720   v7-12, no7; Jan. 1826-Dec. 1831
Reformer and Christian
Reel 720   v12, no8-v14; Feb. 1832-Nov. 1835

720 WORCESTER MAGAZINE AND HISTORICAL JOURNAL. v1-2; Oct. 1825-Oct. 1826.

721-725 PHILADELPHIA ALBUM AND LADIES' LITERARY PORT FOLIO
Album and Ladies' Weekly Gazette
Reel 721   v1; June 7, 1826-May 30, 1827
Philadelphia Album and Ladies Literary Gazette
Reel 721   v2; June 6, 1827-May 28, 1828
Reel 722   v3; June 4, 1828-May 27, 1829
Reel 723   v4, no1-27; Jan. 2-July 3, 1830
Philadelphia Album and Ladies' Literary Portfolio
Reel 723   v4, no28-v5; July 10, 1830-Dec. 31, 1831
Reel 724   v6-7; Jan. 7, 1832-Dec. 28, 1833
Reel 725   v8; Jan. 4-Dec. 27, 1834

725 AMERICAN ANTI-SLAVERY REPORTER. v1; Jan.-Aug. 1834.

725 AMERICAN JOURNAL OF MUSIC AND MUSICAL VISITOR
Musical Visitor
Reel 725   v1-2; July 17, 1840-July 2, 1842
Boston Musical Visitor
Reel 725   v3; Aug. 8, 1842-Oct. 8, 1844
American Journal of Music and Musical Visitor
Reel 725   v4-5; Aug. 29, 1844-Oct. 20, 1846

726-729 AMERICAN JURIST AND LAW MAGAZINE
Reel 726   v1-8; Jan. 1829-Oct. 1832
Reel 727   v9-15; Jan. 1833-July 1836
Reel 728   v16-21; Oct. 1836-July 1839
Reel 729   v22-28; Oct. 1839-Jan. 1843

730-731 AMERICAN LAW JOURNAL
Pennsylvania Law Journal
Reel 730   v1-6; 1842-Sept. 1847
Reel 731   v7; Nov. 1847-June 1848
American Law Journal
Reel 731   v8-11; July 1848-June 1852

732 AMERICAN LAW MAGAZINE. v1-6; Apr. 1843-Jan. 1846.

733 DWIGHTS AMERICAN MAGAZINE, AND FAMILY NEWSPAPER. v1-nsv1; Feb. 8, 1845-July 1, 1851.

734 AMERICAN REPERTORY OF ARTS, SCIENCES, AND USEFUL LITERATURE. v1-3; Aug. 2, 1830-Apr. 1832.

734 ARCTURUS. v1-3; Dec. 1840-May 1842.

734 FESSENDEN'S SILK MANUAL AND PRACTICAL FARMER. v1-2; May 1835-Feb. 1837.

735-736 FRIENDS' INTELLIGENCER
Friends' Weekly Intelligencer
Reel 735   v1-4; Mar. 30, 1844-Mar 25, 1848
Reel 736   v5-6; Apr. 1, 1848-Mar 23, 1850

736 PERIODICAL LIBRARY. v1-3; 1833.

REEL

737 HISTORICAL FAMILY LIBRARY. June 20, 1835-
1841.

738-740 LADIES' COMPANION, AND LITERARY EXPOSI-
TOR
Ladies' Companion, a Monthly Magazine
Reel 738   v1-8; May 1834-Apr. 1838
Reel 739   v9-16; May 1838-Apr. 1842
Reel 740   v17-18; May 1842-Apr. 1843
Ladies' Companion, and Literary Expositor
Reel 740   v19-21; May 1843-Oct. 1844

741 UNITED STATES LAW INTELLIGENCER AND
REVIEW. v1-3; Jan. 1829-Dec. 1831.

741 LITERARY GAZETTE AND AMERICAN
ATHENAEUM
New York Literary Gazette and Phi Beta Kappa
Repository
Reel 741   v1; Sept. 10, 1825-Mar. 4, 1826
New York Literary Gazette and American Athenaeum
Reel 741   v2; Mar. 11-Sept. 2, 1826
Literary Gazette and American Athenaeum
Reel 741   v3; Sept. 9, 1826-Mar. 3, 1827

742 LITERARY UNION. v1-nsv2; Apr. 7, 1849-July 1850.

742 MAGAZINE FOR THE MILLION. v1; Feb. 17-Apr. 27,
1844.

742 MAGAZINE OF USEFUL AND ENTERTAINING
KNOWLEDGE
Mechanics' and Farmers' Magazine of Useful Know-
ledge
Reel 742   v1, no1-2; June 15-July 15, 1830
Magazine of Useful and Entertaining Knowledge
Reel 742   v1, no. 3-v2, no5; Aug. 1830-May 1831

742 MECHANIC APPRENTICE. v1; May 1845-Apr. 1846.

743 MERRY'S MUSEUM FOR BOYS AND GIRLS
Robert Merry's Museum
Reel 743   v1-20; Feb. 1841-Dec. 1850

744 MILITARY MAGAZINE AND RECORD OF THE
VOLUNTEERS OF THE CITY AND COUNTY OF
PHILADELPHIA. v1-3; Mar. 1839-June 1842.

745 MONTHLY CHRONICLE OF EVENTS, DISCOVER-
IES, IMPROVEMENTS, AND OPINIONS. v1-3; Apr.
1840-Dec. 1842.

745 PIONEER. v1; Jan.-Mar. 1843.

746 PORTLAND MAGAZINE. v1-2; Oct. 1, 1834-June 1,
1836.

746 POUGHKEEPSIE CASKET. v1-4; Jan. 2, 1836-Apr. 3,
1841.

747-748 PRAIRIE FARMER
Union Agriculturist and Western Prairie Farmer
Reel 747   v1-2; Jan. 1841-Dec. 1842
Prairie Farmer
Reel 747   v3-8; Jan. 1843-Oct. 1848
Reel 748   v9-10; Jan. 1849-Dec. 1850

748 PRESENT. v1; Sept. 1843-Apr. 1, 1844.

748 PRINCETON MAGAZINE. v1; Mar. 1850-Feb. 1851.

REEL

749-750 PRISONER'S FRIEND
Reel 749   v1-nsv3; Jan. 1, 1845-Aug. 1851
Reel 750   nsv4-9; Sept. 1851-Aug. 1857

751 SCRIPTURAL INTERPRETER. v1-7; Jan. 1831-
Dec. 1836.

752 SPIRIT OF THE PILGRIMS. v1-6; Jan. 1828-Dec.
1833.

753 ZODIAC. v1-2; July 1835-Jan. 1837.

753 SPIRIT OF THE AGE AND JOURNAL OF HUMAN-
ITY. v1; May 23, 1833-Mar. 20, 1834.

Unit 19

754-762 AMERICAN JOURNAL OF SCIENCE
American Journal of Science and Arts
Reel 754   v11-19; Oct. 1826-Jan. 1831
Reel 755   v20-28; July 1831-July 1835
Reel 756   v29-38; Jan. 1836-Apr. 1840
Reel 757   v39-47; Oct. 1840-Oct. 1844
Reel 758   v48-50; Apr. 1845-General Index
(Vols. 1-49)
Reel 758   s2v1-6; May 1846-Nov. 1848
Reel 759   s2v7-14; May 1849-Nov. 1852
Reel 760   s2v15-23; May 1853-May 1857
Reel 761   s2v24-31; Nov. 1857-May 1861
Reel 762   s2v32-40; Nov. 1861-Nov. 1865

763 AMERICAN MECHANICS' MAGAZINE. v2, no41-45;
Dec. 31, 1825-Feb. 11, 1826.

763 BOSTON MEDICAL INTELLIGENCER. v3-5; Jan. 3,
1826-Feb. 12, 1828.

763 CHRISTIAN JOURNAL, AND LITERARY
REGISTER. v10-14; Jan. 1826-Dec. 1830.

764-766 MISSIONARY HERALD AT HOME AND ABROAD
Missionary Herald
Reel 764   v22-30; Jan. 1826-Dec. 1834
Reel 765   v31-37; Jan. 1835-Dec. 1841
Reel 766   v38-46; Jan. 1842-Dec. 1850

767 ADVOCATE FOR THE TESTIMONY OF GOD
Apostolic Advocate
Reel 767   v1-3; May 1, 1834-Apr. 1837
Advocate for the Testimony of God, as it is Written
in the Books of Nature and Revelation
Reel 767   v4-5; May 1837-Apr. 1839

767 ALBANY BOUQUET AND LITERARY SPECTATOR
Reel 767   v1; Apr. 18-Sept. 19, 1835

767 AMERICAN HISTORICAL MAGAZINE. v1; Jan.-June
1836.

768 AMERICAN MAGAZINE OF USEFUL AND ENTER-
TAINING KNOWLEDGE. v1-3; Sept. 1834-Sept. 1837.

768 AMERICAN MONTHLY REVIEW. v1-4; Jan. 1832-
Dec. 1833.

769 AMERICAN MUSICAL JOURNAL. v1; Oct. 1834-
Nov. 1835.

REEL

769   ANTI-MASONIC REVIEW, AND MAGAZINE. v1-2; Jan. 1828-Dec. 1830.

769   AURORA. v1; July 4, 1834-Apr. 25, 1835.

769   BALTIMORE MONUMENT. v1-2; Oct. 8, 1836-Sept. 29, 1838.

770   BALTIMORE PHOENIX AND BUDGET. v1; Apr. 1841-Mar. 1842.

770   BOSTON MUSICAL REVIEW. v1; Sept. 1-Nov. 1, 1845.

770   CONNECTICUT ACADEMY OF ARTS AND SCIENCES, NEW HAVEN. MEMOIRS. v1; 1810-1816.

770   DISTRICT SCHOOL JOURNAL OF THE STATE OF NEW YORK. v1-12; Mar. 25, 1840-Apr. 1852.

771   ELEPHANT. v1; Jan. 22-Feb. 19, 1848.

771   EUTERPEIAD. v1-2; Apr. 15, 1830-Nov. 1, 1831.

771   FAMILY LYCEUM. v1; July 28, 1832-Aug. 10, 1833.

772-776   GODEY'S MAGAZINE
     Lady's Book
       Reel 772   v1-6; July 1830-June 1833
     Monthly Magazine of Belles-Lettres and the Arts, the Lady's Book
       Reel 772   v7-9; July 1833-Dec. 1834
     Lady's Book
       Reel 772   v10; Jan.-June 1835
       Reel 773   v11-19; July 1835-Dec. 1839
     Godey's Lady's Book, and Ladies American Magazine
       Reel 773   v20; Jan.-June 1840
       Reel 774   v21-27; July 1840-Dec. 1843
     Godey's Magazine and Lady's Book
       Reel 774   v28-29; Jan.-Dec. 1844
       Reel 775   v30-36; Jan. 1845-June 1848
     Godey's Lady's Book
       Reel 775   v37; July-Dec. 1848
       Reel 776   v38-41; Jan. 1849-Dec. 1850

777   GRAHAM JOURNAL OF HEALTH AND LONGEVITY. v1-3; Apr. 4, 1837-Dec. 14, 1839.

777   HARVARD REGISTER. no1-12; Mar. 1827-Feb. 1828.

777   ILLUSTRATED FAMILY MAGAZINE
     New England Family Magazine
       Reel 777   v1-2; Feb.-Dec. 1845
     Illustrated Family Magazine
       Reel 777   v3-4; Jan.-Sept. 1846

777   LITERARY CASKET. v1; Mar. 4, 1826-Feb. 3, 1827.

777   LITERARY FOCUS. v1; June 1827-May 1828.

777   MAGNOLIA; OR, LITERARY TABLET. v1; Oct. 5, 1833-Sept. 20, 1834.

778   MONTHLY MISCELLANY OF RELIGION AND LETTERS. v1-9; Apr. 1839-Dec. 1843.

779   SPIRIT OF THE XIX CENTURY. v1-2; Jan. 1842-Dec. 1843.

REEL

779-780   WELLMAN'S MISCELLANY
     Wellman's Literary Miscellany
       Reel 779   v1-4; no2; July 1849-Feb. 1851
     Monthly Literary Miscellany
       Reel 779   v4, no3-v8, no2; Mar. 1851-Feb. 1853
     Western Literary Miscellany
       Reel 779   v8, no3-v9, no1; Mar.-July 1853
     Western Literary Cabinet
       Reel 779   v9, no2-v10; Aug. 1853-June 1854
     Wellman's Miscellany
       Reel 780   s2v1-7; Jan. 1870-Feb. 1873

780-783   AMERICAN LITERARY GAZETTE AND PUBLISHERS' CIRCULAR
     American Publishers' Circular and Literary Gazette
       Reel 780   v1-2; Sept. 1, 1855-Dec. 27, 1856
       Reel 781   v3-7; Jan. 3, 1857-Dec. 5, 1861
       Reel 782   v8; Jan.-Dec. 1862
     American Literary Gazette and Publishers' Circular
       Reel 782   ns2v1-s3v9; Jan. 1863-Oct. 15, 1867
       Reel 783   s3v10-18; Nov. 1867-Jan. 15, 1872

784   AMARANTH. v1; Feb. 20-Dec. 11, 1847.

784   BOSTON WEEKLY MAGAZINE. v1-3; Sept. 8, 1838-Sept. 11, 1841.

Unit 20

785-787   NEW-YORK MIRROR
       Reel 785   v3no24-v10; Jan. 7, 1826-June 29, 1833
       Reel 786   v11-17; July 6, 1833-June 20, 1840
       Reel 787   v18-20; June 27, 1840-Dec. 31, 1842

787   AMERICAN LITERARY MAGAZINE. v1-5; July 1847-Aug. 1849.

788   BOSTON PEARL, A GAZETTE OF POLITE LITERATURE
     Bouquet: Flowers of Polite Literature
       Reel 788   v1-2; June 11, 1831-June 1, 1833
       Reel 788   v3, no1-3; July 6-Aug. 3, 1833
     Pearl and Literary Gazette
       Reel 788   v3; Aug. 17, 1833-Aug. 2, 1834
     Hartford Pearl and Literary Gazette
       Reel 788   v4, no1-8; Aug. 20-Oct. 8, 1834
     Boston Pearl and Literary Gazette
       Reel 788   v4, no9-52; Nov. 8, 1834-Sept. 5, 1835
     Boston Pearl, a Gazette of Polite Literature
       Reel 788   v5-6; Sept. 19, 1835-Sept. 14, 1836

789   CINCINNATI MIRROR, AND WESTERN GAZETTE OF LITERATURE, SCIENCE, AND THE ARTS. v1-5; Oct. 1, 1831-Sept. 17, 1836.

789-791   CONNECTICUT COMMON SCHOOL JOURNAL AND ANNALS OF EDUCATION
     Cumulative Index 1-4; 1838-1842
       Reel 789
     Connecticut Common School Journal
       Reel 789   v1-4; Aug. 1838-Sept. 1, 1842
     Connecticut Common School Journal and Annals of Education
       Reel 790   v5-nsv3; Sept. 1851-Dec. 1856
       Reel 791   nsv4-13; Jan. 1857-Dec. 1866

792   ESCRITOIR. v1; Jan. 28, 1826-Jan. 20, 1827.

REEL

792-794   **EVANGELICAL MAGAZINE AND GOSPEL ADVO-CATE**
Evangelical Repository
Reel 792   v1; Apr. 21, 1827-Mar. 15, 1828
Utica Evangelical Magazine
Reel 792   v2; Apr. 5, 1828-Mar. 21, 1829
Evangelical Magazine
Reel 792   v3; Apr.-Dec. 1829
Evangelical Magazine and Gospel Advocate
Reel 792   nsv1-5; Jan. 1830-Dec. 27, 1834
Reel 793   nsv6-12; Jan. 3, 1835-Dec. 24, 1841
Reel 794   nsv13-19; Jan. 7, 1842-Dec. 29, 1848

795-797   **GENESEE FARMER**
New Genessee Farmer and Gardeners' Journal
Reel 795   v1-5; Jan. 1840-Dec. 1844
Genesee Farmer
Reel 795   v6-13; Jan. 1845-Dec. 1852
Reel 796   v14-s2v22; Jan. 1853-Dec. 1861
Reel 797   s2v23-26; Jan. 1862-Dec. 1865

797   **JEFFERSONIAN.** v1; Feb. 17, 1838-Feb. 9, 1839.

798   **LITERARY AND THEOLOGICAL REVIEW.** v1-6; Jan. 1834-Dec. 1839.

799   **LITERARY GEMS.** v1; Apr. 10-July 1833.

799   **LITERARY INQUIRER.** v1-3; Jan. 1, 1833-Oct. 15, 1834.

799   **LITERARY JOURNAL, AND WEEKLY REGISTER OF SCIENCE AND THE ARTS.** v1; June 8, 1833-May 31, 1834.

799   **NATIONAL MAGAZINE AND REPUBLICAN REVIEW.** v1-2; Jan.-June 1839.

799   **NATIONAL MAGAZINE; OR, LADY'S EMPORIUM.** v1-2; Nov. 1830-July 1831.

800-801   **NATIONAL REGISTER**
Reel 800   v1-8; Mar. 2, 1816-Dec. 25, 1819
Reel 801   v9-10; Jan. 1-Oct. 7, 1820

801   **NATURALIST.** v1-2; Dec. 1830-Dec. 1832.

802   **NEW-ENGLAND MEDICAL REVIEW AND JOURNAL.** v1; Jan.-Oct. 1827.

802   **NEW-ENGLAND TELEGRAPH, AND ECLECTIC REVIEW.** v1-2; Jan. 1835-Dec. 1836.

802-803   **NEW-YORK LEGAL OBSERVER**
Reel 802   v1-4; Oct. 1, 1842-Dec. 1846
Reel 803   v5-12; Jan. 1847-Dec. 1854

804   **NORTH AMERICAN ARCHIVES OF MEDICAL AND SURGICAL SCIENCE.** v1-2; Oct. 1834-Sept. 1835.

804-805   **NORTH AMERICAN MEDICAL AND SURGICAL JOURNAL**
Reel 804   v1-4; Jan. 1826-Aug. 1827
Reel 805   v5-12; Jan. 1828-Oct. 1831

806   **OASIS.** v1; Aug. 12, 1837-July 28, 1838.

806-809   **SOUTHERN AGRICULTURIST, HORTICULTURIST, AND REGISTER OF RURAL AFFAIRS**
Southern Agriculturist and Register of Rural Affairs
Reel 806   v1-5; Jan. 1828-Dec. 1832

Reel 807   v6-9; Jan. 1833-Dec. 1836
Reel 808   v10-12; Jan. 1837-Dec. 1839
Southern Cabinet of Agriculture, Horticulture, Rural and Domestic Economy
Reel 808   v1; Jan.-Dec. 1840
Southern Agriculturist, Horticulturist, and Register of Rural Affairs
Reel 808   nsv1; Jan.-Dec. 1841
Reel 809   nsv2-6; Jan. 1842-Dec. 1846

810   **STRANGER.** v1-; July 3, 1813-June 25, 1814.

810-812   **AMERICAN ALMANAC AND REPOSITORY OF USEFUL KNOWLEDGE**
Reel 810   v1-10; 1830-1839
Reel 811   v11-20; 1840-1849
Reel 812   v21-32; 1850-1861

813   **AMARANTH.** 1847-1855.

814-815   **NATIONAL MAGAZINE**
Reel 814   v1-7; July 1852-Dec. 1855
Reel 815   v8-13; Jan. 1856-Dec. 1858

816   **NEW ENGLAND QUARTERLY JOURNAL OF MEDICINE AND SURGERY.** v1; July 1842-Apr. 1843.

816   **NAVAL MAGAZINE.** v1-2; Jan. 1836-Nov. 1837.

Unit 21

817-830   **AMERICAN JOURNAL OF SCIENCE**
Reel 817   2sv41-48; Jan. 1866-Nov. 1869
Reel 818   2sv49-3sv6; Jan. 1870-Dec. 1873
Reel 819   3sv7-3sv13; Jan. 1874-June 1877
Reel 820   3sv14-3sv20; July 1877-Dec. 1880
Reel 821   3sv21-3sv28; Jan. 1881-Dec. 1884
Reel 822   3sv29-3sv34; Jan. 1885-Dec. 1887
Reel 823   3sv35-3sv40; Jan. 1888-Dec. 1890
Reel 824   3sv41-3sv46; Jan. 1891-Dec. 1893
Reel 825   3sv47-4sv2; Jan. 1894-Dec. 1896
Reel 826   4sv3-4sv8; Jan. 1897-Dec. 1899
Reel 827   4sv9-4sv14; Jan. 1900-Dec. 1902
Reel 828   4sv15-4sv20; Jan. 1903-Dec. 1905
Reel 829   4sv21-4sv26; Jan. 1906-Dec. 1908
Reel 830   4sv27-4sv30; Jan. 1909-Dec. 1910

830-838   **BAPTIST MISSIONARY MAGAZINE**
Missionary Magazine
Reel 830   v31-33; Jan. 1851-Dec. 1853
Reel 831   v34-41; Jan. 1854-Dec. 1861
Reel 832   v42-49; Jan. 1862-Dec. 1869
Reel 833   v50-52; Jan. 1870-Dec. 1872
Baptist Missionary Magazine
Reel 833   v53-57; Jan. 1873-Dec. 1877
Reel 834   v57-65; Jan. 1878-Dec. 1885
Reel 835   v66-73; Jan. 1886-Dec. 1893
Reel 836   v74-79; Jan. 1894-Dec. 1899
Reel 837   v80-83; Jan. 1900-Dec. 1903
Reel 838   v84-89; Jan. 1904-Dec. 1909

839   **ODD FELLOWS' MAGAZINE**
Reel 839   v1, no1-2; Oct. 1, 1825-Jan. 1, 1826
Reel 839   new series; Mar.-June 1828
Reel 839   Oration by Yates; Feb. 22, 1826

839   **ARIEL.** v1-6; Apr. 14, 1827-Nov. 24, 1832.

REEL

839   ATLANTIC JOURNAL, AND FRIEND OF KNOW-LEDGE. v1; Spring 1832-Winter 1833.

840   TRANSACTIONS OF THE LITERARY AND PHILO-SOPHICAL SOCIETY OF NEW-YORK. v1-2; 1815-1825.

840   MUSICAL MAGAZINE. v1-2; May 1835-Apr. 1837.

840   MUSICAL REPORTER. v1; Jan.-Sept. 1841.

841-842   NEW-ENGLAND MAGAZINE
      Reel 841   v1-7; July 1831-Dec. 1834
      Reel 842   v8-9; Jan.-Dec. 1835

842   NEW HAMPSHIRE REPOSITORY. v1-2; Oct. 1845-Jan. 1847.

842   NEW YORK ILLUSTRATED MAGAZINE OF LITERATURE AND ART. v1-3; Sept. 20, 1845-June 1847.

843-844   NEW YORK REVIEW
      Reel 843   v1-7; Mar. 1837-Oct. 1840
      Reel 844   v8-10; Jan. 1841-Apr. 1842

844   NORTHERN LIGHT. v1-4; Apr. 1841-Sept. 1844.

844   OLDEN TIME. v1-2; Jan. 1846-Dec. 1847.

845   PARLOUR REVIEW, AND JOURNAL OF MUSIC, LITERATURE, AND THE FINE ARTS. v1; Jan. 6-Mar. 10, 1838.

845   ROBERT'S SEMI-MONTHLY MAGAZINE FOR TOWN AND COUNTRY. v1-2; Jan. 15, 1841-Jan. 1, 1842.

845   ROUGH AND READY. v1; Dec. 12, 1846-Mar. 13, 1847.

Unit 22

846   AMERICAN MEDICAL REVIEW. v3; Apr.-Aug. 1826.

846-854   PRINCETON REVIEW
      Biblical Repertory
      Reel 846   s2v23-27; Jan. 1851-Oct. 1855
      Reel 847   s2v28-31; Jan. 1856-Oct. 1859
      Reel 848   s2v32-36; Jan. 1860-Oct. 1864
      Reel 849   s2v37-41; Jan. 1865-Oct. 1869
      Reel 850   s2v42-43; Jan. 1870-Oct. 1871
      Presbyterian Quarterly and Princeton Review
      Reel 850   s3v1-3; Jan. 1872-Oct. 1874
      Reel 851   s3v4-6; Jan. 1875-Oct. 1877
      Princeton Review
      Reel 851   s4v1; Jan.-May 1878
      Reel 852   s4v2-6; July 1878-Nov. 1880
      Reel 853   s4v7-14; Jan. 1881-Nov. 1884
      New Princeton Review
      Reel 854   s5v1-6; Jan. 1886-Nov. 1888

855-862   DEBOW'S REVIEW
      DeBow's Review of the Southern and Western States
      Reel 855   v10-13; Jan. 1851-Dec. 1852
      DeBow's Review and Industrial Resources, Statistics, etc.
      Reel 855   v14; Jan.-June 1853
      Reel 856   v15-19; July 1853-Dec. 1855

      Reel 857   v20-24; Jan. 1856-June 1858
      Reel 858   v25-28; July 1858-June 1860
      Reel 859   v29-31; July 1860-Dec. 1861
      Reel 860   v32-34; Jan. 1862-July/Aug. 1864
      DeBow's Review, Devoted to the Restoration of the Southern States
      Reel 860   After the war series 1-3; Jan. 1866-June 1867
      Reel 861   After the war series 4; July-Dec. 1867
      DeBow's Review
      Reel 861   After the war series 5-6; Jan. 1868-Dec. 1869
      Reel 862   After the war series 7-8-June 1880 issue; Jan. 1870-June 1880

862-880   GODEY'S MAGAZINE
      Godey's Lady's Book
      Reel 862   v42-44; Jan. 1851-June 1852
      Reel 863   v45-48; July 1852-June 1854
      Godey's Lady's Book and Magazine
      Reel 864   v49-53; July 1854-Dec. 1856
      Reel 865   v54-58; Jan. 1857-June 1859
      Reel 866   v59-64; July 1859-June 1862
      Reel 867   v65-70; July 1862-June 1865
      Reel 868   v71-76; July 1865-June 1868
      Reel 869   v77-81; July 1868-Dec. 1870
      Reel 870   v82-86; Jan. 1871-June 1873
      Reel 871   v87-91; July 1873-Dec. 1875
      Reel 872   v92-96; Jan. 1876-June 1878
      Reel 873   v97-102; July 1878-June 1881
      Reel 874   v103-105; July 1881-Dec. 1882
      Godey's Lady's Book
      Reel 874   v106-108; Jan. 1883-June 1884
      Reel 875   v109-114; July 1884-June 1887
      Reel 876   v115-119; July 1887-Dec. 1889
      Reel 877   v120-124; Jan. 1890-June 1892
      Reel 878   v125, no745-747; July-Sept. 1892
      Godey's Magazine
      Reel 878   v125, no748-v128; Oct. 1892-June 1894
      Reel 879   v129-132; July 1894-June 1896
      Reel 880   v133-137; July 1896-Aug. 1898

880   RUTGERS LITERARY MISCELLANY v1; Jan.-Dec. 1842.

Unit 23

881   GUARDIAN AND MONITOR. v8-10; Jan. 1826-Dec. 1828.

881   NEW MONTHLY MAGAZINE AND LITERARY JOURNAL. nsv1-3; Jan. 1833-June 1834.

881-884   AFRICAN REPOSITORY
      Reel 881   v27-30; Jan. 1851-Dec. 1854
      Reel 882   v31-40; Jan. 1855-Dec. 1864
      Reel 883   v41-49; Jan. 1865-Dec. 1873
      Reel 884   v50-68; Jan. 1874-Jan. 1892

884-886   BROWNSON'S QUARTERLY REVIEW
      Reel 884   3sv1-2; Jan. 1853-1854
      Reel 885   3sv3-(New York Series)-3 New York Series v3; 1855-1862
      Reel 886   3 New York Series v4-(National Series)-Last Series v1-3; 1863-1875

REEL

886-889 CHRISTIAN REFLECTOR
Reel 886   v1-2; May 1838-Dec. 1839
Reel 887   v3-6; Jan. 1840-Dec. 1843
Reel 888   v7-10; Jan. 1844-Dec. 1847
Reel 889   v11; Jan. 1848-May 1848

889 COMMON SCHOOL ASSISTANT. v1-5; Jan. 1836-Apr. 1840.

889-890 EPISCOPAL WATCHMAN
Reel 889   v1-5; Mar. 1827-May 1832
Reel 890   v6-7; May 1832-Nov. 1833

890-893 HORTICULTURIST AND JOURNAL OF RURAL ART AND RURAL TASTE
Reel 890   v6-10; Jan. 1851-Dec. 1855
Reel 891   v11-17; Jan. 1856-Dec. 1862
Reel 892   v18-27; Jan. 1863-Dec. 1871
Reel 893   v28-30; Jan. 1872-Dec. 1875

893 LADIES' LITERARY PORTFOLIO. v1; Dec. 10, 1823-Dec. 9, 1829.

893-899 LADIES' REPOSITORY
Reel 893   v10-13; Jan. 1850-Dec. 1853
Reel 894   v14-18; Jan. 1854-Dec. 1858
Reel 895   v19-22; Jan. 1859-Dec. 1862
Reel 896   v23-26; Jan. 1863-Dec. 1866
Reel 897   v27-30; Jan. 1867-Dec. 1870
Reel 898   v31-34; Jan. 1871-Dec. 1874
Reel 899   v35-36; Jan. 1875-Dec. 1876

899-903 NATIONAL ERA
Reel 899   v1; Jan.-Dec. 1847
Reel 900   v2-4; Jan. 6, 1848-Dec. 26, 1850
Reel 901   v5-7; Jan. 2, 1851-Dec. 29, 1853
Reel 902   v8-10; Jan. 1854-Dec. 1856
Reel 903   v11-14; Jan. 1857-Mar. 1860

904-912 NEW ENGLANDER AND YALE REVIEW
New Englander
Reel 904   Cumulative Index v1-19; Mar. 1843-Oct. 1861
Reel 904   v9-14; Feb. 1851-Nov. 1856
Reel 905   v15-18; Feb. 1857-Nov. 1860
Reel 906   v19-24; Jan. 1861-Oct. 1865
Reel 907   v25-29; Jan. 1866-Oct. 1870
Reel 908   v30-34; Jan. 1871-Oct. 1875
Reel 909   v35-39; Jan. 1876-Nov. 1880
Reel 910   v40-44; Jan. 1881-Nov. 1885
New Englander and Yale Review
Reel 911   v45-51; Jan. 1886-Dec. 1889
Reel 912   v52-56; Jan. 1890-Mar. 1892

912-913 ROVER
Reel 912   v1-2; 1843-1844
Reel 913   v3-5; 1844-Sept. 1845

913 SELECT JOURNAL OF FOREIGN PERIODICAL LITERATURE
Reel 913   v1-2; 1833
Reel 913   v3-4; 1834

Unit 24

914 BOWEN'S BOSTON NEWS-LETTER. v1-2; Nov. 5, 1825-Dec. 30, 1826.

914 HOPKINSIAN MAGAZINE. v1-4; Jan. 1824-Dec. 31, 1832.

REEL

915 PORT FOLIO. Series 6, v1-2; July 1826-Dec. 1827.

915-916 AMERICAN MASONIC REGISTER AND LITERARY COMPANION
Reel 915   v1-4; Aug. 31-1839-Aug. 26, 1843
Reel 916   v5-8; Nov. 1843-Oct. 1847

916 CAREY'S LIBRARY OF CHOICE LITERATURE. v1-2; Oct. 1, 1835-Mar. 26, 1836.

916-923 CHURCH REVIEW
Church Review, and Ecclesiastical Register
Reel 916   v1-4; Apr. 1848-Jan. 1852
Reel 917   v5-10; Apr. 1852-Jan. 1858
American Quarterly Church Review, and Ecclesiastical Register
Reel 917   v11; Apr. 1858-Jan. 1859
Reel 918   v12-18; Apr. 1859-Jan. 1867
Reel 919   v19-21; Apr. 1867-Jan. 1870
American Quarterly Church Review
Reel 919   v22-23; Apr. 1870-Oct. 1871
American Church Review
Reel 919   v24-26; Jan. 1872-Oct. 1874
Reel 920   v27-35; Jan. 1875-July 1881
Reel 921   v36-45; Oct. 1881-Apr. 1885
Church Review
Reel 922   v46-50; July 1885-Dec. 1887
Reel 923   v51-63; Jan. 1888-Oct. 1891

924 EVERY BODY'S ALBUM. v1-2; July 1836-June 1837.

924 EXPOSITOR. v1; Dec. 8, 1838-July 20, 1839.

924-934 FRIENDS REVIEW
Reel 924   v5-7; Sept. 20, 1851-Sept. 9, 1854
Reel 925   v8-11; Sept. 16, 1854-Sept. 4, 1858
Reel 926   v12-16; Sept. 11, 1858-Aug. 29, 1862
Reel 927   v17-20; Sept. 5, 1863-Aug. 24, 1867
Reel 928   v21-24; Aug. 31, 1867-Aug. 19, 1871
Reel 929   v25-27; Aug. 26, 1871-Aug. 15, 1874
Reel 930   v28-31; Aug. 22, 1874-Aug. 10, 1878
Reel 931   v32-35; Aug. 17, 1878-Aug. 5, 1882
Reel 932   v36-40; Aug. 12, 1882-July 28, 1887
Reel 933   v41-44; Aug. 4, 1887-July 23, 1891
Reel 934   v45-48; July 30, 1891-July 5, 1894

935-937 HUNTRESS
Reel 935   v1-8; Dec. 2, 1836-Feb. 8, 1845
Reel 936   v9-14; Feb. 15, 1845-Feb. 7, 1852
Reel 937   v15-New Series, v1; Feb 14, 1852-July 24, 1854

937 IRISH SHIELD. v1-4; Jan. 1829-Aug. 31, 1831.

938 NEW YORK STATE MECHANIC. v1-2; Nov. 20, 1841-June 17, 1843.

938-939 NORTH AMERICAN QUARTERLY MAGAZINE
North American Magazine
Reel 938   v1-4; Nov. 1832-Oct. 1834
Reel 939   v5; Nov. 1834-Apr. 1835
North American Quarterly Magazine
Reel 939   v6-9; July 1835-June 1838

939-940 NORTH AMERICAN MISCELLANY AND DOLLAR MAGAZINE
North American Miscellany; a Weekly Magazine of Choice Selections from the Current Literature of This Country and Europe
Reel 939   v1-2; Feb.-July 1851

REEL

North American Miscellany and Dollar Magazine
Reel 940   v3-4; Sept. 1851-Aug. 1852

940   OHIO COMMON SCHOOL DIRECTOR. v1; Mar.-Nov. 1838.

940   OLIVER'S MAGAZINE. no1; Oct. 1841.

940-943   THEOLOGICAL AND LITERARY JOURNAL
Reel 940   v1-3; July 1848-Apr. 1851
Reel 941   v4-8; July 1851-Apr. 1856
Reel 942   v9-12; July 1856-Apr. 1860
Reel 943   v13; July 1860-Apr. 1861

943   VIRGINIA HISTORICAL REGISTER, AND LITERARY COMPANION
Virginia Historical Register, and Literary Advertiser
Reel 943   v1-2; Jan. 1848-Oct. 1849
Virginia Historical Register, and Literary Notebook
Reel 943   v3-4; Jan. 1850-Oct. 1851
Virginia Historical Register, and Literary Companion
Reel 943   v5-6; Jan. 1852-Oct. 1853

Unit 25

944   AMERICAN MEDICAL REVIEW
Medical Review and Analectic Journal
Reel 944   v1; June 1824-Apr. 1825
American Medical Review and Journal
Reel 944   v2-3; Sept. 1825-Aug. 1826

944   NEW-ENGLAND JOURNAL OF MEDICINE AND SURGERY. v15; Jan.-Oct. 1826.

944   UNITED STATES LAW JOURNAL
United States Law Journal, and Civilian's Magazine
Reel 944   v1, no1-4; June 1822-Apr. 1823
United States Law Journal
Reel 944   v2, no5-6; Jan.-Apr. 1826

945   ALETHIAN CRITIC. v1; Apr. 1804-1806.

945-973   ECLECTIC MAGAZINE OF FOREIGN LITERATURE
Eclectic Magazine of Foreign Literature
Reel 945   Cumulative Index 1-96
Reel 945   Index to the Engravings (1844-1884)
Reel 945   v22-27; Jan. 1851-Dec. 1852
Reel 946   v28-33; Jan. 1853-Dec. 1854
Reel 947   v34-39; Jan. 1855-Dec. 1856
Reel 948   v40-45; Jan. 1857-Dec. 1858
Reel 949   v46-51; Jan. 1859-Dec. 1860
Reel 950   v52-57; Jan. 1861-Dec. 1862
Reel 951   v58-63; Jan. 1863-Dec. 1864
Reel 952   nsv1-4; Jan. 1865-Dec. 1866
Reel 953   nsv5-8; Jan. 1867-Dec. 1868
Reel 954   nsv9-12; Jan. 1869-Dec. 1870
Reel 955   nsv13-16; Jan. 1871-Dec. 1872
Reel 956   nsv17-20; Jan. 1873-Dec. 1874
Reel 957   nsv21-24; Jan. 1875-Dec. 1876
Reel 958   nsv25-28; Jan. 1877-Dec. 1878
Reel 959   nsv29-32; Jan. 1879-Dec. 1880
Reel 960   nsv33-35; Jan. 1881-June 1882
Reel 961   nsv36-38; July 1882-Dec. 1883
Reel 962   nsv39-41; Jan. 1884-June 1885
Reel 963   nsv42-44; July 1885-Dec. 1886
Reel 964   nsv45-47; Jan. 1887-June 1888
Reel 965   nsv48-50; July 1888-Dec. 1889
Reel 966   nsv51-54; Jan. 1890-Dec. 1891

REEL

Reel 967   nsv55-58; Jan. 1892-Dec. 1893
Reel 968   nsv59-62; Jan. 1894-Dec. 1895
Reel 969   nsv63-67; Jan. 1896-May 1898; Dec. 1898
Reel 970   nsv68; July 1898-Nov, 1898; June 1898
Eclectic Magazine, and Monthly Edition of the Living Age
Reel 970   3sv1-4; Jan. 1899-Dec. 1900
Eclectic Magazine of Foreign Literature
Reel 971   3sv5-8; Jan. 1901-Dec. 1902
Reel 972   3sv9-13; Jan. 1903-June 1905
Reel 973   3sv14-osv148; July 1905-June 1907

973   FAMILY MINSTREL. v1; Jan. 1835-Jan. 1836.

973   NEW ORLEANS MISCELLANY. v1; Dec. 1847-Feb. 1848.

973   NEW YORK LITERARY GAZETTE. no1-24; Feb. 2-July 13, 1839.

973   NORTH AMERICAN. v1; May 19-Nov. 24, 1827.

973   OHIO MEDICAL REPOSITORY OF ORIGINAL AND SELECTED INTELLIGENCE. v1; Apr. 1, 1826-Apr. 18, 1827.

Units 26-28

974-1052   LIVING AGE
Littell's Living Age
Reel 974   Cumulative Index 1-100; 1844-1869
Reel 974   v28-31; Jan. 1851-Dec. 1851
Reel 975   v32-36; Jan. 1852-Mar. 1853
Reel 976   v37-42; Apr. 1853-Sept. 1854
Reel 977   v43-47; Oct. 1854-Dec. 1855
Reel 978   v48-51; Jan. 1856-Dec. 1856
Reel 979   v52-56; Jan. 1857-Mar. 1858
Reel 980   v57-59; Apr. 1858-Dec. 1858
Reel 981   v60-64; Jan. 1859-Mar. 1860
Reel 982   v65-69; Apr. 1860-June 1861
Reel 983   v70-74; July 1861-Sept. 1862
Reel 984   v75-80; Oct. 1862-Mar. 1864
Reel 985   v81-86; Apr. 1864-Sept. 1865
Reel 986   v87-92; Oct. 1865-Mar. 1867
Reel 987   v93-96; Apr. 1867-Mar. 1868
Reel 988   v97-101; Apr. 1868-June 1869
Reel 989   v102-106; July 1869-Sept. 1870
Reel 990   v107-111; Oct. 1870-Dec. 1871
Reel 991   v112-115; Jan. 1872-Dec. 1872
Reel 992   v116-119; Jan. 1873-Dec. 1873
Reel 993   v120-123; Jan. 1874-Dec. 1874
Reel 994   v124-127; Jan. 1875-Dec. 1875
Reel 995   v128-132; Jan. 1876-Mar. 1877
Reel 996   v133-136; Apr. 1877-Mar. 1878
Reel 997   v137-140; Apr. 1878-Mar. 1879
Reel 998   v141-144; Apr. 1879-Mar. 1880
Reel 999   v145-149; Apr. 1880-June 1881
Reel 1000   v150-154; July 1881-Sept. 1882
Reel 1001   v155; Oct. 1882-Dec. 1882
Reel 1002   v156-159; Jan. 1883-Dec. 1883
Reel 1003   v160-163; Jan. 1884-Dec. 1884
Reel 1004   v164-167; Jan. 1885-Dec. 1885
Reel 1005   v168-172; Jan. 1886-Mar. 1887
Reel 1006   v173-176; Apr. 1887-Mar. 1888
Reel 1007   v177-180; Apr. 1888-Mar. 1889
Reel 1008   v181-183; Apr. 1889-Dec. 1889

Reel 1009   v184-187; Jan. 1890-Dec. 1890
Reel 1010   v188-191; Jan. 1891-Dec. 1891
Reel 1011   v192-195; Jan. 1892-Dec. 1892
Reel 1012   v196-199; Jan. 1893-Dec. 1893
Reel 1013   v200-203; Jan. 1894-Dec. 1894
Reel 1014   v204-207; Jan. 1895-Dec. 1895
Reel 1015   v208-211; Jan. 1896-Dec. 1896
Living Age
Reel 1016   v212-215; Jan. 1897-Dec. 1897
Reel 1017   v216-219; Jan. 1898-Dec. 1898
Reel 1018   v220-223; Jan. 1899-Dec. 1899
Reel 1019   v224-227; Jan. 1900-Dec. 1900
Reel 1020   v228-230; Jan. 1901-Sept. 1901
Reel 1021   v231-234; Oct. 1901-Sept. 1902
Reel 1022   v235-238; Oct. 1902-Sept. 1903
Reel 1023   v239-242; Oct. 1903-Sept. 1904
Reel 1024   v243-246; Oct. 1904-Sept. 1905
Reel 1025   v247-250; Oct. 1905-Sept. 1906
Reel 1026   v251-254; Oct. 1906-Sept. 1907
Reel 1027   v255-258; Oct. 1907-Sept. 1908
Reel 1028   v259-262; Oct. 1908-Sept. 1909
Reel 1029   v263-266; Oct. 1909-Sept. 1910
Reel 1030   v267-270; Oct. 1910-Sept. 1911
Reel 1031   v271-274; Oct. 1911-Sept. 1912
Reel 1032   v275-278; Oct. 1912-Sept. 1913
Reel 1033   v279-282; Oct. 1913-Sept. 1914
Reel 1034   v283-286; Oct. 1914-Sept. 1915
Reel 1035   v287-290; Oct. 1915-Sept. 1916
Reel 1036   v291-294; Oct. 1916-Sept. 1917
Reel 1037   v295-298; Oct. 1917-Sept. 1918
Reel 1038   v299-302; Oct. 1918-Sept. 1919
Reel 1039   v303-306; Oct. 1919-Sept. 1920
Reel 1040   v307-310; Oct. 1920-Sept. 1921
Reel 1041   v311-314; Oct. 1921-Sept. 1922
Reel 1042   v315-318; Oct. 1922-Sept. 1923
Reel 1043   v319-323; Oct. 1923-Dec. 1924
Reel 1044   v324-327; Jan. 1925-Dec. 1925
Reel 1045   v328-332; Jan. 1926-June 1927
Reel 1046   v333-335; July 1927-Feb. 1929
Reel 1047   v336-339; Mar. 1929-Feb. 1931
Reel 1048   v340-343; Mar. 1931-Feb. 1933
Reel 1049   v344-348; Mar. 1933-Aug. 1935
Reel 1050   v349-354; Sept. 1935-Aug. 1938
Reel 1051   v355-359; Sept. 1938-Feb. 1941
Reel 1052   v360; Mar. 1941-Aug. 1941

1052   **PITTSBURGH RECORDER.** v3-6; Feb. 3, 1824-
Dec. 25, 1827.

1053-1061   **NEW-ENGLAND HISTORICAL AND GENEALOGI-
CAL REGISTER**
New-England Historical and Genealogical Register
Reel 1053   Cumulative index 1-41; 1847-1887
Reel 1053   Cumulative index 1-50; Jan. 1847-Oct.
1896
Reel 1053   Cumulative index 1-10; 1847-1856
Reel 1053   v1-8; Jan. 1847-Oct. 1854
Reel 1054   v9-10; Jan. 1855-Oct. 1856
Reel 1054   Cumulative index 11-15; 1857-1861
Reel 1054   v11-16; Jan. 1857-Oct. 1862
Reel 1055   v17-22; Jan. 1863-Oct. 1868
**New-England Historical and Genealogical Register and
Antiquarian Journal**
Reel 1055   v23-24; Jan. 1869-Oct. 1870
Reel 1056   v25-27; Jan. 1871-Oct. 1873
New-England Historical and Genealogical Register
Reel 1056   v28-31; Jan. 1874-Oct. 1877
Reel 1057   v32-39; Jan. 1878-Oct. 1885
Reel 1058   v40-45; Jan. 1886-Oct. 1891
Reel 1059   v46-50; Jan. 1892-Oct. 1896

Reel 1060   v51-55; Jan. 1897-Oct. 1901
Reel 1061   v56-59; Jan. 1902-Oct. 1905

Unit 29

1062-1071   **AMERICAN FARMER**
American Farmer, Containing Original Essays . . .
Reel 1062   v7-13; Mar. 25, 1825-Mar. 9, 1832
Reel 1063   v14-15; Mar. 16, 1832-Mar. 7, 1834
Farmer and Gardener . . .
Reel 1063   2sv1-6; May 9, 1834-May 22, 1839
**American Farmer, and Spirit of the Agricultural
Journals . . .**
Reel 1064   3sv1-5; May 29, 1839-May 15, 1844
Reel 1065   3sv6-4sv5; May 22, 1844-June 1850
American Farmer, a Monthly Magazine . . .
Reel 1065   4sv6; July 1850-June 1851
Reel 1066   4sv7-13; July 1851-Jan. 1858
Reel 1067   4sv14-6sv4; July 1858-Dec. 1869
Reel 1068   7sv1, no1-7; Jan.-July 1870
American Farmer and Rural Register
Reel 1068   8sv1-2; Jan. 1872-Dec. 1873
American Farmer
Reel 1068   8sv3-4; Jan. 1874-Dec. 1875
Reel 1069   8sv5-9; Jan. 1876-Dec. 1880
American Farmer; Devoted to Agriculture . . .
Reel 1070   8sv10-9sv3; 10sv10-11sv1; Jan. 1881-
Dec. 15, 1892
Reel 1071   ns, nos25-90; Jan. 1, 1893-Feb. 1897

1072   **FRIEND OF PEACE.** v1-4; 1815-1827.

1072   **GOSPEL ADVOCATE AND IMPARTIAL INVESTI-
GATOR.** v4-7; Jan. 13, 1826-Dec. 26, 1829.

1073-1087   **MEDICAL NEWS**
Medical News
Reel 1073   v9-24; Jan. 1851-Dec. 1866
Reel 1074   v25-34; Jan. 1867-Dec. 1876
Reel 1075   v35-37; Jan. 1877-Dec. 1879
Medical News and Abstract
Reel 1075   v38-39; Jan. 1880-Dec. 1881
Medical News
Reel 1075   v40; Jan.-June 24, 1882
Reel 1076   v41-45; July 1, 1882-Dec. 27, 1884
Reel 1077   v46-50; Jan. 3, 1885-June 25, 1887
Reel 1078   v51-55; July 2, 1887-Dec. 28, 1889
Reel 1079   v56-60; Jan. 4, 1890-June 25, 1892
Reel 1080   v61-64; July 2, 1892-June 30, 1894
Reel 1081   v65-68; July 7, 1894-June 27, 1896
Reel 1082   v69-72; July 4, 1896-June 25, 1898
Reel 1083   v73-76; July 2, 1898-June 30, 1900
Reel 1084   v77-79; July 7, 1900-Dec. 28, 1901
Reel 1085   v80-82; Jan. 4, 1902-June 27, 1903
Reel 1086   v83-85; July 4, 1903-Dec. 31, 1904
Reel 1087   v86-87; Jan. 7-Dec. 30, 1905

1087-1090   **NATIONAL PREACHER AND VILLAGE PULPIT**
Reel 1087   Cumulative Index, 1-38; 1826-1864
**National Preacher; or, Original Monthly Sermons from
Living Ministers**
Reel 1087   v1-2; June 1826-May 1828
American National Preacher
Reel 1087   v3-5; June 1828-May 1831
Reel 1088   v6-21; June 1831-Dec. 1847
Reel 1089   v22-31; Jan. 1848-Dec. 1857
National Preacher and Village Pulpit
Reel 1089   nsv1-2; Jan. 1858-Dec. 1859
Reel 1090   nsv3-9; Jan. 1860-Dec. 1866

REEL

1090-1092 NEW-YORKER
 Reel 1090 v1-2; Mar. 26, 1836-Mar. 18, 1837
 Reel 1091 v3-8; Mar. 25, 1837-Mar. 14, 1840
 Reel 1092 v9-11; Mar. 21, 1840-Sept. 11, 1841

1092 PHILADELPHIA MONTHLY MAGAZINE. v1-nsv1; Oct. 1827-Oct. 1829.

1092 QUARTERLY JOURNAL AND REVIEW. v1; Jan.-Oct. 1846.

Unit 30

1093 AMERICAN MILLENARIAN AND PROPHETIC REVIEW. v2; June 1, 1843-Apr. 1844.

1093 CHRISTIAN REGISTER. v1; June 1822-May 1823.

1093 LADY'S WESTERN MAGAZINE AND GARLAND OF THE VALLEY. v1; Jan.-June 1849.

1093 MECHANICS' MAGAZINE, AND JOURNAL OF PUBLIC INTERNAL IMPROVEMENT. v1; Feb. 1830-Jan. 1831.

1093-1113 METHODIST REVIEW
 Methodist Quarterly Review
 Reel 1093 v33-35; Jan. 1851-Oct. 1853
 Reel 1094 v36-40; Jan. 1854-Oct. 1858
 Reel 1095 v41-45; Jan. 1859-Oct. 1863
 Reel 1096 v46-50; Jan. 1864-Oct. 1868
 Reel 1097 v51-55; Jan. 1869-Oct. 1873
 Reel 1098 v56-59; Jan. 1874-Oct. 1877
 Reel 1099 v60-63; Jan. 1878-Oct. 1881
 Reel 1100 v64-66; Jan. 1882-Oct. 1884
 Methodist Review
 Reel 1100 v67; Jan.-Nov. 1885
 Reel 1101 v68-71; Jan. 1886-Nov. 1889
 Reel 1102 v72-74; Jan. 1890-Nov. 1892
 Reel 1103 v75-77; Jan. 1893-Dec. 1895
 Reel 1104 v78-80; Jan. 1896-Nov. 1898
 Reel 1105 v81-83; Jan. 1899-Nov. 1901
 Reel 1106 v84-86; Jan. 1902-Nov. 1904
 Reel 1107 v87-89; Jan. 1905-Dec. 1907
 Reel 1108 v90-93; Jan. 1908-Dec. 1911
 Reel 1109 v94-97; Jan. 1912-Dec. 1915
 Reel 1110 v98-102; Jan. 1916-Dec. 1919
 Reel 1111 v103-106; Jan. 1920-Dec. 1923
 Reel 1112 v107-110; Jan. 1924-Dec. 1927
 Reel 1113 v111-114; Jan. 1928-June 1931

1114-1120 MONTHLY RELIGIOUS MAGAZINE AND THEOLOGICAL REVIEW
 Monthly Religious Magazine
 Reel 1114 v1-7; Jan. 1844-Dec. 1850
 Reel 1115 v8-15, no1; Jan. 1851-Jan. 1856
 Monthly Religious Magazine and Independent Journal
 Reel 1115 v15, no2-6; Feb.-June 1856
 Reel 1116 v16-23; July 1856-June 1860
 Reel 1117 v24-v25, no1; July 1860-Jan. 1861
 Monthly Religious Magazine
 Reel 1117 v25, no2-v32; Feb. 1861-Dec. 1864
 Reel 1118 v33-40; Jan. 1865-Dec. 1868
 Reel 1119 v41-42; Jan.-Dec. 1869
 Monthly Review and Religious Magazine
 Reel 1119 v43-44, no1; Jan.-July 1870
 Religious Magazine and Monthly Review
 Reel 1119 v44, no2-v46; Aug. 1870-Dec. 1871
 Reel 1120 v47-50; Jan. 1872-Dec. 1873

REEL

 Monthly Religious Magazine and Theological Review
 Reel 1120 v51; Jan.-Dec. 1874

1120 MUSICAL CABINET. v1; July 1841-June 1842.

1120-1123 NEW-ENGLAND GALAXY
 Reel 1120 v9; Jan. 6, 1826-Dec. 29, 1826
 Reel 1121 v10-13; Jan. 5, 1827-Dec. 31, 1830
 Reel 1122 v14-17; Jan. 7, 1831-Dec. 27, 1834
 Reel 1123 v18-20; Jan. 3, 1835-Dec. 31, 1836

1123 NEW JERSEY AND PENNSYLVANIA AGRICULTURAL MONTHLY INTELLIGENCER. v1; May 1825-Oct. 26, 1826.

1124 NEW MIRROR. v1-3; Apr. 8, 1843-Sept. 28, 1844.

1124 OPERA GLASS. v1; Sept. 8-Nov. 3, 1828.

1124 SABBATH SCHOOL VISITANT. v1-2; June 7, 1824-Feb. 1826.

1124 UNITED STATES REVIEW AND LITERARY GAZETTE. v1-2; Oct. 1826-Sept. 1827.

Unit 31

1125-1151 AMERICAN JOURNAL OF THE MEDICAL SCIENCES
 Reel 1125 nsv21-25; 1851-1852
 Reel 1126 nsv26-32; 1853-1856
 Reel 1127 nsv33-38; 1857-1859
 Reel 1128 nsv39-45; 1860-1863
 Reel 1129 nsv46-52; 1863-1866
 Reel 1130 nsv53-58; 1867-1869
 Reel 1131 nsv59-63; 1870-1872
 Reel 1132 nsv64-70; 1872-1875
 Reel 1133 nsv71-76; 1876-1878
 Reel 1134 nsv77-82; 1879-1881
 Reel 1135 nsv83-88; 1882-1884
 Reel 1136 nsv89-94; 1885-1887
 Reel 1137 nsv95-99; 1888-1890
 Reel 1138 nsv100-104; 1890-1892
 Reel 1139 nsv105-109; 1893-1895
 Reel 1140 nsv110-114; 1895-1897
 Reel 1141 nsv115-119; 1898-1900
 Reel 1142 nsv120-123; 1900-1902
 Reel 1143 nsv124-126; 1902-1903
 Reel 1144 nsv127-129; 1904-1905
 Reel 1145 nsv130-132; 1905-1906
 Reel 1146 nsv133-136; 1907-1908
 Reel 1147 nsv137-140; 1909-1910
 Reel 1148 nsv141-143; 1911-1912
 Reel 1149 nsv144-146; 1913-1914
 Reel 1150 nsv147-150; 1915-1916
 Reel 1151 nsv151-153; 1916-1917

Unit 32

1152-1157 AMERICAN JOURNAL OF THE MEDICAL SCIENCES
 Reel 1152 nsv154-156; July 1917-Dec. 1918
 Reel 1153 nsv157-159; Jan. 1919-June 1920
 Reel 1154 nsv160-162; July 1920-Dec. 1921
 Reel 1155 nsv163-164; Jan. 1922-Dec. 1922
 Reel 1156 nsv165-166; Jan. 1923-Dec. 1923
 Reel 1157 nsv167-168; Jan. 1924-Dec. 1924

REEL

1158   AMERICAN SUNDAY-SCHOOL TEACHERS' MAGAZINE AND JOURNAL OF EDUCATION. v1; Dec. 1823-Nov. 1824.

1158   CHRISTIAN BAPTIST. v4-7; Aug. 7, 1826-Aug. 3, 1829.

1158-1166 FLAG OF OUR UNION
Reel 1158	v9-10; Jan. 7, 1854-Dec. 29, 1855
Reel 1159	v11-12; Jan. 5, 1856-Dec. 26, 1857
Reel 1160	v13-15; Jan. 2, 1858-Dec. 29, 1860
Reel 1161	v16-19; Jan. 5, 1861-Oct. 29, 1864
Reel 1162	v20; Jan. 7, 1865-Dec. 30, 1865
Reel 1163	v21; Jan. 6, 1866-Dec. 29, 1866
Reel 1164	v22; Jan. 5, 1867-Dec. 28, 1867
Reel 1165	v23; Jan. 4, 1868-Dec. 26, 1868
Reel 1166	v24-25; Jan. 2, 1869-May 14, 1870

1167-1191 FRIENDS' INTELLIGENCER
Friends' Weekly Intelligencer
| Reel 1167 | v7-9; Mar. 30, 1850-Mar. 19, 1853 |

Friends' Intelligencer
Reel 1167	v10; Mar. 26, 1853-Mar. 18, 1854
Reel 1168	v11-13; Mar. 25, 1854-Mar. 14, 1857
Reel 1169	v14-16; Mar. 21, 1857-Mar. 10, 1860
Reel 1170	v17-19; Mar. 17, 1860-Mar. 7, 1863
Reel 1171	v20-22; Mar. 14, 1863-Mar. 3, 1866
Reel 1172	v23-25; Mar. 10, 1866-Feb. 27, 1869
Reel 1173	v26-28; Mar. 6, 1869-Feb. 24, 1872
Reel 1174	v29-31; Mar. 2, 1872-Feb. 20, 1875
Reel 1175	v32-33; Feb. 27, 1875-Feb. 17, 1877
Reel 1176	v34-36; Feb. 24, 1877-Feb. 14, 1880
Reel 1177	v37-39; Feb. 21, 1880-Feb. 10, 1883
Reel 1178	v40-42; Feb. 17, 1883-Dec. 26, 1885
Reel 1179	v43-44; Jan. 2, 1886-Dec. 31, 1187
Reel 1180	v45-46; Jan. 7, 1888-Dec. 28, 1889
Reel 1181	v47-48; Jan. 4, 1890-Dec. 26, 1891
Reel 1182	v49-50; Jan. 2, 1892-Dec. 30, 1893
Reel 1183	v51-52; Jan. 6, 1894-Dec. 28, 1895
Reel 1184	v53-54; Jan. 4, 1896-Dec. 25, 1897
Reel 1185	v55-56; Jan. 1, 1898-Dec. 30, 1899
Reel 1186	v57-58; Jan. 6, 1900-Dec. 28, 1901
Reel 1187	v59-60; Jan. 4, 1902-Dec. 26, 1903
Reel 1188	v61-62; Jan. 2, 1904-Dec. 30, 1905
Reel 1189	v63-64; Jan. 6, 1906-Dec. 28, 1907
Reel 1190	v65-66; Jan. 4, 1908-Dec. 25, 1909
Reel 1191	v67; Jan. 1, 1910-Dec. 31, 1910

1191-1194 NEW ENGLAND FARMER
Reel 1191	v1-4; Dec. 1848-Dec. 1852
Reel 1192	v5-9; Jan. 1853-Dec. 1857
Reel 1193	v10-15; Jan. 1858-Dec. 1863
Reel 1194	v16-nsv1-5; Jan. 1864-Dec. 1871

1195-1196 NEW YORK FARMER
| Reel 1195 | v1-7; Jan. 1828-Dec. 1834 |
| Reel 1196 | v8-10; Jan. 1835-Oct. 1837 |

1196   PHILADELPHIER MAGAZIN FUR FREUNDE DER DEUTSCHEN LITERATUR IN AMERIKA
Readinger Magazin fur Freunde der Deutschen Literatur in Amerika
| Reel 1196 | v1, no1-12; Jan.-Dec. 1824 |

Philadelphier Magazin fur Freunde der Deutschen Literatur in Amerika
| Reel 1196 | nsv1, no1-10; Jan.-Oct. 1825 |

1196   UNITARIAN. v1; Nov. 18, 1827-Feb. 15, 1828.

REEL

Unit 33

1197   CHRISTIAN TELESCOPE AND UNIVERSALIST MISCELLANY. v2-4; Jan. 1826-Oct. 1828.

1197   INVESTIGATOR AND ADVOCATE OF INDEPENDENCE
Investigator
| Reel 1197 | v1; Jan.-Dec. 1845 |

Investigator and Advocate of Independence
| Reel 1197 | v2; Jan.-Dec. 1846 |

1197-1215 MEDICAL AND SURGICAL REPORTER
Reel 1197	v1-2; Oct. 1858-Sept. 1859
Reel 1198	v3-7; Oct. 1859-Mar. 1862
Reel 1199	v8-13; Apr. 1862-Dec. 1865
Reel 1200	v14-18; Jan. 1866-June 1868
Reel 1201	v19-23; July 1868-Dec. 1870
Reel 1202	v24-28; Jan. 1871-June 1873
Reel 1203	v29-34; July 1873-June 1876
Reel 1204	v35-40; July 1876-June 1879
Reel 1205	v41-45; July 1879-Dec. 1881
Reel 1206	v46-49; Jan. 1882-Dec. 1883
Reel 1207	v50-53; Jan. 1884-Dec. 1885
Reel 1208	v54-56; Jan. 1886-June 1887
Reel 1209	v57-59; July 1887-Dec. 1888
Reel 1210	v60-63; Jan. 1889-Dec. 1890
Reel 1211	v64-66; Jan. 1891-June 1892
Reel 1212	v67-69; July 1892-Dec. 1893
Reel 1213	v70-72; Jan. 1894-June 1895
Reel 1214	v73-76; July 1895-June 1897
Reel 1215	v77-78; July 1897-May 1898

1215   MONTHLY REPOSITORY AND LIBRARY OF ENTERTAINING KNOWLEDGE. v1-4; June 1830-May 1834.

1216   MUSICAL MAGAZINE; OR, REPOSITORY OF MUSICAL SCIENCE. v1-3; Jan. 5, 1839-Apr. 24, 1842.

1216   ORION. v1-4; Mar. 1842-Aug. 1844.

1217-1229 REFORMED CHURCH REVIEW
Mercersburg Review
| Reel 1217 | v3-4; Jan. 1851-Oct. 1852 |

Mercersburg Quarterly Review
| Reel 1217 | v5-7; Jan. 1853-Oct. 1855 |
| Reel 1218 | v8; Jan.-Oct. 1856 |

Mercersburg Review
Reel 1218	v9-13; Jan. 1857-Oct. 1861
Reel 1219	s2v1-5 (14-18); Jan. 1867-Oct. 1871
Reel 1220	s2v6-10 (19-23); Jan. 1872-Oct. 1876
Reel 1221	s2v11-12 (24-25); Jan. 1877-Oct. 1878

Reformed Quarterly Review
Reel 1221	s3v1-3 (26-28); Jan. 1879-Oct. 1881
Reel 1222	s3v4-9 (29-34); Jan. 1882-Oct. 1887
Reel 1223	s3v10-15 (35-40); Jan. 1888-Oct. 1893
Reel 1224	s3v16-18 (41-43); Jan. 1894-Oct. 1896

Reformed Church Review
Reel 1224	s4v1-3 (44-46); Jan. 1897-Oct. 1899
Reel 1225	s4v4-8 (47-51); Jan. 1900-Oct. 1904
Reel 1226	s4v9-13 (52-56); Jan. 1905-Oct. 1909
Reel 1227	s4v14-19 (57-62); Jan. 1910-Oct. 1915
Reel 1228	s4v20-25 (63-68); Jan. 1916-Oct. 1921
Reel 1229	s5v1-5 (69-73); Jan. 1922-Oct. 1926

Unit 34

1230-1231 CHRISTIAN PARLOR MAGAZINE
| Reel 1230 | v1-7; May 1844-Apr. 1851 |
| Reel 1231 | v8-nsv1; 1852-1855 |

REEL

1231   INVESTIGATOR AND EXPOSITOR. v1; July 4, 1839-Oct. 1840.

1231   JOURNAL OF EDUCATION. v1-2; Mar. 1838-Feb. 1840.

1232-1233 LADIES' WREATH
     Reel 1232   v1-7; May 1846-1853
     Reel 1233   v8-17; 1854-1859

1233   LITERARY EMPORIUM. v1-5; Jan. 1845-Jan. 1847.

1234   LITERARY REGISTER. v1-2; June 2, 1828-June 27, 1829.

1234-1237 MEDICAL EXAMINER
     Reel 1234   v1-4; Jan. 1860-Dec. 1863
     Reel 1235   v5-9; Jan. 1864-Dec. 1868
     Reel 1236   v10-14; Jan. 1869-Dec. 1873
     Reel 1237   v15-16; Jan. 1874-July 1875

1237-1245 MISSIONARY HERALD AT HOME AND ABROAD
Missionary Herald
     Reel 1237   v47-51; Jan. 1851-Dec. 1855
     Reel 1238   v52-60; Jan. 1856-Dec. 1864
     Reel 1239   v61-68; Jan. 1865-Dec. 1872
     Reel 1240   v69-76; Jan. 1873-Dec. 1880
     Reel 1241   v77-82; Jan. 1881-Dec. 1886
     Reel 1242   v83-88; Jan. 1887-Dec. 1892
     Reel 1243   v89-94; Jan. 1893-Dec. 1898
     Reel 1244   v95-99; Jan. 1899-Dec. 1903
     Reel 1245   v100-102; Jan. 1904-Dec. 1906

1245   MONTHLY OFFERING. v1-2; July 1840-Oct. 1842.

1245-1254 MUSEUM OF FOREIGN LITERATURE, SCIENCE, AND ART
     Reel 1245   v1; July 1822-Dec. 1822
     Reel 1246   v2-7; Jan. 1823-Dec. 1825
     Reel 1247   v8-12; Jan. 1826-Apr. 1828
     Reel 1248   v13-18; May 1828-June 1831
     Reel 1249   v19-22; July 1831-June 1833
     Reel 1250   v23-26; July 1833-June 1835
     Reel 1251   v27-31; July 1835-Dec. 1837
     Reel 1252   v32-36; Jan. 1838-Aug. 1839
     Reel 1253   v37-42; Sept. 1839-Aug. 1841
     Reel 1254   v43-45; Sept. 1841-Dec. 1842

1254   NEW YORK TELESCOPE
Telescope
     Reel 1254   v1-4; June 5, 1824-May 24, 1828

1254-1257 OHIO CULTIVATOR
     Reel 1254   v1-2; Jan. 1, 1845-Dec. 15, 1846
     Reel 1255   v3-9; Jan. 1, 1847-Dec. 15, 1853
     Reel 1256   v10-16; Jan. 1, 1854-Dec. 15, 1860
     Reel 1257   v17-22; Jan. 1, 1861-Dec. 1866

1257   PARTHENON. v1; Aug. 22-Nov. 7, 1827.

1257-1258 REPUBLIC OF LETTERS
     Reel 1257   v1-4; 1834-1835
     Reel 1258   v5-6; 1836

1258   SARGENT'S NEW MONTHLY MAGAZINE, OF LITERATURE, FASHION, AND THE FINE ARTS. v1; Jan.-June 1843.

1258   SOUTHERN LITERARY GAZETTE. v1-nsv1; Sept. 1828-Oct. 1829.

1258   THEATRICAL BUDGET. nsv1-6; 1828.

1258-1259 UNITED BRETHREN'S MISSIONARY INTELLIGENCER
     Reel 1258   v1-3; 1822-1830
     Reel 1259   v4-9; 1831-1848

1260   WESTERN LITERARY MAGAZINE
Literary Messenger
     Reel 1260   v1-2; June 1840-May 1842
Literary Casket
     Reel 1260   v3, nos1-8; July 1842-Apr. 1843
Western Literary Casket
     Reel 1260   v3, nos9-12; May-Aug. 1843
Western Literary Magazine
     Reel 1260   v4, no1-7; Sept. 1843-Feb. 1844

1260   WESTERN MISCELLANY. v1; July 1848-June 1849.

1260-1262 WESTERN RECORDER
     Reel 1260   v1-2; Jan. 1824-Dec. 1825
     Reel 1261   v3-6; Jan. 1826-Dec. 1829
     Reel 1262   v7-10; Jan. 1830-Oct. 1833

Unit 35

1263-1270 ALBION
     Reel 1263   v35-37; Jan. 3, 1857-Dec. 31, 1859
     Reel 1264   v38-40; Jan. 7, 1860-Dec. 27, 1862
     Reel 1265   v41-43; Jan. 3, 1863-Dec. 30, 1865
     Reel 1266   v44-46; Jan. 6, 1866-Dec. 26, 1868
     Reel 1267   v47-48; Jan. 2, 1869-Dec. 31, 1870
     Reel 1268   v49-50; Jan. 7, 1871-Dec. 28, 1872
     Reel 1269   v51-52; Jan. 4, 1873-Dec. 26, 1874
     Reel 1270   v53-54; Jan. 2, 1875-Dec. 23, 1876

1271   COLUMBIAN STAR. v5-8; Jan. 7, 1826-May 2, 1829.

1271   EVANGELIST. v1-2; Jan. 1824-Dec. 1825.

1272-1273 GENIUS OF UNIVERSAL EMANCIPATION
     Reel 1272   v1-nsv2 [i.e., 5-8]; Jan. 7, 1826-Aug. 30, 1828
     Reel 1273   nsv3-v16 [i.e., 9-16]; Sept. 6, 1828-Mar. 8, 1839

1274-1287 MASSACHUSETTS PLOUGHMAN AND NEW ENGLAND JOURNAL OF AGRICULTURE
     Reel 1274   v1-5; Jan. 15, 1842-Sept. 26, 1846
     Reel 1275   v6-8; Oct. 3, 1846-Sept. 29, 1849
     Reel 1276   v9-29; Oct. 6, 1849-Sept. 17, 1870
     Reel 1277   v30-32; Oct. 1, 1870-Sept. 27, 1873
     Reel 1278   v33-37; Oct. 4, 1873-Sept. 28, 1878
     Reel 1279   v38-41; Oct. 5, 1878-Sept. 30, 1882
     Reel 1280   v42-44; Oct. 14, 1882-Sept. 26, 1885
     Reel 1281   v45-48; Oct. 3, 1885-Dec. 29, 1888
     Reel 1282   v56-57; Oct. 10, 1896-Sept. 24, 1898
     Reel 1283   v58-59; Oct. 1, 1898-Sept. 22, 1900
     Reel 1284   v60-61; Sept. 29, 1900-Sept. 20, 1902
     Reel 1285   v62; Sept. 27, 1902-Sept. 19, 1903
     Reel 1286   v63-64; Sept. 26, 1903-Dec. 30, 1905
     Reel 1287   v65; Jan. 6-Nov. 17, 1906

1287-1288 MEDICAL AND SURGICAL REPORTER
New Jersey Medical Reporter and Transactions of the New Jersey Medical Society
     Reel 1287   v1-4; Oct. 1847-Sept. 1851
     Reel 1288   v5-7; Oct. 1851-Dec. 1854

REEL

New Jersey Medical Reporter
Reel 1288   v8; Jan.-Dec. 1855
Medical and Surgical Reporter
Reel 1288   v9-11; Jan. 1856-Sept. 1858

1289-1291 MUSICAL VISITOR
Reel 1289   v1-13; Oct. 1871-Dec. 1884
Reel 1290   v14-21; Jan. 1885-Dec. 1892
Reel 1291   v22-26; Jan. 1893-Dec. 1897

1292   NEW YORK LITERARY GAZETTE AND JOURNAL
OF BELLES LETTRES, ARTS, SCIENCE, etc. Nov.
15, 1834-Feb. 14, 1835.

1292-1308 PETERSON MAGAZINE
Lady's World of Fashion
Reel 1292   v1-2; Jan.-Dec. 1842
Lady's World
Reel 1292   v3; Jan.-May 1843
Artist and Lady's World
Reel 1292   v3; June 1843
Ladies' National Magazine
Reel 1292   v4-11; July 1843-June 1847
Reel 1293   v12-14; July 1847-Dec. 1848
Peterson's Magazine
Reel 1293   v15-21; Jan. 1849-June 1852
Reel 1294   v22-29; July 1852-June 1856
Reel 1295   v30-36; July 1856-Dec. 1859
Reel 1296   v37-42; Jan. 1860-Dec. 1862
Reel 1297   v43-48; Jan. 1863-Dec. 1865
Reel 1298   v49-55; Jan. 1866-June 1869
Reel 1299   v56-61; July 1869-June 1872
Reel 1300   v62-68; July 1872-Dec. 1875
Reel 1301   v69-74; Jan. 1876-Dec. 1878
Reel 1302   v75-80; Jan. 1879-Dec. 1881
Reel 1303   v81-87; Jan. 1882-June 1885
Reel 1304   v88-93; July 1885-June 1888
Reel 1305   v94-99; July 1888-June 1891
Reel 1306   v100-102; July 1891-Nov. 1892
New Peterson Magazine
Reel 1306   nsv1-2 (103-104); Dec. 1892-Dec.
1893
Reel 1307   nsv3-4 no2; Jan.-Aug. 1894
Peterson Magazine
Reel 1307   nsv4, no3-v6; Sept. 1894-Dec. 1896
Reel 1308   nsv7(113); Jan.-Dec. 1897

1308   ROSE OF THE VALLEY. v1; 1839.

1308   SALMAGUNDI (PAULDING). s2v2-3; Oct. 2, 1819-
Aug. 19, 1820.

1308   UNIVERSALIST. v1; Apr. 1, 1825-Mar. 15, 1826.

1309-1310 UNIVERSALIST WATCHMAN, REPOSITORY AND
CHRONICLE
Christian Repository
Reel 1309   v1-6; July 1820-Dec. 1825
Universalist Watchman
Reel 1309   nsv3-4; Apr. 30, 1831-Apr. 20, 1833
Reel 1310   nsv10-18; June 30, 1838-July 9, 1847

1311-1313 WESTERN LUMINARY
Reel 1311   v1-4; July 14, 1824-June 25, 1828
Reel 1312   v5-8; July 2, 1828-June 27, 1832
Reel 1313   v9-11; Jan. 9, 1833-Dec. 31, 1834

1313   YANKEE AND BOSTON LITERARY GAZETTE. v1-
nsno6; Jan. 1, 1828-Dec. 1829

REEL

Unit 36

1314   JOURNAL OF BELLES LETTRES. v1-17; June 25,
1832-Apr. 1842.

1314-1317 MASSACHUSETTS MEDICAL SOCIETY. MEDICAL
COMMUNICATIONS
Reel 1314   v9-11; 1854-1880
Reel 1315   v12-16; 1881-1895
Reel 1316   v17-19; 1896-1904
Reel 1317   v20-24; 1905-1913

1318-1340 NATIONAL POLICE GAZETTE . . .
Reel 1318   v1-22; Oct. 1845-Aug. 31, 1867
Reel 1319   v23-24; Sept. 7, 1867-Sept. 20, 1879
Reel 1320   v35-36; Sept. 27, 1879-Sept. 18, 1880
Reel 1321   v37-38; Sept. 25, 1880-Oct. 1, 1881
Reel 1322   v39-40; Oct. 8, 1881-Oct. 14, 1882
Reel 1323   v41-42; Oct. 21, 1882-Oct. 13, 1883
Reel 1324   v43-44; Oct. 20, 1883-Sept. 27, 1884
Reel 1325   v45-46; Oct. 4, 1884-Sept. 19, 1885
Reel 1326   v47-48; Sept. 26, 1885-Sept. 25, 1886
Reel 1327   v49-50; Oct. 2, 1886-Sept. 24, 1887
Reel 1328   v51-52; Oct. 1, 1887-Sept. 22, 1888
Reel 1329   v53-54; Sept. 29, 1888-Sept. 21, 1889
Reel 1330   v55-57; Sept. 28, 1889-Mar. 14, 1891
Reel 1331   v59-62; Sept. 26, 1891-May 20, 1893
Reel 1332   v63; Sept. 2, 1893-Sept. 8, 1894
Reel 1333   v65-67; Sept. 15, 1894-Feb. 29, 1896
Reel 1334   v69-75; Sept. 5, 1896-Feb. 10, 1900
Reel 1335   v76-78; Feb. 17, 1900-June 29, 1901
Reel 1336   v79-80; July 6, 1901-June 28, 1902
Reel 1337   v81-82; July 5, 1902-June 27, 1903
Reel 1338   v83-84; July 4, 1903-June 25, 1904
Reel 1339   v85-86; July 2, 1904-June 24, 1905
Reel 1340   v87-89; July 1, 1905-Dec. 29, 1906

1341-1353 PHRENOLOGICAL JOURNAL AND SCIENCE OF
HEALTH
American Phrenological Journal
Reel 1341   Cumulative Index, v1-3
Reel 1341   v1-7; Oct. 1838-Dec. 1845
Reel 1342   v8-18; Jan. 1846-Dec. 1853
Reel 1343   v19-37; Jan. 1854-June 1863
Reel 1344   v38-49; July 1863-Dec. 1869
Phrenological Journal and Science of Health
Reel 1345   v50-57; Jan. 1870-Dec. 1873
Reel 1346   v58-64; Jan. 1874-June 1877
Reel 1347   v65-74; July 1877-June 1882
Reel 1348   v75-83; July 1882-Dec. 1886
Reel 1349   v84-92; Jan. 1887-Dec. 1891
Reel 1350   v93-102; Jan. 1892-Dec. 1896
Reel 1351   v103-112; Jan. 1897-Dec. 1901
Reel 1352   v113-119; Jan. 1902-Dec. 1906
Reel 1353   v120-124; Jan. 1907-Jan. 1911

1354-1357 WALDIE'S SELECT CIRCULATING LIBRARY
Reel 1354   v1-5; Oct. 1, 1832-June 30, 1835
Reel 1355   v6-10; July 7, 1835-Dec. 26, 1837
Reel 1356   v11-15; Jan. 2, 1838-June 1841
Reel 1357   v16-17; July 1841-Apr. 1842

1357-1363 UNIVERSALIST QUARTERLY AND GENERAL
REVIEW
Reel 1357   General Index, v1-48
Reel 1357   v8-11; Jan. 1851-Oct. 1854
Reel 1358   v12-18; Jan. 1855-Oct. 1861
Reel 1359   v19-24; Jan. 1862-Oct. 1867
Reel 1360   v25-30; Jan. 1868-Oct. 1873
Reel 1361   v31-36; Jan. 1874-Oct. 1879
Reel 1362   v37-42; Jan. 1880-Oct. 1885
Reel 1363   v43-48; Jan. 1886-Oct. 1891

Unit 37

1364-1365 AMERICAN ACADEMY OF ARTS AND SCIENCES, BOSTON. MEMOIRS
Reel 1364   nsv5-9; 1855-1867
Reel 1365   nsv10-12; 1868-1902

1365-1367 ATHENEUM
Reel 1365   v19-21; Apr. 1826-Oct. 1827
Reel 1366   v22-29; Oct. 1827-Oct. 1831
Reel 1367   v30-32; Oct. 1831-Mar. 1833

1367   ATLANTIC SOUVENIR. 1826-1832.

1368   BROWN'S LITERARY OMNIBUS
Waldie's Literary Omnibus
Reel 1368   v1; 1837
Brown's Literary Omnibus
Reel 1368   v2; 1838

1368-1370 CUMBERLAND PRESBYTERIAN REVIEW
Theological Medium
Reel 1368   v2-9; Nov. 1846-Oct. 1873
Reel 1369   v11-15; Jan. 1875-Oct. 1879
Cumberland Presbyterian Quarterly
Reel 1369   v16; Jan.-Oct. 1880
Cumberland Presbyterian Quarterly Review
Reel 1369   v17-18; Jan. 1881-Oct. 1882
Reel 1370   v19; Jan.-Oct. 1883
Cumberland Presbyterian Review
Reel 1370   v20; Jan.-Oct. 1884

1370   MESSENGER
Holston Conference Messenger
Reel 1370   v1, no1-18; Jan. 6, 1826-May 5, 1827
Messenger for the Holston Conference
Reel 1370   v1, no19-v2, no52; May 13-Dec. 29, 1827

1370-1371 JESUIT; OR, CATHOLIC SENTINEL
Jesuit; or, Catholic Sentinel
Reel 1370   v1-2; Sept. 1829-Aug. 1831
United States Catholic Sentinel
Reel 1371   v3; Oct. 1, 1831-Sept. 21, 1832
Jesuit; or, Catholic Sentinel
Reel 1371   v4-5; Oct. 1833-Dec. 1834

1371-1388 MAINE FARMER
Reel 1371   v20-21; Jan. 1852-Dec. 1853
Reel 1372   v22-24; Dec. 29, 1853-Dec. 18, 1856
Reel 1373   v25-27; Dec. 25, 1856-Dec. 15, 1859
Reel 1374   v28-30; Dec. 22, 1859-Dec. 11, 1862
Reel 1375   v31-33; Dec. 18, 1862-Dec. 7, 1865
Reel 1376   v34-36; Dec. 14, 1865-Dec. 5, 1868
Reel 1377   v37-39; Dec. 12, 1868-Dec. 2, 1871
Reel 1378   v40-42; Dec. 9, 1871-Nov. 28, 1874
Reel 1379   v43-45; Dec. 5, 1874-Nov. 24, 1877
Reel 1380   v46-48; Dec. 1, 1877-Nov. 20, 1880
Reel 1381   v49-51; Nov. 25, 1880-Nov. 15, 1883
Reel 1382   v52-55; Nov. 22, 1883-Nov. 10, 1887
Reel 1383   v56-59; Nov. 17, 1887-Nov. 5, 1891
Reel 1384   v60-61; Nov. 12, 1891-Nov. 2, 1893
Reel 1385   v62-63; Nov. 9, 1893-Oct. 31, 1895
Reel 1386   v64-65; Nov. 7, 1895-Oct. 28, 1897
Reel 1387   v66-67; Nov. 4, 1897-Oct. 26, 1899
Reel 1388   v68; Nov. 2, 1899-Oct. 25, 1900

1388-1396 MEDICAL TIMES AND REGISTER
Medical Times
Reel 1388   v1; Oct. 1, 1870-Sept. 15, 1871

Philadelphia Medical Times
Reel 1388   v2-3; Oct. 1871-Sept. 27, 1873
Reel 1389   v4-8; Oct. 4, 1873-Sept. 28, 1878
Reel 1390   v9-13; Oct. 12, 1878-Sept. 22, 1883
Reel 1391   v14-17; Oct. 6, 1883-Sept. 17, 1887
Reel 1392   v18-19; Oct. 1, 1887-Apr. 15, 1889
Times and Register
Reel 1392   v20; May 4, 1889-June 28, 1890
Reel 1393   v21-23; July 5, 1890-Dec. 26, 1891
Reel 1394   v24-27; Jan. 2, 1892-June 30, 1894
Reel 1395   v28-30; July 7, 1894-Dec. 28, 1895
Medical Times and Register
Reel 1395   v31-33; Jan. 4, 1896-June 26, 1897
Reel 1396   v34-41; July 10, 1897-Aug. 1903

1397-1404 NEW ENGLAND FARMER, AND HORTICULTURAL REGISTER
Reel 1397   v4-10; July 29, 1825-July 11, 1832
Reel 1398   v11-17; July 18, 1832-July 3, 1839
Reel 1399   v18-24; July 10, 1839-June 24, 1846
Reel 1400   v47-51; Nov. 21, 1868-Dec. 28, 1872
Reel 1401   v57-59; Jan. 5, 1878-Dec. 25, 1880
Reel 1402   v60-63; Jan. 15, 1881-Dec. 27, 1884
Reel 1403   v64-66; Jan. 3, 1885-Dec. 31, 1887
Reel 1404   v68-69; Jan. 5, 1889-Apr. 19, 1890

1404-1406 OHIO MEDICAL AND SURGICAL JOURNAL
Reel 1404   v1-4; Sept. 1, 1848-July 1, 1852
Reel 1405   v5-11; Sept. 1, 1852-July 1, 1859
Reel 1406   v12-nsv3; Sept. 1, 1859-June 1878

1407   PATHFINDER. no2-15; Mar. 4-June 3, 1843.

1407   SOUTHERN AND WESTERN MONTHLY MAGAZINE AND REVIEW. v1-2; Jan.-Dec. 1845.

1407   SOUVENIR. v1-2; July 4, 1827-June 20, 1829.

1407   TEACHER'S GUIDE AND PARENT'S ASSISTANT. no1-24; Nov. 1826-Dec. 1827.

1407   VIRGINIA LITERARY MUSEUM AND JOURNAL OF BELLES LETTRES, ARTS, SCIENCES etc. v1, no1-52; June 17, 1829-June 9, 1830.

1408   WALHALLA. v1-4; July 1845-June 1847.

1408   WEEKLY INSPECTOR. v1-2; Aug. 30, 1806-Aug. 22, 1807.

1408   WESTERN FARMER AND GARDENER
Indiana Farmer and Gardener
Reel 1408   v1; Feb.-Dec. 1845
Western Farmer and Gardener
Reel 1408   v2-3; Jan. 1846-Jan. 1848

1408   YANKEE DOODLE. v1-2; 1846-1847.

Units 38-39

1409-1412 CINCINNATI WEEKLY HERALD AND PHILANTHROPIST
Philanthropist
Reel 1409   v1-3; Jan. 1, 1836-Jan. 15, 1839
Reel 1410   v4-6; Jan. 22, 1839-July 16, 1842
Reel 1411   v7-8, no4; July 23, 1842-Oct. 11, 1843
Cincinnati Weekly Herald and Philanthropist
Reel 1411   v8, no5-v9; Oct. 18, 1843-Aug. 6, 1845
Reel 1412   v10-11; Sept. 17, 1845-Dec. 1, 1846

REEL

1412-1419 FRIEND; A RELIGIOUS AND LITERARY JOURNAL
Reel 1412   v25-30; Sept. 20, 1851-Sept. 5, 1857
Reel 1413   v31-37; Sept. 12, 1857-Aug. 27, 1864
Reel 1414   v38-44; Sept. 3, 1864-Aug. 19, 1871
Reel 1415   v45-50; Aug. 26, 1871-Aug. 11, 1877
Reel 1416   v51-57; Aug. 18, 1877-Aug. 2, 1884
Reel 1417   v58-64; Aug. 9, 1884-July 25, 1891
Reel 1418   v65-71; Aug. 1, 1891-July 16, 1898
Reel 1419   v72-79; July 23, 1898-July 7, 1906

1420-1481 INDEPENDENT . . .
Reel 1420   v3-5; Jan. 2, 1851-Dec. 29, 1853
Reel 1421   v6-7; Jan. 5, 1854-Dec. 27, 1855
Reel 1422   v8-9; Jan. 3, 1856-Dec. 31, 1857
Reel 1423   v10-11; Jan. 7, 1858-Dec. 29, 1859
Reel 1424   v12-13; Jan. 5, 1860-Dec. 26, 1861
Reel 1425   v14-15; Jan. 2, 1862-Dec. 31, 1863
Reel 1426   v16-17; Jan. 7, 1864-Dec. 28, 1865
Reel 1427   v18-19; Jan. 4, 1866-Dec. 26, 1867
Reel 1428   v20-21; Jan. 2, 1868-Dec. 30, 1869
Reel 1429   v22; Jan. 6-Dec. 29, 1870
Reel 1430   v23; Jan. 5-Dec. 28, 1871
Reel 1431   v24; Jan. 4-Dec. 26, 1872
Reel 1432   v25; Jan. 2-Dec. 25, 1873
Reel 1433   v26; Jan. 1-Dec. 31, 1874
Reel 1434   v27; Jan. 7-Dec. 30, 1875
Reel 1435   v28; Jan. 6-Dec. 28, 1876
Reel 1436   v29; Jan. 4-Dec. 27, 1877
Reel 1437   v30; Jan. 3-Dec. 26, 1878
Reel 1438   v31; Jan. 2-Dec. 25, 1879
Reel 1439   v32; Jan. 1-Dec. 30, 1880
Reel 1440   v33; Jan. 6-Dec. 29, 1881
Reel 1441   v34; Jan. 5-Dec. 28, 1882
Reel 1442   v35; Jan. 4-Dec. 27, 1883
Reel 1443   v36; Jan. 3-Dec. 25, 1884
Reel 1444   v37; Jan. 1-Dec. 31, 1885
Reel 1445   v38; Jan. 7-Dec. 30, 1886
Reel 1446   v39; Jan. 20-Dec. 29, 1887
Reel 1447   v40; Jan. 5-Dec. 27, 1888
Reel 1448   v41; Jan. 3-Dec. 26, 1889
Reel 1449   v42; Jan. 2-Dec. 25, 1890
Reel 1450   v43; Jan. 1-Dec. 31, 1891
Reel 1451   v44; Jan. 7-Dec. 29, 1892
Reel 1452   v45; Jan. 5-Dec. 28, 1893
Reel 1453   v46; Jan. 4-Dec. 27, 1894
Reel 1454   v47; Jan. 3-Dec. 26, 1895
Reel 1455   v48; Jan. 2-Dec. 31, 1896
Reel 1456   v49; Jan. 7-Dec. 30, 1897
Reel 1457   v50; Jan. 6-Dec. 29, 1898
Reel 1458   v51; Jan. 5-Dec. 28, 1899
Reel 1459   v52; Jan. 4-Dec. 27, 1900
Reel 1460   v53; Jan. 3-Dec. 26, 1901
Reel 1461   v54; Jan. 2-Dec. 25, 1902
Reel 1462   v55; Jan. 1-Dec. 31, 1903
Reel 1463   v56-57; Jan. 7-Dec. 29, 1904
Reel 1464   v58-59; Jan. 5-Dec. 28, 1905
Reel 1465   v60-61; Jan. 4-Dec. 27, 1906
Reel 1466   v62-63; Jan. 3-Dec. 26, 1907
Reel 1467   v64-65; Jan. 2-Dec. 31, 1908
Reel 1468   v66-67; Jan. 7-Dec. 30, 1909
Reel 1469   v68-69; Jan. 6-Dec. 29, 1910
Reel 1470   v70-71; Jan. 5-Dec. 28, 1911
Reel 1471   v72-73; Jan. 4-Dec. 26, 1912
Reel 1472   v74-76; Jan. 2-Dec. 25, 1913
Reel 1473   v77-80; Jan. 5-Dec. 28, 1914
Reel 1474   v81-86; Jan. 4, 1915-June 26, 1916
Reel 1475   v87-90; July 3, 1916-June 30, 1917
Reel 1476   v91-93; July 7, 1917-Mar. 30, 1918
Reel 1477   v94-100; Apr 6, 1918-Dec. 27, 1919
Reel 1478   v101-107; Jan. 3, 1920-Dec. 31, 1921

REEL

Reel 1479   v108-113; Jan. 7, 1922-Dec. 27, 1924
Reel 1480   v114-117; Jan. 3, 1925-Dec. 25, 1926
Reel 1481   v118-121; Jan. 1, 1927-Oct. 13, 1928

1482-1486 NASSAU LITERARY MAGAZINE
Nassau Monthly
Reel 1482   v1-6; Feb. 1842-May 1847
Nassau Literary Magazine
Reel 1482   v8-20; Sept. 1848-May 1860
Reel 1483   v21-33; Sept. 1860-May 1878
Reel 1484   v34-43; June 1878-Apr. 1888
Reel 1485   v44-50; May 1888-Apr. 1895
Reel 1486   v51-63; May 1895-Mar. 1908

1487-1488 PICTORIAL REVIEW
Reel 1487   v1-5; Sept. 15, 1899-Sept. 1904
Reel 1488   v6-8; Oct. 1904-Dec. 1906

1488-1490 RELIGIOUS INTELLIGENCER. . .
Reel 1488   v15-16; June 5, 1830-May 26, 1832
Reel 1489   v17-20; June 2, 1832-May 28, 1836
Reel 1490   v21-22; June 4, 1836-Oct. 7, 1837

1490   **TENNESSEE FARMER.** v1-4; Dec. 1834-Dec. 1839.

1491-1497 WATCHMAN-EXAMINER, A NATIONAL BAPTIST PAPER
Christian Watchman
Reel 1491   v8-11; Dec. 8, 1826-Dec. 31, 1830
Reel 1492   v12-15; Jan. 7, 1831-Dec. 26, 1834
Reel 1493   v16-19; Jan. 2, 1835-Dec. 28, 1838
Reel 1494   v20-23; Jan. 5, 1839-Dec. 30, 1842
Reel 1495   v24-27; Jan. 6, 1843-Dec. 25, 1846
Reel 1496   v28-29, no19; Jan. 1, 1847-May 11, 1848
Christian Reflector and Christian Watchman
Reel 1496   v29, no20-v29, no42; May 18-Oct. 19, 1848
Christian Watchman and Christian Reflector
Reel 1496   v29, no43-v31; Oct. 26, 1848-Dec. 26, 1850
Christian Watchman and Reflector
Reel 1497   v32-35; Jan. 2, 1851-Dec. 28, 1854

1497   **WESTERN QUARTERLY REPORTER OF MEDICAL, SURGICAL, AND NATURAL SCIENCE.** v1-2; Jan. 1822-1823.

Unit 40

1498-1499 FREE ENQUIRER
New-Harmony Gazette
Reel 1498   v1-3; Oct. 1, 1825-Oct. 22, 1828
Free Enquirer
Reel 1498   s2v1-3; Oct. 29, 1828-Oct. 22, 1831
Reel 1499   s2v4-s3v2; Oct. 29, 1831-June 28, 1835

1499-1501 MERRY'S MUSEUM FOR BOYS AND GIRLS
Robert Merry's Museum
Reel 1499   v21-22; Jan.-Dec. 1851
Merry's Museum and Parley's Magazine
Reel 1499   v23-26; Jan. 1852-Dec. 1853
Reel 1500   v27-34 (nsv4); Jan. 1854-Dec. 1857
Merry's Museum, Parley's Magazine, Woodworth's Cabinet and the Schoolfellow
Reel 1500   v35 (nsv5)-v42(nsv12); Jan. 1858-Dec. 1861
Reel 1501   v51 (nsv21)-v52 (nsv22); Jan.-Dec. 1866

REEL

Merry's Museum and Woodworth's Cabinet
Reel 1501   v53 (nsv23)-v54 (nsv24); Jan.-Dec.
1867
Merry's Museum for Boys and Girls
Reel 1501   v55-60; Jan. 1868-Dec. 1871

1502-1519 MICHIGAN FARMER
Reel 1502   v9-15; Jan. 1851-Dec. 1857
Reel 1503   v16-nsv4; Jan. 1858-Mar. 22, 1862
Reel 1503   s3v2; July 1863-June 1864
Reel 1504   s3v12; Jan. 4-Dec. 27, 1881
Reel 1505   s3v13; Jan. 10-Dec. 26, 1882
Reel 1506   s3v14; Jan. 2-Dec. 25, 1883
Reel 1507   s3v15; Jan. 1-Dec. 30, 1884
Reel 1508   s3v16; Jan. 6-Dec. 29, 1885
Reel 1509   s3v17; Jan. 5-Dec. 28, 1886
Reel 1510   s3v18; Jan. 4-Dec. 26, 1887
Reel 1511   s3v19; Jan. 2-Dec. 29, 1888
Reel 1512   s3v20; Jan. 5-Dec. 28, 1889
Reel 1513   s3v21; Jan. 4-Dec. 27, 1890
Reel 1514   s3v31-34; Jan. 9, 1897-Dec. 31, 1898
Reel 1515   s3v35-38; Jan. 7, 1899-Dec. 29, 1900
Reel 1516   s3v44-47; Aug. 22, 1903-June 24,
1905
Reel 1517   s3v48-50; July 1, 1905-Dec. 29, 1906
Reel 1518   s3v51-osv130; Jan. 5, 1907-June 27,
1908
Reel 1519   osv131; July 4-Dec. 26, 1908

1519-1529 SOUTHERN CULTIVATOR
Reel 1519   v1-9; Mar. 1, 1843-Dec. 1851
Reel 1520   v10-16; Jan. 1852-Dec. 1858
Reel 1521   v17-24; Jan. 1859-Dec. 1866
Reel 1522   v25-28; Jan. 1867-Dec. 1870
Reel 1523   v29-33; Jan. 1871-Dec. 1875
Reel 1524   v34-41; Jan. 1876-Sept. 1883
Reel 1525   v43-48; Jan. 1885-Dec. 1890
Reel 1526   v49-52; Jan. 1891-Dec. 1894
Reel 1527   v53-60; Jan. 1895-Dec. 15, 1902
Reel 1528   v61-63; Jan. 1, 1903-Dec. 15, 1905
Reel 1529   v64; Jan. 1-Dec. 15, 1906

1529-1542 SOUTHERN PLANTER
Southern Planter
Reel 1529   v1-7; Jan. 1841-Dec. 1847
Reel 1530   v8-15; Jan. 1848-Dec. 1855
Reel 1531   v16-19; Jan. 1856-Dec. 1859
Reel 1532   v20-27; Jan. 1860-Dec. 1866
Southern Planter and Farmer
Reel 1532   nsv1-2 (v28-29); Jan. 1867-Dec. 1868
Reel 1533   nsv3-5 (v30-32); Jan. 1869-Dec. 1871
Reel 1534   nsv6-8 (v33-35); Jan. 1872-Dec. 1874
Reel 1535   nsv9 (v36)-38; Jan. 1875-Dec. 1877
Reel 1536   v39-42; Jan. 1878-Dec. 1881
Southern Planter
Reel 1537   v43-47; Jan. 15, 1882-Dec. 1886
Reel 1538   v48-51; Jan. 1887-Dec. 1890
Reel 1539   v52-56; Jan. 1891-Dec. 1895
Reel 1540   v57-61; Jan. 1896-Dec. 1900
Reel 1541   v62-65; Jan. 1901-Dec. 1904
Reel 1542   v66-67; Jan. 1905-Dec. 1906

1543-1545 WORLD AFFAIRS
American Advocate of Peace
Reel 1543   v9-18; Jan./Feb. 1851-Nov./Dec. 1868
Reel 1544   nsv1-15; Jan. 1869-June 1884
Reel 1544   v54-57; June 1892-Dec. 1895
Reel 1545   v58-68; Jan. 1896-Dec. 1906

REEL

Unit 41

1546-1572 YOUTH'S COMPANION
Reel 1546   v1-12; Apr. 16, 1827-May 10, 1839
Reel 1547   v13-24; May 17, 1839-Apr. 24, 1851
Reel 1548   v25-35; May 1, 1851-Dec. 26, 1861
Reel 1549   v37-43; Jan. 1, 1863-Dec. 29, 1870
Reel 1550   v44-48; Jan. 5, 1871-Dec. 30, 1875
Reel 1551   v49-53; Jan. 6, 1876-Dec. 30, 1880
Reel 1552   v54-57; Jan. 6, 1881-Dec. 25, 1884
Reel 1553   v58-60; Jan. 1, 1885-Dec. 29, 1887
Reel 1554   v61-63; Jan. 5, 1888-Dec. 25, 1890
Reel 1555   v64-65; Jan. 1, 1891-Dec. 29, 1892
Reel 1556   v66-67; Jan. 5, 1893-Dec. 27, 1894
Reel 1557   v68-70; Jan. 3, 1895-Dec. 31, 1896
Reel 1558   v71-72; Jan. 7, 1897-Dec. 29, 1898
Reel 1559   v73-74; Jan. 5, 1899-Dec. 27, 1900
Reel 1560   v75-76; Jan. 3, 1901-Dec. 25, 1902
Reel 1561   v77-78; Jan. 1, 903-Dec. 29, 1904
Reel 1562   v79-80; Jan. 5, 1905-Dec. 27, 1906
Reel 1563   v81-82; Jan. 3, 1907-Dec. 31, 1908
Reel 1564   v83-84; Jan. 7, 1909-Dec. 29, 1910
Reel 1565   v85-86; Jan. 5, 1911-Dec. 26, 1912
Reel 1566   v87-88; Jan. 2, 1913-Dec. 31, 1914
Reel 1567   v89-90; Jan. 7, 1915-Dec. 28, 1916
Reel 1568   v91-92; Jan. 4, 1917-Dec. 26, 1918
Reel 1569   v93-95; Jan. 2, 1919-Dec. 29, 1921
Reel 1570   v96-98; Jan. 5, 1922-Dec. 25, 1924
Reel 1571   v99-101; Jan. 1, 1925-Dec. 1927
Reel 1572   v102-103; Jan. 1928-Sept. 1929

1572-1612 ZION'S HERALD
Zion's Herald
Reel 1572   v1-2; Jan. 9, 1823-Dec. 29, 1824
Reel 1573   v3-5; Jan. 5, 1825-Dec. 26, 1827
Reel 1574   nsv6; Jan. 7-Dec. 30, 1835
Reel 1574   nsv7-9; Jan. 6, 1836-Dec. 26, 1838
Reel 1575   nsv10-12; Oct. 9, 1839-Dec. 26, 1841
Zion's Herald and Wesleyan Journal
Reel 1575   nsv13-17; Jan. 1842-Dec. 26, 1846
Reel 1576   nsv18-21; Jan. 6, 1847-Dec. 25, 1850
Reel 1577   nsv22-30; Jan. 1, 1851-Dec. 28, 1859
Reel 1578   nsv31-35; Jan. 4, 1860-Dec. 28, 1864
Reel 1579   nsv36-38; Jan. 4, 1865-Dec. 26, 1867
Zion's Herald
Reel 1580   v45-47; Jan. 2, 1868-Dec. 29, 1870
Reel 1581   v48-49; Jan. 5, 1871-Dec. 26, 1872
Reel 1582   v50; Jan. 2-Dec. 25, 1873
Reel 1583   v51; Jan. 1-Dec. 31, 1874
Reel 1584   v52; Jan. 7.-Dec. 30, 1875
Reel 1585   v53; Jan. 6-Dec. 28, 1876
Reel 1586   v54; Jan. 4-Dec. 27, 1877
Reel 1587   v55; Jan. 3-Dec. 26, 1878
Reel 1588   v56; Jan. 2-Dec. 25, 1879
Reel 1589   v57; Jan. 1-Dec. 30, 1880
Reel 1590   v58; Jan. 6-Dec. 29, 1881
Reel 1591   v59; Jan. 4-Dec. 27, 1882
Reel 1592   v60; Jan. 3-Dec. 26, 1883
Reel 1593   v61; Jan. 2-Dec. 31, 1884
Reel 1594   v62; Jan. 7-Dec. 30, 1885
Reel 1595   v63; Jan. 6-Dec. 29, 1886
Reel 1596   v64; Jan. 5-Dec. 28, 1887
Reel 1597   v65-66; Jan. 4-Dec. 26, 1888
Reel 1598   v67; Jan. 2-Dec. 25, 1889
Reel 1599   v68; Jan. 1-Dec. 31, 1890
Reel 1600   v69; Jan. 7-Dec. 30, 1891
Reel 1601   v70; Jan. 6-Dec. 28, 1892
Reel 1602   v71-72; Jan. 4, 1893-Dec. 26, 1894
Reel 1603   v73-74; Jan. 2, 1895-Dec. 30, 1896
Reel 1604   v75-76; Jan. 6, 1897-Dec. 28, 1898

Reel 1605	v77; Jan. 4-Dec. 27, 1899
Reel 1606	v78; Jan. 3-Dec. 26, 1900
Reel 1607	v79; Jan. 2-Dec. 25, 1901
Reel 1608	v80; Jan. 1-Dec. 31, 1902
Reel 1609	v81; Jan. 7-Dec. 30, 1903
Reel 1610	v82; Jan. 6-Dec. 28, 1904
Reel 1611	v83; Jan. 4-Dec. 27, 1905
Reel 1612	v84; Jan. 3-Dec. 26, 1906

Unit 42

1613-1647 NORTH AMERICAN REVIEW

Reel 1613	v72-79; Jan. 1851-Oct. 1854
Reel 1614	v80-86; Jan. 1855-Apr. 1858
Reel 1615	v87-93; July 1858-Oct. 1861
Reel 1616	v94-99; Jan. 1862-Oct. 1864
Reel 1617	v100-105; Jan. 1865-Oct. 1867
Reel 1618	v106-112; Jan. 1868-Apr. 1871
Reel 1619	v113-120; July 1871-Apr. 1875
Reel 1620	v121-127; July 1875-Dec. 1878
Reel 1621	v128-133; Jan. 1879-Dec. 1881
Reel 1622	v134-139; Jan. 1882-Dec. 1884
Reel 1623	v140-145; Jan. 1885-Dec. 1887
Reel 1624	v146-150; Jan. 1888-June 1890
Reel 1625	v151-155; July 1890-Dec. 1892
Reel 1626	v156-160; Jan. 1893-June 1895
Reel 1627	v161-165; July 1895-Dec. 1897
Reel 1628	v166-170; Jan. 1898-June 1900
Reel 1629	v171-174; July 1900-June 1902
Reel 1630	v175-178; July 1902-June 1904
Reel 1631	v179-181; July 1904-Dec. 1905
Reel 1632	v182-184; Jan. 1906-Apr. 1907
Reel 1633	v185-188; May 1907-Dec. 1908
Reel 1634	v189-192; Jan. 1909-Dec. 1910
Reel 1635	v193-196; Jan. 1911-Dec. 1912
Reel 1636	v197-200; Jan. 1913-Dec. 1914
Reel 1637	v201-203; Jan. 1915-June 1916
Reel 1638	v204-206; July 1916-Dec. 1917
Reel 1639	v207-209; Jan. 1918-June 1919
Reel 1640	v210-213; July 1919-June 1921
Reel 1641	v214-217; July 1921-June 1923
Reel 1642	v218-222; July 1923-Feb. 1926
Reel 1643	v223-226; Mar. 1926-Dec. 1928
Reel 1644	v227-230; Jan. 1929-Dec. 1930
Reel 1645	v231-235; Jan. 1931-June 1933
Reel 1646	v236-241; July 1933-June 1936
Reel 1647	v242-248; Autumn 1936-Winter 1939/40

Units 43-44

1648-1683 BANKERS' MAGAZINE

Bankers' Magazine and Statistical Register

Reel 1648	v6-8; July 1851-June 1854
Reel 1649	v9-12; July 1854-June 1858
Reel 1650	v13-16; July 1858-June 1862
Reel 1651	v17-20; July 1862-June 1866
Reel 1652	v21-24; July 1866-June 1870
Reel 1653	v25-28; July 1870-June 1874
Reel 1654	v29-32; July 1874-June 1878
Reel 1655	v33-36; July 1878-June 1882
Reel 1656	v37-40; July 1882-June 1886
Reel 1657	v41-44; July 1886-June 1890
Reel 1658	v45-48; July 1890-June 1894
Reel 1659	v49; July 1894-Nov. 1894

Bankers' Magazine

Reel 1659	v50; Dec. 1894-June 1895

Rhodes' Journal of Banking and the Bankers' Magazine Consolidated

Reel 1659	v51; July-Dec. 1895

Bankers' Magazine

Reel 1659	v52; Jan. June 1896
Reel 1660	v53-56; July 1896-June 1898
Reel 1661	v57-59; July 1898-Dec. 1899
Reel 1662	v60-62; Jan. 1900-June 1901
Reel 1663	v63-65; July 1901-Dec. 1902
Reel 1664	v66-68; Jan. 1903-June 1904
Reel 1665	v69-71; July 1904-Dec. 1905
Reel 1666	v72-74; Jan. 1906-June 1907
Reel 1667	v75-77; July 1907-Dec. 1908
Reel 1668	v78-80; Jan. 1909-June 1910
Reel 1669	v81-84; July 1910-June 1912
Reel 1670	v85-89; July 1912-Dec. 1914
Reel 1671	v90-93; Jan. 1915-Dec. 1916
Reel 1672	v94-97; Jan. 1917-Dec. 1918
Reel 1673	v98-101; Jan. 1919-Dec. 1920
Reel 1674	v102-104; Jan. 1921-June 1922
Reel 1675	v105-107; July 1922-Dec. 1923
Reel 1676	v108-110; Jan. 1924-June 1925
Reel 1677	v111-114; July 1925-June 1927
Reel 1678	v115-118; July 1927-June 1929
Reel 1679	v119-122; July 1929-June 1931
Reel 1680	v123-127; July 1931-Dec. 1933
Reel 1681	v128-132; Jan. 1934-June 1936
Reel 1682	v133-139; July 1936-Dec. 1939
Reel 1683	v140-146; Jan. 1940-June 1943

1684-1692 EPISCOPAL RECORDER

Philadelphia Recorder

Reel 1684	v1-3; Apr. 5, 1823-Dec. 31, 1825
Reel 1685	v4-8; Apr. 1, 1826-Mar. 26, 1831

Episcopal Recorder

Reel 1686	v9-11; Apr. 2, 1831-Mar. 29, 1834
Reel 1687	v12-14; Apr. 5, 1834-Mar. 25, 1837
Reel 1688	v15-17; Apr. 1, 1837-Mar. 21, 1840
Reel 1689	v18-20; Mar. 28, 1840-Mar. 18, 1843
Reel 1690	v21-23; Mar. 25, 1843-Mar. 14, 1846
Reel 1691	v24-26; Mar. 21, 1846-Mar. 10, 1849
Reel 1692	v27-28; Mar. 17, 1849-Mar. 22, 1851

1692-1696 HEALTH

Herald of Health

Reel 1692	v36-44; Jan. 1864-Dec. 1867
Reel 1693	v48-49, 51; July 1869-Dec. 1892

Health

Reel 1693	nsv50-53; Sept. 1900-Dec. 1903
Reel 1694	nsv55-56; Jan. 1905-Dec. 1906
Reel 1695	nsv57-59; Jan. 1907-Dec. 1909
Reel 1696	nsv60-63; Jan. 1910-Dec. 1913

1696-1700 NEW WORLD

Reel 1696	v1-2; June 6, 1840-June 26, 1841
Reel 1697	v3-5; July 3, 1841-Dec. 31, 1842
Reel 1698	v6-8; Jan. 7, 1843-June 29, 1844
Reel 1699	v9-10; July 6, 1844-May 10, 1845
Reel 1700	Extra series no. 1-38; Oct. 4, 1842-Dec. 1842
Reel 1700	Extra series no. 39-105; Dec. 1842-Jan. 1844
Reel 1700	Folio edition v1-2; Oct. 26, 1839-Dec. 26, 1840

1701-1706 UNIVERSALIST

Universalist Magazine

Reel 1701	v8-9; June 24, 1826-June 28, 1828

Trumpet and Universalist Magazine
Reel 1701	v10-12; July 5, 1828-June 25, 1831
Reel 1702	v13-18; July 2, 1831-June 17, 1837
Reel 1703	v19-22; June 24, 1837-June 19, 1841
Reel 1704	v23-26; June 26, 1841-June 14, 1845
Reel 1705	v27-29; June 21, 1845-June 10, 1848
Reel 1706	v30-32; June 17, 1848-June 7, 1851

Unit 45

1707-1716 **AMERICAN JOURNAL OF PHARMACY**
Reel 1707	v25-30; Jan. 1853-Nov. 1858
Reel 1708	v31-36; Jan. 1859-Nov. 1864
Reel 1709	v37-42; Jan. 1865-Nov. 1870
Reel 1710	v43-48; Jan. 1871-Dec. 1876
Reel 1711	v49-53; Jan. 1877-Dec. 1881
Reel 1712	v54-58; Jan. 1882-Dec. 1886
Reel 1713	v59-63; Jan. 1887-Dec. 1891
Reel 1714	v64-68; Jan. 1892-Dec. 1896
Reel 1715	v69-73; Jan. 1897-Dec. 1901
Reel 1716	v74-79; Jan. 1902-Dec. 1907

1717-1720 **CATHOLIC TELEGRAPH**
Reel 1717	v1-5; Oct. 22, 1831-Nov. 24, 1836
Reel 1718	v6-9; Dec. 8, 1836-Dec. 26, 1840
Reel 1719	v10-14; Jan. 2, 1841-Dec. 25, 1845
Reel 1720	v15; Jan. 1, 1846-Dec. 31, 1846

1720-1726 **PRAIRIE FARMER**
Reel 1720	v11-15; Jan. 1851-Dec. 1855
Reel 1721	v18-23 (nsv2-7); July 1, 1858-June 27, 1861
Reel 1722	v29-34 (nsv13-18); Jan. 2, 1864-Dec. 29, 1866
Reel 1723	v35-36 (nsv19-20); Jan. 5-Dec. 28, 1867
Reel 1723	v43; Jan. 6-Dec. 28, 1872
Reel 1724	v44-45; Jan. 4, 1873-Dec. 26, 1874
Reel 1725	v46-47; Jan. 2, 1875-Dec. 30, 1876
Reel 1726	v48; Jan. 6-Dec. 29, 1877

1726-1733 **RAILWAY TIMES**
American Railway Times
Reel 1726	v1-2; Dec. 1, 1849-Dec. 26, 1850
Reel 1727	v3-5; Jan. 2, 1851-Dec. 29, 1853
Reel 1728	v6-8; Jan. 5, 1854-Dec. 25, 1856
Reel 1729	v9-11; Jan. 1, 1857-Dec. 24, 1859

Railway Times
Reel 1730	v12-14; Jan. 7, 1860-Dec. 27, 1862
Reel 1731	v15-18; Jan. 3, 1863-Dec. 29, 1866
Reel 1732	v19-21; Jan. 5, 1867-Dec. 25, 1869
Reel 1733	v22-24; Jan. 1, 1870-Nov. 2, 1872

1734-1748 **SCIENTIFIC AMERICAN**
Reel 1734	nsv15-20; June 30, 1866-June 26, 1869
Reel 1735	nsv21-26; July 18, 1869-June 22, 1872
Reel 1736	nsv27-32; July 6, 1872-June 25, 1875
Reel 1737	nsv33-38; July 3, 1875-June 29, 1878
Reel 1738	nsv39-44; July 6, 1878-June 25, 1881
Reel 1739	nsv45-50; July 2, 1881-June 28, 1884
Reel 1740	nsv51-56; July 5, 1884-June 25, 1887
Reel 1741	nsv57-62; July 2, 1887-June 28, 1890
Reel 1742	v63-68; July 5, 1890-June 24, 1893
Reel 1743	v69-73; July 1, 1893-Dec. 28, 1895
Reel 1744	v74-78; Jan. 4, 1896-June 25, 1898
Reel 1745	v79-83; July 2, 1898-Dec. 29, 1900
Reel 1746	v84-89; Jan. 5, 1901-Dec 26, 1903
Reel 1747	v90-94; Jan. 2, 1904-June 30, 1906
Reel 1748	v95-99; July 7, 1906-Dec. 26, 1908

Unit 46

1749-1788 **CHRISTIAN ADVOCATE**
Christian Advocate
Reel 1749	v1, no1-27; Sept. 9, 1826-Mar. 10, 1827

Christian Advocate and Journal
Reel 1749	v1, no28-v2, no52; Mar. 17, 1827-Aug. 29, 1828

Christian Advocate and Journal and Zion's Herald
Reel 1749	v3-4; Sept. 5, 1828-Aug. 27, 1830
Reel 1750	v5-7; Sept. 3, 1830-Aug. 23, 1833

Christian Advocate and Journal
Reel 1750	v8; Aug. 30, 1833-Aug. 22, 1834
Reel 1751	v9-18; Aug. 29, 1834-Aug. 7, 1844
Reel 1752	v19-22; Aug. 14, 1844-Dec. 29, 1847
Reel 1753	v23-25; Jan. 5, 1848-Dec. 26, 1850
Reel 1754	v26-28; Jan. 2, 1851-Dec. 29, 1853
Reel 1755	v29-36; Jan. 5, 1854-Dec. 26, 1861
Reel 1756	v37-38; Jan. 2, 1862-Dec. 31, 1863
Reel 1757	v39-40; Jan. 7, 1864-Dec. 28, 1865

Christian Advocate
Reel 1758	v41-42; Jan. 4, 1866-Dec. 26, 1867
Reel 1759	v43-44; Jan. 2, 1868-Dec. 30, 1869
Reel 1760	v45-46; Jan. 6, 1870-Dec. 28, 1871
Reel 1761	v47-48; Jan. 4, 1872-Dec. 25, 1873
Reel 1762	v49-50; Jan. 1, 1874-Dec. 30, 1875
Reel 1763	v51; Jan. 6-Dec. 28, 1876
Reel 1764	v52; Jan. 4-Dec. 27, 1877
Reel 1765	v53; Jan. 3-Dec. 26, 1878
Reel 1766	v54; Jan. 2-Dec. 25, 1879
Reel 1767	v55; Jan. 1-Dec. 30, 1880
Reel 1768	v56; Jan. 6-Dec. 29, 1881
Reel 1769	v57; Jan. 5-Dec. 28, 1882
Reel 1770	v58; Jan. 4-Dec. 27, 1883
Reel 1771	v59; Jan. 3-Dec. 25, 1884
Reel 1772	v60-61; Jan. 1, 1885-Dec. 30, 1886
Reel 1773	v62-63; Jan. 6, 1887-Dec. 27, 1888
Reel 1774	v64; Jan. 3-Dec. 26, 1889
Reel 1775	v65; Jan. 2-Dec. 25, 1890
Reel 1776	v66; Jan. 1-Dec. 31, 1891
Reel 1777	v67; Jan. 7-Dec. 29, 1892
Reel 1778	v68; Jan. 5-Dec. 28, 1893
Reel 1779	v69; Jan. 4-Dec. 27, 1894
Reel 1780	v70; Jan. 3-Dec. 26, 1895
Reel 1781	v73; Jan. 6-Dec. 29, 1898
Reel 1782	v74; Jan. 5-Dec. 28, 1899
Reel 1783	v75; Jan. 4-Dec. 27, 1900
Reel 1784	v76; Jan. 3-Dec. 26, 1901
Reel 1785	v77; Jan. 2-Dec. 25, 1902
Reel 1786	v78; Jan. 1-Dec. 31, 1903
Reel 1787	v79; Jan. 7-Dec. 29, 1904
Reel 1788	v80; Jan. 5-Dec. 28, 1905

1789-1796 **WESTERN CHRISTIAN ADVOCATE**
Reel 1789	v1-3; May 2, 1834-Apr. 21, 1837
Reel 1790	v4-6; Apr. 28, 1837-Apr. 17, 1840
Reel 1791	v7-35; Apr. 24, 1840-Dec. 9, 1868
Reel 1792	v36-41; Feb. 3, 1869-Dec. 30, 1874
Reel 1793	v47; Jan. 14-Dec. 29, 1880
Reel 1794	v48; Jan. 5-Dec. 28, 1881
Reel 1795	v49; Jan. 4-Dec. 27, 1882
Reel 1796	v50; Jan. 3-Dec. 26, 1883

1797-1801 **INDIANA FARMER'S GUIDE**
Indiana Farmer
Reel 1797	v2, 7; Sept. 11, 1852-Aug. 15, 1853; Apr. 18, 1858-Mar. 1859

Indiana Farmer's Guide
Reel 1797	v30 (2d series); Jan. 5-Dec. 28, 1918
Reel 1798	v31 (2d series); Jan. 4-Dec. 27, 1919
Reel 1799	v32 (2d series); Jan. 3-Dec. 25, 1920
Reel 1800	v33 (2d series); Jan. 1-Dec. 31, 1921
Reel 1801	v34 (2d series); Jan. 7-Dec. 30, 1922

1801-1815 OHIO FARMER
Reel 1801	v5; Jan. 5-Dec. 27, 1856
Reel 1802	v6-14; Jan. 3, 1857-Dec. 30, 1865
Reel 1803	v15-16; Jan. 6, 1866-Dec. 28, 1867
Reel 1804	v17-19; Jan. 4, 1868-Dec. 24, 1870
Reel 1805	v20-44; Jan. 7, 1871-Dec. 27, 1873
Reel 1806	v45-51; Jan. 3, 1874-June 30, 1877
Reel 1807	v52-60; July 7, 1877-Dec. 31, 1881
Reel 1808	v61-68; Jan. 7, 1882-Dec. 26, 1885
Reel 1809	v69-86; Jan. 2, 1886-Dec. 27, 1894
Reel 1810	v87-91; Jan. 3, 1895-June 24, 1897
Reel 1811	v92-96; July 1, 1897-Dec. 28, 1899
Reel 1812	v97-101; Jan. 4, 1900-June 26, 1902
Reel 1813	v102-105; July 3, 1902-June 25, 1904
Reel 1814	v106-109; July 2, 1904-June 30, 1906
Reel 1815	v110; July 7-Dec. 29, 1906

1815-1825 REFORMED CHURCH MESSENGER
Weekly Messenger
Reel 1815	v7-8; Sept. 22, 1841-Sept. 13, 1843
Reel 1816	v9; Sept. 27, 1843-Sept. 11, 1844

German Reformed Messenger
Reel 1816	v17-18; Sept. 10, 1851-Aug. 31, 1853
Reel 1817	v19-21; Sept. 7, 1853-Aug. 27, 1856
Reel 1818	v22-24; Sept. 3, 1856-Aug. 24, 1859
Reel 1819	v25-28; Aug. 31, 1859-Sept. 16, 1863
Reel 1820	v29-32; Sept. 23, 1863-Aug. 28, 1867

Reformed Church Messenger
Reel 1821	v33-36; Sept. 4, 1867-Dec. 28, 1870
Reel 1822	v37-39; Jan. 4, 1871-Dec. 24, 1873
Reel 1823	v40; Jan. 7-Dec. 30, 1874

Messenger
Reel 1823	v45-46; Jan. 5, 1876-Dec. 26, 1877
Reel 1824	v47; Jan. 2-Dec. 25, 1878

Reformed Church Messenger
Reel 1824	v58-59, 74; July 3, 1890-Dec. 28, 1905
Reel 1825	v75; Jan. 4-Dec. 27, 1906

Unit 47

1826-1828 CHRISTIAN INDEX
Columbian Star and Christian Index
Reel 1826	v1-3; July 4, 1829-Dec. 25, 1830

Christian Index
Reel 1826	v4-8; Jan. 1, 1831-June 29, 1833
Reel 1827	[s2v5], 60-61, 63; Jan. 5-Dec. 28, 1837; Mar. 23, 1882-Dec. 20, 1883; Jan. 1-Dec. 24, 1885
Reel 1828	v64-65, 79; Jan. 7, 1886-Dec. 24, 1887; Jan. 5, 1889-Dec. 28, 1899

1829-1855 EVANGELIST AND RELIGIOUS REVIEW
New York Evangelist
Reel 1829	v1-7; Mar. 6, 1830-Dec. 24, 1836
Reel 1830	v8-12; Jan. 2, 1837-Dec. 25, 1841
Reel 1831	v13-15; Jan. 6, 1842-Dec. 26, 1844
Reel 1832	v16-19; Jan. 6, 1845-Dec. 28, 1848
Reel 1833	v20-23; Jan. 4, 1849-Dec. 30, 1852
Reel 1834	v24-27; Jan. 6, 1853-Dec. 25, 1856
Reel 1835	v28-30; Jan. 1, 1857-Dec. 29, 1859
Reel 1836	v31-32; Jan. 5, 1860-Dec. 26, 1861
Reel 1837	v33-34; Jan. 2, 1862-Dec. 31, 1863
Reel 1838	v35-36; Jan. 7, 1864-Dec. 23, 1865
Reel 1839	v39-40; Jan. 2, 1868-Dec. 30, 1869
Reel 1840	v41-42; Jan. 6, 1870-Dec. 28, 1871
Reel 1841	v43-44; Jan. 4, 1872-Dec. 25, 1873
Reel 1842	v45-46; Jan. 1, 1874-Dec. 30, 1875
Reel 1843	v47-48; Jan. 6, 1876-Dec. 27, 1877

Reel 1844	v50-51; Jan. 2, 1879-Dec. 30, 1880
Reel 1845	v52-53; Jan. 6, 1881-Dec. 28, 1882
Reel 1846	v54-55; Jan. 4, 1883-Dec. 25, 1884
Reel 1847	v56-57; Jan. 1, 1885-Dec. 30, 1886
Reel 1848	v58-59; Jan. 6, 1887-Dec. 27, 1888
Reel 1849	v60-63; Sept. 19, 1889-Aug. 25, 1892
Reel 1850	v65; Jan. 4-Dec. 27, 1894
Reel 1851	v66; Jan. 3-Dec. 26, 1895
Reel 1852	v67; Jan. 2-Dec. 31, 1896
Reel 1853	v68-69; Jan. 7, 1897-Dec. 29, 1898
Reel 1854	v70-71; Jan. 5, 1899-Dec. 27, 1900
Reel 1855	v72-73, no10; Jan. 3, 1901-Mar. 6, 1902

Evangelist and Religious Review
Reel 1855	v73, no11-30; Mar. 13-July 24, 1902

1856-1874 NEW YORK OBSERVER
New York Observer and Chronicle
Reel 1856	v11-23; Jan. 5, 1833-Dec. 27, 1845
Reel 1857	v24-31; Jan. 3, 1846-Dec. 29, 1853
Reel 1858	v32-35; Jan. 5, 1854-Dec. 31, 1857
Reel 1859	v36-38; Jan. 28, 1858-Dec. 27, 1860
Reel 1860	v39-43; Jan. 3, 1861-Dec. 28, 1865
Reel 1861	v44-46; Jan. 4, 1866-Dec. 31, 1868
Reel 1862	v47-53; Jan. 7, 1869-Dec. 30, 1875
Reel 1863	v54-72; Jan. 6, 1876-Dec. 27, 1894
Reel 1864	v73; Jan. 3-Dec. 26, 1895
Reel 1865	v74; Jan. 2-Dec. 31, 1896
Reel 1866	v75; Jan. 7-Dec. 30, 1897
Reel 1867	v76-77; Jan. 6, 1898-Dec. 28, 1899
Reel 1868	v78-79; Jan. 4, 1900-Dec. 26, 1901
Reel 1869	v80-81; Jan. 2, 1902-Dec. 31, 1903
Reel 1870	v82-83; Jan. 7, 1904-Dec. 28, 1905
Reel 1871	v84-85; Jan. 4, 1906-Dec. 26, 1907
Reel 1872	v86-87; Jan. 2, 1908-Dec. 30, 1909
Reel 1873	v88-90; Jan. 6, 1910-Dec. 28, 1911
Reel 1874	v91; Jan. 4-May 30, 1912

1874-1883 WATCHMAN-EXAMINER
Christian Watchman and Reflector
Reel 1874	v36-39; Jan. 4, 1855-Dec. 30, 1858
Reel 1875	v40-42; Jan. 6, 1859-Dec. 26, 1861

Watchman
Reel 1875	v75; Sept. 20-Dec. 27, 1894
Reel 1876	v76; Jan. 3-Dec. 19, 1895
Reel 1877	v77-78; Jan. 2, 1896-Nov. 11, 1897
Reel 1878	v79-81; Sept. 29, 1898-Dec. 27, 1900
Reel 1879	v82-83; Jan. 3-Dec. 26, 1901
Reel 1880	v84; Jan. 2-Dec. 25, 1902
Reel 1881	v85; Jan. 1-Dec. 31, 1903
Reel 1882	v86; Jan. 7-Dec. 29, 1904
Reel 1883	v87-88; Jan. 5, 1905-Dec. 20, 1906

1884 WEEKLY VISITOR AND LADIES' MUSEUM
Reel 1884	v1-4; Nov. 1, 1817-Oct. 30, 1819
Reel 1884	nsv5-6; May 4, 1822-Apr. 19, 1823

Unit 48

1885-1887 CHRISTIAN INQUIRER
Reel 1885	v1-5; Oct. 17, 1846-Dec. 28, 1850
Reel 1886	v6-12; Oct. 11, 1851-Sept. 18, 1858
Reel 1887	v13-19; Oct. 2, 1858-Dec. 10, 1864

1887-1908 CHRISTIAN OBSERVER
Religious Remembrancer
Reel 1887	v1-3; Sept. 4, 1813-Aug. 24, 1816
Reel 1888	v4-10; Aug. 31, 1816-Aug. 16, 1823

REEL

Christian Observer
Reel 1888   v19 (nsv1); Jan. 2-Dec. 24, 1840
Reel 1889   v20-23; Jan. 1, 1841-Dec. 27, 1844
Reel 1890   v24-27; Jan. 3, 1845-Dec. 30, 1848
Reel 1891   v28-31; Jan. 6, 1849-Dec. 25, 1852
Reel 1892   v32-35; Jan. 1, 1853-Dec. 25, 1856
Reel 1893   v36-39; Jan. 1, 1857-Dec. 27, 1860
Reel 1894   v83-84; Sept. 4, 1895-Dec. 30, 1896
Reel 1895   v85; Jan. 6-Dec. 29, 1897
Reel 1896   v86; Jan. 5-Dec. 28, 1898
Reel 1897   v87; Jan. 4-Dec. 27, 1899
Reel 1898   v88; Jan. 3-Dec. 26, 1900
Reel 1899   v89; Jan. 2-Dec. 25, 1901
Reel 1900   v90; Jan. 1-Dec. 31, 1902
Reel 1901   v91; Jan. 7-Dec. 30, 1903
Reel 1902   v92; Jan. 6-Dec. 28, 1904
Reel 1903   v93; Jan. 4-Dec. 27, 1905
Reel 1904   v94; Jan. 3-Dec. 26, 1906
Reel 1905   v95; Jan. 2-Dec. 25, 1907
Reel 1906   v96; Jan. 1-Dec. 23, 1908
Reel 1907   v97; Jan. 6-Dec. 29, 1909
Reel 1908   v98; Jan. 5-Dec. 28, 1910

1909   CHRISTIAN OBSERVER, CONDUCTED BY MEMBERS OF THE ESTABLISHED CHURCH. v12-42; Jan. 1813-Dec. 1842.

1910   CHRISTIAN SECRETARY. v30-68; Mar. 7, 1851-Dec. 25, 1889.

1911-1924 CONGREGATIONALIST AND HERALD OF GOSPEL LIBERTY
Congregationalist
Reel 1911   v76-78; Jan. 6, 1891-Dec. 28, 1893
Reel 1912   v79; Jan. 4-Dec. 27, 1894
Reel 1913   v80; Jan. 3-Dec. 26, 1895
Reel 1914   v81; Jan. 2-Dec. 31, 1896
Reel 1915   v82; Jan. 7-Dec. 30, 1897
Reel 1916   v83; Jan. 6-Dec. 29, 1898
Reel 1917   v84; Jan. 5-Dec. 28, 1899
Reel 1918   v85; Jan. 4-Dec. 29, 1900
Reel 1919   v86, nos1-20; Jan. 5-May 18, 1901
Congregationalist and Christian World
Reel 1919   v86; May 25, 1901-Dec. 28, 1901
Reel 1920   v87; Jan. 2-Dec. 27, 1902
Reel 1921   v88; Jan. 3-Dec. 26, 1903
Reel 1922   v89; Jan. 2-Dec. 31, 1904
Reel 1923   v90; Jan. 7-Dec. 30, 1905
Reel 1924   v91; Jan. 6-Dec. 29, 1906

1925-1934 HERALD OF GOSPEL LIBERTY
Reel 1925   v75-78; Jan. 4, 1883-Dec. 23, 1886
Reel 1926   v79-82; Jan. 6, 1887-Dec. 25, 1890
Reel 1927   v83-96; Jan. 1, 1891-Dec. 29, 1904
Reel 1928   v97-103; Jan. 5, 1905-Mar. 30, 1911
Reel 1929   v104-106; Jan. 18, 1912-Dec. 31, 1914
Reel 1930   v107-108; Jan. 7, 1915-Dec. 28, 1916
Reel 1931   v109-114; Jan. 4, 1917-Dec. 28, 1922
Reel 1932   v115-117; Jan. 4, 1923-Dec. 31, 1925
Reel 1933   v118-120; Jan. 7, 1926-Jan. 1929
Reel 1934   v121-122; Jan. 3, 1929-Feb. 27, 1930

1934-1935 JOURNAL OF PRISON DISCIPLINE AND PHILANTHROPY
Pennsylvania Journal of Prison Discipline and Philanthropy
Reel 1934   v11; Jan.-Dec. 1856
Journal of Prison Discipline and Philanthropy
Reel 1934   v12-nsv12; Jan. 1857-Jan. 1873
Reel 1935   nsv13-59; Jan. 1874-May 1920

1936   PRAIRIE FARMER. v39-42; July 4, 1868-Dec. 30, 1871.

1936-1947 SATURDAY EVENING POST
Saturday Evening Post
Reel 1936   July 8, 1826-Dec. 27, 1828
Reel 1937   Jan. 3, 1829-Dec. 25, 1830
Atkinson's Saturday Evening Post
Reel 1937   Feb. 5, 1831-Dec. 19, 1835
Reel 1938   Jan. 2, 1836-Nov. 2, 1839
Saturday Evening Post
Reel 1938   Nov. 9, 1839-Dec. 29, 1849
Reel 1939   Jan. 5, 1850-Dec. 26, 1857
Reel 1940   Jan. 7, 1860-Dec. 28, 1861
Reel 1941   Jan. 4, 1862-Aug. 26, 1865
Reel 1942   Jan. 6, 1866-Dec. 25, 1869
Reel 1943   Jan. 1, 1870-Dec. 27, 1873
Reel 1944   Jan. 3, 1874-Dec. 29, 1877
Reel 1945   Jan. 5, 1878-Dec. 31, 1881
Reel 1946   Jan. 2, 1882-Dec. 29, 1883
Reel 1947   Jan. 5, 1884-July 11, 1885

1948   THEOLOGICAL REPERTORY, AND CHURCHMAN'S GUIDE
Washington Theological Repertory
Reel 1948   v8-nsv1; Aug. 1826-Dec. 1828
Theological Repertory, and Churchman's Guide
Reel 1948   nsv2-3; Jan. 1829-Dec. 1830

1948-1959 TOWN AND COUNTRY
Morris's National Press, a Journal for Home
Reel 1948   Feb. 14-Nov. 14, 1846
Home Journal
Reel 1948   Nov. 21, 1846-Dec. 18, 1847
Reel 1949   May 6, 1848-Dec. 28, 1850
Reel 1950   Feb. 8, 1851-Dec. 27, 1856
Town and Country
Reel 1951   v57; Mar. 15, 1902-Mar. 7, 1903
Reel 1952   v58; Mar. 14, 1903-Mar. 5, 1904
Reel 1953   v59; Mar. 12, 1904-Mar. 4, 1905
Reel 1954   v60; Mar. 11, 1905-Mar. 3, 1906
Reel 1955   v61; Mar. 10, 1906-Mar. 16, 1907
Reel 1956   v62; Mar. 23, 1907-Mar. 14, 1908
Reel 1957   v65; Mar. 19, 1910-Mar. 11, 1911
Reel 1958   v66; Mar. 18, 1911-Mar. 9, 1912
Reel 1959   v67; Mar. 16, 1912-Mar. 8, 1913

1960-1961 TRANSYLVANIA JOURNAL OF MEDICINE AND THE ASSOCIATE SCIENCES
Reel 1960   v1-3; Feb. 1828-Nov. 1830
Reel 1961   v4-5; 9; Feb. 1831-Nov./Dec. 1832; Jan.-Dec. 1836

1961-1962 UNITED STATES CATHOLIC MISCELLANY
Reel 1961   v1-5; June 5, 1822-Dec. 28, 1825
Reel 1962   v6-14; July 22, 1826-June 20, 1835

1963-1966 ZION'S HERALD
Reel 1963   v85; Jan. 2-Dec. 25, 1907
Reel 1964   v86; Jan. 1-Dec. 30, 1908
Reel 1965   v87; Jan. 6-Dec. 29, 1909
Reel 1966   v88; Jan. 5-Dec. 28, 1910

AMERICAN PERIODICALS—1850-1900, Civil War and Reconstruction (APS III)

REEL

Unit 1

1-4   **ANDOVER REVIEW**
    Reel 1   Cumulative Index, v1-10; 1884-1888
    Reel 1   v1-5; Jan. 1884-June 1886
    Reel 2   v6-10; July 1886-Dec. 1888
    Reel 3   v11-15; Jan. 1889-June 1891
    Reel 4   v16-19; July 1891-Dec. 1893

4-5   **BAPTIST QUARTERLY**
    Reel 4   v1-2; Jan. 1867-Oct. 1868
    Reel 5   v3-11; Jan. 1869-Oct. 1877

6   **CALIFORNIAN ILLUSTRATED MAGAZINE.** v1-5; Oct. 1891-Apr. 1894.

7   **DIAL.** v1; Jan.-Dec. 1860.

7-12   **GALAXY**
    Reel 7   v1-4; May 1866-Dec. 1867
    Reel 8   v5-8; Jan. 1868-Dec. 1869
    Reel 9   v9-12; Jan. 1870-Dec. 1871
    Reel 10   v13-16; Jan. 1872-Dec. 1873
    Reel 11   v17-20; Jan. 1874-Dec. 1875
    Reel 12   v21-25; Jan. 1876-Jan. 1878

13-15   **JOURNAL OF SPECULATIVE PHILOSOPHY**
    Reel 13   Cumulative Index, v1-15; 1867-1881
    Reel 13   v1-10; 1867-1876
    Reel 14   v11-18; Jan. 1877-Oct. 1884
    Reel 15   v19-22; Jan. 1885-Dec. 1893

15   **PIONEER.** v1-4; Jan. 1854-Dec. 1855.

15-17   **RADICAL**
    Reel 15   v1; Sept. 1865-Aug. 1866
    Reel 16   v2-8; Sept. 1866-July 1871
    Reel 17   v9-10; Aug. 1871-June 1872

17   **RUSSELL'S MAGAZINE.** v1-6; Apr. 1857-Mar. 1860.

18-20   **SOUTHERN REVIEW**
    Reel 18   v1-8; Jan. 1867-Oct. 1870
    Reel 19   v9-17; Jan. 1871-Apr. 1875
    Reel 20   v18-26; July 1875-July 1879

21-25   **UNITARIAN REVIEW**
    Unitarian Review and Religious Magazine
    Reel 21   v1-6; Mar. 1874-Dec. 1876
    Reel 22   v7-12; Jan. 1877-Dec. 1879
    Reel 23   v13-19; Jan. 1880-June 1883
    Reel 24   v20-26; July 1883-Dec. 1886
    Unitarian Review
    Reel 24   v27; Jan. 1887-June 1887
    Reel 25   Cum Index, v27-34; 1887-1890
    Reel 25   v28-36; July 1887-Dec. 1891

Unit 2

26   **BEADLE'S MONTHLY.** v1-3; Jan. 1866-June 1867.

26-28   **HISTORICAL MAGAZINE**
    Reel 26   v1-6; Jan. 1857-Dec. 1862
    Reel 27   v7-2sv6; Jan. 1863-Dec. 1869
    Reel 28   2sv7-3sv3; Jan. 1870-Apr. 1875

REEL

28-30   **HOURS AT HOME**
    Reel 28   v1-2; May 1865-Apr. 1866
    Reel 29   v3-9; May 1866-Oct. 1869
    Reel 30   v10-11; Nov. 1869-Oct. 1870

30-31   **MANHATTAN**
    Reel 30   v1-3; Jan. 1883-June 1884
    Reel 31   v4; July-Sept. 1884

31-32   **NEW WORLD**
    Reel 31   v1-4; Mar. 1892-Dec. 1895
    Reel 32   v5-9; Mar. 1896-Dec. 1900

33-52   **OVERLAND MONTHLY AND OUT WEST MAGAZINE**
    Reel 33   v1-7; July 1868-Dec. 1871
    Reel 34   v8-14; Jan. 1872-June 1875
    Reel 35   v15-2sv5; July 1875-June 1885
    Reel 36   2sv6-10; July 1885-Dec. 1887
    Reel 37   2sv11-15; Jan. 1888-June 1890
    Reel 38   2sv16-20; July 1890-Dec. 1892
    Reel 39   2sv21-24; Jan. 1893-Dec. 1894
    Reel 40   2sv25-28; Jan. 1895-Dec. 1896
    Reel 41   2sv29-33; Jan. 1897-June 1899
    Reel 42   2sv34-39; July 1899-June 1902
    Reel 43   2sv40-44; July 1902-Dec. 1904
    Reel 44   2sv45-49; Jan. 1905-June 1907
    Reel 45   2sv50-54; July 1907-Dec. 1909
    Reel 46   2sv55-59; Jan. 1910-June 1912
    Reel 47   2sv60-64; July 1912-Dec. 1914
    Reel 48   2sv65-69; Jan. 1915-June 1917
    Reel 49   2sv70-75; July 1917-June 1920
    Reel 50   2sv76-82; July 1920-Dec. 1924
    Reel 51   2sv83-88; Jan. 1925-Dec. 1930
    Reel 52   2sv89-93; Jan. 1931-June 1935

52   **RIVERSIDE MAGAZINE FOR YOUNG PEOPLE.** v1-4; Jan. 1867-Dec. 1870.

53   **UNITED STATES SERVICE MAGAZINE.** v1-5; Jan. 1864-June 1866.

Unit 3

54-57   **AMERICAN ANTIQUARIAN AND ORIENTAL JOURNAL**
    American Antiquarian: a Quarterly Journal Devoted to Early American History, Ethnology and Archaeology
    Reel 54   v1-2; Apr. 1878-June 1880
    American Antiquarian and Oriental Journal
    Reel 54   v3-10; Oct. 1880-Nov. 1888
    Reel 55   v11-18; Jan. 1889-Nov. 1896
    Reel 56   v19-26; Jan. 1897-Nov. 1904
    Reel 57   v27-36; Jan. 1905-Dec. 1914

58   **AMERICAN HISTORICAL REGISTER AND MONTHLY GAZETTE.** v1-nsv1; Sept. 1894-May 1897.

59-60   **BAPTIST QUARTERLY REVIEW**
    Baptist Review
    Reel 59   v1-3; Jan. 1879-Dec. 1881
    Baptist Quarterly Review
    Reel 59   v4-7; Jan. 1882-Dec. 1885
    Reel 60   v8-14; Jan. 1886-Oct. 1892

61   **CHAP-BOOK.** v1-9; May 15, 1894-July 1, 1898

REEL		
62-63	**MANIFESTO**	
	Shaker	
	Reel 62	v1-2; 1871-1872
	Reel 62	Cum. Index, v3-5; 1873-1875
	Shaker and Shakeress Monthly	
	Reel 62	v3-5; 1873-1875
	Shaker	
	Reel 62	v6-7; 1876-1877
	Shaker Manifesto	
	Reel 62	v8-13; 1878-1883
	Manifesto	
	Reel 62	v14-16; 1884-1886
	Reel 63	v17-29; 1887-1899
64-65	**OLD GUARD**	
	Reel 64	v1-6; Jan. 1863-Dec. 1868
	Reel 65	v7-8; Jan. 1869-Dec. 1870
65-66	**OUR YOUNG FOLKS**	
	Reel 65	v1-3; Jan. 1865-Dec. 1867
	Reel 66	v4-9; Jan. 1868-Dec. 1873
67	**PHYSICIAN'S MAGAZINE.** v1; Aug. 1885-Mar. 1886.	
67-69	**POTTER'S AMERICAN MONTHLY**	
	Reel 67	v1-7; Jan. 1872-Dec. 1876
	Reel 68	v8-15; Jan. 1877-Dec. 1880
	Reel 69	v16-19; Jan. 1881-Sept. 1882
69-84	**PUCK**	
	Reel 69	v1-3; Mar. 1877-Sept. 4, 1878
	Reel 70	v4-9; Sept. 11, 1878-Sept. 7, 1881
	Reel 71	v10-15; Sept. 7, 1881-Aug. 27, 1884
	Reel 72	v16-21; Sept. 3, 1884-Aug. 24, 1887
	Reel 73	v22-26; Aug. 31, 1857-Feb. 19, 1890
	Reel 74	v27-31; Feb. 26, 1890-Aug. 17, 1892
	Reel 75	v32-37; Aug. 24, 1892-Aug. 14, 1895
	Reel 76	v38-42; Aug. 21, 1895-Feb. 9, 1898
	Reel 77	v43-48; Feb. 16, 1898-Feb. 6, 1901
	Reel 78	v49-54; Feb. 13, 1901-Jan. 27, 1904
	Reel 79	v55-59; Feb. 3, 1904-July 25, 1906
	Reel 80	v60-65; Aug. 1, 1906-July 21, 1909
	Reel 81	v66-71; July 28, 1909-July 17, 1912
	Reel 82	v72-76; July 24, 1912-Jan. 16, 1915
	Reel 83	v77-80; Jan. 23, 1915-Jan. 13, 1917
	Reel 84	v81-83; Jan. 20, 1917-Sept. 5, 1918

Unit 4

85-91	**AMERICAN JOURNAL OF EDUCATION**	
	Reel 85	v1-5; Aug. 1855-Sept. 1858
	Reel 86	v6-11; Mar. 1859-June 1862
	Reel 87	v12-16; Sept. 1862-Dec. 1866
	Reel 88	v17-20; Sept. 1867-1870
	Reel 89	v21-24; 1870-1873
	Reel 90	v25-28; 1874-1878
	Reel 91	v29-32; 1878-1882
92-99	**ARENA**	
	Reel 92	v1-5; Dec. 1889-May 1892
	Reel 93	v6-9; June 1892-May 1894
	Reel 94	v10-14; June 1894-Nov. 1895
	Reel 95	v15-19; Dec. 1895-June 1898
	Reel 96	v20-25; July 1898-June 1901
	Reel 97	v26-32; July 1901-Dec. 1904
	Reel 98	v33-38; Jan. 1905-Dec. 1907
	Reel 99	v39-41; Jan. 1908-Aug. 1909

REEL		
99-100	**CONTINENT**	
	Our Continent	
	Reel 99	v1-2; Feb.-Dec. 1882
	Continent; an Illustrated Weekly Magazine	
	Reel 100	v3-6; Jan. 1883-Dec. 1884
101-108	**CRITIC**	
	Reel 101	v1-7; Jan. 15, 1881-Dec. 26, 1885
	Reel 102	v8-15; Jan. 2, 1886-Dec. 28, 1889
	Reel 103	v16-21; Jan. 4, 1890-Dec. 31, 1892
	Reel 104	v22-26; Jan. 7, 1893-June 29, 1895
	Reel 105	v27-31; July 6, 1895-Dec. 25, 1897
	Reel 106	v32-37; Jan. 1, 1898-Dec. 1900
	Reel 107	v38-43; Jan. 1901-Dec. 1903
	Reel 108	v44-49; Jan. 1904-Sept. 1906
109	**HARVARD REGISTER.** v1-3; Jan. 1880-July 1881.	
109	**INTERNATIONAL MONTHLY MAGAZINE OF LITERATURE, SCIENCE AND ART.** v1-5; July 1850-Apr. 1852.	
110-111	**NATIONAL REPOSITORY**	
	Reel 110	v1-6; Jan. 1877-Dec. 1879
	Reel 111	v7-8; Jan.-Dec. 1880

Unit 5

112-130	**BOOKMAN**	
	Reel 112	v1-5; Feb. 1895-Aug. 1897
	Reel 113	v6-9; Sept. 1897-Aug. 1899
	Reel 114	v10-13; Sept. 1899-Aug. 1901
	Reel 115	v14-17; Sept. 1901-Aug. 1903
	Reel 116	v18-21; Sept. 1903-Aug. 1905
	Reel 117	v22-25; Sept. 1905-Aug. 1907
	Reel 118	v26-29; Sept. 1907-Aug. 1909
	Reel 119	v30-33; Sept. 1909-Aug. 1911
	Reel 120	v34-37; Sept. 1911-Aug. 1913
	Reel 121	v38-41; Sept. 1913-Aug. 1915
	Reel 122	v42-45; Sept. 1915-Aug. 1917
	Reel 123	v46-49; Sept. 1917-Aug. 1919
	Reel 124	v50-54; Sept. 1919-Feb. 1922
	Reel 125	v55-58; Mar. 1922-Feb. 1924
	Reel 126	v59-62; Mar. 1924-Feb. 1926
	Reel 127	v63-66; Mar. 1926-Feb. 1928
	Reel 128	v67-70; Mar. 1928-Feb. 1930
	Reel 129	v71-74; Mar. 1930-Mar. 1932
	Reel 130	v75-76; Apr. 1932-Mar. 1933
130-132	**OLD AND NEW**	
	Reel 130	v1-4; Jan. 1870-Dec. 1871
	Reel 131	v5-10; Jan. 1872-Dec. 1874
	Reel 132	v11; Jan.-May 1875
132-139	**UNITED SERVICE**	
	Reel 132	v1-5; Jan. 1879-Dec. 1881
	Reel 133	v6-10; Jan. 1882-June 1884
	Reel 134	v11-nsv1; July 1884-June 1889
	Reel 135	nsv2-6; July 1889-Dec. 1891
	Reel 136	nsv7-11; Jan. 1892-June 1894
	Reel 137	nsv12-17; July 1894-Apr. 1897
	Reel 138	3sv1-5; Jan. 1902-June 1904
	Reel 139	3sv6-8; July 1904-Dec. 1905

REEL

Unit 6

140   CONTINENTAL MONTHLY. v1-6; Jan. 1862-Dec. 1864.

141-147   AMERICAN ACADEMY OF ARTS AND SCIENCES, BOSTON. PROCEEDINGS
Reel 141   v1-7; May 1846-May 1868
Reel 142   v8-14; May 1868-May 1879
Reel 143   v15-20; May 1879-May 1885
Reel 144   v21-27; May 1885-May 1892
Reel 145   v28-33; May 1892-May 1898
Reel 146   v34-37; May 1898-May 1902
Reel 147   v38-41; May 1902-May 1906

148-151   EVERY SATURDAY
Reel 148   v1-5; Jan. 1866-June 1868
Reel 149   v6-nsv1; July 1868-Dec. 1870
Reel 150   nsv2-3sv2; Jan. 1871-Dec. 1872
Reel 151   3sv3-4sv2; Jan. 1873-Oct. 1874

152-154   INTERNATIONAL REVIEW
Reel 152   Cumulative Index, v1-9; 1874-80
Reel 152   v1-4; Jan. 1874-Dec. 1877
Reel 153   v5-9; Jan 1878-Dec. 1880
Reel 154   v10-14; Jan. 1881-June 1883

155-159   LITERARY WORLD
Reel 155   v1-10; June 1870-Dec. 1879
Reel 156   v11-16; Jan. 1880-Dec. 1885
Reel 157   v17-22; Jan. 1886-Dec. 1891
Reel 158   v23-28; Jan. 1892-Dec. 1897
Reel 159   v29-35; Jan. 1898-Dec. 1904

160-163   NATIONAL MAGAZINE
Magazine of Western History
Reel 160   v1-4; Nov. 1884-Oct. 1886
Reel 161   v5-8; Nov. 1886-Oct. 1888
Reel 162   v9-13; Nov. 1888-Apr. 1891
Reel 163   v14; May-Oct. 1891
National Magazine; a Monthly Journal of American History
Reel 163   v15-19; Nov. 1891-Oct. 1894

164   PUNCHINELLO. v1-2; Apr.-Dec. 1870.

164-167   PUTNAM'S MAGAZINE
Putnam's Monthly Magazine of American Literature, Science, and Art
Reel 164   v1-4; Jan. 1853-Dec. 1854
Reel 165   v5-9; Jan. 1855-June 1857
Reel 166   v10; July-Dec. 1857
Putnam's Magazine. Original Papers on Literature, Science, Art, and National Interests
Reel 166   nsv1-3; Jan. 1868-June 1869
Reel 167   nsv4-6; July 1869-Nov. 1870

167-170   QUARTERLY JOURNAL OF ECONOMICS
Reel 167   Cumulative Index, v1-10; 1886-1896
Reel 167   v1-3; Oct. 1886-July 1889
Reel 168   v4-10; Oct. 1889-July 1896
Reel 169   v11-16; Oct. 1896-Aug. 1902
Reel 170   v17-20; Nov. 1902-Aug. 1906

Unit 7

171-172   AMERICAN EDUCATIONAL MONTHLY
American Education Monthly
Reel 171   v1-4, no9; Jan. 1864-Sept. 1867

REEL

American Educational Monthly, and New York Teacher
Reel 171   v4, no10-v4, no12; Oct.-Dec. 1867
New York Teacher and American Educational Monthly
Reel 171   v5-6; Jan. 1868-Dec. 1869
American Educational Monthly
Reel 171   v7-8; Jan. 1870-Dec. 1871
Reel 172   v9-12; Jan. 1872-Dec. 1875
Schermerhorn's Monthly
Reel 172   v13; Jan.-Dec. 1876

172-173   CALIFORNIAN AND OVERLAND MONTHLY
Californian
Reel 172   v1-2; Jan.-Dec. 1880
Reel 173   v3-6, no33; Jan.- 1881-Sept. 1882
Californian and Overland Monthly
Reel 173   v6, no34-36; Oct.-Dec. 1882

173-186   CHAUTAUQUAN
Reel 173   v1-2; Sept. 1880-July 1882
Reel 174   v3-6; Oct. 1882-July 1886
Reel 175   v7-10; Oct. 1886-Mar. 1890
Reel 176   v11-14; Apr. 1890-Mar. 1892
Reel 177   v15-18; Apr. 1892-Mar. 1894
Reel 178   v19-22; Apr. 1894-Mar. 1896
Reel 179   v23-27; Apr. 1896-Sept. 1898
Reel 180   v28-32; Oct. 1898-Mar. 1901
Reel 181   v33-37; Apr. 1901-Aug. 1903
Reel 182   v38-42; Sept. 1903-Feb. 1906
Reel 183   v43-51; Mar. 1906-Aug. 1908
Reel 184   v52-60; Sept. 1908-Nov. 1910
Reel 185   v61-70; Dec. 1910-May 1913
Reel 186   v71-72; June 7, 1913-May 23, 1914

186   DANVILLE QUARTERLY REVIEW. v1-4; Mar. 1861-Dec. 1864.

187-200   DIAL
Reel 187   v1-9; May 1880-Apr. 1889
Reel 188   v10-17; May 1889-Dec. 16, 1894
Reel 189   v18-24; Jan. 1, 1895-June 16, 1898
Reel 190   v25-30; July 1, 1898-June 16, 1901
Reel 191   v31-37; July 1, 1901-Dec. 16, 1904
Reel 192   v38-44; Jan. 1, 1905-June 16, 1908
Reel 193   v45-51; July 1, 1908-Dec. 16, 1911
Reel 194   v52-58; Jan. 1, 1912-June 10, 1915
Reel 195   v59-64; June 24, 1915-June 6, 1918
Reel 196   v65-69; July 18, 1918-Dec. 1920
Reel 197   v70-73; Jan. 1921-Dec. 1922
Reel 198   v74-78; Jan. 1923-June 1925
Reel 199   v79-84; July 1925-June 1928
Reel 200   v85-86; July 1928-July 1929

Unit 8

201-202   AMERICAN CATHOLIC HISTORICAL RESEARCHES
Reel 201   Cumulative Index v1-29; July 1884-July 1912
Historical Researches in Western Pennsylvania, Principally Catholic
Reel 201   v1; July 1884-Apr. 1885
Catholic Historical Researches
Reel 201   v2-3, no2; July 1885-Oct. 1886
American Catholic Historical Researches
Reel 201   v3, no3-v21; Jan. 1887-Oct. 1904
Reel 202   nsv1-8; Jan. 1905-July 1912

REEL

203-204   **AMERICAN MAGAZINE OF CIVICS**
    American Journal of Politics
      Reel 203   v1-4; July 1892-June 1894
      Reel 204   v5; July-Dec. 1894
    American Magazine of Civics
      Reel 204   v6-9; Jan. 1895-Jan. 1897

205-207   **AMERICAN PRESBYTERIAN REVIEW**
    American Theological Review
      Reel 205   v1-4; 1859-1862
    American Presbyterian and Theological Review
      Reel 206   nsv1-5; Jan. 1863-Oct. 1867
      Reel 206   nsv6; Jan.-Oct. 1868
    American Presbyterian Review
      Reel 207   ns(s3)v1-3; Jan. 1869-Oct. 1871

208-235   **FOREST AND STREAM**
      Reel 208   v1-4; Aug. 14, 1873-Aug. 5, 1875
      Reel 209   v5-8; Aug. 12, 1875-Aug. 2, 1877
      Reel 210   v9-13; Aug. 9, 1877-Jan. 1880
      Reel 211   v14-17; Feb. 1880-Jan. 1882
      Reel 212   v18-20; Feb. 1882-July 1883
      Reel 213   v21-24; Aug. 1883-July 1885
      Reel 214   v25-28; July 30, 1885-July 1887
      Reel 215   v29-32; July 28, 1887-July 18, 1889
      Reel 216   v33-36; July 25, 1889-July 16, 1891
      Reel 217   v37-39; July 23, 1891-Dec. 28, 1892
      Reel 218   v40-42; Jan. 5, 1893-June 30, 1894
      Reel 219   v43-45; July 7, 1894-Dec. 28, 1895
      Reel 220   v46-50; Jan. 4, 1896-June 25, 1898
      Reel 221   v51-54; July 2, 1898-June 30, 1900
      Reel 222   v55-57; July 7, 1900-Dec. 28, 1901
      Reel 223   v58-60; Jan. 4, 1902-June 27, 1903
      Reel 224   v61-63; July 1903-Dec. 1904
      Reel 225   v64-66; Jan. 7, 1905-June 30, 1906
      Reel 226   v67-68; July 7, 1906-June 29, 1907
      Reel 227   v69-71; July 6, 1907-Dec. 26, 1908
      Reel 228   v72-74; Jan. 2, 1909-June 25, 1910
      Reel 229   v75-77; July 2, 1910-Dec. 30, 1911
      Reel 230   v78-80; Jan. 6, 1912-June 28, 1913
      Reel 231   v81-85; July 5, 1913-Dec. 1915
      Reel 232   v86-89; Jan. 1916-Dec. 1919
      Reel 233   v90-93; Jan. 1920-Dec. 1923
      Reel 234   v94-97; Jan. 1924-Dec. 1927
      Reel 235   v98-100; Jan. 1928-July 1930

236-238   **OLIVER OPTIC'S MAGAZINE**
      Reel 236   v1-8; Jan. 5, 1867-Dec. 31, 1870
      Reel 237   v9-14; Jan. 1871-Dec. 1873
      Reel 238   v15-18; Jan. 1874-Dec. 1875

Unit 9

239-240   **ALDINE**
    Aldine Press; a Typographic Art Journal
      Reel 239   v3; 1870
    Aldine, a Typographic Art Journal
      Reel 239   v4-6; 1871-73
    Aldine, the Art Journal of America
      Reel 239   v7-8; 1874-1877
      Reel 240   v9; 1878-1879

240-243   **AMERICAN LAWYER**
      Reel 240   v1-4; Jan. 1893-Dec. 1896
      Reel 241   v5-9; Jan. 1897-Dec. 1901
      Reel 242   v10-14; Jan. 1902-Dec. 1906
      Reel 243   v15-16; Jan. 1907-July 1908

REEL

243   **AMERICAN SOCIALIST.** v1-4; Mar. 1876-Dec. 25, 1879.

244-249   **APPLETONS' JOURNAL**
    Appletons' Journal of Literature, Science and Art
      Reel 244   v1-4; Apr. 3, 1869-Dec. 31, 1870
      Reel 245   v5-8; Jan. 7, 1871-Dec. 28, 1872
      Reel 246   v9-12; Jan. 1, 1873-Dec. 26, 1874
      Reel 247   v13-15; Jan. 2, 1875-June 1876
    Appletons' Journal
      Reel 247   nsv1-2; July, 1876-June, 1877
      Reel 248   nsv3-9; July, 1877-Dec. 1880
      Reel 249   nsv10-11; Jan.-Dec. 1881

249-252   **BALLOU'S PICTORIAL DRAWING-ROOM COMPANION**
    Gleason's Pictorial Drawing-Room Companion
      Reel 249   v1-4; May 3, 1851-June 25, 1853
      Reel 250   v5-7; July 2, 1853-Dec. 30, 1854
    Ballou's Pictorial Drawing-Room Companion
      Reel 250   v8-10; Jan. 6, 1855-June 28, 1856
      Reel 251   v11-16; July 5, 1856-June 24, 1859
      Reel 252   v17; July 2-Dec. 24, 1859

252-253   **BIBELOT**
      Reel 252   Cumulative Index, v1-20; 1895-1925
      Reel 252   v1-10; 1895-1904
      Reel 253   v11-21; 1905-1925

254-264   **BIBLICAL WORLD**
    Hebrew Student: a Monthly Journal in the Interests of Old Testament Literature and Interpretation
      Reel 254   v1-2; Apr. 1882-June 1883
    Old Testament Student
      Reel 254   v3-8; Sept. 1883-June 1889
    Old and New Testament Student
      Reel 255   v9-15; July 1889-Dec. 1892
    Biblical World
      Reel 256   nsv1-6; Jan. 1893-Dec. 1895
      Reel 257   nsv7-12; Jan. 1896-Dec. 1898
      Reel 258   nsv13-18; Jan. 1899-Dec. 1901
      Reel 259   nsv19-24; Jan. 1902-Dec. 1904
      Reel 260   nsv25-30; Jan. 1905-Dec. 1907
      Reel 261   nsv31-36; Jan. 1908-Dec. 1910
      Reel 262   nsv37-42; Jan. 1911-Dec. 1913
      Reel 263   nsv43-49; Jan. 1914-June 1917
      Reel 264   nsv50-54; July 1917-Nov. 1920

264-265   **EMERSON'S MAGAZINE AND PUTNAM'S MONTHLY**
    United States Magazine of Science, Art, Manufactures, Agriculture, Commerce and Trade
      Reel 264   v1-2; May 15, 1854-Apr. 1856
    United States Magazine
      Reel 265   v3-4; July 1856-June 1857
    Emerson's United States Magazine
      Reel 265   v5, no37-39; July-Sept. 1857
    Emerson's Magazine and Putnams Monthly
      Reel 265   v5, no40-v7; Oct. 1857-Nov. 1858

266-268   **JOURNAL OF SOCIAL SCIENCE**
      Reel 266   v1-17; June 1869-May 1883
      Reel 267   v18-34; May 1884-Nov. 1896
      Reel 268   v35-46; Dec. 1897-Dec. 1909

269   **MATHEMATICAL MONTHLY.** v1-3; Oct. 1858-Sept. 1861.

269   **NEW ENGLAND JOURNAL OF DENTISTRY AND ALLIED SCIENCES.** v1-3; Jan. 1882-Dec. 1884.

REEL

270	**PHILOBIBLION.** v1-2; Dec. 1861-Dec. 1863.

270-271	**SHAKESPEARIANA**	
	Reel 270	v1-6; Nov. 1883-Dec. 1889
	Reel 271	v7-10; Jan. 1890-1893

271	**UTAHNIAN.** v1; June 20, 1896-Apr. 1897.

Unit 10

272-293	**FORUM AND CENTURY**	
	Forum	
	Reel 272	v1-5; Mar. 1886-Aug. 1888
	Reel 272	Cumulative Index 1-32; 1886-1902
	Reel 273	v6-10; Sept. 1888-Feb. 1891
	Reel 274	v11-15; Mar. 1891-Aug. 1893
	Reel 275	v16-19; Sept. 1893-Aug. 1895
	Reel 276	v20-24; Mar. 1896-Feb. 1898
	Reel 277	v25-29; Mar. 1898-Aug. 1900
	Reel 278	v30-34; Sept. 1900-June 1903
	Reel 279	v35-40; July 1903-Dec. 1908
	Reel 280	v41-45; Jan. 1909-June 1911
	Reel 281	v46-50; July 1911-Dec. 1913
	Reel 282	v51-54; Jan. 1914-Dec. 1915
	Reel 283	v55-58; Jan. 1916-Dec. 1917
	Reel 284	v59-63; Jan. 1918-June 1920
	Reel 285	v64-69; July 1920-June 1924
	Reel 286	v70-73; July 1924-June 1925
	Reel 287	v74-76; July 1925-Dec. 1926
	Reel 288	v77-79; Jan. 1927-June 1928
	Reel 289	v80-83; July 1928-June 1930
	Forum and Century	
	Reel 290	v84-88; July 1930-Dec. 1932
	Reel 291	v89-94; Jan. 1933-Dec. 1935
	Reel 292	v95-101; Jan. 1936-June 1939
	Reel 293	v102-103; July 1939-June 1940

293-297	**OPEN COURT**	
	Reel 293	v1-3; Feb. 17, 1887-Feb. 20, 1890
	Reel 294	v4-8; Feb. 27, 1890-Dec. 27, 1894
	Reel 295	v9-13; Jan. 3, 1895-Dec. 1899
	Reel 296	v14-17; Jan. 1900-Dec. 1903
	Reel 297	v18-19; Jan. 1904-Dec. 1905

297-309	**OUTING**	
	Outing, a Journal of Recreation	
	Reel 297	v1-2; Oct. 1882-Dec. 1883
	Outing and the Wheelman	
	Reel 297	v3; Jan.-Mar. 1884
	Reel 298	v4-5; Apr. 1884-Mar. 1885
	Outing, an Illustrated Monthly Magazine of Recreation	
	Reel 298	v6-8; Apr. 1885-Sept. 1886
	Reel 299	v9-14; Oct. 1886-Sept. 1889
	Reel 300	v15-19; Oct. 1889-Mar. 1892
	Reel 301	v20-25; Apr. 1892-Sept. 1895
	Reel 302	v26-30; Oct. 1895-Sept. 1897
	Reel 303	v31-34; Oct. 1897-Sept. 1899
	Reel 304	v35-39; Oct. 1899-Mar. 1902
	Reel 305	v40-43; Apr. 1902-Mar. 1904
	Reel 306	v44-47; Apr. 1904-Mar. 1906
	Outing Magazine	
	Reel 307	v48-51; Apr. 1906-Mar. 1908
	Reel 308	v52-55; Apr. 1908-Mar. 1910
	Reel 309	v56-57; Apr. 1910-Mar. 1911

309-313	**SOUTHERN HISTORICAL SOCIETY**	
	Reel 309	v1-4; Jan. 1876-Dec. 1877
	Reel 309	Cumulative Index, v1-10; 1876-1882

REEL

	Reel 310	v5-11; Jan. 1878-Dec. 1883
	Reel 311	v12-19; Jan. 1884-Dec. 1891
	Reel 312	v20-28; Jan. 1892-Dec. 1900
	Reel 313	v29-33; Jan. 1901-Dec. 1905

Unit 11

314-316	**AMERICAN METEOROLOGICAL JOURNAL**	
	Reel 314	v1-4; May 1884-Apr. 1888
	Reel 315	v5-9; May 1888-Apr. 1893
	Reel 316	v10-12; May 1893-Apr. 1896

316-341	**MCBRIDE'S MAGAZINE**	
	Lippincott's Magazine of Literature, Science and Education	
	Reel 316	v1-3; Jan. 1868-June 1869
	Reel 317	v4-7; July 1869-June 1871
	Lippincott's Magazine of Popular Literature and Science	
	Reel 317	v8; July-Dec. 1871
	Reel 318	v9-13; Jan. 1872-June 1874
	Reel 319	v14-17; July 1874-June 1876
	Reel 320	v18-21; July 1876-June 1878
	Reel 321	v22-25; July 1878-June 1880
	Reel 322	v26-30; July 1880-Dec. 1882
	Reel 323	v31-35; Jan. 1883-June 1885
	Reel 324	v36; July-Dec. 1885
	Lippincott's Monthly Magazine	
	Reel 324	v37-39; Jan. 1886-June 1887
	Reel 325	v40-42; July 1887-Dec. 1888
	Reel 326	v43-45; Jan. 1889-June 1890
	Reel 327	v46-49; July 1890-June 1892
	Reel 328	v50-53; July 1892-June 1894
	Reel 329	v54-57; July 1894-June 1896
	Reel 330	v58-60; July 1896-Dec. 1897
	Reel 331	v61-63; Jan. 1898-June 1899
	Reel 332	v64-66; July 1899-Dec. 1900
	Reel 333	v67-70; Jan. 1901-Dec. 1902
	Reel 334	v71-74; Jan. 1903-Dec. 1904
	Reel 335	v75-77; Jan. 1905-June 1906
	Reel 336	v78-80; July 1906-Dec. 1907
	Reel 337	v81-83; Jan. 1908-June 1909
	Reel 338	v84-86; July 1909-Dec. 1910
	Reel 339	v87-89; Jan. 1911-June 1912
	Reel 340	v90-93; July 1912-June 1914
	Reel 341	v94-96; July 1914-Aug. 1915
	McBride's Magazine	
	Reel 341	v97; Sept.-Apr. 1915

342-344	**MONIST**	
	Reel 342	v1-5; Oct. 1890-July 1895
	Reel 343	v6-10; Oct. 1895-July 1900
	Reel 344	v11-15; Oct. 1900-Oct. 1905

Units 12-13

345-367	**CENTURY, A POPULAR QUARTERLY**	
	Scribner's Monthly	
	Reel 345	v1-4; Nov. 1870-Oct. 1872
	Reel 346	v5-8; Nov. 1872-Oct. 1874
	Reel 347	v9-12; Nov. 1874-Oct. 1876
	Reel 348	v13-16; Nov. 1876-Oct. 1878
	Reel 349	v17-19; Nov. 1878-Apr. 1880
	Reel 350	v20-22; May 1880-Oct. 1881
	Century Illustrated Magazine	
	Reel 351	v23-25; Nov. 1881-Apr. 1883

Reel 352	v26-28; May 1883-Oct. 1884
Reel 353	v29-31; Nov. 1884-Apr. 1886
Reel 354	v32-34; May 1886-Oct. 1887
Reel 355	v35-37; Nov. 1887-Apr. 1889
Reel 356	v38-40; May 1889-Oct. 1890
Reel 357	v41-43; Nov. 1890-Apr. 1892
Reel 358	v44-46; May 1892-Oct. 1893
Reel 359	v47-49; Nov. 1893-Apr. 1895
Reel 360	v50-52; May 1895-Oct. 1896
Reel 361	v53-55; Nov. 1896-Apr. 1898
Reel 362	v56-58; May 1898-Oct. 1899
Reel 363	v59-61; Nov. 1899-Apr. 1901
Reel 364	v62-64; May 1901-Oct. 1902
Reel 365	v65-67; Nov. 1902-Apr. 1904
Reel 366	v68-70; May 1904-Oct. 1905
Reel 367	v71; Nov. 1905-Apr. 1906

367-423 NEW OUTLOOK
Christian Union

Reel 367	v1; Jan. 1870-June 1870
Reel 368	v2-3; July 1870-June 1871
Reel 369	v4-6; July 1871-Dec. 1872
Reel 370	v7-9; Jan. 1873-July 1874
Reel 371	v10-12; July 1874-Dec. 1875
Reel 372	v13-15; Jan. 1876-June 1877
Reel 373	v16-18; July 1877-Dec. 1878
Reel 374	v19-21; Jan. 1879-June 1880
Reel 375	v22-24; July 1880-Dec. 1881
Reel 376	v25-27; Jan. 1882-June 1883
Reel 377	v28-30; July 1883-Dec. 1884
Reel 378	v31-32; Jan. 1885-Dec. 1885
Reel 379	v33-34; Jan. 1886-Dec. 1886
Reel 380	v35-36; Jan. 1887-Dec. 1887
Reel 381	v37-38; Jan. 188-Dec. 1888
Reel 382	v39-40; Jan. 1889-Dec. 1889
Reel 383	v41-42; Jan. 1890-Dec. 1890
Reel 384	v43-44; Jan. 1891-Dec. 1891
Reel 385	v45-46; Jan. 1892-Dec. 1892
Reel 386	v47; Jan.-June 1893

Outlook

Reel 386	v48; July-Dec. 1893
Reel 387	v49-50; Jan. 1894-Dec. 1894
Reel 388	v51-52; Jan. 1895-Dec. 1895
Reel 389	v53-54; Jan. 1896-Dec. 1896
Reel 390	v55-57; Jan. 1897-Dec. 1897
Reel 391	v58-60; Jan. 1898-Dec. 1898
Reel 392	v61-63; Jan. 1899-Dec. 1899
Reel 393	v64-66; Jan. 1900-Dec. 1900
Reel 394	v67-69; Jan. 1901-Dec. 1901
Reel 395	v70-72; Jan. 1902-Dec. 1902
Reel 396	v73-75; Jan. 1903-Dec. 1903
Reel 397	v76-78; Jan. 1904-Dec. 1904
Reel 398	v79-81; Jan. 1905-Dec. 1905
Reel 399	v82-83; Jan. 1906-Aug. 1906
Reel 400	v84-85; Sept. 1906-Apr. 1907
Reel 401	v86-88; May 1907-Apr. 1908
Reel 402	v89-91; May 1908-Apr. 1909
Reel 403	v92-94; May 1909-Apr. 1910
Reel 404	v95-97; May 1910-Apr. 1911
Reel 405	v98-100; May 1911-Apr. 1912
Reel 406	v101-103; May 1912-Apr. 1913
Reel 407	v104-106; May 1913-Apr. 1914
Reel 408	v107-109; May 1914-Apr. 1915
Reel 409	v110-112; May 1915-Apr. 1916
Reel 410	v113-115; May 1916-Apr. 1917
Reel 411	v116-118; May 1917-Apr. 1918
Reel 412	v119-121; May 1918-Apr. 1919
Reel 413	v122-125; May 1919-Aug. 1920
Reel 414	v126-129; Sept. 1920-Dec. 1921
Reel 415	v130-132; Jan. 1922-Dec. 1922

Reel 416	v133-135; Jan. 1923-Dec. 1923
Reel 417	v136-138; Jan. 1924-Dec. 1924
Reel 418	v139-142; Jan. 1925-Apr. 1926
Reel 419	v143-147; May 1926-Dec. 1927
Reel 420	v148-150; Jan.-Oct. 17, 1928

Outlook and Independent

Reel 420	v150-151; Oct. 24, 1928-Apr. 1929
Reel 421	v152-155; May 1929-Aug. 1930
Reel 422	v156-159; Sept. 1930-Dec. 1931
Reel 423	v160; Jan.-Feb. 1932

Outlook

Reel 423	v160; Mar.-Apr. 1932

New Outlook

Reel 423	v161-165; Oct. 1932-June 1935

Unit 14

424-429 AMERICAN JOURNAL OF PHILOLOGY

Reel 424	v1-5; 1880-1884
Reel 425	v6-10; 1885-1889
Reel 426	v11-15; 1890-1894
Reel 427	v16-20; 1895-1899
Reel 428	v21-25; 1900-1904
Reel 429	v26-31; 1905-1910

430-450 HARPER'S BAZAAR

Reel 430	v1-2; Nov. 1867-Dec. 1869
Reel 431	v3-4; Jan. 1870-Dec. 1871
Reel 432	v5-6; Jan. 1872-Dec. 1873
Reel 433	v7-9; Jan. 1874-Dec. 1876
Reel 434	v10-12; Jan. 1877-Dec. 1879
Reel 435	v13-15; Jan. 1880-Dec. 1882
Reel 436	v16-18; Jan. 1883-Dec. 1885
Reel 437	v19-20; Jan. 1886-Dec. 1887
Reel 438	v21-22; Jan. 1888-Dec. 1889
Reel 439	v23-24; Jan. 1890-Dec. 1891
Reel 440	v25-26; Jan. 1892-Dec. 1893
Reel 441	v27-28; Jan. 1894-Dec. 1895
Reel 442	v29-30; Jan. 1896-Dec. 1897
Reel 443	v31-32; Jan. 1898-Dec. 1899
Reel 444	v33; Jan. 1900-Dec. 1900
Reel 445	v34-35; Jan. 1901-Dec. 1901
Reel 446	v36-37; Jan. 1902-Dec. 1903
Reel 447	v38-39; Jan. 1904-Dec. 1905
Reel 448	v40-41; Jan. 1906-Dec. 1907
Reel 449	v42-43; Jan. 1908-Dec. 1909
Reel 450	v44-46; Jan. 1910-Nov. 1912

451 NEW YORK GENEALOGICAL AND BIOGRAPHICAL SOCIETY. v1; Dec. 1869.

451-455 NEW YORK GENEALOGICAL AND BIOGRAPHICAL RECORD

Reel 451	v1-10; 1870-1879
Reel 452	v11-20; 1880-1889
Reel 453	v21-20; 1890-1899
Reel 454	v31-37; 1900-1906
Reel 455	v38-41; 1907-1910

456-461 PENNSYLVANIA MAGAZINE OF HISTORY AND BIOGRAPHY

Reel 456	v1-7; 1877-1883
Reel 457	v8-13; 1884-1889
Reel 458	v14-18; 1890-1894
Reel 459	v19-23; 1895-1899
Reel 460	v24-29; 1900-1905
Reel 461	v30; Mar. 1906-Oct. 1906

461-462	ROUND TABLE	
	Reel 461	v1-4; Dec. 1863-Dec. 1866
	Reel 462	v5-10; Jan. 1867-July 1869

| 462 | ROYCROFT QUARTERLY. no1-3; May-Nov. 1896. | |

Unit 15

463-472	AMERICAN LAW REVIEW	
	Reel 463	Cumulative Index, v1-13; 1866-79
	Reel 463	v1-5; Oct. 1866-July 1871
	Reel 464	v6-10; Oct. 1871-July 1876
	Reel 465	v11-14; Oct. 1876-Dec. 1880
	Reel 466	v15-18; Jan. 1881-Dec. 1884
	Reel 467	v19-22; Jan. 1885-Dec. 1888
	Reel 468	v23-26; Jan. 1889-Dec. 1892
	Reel 469	v27-30; Jan. 1893-Dec. 1896
	Reel 470	v31-34; Jan. 1897-Dec. 1900
	Reel 471	v35-38; Jan. 1901-Dec. 1904
	Reel 472	v39-40; Jan. 1905-Dec. 1906

473-476	GUNTON'S MAGAZINE	
	Social Economist	
	Reel 473	v1-9; Mar. 1891-Dec. 1895
	Gunton's Magazine of American Economics and Political Science	
	Reel 474	v10-14, no4; Jan. 1896-Apr. 1898
	Gunton's Magazine	
	Reel 474	v14, no5-v16; May 1898-June 1899
	Reel 475	v17-22; July 1899-June 1902
	Reel 476	v23-27; July 1902-Dec. 1904

477-493	MCCLURE'S MAGAZINE	
	McClures Magazine	
	Reel 477	Cumulative Index, v1-18; 1893-1902
	Reel 477	v1-6; June 1893-May 1896
	Reel 478	v7-9; June 1896-Oct. 1897
	Reel 479	v10-13; Nov. 1897-Oct. 1899
	Reel 480	v14-18; Nov. 1899-Apr. 1902
	Reel 481	v19-23; May 1902-Oct. 1904
	Reel 482	v24-28; Nov. 1904-Apr. 1907
	Reel 483	v29-31; May 1907-Oct. 1908
	Reel 484	v32-34; Nov. 1908-Apr. 1910
	Reel 485	v35-38; May 1910-Apr. 1912
	Reel 486	v39-41; May 1912-Oct. 1913
	Reel 487	v42-43; Nov. 1913-Oct. 1914
	Reel 488	v44-47; Nov. 1914-Oct. 1916
	Reel 489	v48-51A; Nov. 1916-Dec. 1919
	Reel 490	v52-54; Jan. 1920-Feb. 1923
	Reel 491	v55-57; Mar. 1923-Aug. 1924
	Reel 492	nsv1-2; May 1925-Jan. 1926
	McClures, the Magazine of Romance	
	Reel 492	v58-59, no3; June 1926-Sept. 1927
	McClure's	
	Reel 492	v59,no4-6; Oct.-Dec. 1927
	Reel 493	v60; Jan.-June 1928
	New McClure's	
	Reel 493	v61-62; July 1928-Mar. 1929

Unit 16

494-500	AMERICAN ECONOMIC ASSOCIATION. PUBLICATIONS	
	Reel 494	Index; 1886-1910
	Reel 494	General Contents and Index, v1-11; 1886-1896

	Reel 494	v1-6; Mar. 1886-Nov. 1891
	Reel 495	v7-11; Jan. 1892-Aug. 1896
	Reel 496	nsv1-s3v2; Dec. 1897-Nov. 1901
	Reel 497	s3v3-5; Feb. 1902-Nov. 1904
	Reel 498	s3v6-8; Feb. 1905-Nov. 1907
	Reel 499	s3v9-11; Feb. 1908-Dec. 1910
	Reel 500	s4v1; Mar. 1911-Dec. 1911

500-532	LIFE	
	Reel 500	v1-4; Jan. 1883-Dec. 1884
	Reel 501	v5-10; Jan. 1885-Dec. 1887
	Reel 502	v11-16; Jan. 1888-Dec. 1890
	Reel 503	v17-22; Jan. 1891-Dec. 1893
	Reel 504	v23-28; Jan. 1894-Dec. 1896
	Reel 505	v29-33; Jan. 1897-June 1899
	Reel 506	v34-38; July 1899-Dec. 1901
	Reel 507	v39-42; Jan. 1902-Dec. 1903
	Reel 508	v43-46; Jan. 1904-Dec. 1905
	Reel 509	v47-49; Jan. 1906-June 1907
	Reel 510	v50-52; July 1907-Dec. 1908
	Reel 511	v53-55; Jan. 1909-June 1910
	Reel 512	v56-57; July 1910-June 1911
	Reel 513	v58-59; July 1911-June 1912
	Reel 514	v60-61; July 1912-June 1913
	Reel 515	v62-63; July 1913-June 1914
	Reel 516	v64-65; July 1914-June 1915
	Reel 517	v66-67; July 1915-June 1916
	Reel 518	v68-69; July 1916-June 1917
	Reel 519	v70-71; July 1917-June 1918
	Reel 520	v72-73; July 1918-June 1919
	Reel 521	v74-75; July 1919-June 1920
	Reel 522	v76-78; July 1920-Dec. 1921
	Reel 523	v79-81; Jan. 1922-June 1923
	Reel 524	v82-84; July 1923-Dec. 1924
	Reel 525	v85-86; Jan. 1925-Dec. 1925
	Reel 526	v87-88; Jan. 1926-Dec. 1926
	Reel 527	v89-90; Jan. 1927-Dec. 1927
	Reel 528	v91-92; Jan. 1928-Dec. 1928
	Reel 529	v93-94; Jan. 1929-Dec. 1929
	Reel 530	v95-97; Jan. 1930-June 1931
	Reel 531	v98-100; July 1931-Dec. 1933
	Reel 532	v101-103; Jan. 1934-Nov. 1936

Unit 17

533-547	ARTHUR'S HOME MAGAZINE	
	Home Magazine	
	Reel 533	v1-6; Oct. 1852-Dec. 1855
	Reel 534	v7-8; Jan.-Dec. 1856
	Lady's Home Magazine	
	Reel 534	v9-14; Jan. 1857-Dec. 1859
	Reel 535	v15-16; Jan.-Dec. 1860
	Arthur's Home Magazine	
	Reel 535	v17-21; Jan. 1861-June 1863
	Reel 536	v22-28; July 1863-Dec. 1866
	Reel 537	v29-36; Jan. 1867-Dec. 1870
	Arthur's Lady's Home Magazine	
	Reel 538	v37-40; Jan. 1871-Dec. 1872
	Arthur's Illustrated Home Magazine	
	Reel 538	v41; Jan.-Dec. 1873
	Reel 539	v42-44; Jan. 1874-Dec. 1876
	Reel 540	v45-47; Jan. 1877-Dec. 1879
	Arthur's Home Magazine	
	Reel 541	v48-50; Jan. 1880-Dec. 1882
	Reel 542	v51-53; Jan. 1883-Dec. 1885
	Reel 543	v54-57; Jan. 1886-June 1888
	Reel 544	v58-60; July 1888-Dec. 1890
	Reel 545	v61-62; Jan. 1891-Dec. 1892

Reel 546	v63-64; Jan. 1893-Dec. 1894
Reel 547	v65-66; Jan. 1895-Sept. 1897

548-566 **CENTRAL LAW JOURNAL**

Reel 548	Index, v1-54; 1874-1902
Reel 548	v1-3; Jan. 1874-Dec. 1876
Reel 549	v4-8; Jan. 1877-June 1879
Reel 550	v9-13; July 1879-Dec. 1881
Reel 551	v14-18; Jan. 1882-June 1884
Reel 552	v19-23; July 1884-Dec. 1886
Reel 553	v24-27; Jan. 1887-Dec. 1888
Reel 554	v28-32; Jan. 1889-June 1891
Reel 555	v33-37; July 1891-Dec. 1893
Reel 556	v38-42; Jan. 1894-June 1896
Reel 557	v43-47; July 1896-Dec. 1898
Reel 558	v48-53; Jan. 1899-Dec. 1901
Reel 559	v54-59; Jan. 1902-Dec 1904
Reel 560	v60-65; Jan. 1905-Dec. 1907
Reel 561	v66-71; Jan. 1908-Dec. 1910
Reel 562	v72-76; Jan. 1911-June 1913
Reel 563	v77-81; July 1913-Dec. 1915
Reel 564	v82-87; Jan. 1916-Dec. 1918
Reel 565	v88-93; Jan. 1919-Dec. 1921
Reel 566	v94-100; Jan. 1922-Mar. 1927

567-568 **PHYSICIANS' AND SURGEONS' INVESTIGATOR**

Reel 567	v1-8; Jan. 1880-Nov. 1887
Reel 568	v9-10; Jan. 1888-Sept. 1889

568-569 **VANITY FAIR**

Reel 568	v1-4; Dec. 31, 1859-Dec. 28, 1861
Reel 569	v5-7; Jan. 4, 1862-July 4, 1863

Unit 18

570-580 **ALBANY LAW JOURNAL**

Reel 570	Cumulative Index, v1-20; 1870-1879
Reel 570	v1-7; Jan. 1870-June 28, 1873
Reel 571	v8-14; July 5, 1873-Dec. 20, 1876
Reel 572	v15-20; Jan. 6, 1877-Dec. 27, 1879
Reel 573	Cumulative Index, v21-34; 1880-1886
Reel 573	v21-26; Jan. 3, 1880-Dec. 30, 1882
Reel 574	v27-32; Jan. 6, 1883-Dec. 26, 1885
Reel 575	v33-38; Jan. 2, 1886-Dec. 29, 1888
Reel 576	v39-44; Jan. 5, 1889-Dec. 26, 1891
Reel 577	v45-51; Jan. 2, 1892-June 29, 1895
Reel 578	v52-58; July 6, 1895-Dec. 31, 1898
Reel 579	v59-65; Jan. 7, 1899-Dec. 1903
Reel 580	v66-70; Jan. 1904-Dec. 1908

580-585 **ART AMATEUR**

Reel 580	v1-6; June 1879-May 1882
Reel 581	v7-16; June 1882-May 1887
Reel 582	v17-24; June 1887-May 1891
Reel 583	v25-32; June 1891-May 1895
Reel 584	v33-40; June 1895-May 1899
Reel 585	v41-49; June 1899-Sept. 1903

586-589 **BELFORD'S MONTHLY**

Belford's Magazine

Reel 586	v1-4; June 1888-May 1890
Reel 587	v5-6; June 1890-May 1891
Reel 588	v7; June-Aug. 1891

Belford's Monthly and Democratic Review

Reel 588	v8; Sept. 1891-May 1892

Belford's Monthly

Reel 588	v9; June-Nov. 1892
Reel 589	v10-11; Dec. 1892-July 1893

589-590 **PHILISTINE**

Reel 589	Index, v1-20; 1895-May 1905
Reel 589	v1-10; June 1895-May 1900
Reel 590	v11-23; June 1900-Nov. 1906

591-599 **ST. NICHOLAS; AN ILLUSTRATED MAGAZINE FOR YOUNG FOLKS**

Reel 591	v1-5; Nov. 1873-Oct. 1878
Reel 592	v6-9; Nov. 1878-Oct. 1882
Reel 593	v10-13; Nov. 1882-Oct. 1886
Reel 594	v14-17; Nov. 1886-Oct. 1890
Reel 595	v18-21; Nov. 1890-Oct. 1894
Reel 596	v22-24; Nov. 1894-Oct. 1897
Reel 597	v25-28; Nov. 1897-Oct. 1901
Reel 598	v29-31; Nov. 1901-Oct. 1904
Reel 599	v32-34; Nov. 1904-Oct. 1907

Units 19-20

600-649 **AMERICAN ARCHITECT AND ARCHITECTURE**

American Architect and Building News

Reel 600	Decennial Index; 1876-1885
Reel 600	v1-2; Jan. 1, 1876-Dec. 29, 1877
Reel 601	v3-5; Jan. 5, 1878-June 28, 1879
Reel 602	v6-8; July 5, 1879-Dec. 25, 1880
Reel 603	v9-11; Jan. 1, 1881-June 24, 1882
Reel 604	v12-14; July 1, 1882-Dec. 29, 1883
Reel 605	v15-17; Jan. 5, 1884-June 27, 1885
Reel 606	v18-19; July 4, 1885-June 26, 1886
Reel 607	v20-21; July 3, 1886-June 25, 1887
Reel 608	v22-23; July 2, 1887-June 30, 1888
Reel 609	v24-25; July 7, 1888-June 29, 1889
Reel 610	v26-28; July 6, 1889-June 28, 1890
Reel 611	v29-31; July 5, 1890-Mar. 28, 1891
Reel 612	v32-34; Apr. 4-Dec. 26, 1891
Reel 613	v35-37; Jan. 2-Sept. 24, 1892
Reel 614	v38-41; Oct. 1, 1892-Sept. 30, 1893
Reel 615	v42-46; Oct. 7, 1893-Dec. 29, 1894
Reel 616	v47-50; Jan. 5-Dec. 28, 1895
Reel 617	v51-54; Jan. 4-Dec. 26, 1896
Reel 618	v55-59; Jan. 2, 1897-Mar. 26, 1898
Reel 619	v60-65; Apr. 2, 1898-Sept. 30, 1899
Reel 620	v66-70; Oct. 7, 1899-Dec. 29, 1900
Reel 621	v71-75; Jan. 5, 1901-Mar. 29, 1902
Reel 622	v76-80; Apr. 5, 1902-June 1903
Reel 623	v81-85; July 4, 1903-Sept. 24, 1904
Reel 624	v86-88; Oct. 1, 1904-Dec. 30, 1905
Reel 625	v89-90; Jan. 6-Dec. 29, 1906
Reel 626	v91-92; Jan. 5-Dec. 28, 1907
Reel 627	v93-94; Jan. 4-Dec. 30, 1908

American Architect

Reel 628	v95-96; Jan. 6-Dec. 29, 1909
Reel 629	v97; Jan. 5-June 29, 1910
Reel 630	v98-99; July 6, 1910-June 28, 1911
Reel 631	v100-102; July 5, 1911-Dec. 25, 1912
Reel 632	v103-104; Jan. 1-Dec. 31, 1913
Reel 633	v105-106; Jan. 7-Dec. 30, 1914
Reel 634	v107-108; Jan. 6-Dec. 29, 1915
Reel 635	v109-110; Jan. 5-Dec. 27, 1916
Reel 636	v111-112; Jan. 3-Dec. 26, 1917
Reel 637	v113-114; Jan. 2-Dec. 25, 1918
Reel 638	v115-116; Jan. 1-Dec. 31, 1919
Reel 639	v117-118; Jan. 7-Dec. 29, 1920
Reel 640	v119-120; Jan. 5-Aug. 17, 1921

American Architect and the Architectural Review

Reel 640	v121; Aug. 31, 1921-June 21, 1922
Reel 641	v122-124; July 5, 1922-Dec. 19, 1923
Reel 642	v125-126; Jan. 2-Dec. 31, 1924

American Architect
Reel 643   v127-129; Jan. 14, 1925-June 20, 1926
Reel 644   v130-132; July 5, 1926-Dec. 20, 1927
Reel 645   v133-135; Jan. 5, 1928-June 20, 1929
Reel 646   v136-139; July 5, 1929-June 1931
Reel 647   v140-143; July 1931-Nov. 1933
Reel 648   v144-148; Jan. 1934-May 1936
American Architect and Architecture
Reel 648   v148; June 1936
Reel 649   v149-152; July 1936-Feb. 1938

650-660   AMERICAN CATHOLIC QUARTERLY REVIEW
Reel 650   Cumulative Index, v1-25; Jan. 1876-
               Oct. 1900
Reel 650   v1-4; Jan. 1876-Oct. 1879
Reel 651   v5-8; Jan. 1880-Oct. 1883
Reel 652   v9-12; Jan. 1884-Oct. 1887
Reel 653   v13-16; Jan. 1888-Oct. 1891
Reel 654   v17-20; Jan. 1892-Oct. 1895
Reel 655   v21-24; Jan. 1896-Oct. 1899
Reel 656   v25-28; Jan. 1900-Oct. 1903
Reel 657   v29-33; Jan. 1904-Oct. 1908
Reel 658   v34-38; Jan. 1909-Oct. 1913
Reel 659   v39-44; Jan. 1914-Oct. 1919
Reel 660   v45-49; Jan. 1920-Jan. 1924

660-669   COSMOPOLITAN
Reel 660   v1-2; Mar. 1886-Feb. 1887
Reel 661   v3-7; Mar. 1887-Oct. 1889
Reel 662   v8-12; Nov. 1889-Apr. 1892
Reel 663   v13-16; May 1892-Apr. 1894
Reel 664   v17-21; May 1894-Oct. 1896
Reel 665   v22-26; Nov. 1896-Apr. 1899
Reel 666   v27-31; May 1899-Oct. 1901
Reel 667   v32-36; Nov. 1901-Apr. 1904
Reel 668   v37-41; May 1904-Oct. 1906
Reel 669   v42; Nov. 1906-Apr. 1907

669-670   LIBERTY (NOT THE DAUGHER BUT THE MOTHER OF ORDER)
Reel 669   v1-10; Aug. 6, 1881-May 4, 1895
Reel 670   v11-17; May 18, 1895-Apr. 1908

670-674   ONEIDA CIRCULAR
Circular
Reel 670   v1-2; Nov. 6, 1851-Nov. 12, 1853
Reel 671   v3-7; Dec. 6, 1853-Jan. 20, 1859
Reel 672   v8-nsv2; Jan. 27, 1859-Mar. 12, 1866
Reel 673   nsv3-7; Mar. 19, 1866-Dec. 26, 1870
Oneida Circular
Reel 674   nsv8-13; Jan. 2, 1871-Mar. 9, 1876

Unit 21

675-689   AMERICAN MAGAZINE
Frank Leslie's Popular Monthly
Reel 675   v1-4; Jan. 1876-Dec. 1877
Reel 676   v5-8; Jan. 1878-Dec. 1879
Reel 677   v9-12; Jan. 1880-Dec. 1881
Reel 678   v13-16; Jan. 1882-Dec. 1883
Reel 679   v17-20; Jan. 1884-Dec. 1885
Reel 680   v21-24; Jan. 1886-Dec. 1887
Reel 681   v25-28; Jan. 1888-Dec. 1889
Reel 682   v29-32; Jan. 1890-Dec. 1891
Reel 683   v33-36; Jan. 1892-Dec. 1893
Reel 684   v37-40; Jan. 1894-Dec. 1895
Reel 685   v41-44; Jan. 1896-Dec. 1897
Reel 686   v45-48; Jan. 1898-Oct. 1899

Reel 687   v49-53; Nov. 1899-Apr. 1902
Reel 688   v54-57, no4; May 1902-Feb. 1904
Leslie's Monthly Magazine
Reel 688   v57, no5-v58; Mar.-Oct. 1904
Reel 689   v59-60, no4; Nov. 1904-Aug. 1905
American Illustrated Magazine
Reel 689   v60, no5-v62, no1; Sept. 1905-
               May 1906
American Magazine
Reel 689   v62, no2-6; June-Oct. 1906

689-707   CURRENT OPINION
Current Literature
Reel 689   v1; July-Dec. 1888
Reel 690   v2-6; Jan. 1889-Apr. 1891
Reel 691   v7-11; May 1891-Dec. 1892
Reel 692   v12-15; Jan. 1893-June 1894
Reel 693   v16-19; July 1894-June 1896
Reel 694   v20-23; July 1896-June 1898
Reel 695   v24-28; July 1898-June 1900
Reel 696   v29-32; July 1900-June 1902
Reel 697   v33-36; July 1902-June 1904
Reel 698   v37-40; July 1904-June 1906
Reel 699   v41-44; July 1906-June 1908
Reel 700   v45-48; July 1908-June 1910
Reel 701   v49-52; July 1910-June 1912
Reel 702   v53; July 1912-Dec. 1912
Current Opinion
Reel 702   v54-56; Jan. 1913-June 1914
Reel 703   v57-61; July 1914-Dec. 1916
Reel 704   v62-66; Jan. 1917-June 1919
Reel 705   v67-70; July 1919-June 1921
Reel 706   v71-74; July 1921-June 1923
Reel 707   v75-78; July 1923-Apr. 1925

Units 22-23

708   **AMERICAN GEOGRAPHICAL SOCIETY OF NEW YORK. BULLETIN. v1-2; Aug. 1852-1857.**

708-716   AMERICAN GEOGRAPHICAL SOCIETY OF NEW YORK. BULLETIN (formerly JOURNAL)
Reel 708   Cumulative Index; 1852-1915
Journal of the American Geographical and Statistical Society
Reel 708   v1-2; Jan. 1859-1872
Journal of the American Geographical Society of New York
Reel 708   v3-7; 1873-1875
Reel 709   v8-17; 1876-1885
Reel 710   v18-23; 1886-1891
Reel 711   v24-29; 1892-1897
Reel 712   v30-32; 1898-1900
Bulletin (formerly Journal) of the American Geographical Society of New York
Reel 712   v33-35; 1901-1903
Reel 713   v36-39; 1904-1907
Reel 714   v40-42; 1908-1910
Reel 715   v43-45; 1911-1913
Reel 716   v46-47; 1914-1915

716-729   BALLOU'S MONTHLY MAGAZINE
Ballou's Dollar Monthly Magazine
Reel 716   v1-2; Jan.-Dec. 1855
Reel 717   v3-8; Jan. 1856-Dec. 1858
Reel 718   v9-14; Jan. 1859-Dec. 1861
Reel 719   v15-16; Jan.-Dec. 1862